ACRONYMS

NABET National Association of Broadcast Employees & Technicians

NASA National Aeronautics & Space Administration

NABTS North American Basic Teletext Specification

NATPE National Association of Television Program Executives

NBC National Broadcasting Company

NCTA National Cable Television Association

NET National Educational Television

NHK Nippon Hoso Kyokai

NIWS News Information Weekly Service

NPR National Public Radio

NRB National Religious Broadcasters

NTSC National Television Systems Committee

NWIO New World Information Order

O&O Owned & Operated

OWI Office of War Information

PAS Pan American Satellite Corp.

PBS Public Broadcasting Service

PI Per-Inquiry

PICON Public Interest, Convenience, Or Necessity

PIP Picture In Picture

PPV Pay-Per-View

PTAR Prime-Time Access Rule

PTL Praise The Lord

PTT Post, Telephone, & Telegraph

PSA Public Service Announcement

PUP Portable Uplink

PUR Persons Using Radio

RAB Radio Advertising Bureau

RADAR Radio's All-Dimension Audience Research

RCA Radio Corporation of America

RF Radio Frequency

RFE Radio Free Europe

RFP Request For Proposals

RL Radio Liberty

RTNDA Radio-Television News Directors Association

SBS Satellite Business Systems

SCS Subsidiary Communications Service

SCOTUS Supreme Court Of The United States

SESAC Society of European Stage Authors & Composers

SHF Super-High Frequency

SMART Stop Marketing Alcohol on Radio & Television

SMATV Satellite Master Antenna TV

SNG Satellite News Gathering

SRDS Standard Rate & Data Service

SSB Single Sideband

STV Subscription TV

TBS Turner Broadcasting Systems

TCI Tele-Communications, Inc.

TIO Television Information Office

TNT Turner Network Television

TvB Television Bureau of Advertising

TvQ TV Quotient

TVRO Television Receive-Only Antenna

UHF Ultra-High Frequency

UNESCO United Nations Education, Scientific & Cultu. al Organization

UP United Press

UPI United Press International

USCI United Satellite Communications Inc.

USIA United States Information Agency

VBI Vertical Blanking Interval

VCR Videocassette Recorder

VHF Very High Frequency

VH-1 Video Hits One

VJ Video Jockey

VLF Very Low Frequency

VOA Voice of America

VTR Videotape Recorder

WARC World Administrative Radio Conference

WGA Writer's Guild of America

WST World System Teletext

BROADCASTING
IN
AMERICA

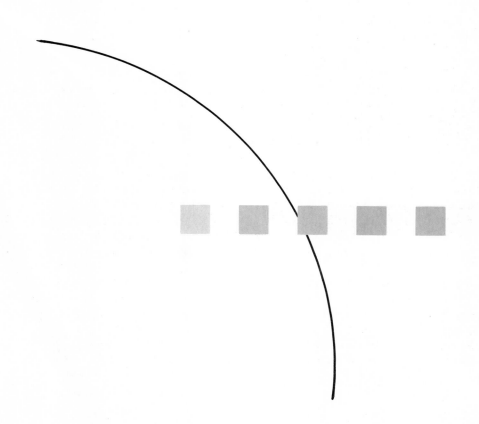

BROADCASTING
IN
AMERICA

A Survey of Electronic Media

SIXTH EDITION

SYDNEY W. HEAD
University of Miami

CHRISTOPHER H. STERLING
The George Washington University

with contributions by
Susan Tyler Eastman, *Indiana University*
Lemuel B. Schofield, *University of Miami*

HOUGHTON MIFFLIN COMPANY **BOSTON**
Dallas   Geneva, Ill.   Palo Alto   Princeton, N.J.

Acknowledgments for photographs on the part opener pages: Declan Haun

Printed in the U.S.A.

Library of Congress Catalog Card Number: 89-80939

ISBN: 0-395-43253-7

ABCDEFGHIJ-M-9543210/89

Cover photograph by Ken Cooper

BRIEF CONTENTS

CONTENTS

LIST OF EXHIBITS

PREFACE

Despite enormous changes in its field of coverage since the first edition, the sixth edition of *Broadcasting in America* retains its original underlying goal of viewing the electronic media in a broad academic perspective. These media, both as products of contemporary social forces and as social forces in their own right, should be seen in context. They impinge on many academic areas, ranging from economics to law, from history to social science. Study of the electronic media can be interesting and rewarding in itself, but also can both enrich the study of other subjects and in turn be enriched by them.

Though retaining the same general outline, the present edition of *Broadcasting in America* introduces changes in keeping with the changing media scene and in response to recommendations of teachers who had used the fifth edition. For example, we have reverted to treating public broadcasting in a chapter of its own, except for some commercial-noncommercial comparisons in the program chapters. The comparison of the American system with systems in other countries now appears as a concluding instead of as a preliminary chapter. The prologue now introduces the book's key concepts.

More generally, the profound changes brought about by cable television, satellites, videocassettes, digital signal processing, and deregulation have been more thoroughly assimilated throughout the text that was possible heretofore. We have also tried to improve the readability of the text throughout and to illustrate it more fully. Many new exhibits have been added, ranging from photos of leading personalities to detailed explanations of technical developments. Also, a new, detailed glossary, prepared by ancillary authors Louise Benjamin and Michael Porter, has been added to the book for easy reference and clearer distinction of broadcasting's many industry terms.

Special Features

▌ The new prologue introduces the key concepts used throughout the book, stripped of the details that might initially confuse readers new to the field. This preliminary overview should help orient readers before they plunge into the more detailed chapters that follow.

▌ Part I has been recast to take into account the longer perspective now available on electronic-media history. This revision has meant sacrificing some of the details of early broadcasting development to enable enlarging on the evolution of cable television, satellite relays, and other later trends.

▌ Part 2 devotes more attention to newer technologies such as satellite relays, digital processing, and high-definition television. At the same time, some of the more intricate aspects of these and other technical matters have been detached from the main text as sidebar features. Those who find that grappling with the physical aspects of the electronic media somewhat daunting can skip over these technical exhibits without losing the main thread of the exposition.

▌ Part 3 fully explores the bottom-line thinking that pervades the industry because of deregulation and the "urge to merge," which have resulted in such industry-shaking events as General Electric's absorption of RCA, and Sony's takeover of both CBS Records and Columbia Pictures. The economic chapters conclude with a down-to-earth analysis of the contemporary media job market with special reference to opportunities for women and minorities.

▪ Part 4 shows how new economic forces have affected programs, programming, and program production, reflecting the emergence of cable television as a major player with its own creative agenda and its own programming strategies. This Part includes an extensive analysis of sports programming and scheduling.

▪ Part 5's presentation of effects research reflects changes in audience research brought about by the introduction of People Meters.

▪ Part 6 takes a more hard-nosed view of the goals and processes of deregulation than heretofore, fully exploring the fall-out from the increased reliance on marketplace competition, consumer sovereignty, and conservative judicial thinking. It takes into account new First Amendment perspectives brought about by technological convergence. The three chapters of this part have been reorganized into what we think is a more easily understood sequence, with chapters focusing respectively on laws and agencies, licensing, and constitutional issues.

▪ Finally, the Epilogue, Part 7, takes into account the changing international role of U.S. media in the face of shifting world forces such as the growing reliance on market-based economies, reflected in the emergence of the Common Market in Europe and *perestroika* and *glasnost* in the Communist World.

Ancillary Support

Michael Porter of the University of Missouri has prepared a wholly new *Instructor's Manual with Test Items*. It includes chapter analyses and summaries, reviews of learning objectives and key concepts, lecture and activity suggestions, and a bank of multiple-choice test items. The manual also includes a series of "Memos to BIA Course Instruc-

tors" from the authors, containing suggestions reflecting their long teaching experience and the goals they had in mind in writing the book.

A *Microtest* program incorporates the multiple-choice test items on a floppy disk for use with IBM, IBM-compatible, and Macintosh personal computers.

Louise Benjamin of Indiana University has written an all-new *Study Guide* for students. It includes chapter-by-chapter lists of learning objectives, key concepts, and practice multiple-choice test items. The test items include analyses explaining why the wrong answers are wrong and the right answers right, with cross-references to the relevant passages in the text.

Contributing Authors and Critics

As in the last edition, the chapters on programs and economics were contributed by specialists in these fields, respectively Professors Susan Tyler Eastman (Indiana University) and Lemuel B. Schofield (University of Miami). Professor Eastman, senior editor of and a contributor to *Broadcast/Cable Programming: Strategies and Practices* (Wadsworth, 3d ed., 1989), has taught "the BIA course" for more than a decade. Professor Schofield, associate dean of the University of Miami School of Communication, combines extensive experience as an attorney and as a television station manager with that of teaching broadcast/cable management courses. In addition to writing the economics chapters, he generously provided program economics data and other material used elsewhere in the book.

The authors and contributors are grateful to the many people in the academic and business worlds who gave valuable expert advice and specialized assistance. We wish to acknowledge in particular the help we received from Erwin Krasnow of Verner, Liipfert, Bernhardt & McPherson (advice on legal material), Stephen Winzenberg of Florida South College (material on religious broadcasting), and Marcia Kreuger of George Washington University (research and computer services).

The teachers listed below reviewed the draft manuscript at the publisher's request. Their unsigned critiques alerted us to errors and offered helpful counsel on both organization and content.

Anneke-Jan Boden, *Eastern Montana College*
Don M. Flournoy, *Ohio University*
Ruane B. Hill, *University of Wisconsin-Milwaukee*
W. Dale Hoskins, *Northern Arizona University*
Alfred Owens, *Youngstown State University*
Norma Pecora, *University of Maryland*
Michael J. Porter, *University of Missouri-Columbia*
Robert T. Ramsey, *Stephen F. Austin State University*

Ted Schwalbe, *SUNY-Fredonia*
Robert Stahley, *Los Angeles City College*
Jack Summerfield, *New York Institute of Technology*

We assume responsibility for the use made of the assistance given by the above and other advisors.

Sydney W. Head   Christopher H. Sterling
Coral Cables, FL   *Washington, DC*

BROADCASTING
IN
AMERICA

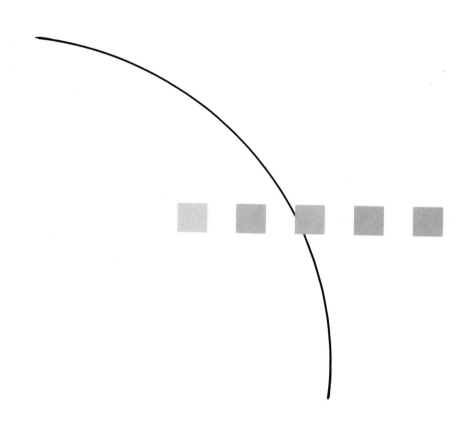

PROLOGUE

THE WORLD OF BROADCASTING

▋▋▋▋▋▋ CHAPTER 1

KEY CONCEPTS

1.1
Why Study Broadcasting?

Why not be a couch potato—just sit back and enjoy programs, as most people do? The very fact that people turn into couch potatoes gives us one reason: *broadcasting has consequences,* effects that spread widely and penetrate deeply. It ranks as the most universal means of public communication, conveying information (or, all too often, misinformation), entertainment, education, and persuasion—all of which, intentionally or not, teach cultural values.

Broadcasting has a pervasive influence throughout the world. Programs can be picked up almost anywhere on the Earth's surface. About 212 countries and dependencies have their own radio broadcasting stations.* About 84 percent of them have their own television stations, but even in the remotest places people who have no stations resort to videocassettes and backyard satellite dishes, to gain access to television.

More homes boast radio and television receivers than any other modern amenity. Millions of people lacking such conveniences as electricity, indoor

plumbing, refrigerators, telephones, and common medicines nevertheless have radio receivers. Travelers often note with astonishment that festering slums bristle with television antennas. Many people spend more time listening to and looking at broadcasts than on any other waking activity.

Virtually everyone, therefore, finds something of interest about broadcasting. Some want to become part of it, as actors, writers, producers, executives. Some want to use it in their business or profession. Some have a scholarly interest in its many facets. Even people with no specialized vocational, utilitarian, or scholarly interest in the medium have a stake in learning about it because we all come under its influence and buy the products it advertises. As consumers, we all need to understand how broadcasting operates and what policies seem most likely to make the medium work for us rather than against us.

This book tries to serve all who need a basic introduction to broadcasting in America, whether as prospective broadcasters, as users, as researchers, or as consumers. It identifies the influences that shape the medium, explores how the system affects society, and analyzes the measures society takes to control it. This chapter gives a foretaste of the main themes developed in the book.

Though focused on broadcasting in America, this book cannot entirely ignore foreign broadcasting. The American system has always strongly influenced

---

*Data on numbers of countries with broadcasting are based on listings in *World Radio TV Handbook,* 1989. Those with no television consist mostly of small islands that lack the resources to support such a service.

other countries—sometimes as a model to be imitated, but often also as a cautionary example of what to avoid. Foreign systems throughout the world draw heavily on American sources for television programs. Satellites and other means of global communication enhance transnational exchange, further magnifying American influence, but also facilitating the reverse—programs and ideas imported from abroad. The concluding chapter of this book reviews broadcasting in a global context, comparing the American system with others and noting how systems around the world interact with one another.

1.2
Some Essential Terms

Writers and speakers often misuse the word *broadcasting,* assuming that any programs and messages transmitted over the air and even over cable constitute broadcasts. But the term has a precise and limited meaning. Its accurate definition has important practical consequences because government controls differ significantly from one medium to another, and broadcasting carries a heavier burden of regulation than other media.

Broadcasting   *To broadcast* means *to send out sound and pictures by means of radio waves through space for reception by the general public.* The phrases "by means of radio waves through space" and "reception by the general public" have key significance. For example, under this definition, *cable television* is not broadcasting. Both use radio waves, but cable sends them through a special type of wire (coaxial cable), whereas broadcasting sends them through the open air. Despite the fact that many cable channels consist of broadcast programs picked up off the air by cable companies and delivered to subscribers, different regulations and physical limitations govern the licensing and operation of these two program delivery methods.

Relays   Both broadcasting and cable companies rely heavily on *relays* to supply them with nationally distributed programs. As used here, the term *relay* refers to either wire or wireless methods of distributing programs simultaneously and privately, without broadcasting them.

Like broadcast stations, satellites and certain other relay devices operate "by means of radio waves." Instead of sending programs out for "reception by the general public," though, they send them *point-to-point* (from one specific source to one intended recipient) or *point-to-multipoint* (to more than one specific recipient). Even though members of the public equipped with suitable receivers can intercept satellite relays—for instance, a network's distribution of its programs to affiliates—the network headquarters *intends* them for reception only by affiliates, not by the general public. Satellite relay links to affiliated stations or cable systems use radio waves, yet relay transmissions do not qualify as broadcasts because their senders *intend* them for reception only at specific points, namely the locations of affiliated stations or cable systems, not for direct "reception by the general public." Thus *intent* plays a key role in defining broadcasting.

Electronic Mass Media*   Traditional broadcasting competes with cable television and other comparatively new methods in delivering programs to the public. Indeed, more than half the television homes in the United States receive broadcast programs indirectly, via cable systems, rather than over-the-air from stations.

Nevertheless, the word *broadcasting* has been retained in the title of this book for its succinctness, even though the book covers nonbroadcast types of transmission that also deliver programs to the public. If the phrase were not so cumbersome, the term *electronic mass communication media* might

---

*Note that the "a" ending means that *media* is a plural noun ("the media *are*"), though careless speakers and writers often use it as a singular when referring to several media. This misuse is more than a petty language error. "Media" used as a singular noun lumps together *all* public media—broadcasting, cable, print, film, and the rest—obscuring the fact that each medium has its own separate identity and unique characteristics.

have been preferable. According to the Communications Act of 1934, which is the federal law that governs transmission of all types of radio and interstate wire communication in the United States:

The term "media of mass communication" includes television, radio, cable television, multipoint distribution services, and other services, the licensed facilities of which must be substantially devoted toward providing programming or other information services within the editorial control of the licensee. [309 USC (1)(3) (C)(i)]*

The phrase "within the editorial control of the licensee" distinguishes mass-media services from *common-carrier* services. For example, the licensee of a public telephone service (a typical common carrier) has no right to say who will make telephone calls or to edit conversations. But those licensed to program electronic mass media not only have the right to select performers and speakers and to edit what they say, they have the legal *obligation* to control the programs that go out over their facilities, selecting and editing so as to conform with the laws under which the particular mass-media service operates.

People sometimes complain that when the operators of stations edit programs, they violate the constitutional guarantee of free speech and press. Such critics forget, however, that the Constitution's First Amendment forbids *government* interference with such freedoms, not private interference. Station executives who censor material in accordance with their or their owners' editorial standards may be guilty of faulty judgment or bad public relations, but not of First Amendment violations.

Telecommunications   Common carriers, along with broadcasting and cable systems, form part of a broad range of services known as *telecommunications*. Telecommunications services transmit voice, video, text, and data by means of wire (including the specialized substitutes for ordinary

---

*For explanation of citations such as this, see p. 420. Multipoint distributions service (MDS) is described in Section 4.3.

wire called coaxial cable and fiber-optic cable) and by means of radio waves. Students of broadcasting need to know something about nonbroadcast telecommunications because most electronic mass media depend heavily on other telecommunications services, especially in relay facilities that make networks possible.

Hybrid Services   Even the foregoing broad distinctions between common carriers and mass media become debatable in the case of certain *hybrid* services that have characteristics of both types of communication. Precise classification is more than legal hairsplitting because the law controls mass media more rigorously than common carriers; owners of hybrid services therefore prefer the common-carrier classification so as to escape regulation as mass media. The Federal Communications Commission also favors calling hybrid services common carriers, in keeping with its current policy of minimizing government regulation.

Even the telephone, the classic example of a common carrier, has become hybridized. For example, it takes on characteristics of a mass medium when used for "dial-it" services, sometimes called "mass announcement services." For a price, listeners can hear and even participate in short audio "programs" by dialing numbers with special prefixes.

Dial-it services first achieved popularity with a service called SportsPhone, which disseminates game scores and sport stories. Dial-it services now include a wide array of subjects such as soap-opera summaries, stock reports, diet advice, contests, horror stories, group conversations, and even a "sound off" service that gives callers a chance to register or listen to personal gripes addressed to no one in particular.

Pornography figures prominently among dial-it services, and objectors often call upon telephone companies to censor "dial-a-porn." But the Communications Act requires common carriers to serve *all* users, without discrimination (47 USC 202). Operators of dial-it services, along with opponents of government interference generally, claim that discrimination against dial-a-porn purveyors violates not only the Communications Act but also the Constitution's First Amendment free-speech clause.

As another example of a hybrid service, satellites usually function as common carriers and therefore escape broadcasting regulations. But the DBS (direct-broadcast satellite) services that are beginning to become available in some parts of the world seem to constitute broadcasting. Homeowners with suitable satellite receiving antennas can pick up DBS programs directly from a satellite as though it were a terrestrial television station. DBS program-service providers scramble their signals, however, so that only subscribers can receive them. Barring the general public thus puts DBS services into the point-to-multipoint rather than the broadcast category. Again, the definition hinges on *intent* rather than on *content*. Does a service intend to reach the general public, or only certain designated recipients?

1.3
Organization of This Book

In the 1990s, the traditional broadcasting services that have evolved since sound radio emerged in the 1920s face profound challenges from new media and new technologies. Will unrelenting competition and irreversible technical change radically alter ordinary broadcasting, even displace it entirely? This survey of broadcasting in America must confront that insistent question at every turn, as suggested by the following part-by-part summary of contents:

■ Part 1: History   What previous forms of communication led to broadcasting? How did these precursors influence its development? How did it evolve as an independent medium, and what new competition does it face?

■ Part 2: Technology   What physical principles govern broadcasting? How do these principles determine both its physical limits and its unique physical advantages? How does technology converge to give rise to newer media?

■ Part 3: Economics   Who owns the broadcasting medium? Who pays for programs? To what extent do economic influences determine the medium's structure and behavior? How does competition

from newer electronic media alter the broadcasting medium?

■ Part 4: Content   What kinds of programs does broadcasting offer? How do they get produced and scheduled? What makes them different from other mass communication products? How do the newer media affect them?

■ Part 5: Impact   How do researchers measure the audiences of broadcasting and related media? What impact do programs have on those audiences?

■ Part 6: Control   What legal concepts, government rules, and social demands have arisen to control the social impact of broadcasting? Does it need different controls than competing media?

■ Epilogue: Global View   Finally, how do broadcasting and related media in America differ from those of other countries? What influence does the American example have on foreign systems, and what of possible benefit to the American system can be learned from analyzing differences among systems?

The remainder of this chapter introduces the key concepts involved in each of these areas of study.

1.4
Part 1   History

Once it was accepted as a commercially supported medium in the late 1920s, broadcasting grew with extraordinary speed. National networks soon became the dominant players in the broadcast scene and have remained so, even though cable television began to challenge them seriously in the late 1970s. Meanwhile, as a minor yet significant strand in the medium's history, a noncommercial alternative to commercial broadcasting gradually evolved into what we now know as public radio and public television stations and their respective national networks, NPR (National Public Radio) and PBS (Public Broadcasting Service).

Evolution of Concept   Broadcasting evolved from prior technologies—the telegraph, the telephone, and wireless (radio) ship-to-shore communication. Services based on these technologies were common carriers, providing *point-to-point* and *point-to-multipoint* communication. Wire and wireless messages carried the addresses of specific recipients or groups of recipients, like first-class mail. Broadcasting introduced a new wireless communication concept—messages without addressees, or in effect messages addressed to "any receiver," something like fourth-class mail sent to "occupant." The verb *to broadcast* was adopted to express this idea of scattered, undefined, anonymous dissemination. It comes from the farmer's way of hand-sowing grain by *casting it broadly*, letting seeds fall where they may (see Exhibit 1–1). When stations broadcast, they scatter "seed" (that is, news, entertainment, advertising, and so on) across the land to fall wherever receivers happen to be turned on and tuned in.

After the first radio broadcast stations began regular operations in about 1920, it took only a few years for this new communication concept to become firmly established. Television broadcasting,* as an extension of the original audio mode, began in earnest in 1948, following a hiatus in development imposed by World War II (1939–1945).

Production Centralization   Individual stations have limited resources for program creation. They need to combine forces to share programs produced centrally. This need for sharing led to the development of *distribution* technologies, the means of transferring programs from production centers to station locations. One distribution method, the *network*, relies on high-quality *relays*, the means for instantaneous distribution from a network's headquarters to affiliates throughout the nation. Network wire relays evolved from simple telephone wire to coaxial and (increasingly in recent years) fiber-optic cable, from terrestrial radio links (microwave relays) to space radio (distribution satellites).

---

*Both audio (sound) broadcasting (commonly called "radio") and sound-with-picture (video) broadcasting ("television") are forms of *radio transmission*, a mode also used for many other types of communication, such as the radio telephone and radio data transmission.

At first networks regarded live programs as their special domain, but live production has drawbacks, among them the need to compensate for different time zones. For example, a live prime-time evening program that started in New York at 8:00 P.M. would start on the West Coast at the unsuitable pre–prime-time hour of 5:00 in the afternoon. Networks at first repeated programs live for the West Coast, holding off adopting the obvious solution of temporarily *storing* programs for delayed broadcast, pending the development of high-quality recording technology.

That technology also furthered the evolution of an alternative distribution method, *syndication*. Distribution companies syndicate recorded programs by making contracts to send them to individual stations on a nonnetwork basis.

Network Dominance   For some 40 years, the three leading national networks, NBC, CBS, and ABC, dominated broadcasting—first radio only, then both radio and television. Their size, prestige, and pioneering developments in the program, business, and technical fields enabled networks to set the standards for the entire industry.

Most *independent* (nonnetwork) stations played a secondary role, relying heavily on syndicated programs (which, with the advent of television, often consisted of old network programs reissued as "off-network" syndicated shows). The introduction in 1952 of UHF television stations, inherently inferior in coverage to VHF stations, contributed to the secondary status of "independents."

As far back as the early 1940s, the FCC (Federal Communications Commission) had become uneasy about the dominance of the national networks (at that time radio only) and began making rules to curb them. It sought to protect affiliate autonomy and to prevent the networks from dominating the talent agency and program production fields. FCC rules limited the television networks' right to produce their own prime-time entertainment programs and to engage in syndication; the prime-time access rule (PTAR) prevented the networks from filling all the best evening hours in the major markets. Partly because of these rules, by the late 1970s, indepen-

EXHIBIT 1–1   Invention of "Broadcasting"

Not only the technology of broadcasting but also its language had to be invented. Prior to 1921 broadcasting was popularly known as "radio telephony" or simply "wireless." The latter term, in fact, prevailed in Britain for many years. In 1926, shortly after its founding, the BBC (British Broadcasting Corporation) began recruiting distinguished literary figures such as George Bernard Shaw and Rudyard Kipling to serve on an Advisory Committee on Spoken English. The committee met several times a year to settle the fate of "debatable words" (Briggs, 1961: 242).

The new verb "to broadcast" itself became one of the debatable words because of doubts as to whether its past tense should take the form "broadcast" or "broadcasted." The committee decided in favor of the irregular past tense, "broadcast," following the precedent of the verb "to cast." Therefore one says "Yesterday he broadcast the news," not "he broadcasted."

Note in the contemporary British cartoon the announcer's formal dress, which the BBC then required, as indeed did NBC when it was founded in the 1920s.

Unrecognized Heroes. The Announcer who said 'broadcasted'.

SOURCE: Asa Briggs, *The History of British Broadcasting*, Vol. I, *The Birth of Broadcasting* (London: Oxford University Press, 1961), I-243.

dent (unaffiliated) television stations began to make inroads into the networks' dominant *audience share* (the percentage of the actual audience at any particular time tuned to a particular program, station, or network).

Cable Competition   Even more damaging to network pre-eminence, however, was the emergence of cable television as a source of program options. Cable television started around 1950, soon after mass television broadcasting itself, but at first it merely extended broadcast station coverage. For years, FCC regulations confined cable primarily to this subservient role. When court rulings and a new Washington philosophy of deregulation finally swept away restrictions in the late 1970s and early 1980s, cable began spectacular growth, reaching half the television sets in the country by 1987.

The introduction in 1976 of the first *superstation* gave crucial impetus to cable growth. An ordinary, nonaffiliated UHF broadcast station (now WTBS–TV) in Atlanta, GA, attained superstation status simply by arranging for satellite distribution of its program schedule to cable systems throughout the country. Cable operators welcomed it as a way to obtain an entire channel of programs without the need to create a new, cable-specific program schedule of their own. Subsequently, over a score of cable-specific channels emerged, including pay-cable services, making the new delivery system a true competitor of broadcasting, not just a parasitic dependent.

As a result of cable's evolution, by 1988 the television broadcast networks' share of the national audience had declined from the 90 percent level, where it had hovered for years, to about 70 percent.* Cable thus contributed to reducing the overwhelming dominance of the broadcast networks. However, this decline in network television preeminence should be seen in perspective: the networks remain by far the leading purveyors of news, entertainment, and advertising to mass audiences. One must keep in mind that the networks' competition is fragmented into hundreds of independent stations and scores of cable channels, no one of which remotely approaches the coverage and prestige of any one of the three major television broadcast networks.

Public Broadcasting Despite several early attempts at setting aside broadcast channels exclusively for educational use, Congress made no provision in the 1934 Broadcasting Act for a special noncommercial class of stations to supplement the commercial stations' somewhat monotonous program diet. Nevertheless, from the beginning, some people felt a need for an alternative service that would take advantage of the educational potential of broadcasting and escape the domination of advertisers.

In fact, educational, religious, and other noncommercial institutions were among the licensees of the early AM radio stations in the 1920s, but most of them failed to keep pace with developments and eventually surrendered their valuable channels to commercial interests. Later, the FCC, recognizing that noncommercial institutions could not compete effectively with commercial organizations for the limited number of channels available, set aside FM and television channels exclusively for noncommercial use. In 1967 Congress bolstered these moves

---

*In estimating the networks' audience percentage, research firms include viewers who receive network programs via cable's redelivery of television station programs.

by amending the Communications Act to create the Corporation for Public Broadcasting, a federal funding and support agency.

1.5
Part 2 Technology

Revolutionary changes in communications technology of the past two decades can be traced primarily to five lines of development:

▌ The use of *satellites* to distribute and deliver programs and messages.

▌ The use of *fiber-optic* conductors in place of copper wire or coaxial cable.

▌ The substitution of *digital* for analog means of encoding signals (sounds, pictures, symbols).

▌ The development of small *computers*, which in turn depend on large-scale *integrated-circuit silicon chips.*

▌ *Convergence,* the tendency for hitherto separate technologies (considerably helped by the developments just named) to combine into new configurations, creating new modes of communication.

Satellites Communication satellites serve broadcasters and cable operators as distribution devices for relaying programs to widely dispersed stations and systems. Public broadcasting pioneered this use of satellites in the late 1970s, and was soon imitated by the commercial networks. Cable television, crucially dependent on satellite distribution, used satellites from the outset of its emergence as a national medium in the mid-1970s.

Satellites have another feature valuable for broadcasting: their ability to span oceans, which is impossible with the relay technology previously available (though fiber-optic cables, first laid on the seabed in 1988, have the potential for challenging satellites as the prime means of transoceanic relaying). Satellite relays make it easy for broadcasters and cable operators to schedule live coverage of news and sports events from all parts of the world.

Satellites later developed DTH *(direct-to-home)* transmission. A DBS *(direct-broadcast satellite)* transmitter can deliver programs to consumers without going through an intervening terrestrial station. Each terrestrial broadcast transmitter, relatively cumbersome and inflexible, reaches only a limited area, so that hundreds of such transmitters must be linked to provide national coverage in a large country such as the United States. A single DBS transmitter in space can serve the entire country.

Despite their advantages, DTH services developed more slowly than satellite relay services; to succeed, DBS needs to entice the mass audience to invest in special satellite reception equipment. In the United States the rapid growth of cable television services removed the incentive for this investment, pre-empting the mass demand for DBS services. In most other countries, cable installation progressed more slowly, making DTH services more attractive to consumers. In the long run, DBS poses a threat to both traditional broadcast television and cable television. It takes advantage, as cable cannot, of broadcasting's unique ability to send programs to any number of receivers without physical connection (Exhibit 1–2). This ability enables reaching the most remote receivers with ease and increasing the number of receivers without increase in transmission costs.

In fact, one increasingly sees the term "terrestrial broadcasting," calling attention to the fact that traditional stations on Earth must expect competition from space-based DBS transmitters. The difference lies not only in the transmitters' locations and coverage areas but also in the frequency bands they use. Channels available for terrestrial broadcasting have become so crowded that little room for expansion remains; the higher-frequency, less-crowded bands used by satellites allow for more growth and flexibility. Another threat to terrestrial broadcasting comes from the possibility of delivering programs to households by means of fiber-optic telephone cables—a universal form of cable television.

Fiber Optics Using light waves guided through hair-thin flexible strands of glass, *fiber-optic cable* offers several advantages over both copper cable and radio relays: small diameter (making for easy installation), enormous capacity, freedom from interference, and transmission efficiency (Exhibit 1–3). Signals sent through coaxial-cable transmission lines quickly lose their strength, requiring frequent reamplification. Signals in fiber-optic channels can travel much farther than those in coaxial cable before needing reamplification. More important, the great capacity of fiber-optic transmission lines ideally suits the needs of the new digital method of signal processing that is transforming communication technology.

From Analog to Digital Processing Radio and television broadcasting and cable television have traditionally used AM (amplitude modulation) and FM (frequency modulation). These are *analog* methods of encoding signals that are rapidly giving way to *digital* methods throughout the electronic world. The term *digital* already has become familiar to music recording enthusiasts in such phrases as "digital sound" and "digital audio tape" (DAT). Widespread use of personal computers has made people aware of such digital concepts as *bit* (*binary digit*) and *byte* (the group of bits that represents a single letter or numeral).

Without going into detail, suffice it to say at this point that digital processing makes possible much higher fidelity than before, along with endless possibilities for manipulating images such as those seen in glitzy television program titles. Many everyday appliances already use digital processing, but its use in broadcast transmission would require much wider bands of frequencies than does the present analog transmission system. Digital conversion may eventually mean new frequency assignments and replacement of existing transmitters, receivers, and related equipment.

Digital technology plays a key role in plans for high-definition television (HDTV), which some producers already use for "mastering" (making original recordings of) new productions. HDTV could vastly improve television reception, filling a wide, wall-mounted receiver screen with pictures equal in quality to those seen in movie theaters. A score of

EXHIBIT 1–2 Direct-to-Home Satellite Broadcasting

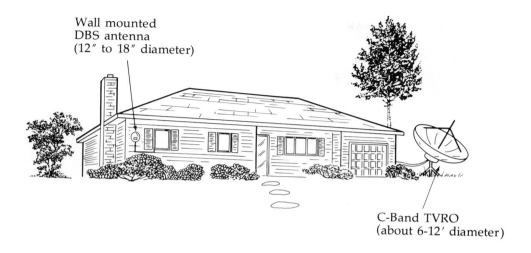

Wall mounted
DBS antenna
(12″ to 18″ diameter)

C-Band TVRO
(about 6-12′ diameter)

Relatively small receive-only television antennas (TVROs) enable homeowners to receive satellite signals directly, without the need of being within reach of a terrestrial television station. This satellite-to-home service began in an unplanned way when hobbyists set up TVROs in their backyards to pick up relay signals never intended for public reception, such as television network feeds to their affiliates and satellite-to-cable program channels. This kind of satellite reception came to be known as C-band direct, *referring to the frequency band used by relay satellites.*

True DBS (direct-broadcast satellite) services use higher power and shorter wavelength Ku-band *frequencies, enabling the use of much smaller antennas suitable for mounting on the side or roof of a house.*

rival high-definition methods has been proposed that would make present receivers obsolete. Other methods seek to enhance the present picture standard, using a *compatible* system that would allow existing sets to continue receiving signals. Contemporary color television is compatible in the sense that monochrome (black-and-white) sets can receive color pictures, reproducing as black-and-white pictures.

Satellites could play a decisive role in HDTV development. To enlarge the existing terrestrial broadcast channels to accommodate HDTV would be difficult if not impossible because of all the other services that crowd the frequency spectrum. Direct-broadcast satellites, however, use frequency bands that have not already been locked into existing standards by long tradition and widespread usage. Thus DBS could make the changeover to HDTV relatively easily.

Computers The utter simplicity of a digital signal's make-up enables easy manipulation of signal content. Viewers often see examples of such manipulation in the infinitely varied permutations of television graphics, often merged with live pictures. Switching around the recorded digital-signal bits

EXHIBIT 1–3   Fiber-Optic Cable

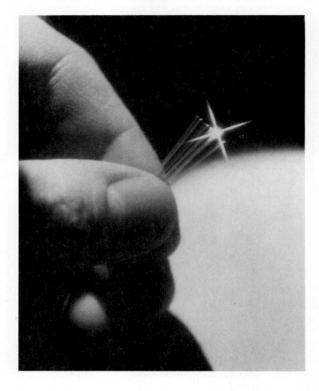

An AT&T fiber-optic cable made up of five pairs of hair-thin glass strands (each pair can carry about 50,000 telephone calls) transmitted on beams of laser light. Capacity is limited not by the small size of the fibers but by the speed of the lasers that generate the information-bearing light beams and the light detectors at the receiving end. Currently, these components can send and receive 3.4 billion bits of information per second.

The small cables may be strung on poles or buried underground or beneath the sea. Other communication enterprises increasingly use fiber-optic conductors to relay all sorts of electronically encoded information. Underwater fiber-optic cables enable telephone calls between Tokyo and Geneva. For broadcasting, television fiber-optic relays are used mostly along the high-density routes between Washington, DC, and Boston. Cable television systems use fiber-optic trunk lines in experimental installations.

SOURCE: AT&T.

makes possible these dazzling video effects. Only *computers* could manipulate picture content with such speed and intricacy.

Television graphics represent just one of innumerable examples that could be cited of the profound effect of computers on broadcasting and on communication generally. The computer's ability to manipulate and store the simple yet incredibly numerous bits and bytes of digitally processed information almost instantaneously has truly revolutionized communication technology.

Convergence   Digital processing provides a common electronic language that encourages interaction among formerly distinct modes of communicating—the telephone, broadcasting, cable television, motion pictures, printing, data storage and transmission, and even mail. Distinctions among these previously separate modes of communication have grown less sharp, and new combinations have emerged. In this process of *convergence,* computers play a central role, bridging the gaps between different functions and technologies. Convergence presents the broadcasting medium with unforeseen challenges that may alter its nature or even eliminate it in its present form.

Examples of convergence: some FM radio stations offer the service of downloading computer software to audience members by means of subcarriers that do not interfere with regular programming. The telephone, formerly devoted only to voice communication, now may tie into a computer modem for transmission and reception of mail, data, and drawings. Telephone lines can provide many other "enhanced" or "value-added" services, subject only to consumer demand and regulatory assent.

ISDN   Fiber optics, computers, and digital processing come together in a marriage that promises to transform the familiar telephone system into an *integrated services digital network* (ISDN). This forbidding name simply refers to converting the conventional network of telephone lines that crisscross the nation to digital signal processing and using the greatly enhanced system to transmit a great variety of different communication services in addition to the plain old telephone (POT, as engineers call it). A *broadband* ISDN could transmit all these services, including radio and television programs, simultaneously. Messages could be sent bi-directionally, both to and from subscribers' premises. Experimental ISDNs have already been installed in limited areas, paving the way for a future national ISDN.

1.6
Part 3 Economics

Such new services will emerge if called forth by *mass demand*. Astronauts landed on the moon not because of any mass demand for such landings but because the U.S. government backed the enterprise without regard to costs. In the mass communication field, however, the needs and desires of the consumer market play a decisive role under the U.S. system. (In many other countries the government pays the way, in part or entirely.)

Technology could create many new wonders that never reach the market or, having been offered for sale, fail for lack of public demand. Examples of projects that found backing but still lost millions of dollars because of public apathy abound, among them two major cable channels devoted to cultural programs (RCA and CBS), a satellite news channel (ABC/Westinghouse), a system for delivering programs to homes at night for automatic VCR recording (TeleFirst), a direct-broadcast satellite program service (United Satellites Communications), and a cable television service that permitted viewers to send messages as well as receive programs (Warner Cable's Qube).

Public Investment   To succeed, a new consumer technology requires two reciprocal conditions: (1) investors must be willing to gamble on being able to generate public demand, and (2) enough early purchasers who are not too particular about cost must respond to justify initiating the mass production that brings the cost down to an affordable level for the majority of consumers.

The television receiver is one of the most remarkable examples of this process: an incredibly complex yet highly reliable piece of sophisticated technology that costs relatively little because it sells in the millions worldwide, year after year. In 1989 the Japanese produced an HDTV receiver that cost $60 thousand. Investors and early purchasers, both relatively insensitive to cost, must be found to take a chance on stimulating the mass market in order for the price to come down to the level affordable by the average consumer.

Compared with the costs of stations, cable systems, networks, and programs, each household invests very little in receivers, videotape recorders, cable installation, and the like. However, millions of households in the aggregate invest billions of dollars in home reception facilities, far outweighing the aggregate investment of station and cable system owners. Only in the case of the electronic mass media does the general public share in this way, making a *capital investment* in media enterprises. The consumer pays for the reception facilities, an essential part of the system without which transmission facilities would be useless. The public's financial stake gives it special claims, different from its claims on newspapers and movie theaters.

Mass demand eventually equipped virtually every home with one or more television receivers—originally bought and maintained just to see broadcast programs. This universal availability of television receivers afforded a unique opportunity for exploitation by nonbroadcast media.

One of the principal beneficiaries of this opportunity was cable television. It differs from broadcasting fundamentally, adding significant installation and subscription costs to the consumer's outlay for broadcast receiving equipment. In return, the subscriber gets a wider choice of programs and (usually) a clearer picture. Also, in the case of pay cable the subscriber benefits from having the option of paying extra for especially desired programs that the cable company could not afford on the basis of basic subscription fees and advertising income alone.

Many other innovative services could take advantage of the ready-made electronic screen available in virtually every home—if set owners found such services worth the price of subscription. For example, *teletext* can broadcast written messages and graphics for display on television screens along with regular broadcast television programs. So far, however, teletext has not proved sufficiently attractive to the American mass audience to warrant extensive development.* *Videotex,* a two-way wired version of one-way, over-the-air teletext, proved even less attractive to set owners because it requires payment of line charges and purchase or rental of a special decoder. American promoters finally gave up trying to persuade the general public to display videotex on television receivers, targeting instead personal computers, another kind of electronic screen already available in many homes.

Sources of Funding Aside from the public's investment in receivers, three primary funding sources support the world's broadcasting systems: advertising, government subsidies, and receiver license fees (paid by all who own sets, in addition to subscription fees for cable television where it exists).

Most countries try to ensure that broadcasters will consider the welfare of the public as well as the welfare of their funding sources; still, the one who pays the piper tends to call the tune, leaving broadcast services to some extent subservient to their funders. United States broadcast law requires station licensees to place "the public interest, convenience, and necessity" ahead of purely commercial interests, but in practice the interests of advertisers tend to dominate.

Economic Pluralism Experience has shown that funding from more than one source best prevents undue subservience to any one money supplier. *Economic pluralism* seems to cultivate broadcasting's beneficent potential to the fullest. Pluralism in this context means more than simply pitting many suppliers of program services against

one another. If the same motivation drives all services, they tend merely to imitate one another. Ideally, under a pluralistic system, more than one motive controls the production, selection, and scheduling of programs. When commercial, profit-driven stations and networks compete on a relatively equal footing with nonprofit, public-service stations and networks, the result is diversified programs, satisfying to minority as well as to majority tastes and preferences.

In the United States, public broadcasting offers a noncommercial alternative to ad-supported broadcasting. But this American pluralism suffers from the weakness of its noncommercial component. The lack of consensus as to its goals, the uncertainty of its funding, and the fact that much of its program underwriting revenue comes from the same firms that advertise on commercial television prevent public broadcasting from competing effectively with its commercial counterpart. Commercial broadcasters have the lion's share, not only of financial resources, but also of channel allotments, hours on the air, and audience size. Moreover, commercial broadcasting gains strength from having a single, clear-cut purpose—the goal of making a profit.

The fact that advertising supports most broadcasting in America, even to some extent so-called noncommercial broadcasting, makes the advertising market a key topic of study in this book.

Centripetal Tendency Economic factors drive broadcasting and other electronic mass media toward centralization. This *centripetal tendency* runs counter to public-service considerations that favor localism. However, local resources alone can generate only a limited range of programs, certainly not the high-quality programs needed to match the output of the rival mass media. In consequence, program production and other functions tend to become concentrated at centers where the best facilities and creative talents can be assembled and where major advertisers, agencies, and other business interests have their headquarters.

After radio broadcasting began in the early 1920s, New York–based national networks soon emerged, along with national distributors of syndicated pro-

---

*Teletext has had somewhat more success among Europe's centralized national broadcasting services than among the more fragmented United States services.

grams. When television developed, Hollywood became the main source of top entertainment programs, with New York remaining the primary source of top news and public affairs programs as well as the business center of the industry.

1.7
Part 4 Programs

Whether profit or public-service goals dominate, the success of electronic mass media enterprises hinges on *programs as motivators*. Programs, after all, stimulate the mass purchase and use of sets, without which the system as we know it could not exist. The word "mass" has important implications for programming. Broadcasting must attract extraordinarily large numbers of people, cutting across age, sex, education, social status, and income differences that usually divide people into separate audiences for communication products. Broadcasting attains this breadth of appeal at the cost of reducing most programs to the least-common-denominator level of audience taste.

In reaction to this "massification" effect, the counter-concept of *narrowcasting* emerged—program services too specialized for the mass audience, deliberately tailored for smaller, more selective audiences. A broadcast television station cannot afford such specialization; its success or failure depends on what it puts on its one channel. Cable television, however, with its many channels, seemed an ideal medium for narrowcasting. Cable can afford to devote entire, full-time channels to *thematic* specializations such as weather, financial affairs, children's interests, sports, and the arts. Though the audience for a thematic channel on a cable system may be small, the system has other channels with other appeals. Moreover, the aggregate of even very small audiences tuned to that same channel on thousands of cable systems throughout the nation can amount to a respectable size.

Formats Broadcasting borrowed existing information, entertainment, educational, and persuasive formats, initially contributing little new of its own. It drew upon stage, press, movies, sports, lecture platforms, pulpits, and parlor games (see Exhibit 1–4).

Trying to identify program formats that are unique to broadcasting makes an interesting analytical exercise. Perhaps the several forms of radio and television talk shows come closest to qualifying as true broadcasting inventions. However, broadcasting made its primary original contribution in another way—by scheduling formats already familiar as isolated events into new, convenient, and intriguing *sequences* of events, and delivering that sequence directly into the home. Even though broadcasting may not have contributed much in the way of new content genres or formats, this ability to deliver a continuous, scheduled service especially adapted to the home environment represented a unique achievement among the mass media.

Consumption Rate The continuousness of broadcasting's service created a supply problem never before faced by an information-entertainment medium. Only by invoking what might be called the *parsimony principle* could broadcasters meet the demand. The parsimony principle calls for using program materials as sparingly as possible, repeating them as often as possible, and sharing them as widely as possible. Producers and program suppliers have developed many parsimonious strategies. Producing programs in series, for example, cuts down on production costs. Sharing programs widely by means of networks and syndicated distribution also helps. *Star Trek* used the same characters, sets, and basic situation in each episode, minimizing casting, writing, and production expense; after a three-year network run it went into syndication, playing on individual stations all over the United States and in dozens of foreign countries as well. For many programs, income from foreign distribution forms an important ingredient in the economics of production.

Program Balance When relatively few stations competed for attention, traditional broadcast sched-

EXHIBIT 1–4   Parlor Games Go Public

In the days before mass entertainment, families relied far more than they do now on self-generated group entertainment at home. Reading aloud, group singing, and parlor games were among the popular leisure-time home activities. Going out to the vaudeville theater was a rare treat for some and entirely beyond the reach of most. Then came the gramophone to supplement home-made music and the movie theater as a more accessible form of boxoffice entertainment. Radio and later television, functioning as home media, completed the displacement of traditional family entertainment. They not only took over much of traditional theatrical and musical entertainment, but also even the lowly parlor game. Audience participation games, in imitation of the old-fashioned fireside contests, have always been a popular form of broadcast entertainment. Pictured here is a scene from Scrabble, one of the leading television game shows, MCd at the time of this photograph by Chuck Woolery.

SOURCE: NBC, Inc.

ules usually offered a *comprehensive* service of entertainment, news, information, education, and inspiration. Too few stations existed at first to allow for much program specialization. The ideal of program *balance** emerged, with regulators and most broadcasters agreeing that each station and network should offer something for everyone in its audience. Even though light entertainment usually won the biggest audiences, the ideal of occasionally balancing sheer entertainment with news, information, education, inspiration, and the arts persisted.

However, as the number of stations grew and newer methods of delivery such as cable television emerged, comprehensive service gave way to *generic* (or *thematic*) services, each concentrating on one particular format or content type. Familiar examples include music and talk radio, and video channels devoted exclusively to specific genres such as art, children's programs, music videos, news, religion, teleshopping, and want-ads. Practically all U.S. radio stations have adopted generic formats, as have some television stations.

The national television broadcast networks clung to the ideal of comprehensive programming, but during the 1980s their traditional commitment to serious news and public affairs programs began to erode. Turnovers of ownership, the growth of huge, conglomerate corporations without commitment to the traditional public-service ideals of old-time network broadcasters, competition from cable, and deregulation that relaxed enforcement of public-interest standards all contributed to this decline. Networks cut back on news department budgets, paying close attention to cost cutting. Although they maintained their news programs, the news took on a more popularized form, emphasizing entertainment as well as information. A new hybrid format emerged, called somewhat derisively *infotainment.*

Real-Time Attribute   News programs especially benefit from broadcasting's ability to deliver reports of events in *real time,* simultaneously with

---

**The term *balance* is also used in a more restricted sense, referring to fair presentation of differing viewpoints on controversial issues.*

their occurrence. Timeliness enhanced the fascination of broadcasting's achievement of delivering sequenced programs to the home. All network programs took advantage of this attribute until the development of efficient, high-quality recording made real-time broadcasts optional. Nevertheless, the most-heard and most-watched programs, the top news and sports events, still derive their impact from their immediacy. Satellites enormously enhance this ability to cover events in real time. Cable television introduced a new flexibility by dedicating entire channels to news and public affairs, enabling coverage of ongoing events for hours—even days—on end.

But satellites also tend to weaken the traditional networks, one of whose major strengths was their ability to capitalize on broadcasting's real-time attribute with their extensive news-gathering facilities, which far exceeded the scope of any individual station's resources. Inexpensive satellite relays, however, enable stations to send back their own individualized real-time reports of distant national events even before network news hits the air. For example, numerous stations send local reporters to the national political conventions, covering local angles via satellite for home-town audiences.

In conveying live events such as news happenings and athletic contests, broadcasting shapes what audiences see and hear, influencing their perceptions of reality. The camera's selectivity, the need to compress, and the stress on visual images all tend to distort television reporting of news and public affairs. As an obvious example, televised football differs from pre-television football because it has to conform to artificial restraints on scheduling and timing to answer the needs of broadcasters and advertisers.

1.8
Part 5 Impact

Television's distorting influence is only one of the many areas of concern about the impact of the electronic media. Questions about impact interest politicians, social scientists, religious leaders, ad-

vertisers, concerned parents, and many others. Virtually every special-interest group claims that television has specific effects. Such groups want either to prevent alleged unfavorable effects or to encourage the presumed favorable effects they hope will promote their goals.

Competing Media Among the first to feel the impact of broadcasting were competing media. By adopting the formats of the competition, the broadcasting medium influenced, sometimes with devastating effect, the existing forms of commercial public entertainment, information delivery, and family recreation. In-home entertainment made available by broadcasting completed the destruction of one of its main entertainment predecessors, live vaudeville, which already suffered from movie competition. Radio almost destroyed a flourishing phonograph business, only to revive and enhance it by stimulating interest in music-listening and by supplying the technology for improved sound recording and reproduction.

Newspaper owners feared that radio would similarly devastate their business, but it turned out that broadcasting helped the print medium by alerting people to news events without giving them all the details they could find in the papers. Though the number of competing daily newspapers has fallen drastically, more specialized new publications have flourished. Television also affected the style and format of news publications, encouraging shorter, punchier stories and the use of color printing. The national newspaper *USA Today* strikingly reflects these influences (Exhibit 1–5).

National general-interest magazines found that television pre-empted their audiences, but television also stimulated the growth of smaller, special-interest magazines (illustrating again the tendency toward generic content specialization).

Television news replaced the filmed newsreels that once preceded every feature attraction in movie theaters. Television entertainment even threatened the survival of movies themselves, but the movie industry soon discovered that television created an inexhaustible new market for the old films that had been gathering dust in Hollywood vaults. Moreover,

EXHIBIT 1–5   Sincerest Form of Flattery

The newspaper USA Today *shows television's influence on a rival medium. Departing from traditional newspaper make-up and editorial style,* USA Today *emulates the brevity, quick cutting, bright hues, upbeat tempo, and other features of news as presented on color television. In 1988, the publisher imitated its imitation by spinning off a television clone of the newspaper, called* USA Today: The Television Show, *produced by GTG Entertainment, one of the more prestigious Hollywood production companies. Drawing chiefly on four of the paper's sections—news, money, sports, and "life"—and emphasizing people more than ideas, it seemed like a natural for television. Over 150 stations contracted to run its 30-minute segments weekdays plus a 60-minute weekend segment, despite never having seen a pilot show.*

SOURCE: USA Today.

television was willing to pay for the Hollywood know-how and facilities needed for the production of new entertainment programs tailored especially for the small screen.

Thus broadcasting media profoundly affected competing communication media; some were put out of business, but on the whole its competition tended to encourage survival through adaptation and innovation.

Audience Measurement   Of more lasting and widespread concern, however, has been the impact of broadcasting on its audiences. Research on this impact depends on preliminary findings about *reach:*

EXHIBIT 1–5   Continued

USA Today: The Television Show *hit the air with great fanfare in late 1988, only to fizzle out. Neither critics nor audiences took kindly to this twice-watered down version of the news, dubbed by some as "news for the MTV age." It was branded superficial and dull: "Almost buried in a blizzard of graphics and factual trivia were brief features of a blandness that would make the networks blush . . ." (Morgenstern, 1989: 26). A* New Yorker *magazine cartoon carried the imitation theme forward to its next logical step, a spin-off into still another medium—the motion picture.*

SOURCE: Cartoon from *New Yorker,* 18 Dec. 1988, 39.

How many people and what kinds of people listen to and watch specific programs and services? How much time do people spend looking at and listening to which programs? Ratings research grapples with these questions.

Of course all media need to research such basic coverage questions, but the broadcasting medium introduced new measurement problems. Researchers can easily count physical entities such as the number of newspapers or movie tickets sold. Difficulties arise when they attempt to measure watching and listening. Watching and listening usually take place in private, beyond the range of direct observation by researchers; these activities can be continuous or intermittent; and viewers can switch rapidly from one program source to another.

Each newspaper, magazine, and movie comes as a separate entity, but broadcasts come in a continuous stream. The very size and varied composition of audiences make for still more complications. Ratings firms such as Arbitron and A. C. Nielsen have devised measurement techniques for dealing with these problems of inaccessibility, intangibility, size, and heterogeneity, but their reliability remains controversial even after a half-century of evolution and the development of sophisticated reporting technology.

The dominant role that advertisers play results in fixation on measuring audience size and composition as revealed by set-tuning behavior to the almost total neglect of other aspects of audience response. Such quantitative set-use measurements do not, as broadcasters often claim, give us an index of audience satisfaction or an adequate guide to future program choices. They merely show what audiences tolerated in the past. Size measurements tell nothing about the *intensity* of audience likes and dislikes, nor do they give any guidance for future program decisions, except perhaps to suggest using either more or less of the already familiar program types.

Behavioral Effects If researchers have difficulty in measuring the size and composition of broadcast audiences, they find the medium's specific impacts on the behavior of the people it reaches even more difficult to assess. Yet most of us take impact for granted, agreeing with Marshall McLuhan, an influential media theorist, who called the mass media marketers "so pervasive in their personal, political, economic, aesthetic, psychological, moral, and social consequences that they leave no part of us untouched, unaffected, or unaltered" (McLuhan & Fiore, 1967: 26).

Certain groups have intense interest in knowing how political advertising affects the outcome of elections; how reactions to television sex and violence influence the outlook and behavior of children; how depictions in dramatic presentations shape our perception of minorities and other groups; how the alleged political biases of a medium affect audience attitudes; how the very presence of cameras affects crowd behavior.

Researchers who make a profession of scientifically studying the media point out the impossibility of isolating and tracing the effects of specific images and messages. Effects may be direct or indirect, immediate or delayed, subjective or overt, intended or accidental. Results may be due to, and certainly will be influenced by, many factors other than the output of a particular medium—the personal characteristics of audience members, their social milieu, their other sources of information, and untold numbers of other internal and external influences.

In fact, media theorists tend to reject as far too simplistic the notion of audience members as passive recipients. They dismiss the concept of direct, one-for-one responses to media stimuli. Researchers prefer to think not of cause and effect, but of how people *use* media information, what kinds of *satisfactions* they get from the media, and how their predispositions interact both with the media and with other sources of information.

Nevertheless, whatever the difficulties of media research, the demand for it continues to rise. Policymakers and rulemakers increasingly rely on research guidance in passing laws and writing rules to control the media—all of which assumes, of course, that products of the media do in fact have an effect upon audiences.

1.9
Part 6 Controls

Most controls imposed on the broadcasting medium by government, public opinion, and the industry itself rest on assumptions about effects, both good and bad. All governments take it for granted that they have an obligation to monitor and moderate the social impact of radio and television. People tend to feel that they should have the right to exercise some control because their government authorizes broadcasting to enter their homes and because they themselves buy and maintain receivers and, in many cases, pay subscription fees.

Constitutional Protection Constitutional democracies, however, put limits on government interference with the media. In the United States the First Amendment to the Constitution gives public communication explicit protection from official interference. But not all the media receive the same degree of protection. The press, broadcasting-cable, and common carriers (telephones and the like) each operates under a somewhat different legal regime, and therefore each has somewhat different First Amendment standing. The freedom to print, hundreds of years in the making, enjoys the most extensive protection. Editors have no legal obligation to publish any particular item; they can choose to print or not print according to their own editorial judgments and personal convictions.

Broadcasting, however, involves the use of a limited public resource, a portion of the electromagnetic spectrum, on license from the government. It enters the intimacy of the home, where even the youngest child hears or sees it. As the new domain of broadcasting law emerged, it responded to these special attributes of the medium, imposing an obligation to operate *in the public interest*. This duty involves, for example, avoiding exposing children to indecency and making time available for political candidates; in the past it required (and may again in the future) scheduling discussions of controversial public issues (the fairness doctrine).* Common carriers, on the other hand, have (or at least used to have) nothing to do with the content of the messages they carried, acting only as neutral purveyors. Basic facilities such as telephone networks would be uneconomical to duplicate; therefore they tended to become legally approved monopolies. In exchange for the advantage of not having to face competition, they surrendered control over their rates to government agencies which were empowered to regulate their activities to protect the public interest.

The previously mentioned tendency of technologies to converge brings into question such distinctions among communication systems because the merging of functions makes it difficult to tell where one medium ends and another begins. For example, if a broadcaster delivers news via teletext or a cable system delivers it via videotex, do those "publishing" acts give them the same First Amendment rights as those enjoyed by newspapers? If a common carrier no longer ignores communication content but enhances it, for example by putting it through a computer to give it some more useful format, should that action bring the common carrier under the same regulations as broadcasting?

Cable television occupies a particularly ambiguous position: most cable systems operate much like common carriers, enjoying local monopolies and relying almost exclusively on materials over which they exert no editorial control. Should these facts put them in the same legal basket as common carriers? Or, since they carry broadcast signals and sometimes originate their own programs in the manner of broadcasters, should they become subject to the same legal obligations that the FCC imposes on broadcasters? Congress answered this question when it adopted the 1984 Cable Act, exempting cable television from common-carrier or broadcasting status.

Several arguments have been used to justify withholding some First Amendment rights from broadcasting, differentiating it legally from the press:

▮ Space in the broadcast frequency spectrum falls short of meeting the demand, suggesting that the government should select those applicants for frequencies who seem best qualified to serve the public interest.

▮ In any event, the "public airwaves," like public parks, should be used more for public benefit than for private profit.

▮ Broadcasting enters the privacy of the home, where it becomes highly accessible to children; therefore, it should be subject to more constraints than the less accessible medium of print.

▮ The universality and ubiquity of broadcasting endow it with such power to influence society that

---

*It was called a *doctrine* because the FCC invented it as an aspect of operation "in the public interest." The FCC deleted the doctrine in 1987, but later Congress gave signs of reviving it as an amendment to the Communications Act.

the government needs to monitor it to protect the public interest.

Deregulation   A case can be made for each of these arguments, but those who support *deregulation* find them unconvincing. Deregulation, a powerful movement that peaked during the 1980s, finds support from most broadcasters and cable operators, from the contemporary appointees to the FCC, and from political conservatives generally. Deregulatory thinking dismisses the frequency-shortage argument as a basis for limiting broadcasters' freedom because more than 12,000 broadcast stations and 8,000 cable systems compete for attention. It rejects the "public-airwaves" argument as false and the "home-environment" argument as irrelevant. Deregulatory thinking holds that the public itself should monitor and control the medium's social influence. If, for example, parents object to programs their children watch, they should prevent the children from watching, rather than expecting the government to prevent the media from disseminating the objectionable programs. If the public gets fed up with too many commercials, it will force moderation by tuning to less heavily commercialized stations.

Deregulation implies, among other things, substituting market forces—economic competition and free consumer choice—for regulation by government bureaucrats. Its supporters base their arguments on an economic theory, currently in the ascendancy in Washington, that tends to regard broadcasting and the other media simply as businesses and programs simply as commodities. Deregulation also has political overtones, emphasizing opposition to "big government."

Deregulatory thinking pervades U.S. media policy, and U.S. officials vigorously promote it in foreign countries. Its influence will be repeatedly noted throughout this book, for it affects even technology (arguing, for example, that the marketplace rather than the FCC should set the engineering standards for new technologies such as stereophonic AM radio). It tends to take literally the Constitution's command that "Congress shall make no law . . . abridging the freedom . . . of the press," seeing no First Amendment justification for treating one medium any differently from any other. Deregulators cite the convergence of technologies previously mentioned; the tendency toward blurring the lines between print, wire, and wireless communication proves, they say, that all media should be equally free of government regulation.

Monopoly Prevention   Another First Amendment principle calls for diversification of media ownership. In an economic system based upon free enterprise and market competition, steps need to be taken to keep a few owners from buying up so many outlets that they dominate the marketplace of ideas. Antimonopoly laws ensure diversification of ideas and information. Democratic governments, depending as they do on informed voters, place a high value on public access to as many different sources of information and conflicting points of view as possible.

This goal implies taking steps to assure access to the air by political candidates and by both incumbent officials and "the loyal opposition," as well as to make political information available through news and public affairs programs. Prevention of monopoly, which has both economic and political goals in view, represents one way of promoting such access. Paradoxically, the deregulatory goal of "getting the government off the back" of commercial enterprises has weakened the enforcement of antimonopoly laws, allowing concentration of media ownership in fewer hands. To the extent that such concentration diminishes competition, it works against the deregulatory goal of an open marketplace.

Localism   Monopoly implies absentee ownership and the neglect of local interests in favor of larger, corporate interests. When radio broadcasting began in the United States, one of its most attractive potentials seemed to be its ability to enhance local democracy by giving communities a common forum for discussion of public issues. Idealists in radio's early days thought the new medium would revive the spirit of the traditional New England town meet-

EXHIBIT 1–6 Pleasures & Perils of Public-Access Cable

New York City's Manhattan Cable TV probably has the most active public-access cable channel in the country, on the air 150 hours a week with "an unpredictable hodgepodge of programs—well-produced and innovative one half-hour, grainy and downright boring the next" (Belkin, 1987). Access shows have included a teacher's showing of media projects created by her class; a puppet called Rapid T. Rabbit who lives in the subway; and a weekly tribute to Frank Sinatra.

Access programs do not always consist of fun and games. Manhattan Cable TV is one of more than a score of systems that have carried *Race and Reason,* a series identified with the White Aryan Resistance movement. The Communications Act allows cities to require access channels in their franchises, but forbids cable operators to impose any "editorial control" over such channels (§47 USC 611). This restriction can cause problems for both cities and cable operators when users to whom they both object exercise their legal right to appear on a designated public-access channel.

In Kansas City, MO, for example, the announcement by the Ku Klux Klan that it planned to produce a weekly series punningly titled "Kansas City Cable" on American Cablevision's public-access channel triggered an outpouring of citizen complaints to the City Council and the cable operator. Barred by the Communications Act from requiring the cable company to censor the access channel's content, the City Council voted to delete the channel entirely in mid-1988, to the evident relief of the cable operator. American Cablevision believed that "forcing a private company such as ours to speak (i.e., through the KKK) may be a violation of *the cable operator's* First Amendment rights"; it feared that the presence of KKK members in its studio would endanger its facilities and staff. American Cablevision substituted a hybrid "community programming" channel permitting "Letters to the Editor" type of access, subject to its editorial control.

The city's action raised what one commentator called "an exquisitely vexing" First Amendment issue. Traditionally the courts have held that highly inflammatory minority views have just as much First Amendment protection as comfortable mainstream views. Even the KKK has rights. The American Civil Liberties Union filed a suit early in 1989 alleging that the City Council had violated the KKK's First Amendment rights. A few months later, concluding that it stood little chance of winning the First Amendment argument, the city voted to restore the access channel. The "vexing" problems of First Amendment rights to use electronic mass media versus majority opinion are discussed at length in Section 18.1.

SOURCES: Lisa Belkin, "A Look Behind the Scenes at Public-Access TV," *New York Times,* 13 April 1987, Y19; David A. Kaplan, "Is the Klan Entitled to Public Access?," *New York Times,* 31 July 1988, H 25A; Carol Rothwell, Director of Public Affairs, American Cablevision, personal letter to the author, 31 Jan. 1989; *New York Times,* "Kansas City Restores Cable Outlet to Which the Klan Sought Access," 16 July 1989, 9.

ing, opening new opportunities for grass-roots citizen participation in community affairs. Early cable television enthusiasts thought along the same lines.

Accordingly, in the United States more than in other countries, lawmakers originally saw broadcasting as a localized rather than as a national service. This view drew support from the U.S. federal form of government, under which states jealously guard local and regional prerogatives. Even today, under the Communications Act (dating in its essential philosophy back to 1927), licensing a station involves defining a specific local service area and proposing program offerings attuned to the needs of that area.

In practice, however, economic forces favoring centralization soon challenged localism. Much of the deregulation of the 1980s consisted of abandoning attempts to force localization, letting centripetal tendencies have their way. Networks won release from some of the rules that curbed their influence, station owners no longer had to work so hard at serving their local coverage areas, and absentee owners could buy up more stations than formerly.

Originally, the FCC expected applicants for licenses to have a serious interest in owning a station to serve the public as well as to make a profit. Many licensees took pride in the feeling that their responsibilities as broadcasters gave them a special mission in life. In the deregulated broadcasting culture of the 1980s, however, huge conglomerate corporations trade stations and networks back and forth, losing sight of public-service obligations in their single-minded drive to please stockholders with favorable profit margins.

Cable television enthusiasts originally offered as a selling point the possibility of designating *local-access channels* especially for nonprofit programs presented informally by local groups and individuals. Most cable franchises in the larger cities require the provision of nonprofit channels, known collectively as PEG (public, educational, and government) channels. In some large cities, local access can claim some success in meeting the idealistic goals of localism (see Exhibit 1–6), but, on the whole, deregulation has had the same centripetal effect on the cable television business as it has had on broadcasting.

1.10
Epilogue: Global View

Foreign broadcasting systems serve local needs even less than the American system does. The governments in these countries play a more dominant role, looking at broadcasting from a national rather than a local perspective.

Nationalism Foreign broadcasting systems generally have both a national and a nationalistic orientation. They consist primarily of highly centralized, national transmitter networks, rather than the numerous stand-alone stations licensed to serve local markets favored in the United States. In other countries, regional and, more recently, local or community stations have only gradually emerged, partly in response to insistent demands to serve local needs and partly in response to the widespread success of unauthorized "pirate" stations.*

Most countries impose quotas on imported programs to limit foreign intrusion and to foster domestic production and employment. In Britain, broadcasters voluntarily limit television entertainment imports to 14 percent of their programs, but in some countries official ceilings allow broadcasters to import as much as 60 percent of all programs. In practice, imports sometimes mount to 90 percent (Exhibit 1–7).

Most nations also impose regulations designed to maintain the dominance and purity of the national language (or languages in the case of multilingual countries such as Canada, Belgium, and Switzerland). For example, laws sometimes require dubbing in the national language and meeting standards of language purity. Most countries also impose strict nationality requirements on owners.†

Role of National Resources A nation's size, in terms of both its population and its gross national product, plays a crucial role in determining the extent to which it can mount a national broadcasting service independent of outside program sources. Broadcasting and the other electronic mass media consume so much program material that only large, prosperous nations can muster enough creative talent, production resources, and funding to achieve program autonomy.

None of the smaller Third World countries have such resources, and even highly developed small

---

*Regionalism has been maintained where federal governments preserve regional autonomy, notably in Switzerland and West Germany, and British broadcasting has always catered to the regional interests of Northern Ireland, Scotland, and Wales.

†In the United States, the Communications Act restricts station ownership to U.S. citizens, limiting to a relatively small percentage the amount of stock in a broadcast company that foreigners may own (§47 CFR 310). However, some deregulation supporters oppose citizenship requirements for owners, regarding such limitations as an unnecessary impediment to free trade.

EXHIBIT 1–7   Extent of TV Program Imports

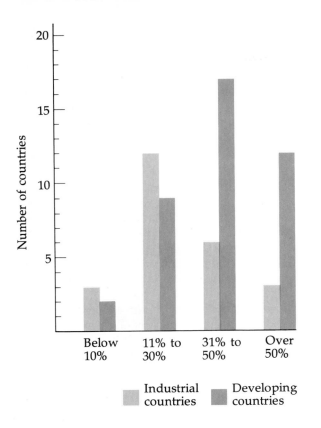

Even most industrialized countries import at least some programs, a few as much as over 50 percent, but developing countries are far more likely to depend on imports. Only five countries fell in the under-10 percent group, with the United States importing the least (2 percent). Ideological and cultural influences as much as economics limited imports in the other four: Japan (6 percent), China, India, and the USSR (all 8 percent). Only three developed countries fall in the over-50 percent group: Singapore (55 percent), Ireland (57 percent), and New Zealand (73 percent). These data predate October 1986; since then significant changes in program export–import levels have occurred because of increased demand for programs to fill cable and satellite channels as well as expanded broadcasting facilities. As an example of countries importing more, both China and the USSR have liberalized their information policies, permitting a higher level of imported programs. New Zealand, on the other hand, has deregulated broadcasting and earmarked receiver license fee income specifically to underwrite increased domestic program production.

SOURCE: Dietrich Berwanger, *Television in the Third World: New Technology and Social Change* (Friedrich Ebert Stiftung, Bonn, West Germany), 1987: 55–56.

countries depend heavily on outside sources. Switzerland, Belgium, and the Scandinavian states produce first-class domestic programs; but to satisfy the demand for program variety and to fill a reasonably long broadcast day, they rely on both program imports and spillover services from neighboring countries (see Exhibit 1–7).

Finances   Worldwide, three basic systems of funding broadcasting occur: government-operated,

public-service, and commercial. *Governments* finance and operate most broadcasting systems, including those of all the Communist regimes and most of the Third World countries, except in Central and South America. The Latin American nations generally adopted the U.S. model of private, *commercial* ownership, later modified to varying degrees by introduction of government-owned services to reach neglected rural areas and to promote national cultures. *Public-service* broadcasting flourishes in parliamentary democracies—Australia, Canada, Japan, New Zealand, Western Europe. Most of these countries have *pluralistic* systems, in which commercial and public-service components operate side by side.

Keeping both government and commercial interests at arm's length, but without necessarily shunning the help of either completely, public-service broadcasting seeks to accomplish goals not likely to be adequately met by commercial services. It tries to serve all citizens equally, giving people in remote rural areas program choices similar to those enjoyed by people in cities. Public-service broadcasting also seeks balanced programming, supplementing light entertainment with programs serving culture, education, public affairs, and minority interests. Commercial broadcasting, in contrast, tends to emphasize the light entertainment that advertisers prefer and to bring an oversupply of services to heavily populated, rich markets and to neglect the thinly populated, poorer markets.

Foreign public-service broadcasting services rely almost universally on *receiver license fees* for a major part of their funding, supplemented in most cases by limited advertising revenue. Those that sell advertising time must usually limit their ad revenue to a relatively small proportion of their budgets, thus avoiding domination by commercial interests. Receiver license fees provide a steady, predictable, relatively neutral source of income, less subject to political pressures than direct government subsidies. Because the public always opposes fee increases, however, politicians never raise fees fast enough to satisfy fully the needs of the broadcasting organizations.

U.S. Influence European public-service broadcasting, often mistakenly regarded disdainfully by American broadcasters simply as *government* broadcasting, consciously strives to resist American influence. Nevertheless, foreign public-service broadcasters buy American programs because they cost so little and are popular with most audiences. American production values and American culture fascinate people nearly everywhere, particularly young people. However, American programs do not necessarily hold the same attractions for government officials and cultural leaders.

Although U.S. syndicated programs dominate the world export market, it does not follow that foreign audiences always prefer U.S. entertainment programs to those produced at home. Once a country gears up professionally, indigenous programs prove more popular than imports. But most countries simply cannot produce enough of their own entertainment to fill all their network and cable system schedules.

United States distributors find an especially ready acceptance with the operators of international cable networks and direct-to-home satellite services, notably those of Europe. Foreign U.S. investments and exported managerial skills also bring American influence to bear. Entrepreneurs, even those in major countries like Britain, France, and West Germany, have difficulty in mounting profitable satellite-to-cable networks on a national basis. The alternative, networks appealing to the whole of Europe or to those parts that share a common language, must surmount conflicting sets of media laws, incompatible technical standards, different copyright and performing rights restrictions, various language and cultural preferences, and erratically drawn coverage areas.

American influence also has grown because the advanced countries have all begun to subscribe in varying degrees to the U.S. deregulatory philosophy of open, competitive markets operating in a minimally regulated environment. The U.S. government actively promotes these goals abroad in order to keep foreign markets open for U.S. programs, communications services, communications hardware, and investments. Deregulation thus has backed the traditional, centralized public-service broadcasters of the European type into a corner. Government after government has begun to question the advisability of protecting these services from the inroads of private entrepreneurs.

The Epilogue of this book returns to these global themes, describing selected foreign systems and foreign reactions to U.S. influence in the world of electronic mass media.

Summary

▌ Broadcasting is a worthwhile subject of study because it interests many different types of specialists and has effects that people want to control for their own or society's benefit.

▌ Differentiating broadcasting from cable television and other communications media matters because regulations differ among the media.

▌ This book treats (in order): history, technology, economics, programs, impact, controls, and a global view of U.S. media compared with those in other countries.

▌ Broadcasting began in the 1920s. Important developments since then include centralization of production, the rise of networks to a dominant place in programming, and the emergence of cable television and satellites.

▌ Technological development has been marked by a process of convergence, assisted especially by satellites, digital signal processing, and computers. Convergence has blurred distinctions among the different telecommunication genres.

▌ Economics drives the broadcasting medium toward centralization of functions; because funding sources tend to control the nature of a service, multiple sources help broaden the program fare.

▌ Programs tend to replicate already existing media formats; program providers increasingly specialize instead of offering diverse program schedules.

▌ The broadcasting medium's ability to attract audiences from competing media has strongly affected those media. Ratings measure audience impact in terms of the program choices they make. These measurements, which play a major role in attracting advertisers, influence the choice of programs to be produced.

▌ First Amendment constraints limit regulation of the media, but hitherto the broadcasting medium has been considered less subject to First Amendment protection than the press. However, the contemporary policy of deregulation tends toward equalizing First Amendment protections. Prevention of monopoly and encouragement of localism have been special regulatory concerns.

▌ Broadcasting in other nations tends to be more nationally oriented and more nationalistic in outlook than in America. Small countries, unable to produce sufficient programs to fill their national channels, find it necessary to import large percentages of their programs.

▌ U.S. programs dominate the international market because of their quantity, their relatively low prices, their production values, and the intense interest American culture elicits in foreign countries. However, well-produced home-grown programs usually outdraw imports.

DEVELOPMENT

PART 1

American broadcasting took a number of decades to develop into the widespread and varied system we know today. The next three chapters trace that evolution: the development of wireless and then radio to 1927 (Chapter 2); the heyday of radio and television for the next half-century (Chapter 3); and the development of competing electronic media services, mainly in the past decade or so (Chapter 4). We consider the inventors who made broadcasting possible, along with the business innovators who made it universal reality, and follow the growth of system and content from the first tentative programs and hookups of the crystal-set era of the 1920s to the cornucopia of electronic media services available in the 1990s.

▌▌▌▌▌ CHAPTER 2

THE RISE OF RADIO

It took a century to introduce photography into general use, the telephone took half a century, radio technology 35 years. That special form of wireless radio called *broadcasting* took only about eight years. The preconditions for its emergence had been evolving for at least a century. Several developments were intertwined: (1) the emergence of social conditions favorable to the development of mass communication (urbanization, better education, more leisure time, and so on), leading to the habit of media consumption; (2) the corresponding growth of industrial and business institutions able to provide consumer goods in quantity (including entertainment and informative media content); and (3) the progress of scientific know-how that made possible new ways of communicating that content.

2.1
Precedents

The habit of mass media consumption had already been cultivated by the popular press, the phonograph, and the motion picture long before broadcasting began. These older media arose from the mechanical inventive tradition of the 19th century and from fundamental social changes brought about by the Industrial Revolution (roughly 1750–1850). For centuries, the primary occupation of the masses of people living in Western countries had been ag-

riculture); but industrial occupations increasingly drew people away from the land until eventually, by the mid-20th century, most people lived and worked in cities.

The concentrations of people in cities became the target of what we now call the "mass media"—those means of communication that use technology to reach large parts of the total population almost simultaneously with the kinds of news and entertainment that ordinary people find attractive, at a price that ordinary people can afford to pay.

The Penny Press Urban concentration, education and rising literacy, and leisure all contributed to changing the print medium from a special amenity provided primarily for the elite to a commonplace product for the masses. The penny press signaled this transformation. After 1833, the New York *Sun* led a new trend toward mass-oriented and mass-produced papers. They sold for a mere penny a copy, first in the thousands and eventually in the hundreds of thousands of copies.

Until that time, newspapers had concentrated on news of commerce, party politics, and other such "serious" subjects. The popular press broadened the range of subjects covered, exploiting news of everyday events, sensational crimes, gossip, human interest stories, and sports—all presented in a breezy, colloquial style that contrasted with the flowery essay style of the past. Popular newspapers widened their appeal by cutting across lines of class, sex, age, political party, and cherished beliefs. By the 1890s some mass-oriented newspapers had circulations of over a million. They helped to create the habit of mass media consumption from which broadcasting would profit in the 1920s.

Vaudeville   Early broadcasting drew heavily from vaudeville, itself a successor to traveling minstrel shows. Immensely popular in the 1880–1920 era, vaudeville featured song-and-dance teams, short plays, Irish tenors, and ethnic comics, and filled established vaudeville theaters in cities large and small. New York had 37 vaudeville houses, Philadelphia 30, and Chicago 22. Hundreds operated in smaller towns across the country. By the turn of the century, vaudeville theaters began showing bits of novelty film as a filler while clearing the house between programs—"an ironic foreshadowing of impending doom" (Nye, 1970: 171). At its peak, the vaudeville circuit sold more tickets than all other kinds of entertainment combined. Then came movies, followed by radio. They could earn more money because they could bring entertainers to national audiences without the cost of transporting troupes and all their baggage, scenery, and musical instruments from town to town. The new media drew on the same vaudeville talent pool. Song-and-patter teams proved especially adaptable to radio. Such famous radio comics as Jack Benny and Fred Allen started in vaudeville. The musical variety shows of network radio and later television had their vaudeville counterparts.

The Phonograph   A late-19th-century invention, the phonograph, helped vaudeville to prepare the public for radio broadcasting. Owning a phonograph accustomed people to investing in a piece of furniture that brought entertainment into the home. By the end of World War I, on the eve of the introduction of broadcasting, some 200 phonograph manufacturers turned out more than two million players each year.

When radio began to develop in the 1920s, phonograph recording still depended on obsolete acoustic methods that were not fundamentally different from those used by Thomas Edison in 1878. Competition from radio broadcasting and the Depression devastated the phonograph industry, and by 1933 it was "practically extinct" (Gelatt, 1977: 265).

Ironically, not long after it drove many phonograph companies out of business, broadcasting began to help them revive. This reversal came about partly as a result of the increased mass appetite for music that radio created, and partly because of improved recording methods made possible by the belated application of radio technology to the phonograph.

Motion Pictures   The cinema evolved side by side with the phonograph. In fact, Edison played a key role in both developments, marketing his "kinetoscope" motion-picture camera in 1889. He modified it slightly in the 1890s to turn it into a peepshow device that enabled viewers, one at a time, to watch brief sequences of pictures in silent motion. Like the phonograph industry, motion pictures had become well established by the time broadcasting began in 1920. The movies catered to a mass audience for information as well as entertainment: newsreels formed an important part of movie theater presentations before television superseded them.

Like the phonograph, motion pictures had something to learn from radio technology—the ability to talk. The need for *synchronized* sound (precise matching of sound and picture) stymied progress toward "talkies." They finally began in earnest in 1928, with several rival sound systems competing for acceptance. One of these had been developed by RCA, the owner of the first national radio network—an example of the many links between broadcasting and motion pictures in the 1920s, long before the advent of television.

2.2
Wire Communication

Although broadcasting benefited from the prior arts of sound recording and the motion picture, its direct technical and industrial antecedents were the telegraph and the telephone—point-to-point rather than mass-oriented communication media. This means that it was electronic technology, rather than the mechanical technology of the early phonograph and the movies that led to the invention of radio and, eventually, to its application to public as well as private communication purposes.

The Land Telegraph   Most people did not feel any urgent need for instant communication beyond the horizon in times of peace until the era of the steam railroad. Then some means of signaling to distant stations became essential for safe and efficient rail operations. To meet this need, the British developed a form of *electrical telegraphy* in the 1820s.* Electrical impulses sent along a wire caused deflections of a pointer in a detecting device at the receiving end. An operator "read" the message by interpreting the movements of the pointer.

An American, Samuel F. B. Morse, after extensive experiments in the 1830s, made significant improvements. His telegraph receiver had the great advantage of automatically recording messages on strips of paper. We still use the term *Morse code* for the system that he and a partner developed for translating the letters of the alphabet into patterns of electrical impulses.

With the help of federal money, in 1844 Morse installed the first operational telegraph line in the United States, linking Washington, DC, and Baltimore. The first message over the forty-mile line suggests the awe the achievement created: "What hath God wrought!"

In most parts of the world, governments still retain the responsibility for operating national telegraphy systems. Congress, however, fearing that the federal Post Office would lose money if the government competed with itself by running the telegraph as well, sold its interest in Morse's line to

---

*The word *telegraphy* ("distant writing") was already in use, referring to the relaying of semaphore (visual) messages through a series of line-of-sight signaling stations. However, today telegraphy and the later term *telephony* refer, respectively, to code and voice communication by wire, unless preceded by the word *wireless* or *radio.*

private investors, retaining only the right of government regulation. By the end of the Civil War, a single company, Western Union, had emerged as the dominant force in the telegraph field.

Submarine Cable   Laying telegraph lines underwater offered a more difficult challenge than overland telegraph. Technological problems and the lack of financial backing frustrated several attempts to lay cable beneath the Atlantic Ocean. Regular transatlantic cable communication began in 1866, and soon Europe and America could exchange information in minutes instead of weeks or months. Accelerated international communication brought profound changes. The first breach had been made in the walls of international isolation, with far-reaching effects on trade, politics, diplomacy, and war.

Submarine cable and telegraphy had an early and lasting association with news. Even before the electric telegraph became available, newspapers had begun to share the costs of news gathering, the first form of media syndication (see Chapter 13). The British news agency Reuters "followed the cable" wherever it led around the globe, establishing one of the first international *news agencies* or *news wire services.* The Associated Press began in New York in the 1840s, and soon other nations followed suit.

Bell's Telephone   Inventors next turned their attention to the transmission of speech itself, eliminating the tedious business of encoding and decoding telegraph messages. Sound, of course, involves much more complex variation of electric current than do the simple "on-off" signals of the telegraph. The problem of the telephone centered on finding a sensitive *transducer,* a modulating device able to convert complex sound energy from one medium (air) to another medium (electric current). Many investigators struggled with this problem and were on the verge of a solution when Alexander Graham Bell filed for the key telephone patent in 1876.

Bell organized his original telephone firm a year later, when he secured a second essential patent. But the inventor and his friends could not raise enough capital to develop the new invention. Control over the patents soon passed to others who went on to develop the company known today as AT&T.

Role of Big Business Rather than spread to ungainly proportions by trying to serve the entire country directly, AT&T adopted a policy of franchising regional operating companies. These firms received the exclusive and permanent right to use the Bell patents. They in turn gave AT&T substantial stock holdings. By the time the Bell patents ran out in 1893–1894, AT&T had controlling interests in the franchise companies. Furthermore, AT&T had developed the *long lines* connecting the central offices of telephone companies with one another. AT&T assured its supremacy in the long-distance field by acquiring a key radio invention, the Audion (Section 2.3), in 1914, making coast-to-coast telephone service possible. With AT&T's 1881 purchase of Western Electric as its manufacturing arm, the whole process of manufacture, installation, and servicing could be kept within the Bell companies.

Thus we see how patent control led to the first great telecommunication monopolies. Western Union, when first offered the fledgling Bell patent in 1877 for a mere $100,000, turned down the chance, regarding telephony as unimportant to its monopoly position. Yet in a few years telephony's expansion had carried AT&T to much greater size and scope than Western Union. Indeed, the telephone firm bought control of its older rival in 1910 and held it until pressured by the government to sell in 1913.

This centralization of control and extensive electronic communication experience allowed AT&T to dominate early radio broadcasting in the 1920s when the company saw broadcasting as a form of telephony (Section 2.8). The need for long-distance relay facilities for network interconnections gave AT&T a continuing role in broadcasting into the 1980s.

During the early 1900s, AT&T's manufacturing arm, Western Electric, ranked as one of the largest industrial concerns in the country. With two other companies, General Electric (GE) and Westinghouse, it largely dictated the direction of the electrical industry and set the tone for the industry's reaction to early wireless communication. GE took an immediate interest in development of the vacuum tube, which would prove crucial to wireless innovation. The company also became a key investor in early radio broadcasting. Its great rival, Westinghouse, owned broadcast stations even before GE, including the pioneer station KDKA (Section 2.7). Westinghouse, GE, and AT&T's Western Electric formed an invincible triumvirate in the fields of electric lighting, power, and transport manufacturing, as well as in communications. Their patent control, economic power, and know-how had a crucial impact on the emergence of wireless and broadcasting.

2.3
Invention of Wireless

The notion that it should somehow be possible to do the job of the telegraph and the telephone without using costly and confining wire connections stimulated the inventive juices of scientists and tinkerers in the last quarter of the 19th century.

Conflicting Claims Inventors in many countries claimed to have been the first to solve the problem of wireless transmission. Most claimants had common access to critically important scientific knowledge about electromagnetic energy that had recently appeared in documents published by two physicists: (1) an 1873 theoretical paper by James Clerk Maxwell, predicting the existence of invisible radiant energy similar to light; and (2) the report of a laboratory experiment by Heinrich Hertz, in which he proved Maxwell's theory by generating and detecting radio energy and measuring its wavelength.

Hertz's 1888 paper *Electromagnetic Waves and Their Reflection* led directly to the invention of radio within a few years of its publication. In recognition of the importance of his contribution, his name, abbreviated Hz, with the meaning "one cycle per second," has been adopted internationally as the standard way to express the frequency of radio waves.

But Hertz sought to verify a scientific theory, not to invent a method of communication. He failed to realize the practical implications of his experiments.

Marconi's "Releasing Touch" It remained for Guglielmo Marconi—more an inventor than a scientist—to supply the "right releasing touch," in the words of a Supreme Court justice (US, 1942: 65). Stimulated by Hertz's paper, the young Marconi experimented with equipment similar to Hertz's, first indoors and then on the grounds of his father's estate in Italy. Endless experiments with different shapes, sizes, and types of antennas, ground systems and other components gradually improved the performance of his pioneering wireless system. Fortunately, Marconi had the leisure for experimentation and the money for equipment. Equally important, he had access through his family to high official and business circles.

As soon as Marconi had convinced himself that wireless was more than a laboratory toy, he offered it to the Italian government, only to be rebuffed. His mother came from the Jameson family, well-known British whiskey distillers. She arranged introductions to important English postal and military officials, the most likely customers in Britain for the invention. Marconi, by then 22, went to London and registered his patent in 1896. In 1897 he launched his own company, with the help of the Jameson family, to manufacture wireless equipment and to offer wireless telegraphic services to the public.

To a remarkable degree Marconi combined the genius of the inventor with that of the business innovator. As an inventor he persisted tirelessly, never discouraged, even by hundreds of failed attempts at solving a problem. As a business manager he had a flair for effective public relations. In the early years of the century, he repeatedly staged dramatic and convincing demonstrations to prove the usefulness of wireless (Exhibit 2–1). In 1909, Marconi shared the Nobel prize in physics with Germany's Ferdinand Braun for achievements in wireless telegraphy.

Among Marconi's business ventures, the U.S. branch of his company, known as American Marconi, had a decisive influence on the development

EXHIBIT 2–1 Guglielmo Marconi (1874–1937)

In a 1902 photo, the inventor examines the paper tape bearing a radiographic message in Morse code. Though radio equipment still remained very crude, well-developed wire telegraphy equipment could be readily adapted to record wireless messages. Seated is George Kemp, Marconi's most trusted engineering assistant.

SOURCE: Courtesy Smithsonian Institution, Washington, DC.

of broadcasting in America. Founded in 1899, American Marconi finally began to realize substantial profits in 1913 with its virtual monopoly on U.S. wireless communication: it owned 17 land stations and 400 shipboard stations. All these facilities used a wireless extension of the telegraph principle—point-to-point communication between ships and shore stations, between ships at sea, and between countries.

Technical Advances For some 20 years, radio waves could be transmitted only in short bursts, suitable for radio telegraphy but not for speech. The *vacuum tube oscillator* finally provided a *continuous* signal effective for transmission of speech.

Another key problem concerned *detection,* or sensing, of incoming signals. Marconi and later inventors worked on a variety of approaches. In 1904, Marconi obtained a U.S. *tuner* patent that enabled his transmitters to restrict their radiation to a limited group of frequencies. Receivers could then select, or tune to, the desired frequencies, excluding simultaneous signals present in other parts of the spectrum.

Early equipment also lacked means of signal amplification. The solution to the problems of signal generation, detection, and amplification came with the invention of an improved *vacuum tube,* which made radio broadcasting possible. For that reason, its inventor, Lee de Forest, felt justified in titling his autobiography *Father of Radio* (1950).

De Forest's Audion   After receiving a Yale Ph.D. in 1899, de Forest worked first as an engineer but soon began to devote all his time to developing his own inventions. Following the leads of Edison's electric light in 1883 and Marconi researcher Ambrose Fleming's vacuum tube patent of 1904, he experimented with the idea of creating a radio detector by using a glowing filament to heat gas within a glass enclosure. Edison and Fleming had both patented devices based upon the then-unexplained fact that an electric current would flow between the hot filament of an electric lamp and a nearby metal plate inside the lamp. Because such lamps or tubes had two elements, the filament and the plate, they were called *diodes.*

De Forest made the crucial improvement by adding a third element to the tube, creating a *triode.* He positioned the new element, the *grid,* between the filament and the plate. A small voltage applied to the grid could control with great precision the flow of electrons from filament to plate. Thus a weak signal could be amplified. De Forest first used the triode, or *Audion,* as one of his associates dubbed it, in 1906.

Development of the Audion and the new circuits to go with it took more than a dozen years. Its first practical application improved not radio, but telephony. In 1913, AT&T purchased telephone rights for vacuum tube repeaters (amplifiers in telephone lines) from de Forest, making the first long-distance service possible two years later.

2.4
Early Wireless Services

During its first two decades, wireless as a business made its money from supplying *point-to-point* and *point-to-multipoint* services. Wireless manufacturing was limited to the specialized needs of the few communications service companies. The mass market for millions of broadcast receivers and thousands of broadcast transmitters lay in the future. Overland wireless services had no appeal because of existing telephone and telegraph lines.

Maritime Services   Naturally, the naval powers of the world took an immediate interest in military applications of wireless. Wireless helped in a maritime disaster as early as 1898. Both the British and American navies began experimenting with ship installations in 1899. The Japanese victory in the Russo-Japanese War in 1904–1905 is ascribed at least in part to the superiority of Japanese Marconi-supplied equipment to that used by the Russian Navy.

Commercial ships at sea became early customers for radio communication. Radio let them communicate with one another over long distances and with coastal stations far beyond the horizon. In 1909, when the S.S. *Republic* foundered off New York, wireless-alerted rescue ships saved all the passengers. Each year the number of dramatic rescues increased (see Exhibit 2–2).

Transoceanic Wireless   Long-distance radio communication across oceans held commercial promise as an alternative to expensive submarine telegraph cables, but because of technical limitations this radio service did not become strongly competitive until the 1920s. In the meantime, the Marconi company, which dominated the transatlantic wireless business, built several high-power coastal

EXHIBIT 2–2   The Titanic Disaster: April 1912

A luxury liner advertised as unsinkable, the *Titanic,* struck an iceberg and sank in the Atlantic on her maiden voyage from Britain to the United States in April 1912. One heroic Marconi radio operator stayed at his post and went down with the ship, although the second operator survived. Some 1,500 people died—among them some of the most famous names in the worlds of art, science, finance, and diplomacy—partially because each nearby vessel, unlike the *Titanic,* had but one radio operator (all that was then required), who had already turned in for the night. Only by chance did the operator on a ship some 50 miles distant hear distress calls from the *Titanic.* It steamed full speed to the disaster site, rescuing about 700 survivors.

The fact that for days radiotelegraphy maintained the world's only thread of contact with the survivors aboard the rescue liner *Carpathia* as it steamed toward New York brought the new medium of wireless to public attention as nothing else had done. Subsequent British and American inquiries revealed that a more sensible use of wireless (such as a 24-hour radio watch) could have decreased the loss of life. Because of such findings, the *Titanic* disaster influenced the worldwide adoption of stringent laws governing shipboard wireless stations. The *Titanic* tragedy also set a precedent for regarding the radio business as having a special public responsibility. This concept carried over into broadcasting legislation a quarter of a century later.

SOURCE: UPI/Bettmann Archive.

spark-transmitter stations in the United States and Canada prior to the outbreak of World War I in 1914.

In 1917, GE installed a 200-kilowatt *alternator* in its New Brunswick, NJ, facility. The alternator, a huge and costly machine, put out a powerful very low frequency (VLF) signal at about 20 kHz. It represented a major improvement in long-distance radio communication. During the 1920s, vacuum tube transmitters displaced alternators. This enabled the development of the short-wave (high-frequency) portion of the spectrum, which turned out to be much more efficient than the lower frequencies that

had previously been used for long-distance communication. A sharp rise in transatlantic radio traffic followed.

Wireless in World War I   When direct American participation in the war began in April 1917, the U.S. Navy took over all wireless stations in the country, commercial and amateur alike, and either dismantled them or ran them as part of the navy's own training and operational programs. The navy already had 35 shore stations. The Army Signal Corps also used radio, as did the Air Service. Some 10,000 soldiers and sailors received training in wireless.

After the war, they helped popularize the new medium, forming part of the cadre of amateur enthusiasts, laboratory technicians, and electronics manufacturing employees. They constituted a ready-made audience for the first broadcasting services.

In order to mobilize the total wireless resources of the country for war, the navy decreed a moratorium on patent lawsuits over radio inventions. Manufacturers agreed to pool their patents, making them available to one another without risk of infringement suits. The war brought about a transition. Previously, the wireless business had been dominated mainly by inventor-entrepreneurs, struggling to market their discoveries while feverishly experimenting on new ones. After the war, big business took over. AT&T had added wireless rights to its original purchase of telephone rights to de Forest's Audion. GE had the powerful alternator patents and the ability to mass-produce vacuum tubes. Westinghouse, also a producer of vacuum tubes, looked for new ways of capitalizing on wireless.

2.5
Radiotelephony Experiments

All the wireless services we have discussed so far used *radiotelegraphy,* not voice transmissions. Throughout this early period, however, eager experimenters sought the key to *radiotelephony,* the essential precursor of broadcasting.

Fessenden's 1906 "Broadcast" Reginald Fessenden made the first known radiotelephone transmission, resembling what we now call a broadcast, in 1906. Using an ordinary telephone microphone and an alternator to generate radio energy, Fessenden made his historic transmission on Christmas Eve from Brant Rock, on the Massachusetts coast south of Boston (Exhibit 2–3). Fessenden himself played a violin, sang, and read from the Bible. He also transmitted the sound of a phonograph recording. Ship wireless operators heard the transmission far out at sea, amazed to hear actual voices and music in earphones that up to then had brought them only static and the harsh staccato of Morse code.

Fessenden (center) stands with some of his associates in front of the building where he made the historic 1906 broadcast. The column in the background is the base of his antenna.

SOURCE: Courtesy Smithsonian Institution, Washington, DC.

EXHIBIT 2–4 Lee de Forest (1873–1961)

The inventor in 1907 with a transmitter of the type used in his famous 1907 broadcast, along with a shipboard receiver of the type that picked up the transmission.

SOURCES: Courtesy Smithsonian Institution, Washington, DC, and Culver Pictures.

Fessenden's historic transmission led a long string of demonstrations that culminated in the start of regular broadcasting services in 1920.

De Forest's Experiments Lee de Forest, the prolific inventor who patented the Audion, also felt the challenge of radiotelephony. A lover of fine music, he naturally turned toward radiotelephony. In 1907, hard on the heels of Fessenden, de Forest made experimental radiotelephone transmissions from a building in downtown New York City (Exhibit 2–4).

By 1916, de Forest had begun using his Audion as an oscillator to generate radio-frequency energy. In doing so, he opted for electronic means of generation rather than the mechanical means of the alternator. He set up an experimental transmitter that year in his Bronx home and began transmitting phonograph recordings and announcements. He even aired election returns in November 1916, anticipating by four years the opening broadcast of KDKA. Many others also made radiotelephone transmissions at university laboratories and in private research facilities during the early years of the century.

2.6
Government Monopoly: The Road Not Taken

During World War I, the military importance of radio, still in its prebroadcast phase, raised the question as to whether the government's control should be made a permanent monopoly. World War I ended in November 1918, yet the navy did not relinquish control of radio facilities until early in 1920. The critical decisions made during this 18-month period profoundly affected the future of broadcasting in America.

The Navy's Claims Was radio too vital to entrust to private hands? The navy thought so. In fact, the navy had always asserted jurisdiction over radio as a natural right, assuming that it was destined to remain primarily a marine service. The navy supported a bill introduced in the House of Representatives late in 1918 that proposed, in effect, to make radio a permanent government monopoly. Despite strong arguments from navy brass at the hearings, the bill failed to pass a committee vote.

Restoration of private ownership in 1920, however, meant returning most commercial wireless communication facilities in the United States to a foreign company, American Marconi. Moreover, that company seemed about to capture exclusive rights to use an important American invention, GE's alternator, which had so greatly improved transoceanic radiotelegraphy during the war. Disturbed at the prospect of American Marconi consolidating its U.S monopoly by capturing the exclusive rights to the alternator, the navy strongly opposed the deal. British Marconi, the parent of the American subsidiary, found itself caught in a squeeze play. With tacit government approval, the board chairperson of GE, Owen D. Young, negotiated the sale of American Marconi stock to American companies.

RCA Founded British Marconi agreed to sell its American subsidiary to GE, which thereupon created a new subsidiary in the fall of 1919 to carry on American Marconi's extensive wireless telegraphy business—the Radio Corporation of America (RCA). Under RCA's charter, all its officers had to be Americans and 80 percent of its stock had to be in American hands.

RCA took over American Marconi's assets on November 20, 1919. Eventually RCA's name became intimately linked with broadcasting, but in 1919 its founders had no plans to enter that field.

Westinghouse and AT&T joined GE as investors in the new corporation. AT&T sold its interest in 1923, but RCA remained under GE and Westinghouse control until 1932, when an antitrust suit forced

them to sell their stock, making RCA an independent corporation.

David Sarnoff, who would play the key RCA leadership role, had started with American Marconi as a radio code clerk and became assistant traffic manager of the company's radiotelegraphy business. When RCA took over in 1919, he stayed on with the new firm and was promoted to commercial manager. He helped to convert the company from a collection of small radiotelegraph firms into a major corporation presiding over numerous subsidiary companies. In 1930, Sarnoff became president of the company, and in 1947 chairperson of the board, finally retiring in 1969. As *Time* said in its 1971 obituary, his was "one of the last great autocracies in U.S. industry."

RCA and its parent companies each held important radio patents, yet each found itself blocked by patents held by the others. In the 1919–1923 period, AT&T, GE, Westinghouse, RCA, and other minor players worked out a series of *cross-licensing agreements,* modeled after the navy-run patent pool of World War I. These allowed the signatory companies to use one another's patents and to carve up the market for radio service and equipment. Within a few years, however, these carefully worked out plans fell into utter confusion because of the astonishingly rapid growth of a brand-new use for radiotelephony—broadcasting.

2.7
The "First" Broadcast Station

Amateur Beginnings In 1920, Dr. Frank Conrad, an engineer with Westinghouse in Pittsburgh, operated an amateur radiotelephone station, 8XK, in connection with experimental work at the factory (Exhibit 2–5). Conrad fell into the habit of transmitting recorded music, sports results, and bits of talk in response to requests from other amateurs. These informal "programs" built up so much interest that they began to be mentioned in newspapers. None of this was unusual—similar amateur transmissions had been made by others elsewhere around the world. What made Conrad's 8XK transmissions

EXHIBIT 2–5   Conrad's 8XK and Its Successor, KDKA

Frank Conrad's transmitter (left) typified the improvised setups used by wireless inventors and experimenters. It contrasts with the first KDKA transmitter facilities (right), with which the Harding-Cox election returns were broadcast on November 2, 1920.

SOURCE: Courtesy Westinghouse Broadcasting Co., Pittsburgh, PA.

different was that they set a unique chain of events in motion.

Horne's department store in Pittsburgh, noting the growing public interest in wireless, sensed that the general public might be willing to buy receiving sets to pick up Conrad's broadcasts. Until then, wireless had been mainly the domain of engineers and technical amateurs. Horne's installed a demonstration receiver in the store and ran a box in their regular newspaper display advertisement of September 22, 1920: "Air Concert 'Picked Up' by Radio Here . . . Amateur Wireless Sets made by the maker of the Set which is in operation in our store, are on sale here $10.00 up."

Opening of KDKA Westinghouse executives saw the possibility of a novel merchandising tie-up: it could manufacture radio receivers and create a demand for the new product by regularly transmitting programs for the general public. Accordingly, Westinghouse ordered conversion of a radiotelegraph transmitter for radiotelephony. It went on the air as station KDKA from an improvised studio at the Westinghouse factory in East Pittsburgh on November 2, 1920.

KDKA's opening coincided with the presidential election of 1920, so the maiden broadcast took advantage of public interest in voting results. This first KDKA program consisted of news about the Harding–Cox election returns, fed to the station by telephone from a newspaper office, interspersed with phonograph and live banjo music. After the election, KDKA began a regular one-hour-per-evening broadcast schedule of music and talk.

The First Listeners Broadcasting would have developed much more slowly had it not been for a ready-made audience of thousands of amateur set builders who created demand for a type of radio service never before supplied as a business—entertainment. In order to appreciate the fascination of the 8XK and early KDKA transmissions for listeners of the day, we have to remember that previously, with rare exceptions, the only signals on the air had been in the monotonous drone of Morse code. To hear music and the human voice instead was a startling and thrilling experience for listeners.

The audience quickly expanded beyond the original nucleus of amateurs. Many enthusiasts built inexpensive homemade crystal sets.* Moreover, the experience of listening in created an insatiable public appetite for receiver improvements: first (after 1922) a detector vacuum tube, then another tube for an amplifier, then more tubes for a superheterodyne circuit, then a loudspeaker. Manufacturers could not keep up with demand.

KDKA's Success Unhampered by competing signals, KDKA's sky wave (Section 5.7) could be picked up at great distances. Newspapers all over the country and even in Canada printed the station's program schedule. To assist the transmission of DX (long-distance—meaning almost any station in another town) to listeners, local stations often observed a "silent night" once a week so as not to interfere with incoming signals from more distant stations.

In its first year of operation, KDKA pioneered many types of programs that later became standard radio fare: orchestra music, church services, public-service announcements, political addresses, sports events, dramas, and market reports. But KDKA lacked one now-familiar type of broadcast material—*commercials.* Westinghouse did not sell advertising, bearing the entire expense in order to promote sales of its own products. Manufacturers took it for granted that each firm that wanted to promote its wares over the air would open its own station.

KDKA meets five criteria that qualify it as the *oldest U.S. station still in operation,* despite many claims based on earlier experiments, demonstrations, and temporary operations. KDKA (1) used radio waves (2) to send out noncoded signals (3) in a continuous, scheduled program service (4) intended for the general public, and (5) was licensed by the government to provide such a service (Baudino & Kittross, 1977).*

Competition Begins Westinghouse did not have the field to itself for very long. Broadcast station operations had strong appeal for department stores, newspapers, educational institutions, churches, and electrical equipment supply dealers. Though the number of stations increased slowly in 1920, with 30 licenses issued by the end of the year, in the spring of 1922 the new industry gathered momentum. In that year alone, 100,000 receivers were sold. By May more than 200 stations had been licensed, and the upward trend continued the next year, with the number reaching 576 early in 1923.

Among those early stations, however, mortality ran high. Would-be broadcasters hastened to get in on the ground floor of—they knew not quite what. Inadequately backed stations soon fell by the wayside. Educational stations in particular lost out in this process of elimination.

---

*A homemade set consisted at the minimum of a hand-wound coil (a round Quaker Oats box was a favorite form on which to wind the coil) with a slide to make contact at various points along the coil as a means of tuning, a crystal, and a pair of earphones. A simple length of wire strung outdoors acted as an antenna.

---

*No *broadcasting* licenses as such existed in 1920. KDKA received a license equivalent to the ones issued to commercial shore stations that exchanged radiotelegraph messages with ships under the Radio Act of 1912 (Section 2.10).

2.8
Emergence of an Industry

No such problems of money or managerial support bothered the two leading New York stations—WJZ, flagship station of the Radio Group (GE, Westinghouse, and RCA), and WEAF, flagship of the Telephone Group (AT&T and Western Electric). They represented two opposing philosophies of broadcasting.

Rival Station Approaches Westinghouse opened WJZ in October 1921. As a manufacturing company member of the Radio Group, Westinghouse first saw WJZ as a way to stimulate interest in its own products. Recognizing that attractive programming motivated people to buy receivers, WJZ from the start assumed responsibility for producing programs.

AT&T's WEAF went on the air August 16, 1922. The company spared no expense. As the country's leading communication firm, AT&T gave WEAF every technical advantage, but explained that it would "furnish *no programs whatsoever* over that station" (Dept. of Commerce, 1922: 7, italics supplied). The telephone company thought of the broadcasting medium as a common carrier, merely a new form of telephony. In a 1922 press release about WEAF, AT&T emphasized the point:

> Just as the company leases its long distance wire facilities for the use of newspapers, banks, and other concerns, so it will lease its radio telephone facilities and will not provide the matter which is sent out from this station (quoted in Banning, 1946: 68).

It soon became clear, however, that the idea of filling the schedule entirely with leased time simply would not work. Advertisers had no idea how to fill their time with program material capable of attracting listeners. The telephone company therefore found itself forced into show business after all—a decidedly uncomfortable role for a regulated monopoly that was extremely sensitive about maintaining a serious and dignified public image.

Thus the two groups started with opposing theories about the way broadcasting should work. In

the end, it turned out that each group was partly right. The Radio Group idea that each company would own a separate station devoted exclusively to promoting that owner's goods was not practicable. The Telephone Group correctly foresaw that the number of stations would have to be limited— that each would have to be used by many different advertisers. It miscalculated, however, in placing the primary emphasis on message senders rather than on the interest of the general public, whose good will (and ears) had to be earned. In this matter, the Radio Group's acceptance of responsibility for providing a program service prevailed. It took about four years for these conflicting ideas to sort themselves out.

"Toll" Broadcasting WEAF called advertiser-leased time "toll" broadcasting. It first leased facilities for a toll broadcast on August 28, 1922. A Long Island real-estate firm paid a $50 toll for ten minutes in which to describe the advantages of living in Hawthorne Court, an apartment complex in the Jackson Heights section of New York City.

True to the telephone company's concept, WEAF at first allowed advertisers to fill all their time with their own sales message. The idea that advertising would occupy only occasional announcements in programs consisting mostly of entertainment came later.

AT&T thought in terms of *institutional* advertising. Nothing so crass as price could be mentioned. In 1923 the first weekly advertiser appeared on WEAF, sponsoring a musical group it called "The Browning King Orchestra"—a handy way to ensure frequent mention of the sponsor's name. The fact that Browning King sold clothing, however, was never mentioned.

"Chain" Broadcasting AT&T interpreted the cross-licensing agreements as giving it the right to prevent other broadcasters from connecting broadcast equipment to its telephone lines. WEAF soon began to capitalize on this advantage.

In 1923, networking began, with the first permanent station interconnection between WEAF and WMAF (South Dartmouth, MA), the latter owned by a rich eccentric who operated WMAF for his own amusement. He persuaded WEAF to feed him both toll (commercial) and nontoll (sustaining) programs, paying a fee for the latter and broadcasting the commercial programs without additional cost to the advertisers.

AT&T gradually added to its "chain" (network) of stations. In October 1924, it set up a temporary coast-to-coast chain of 22 stations to carry a speech by President Coolidge. The regular WEAF network at this time, however, consisted of only six stations, to which WEAF fed three hours of programming a day. Regular AT&T telephone lines linked the stations together. But by 1926 the telephone company began setting aside special circuits for the exclusive use of its radio network.

Refused network interconnection by AT&T, the Radio Group's station turned to the telegraph lines of Western Union, but telegraph lines provide too narrow a band of frequencies for satisfactory broadcast use. Despite these difficulties, in 1923 WJZ opened a station in Washington, DC, and by 1925 it had succeeded in organizing a network of 14 stations.

New Cross-Licensing Agreements The growing market for broadcasting equipment, especially radio receivers, upset the delicate balance of commercial interests that the RCA cross-licensing agreements had devised. Those agreements covered only point-to-point wireless and did not account for broadcasting. Thus there were no rules among the patent partners for manufacture of broadcast transmitters and receivers. "The public appetite for sets was insatiable and not to be filled for years. Queues formed before stores that had any sets or parts. Dealers were a year in catching up on orders" (Lessing, 1969: 111). A federal suit alleging that the patent pool violated antitrust laws (because pool members tried to control manufacture and sale of all radio equipment) added urgency to the need for change. By 1926, AT&T concluded that its original concept of broadcasting as a branch of telephony had been a mistake.

Accordingly, the signatories of the cross-licensing agreements redistributed and redefined the parties'

rights to use their commonly owned patents and to engage in the various aspects of the radio business. Briefly summarized, AT&T kept the rights to two-way telephony but sold WEAF and its other broadcasting assets to the Radio Group in 1926 for $1 million, also agreeing not to manufacture radio receivers. RCA agreed to rent all network relays from AT&T. It would be difficult to overestimate the significance of this 1926 agreement to the future of broadcasting in America. As long as the two groups of major communications companies fought about fundamental policies, broadcasting's economic future remained uncertain. The 1926 agreements removed that uncertainty.

2.9
Network Evolution

A few months after the 1926 settlement, the Radio Group, under Owen Young and David Sarnoff's leadership, created a new subsidiary, the National Broadcasting Company (NBC). NBC thus became the first company organized solely and specifically to operate a broadcasting *network*. Its $4^{1}/_{2}$ hour coast-to-coast inaugural broadcast took place on November 15, 1926. The 25 stations in the network reached an estimated five million listeners. Not until after 1928, however, did coast-to-coast network operations begin on a regular basis.

Starting with the new year in 1927, RCA divided NBC into two semiautonomous networks, the Blue and the Red. WJZ (later to become WABC) and the old Radio Group network formed the nucleus of the Blue; WEAF (later to become WNBC) and the old Telephone Group network formed the nucleus of the Red. This dual network arrangement arose because NBC now had duplicate outlets in New York and other major cities. By tying up two of the best stations in major cities, and by playing one network off against the other, NBC gained a significant advantage over the rival networks that had begun to develop.

In 1927, soon after NBC began, an independent talent-booking agent, looking for an alternative to NBC as an outlet for his performers, started a rival

EXHIBIT 2–6 Sarnoff and Paley

Both of the network broadcasting pioneers came from immigrant Russian families, but there the similarity ceases. Sarnoff (left) rose from the direst poverty, a self-educated and self-made man. In contrast, Paley (right) had every advantage of money and social position. After earning a degree from the Wharton School of Business at the University of Pennsylvania in 1922, he joined his father's prosperous cigar company.

The differences between Sarnoff and Paley extended to their personalities and special skills. Sarnoff was "an engineer turned businessman, ill at ease with the hucksterism that he had wrought, and he did not condescend to sell, but Bill Paley loved to sell. CBS was Paley and he sold it as he sold himself" (Halberstam, 1979: 27).

Sarnoff had been introduced to radio by way of hard work at the telegraph key for American Marconi, Paley by way of leisurely DX listening: "As a radio fan in Philadelphia, I often sat up all night, glued to my set, listening and marveling at the voices and music which came into my ears from distant places," he recalled (Paley, 1979: 32).

Paley's introduction to the business of radio came through sponsoring of programs. After becoming advertising manager of his father's cigar company in 1925, he experimented with ads on WCAU in Philadelphia. Impressed with the results, he explored getting into the radio business and late in 1928 took over the struggling CBS network.

Both men, shown here about 1930, were highly competitive and pitted their companies against each other for 40 years before Sarnoff's retirement in 1969.

SOURCES: Sarnoff, courtesy RCA; Paley, courtesy CBS.

network. It went through rapid changes in owner-ship, picking up along the way the name Columbia Phonograph Broadcasting System as a result of an investment by a record company. The latter soon withdrew, but left behind the right to use the Columbia name. The network's future remained uncertain until September 1928, when William S. Paley purchased the "patchwork, money-losing little company," as he later described it. He had become interested in radio as the advertising manager for his father's Philadelphia cigar business. When he took over, CBS had only 22 affiliates. Paley quickly turned the failing network around with a new affiliation contract. In his autobiography a half-century later he recalled:

> I proposed the concept of free sustaining service . . . I would guarantee not ten but twenty hours of programming per week, pay the stations $50 an hour for the commercial hours used, but with a new proviso. The network would not pay the stations for the first five hours of commercial programming time . . . to allow for the possibility of more business to come, the network was to receive an option on additional time.
>
> And for the first time, we were to have exclusive rights for network broadcasting through the affiliate. That meant the local station could not use its facilities for any other broadcasting network. I added one more innovation which helped our cause: local stations would have to identify our programs with the CBS name (Paley, 1979: 42).

These Paley innovations became standard practice in network contracts. Paley also simplified the firm's name to Columbia Broadcasting System (the corporate name was later further simplified to CBS, Inc.) and bought a New York outlet, now WCBS, as the network flagship station. For the next several years, CBS never faltered, and Paley eventually rivaled Sarnoff as the leading broadcast executive (see Exhibit 2–6).

By 1928, under the pressure of rising operating costs and advertiser interest, advertising on radio became more acceptable and much more common. Because most stations had not yet developed the needed programming and production skills, advertising agencies took over the programming role, introducing the idea of program *sponsorship*. Spon-sors did more than simply advertise—they also brought to the networks the shows that served as vehicles for the advertising messages. Advertising agencies thus became program producers, and during the height of network radio's popularity, they controlled most major entertainment shows on behalf of their advertiser clients.

The agencies evaded early network rules against frequent mention of sponsors by tacking trade names to performers' names. Audiences of the late 1920s heard "The Cliquot Club Eskimos," "The A&P Gypsies," "The Ipana Troubadours," and so on. An opening billboard announcement from this period manages to add four indirect product mentions to the permissible single direct mention of sponsor and product name:

> Relax and smile, for Goldy and Dusty, the Gold Dust Twins are *here* to send their songs *there,* and "brighten the corner where you are." The Gold Dust Corporation, manufacturer of Gold Dust Powder, engages the facilities of station WEAF, New York . . . so that listeners-in may have the opportunity to chuckle and laugh with Goldy and Dusty. Let those Gold Dust Twins into your hearts and homes tonight, and you'll never regret it, for they *do* brighten the dull spots (quoted in Banning, 1946: 262).

Anyone not already aware of the product could hardly guess that the commercial refers to laundry soap powder.

2.10 Government Regulation

One final foundation block remained to complete the story of broadcasting's emergence—the passage of national legislation capable of imposing order on the new medium.

Wire Regulation The federal government's decision to return radio to private control after World War I did not mean abandonment of government oversight. Since the beginning of telegraphy, governments throughout the world had recognized the need for both national and international regulation to ensure fair and efficient operation of telecommunication systems. In 1865, 25 European countries drew up the International Telegraphic Convention, precursor of the International Telecommunication Union, which now provides a cooperative world forum to regulate technical aspects of wire and wireless communication. Thus prior experience in the regulation of the wire services set a pattern for radio regulation.

Maritime Wireless Regulation The first international conference specifically concerned with wireless communication took place in Berlin in 1903, only six years after Marconi's first patent. It dealt mainly with the Marconi company's refusal to exchange messages with rival maritime wireless systems. The conference agreed that humanitarian considerations had to take precedence over commercial rivalries in maritime emergencies. Three years later, at the Berlin Convention of 1906, nations agreed to equip ships with suitable wireless gear and to exchange SOS messages freely among different commercial systems.*

Finally, prodded by the terrible lesson of the 1912 *Titanic* disaster (see Exhibit 2–2), Congress confirmed the 1906 convention rules by modifying a 1910 wireless act requiring radio apparatus and operators on most ships at sea. A few weeks later, the Radio Act of 1912, the first comprehensive U.S. *radio* (not broadcasting) legislation, called for federal licensing of all land transmitters. The 1912 act remained in force until 1927—throughout broadcasting's first years.

Failure of the 1912 Act The new law worked well enough for the point-to-point services for which it was designed. Broadcasting, however, introduced unprecedented demands on the spectrum never imagined in 1912. The act called for the secretary of

commerce to grant licenses to U.S. citizens "upon application therefor," and gave no grounds on which applications might be rejected. In 1912, Congress had no reason to anticipate rejections. Presumably all who had need or reason to operate radio stations could be allowed to do so. After becoming secretary of commerce in 1921, Herbert Hoover made all broadcast stations share time on the same channel. Later that year he allocated the frequency 833 kHz for "news and entertainment" stations, and 618 kHz for "crop and weather report" stations. The practice of time sharing worked well for ships' stations, which needed only occasional exchanges of specific messages and could wait for use of a channel. But broadcast stations, with their need to transmit uninterrupted program services, demanded continuous access to their channels.

The rapid growth in the number of stations soon created intolerable interference. Adding more channels didn't help because still more stations crowded on the air. Some owners then began to freely change frequency, power, times of operation, and even their location at will. These changes created even worse interference, of course, so that decent reception became impossible (Exhibit 2–7).

National Radio Conferences Hoover, an ardent believer in free enterprise, hoped that the radio business would be able to discipline itself without government controls. To that end, he called a series of four national radio conferences in Washington. At the first, in 1922, only 22 broadcasters attended, whereas by 1925 the number had risen to 400. In 1924, Hoover optimistically called these conferences "experiments in industrial self-government" (Dept. of Commerce, 1924: 2), but even then he must have suspected the hopelessness of the experiment. He commented repeatedly on the fact that here was an industry that increasingly *wanted* government regulation to eliminate the interference problem. From year to year, the conferees grew more explicit in their pleas for government action. (These experiences under an earlier Republican administration contrast sharply with the zeal of the 1980s Reagan administration for dismantling the regulatory system that evolved in the 1920s.)

---

*The international distress, or SOS, frequency was set at 600 meters, what we now call 500 kHz. This decision had a bearing on the eventual allocation of the broadcasting band. It would have been more efficient to start the AM band lower in the spectrum, but this was prevented by the need to avoid interference with the distress frequency.

EXHIBIT 2–7   The Secretary vs. the Evangelist

An example of the bizarre regulatory problems facing the secretary of commerce was the station owned by Aimée Semple McPherson, a popular evangelist of the 1920s. She operated a pioneer broadcast station that "wandered all over the waveband" from her "temple" in Los Angeles. After delivering repeated warnings, a government inspector ordered the station closed down. Secretary Hoover thereupon received the following telegram from the evangelist:

> *PLEASE ORDER YOUR MINIONS OF SATAN TO LEAVE MY STATION ALONE. YOU CANNOT EXPECT THE ALMIGHTY TO ABIDE BY YOUR WAVE-LENGTH NONSENSE. WHEN I OFFER MY PRAYERS TO HIM I MUST FIT INTO HIS WAVE RECEPTION. OPEN THIS STATION AT ONCE. (Hoover, 1952: II–142)*

Evangelist McPherson, after being persuaded to engage a competent engineer, was allowed to reopen her station.

SOURCE: UPI/Bettmann Archive.

Zenith Decision   Finally, a 1926 federal court decision completely undermined Hoover's assumed powers of enforcement. A Zenith Radio Corporation station, WJAZ in Chicago, had operated at times and on frequencies different from those authorized in its license. Hoover brought suit under the 1912 act to enforce compliance, but the court found in favor of the station, stating, ". . . Administrative rulings cannot add to the terms of an act of Congress and make conduct criminal which such laws leave untouched" (F 2d, 1926: 618).

The Zenith case illuminates a fundamental concept of the American system of "government by laws, not men." No government official has unlimited authority. Paradoxically, by failing to define the secretary's discretionary powers to enforce the Radio Act, Congress left him powerless.

In less than a year, 200 new broadcast stations took advantage of the government's inability to enforce licensing rules. Meaningful reception had become impossible in most places—the Federal Radio Commission later noted that "the listener might suppose instead of a receiving set he had a peanut roaster with assorted whistles" (FRC, 1927: 11). In New York, 38 stations created bedlam, as did 40 in Chicago. Sales of radio sets declined noticeably. Finally, in a message to Congress in late 1926, President Coolidge said, "The whole service of this most important public function has drifted into such chaos as seems likely, if not remedied, to destroy its great value. I most urgently recommend that this legislation should be speedily enacted" (Coolidge, 1926: 32).

Radio Act of 1927   Coolidge referred to a proposed new radio law, which after long debate Congress finally passed on February 23, 1927. The Radio Act of 1927 embodied the recommendations of Hoover's Fourth Radio Conference and so can be said to represent what most of the broadcasters themselves wanted.

The act provided for a *temporary* Federal Radio Commission (FRC) to put things in order. After two years, though, it became clear that broadcasting and other radio services would need continuing and detailed attention, so Congress made the FRC permanent. The radio commission defined the broadcast band, standardized channel designation by frequency instead of wavelength, closed down portable broadcast transmitters, and cut back on the number of stations allowed to operate at night. (Interference increases after dusk, because AM signals travel farther.)

At last investors in broadcasting could move ahead with assurance that signals would not be ruined by uncontrollable mavericks on the airwaves. The passage of the Radio Act of 1927 and the start of continuing supervison by the FRC meant that the final foundation stone of broadcasting as a new communication service had been laid. The period of stable growth could now begin.

Summary

▌ Among the preconditions for development of broadcasting were the general late-19th-century trends toward urbanization, education, and development of major industries. The penny-press newspaper, vaudeville, the phonograph, and the motion picture gave rise to patterns of mass media production, distribution, and consumption that would soon be followed by radio broadcasting.

▌ The industrial context for radio was the electrical industry, dominated by AT&T's Western Electric, by General Electric, and by Westinghouse, all of which controlled important patents. The immediate technical precursors of wireless were the land telegraph of the 1840s, the submarine cable of the 1860s, and the telephone of the 1880s.

▌ The theories of James Clerk Maxwell in the 1860s led to the experiments of Heinrich Hertz two decades later, and provided the impetus for Guglielmo Marconi's development of a working wireless system in the 1890s.

▌ Wireless was first applied to maritime and transoceanic telegraphic communication early in this century. Only after development of the vacuum tube in 1904 by Ambrose Fleming, and its major improvement in 1906 by Lee de Forest with the Audion, did practical radiotelephony become possible.

▌ World War I accelerated the development of radio technology, bringing about the pooling of crucial wireless patents and the development of radio manufacturing and trained radio personnel. The U.S. Navy took over control of most radio transmitters for the 1917–1920 period.

∎ Under protest, the navy handed back nonmilitary transmitters to private hands in 1920. GE formed RCA to take over and operate the holdings of American Marconi. Major manufacturing firms entered patent cross-licensing agreements in the 1919–1923 period to allow the development of wireless. All of this was directed to point-to-point long-distance service.

∎ The foundation for broadcasting was laid between 1919 and 1927 and included (1) the concept of broadcasting to entertain a general audience, (2) the acceptance of advertising as the means of radio's financial support, (3) the development of competing national networks of stations, and (4) the federal regulation and licensing of stations.

∎ The early development of broadcasting was characterized as well by a basic conflict between the Radio and Telephone Groups of broadcasters. Disagreements centered on the use of pooled patents, rights to sell advertising on the air, and the use of telephone lines for networking.

∎ In 1926, cross-licensing agreements drawn up prior to the development of broadcasting were replaced. AT&T withdrew from broadcasting except to provide network interconnections. The rival networks became NBC Red and Blue, under the overall control of RCA. A rival firm, CBS, was formed in 1927 and was purchased by William Paley two years later.

∎ A wireless act of 1910 was replaced by the Radio Act of 1912, which was not designed to control broadcasting. By 1926, despite the efforts of Secretary Hoover, radio had fallen into a chaotic unregulated state. Congress finally passed the Radio Act of 1927 to complete the final step in laying the foundation of broadcasting in America.

CHAPTER 3

FROM RADIO
TO TELEVISION

For nearly three decades, AM radio dominated the broadcasting business. While other technologies slowly evolved in laboratories, broadcasting developed along the pattern that had been established in the 1920s. Networks matured, the number of stations and receivers increased, and radio became part of the fabric of American life.

These "golden years" of radio's expanding popularity and success coincided with years of extreme social stress—the Great Depression, followed soon by the Second World War. For millions of listeners, radio provided both entertainment that allowed them an escape from reality and news that described the changing world. Changes in older print, film, and recorded media became evident in the 1930s and accelerated rapidly with the inception of commercial television. This chapter covers the transition from radio to television, setting the stage for the even more dramatic changes in later years. The history of educational radio and television is discussed in Chapter 10.

3.1
The Great Depression
(1929–1937)

During the early 1930s, for the first time in broadcasting history, the number of stations on the air actually decreased (Exhibit 3–1). This decline occurred both because of the Federal Radio Commission's efforts to clear up interference among stations and because of the shortage of investment funds during the Depression years. By 1937, however, three-quarters of all U.S. homes had radios, and the number of stations had again begun an upward climb that has continued ever since.

During the 1929–1937 period, a third of American workers lost their jobs; national productivity fell by half. None of the present-day welfare programs cushioned the intense suffering caused by unemployment and poverty. In this time of great trial, radio entertainment came as a godsend, the one widely available distraction from the grim realities of the daily struggle to survive. As little as $15 could buy a vacuum tube receiver. Listener loyalty became "almost irrational," according to historian Erik Barnouw:

> Destitute families, forced to give up an icebox or furniture or bedding, clung to the radio as to a last link to humanity. In consequence, radio, though briefly jolted by the Depression, was soon prospering from it. Motion picture business was suffering, the theater was collapsing, vaudeville was dying, but many of their major talents flocked to radio—along with audiences and sponsors. Some companies were beginning to make a comeback through radio sponsorship. In the process, the tone of radio changed rapidly (Barnouw, 1978: 27).

EXHIBIT 3–1   Growth of Radio Stations, 1920–1990

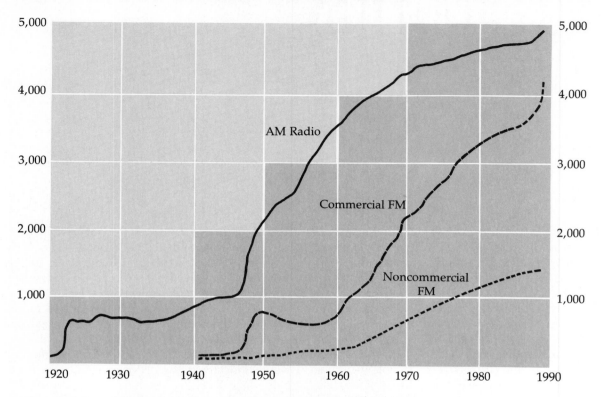

Note that the only downtrends in the growth curves occurred in 1930s AM, when the FRC imposed order on the pre-Radio Act chaos, and in 1950s FM, when its initial promise seemed not to be paying off. The sharp upward trend in the AM growth curve in the late 1940s occurred after the removal of World War II's restraints on consumer goods.

SOURCE: Adapted from Christopher H. Sterling and John M. Kittross, *Stay Tuned: A Concise History of American Broadcasting.* Copyright 1990 by Wadsworth Publishing Co., Inc. Reprinted by permission of Wadsworth Publishing Co., Belmont, CA.

Coming into office early in 1933, Franklin D. Roosevelt proved to be a master broadcaster, the first national politician to exploit the new medium to its full potential in presidential politics. He lifted the nation's spirit with the ringing phrases in his inaugural address ("The only thing we have to fear is fear itself"), broadcast throughout the country by both CBS and NBC, the only national networks in 1933.

Soon Roosevelt's distinctive, patrician voice became familiar to every listener who tuned in to his "fireside chats," the term used to suggest the informality, warmth, and directness of these presidential radio reports to the people—a brand-new phenomenon in American politics. "It was in the most direct sense," wrote David Halberstam, "the government reaching out and touching the citizen . . . Roosevelt was the first professional of the art" (1979: 15).

The FCC Takes Over Roosevelt also had an important impact on the regulation of communications. To correct overlap among the several agencies then dealing with telegraph, telephone, and radio operations, he sent a message to Congress early in 1934 urging the formation of a *communications* commission to pull together the different pieces under one roof. Based on that request, plus its own detailed study of the situation, Congress passed the comprehensive *Communications Act of 1934.*

The act created a seven-member Federal Communications Commission (reduced to five members in 1982) to regulate all interstate electronic communication, including broadcasting. Much of the Radio Act of 1927 survived, however, its text incorporated in the 1934 act. The FCC began operation in mid-1934, one of the many agencies established in the flurry of New Deal government activity. A half century later, FCC Chair Mark Fowler would call the agency "the last of the New Deal dinosaurs," referring to the fact that for years the FCC showed no reluctance to use its licensing powers to force stations to act in what the commission understood to be the public interest instead of only in their own commercial interest.

Broadcast Conservatism Major stations and networks of the 1930s maintained standards of deportment that today would seem absurdly formal. Network announcers were expected to wear dinner jackets in the evening and to speak literate English. Broadcasters and advertisers were sensitive to radio's status as a guest in the home. A public furor erupted in 1937 over some lines read by actress Mae West in a comedy dialogue with Charlie McCarthy, Edgar Bergen's ventriloquist dummy (now on exhibition at the Smithsonian):

West: Why don't you come home with me? I'll let you play in my woodpile. . . . You're all wood and a yard long. You weren't so nervous and backward when you came to see me at my apartment. In fact, you didn't need much encouragement to kiss me.
    Charlie: Did I do that?
    West: You certainly did, and I got marks to prove it, and splinters, too (quoted in *Broadcasting*, 1970: 119).

The FCC had to respond to outraged complaints, and so it lectured NBC on its obligation to maintain proper standards of taste and propriety.

In another controversial case, *The Mercury Theater on the Air,* a series directed by Orson Welles and John Houseman, produced a sensational radio play called "The War of the Worlds" in October 1938. In the form of radio news reports, it simulated an invasion from Mars, causing widespread panic among listeners. Many began to flee the imaginary Martians even though the play had been clearly identified as a Halloween prank. One reason for the extraordinary impact of the play may have been that it came shortly after radio reported the month-long Munich crisis, foreshadowing the outbreak of World War II. Listeners had become so edgy, expecting radio reports of dire events, that even a Martian invasion seemed possible to many. The FCC cleared its regulatory throat over the program, but decided that no overt deception had been intended and took no action.

Programming Excesses Side by side with the self-conscious correctness and conservatism of network radio, however, there existed another, quite different standard of broadcasting. All across the country, radio proved irresistibly attractive to a variety of raffish, offbeat individualists who exploited it as a personal mouthpiece. As pioneer radio critic Ben Gross recalled it,

Tailors, preachers, loan sharks, swamis, and physical-culture men, merchants, nostrum dispensers, and frenzied advocates of odd ideas, such as Colonel Henderson of Shreveport, Louisiana, who combined primitive theology with hatred of chain stores, indulged in a saturnalia of "free speech." . . . In a steady procession, there came before the microphones newscasters who merely read word-for-word items from the daily papers, owners of diploma mills, crystal-gazing fortune-tellers, installment furniture men, conductors of matrimonial bureaus, fakers, nuts and dreamers making merry carnival (Gross, 1954: 68).

In most cases the Federal Radio Commission (FRC) had been able to correct abuses without withdrawing licenses (which at first had to be renewed at six-month intervals). But in two notorious instances in the early 1930s the commission administered the ultimate penalty. In one case, the FRC objected to the broadcasting of medical advice by a "Dr." John R. Brinkley on his station, KFKB, in Milford, KS. Brinkley, though not a qualified physician, prescribed sex-rejuvenation surgery and drugs that he packaged himself and sold by number rather than by name. The FRC refused to renew KFKB's license, saying that Brinkley used the station to sell his quack medicine and attack others (especially the American Medical Association), not in the broader public interest.

The second case involved a religious crusader alleging municipal corruption. The Reverend Dr. Shuler of the Trinity Methodist Church (South) broadcast in Los Angeles over KGEF, a small, shared-time religious station. His fire-and-brimstone personal attacks drew the biggest radio audience in Los Angeles when he was on the air. However, when KGEF's license came up for renewal in 1931, some 90 witnesses appeared in opposition. The FRC turned down the renewal application.

Both the KFKB and the KGEF renewal denials withstood court appeals, establishing in the early 1930s the commission's legal right to review a station's past programming in deciding whether license renewal would be in the public interest. As an indication of the difference between the regulation of the 1930s and that of today, many communication lawyers now agree that in the permissive atmosphere of the 1980s neither station would have lost its license.

The fact that Brinkley and Shuler had broadcast *licenses* made them vulnerable. Most personal exploiters of radio simply bought time on the air. Notable among this group during the 1930s was the Reverend Charles E. Coughlin, a Catholic priest with a charismatic radio appeal. From the unlikely base of a small parish church, The Shrine of the Little Flower, in a suburb of Detroit, Father Coughlin built up a fanatically loyal national radio following. His vitriolic sermons against communism, Wall Street, Jews, labor unions, and other targets generated millions of dollars in small donations from his devoted followers. Because of his pro-Nazi sympathies, his opponents called his church "the Shrine of the Little Führer." He was finally silenced in 1940, not by political opponents or church superiors but by the refusal of networks and most larger stations to continue selling him time (Brown, 1980). With U.S. entry into World War II imminent, his tirades had become an embarrassment to the broadcasting industry.

The downfall of Brinkley, Shuler, and Coughlin did not put other exploiters out of business; it merely caused most of them to lower their profile. Spellbinders, quacks, cultists, zealots, and get-rich-quick schemers have always been part of the broadcasting scene. They cannot be completely suppressed without violating the First Amendment's guarantees of freedom of expression and of religion and the constitutional separation of church and state. The excesses of some of today's notorious "televangelists" illustrate the point.

Network Development William Paley's upstart rival network, CBS, worked for years to overcome its image as the number-two chain, laboring in the wake of NBC. Big advertisers and star performers automatically preferred NBC to CBS whenever they had a choice, regardless of CBS's growing popularity. "We were at the mercy of the sponsors and the ad agencies," wrote Paley. "They could always take a successful show away from us and put it on NBC" (1979: 174).

NBC remained a wholly owned subsidiary of RCA as RCA became a giant diversified corporation with worldwide interests in communications services and manufacturing. Reflecting RCA's high corporate status, NBC tended to assume the role of a dignified elder among the networks. It further enhanced its image in 1933 when it moved into new headquarters in the seventy-story art-deco-style RCA building, part of New York's famed Rockefeller Center.*

---

*CBS achieved its own architectural monument in 1965 when it moved into a splendid Eero Saarinen–designed headquarters tower at the corner of 52nd Street and Sixth Avenue, just two blocks from NBC. Sheathed in elegant dark granite, the CBS building became known as "Black Rock," while NBC was referred to as "30 Rock" for its address, and the more aggressive ABC became "Hard Rock."

The Mutual Broadcasting System started with a different premise from that of the older networks. In the early 1930s there were only two major-market radio stations on clear channels that were not affiliated with CBS or NBC: WGN-Chicago and WOR-New York. They arranged in 1934 to form a network organization to sell time jointly with WXYZ-Detroit and WLW-Cincinnati. The four stations started the network by exchanging programs on a regional network basis. Their chief asset at the start, *The Lone Ranger,* had been introduced by WXYZ in 1933.

Radio Comedy's Success   The first network radio entertainment program to achieve addictive popularity was a prime-time, five-days-a-week situation comedy, *Amos 'n' Andy;* Charles Correll ("Andy") and Freeman Gosden ("Amos") came to radio as a song-and-patter team. At a station manager's suggestion, they tried their luck at a comedy series. The two white performers developed a black dialect show in ghetto English, featuring the ups and downs of the "Fresh Air Taxicab Company of American, Incorporated."

Amos 'n' Andy became the top network show in the early 1930s. Traffic stopped on the main streets of towns across the country and movies halted in midreel at 7:00 P.M. so that people would not miss their nightly 15 minutes of chuckles over the antics of Amos, Andy, the Kingfish, Lightnin', Madam Queen, and a host of minor characters, most of whom Correll and Gosden played themselves.

Today the impersonation of blacks by white actors using exaggerated dialect and comedy situations based on ghetto poverty could not be seriously proposed. A Pittsburgh newspaper asked the FCC to ban the series by 1931, alleging racism, but its defenders had a convincing argument: most blacks seemed to enjoy the program just as much as whites.*

---

*Opposition became more general in the 1950s. CBS ran a television version of *Amos 'n' Andy* (with black actors) from 1951 to 1953, but dropped it because of opposition from the National Association for the Advancement of Colored People. Syndicated showings continued until 1966, when the syndicator finally agreed to withdraw the series from both national and international syndication (Brown, 1977: 16).

3.2
Early Radio Controversies

Live Music Era   The networks and the larger stations relied heavily on music from the very beginning of radio. In the mid-1930s more than half of all radio programming consisted of music, three-quarters of it carried on a sustaining (nonsponsored) basis. Most large stations had their own live musical groups, and the networks even had their own symphony orchestras.

In its early years, CBS devoted a quarter of its entire schedule to music. NBC began regular broadcasts of the Metropolitan Opera in 1931, carrying it mostly on a sustaining basis until 1940. Thereafter Texaco, Inc., began to underwrite the Met broadcasts and has continued to do so ever since—"the longest continuous commercial underwriting of the same program by the same sponsor in the history of radio" (McDowell, 1979). Texaco, which now organizes a special ad hoc 300-station radio network to carry the programs, abstains from commercial interruptions, inserting brief sponsor identifications only at intermissions.

All this had tremendous impact on the musical world, creating vast new public appetites for all sorts of music, old and new, classical and popular. While expanding the market for music, however, radio also created copyright and union-rights problems never before faced by the creators and performers of musical works.

ASCAP and BMI   Under the copyright law,* the playing of a recording in public for profit constitutes a "performance." As such, it obligates the user (in this case the radio station) to pay the copyright holders (who may include composers of the music, lyricists, and music publishers) for *performing rights.*

Music copyright holders cannot possibly personally monitor music performances at tens of thousands of commercial establishments—concert halls,

---

*The present law, passed in 1976 (USC, 17), replaced the 1909 law in effect when radio broadcasting began. Details of the 1976 Act are discussed in Section 16.5.

hotels, nightclubs, and other such public places as well as broadcasting stations. Instead, they rely on *music licensing* organizations to act on their behalf in collecting copyright fees for performances of both live and recorded music. The first U.S. organization of this type, the American Society of Composers, Authors, and Publishers (ASCAP), dates back to 1914. It checks on the public performance of music copyrighted by its members, collects royalty fees, and distributes the net income to the copyright owners.

When radio began, no one could be sure what impact this new way of performing music would have. Would repeated radio performances quickly kill off interest in new musical works, or would they enhance the market for sheet music, recordings, and in-person performances? As early as 1922, ASCAP began making substantial demands for payments by broadcasters for the use of musical works in its catalog, whether broadcast live or from recordings.

These demands imposed a new and unexpectedly heavy financial burden on radio stations. In 1923 station owners formed the National Association of Broadcasters (NAB) to deal with ASCAP's demands on an industrywide basis. Nevertheless, as radio grew, the fees collected by ASCAP also grew, and soon broadcasting contributed the major share of the association's royalties. ASCAP, as the sole U.S. licensing organization, controlled virtually all contemporary arrangements of older compositions on which original copyrights had expired. Radio stations found it impossible to produce listenable music programs without infringing on ASCAP copyrights.

In 1937 broadcasters moved decisively to break the ASCAP monopoly. When ASCAP proposed yet another substantial fee increase, the broadcasters formed their own cooperative music-licensing organization, Broadcast Music, Inc. (BMI), which began operation in 1940. Its first "affiliates," as it calls its copyright owners, composed country, western, and "race" music (black popular music). Most had never registered with ASCAP. Eventually, BMI built up a comprehensive library representing more than a million musical works owned by some 55,000 publishers and writers (see Section 16.5).

Recorded Programs   When radio began, phonograph recordings still used relatively primitive technology. They ran at 78 revolutions per minute, allowing time for only three or four minutes on a side. In 1929 sixteen-inch ETs (*electrical transcriptions*), running fifteen minutes to a side at 33 1/3 rpm, came into use for radio program syndication and for subscription music libraries. The latter provided stations with a basic library of music on ETs, supplemented at regular intervals by additional recordings.

The radio networks, however, scorned recorded programs. They regarded their ability to distribute *live* programming to their affiliates as a major asset. ABC, formed in 1945, broke the recording ban in order to lure Bing Crosby away from NBC in 1946. The singer hated the tension and risks of real-time broadcasting, compounded by the need to repeat each live program in New York a second time for the West Coast to compensate for time-zone differences. Crosby himself financed a then little-known company, Ampex, to make tape recorders based on magnetic tape technology developed by the Germans during World War II. As soon as broadcast-quality audio tape recorders became available, Crosby insisted on recording his weekly prime-time program. CBS and NBC soon followed the ABC lead in dropping the ban on recordings.

AFM Battle Against Recordings   Although the broadcasting medium created many new jobs for musicians, they saw its increasing reliance on recorded music (especially the ETs then used for syndicated programs) as a threat. If stations and networks made use of recordings, many musicians would lose their jobs. In 1922 an implacable opponent of radio's use of recordings, James Caesar Petrillo, became president of the Chicago chapter of the American Federation of Musicians (AFM).

"Little Caesar" Petrillo first built a strong political base locally in Chicago, then went on to become national AFM president in 1940. He threatened to close down transcription makers, forcing syndication firms to pay substantial extra fees for every broadcast transcription made, with the money going

EXHIBIT 3–2 *Broadcasting* Magazine—Radio to Television

Sol Taishoff and Martin Codell began Broadcasting, *now the standard trade weekly, in 1931, on an investment of about $11,000. It appeared biweekly for its first decade, reporting on business and programming news, and the changing regulatory scene. With its strongly pro-industry editorials and its editors who were active in broadcast and regulatory circles,* Broadcasting *often shaped the news it reported of what was then a very small radio industry. In 1935 it published its first annual directory of all stations and ancillary businesses, now called* Broadcasting/Cable Yearbook. *In January 1941, the magazine became a weekly. Taishoff bought out his partner in 1944, and a few years later Codell founded* Television Digest, *a weekly newsletter that is now the chief competitor of* Broadcasting. *Taishoff died in 1982 after more than 50 years at the helm of his magazine, which has always been headquartered in Washington, DC. In 1987, the family sold control to the Times Mirror conglomerate for $75 million, though son Larry Taishoff remained in charge of day-to-day operations. Circulation by 1989 stood at about 38,000.*

SOURCE: *Broadcasting* magazine.

to a union slush fund that Petrillo alone controlled. He succeeded in forcing broadcasters to hire professional musicians as "platter turners" in the control rooms and as librarians in the station record libraries of his home town, Chicago. He demanded that stations increase musicians' pay as much as fivefold. With unprecedented bravado, Petrillo defied the National War Labor Board, President Roosevelt, the Supreme Court, and the Congress of the United States.

Congress finally passed the Lea Act in 1946, adding §506* to the Communications Act of 1934 specifically to bring Petrillo under control. The Lea Act forbade stations to hire unneeded personnel to satisfy union demands, banned union restrictions on the use of transcriptions, and forbade unions to prevent broadcasts by amateur musicians.

Press–Radio "War"   News, no less than music, depends on syndication by *press associations,* or *wire services* (referring to the fact that they first flourished with the telegraph).

Radio disturbed the vested interests of the news agencies and their customary clients, the newspapers. Radio, in bypassing the written word, seemed to threaten the very future of news publications. Who would want to buy a paper to read news already heard on the radio? Who would want to buy advertising space in papers carrying stale news? The newspapers calculated that they could suppress radio competition by denying broadcasters access to the major news agencies, at the time the Associated Press (AP), owned cooperatively by newspapers themselves, the International News Service (INS), and the United Press (UP).

NBC's Blue Network inaugurated regular 15-minute nightly newscasts by Lowell Thomas in 1930, a sign that radio might soon assume a serious competitive role. In response to threats that news agency services would soon be cut off, CBS began forming its own news-gathering organization. Recognizing that they could not hold back the tide, the news-

paper publishers proposed a truce in 1933. The result, known as the Biltmore Agreement, set up a Press–Radio Bureau designed to protect the papers' interests.*

According to the terms of the agreement, CBS suspended its own news gathering, and both networks agreed to confine themselves to two 5-minute press-wire news summaries from the Press–Radio Bureau. These could be aired only after the morning and evening papers had appeared, could be used only on a sustaining (nonsponsored) basis, and had to be followed by the admonition, "For further details, consult your local newspaper(s)." The bureau agreed to issue additional special bulletins on events "of transcendent importance," but such bulletins had to be written "in such a manner as to stimulate public interest in the reading of newspapers" (quoted in Kahn, 1984: 103).

In practice, the Press–Radio Bureau never worked effectively. Only about a third of the existing stations subscribed to it, and several independent radio news services sprang up to fill the gap. Broadcasters also took advantage of escape clauses in the agreement that exempted news commentaries. In consequence, a great many radio newscasters became instant commentators.

United Press broke the embargo in 1935, and was soon joined by International News Service (these two merged to form today's UPI in 1958). The Press–Radio Bureau finally expired, unmourned, in 1940 when the Associated Press began to accept radio stations as members of the association.

As broadcast news matured, it became evident that, contrary to the fears of newspaper publishers, radio coverage actually stimulated newspaper reading instead of discouraging it. The press services eventually acquired even more broadcasters than publishers as customers and began to offer services specially tailored for broadcast stations, including audio feeds ready to go directly on the air. Central to radio's winning of the "war" was the growing strength of the national networks.

---

*The symbol § is used throughout this book to refer to sections of laws and documents *other than* this book.

*CBS and NBC were parties to the agreement, but the nonaffiliated stations were not. The relevant parts of the document are reprinted by Kahn (1984: 101).

Chain Broadcasting Investigation By 1938, radio stations representing 98 percent of the total nighttime wattage were affiliated with either NBC or CBS. Then as now, the great majority of affiliated stations were tied to the networks not by ownership but by contract.

In 1934, the Mutual Broadcasting System (MBS) began to emerge in the Midwest. Frustrated in its attempts to expand from a regional into a national network, MBS complained to the Federal Communications Commission that CBS and NBC unfairly dominated the network field. After more than three years of investigation, the FCC issued its *chain broadcasting* regulations, aimed at relaxing the older networks' hold over affiliates and talent, and freeing affiliates to program more for local needs and interests. Among other things, the new rules forbade dual networks covering the same markets and forced both CBS and NBC to give up the talent-booking agencies they had developed as sidelines. The rules also forbade the networks to force stations to carry programs that they did not wish to accept, or to infringe in other ways on the autonomy of affiliates.

Concerned about the intrusions into their business affairs, CBS and NBC predicted total collapse of the network system if the regulations went into effect. They fought the case all the way to the Supreme Court, but in 1943 the Court finally settled the argument in favor of the FCC (U.S., 1943: 190).* NBC's dual network operation ended in 1943 with the sale of its Blue network, which in 1945 became the American Broadcasting Company (ABC). The predicted collapse of network broadcasting failed to materialize, and even Mutual expanded rapidly. Thus emerged the four-network radio pattern, which endured until the late 1960s.

3.3
Television and FM Radio Emerge

As they tuned in to radio entertainment and news, listeners in the 1930s began to hear and read more about radio-with-pictures, or television, experiments. Rumors of a new kind of radio that eliminated static also surfaced. Both developments took far longer to reach commercial fruition than their backers then suspected.

What Delayed TV? The idea of wireless transmission of pictures occurred to inventors as early as that of wireless sound transmission. However, even after sound broadcasting became a reality, television still remained in the experimental stage.

Television had to wait for a more sophisticated technology. It took even longer to reach agreement on a single national standard specifying the details of the television signal. Standardizing such technical details as the number of lines in a picture (a determinant of picture quality) would freeze development at a particular level. If it turned out later that standards should have been set at a higher level, tremendous waste would occur because change would outmode millions of receivers and much studio and transmitter equipment.

Setting television standards involved finding a compromise among the conflicting interests of patent holders, manufacturers, and government bureaucracies, each with its own economic and political concerns. For these reasons, in the years before 1948 television moved forward slowly as standards were improved bit by bit and the FCC cautiously granted licenses for limited public tryouts.

Television technology went through two phases: that of mechanical scanning and that of electronic scanning. The latter began to take the lead in the early 1930s and had just begun to reach a satisfactory level when World War II (1939–1945) interrupted further development. Accordingly, widespread introduction of modern television had to wait for the war to end.

Experimental television therefore had existed for decades before television became a mass medium. Early systems produced crude pictures that were interesting only as curiosities. Public acceptance

---

*The FCC extended the chain broadcasting rules to television in 1946. In 1977, after radio networks had ceased to play a dominant role, the commission lifted most of the original radio chain regulations. (For details on TV network rules, see Section 8.2.)

EXHIBIT 3–3   First U.S. Television Star

During the early experiments with electronic television, RCA laboratories used, as a moving object to televise, a 12-inch paper maché model of a popular cartoon character, Felix the Cat, posed on a revolving turntable under hot lights. The image at left shows how Felix looked on television in 1929 when picture definition was still only 60 lines per frame.

SOURCE: Courtesy NBC.

awaited pictures with sufficient lack of flicker and sufficient resolution (detail) for comfortable viewing—a standard at least as good as that of the home movies then familiar to consumers.

Early experiments used *scanning discs,* large metal "wheels" perforated with small holes in a spiral pattern. (They were first conceived by Paul Nipkow in Germany in the 1880s, but never developed.) As the "Nipkow discs" spun in front of an aperture, the holes admitted light in successive lines. They made crude pictures made up of 30 lines per frame, compared with 525 lines in contemporary television (Exhibit 3–3).*

Charles Francis Jenkins in the United States and John Logie Baird in Britain demonstrated mechanical systems, and both briefly manufactured and sold receivers. Baird's persistent efforts, along with those of the British Marconi–EMI concern, which had developed a competing all-electronic system, culminated in late 1936 with the BBC's introduction of the first high-definition television service.*

Mechanical television had by the late 1930s reached the peak of what it could offer, and electronic systems, even in the crude stage prevalent at that time, provided far better transmission and reception and much clearer pictures. The BBC soon

---

*A variant of this mechanical television system provided the first pictures of men on the moon in 1969. Scientists reverted to the older system because of its ruggedness, desirable under the conditions of broadcasting from space.

*Formerly *high-definition* television was characterized by pictures consisting of at least 200 scanning lines per frame; the modern high-definition television (HDTV) will have more than 1,000 lines.

dropped Baird's mechanical apparatus and concentrated on electronic developments, but closed down its service when World War II began.

Electronic Television Two inventors figured prominently in electronic television developments in the United States: Philo T. Farnsworth and Vladimir Zworykin. Farnsworth, a self-taught American genius, developed an electronic (nonmechanical) scanning system he called "image dissection." He invented the basic methods that are still used for suppressing the scanning beam retrace path (see Section 6.8) and for inserting synchronizing pulses.

Zworykin emigrated to the United States from Russia in 1919 and worked as an engineer for Westinghouse. In 1923 he applied for patents covering a largely electronic television system, but he immediately found himself embroiled in a seven-party patent interference suit. One of the seven parties, Farnsworth, finally won a key decision on his electron optics patent in 1934. RCA acknowledged Farnsworth's victory in 1939 by paying him a million dollars for the right to use his discoveries. In the interim Zworykin won lasting fame as the inventor of the *iconoscope,* the electronic camera pickup tube (Exhibit 3–4).

In 1930 Zworykin became head of a celebrated research group of more than 40 engineers at the RCA laboratories in Camden, NJ. Formed from a merger of the television research programs of General Electric and Westinghouse with that of RCA, the Camden team systematically investigated all aspects of electronic television development, solving not only technological problems but also the subjective problem of setting the picture quality standards needed to win full public acceptance.

During the 1930s the Camden team tackled and solved all the outstanding problems. They progressed to higher and higher line frequencies, year by year, from the 60-line standard of 1930 (Exhibit 3–3) to 441 lines in 1939. They increased image size and brightness, introduced interlace scanning to suppress flicker, adapted equipment to use the newly opened VHF band, and introduced sets into homes on an experimental basis.

By 1939 the Camden group felt ready for a major public demonstration. RCA chose the 1939 New York World's Fair, with its "World of Tomorrow" theme, as a suitably prestigious and symbolic launching pad for the 441-line RCA television demonstration. For the first time the general U.S. public had a chance to see (and to be seen on) modern television.

Nevertheless, the Federal Communications Commission withheld permission for full-scale commercial operations pending industrywide agreement on engineering standards. This came with the recommendations of the National Television Systems Committee (NTSC), representing 15 major electronics manufacturers. In 1941 the FCC adopted the NTSC standards for black-and-white television, including the 525-lines-per-frame and 30-frames-per-second standards still in effect today.

Within the year the United States was at war with Japan and Germany. With production of civilian consumer electronics halted, television development had to be shelved for the duration.

FM's Troubled Origins For its first quarter century, the word *broadcasting* meant only amplitude-modulated (AM) radio. Edwin Armstrong (Exhibit 3–5) invented a much improved alternative system using frequency modulation (FM) in 1933, but for almost 30 years it languished as a poor relation of the established AM system. Armstrong saw himself as the victim of a conspiracy to kill FM, frustrating his dream of success.

Costly changes in spectrum allocations, favoring television over FM, seemed to Armstrong still more evidence of conspiracy. At the close of World War II the FCC reassigned FM's prewar channels, moving it up to its present VHF location, 88–108 MHz. This 1945 move made obsolete the half million FM receivers that had been built to work on lower frequencies.

Many major AM station owners obtained FM licenses, simply as insurance against the possibility that FM might catch on and make AM obsolete. They made no attempt to take advantage of FM's superior quality or even to program it as a separate service. Instead, they merely simulcast their AM programs on FM transmitters. In the absence of high-fidelity programming, listeners had little incentive to buy, and manufacturers had little incentive to develop, high-fidelity receivers.

Early interest in FM stations, mostly as minor partners in AM/FM combinations, peaked in 1948, with more than a thousand stations authorized. But in that year television's rapid climb to power began, pushing FM into the background. In 1949 alone, 212 commercial FM stations went off the air, and

EXHIBIT 3–5   Edwin Armstrong (1890–1954)

The inventor paces the catwalk of his 400-foot experimental FM antenna, built in 1938 on the Palisades above the Hudson River at Alpine, NJ. He opened station W2XMN on this site in 1939 as the first high-powered FM station; the only previous one had been a low-powered amateur station for demonstration purposes.

SOURCE: *Broadcasting* magazine.

total authorizations continued to decline until 1958 (Exhibit 3–1). There was little reason for listeners to buy often expensive FM receivers, or for advertisers to buy time to reach these listeners. AM's future seemed assured as FM faded away. Inventor Armstrong took his own life in 1954 in despair.

3.4
Broadcasting at War (1938–1946)

The last shackles of the Great Depression fell away only when the country began to increase production in response to the growing threat of war in Europe and the Pacific. Radio developed the first live overseas reports of events in Europe, relayed by short-wave back to New York, and thence to network affiliates. Live reports of Hitler's annexation of Austria in 1938, the invasion of Poland a year later, and finally the 1941 Pearl Harbor attack reached American homes from radio reporters on the scene.

During World War II, radio escaped direct military censorship by complying voluntarily with common-sense rules. For example, broadcasters avoided man-on-the-street and other live interviews and weather reports.* In 1942 President Roosevelt appointed a well-known CBS radio newscaster, Elmer Davis, to head the newly created Office of War Information (OWI). The OWI mobilized an external broadcasting service. Eventually, the OWI became known as the Voice of America. By 1944, even though broadcasting had been declared an essential industry and therefore exempt from the draft, half the broadcast employees in the country had joined the armed forces.

Although wartime restrictions on civilian manufacturing, imposed in 1942, cut back on station construction and receiver production, during this period the number of radio stations on the air more than doubled, reaching just over a thousand by the end of 1946 (Exhibit 3–1). And radio advertising boomed. The government allowed manufacturers to write off advertising costs as a business expense, even though they had no products to sell because

they were devoting their capacity to military needs. This stimulated manufacturers to spend freely to keep their names before the public until consumer products returned after the war. Released from competitive pressures to maximize audiences with sure-fire, mass-appeal material, some invested in first-rate programming.

The networks, too, invested in often highly creative and artistic programs, particularly drama. Radio developed its own playwrights, notably Norman Corwin and Arch Oboler, who won their chief literary fame in broadcasting. CBS commissioned Corwin to celebrate the great moment of Allied victory in Europe with an hour-long radio play, "On a Note of Triumph," in 1945.

This notable program climaxed an extraordinary flowering of radio art—original writing of high merit, produced with consummate skill, and always live, for the networks still banned recordings. With the end of the war years and the artificial support for culture, competitive selling resumed, and this brief, luminous period of radio creativity came to an end.

Radio News Anxious to outdo NBC's developing European news operation, CBS decided on a bold stroke, a half hour devoted to a CBS foreign news "roundup" on the Nazi invasion of Austria, originating live from key points: London, Paris, Rome, Berlin, Vienna. The networks' ban on recordings created tremendous problems of coordination and precise timing. In that historic half hour, anchored by Robert Trout and featuring reports by William Shirer, Edward R. Murrow (Exhibit 3–6), and others, "radio came into its own as a full-fledged news medium" (Kendrick, 1969: 158).

Later in 1938 came the Munich crisis. The Allies abandoned Czechoslovakia to Hitler, climaxing 18 days of feverish diplomatic negotiations among the great powers. During these tense days and nights, pioneer commentator H. V. Kaltenborn achieved fame and fortune by extemporizing a remarkable string of 85 live broadcasts from New York, reporting and analyzing news of each diplomatic move as it came in by wire and wireless. News staffers at CBS would shake Kaltenborn awake (he slept on a cot in a studio) and hand him the latest bulletins;

---

*During World War I, private radio stations had been closed down (though this was before the broadcasting era). During World War II, the president refrained from using his right under §606 of the Communications Act of 1934 to assume sweeping control over all federally regulated wire and radio communications. Currently, broadcasting stations participate voluntarily in the Emergency Broadcasting System, a set of standby procedures that can be put into immediate effect in case of national emergency.

EXHIBIT 3–6   Edward R. Murrow (1908–1965)

CBS news reporter Murrow is seen walking not far from the BBC's Broadcasting House in downtown London during the Second World War. He and other American reporters used a tiny studio located in a sub-basement. Once, when the building took a hit during a German bombing raid, Murrow continued his live report as stretcher bearers carried dead and injured victims of the raid past the studio to the first-aid station.

First employed by CBS in 1935 as director of talks in Europe, he came to the notice of a wider public through his memorable live reports from bomb-ravaged London in 1940, and later from even more dangerous war-front vantage points. Unlike other reporters, he had a college degree in speech rather than newspaper or wire-service experience. The British appreciated his realistic and often moving word-and-sound pictures of their wartime experiences, and American listeners liked the way he radiated "truth and concern," as William Paley put it (1979: 151).

Widely admired by the time the war ended, he became the core of the postwar CBS news organization. He served briefly as vice president for news but soon resigned the administrative post to resume daily news-casting. As an on-the-air personality, he survived the transition to television better than others, going on to appear in *See It Now* and in often highly controversial documentaries. He resigned from CBS in the early 1960s to direct the U.S. Information Agency under President Kennedy.

SOURCE: CBS News.

going on the air immediately, he first read the bulletin, then ad-libbed his own lucid, informed commentary. "Even as I talked," wrote Kaltenborn, "I was under constant bombardment of fresh news dispatches, carried to my desk from the ticker room. I read and digested them as I talked" (Kaltenborn, 1938: 9).

Thanks to CBS's early start, Paley's enthusiastic support, and his good luck in assembling a superlative staff of news specialists, CBS set a high standard for broadcast journalism during the war years, establishing a tradition of excellence that lasted into the 1980s.

Wartime Television   During World War II six experimental stations remained on the air, in New York City (two stations), Schenectady, Philadelphia, Chicago, and Los Angeles. They devoted their brief schedules (they were on the air only four hours a week) primarily to civilian defense programs.

About 10,000 receivers existed, half of them in New York City.

The end of the war in 1945 did not, as some expected, bring an upsurge in television activity, despite a backlog of 158 pending station applications. Investors held back for several reasons. The 1941 decision on standards (Section 3.3) had left the issue of color television unresolved, and many experts believed that all-out development should await adoption of a color system. Moreover, potential investors wondered whether the public would buy receivers that cost many times the price of radios. And would the major advertisers pay the higher cost of television programming? Owners of successful radio stations, accustomed to making money with the greatest of ease, felt little incentive to take on the formidable complexities of this little-known new medium.

Two favorable developments occurred shortly after the war, however: (1) the *image orthicon* camera tube, introduced in 1945, improved camera sensitivity, eliminating the need for the uncomfortably high levels of studio light that the iconoscope had required; and (2) AT&T began to install intercity coaxial cable links (Section 7.4), enabling network interconnection. The New York–Washington, DC link opened in 1946. Finally, in the summer and fall of 1948, the long-predicted rush into television began.

3.5
TV's Growing Pains

In 1948 the number of television stations on the air increased from 17 to 48. The number of cities served by television went from 8 to 23. Set sales increased more than 500 percent over the 1947 level and by 1951 had already surpassed radio set sales. Increased opportunities for viewing in 1948 multiplied the audience in one year by an astonishing 4,000 percent. Also, in 1948, coaxial cables for network relays became available to the Midwest as well as on the East Coast, and regular network service began. Important advertisers started experimenting with the new medium, and large-scale programming emerged.

Freeze Imposed (1948–1952) Television's growing pains had not yet ended, however. The FCC's go-ahead for commercial television had made only 12 VHF channels available to serve the entire United States, compared with 107 AM channels and 100 FM channels.* As more and more stations began to go on the air, it became obvious that (1) the demand for stations would soon exceed the supply of channels, and (2) the FCC had not required enough geographical separation between stations on the same channel to prevent serious cochannel interference.

To forestall a potentially chaotic situation, on 29 September 1948 the FCC abruptly froze processing of further television license applications. The freeze had no effect on applicants whose permits had already been approved. As a result, for the nearly four years of the freeze, 108 "prefreeze" stations had an enviable monopoly.

The freeze did not seriously inhibit television's growth. During the 1948–1952 period, the number of sets in use rose from a quarter-million to more than 17 million. After heavy losses at the outset, by 1951 stations began to earn back their investment. Coaxial cable and microwave networks joined the East Coast to the West Coast in 1951, inaugurating national network television, which soon reached 60 percent of American homes.

Sixth Report and Order (1952) Meanwhile, the FCC held a series of hearings to settle the engineering and policy questions that had brought on the freeze. The long-awaited decision, the charter of present-day U.S. television, came on 14 April 1952, in the historic FCC *Sixth Report and Order* (FCC, 1952: 148).† The new rules expanded the

---

*Originally, the FCC allocated 13 channels, but channel one experienced too much interference from adjacent frequencies. The FCC reassigned it in 1948 to land-mobile communications. The rest were the same VHF channels, numbered 2 through 13, still in use today.

†When faced with complex decisions, the FCC often issues preliminary "reports and orders" for public comment before arriving at a final version. The fact that it took six such reports to decide on the television allotment plan indicates the problem's complexity.

EXHIBIT 3–7 TV Channel Allotment Plan

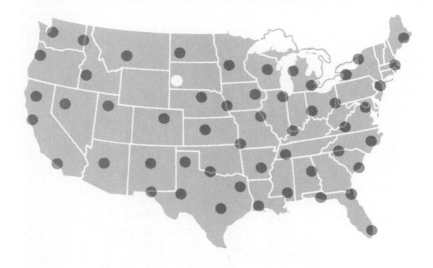

This map shows the occupied *channel 7 allotments, except for 3 outside the 48 contiguous states. They are scattered relatively evenly throughout the country, separated from each other by a minimum of 170 miles. The list of all channels available in one of the cities is shown below. Rapid City, SD, is allotted two UHF channels (one of which went on the air in 1988), but the town gets additional service from translators that bring in signals of several stations allotted to other cities in that region, plus cable television.*

Status of channel allotments in Rapid City, SD in late 1988 (shown by a white dot on the map):

3—occupied by KOTA, an ABC affiliate

7—occupied by KEVN, an NBC affiliate

9—occupied by KBHE, a noncommercial station licensed to the state of South Dakota

15—occupied by KCLO, went on the air in November 1988

21—not on the air

number of channels by supplementing the 12 VHF channels with 70 new channels in the UHF band (the feasibility of using this higher range of frequencies had been demonstrated during World War II).

A table of 2,053 allotments awarded the use of one or more channels to each of 1,291 communities—a sharp contrast with the prefreeze plan, which had allotted channels to only 345 cities. More than 66 percent of the allotments fell in the UHF band. The FCC reserved about 10 percent of the total for noncommercial educational use, mostly in the UHF band. Exhibit 3–7 shows the spacing of cochannel allotments around the country to avoid interference and also gives an example of individual city allotments. The table of allotments has been amended

EXHIBIT 3–8   Growth of Television Stations, 1948–1988

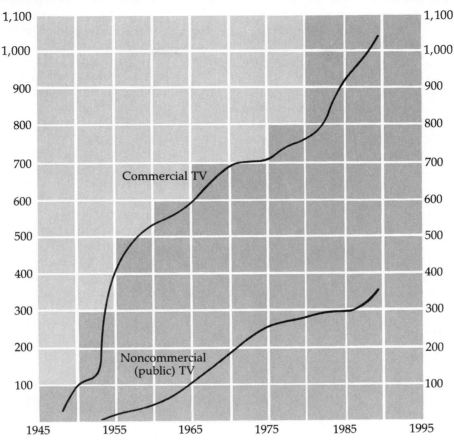

The modern TV era started in 1948, with 16 stations on the air. Just over 100 stations had been authorized when the 1948–1952 freeze imposed a temporary ceiling. After that the number shot up, reaching 400 by 1955. Growth began to slow down at that point, but has never actually stopped. Noncommercial stations developed more slowly, starting with the first two in 1954.

many times, one of the more significant changes being an increase in educational reservations to about 35 percent of the total.*

Tremendous pressures for new stations had built up during the freeze. In less than a year after the thaw, all outstanding uncontested applications had

*Other major changes include reallocating channel 37 to radio astronomy and, in 1970, channels 70 to 83 to land-mobile use. In 1980 the FCC proposed more than 100 additional VHF channel

allotments, to be made available as "drop-ins." These would be shoehorned into the allotment plan by reducing cochannel mileage separations and using directional antennas. In the end, only four such allotments were made.

been granted. The number of stations more than tripled in the first postfreeze year (Exhibit 3–8). Then began the long-drawn-out process of deciding among competing applicants for the few, immensely valuable channels remaining in the most desirable markets.

Despite its long gestation period, the new channel allotment plan had serious defects. For one thing, there were too few channels to give viewers in every market an equal number of choices. Ideally, every viewer should eventually have had a choice among at least five stations: an affiliate of each of the three commercial networks, a noncommercial station, and at least one independent station.

In practice 70 percent of the television *households* in the country can receive nine or more stations off the air (not counting cable TV). But only 8 percent of the *markets* in the country have five or more stations. The entire state of New Jersey, for example, had no VHF station until the 1980s, and only four or five UHF commerical stations.* Yet the two major neighboring markets, New York and Philadelphia, blanketed most of New Jersey. In several of the biggest cities, New York, Los Angeles, and Philadelphia among them, the maximum feasible number of VHF channels had already been licensed before the freeze, making it impossible to designate noncommercial VHF channels in those cities.

UHF Dilemma   The FCC's decision to allot television to both VHF and UHF channels, and, moreover, to *intermix* the two in many localities, made the inequities that much worse. The commission had originally tried to ensure equal coverage potentials for both VHF and UHF allotments by authorizing UHF to use much higher power, hoping in this way to overcome the inherent propagation weakness of UHF waves as compared with VHF. Even if added power could have had the desired effect, however, years went by before maximum-

power UHF transmitters became available.* UHF transmitters cost more than VHF to install and operate. Long after UHF television began, manufacturers still built primarily VHF-only receivers because of national demand for VHF viewing, forcing viewers in UHF-served markets to buy often difficult-to-use converters.

Faced with such overwhelming disadvantages, UHF television began to slip backward, reaching a low point of only 75 stations in 1960. The FCC tried a variety of measures to encourage the failing stations. Its most useful step was to get Congress to require manufacturers to equip all receivers with UHF tuning. This legislation became effective in 1964 (47 USC 303). Still later FCC rules required UHF tuning to be equal in ease to VHF.

By 1956 some of the FCC's efforts had taken effect, and UHF began a steady, though not spectacular, growth. FCC financial reports indicate that until 1974 UHF stations as a group continued to lose money. Thereafter their profit margin increased each year.

In practice it appears that at present UHF stations can at best achieve only 80 to 85 percent of the coverage enjoyed by competing VHF stations, although UHF proponents still hope that improved receivers and antennas—as well as carriage of UHF stations on cable television—will some day equalize coverage with VHF except in areas of rough terrain and in cities with many tall buildings.

Color Standards   RCA's leadership in the original development of black-and-white television gave its subsidiary, NBC, a head start over the other networks. CBS saw an opportunity to counter NBC's advantage by taking the lead in color. During the 1940s, CBS developed a partially mechanical color television system that was *incompatible* with the NTSC black-and-white standards. The FCC actually approved the CBS system for public use in 1950, although few sets reached the market because of

---

*The FCC reallotted WOR-TV, channel 9, to northern New Jersey from New York City in 1982 in response to strong congressional pressure. In return, the licensee, RKO General, was granted a license renewal despite some severe shortcomings. RKO sold the station a few years later. See Exhibit 17–1.

---

*The pioneer commercial UHF station, KPTV (Portland, OR), went on the air in September 1952, using an RCA experimental transmitter. The first *maximum-power* (5 million watts) UHF transmitter did not go on the air until 1974.

the Korean War emergency restrictions on some kinds of manufacturing. Meanwhile, RCA continued working on its own compatible, all-electronic color system.

The rival networks eventually tired of the expensive wrangling, and in 1953 all parties accepted new standards proposed by the NTSC for an electronic system patterned closely on RCA's and thus compatible with sets already in use. This meant that black-and-white receivers already on the market could pick up color signals in monochrome.

But color telecasts on a large scale developed slowly because of the cost of receivers and lack of advertiser interest. Five years after the 1953 FCC adoption of the NTSC standards, only NBC offered programs in color. Full network color production in prime time came only in 1966. By 1972 half the country's homes had color television sets. Virtually all manufacturers now make only color sets, except for small portables.

3.6
Era of TV Dominance

Television grew far more rapidly than had radio two decades before because developers of the new medium could build on the knowledge and capital they had attained from the old. But television had no shoestring operations of the type that got small radio stations on the air: the cost of television programming and the lack of recorded backlog favored the network approach. Television networking, however, had to await development of special coaxial cable and microwave relay links built by AT&T.

Until the early 1950s, television stations had to survive without direct network interconnection. The recorded alternative, called *kinescopes,* consisted of the television pictures as they appeared on the face of a receiver tube. These filmed recordings of network programs became available by 1948, but their poor quality discouraged their use. In 1956 the Ampex Corporation demonstrated a successful *videotape* process, which saw its first practical use that fall on CBS. In a rare spirit of cooperation, competing manufacturers put aside their rivalries and opted for a compatible videotape standard from the outset.

Three Networks   Several factors kept the number of national commercial television networks to three: limitations on the availability of programs, on advertiser support, on hours available at affiliated stations, and, most crucial of all, on the number of broadcast channels in urban areas. To be competitive, a full-service commercial network must have access to affiliates with approximately equal coverage potential in all major markets. The FCC's 1952 *Sixth Report and Order* effectively limited television to three networks, since too few cities had been allotted more than three channels with equal coverage potential. Even if all the independent commercial stations in the country combined to form a fourth network, this network would be able to reach only about 85 percent of the population, whereas the three national networks can reach more than 95 percent of television homes.

Nevertheless, there have always been pressures to create a fourth national television network. When television networking began, Mutual, the fourth radio network, lacked the money to branch into television. But from 1946 to 1955 a fourth chain *did* exist: the DuMont Television Network, founded by Allen B. DuMont, a developer and manufacturer of cathode-ray tubes and a pioneer receiver manufacturer. DuMont survived only while the lack of live interconnection facilities kept networking in check. Once the relays for interconnection became generally available, DuMont could not compete with the larger and older networks.

DuMont's demise prompted the FCC's second network investigation in 1955–1957. Its inquiry concluded that the three remaining television networks (ABC, CBS, and NBC) held too much economic power over their affiliates (House CIFC: 1958). Although it was not a landmark like the first network report of 1941, the 1958 study did lead eventually to substantial rule changes (see Section 8.2).

The "Live Decade" (1948–1957)   If we look back with nostalgia to radio's "golden era" of the 1930s and 1940s, we may justifiably feel the same way about television's first decade. The networks put first priority on stimulating people to buy sets, and only attractive programs could do that:

> It was the only time in the history of the medium that program priorities superseded all others. If there was an abundance of original and quality drama at the time . . . it was in large part because those shows tended to appeal to a wealthier and better-educated part of the public, the part best able to afford a television set in those years when the price of receivers was high (Brown, 1971: 154).

Most programming, local and network, was necessarily live—a throwback to the earliest days of radio. Videotape recording had not yet been invented. Original television plays constituted the most memorable artistic achievements of television's live decade. "Talent seemed to gush right out of the cement," wrote the pioneer *New York Times* critic, Jack Gould (1973: 6).

A more realistic appraisal, perhaps, came from Robert Saudek, producer of *Omnibus,* a prestigious series initiated in 1952 with Ford Foundation support as an experiment in high-quality television. Asking himself whether the benefits of live production really justified the strain, Saudek concluded:

> Any sane observer would have to say no, because it is both efficient and economical to put shows on film or tape. Not only does it provide profitable reruns, but also . . . the scheduling of crews, studios, lights, cameras, sound and all the other hardware can be frozen and stored away like TV dinners to be retrieved and served up on demand (Saudek, 1973: 22).

In short, the economics of television drove it relentlessly toward shared and reused programming, and therefore toward recording, at both the local and the network levels.

Production Moves to Hollywood
Television programs could, of course, have been recorded from the very beginning by making them originally on motion picture film. Economic, technical, and social barriers delayed adoption of this solution.

The slow and cumbersome single-camera production method, traditional in Hollywood, cost far too much for television. It took time to adapt film to the physical limitations of television, with its lower resolution, its smaller projected picture area, and its much more restricted contrast range. Solutions to these problems came slowly because of the motion picture industry's feeling of superiority. It regarded the upstart television medium with a mixture of overt contempt and secret fear.

Moreover, many television specialists and critics counted on television to bring about a new mass entertainment genre, less trite than familiar Hollywood fare. The two points of view were as far apart as their two centers, television in New York and film in Los Angeles. But the economics of the two media drove them ever closer together. Inexorably, as the technical barriers to producing television programs on film fell, the production base for entertainment programming shifted to the West Coast.

In the 1956–1957 season, 63 percent of all network programming still came from New York; nearly all of it was live, whereas most of the West Coast production was on film. But in 1958 NBC moved *Studio One,* for a decade the most prestigious of the New York live television drama series, to Hollywood. It died within months, symbolizing the demise of television's live decade (Exhibit 3–9).

Feature Films
In a replay of the newspapers' earlier fears that radio would undermine the news business, Hollywood withheld its better and more recent theatrical feature films from television for a dozen years. Only pre-1948 films could be seen on television, except for some foreign imports grudgingly released by the film companies in fits and starts. The cutoff year was 1948 because after that year feature-film production contracts contained restrictive clauses taking into account the possibility of release to television.

During the early 1950s, then, television stations had to content themselves with old "B"-grade movies produced by minor companies. Somewhat in the spirit of early radio, when networks disdained to use recorded sound, television networks in the 1950s disdained to use feature films. For the time being, movies served only as fillers in locally programmed hours. Not until the early 1960s did

EXHIBIT 3–9   Early TV Shows

What's My Line? *exemplifies the half-hour panel show (in this case, celebrity panelists tried to identify mystery guests' careers) and the heavy presence of early advertisers.* Lassie *was a long-running Sunday evening program aimed at children. Mary Martin played* Peter Pan *on NBC in 1955, an early example of the "spectacular" or special program telecast live. A 1960 version was replayed in 1989.* The Honeymooners, *starring Art Carney, Jackie Gleason, and Audrey Meadows, was an early half-hour situation comedy built around a bumbling bus driver (Gleason) and an off-the-wall sewer worker (Carney), perennially seen in syndication to this day.*

SOURCES: CBS; except *Peter Pan*, from NBC.

Hollywood conclude that the television bane could also be a boon because networks would pay substantial prices for the "post-48" films that had no value for theatrical release.

Network Rivalries Most of NBC's early programming strategies sprang from the fertile imagination of Sylvester "Pat" Weaver (perhaps best known in the 1980s as the father of film actress Sigourney Weaver). Weaver resigned his job as the broadcasting chief of a major advertising agency in 1949 to become NBC's vice president for television. He left NBC only six years later as chair of the board, but in those few formative years he made a permanent mark on television programming. Though assuredly an intellectual, Weaver had the common touch in mass entertainment without being common. Most presumed television "experts" at that time simply tried to adapt radio or the theater to television. Weaver had a special talent for ridding himself of preconceived media habits to look at television with a fresh vision.

He foresaw, for example, that the single-sponsor show, the hallmark of big-time network radio, simply could not last in prime-time television. Program costs would eventually become far too high for any but a few rich, highly prestigious corporations to bear, and even they would be able to afford full sponsorship only occasionally. Instead, Weaver introduced *segmented sponsorship,* which enabled a number of different advertisers to share the spotlight in a single program. He also introduced the *magazine format,* which combines a number of separate features within the framework of a single program.

Disregarding conventional wisdom about the inviolability of established viewing habits, he disrupted regular schedules to run occasional one-time "spectaculars," 90 minutes long. The other networks refused to take such risks at first, but eventually Weaver's spectaculars became common practice on all networks as "specials."

Weaver, like William Paley at CBS, wanted to recapture commercial entertainment from advertising agencies, who had taken control during radio days (Section 2.9). He recognized that advertiser control meant conservative, no-risk programming. Only the networks, Weaver said, could "gamble on shows, on talent, on projects; and we often will lose in doing this all too often. But only a great network can afford the risk, and that is essentially why the great network service is so important to this country" (1955). As production costs rose, fewer advertisers could afford to supply programs. A study of prime-time program sources in the period 1957 to 1968 showed that advertisers declined as a source from 33 percent of the total to only 3 percent. Independent program packagers increased during the same period, producing 81 percent of all regularly scheduled prime-time programs by 1968 (Little, 1969: 1).

Despite Weaver's success with specific innovations, however, CBS steadily gained in the *overall* ratings race with NBC during Weaver's tenure. In consequence, NBC let Weaver go in 1955. That same year, CBS achieved the number-one-place in the ratings, a place it would hold undisputed for 21 years.

The American Broadcasting Company (ABC) faced tough competition, running well behind NBC and CBS in both radio and television. As the networks entered the television age in 1948, ABC found itself in somewhat the same position that CBS had occupied in the early days of network radio. Top advertisers and performers automatically turned to CBS or NBC, regarding ABC only as a last resort. ABC began to pay more attention to audience demographics, tailoring prime-time shows to the young, urban, adult segments of the audience. This policy meant emphasizing action, violence, and sex. ABC abandoned any serious attempt to offer the more balanced range of programming that the older networks had always thought essential to their national images.

Ironically, a second government-decreed corporate breakup rescued ABC in 1953. The Justice Department had forced a breakup of the big Hollywood motion picture studios. This meant that the studios had to sell off their extensive theater chains. One of the spun-off companies, Paramount Theaters, merged with ABC in 1953 after a long FCC proceeding, injecting much-needed funds and establishing a link with Hollywood that eventually paid off handsomely as ABC grew slowly to equal status with CBS and NBC.

In 1954, Walt Disney, the first of the major studio leaders to make a deal with television, agreed to produce a series of programs for ABC called *Disneyland* (1954–1957). This series was continued on NBC under various titles until it was finally dropped in 1981. The ABC deal gave Disney free advertising for his California theme park (just then opening) and Disney feature films.

3.7
Television's Impact on Radio

For radio, the year 1948 marked both a high-water mark and the beginning of the end for full-service network programming. In that year, radio networks grossed more revenue than ever before or since, excluding profits from their owned and operated stations. For more than 15 years, the networks had dominated broadcasting, but television was about to end their rule.

Network Radio Tries to Adjust After World War II, CBS's William Paley launched an all-out attack on NBC's leadership in radio programming. "I would grant NBC its greater reputation, prestige, finances, and facilities," said Paley, "but CBS had and would continue to have the edge in creative programming" (1979: 174). Paley discovered that star performers could increase their income by incorporating themselves, then selling their corporation's services to a network instead of taking salaries. Corporation profits were taxed as capital gains at only 25 percent, whereas salaries were then taxed as high as 77 percent (Paley, 1979: 193).

Using this leverage, Paley signed up Jack Benny in 1948. Within a short time, Bing Crosby, Red Skelton, Edgar Bergen, George Burns and Gracie Allen, Groucho Marx, and Frank Sinatra all deserted NBC for greener fields at CBS. By the fall of 1949, Paley finally achieved his dream of taking the lead away from NBC, a lead CBS held for the brief remaining life of big-time network radio—and was able to hold in the early decades of television.

By 1948, the network whose complaints against CBS and NBC had precipitated the chain broadcasting investigation, Mutual, had more than 500 affiliates and advertised itself as "the world's largest network." Most MBS affiliates had low power, however, and were outside the major urban centers. Under pressure to survive, MBS introduced innovative business practices, such as network *cooperative advertising*—using local advertisers to support network programming, originally the exclusive domain of national advertisers. Such ingenuity never succeeded in making Mutual financially stable, however, and its whole history has been marked by frequent changes in ownership. During a four-year period in the 1950s its ownership changed six times.

Decline of Radio Networks Through the 1940s, national radio networks supplied a full schedule of programs, much as television networks do today. Advertisers sponsored entire programs, rather than buying scattered spot announcements as they now do in television. But this very identity of sponsors with network programs and stars led to the precipitous decline in radio network fortunes after 1948. Television rapidly captured the mass audience and lured away major advertisers, and with them the major performers. By the early 1950s, the complacent pretelevision days had ended. William Paley, who led CBS through this transition, recalled:

> Although [CBS's] daytime schedule was more than 90 percent sponsored, our prime-time evening shows were more than 80 percent sustaining. Even our greatest stars could not stop the rush to television. Jack Benny left radio in 1958; Bing Crosby left nighttime radio in 1957 and quit his daytime program in 1962. It was sad to see them and other old-timers go. *Amos 'n' Andy*, which had been on radio since 1926 and on a network since 1929, left the air in 1960 (1979: 227).

The ultimate blow came when radio stations actually began refusing to renew network contracts—a startling change, considering that previously a network affiliation had always been regarded as a precious asset. But rigid network commitments interfered with the freedom that stations needed to put their new tailor-made, post-television program formulas into effect. Only a third of the radio stations had network affiliations by the early 1960s. Networks scaled down their service to brief hourly news bulletins, short information features, a few public affairs programs, and occasional on-the-spot sports events.

In 1948, the year television began its phenomenal growth, the radio networks and their few owned and operated stations earned $18 million. By 1958, radio network income had dropped to zero. The total income of the stations dropped from $46 million to $41 million in the same period, but with twice as many stations claiming a slice of the pie. On average, each station earned only half as much in 1958 as it had in 1948.

Rock to the Rescue If music had been important to radio during the pretelevision era, after television began it became all-important. With the loss of network dramas, variety shows, quiz games, and documentaries, radio programming shrunk essentially to music and news/talk, with music occupying by far the majority of the time on most stations. Providentially for radio, this programming transition coincided with the rise of a new musical culture, one that found radio an ideally hospitable medium.

Early in the 1950s, a Cleveland disc jockey (DJ) named Alan Freed gained national recognition:

> [Freed] began playing a strange new sound. A sound that combined elements of gospel, harmony, rhythm, blues, and country. He called it "rock and roll." And people everywhere began to listen. . . . It transcended borders and races. It was enjoyed down South as well as in the North. The music was no longer segmented. Both blacks and whites were able to listen . . . Rock and roll sang to the teen-ager; it charted his habits, his hobbies, his hang-ups (Drake-Chenault, 1978: 1).

Radio proved to be the perfect outlet for this new form of expression. Rock lyrics spread the slogans of the disenchanted and the disestablished in a coded language, in defiance of the stuffy standards that the broadcasting medium had previously sought to maintain.

Top-40 Radio The answer to television came in the late 1950s in the form of "Top-40" program-ming. The name referred to the practice of rigidly limiting DJs to a prescribed *playlist* of current best-selling popular recordings. Gordon McLendon, a colorful sportscaster and station owner, is one of those credited with pioneering the format. Another pioneer, Todd Storz, applied the Top-40 formula to group-owned stations.

Such innovators frequently moved bottom-ranked stations to the first rank in their markets in a matter of months. An hour's monitoring of a Storz Top-40 station in the late 1950s yielded the following statistics: 125 program items in the single hour; 73 time, weather, promotional, and other brief announcements; 58 repetitions of call letters; a $3^1/_2$ minute newscast featuring accidents and assaults, each item averaging two sentences in length. The overall effect was loud, brash, fast, hypnotic—and memorable. The station acquired an instantly recognizable "sound." No other station on the dial sounded anything like a newly programmed Storz station.

The success of the Top-40 formula came as much from its ruthlessness in repelling listeners as from its skillfullness in attracting them. Formula programmers relied on consistency above all else, programming relentlessly for a limited audience segment no matter how many other segments took offense. The second ingredient in Top-40 success was an equally single-minded dedication to ceaseless promotion and advertising. Call letters and dial position had to be indelibly imprinted on the listener's mind.

FM's Triumph FM began to recover from its decade-long slide in 1958. Its success came not only from greater audience interest in its improved sound quality but also from the drying up of AM channel availability and from a deliberate FCC policy of encouraging FM.

For example, in 1961, the FCC approved technical standards for FM stereo. The combination of FM's new stereo capability with its greater fidelity, coming just as public interest in high-fidelity stereo recording reached a peak, gave FM a substantial advantage over AM sound. FM rode that technical lead to become the fastest-growing broadcasting medium of the 1960s.

FCC decisions in 1965–1967 contributed further to FM's success. The *nonduplication rule* required AM/FM owners in major markets to program FM operations independently of AM sister stations at least half the time, giving an important stimulus to independent FM programming.* The rule was gradually expanded to cover smaller markets and more station time. This rule proved crucial in transforming FM from a shadow of AM to an independent service with its own format specialization.

At first, FM suffered from the relative scarcity of FM receivers. In the 1950s *transistor* radios began to make AM a truly portable medium. Car radios dominated the important morning and afternoon "drive time" audiences, and few cars had FM receivers. In search of parity, FM lobbyists tried to persuade Congress to pass an "all channel" bill similar to that passed for television. But growing audience demand for access to both radio services eventually accomplished the same end without legislation. By 1974 the majority of radios had FM, and two years later most car radios could also receive FM signals (Sterling, 1984: 225). By the 1980s few radios were sold that could not receive both bands.

3.8
Ethical Crises of the 1950s

The explosive growth of broadcasting and the potential for vast profits created many temptations. A series of ethical crises occurred in the 1950s: fraudulence in programming (including *payola*, payoffs to radio DJs for playing certain records), political blacklisting, and malfeasance in office by FCC commissioners.

Quiz Scandals In the mid-1950s, high-stakes television quiz programs captured national attention. They dominated prime-time ratings, becoming

*As part of its deregulation of radio and television, the FCC dropped the nonduplication requirement in 1986, by which time most FM stations were profitable largely because of their separate formats. The rule was no longer needed—marketplace competition would continue to assure that few AM/FM combinations were programmed alike.

EXHIBIT 3–10 Quiz Scandals

Then a Columbia University English instructor, Charles Van Doren is seen in one of the "isolation booths" used in the quiz programs to prevent the contestant from getting tips from the studio audience. In the investigation that followed a disclosure of rigged winning or losing outcomes, Van Doren received a suspended sentence after pleading guilty to charges of perjury. He also lost his jobs with both Columbia University and NBC television, where he had been a member of the Today *show cast.*

SOURCE: AP/Wide World Photos.

an obsession for audiences and programmers alike. The first big-time quiz show, *The $64,000 Question,** premiered on CBS in 1955, followed in 1956 by NBC's *Twenty-One* and then by dozens of others. At the height of the fad, five new quiz shows hit the air in a single day.

Producers milked the contests for the last possible drop of suspense. Thousands of dollars hung in the balance as audiences awaited crucial answers from contestants enclosed in "isolation booths" to prevent prompting. Most glamorous of the con-

*In 1989 dollars, the top prize would have been worth closer to $325,000.

testants on *Twenty-One* was Charles Van Doren, a bachelor in his twenties and a faculty member at Columbia University. For 15 breathless weeks Van Doren survived one challenge after another. By the time he finally lost, he had won $129,000 and had become a media supercelebrity.

But Van Doren, along with most other contestants, had been faking all the time, conniving with program producers to rig the outcome. The drive to raise advertising rates by garnering the largest possible audiences seduced producers into rigging the quiz in order to keep crowd-pleasing contestants on the air as long as possible (Exhibit 3-10).

The first hints of quiz rigging began to surface in 1956, when several unsuccessful contestants began to speak out. Despite pious disclaimers from other contestants, producers, advertisers, and network officials, the New York district attorney began an investigation late in 1958. Ultimately, ten persons pleaded guilty to having perjured themselves by denying complicity in quiz rigging. By the time official confirmation of fraud came in July 1959, the quiz craze had run its course, for the time being, having earned millions of dollars for drug and cosmetic sponsors. Van Doren and others indicted by the grand jury received suspended sentences.

The ripples spread far and wide. President Dwight D. Eisenhower requested a report from the U.S. Attorney General. Congress amended the Communications Act of 1934, threatening fines and/or jail for complicity in rigging "contests of intellectual knowledge, intellectual skill or chance" (47 USC 509). Also, the networks moved to take back some degree of programming control from advertisers— a move reinforced by the rising cost of television time, which made sponsorship of entire programs too costly for advertisers. For a time, network officials spoke in glowing terms of an increase in public-affairs and documentary programming, and the industry set up the Television Information Office (TIO) to give broadcasting a better public image.*

The quiz scandals dramatized divergent views of broadcasting's role. To some, the quiz deceptions seemed a massive betrayal of public trust, a symptom of widespread moral decay. But to others, the rigging seemed no more fraudulent than a stage pistol with blanks rather than real bullets. In response to an opinion survey taken just after the disclosure of the quiz rigging, a quarter of the respondents saw nothing wrong with the deception (Kendrick, 1969: 130).

Blacklisting   The social role of broadcasting came into question from another perspective during the late 1940s and 1950s. During this Cold War period, some Americans feared imminent Russian takeover. There was an intensive hunt for evidence of pro-communist, subversive influences. People in the news and entertainment media became favorite targets of the hunters. Many performers and writers suspected of leftist sympathies found themselves on *blacklists*—privately (and sometimes publicly) circulated rosters compiled by zealous, usually self-appointed investigators. The listmakers searched through newspaper files and other records for evidence of people's associations with causes and organizations suspected of having subversive intentions.

People whose names appeared on such lists lost their jobs suddenly and thereafter found themselves unemployable, usually with no explanation or opportunity for rebutting the evidence. Actors found themselves especially vulnerable because a few years before, during World War II, they had often been asked to appear at benefit performances and rallies in support of the war effort. As a wartime ally of the United States, the Soviet Union sometimes benefited from such appearances, making it easy to accuse the actors of communist leanings.

After news of a few arbitrary dismissals became embarrassingly public, the networks and advertising agencies "institutionalized" blacklisting in order to avoid unfavorable publicity. According to a study

---

*The networks and the National Association of Broadcasters closed the TIO in 1989 because of "changing industry patterns, dupli-

cation of efforts by industry organizations, and declining membership," they said. The FCC's deregulation policy and lowered public expectations also made such expensive public relations efforts less essential.

commissioned by the Fund for the Republic, they assigned top executives to comb through blacklists and to compile their own "black," "gray," and "white" lists as guides to safe casting and job assignment decisions (Cogley, 1956). They found plenty of names in such publications as *Red Channels: The Report of Communist Infiltration in Radio and Television,* published by Counterattack in 1950. Scores of writers, performers, newspersons, and other broadcast employees found their careers abruptly halted. Many innocent people suffered permanent damage; some even committed suicide.

Proving the falsity of accusations or disclaiming any communist leanings did not suffice to "clear" names once clouded. Mere innocence was not enough. Private anticommunist "consultants" demanded that suspects purge themselves of "dangerous neutralism." AWARE, Inc., one of the self-appointed blacklist groups, published *The Road Back: Self Clearance.* It advised those who wanted to clear their names to "support anti-Communist persons, groups, and organizations" and to "subscribe to anti-Communist magazines, read anti-Communist books, government reports and other literature." Religious conversion also counted as a favorable sign of political redemption (quoted in Cogley, 1956: 136).

The broadcasting industry knuckled under with scarcely a murmur of public protest. However, when the Fund for the Republic polled broadcasting executives, it found that only 11 percent regarded the blacklisters as "sincere and patriotic." Other executives referred to them as "misguided," "crazy," "profiteers," and "pathological." Sixty-seven percent of the industry members interviewed believed that professional jealousy motivated the blacklisters (Cogley, 1956: 242).

Among the talent unions, only Actors' Equity took an antiblacklisting stand. The American Federation of Television and Radio Artists (AFTRA) failed to come to the aid of its accused members.

The Faulk Case   One AFTRA member fought back. John Henry Faulk, a successful radio personality at CBS, had helped to organize an antiblacklist (but also anticommunist) ticket for the New York

AFTRA chapter, and had won election as second vice president. The pro-blacklist faction included several officers of AWARE, Inc. Following the defeat of its slate in the AFTRA election, AWARE published a report accusing Faulk of seven instances of activities it considered politically suspect.

He brought suit against the blacklisters in 1956. Later that year, CBS abruptly discharged Faulk while he was out of the country on vacation. Upon his return, he found his career at an end.

Alleging a malicious conspiracy to defame him, Faulk proved each of AWARE's seven charges false. The viciousness of the libel so appalled the jury that it awarded even more damages than Faulk asked— a total of $3.5 million. On appeal, the defendants received another stinging rebuff when a five-judge New York appellate court unanimously upheld the guilty verdict, remarking that "the acts of the defendants were proved to be as malicious as they were vicious." The court did, however, reduce the damages to $550,000 (AD, 1963: 464), most of which Faulk never collected. Louis Nizer, Faulk's lawyer, concluded his own story of the case by saying, "One lone man had challenged the monstrously powerful forces of vigilantism cloaked in super patriotism" (1966: 464).

In point of fact, the blacklisters only seemed monstrously powerful. They gained their strength from the timidity of the broadcasters, advertisers, and agencies, who generally surrendered meekly in order to avoid controversy.

Murrow Confronts McCarthy   Another episode in the 1950s exemplified broadcasters' acceptance of journalistic responsibility. The best-known exponent of the blacklisting style of patriotism was Senator Joseph R. McCarthy (R-Wisconsin). As chair of a Senate subcommittee on investigations, McCarthy staged a series of flamboyant witch hunts. His methods caused the term *McCarthyism* to enter the language as a synonym for public character assassination based on unfounded accusations.

Edward R. Murrow, a CBS newsman, took the risk of openly opposing McCarthy. In television documentaries and radio commentaries, Murrow had criticized specific instances of McCarthy's unfairness, but not until March 9, 1954, did he mount a direct attack on McCarthy's methods as a whole. That night, Murrow devoted his entire *See It Now* program to a devastating critique of McCarthyism.

To create the program, Murrow and his producer, Fred Friendly, needed to do little more than draw upon their film files. McCarthy's outrageous, inconsistent, illogical, opportunistic, and devious methods themselves condemned him. McCarthy accepted CBS's offer of rebuttal time, filming his reply on a Fox Movietone sound stage at a cost of $6,000, which CBS paid. With his usual wild rhetoric, McCarthy called Murrow "the leader and the cleverest of the jackal pack which is always found at the throat of anyone who dares to expose individual Communists and traitors" (quoted in Friendly, 1967: 55). Later in 1954, television dealt another blow to McCarthy by broadcasting in full the 36-day hearings of his Senate subcommittee, during which he attacked the patriotism of the U.S. Army.* As in the *See It Now* broadcast, on camera McCarthy turned out to be his own worst enemy.

Murrow himself never claimed that the *See It Now* analysis played a decisive role in McCarthy's subsequent decline. Press criticism was already on the rise, and the mood of the country was changing. In any event, within the year McCarthy's career effectively ended when the Senate passed a motion of censure against him.

In doing its part to expose McCarthy, broadcasting to some extent redeemed itself for having given in so tamely to the demands of the blacklisters. Nevertheless, as Murrow said, looking back five years after the event, "the timidity of television in dealing with this man when he was spreading fear throughout the land is not something to which the art of communications can ever point with pride. Nor

should it be allowed to forget it" (quoted in Kendrick, 1969: 70).

FCC Payoffs   In the late 1950s, two FCC commissioners were forced to resign under pressure. In March 1958, Commissioner Richard Mack withdrew when it became known that he had accepted a bribe to vote for a particular applicant for a potentially lucrative television license in Florida. Two years later, FCC chair John Doerfer left office over charges of having accepted cruises on the yacht of the owner of a group of stations and of having submitted double and triple bills for official travel.

These and other FCC transgressions led to a series of intensive congressional investigations of FCC operations. Part of the problem lay in the quality of the appointments made to the FCC and similar government agencies. Presidential appointments to these relatively minor bureaucratic posts notoriously served as political payoffs. Cynically self-serving regulator–industry relationships also played a part in an era when the FCC often actually regulated. With later deregulation, however, the commission took the broadcasters' side against the Communications Act (that "last of the New Deal dinosaurs"), and identification of regulators with industry interests became commonplace rather than scandalous. We return to this theme in Chapter 17.

Summary

▌ Over the four decades covered in this chapter, broadcasting expanded from a small prewar business of 800 AM stations to a modern industry of nearly 9,000 radio and television stations. Throughout, first in radio and after 1948 in television, the three national networks dominated broadcast programming and economics. Early concern about broadcasting's competitive impact was evident in the 1930s battles over music licensing, union battles against use of recordings, and the brief press-radio war.

▌ RCA spearheaded the U.S. television system that was finally approved by the FCC in 1941. FM radio,

---

*In those days the networks, especially the weaker ones, could find time for such extended coverage without undue sacrifice. Both the DuMont network and ABC carried the 187 hours of hearings in full, although ABC did not at that time have complete coast-to-coast coverage. NBC carried a few days of the hearings, and CBS showed film clips in the evenings.

the brainchild of inventor Edwin Howard Armstrong, was also approved for commercial operation in 1941 but saw only limited growth until the 1960s.

▮ Though the radio industry grew little in size during World War II, it gained enormously in stature as it reported from the world's battlefronts, laying the ground for postwar broadcast journalism.

▮ Postwar network radio reached its height of rivalry as CBS surpassed NBC in popularity. ABC, which developed from the sale of NBC Blue, continued to struggle, and Mutual developed its small market affiliations.

▮ Commercial television began in earnest with the inception of network service in 1948, although coast-to-coast interconnections did not come until 1951.

▮ Demand for station assignments became so heavy that the FCC was forced to reevaluate its entire allotment scheme. A freeze on licensing was implemented from 1948 to 1952, ending with the *Sixth Report and Order,* which opened up UHF frequencies and set aside reserved assignments for noncommercial operation. Channel assignment and the problems of limited UHF coverage were dominant industry issues in the 1950s.

▮ After years of developmental work by CBS (on a mechanical system) and RCA (on an electronic system), the FCC approved color television operations late in 1953. But color did not take off commercially for another decade, largely because of its high cost.

▮ Networks patterned on the radio model dominated the first decades of television operation. Though NBC pioneered many original practices, CBS soon dominated audience ratings. ABC struggled in a weak third place, and DuMont, the fourth network attempt, failed in 1955, since too few markets had four stations.

▮ Production of network programming moved from New York to the West Coast, providing a closer alliance with the film industry. In 1956 videotape was introduced, making possible greater production and scheduling flexibility.

▮ As viewers and advertisers flocked to television, the old radio network system fell apart. The development in the mid-1950s of rock music, formula Top-40 radio formats, and portable transistor radios helped to build a new identity for radio.

▮ FM radio became the fastest-growing broadcasting medium of the 1960s, encouraged by FCC decisions that established stereo standards, and that required separate AM and FM programming from owners who operated both kinds of stations. In addition, the general overcrowding in AM contributed to FM's growth.

▮ Rapid change and expansion of the broadcast industry, and the potential for fast and vast profits, led to several ethical crises late in the 1950s. Rock radio was shaken by DJ payola, popular TV network quiz shows turned out to be largely rigged, political blacklisting was widespread, and two FCC commissioners were forced to resign because of malfeasance in office. Yet the industry showed what impact television could have as CBS's Edward R. Murrow took on demagogue Senator Joseph McCarthy in a hard-hitting documentary that helped end the senator's reign of political terror.

▮ Throughout this period, broadcasting had little competition, except from established newspapers. Radio and television stations were often money machines for owners. Network-dominated television appeared likely to dominate leisure time for decades to come. But dramatic changes were in the offing.

CHAPTER 4

ERA OF NEW COMPETITION

Through the 1970s, traditional television and radio broadcasting continued to grow and prosper, not much changed in outline from a decade or two earlier. But rival delivery systems began to gather strength in the late 1970s and 1980s, posing unprecedented challenges to the system of broadcasting that had evolved over the previous half century. Audience demand for more viewing options, technological progress, and important changes in regulatory thinking favoring marketplace solutions all combined to create the fast-changing electronic media scene of the 1980s.

4.1
Emergence of Cable TV

The 1952 *Sixth Report and Order* planted the seeds of future change. The television channel allotment table set up by that watershed FCC decision severely limited the number of television signals that could be received, even in the largest cities. The table left large *white areas*, those devoid of television service. Most homes that could receive television at all had only three to five channels to choose from, even after activation of the UHF channels that the 1952 decision made available. Pent-up public demand thus set the stage for additional and alternative modes of program delivery.

Extending TV Coverage   Several types of low-power repeater transmitters emerged to extend television station coverage by retransmitting signals to local areas without service. The most common type, *translator* transmitters, extended signals by "translating" the original signal, usually from UHF to VHF, to service white areas. From some 300 operations in 1960, these increased to 2,500 by 1970 and more than 4,000 by 1980. A few low-power *booster* transmitters filled holes in station coverage by rebroadcasting signals on the same channel as the main transmitter. *Satellite* stations offered some local programming of their own, but generally rebroadcast programs (just like a network affiliate) from a station under the same ownership located in a larger market. All three approaches were attempts to provide more coverage without adding interference.

But these services, some quite controversial at the time,* merely expanded the coverage of existing stations, one signal at a time. Such repeaters still have a role to play; more than 5,000 were operating in 1988. They also laid the groundwork for a future service in the 1980s, *low-power television* (LPTV).

Community Antenna TV   Another alternative, *community antenna television* (CATV), emerged

---

*At first, these small repeaters operated without benefit of an FCC license, since they didn't fit into the scheme of its *Sixth Report*. The commission tried to force them off the air, but the governor of Colorado, formerly an influential senator, used his contacts in Congress to pressure the FCC to license the translators (in 1956) and boosters retroactively.

soon after broadcast television began commercial service. One early system began in 1950 at Lansford, PA, about 80 miles northwest of Philadelphia, the nearest large market. Lansford residents could not receive Philadelphia stations because of hilly terrain. The CATV system used a special antenna on a nearby hilltop to pick up three Philadelphia stations, then delivered the signals to subscribers below by means of a coaxial cable connection direct to their homes.

During their first decade, CATV systems remained primarily a local concern. Initial regulation, if any, came from municipal governments, which granted permission to run cables over or under public property. These authorities granted cable operators *franchises* to install and operate their systems for a fixed number of years (usually 15). Early systems carried only five or six channels, devoted entirely to off-the-air signals of stations in nearby cities. Most served from a few dozen to a few hundred subscribers.

As long as cable acted as a neutral redelivery service, filling in unserved areas, beefing up fringe reception, and overcoming local interference, broadcasters welcomed it. Some stations eventually found their signals carried by dozens of cable systems, so that they reached substantially larger audiences than before.

Program Augmentation After their initial success in enabling reception of broadcast television, CATV operators began to seek ways to enhance their service to make subscriptions more salable. After a system had repaid the installation costs, new services could be added at a small additional expense. *Augmentation* took several forms. The number of programs could be increased by importing signals of distant stations* via microwave relay. With *local origination,* original programming on one or more cable channels was provided at no extra subscriber cost. A third type of augmentation, eventually crucial to cable de-

velopment, involved offering feature films, sports, and special events from nonbroadcast program sources at extra cost to subscribers.

When cable pioneers began to consider more ways to expand their business, they looked toward larger towns and cities, where concentrations of potential subscribers could be found. Big-city dwellers might have several local over-the-air services, but they often had difficulties with direct reception because of interference. Cable operators could sell them clearer reception, but they wanted to entice subscribers with more options—imported distant signals, local origination, and sometimes extra-cost services.

By the mid-1960s, as cable expanded, broadcasters began to see it more as a dangerous predator than as a benign extender of their audiences. The growing practice of importing signals tended to obliterate the fixed market boundaries imposed by the coverage limitations of over-the-air broadcasting. A network affiliate might find its network programs duplicated in its viewing area on a cable-imported distant station, thus dividing its audience. Cable tended to fragment audiences, leaving broadcast stations with lower ratings and thus less appeal for advertisers. By this time, benign community antenna television had emerged as a full-fledged competitor known simply as *cable television.*

Protectionist Regulation Broadcasters began to appeal to the Federal Communications Commission for protection. At first the FCC demurred, seeing cable systems merely as extensions of the viewer's own antenna. As cable's economic impact on broadcasting increased, however, the FCC began to intervene. Having nurtured UHF television for years, the commission could not afford to see its shaky foundation undermined by cable expansion, which hurt the weakest stations first. Even educational stations expressed concern about imported noncommercial signals from other markets, claiming that cable competed unfairly for their already-small audiences.

In 1962, persuaded by broadcasters' concerns, the commission began to impose case-by-case restrictions on cable systems that applied for micro-

---

*The term *distant stations* acquired a legal meaning as the FCC began regulating cable: broadcast stations not receivable over the air in the cable television system's market, not necessarily stations at an extreme distance.

wave relay licenses to bring in distant stations, and were thus engaged in radio communication. In 1966 it extended regulation to all cable systems, beginning a period of pervasive control of cable.

The FCC made cable systems carry all local television stations (the *must-carry rule*) and refrain from duplicating network programs on the same day the network offered them. No new signals could be imported into any of the top 100 markets without a hearing on the probable effect of such importations on existing broadcast stations. The Supreme Court upheld the FCC's growing intervention (U.S., 1968a: 157).

The FCC, broadcasters, and cable operators carried on a three-way debate about cable's role in the top 100 markets, which include about 80 percent of the country's people and have sufficient off-the-air broadcast service. Broadcasters feared unrestricted invasion by augmented cable. They spread scare stories about *siphoning,* the draining of hitherto "free" broadcast programs by cable systems able to outbid broadcasters for transmission rights. They warned that network news and local-station public-service programs would decline if cable cut deeper into broadcasters' revenues.

Such tactics resulted in the so-called definitive FCC cable regulations of 1972 (FCC, 1972b: 143). The rules severely restricted the type and number of signals that cable could bring into the largest cities. Cable had to provide, on request, *access channels* for local governments, educational institutions, and the general public. As long as cable served primarily to expand coverage of television stations or to provide new kinds of programs, it would be allowed. However, this regulatory cage built to contain cable soon began to fall apart.

Deregulation Only five years after the FCC "definitive" rules appeared, a Court of Appeals decision held that the commission "has in no way justified its position that cable television must be a supplement to, rather than an equal of, broadcast television" (F, 1977d: 9). This rebuff, plus a change in administration (at the White House and consequently in the FCC chair), led to FCC reconsider-

ation. Under court orders as well as its own initiative, the commission removed itself step by step from cable regulation. No longer would the FCC oversee local cable franchise standards, nor would systems have to meet federal construction standards. Large cable systems no longer had to originate at least some programming locally.* Under the triple pressures of court review, its own economic analysis, and a changed political outlook on regulation, the commission had turned completely around in its perception of cable's role (see Exhibit 17–7).

At the same time, satellite-to-cable program services gave cable systems an increasingly wide choice of national programs. This diversity coincided with long-time FCC broadcast programming objectives. In short, the commission no longer sought to protect broadcasting from cable, but rather encouraged competition between the two. Cable grew accordingly (Exhibit 4–1).

4.2
Cable Becomes a Major Player

Three further developments in the 1970s played major roles in the evolution of CATV into cable television as a mature and independent service: (1) the proliferation of domestic satellite relays, (2) the development of the television "superstation," and (3) the introduction of pay-cable services. In the 1980s came a fourth development, the provision of cable-specific original program material.

Role of Domsats International communication satellites came into use for broadcast relays in the 1960s. They answered the demand for transoceanic programming, enabling television to bring foreign events to the television screen instanta-

---

*The impact of this regulatory cycle shows up in FCC employment records. With the issuance of the 1972 rules, the commission established a new bureau to oversee cable. Within a year, the bureau had grown to some 300 employees. A decade later, with the decline in the FCC's cable role, only 30 persons remained when the FCC folded the operation into its new Mass Media Bureau.

EXHIBIT 4-1   Cable TV Growth Indicators: 1960–1988

Year	Number of systems	Number of subscribers	Average subscribers per system	Percentage of homes with cable	Percentage of systems with 13 or more channels*
1960	640	650,000	1,016	1.4	N/A
1965	1,325	1,275,000	962	2.4	N/A
1970	2,490	4,500,000	1,807	7.6	3
1975	3,506	9,800,000	2,795	14.3	22
1980	4,225	16,000,000	3,787	20.0	29
1985	6,500	35,000,000	5,385	41.1	29
1988	8,413	43,790,000	5,205	49.4	N/A

*Data on system channel capacity for 1980 and 1985 actually reflect data for 1979 and 1984, respectively

As cable TV grew, system size and channel capacity both increased. After 1975, pay cable spurred basic cable growth.

SOURCES: Christopher H. Sterling, *Electronic Media: A Guide to Trends in Broadcasting and Newer Technologies, 1920–1983*, pp. 28, 30. Copyright © 1984 by Christopher H. Sterling. Reprinted and adapted with permission of Praeger Publishers; 1985 and 1988 data from National Cable Television Association, citing *TV Factbook*.

neously. The existence of a well-developed national system of microwave and coaxial cable relays postponed a similar demand for *domestic satellites (domsats)* designed to relay programs within the country.

In 1972, however, a key FCC deregulatory move stimulated that demand: its "open skies" policy, which allowed any business firm with the requisite financial and technical resources to launch one or more domsats (FCC, 1972a: 844). Western Union's Westar I became the first American domsat in 1974. The FCC regulates satellite operators as *common carriers* (point-to-point, rate-regulated communication services). Carriers lease or sell transponders (combination receiver-transmitters) to brokers and program distributors.

A second key FCC decision, issued in 1979, deregulated television receive-only (TVRO) antennas, eliminating a cumbersome and expensive licensing process. The dropping of regulatory barriers opened the way for widespread use of satellites to relay program services to cable systems—and soon to broadcast stations—at less cost than with traditional land lines. Increased sales led to greater TVRO production and lower prices.

Emergence of Superstations   TVROs gave cable systems a relatively efficient and inexpensive way of obtaining nationally distributed program services with which to attract new subscribers. But the programs themselves remained in short supply until Ted Turner came upon the scene (Exhibit 4–2). An innovative entrepreneur who thought little of broadcast network programming and had faith in cable's future, Turner invented a way of combining local broadcasting with national cable program needs—what came to be called the *superstation*. He had bought the lowest-ranked outlet in the five-station Atlanta market, UHF channel 17, which became WTBS. In 1976, he contracted with Southern Satellite Systems (SSS), a satellite capacity resale company, to *uplink* WTBS programs to RCA's Satcom I for distribution to cable systems (Exhibit 4–3, page 86). He enticed cable systems to invest in their own TVROs to downlink WTBS, offering systems a full schedule of sports and movie program-

EXHIBIT 4–2   Ted Turner—"Captain Outrageous"

No more colorful a character bestrides the world of electronic media than Ted Turner, chairperson of the board and president of Turner Broadcasting Systems (TBS). TBS owns and operates SuperStation WTBS, Cable News Network, Headline News, Turner Network Television (TNT, a satellite-to-cable program network), Turner Program Services, and two professional sports teams: the Atlanta Braves (baseball) and Atlanta Hawks (basketball).

Referred to variously as "Terrible Ted," "Captain Outrageous," and "The Mouth of the South," Turner is known for his outspoken opinions, his willingness to challenge the establishment, his aggressive and entrepreneurial spirit ("Lead, follow, or get out of the way"), his driving ambition ("My desire to excel borders on the unhealthy"), and his ego (he once told an interviewer, "If I only had a little humility, I'd be perfect"). Physically, he is the prototype of the southern gentleman: tall, lanky, with silver-streaked hair and mustache, cigar-smoking, speaking with more than a bit of Georgia drawl. He loves the movie *Gone With the Wind* so much he named one of his five children Rhett.

Turner attended Brown University, where he was vice president of the Debating Union and commodore of the Brown Yacht Club. College yachting experience later served him in good stead when in 1977 he won the prestigious America's Cup race. Brown threw him out of college twice and his fraternity once dropped him for burning down its homecoming display.

Turner began his business career as an account executive with his father's advertising company in Savannah, later joining the company's office in Macon, GA, as general manager. In 1963, he became chief executive officer of the various Turner companies with headquarters in Atlanta. His interest in broadcasting began with his 1970 acquisition of Atlanta's Channel 17, then a failing independent operation. There he dreamed up the superstation concept six years later (Exhibit 4–3). The station beams its signal by satellite-to-cable relays, making its programs nationally available to millions of viewers.

On 1 June 1980, Turner launched Cable News Network (CNN), the first live, 24-hour-a-day, all-news cable network. Knowledgeable observers predicted its early demise (some dubbed it the "Chicken Noodle Network"), but by 1988 over 8,000 cable systems carried CNN to a potential 40 million homes. Millions more see it in over 50 foreign countries. In 1981, Turner began a second cable news service, CNN-2, now called Headline News, a continuously updated 30-minute cycle of hard news carried both by cable systems and some television stations. In 1982, he formed CNN Radio, a 24-hour all-news cable network with affiliates across the country.

ming practically free; cable systems paid SSS only ten cents per subscriber (Turner's revenues came from higher advertiser rates on WTBS, which he began charging in 1979).

WTBS programs went at first to only about 20 cable systems. By the end of 1978, more than 200 systems downlinked WTBS; a year later, there were ten times that many. Improved TVRO technology that made the dishes smaller and cheaper helped this record growth.

Pay Cable   The second innovation in cable programming came with *pay cable,* led by Home Box Office (HBO) in 1972. It introduced the idea of offering subscribers a special channel of superior entertainment for which they would pay an added fee over the *basic* fee charged for run-of-the-mill channels. HBO started in Wilkes-Barre, PA, supplying a channel of pay-cable movies to several cable systems in the Northeast and delivering its programs to cable companies by mail or microwave relays. Lack of cost-effective relay facilities held back pay-cable progress until 1975, when HBO announced that it had leased a transponder on RCA's Satcom I and would offer its programs to any system in the country that was able to buy or lease a TVRO antenna. Satellite delivery reduced distribution costs

EXHIBIT 4–2 Continued

In 1984, Turner stumbled when he tried to compete with Music Television (MTV). His Cable Music Channel lasted only 36 days, failing to achieve the 10 million subscribers needed to survive (he originally claimed 2.2 million, but that later fell to about 350,000). MTV bought some of its assets for about $1 million plus free advertising on Turner's other cable services.

SOURCE: Photo courtesy Turner Broadcasting Systems, Inc.

His biggest battle came in 1985 when he tried to take over the CBS broadcast network. Although he lost that fight, he came up within a year as the new owner of MGM's film library, including his beloved *Gone With the Wind* for use on his superstation and the projected TNT cable network. The purchase pushed TBS deeply into debt, forcing Turner to accept a consortium of large cable system operators as partners. They received positions on his board of directors, in return for their investment in TBS. Three years later he scheduled *Gone With the Wind* for the October 1988 debut of Turner Network Television (TNT). He promoted TNT as the first cable network designed expressly to challenge the three broadcast networks. Initially able to reach about 17 million homes, the service offered mostly movies but promised 200 original programs a year by 1992. Early projects included *The Story of Billy the Kid, The Story of Michelangelo,* the plays of William Shakespeare, and the historionics of his newly acquired National Wrestling Alliance. To attract more viewers to both TNT and WTBS, Turner backed the "colorization" of black-and-white films from the MGM film vaults. This computer process, which adds color to old films, involved Turner in more controversy with critics who accused him of ruining classic movies. But Turner was already looking to his next project. . . .

and enabled simultaneous scheduling, which made possible national promotion of the service. This one move transformed the cable business:

> Rarely does a simple business decision by one company affect so many. . . . In deciding to gamble on the leasing of satellite TV channels, Time Inc. [by then the owner of HBO] took the one catalytic step needed for the creation of a new national television network designed to provide pay TV programs (Taylor, 1980: 142).

HBO charged a flat monthly payment rather than the complicated pay-per-view fee used in earlier pay-cable experiments. At first, subscribers complained about the quality of the films, but after 1978,

when HBO began making a profit (and when some restrictive FCC rules were dropped), it began to show newer and better movies. Vigorous promotion increased audience demand for pay-cable services, stimulating entry of entrepreneurs into the new programming market.

Fewer than 200 cable systems had TVROs in 1977, but within a decade some 8,000 had them, with many systems using two or more to pick up different satellites. The superstation and pay-cable innovations pioneered by Turner and HBO stimulated explosive cable system growth. Only a quarter of all cable systems carried a pay-cable channel in 1977, but by the mid-1980s, virtually all did.

EXHIBIT 4–3   Satellite Distribution

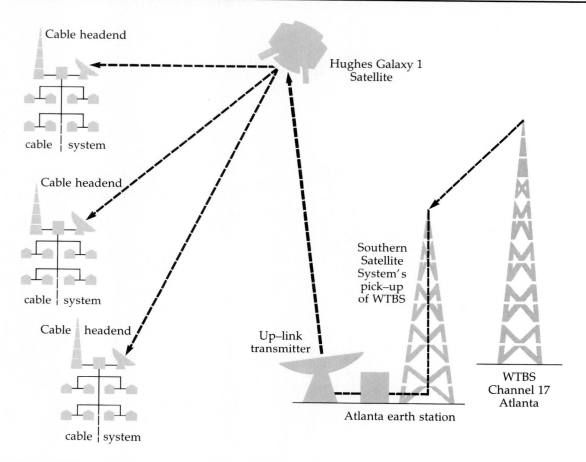

This diagram illustrates how Atlanta "SuperStation" WTBS gets its signal to cable systems all over the United States. The programming is picked up off the air by a satellite carrier, in this case Southern Satellite System, and is now sent to a Hughes Galaxy 1 satellite transponder by means of a large uplink Earth station about nine miles from the television station. The signal is then beamed down by the transponder for pickup at receive-only earth stations located near the headends of cable systems across the country.

SOURCE: Turner Broadcasting Systems, Inc.

Program Innovation   Until 1980, cable remained basically a parasitic medium, providing preexisting broadcast programs and motion pictures to home TV sets without adding much new or original programming of its own. HBO led the way in the development of *cable-specific* programming, new programs produced especially for showing on cable. HBO, soon followed by other services, taped special stage shows and sports events, and commissioned original program material to expand pay-cable services beyond just movie packages.

In the late 1960s, writers predicting cable's future had expected that cable-specific programming would develop early and would serve a wide variety of special audience interests. The regulatory barriers of the 1970s and the initial cost of building cable systems delayed development of such original programming until the proliferation of satellite networks in the early 1980s made specialization financially possible.

One of the first to offer a format unavailable on broadcast television was Ted Turner, whose 24-hour Cable News Network (CNN) aired amid predictions that such a national cable news service would cost far more than it could earn (see Exhibit 4-2). The pundits were wrong. Once again, Turner's flare for daring experiments paid off. He even helped to change broadcasting because stations and networks had to expand their news programming to meet the competition from cable. Turner added CNN Headline news just 18 months later, giving news junkies two 24-hour choices. Turner may have gotten some of the news idea from a cable consortium effort, C-SPAN (Cable Satellite Public Affairs Network), which beginning in 1979 had provided coverage of floor proceedings of the U.S. House of Representatives as well as hearings and other public-affairs material, all supported by the cable industry rather than advertising.

Another cable-specific program innovation combined radio's music with television's pictures. MTV (Music Television) began in August 1981, providing 24 hours of hit recordings with matching video images, tied together by video disc jockeys. Early in 1982 the Weather Channel began to provide 24-hour weather and environmental programming. As the decade wore on, other specialized cable-only channels appeared: evangelical religious networks' constant fund-raising, the Nashville Network's focus on country music and variety, Nickelodeon's programming for children, and ESPN's coverage of sporting events. In the mid-1980s a flurry of *home shopping* networks gave viewers a chance to order jewelry and gadgets by telephone.

By late 1988, cable system operators could choose among more than 60 satellite-distributed program channels offered by 5 major superstations, 6 pay-cable services, 6 pay-per-view networks, and 44 basic program services.

Scrambled Signals As extra-pay options increased, so did *piracy*—unauthorized reception by nonpaying viewers who could defeat the simple devices used to block such reception. Indeed, cable "traps" could not possibly block most freeloaders because they went directly to the source—the satellites that relay the programs to cable headends—and downlinked programs to their own backyard TVROs. The number of personal TVROs in service rose from about 4,000 in 1980 to about 2 million by 1988, many in rural areas with little or no television service, whether over-the-air or cable. Until 1986, these backyard dish owners could freely view any satellite signals. HBO pioneered again by electronically scrambling its video and audio signals. TVRO owners then had to purchase a decoder box and pay a monthly subscription fee to obtain clear signals. Soon not only most cable networks but also broadcast networks scrambled their signals (Exhibit 4–4).

In 1984, several national *pay-per-view* (PPV) services began, a throwback to the per-program payments originally used in over-the-air pay-television schemes. PPV used scrambling from the start.

4.3
Niche Options

Several alternative services fill specific niches in the program delivery business, supplementing broadcasting and cable television. Even late in the 1980s, their success had been spotty at best, yet one had been touted for nearly four decades.

STV A means of converting broadcast television into a pay service known as *subscription television* (STV) had been proposed in the late 1940s, long before cable and HBO appeared. Despite vigorous promotion by Zenith and other manufacturers, lobbyists from the broadcasting and theater industries stymied its development. Fearful of new competition, the lobbyists persuaded the FCC and Congress to delay authorizing STV. They played upon fears that STV would *siphon* programming, especially big-ticket sporting events, away from "free TV." Siphoning would be contrary to the public interest, critics argued, because many viewers could not afford to start paying for the very programming they formerly saw without charge on broadcast television. On the other hand, weak independent UHF stations saw STV in the 1950s as a life-saving additional source of revenue, supplementing anemic advertiser revenue with direct viewer payments for premium entertainment.

The FCC finally authorized STV in 1968, but under rules so restrictive as to discourage applicants. Only in 1977, as part of deregulation, did the FCC ease STV rules, prompting the first stations to go on the air in Los Angeles and New York. By 1983, 27 stations served about 2 million viewers, only a tenth the number of pay-cable viewers at the time. Ironically, widely advertised pay-cable programs created a temporary market for STV carriage of those same programs in cities not yet wired for cable's multiple channels.

Typically, STV stations operated as normal television outlets in the daytime, seeking to attract viewers with nonsubscription programs. Then they would start scrambling their signals for the pay programs during prime time. But as cable services expanded, markets in which single-channel STV could survive declined; the last STVs closed down in 1986. The failure of STV made it clear that once multichannel pay cable became available in a market, single-channel services such as STV could not compete.

"Wireless Cable" or MMDS Operating on far higher frequencies than regular television channels, *multipoint distribution service* (MDS) developed after 1970 as a variant of the STV idea. It is a common-carrier delivery service, transmitting by microwave from one point to multiple points of reception within direct line of sight of the transmitter. *Downconverters* translate the super-high-frequency MDS signals to normal television frequencies viewable on any set (Exhibit 4–5).

The FCC first authorized MDS for business services as a common carrier in 1962. Eight years later, it allowed MDS to transmit television entertainment, making two channels available in each of the 50 largest U.S. cities. MDS began to expand in the 1980s, sparked by the same increased demand for movies and special events made popular by national promotion of pay-cable services that pushed STV in cities that were not yet fully cabled.

Although an MDS unit costs less to build and operate than a regular broadcast station or a cable system, the FCC regulates it as a common carrier. Thus license holders may not themselves provide programming. Instead, they contract out the programming function, often to HBO or some other pay-cable provider. MDS thus has the distinction of being the only electronic entertainment medium in which the owner does not directly program the service. On the other hand, the less cumbersome licensing procedures for common carriers compared with broadcasters and cable systems allow for faster market entry for new MDS services.

Until 1983, MDS, like STV before it, remained a single-channel service, limited to a few large markets and facing increasing multichannel competition from cable. To enhance the ability of MDS to compete with cable, the FCC authorized *multichannel MDS* (MMDS) in major markets, allowing two MMDS operators to offer up to six pay channels each, two leased from licensees of *instructional television fixed services*. This FCC decision caused a boom in applications for what became known as *wireless cable*. Faced with 16,000 applications for about 1,000 available MMDS channels, the FCC announced plans to choose licensees by lottery. The first MMDS service, Capital Connection of Arlington, VA, began operation in December 1985.

But wireless cable faced problems that by the late 1980s appeared to doom it to only a minor role. Licensees first have to assemble enough channels to compete effectively with cable—sometimes ten or more—by leasing unused capacity from other commercial and instructional operations. Then they

EXHIBIT 4–4   Satellite-to-Home Viewing

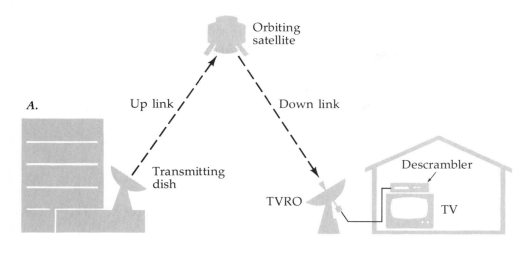

(A) Satellite delivery of programs directly to viewers' homes depends on a reliable means of scrambling the video and sound signals, to be descrambled by devices supplied only to homes that pay monthly subscription charges for the service. (B) The descrambling device, in this case a VideoCipher II along with its hand-held remote control unit, the industry standard in the late 1980s, is installed between the viewer's TVRO and the television receiver.

SOURCES: Descrambler courtesy General Instrument. TVRO courtesy Eric A. Roth.

must battle for programming from the same suppliers that cater to cable television. But the most popular services generally refuse to deal with MMDS operators, since they depend primarily on MMDS' competitors, the cable companies, for their income. Meanwhile, cable continues to expand in the last of

EXHIBIT 4–5   Niche Pay-TV Services

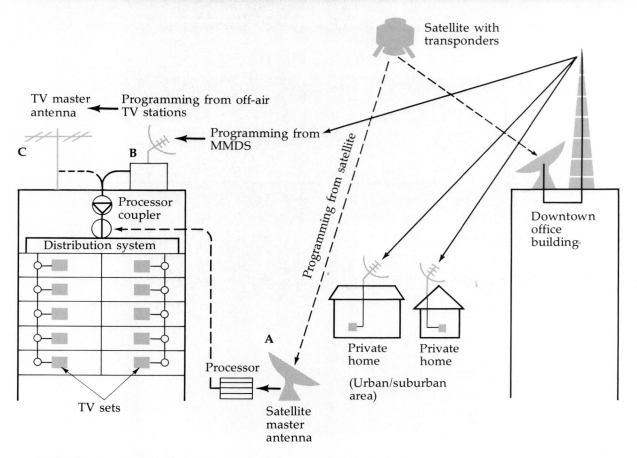

Satellite with transponders

TV master antenna

Programming from off-air TV stations

Programming from MMDS

Programming from satellite

C

B

A

Processor coupler

Distribution system

TV sets

Processor

Satellite master antenna

Downtown office building

Private home

Private home

(Urban/suburban area)

Viewers living in apartment buildings often receive their television signals by means of (A) a satellite master antenna television system, (B) a multichannel multipoint distribution service, or (C) a master antenna picking up off-the-air signals. Each supplies a cabled distribution service within the building. SMATV reception comes from a satellite TVRO located next to or on top of the building, whereas MMDS service, which is a pay subscription service, comes from a small terrestrial receiving antenna on the building roof. Individual homes also can subscribe to MMDS services. Cable system operators pressure local franchise authorities to eliminate various MATV options—or at least to allow cable access to such buildings.

the major markets, closing the "window of opportunity" for MMDS competition. MMDS seems likely to be limited to specialized services (as to hotels) and some markets with limited cable availability.

MATV/SMATV   The first SMATVs (*satellite master antenna television* systems) began to appear around 1980. The fact that they operate on private property and service only subscribers on that property (usually an apartment or condominium complex) exempts SMATV both from regulations imposed on cable systems and from broadcast rules. The building-top TVRO may tie into existing master antenna television (MATV) cabling, or special cabling may be installed (Exhibit 4–5).

Cable system operators, who seek to sign up as many households as possible in their franchise areas, oppose SMATV competition. Applicants for cable franchises often pressure the municipalities granting the franchises either to dismantle existing SMATVs or to give cable operators equal access to SMATV buildings. SMATV competes with cable even more directly: each has several channels of pay programming, usually delivered by satellite. And both also compete with regular broadcasting.

DBS Widely touted when it was first announced in 1980, dismissed by mid-decade, then once again looking promising for the early 1990s, *direct-broadcast satellite* (DBS) services threatened to make land-based delivery systems obsolete by sending programs directly to consumers without the need for any intervening station or cable system. Each subscribing home would have its own small TVRO antenna to downlink signals directly from specially designed DBS satellites. In 1980, a subsidiary of the Communications Satellite Corporation (Comsat) applied to the FCC for permission to design and launch a DBS service providing three channels of programming to the eastern part of the country. Designed for those who were unable to get cable or off-the-air services, the Comsat DBS would have interested mainly rural residents. Construction cost estimates ran as high as $750 million, including satellite design, satellite launch, and initial program expenses. Eight other firms soon announced similar plans.

The FCC authorized commercial DBS operations in June 1982—a remarkably fast regulatory go-ahead for a totally new service. Critics (including broadcasters, who took alarm at the specter of a system that would do away with the need for terrestrial stations and networks) questioned whether a service aimed mainly at rural audiences and competing in other areas with cable and other services could ever recoup its costs.

The answer came in 1984, when United Satellite Communications (USCI) inaugurated America's first DBS service from Indianapolis using a temporarily rented transponder on a Canadian satellite. USCI was said to have committed $178 million for equipment, marketing, programming, and customer service. USCI had only about 7,000 subscribers, far below expectations, when it shut down in April 1985. In the meantime, Western Union, CBS, and the Comsat subsidiary that had started it all had backed away from their DBS plans.

This dim record, produced in equal part by the expansion of cable and home VCR sales and by a lack of a clear program role, killed the economic viability of DBS. Far more attention had been paid to DBS technology than to services. In the United States, at least, DBS seemed to offer nothing sufficiently different from other media to make it likely to succeed. Any of the DBS proposals contrasted unfavorably with the large assortment of basic and pay channels that cable could offer. Moreover, in rural areas beyond the reach of stations and cable, the potential demand for DBS had been largely satisfied by home TVRO *C-band direct* reception from satellite channels that were intended as relays rather than for home reception. The fact that C-band satellites require larger and more expensive receiving antennas than would higher-powered DBS satellites did not discourage their installation by some 2 million households.

By the end of the decade, however, technological advances had revived interest in DBS. Once again, the FCC had several applications from potential DBS system operators to consider, all proposing services that would begin in the early to mid-1990s. Applicants then focused on less-expensive lower-power satellites, thanks to advances in the design of small earth receiving antennas. Plans for U.S. systems drew on increasing experience with DBS systems in Europe and the Far East, in both of which DBS faced fewer competing terrestrial channels than it did in the United States. Plans for the 1990s place a higher priority on offering program alternatives rather than merely focusing primarily on technology, as the first-generation DBS system applicants had done.

4.4
Home Entertainment Center

Along with the emergence of new delivery systems came viewers' increasing ability to control their home electronic media environment. Home video recorders and players allow viewers to purchase and copy programs of their own choosing and use them at leisure, instead of having to accept common signals sent to large, undifferentiated, widely dispersed audiences. Home video and other developments of the last 15 years rely heavily on computers, which in turn rely on integrated circuits engraved on silicon chips.

Microelectronic Revolution   We left the evolution of electronics at the stage where de Forest's improvement of the electronic tube had opened the way to broadcasting. A far more efficient means of manipulating electrons, the *transistor,* has supplanted the thermionic tube for most applications. The fragile, bulky, power-hungry tube has given way to tiny solid blocks of crystal—hence the term *solid-state* devices for the transistor and its successors.

A trio of Bell Laboratories engineers—John Bardeen, Walter Brattain, and William Shockley*—invented the transistor in 1947, collectively receiving the Nobel Prize in Physics in 1956. In a few years, their device transformed the electronics industry. The transistor radio, one of the first mass-produced products based on the transistor, appeared in 1954, quickly becoming the best seller in consumer product history (Exhibit 4–6).

The transistor made possible the development of the prime electronic artifact of the late 20th century, the *computer*. Early experimental computers used electron tubes, but they needed thousands of them, plus miles of wires. The tubes generated so much heat that attendants had to stand by to replace the ones that blew out. Transistors solved this problem, at the same time enormously increasing computer speed and memory capacity.

Small computers remained impractical, however, so long as thousands of separate transistors had to be meticulously wired together with hand-soldered connections. True miniaturization became possible with the invention of the *integrated circuit,* or computer "chip" (Exhibit 4–6). Two engineers working separately arrived at this solution six months apart, Jack Kilby in 1959 and Robert Noyce in 1960. Each one's version had certain advantages over the other, but Kilby won the rights to the invention in a lengthy patent suit (F, 1969: 1391). Today, the two regard each other in friendly fashion as co-inventors of the chip. Curiously, these heroes of modern electronics remain unsung:

> Twenty-five years after they came up with the idea that changed the world and launched the microelectronic revolution—a revolution that has become a part of daily life for everyone on Earth—both Robert Noyce and Jack Kilby are cloaked in almost total obscurity (Reid, 1984: 195).

Their epochal invention uses a crystalline material, often silicon (hence the name Silicon Valley for the area south of San Francisco where much of the U.S. electronics industry is concentrated), to make each of the main electrical components needed in most circuits. Zenith first used such chips commercially in a miniature hearing-aid amplifier marketed in 1964. The chip's ability to concentrate many electronic functions in a tiny space made possible an explosion of devices such as digital watches and hand-held calculators. The personal computer, developed and first effectively marketed by Apple and others, then popularized by IBM, began to transform the work scene (including daily operations in broadcasting systems and cable operations) in the early 1980s. The chip and the personal computer have been fundamental in transforming electronic communications. Many of these new possibilities come together in the VCR.

VCRs: Viewer Control   The home video recorder dates back to at least 1972, when Sony introduced the first *videocassette recorder* (VCR), the U-Matic, for educational and business applications. Three years later the same firm marketed its Beta-

---

*Shockley's name is the best known of the three because of his later espousal of controversial theories about intelligence and race.

EXHIBIT 4–6   Changing Definitions of "Portable"

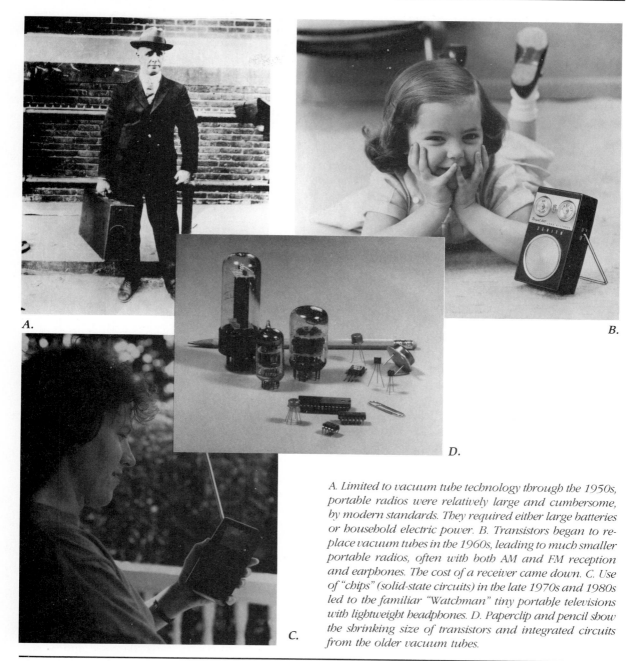

A.

B.

D.

C.

A. Limited to vacuum tube technology through the 1950s, portable radios were relatively large and cumbersome, by modern standards. They required either large batteries or household electric power. B. Transistors began to re-place vacuum tubes in the 1960s, leading to much smaller portable radios, often with both AM and FM reception and earphones. The cost of a receiver came down. C. Use of "chips" (solid-state circuits) in the late 1970s and 1980s led to the familiar "Watchman" tiny portable televisions with lightweight headphones. D. Paperclip and pencil show the shrinking size of transistors and integrated circuits from the older vacuum tubes.

SOURCE: Photos A and B courtesy Zenith Electronics Corporation; photos C and D by Janna Olson.

EXHIBIT 4–7   VCR Growth: 1978–1988

Year	VCRs sold	Average price	VCR households	% of TV homes	Titles available	Blank tape sales
1978	402	$1,200	200	—	N/A	N/A
1980	805	1,080	840	1%	3,000	N/A
1982	2,035	900	2,530	3	4,000	$33,529
1984	7,616	680	18,880	11	7,000	133,088
1986	12,005	432	30,920	36	N/A	296,253
1988	10,748	377	51,390	58	N/A	296,947

By 1988, nearly 60 percent of the nation's homes had VCRs. As prices dropped, sales shot up. By the end of the 1980s, prices stabilized, with the least expensive VCRs costing under $300. At the same time tape rentals slowly began to give way to tape sales as prices of theatrical films on videotape dropped. Sales of blank tapes give an indication of the extent of off-air taping.

SOURCES: Sales data from Electronic Industries Association; household and percent of homes with VCRs from Television Bureau of Advertising.

max machine for the home market at an initial price of $1,300. Futurists predicted a new video revolution, now that consumers could choose not only *when* they would view something but also *what* they would view at that time—broadcast or cable programs, prerecorded cassettes, or their own home-recorded sources.

Sony's monopoly ended in 1977 when Matsushita introduced a technically incompatible cassette format, the VHS system, also developed in Japan. The new system gradually monopolized the home VCR market (Exhibit 4–7). Various "bells and whistles" stimulated sales, bringing prices down from an average of more than $1,000 in the late 1970s to about a third of that amount a decade later.

By the mid-1980s, several trends combined to create the long-promised home video revolution. Sales of VCRS since 1975 have closely paralleled the 1959–1966 "take-off" years of color television receiver sales. As VCR penetration rose, Hollywood recognized a new market for viewing motion pictures. Soon thousands of films could be bought or, more often, rented for home showing, further en-

couraging VCR sales. VCR users could easily duplicate tapes, leading to widespread piracy. Film distributors changed their marketing strategies to forestall illicit copying. Outlets rented films for just a dollar or two a night—cheaper than copying. Such inexpensive rentals encouraged still more VCR buying. By late in the 1980s, prices of leading motion pictures for purchase had dropped from $80 and more to $30 and less, encouraging more film purchases—and VCR use. When the blockbuster film *E.T.* finally reached the home-sale market, a record 14 million were sold at $29.95.

VCRs encouraged *timeshifting,* the recording of broadcast or cable programs not to keep but mainly to view at a later time. Research shows that most recording occurs in prime time (41 percent) and weekday daytime, particularly serials (29 percent). VCR owners take two-thirds of all their recordings from network affiliates, 16 percent from independents, and the remainder from public TV stations and both basic and pay-cable channels (Nielsen, 1988: 12). VCRs have an important psychological effect—the viewers can control what they see and when.

Furthermore, the machines make it easy to cut out commercials during recording (*zapping*) or playback (*zipping*)—a selling point for VCRs, but hardly popular with broadcasters and advertisers.

Cable interests view VCRs as competitors. HBO and other pay-cable services saw little audience growth after the mid-1980s, largely because of the competition from VCR film rentals. The rise of pay-per-view channels represents one cable response to the VCR threat.

Videodiscs and CDs Magnavox introduced the videodisc in 1978. Although it could be used for playback only, not for home recording, it cost about half what a VCR then cost and offered a superior picture. Several incompatible formats, using either laser or capacitance (nonlaser electronics) technology, soon came on the market. RCA bet on the latter approach, introducing its Selectavision in 1981. But mass marketing brought down the price of VCRs faster than expected, wiping out the cost advantage of videodiscs. Coupled with the inability to record, price competition from VCRs proved fatal to the home-market potential of videodisc machines, although they continued to play a role in training for education and business. In 1984, RCA pulled Selectavision out of the home videodisc market, taking a loss of some $500 million. The videodisc appeared to be another consumer product washout.

Once again, however, technology came to the rescue. Starting in 1983, the first new audio product since the tape recorder, the compact disc (CD) record player, appeared on the market. As discussed further in Section 7.2, the CD uses digital recording methods and a laser beam to play back the musical signal, achieving nearly perfect sound reproduction with no surface noise or distortion. They were expensive at first (players cost about $800 and discs at least $20 each), but mass production caused prices to drop (to about $150 for players and under $10 for some discs), so that by the late 1980s the CD could be said to "have had the most successful product introduction in consumer electronics history" (EIA, 1988: 31). By 1989, about 10 percent of homes owned a CD player.

By the end of the decade, the CD boom affected home video. Videodisc players capable of playing either audio or video appeared, and videodisc programs—mainly motion pictures—became more readily available. The merger of devices to entertain and to inform (the home computer especially) offered new combinations for consumers to consider (Exhibit 4–8).

Interactive Information Services Visionaries of the 1970s foresaw as an integral part of the home video or home information center the ability of the set owner to talk back. Two-way or *interactive* cable would let customers hold a dialogue with the cable operator, who could forward communications to stores, banks, public utilities, safety agencies, and others.

In 1977, Warner Cable, one of the large multiple-system cable operators (MSOs), began to offer an interactive service called Qube on its Columbus, OH, system. Qube provided ten special channels over which viewers could respond by means of a touch-pad to questions aired during programs. At the height of the experiment, Qube asked viewers to respond to questions about ten times a day. Limited public demand and the difficult economic situation of the early 1980s brought Qube, which had consistently lost money in its three years to an end. Too few in the audience had made sufficient use of the interactive feature to warrant its cost.

Numerous other two-way experiments took place, often supported by research grants from government agencies or foundations. But when the support lapsed, most of these experiments also ended, since they lacked enough subscribers to cover their costs.

Another information service, this one based on broadcast transmission, *teletext,* delivers print and graphic materials to television screens in homes and offices (Exhibit 6–13). The teletext material goes out from regular broadcast television transmitters, occupying an unused portion of the channel, the vertical blanking interval (VBI). Viewers use a keypad to order up specific "pages" or screens of data from perhaps 200 screens constantly transmitted

EXHIBIT 4-8   Home Video Center

Reception
(Typically *one* of these)

In home use
(any or all of these)

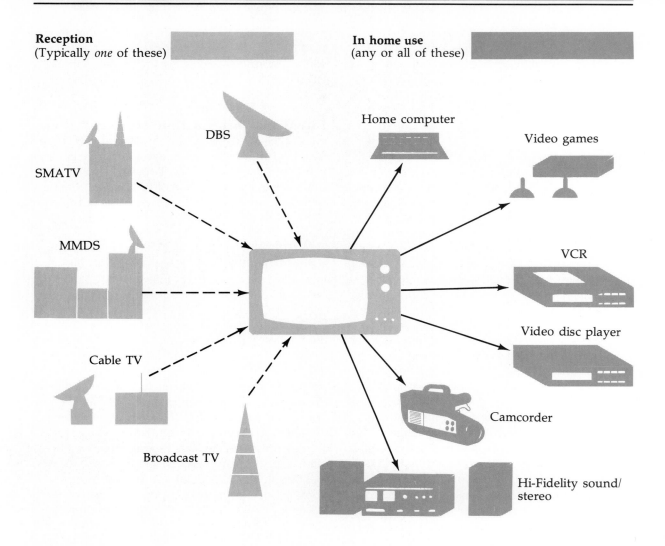

SMATV

DBS

Home computer

Video games

MMDS

VCR

Cable TV

Video disc player

Broadcast TV

Camcorder

Hi-Fidelity sound/ stereo

By the late 1980s, the home television receiver became the reception center for an increasing variety of video distribution channels (left side of diagram—typically only one reception unit being used per household); and in-home inputs (right side of diagram—several, if not all, devices are often connected with the one reception set).

(and updated) from the station. The FCC authorized teletext in 1983, but failed to mandate technical standards, partly because of uncertainty about its appropriate role: should teletext offer services to the mass consumer market or, as in Europe, aim largely at a narrower business and institutional market? For a while in the early 1980s, experts touted teletext as the core of a developing home information center built around the television or computer screen.

Teletext should not be confused with *videotex,* a similar service with important differences. Videotex offers *two-way* communication over telephone or cable lines, not broadcast stations. Thus common-carrier firms usually control the videotex delivery "gateway" and delivery system.* Two large market tests, one in Los Angeles and the other in Florida, closed down early in 1986, having lost some $90 million because of insufficient consumer and advertiser appeal. By then it appeared that the home computer would be used more frequently than the television screen for interactive information retrieval from such sources as Compuserve and The Source.

4.5
Impact on Broadcasting

The services previously described naturally had an impact on the broadcasting industry. Broadcasters had to battle both new and old competitors to maintain their traditional dominance in an ever more fragmented market. The FCC came to their aid by relaxing regulatory restraints, giving broadcasters a chance to maximize revenues. Technology also helped by improving production tools and reception quality. Cable television and VCRs—both available in more than half the nation's homes by

---

*The *Minitel* videotex system has become highly successful throughout France. The ministry of telecommunications gave away simple terminals and offered electronic updated Yellow Pages service to encourage use. By 1988, thousands of independent information providers bought pages on Minitel, and subscriber usage was growing.

1987—had the most perceptible impact on broadcast audience shares and revenues.

The number of broadcast stations continued to grow after 1975, but at a slower rate. The networks' share of prime-time viewers declined from over 90 percent in 1978 to about 70 percent by 1988, and seemed likely to dip further. All three networks changed hands (the first such changes since 1953), and all trimmed down by laying off thousands of workers, the better to meet competition.

Deregulation   In the late 1970s, broadcasters, faced with rising competition from less heavily regulated cable systems and newer delivery options, argued for *regularity parity,* or what some called a level playing field. As discussed further in Section 17.6, the FCC and Congress began coming around to the broadcasters' thinking, responding to conservative political ideology, market-oriented economic theory, and the many competing technologies. Congress extended license terms in 1981 to five years for television and seven for radio. The FCC dropped many operational regulations, such as detailed log requirements, regular reporting of financial data, ascertainment of community needs, and even some engineering rules. In a highly controversial move, the FCC in 1987 rescinded the Fairness Doctrine, which it had spottily enforced for some four decades. But the newer services also benefited from deregulation. In most cases, the FCC decided to regulate them either minimally or not at all, trusting to marketplace competition to keep all players in line. Thus, even after the removal of many rules, radio and television stations remained by far the most regulated of media, and so the quest for further deregulation remained a top broadcast industry priority throughout the 1980s.

Network Competition   Network changes in the 1980s give a good feel for what was happening in broadcasting. On the eve of significant new media competition, ABC finally achieved competitive equality with CBS and NBC. Only in the 1970s did the third-ranking network gain an affiliate lineup equaling those of the two older networks. It expanded its evening news to a half hour and went fully into color. Late in the decade, ABC led in network ratings for several seasons in succession.

NBC tried to move to the number-one slot by hiring away ABC's program chief, Fred Silverman, as president. But NBC remained in third place until former independent producer Grant Tinker took the network presidency for five years, piloting NBC into the top spot (for the first time) by 1985. The CBS story after 1970 centers largely on the search for William Paley's replacement. After a half century at the helm, Paley brought in a string of potential successors, only to tire of each and force him out. Paley finally retired in 1983, making Thomas Wyman the CBS chief executive officer, only the second one in the network's 55-year history.

But these boardroom battles and the constant search for ratings success with look-alike programming masked the underlying changes that were in process. Signs of those changes emerged in the results of the FCC's third (and probably last) broadcast network investigation. From 1978 to 1980, a team of lawyers and economists assessed the regulatory status of networks in light of developing technologies. The Department of Justice had previously settled, with consent degrees, antitrust suits against all three networks, loosening their control over independent programmers and barring them from acting as sales representatives for their affiliates. The FCC study concluded that most FCC network rules had little value in the rapidly changing contemporary marketplace. They merely restricted legitimate business interaction between networks and their affiliates without actually protecting the stations from network dominance. The best way for the FCC to deal with decades of dominance by the three networks, the report concluded, would be to eliminate what barriers it could to the formation of *new* networks.*

The essential conclusions of the report seemed vindicated when international publisher Rupert Murdoch announced in 1985 his acquisition of six independent television stations to complement his purchase a year earlier of half ownership of the 20th Century Fox film studio. Late in 1985 he announced plans to start a fourth television broadcast network—the only attempt since 1967, when an underfunded Overmyer/United Network effort lasted all of a month (Exhibit 4–9).

The new Fox network was too small to be subject to the FCC's national network rules, and so it escaped the restrictions on producing its own entertainment programs that faced the traditional networks. This freedom enabled Fox to capitalize on its unique vertical integration of a Hollywood production facility with network distribution facilities. Whether the venture would succeed was still very much in doubt in 1989.

Network Ownership Changes After more than three decades of stable ownership, the three established television networks all changed hands in less than two years. This sudden break with a 30-year tradition was the result of several developments that happened to coincide: retirement of long-time leaders, declines in ratings, poor financial performance, and FCC deregulation of station ownership.

ABC went first. In 1985, Capital Cities Communications* announced that it would acquire American Broadcasting Companies, parent of the ABC network, in a friendly deal valued at more than $3.5 billion. Long-time ABC Chair Leonard Goldensen, moving toward retirement, wanted the network to have a larger financial base. The change in control created a conglomerate worth some $4.5 billion (the 1953 merger of ABC with Paramount Theaters, also engineered by Goldensen, had been valued at

*The study concluded that there were only three broadcast networks not because of broadcaster greed, but because of channel allotment decisions made in the 1952 *Sixth Report*. Those markets that were allotted only three or more commercial television channels include virtually all the country's population, but larger markets that were allotted *four* stations, taken as a whole, include only about 75 percent of the population; markets with *more than*

four stations include an even smaller proportion of the audience. Thus would-be fourth or fifth television networks can never achieve coverage parity with the existing three, and this might result in economic failure.

*Referred to in the industry as "Cap Cities," the name is derived from the fact that the company's first two stations were located in state capitals: Albany, NY, and Raleigh, NC.

$25 million). The combined firm had to shed its cable interests and several TV stations to meet FCC ownership rules.

Within weeks after the Cap Cities/ABC announcement, Ted Turner announced plans for an unfriendly takeover of CBS in a complex deal valued at about $5 billion. Instead of cash, he offered CBS stockholders "junk bonds" (high-risk, high-yield debt securities secured by the resources of the target company) and stock in Turner Broadcasting in exchange for a controlling two-thirds of CBS. The network thwarted his effort by purchasing 21 percent of its stock from the general public, for which it went deeply into debt. Turner withdrew his offer, but left CBS reeling from debt and internal dissension. Severe cutbacks resulted, and in late 1985 the network sold one of its owned and operated stations.

CBS network management seemed relieved when Laurence Tisch, chairperson of the Loews entertainment and investment conglomerate, bought 12 percent of the network's stock and took a position on the board. Later in the year, Tisch enlarged his holdings to just under 25 percent and edged out Thomas Wyman as network chief executive officer. William Paley came back from retirement as a figurehead chairperson. Over the next two years, Tisch sold off virtually all the network subsidiaries, including extensive publishing interests, culminating with the sale of Columbia Records (the world's largest record company) to the huge Japanese manufacturer Sony in 1988 for $2 billion. CBS then looked for stations to purchase with its cash hoard, buying its first in the Miami market and looking for still more as it focused its attention on broadcasting. Although Tisch touted CBS's broadcasting-only future, critics wondered how the company could compete as technologies continue to evolve.

In December 1985 came NBC's turn. Its parent company, RCA, had been weakened by years of inept management and huge losses from unsuccessful forays into the computer and videodisc markets. RCA welcomed General Electric's offer. RCA—and its then top-rated NBC subsidiary—went for $6.28 billion, then the biggest non-oil acquisition ever made in the United States. The sale made NBC a part of the nation's second largest industrial corporation (excluding car manufacturers), with annual sales of over $40 billion. New management at NBC sold off the NBC radio network and then, in separate deals, the individual NBC radio stations, thus ending nearly seven decades in that business. "Radio City," NBC's long-time New York home, no longer housed a radio network, and the RCA building, centerpiece of Rockefeller Center, became the GE building. WNBC radio, developed from AT&T's WEAF commercial broadcast pioneer, left the air late in 1988, replaced by an all-sports station.

For months after the takeovers, news from the three networks seemed all bad. Profits fell, audience shares slipped, and employees by the thousand lost their jobs. The new owners made it clear that the days of cushy network jobs and fat expense accounts were gone. From the public-interest standpoint, the network takeovers raised serious and long-range concerns about increasing concentration of economic and editorial control in communications. The neutrality of network news seemed at risk as huge conglomerates with major military and other government-funded contracts that could create conflicts of interest took control.

Telephone Company Competition This trend toward centralization followed a highly successful model. For some 75 years, AT&T had operated as a *regulated monopoly* under the supervision of the FCC. AT&T (the "Bell System") had created a widely admired telephone service, keeping local telephone service rates low through a subsidy from long-distance earnings, mainly from business users. AT&T also earned substantial revenues by providing land-line interconnections for radio and television networks. The 1926 agreements between AT&T and the broadcasters described in Section 2.8 had worked well for a half century.

The development of microwave and later satellite relay technology, along with a general trend toward electronic miniaturization, began to revolutionize the telephone and business communications industries in the 1970s. Firms offering specialized long-distance services began to compete with AT&T. The government grew concerned about AT&T's monop-

EXHIBIT 4–9   Rupert Murdoch and a New Network

In 1985, Australian publisher Rupert Murdoch became a United States citizen almost overnight in order to acquire Metromedia's six independent major-market television stations (WNEW-TV, New York; KTTV-TV, Los Angeles; WFLD-TV, Chicago; WTTG-TV, Washington, DC; KNBN-TV, Dallas; and KRIV-TV, Houston) and one network affiliate (WCVB-TV, Boston) for $2 billion. He resold (*spun off*) WCVB-TV to the Hearst Corporation for $450 million, but picked up another Boston station, WFXT-TV.

Having purchased half ownership of 20th Century-Fox film corporation in 1984 for $250 million, Murdoch acquired the remaining half in 1985 (after the Metromedia deal) for $325 million. He thus gained complete control over a company with an extensive film library (including such hits as *Cocoon* and *Aliens*) and rights to numerous television series (*L.A. Law* and *M*A*S*H,* for example). With this as his presumed programming base, in October 1985 Murdoch announced plans to form a new national television network, Fox Broadcasting Company. The six stations he owned (reaching about 20 percent of all U.S. television households) served as the network core. This was to be the first competition for ABC, CBS, and NBC since the 1960s (when the United Network opened and shut within one month).

To the surprise of many, Murdoch did not turn to the Fox vaults for his network programming. Rather, the upstart service premiered in October 1986 with *The Late Show,* starring comedienne Joan Rivers. Rivers, who had been the primary substitute host on Johnny Carson's *Tonight Show* on NBC, had credited Carson for much of her success. She became the object of Carson's ire when she switched from friend and col-

laborator to competitor and challenger in his time period. The Rivers show lasted only seven months. Fox tried several other programs before giving up on the late-night time period altogether in order to concentrate on other parts of the day.

In its first season, Fox averaged between 2 percent and 6 percent of the national audience. Fox programs typically languished at the bottom of the Nielsen list, although some fared better; for example, the network's 1988 Emmy Awards telecast attracted an 18 percent share of the viewers.

The quality of the Fox affiliate lineup remained one of the network's biggest problems. More than 120 stations carried Fox programming, but most were UHF, some were only low-power television stations, and nearly all were the weakest stations in their markets. The network lost about $80 million in its first year of operation.

Nevertheless, in 1988, Jack Otter, a senior vice president of McCann-Erickson advertising agency and former NBC network executive, found the network "just about where they and we expected them to be at this time." Fox president Jamie Kellner admitted: "When you're going against companies that have the power of ABC, CBS, and NBC, you're taking on a pretty heavy job. It's like climbing Mount Everest" (*Time,* 28 Mar. 1988).

Not that Murdoch had only Fox on his mind, however. Already the publisher of *New York* and *New Woman,* his acquisition in 1988 of Triangle Publications (publisher of *TV Guide*) for $3 billion brought his U.S. magazine empire to about the same level as that of Time Inc., the largest magazine publisher in America. Indeed, Murdoch appeared well on his way

olistic response to these competing firms and its apparent suppression of some promising new technologies.

In late 1974, the Department of Justice brought suit to break up the Bell System on antitrust grounds. An earlier attempt had led to an out-of-court settlement in 1956 that changed little. After years of wrangling and a year-long court battle, a *consent decree*

settled the case in 1982.* AT&T admitted no wrongdoing, but agreed to major changes, including (1) divestiture of its regional operating companies (thereafter known as "Baby Bells"),

---

*Often called the *MFJ* for *modified final judgment,* the 1982 agreement was legally a modification (actually a replacement) of the 1956 "final judgment."

EXHIBIT 4–9   Continued

to developing the most powerful communications empire in the world. He controlled 60 percent of metropolitan newspaper circulation in Australia and 36 percent of the national distribution in Britain; he also had part ownership in ten book publishers. His Sky Channel, a satellite broadcasting service for cable TV viewers, reached more than 13 million homes in 22 European countries. He had interests in printing plants, real estate, an airline, even sheep farms. He lacked Ted Turner's style and notoriety, but when it came to business, Murdoch made the man from Atlanta look like an amateur.

SOURCE: Courtesy The News Corporation Ltd. and Fox Broadcasting Co.

(2) complete withdrawal from all telephone service other than long distance, and (3) continued ownership of manufacturing facilities and the country's premier industrial research operation, Bell Laboratories. On January 1, 1984, the now-independent Baby Bells began operation as seven separately owned regional holding companies. Each began to seek a wider role in the information market.

Under the provisions of the consent decree, the Baby Bells could neither manufacture telephone equipment nor engage in most activities involving provision of information. By the end of the 1980s, pressure had built in Congress as well as among telephone firms to modify the 1982 decree to allow the Baby Bells to become providers of information services, including cable or broadcasting. The specter of the powerful telephone companies entering the electronic media field drew the broadcast and cable businesses together in common fear of telephone competition.

In the late 1980s, the telephone companies proposed to go into the cable television business, but the FCC and Congress had banned such services by telephone companies since the 1970s if both telephone and cable services overlapped. Both businesses provide direct wire connections (with telephone companies converting to wideband optical fiber in the late 1980s) to homes, although their *system architecture* differs (telephone systems consist of switched multipoint-to-multipoint linkages, whereas cable systems usually link single points to multipoint destinations). As telephone firms became interested in advanced information services, such as videotex, and cable systems expanded beyond mere entertainment into various kinds of home and business services, the overlaps in content and role became more evident. Cable feared that the deep pockets of the telephone companies would mean unfair competition. Telephone officials, on the other hand, have had little experience with media. The changing telephone-broadcasting-cable relationship became one of the key policy problem areas of the 1990s.

Radio   Amidst all the new competition, radio continued to expand, dividing its audience into ever-smaller segments. The growth came in part from FCC relaxation of restraints on ownership and deregulation of other aspects of the business. The number of FM stations rose to match that of AM by the mid-1980s (Exhibit 3–1). But with its better sound and often fewer commercials, FM passed AM in national audience popularity by the late 1970s. By 1988, FM had three listeners for every AM listener. AM pressed the FCC for a variety of technical and ownership rule changes to even the competitive odds.

In 1981 the FCC approved stereo broadcasting by AM stations, but declined to choose among five competing technical systems that had emerged. This refusal set a precedent, for the FCC had usually picked national standards for new technologies from among those recommended by industry committees. The commission, now controlled by marketplace ideology, argued that competition rather than government should select new standards. Individual stations should pick whichever system they wanted,

and consumers could buy AM stereo sets to match. The FCC would get involved only if interference resulted. Broadcasters argued that lack of a recognized standard would delay the spread of AM stereo as stations and manufacturers alike waited to see what the marketplace would do. By 1988, seven years after the "decision," only about 20 percent of AM stations broadcast in stereo, most using a Motorola-developed standard.

But AM's problems went too deep for any technological fix. Too many stations chased too few advertising dollars and listeners. Many listeners perceived AM as being full of advertising and talk (although some listeners liked the call-in formats). Several stations that had been on the air for decades closed down under the competitive pressure, and long-term owners sold others. The end of the NBC radio network's flagship station, WNBC–AM, in 1988 after two-thirds of a century on the air seemed indicative of the deep problems faced by AM radio.

Technological Improvements   Throughout the era of increasing competition, technological developments in transmission and reception continued; these are discussed in detail in Chapter 6. Manufacturers added attractive new features to receivers, making them easier to use: digital tuning, vastly improved sound, tiny portable radios and then television sets, larger-screen sets (from the standard 21 inches of the 1960s to sets approaching 30 inches diagonal measure in the late 1980s), sets better able to accommodate cable's increased number of channels, sets allowing two pictures to be shown at a time, and so on.

All these new features had to be *compatible* with existing standards—those developed in the 1920s for AM and those developed two decades later for FM and television. An FCC attempt to increase the number of AM stations on the air (not, perhaps, just what the business needed) in the early 1980s by reducing channel spacing from 10 kHz to 9kHz (the standard in all countries other than those in the Western Hemisphere), for example, foundered largely on fears of receiver obsolescence and the costs of adjusting thousands of transmitters. Yet a system of stereo sound for television received quick

EXHIBIT 4–10 The AM-Radio Talk Show

Boston talk show host Jerry Williams exemplifies a radio programming staple in the 1980s—the highly opinionated and often purposely rude talk show host who takes on all comers. In the business for three decades, Williams is boosted by his station as "radio's last angry man" to highlight his approach to the controversial issues discussed.

SOURCE: *The Boston Globe.*

industry agreement and FCC approval in 1984. Manufacturers, who had already generally agreed upon a common technical standard, announced the availability of decoders to pick up the stereo sound. The first stereo network transmissions came in the 1984–1985 television season.

On the other hand, a significant step forward quickly brought engineers and policymakers up against the barrier of old standards and the inertia represented by the millions of existing sets in viewers' hands. Demonstrated in the United States for the first time in 1981, *high-definition television*

(HDTV) promised a picture resolution twice as good as the American standard, but at the cost of incompatibility with existing receivers. By the end of the decade, at least 12 different proposed technical standards for the production and transmission of HDTV vied for approval, with billions of dollars in mass consumer sales riding on the outcome. It appeared that HDTV might first be used in production for and exhibition by cinemas and VCRs, leapfrogging the spectrum-bound broadcaster—another reason for pessimism about the future of broadcasting.

Too Much Competition?   Development of new delivery systems and improvements on older systems raised questions for manufacturers, broadcasters, competing systems, and policymakers. What should be concluded from the highly expensive failures of the 1980s, such as RCA's videodisc, Comsat's initial DBS proposal, several teletext and videotex experiments, STV, and Warner's Qube interactive cable system, among others?

Some argued that too many competitors overtaxed program creativity and too few consumer dollars. Did all these options offer a real choice, or simply new means of receiving the same old programs long provided by traditional broadcasting? Do marketplace pressures encourage the wrong kind of media investment—overlapping services that provide nothing really new?

The preference for marketplace rather than government control increased after 1970. Services developed since then (pay cable, MMDS, SMATV, DBS, and VCRs) had little or no regulatory oversight— and brought little new programming to viewers. With its AM stereo "nondecision," the FCC began to abandon its traditional role of helping to shape electronic media by mandating standards. Thus far, all the technological jockeying has primarily offered a variety of delivery methods rather than a genuine choice among abundant new programs. Channel diversity has not been matched by comparable variety in content. The chapters that follow provide more detail on why improvements in program services failed to keep pace with improvements in technology.

Summary

▌ Since 1970, broadcasting has faced increasing competition from new delivery systems that grew out of limitations on over-the-air television coverage, most of them traceable to the 1952 *Sixth Report* decision on television channel allotments.

▌ Community antenna television, later to become cable television, began in several rural mountain communities in the late 1940s, using a common antenna and direct cable connection to provide TV signals to subscriber homes.

▌ Cable augmented the provision of broadcast signals with distant signal importation and some original programming by the 1960s. This concerned broadcasters, who pressured the FCC to limit cable expansion. The early 1970s saw the peak of FCC and state regulatory control of cable.

▌ Cable continued to expand despite regulation because of the development after 1975 of domestic-satellite-distributed network services, such as the pioneering use of domsats by Ted Turner's superstation and HBO's pay-cable service.

▌ Several minor or niche delivery alternatives developed, including subscription television (STV) and multipoint distribution services (MDS), but these single-channel options gave way in the face of multiple-channel competition from cable, master and satellite antenna systems (MATV and SMATV), and multichannel MDS. None except cable served more than a tiny portion of the total audience.

▌ Direct-broadcast satellites (DBS), heavily touted in the early 1980s, turned out to be economically unviable in the face of widespread terrestrial competition, but may enter the marketplace in the 1990s offering new programming.

▌ Development of the integrated circuit after 1959 led to many consumer products, notably the videocassette recorder (VCR), first introduced in 1975 and in more than half of the nation's homes by 1988. The VCR changed film distribution patterns and enabled viewers to time-shift their viewing. It also provided competition for pay-cable channels, resulting in the introduction of pay-per-view services.

■ Two-way or interactive cable and videotex experiments proved uneconomical. On the other hand, basic cable networks continued to expand and move into the black in the 1980s, with services like Turner's CNN seen as competitive to broadcast network offerings.

■ After 1975, Congress and the FCC increasingly viewed the regulation of broadcasting as excessive, especially in view of the many competing delivery systems. Political ideology and market-oriented economic thinking motivated the loosening or outright removal of many former controls on radio and television.

■ The FCC conducted its third investigation of networks and concluded that most rules limiting television network behavior should be eliminated.

■ All three networks, beginning with ABC and concluding with NBC, changed hands in the mid-1980s after three decades of stable control. The change-overs resulted in part from options opened by deregulation and concern over network television's future amidst rising competition.

■ Potential telephone company entry into the information industries, especially cable television, promised to be an important policy question of the early 1990s.

■ The potential of high-definition television (HDTV) and related systems appeared promising for introduction in the 1990s, though major questions of standards and compatibility with existing receivers had yet to be resolved.

■ Critics noted that too few new program ideas emerged to match the new technological options.

TECHNOLOGY

The next three chapters provide the essential background for understanding the physical aspects of how the electronic media work. One needs to master the basic terms and concepts in order to understand broadcasting and its relation to newer technology, such as cable television and satellites. It is the physical basis of electronic communication media that determines their potentialities and their limitations. Where and how far signals will travel, how much information they can carry, their susceptibility to interference, the need for technical regulation—all depend on their physical nature.

Chapter 5 surveys in lay terms the basic concepts involved in using radio energy for communication. Chapter 6 uses these concepts in surveying the technology of the traditional broadcasting system. And finally, Chapter 7 also uses the basic concepts of Chapter 5 in surveying the supporting technologies for networking and recording, along with cable television and related methods of delivering programs, and the interaction of all these with traditional broadcasting.

▌▐▐▐▐ CHAPTER 5

BASIC PHYSICAL CONCEPTS

Technology need not overawe the layperson if it is approached step by step in terms of familiar, everyday experiences. The layperson without an engineering background has to accept some of the more arcane concepts on faith, to be sure, but the basic ideas need not be difficult to master.

This chapter simplifies the task of understanding communication technology by focusing on the fundamental terms and concepts, leaving the complications of practical applications to the succeeding chapters. A solid grounding in the basics surveyed in this chapter should make it easier to grasp the physical nature of AM, FM, and television broadcasting; of networking, relaying, and recording; and of cable television, satellites, high-definition television, teletext, and other new services.

5.1
Electromagnetism

Four fundamental forces exist in nature—two esoteric atomic forces and two more familiar forces, gravity and *electromagnetism*. The last, electromagnetism, makes possible a host of communication services, among them broadcasting. Radio,* an

invisible form of electromagnetism, has the unique ability to travel through empty space, going forth in all directions without benefit of any conductor such as wire or air. This ability gives radio its most significant advantage over other ways of communicating. Radio waves can leap over oceans, span continents, penetrate buildings, pass through people, go to the moon and back.

All forms of radiant electromagnetic energy share three fundamental characteristics: in traveling, they all (1) move at the same high *velocity,* (2) assume the properties of *waves,* and (3) *radiate* outward from a source without benefit of any discernible physical vehicle.

Radio energy cannot be seen, but light, a visible form of electromagnetic energy, can. Light therefore serves to illustrate some of the main characteristics of radio. Turn on an electric bulb and light radiates into the surrounding space, traveling 186,000 miles (300 million meters) per second.* Both radio and light energy can be reflected, and both lose their strength as they travel away from their source. Radio and light differ, however, in wavelength and wave frequency: light has much shorter waves with much higher frequency.

---

*As used in this chapter, the word *radio* means not just sound (audio) broadcasting but the *method* of communicating without wires. In this sense, radio transmits sounds, pictures, streams of coded data, and many other types of content, even sheer noise.

*Nothing else known in the universe matches the speed of light, which makes the velocity of electromagnetic energy a fundamental physical benchmark. In Einstein's famous equation for atomic energy, $E = Mc^2$, the c stands for the speed of light.

Frequency refers to the fact that all electromagnetic energy has an *oscillating* (vibrating or alternating) motion, depicted in terms of waves. The number of separate wavelike motions produced each second determines a particular wave's frequency— a key concept because differences in frequency determine the varied forms that electromagnetic energy assumes.

5.2
Electromagnetic Spectrum

A large number of frequencies visualized in numerical order constitutes a *spectrum*. The keyboard of a piano symbolizes a sound spectrum, starting at the left with keys that produce low sound frequencies and progressing through higher and higher frequencies to the right end of the board. You can see a visible spectrum when a rain shower, acting as a prism, breaks up sunlight into its component colors. Sunlight, though seemingly colorless, actually combines "all the colors of the rainbow," and colors differ because their frequencies differ.

To the human eye, the lower frequencies of light seem red in color; as frequency increases, we see light as yellow, green, blue, and finally violet, the highest visible frequency. Above violet come *ultraviolet* frequencies; below the frequency visible as red come *infrared* frequencies.

Exhibit 5–1A shows the frequencies of different types of energy in the electromagnetic spectrum. Note that as frequency *in*creases, wavelength *de*creases. Frequencies usable for radio communication occur near the lower end of the spectrum, the part with the lower frequencies and longer wavelengths (Exhibit 5–1B). Communication satellites use the highest frequencies useful for broadcasting, mostly in the range 3 GHz (3 *billion* oscillations per second) to 15 GHz. These frequencies still come nowhere near those of light. As frequency increases, the practical difficulties of using electromagnetic energy for communication also increase. As communication technology has improved, the upper limit of usable frequencies has been pushed higher and

higher. Still, there comes a point on the frequency scale at which electromagnetic energy can no longer be used for communication.*

So far, radio has been introduced as a form of radiant energy that travels through space at the same velocity as light, 186,000 miles per second, in the form of waves that have characteristic frequencies and lengths. The position of radio waves in the frequency–length scale tells us how particular waves behave, as indicated in Exhibit 5–1A.

5.3
Sound Waves

Although sound energy differs from electromagnetic energy in fundamental ways, it too originates from oscillating sources and can be depicted as traveling in a wavelike manner. Sound therefore can be used to illustrate the characteristics of waves in an understandable way, since we can actually *hear* differences in frequency and other wave characteristics. Radio waves become perceptible to us only after they have been detected by a receiving device.†

Wave Motion The example of a conversation between two people at a party can illustrate the sound-wave motion principles. A speaker's vocal cords vibrate, producing word-sounds; these oscillations of the vocal cords set molecules of air into wavelike motion. The sound waves travel through the air to a listener's eardrums, which respond by

---

*Fiber-optic technology enables light itself to be used to carry communications, but not in open space like radio waves; the light is enclosed in hair-thin strands of glass bundled together in a fiber-optic cable. Of course, light as such has long been used to communicate visually at a distance through the open air by means of semaphores, lighthouses, and other such signaling devices.

†Occasionally people located near powerful transmitters do pick up radio signals without benefit of receivers. It was reported, for example, that a person's dental fillings acted as a receiver, condemning that person to hear radio programs constantly. Occasionally external objects such as iron fences also pick up radio signals and reproduce them audibly.

EXHIBIT 5–1   Uses of the Electromagnetic Spectrum

A.

Electromagnetic phenomena	Examples of uses	Frequency ranges	Typical wavelengths
Cosmic rays	Physics, astronomy	10^{14} GHz and above	Diameter of an electron
Gamma rays	Cancer therapy	10^{10}–10^{13} GHz	Diameter of smallest atom
X rays	X-ray examination	10^8–10^9 GHz	Diameter of largest atom
Ultraviolet radiation	Sterilization	10^6–10^8 GHz	1 hundred-millionth of a meter
Visible light	Human vision	10^5–10^6 GHz	1 millionth of a meter
Infrared radiation	Photography	10^3–10^4 GHz	1 ten-thousandth of a meter
Radio waves	Radar, microwave relays, satellites, television, short-wave radio, AM and FM radio	300 GHz to 150 kHz	1 centimeter to 20,000 meters

Note that, reading from the top down, frequency decreases as wavelength increases. Radio occupies the lower frequencies; the higher the frequency (or the shorter the waves), the more dangerous the manifestations of electromagnetic energy become. But even some of them can be useful, as in the case of X rays.

The following table breaks down the radio-frequency portion of the spectrum into large bands, as designated by international agreement. Low-frequency radio, a long-distance form of AM broadcasting, is used in Europe but not in the United States.

B.

Name of frequency band	Frequency range	Broadcast-related uses
LF (low frequency)	30–300 kHz	LF radio (Europe)
MF (medium frequency)	300–3,000 kHz	AM radio
HF (high frequency)	3–30 MHz	Short-wave radio
VHF (very high frequency)	30–300 MHz	VHF TV, FM radio
UHF (ultra high frequency)	300–3,000 MHz	UHF TV, microwave relays, satellites
SHF (super high frequency)	3–30 GHz	Satellites
EHF (extremely high frequency)	30–300 GHz	Satellites

Note how the bands grow progressively larger as frequency increases. Changes in frequency nomenclature avoid awkwardly long numbers: a kilohertz (kHz) = 1,000 Hz (hertz, or cycles per second); a megahertz (MHz) = 1,000 kHz; a gigahertz (GHz) = 1,000 MHz. Broadcasting uses only parts of these bands, which accommodate many types of nonbroadcast services as well. Exhibit 6–8 shows the specific portions of the bands used by AM and FM radio and VHF and UHF television.

vibrating in step with the wave motion of the air molecules. Eardrum vibrations stimulate nerve fibers leading to the listener's brain, which interprets the vibrations as words. Eardrums, unlike broadcast receivers, cannot "tune out" other voices using different frequencies; competing conversations may therefore interfere with comprehension. In this case, the speaker can increase the volume of speech (producing stronger waves) to overcome the interference.

The chief wave-motion concepts can be deduced from this sequence of events. At each step in the sequence, vibration (alternation, oscillation) occurs. Vibration in one object (vocal cords) causes corresponding vibratory motion in other objects (air, eardrums). The medium of vibrating air molecules carries meaning invisibly from one point to another.

Wave Motion Analyzed   As waves travel outward, they go through a *cycle* of motion. That cycle is conventionally visualized as a wheel (which is what *cycle* means). To break a wave down into its components, consider the motion of a point on the perimeter of a revolving wheel, as depicted in Exhibit 5–2. A tracing of that motion results in a waveform illustrating *amplitude, length, frequency,* and *velocity.* Distance above and below the level of the axle represents *amplitude,* which in the case of sound we perceive as loudness. We can measure the distance the wheel travels in one revolution, which corresponds to the *length* of the wave. We can count the number of revolutions the wheel makes in a second, which tells us the *frequency* of the wave, heard in terms of pitch (either length or frequency represents a measurement of a sound's pitch). Finally, the distance traveled in a unit of time (in this case a second) yields a measure of *velocity.*

Phase   As the wheel in Exhibit 5–2 goes through its first half revolution (180 degrees), the waveform rises to a maximum and then drops back to its starting level; then, during the second half of the wheel's revolution, the waveform goes through an opposite motion. Each half constitutes a *phase,* and together they make up a complete *cycle.* Thus a

wave consists of two opposite phases, forming a cycle. Frequency is expressed in terms of *cycles per second.*

These opposing phases of a wave cycle may be regarded as positive (plus) and negative (minus) aspects of the wave. If the positive aspects of two simultaneous waves coincide, their energies combine to make a larger total amplitude at that point. If, however, a negative and a positive aspect of two nonsynchronous waves coincide, the smaller subtracts from the larger, making a smaller total amplitude at that point. When two waves of the *same frequency* exactly coincide, they are said to be *in phase.* If each has the same amplitude, their combined amplitude is double the amplitude of just one. Conversely, if two waves of the same amplitude that are exactly half way (180 degrees) *out* of phase combine, they cancel each other completely.

Phase plays an important role in many practical applications throughout electronic systems. For example, two or more microphones fed to the same amplifier must be phased correctly to prevent their signals from interfering with each other; television relies on phase differences in processing color information; some directional transmitting antennas use phase reinforcement and cancellation to strengthen radiation in one direction and weaken it in another.

Overtones   Phase also has an important bearing on sound quality. A sound with a perfectly smooth, symmetrical waveform consists of a single frequency, a pure tone. Pleasing musical tones and natural sounds, however, consist of many different frequencies of varying amplitudes, all produced at the same time. When these frequencies combine, their phase differences result in a single complex wave with an irregular pattern, as shown in Exhibit 5–3.

Complex sounds have *overtones* (also called *harmonics*). The frequency we hear as "the" pitch of a sound is its *fundamental* frequency. The fundamentals of human speech have quite low frequencies, from 200 to 1,000 cycles per second (cps) for women and from 100 to 500 cps for men. (The overall range of human hearing is from about 20

EXHIBIT 5–2 Wave-Motion Concepts

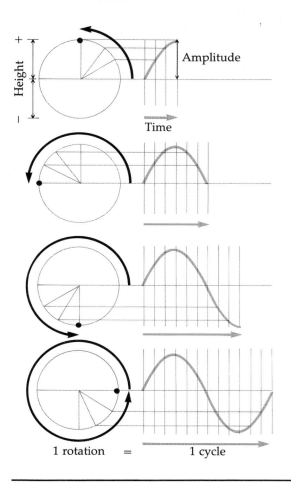

Height
+

Amplitude

Time

1 rotation = 1 cycle

Tracing the rise and fall of a spot on the rim of a revolving wheel illustrates the concepts of cycle, phase, amplitude, *and* velocity. *The spot starts at the level of the axle and moves first up, then down, then up again. The changing distances of the spot above and below the axle level represent changes in amplitude.*

One complete revolution of the wheel represents one cycle of wave movement.

If we regard movement above the level of the axle as positive and that below the axle as negative, we can say that each cycle consists of two opposite halves, or phases.

The distance covered during the time the wheel takes to make one revolution can be used to calculate its speed of travel, or velocity. For example, a wheel that revolved ten times a second and traveled four feet for every revolution would have a velocity of 10 × 4, or 40, feet per second.

SOURCE: Adapted from John R. Pierce, *Signals: The Telephone and Beyond* (San Francisco: W. H. Freeman, 1981), p. 35.

to 20,000 cps, but it varies a good deal from one person to another.) The overtones that give voices their distinctive timbres have higher frequencies, multiples of the fundamentals. Thus middle C, with a fundamental of 264 cps, may have overtones at 528 cps, 792, 1056, and so on.

Differences in the distribution and amplitudes of overtones account for qualitative differences among sounds with the same pitch. One can distinguish a violin from a clarinet, even when they produce ex-actly the same note at the same volume, because their overtones differ. Overtones have relatively high pitch; therefore accurate sound reproduction requires equipment that can reproduce the higher sound frequencies. Hi-fi equipment has, among other things, the ability to capture overtones by reproducing sound frequencies up to 15,000 cps or higher.

Acoustic Environments Sound waves, once launched into a given environment, begin to *atten-*

EXHIBIT 5–3   Analysis of a Complex Wave

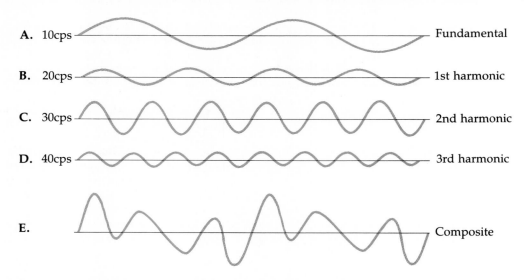

A.	10cps	Fundamental
B.	20cps	1st harmonic
C.	30cps	2nd harmonic
D.	40cps	3rd harmonic
E.		Composite

A method called Fourier analysis can be used to break down a complex wave into its component frequencies. For example, a Fourier analysis of the complex wave E yields the simple waves A through D. Wave A represents the fundamental *frequency of the complex wave, vibrating at 10 cycles per second (Hz). Waves B, C, and D represent* harmonics *of that fundamental, waves with frequencies of 20, 30, and 40 Hz, respectively. Waves A through D combined produce the composite wave E.*

SOURCE: Adapted from Paul Davidovits, *Communication* (New York: Holt, Rinehart & Winston, 1972), p. 129, Fig. 11–1.

uate, or gradually lose their energy, as they travel. Draperies, human bodies, clothing, and other soft, irregularly shaped objects tend to *absorb* sound energy, increasing the rate of attenuation. Hard, flat room surfaces *reflect* sound waves, causing reverberations or echoes (reverberations are echoes that are too closely spaced in time to be heard as separate sounds). Excessive sound absorption gives a room a "dead," uninteresting sound; reflections produce "live," bright sounds. Acoustic engineers design studios and auditoriums with the optimum degree of reverberation. Often they call for adjustable reflective and absorptive panels so that reverberation can be increased or lessened, depending on the needs of particular performers and instruments.

The shorter the waves, the more easily small objects block their path. Long waves tend to "bend" around objects in their path. One can verify this fact by listening to music in another room or from around the corner of a building. As soon as one turns the corner into the area where the music originates, it immediately brightens because one begins hearing the shorter-wave (that is, higher-pitched) sounds that could not get around corners as readily as the longer-wave sounds.

In summary, this section has used aspects of sound that can be personally experienced to introduce the basic characteristics of wave motion—oscillation, amplitude, wavelength, wave frequency, wave velocity, phase, and the overtones found in complex waves. This section also introduced the concepts of wave attenuation and reflection. Although sound and radio are entirely different forms of energy, all these sound-wave concepts also apply to radio.

5.4
Radio Waves

Like sound waves, radio waves behave in characteristic ways, depending on their frequency and phase relationships. Radio waves attenuate, can be absorbed or reflected, and produce echoes. For example, visual echoes from reflected signals account for the "ghosts," or double images, sometimes seen in television pictures.

Keep in mind, however, that radio waves differ fundamentally from sound waves, especially in terms of frequency, velocity, and mode of travel. Limitations of the ear confine audible sound to a frequency range of about 20 to 20,000 cps (people's hearing acuity varies a good deal, especially at the upper frequencies). In contrast, the radio spectrum runs from a few thousand cycles per second into the billions. Radio waves travel at 186,000 miles per second, the speed of light (which is the visible form of electromagnetic energy), or about 900,000 times the speed of sound in air.

Finally, radio waves need no intervening medium, such as air, in which to travel. Indeed, they travel best in a total vacuum. Sound, on the other hand, must have air, water, or some other physical conductor. A favorite elementary physics experiment shows how an electric bell ringing in an airtight bell jar is gradually silenced as the air is drawn out of the jar, creating a vacuum.

Frequency–Wavelength Relationship The phrase "cycles per second" has been shortened by international agreement to *hertz** (abbreviated Hz), meaning a frequency of *one cycle per second*. The number of hertz in the frequencies of the higher radio bands rises into the billions, making for awk-

*So named to honor a pioneer radio physicist, Heinrich Hertz (1857–1894). His contribution is discussed in Section 2.3.

wardly long numbers. Prefixing the term *hertz* with the standard metric multipliers *kilo-* (thousand), *mega-* (million), and *giga-* (billion) simplifies the numbering system. Exhibit 5–1B shows the use of these metric terms in defining the radio-frequency spectrum's major subdivisions (*bands*) and the abbreviations, such as VHF and UHF, used to identify these bands.

As Exhibit 5–1 suggests, the location of any wave in the electromagnetic spectrum can be stated in terms of either its frequency or its wavelength (Exhibit 5–4 shows how to convert from one to the other). For example, the term *microwaves* identifies a group of waves by their length, but the term *VHF* identifies a group by frequency. The number 600 (often abbreviated to 60) on a standard (AM) radio receiver dial identifies a carrier frequency of 600 kHz; an FM station's dial number refers to megahertz (98.9, for example, means a carrier frequency of 98.9 MHz). Television stations, however, have different carrier frequencies for their video and audio components; for the sake of convenience we identify them by channel number rather than by wavelength or frequency. For example, "channel 6" means a station using the 82–88-MHz channel, with a video carrier-wave frequency of 83.5 MHz and a sound carrier-wave frequency of 88.75 MHz.

Carrier Waves Recall that sound production needs some physical *vibrating* object—vocal cords, drum head, saxophone reed, guitar string, or the like. Radio-wave production, too, depends upon vibration (oscillation), but of an electric current rather than a physical object. An oscillating current can be envisioned as power surging back and forth (alternating) in a wire, rising to a maximum in one direction (one phase), then to a maximum in the other direction (the opposite phase).

When current alternates in any electric circuit, even in the wiring of one's home, it releases electromagnetic energy into the surrounding space. The 60-cycles-per-second oscillation of household electric power causes radiations that a broadcast receiver would pick up and reproduce as a 60-Hz audible hum were it not for shielding that cuts off

EXHIBIT 5–4   Finding Wavelength from Frequency (and Vice Versa)

Wavelength and frequency have an inverse relationship: as frequency increases, wavelength decreases. Both are related to velocity, the rate at which electromagnetic energy travels through space, which is a fixed quantity of about 300 million meters (186,000 miles) per second.

To put it in more familiar terms, imagine a soldier marching at 120 steps per minute. If he or she covers 3 feet with each step, the rate of travel (velocity) will be 3 × 120, or 360, feet per minute. If the soldier wants to keep up the same velocity but take fewer steps, he or she can do that by taking longer steps. For example, if each step covers 4 feet instead of 3, the soldier can cover 360 feet in a minute with only 90 steps (4 × 90 = 360).

Applying this analogy to electromagnetic energy, step length equates with wavelength, and steps per minute equates with frequency. We now deal with much larger numbers, however. An AM radio station at 600 on the dial radiates a basic wave frequency of 600 kHz, which means 600,000 hertz (waves per second). To find the length of each wave emanated by that station, divide velocity by frequency:

300,000,000 meters per second divided by 600,000 hertz = a wavelength of 500 meters.

Conversely, given a wavelength of 500 meters, you can find its frequency the same way:

300,000,000 divided by 500 = 600,000.

In summary, to find wavelength in meters, divide frequency in hertz into velocity in meters; to find frequency in hertz, divide wavelength in meters into velocity in meters. Put another way, velocity (treated as a constant of 300,000,000 meters per second) is the product of wavelength in meters times frequency in hertz.

the emissions. The tendency of alternating current to radiate energy increases with its frequency—the higher the rate of alternation, the more radiation takes place. Dangerous radiations such as x-rays occur at frequencies far above radio frequencies, but even the much lower-frequency *microwaves* used in some forms of broadcasting (as well as in microwave ovens) can be harmful to humans close to high-power transmitters (or ovens that leak wave energy).

A broadcast transmitter generates *radio-frequency* energy, feeding it to a transmitting antenna for radiating into space. The basic emission, the transmitter's *carrier wave,* oscillates at the station's allotted frequency, radiating energy at that frequency continuously, even when no sound or picture is going out.

To review, this section has emphasized the contrast between sound and radio waves in terms of frequency, velocity, and mode of propagation. It has introduced the radio-frequency spectrum and the names of its several bands, within which stations radiate their assigned carrier waves.

5.5
Modulation

The next basic concept, *modulation,* concerns the method of impressing information on a transmitter's carrier wave to enable its antenna to radiate programs.

Signals as Energy Patterns   We can modulate a flashlight beam merely by turning it on and off. A distant observer could decode such a modulated light beam according to any agreed-upon meanings—a pattern of short flashes might mean "All OK," whereas a series of short-long flashes might mean "Having trouble, send help." Thus modulation produces a *pattern* that can be interpreted as a meaningful *signal*. Any patterned physical variation can become a signal—light changing from green to red, a head nodding up and down, a finger pointing.

When radio waves are used to signal words, sounds can be visualized as consisting of amplitude patterns (loudnesses) and frequency patterns (tones or pitches). A microphone, responding to variations in air pressure, translates these pressure patterns into corresponding electrical patterns, a sequence of waves with amplitude and frequency variations that approximately match those of the sound-in-air pattern. Ultimately, those *audio*-frequency electrical variations modulate a transmitter's *radio*-frequency carrier, causing its oscillations to assume the same pattern. At last we have a radio signal—patterned variations that convey information by means of a modulated carrier wave.

Note that modulation involves frequencies in two widely different ranges—the low frequencies of the signal (sound frequencies in this instance) and the much higher frequencies of the carrier (radio frequencies). In order to reproduce the signal pattern, the carrier's own frequencies must be much higher than those of the signal. As an analogy, imagine arranging a large number of small pieces of tile into a mosaic picture. The pieces of tile must be much smaller than the picture if they are to render an image. So it is with the frequency of the signal waves (the tiles) in comparison to that of the radio waves (the picture): a large quantity of radio waves (that is, a high frequency) is needed to depict the shape of sound waves (Exhibit 5–5).

Transduction

At each point where a transfer of energy from one medium to another takes place, a *transducer* (literally a "leader across") does the job. A microphone as a transducer changes sound patterns into electrical patterns. A television camera transduces light patterns into electrical patterns. A transmitter transduces electrical frequency patterns into a higher-frequency domain, that of *radio-frequency* (RF) energy. Even the keyboard on a computer acts as a transducer, changing the physical energy of striking the keys into electrical pulses.*

Sidebands

The single radio frequency that identifies a carrier wave can carry little information each second, but broadcast signals require many pieces of information each second. To convey a 500-cycles-per-second sound tone would entail sending 500 pieces of information a second. Thus modulating the carrier's single frequency involves the use of adjacent frequencies. These additional frequencies constitute *sidebands,* frequencies that extend both above and below the carrier frequency. The more information conveyed, the wider the sidebands and therefore the wider the channel.

Because the upper and lower sidebands simply mirror each other, either one can convey all the information imposed on a carrier wave. Many radio services—for example, sound broadcasting—nevertheless transmit both sidebands. That wastes spectrum space, but suppressing one of the sidebands would add considerably to the cost of both sending and receiving equipment.

However, because of the vital importance of conserving frequencies, some services economize on spectrum usage by suppressing one sideband, either fully or partially. Suppression results in *single-sideband* (SSB) or *vestigial-sideband* (VSB) transmission.† Television needs such wide channels that transmitting both sidebands would be extremely costly in spectrum space, seriously limiting the number of channels that could be allocated to television. Therefore one of the television signal's side-

---

*Computers often come equipped with another type of transducer, a *modem* (modulator-demodulator). When a computer sends out messages over a telephone line, its modem changes (transduces) the computer's digital bits and bytes into corresponding analog audio signals for transmission over the telephone line; when the computer receives messages over the telephone line, it reverses the process, changing the audio signals back into its own digital language.

†The worldwide demand for short-wave radio channels far exceeds the supply, causing much interference and requiring expensive measures to overcome the interference. Serious thought is being given to converting all short-wave transmissions to the single-sideband mode, although this would outmode millions of receivers and thousands of transmitters built to operate only in the double-sideband mode.

EXHIBIT 5–5   How Amplitude and Frequency Modulation Work

A microphone produces variations in voltage called a baseband *signal. When depicted graphically, a baseband audio signal assumes a wavelike form with positive and negative voltages, like this:*

A.

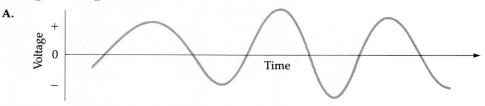

In preparation for amplitude modulating the station's carrier wave with this waveform, the transmitter artificially increases the baseband voltages (amplitudes), turning the entire signal into a pattern of positive voltages:

B.

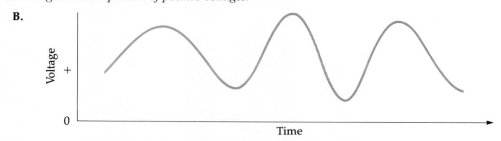

The transmitter imposes this positive voltage pattern on the carrier wave, modulating *it, or causing formation of an* envelope *that outlines the shape of the original audio waveform. The lower half of the modulated carrier mirrors the upper half, the two halves constituting* sidebands *that extend above and below the carrier frequency. Note that in order to form an envelope, the carrier frequency must be* higher *than the baseband frequency.*

C.

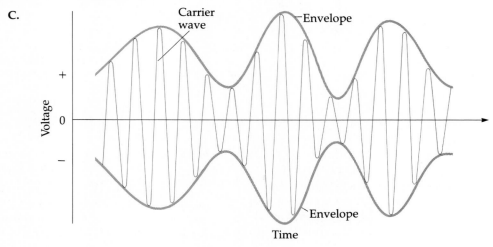

EXHIBIT 5–5   Continued

An unmodulated *carrier wave has constant amplitude and frequency, like this:*

An *unmodulated* carrier wave emitted by a transmitter has an unchanging frequency and amplitude pattern:

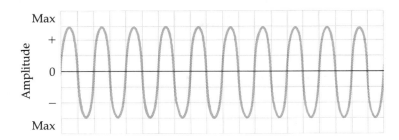

An amplitude-modulated carrier changes amplitudes to represent the signal pattern, like this:

An AM carrier wave, modulated by a pattern of *amplitude* changes representing a signal:

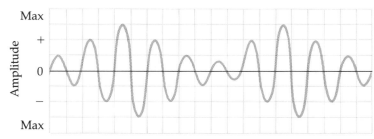

But a frequency-modulated carrier has constant amplitude, with frequency changes conveying the signal pattern:

An FM carrier wave, modulated by a pattern of *frequency* changes representing the same signal:

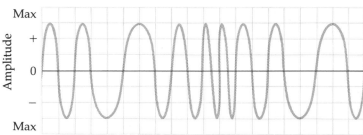

SOURCES: John R. Pierce, *Signals: The Telephone and Beyond* (San Francisco: W. H. Freeman & Co., 1981), p. 61; Federal Communications Commission (FCC).

bands is partially suppressed, leaving only a vestigial lower sideband, as shown later in Exhibit 6–7.

Channels   Because of the need for sidebands, it is necessary to allot each station a group of frequencies in addition to its designated carrier frequency. This group constitutes its *channel.* One can visualize a channel in terms of a water-supply system: a very thin pipe could eventually fill a big reservoir with its slow trickle of water, but a gush of water from a large-diameter pipe would be needed to fill the reservoir rapidly.

In radio communication, channel width determines information capacity, just as pipe diameter determines water capacity. Broadcasting needs large pipes, or channels, because we want immediate, "real-time" results. Some nonbroadcast radio services, however, trade slow delivery for economy in channel width. Certain pictorial news services, for example, deliver video information over narrow radio channels, taking several seconds to build up a single black-and-white still picture. The VisiTel picture-telephone service introduced in 1987 takes 5 seconds to deliver a caller's picture to a small screen beside the telephone.

A taxi radio-dispatching service needs immediate delivery, but it can tolerate narrow channels because it needs only voice intelligibility, not voice quality. Radio broadcasting needs wide channels because sound quality matters and quality comes from overtones, so that radio needs the ability to reproduce higher frequencies. Television channels need vastly greater information capacity in order to pour forth instantaneous pictures as well as sound.

Modulation Methods Recall that modulation means imposing a meaningful pattern of variations on an otherwise unvaried stream of energy. The chief methods for imposing patterns on broadcast carriers involve varying either *amplitude* or *frequency*. Exhibit 5–5 shows how they work. To visualize the process, picture a transmitter being fed a sound that has the pitch of middle C—acoustic vibrations of 264 cycles per second. Such a sound would cause an amplitude-modulated carrier wave to change its *amplitude* (level of energy) 264 times a second. The same sound would cause a frequency-modulated carrier wave to change its *frequency* 264 times a second.

We call standard radio AM because it uses amplitude modulation, whereas FM radio uses frequency modulation. Television uses both methods: AM for the video signal and FM for the audio signal.

AM radio has the disadvantage that electrical interference can distort reception when receivers pick up unwanted radio energy, such as that caused by lightning or electrical machinery as well as by interfering signals from other transmitters. These intrusive signals interact with the transmitted RF energy, distorting the modulation pattern. Listeners hear such distortions in the received signal as *static* and other forms of "noise." Electrical interference has no effect on FM carriers, however. They rely on frequency rather than amplitude modulation patterns.

AM and FM signal processing methods depict the original signal pattern *continuously*. They form an *analog* pattern, a continuously changing pattern that corresponds to the continuous flow of sound or images that impinges upon microphone or camera. Analog signals have an inherent susceptibility to distortion during transmission, reception, recording, and playback. The previously mentioned example of static is only one of many distortion-causing influences that limit the ability of analog systems to process information with fidelity. A newer method, *digital processing,* not only eliminates this problem but also affords many other important advantages.

5.6
Digital Signal Processing

Traditional clocks and watches tell time by the *analog* method, using continuously rotating hands to represent the uninterrupted flow of time.* The now-familiar *digital* timepiece tells time directly in numbers, jumping from one number to the next instead of telling time by means of gradually moving hands.

Encoding Digital signal processing has this same property of jumping from number to number (digit to digit). It breaks down an incoming signal into a stream of separate, individual energy pulses and assigns a numerical value to each pulse. It somewhat resembles cutting up a picture (the analog signal)

---

*Traditional timepieces are derived from the sundial, whose continuously moving shadow forms an analog of the sun's uninterrupted movement across the sky.

into thousands of tiny pieces and assigning a number systematically to each piece. It would then be possible to transfer the picture piece by piece to another location and reassemble it there.

Digital processing breaks down an analog signal into many tiny pieces by *sampling* it at such high speed that the resulting digitized version *seems* continuous to an observer. In fact, however, the signal has been converted into a stream of separate pulses of energy. Each pulse is identified by a set of digits: hence the term *digital*.

One speaks of *digital encoding* because each pulse receives a digital code number. These code numbers consist of nothing more than the digits "zero" and "one" in various combinations. They employ the *binary code,* a term familiar to those who use computers.* As an example, signals modulated by a microphone have a continuously varying electrical amplitude (that is, voltage). A digital processor samples this continuous (analog) amplitude pattern, breaking it down into a series of small, discrete amplitude values. An encoder *quantizes* each value by assigning it a binary number representing the momentary amplitude. The output consists of nothing more than a pattern of "power off" signals (zeros) and "power on" signals (ones).

For those who are interested in more details of digital processing, Exhibit 5–6 (pages 122–123) shows how it works. For others, it is enough to accept the idea that digital processing converts a continuous signal into a series of binary numbers.

Advantages The extreme simplicity of digitized signals protects them from the many extraneous influences that distort analog signals. Recording, relaying, and other manipulations of analog information inevitably cause quality loss; each new manipulation of the signal introduces its own distortions. Digital signals, being simply raw pulses of energy interspersed with moments of no energy,

resist distortion as long as the elementary difference between "off" and "on" can be discerned.

Digitally processed signals need wider channels than the same signals in analog form because it takes a string of binary digits to identify each tiny sample. The first communication modes to use digital processing, therefore, were those with relatively simple signals that made no great demands on the spectrum, for example, data processing and telephone calls. The need for high-capacity channels has delayed the application of digital methods to broadcast transmission and reception. However, numerous electronic consumer items, notably compact-disc (CD) audio recording and digital audio tape (DAT), use the digital method. It has also been applied to studio recording and other production functions, revolutionizing prebroadcast phases of program preparation and increasing enormously the range of effects available to video directors.

5.7
Wave Propagation

However they may have been processed, modulated signals travel from the transmitter to its *antenna,* the physical structure from which signals radiate into surrounding space. The traveling of signals outward from the antenna is called *propagation*. In traveling, radio energy *attenuates,* growing progressively weaker as it covers a larger and larger area. Attenuation also results from absorption of radio energy as it passes through the atmosphere; this absorption becomes more and more pronounced as frequency rises.

Coverage Contours An omnidirectional (all-directional) antenna would theoretically radiate signals over a circular area. In practice, however, coverage patterns usually assume uneven shapes. How far and in which directions energy travels depend on a number of variables, among them transmitter power and frequency, antenna efficiency and directionality, and the varying conditions encountered in the propagation path. Physical objects and

---

*Computer users encounter the term *bit,* meaning *binary digit,* and *byte,* meaning a group that is sufficient to represent a letter of the alphabet, a number, a punctuation mark, or a symbol such as the dollar sign.

EXHIBIT 5–6   More About Digital Signal Processing

Digital signal processing has become so pervasive in contemporary life that it's worth a little effort to learn how it works.

Actually, digital signal processing began with the first of the electrical communication systems, the 19th century telegraph. The American telegraph pioneer, Samuel F. B. Morse, invented a signaling code, known ever since as the Morse code. Telegraph operators sent messages in Morse by means of an on-off key that controlled electricity going down the telegraph wire. The code consists simply of varying lengths of "on" and "off," presented to the ear or eye as dots, dashes, and spaces, which in turn represent letters of the alphabet, punctuation marks, and numbers.

Modern digital signal processing also employs simple on-off signals. They represent the elements of a *binary code,* a two-digit number system that requires only two code symbols, conventionally written as 0 and 1. Numbers of the everyday zero-to-nine decimal system, the letters of the alphabet, punctuation marks, conventional signs, and picture elements all can be represented as groups of binary digits. Thus all communication content can be reduced to nothing but strings of zeros and ones.

In an electric circuit, "power off" can represent "0" and "power on" can represent "1." Thus a system that communicates digitally needs to make only one elementary distinction. "On" and "off" differ so obviously that they leave little chance for ambiguity. That simplicity makes digital signals extremely "rugged"—able to withstand external interference and imperfections in transmission and copying systems.

The two-digit or binary number system contrasts with the ten-digit *decimal* system (0 through 9) of everyday life. In that familiar system, the values of digits depend on their *positions* relative to one another, counting from right to left. Each new position increases a digit's value by a multiple of 10. Thus the number 11 means (counting from right to left): one 1 plus one 10 ($1 + 10 = 11$). The binary code also relies on position, but each digit's position, again counting from right to left, increases by a multiple of 2. Thus in binary code the decimal number 11 becomes 1011, which means (counting from right to left)

one 1 plus one 2 plus no 4 plus one 8 ($1 + 2 + 0 + 8 = 11$). Here's an example converting the three-digit decimal number 463 to binary form:

Multipliers: 8 4 2 1 0

Binary numbers:
$$0\ 1\ 0\ 0\ 0 = 0 + 4 + 0 + 0 + 0 = 463$$
$$0\ 1\ 1\ 0\ 0 = 0 + 4 + 2 + 0 + 0 =$$
$$0\ 0\ 1\ 1\ 0 = 0 + 0 + 2 + 1 + 0 =$$

As the examples indicate, it takes more digits to express a number in the binary system than in the decimal system. Thus, although the simplicity of digital transmissions makes them less subject to error, they have the disadvantage of needing larger channels than analog transmissions. *Bit speed,* the number of bits (binary digits) a channel can handle each second, therefore becomes an important consideration in specifying digitized information channels. A digital telephone circuit, for example, needs a bit speed of 64,000 bits per second, which requires a 32-kHz bandwidth for transmission—many times the width of an analog telephone channel.

The high bit speed required for encoding complex information translates into a need for correspondingly wide frequency channels; for this reason, spectrum shortages bar conversion of broadcasting to digital processing. Closed-circuit communications, since they do not require spectrum allocations, do not have this problem. Digital recording, both audio and video, has already become routine, for example.

Conversion of an analog to a digitized signal involves *quantizing* the analog signal, that is, turning it into a number sequence. Quantizing consists of rapidly sampling an analog waveform and assigning a binary numerical value to the amplitude of each momentary item in the sample. The graph at right depicts a segment of an analog waveform, showing (A) the points at which sampling occurs, (B) the decimal values assigned to amplitude levels, and (C) the binary expressions ("bytes") equivalent to the decimal values.

Along the bottom of (A), t_1, t_2, t_3, and so on, represent the sampling points. You can use the amplitude scale at the left to estimate the decimal number value of

EXHIBIT 5–6 Continued

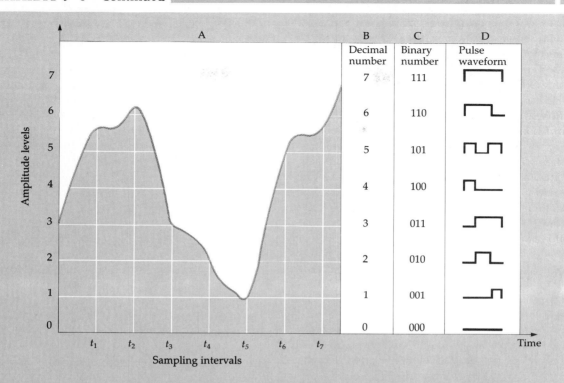

	B	C	D
	Decimal number	Binary number	Pulse waveform
	7	111	
	6	110	
	5	101	
	4	100	
	3	011	
	2	010	
	1	001	
	0	000	

each point. Note that the digital wave, depicted in column D, can have only two conditions, either "on" or "off," with the *time* as an additional variable. Continuous "on" for the entire time period allotted to one item represents the binary value 111; continuous "off" for the entire period represents 000. To represent the binary number 101, the wave shows "on," "off," and another "on" within a single time segment.

Above you see the modulated signal representing the digital version of the analog wave in the previous drawing. The signal consists simply of a train of pulses representing digitally expressed values that give the amplitude level at each of the sampling points. Note

that quantizing involves some rounding off: the signal level at t_1 actually falls between 5 and 6 on the amplitude scale but appears in the digitized signal as level 6. You can understand from that compromise that the higher the sampling rate, the greater the fidelity of the digitized signal. There is an equation for calculating the sampling rate necessary to avoid distortion; it usually calls for sampling thousands of times per second. The intervals marked "S" in the pulse-train diagram represent moments of zero amplitude inserted to separate each of the time periods occupied by a single item of digitized data.

Pulse waveform train

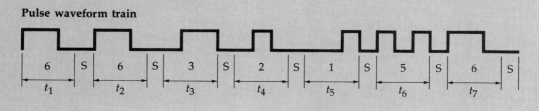

electrical interference in the transmission path, interference from other stations, the time of day, and even seasonal sunspot changes can affect propagation distances and patterns. Waves may be *refracted* (bent), *reflected, absorbed,* or *ducted* (propagated over abnormally long distances because they are trapped between layers of air of differing temperatures).

The higher the frequency of waves, the more the atmosphere absorbs their energy and therefore the shorter the distance they will travel. Objects that are wider than a wave's length tend to block its propagation, causing "shadows" in coverage areas. Higher-frequency waves (that is, those of shorter length) can be interrupted by buildings and trees. VHF, UHF, SHF, and EHF waves (explained in Exhibit 5–1) have such short lengths that even smaller objects can interfere with their propagation. The shortest waves can be blocked by objects as tiny as raindrops.

All these variables combine to make irregular coverage-pattern shapes called *coverage contours.* Engineers draw contours on maps by measuring signal strength at various points surrounding a transmitter, showing lines of equal received power.

As previously noted, how much and in what ways specific conditions along a propagation path affect signal coverage depend largely upon the frequency band the signal occupies. Just as the behavior of electromagnetic radiation differs markedly from one range of frequencies to another across the spectrum, so does radio-frequency energy differ according to band. Frequency management strategies take these facts into consideration, seeking to match frequency-band allocations with the needs of particular services.

Frequency-related propagation differences can be summarized by dividing waves into three types: direct, ground, and sky waves. Each type has advantages and disadvantages that must be considered in matching frequency bands with service needs. Thus services such as international radio broadcasting need waves that are capable of traveling long distances, whereas services such as domestic television can use waves that travel only relatively short distances.

Direct Waves   At the frequencies used by FM radio and television (that is, VHF and UHF frequencies), waves follow a line-of-sight path. Called *direct waves,* they travel directly from transmitter antenna to receiver antenna, reaching only as far as the horizon (Exhibit 5–7). Line-of-sight distance to the horizon from a 1,000-foot-high transmitting antenna propagating over a flat surface reaches about 32 miles; the signal does not cease abruptly beyond that point, but fades rapidly.* Engineers place direct-wave antennas as high as possible in order to extend the apparent horizon. By the same token, raising the height of a receiving antenna also extends the horizon limit.

Ground Waves   The medium-frequency waves used by AM radio travel as *ground waves,* propagated through the surface of the Earth. They can follow the Earth's curvature beyond the horizon, as shown in Exhibit 5–7. Ground waves therefore have the potential for covering wider areas than direct waves. In practice, however, a ground wave's useful coverage area depends on several variables, notably soil conductivity. Dry, sandy soil conducts radio energy poorly, whereas damp soil conducts it well.†

Sky Waves   Most radio waves, when allowed to radiate upward toward the sky, lose much of their energy to atmospheric absorption. Any remaining energy dissipates into space. However, waves in the medium-frequency (AM radio) and high-frequency

---

*Upon reaching the horizon, most of the energy in direct waves flies off into space. However, the atmosphere causes a certain amount of energy scattering, so that weak rays of energy stray beyond the horizon. Some intermediate-distance relay systems rely on *scatter propagation* to leap over bodies of water to destinations below the horizon, using very large receiving antenna structures to gather in the thinly scattered energy.

†The FCC publishes a map showing soil conductivity throughout the United States (47 CFR 73.190). The most conductive soils have 30 times the conductivity of the least conductive. Salt water, by far the best conductor, sometimes helps to propagate signals for long distances along shore lines.

EXHIBIT 5–7   Direct and Ground-Wave Propagation

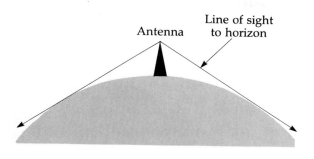

Line of sight to horizon

Antenna

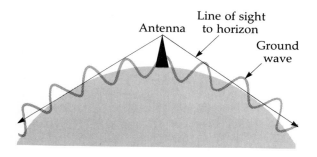

Line of sight to horizon

Antenna

Ground wave

Direct waves *travel straight out, like light, from small radiating elements atop an antenna support. Television antennas radiate their waves downward toward the reception area, blocking off radiation that would otherwise travel upward and outward into space. The distance to the apparent horizon limits the coverage area of direct-wave transmissions. One speaks of the "apparent" horizon because its distance varies in accordance with the heights of the sending and receiving antennas.*

Ground waves *travel along the surface of the Earth, whose electrical conductivity affects the distance they can travel. Given good soil conductivity and sufficient power, ground waves outdistance direct waves, reaching well beyond the horizon.*

(short-wave radio) bands, when they encounter the *ionosphere,* tend to bend back at an angle toward the earth in the form of *sky waves.*

The ionosphere consists of several atmospheric layers from about 40 to 600 miles above the Earth's surface. Bombarded by high-energy solar radiation, the ionosphere takes on special electrical properties, causing sky waves to *refract* (bend) back toward the earth. Under the sun's influence, ionosphere layers move up and down daily and also vary according to season of the year. Different layers of the ionosphere affect different frequencies; therefore, because of differences in the height of layers, angles of refraction vary according to frequency.

Under the right frequency, power, and ionosphere conditions, refracted sky waves bounce off the surface of the Earth, travel back to the ionosphere, bend back again, and so on, following the curvature of the Earth and traveling thousands of miles (see Exhibit 5–8).

The ionosphere's effectiveness varies with time of day and with frequency. Services that rely on sky waves vary accordingly. Some services, such as AM radio, generate sky waves only at night, covering wider areas then than in the daytime; short-wave services can switch frequency several times throughout the 24 hours of the day to take continuous advantage of the ionospheric refraction.

Propagation and Frequency in Summary

Several summarizing generalizations can be made concerning the interaction of frequency with other factors that affect coverage:

- Ground waves are most useful at lower frequencies, sky waves in the middle frequencies, and direct waves at higher frequencies.
- Atmospheric noise affects the lower frequencies most; electron noise in electrical components affects the higher frequencies.
- The higher the frequency, the more power is needed to generate a usable signal. Thus a channel located at a lower point in the frequency spec-

EXHIBIT 5–8 Ionosphere and Sky-Wave Propagation

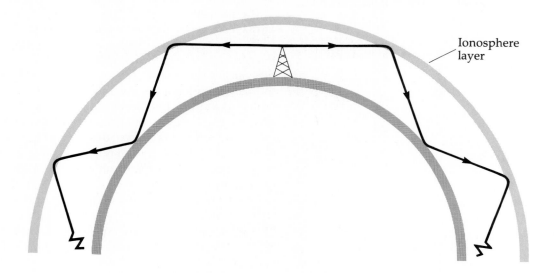

Ionosphere
layer

Usually when radio waves radiate skyward, any energy not absorbed by the atmosphere eventually dissipates into space. Waves in the MF and HF (medium- and high-frequency) bands, however, have the peculiar property of bending back toward Earth when they encounter the ionosphere. This consists of a series of atmospheric layers that react to radiations from the sun, taking on the special electrical property that causes waves to bend back toward Earth in the form of sky waves. A return wave may bounce off the Earth back to the ionosphere, return to Earth, and so on, in a series of skips. Alternate heating and cooling of the ionosphere as the sun rises and sets change its height and reflective properties, so that it reflects different frequencies at different times of the day and night.

SOURCE: Excerpted from Stanley Leinwoll, *From Spark to Satellite*, copyright © 1979 by Stanley Leinwoll. Reprinted with permission of Charles Scribner's Sons.

trum is always preferable, other things being equal, to one at a higher point.

■ The shorter the waves (meaning the higher the frequencies), the more directional propagation becomes and the more easily obstructions block wave propagation.

■ Medium-frequency waves (the ones AM radio uses) produce usable sky waves only after sundown, when the ionosphere cools; high-frequency waves (used by short-wave services) can use the ionosphere during the daytime but must change

frequency periodically to match changing ionospheric conditions.

5.8
Antennas

Antennas launch signals on their way at the transmitting end and pick them up at the receiving end. Antenna size and location can have a critical influence not only on the efficiency of transmission but also reception.

Reception In AM radio, small receiving antennas built into the set are sufficient to pick up strong signals. The higher the frequency, however, the more elusive the signal, and the more essential an efficient outdoor antenna becomes. Thus in many locations, indoor rabbit ears suffice for VHF television signals, but UHF signals may require a more efficient outdoor antenna. The size difference between a television VHF rabbit-ear receiving antenna and the small wire ring used for UHF reception reflects the difference in wavelength. Satellites, which use still higher frequencies and radiate relatively very low-power signals, need highly efficient outdoor receiving antennas.

Transmission Transmitting antennas vary widely in size because, if they are to work efficiently, their length must be mathematically related to that of the waves they radiate. Broadcast transmitter antennas usually measure one-half or one-quarter of the wavelength they radiate. Waves at the lower end of the AM band (540 kHz) have a length of about 1,823 feet; at the upper end of the AM dial (1,600 kHz), they measure only 593 feet. Channel 2 (VHF) television transmitters radiate 20-foot waves, whereas television channel 48 (UHF) waves are less than 2 feet long.

Directionality Much as light from flashlights and headlamps can be focused by reflectors, transmitting antennas can be designed to block propagation in some directions and reinforce it in others. In most cases, propagation in all directions, upward as well as outward, would be wasteful because much of the energy would never reach receivers. Directional propagation also has value for preventing interference with other stations and for beaming signals toward inhabited areas.

Concentration of radiated energy increases its effective strength. This increase, called *antenna gain,* can be very great. A microwave relay antenna concentrates its energy into a narrow beam, aimed at a single reception point. Such a beam can achieve a gain of 100,000 times the effective radiated power of an omnidirectional antenna. Indeed, because microwave signals attenuate rapidly, they would be of little use without this high gain, which enables them to punch through the atmosphere.

5.9
Spectrum Conservation

Limitations on the available spectrum make efficient use of allocated frequencies essential. A huge and ever-growing number of radio transmitters of many different kinds share the radio-frequency spectrum. The threat of interference among stations, the demands for spectrum allocations by new services, and the growth of established services make efficient spectrum management on a worldwide scale vitally important.

Frequency Allocation Through the International Telecommunication Union (discussed in detail in Section 19.3), national communication authorities worldwide agree on the division of the spectrum among the various telecommunication services. This process, called *allocation,* involves designating specific segments (bands) of the spectrum for the use of specific services, sometimes on a shared basis.

Allocation strategies seek to match the needs of a service with the part of the spectrum that has the appropriate propagation characteristics. Thus terrestrial long-distance services make high demands on the HF band in order to capitalize on sky waves. A local service that needs to make only line-of-sight contacts can use VHF or higher frequencies. Some services require exclusive use of their channels to enable around-the-clock communication, whereas with others many users can share channels because they require only occasional contacts. Some, like radiotelephones, can use relatively narrow channels; others, like television, must have very wide channels.

Demands on Spectrum Many services other than broadcasting need frequency allocations. Civilian nonbroadcast users include personal services (citizens band radio, for example), private land mobile services (ambulances, news-gathering units), marine services, aviation services, public-safety services (police, fire), common carriers (radio-telephones, microwave relays), land transportation (taxicabs, railroads), and satellite services. Broadcasting, though it represents less than 1 percent of all transmitters authorized in the United States, makes especially heavy demands. Nearly 12 thousand primary radio and television stations need continuous access to relatively large channels.* Moreover, broadcasters use many auxiliary facilities, such as subsidiary repeaters (translators) and studio-to-transmitter links. Broadcasting also uses radio relays, both terrestrial and satellite, making still more demands on spectrum space. In fact, broadcasting uses more than 80 percent of the radio spectrum below 1 GHz, the region of the spectrum most in demand for all forms of terrestrial radio communication.

Conservation Measures The need to conserve radio frequencies encourages spectrum-saving technologies. One of the most common, *multiplexing,* allows the transmission of two or more independent signals in the same channel. For example, *frequency-division* multiplex divides a channel into two or more subchannels, each with its own carrier and signal. Another type, *time-division* multiplex, rapidly samples each of several signals, sending short bursts of each through the same channel; this method enables the filling in of otherwise wasted time, for example, the pauses that occur between words and phrases in telephone speech.

Another spectrum-saving measure, *band compression,* economizes on frequencies by selective omission. For example, in any video transmission, not all pictures change totally from frame to frame. Some picture elements remain the same over a series of frames. One method of band compression

transmits information only about elements that *do* change, thus reducing the average amount of new information that has to be processed each second. In the future, such band-compression measures may enable better-quality television pictures to be transmitted without enlarging the picture channel.

Guided Waves Spectrum conservation can be achieved by using a portion of the spectrum in enclosed spaces where interference does not normally occur. Radio energy can be propagated through *guides* or pipes, such as coaxial copper and fiber-optic cables. Confining radio energy within an artificial environment eliminates the need for antennas, the problems of cochannel interference, and the varying behaviors of direct, ground, and sky waves. Radio energy enclosed in wave guides can be modulated and propagated; it retains all the characteristics already described, except those that arise from its being in open space. However, radio energy traveling through wave guides other than optical fibers attenuates rapidly, making it necessary to reamplify signals at frequent intervals, which adds to the expense of transmission.

Cable television, a conspicuous example of a wave-guide system, uses the same radio-frequency energy as broadcasting, subject to the same fundamental physical laws. Delivering programs by cable avoids interference problems and the vagaries of different propagation paths. Thus cable enables scores of channels to be delivered in a single area where interference would limit open propagation to only a few channels.

Cable as an alternative has its costs, however. Not only does it literally cost the audience the price of subscriptions, it also sacrifices the miraculous asset of true radio communication—the unique ability to reach audiences without the aid of physical connections. Broadcasting ignores many of the physical and political barriers that curb the reach of all other means of communication.

Summary

∎ An understanding of the physical basis of electronic communication helps in understanding the

---

*Up-to-date figures on stations can be obtained from the weekly feature "Where Things Stand" in the trade magazine *Broadcasting*. In early 1989 it listed approximate on-air figures as follows: 10,439 radio stations, 1,369 of them educational FM; 1,388 television stations, 335 of them educational. In addition, 455 low-power television stations were on the air, and there were nearly 6,500 low-power translators (low-power repeater stations).

benefits and problems that arise from radio's physical nature. To appraise the new media, one needs an understanding of their underlying technology.

▌ Radio communication (including sound, pictures, and other types of material) employs a form of electromagnetic energy that has some of the characteristics of sound and visible light.

▌ Like sound, radio energy originates from an oscillating source and can be described in terms of waves that have length, frequency, phase, and velocity. These waves are subject to attenuation, refraction, reflection, absorption, and interference.

▌ However, sound waves differ significantly from radio waves in their velocity, frequency, and mode of travel.

▌ Radio frequencies occupy part of the electromagnetic spectrum; their characteristics vary according to their position in that spectrum. International agreements have grouped the radio-frequency range into bands, designated by frequency: low (LF), medium (MF), high (HF), very high (VHF), and so on. Waves behave somewhat differently in each band.

▌ The basic emission of a broadcasting station, its carrier wave, may be propagated as a ground wave (reaching beyond the horizon), a direct wave (reaching only to the horizon), or a sky wave (reaching long distances because of ionosphere refraction).

▌ Modulation imposes information on a carrier wave, creating sidebands that collectively occupy a group of frequencies called a channel. The more information a channel must deliver simultaneously, the wider it must be.

▌ In traditional broadcasting, modulation of a carrier wave's amplitude (as in AM) or its frequency (as in FM) occurs in a manner described as analog signal processing.

▌ A more sophisticated method, digital processing, converts original continuous analog signals into discontinuous pulses of energy. Digitally processed signals, though more resistant to distortion and highly manipulable, require wider frequency channels than analog signals.

▌ Modulated carrier waves, upon being piped to an antenna, are radiated as electromagnetic energy. The length of a transmitter's antenna is proportional to the length of the waves it radiates. Directional antennas control the spread of signals, increasing signal intensity in desired directions.

▌ Demand for radio frequencies exceeds supply. Good spectrum management practices match service needs with the characteristics of the various frequency bands. Multiplexing helps conserve frequencies by making it possible to modulate more than one carrier in a single channel. Band compression is another conservation measure.

▌ Broadcasting shares the spectrum with many other radio services. It consumes much spectrum space because it needs continuous access to relatively wide channels. Moreover, primary broadcasting stations depend on a variety of auxiliary transmitters, including some in satellites, adding to the burden the medium imposes on the spectrum.

▌ Cable television uses the same waves and channels as broadcasting, but encloses them within a conductor (usually coaxial cable, but increasingly fiber-optic cable). A single cable can conduct many channels simultaneously, in contrast with broadcasting's single channel per station.

CHAPTER 6

TRADITIONAL BROADCASTING TECHNOLOGY

This chapter uses the basic terms and concepts laid out in Chapter 5 to describe the technology of the traditional broadcasting services: standard (AM) radio, FM radio, and television. It assumes that you have read the previous chapter, and that you already understand generally the nature of the radio spectrum and the behavior of radio waves.

6.1
Gaining Access to the Spectrum

To use the spectrum for communication, formal technical access rules must be adopted, both nationally and internationally. Such rules are essential to assure efficient use of this limited resource and minimize interference among users.

Spectrum Regulation   Most countries belong to the International Telecommunication Union (ITU), the body that coordinates worldwide radio-frequency spectrum use. The ITU defines three steps in parceling out frequencies:

■ *Allocation,* the setting aside of groups (bands) of frequencies for the use of specific communication services. The ITU allocations apply to all countries, with slight differences among the three ITU

regions (roughly the Americas, Europe-Africa, and Asia).

■ *Allotment,* the distribution of the allocated frequencies to specific countries or regions.

■ *Assignment,* the designation of specific frequencies for the use of individual stations, usually through *licensing.* The group of frequencies assigned to a station constitutes a *channel.* Each service requires channels whose bandwidth suits the amount of information they need to carry.

Channel Allotments   In the United States, the Federal Communications Commission (FCC) has the responsibility for licensing stations in accordance with ITU rules. It compiles *allotment tables* designating specific FM and television channels for use in specific communities. A would-be licensee looks through the relevant allotment table to see whether there is an unused channel in the proposed service area.* However, the FCC assigns AM channels on an ad hoc basis. A would-be AM licensee must search for an unoccupied channel at the desired location, then perform an engineering study to find out whether that channel could be activated without causing interference with existing stations.

---

*The allotment tables can be found in 47 CFR 73.202 and 73.606.

6.2
Interference

The factor of mutual interferences among stations severely limits the number of stations that can be licensed in any particular market. The primary troublemaker, cochannel interference, comes from other stations operating on the same channel. Adjacent-channel interference also occurs among stations in the same locality.

Cochannel Interference Two stations operating on the same channel must be sited far enough apart geographically to prevent their coverage contours from overlapping and causing *cochannel interference.* Signals that are too weak to provide reliable service to an audience may nevertheless cause such interference; a station's interference zone therefore extends far beyond its service area.

The changing daytime and nighttime coverage areas of AM stations, caused by sky-wave propagation at night, complicates prevention of AM cochannel interference. The FCC tries to prevent such sky-wave interference by requiring many AM stations to use lower power at night.

The FCC could prevent all cochannel interference simply by licensing only one station on each channel, but this would limit the number of operating stations too drastically. U.S. regulatory policy calls for allowing as many local communities as possible to have their own stations; the FCC therefore makes cochannel separation rules as liberal as possible.

Adjacent-Channel Interference In the vicinity of a transmitter, the radiation is so powerful that the sidebands spread far beyond the nominal channel limits, spilling over into *adjacent channels.* The possibility of such interference limits the number of stations that can be licensed in any one locality; you will not find consecutively numbered channels licensed in a single market.*

*The fact that the frequencies of the television band do not run consecutively without interruption makes for exceptions: channels 6 and 7 can operate in the same market because the FM band intervenes between them; a nontelevision group of fre-

Distance rapidly attenuates signals as they travel from the transmitter, however, so that adjacent-channel stations need be separated only by about the radius of their service areas. For example, the FCC imposes an adjacent-channel separation distance of only 60 miles for VHF television stations.

6.3
AM Stations

As the first broadcasting service to develop, AM radio came to be called *standard broadcasting.* "AM" as a class name is somewhat misleading because the term means simply *amplitude modulation,* a type of modulation used by many services other than standard broadcasting. The video component of the television signal, for example, is amplitude-modulated.

Location in Spectrum By international agreement, AM channels occupy a segment of the MF band. In the United States the AM broadcasting segment of that band runs from 535 to 1,605 kHz, affording a total bandwidth of 1,070 kHz. In 1988, ITU members finalized an agreement to extend the upper limit of the AM band to 1.705 kHz. Receivers must be redesigned to extend their tuning range to pick up the new channels, and the FCC did not expect to begin licensing them until 1990. The discussion that follows describes AM as it existed before the new channels were added.

The ionosphere refracts waves in the MF band, but only at night. After sundown, therefore, AM stations can produce sky waves that reach far beyond their daytime coverage contours. However, unless they are protected from cochannel interference, AM stations do not necessarily get improved nighttime coverage from sky waves. Indeed, sky waves from distant cochannel stations may intrude, shrinking an AM station's nighttime coverage. The FCC de-

quencies similarly intervenes between channels 4 and 5; and a jump between VHF and UHF frequencies occurs between channels 13 and 14. Exhibit 6–8 shows the details of these discontinuities.

vised a system of station and channel classifications (described below), one of whose purposes is to compensate for the disparity between daytime and nighttime coverage.

Channel Width Recall that in deciding on the channel width for a service, planning authorities must consider the information capacity the service needs to fulfill its purpose. They must find a compromise between *ideal* quality (requiring wide channels and expensive equipment) and reasonably satisfactory quality (getting by with narrower channels and more moderate equipment costs).

Telephones, whether wire or wireless, require a bandwidth of about 2,500 Hz, for example. This width allows voice intelligibility, but it cannot convey the aesthetic aspects of speech and music. Ideally, sound broadcasting channels would be wide enough to encompass the full range of overtone frequencies detectable by the keenest human ear— a bandwidth on the order of 15,000 Hz, six times the telephone bandwidth. However, AM stations in the United States make do with only 5,000 Hz.

In practice, the FCC spaces AM channels 10 kHz apart.* This spacing allows for 107 channels (that is, 1,070 divided by 10). A station's carrier-wave frequency, expressed in kilohertz, identifies its channel—540, 550, 560, and so on up to 1,600 kHz. The 10-kHz spacing means that channels extend 5 kHz above and below their carrier frequencies. For example, a station at 540 on the dial occupies a channel that runs from 535 to 545 kHz.

The 10-kHz spacing allows only 5 kHz for the actual signal, because modulation generates mirror-image sidebands on each side of a carrier frequency. One 5-kHz sideband contains all the useful information. This limitation makes AM less adequate for music than is FM. True, the 10-kHz limit refers to channel *spacing* rather than to maximum channel width. Stations may modulate beyond 5 kHz on either side of their carrier frequencies if they can do so without causing interference, and many do. For most listeners this wider channel does not result in improved sound, however, because the loudspeakers in inexpensive AM receivers cannot reproduce the audible range that even a 5-kHz signal can provide.

Channel Classes The FCC classifies AM channel as *local* (6 channels), *regional* (41 channels), and *clear* (60 channels). By defining varying areas of coverage according to need, channel classification helps the FCC to license the maximum number of stations. Local-channel stations serve small communities or parts of large metropolitan regions, regional-channel stations serve metropolitan areas or rural regions, and clear-channel stations serve both large metropolitan areas and, at night, distant rural listeners. These channels have been "cleared" of interfering cochannel nighttime signals to enable sky-wave reception in remote areas. Exhibit 6–1 shows AM channel classes in relation to station classes.

Station Classes Sky-wave coverage also influences the FCC's *station* classification system. In the interest of licensing the maximum possible number of outlets, the FCC divides AM stations into four classes, designated I, II, III, and IV (shown in relation to channel classes in Exhibit 6–1). Class I stations (about 1 percent of the total) have "dominant" status on clear channels.*

Secondary stations on clear channels, designated as Class II (about a third of the total), must avoid interfering with the Class I stations whose frequencies they share. Class II stations avoid interfering mainly through their wide geographic separation

---

*Many countries use only 9-kHz spacing. In 1980 and 1982, ITU regional radio conferences (RARCs) for the Americas considered increasing the number of AM channels by reducing channel separation to 9 kHz. The U.S. delegation at first favored the change, but under pressure from U.S broadcasters, concerned about conversion costs and the prospect of more competition, the United States reversed its position.

---

*Originally, the FCC gave dominant stations on clear channels nationwide protection from interference, but the demand for still more licenses and the spirit of deregulation led to erosion of the clear-channel principle. Since 1980, Class I stations on clear channels sometimes have to share their frequencies with other primary stations in distant parts of the country. For lists of channels by class and the classification of stations on each channel, see the most recent issue of *Broadcasting-Cablecasting Yearbook*.

EXHIBIT 6–1   AM Radio Stations by Channel and Station Class

Station class (Power range)	Percentage of stations on channels (number of channels)		
	Clear channels (60)	Regional channels (41)	Local channels (6)
Class I (10,000–50,000 W)	1%	—	—
Class II (2,500–50,000 W)	33%	—	—
Class III (500–5,000 W)	—	46%	—
Class IV (250–1,000 W)	—	—	22%

A relatively large number of clear channels have been designated because each has only one dominant Class I station, which provides long-distance sky-wave signals at night to remote areas. Class I stations have A and B subclasses, with the 1-Bs mostly on foreign clear channels. The Class II stations also occupy clear channels, but they have secondary status; they often must reduce power at night and use directional antennas to protect cochannel Class I stations. Although there are only 6 local channels, a large number of Class IV stations occupy them; because of the low power of Class IV stations, many can operate on each local channel without causing cochannel interference.

To minimize interference, most AM stations must use directional antennas (with day directions often differing from night directions). In addition, about half the AM stations must leave the air at the time of local sunset so as not to generate sky-wave interference. By about 1990 the FCC was expected to complete plans for phasing in 10 additional channels, made possible by the 100-kHz extension of AM band authorized by the International Telecommunication Union.

See Broadcasting/Cablecasting Yearbook *for a list of all AM stations by channel, location, power, and antenna pattern. For details of FCC rules on station and channel classes, see 47 CFR 73.21 ff.*

from cochannel Class I stations; often they must also restrict their output by using directional antennas (sometimes with different patterns for night and day) and by either reducing power or closing down entirely at night.

Class III stations (46 percent of the AM total) occupy regional channels; Class IV, local channels. Although the local-channel class comprises only 6 of the 107 AM channels, the Class IV stations as-

signed to them amount to 22 percent of the AM stations on the air. They have such low power (and therefore such short range) that many can use the same channel without interfering with one another.

Power   Transmitter power plays an especially important role in AM radio. High power not only improves the efficiency of both ground-wave and sky-wave propagation, it also overcomes static. Furthermore, station owners find the claim of high power useful in persuading advertisers that their stations have strong audience impact.

Power authorizations for domestic U.S. AM broadcasting run from 250 watts (W) for the smaller Class IV stations on local channels to a maximum of 50,000 W (50 kW) for Class I and II stations on clear channels. The 50-kW ceiling is low relative to the maximum in other countries, which tend to favor centralized control of broadcasting. Limiting power to 50 kW makes it possible to license more stations and prevents those with high power from getting too much of a competitive edge over those with less power.

Antennas   AM stations usually employ quarter-wavelength transmission antennas. The entire steel tower acts as the radiating element. In choosing sites, engineers look for good soil conductivity, freedom from surrounding sources of electrical interference, and avoidance of the flight paths of aircraft approaching and leaving airports. Because ground waves propagate through the Earth's crust, AM antennas must be extremely well grounded, with many heavy copper cables buried in trenches radiating out from the base of the antenna tower (Exhibit 6–2 shows an array of AM antennas under construction).

Carrier Current   There is a nonbroadcast AM service that permits colleges and universities to operate on-campus stations, and several hundred do so. Low-power AM signals can be fed into the steam pipes or power lines of buildings as distribution grids. The signals radiate for a short distance into the space surrounding these conductors. Such services, called *carrier-current* stations, combine elements of both wire and wireless propagation. They require no licenses and, unlike educational FM stations, may sell advertising.

A licensed carrier-current service, Travelers Information Service (TIS), uses radiation from wires strung or buried alongside highways. TIS supplies traffic information to motorists on the approaches to airports and similar congested thoroughfares. Road

EXHIBIT 6–2   AM Transmitting Antennas

The entire steel tower of an AM radio antenna serves as its radiating element. For efficient propagation, its length must equal a quarter the length of the waves it radiates. Propagation also depends on soil conductivity, among other things. Heavy copper ground cables, buried in trenches radiating from the tower base, ensure good ground contact. The photo shows an array of antenna towers (for obtaining directional propagation) nearing completion, with the ground-cable trenching still visible.

SOURCE: Courtesy of Stainless Steel, Inc., North Wales, PA.

signs instruct motorists to tune to the relevant AM channel.

6.4
FM Stations

The term *standard broadcasting* has become something of a misnomer, because FM's inherently superior quality has enabled it to forge ahead of AM in numbers of listeners and stations (if one counts noncommercial stations).*

FM Channels U.S. frequency-modulation broadcasting occupies a 20-MHz block of frequencies in the VHF band, running from 88 to 108 MHz. The 20-MHz block allows for 100 FM channels of 200 kHz (0.2 MHz) width. The FCC identifies them by the numbers 201 to 300, but licensees prefer to identify their stations by their midchannel frequency (in megahertz) rather than by channel number (88.1 for channel 201, 88.3 for channel 202, and so on). The FCC reserves the first 20 FM channels for noncommercial, educational use.

FM needs relatively generous channel width (20 times that of AM radio), because frequency modulation inherently uses more frequencies than AM. Moreover, the FCC left room for multiplexing additional carriers in the channel, both for stereo and for nonbroadcast services.

Coverage Stations using the VHF band radiate direct waves, so that FM reaches only to the horizon. Because of this limitation to direct-wave propagation, FM escapes the nighttime sky-wave problem that complicates AM station licensing. An FM station has a stable coverage pattern, night and day, its shape and size depending on the station's power, the height of its transmitting antenna above the surrounding terrain, and the extent to which obtrusive terrain features or buildings block wave paths. The ability of FM signals to blank out interference from other stations more effectively than do AM signals also contributes to coverage stability. An FM signal needs to be only twice as strong as a competing signal to override it, whereas an AM signal needs to be 20 times as strong.

FM's short (VHF band) wavelength calls for short radiating and receiving antenna elements. In keeping with the horizontal polarization standard,* these antennas are mounted horizontally (which puts FM automobile reception at a slight disadvantage because most auto antennas are mounted vertically). To take best advantage of FM's direct-wave propagation, station owners mount antenna towers on high buildings or hilltops to extend the apparent horizon as far as possible. The FCC has not authorized FM stations to use directional antennas as AM stations do, although some owners have asked the FCC to consider them for stations in major markets.

Station Classes Because of FM's coverage stability and uniformity, the FCC needs no elaborate channel and station classification systems such as it uses for AM. The commission simply divides the country into zones and FM stations into three groups according to coverage area: Classes A, B, and C, defined in terms of power, antenna height, and zone. Class A station power/height combinations enable a station to cover a radius of about 15 miles; Class B, about 30 miles; and Class C, about 60 miles.† The maximum power/height combination permits 100,000 W of power (twice the maximum AM station power) and a 2,000-foot antenna height.

Signal Quality Good FM receivers with suitable loudspeakers can reproduce sound frequencies as high as 15,000 Hz. For discriminating listeners, this frequency range enables the reproduction of the overtones necessary for high-fidelity sound, giving FM a major quality advantage over AM radio.

Moreover, frequency modulation is inherently static-free, because the signal depends on variations in frequency rather than in amplitude. Static comes

---

*FM also benefits from the fact that increasing interference in the AM band has degraded the quality of AM signals. The FCC's eagerness to license more and more stations and its failure to vigorously police external sources of interference have thus compounded AM's inherent disadvantages.

Polarization refers to the fact that radio waves oscillate *across* their propagation paths. Transmitter antenna orientation determines the direction of oscillation. Usually polarization is either horizontal (causing back-and-forth oscillation) or vertical (causing up-and-down oscillation), but circular polarization is also used.

†A fourth class, D, consists of very low power (10-W) FM educational stations, but since 1980 the FCC has sought to displace them if other, full-powered candidates for their noncommercial channels exist. The 10-W stations have several options for moving to other channels if they do not interfere with full-power stations. See 47 CFR 73.512 for details.

EXHIBIT 6–3 Short-Wave (HF) Broadcast Bands

Band designation		Band limits
Meters	Megahertz	Kilohertz
49	6	5,950–6,200
41	7	7,100–7,300
31	9	9,500–9,775
25	11	11,700–11,975
19	15	15,100–15,450
16	17	17,700–17,900
13	21	21,450–21,750
11	25	25,600–26,100

International broadcasters use these bands to reach distant targets by means of sky waves. Additional HF broadcast bands in the 5-MHz range have been allocated for domestic services in the tropical zone, where atmospheric interference caused by storms limits the usefulness of the MW frequencies normally used for domestic radio broadcasting. The entire HF band runs from 3,000 to 30,000 kHz. Marine, air, land mobile, amateur, and other services use the rest of the band, which is in high demand because of its long-distance capability.

from amplitude distortions caused when extraneous sources of electromagnetic energy interact with the AM signal. This advantage of FM is particularly noticeable in the southern part of the country and in large cities. Subtropical storms in the southern latitudes cause much natural static, and in cities concentrations of electrical machinery and appliances cause humanmade static.

FM radio also has greater *dynamic range* (the loudness difference between the weakest and strongest sounds) than AM. Sound reproducing systems do not easily match the human ear's capacity to accept extremes of loudness and softness. Very soft sounds tend to get lost in the electron noise of the apparatus, and very loud sounds overload the system, causing distortion. AM broadcasting has much less dynamic range and even sacrifices some of that

by artificially compressing the signal in order to maximize average power output.

Multiplexed FM Services   FM's generous 200-kHz channel width makes it easy to enhance the quality of FM still more by multiplexing a second carrier to furnish stereophonic sound.* Put in simple terms, stereo works as follows: two parallel sets of equipment, corresponding to the listener's left and right ears, pick up and amplify two versions of the sound source. One component modulates the regular FM carrier wave, the other a subcarrier within the FM channel. A stereophonic receiver, also equipped with parallel sound channels, separates the signals for delivery to the left and right speakers.

In addition to stereo sound, FM can also multiplex secondary services. A licensed *subsidiary communications service* (SCS), such as readings for the blind or background music for offices and stores, requires attaching a converter to the ordinary FM receiver to enable reception.

6.5
Short-Wave Broadcasting

The general public in the United States makes little use of short-wave broadcasting, though it plays an important role in the domestic broadcasting of some countries. The United States does use it extensively for international diplomacy. Short-wave services use amplitude modulation and can reach distant areas by exploiting the sky waves bounced back from the ionosphere.

Propagation   Parts of the HF band between 6 and 25 MHz have been designated by the ITU for international short-wave services (Exhibit 6–3). The ionosphere tends to refract waves in this band both day and night, enabling round-the-clock coverage

---

*AM radio can also transmit stereophonic sound, but its narrow channel makes the technology more difficult. Moreover, the absence of a universally accepted AM stereo technology has discouraged station owners from converting (see Section 3.7).

thousands of miles away. However, the electrical properties of the ionosphere layers constantly change under the impact of the sun's rays; also, the layers lose altitude as they cool off at night. For these reasons, a frequency that works well when propagated at a given angle over a given wave path at ten in the morning might be entirely useless by four in the afternoon. Seasonal changes also occur, making frequencies that reach a given target area in the spring useless for that area at other seasons.

Propagation theory predicts ionospheric shifts, enabling short-wave engineers to schedule frequency changes throughout the day and from season to season. Unlike domestic AM stations, therefore, short-wave international services need to feed their outputs to several different antennas, each designed to radiate a different frequency. Short-wave antennas are usually directional, beaming their signals toward specific target areas. The radiating elements consist of extensive arrays of suspended cables, as shown in Exhibit 6–4; the steel towers serve to support the cables, not to radiate the signal.

Though short when compared with MF waves, HF broadcast waves nevertheless vary from 11 to 49 meters (about 36 to 160 feet) in length. Radiating elements must therefore be relatively long, as suggested by Exhibit 6–4. Major short-wave antenna installations such as the Voice of America antenna sites occupy hundreds, even thousands, of acres because not only are the antenna arrays very large, but each requires equally large reflecting elements for directional propagation.

U.S. Short-Wave Stations

In the United States, short-wave (HF) stations provide international, not domestic, services, although many foreign countries do have domestic HF transmitters.* Only a few privately operated international short-wave stations exist in the United States, mostly evangelistic religious outlets operated noncommercially. However, elsewhere in the world a number of international com-

_____

*The ITU allocates certain HF bands for domestic broadcasting in the tropics, where atmospheric noise makes standard AM radio largely ineffective during the rainy season.

EXHIBIT 6–4 Short-Wave Transmitting Antenna

The Voice of America uses scores of short-wave antennas such as this. The steel towers support the cables that function as radiating elements. Each VOA site has many antennas to feed different frequencies in the HF band, along with other suspended wires that act as reflectors to beam signals in specific directions to reach designated overseas target areas.

SOURCE: Courtesy Voice of America, Washington, DC.

mercial stations use short waves, and a trend toward such stations may be emerging in the United States. In 1980, WRNO pioneered an international short-wave commercial station in New Orleans, targeting commercial messages to Canada and Europe. It can, of course, also be heard on short-wave receivers in the United States.

The U.S. government's official external service, the Voice of America (VOA), operates more than a hundred short-wave transmitters, located both within the country and overseas.* It also leases time on international satellites to relay programs to overseas transmitters. Foreign listeners can pick up short-wave VOA broadcasts directly or hear them on strategically located overseas short- and medium-wave VOA rebroadcast transmitters.

6.6
Pictures in Motion

Television technology can be more easily described if we look first at the principles developed for the cinema, the original technology of pictures in motion.

Picture Elements   Most photographic systems represent scenes by breaking reality down into many tiny *pixels* (picture elements). Basically, the size and distribution of pixels govern picture *resolution* (also called *definition*). These terms refer to a picture system's fineness of detail, specifically its ability to distinguish two small, closely adjacent objects as separate objects. Resolution in photography parallels information capacity in radio communication. High-resolution pictures demand a broadband channel, one able to handle a great many pixels each second.

The information capacity of motion picture depends not only on film resolution but also on the size of the picture area available for each frame in the film strip and on the rate (stated in frames per second) at which the film moves through the camera. Three quality standards have emerged, based on the width of film stocks (stated in millimeters): 35 mm, 16 mm, and 8 mm. Along with some larger formats for wide-screen projection, 35 mm represents the professional theatrical standard. The intermediate size, 16-mm film, was originally the

amateur standard, but television's great appetite for film stimulated the evolution of 16-mm technology to a professional level. The less expensive 8-mm format became the amateur, home-movie standard.*

In all cinema formats, some film area must be reserved for sprocket holes, for between-frame spaces, and (usually) for a soundtrack. In television channels, some frequencies must similarly be reserved for sound and auxiliary information.

Frame-Frequency Standards   In cinema, what appears to be motion actually consists of still pictures (*frames*) projected in rapid succession. Each frame freezes the action at a slightly later moment than the preceding frame. The human eye retains the image of an object briefly after the object has been removed. This *persistence of vision* blends together the images in successive frames. Thus the motion of motion pictures exists only "in the mind's eye" as an optical illusion.

A fairly satisfactory illusion of natural motion occurs if a projector displays at least 16 frames per second (fps). For that reason, during the silent era the motion-picture industry adopted 16 fps as the standard frame rate. At 16 fps, however, the soundtrack along the edge of the film passes too slowly over the projector's sound pickup head for adequate sound quality. The industry therefore adopted the higher rate of 24 fps for sound motion pictures. The difference between the frame rate of silent and sound films accounts for the comic jerkiness of silent films shown on modern projectors; these projectors increase the original projection rate by 50 percent, speeding up the action to an unnatural degree.

Flicker Prevention   Although 24 fps gives the illusion of continuous action, at that projection rate the eye still detects the fact that light falls on the screen intermittently. After each frame flashes on the screen, a moment of darkness ensues while the

---

*As an exception to the ITU rule designating MW stations exclusively for domestic services, the VOA also uses some MW (standard broadcasting) transmitters for international broadcasting, notably one at Marathon in the Florida Keys, designed to reach Cuba. Other countries also use MW transmitters for external services.

---

*Note that although high-definition television (HDTV) reaches 35-mm quality, the present (NTSC) television standard falls well below the quality level normally expected for theatrical projection. HDTV is discussed in Section 6.11.

machine pulls the next frame into position for projection. The eye reacts more sensitively to these gross changes from illumination to blackout than to the small changes in positions of objects from frame to frame. A sensation of *flicker* results. In fact, early movies earned the name *flicks* because their low frame rate made them flicker conspicuously.

Increasing the frame frequency can overcome the flicker sensation, but because the 24-fps rate gives all the visual and sound information required, such an increase would be wasteful. Instead, modern projectors show each frame *twice:* when the projector pulls a frame into place, it flashes the picture on the screen, blacks out the screen, then flashes the *same frame again* before blacking out to pull the next frame into position. Although it projects only 24 separate pictures, it illuminates the screen 48 times per second, thus avoiding the flicker sensation. Television uses a similar trick, illuminating the screen twice as many times as the number of complete pictures shown each second.

6.7
Electronic Pictures

Analysis of cinema methods suggests that an electronic analog must meet four requirements: it must (1) analyze pictures into electronic pixels; (2) generate enough frames per second for the illusion of motion; (3) suppress the sensation of flicker by doubling frame frequency, without increasing information load; and (4) provide a channel wide enough to transmit all this information in real time (that is, without perceptible delay), including simultaneous sound and auxiliary signals.

Pickup Tube The heart of the television system, the *pickup tube,** is a transducer for converting light energy into electrical energy. It breaks down each image into thousands of picture elements (pix-

els). The pixels start as bits of light energy distributed throughout the image; the picture tube picks them up systematically as a sequence of dotted lines, each dot representing a pixel. The picture tube converts each line of pixels into a stream of electrical impulses (voltages). An ordinary photographic camera lens focuses the live or filmed televised scene on the face of the pickup tube. Thereafter, electrons take over. Without the speed and exquisite precision of electrons, television with satisfactory definition would be impossible.

Pickup tubes have come in various shapes and sizes, as shown in Exhibit 6–5. In principle, they work as follows: the camera lens focuses an image on the *target plate* within the tube. The target plate, covered with thousands of light-sensitive specks, represents a single picture or *frame*. Each speck converts the light energy that falls on it into an electric charge of corresponding intensity. Thus each of the thousands of pixels on the target plate takes on an electric charge proportionate to the amount of light it has stored. Next, the tube releases each of the momentarily stored charges, one at a time.

Electrons come into play as the releasing agent. At the end of the tube opposite to the target plate, an *electron gun* shoots a stream of electrons toward the back of the plate. As the electrons fly down the length of the tube, they pass through magnetic fields generated by external *deflection coils* surrounding the body of the tube (Exhibit 6–5). Magnetic forces attract and repel the electron stream, making it move systematically in a *scanning* (reading) motion, left to right, line by line, top to bottom. Thus the electron beam "reads" the information on the target plate. The string of electric pulses that results constitutes the pickup tube's output (Exhibits 6–6 and 6–7, pages 141 and 142, give more details).

The pickup tube has no moving parts. Its electron gun remains fixed. Special circuits that send appropriate electrical messages to the deflection coils control the scanning movements of the electron beam. A film camera must have a revolving shutter to interrupt the scene each time it draws a new film frame into place for exposure. The television camera needs no shutter, for the video picture never exists as a complete frame, only as a sequence of

---

*Some specialized situations, such as slow-motion sports coverage, call for the use of a solid-state imager, a tubeless camera based on a more recent technology, the CCD (*charge-coupled device*). These devices have not yet been generally adopted for professional use, but have been for home video cameras.

EXHIBIT 6–5   TV Pickup Tube

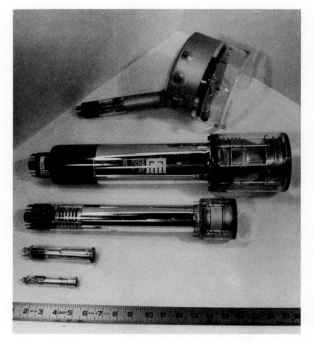

A.

A. As technology improved, tubes became smaller. Commercial broadcasters first used the iconoscope, the odd-shaped tube at the top. Then image orthicons, with 3-inch and 4.5-inch faces, replaced iconoscopes. Smaller tubes such as the vidicon and plumbicon in turn replaced the image orthicon.

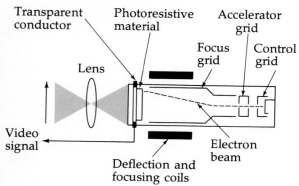

B. The main components and functions of the vidicon type of tube are as follows: a lens focuses the image on a photoresistive plate whose electrical resistance varies with the amount of light striking its surface. At the base of the tube, three components called grids help generate and shape the electron beam. As it leaves the focus grid, it enters magnetic fields created by coils surrounding the neck of the tube. Changes in the magnetic fields, caused by changes in the voltage fed to the deflection coils, sweep the electron beam back and forth in the prescribed scanning pattern. As the electron beam scans the rear side of the plate, it causes the electric energy stored in each pixel to flow to the conductor plate as an electrical voltage. The varying amplitudes of those voltages, led by wire away from the plate, constitute the video signal (illustrated in Exhibit 6–7).

SOURCES: Photo by Frank Sauerwald, Temple University. Drawing adapted from A. Michael Noll, *Television Technology: Fundamentals and Future Prospects* (Norwood, MA: Artech House, 1988), Fig. 7–8, p. 67.

pixels. Television relies on persistence of vision to blend the pixel sequence into a seemingly unbroken image in the mind's eye.

Scanning Standards   Recall that motion pictures have two frequency standards: 24 fps for continuity of motion, and 48 fps for continuity of illumination (to eliminate flicker). It would have saved some problems in televising film had television adopted the same standards. However, the television camera does not "take" a complete picture all at once, so television could use cinema's antiflicker

EXHIBIT 6–6   Scanning

A.

B.

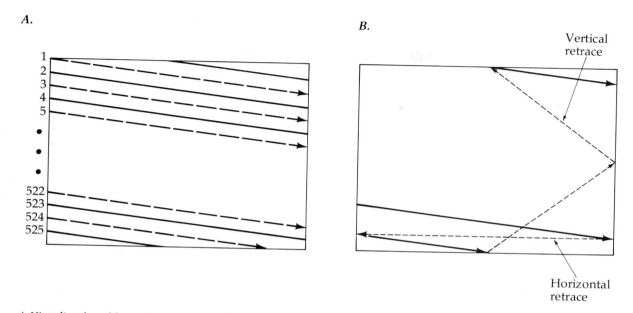

A. Visualize the odd-numbered lines (depicted as broken) as scanning the first field, leaving room for the even-numbered lines (depicted as solid) to scan the second field. Together the lines of the two fields "interlace" to make up the complete frame of 525 lines. B. At the end of each line and of each field, the electron beam must fly back to start a new line or new field. During these horizontal and vertical flyback, or retrace, times, a blanking signal prevents the beam from activating any picture elements. The horizontal retrace path runs directly from the end of one line back to the start of the next, but for reasons of technological convenience the vertical retrace path makes a jog before it reaches the starting point of the next field at the top of the frame. The vertical retrace time, equivalent to the time needed to scan 21 normal lines, is called the VBI (vertical blanking interval); during this period, nonpicture information can be transmitted, such as closed captions and teletext (see Exhibit 6–13).

strategy of repeating each entire frame only at the unacceptable price of nearly doubling the television channel size.

Instead, television splits each frame into two parts by scanning first the odd-numbered lines, then the even-numbered lines. Each scanning sequence, called a *field,* illuminates the receiver screen from top to bottom, but each field picks up only *half* the pixels in the frame. This method, known as *offset* or *interlace* scanning, causes the electron beam to scan line 1, line 3, line 5, and so on to the bottom of the field, then fly back to the top of the field to fill in line 2, line 4, line 6, and so on (Exhibit 6–6). Thus instead of film's repetition rates of 24 and 48, tele-

EXHIBIT 6–7 TV Channel Architecture and Signal Formation

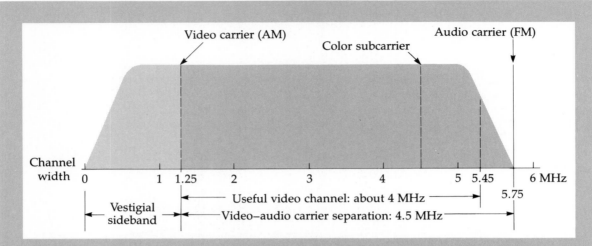

This diagram shows the architecture of the 6-MHz television channel. A vestigial lower sideband takes up the 1.25 MHz below the video carrier frequency because the sideband cannot be cut off abruptly. A subcarrier, higher in the video portion of the channel, conveys the color information. When modulated by the black-and-white video (luminance) information, the main video carrier's upper sideband overlaps the sideband of the color subcarrier. *Interleaving* minimizes conflict. Uneven distribution of frequencies carrying the luminance signal makes such interleaving possible. If the teeth of a comb are visualized as the frequencies occupied by the monochrome information, the color information occupies frequencies represented by the spaces between the teeth.

A 100-kHz subchannel accommodates the audio information, located near the upper end of the channel. A buffer zone above the audio subchannel intervenes before the next higher contiguous 6-MHz channel begins.

Above is a portion of a video signal, representing in simplified form the last field of one frame (L) followed by the vertical blanking interval and then the first two fields of the next frame (L' and L"). At L occurs the last line of a frame, represented by the varying voltage amplitudes released by the electron beam as it scans the line. At the end of the line, amplitude is increased artificially to a level above "picture black," a region known as "blacker than black" because it is not visible on the receiver screen. The vertical blanking and synchronizing signals follow (depicted here as an unvarying am-

vision uses 30 (frame frequency) and 60 (field frequency).* Engineers chose these rates to take advantage of the precise, universal timing standard already available throughout the United States: the 60-Hz alternating electric current in homes.

Modern television no longer depends on that source for its time base. Nevertheless, the fact that much of the world uses 50-Hz house current accounted originally, in part at least, for differences between U.S. television technical standards and those of many other countries. Fifty-hertz countries standardized frames and field frequencies at 25 and 50. The 50/60 disparity continues to stand in the way of adopting a world television standard for the emerging, more advanced television technologies.

---

*Special television film projectors solve the mismatch between film and television field-frequency standards (48 versus 60 fps) by displaying every fourth film frame an extra time, thus adding 12 projections per second to film's normal 48 fields to bring the projection rate up to television's 60-field standard. Standards experts have discussed changing film standards to 30/60, which would greatly improve the quality of 16-mm film.

EXHIBIT 6–7   Continued

plitude but in actuality consisting of complex variations in amplitude). This period is the VBI, the vertical blanking interval, during which the electron beam flies back to start the next field. L′ represents the voltages generated by the first line of that field, followed by a briefer blacker-than-black interval to cover the shorter period during which the beam flies back to the start of the next line, depicted by L″.

The brightest parts of the picture generate the highest amplitude levels, but for several practical reasons, such as the need for the blacker-than-black retrace intervals,

reverse modulation inverts the signal so that low amplitude represents light and high amplitude represents dark picture elements. This reversal becomes evident to the viewer at times, for example, when the receiver picks up interference caused by an automobile ignition that creates static. The spark plugs emit radiation when they fire, *adding* amplitude to the intended picture signal. Were it not for reverse modulation, these higher-than-normal amplitudes would show up as lines of white dots in the picture; in fact, ignition interference appears as lines of black dots.

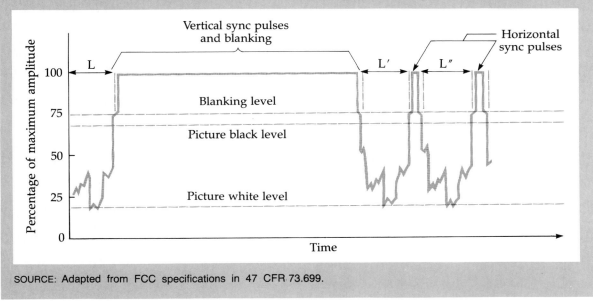

SOURCE: Adapted from FCC specifications in 47 CFR 73.699.

6.8
The TV Signal

You can see from the foregoing description that the television receiver reconstructs an electronic picture consisting of pixels arranged in lines, fields consisting of lines, and frames consisting of fields. All this requires the utmost precision in timing, made possible only by electronic means.

Picture Definition   The number of lines per frame makes a convenient index of a system's level of *resolution,* or definition. The U.S. standard of 525 lines per frame determines a picture's *vertical resolution.* However, not all 525 lines can be used to convey picture information. Some time that would otherwise be occupied with transmitting lines must be devoted to auxiliary picture information. Also, receivers vary in the way they present the picture, necessitating the use of a *mask* to standardize the visible television image. In practice, black-and-white pictures depend on only about 340 lines per frame. The color component consists of even fewer lines, about 280. This low resolution does not degrade color-picture quality, however, because the fine details in color pictures appear only in black-and-white. By way of comparison, a theatrical quality 35-mm film frame has the equivalent of 1,000 lines. However, high-definition television, discussed at the close of this chapter, will eventually match the best film standard.

Auxiliary Signals Vitally important auxiliary signals called *sync pulses* keep the scanning in the receiver tube in step (synchronized) with the scanning in the camera. This synchronizing function is comparable to film *registration* mechanisms in movie cameras and projectors. They have toothed wheels (sprockets) that engage the sprocket holes along the edges of film, moving it forward at the right speed and holding each frame accurately positioned when stopping to record or project an image.

Television sync pulses, originated by a special timing device in the studio (see Exhibit 6–9), ensure that each pixel in each line will appear on the receiver screen in the same location it had in the pickup tube. Even a slight loss of synchronization renders received pictures unusable. For this reason, lightweight portable television equipment could not be used outside the studio until development of the *time-base corrector* made it possible to maintain precise synchronization between field and studio equipment.

Another type of auxiliary signal cuts off the scanning beam during *retrace* intervals, the time the electron beam needs to fly back diagonally from the end of one line to the beginning of the next (horizontal retrace) and from the bottom of one field back to top of the next field (vertical retrace, shown in Exhibit 6–6). During these breaks in scanning, also called *blanking* intervals, auxiliary signals prevent picture pickup so that the electron beam's retrace paths will not destroy the orderly scanning pattern.

Sound U.S. television uses frequency modulation (FM) for the sound carrier; the 100-kHz sound channel is located in the upper part of the television channel (Exhibit 6–7). No synchronizing signals are needed to keep sound and picture in step, since they occur simultaneously and go out in real time.

Color In approving television color standards, the FCC insisted on *compatibility* to assure that people with monochrome receivers could continue to receive pictures after transmitters converted to color. At the same time, the system had to be capable of adding color information without enlarging the established 6-MHz monochrome channel. A committee of major U.S. manufacturers met these criteria with the system known as *NTSC* (National Television System Committee) color.*

The television signal mixes three primary-color signals to produce all other colors. Filters separate the primary color information (red, blue, and green) before the image reaches the camera tube. In addition to *hue* (what we perceive as color), all colors also have a brightness attribute, *luminance*. The noncolor luminance component contributes all the fine detail in color pictures. A monochrome receiver interprets a color picture using the luminance signal alone and thus can display it in black and white. Multiplexing enables a color carrier to be added without enlarging the television channel, fulfilling the compatibility criterion. Exhibit 6–7 shows the location of the color subcarrier.

6.9
The TV Channel

Television's heavy information load requires a broadband channel. U.S. standards call for a 6-MHz channel—600 times the width of an AM radio broadcast channel (Exhibit 6–8). Indeed, *all* the AM and FM broadcast channels together occupy less spectrum space than only four television channels. Even so, the NTSC standards allow for only fair picture resolution. In the near future, HDTV (high-definition television) may significantly improve resolution and other aspects of the broadcast picture.

---

*Nearly three-quarters of foreign television services use PAL (West German) or SECAM (French) color. PAL is the most widely used.

EXHIBIT 6–8 Summary of Broadcast Channel Specifications

Broadcast service	Channel width	Number of channels	Channel identification numbers	Band	Allocated frequencies
AM (standard) radio	10 kHz	107[a]	54–160[b]	MF	535–1605 kHz[a]
VHF television	6 MHz	3	2–4[c]	VHF	54–72 MHz
		2	5–6	VHF	76–88 MHz[d]
FM radio	200 kHz	100	201–300	VHF	88–108 MHz
VHF television	6 MHz	7	7–13	VHF	174–216 MHz
UHF television	6 MHz	56[e]	14–69	UHF	470–806 MHz

[a]AM channels are not numbered but are denoted by midchannel frequencies at 10-kHz intervals—540, 550, 560, . . . up to 1600. Receiver dials often omit the last zero, reading 54, 55, 56, and so on.
[b]The AM band is due to be expanded to 117 channels running up to 1705 kHz in 1990.
[c]Originally there was a channel 1, located at 44–50 MHz. However, it interfered with other services, and in 1948 the FCC reallocated that group of frequencies to nonbroadcast services but retained the original number scheme.
[d]Note that VHF channel 6 comes immediately before the start of the FM band. This proximity sometimes causes TV–FM interference.
[e]Because of the high demand for UHF frequencies among other services, not all the 56 UHF channels have been allotted to actual TV use.

This table consolidates scattered information in the text to enable the primary channel specifications for all three broadcast services to be compared. Note that the television allocation is fragmented into four different frequency groups in two different bands.

Channel Width and Picture Quality The NTSC television channel allots 4 of the 6 MHz to picture information, including auxiliary signals. The vestigial lower sideband, the audio channel, and guard bands (buffer zones to prevent side-by-side signals from interfering with each other) occupy the remaining 2 MHz (details are shown in Exhibit 6–7).

Even the relatively large 4-MHz picture television channel achieves relatively low picture resolution by the standards of theatrical motion pictures and good-quality still photography. The average home receiver displays about 150,000 pixels per frame. A projected 35-mm film frame has about a million, an 8 × 10-inch photoengraving about two million. Magnifying the television picture by projection makes it possible to sit farther from the screen but adds no detail; in fact, some of the detail gets lost in the projection process.

Current television resolution standards represent compromises based on research aimed at determining the lowest quality that most viewers could tolerate. Quality had to be kept to a minimum to avoid using too much spectrum space. The same spectrum-saving goal motivated the suppression of the lower sideband produced by the television channel.

Location in Spectrum When the time came to allocate frequencies for television, much of the most suitable spectrum region, the VHF band, had already been allocated to other services. Room remained for only 12 (originally 13) VHF channels, numbered 2 through 13.*

*Finding that the original channel 1, 44–50 MHz, interfered with other services, in 1948 the FCC reassigned it to nonbroadcast uses, but kept the original numbers for the remaining 12 VHF channels.

EXHIBIT 6–9 Operational TV System Components and Signals

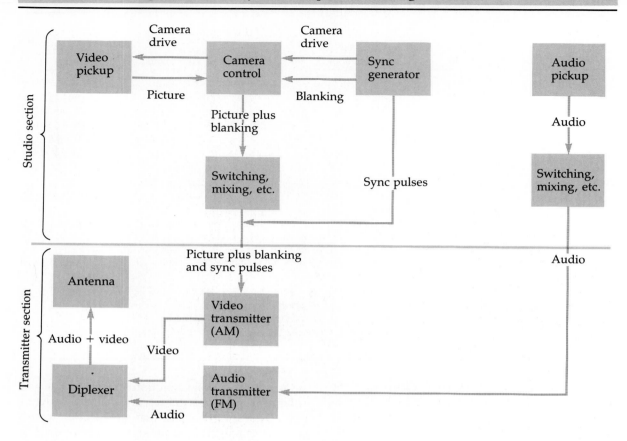

Each block stands for a function that in practice may involve many different pieces of equipment. The upper half of the diagram represents the basic items and functions involved in studio operations; the lower half, those involved in transmission operations. Separate sets of equipment handle the video and audio components all the way to the diplexer, the device in the transmitters that finally marries the two signals so that they can be transmitted as a composite. (Exhibit 6–7 shows how the audio and video components are multiplexed in a single channel.)

SOURCE: Harold E. Ennes, *Principles and Practices of Telecasting Operations* (Indianapolis: Howard W. Sams, 1953).

To find room for even those few channels, the FCC had to put VHF television into three different blocks of frequencies, as shown in Exhibit 6–8. After discovering that 12 channels could not satisfy the demand for stations, the FCC in 1952 added 70 additional channels in the UHF band, numbered 14 through 83 (later reduced to 56 UHF channels numbered 14 through 69). A table allots specific channels by number to specific towns and cities throughout the United States (found in 47 CFR

73.606). For purposes of setting TV cochannel separations, the FCC has different standards for three geographic zones (essentially, northern, midland, and south) and two channel types, VHF and UHF. As an example of the VHF-UHF distinction, in Zone 1, stations on VHF channels must be about 170 miles apart, whereas those on UHF must be about 155 miles apart. For details of these rules, see 47 CFR 73.609–613.

6.10
Transmission and Reception

The directional nature of the waves used by television and the need to keep the pickup tube in exact synchronization with the receiver complicate the processes of transmission and reception.

Studio As Exhibit 6–9 suggests, the *sync generator* plays a major role in the television control room, ensuring synchronization of pickup and receiver tubes. It controls picture scanning by generating the precise timing signals for driving the camera's deflection coils and inserting the blanking signals. The sync generator also controls the timing of such additional video sources as tape recorders, video disc recorders, computer memories, film projectors, and network feeds. A completely independent set of audio equipment handles the sound component of the program.

Transmission The video and audio signals are fed independently to the transmitter, which may be located miles away from the studio at a suitable antenna site. There the two signals modulate separate audio and video transmitters. Because of its greater information load, the video component needs up to 20 times as much power as the audio. A station's power is usually stated in terms of the *effective radiated power* (ERP) of its video signal.

Signals from the video and audio transmitters meet for the first time at a *diplexer,* a device that combines them into a composite signal to feed the antenna (Exhibit 6–9).

Because television relies on direct waves, engineers seek the highest possible locations for an-

EXHIBIT 6–10   Television Antenna

Because of the importance of height to maximize television's line-of-sight coverage, Boston's WQTV (TV) chose the roof of the 55-story Prudential Center as its antenna site. A helicopter lifts the antenna assembly into place atop the supporting tower. The radiating elements are mounted in a spiral pattern, denoting circular polarization of the signal.

SOURCE: Courtesy CETEC Antenna Corporation.

tenna sites, such as mountain peaks, the roofs of tall buildings, or the tops of tall steel towers (Exhibit 6–10). Direct-wave antenna towers do not radiate the signal as do AM towers; they simply support the

EXHIBIT 6–11   TV Propagation Paths

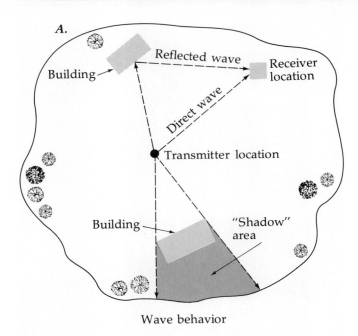

A.

Reflected wave

Building

Receiver location

Direct wave

Transmitter location

Building

"Shadow" area

Wave behavior

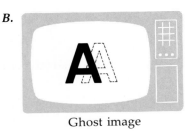

B.

Ghost image

A. Simplified coverage pattern of a television station, showing some characteristics of direct-wave propagation: the waves carry only to the horizon; some may encounter surfaces that reflect signals; some may encounter obstructions that cause "shadow" areas in the coverage pattern. B. When a receiver detects both a direct wave and a reflected wave, the reflected wave will have traveled over a longer path, and will therefore arrive at the receiver slightly later than the direct wave. When the receiver displays the signal of the delayed reflected wave, the image lags slightly behind that of the direct wave, appearing as a "ghost."

radiating elements, which are quite small, in keeping with the shortness of the VHF and UHF waves. Because of *horizontal polarization,* both transmitting and receiving antenna elements are mounted horizontally with reference to the ground below. Some television transmitting antennas emit *circularly polarized* waves, which travel with a corkscrew motion. When circularly polarized television signals are reflected by obstructions, the direction of rotation becomes reversed, causing the receiving antenna to reject the reflected signals. This rejection

helps reception in large cities, where reflections from tall buildings appear on the screen as "ghosts" (Exhibit 6–11).

The television transmitting antenna propagates directionally *downward* toward the line-of-sight coverage area, cutting off the energy that would otherwise shoot off into space above the horizon.

In setting television power limits, the FCC uses a formula that takes antenna height into consideration, as in the case of FM, which also uses VHF waves. VHF television signals have inherent advantages over UHF. Waves in the UHF band, being shorter than VHF waves, can be more easily blocked by objects in their path. Moreover, they attenuate more rapidly than VHF waves. For these reasons, the FCC allows UHF television to use very high power (up to 5 million watts) to compensate to some extent for its coverage limitations.*

Reception Television coverage, limited essentially to the distance to the visible horizon, depends also on receiving antenna efficiency and height, obstructive terrain features, transmitter frequency, and power. Within about 20 miles of a powerful transmitter, indoor antennas usually suffice. At about 30 miles, outdoor antennas become essential.

For commercial and regulatory purposes, the FCC classifies television station coverage in terms of Grade A and Grade B contours. Grade A contours enclose an area in which satisfactory service can be received 90 percent of the time; Grade B contours enclose an area in which reception is satisfactory only 50 percent of the time.*

A transmitting antenna can be sized ideally for its specific channel, but receiving antennas must be designated to pick up either all channels or all channels in one of the bands (VHF or UHF). Since receiving antennas are highly directional, they must be pointed toward the transmitters. In areas where the viewer must look toward widely different points of the compass to find transmitters, a rotatable outdoor antenna may be necessary.

Like transmitters, receivers process the video and audio parts of the signal separately. In conventional receivers, the video information goes to a type of cathode ray tube (CRT), the *kinescope*. A phosphorescent coating on its inside face glows when bombarded with electrons. Within the neck of the kinescope an electron gun, a larger analog of the one in the pickup tube, shoots electrons toward

the face of the tube. Guided by external deflection coils, the electron beam scans the tube face, releasing pixels of varying intensity line by line, field by field, and frame by frame. The synchronizing signals originated by the sync generator in the studio activate the deflection coils, keeping the receiver scanning sequence in step with the sequence in the pickup tube at the studio.

Phosphors that glow in the three primary colors, arranged either in narrow parallel stripes or triads of dots, coat the inside of color kinescopes. Receiver circuits decode the video signal into components representing the energy levels of the three primary colors in each pixel. Data for each color strike the tube face separately, using one or more electron guns (see Exhibit 6–12). Only the primary colors appear on the kinescope. Normally the eye sees various hues as a result of the mix of primaries provided by varying energy levels in the color tube outputs. However, if one looks at part of a color picture on the face of a kinescope with a small magnifying glass, only the three primary colors can be seen.

In principle the kinescope displays only one pixel at a time, but because it takes a while for the activated phosphor to lose its glow, several pixels remain visible at any given instant. Considering the speed and precision with which the primary color pixels, lines, fields, and frames must be delivered each second to create the illusion of realistic moving pictures, the achievement of television seems truly remarkable.

6.11
Technical Innovations

Improvements in this remarkable performance nevertheless continue at an accelerated pace. Following are a few examples of technical innovation.

Ancillary Signals Several possibilities exist for multiplexing additional signals in the existing 6-MHz television channel. For example, no picture information goes out during the *vertical blanking interval* (VBI), the time during which the pickup tube's scanning beam returns from the bottom of

---

*For details on power/height regulations, see 47 CFR 73.699, Fig. 3.

*These contours have no meaning for cable television subscribers, who receive their local television stations as well as cable-specific programming via cable and no longer depend on receiving antennas—although they may still need antennas during cable system outages.

EXHIBIT 6–12 Color Kinescope Tube

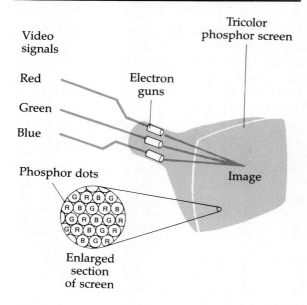

Video signals

Tricolor phosphor screen

Red

Green

Blue

Electron guns

Phosphor dots

Image

Enlarged section of screen

Some receiver tubes use three electronic guns and tricolor phosphor dots. Varying amplitudes in the modulated currents fed to each of the electron guns cause the dots to glow with varying intensities; though only the red, green, and blue primary colors appear on the kinescope face, the eye blends them together to make all the various hues.

SOURCE: Paul Davidovits, *Communication* (New York: Holt, Rinehart & Winston, 1972), p. 114.

the picture to the top to start scanning a new field (shown in Exhibit 6–6).* That interval occupies about 8 percent of the 1/60 second devoted to each field, or the equivalent of 21 picture lines.

Teletext, one of the several users of the VBI, delivers textual matter (including rather crude maps and drawings) to the television screen. A television station equipped to transmit teletext stores up to about 200 pages (picture frames) of information in digital form and transmits them in rotation during the VBI. At the home receiver, the user requests

---

*When a receiver's vertical hold is slightly mistuned, the VBI appears on the screen as a black bar between fields.

specific pages by means of a key pad. The key pad activates a minicomputer that "grabs" the requested frames as they go by, transmitted in rotation; the computer then displays them on the television screen (Exhibit 6–13). The viewer may have to wait several seconds before the selected page comes up in the rotation. Teletext pages can temporarily displace the television picture, or they can be superimposed over the picture.

Closed captioning, a specialized form of teletext, superimposes captions over regular television programs for the benefit of the hearing impaired. Only viewers with a decoder can display the captions; hence the term "closed" for this type of teletext.

Teletext technology has not been standardized, leaving several rival systems to compete for acceptance. In the United States two formats have been tried, NABTS (North American Basic Teletext Specification) and WST (World System Teletext). NABTS resembles systems developed in Canada and France, whereas WST is based on the somewhat simpler system used in the United Kingdom, which pioneered the technology.*

Another ancillary television signal, an audio subcarrier, enables the telecasting of stereophonic and bilingual sound. Receivers with the necessary double speakers came on the market with MPX (multiplex) terminals on the back for plugging in the converters needed to extract the subcarrier signal.

Miniaturization Starting in the 1950s, the changeover in electronics from dependence on vacuum tubes to solid-state devices profoundly affected television technology, as it did all media—even the press, which makes extensive use of computers and radio relay. Vacuum tubes (so called because they provide an enclosed space for the manipulation of electrons in a near vacuum) are bulky, power-hungry, hot, and easily damaged. A rack of equipment containing scores of tubes takes up a great deal of space and has to be artificially cooled.

---

*A nonbroadcast type of text display called *videotex* differs from teletext: (1) it comes to the home by telephone wire rather than over the air; (2) not being limited to the VBI, it can provide unlimited numbers of pages; and (3) it is an interactive system, so that the subscriber can send back requests or messages to the source.

EXHIBIT 6–13   Using the VBI: Closed Captions and Teletext

The VBI (vertical blanking interval) in the television signal occupies channel space equivalent to 21 picture lines but conveys no picture information. Only 9 of the lines need to be used for the sync pulse and related information. Each VBI line can carry 320 bits of digitized information, permitting transmission of 8 letters per line. The 60-per-second field frequency therefore allows sending 240 characters per second. Viewers must equip their sets with adapters to see material transmitted in the VBI. Left photo: the VBI permits sending superimposed captions, such as those for the hearing impaired. Right photo: teletext also uses the VBI to send simple text and graphics, such as this sports scoreboard.

SOURCE: Courtesy CBS Television Network.

Solid-state devices eliminated these problems in most applications, although some vacuum tubes persist, notably the kinescope receiver tube and the traveling-wave tube, the primary source of on-board power in satellites.* The solid-state revolution started with *transistors,* which made possible the manipulation of electrons in a piece of solid material instead of within the relatively large vacuum chamber of a tube.

The second generation of solid-state devices, silicon chips, became familiar from their use in mi-

crocomputers. The latest version of this technology, the very large-scale integrated circuit (VLSIC), enables complex circuitry incorporating thousands of transistors and other components to be etched on a single chip an eighth of an inch in diameter. Integrated-circuit technology marries ideally with digital signal processing, on which the electronic future rests. Miniaturization, microprocessing, and digital techniques have been applied extensively to the field of sound and video recording, which is discussed in the next chapter.

Remote Equipment   ENG (electronic news gathering) and EFP (electronic field production) are examples of benefits made possible by miniaturization. Formerly, when covering outside news events

*In fact, vacuum tubes may make a comeback in the form of *vacuum microelectronics* because electrons flow fastest in a vacuum, and this may be useful in the design of new, flat-panel video display devices (Fisher, 1987).

EXHIBIT 6–14   Television Remotes: Electronic News Gathering Facilities

A.

B.

A. The unwieldy remote vehicle in the background contrasts with the compact, lightweight ENG (electronic news-gathering) van in the foreground. The machine-gun-like object atop the van is a microwave relay antenna for relaying pictures back to the studio. Microwave relays must have a line-of-sight view of the studio receiving antenna or an intermediate relay antenna. B. News gathering by satellite (NGS) greatly extends the reporter's range. A mobile earth station is used to uplink signals to a satellite.

SOURCES: Photo A courtesy WTVJ–TV, Miami, FL; Photo B courtesy WTVT, Tampa, FL.

or when producing on-location program segments and commercials, television crews had to use cumbersome *remote vehicles* (Exhibit 6–14). Miniaturization enables outside coverage using lightweight, portable equipment that is easily carried and operated by one or two persons.

The key to this development, the *time-base corrector,* contains a microcomputer that supplies accurate synchronization, freeing remotely operated portable equipment from dependence on the studio sync generator. Before the time-base corrector became available, synchronizing errors plagued remote operations, showing up as jittery pictures, skewing, and color breakup.

News gathering by satellite (NGS, also known by the registered trademark, SNG), using portable earth stations, started in the mid-1980s, making it possible to relay television reports from any location outside the studio. Previously, live remotes depended on microwave-relay links, which require unobstructed line-of-sight paths between studio and remote unit. NGS-equipped stations (Exhibit 6–14) obtain short-term access to Ku-band satellite transponders (those permitting the smallest uplink dishes) through firms that specialize in selling satellite capacity at retail.

Receiver Improvements Solid-state devices have made broadcast receivers lighter, cooler, less demanding of power, and less expensive to operate. Television sound reception, long a neglected element in receiver design, improved with stereophonic sound, which the FCC authorized in 1984.

EXHIBIT 6–14 Continued

C.

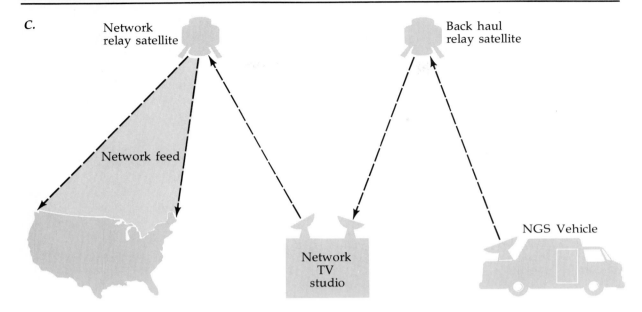

C. Using satellite relays to send program material from a news site back to the studio is called backhauling. When a broadcast network broadcasts a live on-the-spot event, it backhauls the coverage from an NGS vehicle to the studio, using leased short-term satellite capacity. From the studio, the program goes to the network's satellite uplink facility, and then to the permanently leased or owned satellite transponder that relays the program to the network's affiliates throughout the country.

The first stereo sets needed adapters, but manufacturers soon marketed sets with built-in stereophonic capability.

Small computers using digital processing improved picture quality in IDTV (improved definition television) receivers. They improve *apparent* definition by doubling the line frequency, filling in the blank lines normally left by interlace scanning to display a full frame 60 times a second instead of only 30. They filter out ghosts (Exhibit 6–15, page 154) and static, preventing them from distorting the picture. Advanced receivers also offer options such as PIP (picture in picture), freeze frames held in memory, zoom picture enlargement, and special interfaces with cable services and videocassette tape recorders.

Despite predictions that it may soon give way to more advanced technology, the bulky, power-hungry kinescope tube at the heart of the television receiver still offers the best method of displaying electronic pictures. The kinescope tube "has indeed withstood the test of time, and even in this current high-technology age has no equal" (Noll, 1988: 57). The next expected major breakthrough in image display may be a flat, solid-state picture device that can be hung on the wall. It will offer better quality with improved aspect ratio (Exhibit 6–15).

**EXHIBIT 6–15   TV Receiver
Aspect Ratios**

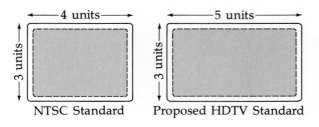

The FCC adopted the National Television Systems Committee's recommendation in the 1940s, standardizing on a 4 by 3 aspect ratio for the television receiver screen (left). A mask over the receiver kinescope (dotted lines in the drawings) cuts off about 10 percent of the picture area at the edges in order to provide a standard picture despite slight variations in picture size. The 4 by 3 aspect ratio (4 units wide by 3 units high) corresponds to that of the original theatrical motion picture standard, although in response to television competition, producers enhanced theatrical films by altering the ratio, using wide-screen lenses.

High-definition television (right) will also adopt a wide-screen aspect ratio, on the order of 5 units wide by 3 units high (the Japanese MUSE system widens the picture even more, using a 16 by 9 aspect ratio).

Flat screens can already be found in tiny, portable receivers. One type uses LCD (*liquid crystal display*) technology, which employs liquid crystal molecules in an ambiguous liquid/solid state. They change from opaque to transparent when hit with an electric charge. Several other alternatives to the kinescope tube are also under development.

HDTV   Larger screens are expected to be one of the benefits from *high-definition* television (HDTV). Japanese engineers have made the most progress with HDTV, experimenting extensively with a 1225-line picture with a 9-to-16 aspect ratio (Exhibit 6–15). This system, called MUSE, has links with the development of direct-broadcast services (DBS). The MUSE system originally called for wider channels

than the U.S. NTSC 6-MHz standard and therefore would outmode all present receivers and transmitters; however, the Japanese also offer a MUSE version that is compatible with present equipment. Since there is no additional spectrum space available in the present terrestrial television bands, HDTV must either conform to present channel specifications or move to the higher-frequency band allocated to direct-to-home satellite transmission.

HDTV of the MUSE type matches the quality of theatrical motion pictures and therefore lends itself to projected display. Ideal viewing of conventional 525-line television calls for a viewing distance of at least six times the picture height; moving closer can cause eyestrain because the viewer strives to see nonexistent detail. HDTV allows comfortable viewing at a distance of only three times the picture height and can also be viewed at a much wider angle from the screen than can existing television. HDTV permits multiple sound tracks, facilitating not only stereophonic sound but also sound in several languages.

The FCC felt some urgency about adopting at least tentative U.S. HDTV standards because of the need to ensure the ability of U.S. terrestrial broadcasting (1) to keep up with the Japanese and Europeans in the race toward improved television, and (2) to keep abreast of domestic cable, VCR, and DBS improvements. Those nonbroadcast services, not being subject to the NTSC 6-MHz channel constraint of broadcast television, could forge ahead with their own nonbroadcast version of HDTV without waiting for a compatible broadcast version to emerge. By 1988, several producers, in the United States and abroad, already had programs in production using MUSE-type HDTV cameras and recorders. This advanced equipment, employed as a "mastering medium," has economic and quality advantages over film.

Producers of HDTV programs convert them to the older television standards, retaining the masters pending the evolution of HDTV home receivers. Once these receivers become common, cable television and videocassette producers could move into HDTV production without waiting for broadcast HDTV to develop.

The explosive growth in technology has made possible these and many other innovative developments. If technological ability alone controlled growth, many more new services and improvements on old ones would have emerged, but technology must wait for consumer demand, awakened by creative entrepreneurial activity.

Summary

▌ Each broadcasting service is allocated certain frequency bands, within which each station is licensed to use a specific channel. Cochannel stations may interfere with each other, as may, at lesser distances, stations on adjacent channels.

▌ The FCC classifies channels and stations according to rules calculated to maximize the number that may operate without causing mutual interference. These classifications take into consideration the propagation characteristics of the frequency band in which each service operates.

▌ It is easier to prevent FM radio and television stations from interfering with each other because they do not generate sky waves at night, as do AM stations.

▌ The wide channels of FM and television readily accommodate multiplexing of additional information on subcarriers. Stereophonic sound and SCS services such as background music are examples of FM subcarrier services; teletext is a television example.

▌ Short-wave stations attain distant coverage by means of sky waves. Unlike domestic stations, international short-wave stations usually use several different frequencies and correspondingly different antennas to adjust to varying sky-wave behavior throughout the broadcast day.

▌ Television technology has analogies with cinema, in that it uses similar strategies for creating the illusion of continuous motion and preventing flicker.

Electronic pictures consist of pixels, lines, fields, and frames, transmitted one pixel at a time in the form of amplitude-modulated analog signals. U.S. standards call for 525-line frames, transmitted at the rate of 30 per second, with interlaced fields transmitted at the rate of 60 per second.

▌ The sound and vision aspects of television rely on separate equipment components in both studio and receiver. The sound signal modulates an FM subcarrier within the television channel, whereas the video signal modulates an AM carrier.

▌ To limit the information load, color television reduces color information to three primary colors. When mixed in appropriate proportions, they depict all the different hues. These three primary colors are multiplexed in the same size channel as that used for monochrome television, thus assuring compatibility (the ability of monochrome receivers to pick up color transmissions in black and white).

▌ Television channels occupy parts of both the VHF and UHF bands. Because UHF waves attenuate more quickly than VHF waves, UHF stations generally have smaller coverage areas, despite the FCC's attempt to compensate by allowing UHF higher power than VHF.

▌ Television receivers repeat the scanning sequence of the camera pickup tube, kept in step by synchronizing signals. The picture is displayed on the face of a kinescope tube. An electron scanning beam activates the tube's phosphorescent coating.

▌ Teletext uses an otherwise idle part of the television signal, the vertical blanking interval, to transmit text and graphics to home television receivers equipped with special decoders.

▌ Current technological innovations in television include miniaturization of receivers and production equipment through the use of solid-state devices; stereophonic sound; and the prospect of high-definition television, which attains theatrical film quality.

▮▮ ▮▮ ▮ ▮ CHAPTER 7

PROGRAM STORAGE, DISTRIBUTION, AND DELIVERY

The electronic media have entered an innovative era, with technology offering a confusing array of new options that profoundly affect traditional broadcasting. To follow these developments, it helps to think of the technology in terms of three basic functions: the *storage, distribution,* and *delivery* of programs. This chapter describes the traditional ways of carrying out these functions and the changes that new technologies have brought.

7.1
Roles of Storage and Distribution

By their very nature, broadcast stations and cable television systems function essentially as *local delivery* mechanisms. They retail to nearby audiences programs that come mostly from distant wholesale sources. Without recordings and means of distributing them rapidly and efficiently, stations and cable systems would be limited to live programs. And without network organizations and the means of interconnecting them with local outlets, live programs could not rise above the limitations of purely local resources.*

Broadcasting and cable succeed as they do only by rising above local limitations and drawing upon national and even international program providers. Without such external sources, there could be no mass-appeal programs, no costly entertainment, no timely world news roundups, no superstar performers, no round-the-clock schedules.

Storage Thus broadcasting and cable television depend on *storing* programs, warehousing them for later release and for repeated re-release still later. Means of storage include disc and tape recordings, still and motion picture films, and computer memories. Virtually all programs, except for some news items, live sports, and some special events, come to listeners and viewers prerecorded. National networks record even "live" materials for *delayed broadcast* to compensate for time differences among geographic zones. Network affiliates also sometimes record live network feeds for later release. Most programs, even timely ones, thus go through one or more recording steps before reaching the public.

---

*A few exceptions prove the rule. Though some radio stations subsist on local talk shows, they supplement them extensively with outside news sources and telephone interviews with distant celebrities. Class I (clear-channel) radio stations furnish service to communities remote from their cities of license, but only at night. And a few television superstations distribute their programs to cable systems in distant markets, but in doing so they function not as stations but as satellite-to-cable networks, distributing mostly recorded material.

Distribution   Storing programs at production centers would be useless without an efficient means of *distributing* them, nationally and internationally. Two mechanisms make centralized production feasible by getting programs efficiently to stations and cable systems: *syndication* and *networking*. These mechanisms enable the wholesaling of expensive program materials, dividing the heavy costs among many local delivery systems (broadcasting and cable), which pass the materials on to end users (listeners and viewers). The economic factors that make syndication and networking essential and the organizational requirements for their operation are discussed elsewhere; here we focus on the technology that makes them physically possible.

International news agencies pioneered the syndication principle, enabling newspapers, and later stations and cable television systems, to furnish consumers everywhere with expertly reported and edited news gathered from the far corners of the Earth. Centrally processed and pre-edited for easy incorporation into local offerings, agency news depends on maintaining worldwide staffs of reporters and editors as well as on leasing communication channels. Only because thousands of outlets share in defraying production and distribution costs does such an elaborate news-gathering process become feasible. Symptomatic of technology's key role, news agencies first burgeoned with the pioneer electronic communication medium, the telegraph. To this day they are called news *wire* services, although for most purposes radio circuits have long since displaced wire.

Broadcasting networks, though distinguished from syndication in business terms, actually function as a novel form of syndication—*instant* program distribution and delivery. News, motion picture, and music syndication methods already existed when broadcasting began, but broadcasting soon introduced its own unique distribution/delivery method, the *network*. Networks accomplish the same distribution function as syndication with important advantages: simultaneous delivery to retail outlets and thence simultaneously to consumers; and a close, symbiotic working relationship between networks and their affiliates.

A *broadcast network,* reduced to its simplest terms,
consists of two or more stations *connected* to each other so that they can put identical programs on the air in more than one market *simultaneously*. Thus networks take advantage of broadcasting's unique instantaneous delivery attribute. They use this attribute best when they cover real events in real time. Even for recorded material, however, network simultaneity has great value: it gives networks their unique identities, adds to the effectiveness of advertising, and enhances networks' ability to promote their programming nationally.

A broadcast network can bind an unlimited number of local voices into a single, unified national voice. Uniquely, broadcast stations can function at times as affiliates of one or more networks and at other times as independent, local outlets. This ability to function locally, regionally, nationally, and indeed even internationally, and to switch instantaneously from one type of coverage to another, gives broadcasting a flexibility shared by no other medium.

Convergence   Syndicated program materials may be sent to buyers by mail, by courier, or increasingly, by the same kinds of relays used by networks. It has therefore become difficult in some cases to say whether a firm is functioning as a syndicator or as a specialized network when it distributes programs to stations or cable systems. Improved technology opens up possibilities for combining old and new functions into innovative configurations.

Such *convergence,* a coming-together process, blurs traditional distinctions among delivery, distribution, and storage functions, as well as between networks and syndicators. The superstation, familiar to cable subscribers, combines operations that once stood apart: although it is licensed as just an ordinary, single television station, it uses broadcast-network methods, linking up hundreds, even thousands, of cable systems instead of stations. However, unlike a broadcast network, superstations use mostly syndicated programs.

As another example, television broadcast receivers have become general-purpose display terminals for cable television, teletext, videotex, satellite downlinks, videocassette recorders, video games, home videocameras, and computers as well as for their original purpose of showing broadcast programs.

Computers play a vital role in convergence, handling the complex switching and other interactions among the elements of hybrid systems. Large-scale integrated circuits on microchips and digital signal processing in small computers bond different elements together into the new configurations, memorizing complex instructions and storing material temporarily for special processing. Thus computers at both sending and receiving ends store and retrieve the pages of teletext that some television stations broadcast along with their regular programs. Much of what you see in broadcast programs has been extensively modified by computers built into production equipment.

7.2
Sound Recording

Turning now to specific technologies, we start with the first to emerge, the prebroadcast art of *sound recording*. Phonographs had wide public acceptance in the two decades before broadcasting, and phonograph music furnished much of broadcasting's earliest programming.

Discs In conventional disc recording, a sound source causes a *stylus* to vibrate as it cuts a concentric groove in a revolving master disc. The stylus transforms the frequency and amplitude patterns of the sound source into corresponding patterns in the form of minute deformations in the grooves. Molds derived from pressings of the master disc can be used to mass-produce copies.

In playback, the grooves cause vibrations in a pickup-head stylus, which converts the movements into a modulated electric current. These analog voltages, after suitable amplification, complete the operation by causing vibrations in a loudspeaker. Audio disc fidelity depends on many variables, among them the sensitivity of the recording and pickup styli, their accuracy in tracking grooves in the disc, the speed with which the disc revolves, and the quality of the electronic components. Each operation inevitably causes imperfections, which mount incrementally.

The distortions inherent in the analog method of disc recording can be avoided by digital signal processing (described in Section 5.6). In addition, substituting *laser** beams for mechanical tracking by styli eliminates the wear and tear inflicted by the physical contact of stylus on disc (Exhibit 7–1). Digitally processed sound in *compact disc* (CD) format has largely replaced stylus recording and playback. Sealing CDs in plastic covers makes them impervious to damage. They have enormous storage capacity, recording an hour's stereo sound on a 4-3/4-inch disc, smaller than a 45-rpm stylus recording holding only three or four minutes of music. CDs represent the first widely mass-marketed digital consumer device of any complexity.

Tape Another storage technology, *magnetic recording,* also avoids the distortions inherent in revolving turntables and stylus-and-groove contact. It combines recording and playback functions and provides portability. In magnetic recording, the reusable storage medium consists of minute particles of metallic compound coating a plastic tape. The smallness of the particles and the number available per second of running time, as determined by the tape's width and velocity, define storage capacity. Master sound recordings on quarter-inch tape usually call for a tape speed of 15 or 30 inches per second. In broadcasting, a playback speed of 7 1/2 ips usually suffices. Much lower speeds can be used when quality matters less, as in office dictation and station output monitoring. Multitrack master recording and other specialized tasks call for still wider tape stock.

The modulated electric current from a microphone varies a magnetic field in a recording head over which the tape passes. Variations in the magnetic field induce patterned arrangements of the metallic particle molecules. On playback, the tape passes over another electromagnetic head in which the tape's magnetic patterns induce a modulated

---

*A laser (light amplification by stimulated emission of radiation) produces coherent light, a highly concentrated beam at a single frequency (or very few frequencies). In addition to their role in videodiscs, lasers supply light for transmission through fiber-optic channels and enable experimental three-dimensional television (holography).

EXHIBIT 7–1   Compact Disc (CD) Playback System

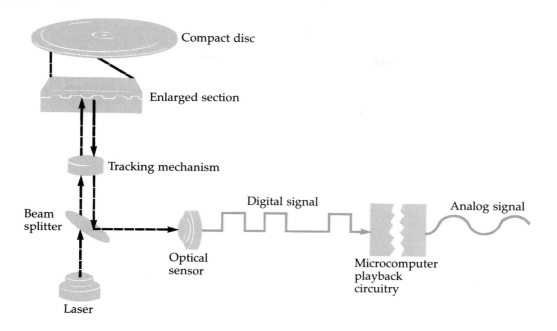

Sound has been recorded on the revolving disc in the form of microscopic pits representing a digitally encoded version of the original signal. A laser beam, guided by a supersensitive tracking mechanism, strikes the pits; they reflect the beam back as a modulated digital signal to an optical sensor. The sensor feeds its digital output to a microcomputer that has a transducer for converting the digital information into analog form for delivery to the audio reproducing system.

electric current for delivery to amplifiers and loudspeaker. Running the tape over a third electromagnet, the erase head, rearranges all the molecules, neutralizing the stored magnetic patterns so that the same tape can be used repeatedly. Digital processing has overtaken analog processing in tape, as it has in disc recording. DAT (digital audio tape) can be copied many times in the course of editing or mass production without the quality losses that occur in duplicating analog tapes.

Originally all tape recorders had a reel-to-reel configuration, with each reel separate and accessible. Now, however, enclosed cassettes or cartridges protect the tape and are more convenient to use

than open reels. A cassette incorporates double hubs, one each for feed and takeup reels, in a single housing. After playing, the cassette must be rewound, or, in the case of half-width recordings, the cassette may be flipped over to play a second "side."

A cartridge, commonly referred to as a *cart,* has a single hub and contains an endless tape loop that repeats itself. Radio stations of all types use carts, but automated stations find them especially convenient. Many carts can be loaded into an automated player, with each cart containing a single program item. Inaudible cues recorded on the tape tell the playback unit to stop at the end of the item and to recue the tape for subsequent replay.

7.3
Picture Recording

The need to vastly increase tape's information capacity delayed its adaptation to picture recording. The first commercially successful *videotape recorder* (VTR), designed for studio use, came on the market in 1956. Before that, pictures could be stored only on film.

Kinescope Recording Surviving recordings of the earliest television shows can be seen in the form of *kinescope recordings* ("kines" for short, pronounced like "kiddies"). A film camera, specially adapted for television's different picture-repetition rate, photographed programs by focusing on the face of a black-and-white picture (kinescope) tube. Kinescope recording lost much of television's already skimpy detail: when played back, programs looked flat and hazy, far from satisfactory for use on the air. Good broadcast quality had to await the VTR.

Videotape That adaptation came in 1956 with the first *quadruplex* videorecorders, developed by Ampex. The early VTRs were costly studio recorders, nothing like the home VCR (videocassette recorder), which came much later. VTR designers needed to greatly increase the speed at which tape passes over the head to enable processing of the large amount of information entailed in pictures plus sound. They solved the tape-speed problem by mounting *four* recording heads on a revolving drum (hence the name *quadruplex*). The drum rotated rapidly *transversely* (across the width of tape) while the tape itself simultaneously moved longitudinally, as it does in sound recording (Exhibit 7–2A). Suction held the two-inch tape against the curvature of the revolving drum to maintain head contact. The combined movements of heads and tape produce an effective head-to-tape speed of 1,500 inches per second. If the tape itself moved at that speed, it would soon wear out the pickup heads; moreover, it would require such enormous spools of tape as to be impractical.

Subsequently, simpler, less expensive professional videotape recorders using one-inch and smaller tape stock came on the market. They retain the principle of combining head and tape movements, but use fewer heads. Instead of laying down the track transversely, the heads cross the tape at an angle, producing a *slanted* track, as shown in Exhibit 7–2. Slant-track recording allows the head to make a longer sweep than would be possible if it moved across the narrow tape transversely. The heads spin on a disc mounted inside a stationary drum or capstan. The tape wraps around the drum in a spiral (helical) path, hence the name *helical* for slant-track recorders.

For portable equipment, broadcasters opted first for three-quarter-inch tape (called *U-matic*), but as tape technology improved, half-inch, 8-mm (about one-third of an inch) and even quarter-inch video formats evolved. Lack of standardization among competing equipment manufacturers delayed widespread professional adoption of the smaller formats, despite their greater convenience and reduced cost.

Professional *digital* videotape recording has evolved three standards. The D1 standard provides the best quality because it handles the color components and the brightness component of the signal separately, each with its own channel. D2 uses *composite* color, meaning that it multiplexes signal components in a single channel in the manner of the analog broadcast signal. D3, the newest standard, also using composite color, reduces tape width from 3/4-inch to 1/2-inch, making it more adaptable for lightweight field equipment. Of course the output of all digital recorders must be converted to analog form for transmission and display on receiver screens.

VCRs Videotape recording formats for home use enclose the tape within cassettes; hence the term *VCR* (videocassette recorder). Older models record sound along the edge of the tape, as in the formats shown in Exhibit 7–2B. More recent models incorporate high-quality stereophonic sound, interleaving slant tracks for sound with the picture tracks.

VCRs depend on the user's home television set for playback display, but contain their own tuners to enable recording off the air while the owner watches a different program on the set. VCRs can

EXHIBIT 7–2 Videotape Recording Formats

A. Transverse Quadruplex Format.

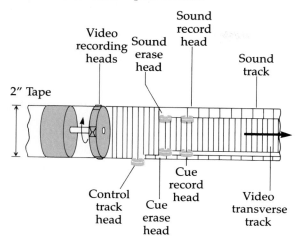

C. One-inch Format.

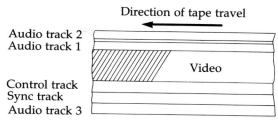

Type C Format

B. Helical Format.

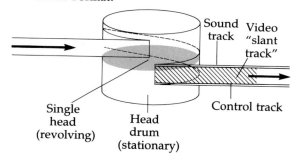

A. Transverse quadruplex format: four video recording heads mounted on a rapidly spinning wheel, shown at the left, lay down transverse tracks across the width of the two-inch tape. Sound is recorded longitudinally along one edge, auxiliary information along the other edge.

B. Helical format: the tape spirals around a large, stationary drum. Within the drum, the videorecording head spins on a revolving disc, making contact with the tape as it slips over the drum's smooth surface. Because of the spiral wrap, the tape moves slightly downward as well as lengthwise, so that the combined movements of tape and recording head produce a slanting track, as shown. Some helical recorders use two heads, some use different wraparound configurations.

C. One-inch format: this is an example of one of the smaller formats. Still narrower VTR tapes are used—3/4-inch, half-inch, 8-mm, and even 1/4-inch.

SOURCE: Courtesy Ampex Corporation.

also record the output of home videocameras (*camcorders*) and can display rented or purchased feature films that have been transferred to tape. Equipped with many sophisticated computer-assisted features, such as the ability to be programmed days in advance to pick up a sequence of shows on different stations, modern digital VCRs are one of the most versatile and popular of the ancillary consumer electronic products. Some provide "windows" to monitor as many as nine channels at once on the screen, freeze-frame storage,

and a "mosaic" function that changes the image into patterns of colored squares.

Role of Computers Minicomputers enable VCRs to perform the feats just mentioned. They convert many functions of both home and studio equipment from analog to digital mode. Digitized studio equipment includes such production aids as character generators, electronic frame stores, and digital effects units. These computer-based aids enable electronic insertion of text and graphics into ongoing programs and the manipulation of images to produce an endless repertoire of visual transformations, familiar especially in animation and title sequences.

Laser Video   The laser recording principle used in the previously mentioned CD audio discs has been applied to picture recording, resulting in *laser video* playbacks with better quality than VCRs and improved freeze-frame and slow motion functions. A combination laser playback unit that reproduces both CD sound discs and laser video discs of movies and other materials has been marketed. Laser technology may eventually displace most other types of home information storage, including the magnetic floppy disks used in home computers. A single computer laser disk has 660-megabyte capacity, many times that of a computer floppy or even most hard disks.* It remained to develop a simple method for home recording on laser discs before they could fully rival the versatility of videotape and floppy disks.

7.4
Terrestrial Relays

Electronic distribution facilities make possible networks and *remote pickups* (for on-the-spot coverage of live events). The key network technology, the "net" of a network, consists of interconnecting *relay* links. A relay station passes on electronic signals, much as relay runners pass on batons at a track meet; networks use wire, cable, microwave, or satellite "runners." Normally, relay signals consist of point-to-point or point-to-multipoint transmissions, closed to the general public. However, *pirates* of various kinds, including backyard satellite dish owners and intelligence services, routinely intercept relay traffic.

Interconnection   Network relays feed centrally produced and scheduled materials to *interconnected* affiliated stations for delivery to consumers

simultaneously in many different markets—more than 200 in the case of each national television network. Some organizations that supply programs to groups of stations use such paradoxical terms as *unwired networks*. Since they lack interconnection with their affiliates, they constitute, in both legal and practical terms, only *pseudonetworks*.

Any point-to-point wire or radio circuit can function as a relay. The channel capacity of the circuit determines which types of relays can be used for specific types of material. Ordinary telephone circuits (specially equalized to compensate for the rapid attenuation of higher frequencies over distance) suffice for radio programs but cannot satisfactorily handle the wide frequency band used by television.

Coaxial Cable   When fed through an ordinary copper wire, high-frequency radio energy tends to radiate from the wire and dissipate rapidly. *Coaxial cable* prevents this loss, trapping the energy and conducting it through an enclosed space. The cable consists of two conductors, a solid wire running down the center of a hollow metal tube. Air or some nonconductive material insulates the wire from the tube, as shown in Exhibit 7–3. Attenuation still occurs, as it must when any radio signals travels, but repeater amplifiers, inserted at frequent intervals, compensate for this loss.

Coaxial cables cost a lot to manufacture and install. In mountain terrain, installation can become prohibitively expensive. Nevertheless, U.S. television networks originally reached their affiliates through nationwide coaxial cable interconnection. The American Telephone and Telegraph Company (AT&T) supplied the coaxial facilities, just as it had the telephone wire facilities for network radio.

Cable television got its name from coaxial cable, which it employs to feed programs to subscribers' homes (but remember that cable television's coaxial lines constitute *delivery* circuits rather than relay circuits). Relay cables usually run underground, but cable television companies string their cables on

---

*The computer version of laser video, known as CD-ROM (compact disk read-only memory) can store hundreds of thousands of pages of information. CD-ROM products on the market supply small libraries of reference works on a single disk. All 12 volumes of the *Oxford English Dictionary* can be obtained on a CD-ROM disk; far more versatile than the printed version, the laser recording permits searching for any word or combination of words within the dictionary's word definitions.

EXHIBIT 7–3   Coaxial Cable

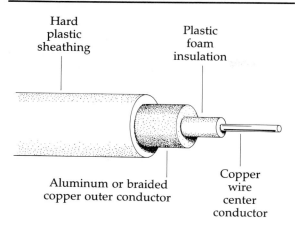

Hard plastic sheathing

Plastic foam insulation

Aluminum or braided copper outer conductor

Copper wire center conductor

Coaxial cable gets its name from the fact that it has two conductors with a common axis: a solid central conductor surrounded by a tubelike hollow conductor. The radio energy travels within the protected environment of the space between the two conductors. Cable television relies on this type of conductor, as do many terrestrial relay links that convey television signals, telephone calls, data, and other types of information.

SOURCE: Adapted from illustration in Walter S. Baer, *Cable Television: A Handbook for Decision Making* (Santa Monica, CA: The Rand Corporation, 1973), p. 4.

existing utility poles,* except in large metropolitan areas where laws require keeping them out of sight beneath the streets.

Microwave Relays   After techniques for efficient transmission of very short waves had been developed, AT&T supplied *microwave relays* for television networking. Located in the VHF band and above, microwaves vary in length from one meter down to a millimeter. Waves this short attenuate in the atmosphere so rapidly that at first they seemed unusable for communication over long distances. When a microwave signal is focused into a narrow, concentrated beam, however, its power can be increased by a factor of a hundred thousand. With

this much strength, microwaves can punch through 30 miles of atmosphere without excessive attenuation. Because of the waves' short length, relatively small sending and receiving antennas can be used (Exhibit 7–4).

A microwave relay system uses a series of towers spaced about 30 miles apart, each keeping the previous and the next tower in the series within line of sight. *Repeater* equipment on a tower receives a transmission from the previous tower, reamplifies it, then passes it on to the receiver on the next tower in the series. It takes more than a hundred such towers to span the continental United States from coast to coast.

Microwave relay networks, unlike coaxial cable networks, have no need to obtain right-of-way easements. Rugged terrain actually favors microwave transmission by providing high points that help in laying out line-of-sight transmission paths. Before the advent of space relays, all television networks came to use microwave relays except for short local coaxial links.

Fiber-Optic Cable   For some relay applications, cable has come back into favor in a new form, *fiber-optic* conductors. A hair-thin strand of extremely pure glass in a fiber-optic cable can transmit modulated light. The tremendously high frequency of light provides a bandwidth in the thousands of megahertz. A single glass filament has more than 600 times the information-carrying capacity of a coaxial cable (see Exhibit 1–4).

The bundle of frequencies present in ordinary light will not travel efficiently through an optical fiber. Instead, *lasers* or *light-emitting diodes* (LEDs) must be used to generate a "coherent" light source. The modulated light does not run straight down the glass fiber like water through a pipe, but reflects at an angle back and forth within the fiber. For this reason, fiber-optic glass must be extraordinarily pure, devoid of impurities that would randomly change the angle of reflection.

Optical fiber cables have many advantages for relay links, especially those carrying very heavy traffic. Little attenuation loss occurs, so that the number of repeater amplifiers needed is reduced; the cables are small in size and light in weight; the cables

*Cable television links can be recognized because of their thickness compared with other overhead wires. At frequent intervals, bulges in the cables indicate the location of repeater amplifiers.

EXHIBIT 7–4   Microwave Relay Antenna Designs

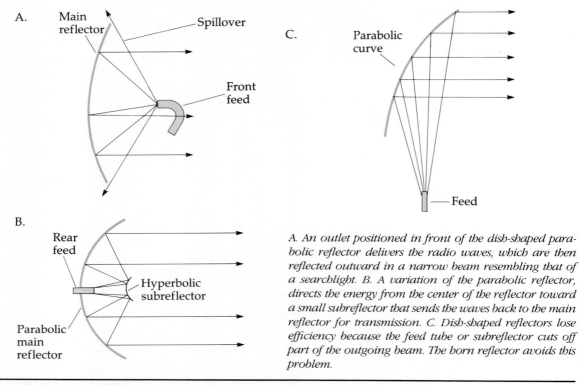

A. *An outlet positioned in front of the dish-shaped parabolic reflector delivers the radio waves, which are then reflected outward in a narrow beam resembling that of a searchlight.* B. *A variation of the parabolic reflector, directs the energy from the center of the reflector toward a small subreflector that sends the waves back to the main reflector for transmission.* C. *Dish-shaped reflectors lose efficiency because the feed tube or subreflector cuts off part of the outgoing beam. The horn reflector avoids this problem.*

SOURCE: Graham Langley, *Telecommunications Primer*, 2nd ed. (London: Pitman Books, 1986).

neither radiate energy to interfere with other circuits, nor receive interference from the outside; and the cables consist of one of the cheapest and most abundant natural materials. The 1984 Los Angeles Olympic Games employed fiber-optic cables to handle the heavy communication load within the Olympic precincts. Fiber-optic cables have been permanently installed on heavy-traffic telephone routes and are even used for the main distribution routes of large cable television systems. Eventually, fiber-optic cables will probably replace most of the conventional copper wire that the telephone has relied on for more than a hundred years.

Fiber-optic cable began supplementing existing undersea copper cables in the late 1980s. A consortium dominated by AT&T opened its 4,000 + -

mile TAT-8 transatlantic submarine fiber-optic cable in 1988. A single fiber can handle 8,000 telephone circuits. TAT-9 was planned for 1991. Such cable facilities could offer an alternative to Intelsat and other satellite systems for transoceanic television relay business.

7.5
Satellite Relays

Because they depend on ground-based towers, microwave relay networks cannot span oceans, as submarine cables can. Prior to the opening of TAT-8, transoceanic undersea cables had limited capacity; they were suitable for telegraph and telephone communication, but not for television. Transoceanic television became possible only when *communication satellites* began to function as relay stations in space.* Far beyond the Earth's attenuating atmosphere, a satellite has line-of-sight access to some 40 percent of the globe's surface (Exhibit 7–5A).

Space Relay Advantages Although they are often likened to microwave towers thousands of miles in height, communication satellites differ fundamentally from the older relay technology. A microwave repeater can link one specific location with only two others—the next sending and receiving points in the relay network; a satellite, however, links a group of relay stations (the satellite's receive-transmit units) to an *unlimited number* of receiving Earth stations. Adding more Earth stations adds nothing to transmission costs, whereas linking up new destinations for microwave networks does.

Satellites also have the advantage of being "distance insensitive," able to reach Earth stations at *any distance* within the satellite's *footprint* (coverage area). In addition, microwave signals lose quality as they go through dozens or scores of reamplifications in being passed on from one repeater station to the next. Satellite relays, however, amplify a signal only once before sending it down to its destination. For an example of how space and terrestrial relays combine in televising a major international event, see Exhibit 7–6 (page 168).

Geostationary Orbit If satellites stay in the same spot in the sky with reference to their target ground stations, there is no need for costly tracking mechanisms to point receiving antennas at a moving signal source. Such satellites operate in *geostation-*

ary (or *geosynchronous*) *orbit*. At about 22,000 miles about the equator, objects revolve around the Earth at the same rate that the Earth revolves around its axis. The centrifugal force tending to throw a satellite outward cancels the gravitational force tending to pull it back to Earth, keeping it apparently suspended in space.

The geostationary orbit, then, consists of an imaginary circle in space, 22,300-plus miles above the equator. Though satellites in that enormous orbit actually move through space at about 7,000 miles an hour, from the perspective of an observer on Earth they appear to stay in one place, keeping in step with the Earth as it rotates. Actually, geosynchronous satellites tend to drift out of position, but ground controllers activate small on-board jet thrusters, making adjustments to keep them in place.*

Through the International Telecommunication Union, the nations have agreed to allot each country one or more specific slots in the geosynchronous orbit for use of its domestic satellites. The ITU identifies positions in degrees of longitude, east or west of the prime meridian at Greenwich, England.† Exhibit 7–5 shows the slots occupied by U.S. domestic satellites.

Each degree of arc in the geostationary orbit represents a separation of about 450 miles. Spacing for C-band satellites (defined in the next subsection) has been reduced from the original four degrees separation to only one degree in order to crowd more satellites into the high-demand portion of the

---

*From time to time, balloons and aircraft had been used as high-elevation television transmitter platforms. In 1988 Congress authorized funds to experiment with a balloon tethered in the Florida Keys to transmit programs over the water to Cuba, supplementing Radio Martí, an existing U.S. government radio service transmitted from a location in the Keys. Its signal would be directly receivable on Cuban television sets, without the need for the ancillary receiving equipment that direct-broadcast satellites require.

---

*Fuel accounts for most of an orbiting satellite's weight; in turn, the amount of thruster fuel a satellite can carry limits its operational life (current communication satellites last about 10 years). It would take too much fuel to keep geosynchronous satellites *exactly* in place; ground controllers therefore let them drift in and out of position, describing a small figure-eight pattern.

†The meridians, imaginary lines dividing the Earth's surface, run north and south, meeting at the north and south poles and crossing the equator at right angles. The circle of the equator, divided into 360 degrees, enables the identification of meridian positions, numbered 1 to 180 degrees east and 1 to 180 degrees west of Greenwich. ITU orbital slot allotments take into consideration the need for a satellite in a given orbital position to look down toward the general zone of the satellite's intended target area.

EXHIBIT 7–5 The Geostationary Satellite Orbit

A.

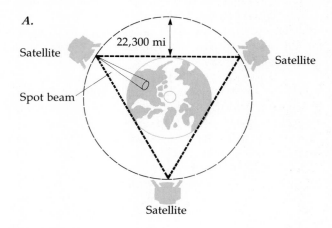

A. Looking down from space on the Earth's north pole, one can see how three equidistant satellites poised above the equator could "see" most of the Earth's surface (only "most" because their signals fade out at polar latitudes). Signals can be intensified when concentrated in a "spot beam" directed at a specific region. The satellites appear to remain stationary with reference to the Earth when positioned at a height of 22,300 miles. INTELSAT, the West's worldwide international satellite system, maintains such satellites over the Atlantic, Pacific, and Indian Oceans.

B.

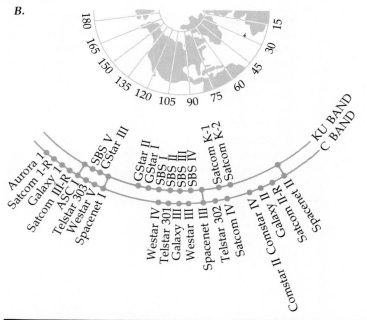

B. Each satellite has its assigned position, expressed in degrees of a half-circle either east or west of the prime meridian at Greenwich, in the segment of the geosynchronous orbit approximately in the longitude of the target area. Because the orbital segment allotted to the United States is so crowded, Ku-band satellites are shown at a different height than the C-band satellites; actually, all occupy the same orbit, 22,300 miles above the equator. Note that the Aurora 1 occupies the position farthest west, at 143°; Spacenet II occupies the position farthest east, at 69° west. The linkages between bands for Spacenet I and others indicate that those satellites carry both Ku-band and C-band transponders. The drawing shows the U.S. satellites and their positions as of mid-1989.

SOURCE (Satellite orbital locations): "Satellite Guide to the Sky," *Broadcasting*, 18 July 1989, p. 44.

orbit.* Even so, demand for orbital allotments has created a potential slot scarcity analogous to the scarcity of spectrum space that holds down the number of terrestrial transmitters that can be authorized.

---

*Orbital separation prevents signal interference, not physical collision. Indeed, some satellites are *co-located,* sharing the same slot. Power, directional antennas, signal polarization, frequency differences, and Earth-station sensitivity all help in preventing satellite signals from interfering with one another. Ku-band satellites designed for direct broadcasting to homes (DBS) have wider spacing because their high power would otherwise cause interference among their downlink transmissions.

Spectrum Allocations   Like Earth-based transmitters, those on satellites need ITU-allocated channels. Satellites used in broadcasting occupy microwave frequencies between 3 and 15 GHz, most of them in the 3–6-GHz region (*C band*) and the 11–15-GHz region (*Ku band*). Most existing operational satellites use the C band.* Newer, more powerful satellites, intended primarily for direct reception by small home antennas, use the higher Ku band. The many terrestrial services that also use microwaves cause interference at Earth stations receiving C-band signals. Ku-band signals escape this drawback, but small objects such as raindrops in heavy downpours can interfere with Ku-band waves.

Each satellite needs two groups of frequencies, one for uplinking (on-board reception) and one for downlinking (on-board transmission). These frequency groups must be far enough apart to prevent interference between uplink and downlink signals. Thus satellite bands come in pairs—4/6 GHz, 12/14 GHz, and so on, with the lower frequencies used for uplinking.

The downlink frequency bands must be large enough to accommodate a number of different channels for simultaneous transmission by the satellite's *transponders* (combination receive-transmit units). Most C-band satellites carry 24 transponders; each transponder can transmit two channels with opposite polarizations, making a capacity of 48 television channels per satellite (or many more narrowband channels such as telephone or radio transmissions, of course). Ku-band satellites usually carry fewer transponders, because high power means more weight per transponder. Some satellites combine both C- and Ku-band transponders for maximum flexibility. Signals may be exchanged between transponders aboard satellites by a procedure called *cross-strapping,* initiated by ground-controllers.

Transmission   Satellite transmitting antennas focus their output into beams to create *footprints* of varying size (Exhibit 7–7). *Global beams,* serving about 40 percent of the Earth's surface, provide transoceanic and continental coverage; *hemispheric beams,* serving about 20 percent of the surface, provide regional coverage; and for smaller footprints, *spot* beams cover about 10 percent. The narrower the beam, the higher the power at reception points, because directionality causes signal gain.

Reception   The bowl-shaped antennas of satellite Earth stations have become familiar sights, but square-shaped satellite receiving antennas ("squareals") exist and may become the standard for direct-broadcast reception in homes. Antenna diameters vary from over a hundred feet down to less than one foot. The larger antennas, used for both transmission and reception, originally represented a deliberate trade-off: massive Earth stations made possible lightweight satellites, which were necessary because of the limitations of early launch rockets. As launch capabilities improved, satellites grew more powerful, permitting smaller ground antennas.

Cable television systems pick up their satellite-fed programs with TVROs (television receive-only antennas) 12 to 15 feet in diameter (Exhibit 7–8). Reception points near the margins of footprints need larger diameters because of signal attenuation (Exhibit 7–7). Less conspicuous components of Earth stations include *low-noise amplifiers* (LNAs), especially sensitive amplifiers that are capable of magnifying without distortion the extremely weak satellite signals that reach the antenna (increasing them by a factor as high as a million); *tuners* to select the desired transponder channels; and *downconverters* to translate satellite frequencies into the range usable by television receivers.

Satellite Construction   Communication satellites need five essential component groups: (1) *transponders,* the receive-transmit units that pick up programs, amplify them, and transmit them back to Earth; (2) *antennas* for receiving uplink signals and transmitting downlink signals (for both program material and telemetering information); (3) *power supplies,* consisting of arrays of solar cells and storage batteries; (4) *telemetering devices* for reporting the satellite's vital signs to, and for receiving instructions from, the ground controllers;

*In 1989, U.S. domestic satellites in orbit numbered 29, of which 4 combined C- and Ku-band transponders; 10 used the Ku band only.

EXHIBIT 7–6   International Broadcast Relays: Seoul Olympic Games

Television coverage of a major international event such as the Olympic Games makes extraordinary demands on relay facilities. A world audience of 2 billion saw the 1988 Seoul Olympics from South Korea. Broadcasters from all over the world used 30 Earth stations to uplink feeds to their home broadcasters.

NBC's routing plan indicates how pervasively satellites have been integrated into network television broadcasting. For its 186 hours of coverage, NBC used 130,000 miles of relay paths, employing microwave, fiber-optic, and satellite links. It used transponders on three different satellites, two international and one domestic. To cover itself in case of interruptions in service, NBC fed its signals through two separate channels, designated as the Red and Blue feeds. Not shown in the chart are the audio linkages, which for the first time enabled stereo sound to be provided for the entire Olympic coverage.

The video portion of the NBC coverage went from cameras at the various events to the Seoul IBC (International Broadcasting Center). From there the Red feed went via fiber-optic relay to a transportable Ko-rean Telecommunications Authority (KTA) ground station, which relayed it to a California spaceport via an INTELSAT international satellite located over the Pacific Ocean. At the spaceport, Comsat (INTELSAT's U.S. partner) received the signal and passed it on to an NBC transportable antenna that uplinked it to the GE American K-2 domsat satellite. This is the Ku-band satellite that NBC uses for distributing its programs to affiliates and for other relay functions.

Meanwhile, the identical Blue feed went from the Seoul center to a Korean transportable Earth station for uplinking to a second INTELSAT satellite over the Pacific. Another California teleport received the signal and passed it on by microwave to NBC's Burbank studios. Burbank relayed it to the NBC distribution satellite and also received the Red feed via that same satellite.

NBC–New York at Rockefeller Plaza also received both the Red and Blue feeds. There NBC inserted the commercials before sending the programs up to the Satcom distribution satellite once more for relay to NBC affiliates throughout the United States.

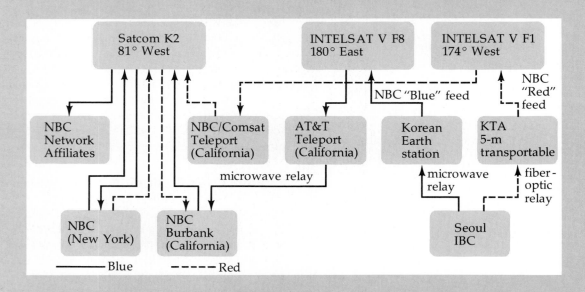

EXHIBIT 7–7 Satellite Footprints

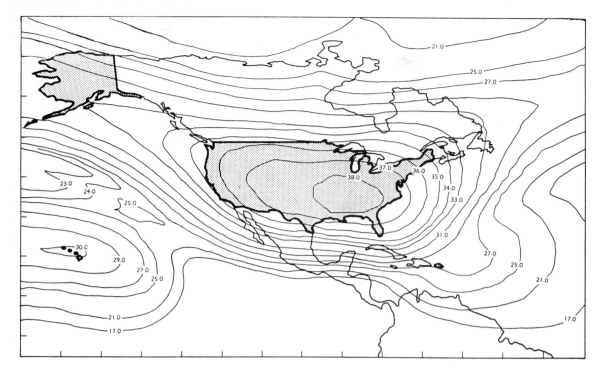

A satellite's usable coverage area, known as its footprint, *is depicted on a map in terms of various levels of signal strength. The inner contour defines the satellite's* boresight, *its area of maximum signal strength, where the smallest receiving antennas can be used. The outermost contour defines its* beam-edge *power, the region beyond which satisfactory reception cannot be expected even with large receiving antennas. The numbers associated with contour lines are signal-strength measurements.*

The map shows one of the footprints of Westar IV, a Western Union C-band domestic satellite, located at 99° west longitude. The map looks foreshortened because the satellite views the United States from a point far to the south, a position above the equator in the vicinity of the Galapagos Islands. Note that this particular transponder emits two beams, a relatively wide beam that focuses on the eastern portion of the United States mainland and a smaller one directed at the Hawaiian Islands. Among Westar IV's users are the PBS and CNN networks.

SOURCE: Hughes Communications.

and (5) small *thrusters* for orienting the satellite and holding it in its assigned position, activated on command from ground controllers (Exhibit 7–9).

Orientation matters because a satellite's antennas must always point in the target direction and its arrays of solar collectors, located on the satellite's body or on extended wings, must receive direct rays from the sun. Most satellites hold stable orientation by means of gyroscopic *spin stabilization*.

The solar collectors charge on-board batteries

7.5 Satellite Relays   169

EXHIBIT 7–8   TVRO Earth Station

Relatively inexpensive television receive-only *(TVRO) Earth stations (antennas) are usually dish-shaped, ranging in size from about 15 feet in diameter (such as the ones used by cable systems to pick up their program networks) down to about one foot (used for direct-to-home reception of DBS signals). The TVROs known as "backyard dishes," on the order of 8 to 12 feet in diameter, are widely used for "C-band-direct" reception, referring to private reception of C-band satellite signals not originally intended for the general public. The TVRO antenna shown here concentrates the weak satellite signal into a narrow beam directed at a small second reflector mounted on the tripod. This secondary reflector beams the signal into a horn at the center of the TVRO dish, from which it is fed, still as a very weak signal, to a low-noise amplifier (LNA).*

SOURCE: Eric A. Roth.

that take over during periods when the Earth's shadow interrupts sunlight. Satellites operate at extremely low power relative to terrestrial relays—power per transponder varies from about 10 watts to 400 watts (the higher power for Ku-band satellites designed for DBS reception). Most satellite transmitters use no more wattage than ordinary electric light bulbs.

Since atmospheric absorption causes attenuation, it may seem paradoxical that satellites send signals such great distances and yet have very low power. However, for most of their 22,000-mile journey, satellite signals travel through the near vacuum of space. When they do encounter the Earth's relatively thin atmospheric envelope, they pass almost straight down through it. Terrestrial radio signals, in contrast, travel nearly parallel to the Earth, impeded by atmospheric absorption along their entire route.

Launching Satellites   A critical moment in the life of every satellite occurs when it first leaves the Earth. Dwarfed by the enormous launch rocket needed to overcome gravity and atmospheric friction in order to attain escape velocity, the fragile satellite starts its journey as a mere passenger. Only after it gets two or three hundred miles high do its own rocket motors take over to loft it into the high geosynchronous orbit.

Most U.S. communication satellites have been launched from Cape Canaveral, FL, by NASA (the National Aeronautics and Space Administration), a government agency charged with nonmilitary development of aviation and space travel. Television viewers have become familiar with the spectacular launches of the NASA *shuttles,* the reusable winged vehicles that carry satellites in their holds for the first stage of the journey. When the shuttles reach their low-orbit stations, they release satellite payloads, which then fire their on-board rockets to reach geosynchronous orbit. Exhibit 7–10 (pages 174–175) gives more details about NASA shuttles and their role in launching satellites.

7.6
Over-the-Air Hybrids

Communication satellites, along with other technologies for relay, storage, and delivery of programs, can be regarded as versatile building blocks, capable of being assembled into many different configurations that adapt them to serve varied purposes. Under the impact of this *technological convergence,* broadcasting increasingly finds itself involved in, and affected by, nonbroadcast communication ser-

EXHIBIT 7–9 Satellite Construction

Many cable network channels use the Galaxy series of domestic satellites, built by the Hughes Aircraft Company. A Galaxy starts out only about 9 feet long at launch because some of its fragile components are retracted to avoid damage during the trauma of the lift-off; once in space, the satellite extends its antennas and the lower solar panel, reaching a length of nearly 22 feet.

Construction features shown in drawing A. include:

Telemetry & Command Antenna—The receive-transmit antenna sends performance data to the ground control center and receives commands from the center.

Antenna Feeds & Antenna Reflectors—Feed horns direct signals for transmission toward reflectors, which

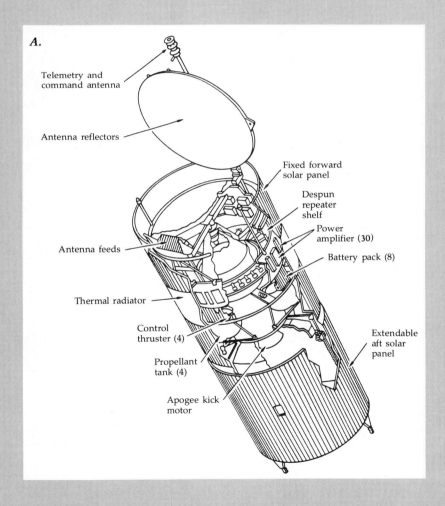

A.

Telemetry and command antenna

Antenna reflectors

Fixed forward solar panel

Despun repeater shelf

Power amplifier (30)

Antenna feeds

Battery pack (8)

Thermal radiator

Control thruster (4)

Propellant tank (4)

Extendable aft solar panel

Apogee kick motor

(Exhibit is continued on next page.)

EXHIBIT 7–9 Continued

redirect the signals back toward Earth. Reflectors function like the microwave antennas depicted in Exhibit 7–4.

Fixed Forward & Extendable Aft Solar Panels—Cylindrical panels hold the solar cells that convert sunlight into electric energy to power the satellite. The sleevelike lower panel at first surrounded the main body of the satellite; after launch it extended downward to expose the upper panel.

Power Amplifiers—Galaxy I, II, and III use TWTAs (traveling-wave tube amplifiers) for on-board signal amplification. Note that Galaxy has 30 amplifiers but only 24 transponders. Spare TWTAs must be carried because they are a satellite's most vulnerable component. The newest Galaxy will use solid-state amplifiers.

Despun Repeater Shelf—To give the satellite gyroscopic stability, the solar panels spin at about 50 revolutions per minute. The shelf supporting the transponders and antennas is "despun" by revolving at the same rate in the opposite direction. This motion cancels the rotation, enabling the antennas to keep pointing in the desired direction.

Battery Pack—Solar panels charge storage batteries, the satellite's only power source when its solar cells temporarily cease functioning as the satellite passes through the Earth's shadow.

Thermal Radiator—About two-thirds of a satellite's power is lost in the form of heat. Unless dissipated by radiation into space, the heat would build up internally and destroy the satellite.

Control Thrusters—A satellite tends to drift out of its assigned orbital slot. Control thrusters, activated on command from the Earth, nudge it back into position.

Propellant Tank—The liquid propellant needed by the control thrusters represents a significant portion of the satellite's weight and plays a major role in limiting a satellite's life span: once its control thrusters stop functioning, a satellite cannot be maintained in orbit.

Apogee Kick Motor—The satellite's on-board rocket motor gives it the final "kick" to move it out of its initial "parking" orbit into geosynchronous orbit, as shown in diagram B. below:

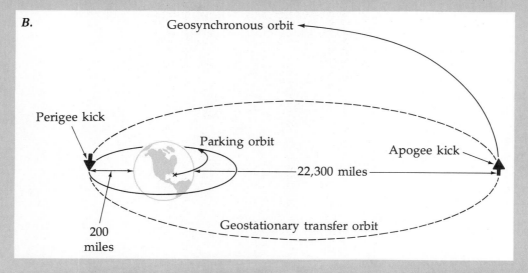

B.

Geosynchronous orbit

Perigee kick

Parking orbit

Apogee kick

22,300 miles

200 miles

Geostationary transfer orbit

SOURCE: Satellite drawing courtesy Hughes Aircraft Company.

vices. This cross-fertilization, characteristic of contemporary electronic communication, results in the formation of the *hybrid* configurations that form the subject of the rest of this chapter. In this context, the term *hybrid* has no pejorative implication; it merely identifies technologies that blend together functions that previously had been distinct and separate.

Direct-Broadcast Satellites (DBS)

Communication services that depend on satellite *relays* can afford large, relatively expensive TVROs (television receive-only antennas) whose size compensates for the low power of C-band satellite transponders. An unexpected bonanza for TVRO antenna manufacturers came when hobbyists, high-tech enthusiasts, and people hungry for video programs but beyond the reach of either television stations or cable systems began installing "backyard dishes." About 2 million such dishes, on the order of 6 to 10 feet in diameter, had been installed in the United States by 1989. They can pick up as many as 150 different programs from domestic satellites, many of them private relays, such as news feeds, not intended for public consumption. These home pickups became known as *C-band direct* reception because C-band satellite users normally intend their transmissions for designated intermediate addressees, not for direct reception by the general public.

Theoretically, private users should have waited for *direct-broadcast satellite* (DBS) services designed specifically for home reception. DBS, a hybrid service combining relays and delivery functions, uses Ku-band frequencies and carries transponders ten times the power of C-band transponders (planned U.S. DBS projects promise from 100 to 230 watts per television channel). The DBS uplink leg acts like a broadcast relay, but the downlink leg acts like a broadcasting station, delivering programs directly to consumers without the intervention of terrestrial transmitters. The high power and shortness of the Ku-band waves favors the use of receiving antennas suitable for mounting on private dwellings—in some cases only a foot in diameter, but in any case not more than three feet (Exhibit 7–11, page 176).

Rebroadcasting

Though it is not a recent development, *rebroadcasting* illustrates hybridization, since it combines the delivery and relay functions in a single operation. If broadcast station A originates a program, station B can pick up A's signal and retransmit it to its own audience on B's own frequency; station C picks up B and retransmits the program on C's frequency, and so on. Some regional FM networks dispense with relays by using rebroadcasting.

However, using rebroadcasting in place of separate relay facilities has drawbacks. Each time a program goes through the broadcast-receive-rebroadcast cycle, it loses some of its original quality; a series of such losses can degrade the signal below the standard expected of broadcasting. Also, audience availability governs the siting of broadcast transmitters, whereas relay stations might require quite different geographical distribution. Moreover, at times when affiliates air local programs, true networks often use their otherwise idle relay facilities to send their affiliates information, preview material, and programs and news items to record for later broadcast—amenities impossible when interconnection depends on rebroadcasting.

Translators

A specialized type of rebroadcasting extends the coverage of television stations and, to a lesser extent, FM stations. Low-power, unattended repeater stations called *translators* may be used to fill in dead spots in a station's coverage area or to reach isolated communities beyond the station's normal reach. Using a sensitive receiver located at a high point in the terrain (sometimes, if too distant for direct rebroadcast, linked to the originating station by microwave relay), the translator picks up its parent station's broadcast signal to rebroadcast it in an otherwise uncovered area. Translators shift ("translate") the parent station's signal to a different channel to prevent cochannel interference between the two.

Local groups desiring to receive television programs usually build and maintain translators, although the consent of the originating station must be obtained. Of the more than 5,000 translators in the United States, many bring signals to sparsely

EXHIBIT 7–10 Satellite Launches: Triumphs and Disasters

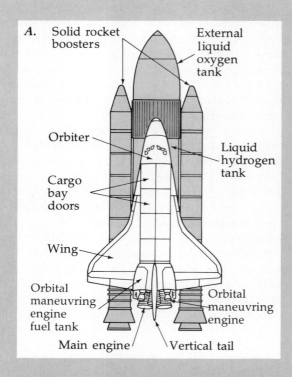

A.
Solid rocket boosters

External liquid oxygen tank

Orbiter

Liquid hydrogen tank

Cargo bay doors

Wing

Orbital maneuvring engine fuel tank

Orbital maneuvring engine

Main engine

Vertical tail

A critical moment in the life of every satellite occurs when it first leaves the Earth. Dwarfed by the enormous launch rocket(s) needed to overcome gravity and atmospheric resistance and to attain escape velocity, the fragile satellite starts its journey as a mere passenger. Only after it reaches an elevation of about 200 miles does a satellite ignite its own rocket motor to loft itself into geosynchronous orbit.

Most launches start with the satellite perched precariously atop a giant, unmanned first-stage rocket that helps it to reach initial low orbit. In 1981, however, NASA introduced the first of a series of reusable launch vehicles, known as orbiters or space *shuttles*.

A. Aided in the first stage by towering strap-on booster rockets and by a huge external, disposable tank to fuel their own motors, shuttles reach a low orbit about 200 miles above the Earth. They stay in orbit only a few days before they return to Earth, gliding on stubby

wings to a landing after surviving the intense heat created by atmospheric friction upon re-entry.

While in orbit, the shuttle opens its cargo bay to release one or more satellites that may form part of its payload.

B. In the drawing depicting the main steps in a shuttle-assisted satellite launch, *perigee* refers to the low orbit the shuttle reaches after release and *apogee* the final geostationary orbit.

Failure of a satellite's on-board motors to ignite and other such difficulties can leave hardware worth $70 million or more stranded uselessly in low orbit. In a remarkable rescue, astronauts on a shuttle mission in 1984 retrieved two errant communication satellites that had been drifting in low orbit for nine months because their on-board motors had failed. Two astronauts in space suits captured the satellites and stowed them aboard the

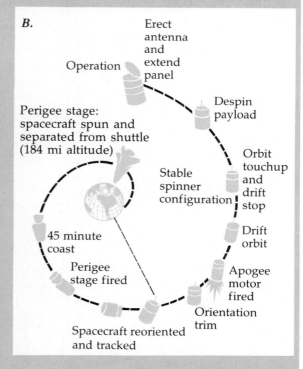

B.

Operation

Erect antenna and extend panel

Despin payload

Perigee stage: spacecraft spun and separated from shuttle (184 mi altitude)

Stable spinner configuration

Orbit touchup and drift stop

Drift orbit

45 minute coast

Perigee stage fired

Apogee motor fired

Orientation trim

Spacecraft reoriented and tracked

EXHIBIT 7–10   Continued

shuttle, which returned them to Earth for repairs. In another demonstration of the shuttle's versatility, astronauts worked out of the cargo bay in space for four hours,

capturing a faulty satellite that had been stranded in low orbit and repairing it on the spot.

C. Satellite launches involve such complex machinery and unleash such enormous power that they sometimes fail. The most spectacular failure, viewed live by millions on television, occurred in 1986 when the *Challenger* shuttle exploded 70 seconds after blast-off at Cape Canaveral.

The accident killed all six crew members and a civilian passenger, a 36-year-old high school teacher, who had been selected as a "citizen observer" from among more than 10,000 applicants for the hazardous ride. Her unnecessary death, regarded by many as an ill-advised public relations stunt to win popular support for spending more money on the space program, added poignancy to the tragedy.

The *Challenger* accident halted NASA shuttle launches until 1988, creating a backlog of delayed satellite launch contracts. Europe's rocket launcher, Ariane, located in French Guyana on the north coast of South America, despite some failures of its own, took up some of the slack. After the *Challenger* disaster, the U.S. government barred NASA from further commercial satellite launch contracts, at least for the time being, reserving the shuttle for official launches. However, private American satellite companies not only have access to Ariane's launch facilities, but can also use rockets made by four private U.S. firms, and, subject to U.S. government approval, facilities offered commercially by the Chinese and Soviet governments.

SOURCE: Courtesy NASA.

settled, mountainous areas. KREX–TV in Grand Junction, CO, for example, benefits from the added coverage provided by 39 translators.

A special class of television stations, *low-power television* (LPTV), uses the same kind of transmitters as translators. Limited to power of 10 watts (1,000 watts if UHF), LPTV stations must avoid interfering with full-power television outlets on the same or adjacent channels.

Teletext   Teletext, as a hybrid service, blends elements of television broadcasting and the print medium. It consists of low-definition "pages" of textual and graphic matter displayed on the television screen. Television stations broadcast the pages in short bursts of data transmitted 60 times a second during the television *vertical blanking intervals* (VBIs). Section 6.11 contains further details on how teletext operates. Cable television can also piggy-

EXHIBIT 7–11 Hypothetical Direct-to-Home Satellite Broadcasting System

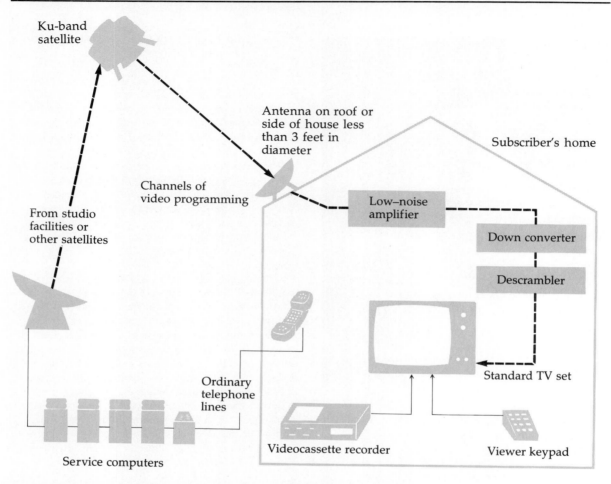

Ku-band satellite

Antenna on roof or side of house less than 3 feet in diameter

Subscriber's home

Channels of video programming

Low–noise amplifier

From studio facilities or other satellites

Down converter

Descrambler

Ordinary telephone lines

Standard TV set

Service computers

Videocassette recorder

Viewer keypad

Direct-broadcast satellite (DBS) services, although already operating in Europe, were not expected in the United States until about the mid-1990s. Customers would pay for DBS program services, necessitating descrambling devices on the customers' premises. DBS program providers need headends comparable in function to those of cable television systems to feed programs to the uplink facility and keep track of customer orders and billing, which will probably be handled in part by telephone. DBS subscribers have a choice of channels corresponding to the number of transponders available on the DBS space vehicle, but not as many choices as are available to subscribers of the more advanced cable systems. Once it is picked up by the subscriber's antenna, the weak satellite signal goes to a low-noise amplifier before being downconverted from the frequencies used by satellites to those tunable by a television receiver.

SOURCE: Adapted from FCC diagram.

back teletext on the television signal, but cable operators usually devote entire channels to *cabletext,* displaying automated news, weather, and other textual information. A similar hybrid service, *videotex,* blends elements of the telephone and the print medium. Videotex uses *wire* instead of broadcast signals to reach consumers, providing an *interactive* service that enables subscribers to access unlimited numbers of pages.

7.7
Cable Television

The broadcast hybrids discussed in the previous section suffer from all the problems of spectrum crowding and interference that are inherent in radio communication conducted "over the air." Cable television avoids these problems by sending signals through the artificial, enclosed environment of *coaxial cable* (Exhibit 7–3). Within the cable, a wide band of frequencies—up to 400 MHz—can be exploited without causing or receiving undue interference.*

Coaxial cable originally had a *distribution* function, having been designed as a broadband device for relaying television broadcast network programs and other signals that needed wider frequency bands than ordinary wires can carry. Cable television changed this usage, blending the distribution and the delivery functions into a new, hybrid service. Moreover, since cable signals do not interfere with existing on-the-air services, cable can employ VHF channels above and below the broadcast VHF portion of the spectrum—frequencies that are denied to broadcasting because they have been assigned to nonbroadcast services.

The translators mentioned earlier in this chapter afford only a partial solution to the problem of extending television station coverage. Each translator rebroadcasts only a single channel, but viewers want a choice of channels. Coaxial cable gives viewers this choice, usually feeding 30 or so program channels, but sometimes over a hundred.

Cable TV System Components *Cable television,* put simply, assembles programs from various sources at the system's *headend* and delivers them via coaxial cable to subscriber homes. Program sources include over-the-air signals from both nearby and distant television stations, locally produced or locally procured material, and program services relayed by satellite-to-cable networks.

To enable cable systems to pick up stations outside their local market, the FCC authorized a special microwave relay service, CARS (Community Antenna Relay Service), that cable television systems may install to bring in programs from stations that are too far away for off-the-air pickup. In addition, cable systems receive the programs of a few broadcast stations, known as *superstations* because they transcend normal broadcast coverage limitations by feeding their programs to numerous cable systems throughout the country via satellite.

The technician who installs cable service in a home usually disconnects the home's outside television antenna, if one exists; the cable system itself picks up television station signals at its headend and delivers some or all of them as part of its basic package of program channels. Unless the installation includes an *A/B switch* to enable the cable connection to be bypassed, the subscriber cannot readily switch back to the outside antenna. Yet the subscriber may need the antenna at times for direct television station reception, either to pick up stations not carried on the cable or to pick up cable-carried stations when the cable system goes down.

Besides reception facilities, a headend contains equipment for reprocessing the incoming signals, equalizing them, and feeding them to a modulator for transmission over the system's coaxial-cable delivery network, assigning each program source to a specific cable channel.* Also at the headend or nearby

---

*Coaxial cable does not enjoy total immunity from interference. When a cable runs near high-power transmitting antennas broadcasting on the same channels used in the cable, "ingress" from the transmitter can cause a double cable image at the home receiver.

*The cable operator can assign channel numbers arbitrarily, without reference to the over-the-air channel numbers of the broadcast stations it delivers. Broadcasters prefer to have the same channel number on cable as on the air, but cable operators often *reposition* them, changing channel numbers to suit their own programming strategies.

EXHIBIT 7–12   Cable Television System Plan

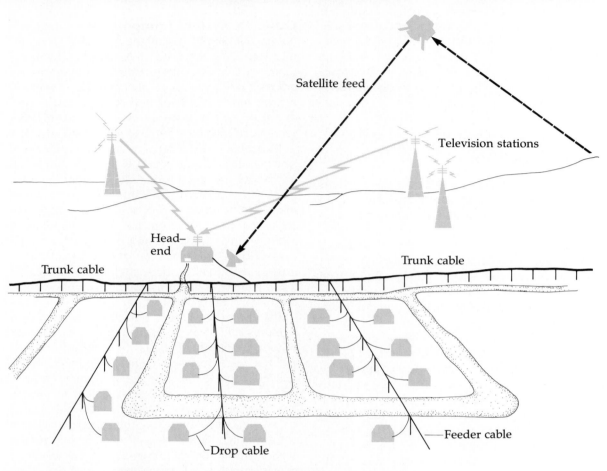

Satellite feed

Television stations

Head–end

Trunk cable

Trunk cable

Feeder cable

Drop cable

The headend of a cable system contains the amplifiers and local origination facilities of the system (if any). The headend receives off-the-air TV station signals picked up by special antennas, and possibly also signals from more distant stations fed by microwave relay. The most important input adjunct is a small Earth-station receiving antenna for picking up satellite signals relayed from a variety of program sources. Trunk and feeder distribution cables, shown mounted on poles in the sketch, would often be run underground within cities.

will be found local-origination facilities, varying in complexity from simple alphanumeric news-and-weather displays to full-scale production studios.

Cable distribution/delivery networks have a *tree-and-branch* pattern. As Exhibit 7–12 shows, *trunk cables* branch to lighter *feeder cables* that carry the signals to clusters of homes, where still lighter *drop cables* connect the system to individual homes. A headend can feed programs over a radius of about five miles; covering wider areas requires subsidiary headends that receive the programs via special *supertrunk* coaxial (or nowadays sometimes fiber-optic) cables or via microwave relays.

Cable television uses the same type of radio-frequency energy as over-the-air transmitters, but this energy attenuates much more rapidly in cable than in the atmosphere. The higher the frequency, the more drastic the attenuation. In the VHF frequency range used by cable, signals lose half their strength traveling a mere 200 feet. Booster amplifiers and equalizers (the latter to compensate for the different rates of attenuation at different frequencies) must be inserted in the cable at frequent intervals to keep the signals up to strength and at the same level on all channels. The battle against attenuation therefore adds considerably to the already high cost of the cable itself.

Where possible, cable firms mount cables on existing utility poles, but within cities the cables must go underground in conduits and tunnels at even greater expense. Cable installation over long distances to reach thinly scattered rural populations would cost too much to make it practicable in remote areas.

Cable Channels Exhibit 7–13 shows the breakdown of the broad band of frequencies fed through a 60-channel coaxial cable. Systems with only 12 channels rely on the VHF tuners in subscribers' television receivers. Systems with more channels must supply customers with an adapter unit that has its own tuning facility. It feeds into one of the channels on the receiver's tuner (usually channel 2, 3, or 4). In effect, the adapter contains an expanded VHF tuner to avoid resorting to the receiver's UHF tuner. UHF attenuates too rapidly to be practicable for cable use. Within the closed environment of coaxial cable, however, cable-system operators can use additional VHF channels that are not available for over-the-air transmission because they have been assigned to other over-the-air services.

Cable television assigns no television signals to the VHF band segment allocated to FM radio but retains those frequencies for delivering audio services. Cable firms obtain audio programming from subcarriers on satellite-delivered television channels as well as from radio broadcast stations.

Encryption and Addressability Cable operators charge a fee above the regular subscription rate for certain premier channels (pay channels) and, in some cases, *pay-per-view* (PPV) programs. Cable operators need to prevent unauthorized viewers from seeing these channels or programs. Program providers, such as networks that relay their products by satellite and direct-to-home services on DBS satellites, also need to control access.

Encryption (scrambling) answers these needs. Several encryption methods exist, but pirates always succeed in defeating even sophisticated scramblers that frequently change the decoder key. Sellers of bootleg descramblers have even held an international conference to promote their wares. In the long run it appears that only harsh laws and vigorous prosecution of manufacturers and sellers of unauthorized descramblers can control piracy.

Pay services ideally need a flexible method of turning encryption on and off so that customers can order pay channels or individual PPV programs on short notice. This calls for *addressability,* a way to control individual customer access to programs and also to receive and execute orders from each customer. At the simplest level, the customer merely telephones the headend to order a service, whereupon the cable company turns on the descrambler for that particular address. However, telephone orders tend to pile up, delaying execution and interfering with impulse buying. More sophisticated addressable systems permit the customer to use a touch-pad to send orders back up the cable itself. Computers at the headend not only execute orders but also carry out the record-keeping and billing operations.

Interactivity Such amenities belong in the general category of *interactive* (two-way) cable systems. Interactivity uses a block of frequencies at the lower end of the coaxial cable frequency band for return, or upstream, messages (see Exhibit 7–14). There are several methods for returning messages, but they all depend on microcomputers to carry on a

EXHIBIT 7–13 Cable TV Spectrum Architecture

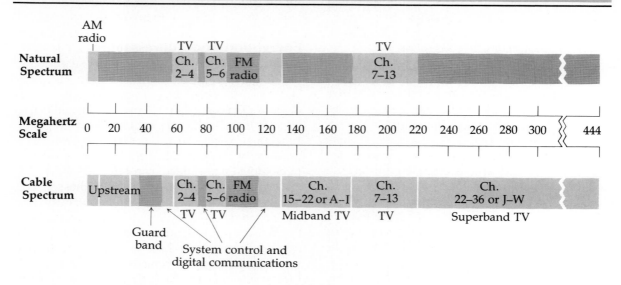

Cable television in effect isolates the spectrum from its natural surroundings by operating within the confines of coaxial cables. This insulation from nature largely eliminates the possibility of interference, always a serious problem when using the natural spectrum; it also enables cable to use segments of the spectrum that have been allocated to nonbroadcast services. Note that cable retains the VHF channel frequencies and numbering system, but positions what it calls "midband" channels (numbered 14 to 22) and "superband" channels (numbered 23 to 60) in frequency bands allocated in the natural spectrum to nonbroadcast services, below the frequencies allocated to over-the-air UHF television. Cable can manipulate signals more easily at these lower frequencies.

SOURCE: Adapted from Thomas F. Baldwin and D. Stevens McVoy, *Cable Communications* (Englewood Cliffs, NJ: Prentice-Hall, 1983), p. 28.

dialogue between the subscriber's converter and the headend. Subscribers communicate via a key pad linked to the computer in the converters attached to the receivers. A better alternative is to build the computers into the receivers, but lack of standardized encryption and addressing technology leaves manufacturers in doubt as to which system to install. The *peritelevision socket* deals with this problem; it is a combination input-output socket on the receiver that both feeds the television signal out to an external converter or descrambler and then feeds the cleaned-up signal back to the receiver for display.

Hybrid Cable Services Already a hybrid service itself, cable television has stimulated still further hybridization, so-called *niche* services that meet the program needs of viewers in specific, limited situations. (The development of these services was described in Section 4.3.) People living in a large apartment house may receive over-the-air broadcast programs via a common antenna mounted atop the building. This form of reception, called MATV (*master antenna television*), becomes *satellite MATV* (SMATV) when the MATV operator supplements the broadcast antenna with a TVRO to pick up satellite-delivered cable network services.

A second niche service, MDS (*multipoint distribution service,* serves receivers either clustered in buildings or located in single homes. Instead of being confined to a single building or contiguous group, as SMATV is, MDS can serve any number of buildings within reach of its short-range, line-of-sight, radiated signals. However, home receivers cannot pick up the signals directly. MDS employs frequencies in the upper reaches of the UHF band, above the frequencies used for broadcast television. The signals must be *downconverted* to the range tunable by receivers before being sent by cable to reception points within buildings.

Originally, the FCC treated MDS as a common-carrier data-delivery facility rather than as a means of delivering entertainment. Accordingly, MDS had too few full-time channels at its disposal to make it competitive with cable television or SMATV. Subsequently the commission made more channels available,* converting MDS into *multichannel* MDS (MMDS), enabling it to compete with cable by delivering as many as 30 channels. Because it closely resembles cable television, except for its use of over-the-air propagation instead of coaxial cable linkage, MMDS has earned the nickname *wireless cable.*

Summary

▮ Broadcast stations function as local delivery mechanisms, highly dependent on storage and distribution technologies for syndication of mass appeal programming. These technologies include disc and tape recording, computer memories, terrestrial relays, and space relays. All these technologies are moving increasingly into digital signal processing.

▮ Compact disc audio recording, using laser light and digital processing, represents a major advance over conventional disc and tape recording.

▮ Kinescope recording, the earliest means of television picture storage, gave way to two-inch quadruplex magnetic tape. For portable recording, professionals use smaller, slant-track formats. The latest home videocassette recorders have stereophonic sound and other advanced features. Video disc recording, an application of audio CD technology to visual materials, greatly increases storage capacity.

▮ Small computers play a vital role in new storage technologies. Television production aids using computer storage in digital form provide virtually unlimited scope for manipulating video images.

▮ Networks use relays for program distribution. Terrestrial distribution systems employ telephone wire (for radio), coaxial cable, and microwave relays (for television). Optical fiber is replacing coaxial cable in heavy-traffic circuits.

▮ Space relays by satellites in geosynchronous orbit have greater flexibility than terrestrial relays. Such satellites need orbital slot allotments and separate frequency allocations for uplink and downlink legs. Cable television systems and backyard dish owners use 15-foot receive-only antennas, whereas 3-foot and smaller dishes suffice for direct broadcast satellite reception.

▮ NASA has launched most U.S. satellites, first by rocket, then via the space shuttle. After the *Challenger* shuttle disaster, the U.S. government withdrew NASA from the private launching business, leaving it to private launchers in the United States and abroad.

▮ Convergence of technologies produces hybrid over-the-air program delivery systems. Cable television, a wire hybrid, uses a relay facility, coaxial cable, as a delivery mechanism. Cable operators use scramblers to control customer access to extra-pay channels and programs.

▮ Cable television employs part of the VHF spectrum in the closed environment of coaxial cable. A single cable can handle many television channels, along with audio and response channels.

▮ Cable television can deliver videotex, although videotex usually uses telephone lines; cable can also use full channels for text material and can emulate teletext by sending text on subcarriers.

▮ Satellite master antenna television and multichannel multipoint distribution service ("wireless cable") are hybrid delivery systems serving so-called niche audiences.

*The commission allowed MDS to borrow channels from ITFS (*Instructional Television Fixed Service*), which it allots to educational authorities for sending educational programs from campus to campus or from campus to sites set aside for adult education.

ECONOMICS

PART 3

The economic basis of a country's broadcasting system largely determines the kind of system it develops. Unlike other Western democracies, the United States allowed commercial motives to dominate the system almost from the beginning. Advertising's primary role in financing most electronic mass media has had a profound impact on the types, number, and variety of program services offered. Cable television introduced subscription as an alternative source of support, but advertising plays an ever-increasing, if secondary, role in that medium as well. Commercial broadcasting and cable are businesses; as such, their primary motivation is to make money. As in any business, the way to make money is to offer a salable product and to have revenues exceed expenses. Part III describes the economic organization of broadcasting in America and the role commercialism plays, then compares commercial with noncommercial systems.

CHAPTER 8

ORGANIZATION: OPERATIONS AND FINANCE

The basic economic unit of electronic mass media is the individual delivery outlet—a broadcast station, a cable television system, or some other entity that delivers programs directly to consumers. However, economic efficiency favors centralization, with individual delivery units combined into networks or other groupings. For still greater efficiency, these groups tend toward *vertical integration,* combinations of program producers, distributors, and delivery outlets. The large organizations that result increasingly dominate the media economy.

8.1
The Commercial Broadcast Station

In the United States, the traditional commercial broadcast station can be defined as an entity (individual, partnership, corporation, or nonfederal governmental authority) that:

▪ Holds a license from the federal government to organize and schedule programs for a specific community in accordance with an approved plan.

▪ Transmits those programs over the air using designated radio facilities in accordance with specified standards.

▪ Carries commercial messages that promote the products or services of profit-making organizations, for which the station receives compensation.

Although an individual owner may legally control more than one station, each outlet must be licensed separately to serve a specific community. Moreover, each license encompasses both transmission and programming functions. A station therefore normally combines three groups of facilities: business offices; studios; and transmitter, tower, and transmitting antenna. Often the transmitting facilities, which ideally should be away from obstructions, may be set up at a distance from the offices and studios, which are typically located in the business district for easy access. Usually all facilities come under common ownership, although in a few cases stations lease some or all of them.

Station Organization Broadcasting station makeup varies enormously, conforming to no standard table of organization. Nevertheless, all stations need to perform four basic functions: (1) general and administrative, (2) technical, (3) programming, and (4) sales. These functions are so basic that noncommercial as well as commercial stations must carry them out (although the former call the money-gathering function "development" instead of "sales").

Exhibit 8–2, page 186, shows some of the subordinate functions that fall under the four main headings. References in the chart to contractual services indicate the extent to which stations depend upon syndication in its various forms (Chapter 13). Not only do stations obtain program materials from external sources, they also obtain the expertise of consultants on problems of finance, management, programming, promotion, sales, technical operations, and legal concerns. More than a thousand firms offer such program and consulting services. Whether they do the work themselves or call on outside assistance, all radio and television stations perform the following functions:

1. *General/administrative* functions include the services that any business needs to provide to create an appropriate working environment. Services of a specialized nature peculiar to broadcasting usually come from external organizations, such as engineering-consulting firms and program syndicators. For a network affiliate, the main such external contract is with its network.

Broadcasters tend to be tireless *joiners* because they need to keep abreast of rapidly evolving program trends, regulations, and technical developments. Innumerable trade and professional organizations serve this need.* Managers usually join such groups as the National Association of Broadcasters, the Television Bureau of Advertising, and the Radio Advertising Bureau. Specialized station associations serve independent television, UHF, and state networks; and farm, religious, and Spanish-language broadcasters. Individuals can join associations of engineers, program executives, promotion specialists, pioneer broadcasters, women broadcasters, and many others.

2. *Technical* functions center on transmitter operations, which must follow strict FCC rules. The station's chief engineer heads technical operations. In the smallest stations, the chief engineer may be the only staff member with much technical expertise, but in most cases he or she supervises a staff of operational and maintenance personnel. Chief engineers at large television stations spend most of

---

*The 1988 *Broadcasting-Cablecasting Yearbook* lists more than 200 national trade professional associations and societies; in addition, each state has its own broadcasting association. Most of these groups hold annual meetings, often with elaborate hardware and software exhibits by vendors and distributors. Major management-oriented associations lobby Congress and state legislators for and against legislation that affects their interests.

EXHIBIT 8–1	Dimensions of The Broadcast and Cable Industries

Total U.S. Population	245.1	million
Total U.S. Households	92.0	million
Total U.S. Television Households (TVHH)	90.4	million
Commercial AM stations	4,950	
Commercial FM stations	4,192	
Educational FM stations	1,390	
Total radio stations on the air	10,532	
Commercial VHF TV stations	547	
Commercial UHF TV stations	523	
Noncommercial VHF TV stations	121	
Noncommercial UHF TV stations	218	
Total TV stations on the air	1,409	
VHF low-power TV stations	300	
UHF low-power TV stations	324	
Total low-power stations on the air	624	

Television Network Affiliates

ABC	220
CBS	193
NBC	207
FOX	122
PBS	336

Cable Systems	10,172	
TVHH passed by cable	84%	
TVHH subscribing to basic cable	54.8%	
TVHH subscribing to pay cable	32%	
Addressable cable homes	14.6	million
Pay-per-view cable homes	5.9	million
TVRO satellite dish households	2.2	million
TVHH with color television sets	97%	
TVHH with two or more television sets	63%	
TVHH with videocassette machines (VCRs)	64%	
TVHH with remote control	66%	
TVHH with home computer	21%	

Although the numbers change almost daily, the data given here are representative for 1989.

SOURCES: *Broadcast Marketing & Technology News,* National Association of Broadcasters, December 1988; *Broadcasting,* 28 Nov. 1988, 27 Feb. 1989, 6 Mar. 1989, 8 May 1989, 22 May 1989, and 29 May 1989; Miami *Herald,* 5 Oct. 1988; and *Broadcasting/Cablecasting Yearbook 1988.*

EXHIBIT 8–2   Station Functional Organization

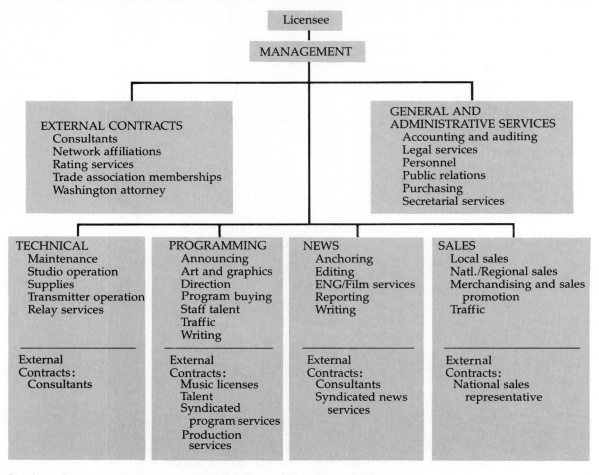

The chart does not represent any particular station, but rather depicts major functions usually performed by all stations. In smaller operations, several functions are often carried out by a single employee. Stations also vary widely as to the types and the extent of the services they obtain under contract from outside sources.

their time on administration and on keeping up with rapidly developing technology. Some small stations share a chief engineer; others use an outsider on a contractual basis.

3. *Program* functions involve planning and implementation phases. Major program planning decisions usually evolve from interplay among the programming, sales, and management heads. Most stations produce few programs locally, so that the program department's major role becomes the selection and scheduling of prerecorded material—music for radio stations, and syndicated series delivered on film or tape or via satellite for television and cable. The *production* department implements

program decisions, carrying out the day-to-day tasks of putting the program schedule on the air.

News, although a form of programming, usually comprises a separate department, headed by a news director who reports directly to top management. This separation of news from entertainment makes sense because of the timely nature of news and the unique responsibilities news broadcasting imposes on management. Usually, the news department also produces station editorials, if any, and public affairs programming.

4. *Sales* departments employ their own staff members to sell time to local advertisers. To reach regional and national advertisers, however, most stations contract with a national sales firm to represent them in out-of-state centers of business. A network affiliate benefits from a third sales force, that of its network.

Coordination of the sales operation with programming requires the processing of a vast quantity of detail—the job of the *traffic* department. It prepares the daily *program pre-log* (usually called simply the *log*), which schedules facilities, personnel, programs, and announcements. As the broadcast day progresses, operators in the station's control room "keep the log" by making entries on the pre-log to record when the scheduled events actually took place. At the end of the day, the program pre-log, with any schedule changes that have occurred incorporated, becomes the final log, providing a record of the day's broadcasts. Traffic personnel make sure that advertising contracts are fulfilled and that spot schedules start and stop on time; they also arrange for *make-goods,* the rescheduling of missed or technically inadequate commercials.

In addition, the traffic department maintains a list of *availabilities* (or, simply, *avails*). This list gives sales personnel up-to-date information on commercial openings in the schedule as they become available for advertisers. Traffic personnel usually fill unsold openings with public-service or promotional announcements. At many stations, computers handle much of the complex work of the traffic department, including generating the program pre-log; in some control rooms, computers keep the log as well (see Exhibit 8–8, page 200).

Low-Power TV Stations The organizational patterns of low-power television (LPTV) stations often differ from those of full-power stations. Some LPTV owners elect to organize and operate their stations in traditional fashion, though with fewer employees. Others simply retransmit the signal of a full-power station. Some affiliate with specialized low-power networks; still others belong to commonly owned groups of LPTV stations, all of which carry the same programs simultaneously—perhaps distributed by satellite.

An LPTV station's role determines its organization. If it competes with other stations in its market, or if it functions as a "mother" station, providing services for its retransmitting stations, its structure usually follows traditional lines. If it operates simply as a rebroadcaster, its entire staff might consist of a single, outside contract engineer who maintains the retransmitter's technical facilities.

Group-Owned Stations Like other enterprises, broadcasting businesses benefit from *economies of scale.* Ownership of several stations enables a company to buy programs, supplies, and equipment in bulk, to spread the cost of consultants across several stations, and generally to share experiences and new ideas.

Were it not for legal constraints, large chains of commonly owned stations would doubtless have evolved, just as in the newspaper business. For reasons of public policy, however, the FCC limits broadcast ownership (with some minor exceptions) to a maximum of 12 AM, 12 FM, and 12 television stations. These numbers do not mean that every group owner has 36 stations. Of the more than 550 commonly owned station groups, most consist of three to five stations (licensees of single AM/FM or AM/FM/TV combinations do not count as group owners); even the most powerful groups fail to reach the ownership ceiling. However, the trend is toward concentration of ownership: 30 years ago, groups owned only half of all VHF television stations in the 100 largest markets, whereas by 1988 they owned about 90 percent.

Group-owned stations do not necessarily all affiliate with the same network, or for that matter with

	GENERAL MANAGER	PROGRAM DIRECTOR	GENERAL SALES MANAGER	NEWS DIRECTOR
8:30	Open mail; dictate letters and memos.	Check Discrepancy Reports for program and equipment problems; take appropriate action.	Check Discrepancy Reports for missed commercials; plan make-goods.	Meet with Assignment Editor and producer; plan the day.
9:30	Discuss financial statements with Business Manager.	Call TV Guide with program updates.	Local sales meeting; discuss accounts and quotas.	Meet with Union Shop Steward; discuss termination of reporter.
10:00	Call group headquarters regarding financial status.	Prepare weekly program schedule.	Accompany local account executive on sales calls.	Read mail; screen tape of last night's 11:00 PM news.
10:30	Meet with civic group angry about upcoming network program.	Select film titles for Saturday and Sunday late movies.	More sales calls.	Discuss noon news rundown with show producer.
11:00	Call network; ask for preview of questionable show.	Meet with Promotion Manager regarding TV Guide ad for local shows.	Call collection agency; discuss delinquent sales accounts.	Meet with Chief Engineer regarding SNG failure.
12:00	Lunch with major advertiser.	Lunch with syndicated program saleswoman.	Lunch with major advertiser.	Monitor noon news; lunch at desk.
2:00	Department heads meeting.	Department heads meeting.	Department heads meeting.	Department heads meeting.
4:00	Meet with Chief Engineer regarding new computer system in master control.	Meet with producer/director to plan local holiday special.	Prepare speech for next week's Rotary club meeting.	Meet with producer and director; plan rundown of 6:00 PM newscast.
6:00	Dinner with Promotion Director job candidate.	Attend National Academy of Television Arts & Sciences annual local banquet.	To airport; catch flight to New York for meeting with National Sales Rep.	Monitor 6:00 PM news.

Not all television station executives work 10- or 12-hour days, but many do, especially as competition from cable and the other new media increases.

any network, except for the groups owned by the networks themselves, known as network *owned-and-operated* (O&O) stations. Each national television network O&O group reaches between 20 and 25 percent of the nation's television households (Exhibit 8–4), assuring the networks their own prestigious outlets in major markets.

Networks have administration for O&O groups separate from their network operations. A vice president heads each O&O station as general manager. She or he has a good deal of operational autonomy to ensure compliance with the FCC requirement that each station must serve its own community of license. Managers of O&Os have sufficient independence to reject network programs that they judge would be contrary to the interests of their local communities, though they rarely use that power.

EXHIBIT 8–4 Top 10 Television Group Owners

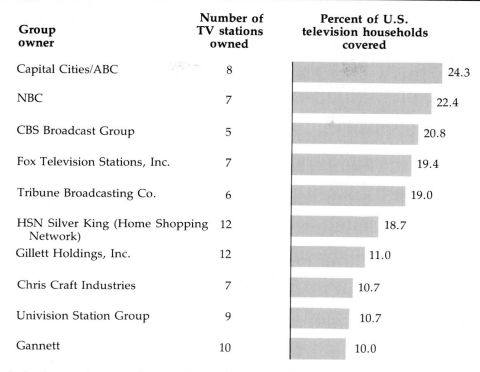

Group owner	Number of TV stations owned	Percent of U.S. television households covered
Capital Cities/ABC	8	24.3
NBC	7	22.4
CBS Broadcast Group	5	20.8
Fox Television Stations, Inc.	7	19.4
Tribune Broadcasting Co.	6	19.0
HSN Silver King (Home Shopping Network)	12	18.7
Gillett Holdings, Inc.	12	11.0
Chris Craft Industries	7	10.7
Univision Station Group	9	10.7
Gannett	10	10.0

In 1989 only the three major networks owned enough major-market stations to reach more than 20 percent of America's television homes, and only these ten groups reached as much as 10 percent.

SOURCE: *Broadcasting*, 22 May 1989, p. 50.

8.2
Commercial Television Networks

Two or more stations interconnected by some means of relay (wire, cable, terrestrial microwaves, satellite) so as to enable simultaneous broadcasting of the same program constitute a minimal *network*. In the 1980s, radio satellite syndicators joined radio networks in providing programming to local stations. Television and radio networks usually provide their affiliates with programs in exchange for the stations' agreement to carry network commercials within those programs. Television networks nearly always, and radio networks in some cases, also pay stations to carry their programs (Exhibit 8–5 lists some of the better-known networks.)

Only three major national commercial television networks exist—ABC, CBS, and NBC—supplemented by Fox, a would-be fourth national network, and over 100 smaller networks. Most of the latter operate part-time, usually sharing programs within a region or a single state. Some have a common program orientation, such as religion (the Moody Broadcasting Network), language (Univision), or sports (Hughes). Those formed for a limited time or special purpose are often referred to as *ad hoc* networks.

EXHIBIT 8–5   Examples of Radio Networks

Network	Number of affiliates	Format
ABC Contemporary	251	Young adult
Entertainment	580	Adult
Information	619	News and commentary
Talkradio	124	Telephone talk, with news and commentary
Associated Press	1,025	Live news, features, interviews
Caballero	72	Spanish-language news, sports, and entertainment
CBS Radio Network	400	Adult
RadioRadio	150	Young adult
National Black Network	116	Black-oriented news, features, talk, and interviews
Wall Street Journal Radio Network	85	Economic, financial news
Mutual	700	News, sports, music, interviews

Modern radio networks offer many different formats and may serve more than one station in the same city. Some stations utilize the services of syndicated, satellite-delivered radio format providers. Examples include Bonneville Broadcasting System (easy listening formats), Far West Communications Inc. (Gold Plus, Adult/Contemporary Hit Radio, True Country), and Drake-Chenault Radio Consultants (11 different program formats).

SOURCES: *Channels Field Guide 1988,* p. 94; and *Broadcasting/Cablecasting Yearbook 1988,* pp. F74–76.

Some station groups and program syndicators operate ad hoc networks to share special programs and feature films or to program specific parts of the broadcast day. Here, however, we focus on the three national *full-service television networks,* ABC, CBS, and NBC.* Each of the three has about 200 affiliates, through which they can reach virtually all the television homes in the United States.

Network Organization Like stations, networks vary in their organizational structure, yet each

---

*The FCC uses varying definitions of *network,* depending on the context. FCC rules dealing with television affiliation agreements define a network as "a national organization distributing programs for a substantial part of each broadcast day to television stations in all parts of the United States, generally via interconnection facilities"; in its prime-time access rule, it defines a network as an entity "which offers an interconnected program service on a regular basis for 15 or more hours per week to at least 25 affiliated television licensees in 10 or more states" (47 CFR 73.658).

must fulfill the same four basic functions as stations—administration, programming, engineering, and sales. Networks, however, enjoy the luxury of a much higher degree of specialization than do stations. NBC, for example, has separate units, each with its own president, for operations, entertainment, news, sports, radio, the television network, and the O&O stations.

The networks appoint droves of vice presidents. At NBC, for example, VPs head up units dealing with finance, business affairs, personnel, research, law, corporate communications, advertising and promotion, press and publicity, and corporate planning. In NBC Television's Entertainment Division, vice presidents supervise units specializing in children's programs, daytime programs, specials and variety programming, game shows, movies, and miniseries; others head the story, drama, and comedy development units.

Distinctive network responsibilities include arranging the relay facilities that deliver programs to stations and maintaining good relations with the affiliates. NBC's Affiliate Relations Department keeps five vice presidents busy. In addition, an advisory board representing NBC's television affiliates helps maintain the working relationship. In the spring, each television network organizes a convention for its affiliated stations, at which it shows pilots of new shows and unveils program plans for the coming season.

Affiliation vs. Independence

About 60 percent of all full-power commercial television stations affiliate with a major network. Most function as *primary affiliates,* serving as *the* affiliate of ABC, CBS, or NBC in a particular market. *Secondary affiliates* share affiliation with more than one network; for example, Butte, MT, has only two stations, one a primary affiliate of CBS, the other a primary affiliate of NBC; both also have secondary affiliations with ABC. A few markets have only a single station. Affiliates in Watertown, NY, and Presque Isle, ME, for example, have the unusual privilege of picking and choosing programs from all three networks.

Affiliation does not mean that a network owns or operates the affiliated stations. ABC, CBS, and NBC do, of course, own television stations. But they contract with hundreds of other television affiliates, agreeing with each to offer it the network's programs before offering them to any other station in the same market. The station agrees to *clear time* for the network schedule, but may decline to carry any particular program, or may offer to carry it at a time other than the time of network origination. The network may or may not agree to the last option.* An affiliate devotes approximately 65 percent of its time to network programs, time for which the network nearly always pays its affiliates.

Networks must buy affiliates' time in order to reach their audiences. Affiliates sell their time to networks at a discount; in exchange, a broadcasting network offers its affiliates five basic services:

▌ A structured *program service.*

---

*As an example of nonclearance, NBC's *Tonight Show* has aired at various times in Nashville, TN, on both the NBC and ABC affiliates, as well as on an independent station.

▌ A means of *program distribution* so that the service can be received by all affiliates at the same time.

▌ An *advertising environment* that appeals to local advertisers.

▌ *Monetary compensation* to the stations based on audience size.

▌ A *sales organization* that finds national clients to purchase network advertisements that occupy part of the affiliates' commercial time.

Approximately 400 stations, most of them UHF and known as *independents,* do not affiliate with any of the three major networks, although they may affiliate with Fox or one of the smaller networks. Independents have had a remarkable rags-to-riches history. Until the late 1970s, most nonaffiliated stations struggled just to survive, unable to compete with network affiliates in attracting audiences. As a group they lost money until 1975, when they first averaged a small profit. In that year, independent stations received 16 percent of all nonnetwork advertising dollars spent in television; by 1980, their share had grown to 20 percent, and by 1987, to 25 percent. In terms of audience, during the 1977–1978 television season, independent stations attracted only 9 percent of the viewers; by the 1987–1988 season, their proportion had reached 25 percent.

Several factors combined to turn at least some independents into profit-makers. The FCC helped by adopting the *prime-time access rule* (PTAR), which gave independents their first chance to counterprogram effectively against network affiliates in the 7:00–8:00 P.M. (Eastern and Pacific) period. PTAR gave independents the advantage of rerunning network series during that hour, a program option that PTAR denied to affiliates in the major markets. Independents gained strength in other time periods with live coverage of sports events, by successfully bidding against affiliates for exclusive rights to popular syndicated program series, and by using aggressive promotion campaigns.

Establishment of the Association of Independent Television Stations (INTV) in 1972 also helped. In 1977 an INTV-sponsored Arbitron study provided much-needed favorable evidence about the size and character of the independent stations' audience, helping them to overcome the negative image of independents in the minds of advertising-agency time buyers. Cable television also helped by making the signal quality of UHF independent stations equal in the eyes of cable viewers to that of the more powerful over-the-air signals of VHF affiliates.

By 1987, however, the independent rose had lost some of its bloom. One reason: in that year a decision by the U.S. Court of Appeals eliminated the *must-carry rules* that had required cable systems to carry all the over-the-air stations broadcasting in their markets. Without must-carry restrictions, cable systems could decide which local stations to carry and which not to carry. UHF stations that are not carried lose the "VHF equality" that cable provides; more important, all-stations that are not carried lose their ability to reach cable subscribers at all, unless the cable homes install *A/B switches* that allow viewers to switch easily from cable to antenna for off-the-air reception. Broadcasters, cable operators, and members of Congress debated into the late 1980s the possibility of restoring the must-carry rule in some form acceptable to all parties.

Some newer independents also brought problems on themselves by building in markets too small to support an independent or entering markets in which established, strong independents already operated. But perhaps the heaviest blow to independents was a staggering increase in program costs. In only two years, from 1984 to 1986, with growing competition from expanding media outlets, the cost of buying programming and producing local newscasts more than doubled. Some stations, in an effort to compete, allocated nearly 50 percent of their total revenue to the acquisition of syndicated programs. By 1987, when prices had begun to level off, some 20 independent television stations had gone bankrupt. Some surviving independents tried specializing in Spanish, religious, or shop-at-home programming. A few even tried all-music-video or expensive all-news formats.

Despite the profitability of some independents, network affiliates continue to dominate television viewing. Affiliation with a national network remains one of the most valuable assets a television station can have. The prices paid for television stations dramatize the value of affiliation. In the late 1980s, VHF independents sold on the average for amounts equal to $75 to $80 for each television household in a station's market area; in contrast, the sales prices of VHF affiliates sometimes exceeded $250 per television household.

Network–Affiliate Contract Networks and their affiliates formalize the economic link between them through an *affiliation contract*. A clause at the heart of such a contract defines the terms on which the network will pay the station for the right to use the station's time. Called *network compensation,* this payment represents in effect a discount price conceded by the affiliate in return for the network's services in obtaining and promoting programs, selling advertising, and relaying both to the station.

Each television network uses a slightly different formula for calculating compensation, but they all arrive at about the same rate of payment. The contract assigns a hypothetical base value to an hour of each affiliate's time. This rate varies from station to station, reflecting differences in market size, station popularity, and other factors. Rates in top markets such as New York and Los Angeles run into the thousands of dollars per hour; they go down to as low as $50, and some affiliates receive no compensation at all.

A complex formula applied to the station's base hourly rate determines the actual amount the network pays for each of its programs an affiliate carries. That formula takes into account (1) the fraction of an hour occupied by the program, (2) the number of commercials sold by the network within the program (compared with the total commercial time available for sale), and (3) the time of day the program airs. The last factor reflects the drastic variation in audience potential from one daypart to another. On the average, network compensation to an affiliate—the amount in dollars actually received by the station—equals only about 15 percent of the affiliate's theoretical network hourly base rate. In the late 1980s, the three major networks combined paid their affiliates about $400 million a year to carry their programs.*

Network compensation represents a surprisingly small percentage of the gross revenues of network-affiliated stations—on the average less than 5 percent. But stations measure the value of affiliation less in terms of compensation than in terms of the audiences that network programs attract. Affiliates profit from the sale of spots in the 90 seconds or so the network leaves open for affiliate station breaks in each prime-time hour of network programming and the seven or eight minutes made available at other times. And the stations' own programs (whether locally produced or syndicated) benefit from association with popular and widely promoted network programs.

Affiliation Contract Regulation Unable to control networks directly (because it does not license them), the FCC exercises control indirectly through rules governing the affiliation contract. Present FCC rules forbid stations from entering into contracts with networks that restrict affiliates' freedom of action in several ways:

1. *Exclusivity.* A network contract may not contain *exclusivity rules* aimed at preventing an affiliate from accepting programs from other networks, nor may an affiliate prevent its network from offering rejected programs to other stations in its market. In practice, independent stations often enter into agreements with networks to have first call on programs that affiliates in their markets reject. For all practical purposes, however, most affiliates and their networks consider their relationships as in fact exclusive.

2. *Length of affiliation contract.* Until 1989, affiliation agreements could last no longer than two years between renewals and had to bind the two

parties equally. (In the 1930s the radio networks had tied up affiliates for five years but themselves for only one.) In that year, the FCC deleted its 44-year-old "two-year rule," finding it to be an anacronism that no longer served its purpose of encouraging new networks.

3. *Network ownership.* A single owner may not own two or more networks covering the same territory (aimed at the 1930s NBC Red-Blue radio network combination).

4. *Program rejection.* A network may not coerce an affiliate in any way to ensure clearance of time for its programs. Stations may cite broad reasons to justify rejection. They might judge programs as "unsatisfactory or unsuitable"; "contrary to the public interest"; or occupying time needed for other programs "of outstanding local or national importance." Theoretically, at least, the affiliate has complete freedom of program choice.

5. *Rate control.* A network may not influence an affiliate's nonnetwork advertising rates. (At one time the radio networks tried to ensure that network advertising would be more attractive to national advertisers than spot [nonnetwork] advertising arranged by direct contracts with stations.)

6. *Sales representation.* A network may not function as national spot sales representative for any of its affiliates other than its O&O stations.

In 1977, recognizing that the original chain broadcasting rules no longer had much relevance to modern radio networks, the FCC dropped most of the old radio rules, the main exception being the exclusivity rule.* At the same time the commission broadened the definition of *radio network* to include the audio news services offered on an interconnected basis by news agencies (63 FCC 2d 674, 1977). Although it gave radio networks more freedom, however, the FCC retained its regulations affecting television networks and imposed still more restrictions on them (such as the prime-time access

---

*Some programs require special compensation adjustments. For example, NBC pays no direct compensation for the two-hour, early-morning *Today* program. Instead, affiliates earn their compensation by selling advertising in the first and third half-hours, retaining all the income; the network, in turn, keeps all the income from sales that it makes in the second and fourth half-hours.

*Radio networks may now offer more than one service in the same market. For example, several of ABC's seven different services, targeted to different demographic groups, may find outlets in the same market.

rule), again through regulation of the network-affiliation agreement.

Affiliate Relations   Networks and their affiliates experience a somewhat uneasy and paradoxical sharing of power, complicated by political and economic factors too subtle for contracts to define. In one sense the networks have the upper hand. Affiliation can play a vitally important role in an affiliate station's success. Although the law states that a network may not coerce stations into accepting programs, networks in fact use every method at their disposal to ensure clearances. This includes veiled suggestions of reductions in network compensation rates and telephone calls to station managers from powerful advertising agencies whose clients had spots on uncleared programs.* And the ultimate reprisal, nonrenewal of network contracts, though rarely carried out, poses an ever-present threat.

On the other hand, without the voluntary compliance of affiliates, a television network amounts to nothing but a group owner of a few stations rather than the main source of programming for some 200 stations. In that sense affiliates have the upper hand, and woe to the network that fails to please them. The defections from other networks that occurred when ABC first forged into the ratings lead in the late 1970s showed what could happen. At the end of a three-year period, ABC not only equaled or topped its rivals in audience size, it also matched them in number of affiliates, having picked up more than 30 stations. However, much of ABC's success in convincing stations to change affiliation resulted from its offering substantially higher compensation, rather than to affiliates' dissatisfaction with their previous network's program performance.

Networks prefer to have their programs carried by the strongest station in each television market. ABC, for example, moved in 1980 from WJKS-TV, a UHF station in Jacksonville, FL, to WLTV, a VHF sta-

tion in the same city. In 1987, ABC reduced WLTV's network compensation rate by about 25 percent. In 1988, when NBC led in the ratings, WLTV returned to NBC, and ABC had to go back to WJKS, the weaker and less desirable UHF station.

Networks cannot always predict audience reactions to affiliation changes. In 1982, for example, when NBC experienced some of the lowest ratings in its history, it affiliated with KCBJ-TV, a UHF station in Columbia-Jefferson City, MO, after ABC dropped KCBJ-TV in favor of a VHF station, KOMU-TV. Unexpectedly, in the first rating period following the switch, the new NBC affiliate increased its share of the prime-time audience in that market by 22 percent (see Exhibit 8–10).

Network Clearance   The complex relationships between networks and their affiliates hinge on the act of *clearance*—the voluntary agreement by an affiliate to keep clear in its program schedule the times the network needs to run its programs. However, even after an affiliate has cleared time for a network series, it still has the right to *pre-empt* individual episodes in that series to substitute programs from other sources.

Networks rely on affiliates not only to carry their programs, but also to carry them *as scheduled*. Delayed broadcasts by affiliates reduce a network's immediate audience for the delayed programs, in consequence reducing their national ratings. Moreover, networks need simultaneous coverage throughout the country to get the maximum benefit from their efforts to promote and advertise their program offerings.

In practice, affiliates accept about 90 percent of all programs offered by their networks, most of them on faith. Stations usually feel no need to preview all network offerings, despite the fact that they as licensees, not the networks, have the ultimate legal responsibility for programs. Because most television programs come in series, however, affiliates know their general tone, so that the acceptability of future episodes can usually be taken for granted. Affiliates can screen questionable or controversial programs in advance, but such previewing occurs infrequently.

---

*In the early 1980s, before his successful late-night program on NBC, David Letterman hosted a daytime program on the same network. Faced with low ratings and poor station clearances, Letterman sometimes made unannounced personal telephone calls to station general managers in an effort to persuade them to carry his show—usually without success.

Thus, realistically, affiliates have little or no influence over the *day-to-day* programming decisions of their networks. In the long run, however, they exert a powerful influence. Network programming strategists take very seriously the feedback that comes from their affiliates. It comes to them from affiliate-relations departments, station advisory boards, annual affiliate conventions, and individual contacts with managers and owners, reinforced by the statistics of affiliate refusals to clear time.

An affiliate might fail to clear time or might preempt already cleared time for several reasons. Often a station simply wants to increase the amount of commercial time available for local sale beyond that which the network programs leave free. It can run more commercials than the network allows by substituting a syndicated program or a movie. Such pre-emptions occur especially during the year-end holiday period, when advertiser demand peaks. Sometimes stations opt to skip low-rated network programs in favor of syndicated material to keep audiences from flowing to competing stations. At other times affiliates want to protect their local audiences from what they regard as morally or politically offensive network offerings. Less frequently, affiliates take the risk of offending their networks and losing audience members in order to schedule locally produced programs in a desirable time that is normally cleared for their network.

One study of affiliate pre-emptions suggested as the dominating motive the drive to increase sales: more than half the replacement programs in a sample month of pre-emptions consisted of either syndicated shows (35 percent) or movies (21 percent). Sports replacements ranked third (16 percent). Local programs came at the bottom of the list, representing only 9 percent of the replacements for network programs (Osborn et al., 1979).

Low-rated network programs traditionally consist, almost by definition, of public-affairs and other nonentertainment offerings; these, therefore, most often fail to get clearance. ABC's evening news ran a poor third to CBS and NBC in the 1960s and early 1970s, in part because more than a score of ABC's major affiliates failed to clear time for it; this guaranteed continued low ratings for ABC's news by denying it access to some 14 percent of the network's potential audience. CBS could persuade less than half its affiliates to clear time even for the highly respected, though often controversial, news documentaries of Edward R. Murrow.

Changes in Network–Affiliate Relations

The foregoing description of the network–affiliate relationship rebuts the image of network programmers as all-powerful dictators, imposing their will on helpless affiliates. Far from being helpless, affiliates in the final analysis have the upper hand when they mobilize their collective strength.

Indeed, beginning in the late 1980s, when rising costs and increasing competition combined to weaken ABC, CBS, and NBC, the network–affiliate relationship began to crack under the strain. Many affiliates turned against their network partners, contributing to the network decline that some in the industry predicted would cause the eventual demise of one or more of the three giants.

Both the networks and their affiliates questioned compensation rates. Affiliates felt that network compensation failed to reflect the real value of their time to their networks. NBC at first complied with the demand for higher compensation, but in 1989 announced a plan to make local-station audience delivery the primary criterion in determining compensation rates. ABC and CBS cut the compensation of many of their affiliates, for some reducing it to zero.* The networks increased the amount of precious advertising time available to themselves in their schedules, a move resented by their affiliates. Pre-emptions reached all-time highs. Some 11 affiliates pre-empted ABC at 8:00 P.M. on weekend nights in order to carry the syndicated *Star Trek: The Next Generation*; as many as 40 CBS affiliates failed to clear all or part of that network's 10:00 to 11:00 A.M. programs in the first quarter of 1987. In 1988 the average ABC affiliate pre-empted one prime-time network hour each week. In response, ABC suggested that the network might begin to cut back

---

*In 1988, in what some broadcasters feared might start a trend, WPBF-TV in West Palm Beach, FL, agreed not only to waive network compensation but also to *pay* ABC for affiliation.

on the number of hours it programmed in prime time as well as in other dayparts. In all, pre-emptions cost the networks tens of millions of dollars in lost revenues.

Technology has freed many affiliates from their almost total dependence on the networks for non-local news. Using satellites and minicams, stations can now cover not only local but also regional, national, and even international news. For example, more than 4,000 anchors, correspondents, editors, photographers, and others, representing nearly 400 television and 300 radio stations, attended the 1988 Democratic convention in Atlanta. About 80 television stations belong to Hubbard Broadcasting's Conus Satellite Cooperative, a relatively inexpensive way of acquiring satellite news feeds. Some member stations purchased their satellite news-gathering trucks with financial help from Conus. All members have access to the cooperative's satellite transponders and serve as contributors to the Conus video pool when news in their areas holds interest for stations in other markets.

To minimize adverse effects of local-station self-sufficiency in news, the three major networks set up news-gathering arrangements with their affiliates similar to those of Conus: ABC with ABSAT, CBS with NewsNet, and NBC with Starcom.* In fact, roles have partially reversed, making the networks dependent on their affiliates. Working with reduced staffs and budgets, the networks look to the local stations for coverage of events that before would have been covered by now-fired network correspondents or by now-closed network news bureaus. The closing credits of a network evening newscast, listing the stations that contributed to that night's program, reflect the trend.

8.3
Cable Television

The economic organization of cable television systems and networks differs substantially from that of broadcast stations and networks. The franchises that

municipalities award to cable systems regulate the systems more loosely than the regulations governing the licenses the FCC awards to broadcast stations. Cable depends primarily on subscriber fees for revenue, so it owes allegiance only to that fraction of the television households in a franchise area that chooses to subscribe (in 1989 as high as 87 percent in some areas, but averaging about 55 percent).

A commercial broadcaster depends almost entirely on advertisers and has an obligation to serve the total audience in its market area, which is usually much larger than that of a cable system. A major television station may serve an entire metropolitan area, but most large cities are divided up into several different cable franchises. Cable systems therefore outnumber commercial television stations nearly 10 to 1. But whereas most households can tune in a number of local radio and television stations, almost without exception there is only a single cable system to which they can subscribe. The distinction between affiliates and independents does not exist in cable—all systems depend almost entirely on television stations and cable program networks to fill their channels.

Basic Unit: The System   By the late 1980s more than 10,000 *cable systems* served 23,000 communities in the United States. Three out of 4 cable subscribers had access to 30 or more channels; 15 percent could see 54 or more; some could view over 100. This diversity makes it nearly impossible to generalize about system organization and structure. Nevertheless, whether small, with a few hundred subscribers, or large, with thousands, each performs the same four basic functions as do broadcast stations.

1. *General/administrative* functions in cable differ little from those same functions in broadcasting (or any other business). However, rather than having an affiliation agreement with only one major television network (or at most three), cable systems often contract with a dozen or more cable networks to fill their numerous channels. People who work in the cable industry also tend to be joiners, the

---

*CNN offers its broadcast and cable affiliates a similar service, Newsource.

major trade group being the National Cable Television Association (NCTA).

2. *Technical* functions at a cable system differ somewhat from those at a broadcast station. First, of course, cable has no transmitter to operate and maintain. It does, however, use a complex array of equipment to receive signals from program suppliers at the *headend* and to send those and other signals, simultaneously, through a network of coaxial cables to homes throughout the system's service area. Broadcast technicians finish their jobs when they have done everything possible to ensure that a good signal leaves the transmitter; they normally have no concern with the equipment at the receiving end. Not so with cable, which typically places in each subscribing home some sort of *converter* that provides an interface between the subscriber's receiver and the system's wire network. Because of concern for the integrity of the entire sending and receiving system, cable organizations often have both *inside-* and *outside-plant* personnel; the first group concerns itself with equipment in the cable system's studio and headend, and the second group handles installation and service of subscriber equipment.

3. *Programming* functions at a cable system differ in scope from those at a broadcast station. A radio or television station programs a single channel. A cable system, on the other hand, programs a multitude of channels. At smaller systems, the general manager may make program decisions, usually in consultation with the director of marketing. Multiple-system operators may divide the programming function into specific areas, such as satellite programming and local origination, often under the direction of a marketing vice president.

Some cable systems produce their own local programming, much of it on channels programmed by community or educational organizations. Although some cable companies, such as Colony Communications, headquartered in Providence, RI, have made a commitment to locally produced news, most systems defer to broadcast radio and television in this expensive and personnel-intensive area.

4. *Sales* at a cable system might better be called *sales and marketing*. Although some systems do sell commercial time on some of their channels, marketing the cable service to subscribers ranks as the more important function. Monthly fees paid by subscribers represent the principal source of any cable system's revenue.

The marketing department has the task of trying to convince nonsubscribers to subscribe and current subscribers not to *disconnect*. Operators use the word *churn* to describe subscriber turnover—new customers signing up for service as others cancel. They calculate churn as a percentage, dividing a current month's disconnects by the prior month's total subscribers and multiplying the result by 100. The rate of churn for basic services may run from as low as 5 percent per year for established systems in stable neighborhoods to 60 percent or higher for newer systems or those in areas with more transient populations. Pay-cable networks average about 50 percent churn over a year.

Customer service representatives (CSRs), working out of the marketing department, have daily contact with present and potential subscribers. CSRs answer telephones for eight or more hours a day, responding to complaints from subscribers and questions from potential customers. A system's ability to handle these calls skillfully can have a profound effect on its financial success and even on whether it keeps or loses its franchise.

System Interconnection   Often several cable systems in a large market interconnect so that materials originated by one system can be seen on all the others, providing combined advertising coverage equivalent in reach to that of the area's television stations. System interconnection may involve physically linking the systems by cable, microwave relays, or satellite (*hard* or *true* interconnections), or it may depend simply on the exchange of program and commercial tapes (*soft* interconnection).

This type of local interconnection differs from the national interconnectivity by satellite for the distribution of program networks; system interconnection functions mainly to distribute commercials. Videopath, the cable industry's first electronic advertising interconnect, began in 1983. Using a microwave network centered in McCook, IL, it delivered commercials to 13 cable companies with a total of 376,000 subscribers. In 1988, Adlink, in Los Angeles, became the first to deliver commercials by satellite.

System interconnection for program distribution occurs when the municipality stipulates as a condition of its franchises that the entire municipal area have the benefit of certain public-service programs available on specific systems.

Multiple-System Operators Cabling large urban areas becomes a capital-intensive proposition, beyond the financial means of small-system operators. The only firms that can provide the large initial investments required are too large to be attracted by the limited potential of a single franchise. Thus emerged a trend toward *multiple-system operators* (MSOs), firms that gathered scores and then hundreds of systems under a single owner. Only such firms could put up the huge sums required to secure franchises and construct cable systems in major metropolitan areas.

Some 350 MSOs operate in the United States. Exhibit 8–6 shows the top 10 MSOs ranked by number of subscribers and by revenue per subscriber. Impressive though these numbers may be, it should be noted that even the largest MSO serves only about 10 percent of all U.S. cable homes and less than 16 percent of all television homes. By contrast, the largest television station group owners can reach nearly 25 percent of all television homes.

In the late 1980s, the top MSO owners included broadcasters (Cox), television program industry companies (Viacom), magazine and newspaper publishers (Time, Times Mirror), and conglomerates (Warner). Nearly 32 percent of all cable systems had ties with broadcast interests, more than 20 percent with program producers, and approximately 18 percent with newspapers. Cable, unlike radio and television, has no limit on the number of systems or subscribers that may be served by a single MSO.

Cable Program Services Cable systems offer the signals of local television stations. Some import the signals of more distant stations as well, and some offer access channels for local programs produced by others. Smaller systems may be able to handle no more than these services. But increased channel capacity has been the trend, creating a demand for additional program sources.

Systems draw upon three main types of cable program providers: basic cable networks, superstations, and pay-cable networks. Cable program networks offer their affiliated systems benefits similar to those provided by broadcast networks: *basic cable networks* offer structured program services, simultaneous program distribution by satellite, and, in many cases, advertising environments that appeal to local advertisers. *Superstations* offer the first two benefits. *Pay-cable networks* also provide the first two benefits and bring cable systems revenue in the form of monthly subscriber fees. More details on the three major types of cable program providers follow.

▮ *Basic Cable Networks.* Cable systems typically program a selection from the approximately 50 available *basic cable networks* in their regular monthly subscription price. Most basic services are *advertiser-supported,* depending on the sale of commercial time for the bulk of their revenue. Cable systems usually pay each network a per-subscriber fee for the right to carry that network's programs. Fees may range from 1 or 2 cents up to 25 cents per subscriber per month. In addition to the time they devote to their own advertising clients, ad-supported networks usually make about two minutes of advertising time per hour available to cable systems for local sale. Exhibit 8–7 (page 200) lists some of the better-known basic cable program services.

Although organized similar to broadcast television networks, advertiser-supported cable networks do differ. First, they have smaller staffs than ABC, CBS, or NBC, and they reach smaller audiences. Second, although they maintain departments that sell commercial time, they must also sell *themselves* to cable systems. Broadcast television networks often compete among themselves for certain specific affiliates, but enough stations exist and network affiliation holds enough value that each network can find an outlet in almost every market. Cable networks have no such assurance of finding affiliates.

EXHIBIT 8-6 Top Ten Cable MSOs

Ranked by basic cable subscribers

Rank	Multiple system operator	Subscribers*	Rank by revenue per subscriber
1	Tele-Communications	4,192,400	57
2	ATC (Time Inc.)	3,776,800	43
3	Continental Cablevision	2,186,500	21
4	Storer	1,480,000	4
5	Cox Cable	1,441,800	9
6	Warner Cable	1,432,800	19
7	Comcast Cable	1,359,300	26
8	United Cable TV	1,186,700	54
9	Newhouse	1,081,600	37
10	Viacom	1,080,400	36

Ranked by per-subscriber revenue

Rank	Multiple system operator	Monthly revenue per subscriber*	Rank by basic cable subscribers
1	Cablevision Systems	$35.92	12
2	Media General	31.94	48
3	TeleCable Corp.	31.13	21
4	Storer	30.72	4
5	Prime Cable	29.99	29
6	Sonic Cable	28.85	60
7	American Cable	28.71	22
8	United Video Management	28.24	66
9	Cox Cable	28.10	5
10	Maclean Hunter	27.72	34

*Basic subscribers as of March 31, 1988; Monthly revenue per subscriber as of December 31, 1987. In May 1989, United Artists Communications merged with United Cable, thus becoming the nation's third-largest cable television operator, based on the number of subscribers served (I–R Daniels Partners First Quarter Report, Denver CO, 1989, p. 1). In July 1989, Time Inc. (owner of ATC) and Warner Communications (owner of Warner Cable) merged, creating Time Warner Inc., the world's largest media and entertainment company, with operations in movies, cable, programming, publishing, and music (*Broadcasting,* 31 July 1989, p. 19).

Although the United States has more than 300 multiple-cable system operators, the 10 largest MSOs together serve about 44 percent of all cable subscribers. However, ranking as a top-10 MSO does not ensure the highest revenue per subscriber. Only two, Storer and Cox, appear on both lists.

SOURCE: *The Kagen Cable TV Financial Databook,* Paul Kagen Associates, June 1988.

EXHIBIT 8–7   Examples of Satellite-Distributed Program Services

Basic channels

Name (Owner & launch date)	Homes reached (millions)	Prime-time rating	Content
Entertainment & Sports Programming Network (ESPN) Capital Cities/ABC (9/79)	48.8	2.5	College and NFL football, college basketball, auto racing, golf, other sports
Cable News Network (CNN) Turner Broadcasting System (6/80)	47.1	1.1	24-hour in-depth news
USA Network Paramount Pictures, MCA Inc. (4/80)	46.2	2.1	Broad-based entertainment, sports
CBN Family Channel Christian Broadcasting Network (4/77)	43.0	1.2	Family entertainment, comedies, westerns, children's shows, religious programs
Music Television (MTV) MTV Networks (Viacom Int. Inc.) (8/81)	42.6	0.8	24-hour music videos, with interviews and concerts; some original programming
C-SPAN (nonprofit corporation of cable companies and others) (3/79)	38.0	NA	Live coverage of U.S. House of Representatives, public-affairs programs, congressional hearings

Superstations

WTBS Turner Broadcasting System (12/76)	45.6	2.6	Family programming, including classic movies, sitcoms, sports
WGN The Tribune Co. (10/78)	24.8	NA	Children's shows, sports, syndicated programs, movies

A single cable network might affiliate with several cable systems operating in different geographical areas within the same market. Conversely, other networks might find that in some markets they have no outlet at all, because competing networks have filled all available cable channels. And some cable systems simply elect to carry some program services and not others, even though some of their channels remain empty. A program provider's marketing department must address these problems in trying to persuade cable systems to carry its programs.

Cable networks also differ from broadcast television networks in not producing news (with the obvious exceptions of the Cable News Networks

EXHIBIT 8–7   Continued

Pay services

Name (Owner & launch date)	Subscribers (millions)	Content
Home Box Office (HBO), Time Inc. (11/72)	16.5	Movies, variety, sports, specials, documentaries, children's programming
Showtime Viacom (7/80)	6.1	Movies, variety, comedy specials, Broadway adaptations
Cinemax, Time Inc. (8/80)	5.1	Movies, comedy, music specials
The Disney Channel, Walt Disney Co. (4/83)	4.0	Original feature films, specials, series, classic films, Disney cartoons
The Movie Channel, Viacom (12/80)	2.5	Double features, film festivals, movie marathons

Home shopping networks

Name	Subscribers	Content
Home Shopping Network (includes HSN II), Home Shopping Network Inc.	77	Electronics, jewelry, housewares, clothing, cosmetics, health products, collectibles
Cable Value Network, CVN Companies Inc.	20	Electronics, tools, jewelry, toys, clothing

Pay-per-view networks

Name	Addressable homes
Request Television and Request-2	3,700,000
Viewer's Choice I and Viewer's Choice II	3,500,000
Home Premier Television	1,400,000

Satellite technology has made it possible to offer an almost bewildering variety of program options to those viewers (in more than half of U.S. television households) who subscribe to cable.

SOURCES: Rating data from *Broadcasting,* 9 Jan. 1989, 96; all other data from *Channels 1989 Field Guide,* 90–102.

and, to a limited extent, the religiously oriented CBN Family Channel). Avoiding the enormous costs of running a national news service enables cable networks to increase their profit potential.

■ *Superstations.* The *superstation* is a paradoxical hybrid of broadcasting and cable television—par-adoxical because, although the FCC licenses each broadcast station to serve only one specific local market, superstations also reach hundreds of other markets throughout the country by means of satellite distribution to cable systems.

Cable systems that buy a superstation satellite feed include it in their basic package of channels, paying only a few cents per subscriber per month for the service. The money pays for the satellite uplink and for the use of the satellite transponder. The station gets its share of the pie through higher advertising rates, justified by the increase in audience represented by the cable subscribers. By 1988 cable systems serving 46 million subscribers, about half of all U.S. television homes, carried Ted Turner's WTBS, the first superstation.

A score of superstations exist. Not all of them welcome the designation, but they cannot prevent satellite distribution of their signals to cable systems as long as the systems pay the mandatory copyright fee. Major superstations include, in addition to WTBS, WGN, in Chicago, owner of the Chicago Cubs baseball team; WWOR, in the New York City area, which carries more sports than any other station in the country; WPIX, also in New York, which features Yankee baseball games; and WTVT, in Dallas.

The television superstation's huge extension of the normally limited broadcast station coverage area created vexing copyright problems. Hitherto, copyright holders selling syndicated programs to individual stations had based their licensing charges on the assumption that each station reached a limited, fixed market. Syndicators formerly licensed WTBS to reach only the Atlanta audience, but as a superstation it now reaches audiences in hundreds of other markets, in many of which television stations may have paid copyright fees for the right to broadcast the very same programs. A law mandating copyright licensing to cable systems compensates owners for this additional coverage, but the law satisfies no one and is the subject of ongoing negotiations within the industry (see Chapter 16 for more on copyright law).

Responding to complaints about inequities created by superstation distribution of copyrighted programs, the FCC in 1988 reimposed its *syndicated exclusivity* rule, known as *syndex*. It allows television stations to negotiate *exclusive* rights to syndicated programs, preventing duplicating of those programs by either competing stations in the same market or cable systems carrying superstations from distant markets. If upheld, this rule could under-

mine the future economics of some superstations: forced to the inconvenience of blacking out programs carried by a superstation, cable systems may elect not to carry that superstation at all. Stations that could be vulnerable under syndex include WWOR-TV (it owns *The Cosby Show*) and WGN-TV (with *Cheers*). WTBS, however, planned a "blackout-proof" schedule, free of all programs currently in syndication to stations, that would give its cable systems no problem programs.

Some cable systems also carry the signals of *radio* superstations, notably Chicago's classical music station WFMT, carried by 360 cable systems serving more than 1.3 million subscribers. Subscribers who pay an extra fee to the cable system operator can receive such radio stations, as well as other audio services, which go through a special cable connection to their home high-fidelity stereo systems. Many cable systems also carry local radio stations as background music for some of their information channels. By 1988, about 40 percent of all commercial radio stations could be heard as audio services on at least one cable system.

Pay-Cable Networks. Subscribers must pay a monthly fee or *premium* in addition to the fee paid for the basic cable service in order to receive *pay-cable networks.** The amount of that subscriber fee varies from system to system and network to network but averages about $10 per month for each of the more popular pay-cable networks. The cable operator negotiates the fee with the program supplier, usually splitting fee revenue 50/50.

In 1972, HBO, the first national pay-cable network,† owned by Time, Inc., began offering cable subscribers commercial-free theatrical motion pictures. It soon entered into movie-rights purchasing in a big way, buying the cable exhibition rights to

---

*Pay cable should not be confused with subscription television (STV), which was once carried by broadcast stations, not cable systems.

†The first experimental pay-cable service, or *toll TV* as it was then called, began as early as 1957, when residents of Bartlesville, OK, paid $9.50 a month to watch movies delivered to their television sets by coaxial cable.

hundreds of old and new Hollywood feature films, as well as many short films. Having attained dominance in pay cable, serving more subscribers than its two largest competitors combined, HBO can all but dictate to Hollywood producers the prices for film rights. HBO calculates the prices it will pay on the basis of a certain amount of money per subscriber (usually about 20 cents), plus a flat fee determined by the value of the specific film to HBO in terms of subscriber appeal. Hollywood producers have long felt that HBO pays too little for film rights, but (aside from withholding films from sale altogether) producers have no options.

The formation in 1978 of Showtime, a pay-cable service that also uses satellites to distribute its films and other programs, somewhat weakened HBO's bargaining power. In 1979, Viacom, the operator of Showtime, sold a half interest in the network to the then-leading MSO, Teleprompter, providing more cable systems and more financial clout for Showtime. (Since 25 Teleprompter systems had previously contracted with HBO, HBO suffered a direct loss.) Nevertheless, HBO had become so firmly established that, despite aggressive marketing, Showtime remained far behind HBO in total subscribers (see Exhibit 8–7).

In 1980, in part to offset the impact of Showtime, HBO began a second service, Cinemax, and the following year expanded its own schedule to 24 hours a day. Cinemax offered programming somewhat different from HBO's and closer to Showtime's. HBO's second service also satisfied the demand among some cable systems for a companion pay service to HBO.

Continuing its efforts to compete effectively with HBO, Showtime in 1983 merged with another pay-cable network, The Movie Channel, although the two continued to operate as separate services. The merger somewhat improved the combination's ability to negotiate with program sources, but HBO continued to dominate in the 1980s, having nearly twice as many subscribers as Showtime and The Movie Channel combined.

Pay-cable networks that take advantage of cable's multichannel-based ability to target specific audiences include the Disney Channel (all-family programming), the Playboy Channel (adult fare), Bravo (cultural programs), and American Movie Classics (a sister service of Bravo offering classic films).

Like the advertiser-supported cable services, pay-cable networks do not yet have staffs the size of those of ABC, CBS, and NBC. HBO, for example, had about 1,400 employees in 1988, compared with about 3,000 at each of the broadcast networks. Unlike the ad-supported networks, pay-cable services do not, of course, need sales forces to sell commercial time. They do, however, have extensive marketing departments that sell the network's service to cable operators and, often in partnership with the cable systems, convince potential customers to subscribe. As with the broadcast television networks, outside companies produce most programs, even original series, carried by pay-cable networks.

Vertical Integration   The owner of a roadside hot-dog stand might find it more efficient and more profitable to produce the hot dogs and rolls he sells, rather than buying them from others; he might find it even more profitable to raise the animals and the wheat used to produce the hot dogs and rolls. Were he to enter the businesses of raising cattle and grain, manufacturing hot dogs, and baking rolls, while continuing to operate his stand, he would have a *vertically integrated* operation. So it is with much of business.

The entertainment industries find vertical integration especially attractive. The motion picture industry set the pattern, with movie producers owning companies that distributed films and theaters that exhibited them. The federal government declared this practice to be in violation of antitrust laws and, after years of legal wrangling, prohibited much of the movies' vertical integration.

Broadcasting, however, has only limited vertical integration. Networks, as program distributors as well as producers of some programs, own some stations (the equivalent of movie exhibitors). However, antitrust law limits both the amount of programming a network may itself produce and the number of stations it may own. The Fox network, because it has not yet achieved full-scale network status as defined by the FCC, practices vertical integration. Ownership ties integrate a program producer (20th Century Fox) with a program distributor (the Fox network) and the program exhibitors (the Fox O&O stations). Other examples include MCA's acquisition of New York superstation WWOR and the Disney organization's acquisition of KHJ-TV in Los Angeles.

Such integration flourishes in the cable industry, which escapes the restrictions imposed on broadcasting. As cable matures and seeks to improve business efficiency, vertical integration increases. Tele-Communications, Inc. (TCI) provides the best example. As an MSO, TCI operates the nation's largest group of cable systems. It also owns parts of a program producer (United Artists), several cable networks (Black Entertainment Television, the Discovery Channel, American Movie Classics, the Fashion Channel), a satellite program distribution service (Netlink USA); and an already vertically integrated program producer/distributor/exhibitor (the Turner Broadcasting System).

8.4
Capital Investment

The broadcast and cable industries, though not as capital intensive as the automobile business, for example, nonetheless require very high investments for constructing new facilities or acquiring and maintaining existing ones.

Broadcasting   The FCC license permitting a station to operate constitutes the owner's most valuable asset. To use a license, an owner must buy equipment to receive, originate, and transmit programming, along with associated buildings and office facilities.

Radio station construction costs range from $50,000 for a simple, small-market AM or FM station to several million dollars for a sophisticated radio facility in a major market. A station in the low-power tele-

vision (LPTV) class that is able to produce local programs may, under ideal conditions, cost no more than $300,000, but a full-power, major-market television facility may cost 100 times that much. Stations that plan to originate secondary services such as teletext need to invest an additional $200,000 for that technology alone.

Operating stations must maintain and, to remain competitive, upgrade their facilities. The median equipment budget for a television station runs to about $300,000 annually; that for a radio station, about $20,000. Major equipment purchases can quickly spend those budgets, and more: satellite news-gathering vans cost between $300,000 and $500,000; newsroom computer systems run between $100,000 and $450,000; weather graphics equipment costs about $20,000. And the future cost of converting a major-market station's facilities to an incompatible high-definition television system runs about $10 million.

Unlike other media, electronic mass media rely on the general public—the consumer—to supply the largest part of the basic capital equipment, the broadcast receivers. The public's capital investment in broadcasting amounts to many times the total investment of the industry itself. In fact, some estimates place the public's investment at more than 90 percent of the total. This public involvement imposes on the broadcast industry a unique obligation to its audiences.

Cable   On a cost-per-home-served basis, a cable system costs even more to construct than a broadcast facility because each home must be physically connected to the cable system. The costs of installing cable on existing utility poles range from $10,000 per mile for rural areas to $100,000 per mile for urban areas, and up to $300,000 per mile for underground cable. To *upgrade* a system—that is, to increase its channel capacity—costs between $10,000 and $15,000 per mile.

As with a television station, a local cable system's origination equipment costs depend on the owner's operating philosophy and desired level of sophistication. A simple monochrome studio may be constructed for as little as $30,000, but a reasonably equipped color facility will cost $200,000 or more. The hardware needed to handle pay-per-view services costs about $10,000. Estimates for headend conversion to HDTV run as high as $1,000,000.

Satellite Services   Because they relay programs more efficiently and cost-effectively than terrestrial relay facilities, communication satellites have reduced the operating costs of stations, systems, and networks. Satellites, more than any other technology, have made it possible for modern cable and other media to flourish.

Although they are more economical for long-distance signal relay than traditional telephone lines and microwave relays, satellites and the equipment associated with them remain expensive. For example, Hughes' Galaxy I satellite, reserved for cable industry use, cost about $30 million to construct, plus another $40 million to launch and insure against possible loss. However, the sale of transponders aboard the satellite for a reported total of $195 million more than offset this $70 million cost.

Early satellite launches by NASA rockets cost about $70 million each. Later, use of the space shuttle brought launch costs down to about $30 million. But the 1986 U.S. government decision to reserve the NASA shuttle for noncommercial uses, combined with higher manufacturing costs, brings the total package for an orbiting satellite to about $200 million. Early geosynchronous satellites had a useful life of only about eight years, but designers expected those manufactured in the late 1990s to last as long as 16 years.

Users may lease transponders for between $25,000 and $200,000 a month, depending on the length of the contract and the location of the satellite. Occasional use [for example, by a television station to *backhaul* (bring home) live coverage of an out-of-town baseball game] costs as little as $200 for one hour. Networks sometimes make their transponders available to their affiliates; NBC rents theirs to affiliates for $14 per minute.

Earth stations that send signals up to satellites (*uplinks*) range in price from about $600,000 to $750,000. Users that need transmission facilities only occasionally may rent Earth stations for as little as $396 an hour for transmission to C-band satellites, or $480 an hour for transmission to Ku-band satellites. Wold Communications, one of several companies that provide portable uplinks (PUPS), brings them to the user's site and rents them for between $3,000 and $5,000 a day, depending on whether the user needs C-band or Ku-band capacity.

TVRO (*television receive-only*) dishes* that cable systems, television stations, or other users employ to downlink satellite signals cost from as little as $1,000 for simple units for residential use, to $40,000 or more for professional models capable of "looking at" several satellites.

SMATV and MMDS   Satellite master antenna television (SMATV) construction costs depend on the size of the multiple-dwelling building and the sophistication of the installation. An average 300-unit system might cost about $80,000, including $35,000 for Earth station equipment but excluding cabling. Cable and connection costs depend on the age and construction of the building (many new complexes come prewired for cable) and on the number of tenants subscribing.

Multichannel multipoint distribution systems (MMDS), sometimes referred to as *wireless cable,* operate from a single transmitter that usually serves large apartment buildings or condominiums. Capital costs for such a system approximate $600 per subscriber.

8.5
Ownership Turnover

In the 34 years from 1954 through 1988, more than 16,000 radio stations and nearly 1,300 television stations changed ownership. The total value of these transactions approximated $38 billion. No governmental agency requires reporting of cable-system

---

*Although still referred to as "dishes," many satellite receiving antennas no longer have that characteristic shape.

EXHIBIT 8–8   How Did We Ever Get Along Before Computers?

Radio and television stations got along well without computers for years, of course. Some still do. But more and more the broadcast and cable industries depend on computer systems to increase efficiency, improve performance, reduce staff sizes, and raise profits.

In the *newsroom* computers serve as word processors for writing news scripts and for editing, organizing, producing newscasts, and making changes minutes before air time. Stations keep (*archive*) past news material and news wire services in computer storage, giving reporters speedy access to background information. Computers make daily assignments of reporters and equipment, act as a message center and automatic telephone dialing service, and even feed news scripts electronically to camera-mounted teleprompters.

In the *sales department* computers monitor commercial availabilities, store market and rating data for use in sales presentations, and make audience and cost projections. They analyze the efficiency of commercials already run by checking against rating data. And they schedule (*traffic*) commercials, watching to ensure contract fulfillment and keeping ads for competing products from running back to back.

Program departments generate daily program pre-logs by computer. They use them, with rating data

entered, to analyze proposed syndicated program acquisitions and to schedule programs and movies already owned. Computers store program contracts, generate graphics (as in the photos on the opposite page), keep track of monthly program costs, and supply reports showing sales revenue for each program aired. Radio stations enter music playlists on computers.

In the *business office,* computers maintain records of advertisers and agencies, their credit history, and the status of their accounts. Computers calculate costs, send out bills (to advertisers and, in the case of cable, to subscribers), and follow up on receiving payment (*collections*). They store personnel files, handle payroll, and help to prepare and, once prepared, to monitor station budgets.

In the *control room,* computers execute program schedules by automatically rolling program and commercial audio cassettes or videotapes, and by inserting commercials at the right spots in cable or broadcast network programs. They make automatic entries on the daily program log, indicating which events ran when (and which didn't and why), and they insert closed captioning for the hearing impaired.

In the *studio,* robotic cameras take live electronic pictures of newscasters in their news sets. Operated

---

transactions comparable to the FCC's requirement for broadcasters; thus no accurate data on cable exist. Industry estimates place total sales of cable systems for 1988 at more than $10 billion. The industry trade journal *Broadcasting* regularly lists stations and cable systems for sale and others already sold.

Broadcast stations and cable systems offer better opportunities to make more money than many other businesses. Supermarkets, for example, have a notoriously low *profit margin* of perhaps 1 or 2 percent. Broadcast station profit margins can reach as high as 50 percent or more. For this reason, large, multifaceted *conglomerates,* many of which have no prior broadcast ownership experience, often choose to invest in this industry. Conglomerates,

however, by definition participate in several types of businesses rather than just one or two. Should one of their businesses suffer setbacks, the effect on a conglomerate would be limited.

Restrictions on Ownership   A company may own as many cable systems as it likes. Not so for broadcasting. A single entity may own as many as 12 AM radio stations, 12 FM stations, and 12 television stations, provided that the 12 TV stations do not together reach more than 25% of all U.S. television households. Minor exceptions to this standard are discussed in Section 17.5.

Before any sale of a radio or television station can become final, it must first receive FCC approval. Usually a municipality controls the sale of a cable

EXHIBIT 8–8   Continued

by control room engineers or as part of the newsroom computer system, these cameras sometimes hang from the studio ceiling, providing shots unavailable from a traditional, human-operated camera.

Over years computers save time and money. But they require a substantial initial investment. For ex-ample, a large-station newsroom computer system with 40 terminals and assorted printers and accessories costs an average of $450,000. By 1988 only about 10 percent of television stations had made that investment.

SOURCE: Photos courtesy of Molly Lynch/WCVB-TV 5, Boston.

system operating under that community's franchise. (For details on legal controls and other influences on sales of broadcast and cable properties, see Section 17.5.)

Station Sales   Although not all radio and television stations are sold at a profit, few are sold at a loss.* David E. Schutz, an independent consultant on broadcast mergers and acquisitions, analyzed 212 radio station sales made in 1985. Of those 212,

157 (74 percent) sold for the same or a higher price than originally paid for the station; only 55 (26 percent) sold at a lower price, most of them AM *stand-alones* (without co-owned FM stations). In recent years AM stations have declined in value compared with FM stations and AM/FM combinations. The 212 transactions showed that station values had increased at 10 percent compounded annual rate (*Broadcasting,* 27 Jan. 1986, 107). Like real estate agents, station brokers bring buyers and sellers together. They usually receive a 5 percent commission but earn somewhat less on major transactions.

Pricing Methods   No reliable formulas exist for determining the appropriate selling price of a station. Several factors influence what a buyer should

---

*One example of a major loss involved Taft Broadcasting's $760 million acquisition of Gulf Broadcasting's five independent stations in 1985, a time when "indies" enjoyed record profits. After two years that proved difficult for many independent stations, Taft sold the group to TVX for $240 million—a loss of some $520 million.

pay or a seller should ask: market size, market location (depressed industrial city or expanding Sunbelt area), radio format or television network affiliation, equipment, competitive position within the market, financing arrangements, and so on.

As a rule of thumb, however, the selling price of an FM station or an AM/FM combination should come to about 2.5 times the station's annual gross revenue, or 10 times its annual cash flow (operating revenues less operating expenses); for a stand-alone AM station, the price would be closer to 1.5 times gross revenue or 5 times cash flow. Formulas for estimating prices for television stations include multiplying gross revenue by 2.5, cash flow by 12, and the number of station viewers by $2,000.

As shown in Exhibit 8–9, the average price for an operating AM radio station in 1988 came close to $900,000, whereas the FM station price exceeded $4 million. By 1989 the top radio station price had reached $75 million, the amount Legacy Broadcasting received in 1988 from Command Communications for KJOI-FM in Los Angeles. The latter company paid the most ever for an AM station, $50 million, when it bought KRLD, Dallas, from Metropolitan Broadcasting. In 1987, Infinity Broadcasting Corp. paid $82 million for KVIL in Dallas, the record for an AM/FM combination.* Then, setting the record for a group, Infinity's 1988 sale of its 15 radio stations cost an investor group, made up of three of Infinity's senior executives, $484 million.

The average price for a television station in 1988 exceeded $25 million. At one time, independent television stations sold for much lower prices than network affiliates. In the mid-1970s, some independents began to increase in value. KTLA-TV, an independent station in Los Angeles, sold in 1983 for $245 million; two years later, Golden West Stations sold it to Tribune Broadcasting for a record-setting $510 million, an increase in value of some $280,000 for *each day* Golden West had owned the station. It was the highest price ever paid for any television station—affiliate, or independent.

---

*Because KVIL-AM accounted for only about $1 million of the price, the deal actually set the FM record price of $81 million.

EXHIBIT 8–9 Radio and Television Station Trading

	Radio		Television	
	Number	Average price	Number	Average price
1978	586	$565,797	51	$5,680,804
1980	424	$801,024	35	$15,261,428
1982	597	$788,480	30	$17,589,180
1984	782	$1,249,391	82	$15,268,582*
1986	959	$1,553,838	128	$21,168,093
1988	845	$2,179,444	70	$25,427,971

*Of the 82 television transactions in 1984, 31 involved only construction permits, not operating stations. If the former (valued at less than $1 million each) are discounted, the average price per station was nearly $24.6 million.

Prices for individual stations vary widely, depending on market size and such other factors as whether a radio station is AM or FM (in 1988 the average AM station sold for $894,294; the average FM station for $4,147,014; and the average AM/FM combination for $3,842,030) and whether a television station is VHF or UHF, affiliate or independent.

SOURCE: *Broadcasting*, 13 Feb. 1989, pp. 42 and 54.

Cable System Sales A rule of thumb for measuring the price of a cable system involves assigning a dollar value to each household that subscribes to the system. In the early 1980s that figure averaged about $300 per subscriber. By the late 1980s the combination of cable deregulation, the financial problems of some independent television stations, and the record-high prices being paid for some broadcast properties made cable the most widely trafficked of the electronic media. As a result, the per-subscriber price for cable systems reached $2,000 and, in several instances, even higher. Like similar formulas for determining selling prices for radio and television stations, this per-subscriber method yields only very rough estimates. It ignores such factors as geographical locations, number of homes passed by the system (which represent potential subscribers), age and channel capacity of the system, amount of system construction remaining, number of pay-channel subscribers, level of subscription rates, and the influence of franchise conditions and expiration date.

A method of establishing value that does account for some of the above-mentioned factors involves projecting a system's cash flow (operating revenues less operating expenses) for the first year of operation following the proposed sale. Recent selling prices have, on the average, been about 12 times the first year's projected cash flow.

As with radio and television station sales, brokers arrange most cable-system sales, taking fees of 2 to 6 percent of the purchase price or, in some cases, accepting part ownership of a system in lieu of a cash commission.

As of the end of 1988, the largest cable-system transaction was the purchase of Storer Communication's cable systems by Tele-Communication Inc., Comcast Corp., and Knight-Ridder Inc. for about $2.8 billion. The price equaled a cost per subscriber of about $2,050 and a cash flow multiple of slightly less than 12.5.

Cable Network Sales The cable industry's settling and maturing process in the 1980s gave rise to a number of sales and mergers of cable networks. In 1983 Showtime and The Movie Channel merged but continued to operate as separate networks; the owners hoped that the combination would compete better with the leading pay service, HBO. The following year, Showtime/The Movie Channel bought out a competing service, Spotlight, a pay-cable network founded in 1981 by Times Mirror, and absorbed Spotlight's subscribers. Finally, after six years of operation, Showtime/The Movie Channel showed a profit in 1984.

The inability of advertising to support more than a limited number of cable program services led to mergers and acquisitions. For example, in 1984 Daytime and the Cable Health Network combined to create a new advertiser-supported service called Lifetime. In the same year, ABC, which already owned 15 percent of ESPN, purchased the remaining 85 percent for $202 million, selling 20 percent of the

service four months later to Nabisco for $60 million. Also in 1984, HBO acquired a 15 percent interest in BET (Black Entertainment Television), a struggling cable network specializing in minority programming, assuming responsibility for marketing it to cable systems and advertisers.

In 1985, in a complex series of deals valued at $690 million, Viacom (a major MSO, programmer, and syndicator and half-owner of Showtime/The Movie Channel) acquired full ownership of Showtime/TMC and of MTV Networks (operator of three basic cable services: MTV, VH-1, and Nickelodeon). These acquisitions made Viacom the largest cable programmer, and the only programmer with significant stakes in both basic and pay-cable services.

Early cable television owners promised that their new services, with their many channels, would deliver programming not regularly offered by the commercial television networks, such as cultural programs, attractive to select, rather than mass, audiences. They spoke of *narrowcasting* as superior to broadcasting. Over time, however, economic reality made it impossible for cable to deliver fully on its cultural promises. For example, in 1982, after sustaining some $30 million in losses, CBS closed down its cultural channel, CBS Cable, for lack of advertiser support. In 1984, hoping to consolidate resources and advertiser dollars, two other cultural programming networks, Arts and the Entertainment Channel, merged to form the new Arts & Entertainment network.

Other specialty cable program services suffered as well and began merging to survive. For example, in 1988 Cable Value Network, the largest cable home shopping service, took over the bankrupt America's Shopping Channel and Fashion Channel Network, which had sustained annual losses of more than $18 million.

8.6
Personnel

The number of people employed in an industry usually gives some indication of its importance. However, although the electronic media employ

EXHIBIT 8–10   South Florida Merry-Go-Round

In Miami, FL, in 1988, for the only time in television history, one of the big three television networks owned and operated a local station that had primary affiliation with one of the other networks.

The bizarre scenario began in 1983 with the death of Mitchell Wolfson. Wolfson had founded WTVJ(TV), the Miami CBS affiliate, in 1949 and, although it was only a part of his Wometco conglomerate, he maintained a personal involvement in the station. For example, the news director reported not to the station general manager but directly to Wolfson, the owner, an arrangement unheard of elsewhere.

After Wolfson died, surviving family members in 1984 sold Wometco, including WTVJ, to the investment firm of Kohlberg, Kravis, Roberts (KKR) for $842 million. Lorimar-Telepictures agreed in May 1986 to buy just the station from KKR for a staggering $405 million, but backed out of the deal five months later.

Meanwhile, the CBS television network, by that time with only four owned-and-operated stations that together reached less than 20 percent of U.S. television households, was looking to enlarge its portfolio. When the Lorimar-Telepictures deal fell through, CBS offered to buy WTVJ(TV), but bid only $170 million.

While continuing to negotiate with KKR, CBS also began talks with TVX, owner of WCIX(TV), a Miami VHF independent station on channel 6. If CBS bought WCIX and moved its affiliation there, the value of WTVJ would drop dramatically. Although this threat gave CBS a strong bargaining position, KKR also realized that WCIX suffered from a signal problem (because of potential interference on channel 6 from Orlando 250 miles to the north), making WCIX a less attractive investment for CBS.

But while CBS negotiated with both KKR and TVX, KKR also carried on talks with another network, NBC. For some time NBC had been trying to buy its Miami affiliate, WSVN(TV), but the owner had refused to sell. The big surprise came in January 1987, just 15 days after WSVN had renewed its NBC affiliation agreement for another two years, when NBC announced its purchase of WTVJ, the CBS affiliate, for $270 million. WSVN's owner, Edward Ansin, outraged at the threatened loss of his NBC affiliation, complained to the FCC and filed suit against everyone involved, claiming violation of antitrust laws. But to no avail. Thus, when the deal closed in September of that year, NBC owned and began to operate a station *still affiliated with CBS*.

The story does not end there, however. WSVN, which had been an NBC affiliate since 1962, faced the prospect that NBC would switch its affiliation to WTVJ as soon as its contract with WSVN expired. Ansin began affiliation talks with CBS but refused to give up his NBC affiliation until his contract expired in 1989. He wanted to stay with the number one network as long as possible, especially to benefit from NBC's 1988 Olympics and World Series coverage.

Fearing that Ansin's delaying tactics might leave it in the end with no affiliate at all, in August 1988 CBS bought WCIX for $59 million—not an unreasonable price for an independent, but a steal for a station that would in fact become a network affiliate. Still, WCIX did have those signal problems, particularly in the rapidly growing areas north of Miami. Early speculation had it that CBS would make a large donation to WPBT(TV), Miami's channel 2 public station, in exchange for WPBT's agreement to swap channels. When WPBT turned down that proposal, CBS convinced WPEC, the ABC affiliate in West Palm Beach, 60 miles north of Miami, to change its affiliation to CBS, thus assuring the network good coverage in the northern areas not served by WCIX. To convince WPEC to make the switch, CBS made a cash payment to the station for new equipment and increased its network compensation rate.

relatively few people, they nevertheless loom large because of the significance of media work.

Work Force Size   The broadcast and cable industries in the aggregate employ 600,000 people full time. This contrasts with General Motors, for example, a single corporation with more than 900,000 employees. However, many highly specialized creative firms undergird the media, producing materials ranging from station identification jingles to prime-time entertainment series. These firms offer more opportunities for creative work than the me-

EXHIBIT 8–10   Continued

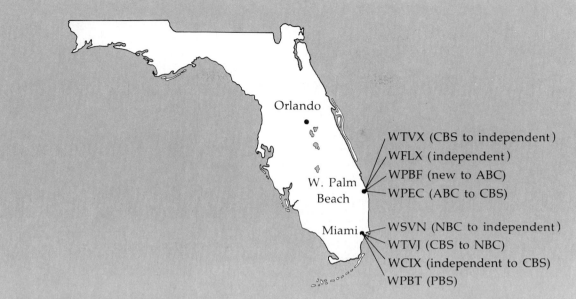

Orlando

WTVX (CBS to independent)
WFLX (independent)
WPBF (new to ABC)
WPEC (ABC to CBS)

W. Palm
Beach

WSVN (NBC to independent)
Miami   WTVJ (CBS to NBC)
WCIX (independent to CBS)
WPBT (PBS)

This left WSVN as the odd party out. The affiliation loss had reduced the value of the station, once estimated at perhaps $300 million, by half or more. Ansin had to face becoming an independent station operator after a quarter-century as an NBC affiliate. He vowed to maintain his affiliate-quality local news operation and, in October 1988, worked out details of an affiliation agreement with the emergent Fox network, formerly carried by WCIX.

But even that does not end the story. Observers expected WTVX, the former CBS UHF affiliate serving West Palm Beach, to pick up that city's ABC affiliation now that WPEC planned to switch to CBS, but the WTVX owners miscalculated. WTVX tried for the ABC contract, as did WFLX, a West Palm Beach independent. But ABC affiliated instead with WPBF-TV, a Palm Beach UHF station not yet even on the air. Actually, the network *sold* the affiliation—a first in network–affiliate relations history. WPBF agreed to waive all network compensation, making a financial deal with ABC that was undisclosed as to details but that represented an estimated overall benefit to the network of at least $1.5 million a year.

Early in the morning of January 1, 1989, the switches went into effect. WTVJ, channel 4 in Miami, went from CBS to NBC. WCIX, channel 6, went from independent to CBS. WSVN, channel 7, went from NBC to independent. WPEC, channel 12 in West Palm Beach, went from ABC to CBS. WPBF, channel 25, went on the air as the Palm Beach ABC affiliate. WTVX, channel 34, went from CBS to independence. And viewers throughout south Florida went to their *TV Guides* to try to sort the whole mess out.

dia themselves—performing, writing, directing, designing, and so on. Many other types of related work take place in advertising agencies, sales representative firms, program-syndicating organizations, news agencies, common carriers, and the motion picture business. Exhibit 8–11 gives employment statistics for the various nonnetwork units of the broadcast and cable industry.

Aside from the major television networks, most broadcast and cable organizations have small staffs. The number of full-time employees at radio stations ranges from fewer than 5 for the smallest markets

EXHIBIT 8–11   Broadcast and Cable Employment

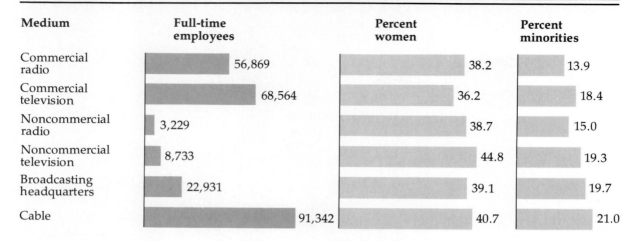

Medium	Full-time employees	Percent women	Percent minorities
Commercial radio	56,869	38.2	13.9
Commercial television	68,564	36.2	18.4
Noncommercial radio	3,229	38.7	15.0
Noncommercial television	8,733	44.8	19.3
Broadcasting headquarters	22,931	39.1	19.7
Cable	91,342	40.7	21.0

These statistics represent broadcast and cable employment, based upon reports from only those nonnetwork units that have five or more full-time employees.

Although much smaller than broadcasting's, the younger cable industry's work force is growing more rapidly, and the representation by women and minorities in cable exceeds that in commercial radio and television.

SOURCES: FCC, *Broadcast and Cable Employment Trend Reports,* Washington, DC, 13 Jan. 1989 (broadcast) and 29 Dec. 1988 (cable).

to about 60 for the largest, with the average being 15. Television stations have between 20 and 300 employees, with a typical network affiliate employing about 90 and an independent station about 60 full-time people.

Cable systems average about 30 full-time employees but range from family-run systems in small communities with perhaps five or six employees to large-city systems with staffs of well over 100. Cable MSO headquarters units average about 55 full-time employees. Cable networks, too, vary in staff size depending on several factors, including subscriber count, the amount and type of original programming offered, and whether or not the service relies on advertising for support.

Salary Scales   The huge salaries reported in gossip columns go to top talent, creative persons, and executives, working mostly at network headquarters and the production centers of New York and Hollywood.* Average salaries for jobs at most stations and cable systems rank as moderate at best, governed by basic laws of supply and demand. Typically, those working in sales earn the highest incomes at broadcast stations. Sales executives sometimes have higher incomes than many others in management. At the department-head level, general sales managers usually make the most money and promotion managers tend to make the least, with program managers falling somewhere between the two. Exhibit 8–12 offers information about starting salaries for new college graduates in media

---

*In 1989, Dan Rather of CBS news reportedly earned the highest salary of any broadcast nonentertainment personality: $2.5 million per year. Laurence Tisch, president and chief executive officer of CBS (and, thus, Rather's boss) earned just over $1 million.

EXHIBIT 8–12 Median Starting Salaries for New College Graduates

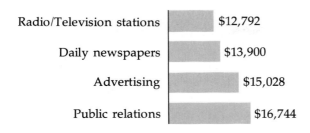

Radio/Television stations	$12,792
Daily newspapers	$13,900
Advertising	$15,028
Public relations	$16,744

The significantly higher salaries earned by college graduates taking their first jobs in public relations and advertising may account for the increasing popularity of those majors at colleges throughout the United States.

SOURCE: Based on a survey, conducted by the Ohio State University School of Journalism, of 1,252 bachelor's degree recipients who completed their programs in journalism and mass communication in May or June of 1987 at one of the 53 schools participating in the survey.

or media-related jobs, whereas Exhibit 8–13 gives average salaries for those already working in broadcasting.

News jobs rank among the better-paying non-supervisory positions in television. A 1987 survey conducted for the Radio-Television News Directors Association found that television news reporters earned a median annual salary of $16,900; anchors earned between $26,000 and $38,000. Radio paid a good deal less, with reporters at $13,000 and anchors at $16,000. Median annual salaries for television and radio news directors showed the same disparity, with TV at $38,000 and radio at $16,800.

Employee benefits can represent a significant addition to a worker's income. About 98 percent of all television stations contribute to employees' health insurance, 88 percent pay for at least part of a life insurance policy, and 64 percent have retirement or pension plans. Radio stations, on the other hand, provide considerably less: only 80 percent contribute to an employee's health insurance, 58 percent

contribute to life insurance, and just 18 percent have retirement or pension plans.

Employment of Women   The FCC enforces Equal Employment Opportunity (EEO) Act standards for broadcast stations, cable systems, and headquarters operations with five or more employees. These standards require an annual report (FCC Form 395) classifying employees according to nine major job categories and according to sex and minority status.

In its annual employment study of all broadcast stations with five or more employees, the FCC reported that in 1988 women occupied more than 38 percent of all jobs, up from 32 percent in 1979. Perhaps more important, women represented 31 percent of the employees classified as *Officials and Managers* (up from 23 percent in 1979) and 49 percent of those classified as *Sales Workers* (up from 31 percent in 1979). (Exhibit 8–11 offers a more detailed analysis of the FCC report.) A 1988 survey by American Women in Radio and Television, however, found less than 10 percent female representation among broadcast station general managers and owners (*Broadcasting,* 20 June 1988: 55).*

For cable systems with five or more employees in 1988, FCC reports reveal similarities with broadcasting. Women constituted nearly 41 percent of all employees and more than 34 percent of officials and managers. The potentially lucrative area of sales saw major improvement; women held nearly 45

*A widely publicized sex-discrimination case involved Christine Craft, hired in 1980 as co-anchor at KMBC-TV, the Metromedia station in Kansas City, MO. Craft claimed that, although she had been assured that her position depended on journalistic talent and not on her appearance, when her bosses critiqued her performance they spent most of their time picking apart her makeup and clothes. The station replaced her in 1981, explaining, she alleged, that she was "too old, too unattractive and not deferential to men." Craft sued for $3.5 million and in 1984 won $225,000 in actual and $100,000 in punitive damages. The court based the award on a finding of fraud; she lost on her claims of sex discrimination and equal-pay violations. In 1985, an appellate court overturned the award, and in 1986 the U.S. Supreme Court closed the case by refusing to hear Craft's appeal. Only one Supreme Court Justice—Sandra Day O'Connor, the sole woman on the court—voted to hear the case.

EXHIBIT 8–13 Television and Radio Station Average Annual Salaries

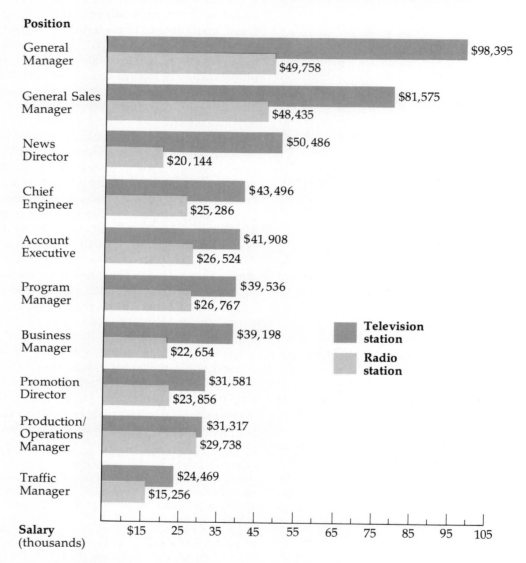

Position

General Manager — Television $98,395 / Radio $49,758

General Sales Manager — Television $81,575 / Radio $48,435

News Director — Television $50,486 / Radio $20,144

Chief Engineer — Television $43,496 / Radio $25,286

Account Executive — Television $41,908 / Radio $26,524

Program Manager — Television $39,536 / Radio $26,767

Business Manager — Television $39,198 / Radio $22,654

Promotion Director — Television $31,581 / Radio $23,856

Production/Operations Manager — Television $31,317 / Radio $29,738

Traffic Manager — Television $24,469 / Radio $15,256

Television station

Radio station

Salary (thousands) — $15 25 35 45 55 65 75 85 95 105

All jobs at television stations command higher average annual salaries than comparable positions at radio stations.

SOURCES: Based on data in *Television Employee Compensation & Fringe Benefits Reports,* National Association of Broadcasters (Washington, DC, 1988) and *Radio Employee Compensation & Fringe Benefits Report,* National Association of Broadcasters (Washington, DC, 1988).

percent of those jobs in 1988, up from only 30 percent in 1983.

Minority Employment

Minority Employment   EEO rules also require stations to report on their efforts to upgrade the employment opportunities of minority-group members. Their progress has been slower than that of women. The FCC reported that in 1988 minorities represented almost 17 percent of all broadcast employees, an improvement of only 3 percentage points over 1979. The percentage of minority members holding sales jobs increased from just over 8 percent in 1979 to more than 10 percent in 1988. The report for officials and managers turned out somewhat better in terms of progress, if not in terms of absolute numbers: in 1988 minorities held nearly 11 percent of the top jobs, up from just under 8 percent in 1979.

FCC enforcement of EEO rules has been somewhat less vigorous for cable than for broadcasting. Still, cable has outpaced broadcasting in terms of its total workforce. Of all workers at cable systems in 1988, minorities amounted to about 21 percent, compared with less than 12 percent in 1979. Of those classified as officials and managers, minorities held more than 10 percent of the jobs, an increase from less than 7 percent five years earlier.*

Unions

Unions   Unionization in broadcasting and cable prevails at the networks, the national production centers, and most large-market network television affiliates, but not at the smaller-station and cable system level. The fragmentation of the industry into so many units—mostly, as we have seen, with relatively small staffs, some of whose people perform more than one type of job—usually makes unionization of small stations impracticable. For example,

a small radio station cannot afford to assign two employees to record interviews, paying one as a technician to operate the equipment and the other as a performer to do the talking, when the job could just as easily be done by one employee.

Unionization of electronic media reflects the fact that these media draw upon types of personnel first unionized in older industries—electrical work, music, motion pictures, stage, and newspapers. Most of the 40-odd unions to which broadcasting and cable employees belong cover workers in other media as well. Thus the American Federation of Musicians, whose marathon battle to control the use of recorded music is described in Section 3.2, represents every kind of professional musician, from players in symphony orchestras to pianists in bars.

People who work in broadcasting and cable can be grouped into two broad categories, the creative/performing group and the crafts/technical group. Unions divide along similar lines; those representing the former usually avoid the word *union,* calling themselves guilds, associations, or federations.

The first pure broadcasting union, American Federation of Television and Radio Artists (AFTRA), began (originally as AFRA) in 1937, representing that universal radio performer, the announcer. Most of the creative/performing unions, however, came from the stage and motion pictures. Examples include the Writers Guild of America (WGA), the American Guild of Variety Artists (AGVA), and the Screen Actors Guild (SAG). When videotape came to rival film as a medium of production, SAG and AFTRA both claimed jurisdiction over performers recorded by the new medium. AFTRA finally won. Many actors now belong to both unions, each of which has about 70,000 members.

The creative unions have played a significant role in forcing adaptation of contract terms to take belated account of developments in technology. The fact that filmmaking contracts had no provisions covering television kept feature films off the air in the 1950s. SAG went on strike in 1960 (when Ronald Reagan was president of the union) to force higher scales for *residuals,* the payments made to performers and others for repeated showings of recorded programs on television. SAG has collected residuals

---

*Broadcasters and cable system operators also must avoid discrimination on the basis of age. In 1980 an Illinois radio station fired a 51-year-old disc jockey after changing its format from beautiful music to MOR/adult contemporary. He had been with the station for 9 1/2 years. Claiming that he had been terminated because of his age, he brought suit against the station. The jury in his 1984 trial agreed and awarded him $194,000 in damages, double the amount of his back pay (*Broadcasting,* 19 Nov. 1984).

EXHIBIT 8–14   A Woman's Place Is in the Newsroom

The path for women to equal job opportunity in broadcasting has been bumpy and long, but some progress has been made.

In 1948 ABC hired Pauline Frederick as the first woman network news correspondent. She remained the sole female hard-news network reporter for the next 12 years. In her early years, when assigned to interview the wives of presidential candidates at national political conventions, she was also required to apply their on-camera makeup. Later she became famous for her coverage of the UN, first as a correspondent for ABC, then with NBC.

In 1976 ABC hired Barbara Walters as the first woman anchor on a weekday evening network newscast. She shared the anchor desk with Harry Reasoner. Her salary: $1 million a year ($500,000 for anchoring and $500,000 for producing and hosting four entertainment specials a year), plus perquisites (a private office decorated to her taste, a private secretary, a makeup consultant, and a wardrobe person). Walters had established her reputation as co-host of NBC's *Today* show and as a successful, if sometimes controversial,

interviewer of famous personalities as diverse as Princess Grace of Monaco, Fred Astaire, Ingrid Bergman, and Fidel Castro. Her tenure as anchor ended in 1977, and she moved on to more celebrity interviews and to ABC's news magazine *20/20.*

After earning a journalism degree in 1969, Connie Chung worked at a Washington, DC, independent station. In 1971 she was hired by CBS as a Washington correspondent. Five years later she became news anchor at CBS's O&O station KNXT in Los Angeles and was reportedly the highest paid local anchor in the country. She joined NBC in 1983 as early morning anchor, took over the Saturday *Nightly News,* and became the regular substitute for Tom Brokaw on the weekday evening newscast. In 1989 she rejoined CBS, this time as anchor of its Sunday evening newscast and of her own program, *Saturday Night with Connie Chung,* serving also as one of Dan Rather's substitutes on the CBS weekday evening news.

SOURCES: Wide World Photos (Frederick); © 1989 Capital Cities/ABC, Inc. (Walters); CBS News Photo (Chung).

Pauline Frederick   Barbara Walters   Connie Chung

for members since 1954, much as ASCAP and BMI collect copyright payments on behalf of composers. In fact, some performers lucky enough to appear in particularly popular syndicated series became known as "residual millionaires."

New technology triggered strikes in 1980–1981 involving several unions. This time they fought over the income from the sale of recorded programs to the pay-television, videocassette, and videodisc markets. Videocassette revenue and residuals again played a role in 1985 and 1988 Writers Guild strikes. Although they also wanted greater creative control over their product, Guild members sought primarily to prevent program producers from reducing payments to writers for reruns of hour-long series sold in syndication. The 1988 strike lasted 22 weeks, causing a delay in the start of the fall television season and a further drop in network audiences.

Technical unions became active in broadcasting early in its history. The first successful strike against a broadcasting station may have been one in St. Louis in 1926, organized against radio station KMOX by the International Brotherhood of Electrical Workers (IBEW), a technicians' union founded in the late 19th century by telephone linemen.

In 1953 NBC technicians formed a separate association of their own that ultimately became the National Association of Broadcast Engineers and Technicians (NABET), the first union exclusively for broadcasting technicians. Later the union changed the word *Engineers* to *Employees* to broaden its scope. Competition between NABET and IBEW has caused many jurisdictional disputes. A third technical union, an old rival of IBEW, the International Alliance of Theatrical Stage Employees and Moving Picture Machine Operators of the United States and Canada (IATSE), entered the television scene from the motion picture industry.*

Employment Opportunities   Surveys of students enrolled in college electronic media programs indicate that most want to work either in on-camera or on-mike positions, or in creative behind-the-camera positions. The oversupply of candidates makes these the *least* accessible to beginners. The delegation by broadcast stations and cable systems of creative work to outside production companies means that such work concentrates in a few major centers, where newcomers face fierce competition and where unions control entry (see Exhibit 8–15).

News, the one field in which *local* production still flourishes, offers an exception to the dearth of production jobs at stations and systems. Nearly all broadcast stations and some cable systems employ news specialists. According to the National Association of Broadcasters, in 1987 the average radio station had 6 news people and the average television station had 30.

Sales offers another employment area likely to expand. All commercial networks and stations, as well as a growing number of cable systems, employ salespeople; moreover, the highest managerial positions historically have been filled from the ranks of sales personnel (although, in recent years, more and more general managers have come out of news). Advertising agencies and national sales representative firms offer entry-level employment opportunities. Nevertheless, personnel directors frequently complain that college-trained job applicants fail to comprehend the financial basis of the industry and its profound influence on every aspect of operations.

Promotion represents another area of potential growth. Stations, systems, and networks promote themselves both to the public and to potential advertisers. Cable networks also use promotion to help persuade cable systems to buy their offerings. As technologies proliferate and competition intensifies, so does the need for creative and effective promotion.

---

*Other unions not normally associated with broadcasting occasionally look to radio or television for new members. In 1974 the locally powerful Teamsters Union organized the NBC affiliate in Chattanooga, TN. The union contract covered all employees at the station except management and a security guard. It included not only engineers and technicians but also the clerical staff, news reporters, and even salespeople. After some early stormy years during which several strikes occurred, employee support diminished, and by the early 1980s the union no longer had a contract with the station.

EXHIBIT 8–15   Advice for Job Seekers

The International Radio and Television Society, The Radio-Television News Directors Association, and The National Association of Television Program Executives commissioned The Roper Organization to conduct a survey of media executives' attitudes concerning the educational preparation received by students seeking careers in broadcasting and cable. Some examples of their opinions:

■ Entry-level job applicants often have unrealistic career expectations. They expect too high a starting salary, they expect to advance too quickly, and they come to the job with a misguided impression of the industry.

■ Recent college graduates will find their best opportunities in *sales* (cited by 49 percent of those responding), *news* (cited by 32 percent), and *production* (28 percent).

■ Nonacademic considerations receive more weight than academic and formal credentials when broadcasters evaluate a candidate for an entry-level position. They regard as most important the applicant's *general presentation, writing skills and style, experience in the industry, and hands-on experience* in actual work situations.

■ Nearly three-fourths of the respondents ranked a four-year undergraduate education as either *essential* or *important.* They placed less importance, however, on a graduate degree.

■ Two-thirds of the executives considered a journalism or a communication degree as an important consideration in evaluating a prospective employee; almost half felt that way about a liberal arts background.

■ Broadcasters generally expect students to come to the job knowing the *basic* elements required for work in the industry—*writing skills,* the *basics of broadcasting, knowledge of equipment operation,* and *communication skills.*

Not everyone agreed with all the findings. For example, Professor Robert O. Blanchard, chairman of the Department of Communication at Trinity University, argued that:

The worlds of the media professionals and mass communication educators overlap only minimally. The obsession of professionals, by nature, is with the present or, more likely, with the immediate past. . . . What they do is based on what worked, or didn't work, last season. The university tradition reflects concern with identifying, assessing and transmitting enduring skills, principles and values, and understanding what they hold for the future. . . . The future for us is symbolized for our times with the advent of the 21st century, where today's students will be living and working most of their adult lives. It will be conceptual skills and principles and values, not last season's entry-level skills, that will guide them through our fast-changing and expanding information society (Robert O. Blanchard, "Put the Roper Survey on the Shelf—We Have Our Own Agenda," *Feedback,* Broadcast Education Association, Summer 1988).

SOURCE: The Roper Organization Inc., "Electronic Media Career Preparation Study," Executive Summary, December 1987.

Although approximately two-thirds of all jobs in cable fall in the technical category, emphasizing electronics and engineering, other areas also have high priority. Marketing, marketing research, and advertising stand at the top of this list. The need for creative people will also increase as more cable systems gear up for public access and local origination programming.

But if applicants look only to broadcasting and cable as their suppliers for jobs, they will seriously limit their employment opportunities. The electronic media have become so pervasive in our American society that virtually every large organization that has any contact with the public uses them in one form or another. Opportunities for production and writing jobs exist at manufacturing and retail firms, religious institutions, educational and health organizations, foundations, government agencies, the armed services, and specialized production companies.

Many such organizations make extensive in-house use of closed-circuit television. Some firms, such as IBM, use teleconferencing networks. The Ford Motor Company produces daily newscasts, complete with field reporters, for its Ford Communications Network, beaming them by closed-circuit television to 180,000 employees in 270 factories and offices in North America. Automotive Satellite Television Network provides 40 hours of programming each month to about 3,000 car dealers.

These and others in the rapidly growing field of *industrial video* apply broadcast techniques to job-skills training, management development, sales presentations, and public relations. Such nonbroadcast uses of television require trained personnel for production, direction, writing, studio operations, program planning, and other tasks that originated as occupational specialties of broadcasting.

Summary

▌ Broadcast stations fulfill four functions: general and administrative, technical, programming, and sales. Station organization follows the same pattern, with subheadings for news, production, traffic, and other specialized functions.

▌ Stations differ according to whether they are network affiliates or independents and whether they are individually owned or part of a group.

▌ Broadcast networks organize along lines similar to stations, with added responsibilities for program distribution and station relations. Most affiliates are not owned by networks; rather, they have a contractual relationship with networks. Each network has a few highly profitable owned-and-operated stations.

▌ The most important provision of affiliated contracts specifies station compensation for time used for network programming. Such compensation amounts to only a small percentage of affiliates' revenues.

▌ Affiliates have the legal right to refuse to clear time for network programs; the prime-time access rule limits the amount of prime time that affiliates in the top 50 markets may clear for network programs.

▌ Cable systems perform the same four functions as commercial broadcast stations, plus marketing the systems' services to subscribers. The programming function is more extensive than at a broadcast television station because of multiple cable channels.

▌ Cable networks are of two types: advertiser-supported (or basic) and pay. Subscribers usually receive ad-supported networks at no additional cost as part of the system's basic package of programming. They pay an extra monthly fee for commercial-free pay networks.

▌ Many cable systems also carry the programming of superstations, independent television stations that distribute their signals by satellite throughout the country.

▌ Capital expenditures in broadcasting and cable range from a few thousand dollars for a small radio station to many millions for cable and satellite operations. A significant portion of the total industry capital investment is made by the consumer through the purchase of radios and television sets.

▌ Some of the profit in broadcasting and cable comes from the buying and selling of stations and systems. Investors are attracted to the industry because of its typically high profit margin.

▌ Many factors influence the price of a station or cable system, but rough estimates are made using various formulas such as multiples of projected cash flow.

▌ Relative to their social impact, broadcasting and cable have small work forces.

▌ The percentage of broadcasting jobs held by women and minorities has increased in recent years but still falls far short of the percentage held by white males.

▌ Broadcast employees are unionized at the network level and in major production centers, but most stations and cable systems are not targets for unionization because their employees are few in number and often do several jobs.

▌ News and sales offer the best employment chances for newcomers to broadcasting. Technical and marketing people are most in demand in the cable industry. Other opportunities exist in industrial, nonbroadcast video.

CHAPTER 9

REVENUE SOURCES
AND PROFITS

Radio and television broadcasting is the largest *national* advertising medium. Only newspapers surpass television in *total* advertising volume. Radio comes fourth in total advertising dollars, after direct mail but ahead of magazines. Advertising on cable, although rapidly increasing, remains small relative to other electronic media (Exhibit 9–1). The remarkable overall profitability of broadcasting and cable television (despite many instances of loss and failure) invites the attention of major financial interests. A great deal of buying and selling went on during the 1980s, often involving mergers of large companies and the growth of conglomerate corporations with interests in many different aspects of the media. The deregulatory stance of the Republican administration in Washington during this period, coupled with its disinclination to invoke antimonopoly laws, encouraged these trends. One result has been a decline in the older commercial broadcasting culture, which at its best prided itself on its concern for the public interest and its role as the premier medium of public expression in a democratic society. Critics charge that in its place has come a "bottom-line mentality," focused not on making money while doing good, but just on making money.

9.1.
Advertising

Broadcasting and cable offer advertisers unique advantages, such as broad audience reach, immediacy, and flexibility. Advertising can be as local as the area covered by a single station or cable system, or as broad as a national network with virtually universal coverage. As an alternative to local or network coverage, advertisers can choose the national spot mode, which enables them to put together individual stations with any combination of coverage areas, station types, and program vehicles desired.

Coverage   Broadcast advertising falls into three categories in terms of coverage areas and image: Local, network, and national spot.

All stations, even network affiliates, function essentially as *local* advertising media, covering single markets, although their individual coverage areas vary a great deal.* As Exhibit 9–2 shows, radio de-

---

*For this reason the phrase "*local* station" can be regarded as redundant, except perhaps when used to distinguish between a low-power AM station on a local channel and stations on regional and clear channels.

EXHIBIT 9–1 Advertising Volume of Major Media, Local vs. National*

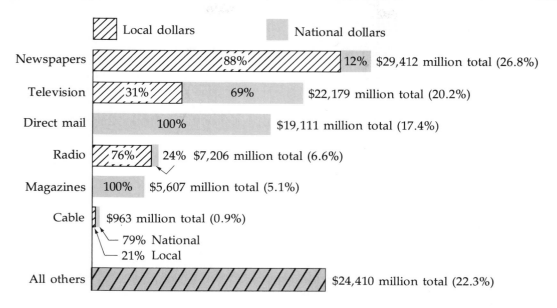

*Numbers in parentheses are percentages of total advertising expenditures in all media.

Newspapers retain the lead as the principal medium for local advertising, television leads in nonlocal advertising, and cable lags far behind all other media.

SOURCE: Based on 1987 data prepared by Robert J. Coen, McCann-Erickson, Inc.

pends on local advertising for most of its revenue, whereas television derives nearly half of its revenue from national spots. This difference reflects the historical fact that television captured most of the national advertisers, driving radio to cultivate local sources of revenue. Moreover, since radio costs far less, small local businesses find it more affordable.

Daily newspapers, broadcasting's chief rival for local advertising dollars, have far less flexibility of coverage. Most communities have only one daily newspaper. Large daily newspapers attempt to adapt their coverage to advertisers' needs by using add-on neighborhood supplements, but in many a one-newspaper town, local advertisers may choose from among two dozen or more radio and television stations with varying coverage areas.

Local broadcast advertisers consist chiefly of fast food restaurants, department and furniture stores, banks, food stores, and movie theaters. When such local firms act as retail outlets for nationally distributed products, the cost of local advertising may be shared between the local retailer (an appliance dealer, for example) and the national manufacturer (a maker of refrigerators, for example). This type of cost sharing, known as local *cooperative advertising,* or just "local co-op," supplies radio with a major source of its revenue, so much so that some stations appoint a special staff member to coordinate cooperative advertising.

When a station connects to a network, it instantaneously converts from a local to part of a regional or national advertising medium. For advertisers of

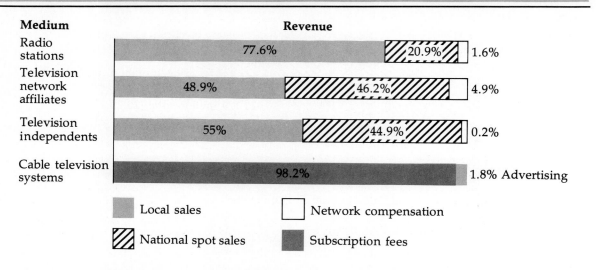

Medium	Revenue

Radio stations: Local sales 77.6%, National spot sales 20.9%, Network compensation 1.6%

Television network affiliates: Local sales 48.9%, National spot sales 46.2%, Network compensation 4.9%

Television independents: Local sales 55%, National spot sales 44.9%, Network compensation 0.2%

Cable television systems: Subscription fees 98.2%, 1.8% Advertising

Legend: Local sales · Network compensation · National spot sales · Subscription fees

Subscription fees include payments for basic and pay program services, installation, and, where available, home security and pay-per-view events.

SOURCES: Based on data in *Television Financial Report* and *Radio Financial Report,* both National Association of Broadcasters, Washington, DC, 1988; and *The Kagan Cable TV Financial Databook,* Paul Kagen Associates, Inc., Carmel, CA, 1988.

nationally distributed products, *network advertising* has five significant advantages:

▪ In a single transaction, the national network advertiser can place messages on more than 200 stations of known quality, strategically located to cover the entire country.

▪ Network advertisers can have centralized control over their advertising messages and assurance that they will be delivered at the times and in the program environments of their choice.

▪ Network advertisers benefit from sophisticated audience research analysis by their networks.

▪ Networks provide convenient centralized billing for commercial-time costs.

▪ Advertisers benefit from the prestige attached to the very fact of being network advertisers.

National spot advertising supplies an alternative to network advertising for clients who need to reach national audiences but who find networks too costly or too inflexible to meet their needs. The stations that participate in a national spot advertising campaign act in concert but do not constitute a network, which consists of *interconnected* stations. Working through their advertising agencies and the stations' national sales representatives (see Section 9.5), national spot advertisers use ad hoc collections of nonconnected stations chosen to meet particular objectives. Advertisers may choose network affiliates (of one or more networks) as well as independents to participate in national spot campaigns. The commercial announcements go out to each of the chosen stations by mail or by satellite. This means, of course, that spot advertisers lack some of the centralized control of message, timing, program environment,* and billing that network advertisers enjoy.

The national spot advertiser assembles the combination of stations that best fits the needs of the

---

*However, *barter syndication,* discussed in Section 13.2 as a form of national spot advertising, arose in part to give bartering advertisers control over the program environment in which their commercials appear.

advertised product or service. But rather than negotiating (at long distance) directly with television stations, the advertiser places an order with two or three national reps (who have offices in or near the advertiser or agency's city) for commercial time on perhaps a hundred individual stations handled by those reps.

Spot advertisers may select any program vehicles that suit their needs. This could mean spots within or between network programs, sponsorship of either local or syndicated programs, or participating spots in local or syndicated programs. National spot enables advertisers to capitalize on *local* program interests, something the network advertiser cannot do. Most of the largest national advertisers use spot and network in combination, as shown in Exhibit 9–5, to achieve better coverage than either could yield on its own.

Advantages Radio and television advertising enjoys advantages unique to those media that make them especially attractive to, and effective vehicles for, advertisers.

- Because virtually all homes have radio and television receivers, broadcasting has unrivaled access to all family members under the changing circumstances of daily living. Moreover, car and portable radios allow broadcasting to compete with magazines and newspapers as a medium that can travel with the consumer outside the home. Above all, the constant availability of broadcasting as a companion that provides entertainment and information gives it a great psychological advantage.

- Then too, programming proceeds continuously. This attribute offers advertisers a unique advantage, letting them time their messages to coincide with activities relevant to their products. For example, commercials for household products can be shown at a time of day when consumers of those products actually use them; sportswear commercials can be aired while fans are tuned to their favorite events.

- Television is the only medium that can reveal how a product works and how it affects the consumer. For example, advertisers can use vivid demonstrations to "prove" claims made for their products. Color adds to the effectiveness of demonstrations, as does participation by celebrity endorsers.

- Commercials often take the form of tiny plays that exploit all the entertainment values of the theater—character, conflict, suspense, and resolution. The wry comment that commercials often entertain more than programs contains a grain of truth. If the skill, careful crafting, attention to minute details, and lavish expenditure of money that go into creating the best commercials went into the production of programs, the vast wasteland of programming might be made to bloom. Unfortunately, multiplying the cost of making a top-quality commercial (in 1988, nearly $5,000 per second) by the number of seconds in programs would make an ordinary situation comedy as costly to produce as a major motion picture. In any case, a commercial once produced may air as a local, national spot, network, or even cable announcement.

A great deal of research and planning go into planting commercial messages at precisely the right moments to maximize their chances of being seen or heard. The newspaper reader can skip over advertisements; the commuter can ignore billboards; mail addressed to "occupant" can be dropped unopened into the wastebasket. But listeners or viewers, once their attention has been engaged, find skillfully placed broadcast commercials less easy to evade.

- The very fact of being advertised in a major medium confers a certain status on a product. Some of the feeling of confidence that people have in a medium may be unconsciously transferred to the products it advertises. Taking advantage of this transference, advertisers sometimes use the phrase "As seen on television" in newspaper ads and in supermarket point-of-sale displays.

- In addition to its psychological advantages as an advertising medium, broadcasting has the geographical advantage of functioning almost equally well locally, regionally, or nationally. The same stations that at one moment serve as local outlets may at another moment serve as outlets for national or regional networks.

Drawbacks Television's unique combination of sight, sound, movement, and color makes it the most effective and persuasive of all advertising media. But television and radio also have disadvantages that make other media more attractive for some messages. Despite their flexibility as advertising media, radio and television stations do have rigidity of defined coverage areas; many small advertisers find broadcast spots simply too expensive; the transience of broadcast spots can be a drawback; and time limitations and broadcast standards forbid or discourage some types of products and presentation styles.

■ Although the broadcast media offer wide flexibility in terms of local, network, and national spot options, their very structure presents other limitations to frustrate advertisers. Networks cover virtually the entire country through a fixed number of affiliates. Yet some advertisers would rather concentrate their messages in certain regions. A company might have limited distribution of its product or might wish to introduce a new line in specific test markets. In some circumstances (regional feeds of football games, for example) an advertiser may be able to limit the geographical exposure a network gives to its commercial. But in most cases the client must take all stations in the network lineup or none at all.

Local advertising and national spot advertising offer one solution, but even they sometimes force the advertiser to pay for superfluous audiences. The owner of an appliance dealership in a suburban mall cannot realistically expect customers to come from the entire metropolitan area. Yet the store's commercials, seen or heard throughout a broadcast station's coverage area, will reach many thousands of people who never visit that mall. In such cases, other advertising methods, such as cable, suburban newspapers, neighborhood inserts in metropolitan dailies, or direct mail brochures addressed to appropriate Zip codes, may prove more efficient.

■ The combination of limited *commercial inventory* (the list of commercial slots in the station's schedule), high demand, and large audience delivery puts television commercial prices beyond the reach of many advertisers. A 30-second announcement in the 1989 Super Bowl cost $675,000—affordable obviously by only the largest national advertisers. Even at the station level, television commercials, particularly those within or adjacent to programs that deliver large audiences, cost too much for small and medium-size businesses. Radio and some independent television stations offer lower-priced spots, but with the lower cost comes a smaller audience.

■ Brief though they may be, commercials irritate some viewers, and technology has made it all too easy (from the advertiser's viewpoint) to avoid them. Commercials typically have about a 20 percent smaller audience than the program in which they appear. And no wonder. With television remote control devices, viewers can *zap* commercials by muting the sound or changing channels when an advertising cluster begins. Or they can *flip* from channel to channel to sample other programs (a practice sometimes called *grazing*), often missing both the original program and its commercials. Viewers with "pause" and "fast forward" features on their videocassette recorders zap commercials by putting their VCRs in "pause" when the ads run, or by intermittently speeding up their machines during playback, thus *zipping* through the messages.

The practice of scheduling several commercials together in *pods* can reduce their impact on viewers who have not resorted to zapping, zipping, flipping, or grazing. During one break in its 8:00 P.M. movie in July 1988, a Miami independent television station ran 18 consecutive nonprogram events (commercials, promotional announcements, etc.) for a total of 6 minutes and 40 seconds. Advertisers who are displeased at the prospect of their commercials being buried in a pod can get the preferred positions of first or last spot in the pod—for about twice the regular price. Some (Excedrin was one of the first to use this ploy) now produce 30-second announcements in two 15-second segments, scheduling the first part at the beginning of a commercial break and the second half at the end. Broadcasters refer to these commercials as *bookends.*

▪ Broadcast commercials must make their point quickly and, if possible, memorably. The listener or viewer cannot linger over the advertisement, pondering whether or not to buy; or clip out the ad to consult it later. Most radio commercials last 60 seconds, most television commercials 30 seconds with a growing trend toward 10 and 15 seconds. Even the longest spot cannot duplicate the impact of a large-display department store ad or a supermarket ad with clip-out coupons. Nor can broadcasting compete effectively with the classified sections of newspapers. Some broadcasters and cable systems offer "want-ad" and "home shopping" segments in their programming, but these lack the convenience of newspapers: viewers must sit through all the announcements to find the one or two that interest them.

A broadcasting station has only 24 hours of "space" each day, putting a limit on its commercial inventory. Moreover, only so many commercials may be scheduled without alienating the audience. Print media, on the other hand, can expand advertising space by adding pages without alienating readers. Nor does broadcasting have anything comparable to the multipage inserts that advertisers buy in newspapers and magazines.

▪ Broadcasting also suffers from the drawback of being unavailable to advertise some products. Congress forbade cigarette advertising, and broadcasters themselves find it expedient to ban such products as hard liquor and X-rated movies.

9.2
Commercial and Other Announcements

For both legal and financial reasons, "nonprogram materials"—commercials and various other kinds of announcements—call for careful definition, scheduling, and record keeping.

Scheduling   Once a salesperson concludes an advertising sale, the contract goes to the *traffic department,* which schedules the requisite commercials and includes them in the daily log of on-the-air activities. This department's role led to the term *trafficking,* referring to the scattering of spots at scheduled times throughout the broadcast day, both between and within programs.*

Commercial placement in relation to programs, to other commercials, and to other types of announcements concerns both advertisers and programmers, giving the trafficking of commercials considerable importance. It requires specific, predictable points at which commercials can be logically inserted into the program flow.

Part of the job of scheduling commercials involves ensuring that announcements for competing products do not appear next to each other. A Buick dealership, for example, does not want its commercial immediately followed (and thus diluted) by an ad for Chevrolets. This concern applies also to *antithetical* products, which may be considered in conflict with one another, even though not directly competitive (beer and milk, for example). Today, at least at the large stations, computers automatically make these and many other scheduling decisions.

Sponsorship   Once the principal type of network advertising, *sponsorship* had the advantage of giving advertisers control over, and identification with, the sponsored programs and their stars. But sponsorship all but disappeared from network radio after television drained away national advertising. It faded from television too during the 1960s, when programs became too expensive for most advertisers to sponsor and when most advertisers, for strategic reasons, decided to scatter their messages over several programs. The term *sponsor* now usually means *any* advertiser, although historically it

---

*Some foreign systems *block schedule* commercials, concentrating them into one or two special blocks of time. This system explicitly segregates commercial from program matter, preventing interruptions in the flow of programs. It also encourages creative ads so that viewers remember them amidst so many others.

meant only one who assumed responsibility for an entire program. Today sponsorship in the original sense survives only for some daytime programs and for occasional specials, underwritten by large corporations that desire a particular type of image-building exposure.

Participation Programs   When stations took over from advertisers the responsibility for programs, they at first maintained the fiction of sponsorship by referring to advertisers whose commercials appeared during program breaks as "participating sponsors," leading to the term *participations* (or *participating spots*). Vestiges of this concept survive in *billboards* shown at the open and close of some television programs, which mention "participating" advertiser names at no added cost as an incentive to spot buyers. Billboards often introduce major sports events for which spot buyers pay premium prices; the higher prices entitle them to special treatment, such as the extra exposure they get from billboard listings.

Today most stations sell advertising simply as *spot announcements* (more briefly, *spots*). Most advertisers use *scatter-buying* strategies, distributing their spots over a number of different programs. In this way, they avoid risking too much on any one program and also gain the advantage of exposure to varied audiences. Some programs have natural breaks where spots can be inserted without interrupting the flow—the breaks between rounds of a boxing match or between record cuts on a radio show, for example. In other cases the break must be artificially contrived. Part of the art of writing half-hour situation comedies lies in building the plot to suspenseful but nevertheless logical break-off points part way through for insertion of commercials.

Opinions on what qualifies as a "natural" break differ. The industry now regards breaks between stories in newscasts as natural, but at one time interrupting news with commercials seemed not only unnatural but also highly unprofessional. Viewers often complain about the arbitrary breaks made in theatrical feature films, whose scripts do not, of course, provide seemingly natural climaxes in the action every 10 minutes. Some viewers also object

to the "television time-outs" taken during football games for the convenience not of players but of advertisers.

Sustaining Programs   Programs neither sponsored nor subject to participating spot insertions constitute *sustaining* programs, limited almost exclusively to public-affairs programs of a type that could not be commercialized without a serious breach of taste—presidential addresses and state funerals, for example. Some programs are not intended to be sustaining but become so by default: most advertisers tend to stay away from documentaries and to avoid controversy. In 1988, unable to achieve requested content changes, some sponsors at the eleventh hour pulled some $2 million worth of commercials from Geraldo Rivera's controversial but highly rated special on NBC, *Devil Worship: Exposing Satan's Underground*.

Station Breaks   Partly as a matter of law and partly as a matter of custom, stations insert *identification announcements* (IDs) between programs and between the major segments of very long programs.* Because ID announcements represent breaks in the program sequence, they are called *station break announcements*. Networks observe the ID requirement by interrupting their program feeds periodically to allow affiliates to make station identification announcements. Networks therefore schedule programs a bit short to allow affiliates time not only for ID announcements but also for one or more commercial announcements.

Promos and PSAs   Two quasi-commercial types of announcements also figure in programming at

---

*The FCC requires IDs, consisting of station call letters and the name of the community of license, at sign-on and sign-off and at hourly intervals, or at a "natural break" if a program runs longer (47 CFR 73.1201). Earlier regulation required more frequent IDs to aid in tracking down improperly operated and unauthorized stations. Today, many stations air many more IDs than are legally required as a promotional device. Sometimes a television station schedules extra IDs to reduce viewer confusion over which station they are watching on cable systems that carry stations on channel numbers other than the station's own—particularly important for viewers keeping rating diaries.

the junctures where commercials normally appear: promotional and public-service announcements.

Promotional announcements (promos) call attention to future programs of networks and stations. Although not technically commercials, they do in fact advertise stations and networks. Most broadcasters consider on-air promotion their most effective and cost-efficient audience-building tool.

Public-service announcements (PSAs) resemble commercials but promote noncommercial organizations and causes. Stations and networks broadcast them without charge. They give broadcasters a way of fulfilling some of their public-service obligations and, along with promos, also serve as fillers for unsold commercial openings.

9.3
Cable Advertising

By 1987 total cable advertising revenue reached nearly $1 billion. National networks generated about 80 percent; local systems only about 20 percent. Cable nevertheless had a long way to go to challenge the older media. In 1987 broadcasting and newspapers each accounted for about one-fourth of all advertising expenditures in all media. Cable received less than 1 percent.

Advantages   Cable shares many of television's advantages and disadvantages, with some variations of its own.

▌ *Coverage flexibility.* Cable offers varied advertising opportunities. Local firms can run commercials in cable systems' locally originated programs. Firms with several retail outlets can schedule messages on several interconnected systems. Others can buy slots made available for local insertions in ad-supported cable networks. National advertisers may place ads on more than 40 national cable networks and superstations.

▌ *Low cost.* Cable channels have smaller audiences than broadcast television, both because of smaller coverage areas and because cable's many channels fragment the audience. Cable therefore

charges less than broadcast television, though in some cases not less than radio stations.

▌ *Audience targeting.* Cable subscribers tend to be better educated and more "upscale" than the average television viewer. Cable's program specialization enables an advertiser to target a specific audience: ESPN delivers avid sports fans, MTV music-oriented teens, CNN news viewers.

▌ *Variable commercial lengths.* Although cable usually conforms to broadcasting's traditional short-length spots, cable offers opportunities for longer messages giving detailed product explanations or demonstrations. These so-called "infomercials" may run 2, 5, or even 30 minutes.

Drawbacks   Ad-supported cable has suffered from a prolonged wariness on the part of advertisers and agencies, and thus has grown less rapidly as an advertising medium than originally expected.

▌ *Viewer resistance.* Cable originally promised viewers "uncut, uninterrupted, commercial-free" television. Pay-cable networks have kept that promise, but even they may eventually find irresistible the temptation to boost their revenue by adding advertising. Surveys indicate that most cable subscribers would be willing to accept commercials as the price of lower subscriptions rates.

▌ *Poorly produced commercials.* Larger advertisers accustomed to paying their advertising agencies to produce commercials for traditional television can easily supply these commercials to cable as well. But small, local firms may have difficulties producing commercials, even simple ones, and if done poorly they can be counterproductive. To alleviate this problem, some cable systems offer local companies commercial production services free or at reduced cost as an inducement to advertise.

▌ *Commercial origination difficulties.* Radio and television stations can easily insert local commercials at scheduled points in their single program channels. Cable systems face the more complex challenge of inserting commercial messages in different program services, not only in locally originated channels but also in advertiser-supported network schedules. Broadcasters usually assign a single operator to integrate commercials and programming, but a cable system cannot afford a separate commercial integrator for each channel. Some cable systems use computer equipment triggered by electronic signals originated by cable networks to insert commercials automatically. But such expensive hardware has often proved imprecise and unreliable, sometimes rolling commercials late or even not at all.

Inadequate audience measurement. Perhaps more than anything else, lack of adequate statistical information about cable's audiences impedes the growth of cable advertising. Most advertisers measure the efficiency of their advertising by how many and what kind of people see or hear their ads. But cable's multiplicity of program choices so fractionalizes its audience that few channels attract viewers in sufficient numbers to produce statistically valid results. Rating services make some information available for the more popular national cable networks, but not for most cable channels.

9.4
Advertising Rates

Time has value for advertisers only in terms of the audiences it represents. Audiences constantly change in size and vary widely in demographic composition. As a result, so does the value of time to the advertiser.

Pricing Factors   Three relatively stable factors affect the prices advertisers pay for broadcast time: *market size, station facilities* (frequency, power, antenna location, and other physical factors that influence coverage), and *network affiliation,* if any. Station managers have no day-to-day control over any of these factors.

Three major dynamic variables exist that make one station successful and another less so: *programming, promotion,* and *sales.* Good management can lure demographically desirable audiences

away from competitors by offering attractive programs supported by effective promotion, and an efficient sales department can lure advertisers away from competitors with persuasive arguments and solicitous attention.

No standard formula for using all these variables to set appropriate broadcast rates exists. Market forces, however, eventually tend to bring prices charged for advertising to an economically rational level. The main test of reasonableness of a price is *cost per thousand* (CPM). CPM represents the cost of reaching 1,000 households or people (or any defined target group, such as men or teens or women aged 18–34). As shown in Exhibit 9–3, you calculate CPM by dividing the audience (in thousands) reached by a commercial message into the amount the broadcaster charged for that commercial. In 1987, advertisers paid an average CPM of $8.10 for a prime-time spot on one of the three major networks.

CPM helps in comparing one medium with another, one station with another, and even one program with another. CPM measurements do, however, have their limitations: they can be no better than the research on which they are based, and in any event they normally reflect past, not future, performance. Occasionally stations and networks make sales "on the come," predicting and in some cases even guaranteeing a specific CPM in advance.* Nevertheless, in the long run advertisers and advertising agencies bypass stations whose CPM gets seriously out of line with the CPMs of competing stations.

Radio Station Rates   Broadcast advertising depends for its effectiveness on cumulative effect. A buyer therefore contracts for spots in groups (a *spot schedule* or a specially priced *spot package*). Thus the *Broadcasting/Cablecasting Yearbook,* in listing sample rates of radio stations in its directory, gives the rates for one-minute spots scheduled 12 times

---

*In 1988 NBC gave advertisers extra, unpaid commercials when ratings for its Olympic programming did not meet original CPM projections. Later that year ABC faced the same problem, caused this time by disappointing ratings for its ambitious mini-series *War and Remembrance.*

EXHIBIT 9–3 Calculating CPM

The standard measure of the cost of commercial time, CPM, means *cost per thousand* (the *M* being the Roman numeral for 1,000). A commercial in television station A's evening news might, for example, cost $800; in station B's evening news, the price might be $900. But this does not necessarily mean that station A offers the preferred advertising buy. Station B might have a much larger audience than its competitor, so that, even at the higher price, its commercial might be more *cost-efficient*.

To make a valid comparison, one calculates the cost of reaching the same number of people or homes or desired demographic groups on each station. Here is the formula:

$$\frac{\text{Cost of a commercial}}{(\text{Average audience delivered} \div 1{,}000)}$$

Thus, if station A's news had an average audience of 200,000 homes, the CPM for a commercial in that program would be

$$\frac{\$800}{(200{,}000 \div 1{,}000)} = \frac{\$800}{200} = \$4$$

By comparison, if Station B delivered 300,000 homes, the CPM for a spot in its newscast would be:

$$\frac{\$900}{(300{,}000 \div 1{,}000)} = \frac{\$900}{300} = \$3$$

This calculation makes the greater cost efficiency of a commercial on station B readily apparent.

Here is an example from real life: NBC estimated that 82 million people watched the 1989 Super Bowl. A 30-second commercial in that game cost $675,000. Although an ad costing well over half a million dollars sounds expensive, the price seems less overwhelming when stated in terms of CPM: only $8.23 to reach 1,000 people. This represented an increase over the $5.91 CPM commanded by the 1988 Super Bowl and 1982's CPM of $3.24.

---

a week in four different time segments of the broadcast schedule, called *dayparts*. For example, a small, rural station in Georgia charges $4 per spot in any daypart, whereas a metropolitan station in Ohio varies its charges from a high of $95 per spot in the 6 A.M.–10 A.M. daypart (morning *drive time*) to a low of $35 in the 7 P.M.–midnight daypart.

The small station does not bother to price dayparts differently because it would hardly pay to keep track of different rates with the basic charge so low. The larger the station and market, the more expensive the time and the more refined rate differences become, reflecting even hour-to-hour changes in audience size and composition.

For detailed radio rate information, buyers consult either individual station rate cards or *Spot Radio Rates and Data,* a bimonthly publication of Standard Rate and Data Service (SRDS). This publication gathers rate-card information from some but not all stations throughout the country and presents the data in a standardized format. In addition to rates, rate cards contain such information as the following:

- *Time classes.* Typically radio stations divide their time into specific dayparts, and even subclasses of dayparts, with different prices for each.

- *Spot position.* Subclasses within dayparts usually depend on the way spots are scheduled. *Fixed-position* spots have an assured place in the schedule and earn a premium rate. *Run-of-schedule* (ROS) spots may be scheduled by a station anywhere within the time period designated in the sales contract. Some stations *rotate* spots, both *horizontally* (over different days) and *vertically* (through different time periods) to give advertisers the benefit of varying exposures for their commercials.

- *Pre-emptibility.* The price of spots may vary with the degree of *pre-emptibility* risk they face. Pre-emptible spots sell at a lower rate than fixed-position spots; the station can cancel them when a higher-paying customer wants those commercial positions. Spots sold as pre-emptible-with-no-advance-notice sell at an even lower rate than spots pre-emptible-with-advance-notice. Advertisers do not, of course, pay for a pre-empted spot. Often, when a pre-emption does occur, the station will try to get the pre-empted advertiser to accept a spot at another time. When this happens (or if a commercial does not air for technical reasons and the advertiser agrees to run it on a subsequent date), the rescheduled spot is called a *make-good*.

▌ *Package plans.* Radio and television stations offer a variety of *packages,* which may include several spots scheduled at various times and on various days or may, for example, include announcements on both an AM and a co-owned FM station. The cost of such a package totals less than the sum of the individual spots, a feature emphasized by salespersons negotiating with small local firms that have little experience in designing broadcast advertising campaigns.

▌ *Special features.* Spots associated with particular programs often earn a higher rate. Many stations list a number of features, such as live sporting events, including both local programs and certain network programs that give affiliates the right to sell spots.

TV Station Rates Listings in the SRDS *Television Spot Rates and Data* books resemble those for radio, but many television stations decline to list their rates. Most listed stations vary their rates far more than do radio stations. A television station may list more than a hundred different prices for spots, using a device known as a *rate grid.* For example, a station might list 20 different time periods or program titles down the left side of its grid. Across the top it might list 6 different rate levels, numbered I through VI. This arrangement would create 120 cells or boxes into which specific prices can be entered.

Rate levels can be defined quite arbitrarily, enabling the station to quote six different prices for the same spot. Such a grid gives sales personnel great flexibility in negotiating deals without having to resort to under-the-table rate cutting. The grid also permits a station to use the same rate card for longer periods, despite changes in audience or in advertiser demand: sales management can simply direct salespersons to negotiate within one area of the grid rather than another. The station sells spots at a higher-priced grid level at times of strong advertiser demand, and at a lower level when demand drops. Using a grid also helps in setting levels of pre-emptibility at which a commercial is likely to "hold" and not be pre-empted by a higher-paying advertiser.

Brief information on some television station rates can also be obtained from the *Broadcasting/Cablecasting Yearbook*'s station directory, but most stations prefer not to quote hard-and-fast rates for entire dayparts, especially in a publication that comes out only once a year. In fact, some television stations refrain from publishing rates in *any* form, relying instead on their sales personnel to negotiate rates with each individual client. For an idea of the range of television rates, examine Exhibit 9–4, which compares prices for television spots in markets of varying size.

Network Rates Extreme differentiation in rates occurs especially in network television. The rate for the same spot position in the same program will change even over the course of a single season if the audience for the program changes significantly. In 1988 the cost for one showing of a 30-second network spot in a regular prime-time television program averaged about $100,000; low-rated programs commanded about $50,000 per spot, whereas high-rated shows sold at $400,000 or more. Remember that these amounts represent *average* rates. Rates for specific spots in specific time slots vary widely. ABC, for example, charged $275,000 for one ad in its 1988 miniseries *War and Remembrance.* The rates cover only time charges, not commercial production costs.

Radio network ad rates also move across a wide range, influenced by daypart and audience reach. In the late 1980s, the average spot on the Westwood

EXHIBIT 9–4 Influence of Market Size on TV Rates

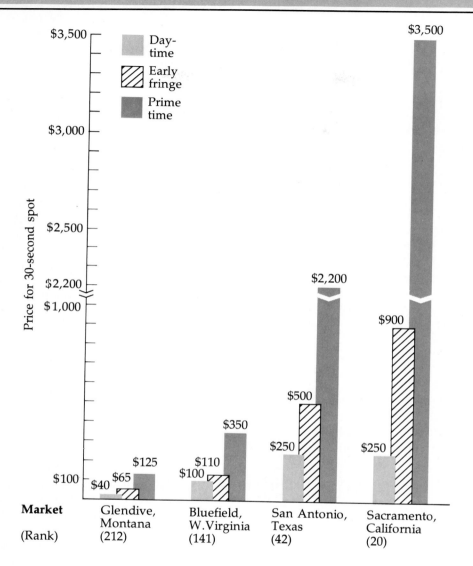

Prices refer to a specific station in each market and to rates for national advertisers. The graph shows the strong correlation between market size and rates. Because TV audiences vary more in size according to daypart than do radio audiences, TV rates vary more widely by daypart than do radio rates. Unlike small-market ratio stations, even very small-market TV stations vary rates according to daypart.

SOURCE: Based on data in station directory in *Broadcasting/Cablecasting Yearbook, 1988,* Broadcasting Publications, Inc., Washington, DC, 1988.

One network cost $900 and on ABC more than $1,000.*

Cable TV Rates

As with broadcasting, cable advertising rates vary with the size and composition of the audience exposed to the commercial. Although wide variations in audience occur within each of the three levels of the industry—local cable systems, interconnected systems, and cable networks—the most clear-cut pricing distinctions reflect those levels.

▌ *Local cable systems* offer many advertising opportunities in both locally originated programs and national program services. In 1988, about 20 percent of all cable systems accepted local ads. Rates for 30-second commercials ranged from as little as $2 up to $400 and sometimes higher.

▌ *Interconnected cable systems* combine to deliver a composite audience throughout a geographic region. The area covered by such a group of systems, called a *cable market of opportunity* (CMO), may represent anywhere from about 55,000 subscribers in the Fort Wayne, IN, CMO to more than 2 million in the New York City CMO. Several spots in selected advertiser-supported cable network programs in Fort Wayne cost as little as $24, whereas a single spot in a sporting event shown in New York City costs $2,000. The Cabletelevision Advertising Bureau publishes a directory of interconnected (but not individual) systems with coverage areas and total subscribers.

▌ *Cable networks* and *superstations,* although national in scope, do not necessarily command the highest advertising prices. Again, audience size and composition determine price. In 1988, during prime time, less than 3 percent of U.S. television households tuned in to WTBS, the highest-rated cable program service. With that rating record, WTBS could charge anywhere from $800 to $15,000 per spot. Other networks, such as The Discovery Channel and Arts & Entertainment, with prime-time ratings of less than 1, had much lower rates. Other examples: in 1988 a 30-second spot on Cable News Network cost as little as $270 during the 9 A.M.–Noon daypart and as much as $4,000 during the network's weekday morning *Moneyline* program. Commercials on MTV averaged $2,500, and on MTV's second music channel, VH-1, $400. In 1988 USA sold spots in reruns of *Miami Vice* and *Murder She Wrote* for an average of $5,500 each.

Variant Rate Practices

Three types of commercial practices used by both broadcasters and cable operators fall outside normal rate practices: trade deals, time brokerage, and per inquiry.

In the most common *trade deals* (also called *tradeouts*), stations exchange commercial time for advertiser goods and services. These might include such items as office space, office supplies, or news department vehicles.

In a more specialized type of trade deal, the advertiser exchanges game-show prizes for 7- to 10-second mentions (or *plugs*) during the show. In exchange for costly prizes, the advertiser receives one or more of the short plugs; in exchange for less expensive prizes, the advertiser must pay an additional fee to receive a single plug. This practice invokes FCC-required *sponsor identification,* usually in the form of visual or *voice-over* credits at the end of a program, ironically constituting yet another plug for the products.

A recent variation involves the donation of items for use during the production of dramatic and comedy programs. By 1988 at least half a dozen specialized *placement companies* offered producers such products as food, beverages, jewelry, and appliances at no cost in exchange for the item's on-camera appearance. The production companies save money by accepting these donations, the manufacturers receive free (or at least low-cost) advertising, and the placement companies make their money in fees paid to them by the manufacturers. This practice escapes the sponsor identification requirement because sponsors donate products that have a reasonable place in the show's story line.

*SRDS once published a booklet on radio and television network rates and data, but because the major networks stopped releasing rate details, publication ceased in 1986.

Stations that practice *time brokerage* sell time in blocks to brokers, who then resell it at a markup. Foreign-language programmers often use brokered time. The FCC once regarded time brokerage as a questionable practice because it could mean surrender of licensee control over programming, in violation of one of the FCC's most emphatic rules. However, in its 1981 report affirming radio deregulation, the FCC approved of time brokerage as a means of giving special groups access to air time. Those who could not afford to operate a station might at least be able to afford to buy a few hours of air time each week for their own use.

Per inquiry (PI) deals, favored by mail-order firms on some cable networks and in cut-rate, late-night time periods on television stations, commit the advertiser to pay not for time but for the number of inquiries or the number of items sold in direct response to PI commercials. Among the most successful PI promotion items have been record albums, audio tapes, and magazine subscriptions. Most broadcasters and cable operators oppose PI advertising in principle because it underrates the value of their advertising services. Advertising's worth cannot be judged fairly by direct sales alone because well-presented commercials can also result in intangible benefits: they can create a favorable image of the advertiser and product and imprint trade names in the audience's consciousness, thus leading to sales at a later time.

9.5
Advertising Sales

Local advertising sales practices differ somewhat from regional and national practices, with each posing its own problems. *Advertising agencies* play a key role in national sales and a major role in local sales, but national sales require additional services from network sales departments and *sales representatives*.

Local Sales The public perceives the performers as the stars of commercial broadcasting, but the broadcasting and cable businesses regard the sales-people who generate the revenue to pay the performers as the real stars. Indeed, salespeople (sometimes called "account executives") typically earn the highest incomes among radio and television employees.

Salespeople usually work on a *commission* basis, keeping a percentage of all advertising dollars they bring in. This arrangement gives them both an incentive to sell as much commercial time as possible and the opportunity to raise their income without depending on annual salary increases.

One variation of the straight-commission plan, called *draw against commission,* pays the account executive a stipulated weekly sum in anticipation of future sales. Some companies treat this arrangement as salary, whereas others consider the payments to be salary advances, repayable by the employee. Some stations pay the commission upon consummation of a sale; others wait until the commercial actually airs. Still others pay only when the station gets paid by the advertiser.

Most television sales departments employ a general sales manager, a local (and sometimes also a national) sales manager, account executives, and support staff. The number of account executives varies from station to station; about six salespeople usually suffice for a medium-market station. At some stations a sales assistant or even a secretary does all the support work; other stations also employ research people and commercial (*continuity*) writers.

Sales managers hire, fire, manage, and train salespersons, assigning them specific advertisers and ad agencies. Beginning salespeople sometimes start without benefit of an *account list* (except, by industry tradition, the telephone Yellow Pages) and must develop their own accounts by making *cold calls* on potential new advertisers.

In addition to the personal qualities needed for success in any sales job, an account executive needs one indispensable sales tool—*audience research.* He or she must reduce the myriad numbers contained in rating reports to terms understandable to a client and must present them in such a way as to show the station in the best possible light. Armed with these data (often printed up in attractive brochures), along with a list of commercial availabilities supplied by the traffic department, the local rate card (if one exists), and information on the advertising needs and history of each prospect, the salesperson sallies forth to do battle.

Radio stations compete among themselves for "radio dollars," television stations compete for television advertising budgets, and both compete with each other and with media. The cable salesperson tries to convince broadcast advertisers to allocate portions of their budgets to cable. The broadcast salesperson suggests to newspaper advertisers that some of the money they pay newspapers would draw more customers if it were diverted to radio or television commercials.

Selling ads available to the local sales department include the services of the Radio Advertising Bureau (RAB), the Television Bureau of Advertising (TvB), and the Cabletelevision Advertising Bureau (CAB). These New York–based organizations supply sales ammunition, such as specialized audience and product data and sales-promotion materials, for their respective subscribers.

In a sense the salesperson's real job begins *after* a client signs the first contract. Thereafter the salesperson nurtures the client's interest in the medium through *account servicing,* seeking to ensure renewal of the first contract and, better still, to bring in bigger contracts in the future. Such servicing includes ensuring timely station receipt of the client's commercial materials, advising the client whenever a commercial airs improperly, arranging make-goods, and informing the client of special advertising opportunities.

Regional and National Sales Stations gain access to national advertising business through *national sales representative* firms ("reps" for short) and, in the case of affiliates, network sales departments. Some stations also have *regional reps* for nonnational sales outside the station's service area. A rep contracts with a string of stations, selling their clients' time in the national and regional markets and functioning as an extension of the stations' own sales staffs. Television reps have only one client

station in any market, whereas radio reps often have more than one.

Cable systems also use sales representatives. Specialized cable reps sell local or regional advertising on individual and interconnected systems. Others, like radio and television reps, sell time on local systems to national spot advertisers.

Reps perform many services other than sales. Their national perspective provides client stations or systems with a broader view than that of merely local markets. Reps often advise clients on programming, conduct research for them, and act as all-around consultants. In return for their services, rep companies collect a commission of from 8 to 15 percent on the spot sales they make for their clients.

A list of the largest national sales reps includes Blair Television (about 130 stations); Katz Television Group (about 190 stations); Petry Television (about 90 stations); and Seltel (about 100 stations). Reps specializing in radio include Interep (about 1,200 stations) and Katz Radio Group (about 1,400 stations).

The 1980s saw the introduction of a new television sales medium: the *unwired network.* Under this concept, companies buy commercial time, usually in bulk and at a discount, from television stations throughout the United States, then sell it, at a markup, to national advertisers.* One such organization, Independent Television Network, offers a package of spots in prime-time movies on independent stations around the country, selling to clients in a one-invoice transaction. Group W Television Sales' Premier Announcement Network sells commercial time in the local news of top-50-market network affiliates. USA Network, working with Corinthian Broadcasting, combines the reach of top-50-market independent stations with the nearly 50 million homes of its cable network. Traditional sales reps strongly oppose the unwired concept, viewing it as a threat to their exclusive national representation of client stations.

---

*This practice differs from time brokerage (discussed in Section 9.4) in that here the purchase/resale is of commercial availabilities, not of program time blocks.

EXHIBIT 9–5 How Top Advertisers Spread Their Budgets

Rank	Advertiser	Total est. ad expend. (millions)	Percent of expenditure allocated to:								
			Network TV	Spot TV	Network radio	Spot radio	Network cable	News-paper	Maga-zines	Out-door	Other
1	Philip Morris	$1,558	21	7	*	2	1	3	16	3	47
2	Procter & Gamble	$1,387	27	17	2	*	2	*	6	*	46
3	General Motors	$1,025	27	10	2	3	*	17	15	*	26
4	Sears, Roebuck	$887	18	3	6	2	*	NA	2	*	NA
5	RJR Nabisco	$840	25	4	*	1	2	2	13	8	45

*Less than 1 percent
NA = Not available

All these premier advertisers chose network television for their major expenditures. Even Philip Morris, prohibited by law from advertising its cigarettes on radio or television, sells other products in sufficient quantity to warrant allocating more than 20 percent of its ad budget to the networks. Among these five firms, only three spent much on cable.

SOURCE: Based on 1987 data reported in *Advertising Age*, 28 Sept. 1988.

Major national advertisers use many different media, so that any medium must persuade advertisers and their agencies to divert as much of their advertising budgets as possible in that medium's direction. Exhibit 9–5 shows how the nation's five largest advertisers, three of which had annual expenditures of more than a billion dollars, allotted funds to the major media. Allocations differ widely, but no advertiser puts all its advertising money into a single medium. Advertising agency media directors decide on the right *media mix.*

Advertising Agencies All regional and national advertisers, and most large local advertisers as well, deal with the media through *advertising agencies.* Hundreds of such agencies exist in the United States, although the 1980s saw a trend toward mergers and consolidation, sometimes involving foreign ownership. Some firms have their own in-house agencies, but most rely on independent agen-

cies staffed with specialists able to handle a number of clients (Exhibit 9–6).

Advertising agencies employ a variety of specialists to advise clients on how to get the most out of their advertising dollars. They conduct research; design advertising campaigns; create commercials; buy time from cable systems, broadcast stations, and cable and broadcast networks; supervise the implementation of and evaluate the effectiveness of ad campaigns; and pay the media on behalf of advertisers. Agencies become intimately familiar with each client's business problems, sometimes even assisting in the development of new products or the redesigning and repackaging of old ones.

Large advertisers rely almost entirely on advertising agencies for creating commercials. Indeed, designing and producing commercials can be an agency's most crucial function. Anyone who doubts that making commercials rates as a highly developed art need look no further than the homemade

EXHIBIT 9–6 Broadcast and Cable Billings of Top Advertising Agencies*

Rank	Agency	Annual broadcast billings as percentage of agency total	Annual cable billings as percentage of agency total
1	Young & Rubicam	70.0	2.0
2	Saatchi & Saatchi DFS	77.5	2.1
3	Leo Burnett	71.0	1.3
4	J. Walter Thompson	59.0	0.0
5	BBDO	58.2	1.7

*In 1987, the London-based WPP Group acquired the JWT Group (including J. Walter Thompson) and, in 1989, announced plans to acquire the Ogilvy Group. The latter deal would make WPP the largest advertising-based company in the world with revenues near $2 billion, operating 645 offices in more than 50 countries, and boasting as clients more than half of the *Fortune* 500 companies (*Broadcasting,* 22 May 1989: 65).

Billings *refers to the amounts billed to clients by the agencies for media services. Each of the top three agencies billed over a* billion *dollars in a single year. Cable advertising billings increase each year but still lag far behind those for broadcast.*

SOURCE: Based on 1987 data in *Broadcasting,* "Broadcasting's Top 50 Advertising Agencies," 21 Mar. 1988, p. 34, reprinted by permission of Broadcasting Publications, Inc.

commercials of small radio and television stations for evidence. The most convincing proof can be found in commercials that star local advertisers in person. Though the weird performances of used-car dealers and discount store owners sometimes achieve a kind of bizarre local notoriety, they testify that creating advertising requires a special kind of talent.

Ad agencies traditionally receive a 15 percent commission on *billings*—the amount charged by the advertising media. An agency bills its client the full amount of advertising time charges, pays the medium 85 percent, and keeps 15 percent as payment for its own services. Variations in payment method arise because a firm's own advertising department may do some of the work or may retain specialist firms to do specific jobs, such as research, time buying, or commercial production. Some agencies accept less than 15 percent commission or charge fees in addition to commission, some work

on a straight fee basis, and some work on a cost-plus basis.

In any event, the fact that the media allow a discount on business brought to them by agencies creates an odd relationship: the agency works for its client, the advertiser, but gets paid by the medium in the form of a discount on time charges. The travel business operates similarly: a travel agency works, at least theoretically, for the traveler, but gets paid by the hotel or airline in discounts on charges.

The fact that the ad agency actually makes the payments for time to the medium (as an agency service, but also in order to deduct agency commission) can create problems if an agency falls on hard times. In the 1970s one of the nation's largest agencies collected money an advertiser owed to CBS, but went bankrupt before passing on the payment, leaving CBS empty-handed. A court ruled that CBS could not collect from the advertiser, and the network had to write off the debt. Taking a lesson from the CBS case, the media now require the signature of both the advertiser and the agency on all contracts made with agencies deemed less than solid.

The CBS incident reinforces the point that the agency works *for the advertiser,* not the advertising medium. That being the case, it may seem odd that a medium would be willing to accept a lower payment for its services when an agency brings business to it. But this seeming generosity makes sense. Without agency services, the media themselves would have to do many specialized jobs that their regular personnel might not be qualified to perform. This method of payment also benefits the media because the agency assumes the burden of judging an advertiser's ability to pay. Some media compensate for the discount on agency-supplied advertising by paying their own sales executives a lower commission for sales made through agencies than for *direct* sales, those made directly by the medium to the advertiser.

Advertiser-supported cable networks deliver relatively small audiences compared with the three major broadcast networks. To address the bothersome task of buying commercial time on those networks, organizations such as Cable One, a time buyer formed in 1987, negotiate deals on behalf of advertisers for spots on all or any combination of cable networks.

Proof of Performance Advertisers and their agencies need evidence to show that contracts have been carried out. The FCC eliminated its rules requiring broadcast stations to keep daily program logs in the 1980s, but station logs continue to supply the most universal documentation of broadcast performance. Logging the time, length, and source of each commercial at the time it airs provides documentary proof of contract fulfillment. A station's sales department relies on logs when it prepares proof-of-performance warranties to accompany billing statements. At many stations today, computers do the logging automatically. Some stations also make slow-speed audio recordings of everything they air as backup in the event of a dispute.

Advertisers and agencies can get independent confirmation of contract fulfillment by subscribing to the services of Broadcast Advertising Reports (BAR), a firm that conducts systematic studies of radio and television commercial performance. BAR checks on commercials by recording the audio portion of television programs in 75 markets, sending the recordings to central offices for processing, and actually viewing commercials in some markets.

Commercial Tracking Two newer commercial tracking systems announced their services in the late 1980s. The A. C. Nielsen Company began testing its Monitor-Plus service in 1986. Monitor-Plus would use computer technology to recognize each television commercial's unique combination of images and sounds. In 1988, Arbitron said its similar new service would begin the following year. Called ScanAmerica, it would combine the peoplemeter ratings of television viewing with a record of products purchased by viewers, logged by respondents using a wand that scans universal product codes. The annual cost for Arbitron's new service was to be about $4 to $5 million to networks, about $200,000 apiece to advertising agencies, and about $75,000 each to advertisers for data on a specific product category.

9.6
Advertising Standards

Advertising raises touchy issues of taste, legality, and social responsibility. Some critics think the FCC should involve itself in setting standards. The Communications Act makes the FCC responsible for ensuring that broadcasters operate in the public interest, and formerly the FCC used this mandate to justify advertising guidelines. However, deregulation brought a hands-off policy. Even the industry's mild attempt at setting up industrywide standards through the National Association of Broadcasters' radio and television codes collapsed in the face of allegations that by recommending concerted industry action, the codes violated antitrust laws.

Sponsor Identification Section 317 of the Communications Act of 1934 requires reasonably recognizable differences between radio and television commercials and programs. A station must disclose the source of anything it puts on the air for which it receives payment, whether in money or some other "valuable consideration." This *sponsor identification* rule attempts to prevent disguised propaganda or "disinformation" from unidentified sources deceiving the public.

Of course, ordinary commercials make their sources self-evident. Anonymity is the last thing commercial advertisers desire. But propagandists who use *editorial advertising* (sometimes called "advertorials") may not always be so anxious to reveal their true identity; nor do those who make under-the-table payments to disc jockeys or others for on-the-air favors wish to be identified. Integration of commerical matter into programming must be handled systematically, not only to ensure compliance with the Communications Act, but also to satisfy the practical record-keeping needs of sales departments.

Evolution of Time Standards Time standards for commercials constantly evolve, reflecting increases both in permissiveness and in media competitiveness.

Constant tension exists between the urge to cram ever more commerical material into the schedule and the need to avoid alienating audiences—and advertisers as well—by intolerable levels of interruption. Here, too, audience tolerance seems to have grown over the years.

The National Association of Broadcasters, in its radio and television codes, had set industry standards for both advertising* and programs. But in 1984 the Justice Department charged that industry efforts to set guidelines for the conduct of its business violated antitrust laws, and the NAB codes became legal history.

---

*Although full of exceptions and qualifications, the NAB Codes— still largely adhered to—set nominal limits on commercial material per hour as follows: radio, 18 minutes; network television affiliates, 9 1/2 minutes in prime time, 16 minutes in all other times; independent television stations, 14 minutes in prime time and 16 minutes in all other times.

Contrary to what many people think, the FCC never set a maximum number of commercial minutes per hour of programming. True, the commission once proposed to start regulating the amount of commercial time, but quickly dropped the idea when an industry-inspired bill to forbid such regulation was introduced into Congress (House CIFC, 1963). Until 1981, broadcast license applications and renewal forms required applicants to state the number of commercial minutes per hour they planned to allow, or had allowed in the past. The FCC then might ask applicants who exceeded the time standards in the industry's own codes to justify the excess. Neither the FCC nor any other authority ever suggested any time limits for commercials on cable television.

The FCC also once prohibited what it called *program-length commercials,* productions that interwove the noncommercial segments of a program so closely with the commercial messages that the program as a whole promoted the sponsor's product or service.

The FCC abandoned the commercial guidelines and dropped the program-length commercial ban in 1981 for radio and in 1984 for television. The commission argued that the marketplace could best control the amount of commercial time. Apparently deregulation of time standards did not produce a massive increase in commercial time during ordinary programming. According to *Broadcast Advertising Reports,* in 1988 network-affiliated television stations averaged nearly 12 minutes of commercial time in each broadcast hour (independent stations slightly less), and just under 6 minutes per hour during network time.

However, a flood of program-length commercials, often questionable in public-interest terms, overran the less desirable hours on both broadcast and cable television. FCC Chairperson Mark Fowler was quoted on these as saying, "What's really at issue here is whether the government trusts the common man to make up his own mind about what to watch or not to watch. If a half-hour TV shop-at-home service is an annoyance, he will choose to watch—or do—something else" (*Broadcasting,* 2 July 1984, 32).

Home-shopping networks, mostly on cable but some on broadcast stations,* generated more than $1 billion in revenue in 1987, with prospects of reaching $2 billion by 1990. Saturday morning television program schedules began featuring children's programs that critics charged amounted to 30-minute toy commercials. *TV Guide,* which identifies programs by types in its listings, began to include many late-night and even daytime television and cable half-hour offerings, explicitly labeled as commercials, featuring sunglasses, real estate get-rich-quick schemes, weight-reducing nostrums, and hair-loss remedies.

Taste Standards   Some perfectly legal products and services that are not usually advertised on the electronic media nevertheless appear in print ads. This double standard of taste evidences the special obligations society imposes on broadcasting and, to a somewhat lesser degree, on cable because they come directly into the home, accessible to all. Nevertheless, canons of acceptability constantly evolve. By the 1980s, formerly unthinkable ads, such as those featuring contraceptives and those showing brassieres worn by live models, became commonplace.

As its most conspicuous example of self-imposed advertising abstinence, broadcasting generally refuses commercials for hard liquor. (On rare occasions hard liquor ads have been broadcast, although industry practice and distilling-industry codes prohibit them.) Most broadcasters decline to carry them for fear of giving added ammunition to opponents of wine and beer advertising.

Beer and wine ads have always been accepted, although various organizations have tried to remove even them from the air. One of most ambitious, SMART (Stop Marketing Alcohol on Radio and Television), conducted a nationwide campaign in 1984 and 1985, collecting thousands of signatures to pressure Congress into banning all alcohol ads. Although the campaign attracted a great deal of

attention and represented the most serious challenge to such ads in years, neither Congress nor the FCC took any final action. The campaign did, however, result in increased industry self-restraint and a public-service announcement campaign, organized by the NAB, to combat alcohol abuse.

Another advertising taboo forbids the display of the unclothed human body. Broadcasters generally felt that nudity might be acceptable in a *National Geographic* special, but not in an ad for women's lingerie. But in 1983 the first United States television commercial with nudity premiered on the USA and Cable Health networks; it showed a nude young woman, back to the camera, donning her $16 bra and $9 panties and then rising and turning to reveal the sponsor's product. This commercial seemed to predict that cable would depart further from broadcast advertising standards, and raised the question as to whether broadcasters will ease standards in order to meet cable competition. Indeed, such relaxation did occur in 1988, when for the first time all three networks permitted lingerie commercials featuring live models.

In any case, in the absence of voluntary industry codes and externally applied regulation, individual broadcasters and cable programmers must gauge the tastes of the audiences they serve and set their standards accordingly.*

Network Self-Regulation   For years the three major television networks, and some group broadcasters, set and enforced both program and advertising standards through separate departments, variously called *Continuity Acceptance, Broadcast Standards,* or *Program Practices.*

At NBC, for example, the Broadcast Standards Department in 1934 began reviewing program and commercial materials to maintain standards of taste and propriety. In a typical television season, department editors made judgments on more than

*In 1989 Home Shopping Network ranked fifth among all television group owners, with its 12 stations covering 19 percent of U.S. television homes.

*A most unusual arrangement at ABC made a program's author the arbiter of good taste. Herman Wouk held control over the length and content of commercials shown during the 1988 miniseries *War and Remembrance,* based on his novel. He barred all 15-second commercials and all ads for laxatives, foot powders, and feminine hygiene products.

2,000 entertainment outlines and scripts and about 50,000 commercials. ABC and CBS used much the same procedures.

The three networks caused concern to some in the industry in the late 1980s, when ABC and CBS reduced the number of employees assigned to standards and practices departments cutting back from about 85 per network to about a third that number, and NBC eliminated its department entirely. Advertisers, agencies, and others expressed fears that these moves might result in an overall lowering of standards, followed by adverse public reaction, and perhaps even attempts at governmental intervention.

Cable networks have not felt it necessary to pay much attention to self-regulation. For example, whereas ABC has a commercial standards guidebook about an inch thick, ESPN (80 percent owned by Cap Cities/ABC) prints its standards on a single page. Other cable networks issue no written standards at all specifically for their services.

Deceptive Advertising   Prosecution for outright deception in advertising falls under the jurisdiction of the Federal Trade Commission (FTC) rather than the FCC. However, use of fraudulent advertising by a broadcaster can be cited by the FCC as showing lack of the character qualifications required of licensees. The FTC's responsibilities extend to all media and all types of unfair trade practices, not just deceptive advertising.

Instances of possible false advertising may be brought to the FTC's attention by consumers, competitors, or the commission's staff. Under its *Advertising Substantiation Program,* the FTC may require the advertiser to provide proof—often based on scientific testing—of the correctness of its advertising claim. If the proof satisfies the FTC, that ends the matter. If not, the FTC may proceed with various sanctions.

The FTC settles most cases of alleged advertising deception by *stipulation,* an informal (and hence time-saving) way of getting advertisers to drop objectionable practices voluntarily. If a formal complaint becomes necessary, the FTC can seek a *consent order,* another nonpunitive measure under which the advertiser agrees to stop the offending practice without admitting guilt. Actual guilt has to be proved before the FTC can obtain a *cease and desist order* forcing compliance with the law. These orders can be appealed to the courts, which usually means considerable delay in bringing the objectionable advertising to a halt.

However, the Reagan administration's 1981 appointee as FTC chairperson said that market forces, rather than government regulations, should impel businesses to work for consumer benefit. In 1983 the FTC revised its policy on deceptive advertising by requiring proof that a "reasonable consumer" had *actually been harmed* before an advertiser could be charged with deceptive advertising. Deceptiveness alone no longer sufficed.

Children's Advertising   Consumer groups, notably Action for Children's Television (ACT), contend that because young children have not yet learned to understand the difference between advertising and entertainment, they need special protection from commercial exploitation. After conducting hearings on this and related questions in 1974, the FCC declined to issue rules, instead making a policy statement and recommending that broadcasters voluntarily adopt special standards for children's advertising in four areas:

▪ *Time standards.* Nonprogram material in children's non-prime-time programs should be limited to 9 1/2 minutes per hour on weekends and to 12 minutes on weekdays.

▪ *Separation.* Care should be taken to separate commercial from program materials clearly.

▪ *Host selling.* The host of a children's show should not deliver commercials within that program.

▪ *Product tie-ins.* Gratuitous product mentions within children's programs should be avoided.

In 1983 the FCC watered down the broadcasters' obligation to carry children's programming, but left children's-advertising standards intact. The FCC's 1984 deregulation of television eliminated all commercial time guidelines, including those applicable to children's programs, but had no effect on the other guidelines for children's advertising.

In 1984 ACT complained to the FCC that sponsors designed programs such as *He-Man* and *G.I. Joe* more to sell dolls and accessories than to entertain children. ACT also objected to program syndication deals, such as that used with *Thunder Cats,* in which stations carrying the program shared profits from the sale of Thunder Cat products. In 1985 the FCC, noting the absence of any evidence that these practices in fact produced any specific harm, rejected ACT's complaints. In the same year the Commission denied yet another ACT request, refusing to require broadcasters and cable operators to insert signals into their programs that would activate special devices to delete commercials directed at children.

In 1987, an appellate court, acting on an appeal brought by ACT, reversed the FCC and ordered the agency to reconsider its children's-advertising guidelines. While the Commission reconsidered, in 1988 Congress passed a bill that would restore time limits on "kidvid" advertising. Beginning in 1990, broadcasters would have to restrict these ads to 10 1/2 minutes per hour on weekends and 12 minutes per hour on weekdays. In addition, the new legislation required stations to serve the "educational and informational needs" of children in their overall programming. President Reagan vetoed the bill, saying that such a law "simply cannot be reconciled with the freedom of expression secured by our Constitution." Peggy Charren, president of ACT, responded by calling Reagan's action "ideological child abuse." Supporters did not give up, however, but reintroduced the legislation once Reagan was out of office.

Unethical Practices Several areas of commercial abuse in broadcasting have been the subject of FCC and even congressional action. Four types of unethical deals have been particularly troublesome: plugola, payola, fraudulent billing, and clipping.

▪ A conflict of interest occurs when a station or one of its employees uses or promotes on the air something in which the station or employee has an undisclosed financial interest. This practice, called *plugola,* usually results in an indirect payoff. A disc jockey who, on her or his program, gives unpaid publicity to a flying school in which she or he owns an interest would be an example.

▪ Direct payments to the one responsible for inserting plugs usually constitutes *payola.* It typically takes the form of under-the-table payoffs by recording company representatives to disc jockeys and others responsible for putting music on the air.

Plugola and payola violate the *sponsor identification* law. After an investigation uncovered a wide range of both plugola and payola practices, Congress strengthened the sponsor identification law in 1960 by adding Section 507 (formerly 508) to the Communications Act, prescribing a $10,000 fine or a year in jail (or both) for each payola violation. Despite these efforts, payola scandals reappear every few years.

▪ Local cooperative advertising sometimes tempts stations into *double-billing* practices. Manufacturers who share the cost of local advertising of their products by their dealers must rely on those dealers to handle co-op advertising. Dealer and station may connive to send the manufacturer a higher bill for advertising than the one the dealer actually paid. Station and dealer then split the excess payment. In the past, some stations have lost their licenses for double-billing frauds when they were compounded by misrepresentations to the FCC.

▪ Network *clipping* occurs when affiliates cut away from network programs prematurely, usually in order to insert commercials of their own. Clipping constitutes fraud, since networks compensate affiliates for carrying programs in their entirety with all commercials intact.

In keeping with its deregulation policy, in 1986 the FCC redefined billing frauds as civil or criminal matters, not FCC violations, and left the networks to solve clipping problems. The FCC did say, however, that it would consider false billings when judging a licensee's character during licensing proceedings.

9.7
Alternative Revenue Sources

Although advertising provides the largest percentage of electronic media revenue by far, cable television introduced an alternative source, subscription fees. Several niche services also rely on subscription fees. Home shopping networks provide another revenue variation. C-SPAN, cable's public affairs network, looks to the cable industry itself to meet its expenses. Finally, broadcast stations increasingly provide auxiliary nonbroadcast services for additional revenue.

Cable Subscription Fees Monthly subscription fees paid by cable subscribers provide about 90 percent of cable television revenue. Some small cable systems charge a single monthly rate. Others offer several levels of program service, called *tiers,* with a separate fee for each level, as well as for "extras" such as FM stereo and hookups for videocassettes and second sets. Under current interpretation of the Cable Act of 1984, the municipalities that franchise cable systems have no authority to regulate the level of such fees.

Most modern systems offer a *basic* service that includes local television stations, one or more distant superstations, and some advertiser-supported cable networks. The monthly fee for this basic package can vary from a few dollars to $25 or more. Industry expert Paul Kagan estimated that in 1987 the average fee for basic services was $13.20 per month.* Some systems with greater channel capacity break their basic service into two tiers. For example, some of the more popular ad-supported networks (such as MTV and ESPN) may be pulled out of the basic package and offered separately as an *expanded basic* service at extra cost. According to 1987 estimates, the monthly fee for expanded basic service averaged $5.65.

The next level of service includes *pay-cable* channels, such as HBO, Showtime, and Disney. By 1987

about 31 million homes subscribed to pay cable, more than half of all cable households. Usually, subscribers must pay a separate fee for *each* pay service they select. Such fees range from about $2 to $20 or more per service per month, with the average about $10. Some systems package two or more pay services and offer them at a price lower than the cumulative price for the individual services. A system in Carlsbad, CA, for example, offered a package consisting of Cinemax, Bravo, American Movie Classics, and a choice of Disney or Playboy for $15.95, compared with the usual price of $9.95 each.

Cable systems averaged about $25.00 total monthly revenue per subscriber in 1987. At that rate, a hypothetical system with 5,000 subscribers generates more than $1.5 million in fees each year. In contrast, the estimated average monthly advertising revenue of cable systems in 1987 amounted to only 47 cents per subscriber; at this rate, our hypothetical 5,000-subscriber system realizes only $27,000 in annual advertising income.

In addition to monthly fees, most cable systems also charge a one-time installation fee. They may also add a "connection" charge when a subscriber elects to add a new pay-cable channel. To induce homeowners to sign up, cable operators frequently offer reduced rates or waive these charges entirely.

Cable systems with *addressable* converters offer special programs on a *pay-per-view* (PPV) basis. With PPV, the subscriber pays a one-time charge to see a single program, either a movie or a special event such as a boxing match or a rock concert. In 1987 approximately 4.5 million PPV subscribers typically paid between $4 and $6 to see each movie and $15 to $25 for each special event.

PPV programs come in one of two ways. First, individual cable systems—so-called *standalones*—can negotiate for and themselves originate a PPV event. Second, national program services can acquire PPV rights to programs and distribute them to cable systems under an arrangement that splits revenue between the program service and the cable systems. Examples of the latter include Pay-Per-View Network, a joint venture of several cable MSOs, and Request Television, owned by Reiss Media Enter-

---

*Estimates of cable fees, subscribers, and revenues in this section come from *The Kagen Cable TV Financial Data Book,* Paul Kagan Associates, Inc., Carmel, CA, 1988.

prises. Cable networks also operate in the PPV arena. Showtime owns Viewer's Choice, which offers movies and supporting events on a PPV basis; Playboy Enterprises' Private Ticket has been in operation since 1985.

Initially, the absence of special electronic hardware, both for distributing PPV programs to subscribers and for handling the flood of impulsive last-minute telephone orders, slowed the growth of PPV. But reliable equipment to meet these needs became available and economical in the late 1980s. By 1988 more than 14 million homes had PPV addressable hardware. Between 500,000 and 600,000 of those homes paid approximately $35 each to watch the 91-second heavyweight championship fight between Mike Tyson and Michael Spinks on June 27, 1988, producing more revenue for promoters and rights holders than did that year's Super Bowl. The subscriber record for a PPV event, though, had been set three months earlier when viewers in 900,000 homes paid between $20 and $25 each to watch *Wrestlemania IV*.

A few cable systems with two-way capability offer ancillary services, such as burglar and fire alarm protection. In some systems, a triggered sensor alerts an operator at the cable headend, who, after calling the homeowner for verification, notifies the police or fire department. In others, signals go directly to the appropriate municipal authority.

Home Shopping Networks The FCC's removal of its long-standing prohibition of program-length commercials produced a new revenue-generating scheme for broadcast and cable: *home shopping* services. By 1988 more than 30 national and regional home shopping networks operated as many as 24 hours a day, 7 days a week, selling mainly jewelry, appliances, clothing, and housewares. Some services offer their products on cable, some on low-power television, some on full-power television, and some on all three. Whatever the medium, the method is the same: viewers see merchandise, usually offered at what the network describes as huge discounts, and call the network to place an order, paying for the goods with a credit card. Revenue for the industry exceeded $1 billion in 1987, or, for

those services operating on cable, about $38 per subscribing household.

Other Subscription Services Other fee-dependent media include multichannel multipoint distribution services (MMDS), satellite master antenna television (SMATV), and home television receive-only satellite receivers (TVROs).

In the 1980s, the MMDS monthly subscriber fee averaged about $15 plus installation, perhaps low enough to make it competitive with some cable systems. But the service did not attract many viewers (fewer than 100,000 as 1990 approached).

Satellite master antenna television operates as a cable system confined to private property. Many operators divide the programming into a basic service and one or more tiers. Basic subscriptions usually range from about $6 to $20 a month, with the full package of basic service and added tiers priced at around $35 a month. Some building owners operate SMATV systems themselves rather than using independent suppliers, offering the service free or at cost to entice new tenants.

Showtime and others package programs for home satellite receiver (sometimes referred to as *backyard dish*) owners who have each paid $400 or so for a device to *decode* or *unscramble* cable network signals. The 1988 Showtime package offered 13 basic-cable networks, plus Showtime or the Movie Channel, for $17.95 a month. Eastern Microwave packaged the signals of three superstations for as little as $36 a year.

Support for C-SPAN One cable network has the distinction of being neither wholly advertiser-supported nor dependent upon subscriber fees. Cable system operators began C-SPAN (Cable-Satellite Public Affairs Network) in 1979 to build a favorable image for cable, both in Washington and in local communities. Operating 24 hours a day, it carries live coverage of congressional proceedings and other public-affairs programming.

About 3,000 participating cable systems with more than 39 million subscribers meet most of C-SPAN's $13 million annual budget by paying four cents or less a month per subscriber to carry the service.

About 10 percent of C-SPAN's revenue comes from corporate underwriting, services (such as production of videotapes and sublease of satellite transponder time), and corporate image messages, usually 10 to 15 seconds long, between programs.

Ancillary Services   Radio and television station signals can be used to deliver ancillary (secondary) commercial services. AM stations may multiplex inaudible secondary signals on their channels. For example, some electric power companies have arranged with AM stations to send multiplexed signals to special receivers at various business locations that would turn off air conditioning units during periods of high demand. FM channels may offer subsidiary communications authorization (SCA) services.* Early SCAs provided Muzak and other background music services, and a few stations offered farm news or business and financial information. The FCC further expanded SCAs in 1983, permitting FM stations to use up to three subcarriers. Stereophonic sound usually occupies one, leaving two available for lease. Many noncommercial radio stations transmit special programming for the visually impaired and some foreign-language material. Others use SCAs for slow-scan video. This service transmits still pictures to educational and other institutions for teleconferencing, instruction, and information distribution. Broadcasters either lease subcarriers to producers of slow-scan or become producers themselves. Despite the variety of SCA uses, less than half of all FM broadcasters utilize the service.

In 1983 and 1984 the FCC authorized television stations to exploit their unused signal capacity, making possible television stereophonic sound and simulcasts of foreign-language audio to accompany English-language television programming. Television stations have the further option of using their vertical blanking intervals (VBIs) to send closed-captioned subtitles to the hearing impaired. Stations derive no direct revenue from their closed-cap-

tioned signals, seeing this activity primarily as a public service.

Production as a Revenue Source   Rather than serving as sources of added income, most locally produced programs add to expenses. Stations, cable systems, and networks produce only a very small percentage of their programs in-house. Most programs come from independent production companies or syndicators. As for commercials, a few television stations and cable systems have production departments that pay for themselves, and sometimes even earn a profit. But most produce commercials at a loss or on a barely break-even basis, treating this service as a necessary cost incurred to help sell advertising time.

9.8
Profit and Loss

From the public-interest standpoint, stations, cable systems, and networks need to earn profits; when they operate at a loss, programs tend to be the first to suffer. Moreover, the lowering of standards by firms that are losing money can be contagious, for rival firms tend to reciprocate by lowering their standards in order to compete in the marketplace.

A Money Machine?   Broadcasting seems so profitable that some have called it a "license to print money." This is only partially true for stations, and even the television networks, historically immune from the financial ups and downs that affect most businesses, have begun to feel the impact of rising costs and increasing competition. For years the networks were highly profitable. In 1983, for the first time, each of the three major commercial television networks generated revenues in excess of $2 billion dollars. In 1984, ABC became the first to exceed $3 billion.

The network decline began in 1985, when revenues fell slightly for the first time since 1971; however, even in that year the three networks attracted more than $8.3 billion in advertising and produced profits exceeding $1 billion. By 1987, however, total

---

*The term has been officially changed to *subsidiary communications services* (SCS), but most in the industry continue to refer to "SCA."

net revenues for ABC, CBS, and NBC had dropped to $6.8 billion. NBC, riding the crest of ratings leadership, showed an increase in profits over 1986; CBS, for the first time in its television history, recorded a net loss in the first quarter of 1987, but was able to end the year in the black; ABC lost about $15 million. All three major networks embarked on an austerity program, cutting budgets and laying off personnel. The emergent Fox network, meanwhile, struggled to stay in the race, losing about $90 million in its 1988 fiscal year and projecting losses at about $20 million in 1989. Nor did the future outlook appear any better. Robert Wright, president of NBC, told a gathering of his affiliates in June 1988 that the network business was getting "worse and worse"; in the same month the New York *Times* quoted him as saying that "there may not be enough advertising money in the marketplace to support two broadcast networks, much less three or four" (Boyer, 1988).

In July 1988, Standard & Poor's (S&P), the firm that rates corporations' financial condition, said that "Business risk is trending upward for the three principal television networks . . . amid growing entertainment alternatives. . . ." Pointing to increasing program costs and the drop in the three networks' combined share of audience (from about 90 percent in 1980 to about 80 percent in 1986, to below 50 percent during some weeks in 1988), S&P saw declining profit margins for all three networks (S&P *CreditWeek,* 4 July 1988, p. 16).

A 1988 Writers Guild strike further weakened the networks' position. Without new episodes of many of the most popular series, the networks' patchwork programming that fall drove viewers to sample alternative entertainment, mostly cable and videocassette.

As a hedge against increasing profit erosion, two of the major networks stepped up their involvement in cable. For example, Cap Cities/ABC had ownership interests in ESPN and, with General Electric (NBC) and others, in Arts & Entertainment. NBC bought a 50 percent interest in Cablevision Systems' Rainbow Program Enterprises in 1988, and began its new Consumer News and Business Channel (CNBC) in 1989.

The networks, like all group owners, also looked to their owned-and-operated stations to shore up their corporate financial positions. A survey by the National Association of Broadcasters found that in 1987 the average network-affiliated television station had a pretax profit of about $3.4 million.

Although the average independent station in the 10 largest markets produced a $5.5 million pretax profit, independents as a group showed an average pretax *loss* of about $130,000 (NAB Television 1988). Whereas the average FM radio station showed a 1987 pretax profit of about $63,000, the typical full-time AM station reported a loss of nearly $20,000 (NAB Radio 1988).

Unprofitable stations may continue to operate, first, because many so-called losses exist only on paper. Corporations pay income taxes on profits, not on revenues; often owners avoid taxes by keeping profits to a minimum through the use of "creative" (though legal) accounting procedures. Second, even genuinely unprofitable stations tend to hang on because the owners or prospective owners remain optimistic about an eventual payoff. Despite these considerations, however, every year some stations file for bankruptcy. A few cease operation, others survive a court-approved reorganization, and still others are sold.

The fact that most FM radio and UHF television stations became profitable only after years of losing money shows that in broadcasting it often pays to keep trying against formidable odds. Failing broadcast properties attract investors for three related reasons: first, owners have faith that losing stations can be turned into money machines, if only the right formula can be found. Second, owners who wait long enough may eventually realize a profit by selling their stations. Third, station ownership satisfies an owner's ego by conferring an aura of glamour and community prestige.

Cable TV Cable, which in five years went from a $200 million loss (1982) to an estimated $279 million profit (1987), also has its share of winners and losers. Newer systems with high construction costs and low subscriber penetration experience sizable losses, at least initially. But many of the established systems regularly generate handsome profits.

Multiple cable-system operator (MSO) profits and losses, influenced by subscription rates and construction costs, vary widely. Tele-Communications Inc. (TCI), the nation's largest MSO, had a 1987 net income about 88 percent lower than its net income for the previous year. On the other hand, ATC, the second largest MSO, enjoyed 1987 profits 23 percent higher than in 1986.

During the franchise application process, when several companies were bidding competitively, applicants often proposed unrealistically expensive systems, agreeing at the same time to charge unrealistically low subscriber fees. For example, in 1983 several firms seeking Philadelphia franchises proposed as many as 130 channels and subscriber rates as low as $1.95 per month for a 36-channel basic package; in 1984 the city granted permits to four systems with mandatory 82-channel capacity. In Sacramento the bidding frenzy reached new heights, with the winner promising to plant 20,000 trees throughout the city.

Some franchise winners, having saddled themselves with unrealistic promises, attempted to renegotiate their franchises. Warner Amex, for example, first proposed a dual-cable, 108-channel system in Milwaukee, but later obtained the city's permission to cut back to a 54-channel, single-cable system. The company also modified its previous promises regarding local origination facilities and subscriber rates.

By the mid-1980s pay-cable network subscriber growth rates had slowed, and some networks even suffered a net loss in total subscribers. Some did not survive at all. In 1987, Group W shut down Home Theatre Network, one of the oldest cable services but one with only about 325,000 subscribers (it featured only movies rated G or PG).

The home videocassette recorder seemed to play an increasingly important role in competition for the video dollar. Viewers buy millions of prerecorded videocassettes each year and rent countless more for as little as a dollar a day—strong competition for the cable operator trying to market premium channels at $10 a month. By 1988, in fact, far more American homes owned VCRs (about 58 percent of all television households according to Nielsen, but about 65 percent according to the Gallup organization) than subscribed to a pay-cable service (about 29 percent). In the late 1980s, however, the subscriber growth curve turned upward, at least for some networks, particularly HBO, Showtime, Cinemax, and the Disney Channel. The Movie Channel and Playboy continued to lose subscribers.

Only the strongest advertiser-supported cable program services succeeded. MTV and CBN became profitable by 1984. Although superstation WTBS had been profitable for several years, the other Turner Broadcasting services, CNN and CNN Headline News, remained in the red until 1986 (Turner's Cable Music Channel lasted barely a month). Even some program services with solid financial backing and entertainment expertise failed. CBS Cable offered quality cultural programming, but attracted too few advertisers and folded in 1982 after only a year's operation, losing an estimated $30 million. You-TV, a service devoted to fitness and health, died in 1988, the same year The Fashion Channel filed for bankruptcy. Other networks sold out or merged with surviving services. Still, the strong survived. In fact, in 1988, ESPN, TBS, and CNN each generated greater profits than either ABC or CBS.

The more recent shop-at-home services had their share of ups and downs. Home Shopping Network had net income of $29.5 million in 1987, a 174 percent increase in only one year. Conversely, Horn & Hardart and Crazy Eddie canceled their home-shopping plans, and the Telephone Auction Network filed for bankruptcy.

Pay-per-view, despite high expectations and some single-event successes, still had a long way to go to reach maturity and stability. By 1988, none of the six national PPV networks had shown a profit.

Influences on Profit   The larger the organization, the more probable its ability to achieve a higher profit margin than smaller organizations.*   A

---

*Profit margin means the percentage of net revenues (after sales commissions but before operating expenses have been deducted) represented by pretax profit. Thus, for example, if a

company may raise profit margins by increasing revenue and/or by reducing expenses. Group owners, and to a lesser extent MSOs, often achieve savings through bulk purchase of equipment, supplies, and programs and by sharing of employees and ideas. Thus, they realize *economies of scale.*

Broadcasters, ad-supported cable networks, and some cable systems also benefit from the fact that they sell an intangible, air time. Expenses do not increase in step with sales. For example, if an appliance dealer buys a television set for $500 and sells it for $750, the dealer makes a $250 profit. Selling a second set yields another profit of $250. For every $750 in sales, the dealer must spend $500 in order to make the $250 profit. By contrast, if it costs a television station $500 to run one episode of *Three's Company,* and if one 30-second commercial within the program sells for $750, the broadcaster makes a $250 profit. But a second spot sold at the same price does not incur a second expense: the cost of the program has already been accounted for, so the entire $750 in revenue counts as profit. A third $750 sale again counts as profit. And so on.

This simplistic hypothetical example does not, of course, account for the many expenses other than direct costs, such as overhead and sales commissions. But it illustrates the advantage broadcasting has over businesses that incur additional costs with each sale. NBC's 51 percent profit increase in 1987 over the prior year, on only an 8 percent increase in sales, offers a real-world example.

Role of Market Size   Profitability in broadcasting depends on market size, which affects all aspects of an enterprise. The larger the market, generally speaking, the larger the station staff, the higher the salaries, the longer the program day, and the more local production occurs—and, of course, the higher the sales revenue and, most likely, profits. Exhibit 9–7 compares markets of widely differing size, showing, for example, that the average tele-

television station has net revenues of $2 million and a pretax profit of $400,000, it would have a profit margin of 20 percent ($400,000 divided by $2 million).

vision station in the top 10 markets earns more than 58 times as much as the average station in markets ranked 81 through 90. These figures do not prove an absolute correspondence between market size and profitability, however. Economic conditions vary among markets, as do the efficiencies of broadcast managements.

9.9
Bottom-Line Broadcasting

Encouraged by federal deregulation and by loose interpretation of antitrust laws, the broadcast and cable industries have in recent years been characterized by acquisition, merger, takeover, vertical integration, and consolidation. The emphasis has been on the economic aspects of the media, often with little apparent concern for public service—the *bottom-line* mentality that focuses exclusively on profit-and-loss figures. Cable, not required to operate in the public interest, convenience, and necessity, made no effort to mask its profit-driven goals. Broadcasting, which does have such a mandate, and which FCC rules formerly kept mostly in the hands of professional broadcasters, fell increasingly into the grasp of conglomerate officials with no broadcasting background.

The FCC's *trafficking* rule, designed to prevent station trading at the expense of public service, had required the holder of a broadcast station license to keep it a minimum of three years before transferring it. But the 1982 deletion of this rule facilitated entry into and quick exit from the broadcast business whenever profit-taking dictated. Many first-time broadcast buyers specialized in *leveraged buyouts* of television stations; the huge debts incurred in these deals, repaid out of station profits, left little money for quality public-affairs programming or other efforts in the public interest. Stations saved money by no longer supporting (and in 1988 deciding to close) the Television Information Office, which had been the industry's public relations arm but which they no longer needed in the deregulatory age. More and more stations turned to a burgeoning source of easy income, the program-length

EXHIBIT 9–7   Television Station Profit and Market Size

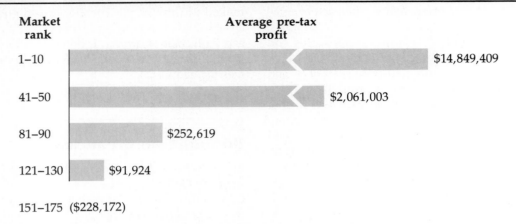

As market rank (in terms of number of television households in the market) goes down, so does the average income for television stations. The parentheses symbol ( ) indicates loss.

SOURCE: *Television Financial Report,* National Association of Broadcasters (Washington, DC, 1988), using 1986–1987 Arbitron Area of Dominant Influence (ADI) market ranking.

commercial, termed by some "video junk mail." Programmers tested the limits of good taste with such network specials as *Favorite Son* and *The Sex Tapes;* series such as the Fox Network's *Married With Children;* and syndicated shows such as *Geraldo, Morton Downey, Jr.,* and a seemingly endless supply of tabloid magazine shows.

A 1987 survey by *Broadcasting Engineering,* an industry magazine, found widespread concern among engineers and technicians about the current quality of the broadcasting product. As the respondents saw it, the driving concern for making a profit had reduced product quality. Some blamed the bottom-line approach to decision making, characteristic of owners with no broadcast background; others pointed to the increased debt burdens and reduced station resources that result when a station changes owners repeatedly in a short space of time (Dick, 1987).

Nowhere did the trend become more evident than at the three major networks. Beginning in the mid-1980s, the once all-powerful networks experienced a decline. Cable, reaching more than 50 percent of all U.S. television households, displaced over-the-air stations as the principal distributor of television programming. And with cable came added competition for viewers' attention. In 1976 the networks routinely captured about 91 percent of the prime-time audience; by 1988 that number had dropped into the low 60s, and even below 50 percent in some heavily cabled markets. The emergent Fox network, while far from reaching parity with the established networks, nonetheless competed for the national broadcast audience. Program costs soared, exacerbated by labor union problems. Network commercial rates rose rapidly in response to rising costs, driving advertisers to seek out alternative vehicles.

In the mid-1980s, new management took over at ABC, CBS, and NBC. With these changes came the call for operating-cost cutbacks. The networks laid off between 2,000 and 3,000 employees and persuaded others to take early retirement.

The new austerity took its heaviest public-service toll in the area of network news. News division budgets, roughly $85 million for each network in 1980, had grown to $300 million by 1986. This $900 million three-network total loomed especially large

EXHIBIT 9–8   Media Ethics (or is that an oxymoron?)

"The most pressing ethical issue facing many media executives is the continuing conflict between making money and serving the public." That was the dilemma most often cited by the 144 readers who responded to a business ethics survey conducted by *Electronic Media,* an industry magazine. Although many of the responses prove fascinating, the disappointingly low response rate puts into question the generalizability of the results.

Respondents included television and radio general managers, multiple-cable-system operators, sales managers, news directors and reporters, syndication sales executives, and television program directors.

Some specifics:

■ 98 percent agreed with the statement that "Generally speaking, good ethics is good business," but 65 percent said that they considered some generally ac-

cepted practices in their field of business to be unethical.

■ 32 percent felt that ethical standards in the television business world were lower than they had been ten years ago.

■ 87 percent believed that most people they knew would be willing to "bend the rules" to achieve success in business so long as their actions hurt no one.

■ 69 percent considered it all right to do a certain amount of "hypoing" during rating periods.

■ 73 percent expressed belief in the honesty of corporate executives.

■ 34 percent said an employee should be fired for filing an expense account with $10 of falsified expenses; and 36 percent admitted they had done exactly that.

SOURCE: *Electronic Media,* 29 Feb. 1988, p. 1.

---

when viewed in the light of news division revenues of only $830 million. A typical network operation included, for example, 8 domestic and 15 foreign news bureaus, staffed by a total of 100 correspondents, each of whom earned an average of $150,000 a year. A consultant's survey found that one-fifth of NBC's correspondents appeared on less than 3 percent of the *NBC Nightly News* air time. Something had to give.

ABC cut its 1,200-person news staff by some 60 people. Laurence Tisch, who took over as president and chief executive officer of CBS in January 1987, said, "I can guarantee you that the one area I will never interfere with is the delivery of news" (Vitale, 1988). He soon thereafter cut the news division's budget by $30 million and fired more than 200 employees, including veteran reporters such as Ike Pappas and Fred Graham. Despite his efforts, the first quarter of 1987 became the first in the network's history to record an overall net loss.

Reactions came swiftly. Congressmen Dennis Eckart of Ohio and John Bryant of Texas called for (and got) hearings in the U.S. House of Representatives. Eckart and Bryant argued that, "The wave of cut-

backs and layoffs that is sweeping all three networks is alarming. . . . The American People deserve to know what the bottom line is where their news programming is concerned." Eckart said, "In this rush for profits, the public interest has been trampled on." Bryant added, "The root of my concern is that these corporate takeovers have made America's principal source of information the subject of giant corporate poker games" (*Broadcasting,* 16 Mar. 1987, 39). Although these hearings created publicity for Eckart and Bryant, they produced little action. No legislation resulted from all the talk.

Making an unprecedented public criticism of his own network, *CBS Evening News* anchor and managing editor Dan Rather wrote a piece for the New York *Times* entitled "From Murrow to Mediocrity," in which he pointed out that Chairperson Tisch "told us when he arrived that he wanted us to be the best. We want nothing more than to fulfill that mandate. Ironically, he has now made the task seem something between difficult and impossible." He added that "news is a business, but it is also a public trust. . . . We have been asked to cut costs and work more efficiently and we have accepted that challenge. What we cannot accept is the notion that the bottom line counts more than meeting our responsibilities to the public. Anyone who says network news cannot be profitable doesn't know what he is talking about. But anyone who says it must *always* make money is misguided and irresponsible" (Rather, 1987).

Summary

▮ Broadcasting achieved relatively rapid success as an advertising medium because of its unique psychological advantages, combined with great flexibility in serving local, regional, and national advertisers.

▮ The effectiveness of broadcast advertising is offset for some users by its costs, by the fact that it often reaches more people than desired, and by limits on commercial length and content.

▮ Commercial practice has shifted from sponsorship to insertion of spots within and between programs over which advertisers have no direct control.

▮ A station's traffic department schedules commercial announcements, preventing back-to-back advertising of competitive products.

▮ Cable enjoys many of television's advantages but suffers from the difficulty of physically inserting commercials in its numerous channels and from the absence of audience research comparable to broadcast rating reports.

▮ Advertising rates reflect the fact that advertisers buy time only as a means of getting access to audiences. Because audiences change with programs and services as well as with times of the day and days of the year, prices for spots tend to change accordingly.

▮ Sales representatives and (for affiliates) network sales organizations supplement broadcast and cable sales departments in reaching some advertising clients.

▮ Advertising agencies plan most advertising campaigns and select media outlets.

▮ The media provide proof of performance through their daily program logs, but agencies also hire specialized firms to check the fulfillment of advertising contracts.

▮ No laws limit the amount of commercial time in and between programs. Formal industry guidelines fell with the NAB codes, so that today only individual station and network standards and market pressures limit advertising time.

▮ Standards of taste continue to evolve with changes in competition and the attitudes of society.

▮ The Federal Trade Commission has authority over deceptive advertising practices, although there has been little enforcement in the 1980s.

▮ Offenses that can jeopardize station licenses include network clipping, double billing, plugola, and payola.

▮ Cable and some other services rely more on subscription fees than on advertising for revenue; some cable systems also offer pay-per-view programs.

▮ Most segments of the American broadcasting and cable industries are structured to make a profit.

▮ The major television networks no longer enjoy the healthy profits they once did. Nationally, affiliated television stations and FM radio stations show profits; independent television stations and AM radio stations do not.

▮ The cable industry as a whole is profitable, although some system operators and program services suffer annual losses.

▮ Increasing competition, rising costs, and dwindling revenue have resulted in some broadcasters operating more in the interest of profit than in the interest of the public.

CHAPTER 10

THE NONCOMMERCIAL ALTERNATIVE

Most of this book deals with commercial radio and television because they form the backbone of broadcasting in America. But here, as in most countries, commercial broadcasting's overwhelming emphasis on mass-appeal light entertainment has failed to meet the full potential of the medium. The profit motive alone cannot be counted on to fulfill all the national cultural, educational, and informational needs that broadcast media could serve. Hence arises the concept of *noncommercial broadcasting,* based on motives other than profit. The best-known noncommercial operators are *public broadcasting* stations.

10.1
From "Educational Radio" to "Public Broadcasting"

What we know today as noncommercial broadcasting started as a more narrowly defined service devoted primarily to education. Indeed, the Federal Communications Commission still refers officially to *noncommercial educational* licensees, even though the 1934 act has been amended by the Public Broadcasting Act of 1967, denoting a broader aim than "education" alone implies.

Rise of Educational Radio Several colleges experimented with wireless telegraphy in the years before World War I. Members of the University of Wisconsin's physics department, for example, began tinkering in 1902, built an operating experimental transmitter by 1909, and progressed to a licensed wireless telegraphy station, 9XM, by 1915. During World War I, 9XM remained in service to assist in training of navy personnel. A few other schools experimented with broadcasting as well.

When license applications boomed in the 1920s, educational and religious institutions joined in the rush. They pursued varied goals: classroom and extension education, school or church promotion, fund raising, cultural betterment, voter awareness, and so on. Most of the pioneer stations operated on a shoestring for only a few hours a week.

With broadcasting's growing financial success in the late 1920s, commercial interests began to covet the AM channels tied up by educational licensees. Some schools surrendered their licenses in return for promises of air time for educational programs on commercial stations—promises that faded with the rising value of air time. Educational stations that held on found themselves confined to low power, inconvenient hours (often daytime only, useless for adult education efforts), and constantly changing frequency assignments. A majority simply gave up the struggle and left the air. In 1927, there were 98 noncommercial stations operating, but by 1933 only 43 remained on the air. By 1945, the number had fallen to about 25. They struggled for local and state support with little success. A commentator suggested why—a weakness of the system that persisted four decades later: "commercial stations made money, convertible into political power; educational stations cost money. If their programming was not popular enough to attract sizable audiences, they were hard to justify politically" (Blakely, 1979: 55).

The failure of most educational institutions to defend their licenses against the raids of commercial interests confirmed what some had said from the first: at the very outset a share of the AM frequencies should have been set aside exclusively for educational use. Educational interests could not be expected to compete for radio channels with commercial interests in the open market.

Channel Reservations   Faced with mounting evidence that commercial stations gave far too little time to meet school needs, the FCC finally accepted the channel reservation principle when it first authorized FM service in 1941, reserving the five lowest channels for noncommercial use. In 1945, the commission set aside 88 to 92 MHz—the lowest 20 of the 100 channels on FM's new higher band—for educational use. Disappointed by inadequate use of these reserved channels, the FCC liberalized its rules in 1948, allowing noncommercial outlets to operate on power as low as 10 watts. With little program exchange and no network, educational FM stations and the 25 or so AM educational survivors from the 1930s depended almost totally on local resources. A research team that studied educational radio stations in 1971–1972 admitted to being confused because "no two stations are alike, and there are almost no models to which to point" (Robertson and Yokom, 1973: 115).

During the 1948 television freeze, commercial interests made a concerted effort to block proposed educational television channel reservations. The Joint Committee on Educational Television spearheaded a counterlobbying effort, asking the FCC not to end the freeze without adopting a channel reservation scheme. Commercial interests argued that reserved channels would go unused while educators tried to get together funds to put stations on the air, whereas commercial firms stood ready to build stations as

soon as the freeze ended. Operating and potential commercial licensees promised free time on the air for educational programs—just as they had for AM radio in the 1930s.

Finally, when the FCC ended the freeze with its 1952 *Sixth Report and Order,* it reserved 242 educational television (ETV) channel allotments, 80 VHF and 162 UHF—but only for a limited time: "long enough to give . . . reasonable opportunity . . . [but] not so long that the frequencies remain unused for excessively long periods of time" (Blakely, 1979: 89). Over the years, however, the FCC made the reservations permanent and increased their number to about 600.

In the decade from the end of the freeze to the passage of the first noncommercial television federal funding legislation of 1962, the service grew very slowly despite concern over possible loss of the reservations (Exhibit 10–1). The few stations on the air depended largely on local production and filmed programs, and stayed on the air about half as long as commercial stations. After 1959, a program cooperative, National Educational Television (NET), provided a few hours a week of shared programs, sent to stations by mail.

Conflict over ETV Philosophy   In the fight to achieve noncommercial channel reservations, the noncommercial television constituency grew larger and more diversified. Traditional educational radio leaders, who had kept the faith over many lean years, now found themselves jostled aside by the newly saved—the national educational establishment, politicians, the Washington bureaucracy, and activist citizen groups.

Out of this matrix of forces emerged conflicting views on the form a noncommercial service should take. One group took "educational television" to imply a broadly inclusive cultural and information service; another construed it more narrowly as a new and improved audiovisual device, primarily important to schools. Some favored a strong national network and a concern for audience building, following the model of commercial broadcasting. Others stressed localism and service for more limited or specialized audiences. Some wanted to stress

EXHIBIT 10–1   Growth of Noncommercial Broadcasting: 1925–1985

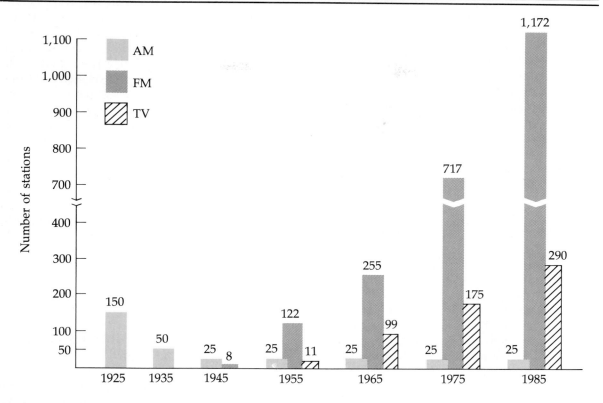

After a steady decline in the number of educational AM stations to 1945, educational radio growth switched to the new FM service, and eventually to television. Only a small proportion of the FM stations qualify for affiliation with NPR—about 170 in 1975, and about 220 in 1985. Data refer to January 1 of each year. The figures for AM educational stations are estimated because there is no official count of such operations.

SOURCE: FCC.

high culture and intellectual stimulation; others wanted to emphasize programs of interest to ethnic minorities, children, and the poor.

As an expert who would help draft landmark 1967 legislation put it later, "It was hardly a system we were seeking to nurture at all, but rather a variety of broadcasting arrangements bearing a common name and yet widely differing in structure, financing, concept of role and degree of independence" (Cater, 1972: 10). The issue of whether the national organizations or the stations should have the dominant role in this debate added to the confusion.

Carnegie Study   Watershed events in noncommercial broadcasting came in 1967 with the report of the *Carnegie Commission on Educational Television* (CCET) and resultant legislation. Made up of top-level representatives from higher education, media, business, politics, and the arts, the commission proposed that Congress establish a corporation for public television. The commission used the word *public* rather than *educational* to disassociate itself from what many regarded as the "somber and static image" projected by the existing ETV services. It also felt that "public" would differentiate instructional or classroom television from a broader noncommercial service intended for general viewing.

The basic structure advocated in the 1967 Carnegie Commission report and the legislation it inspired six months later as part of Lyndon Johnson's "Great Society" program have survived, though with changes in detail. The report did not, however, anticipate the complex struggle for control that would ensue among the major players.

10.2
National Organization

The battles that have shaped public broadcasting since 1967 can be seen as a continuation of the earlier struggle for power among several national organizations, and between them and the local authorities who controlled a growing number of noncommercial radio and television stations. In all this, a government-formed, nonprofit corporation played a pivotal role.

Corporation for Public Broadcasting (CPB)
Congress amended the Communications Act with the Public Broadcasting Act of 1967 (*broadcasting* because Congress added public radio at the last minute), creating the *Corporation for Public Broadcasting* (CPB). The Carnegie Commission had recommended that the president of the United States appoint only half the CPB board, but Congress gave all the appointive power to the president. Congress, wanting to retain close control, declined to legislate long-term financial support as recommended by the Carnegie report. These two departures from the Carnegie plan left the CPB at the mercy of presidential politics, sometimes with unfortunate consequences for the CPB's impartiality (Exhibit 10–2).

The act gave the CPB the right to dispense federal funds to stations and program producers, but not

to own or operate stations. The act describes the corporation's role as also including:

- Facilitating "full development of educational broadcasting in which programs of high quality, obtained from diverse sources, will be made available to ... stations with strict adherence to objectivity and balance in all programs or series of programs of a controversial nature."

- Assisting in setting up network interconnection so that all stations "that wish to may broadcast the programs at times chosen by the stations." (The act authorized common carriers to give free or reduced-rate service to such networks.)

- Carrying out its work "in ways that will most effectively assure the maximum freedom ... from interference with or control of program content or other activities."

- Establishing and maintaining a library and archives.

- Encouraging development of new stations.

- Conducting research and training.

The Battle over PBS's Role
After a good deal of political wrangling arising from fears that a national network might unduly centralize authority over program selection and scheduling functions, CPB launched a national network, the *Public Broadcasting Service* (PBS), in 1969–1970. PBS operates the television interconnection, but, unlike commercial television networks, does not select programs. PBS also initially served as the lobby for public television. Relationships between PBS and the stations as program users—or, in some cases, as major program producers—underwent constant upheaval as the network struggled to establish its identity and to develop a working style.

Disagreement focused on the role PBS should play in setting national programming policy. The Carnegie report had stressed both the vital importance of network interconnection and the need to avoid the kind of program centralization represented by the commercial network model. Public broadcasting was to differ from commercial broadcasting in having "a strong component of local and

EXHIBIT 10–2 Political Manipulation of CPB

Incidents during two conservative presidential administrations provide textbook illustrations of the difficulty of insulating a broadcast service from politics when it depends on government for substantial economic support. Section 398 of the Communications Act, added by the 1967 public broadcasting law, tries to prevent political influence by expressly forbidding any "direction, supervision, or control" over noncommercial broadcasting by officials of the U.S. government. This legal detail did not stop the Nixon administration in the 1970s nor the Reagan administration a decade later from manipulating CPB for its own ends.

When the Public Broadcasting Service (PBS) network began beefing up its news and public-affairs programming around 1970 by hiring ex-commercial-network personnel, the White House took umbrage. Regarding the PBS network as far too liberal, the administration objected to public television's concern with national affairs when, according to the administration's interpretation, it should be focusing on *local* needs. This view struck a chord with some of the station managers, who were already resentful of the increasing centralization of program decision making by PBS and CPB. In 1973, the administration sent a

more direct message when President Nixon vetoed a two-year funding measure for CPB. Several board members—ironically, all presidential appointees—resigned in protest. Long-range federal funding legislation did not finally pass until 1975.

By 1981, when the Reagan administration took office, the CPB board, never high on the priority list of political appointees, had become fertile ground for political gamesmanship. Reagan appointed several hard-right conservatives to the CPB board. In 1986, the Reagan-appointed CPB chair, Sonia Landau, dismissed Edward Pfister as CPB president in a dispute over a proposed trip to the Soviet Union to trade programming. Less than a year later, Pfister's replacement also left CPB, which had developed a reputation for constant political infighting. Another Reagan CPB appointee advocated making a content study to determine whether public television programming leaned too far to the left. Opponents of the research felt that its sponsors merely wanted to send a signal to public broadcasters that they should adopt a more conservative agenda. The study never materialized, but the legally mandated political impartiality of the CPB had been seriously undermined.

---

regional programming." It would "provide the opportunity and the means for local choice to be exercised upon the programs made available from central programming sources" (CCET, 1967: 33).

The Carnegie report failed to appreciate the practical problems of asking the national network (PBS) to provide a smorgasbord of programs from which affiliates would pick and choose at will. A variety of divisive problems emerged:

▌ "Turf" battles arose as people tried to protect the personal roles they had in their own organization. Overlap in functions between CPB and PBS lasted for years, with neither organization being willing to give way to the other.

▌ Licensees, operating under varied ownership and funding restrictions, worried more about survival

than about which national group programmed what. Most stations sided with "their" organization, PBS, against CPB, which they saw as a creature of Washington politics.

▌ Disagreements over basic program philosophy continued to be the critical issue. The "proper" role that public television should play within a largely commercial/entertainment system should dictate programming decisions, but the parties could not agree on a common definition of that role.

▌ Finally, at the heart of most arguments always lurked the funding crisis. Who should get how much money, for what purposes, and with what kind of accountability? The parties could agree on only one thing: public broadcasting always needed *more* money.

Definition of the present PBS role came largely from PBS President Lawrence Grossman (1976–1984). Grossman came from (and would return to) commercial broadcasting. Previous PBS heads had come from public-service and public broadcasting backgrounds. Grossman wanted primary emphasis on programming. PBS offices blossomed with wall-size scheduling boards showing PBS offerings against the commercial networks' fare, suggesting that at last the public system, at least on the national level, had begun to think competitively. Grossman pushed the use of American productions instead of relying as heavily on British material as his predecessors had. He also arrived in time to shape the switch to satellite relays.

Sparked mainly by the wider opportunities made possible by the use of satellite distribution after 1978, the stations reorganized PBS to enhance its programming function, as described in the next subsection. PBS spun off its ancillary activities of station representation (lobbying, research, and similar functions) to what became the National Association of Public Television Stations (NAPTS).

PBS Network Operations By 1988, PBS served 170 noncommercial licensees operating 327 member stations—virtually all public TV stations on the air. Its 35-member board consisted of members of the general public drawn from station boards and professional station managers. PBS staff totaled about 300 in Washington (actually Alexandria, VA), New York, and Los Angeles offices.

PBS practices differ sharply from those of commercial networks. Affiliates sign contracts with PBS agreeing to pay varying levels of dues, determined by each affiliate's budget and market size. Rather than being paid by the network for use of their time, as is the case with commercial services, public stations pay their network for programs. Unlike commercial networks, PBS produces no programs of its own. It provides a distribution service for programs produced by others, most of them selected not by the network, but by member stations (Exhibit 10–3).

Selection occurs through a funding mechanism developed in 1974, the *Station Program Cooperative* (SPC). PBS offers a list of proposed programs for the coming season, categorized as follows: (1) those fully underwritten by business corporations or foundations, (2) those partially funded by those sources, and (3) those lacking financial support of any kind. PBS will carry programs from categories two and three only if a sufficient number of stations vote (and agree to pay) for those programs in a series of voting rounds during which stations commit their programming dollars. Stations make commitments based on their judgment as to which programs will appeal to local viewers, which programs will attract local underwriters, and, perhaps most important, which programs they can afford. PBS prorates each station's share of the cost of each program in categories two and three on the basis of station size and the number of stations voting to participate in the cost of that program. The 1987 SPC led to station funding for some 900 hours of programming at a total cost of nearly $50 million. The remaining programs came from a variety of other sources, discussed in Section 10.5.

The SPC system has been both praised for increasing democracy in the program selection process (at no other network do the affiliates have such a say) and criticized for its emphasis on minimizing financial risk, limiting program innovation, and fostering continuation of "the safe, the cheap, and the known" (Reeves and Hoffer, 1976). The SPC supplies about half of the PBS national schedule, including such well-known staples as *Sesame Street, NOVA,* and *The MacNeil/Lehrer Newshour.* Businesses and other sources underwrote the other half of PBS programming (see Section 10.4).

By 1989, PBS was moving to strengthen the appeal of its prime-time schedule to allow enhanced promotion to increase audiences and raise more program underwriting funds (see Section 10.4). Under the plan, PBS would require at least one public TV station in each market to carry the same program schedule from 8–10 P.M. Sunday through Friday, leaving the 10–11 P.M. hour and all Saturday evening under station control.

Satellite Interconnection Public television pioneered in the use of satellites for network relays. The idea of using communications satellites instead

EXHIBIT 10–3   Public TV Program Sources and Channels

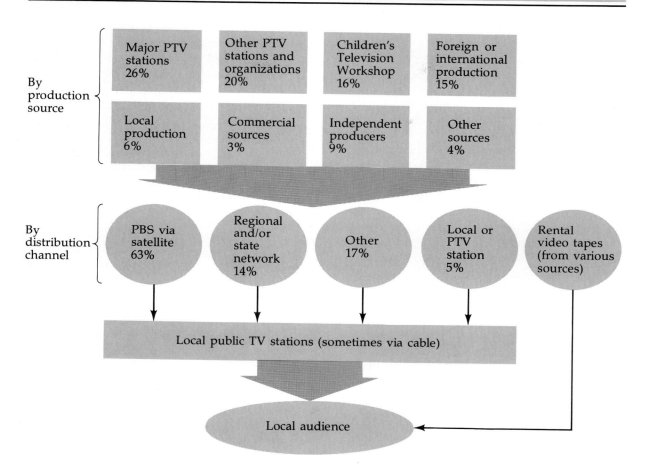

By production source:
- Major PTV stations 26%
- Other PTV stations and organizations 20%
- Children's Television Workshop 16%
- Foreign or international production 15%
- Local production 6%
- Commercial sources 3%
- Independent producers 9%
- Other sources 4%

By distribution channel:
- PBS via satellite 63%
- Regional and/or state network 14%
- Other 17%
- Local or PTV station 5%
- Rental video tapes (from various sources)

Local public TV stations (sometimes via cable)

Local audience

Public television programs come primarily from the eight sources shown at the top of the diagram, and are distributed to public television stations by the four means shown in the middle. Note that the percentages, which vary only marginally from year to year, add to 100 for production source, and also to 100 for distribution source. Cable and home video, of little importance in the 1970s, were growing in distribution importance by the late 1980s.

SOURCE: Corporation for Public Broadcasting.

of AT&T's microwave facilities for relaying public television programs goes back to a Ford Foundation proposal in 1966. A decade later, with government funding support, PBS announced a plan to inter-connect public television stations by means of transponders on a domestic communications satellite. Benefits claimed for the system included better-quality reception, ability to relay signals both east and west as well as variously within given regions, transmission of several signals at a time to allow stations to pick and choose among a wider variety, and cost savings. Stations had to contribute about $25,000 each (a hefty sum for most) to install earth stations, but in a decade would have full ownership of their TVRO antenna.

PBS stations worried not only about the cost but also about the increased centralization that satellite relays would bring. After considerable debate over how the satellite scheduling process should be controlled, the stations set up a Transponder Allocation Committee, ostensibly part of PBS, but in reality controlled directly by the licensees. The stations thus determined the use of transponders. During 1978, public television stations sequentially disconnected themselves from the terrestrial network and began using the satellite interconnection—the first national television network to do so.

PBS's relay system relies on 150 receive-only ground antennas owned by the stations. There are 21 ground stations that can uplink programs to the satellite as well as receive them. One uplink facility, near Washington, provides the main PBS feed; the other uplinks serve regional networks from centers in Colorado, Nebraska, Florida, South Carolina, and Connecticut.

The satellite distribution system, contrary to initial worries, actually enhanced the autonomy of the PBS member stations. They attained greater control over what they receive and use by being able to pick and choose among varied program offerings. They have been largely freed from the time and schedule constraints of a single-feed network. The satellite facilities have improved technical quality, and opened new fund-raising possibilities through the sale of unneeded satellite capacity to other users.

In 1988, PBS asked for bids for a replacement satellite system costing $240 million, to be in place by 1992. The new satellite will offer either four C-band and two Ku-band transponders, or six Ku-band. The higher-frequency Ku-band option, although costing more initially, would allow smaller earth antennas and provide for more system technical flexibility and possible HDTV applications. Congress authorized $200 million toward this re-

placement satellite in late 1988, with the stations being responsible for defraying the remaining costs.

National Public Radio (NPR) Public radio provides an interesting contrast. In 1970, CPB set up *National Public Radio* (NPR) both to interconnect stations (like PBS) and to produce programs (unlike PBS). As a second Carnegie Commission report noted in 1979, NPR:

combines national production and distribution capability with political representation, in a way which many feel is unthinkable for television. In addition, the production activities of NPR are funded directly by CPB and are not, therefore, entirely controlled by the licensee. Unlike the situation in public television, the public radio stations have been quite willing to have national program production and distribution centralized and under the financial oversight of CPB. Public radio stations supported the creation of NPR from the beginning, and they retain control over it through its board. Sorely underfinanced, the stations have recognized the benefits of centralizing program functions. (CCFPB, 1979: 61).

The fact that the NPR network can pick and choose from among a large pool of potential affiliates gives it more clout as a network than PBS. The latter has to admit any noncommercial television station, regardless of its status or policies.

NPR provides its affiliates with about 22 percent of their daily programs. They do not have to carry any set amount of programs. NPR also provides station representation (lobbying) as well as satellite interconnection coordination, with 21 uplinks and over 300 downlinks, most shared with PBS. Satellite distribution began in 1980 (the world's first radio network distributed by satellite) with four audio channels, increased by 1988 to 12 channels. As with the television system, NPR can now send out a variety of simultaneous programs, allowing stations to pick and choose from among more material than before.

Like PBS, NPR has had its financial problems. In 1983–1984, faced with the Republican administration's plans to cut all funding of public broadcasting, NPR's leadership embarked on an ill-fated series of ventures to develop independent funding. NPR's financial status became so precarious by 1984 that the network could save itself only by laying off 140 persons, trimming all but morning and evening news programs for several years, and borrowing $9 million dollars from CPB, which member stations eventually repaid. Some large NPR stations dropped out of the network at this stage.

In 1987, however, NPR's relation with its affiliate stations, which had been under strain during the financial crisis, changed for the better. All CPB radio program funds then began to go directly to the stations, which support NPR by subscribing to (paying for) morning news (including *Morning Edition,* which began in 1979, and *Weekend Edition,* which debuted in 1985), afternoon news (including *All Things Considered,* which began in 1971), and/or NPR's musical and cultural performance programs. More than 90 percent of the member stations subscribe to both news services. At the end of the 1980s, NPR began developing new program ideas in all these categories as stations saved money by increasingly moving to part-time rather than full-time affiliation. Stations, which had paid little or nothing for NPR programs before 1984, began paying anywhere from $25,000 to over $300,000 annually for the network program service. Even stations choosing no network programs pay a fee for NPR's representation or lobbying role.

American Public Radio (APR) A second public radio network, *American Public Radio* (APR), began in 1981; it was formed by Minnesota Public Radio chiefly as a distribution channel for the popular *A Prairie Home Companion,* featuring Garrison Keillor. By 1985, it claimed to be the largest distributor of public radio programming. *Companion* left the air in 1987 when Keillor tired of it, although APR continued the idea with *Good Evening.* Keillor returned to public radio with a new program in the Fall of 1989. APR provides more than 200 hours of material each week to 327 affiliate stations. Unlike NPR, APR provides programs to only one station per market, much like commercial networks. It does not produce programs as NPR does, but rather acquires them from the stations much like PBS. APR distributes original musical performance programs and in 1987 began to feed *MonitoRadio,* a new half-hour weeknight news and feature program of the *Christian Science Monitor* newspaper.

10.3
Stations

Public radio and television stations vary enormously not only in size and resources, but also in goals and philosophy. Though nominally all qualify as "noncommercial educational" stations to the FCC, some flirt with commercialism and many play no discernible educational role. The main source of variation comes from the different types of station ownership. All noncommercial stations are exempt from the ownership limits placed on commercial licensees.

Television Public television stations are of four basic types: (1) state- or municipally-controlled stations, (2) college and university stations, (3) public school system stations, and (4) community stations. The four types tend to differ, even conflict, in their philosophies.

More than 122 stations (or about 38 percent) come under state or municipal control; many of these operate as parts of state educational networks. Among such networks, usually one station located in the state capital does most of the programming; the others serve, in effect, as repeaters. Alabama began what became a nine-station network in 1955; Georgia, Kentucky, Mississippi, Nebraska, South Carolina, and others soon followed its example. In some states, such as Pennsylvania, stations licensed to various (usually local) groups have joined in informal networks.

Some 82 stations, or 25 percent of all public television facilities, belong to institutions of higher learning, most of them publicly supported. They usually have close ties to college curricula and often complement long-established university educational radio stations. The University of Wisconsin's WHA-TV on channel 21 in Madison, for example, went on the air in 1954, building on four decades of prior radio experience. University stations, often staffed largely by students or interns, serve as training grounds in addition to offering program services.

University administrations usually give only general oversight, refraining from direct meddling in station operations. Respect for academic freedom tends to prevent politically inspired interference. A notable exception to this general practice occurred at the University of Houston in Texas when it scheduled the 1980 PBS program *Death of a Princess,* a documentary about the execution for adultery of a Saudi Arabian princess and her commoner lover. Fearing adverse oil industry reactions, the university's vice president for public information canceled a scheduled telecast of the program on the university station, countermanding station management. When viewers mounted a legal challenge to such censorship, an appellate court upheld the university, finding no violation of viewers' First Amendment rights.

Stations operated by, or as auxiliaries of, local school systems or school boards constitute much the smallest category of public television broadcasters—only 14 stations, or just over 4 percent. Such stations naturally focus on in-school instructional programs produced by and for the school system. As school budgets became tighter, several such stations left the air or were transferred to other licensees.

Organizations made up of representatives from various community groups, including schools, colleges, art and cultural organizations, and the like, control 105 public TV stations—a third of all outlets. These nonprofit operations usually receive no direct tax support, depending on foundation, business, and listener funding.

The four ownership structures with their differing funding mechanisms and program goals lead to correspondingly different philosophies. The school- and university-run stations tend to stress education and instruction, whereas the community stations provide a broad mix of cultural, entertainment, and educational programs aimed at more general audiences.

Radio   The best known noncommercial radio stations are the 300 NPR affiliates, all but 28 on the FM band. Those public radio licensees fall into the same categories as public television stations, with universities and schools holding 65 percent, community groups 31 percent, and states and municipalities just over 4 percent of all "CPB-qualified" stations. A much larger group of about 900 "have-not" noncommercial stations either do not qualify for NPR affiliation or do not wish to join the network.

CPB decided to base the national noncommercial radio network on a cadre of professionally competent, full-service stations, referred to as "CPB-qualified." Such stations must meet prescribed minimum standards, among them FM power of at least 3,000 watts, at least one production studio and a separate control room, at least five full-time employees, an operational schedule of 18 hours a day, and an operating budget of at least $150,000 per year. In 1988, only 300 outlets, about a quarter of all the noncommercial radio licensees, qualified for CPB grants and for affiliation with NPR by meeting or exceeding those standards. The other 900 or so stations provide local, often very limited, services.

The FCC's 1948 decision to stimulate growth of noncommercial educational FM by licensing stations to operate on the very low power of 10 watts proved an impediment to the growth of a strong NPR network. Several hundred low-power stations had gone on the air by the 1970s, often taking up frequencies for "electronic sandboxes" instead of giving serious broadcast training or service. Faced with growing demand for public radio licenses, the FCC in 1978 began reversing its course by ordering 10-watt stations to either raise their power to a minimum of 100 watts or assume a secondary status on a commercial frequency, with the possibility of having to give way entirely to an applicant for full-power service.

10.4
Economics of Public Broadcasting

Ask noncommercial broadcasters to name their most serious problem and they invariably answer, insufficient funding. Exhibit 10–4 compares the finances of commercial and public television. It highlights

EXHIBIT 10–4 Funding of Public Broadcasting: A Comparison

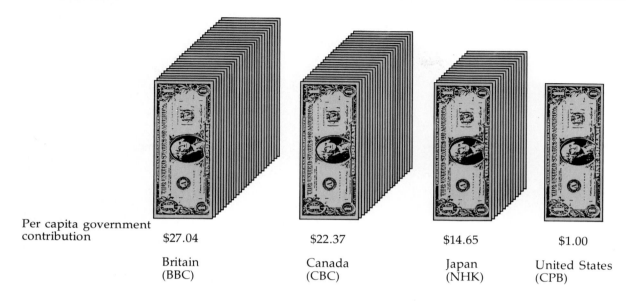

Per capita government
contribution

$27.04	$22.37	$14.65	$1.00
Britain (BBC)	Canada (CBC)	Japan (NHK)	United States (CPB)

A comparison of the per-capita funding for U.S. public broadcasting with that of the noncommercial services in three other countries that also have competing public-service and commercial broadcast systems shows the woefully inadequate funding in the United States. Not shown in the U.S. figure is income obtained by about 800 noncommercial FM stations outside the CPB system.

SOURCE: Corporation for Public Broadcasting.

the inadequacy of funding for the public stations—the *best* funded of the noncommercial licensees. Public television revenue of all kinds in 1986 amounted to $1.13 billion, or $4.70 for every person in America, whereas in the same year commercial television grossed $22 billion, or over $92 per person. Exhibit 10–5 shows the diversity of public broadcasting's funding sources (*not* including the stations outside of CPB's purview, mainly those 900-plus noncommercial radio outlets). Each source brings different obligations with its funding, and each has its own biases. To accommodate the conflicting goals of their numerous and varied contributors, public broadcasters often resort to bland, noncontroversial programs—also a notorious weakness of commercial programming. A monopoly source of funding could also be unduly re-

strictive, of course, but as things stand, public broadcasting executives have to serve too many masters. They spend an inordinate amount of time on fund raising and have too little financial stability to plan effectively.

Congress, citizen groups, and think tanks have long considered alternative ways of funding noncommercial broadcasting. Suggested sources have included an excise tax on the sale or license fees for the use of television receivers (suggested by the first Carnegie Commission), acceptance of limited advertising, conversion of public television to a subscription television (STV) operation, a tax on commercial broadcast revenues, leasing or auctioning spectrum space, and ownership and leasing of a satellite.

None of these proposals has received unanimous

EXHIBIT 10–5 Public Broadcasting Revenue by Source: 1987

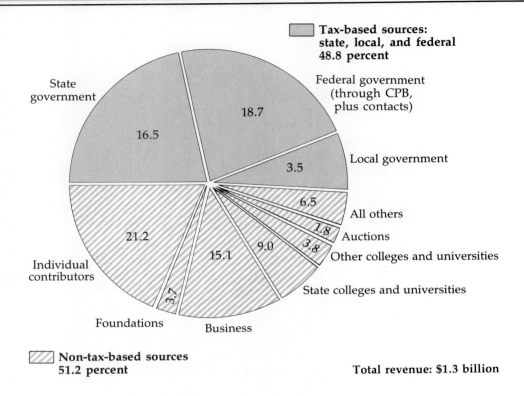

State government 16.5

18.7 Federal government (through CPB, plus contacts)

Tax-based sources: state, local, and federal 48.8 percent

3.5 Local government

6.5 All others

1.8 Auctions

3.8 Other colleges and universities

9.0 State colleges and universities

15.1 Business

3.7 Foundations

21.2 Individual contributors

Non-tax-based sources 51.2 percent

Total revenue: $1.3 billion

During the 1980s, public broadcasting depended increasingly on nontax sources of revenue. At the start of the decade, tax-based sources provided more than two-thirds of all revenue; by 1987 they provided only about one-half.

SOURCE: Corporation for Public Broadcasting.

support, but all concerned agree on the need for (1) *insulating* noncommercial broadcasting from the political pressures of annual congressional funding, (2) an *amount* of funding adequate to allow growth, (3) year-to-year *stability* of revenue, and (4) funding over the *long term,* generally defined as five or more years, to allow more orderly planning of program and technical development. Actual sources of money so far have included foundations, tax support, corporate donations and underwriting, an advertising experiment, and listener contributions, none of which meet the four criteria.

Foundation Grants Next to tax sources, *foundations* provided the largest share of noncommercial broadcasting support up to 1962. During the formative years of educational television, the chief support came from the Fund for Adult Education, an arm of the Ford Foundation. The fund's areas of concern—American history, social anthropology, international understanding, and community self-development—automatically became educational television's topics of concern as well. The economic power of the fund determined the very nature of educational television. The fund also played a crucial role in securing reserved TV channels by helping the groups pressing for channel reservations, by supplying early stations with substantial equipment grants, and by providing a small core of nationally distributed programs for initial operations.

Without the backing of the Ford Foundation, educational television might not have survived its first decade. From 1951 through 1962, the foundation gave some $82 million. In addition to the aforementioned grants, money also went to television instruction, including in-school experiments in several communities. After 1963 and the beginning of federal equipment grants, Ford funds strengthened the national program distribution effort and supported stations with direct grants.

The foundation planned from the start to furnish only seed money—initial start-up grants to help a station or a service run for a few years in the hope that permanent means of support would evolve. Other foundation money, especially from local groups to support stations, was contributed in the 1950s, but the Ford support was crucial. By 1983, by which time its direct role had been largely phased out, Ford grants to noncommercial broadcasting had totaled more than $300 million.

In 1981, the largest single gift ever made to public broadcasting came from Walter Annenberg, publisher of *TV Guide*. He donated $150 million, spread over 15 years, to fund a project to create innovative college-level courses and programs. Organized under CPB, the Annenberg/CPB project annually funds projects selected from dozens of applications. Some are aired on public TV stations.

Government Support From the beginning of educational FM broadcasting in the 1940s, local and state governments supported it at the station and state-network levels. By the mid-1960s, local and state tax funds provided about half of all public broadcasting income. In the face of rising budget problems, however, state support declined to about 30 percent of total system income by the mid-1980s. Local government (mainly school board) support fell to under 5 percent.

In contrast to local and state governments, the federal government at first gave no financial assistance. The FCC set up the noncommercial FM and television educational class of licensees by administrative ruling, but licensees received no legislative recognition until the Educational Television Facilities Act of 1962. This amendment to the Communications Act explicitly acknowledged a federal role in supporting noncommercial broadcasting. It authorized $32 million for awards over a five-year period by what was then the Department of Health, Education and Welfare for the construction, but not operation, of educational television stations. (This function was later transferred to the Department of Commerce's National Telecommunications and Information Administration.) This law was a delayed response to the need to get such stations on the air to protect the reserved channels against commercial pressures for reclassification.*

Limited to a maximum of a million dollars for any one state, federal funds have to be matched by funds from other sources—one federal dollar for each dollar raised locally. This act, extended and revised, continues to assist equipment and facility funding for public broadcasting in the late 1980s, despite several Republican administration attempts to close the program down.

The Reagan administration (1981–1989) did nothing to ease public broadcasting's shortage of funds. Although supporting public broadcasting in principle, Reagan said that the service should look more to the private sector and less to the federal government for funding. This preference echoed the conservative reliance on the marketplace: those who wanted public broadcasting should be willing to pay for it more directly than through tax-supported congressional appropriations. Reagan's policy sub-

---

*Some commercial stations assisted noncommercial outlets by donating broadcast equipment and tower space for antennas—not always for altruistic reasons, however, but more often to keep the educational channels from turning into commercial competitors. In New York City, local commercial stations bought up a vacant commercial channel in 1961 and gave it for use as an educational outlet—WNET-TV on channel 13—thus effectively removing a possible VHF-channel commercial competitor.

verted plans for much needed "long-range" funding from Congress.

Similar earlier attempts to persuade Congress to fund the Corporation for Public Broadcasting for longer than the usual single-year budget cycle fell victim to President Nixon's dislike of the service in the early 1970s (see Exhibit 10–2). He vetoed several bills calling for two- to three-year funding.

During the Ford administration (1974–1977), Congress first authorized funds for more than a single year in the Public Broadcasting Financing Act of 1975, although the legislators actually appropriated money for only three.* The new act upped the matching formula—federal money had to be matched at the ratio of $1.00 for every $2.50 raised by the public broadcasters.

The multiyear appropriations gave PBS sufficient time and funds to initiate serious planning for a satellite interconnection, as well as long-term program commitments. Congress renewed the three-year appropriations cycle again in 1978, 1981, and 1984. Then a new threat appeared. Faced with increasing budget deficits and the Reagan administration's quest to reduce or eliminate federal funding for public television, Congress began to *rescind* public broadcasting appropriations to which it had already agreed. In 1984, Reagan vetoed attempts by Congress to raise CPB funding; finally the Senate and House agreed to bills with the lower amounts he sought.

In 1988, while passing yet another funding bill and unhappy with the continued bickering among public broadcasters, Congress considered giving most appropriations directly to stations, bypassing CPB. In the end, the House and Senate authorized increased spending for public broadcasting through the normal CPB channels, from $245 to $285 million over 1991–1993, and authorized NTIA's facilities funding program to provide $36 to $42 million over the same period. This history of uncertain commitment by Congress to long-term funding levels has made it difficult for public broadcasters to plan for the future. Some seek continued federal funding only until some other method of support can be found. Most promising thus far has been the underwriting of programming.

Program Underwriting A limited form of sponsorship called *underwriting* enables program producers to secure grants from business concerns to defray production costs of specific projects. FCC regulations allow companies brief identifying announcements at the beginning and end of such programs. After 1981, the FCC also allowed corporations to show their logos or trademarks. Sometimes several firms share in underwriting a single series, but more often, as with the well-known Sunday evening *Masterpiece Theatre,* one company, in this case Mobil, underwrites the entire production cost. Stations also seek *local* underwriting to cover their acquisition costs.

Underwriters usually prefer programs that attract sizable audiences (at least in public television terms) rather than the more specialized or controversial programs that might be less popular but are nevertheless the kind of programs an alternative service should provide. Most underwriters will associate themselves only with relatively bland programs, making challenging public-affairs offerings difficult to fund. It took Boston's public television station, WGBH, more than six years to find the $5.6 million needed to produce its controversial *Vietnam: A Television History,* which became the highest-rated documentary of 1983 and won several awards—as well as hostile criticism from conservatives.

By 1986, corporations paid the largest single portion—37 percent—of PBS's annual budget for original broadcast hours, just over $73 million. PBS affiliates paid 27 percent, and CPB provided 15 percent. From 1973 through 1986, corporate support rose by more than 2000 percent.

*In the congressional budget process, the House and Senate first *authorize* a spending ceiling, then later *appropriate* an actual spending level. The second decision, to actually release money, is the decision that really matters. In the 1980s, under pressure from the Reagan administration, Congress created a third step in the budget process, going back to *rescind* funds that were already appropriated but had not yet been spent. It was here, as noted in the text, that public broadcast funds were trimmed back.

Commercial Experiments   As far back as the 1930s, some educational broadcasting advocates proposed *nonprofit* rather than noncommercial radio, with commercials defraying operating costs. During the FCC's 1952 hearings on television channel reservations, educational interests realized that their hopes rested on complete disassociation from commercialism. However, nearly 30 years later, in 1981, Congress temporarily set aside the ban on advertising for noncommercial stations, establishing a Temporary Commission on Alternative Financing for Public Telecommunications (TCAF) to supervise an experiment with commercials on noncommercial stations. An FCC commissioner chaired the TCAF, which included U.S. senators, members of Congress, and public broadcasting representatives among its members.

In January 1982, 10 public television stations volunteered to take part in a 15-month trial of on-air-advertising. Public radio stations decided not to participate. The legislation authorizing the test stipulated that ads could not interrupt programs, could not exceed two minutes in length, and could not promote political, religious, or other ideological points of view. Station managers also maintained a watchful eye to avoid commercials whose content might be considered inappropriate for a public-service medium. Station WTTW-TV in Chicago earned the most advertising income of the 10 participating stations—more than a million dollars in 1982–1983, or nearly 10 percent of its revenue that year. Following completion of the test, the TCAF concluded:

▮ Limited advertising added significant revenues only if labor unions and copyright holders did not demand full equity with commercial stations.

▮ Advertising produced no negative impact on viewing patterns, numbers of subscribers to public television, or other contributions.

▮ Advertising had no effect on programming.

Still, the TCAF concluded that most public television stations would not carry advertisements because of legal restrictions, local economic considerations, or concerns about advertising's impact on the character of public broadcasting. It added that although the experiment eliminated the worst concerns about the impact of advertising on other funding sources for public broadcasting, no experiment could show that advertising would not eventually cause loss of subscriber, underwriter, or government support (TCAF, 1983).

In 1984, the Senate Communications Subcommittee held hearings to examine whether advertising on public broadcasting should be resumed. Several station executives argued for the proposal, but most representatives from CPB opposed the concept (as did the National Association of Broadcasters, concerned about further competition). Eventually Congress shelved the idea, at least for the time being.

In the same year, perhaps influenced by the TCAF recommendations, the FCC authorized "enhanced underwriting," allowing some stations to carry what PBS President Bruce Christensen called "almost commercials" (Smith, 1985). Stations may sell 30-second announcements mentioning specific consumer products. The four-station New Jersey Network, for example, permitted advertisers to talk about products, services, and locations, but drew the line at statements about product superiority. In 1985, a commercial scheduled between the nightly news and the network's weekly drawing for the state lottery cost $350. Enhanced underwriting increased the New Jersey network's income from corporations threefold in just three years—to $900,000 in 1985. New York City's WNET-TV began selling 30-second *general support announcements* (GSAs) for between $1,000 and $1,500 each. They could include the company logo, location, brand and trade names, and a description of a product or service.

Such commercial inroads led to both pressure to open the advertising door even wider and concern by critics and the FCC that some stations had crossed the line from enhanced underwriting to outright commercialism. In 1986, the commission warned that it would enforce the limitations spelled out in its underwriting rules.

Critics charge that the creeping commercialization of public television cannot be justified. The need for an alternative service to commercial broadcasting rests on the fact that commercial motives inevitably tend to influence program choices, over-emphasizing some types and neglecting others. Subjecting public broadcasting to these same motives defeats the goal of a true alternative service.

Public Subscription Individual members of the public contribute about 22 percent of total public broadcasting system revenue, and just over 22 percent of public television revenue, sharing with state governments (just under 22 percent) the key funding role.

The constant search for money to meet the federal "match" requirements for both facilities funding from NTIA and CPB long-range general funding has driven many public television stations to push membership drives to the saturation point. Declining income from local tax-supported sources, such as school boards, has also forced more aggressive solicitation of viewers. Several times a year, at some stations, station staff and volunteers operate banks of telephones while on-air personalities plead for donations in the form of paid memberships. The hard sell of these "begathons" matches the excesses of commercial stations. Polls indicate that viewers disapprove of marathon fund-raising.

Over-the-air auctions (the source of just over 2 percent of public television revenue) can be even more objectionable. Auctions promote donated articles and services (often from commercial sources) so blatantly and at such length that they amount to program-length commercials, once illegal in commercial television. Reacting to criticism, some stations have reduced their on-air campaigns. Miami's station, for example, "bribes" viewers by promising to shorten or even forgo auctions if they meet gift quotas without waiting to be strong-armed into giving.

Other Funding Sources Other expedients considered or actually used to raise funds for non-commercial broadcasting include:

▪ Selling commercial rights to merchandise associated with programs (the Children's Television Workshop obtained a third of *Sesame Street*'s total revenue by the mid-1980s from such sales).

▪ Offering closed-circuit seminar services to business for substantial fees that exceed the actual production costs.

▪ Selling newly produced programs to commercial television or pay cable for initial showing before they are released to public television.

▪ Renting station facilities (usually studios) to commercial producers.

▪ Selling videotapes and other items to viewers.

▪ Participating in commercial tie-ins with programs (PBS gets a portion of the income derived from the many "companion" books sold to parallel PBS series).

▪ Trading a low-number educational UHF channel for a higher UHF commercial channel in the same market, gaining an often substantial cash payment from the commercial broadcaster. (The FCC has thus far disallowed trades of UHF for VHF channels.)

▪ Charging commercial broadcasters a tax or fee to help pay for public broadcast needs.

▪ Selling FM subcarrier or TV vertical blanking interval access for private uses.

▪ Auctioning commercial spectrum space, with proceeds going to develop a fully competitive public broadcasting system.

10.5
Program Sources

Although noncommercial broadcasting has the basic mission of supplying an alternative to commercial broadcasting, program overlap necessarily occurs, and there is even a certain amount of competition for programs. Noncommercial stations often show feature films and syndicated series obtained from the same distributors that commercial stations use. On the other hand, noncommercial outlets do more local production, more experimental programming, more documentaries, more literary-artistic-cultural material, and certainly more instructional/educational telecasts than do commercial broadcasters. Exhibit 10–6 shows the program flow in the noncommercial system.

EXHIBIT 10–6 Public Television Funding Flow

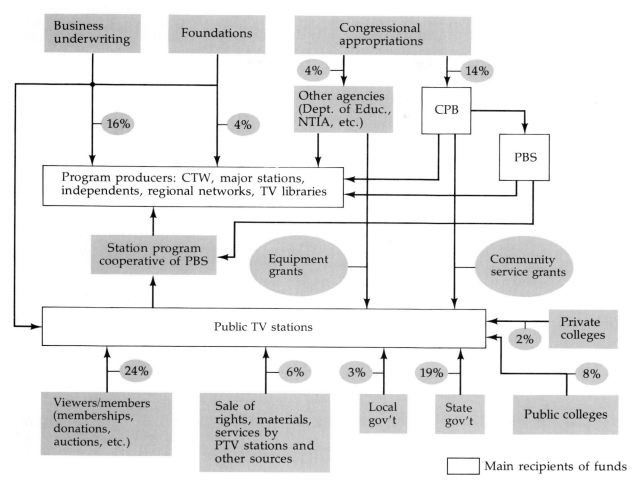

The complex flow of money among institutions in public television is illustrated here. A chart for public radio would be similar, but would show a larger federal share.

SOURCE: Data from Corporation for Public Broadcasting.

Stations as Producers Several production-oriented stations act as network producers for PBS. Among the contributing producer stations, WGBH-Boston, WNET-New York, and KQED-San Francisco stand out. Each has a long history of creative innovation in public television. WGBH introduced Julia Child's *The French Chef,* one of the first nationally recognized public television series, and now produces *Masterpiece Theatre.* Washington, DC, station WETA supplies timely news and public affairs programs, receiving direct support from CPB, among others. In 1986, nearly 38 percent of all public television programming came from such major producer stations.

Independent TV Producers   PBS buys about a tenth of its programs from independent producers, some of whom have complained that the network does not give them the opportunities they merit. They argue that a service dedicated to enhancing program diversity should be especially supportive of innovative producers. Congress recognized this goal when it extended CPB funding in 1988 by requiring that CPB fund an Independent Production Service, separate from CPB, to encourage still more independent program sources.

One nonprofit independent producer, Children's Television Workshop (CTW), won international fame for its *Sesame Street* series, which began in 1969. CTW's initial funding came from government and foundation grants. By the late 1980s, two-thirds of its budget came from ancillary commercial ventures, such as merchandising items using the program name and characters. It even produced a pay-cable series to generate revenue. Because of its independent funding, CTW rose above station-PBS quarrels, sticking to its own research-based agenda. In the mid-1980s, CTW, as discussed further in Section 12.4, provided just over 15 percent of all public TV programming.

TV Syndicators   Public television buys from many of the same syndicated program distributors as commercial television. In its search for alternative types of programs, however, public television draws heavily on foreign sources, notably Britain's BBC and Independent Television (the British commercial program companies). One of PBS's most successful long-running series, *Masterpiece Theatre,* comes from Britain, co-produced by Boston's WGBH (which selects the material and provides the opening and closing remarks by Alistair Cooke) and British independent television companies.

Except for Spanish-language imports, American commercial television stations rarely buy syndicated programs from foreign suppliers. Not so cable television: as specialized cable networks such as Arts and Entertainment and The Discovery Channel emerged, cable competed directly with public television for foreign documentaries, drama series, and feature films. Imported programs previously seen only on public television have now become standard fare on these and other cable channels, reducing public television's once unique role.

In carrying out their classroom instruction mission, public television stations draw upon several large libraries of instructional materials that act as syndicators. Notable examples include the Agency for Instructional Television in Bloomington, IN, and the Great Plains National Instructional Television Library of Lincoln, NE. Both produce, archive, and distribute series of instructional programs for all levels of education.

Local TV Production   The typical noncommercial television station produces and uses more local material than do commercial stations. Locally produced programs consist mainly of news and public affairs, along with some educational/instructional material telecast in daytime hours for in-school use. Just as it has with commercial television stations, the amount of public television local production has declined by half from the mid-1970s to the late 1980s, averaging just over 5 percent of their schedules.

Noncommercial Radio   The typical public radio station affiliated with NPR and/or APR took about two-fifths of its weekly airtime (an average of 146 hours per week, or about 21 hours a day) from these networks and other syndicated sources. Stations produced most of the remaining hours—in many cases in the form of recorded music programs. The increasing number of public radio stations duplicating NPR programs in some major markets led in the late 1980s to some stations leaving the network. By going it alone, they felt, they could more readily specialize and attract at least niche audiences. Such specialization has become the name of the game for some of the approximately 900 noncommercial FM stations that are *not* funded by CPB or affiliated with NPR.

10.6
Rethinking the Role of Noncommercial Broadcasting

Noncommercial broadcasting faced a problem of survival by the 1990s. Despite what nearly all public broadcast spokespersons say, the lack of money does not seem to be the central issue. The noncommercial media face a more basic question: what should noncommercial broadcasting do in times of rapid change in electronic media to justify its existence? Years of bickering and disagreement over mission have ill prepared the noncommercial media to face new competition. The perceived differences among stations and between television and radio now become very important.

Traditional Defense   Those long active in or newly won over to public television claim for it many public benefits, notably the provision of programs usually unavailable on commercial stations: fine arts, music, dance, important foreign-language films, superior drama, public-affairs discussions, and other program categories neglected by commercial networks and stations. Proponents argue that public television does better than commercial television at meeting the needs of subgroups in society, such as ethnic minorities and children. Finally, many see public stations as the last bastion of localism, reflecting and projecting their local communities rather than merely passing on network or syndicated material from distant centers. Public TV station and national organization officials say that public participation in station and system advisory groups helps to define the differences between the goals of public and commercial services. The very existence of disagreements about the role of public television, defenders argue, indicates its openness. Naturally, defenders also see their service as an essential relief from the ever-increasing hard sell content of commercial networks, stations, and cable systems.

Noncommercial radio supporters appear to have a stronger case than supporters of noncommercial television. The CPB-qualified stations affiliated with NPR provide radio's best news and public-affairs programs and attract consistent and loyal audiences. The 900 or so noncommercial FM stations that are not part of the larger CPB/NPR-led elite offer an almost infinite variety of programs and services. The fact that they can often rely totally on listeners and community groups for support attests to their value. When it comes to financial support, radio simply provides "more bang for the buck."

Critical Views   Changes in the electronic media scene, however, have shifted the ground for debate over the future of noncommercial communications. Development of cable networks and other technologies such as VCRs has weakened a major argument for public television by co-opting its once-unique programming, with the possible exception of most in-class instruction. Children's cable services such as Nickelodeon and several ethnic-oriented services aimed at minority audiences have taken over provinces once considered public television's turf. Some critics regard public participation in public television as a mere sham because professional managers make most decisions, just as they do in commercial operations. In short, public television has difficulty in sustaining its traditional claim to offer unique service.

Critics also deride public television for not being able to attract larger audiences. They argue that public television's vaunted fine arts and high culture merely serve privileged groups that are easily able to afford such material without resorting to publicly supported broadcast channels. Critics liken tax support of public broadcasting, dwindling though it is, to the government subsidies that once sustained passenger ships that only the rich could afford to patronize.

Critics hark back to the educational origins of noncommercial broadcasting in emphasizing the value of television and radio for instruction and informal education, often citing *Sesame Street* as an example of what can be accomplished in this genre. The resultant policy question becomes how to preserve and improve this educative role if other services continue to co-opt public broadcasting's broader "alternative" cultural programming function.

Critics sum up by dismissing the funding problem always cited by public broadcasters as a mere evasion, saying that lack of sufficient audience appeal rather than a lack of money lies at the root of their problem. They see the funding crisis as a *result* of the system's limitations rather than a *cause* of those problems. Given the increasing number of viewing and listening options available to most people, critics argue, narrow-appeal services will have to find their own audience support, probably in some form of direct payment from viewers for the services they choose. The rationale for public assistance to a once-unique alternative no longer holds up.

Such arguments largely reflect the deregulatory philosophy that was injected into discussions of U.S. media policy during the conservative political ascendancy of the 1980s (discussed at length in Sections 17.7 and 18.7). Similar attacks on public broadcasting surfaced in other countries, also stimulated by a market-oriented, laissez faire approach to media regulation. Even so widely esteemed a service as that of the BBC came under attack as elitist and lacking in the fiscal responsibility that, according to deregulatory theory, only the "discipline of the market" can impose.

In Europe, as in the United States, these attacks raise a basic question: should all broadcasting be regarded strictly as an economic undertaking, with programs treated as ordinary consumer goods? Or should at least a significant part of any national broadcasting system be regarded as a cultural undertaking, with programs treated as a significant aspect of national culture? Must everything depend on that shibboleth of free marketers, "consumer choice"? Not every consumer chooses to attend the great museums, galleries, and libraries that public funds support in locations not so distant from festering slums, yet few would advocate dismantling all such cultural treasures and diverting their government grants to public housing.

Outlook   Nevertheless, the wave of market-oriented thinking and the deregulatory policies that ride its crest cannot be ignored. As the decade of the 1980s came to an end, leaders of the national public-service broadcasting organizations prepared for the 1990s with a keen sense of the need for profound self-assessments. CPB had a five-year plan in the making, constantly under revision. NPR undertook an in-depth review of its role and its options. PBS tightened control over the public network's prime-time program scheduling, seemingly modeling itself more closely on the national commercial networks than before.

Meanwhile, in 1988, an informal working group consisting of those active in or familiar with public broadcasting made a study of the scene and came up with a proposal for a radical restructuring. It would combine the functions of CPB and PBS into a single Independent Public Broadcasting Institution with a mandate to focus on program production, acquisition, and distribution. Funding would come from a 2-percent levy on consumer electronics purchases. Half the resulting revenues would go to the new Institute, the rest directly to the stations to spend as they saw fit. A pipe dream perhaps, but it dramatized what public broadcasting needs in order not simply to survive, but to fulfill its role as an effective alternative service: an end to bickering, overlapping jurisdictions, and contradictory policies; and relief from the chaotic political shenanigans that inevitably come from not having a federally assured but relatively neutral source of revenue.

Summary

▌ Noncommercial broadcasting includes the public radio and television system, but also hundreds of other radio stations supported by communities, religious groups, and others. All share a nonprofit goal of providing programs that are alternatives to the commercial system.

▌ Educational radio traces its beginnings back before World War I. After a brief boom in the 1920s, the number of noncommercial AM stations had declined by 1945 to about 25.

▌ The FCC first reserved channels for noncommercial radio in 1941 for FM, a reservation retained when FM changed frequency bands in 1945. After a long debate, the FCC extended the reservation idea to television in 1952's *Sixth Report and Order*.

▌ A policy debate about the proper mission of noncommercial broadcasting began in the 1950s and still continues. Many argued for a fairly narrow educational role built around individual stations, whereas others pushed for broader audience appeal, with cultural and entertainment programming disseminated though a centralized authority much like a commercial network.

▌ The landmark Carnegie Commission report of 1967 led directly to legislation late that year that established the Corporation for Public Broadcasting, which in turn set up the Public Broadcasting Service and National Public Radio.

▌ The early years of the new system were marked by a struggle for power between the stations and the new national entities, a search for expanded federal funding, and political interference by Congress and the White House.

▌ By the late 1970s, pushed in part by the opportunities made available by the first broadcast use of satellite interconnection, PBS had settled into a station-controlled program distribution role, with lobbying and other functions moved elsewhere. PBS administers the annual Station Program Cooperative, which funds the most popular national program series.

▌ National Public Radio produces as well as distributes its news and entertainment programming. Numerous changes and a financial crisis resulted by the late 1980s in a public radio system funded and controlled by the stations. American Public Radio is another distributor of programs for noncommercial stations.

▌ Noncommercial television stations are of four types: (1) state- or municipally-controlled stations; (2) college and university stations; (3) public school system stations; and (4) community stations. They differ in approach and funding.

▌ Radio stations are broken into two groups—about 300 "elite" stations that are funded by CPB and belong to NPR, and another 900 or so that are not "CPB-qualified."

▌ Financial support of noncommercial broadcasting has always been a problem. The Ford Foundation and others supported early educational radio and television.

▌ The federal government first made tax funds available in 1963, and initiated long-range funding cycles in 1975. Government support has raised concerns about the adequacy of the insulation between funding and programming decisions. After 1981, under Reagan administration budget pressure, Congress often rescinded funds already approved for public broadcasting.

▌ Nongovernment funding of noncommercial broadcasting—the largest portion of system income—comes from several sources. Business entities often underwrite specific programs or series. Enhanced underwriting results in messages that look very much like commercials. Experiments in advertising on noncommercial stations, however, have not developed into a full-scale funding option.

▌ About a fifth of all noncommercial funding comes from the public through solicitation for memberships, fund-raising "begathons," and the like.

▌ Sources of programming vary widely and include individual stations, independents, syndicators, and instructional program libraries.

▌ Defenders of noncommercial broadcasting stress its services to those underserved by commercial radio and television: minorities, children, and those with cultural interests. Critics, on the other hand, argue there are now other technical and financial options for supplying the services provided by public broadcast stations and that thus the basis of the system set up in 1952 (TV channels) and 1967 (the current national structure) needs to be revised.

PROGRAMMING

PART 4

The collective term *programming* refers to the set of practices used in selecting, scheduling, and evaluating programs. Program decision making involves risks and uncertainties not characteristic of other businesses, operating as it does in the twin spotlights of intense public fascination and critical press reaction. Chapter 11 describes program decision-making problems and practices, the sources of programs, and the scheduling strategies commonly used by programmers. Chapter 12 reviews network programming practices of both broadcasting and cable television. Chapter 13 looks at syndicated and local television and radio programming. Together, these chapters show the options open to programmers and the considerations that govern program choices.

CHAPTER 11

PROGRAMMING BASICS

Programming involves the tasks of choosing programs, scheduling them in a meaningful order, and evaluating their degree of success or failure. All three processes interact constantly: any program schedule will have some hits, some outright failures, and many borderline successes that may tip over into failure at any time. The programmer obtains new shows to replace the canceled shows, adjusts the order of programs with a strategy in mind, and tracks the ratings of all shows continuously. For those responsible for prime-time broadcast network programs, success means attracting at least 15 million television households; for small-market radio station programmers, success may mean capturing a few hundred listeners.

Whether viewed from the perspective of the network, the system, or the station, the overriding purpose of commercial programming is to attract advertisers by delivering audiences of sufficient size and appropriate composition. Other purposes, such as improving or informing the public, are usually secondary. Programmers face a chronic shortage of programs that are both suitable and affordable. So many services clamor for programs that programmers never end their search for "product," as they call it—a term that hints at their point of view regarding program quality. Product that can attract audiences of desirable size and composition costs so much that filling all the channels continuously with brand new, not to mention "good," programs would be an economic impossibility.

11.1
Economic Constraints

Commercial programmers find themselves constrained economically in three ways: (1) programs are exceedingly costly and prices constantly rise; (2) programmers need so much of this costly material that they must devise ways of using it parsimoniously; and (3) programmers depend on advertisers to defray the cost, and so programs must be chosen with a view to attracting the specific audiences advertisers want to target.

Program Costs   The three major networks spend about $4.5 billion a year for the rights to limited use of programs. Nearly $3 billion of that goes for prime-time programs alone. Networks spend more than $150 million each year on pilots for new program series, of which three-quarters fail.

In the late 1980s, the license fees producers charged the commercial networks for a one-hour prime-time drama or action/adventure program averaged $850,000 per episode. Lower-priced series cost as little as $600,000, but higher-priced ones, such as *Dallas, Dynasty,* and *Miami Vice,* cost over $1 million an hour. For 30-minute shows, producer/distributors charged somewhat less than half as much as for 60-minute shows—an average of about $350,000 per episode. Half-hour shows cost less to produce, mainly because most can be shot on permanent, in-studio sets rather than on location, which is much more costly. In addition, producers shoot most 30-minute shows on videotape rather than film, at a saving of about $100,000 per episode.

High as these prices seem, they rarely cover the full cost of production. Producers of prime-time entertainment series count on subsequent syndication fees to bring in the profits. This maneuver, known as *deficit financing,* capitalizes on the peculiar dynamics of the syndication market. Initial network showing enhances the future value of a series because such exposure gives a series the prestige and track record it needs for successful syndication in both foreign and domestic markets.

Part of network program budgets also goes to purchase the rights to sports events. Together, ABC and NBC paid a total of $1.2 billion for the rights to major league baseball in the six years 1984 to 1989; all three broadcast networks and ESPN shared three years of NFL professional football (1988 to 1990) for $1.4 billion; CBS paid $166 million for three years of NCAA post-season basketball tournaments for the early 1990s; and NBC agreed to pay $401 million for the 1992 Summer Olympics in Barcelona, Spain.

Cable networks often compete directly with the broadcast networks for rights to theatrical motion pictures and sporting events and with stations for syndicated programs. Their budgets, however, do not yet approach those of ABC, CBS, or NBC. In 1988, basic cable networks as a group spent about $716 million for programs and were increasing their budgets by about $100 million each year. In all, cable collectively spends about $1.6 billion for programs annually, compared with $1.5 billion annually for *each* of the three broadcast television networks.

At the station level, nonnetwork programs are priced according to market rank, prior program performance, and other factors such as how often they have been rerun. Large-market stations commonly pay more than $10 million for 4 plays of a hundred or so episodes of newly released network shows, though small-market stations might pay as little as $100,000 for the same series. Hits such as *Cosby* and *Who's the Boss?* commanded very high per-episode prices from stations in the late 1980s. Competition between basic cable networks and broadcast stations for the same programs has made former network properties increasingly valuable. In 1988, for example, USA Network paid $30 million for the CBS series *Murder, She Wrote,* a record price for that network. Unlike the broadcast networks, cable networks do not always buy program rights on an *exclusive* basis. Producers often sell movie rights to more than one cable network simultaneously, with the result that the same film may appear on competing channels at the same time. Some networks do buy exclusive rights, however. HBO paid about $300 million in 1988 for the exclusive cable right to all Twentieth Century-Fox films produced between 1989 and 1991 and also made exclusive deals with Paramount, Warner Bros., and Columbia.

Parsimony Principle   To cope with the shortage of programs and their high cost, programmers resort to a variety of strategies based on what might be called the *parsimony principle.* This basic rule dictates that program product be used as sparingly as possible, repeated as often as possible, and shared as widely as possible.

Sparing use of product means, for example, using standardized openings, closings, and transitions in daily newscasts and weekly dramatic programs. It also means spinning out plot lines for as long as possible, as soap operas do, reusing sets and contest ideas, as game shows do, and relying on stereotyped character relationships, as situation comedies do.

Writers and programmers stretch resources by *repeating* program material, using formats that recycle much of the same material from day to day or week to week. All-sport radio stations and all-weather or all-news cable services embody this idea. Other examples include summer reruns, scheduling the same pay-cable movie in many time slots, the play lists of radio music formats, and recap, highlight, and other retrospective program formats ("The Best of . . . "). The weekend *Entertainment This Week,* recycles items from the daily *Entertainment Tonight* with updates and highlights. *Sesame Street* often repeats segments, placing them amid new surroundings. *60 Minutes* repeats stories, adding a tag that tells what has happened since the segment was first aired. Close monitoring of a station, network, or cable service will disclose a surprising amount of sheer repetition.

Program *sharing* relies on distribution mechanisms, broadcast/cable *networks* and *syndication*, that permit many individual outlets (stations and cable systems) to deliver the same programs to different audiences. This sharing usually occurs simultaneously in the case of networks, though normally not in the case of syndication. Sharing by networking or syndication spreads program costs among many outlets. An identical program appears as something fresh to viewers in each of the more than 210 television markets when carried by all affiliates of a broadcast network. A cable program that is distributed on one of the most popular cable networks can reach viewers in more than 8,000 cable franchise areas. The same syndicated program can be purchased by many independent or affiliated stations and be shown in as many as 210 markets.

Audience Targeting   Not only must commercial programmers use program materials as frugally as possible, they must also seek programs that are capable of attracting *large* audiences—but not just *any* large audiences. They need to attract the kind of people that advertisers want to reach. Advertisers will not pay for people who have no money to spend on their products or for people who have no interest in the products they sell.

To reach the audiences that advertisers want, broadcasters use the strategy of *targeting*, choosing programs that appeal to those subsets of the mass audience that are most likely to buy the advertisers' products. The need to reach large numbers of the people willing and able to pay the bills, whether as advertisers or subscribers, has led to targeting and segmentation throughout the electronic media.

The broadcast television networks target the largest single group of viewers, predominantly women between the ages of 25 and 54. Some cable networks target the same broad audience; others program for more narrowly defined groups. Each service defines

its audience in terms of *demographics* (age and gender) and/or *psychographics* (lifestyle and interests). Targeting women 18 to 34 years is a demographic goal; targeting sports fans is a psychographic goal.

Radio has further refined the process of targeting by using *segmentation*, defining extremely narrow subsets of the potential radio audience. Radio usually defines market segment in both demographic and psychographic terms: teenagers-who-want-to-hear-only-hit-songs or 25-to-44-year-old adults-who-prefer-the-music-of-the-1960s. At the same time, radio stations also solicit advertisers that want to reach the station's listener group and adjust advertising and other on-air material to appeal explicitly to that target group. For example, Coca-Cola commercials on rock music stations use rock music backgrounds; the same ads for the same product on country or middle-of-the-road stations use background music appropriate to the listeners of those formats.

Noncommercial broadcasting and pay cable also target specific audience groups. Although they are not constrained by advertisers' goals, they need to attract the audience segments most likely to offer financial support or to pay subscription fees. Public television tends toward programs that appeal to middle- and upper-income and high-educational-level families; pay cable tends to select movies that attract women or families with children.

11.2
Types of Programs

No entirely consistent way of classifying programs by type has been found, but programmers, critics, and viewers commonly accept distinctions based on a broad division between information and entertainment as well as narrower distinctions based on scheduling (frequency and time of day), service format, and genre.

Entertainment-Information   Dichotomy
Nearly all programs fall readily into either the in-

formation or the entertainment category. Although the great bulk of programs qualify primarily as entertainment, information programs receive special attention and deference because they lend the electronic media social importance.

Information programs have two main subtypes: *news* and *public affairs*. News includes news specials as well as the regularly scheduled news-of-the-day programs. Public-affairs programs take such forms as interviews, panel discussions, and documentaries. At one time, documentaries were a major and prestigious type of broadcast network program, but during the 1980s they all but disappeared from the networks, although they became more visible in public television and on specialized cable networks such as Arts & Entertainment and The Discovery Channel. The commercial networks instead emphasize *news specials,* which treat current news events in detail but usually in less depth and with a less defined viewpoint than documentaries. Hot topics in the news that are likely to interest especially large audiences attract network attention as subjects for news specials. News and public-affairs programs are discussed in further detail in Sections 11.4 (news sources), 12.5 (network level), and 13.5 (local level).

Some viewers argue that *sports* programs should be classed as information rather than as entertainment. However, programmers classify programs according to the responsible station or network department and their purpose in the overall program schedule, not according to audience preferences. Programmers regard sports as primarily entertainment, not information. The respective departments differ in purpose, style, and types of personnel.

Television programs also tend to be divided according to scheduling frequency into *series* and *specials*. The story line of an entertainment series continues from one episode to the next, whereas a special stands alone as an isolated program. Specials often mark holiday seasons in the manner, for example, of *Charlie Brown's Christmas Special.* Movies, though they are not scripted as series with continuing story lines, may be scheduled as thematic series—a "horror week" or "western weekend" series, for example.

Scheduling Typology   Programs are also classified according to the part of the day in which they are customarily scheduled. *Prime-time* programs have distinctive qualities, as do other programs associated with specific schedule positions. The same type of program scheduled in two different parts of the day takes on different colorations. Thus a daytime soap opera differs from a prime-time soap opera, and prime-time sports shows may differ from weekend sports shows.

For scheduling purposes, programmers break the 24-hour day into blocks they call *dayparts*. Radio programmers generally divide the day into *morning drive, midday, afternoon drive, night,* and *overnight* segments. Morning and afternoon drive periods have the largest audiences for most radio stations, although some music stations draw more listeners at night.

In television, broadcast and cable network programmers divide the day into a dozen or so parts, as shown in Exhibit 11–1. The most important segment, *prime time,* commands the most viewing. *Access time,* the hour just prior to the network's prime-time programs, during which the networks may not schedule entertainment programs, gives syndicators and station programmers their only access to large audiences. (The rules governing access time are explained more fully in Section 13.1 and Exhibit 13–2.) Network-affiliated stations stack the 6 P.M. to 7 P.M. hour with local and network newscasts. Many major-market stations start local news a half-hour or even an hour earlier than that. The entire segment devoted to news, which differs in length in different markets, constitutes the *news block.* Meanwhile, *fringe time* refers to the hours preceding and following prime time when audiences, though quite large, are either building up to prime levels or dropping off from those levels. Local television programmers call the late afternoon segment, prior to the evening news block, *early fringe* and the period after the end of network prime time *late fringe.* After late fringe comes *late night,* the domain of talk and movies, and then *overnight,* a time period that in large markets is increasingly filled with a mix of network news and locally scheduled

EXHIBIT 11-1   Television Dayparts

Time	Daypart
6-7 AM	Early Early Morning
7-9 AM	Early Morning
9-12 NOON	Morning
12-1 PM	Noon
1-4 PM	Afternoon
4-6 PM	Early Fringe
6-7 PM	News Block (varies)
7-8 PM	Access
8-11 PM	Prime Time
11-12 MID.	Late Fringe
12-2 AM	Late Night
2-6 AM	Overnight

Television and radio use different names for the major dayparts. Television dayparts focus on prime time and the surrounding hours; radio daypart-names focus on morning and afternoon drive, the periods of biggest audiences for radio. The length of the local TV news block varies from market to market and station to station, running as long as two or three hours on some major-market TV stations and as short as an hour elsewhere.

movies. *Daytime* is subdivided into *early morning, morning,* and *afternoon.*

At the network level, prime-time entertainment, daytime series, sports, and specials are handled by different departments, each with its own guidelines, goals, and responsibilities. The prime-time entertainment vice president is in charge of situation comedies and dramatic series, genres that will be discussed in more detail in Chapter 12. Daytime network television includes morning talk shows, game shows, and soap operas; this department is headed by a vice president concerned only with daytime entertainment. This vice president often also has responsibility for children's programming. The networks fill many of their weekend hours with sports, including pre-game talk shows, game play-by-play, post-game analyses, sports highlights, player or coach retrospectives, and so on; these are handled entirely separately from other entertainment programs.

Service Formats   An entire broadcast or cable service devoted to one particular style or type of program acquires a recognizable *format.* Nearly all radio stations have adopted distinctive formats, such as MOR (middle-of-the-road) music, classical music, or call-in talk. In television, CNN developed an all-news format, ESPN an all-sports format, MTV a video music format. Television stations and television broadcast networks tend to offer more generalized services because they cannot afford to narrow their audiences to followers of a particular format.

Program Genres   Borrowing the term from literature, broadcasting and cable programmers use the word *genre* to identify particular types of programs. Usually a program's content identifies its genre, but sometimes, as in the case of children's programs, the target audience rather than the type of content identifies the genre. Familiar entertainment genres are the *situation comedy,* the *game show,* the *western,* and the *soap opera.* Identifying a program by genre is a shorthand way of conveying a great deal about its probable length, seriousness, subject matter, visual approach, production method, and audience appeal. Programs that fall outside normal genre classifications often overlap two genres, leading to terms such as *dramedies* and *docudramas.* Exhibit 11-2 shows further uses of genre terminology.

11.3
Sources of Entertainment Programs

Few broadcast stations or cable systems produce their own entertainment programs, obtaining them instead from networks and syndicators. The broadcast and cable networks, in turn, obtain most of their new shows from Hollywood studios and independent producers.* Seven major Hollywood studios, a few smaller studios, about a dozen major independent producers, and many specialized independent producers create the programs and reap most of the profits. A few programs, seen mostly on cable networks and public television, come from other countries. Exhibit 11–3 illustrates the usual process of developing a new, prime-time program idea.

Television stations produce their own local newscasts and occasional public affairs or holiday programs, but little else. The major television networks produce their own early morning and late night talk and news programs, evening newscasts, and some soap operas and specials, but little else. *Moonlighting,* a prime-time series produced by ABC, was one of the rare exceptions. The fact that the cable networks rely on the same sources as the broadcast networks for their entertainment programs contributes to both program shortages and lack of variety.

Major Hollywood Studios The television networks and stations value movies not only because they fill large amounts of time and generally hold the interest of audiences from beginning to end, but also because most movies appeal especially to the youthful female audiences that advertisers target. When television began, the major motion picture studios attempted to starve the fledgling television industry by withholding their backlog of theatrical movies. But Hollywood soon changed direction, becoming the networks' main source for prime-time television series as well as for movies.

---

*Broadcast networks buy rather than produce most of their entertainment programs as the result of the FCC's "financial interest" rule, which limits production by networks, as explained in Section 17.1

EXHIBIT 11–2 Genres, Formats, and Dayparts

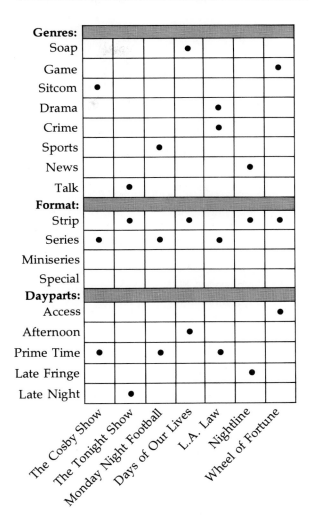

	The Cosby Show	The Tonight Show	Monday Night Football	Days of Our Lives	L.A. Law	Nightline	Wheel of Fortune
Genres:							
Soap				●			
Game							●
Sitcom	●						
Drama					●		
Crime					●		
Sports			●				
News						●	
Talk		●					
Format:							
Strip		●		●		●	●
Series	●		●		●		
Miniseries							
Special							
Dayparts:							
Access							●
Afternoon				●			
Prime Time	●		●		●		
Late Fringe						●	
Late Night		●					

Particular television shows can be classified by their content (genre), *the way they are usually scheduled on the networks* (format), *and the time of day they are typically scheduled on the networks* (daypart). *In syndicated reruns, the methods of scheduling and daypart often differ from the original network run.*

Prime-time television series start earning the producing studios substantive profits only after they have been aired on a network for several years.

EXHIBIT 11–3 Concepts to Programs

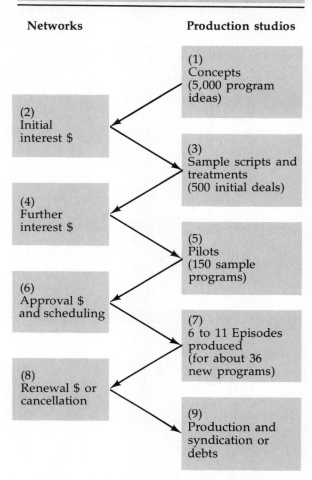

Networks   **Production studios**

(1)
Concepts
(5,000 program
ideas)

(2)
Initial
interest $

(3)
Sample scripts and
treatments
(500 initial deals)

(4)
Further
interest $

(5)
Pilots
(150 sample
programs)

(6)
Approval $
and scheduling

(7)
6 to 11 Episodes
produced
(for about 36
new programs)

(8)
Renewal $ or
cancellation

(9)
Production and
syndication or
debts

The four networks consider several thousand ideas for new programs over the course of a year. These concepts may be newly submitted by studios and independent producers or carry-overs from previous years. If a network shows interest in an idea, it advances funds for sample scripts (or treatments), and if it continues to be interested, the network advances funds for a pilot episode. Out of all the ideas considered, only about 30 to 36 new programs appear in prime time each year.

Then the revenue from syndication starts to roll in, virtually all profit.

In the 1970s, the cable television industry began aggressively acquiring movies, bidding up prices and creating an even greater shortage of programs for broadcasters. Insatiable demands for more movies by the cable networks, television stations, and videocassette rental and sales outlets caused the studios to alter their production and release practices. They began producing more movies, aiming them at a wider variety of audiences, and releasing them not just in summer, as formerly, but throughout the year.

Today's movie fans have many options. They can see movies in theaters or on pay-cable services, broadcast networks, basic cable networks, or local television stations; or they can rent or buy videocassettes to watch at home. As Exhibit 11–4 shows, Hollywood movie studios normally release a feature film initially to movie theaters and shortly thereafter to the VCR market. Within a year, distributors usually make it available to the pay-per-view and pay-cable networks. Many movies that failed at the box office appeal sufficiently to pay-cable viewers to earn a profit. After another year or more of theatrical and VCR distribution, the movie becomes available to the broadcast networks. The networks, however, select only a few movies for airing because many have exhausted their appeal on pay cable or the audience they target is too limited for network television. By the time a broadcast network shows a movie, it has already been on display in other media for over two years. Movies already four or five years old, whether aired by the broadcast networks or not, show up again on pay-cable television schedules to attract repeat viewers and those who missed them on the first go-round. Finally, movies become available in the domestic and foreign syndication markets and may be licensed to television stations or basic cable networks in this country and to television, cable, and DBS services in other countries.

Most of the major movie studios produce original series programs for the broadcast and cable networks. As examples, Warner Bros. produced *Night Court* and *Head of the Class;* Paramount, *Cheers, Family Ties,* and *Dear John;* MCA/Universal, *Murder, She Wrote, Miami Vice, Coach,* and *The Equalizer.* Producing prime-time television programs requires large resources and high risk, whereas daytime net-

EXHIBIT 11–4   The Movie Distribution Sequence

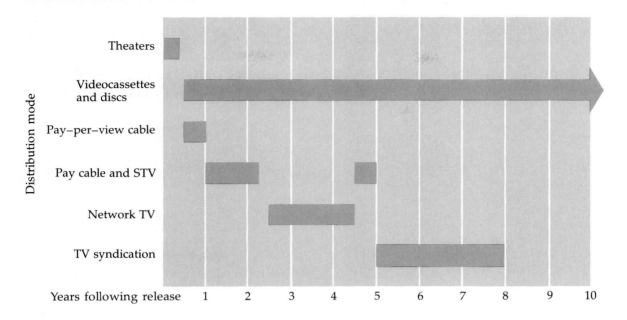

Movies appear first in theaters, then on television. Historically, the networks had first choice of theatrical firms, after their initial theatrical run. Distributors leased the left-overs to individual stations. During the 1980s, however, cable television and home videocassette players changed this pattern. Movies go to the videocassette market soon after theatrical release. In addition, the pay-per-view and pay-cable networks are offered brief windows (short periods of availability) before and after a movie is offered to the broadcast networks. The VCR and cable markets are substantial sources of income for movie (and some television series) distributors. Foreign syndication occurs alongside domestic syndication and is also a major source of profits.

SOURCE: Figures from *Channels' Field Guide to the Electronic Media,* 1985. Copyright Marian Chin, 1985.

work television shows contribute a substantial portion of studio profits at low risk. Later in this chapter, Exhibit 11–6 shows the prime-time program hours produced by the most prolific program producers in 1988–1989.

Lured by the staggering profits from the distribution side of the business, several studios have turned more of their attention to syndicating television programs than to producing them. Series that remain on a network for five or more years, which are successful by definition, move rapidly into syndication in most of the approximately 210 television markets in the United States and in dozens of foreign markets. The movie studios make more money from television, cable, videocassette, and foreign rights than from American theatrical exhibition. In both television and movie production, a few hits have to carry the dead weight of many failures; however, a quickly canceled television series may lose only $1 or 2 million, whereas losses from a single

EXHIBIT 11–5 Hollywood's Big Seven

Seven Hollywood studios dominate movie and television program production and syndication: Twentieth Century-Fox, Paramount, Columbia, MGM, Universal, Warner Bros., and Disney. In the early 1980s, Twentieth Century-Fox became one of the most tenacious and financially successful studios in the television business. In addition to financing big box-office hits such as *Star Wars* and its sequels, Fox produced *M*A*S*H* and *Trapper John* for television. Traditionally, however, Fox bought distribution rights from independent producers rather than financing its own productions, making handsome profits syndicating hundreds of programs and movies during the 1980s.

Rupert Murdoch's purchase of Twentieth Century-Fox in 1986 signaled a new role for Fox in program production for the 1990s. The movie studio will supply programming for the Fox network (FBC), which competes with ABC, CBS, and NBC. By 1990, although still a part-time network, Fox supplied about 100 affiliates with a weekend evening schedule and was moving slowly into weeknight programming. Most of its new shows earn profits for Fox as syndicated programs, even if unsuccessful on the network.

Warner Bros. and Columbia Pictures, after a slump of several years, surged ahead in the mid-1980s with such box-office successes as *Gremlins* and *Ghostbusters,* but they had few successful network series to syndicate. Disney, the newest of the Big Seven, expanded from children's movies into adult productions, mostly for its pay-cable network, The Disney Channel, and for the Fox television network. It produced *Golden Girls* and *Empty Nest* for prime-time television, and

also syndicates cartoons and older television series and produces many made-for-TV movies.

Among the major studios, Paramount was one of the biggest success stories of the 1980s. It had long-term commitments to both television and movies, producing the ongoing hit *Cheers,* syndicating former network series such as *Webster* and *Happy Days,* producing miniseries such as *Shogun* and *Winds of War* for the networks, and producing first-run syndicated shows such as *Entertainment Tonight* and *Solid Gold.* Paramount pioneered in producing on videotape instead of film, reducing overhead costs. It also developed a profitable first-run syndication arm and distributed such box-office blockbusters as *Raiders of the Lost Ark* in 1983; its 1984 sequel, *Indiana Jones and the Temple of Doom;* and its 1989 sequel, *Indiana Jones and the Last Crusade.*

The revenues from such megahits keep the Big Seven on top of the movie and video production business. The broadcast and pay-cable networks must deal with them to get hit movies, and the stations and basic cable networks must deal with them to get former network shows and packages of older movies. Small producers make money only on production; generally they cannot profit from domestic and international distribution of their products. The Big Seven employ huge and experienced staffs and handle most of the distribution and syndication business, getting a cut of the profits. In the 1990s, the studios will also move increasingly into television station ownership and financial participation in cable network programming, giving them additional sources of revenue and intertwining the production, distribution, and delivery aspects of the television business ever more tightly.

SOURCES: Logo photographs: the Universal Globe is a registered trademark of Universal City Studios, Inc.; ® Paramount Pictures; ™ Twentieth Century Fox.

movie failure can run into the tens of millions. The average Hollywood movie costs more than $20 million to produce and another $10 million to $20 million for promotion. Exhibit 11–5 looks at some of the most powerful movie studios.

Independent Producers At least half the prime-time series shown on network television come from *independent producers*. Their creative ideas influence the networks' prime-time production agendas. The second major force in television programming, the independent producers range in size from large firms such as Spelling and MTM, which usually have several series in production simultaneously, to small producers with only a single series under contract at any one time. In the 1970s, some of the independent producers, not connected with any studio, created innovative television series, such as *All in the Family, The Mary Tyler Moore Show, Laverne & Shirley,* and *Dallas.* By the late 1980s, independent producers such as Spelling, Goldberg, Lorimar, Lear, Tandem, MTM, and Steven J. Cannell produced the bulk of prime-time series. Goldberg, for example, originated *Family Ties;* Steven J. Cannell produced *Magnum, P.I.;* Lorimar produced *Dallas.* Movies and daytime television, however, remained largely the province of the Hollywood Big Seven.

Independent producers have several advantages over the big Hollywood studios. Because they lease production facilities, their overhead costs are usually below those of the big studios with which they compete. Lower costs in turn allow independents to charge lower license fees; this is especially advantageous when they are competing to have their pilot episodes selected for trial by a broadcast network. Independents also avoid the traditional movie industry's unwieldy decision-making structures and corporate demands for quick, high profits.

Movies, however, are still the ultimate production challenge. They escape the rigid half-hour and hour structures of commercial television. They demand higher technical and script quality than television shows, allow greater freedom in choice of content, and appeal to top-notch actors who would not consider appearing regularly on television. Both critics and producers place higher value on theatrical film-making than on television program production. Because the Hollywood movie studios dominate the movie business, most independent cable producers got their start producing television series. But a few successes can give an individual or small corporation access to the millions of dollars from banks and other backers needed to finance a theatrical movie (the budget for a single major motion picture generally exceeds the amount spent for an entire year of one-hour network television episodes by millions of dollars).

Movies take more than writing, casting, directing, and editing, however. They also need *distribution.* Reaching theaters and domestic and international television outlets requires staff, marketing know-how, and expert legal (and, in some countries, also political) backup. The distribution problem forces independent producers to surrender part of their profits to studios that can handle distribution/syndication. Because of their large size and great financial reach, the Big Seven seem likely to dominate the producing game for the foreseeable future.

Cable-Only Production The growth of cable program services created an insatiable demand for more movies. The pay-cable leader, HBO, alone demands more than 200 new movies a year. In some years, HBO has laid claim to more than a third of all films in production, obtaining enormous influence over movie producers. In addition, several basic cable services—notably TNT, American Movie Classics, and USA Network—schedule hundreds of older movies, competing with about 400 independent broadcast stations and some affiliates to obtain licenses to use them. Other cable networks capture former network series. Lifetime increased its audiences with *Cagney & Lacey* and *Spenser for Hire;* USA Network did well with *Murder, She Wrote* and *Miami Vice.* Distributor license fees for national services such as the basic or pay-cable networks far exceed the fees paid by individual television stations for the same movies. However, the collective audience for a successfully syndicated former network show may include viewers in 150 or more markets, often exceeding the reach of—and thus the aggregate licensing fee paid by—any cable network.

EXHIBIT 11–6   Sample Prime-Time Programs Produced for Television in the 1988-1989 Season

Producers	Programs for Broadcast Networks	Programs for First-Run Syndication and Cable Networks
Warner Brothers	*China Beach, Growing Pains, Murphy Brown, Night Court*	*Superior Court, People's Court, Mama's Family, Gumby, She's the Sheriff*
Paramount	*Cheers, Dear John, Dolphin Bay, Family Ties, MacGyver, Mission Impossible*	*The Arsenio Hall Show, Entertainment Tonight, Star Trek: The Next Generation, Webster*
Walt Disney	*The Magical World of Disney, The New Adventures of Winnie the Pooh*	*Live with Regis and Kathie Lee, Win Lose or Draw, Siskel & Ebert, Chip'N'Dale's Rescue Rangers*
20th Century Fox	*Have Faith, L.A. Law, Mr. Belvedere, Hooperman*	*9 to 5, Small Wonder, P.M. Magazine, Hour Magazine*
MCA/Universal	*Almost Grown, Coach, Miami Vice, Murder, She Wrote, Columbo*	*Out of This World, My Secret Identity, The Morton Downey Jr. Show*
Columbia	*Police Story, Designing Women, Married . . . With Children, Who's the Boss?*	*Wheel of Fortune, Jeopardy*
MGM/UA	*thirtysomething, 48 Hours, Knightwatch, Dream Street*	*Twilight Zone, Group One Medical, Kids Inc.*

Syndicators therefore usually prefer to sell former network shows to broadcast stations.

To increase the program supply and to gain a distinctive image, pay-cable services such as HBO/Cinemax and Showtime/The Movie Channel *co-finance* movies with producers. This investment gives them *exclusivity,* the right to show the product first on cable. A few of these cable-co-financed movies, such as *On Golden Pond* and *Sophie's Choice,* also had some box-office success in theaters. HBO's parent corporation, the magazine publisher and cable MSO, Time Inc., became Hollywood's largest financer of movies in the 1980s. About one-third of Showtime's schedule and nearly half of The Disney Channel's programs consisted of original cable material.

Each year, basic as well as pay-cable services increase such production activities, developing dramatic and comedy series and variety programs for *first-run cable* use. In 1988, for example, cable networks committed more than $500 million for original production, as compared with $2 billion by the broadcast networks. In 1988, USA Network committed about $65 million for the production of 24 cable-original movies. ESPN consists almost entirely of live events or original cable-only shows; Nickelodeon introduces new programs for children every year; and most other cable networks underwrite at least 10 percent of their schedules annually. Some of the new products qualify as wholly cable-only in concept; others simply add episodes to existing television series, such as more episodes of *Airwolf* on USA Network or more of *Fame* on Showtime. Growing demand for new programs for cable has increased the number of small studios and independents who can stay in business.

Cable-only programs counteract the image of cable as a mere parasite on broadcast television. Moreover, such productions enable each cable service to distinguish itself from its competitors and to gain subscribers who are attracted by programs that are not available on broadcast television. Cable-originated productions also have the potential for helping to fulfill cable's promise to enhance program diversity. The gain in diversity is limited, however, by the fact that most programs originated by cable companies come from the usual Hollywood movie-studio and independent providers of broadcast programs (see Exhibit 11–6).

Co-Production   Program creators have increasingly turned to *co-production* as a way of coping with constantly rising production costs. In co-production, two or more stations, networks, or producers agree to share the financial burden. Co-productions are especially attractive when the parties concerned come from different countries, as this automatically extends the market for the product. As the program market becomes increasingly internationalized, deals between U.S. and foreign producers are growing more common. Often deals involve the use of foreign locations, where costs are generally lower than in the United States.

In noncommercial television, co-productions have been the rule for years, often integrating people and facilities from several television stations, networks, and production houses. More than three-quarters of the PBS network schedule consists of co-productions, many of them international.

11.4
News and Sports Sources

Although they rely on outside producers for most of their entertainment programs, the broadcast networks retain tight control of news and public-affairs production. At one time, the networks also produced their own sports programs, but they eventually found that regional sports production companies could handle the camerawork and satellite transmission at lower costs. News and public affairs remain the one bastion of network television production.

Network News   Each commercial network operates a news division separate from its entertainment division, each employing nearly a thousand people. In the late 1980s, the three networks cut back on their news department operating budgets and reduced staffs (from around 2,000 employees each). Some observers questioned their ability to maintain their traditional news standards, but CNN (Cable News Network) had paved the way by succeeding on a significantly smaller budget (with perhaps only 500 employees), managing to attain high quality, despite a grueling 24-hour schedule.

On the international level, the major news services, Associated Press, United Press International, Reuters, Agence France Presse, TASS, and others, often participate in *pools,* rotating coverage of major public events such as important press conferences and speeches by heads of state. They supply text, video footage, and still pictures to the American television networks, stations, and newspapers. Nonetheless, each of the American television networks still supports foreign news bureaus in the major world capitals, staffed by correspondents with in-depth knowledge of the cultures and political processes they cover. In 1988, NBC purchased part ownership of Reuters, aiming to reduce its foreign bureau costs while still maintaining its international news presence. Until that move, the American television networks had always competed head-on with the international news services.

The broadcast networks traditionally disdained news footage or documentaries from outside sources. Independent news producers criticized this policy, but the networks maintained that in order to shoulder responsibility for news coverage, they had to control news production. This high-minded policy began to erode in the 1980s, however, when the networks began buying news footage from affiliates and from pool feeds in order to cut costs and enliven their coverage. Unconstrained by the broadcast network traditions and lacking their plush resources, CNN uses material from a wide variety of sources, putting competitive pressure on the networks.* To be fair in comparing CNN's performance with that of the networks, however, one must bear in mind that CNN stays on continuously, whereas the broadcast networks focus their primary efforts on half-hour newscasts.

Network Sports Except for professional football games, the broadcast networks rely increasingly on production companies that specialize in televising sports. In effect, these companies syndicate their productions to the networks, reserving replay rights and selling time within the "in" shows in regional markets. The networks pay for the national rights to the events, the cost of producing live games, and their own announcers' salaries and travel costs. Mega-events such as the World Series and the Super Bowl and regular-season NFL football remain the exceptions to this trend. These events bring in so much revenue that the broadcast networks can still make enormous profits after paying for the most elaborate production, using numerous cameras and instant replay machines, gigantic booms and cranes, and other specialized equipment. Sports production companies are also employed by cable networks and individual broadcast stations. ESPN, however, produces most of the games it carries.

For smaller, single-sponsor events, such as golf and bowling tournaments, sponsors pay for production in addition to buying advertising time. The networks supply only the play-by-play and color announcers. Sponsors usually participate in organizing these events, lining up participants and celebrity guests, doing promotion, and even selling tickets. They hire local television stations or sports production companies to televise the events and sell radio and cable rights. Both sides benefit from this division of labor. Sponsors retain control of costs and can ensure maximum promotional value; networks gain hundreds of program hours of minor sports events that they could not cover themselves without too much financial risk. Even though such events usually get low ratings, they can be profitable because costs are usually negligible and the advertising spots are presold. The broadcast and cable networks' willingness to accept fully sponsored, preproduced sports events greatly increases the number of minor-event programs they can afford to carry.

Station News Sources The advent of electronic news gathering (ENG) during the 1970s enabled local news teams to fill longer newscasts and to provide more on-the-scene coverage of local events. An ENG unit can travel quickly and economically by car or helicopter to the scene of an event and feed an on-the-spot news story to the studio by means of a microwave or satellite relay link. Alternatively, the ENG unit can record material for later editing at the studio. Only 3 percent of the commercial television stations used ENG in 1973; by 1989, 90 percent used it, mostly in conjunction with satellite relays.

Both television and radio affiliates can obtain what amounts to syndicated television news services from their own networks. Provided by the networks' news divisions, these services feed hard news items and features over regular network relay facilities during hours when these facilities carry no scheduled network programming. Affiliates can record these feeds, selecting items for later insertion in local newscasts. They pay the networks a fee for the service. They can also obtain the right to record regular network news programs as sources of stories for insertion in their local programs.

In 1980 Independent News Network (INN), a syndicated news program service, began relaying packaged half-hour newscasts live via satellite to subscribing independent stations during the hour preceding network affiliates' late-evening newscasts. Thus, independent television stations could program a half hour of INN and a half hour of local news earlier than affiliates could schedule

---

*CNN has even introduced systematic recruitment of amateur reporters, inviting them to call an 800 number when they have captured news events on home camcorders and giving out "News Hound" stickers for their cameras. Many local broadcast news departments also encourage amateurs to contact them about selling original news footage. Section 13.5 gives more details on local news operations.

late evening news. Affiliates cannot compete by pre-empting the network entertainment programs in order to move late local news to an earlier hour. Thus, independents gain the advantage of attracting viewers who prefer not to wait for late news on the affiliates.

Satellite relays increase the number of news suppliers, freeing affiliates from dependence on their networks for national and international stories. Exhibit 11–7 shows some of the stations' news sources. Independent stations, too, can call upon these suppliers if their news budgets permit. Besides obtaining national and international news from their own ENG facilities and from the major networks or INN, stations can buy news from several other news syndicators, including the Associated Press news service, the United Press/Independent Television News agency, Group W's News Information Weekly Service, Turner's CNN, and Conus Communications. Low-cost satellite feeds enable locally produced newscasts to compete in major markets with network newscasts, diluting the near-monopoly on national and international video coverage that the networks once had.

11.5
Scheduling Practices

Whatever their program sources, stations and networks strive to organize their offerings into coherent *schedules*. Effective scheduling requires coordinating the program sequence with the daily life of audience members, complementing typical audience activities with appropriate programs. For example, light, up-tempo treatment of news and weather suits the busy early morning period when listeners and viewers prepare for their day at work, at school, or in the home. A more in-depth treatment and slower tempo suit the relaxed evening period. Scheduling also serves as a competitive weapon to draw audience members away from rival channels and to prevent rival program services from enticing away some of one's own audience.

Audience Flow Programming strategies center on controlling *audience flow,* the movement of viewers or listeners from one program to another. Movement occurs mostly at the junctures between programs or, on radio, after one block of songs ends and before the next begins. Audience flow includes both *flowthrough* on the same station and *outflow* or *inflow* to and from competing stations or networks.

Researchers calculate the extent of audience flow in prime-time network television. Nielsen studies in the late 1980s showed that, on the average, 85 percent of a network's audience flowed through from one half-hour to the next when the same program continued. However, flowthrough dropped to about two-thirds of the audience when a new program of similar type followed in the next half hour, and to only half the audience when a program of a different type started in the next half hour. Cable systems, VCRs, and increasing numbers of broadcast stations give audiences ever-wider ranges of choice. Remote control key pads make it easy for viewers to switch television channels at will. About two-thirds of households have videocassette players, and three-quarters have remote-control channel selectors. A special vocabulary has evolved to describe how some audience members use remote controls and VCRs: they *graze* through the available channels, *zap* unwanted commercials, *jump* between pairs of channels, *flip* around to see what's happening on nearby channels, and *zip* through the boring parts of prerecorded cassettes. Not all viewers take advantage of this new freedom, however, and programmers continue to employ scheduling strategies designed to control audience flow.

Scheduling Strategies Most media products reach consumers in individually packaged physical units—a videocassette, a phonograph record, a compact disc, an edition of a newspaper or a book, or an issue of a magazine. Only broadcasting and cable television offer the consumer a *continuous* experience. Television and radio programming unfolds, providing not merely a succession of unrelated media packages but a coherent program

EXHIBIT 11–7 **National News Sources For Stations**

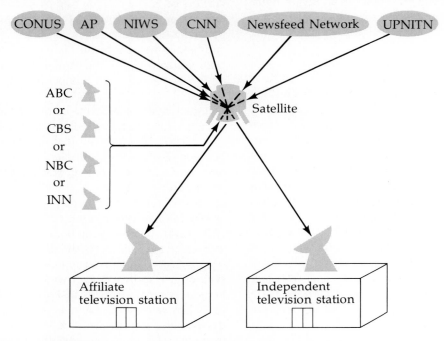

News in written form has long been provided to broadcasters by the established "wire services," news agencies that originally delivered stories to newspapers via telegraphic printers. Television's need for pictures posed new reportorial and distribution problems for such agencies, opening the way to specialized video services. The traditional agencies such as AP (Associated Press) supplemented their wire copy with some video material, but many stations also subscribe to services tailored specifically to video needs. These agencies include UPITN, a combined operation of United Press International (UPI) and Britain's Independent Television News (ITN), which is jointly owned by British commercial television program companies. Some stations also subscribe to News Information Weekly Service (NIWS), a national news service that supplies weekly summaries of news events and feature material. CNN, the cable news network, also acts as a syndicated news source for broadcasters. It exchanges news stories with television stations and supplies stations with CNN Headline News in 5-minute or 30-minute units or continuously from midnight to dawn for an overnight service. Many stations draw on Group W Television's Newsfeed Network, an interactive service that supplies breaking news coverage of major events, the option of live stories from Washington, DC, and access to Group W's library of news footage. An even more highly specialized service, Conus Communications, coordinates Ku-band satellite news gathering by over a score of stations, facilitating exchange of news footage and stories; it also supplies subscribing stations with satellite relay of unedited television coverage of White House press briefings and other executive branch events that are open to news cameras.

service. When devising schedules for this service, programmers take into account changing audience availability, changing work patterns, and changing needs and interests as the cycles of days, weeks, and seasons progress.

Programmers also take into account competition from other program services, using scheduling changes as a primary competitive weapon. Some typical scheduling strategies used by both networks (television, cable, and radio) and individual systems and stations to exploit audience flow follow:

▪ **Counterprogramming** seeks to attract the audience toward one's own station (or network) and away from the competition by offering programs different from those of the competition. For example, an independent station might schedule situation comedies against news programs on the network affiliates in its market.

▪ **Block programming** seeks to maintain audience flowthrough by scheduling programs with similar appeal next to each other—for example, by filling an entire evening with family-comedy programs.

▪ **Stripping** tries to create the habit of daily viewing by scheduling episodes of a series at the same time every day of the week, usually for months on end. For example, affiliates frequently strip situation comedies at 4:30 P.M. and 5 P.M., running a new episode each day of the week.

▪ A **strong lead-in** seeks to attract the maximum initial audience size by starting a daypart with a particularly strong program. An example would be to schedule a one-time hit network show just before local news as a lead-in to the newscast.

▪ A **hammock** tries to establish a new program, or to recover the audience for a show slipping in popularity, by scheduling the program in question *between* two strong programs. Flowthrough from the previous (lead-in) program may enhance the initial audience for the hammocked program, and viewers may stick with the weak (or unfamiliar) show in order to see the strong following program, bolstering the audience for the hammocked program.

▪ **Bridging** attempts to weaken the drawing power of a competing show by scheduling a one-hour (or longer) program that overlaps the start time of the competing show. A two-hour movie scheduled at 7:00 P.M. on a pay-cable network or independent station, for example, *bridges* the 7:30, 8:00, and 8:30 P.M. program changes on competing channels.

▪ **Repetition** tries to make watching a program, especially a movie, convenient for viewers by scattering repeat showings, so that among the many opportunities to watch, each viewer can find an acceptable time. Cable television and public broadcasting use this strategy so that viewers, even though temporarily lured away by popular broadcast network programs, can still catch a particular movie or series episode.

▪ **Stunting** seeks to keep the opposing networks off balance in the short term by such tactics as making rapid schedule changes, opening a new series with an extra-long episode, and interrupting regular programming frequently with heavily promoted specials. Networks tend to use stunting especially during ratings periods.

Television Station Schedules   After clearing time for its network's programs, an affiliated station has about 30 percent of its schedule left to fill with syndicated and local programs. The affiliate programmer's most important decisions concern scheduling in the early fringe and access periods. Programmers at unaffiliated stations, which make up nearly 40 percent of commercial television stations, have many more scheduling options than their counterparts at network affiliates; their chief stratagem, counterprogramming, capitalizes on the inflexibility of the network affiliate's schedule because of time committed to network programs. For example, an independent station's scheduling freedom enables it to air sports events at times when affiliates carry major network shows. Networks can afford to devote prime time to only a few top-rated sports events of national interest. Independents, however, can schedule sports events of lesser interest, even during prime time.

Most of the 630 or so affiliates and the nearly 400 independent stations strip syndicated and local programs *daily*, except for the Saturday and Sunday programs, which are scheduled only weekly. Monday-through-Friday stripping has three advantages for stations: daily same-time scheduling encourages the audience to form regular viewing patterns, such as the 6 P.M. news habit. Second, a station can use a single promotional spot to publicize an entire week's schedule in a given time slot. Finally, purchasing many episodes of syndicated series in a single transaction earns quantity discounts from syndicators.

The practice for stripping off-network programs daily "across the board" has led to an enormous demand for television programs series with many episodes "in the can" (stripping requires 130 episodes for a half-year run). Among the best known long-running series are *Happy Days, M*A*S*H,* and *The Cosby Show.* Series that have generated large numbers of episodes command very high prices in syndication. As Exhibit 11–8 shows, when the prices paid by all station buyers are combined, a series with hundreds of episodes can make millions of dollars in aggregate revenue for syndicators. Network megahits also foster intense bidding among stations for the first syndication rights. Some stations paid more for *The Cosby Show* than for all the rest of their syndicated programs in the year of its first release. Actually, most stations purchasing *Cosby* could not hope to recoup the show's cost from sale of the commercial time within it, but the expectation that it would lead to higher ratings for adjacent programs, especially local newscasts, justified the expense.

Most very long-running series, however, date back to the 1960s and early 1970s. Hits such as *Gunsmoke* and *Marcus Welby, M.D.* seemingly ran forever, whereas most subsequent network series had relatively short runs, building up too few episodes for effective strip scheduling. Exhibit 11–8 lists examples of shows that had enough episodes to attract lots of station buyers.

Broadcast Network Schedules In broadcast television, each of the three major national net-

works offers its affiliates approximately a hundred hours of programs per week, filling about 70 percent of the average affiliate's schedule. The main arena of network rivalry is the weekly 22 hours of *prime time*—the three hours from 8:00 P.M. to 11:00 P.M. each night of the week in the eastern and western time zones, an hour earlier in the central and mountain time zones, plus the extra hour from 7:00 P.M. to 8:00 P.M. on Sundays (EST/PST). Actually, networks make more money on daytime programs than on prime-time programs because of the extraordinarily high cost of prime-time shows. Nevertheless, a broadcast network's performance in prime time establishes its prestige and defines its leadership role.

Prime time affords access to the largest and most varied audiences in any medium and therefore contains the programs with the broadest appeal. In the early 1980s, most cable networks concentrated on reaching demographic subgroups in prime time, showcasing their best product in other time periods. But by the mid-1980s, the largest cable networks, such as ESPN, USA Network, CBN, WTBS, HBO, and Showtime, began to attract large portions of the prime-time mass audience to their programs. They changed strategies accordingly, competing directly and aggressively with the broadcast networks in prime time. During the 1980s, the broadcast networks' average share of the television audience declined to under 70 percent as viewers defected to cable networks, independent stations, and home videocassettes.

Because the networks pay so much for prime-time programs and because they need scheduling maneuverability, they normally schedule prime-time series weekly. If they stripped all of prime time with half-hour programs, each network would have only six weeknight programs to schedule, giving too few chances to capture the number-one position. In other dayparts, however, the broadcast networks strip most of their shows Monday through Friday. Network morning talk programs, soap operas, and evening newscasts, for example, occur at the same times each weekday.

Cable Network Schedules Pay-cable networks rely heavily on the strategy of repetition, fre-

EXHIBIT 11–8   Syndicated Revenues from 1987 to 1991

Syndicator	Off-Net Series	Year Available	Estimated Revenue Per Episode
Paramount	*Cheers*	1987	$1,650,000
Paramount	*Family Ties*	1987	1,400,000
MCA	*The A-Team*	1987	950,000
Victory/MTM	*Hill Street Blues*	1987	1,100,000
Columbia/Embassy	*Silver Spoons*	1987	1,200,000
Paramount	*Webster*	1988	1,400,000
Viacom	*The Cosby Show*	1988	4,800,000
MCA	*Kate & Allie*	1988	1,200,000
Warner Brothers	*Night Court*	1988	1,100,000
Lorimar	*Mama's Family*	1988	515,000
Columbia/Embassy	*Who's the Boss?*	1989	2,500,000
Warner Brothers	*Growing Pains*	1989	910,000
Warner Brothers	*Head of the Class*	1990	950,000
Lorimar	*Alf*	1991	1,500,000
Lorimar	*Perfect Strangers*	1991	1,500,000

quently repeating their movies and variety shows to build audiences cumulatively for each program. Each movie plays several times on different days with different start times. A movie may be recycled as many as a dozen times a month. For this reason, and also because cable program guides come out once a month and cable companies need to encourage monthly subscription renewals, the pay networks plan their schedules in monthly blocks.

Pay cable also uses the bridging strategy, scheduling across the start times of other programs. HBO and Showtime movies, for example, usually start at 8 P.M. and span the 9 P.M. time period, when the largest audience watches television. If a movie ends before 10 P.M., however, HBO usually adds filler material to complete the hour in order to start a new program when viewers may be hunting for something to watch. Sometimes the pay movie networks try to get the jump on the broadcast networks by starting their movies earlier in the evenings (at 7 or 7:30 P.M.). This strategy works best when broadcast schedules have been disrupted by late-running sports or political programs.

Basic cable networks, on the other hand, commonly adopt habit-forming strategies to build loyal audiences. The broad-appeal cable services strip their programs across the board in daytime and prime time. USA Network and Lifetime, for example, stripped costly former network series such as *Miami Vice* and *Molly Dodd* in prime time, hoping to attract repeat viewers away from the broadcast channels to those series and build a cable-watching habit among first-time viewers. ESPN, the sports network, strips a daily sports quiz show and a sports talk show; MTV and VH-1 strip videos; Nickelodeon strips cartoons. Basic cable networks also use counterprogramming and time-period blocking. Superstations, for example, tend to counter mass-appeal adult programs on the broadcast networks with children's shows and movies. The cable shopping and religious networks block several hours of similar programs to hold interested viewers for as long as possible with an alternative to the broadcast network shows.

The theme cable services—also called the *niche services*—have borrowed a leaf from radio, frequently rerunning program materials. Cable networks such as CNN Headline News and The Weather Channel recycle news or weather elements every half-hour or hour in the manner of many all-news radio stations. C-SPAN and local cable access channels also use the repetition strategy.

Radio Scheduling Practices Radio stations use the strategies of counterprogramming, stripping, and blocking even more than television stations. Typically, radio programmers try to choose formats that appeal to groups that are not adequately reached by rival stations. Most stations schedule their program elements, whether songs or news stories, in hourly rotations, creating 60-minute cycles, modified according to daypart. Exhibit 11–9 shows an hourly plan for a jazz music format. Radio stations tend to stick with the same rotation pattern for an entire daypart, a form of blocking.

Satellites relay a variety of program services from which radio stations can draw for news, sports, and entertainment programs. In radio, programmers distinguish between *syndicated features* and *syndicated formats*. A station can obtain a license to use a syndicated country music format, for example, then supplement it with news and entertainment features from other commercial sources, creating a unique mix of programming made up largely of syndicated elements. Radio programming is discussed in more detail in Sections 13.3 and 13.6.

11.6
Program Promotion

Having the best programs in the world avails little if audiences don't know about them. Stations and networks therefore invest liberally in both on-air and printed promotional efforts, and cable systems follow their lead.

Television stations and broadcast and cable networks consider on-air promotional spots the most cost-efficient way to advertise their programs. Most breaks between programs contain **promos** for upcoming programs, short spots urging viewers to stay tuned or come back soon for another wonderful program. Stations and broadcast networks also air teasers for their newscasts, brief mentions of upcoming news stories, in the hour preceding the newscast, to entice viewers to stay tuned. Most cable networks follow this pattern, using breaks in programming to announce upcoming programs. HBO schedules elaborately preproduced billboards of upcoming programs as filler between the end of one show and the start of the next. Special companies produce and schedule cross-promotional announcements among cable services. For example, Prime Time Tonight schedules promotional spots for several cable networks on such basic cable services as The Weather Channel and CNN.

To reach nonviewers, networks and stations also advertise in newspapers and magazines, on radio, on outdoor billboards, and in other media. Radio stations promote television programs, and television stations carry spots promoting radio stations—all paid advertising unless the services are co-owned.

Probably the most important forms of program promotion are program listings and guides. Some cable systems dedicate an entire channel to program listings; others mail customized program guides to their subscribers. Some cable networks offer their own program guides (Arts & Entertainment has one, for example, available at $18 a year). Some cable systems send pay-cable subscribers free printed guides (purchased in bulk by the operator) along with monthly bills. *Cable Guide* has nearly 8 million subscribers, the most of any generic cable-only guide.

EXHIBIT 11–9   An Hourly Music Rotation

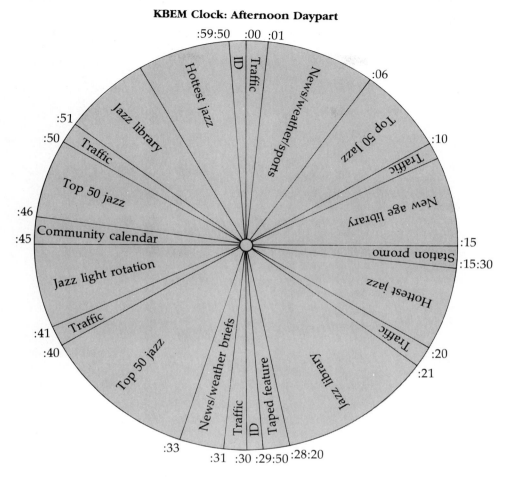

KBEM Clock: Afternoon Daypart

Commercial and noncommercial radio stations follow rotating patterns for their program elements, usually depicted as a wheel or clock. Music stations predetermine the exact times for commercials, public service announcements (PSAs), program promos, identifications (IDs), new headlines, traffic and weather reports, call-in contests, and other elements. News/talk stations often program just news elements during the morning drive daypart, filling their wheels with network headlines, local headlines and stories, features, sports scores, weather and traffic reports, IDs, and so on.

SOURCE: KBEM–FM 88.5 Stereo, Minneapolis Public Schools.

Home satellite dish owners turn to magazines such as *Satellite Orbit* to help determine which transponders carry which services.

Daily newspapers and Sunday supplements devote considerable space to broadcast and cable television listings. Some newspapers gather the data themselves; others hire outside organizations to do the job. The most widely recognized published source for program information, the granddaddy of them all, *TV Guide,* publishes a hundred different edi-

EXHIBIT 11–10   TV Guide

Every week about 20 percent of all U.S. television households turn to *TV Guide* to see what's on television, to decide what to watch, and to read articles and gossip about the television and cable industries. *TV Guide* comes in a distant third, behind weekly TV supplements and daily listings in newspapers, as the source of program information most frequently cited by viewers. But these local publications cannot match *TV Guide*'s estimated national readership of 42 million.

Walter Annenberg (later a U.S. ambassador to Great Britain) combined three local weekly television program guides to create the first edition of *TV Guide* in 1953. He began with 10 regional editions and a circulation of 1.5 million subscribers. By 1988 the magazine offered 106 regional editions with a circulation of about 17 million (down from its 1977 peak of nearly 20 million), the highest of any magazine. Each of the regional editions offers the same national pages of articles and news, plus special pages inserted for that region's cable and station program listings. Nearly half of all *TV Guide* copies are sold at newsstands, mostly in supermarkets.

Media baron Rupert Murdoch took control of *TV Guide* in 1988 when he paid $3 billion for its parent company, Triangle Publications. Murdoch already owned half of *TV Guide*'s Australian counterpart, *TV Week*.

TV Guide is designed for readers, not for the electronic media. Indeed, the magazine includes stories critical of the industry, avoiding the fan magazine image and dwelling less on personalities and more on television's relationship with, and impact on, society. A look at some of the contributing authors supports its claim of serious journalism: Arthur Schlesinger, Jr., Pulitzer Prize-winning historian; Lee Loevinger, former FCC commissioner; Alvin Toffler, author of *Future Shock* and *The Third Wave;* Alexander Haig, Jr., former Secretary of State.

Each week, television stations throughout the country send in upcoming program schedules, and each

week editorial representatives of the magazine call stations to update program information. Often, through its direct contacts, *TV Guide* learns of network program changes before the network's affiliates do—an occasional source of embarrassment to the stations and a subject for acrimonious network/affiliate discussions. The magazine's computers store summaries of more than a quarter of a million syndicated episodes and some 36,000 movies. When a station or network tells *TV Guide* it plans to show a certain episode of a series on a certain day, the editors call up the appropriate summary for inclusion in the listings.

TV Guide does not list all stations and cable program services. A new station must acquire a substantial

tions weekly just within the continental United States, as well as many localized editions for other countries. But it even cannot provide full details on all available programs in households with access to two or three dozen channels or more (Exhibit 13–10).

EXHIBIT 11–10 Continued

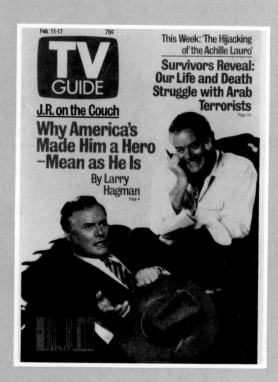

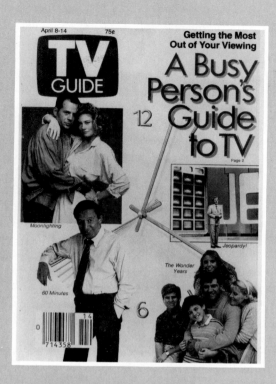

audience before it can get its program schedule included—frustrating problem for operators of new stations. As for cable, dozens of systems, many with 30 channels or more, may operate within a region covered by a single *TV Guide* edition. Since those systems often carry quite different channel lineups, it is impractical for the magazine to include everything. It therefore lists cable programs not by system channel but by program service. Still, there are more cable networks and superstations than could reasonably be listed in a magazine of acceptable size and price. *TV Guide* solves this problem by including only the most-watched services. Rarely, for example, does it offer program information for C-SPAN, Country Music Tele-

vision, MTV, or Financial News Network. It never listed RCA's Entertainment Channel, now out of business, because the service attracted only about 50,000 subscribers. However, *TV Guide*'s policy creates a Catch-22 situation: If potential viewers don't know that a service exists or what programs it carries, the service has little chance of survival. Inclusion in newspaper listings and supplements and *TV Guide* is a crucial step toward solvency for new program services.

SOURCE: *TV Guide* covers reprinted with permission from *TV Guide* magazine. © 1989 by News America Publications Inc., Radnor, PA.

Summary

▌ Broadcast and cable programmers face problems of high program costs, scarcity of materials, and advertisers' demands for effective commercial vehicles.

▌ The prices broadcast networks pay for premiere entertainment programs rarely cover full production costs, but the prestige conferred by network exposure makes such programs highly salable in domestic and international syndication markets.

▌ Programs are commonly classified according to several systems: by the entertainment-information dichotomy, by scheduling conventions, by service formats, and by genre.

▌ Entertainment programs come from the traditional Hollywood "Big Seven" studios, from independent producers, and to a small extent from foreign sources.

▌ The big Hollywood studios retain a large measure of control over the motion picture market through their dominance over the distribution system.

▌ Expanding demand has stimulated production of more feature films than formerly, and the timing of their release to the theater, cassette, broadcast, and cable markets has been revised.

▌ Programs produced especially for cable television services generally come from the same production sources as those for broadcast networks.

▌ Co-production eases the problem of escalating costs to some extent.

▌ Broadcast networks retain control of network news and public-affairs production. But, except for the most prestigious events, the networks have turned to specialist companies for the production of sports programs.

▌ Scheduling strategies that programmers use to influence audience flow include counterprogramming, blocking, stripping, bridging, repeating, and stunting. However, remote tuners enable some audience members to change channels with ease, somewhat undermining the effectiveness of scheduling strategies.

▌ The broadcast networks schedule prime-time programs in weekly cycles, but in other dayparts (except for weekends) they strip programs in daily cycles. Broad-appeal cable networks use the same scheduling conventions.

▌ However, cable theme (niche) networks and radio stations schedule program items in repetitive cycles in various dayparts, aiming for demographically or psychographically similar audience subgroups.

▌ Audience promotion, using on-air announcements, advertising in other media, and program guides, is an essential component of successful programming.

CHAPTER 12

NETWORK TELEVISION AND RADIO PROGRAMS

In both broadcasting and cable, a *network* simultaneously distributes high-cost programs by means of relays to many delivery units (stations and cable systems). Networks can be linked by satellite or microwave, or a combination of both, according to the needs of particular geographic areas, but the key elements are national (sometimes regional) distribution, high-quality programs, and national commercials (or, in the case of public broadcasting, underwriting messages) embedded in the programs.

Networks play such a dominant role in both broadcasting and cable that they need to be analyzed from several points of view. Their technology, organization, and economics have already been discussed in this book; regulations governing networks will be discussed later. In the previous chapter, we examined types of programs, where they come from, and the scheduling strategies networks and stations typically use. At this point we look at specific programs that the commercial and noncommercial networks carry and some major issues associated with network program practices. The networks discussed in this chapter include the three full-service national television broadcasting networks—ABC, CBS, and NBC; one aspirant network not yet offering full service—Fox; PBS, the noncommercial television network; mixed broadcast and cable networks such as WTBS, Univision, and Telemundo; and the sixty-odd

cable networks, especially basic and pay cable's largest services—including USA Network, ESPN, MTV, CNN, HBO, Showtime, and The Disney Channel. Finally, we devote some attention to the radio networks, both the news-and-talk suppliers and the music suppliers.

12.1
Prime-Time Entertainment

During the 22 hours of prime time each week, the three full-service national television broadcast networks vie for huge audiences, larger than any in the previous history of entertainment. Collectively, for nearly three decades, the broadcast networks captured more than 90 percent of the prime-time viewing audience. In the late 1980s, however, with the growth of cable networks, improved independent station programming, and widespread use of home VCRs, the combined network audience prime-time share decreased to less than 65 percent. Nevertheless, major news events carried by all three networks can still reach as much as 90 percent of the adult U.S. population. Unusually popular episodes of entertainment programs sometimes capture more than half of all television homes for an hour or so. Most industry experts expect the broadcast networks collectively to retain at least half of prime-time viewing, but that may entail cutbacks if as many as three full-service television networks are to be profitable.

Prime-time entertainment programs come as weekly series, as movies, and as occasional specials. As explained in Chapter 11, a *series* continues from week to week with the same characters in the same setting, usually as 30-minute situation comedy episodes or one-hour dramas. A series with eight or fewer episodes is known as a *miniseries*. Networks strip their morning and daytime shows daily, but schedule most evening entertainment programs once a week. *Movies* may be theatrical feature films licensed for network showing or *made-for-TV* movies commissioned by networks to fill specific time slots. A theatrical film usually occupies two hours of airtime, but made-for-TV movies may last only 90 minutes, though most last two or more hours. An *entertainment special* is a one-time-only show. It may be a yearly event, such as the annual Academy Awards show, or a comedy/variety or musical holiday extravaganza showcasing a well-known star, often one not commonly seen on television.

Situation Comedies   Long a staple of prime-time network television, *situation comedies* (*sitcoms*) remain highly popular with women 18 to 49, a key demographic group that many advertisers want to reach. After their network run, sitcoms go into syndication for sale to stations as *off-network* series. Stations welcome off-network shows because they want to appeal to the same target group as the networks; moreover, stations like off-network sitcoms because they lend themselves to strip scheduling and effective promotion, and, if unsuccessful, only "stick" the station for a half hour rather than a full hour. More crucial, scheduling half-hour shows such as sitcoms in early fringe allows stations to attract new viewers every 30 minutes. Stations prefer former-network shows to first-run syndicated material because they can better estimate the likely ratings for an off-network program.

After declining in popularity in the early 1980s, sitcoms began a comeback in 1985. By the late 1980s, such shows as *The Cosby Show, Growing Pains, Night Court,* and *A Different World* topped the charts.

Such ratings swings show that audiences eventually tire of almost any program genre, but that a fresh and exciting treatment of an old genre can bring viewers back. Individual hit sitcoms command 30 to 40 percent of the audience and tend to rate higher than hour-long shows. The enormous success of *The Cosby Show* renewed the networks' faith in family-oriented comedy and led to fresh efforts to develop more sitcoms. Such hits as *Cheers* (Exhibit 12–1), *Newhart,* and *Night Court* succeeded in contexts other than family situations, but most sitcoms focus on families.

Networks use two main formulas for prime-time family sitcoms. One features a single dominant star in a traditional family setting; the other treats a nontraditional household situation humorously. As an example of the former, *The Cosby Show*'s success hinges on one outstanding actor who carried a cast of unknowns (though success soon made them well known). The program revolved around a father and mother, both in the professional class, with children facing amusingly treated domestic problems.

On the other hand, responding to pervasive changes in work and family patterns, television series increasingly explore new social relationships, probing the boundaries of acceptable television. *Kate & Allie* typifies a nontraditional family situation: two divorced women with children attempt to make a go of a fatherless, two-mother household. Other nontraditional sitcoms showcase single fathers (*Dear John* and *Bensen*), multiple fathers (*My Two Dads*), middle-aged all-women households (*Golden Girls* and *Designing Women*), second marriages combining two sets of offspring, and other odd combinations of parents of young and full-grown children. The "slobcom" variant emphasizes the less idealistic aspects of family life. The family in Fox's *Married . . . with Children* consists of an unhappy housewife, a poor provider of a husband, and children who seem about to murder each other. ABC's highly successful effort with a less-than ideal family, *Roseanne,* depicts an earthy working-class family.

Because failure costs so much, the networks generally avoid the risk of real innovation. Instead, they incessantly repeat previously successful formats, recycling winning series ideas. A hit sitcom with a

EXHIBIT 12–1 *Cheers*

Set in a below-street-level pub in downtown Boston, the prime-time hit series Cheers *has been popular since it was launched by NBC in 1982. Some characters have shifted since then, but salt-of-the-earth New Englander characters, such as waitress Carla and mail carrier Cliff, help to make* Cheers *an Emmy-award winner.* Cheers *has remained one of the top-rated programs, and its syndicated version is in great demand.*

SOURCE: NBC, Inc.

new angle instantly begets brazen imitations. Programmers call such copies "spinoffs" and "clones." A *spinoff* stars secondary characters from a previous hit on the same network, placing the characters in a new situation: for example, *The Cosby Show* spun off *A Different World,* and *Golden Girls* spun off

Empty Nest. The exceptional popularity of both *Cosby* and *Golden Girls* promised even more spinoffs.

A *clone* program, on the other hand, closely imitates an already popular program on another network, changing only the stars and details of plot and setting. Networks usually clone their rivals' success to blunt a hit's uniqueness while attracting some of the hit's audience. Sitcoms frequently spin off new sitcoms, whereas hour-long programs tend to generate clones. Attempts to capitalize on the success of *Magnum P.I.,* number three in prime time in the early 1980s, led to *Finder of Lost Loves, Hawaiian Heat, Hunter, Miami Vice,* and *Partners in Crime*—all in a single year. Only two of these clones, *Hunter* and *Miami Vice,* survived to become successes in their own right. In subsequent seasons, the networks cloned *Spenser for Hire* and *MacGyver* to attract the same audience. *Spenser* later spun off *A Man Called Hawk.*

In the past, viewers looking for humorous entertainment in a series format on the broadcast networks had to watch sitcoms. But in the early 1980s, producers injected large doses of comedy into action-adventure shows. Series such as *Magnum P.I., Moonlighting,* and *Remington Steele* included light-hearted comic scenes as well as warm-hearted relationships. Late-1980s shows *thirtysomething* and *Beauty and the Beast* magnified these elements, adding nostalgia and fantasy to the mix. In the 1980s, critics referred to some shows as "dramedies," hour-long dramas featuring comedic elements. The use of sitcom elements in diluted dramatic content may have contributed to a slide in sitcom popularity, but once the practice became common, it lost its impact on ratings. By 1990, warm-heartedness in both sitcoms and dramas garnered high ratings.

Dramatic Series   Dramatic series range from *Dallas* to *Beauty and the Beast,* but crime dramas were the most popular throughout the 1980s. Police, lawyer, and detective dramas had previously peaked in the ratings around 1960 (for example, *Dragnet* in the late 1950s and *Perry Mason* in the 1960s), then faded until the mid-1980s, when a new breed of more authentic crime shows captured huge ratings. *Hill Street Blues, L.A. Law,* and *Cagney & Lacey* represent a trend toward dramas dealing with tough social issues using complex plots interweaving large casts of characters (Exhibit 12–2). All these shows use character-oriented plots, focusing on the human-interest appeal of personal moral dilemmas, rather than action-oriented gunfights or car chases.

Miami Vice capitalized on the seamier sides of crime, exploring the sordid underlife beneath big-city glamor. In comparison to *L.A. Law, Miami Vice* and *The Equalizer* exhibited a simplistic, black-and-white view of the world; in these shows, good guys generally stay good guys, though they rarely wear white hats, and bad guys have no redeeming qualities to confuse viewers. In the 1980s, the *Miami Vice* characters influenced music and styles of dress, especially among young people. *The Enforcer* blended Superman and Rambo into an unlikely hero on the side of the little guy in need of help or vindication. This program catered to the all-too-human taste for vengeance, using classical crime and retribution plot lines in modern settings. At another extreme, *Murder, She Wrote* employed sanitized homicide mysteries, usually in upper-class settings, solved by an unlikely detective, a middle-aged mystery story writer.

Movies and Miniseries   By the 1970s the television networks paid astronomical prices for licenses to run outstanding theatrical films. The classic *Gone With the Wind* cost NBC about $5 million for a single showing in 1976, a record price justified by its 65 percent audience share. In 1983, a showing of *Star Wars* cost more than $10 million but attracted only 35 percent of the audience and finished second to a made-for-TV movie. In the mid-1980s, ABC set a new record by paying $15 million for the right to air *Ghostbusters,* even though it had already played for two years in theaters and on pay cable. By 1989, however, the network's average movie licensing price had dipped to about $3 million, because throughout the 1980s home VCRs and pay cable had increasingly depleted the drawing power of most movies on television.

Nevertheless, both broadcast and cable networks still pay huge fees for movie *blockbusters,* the biggest theatrical hits. These costly superhits usually cannot earn back their full rental fees in advertising revenue for a television network, but their indirect rewards may justify the loss. Films are especially useful for clobbering the opposing broadcast networks during February and May *sweep weeks,* periods when ratings services collect viewing data in all the local markets. During the November sweeps,

EXHIBIT 12–2   Tough Issues on
Television

In prime time shows such as L.A. Law, Hill Street Blues, *and* Cagney & Lacey, *characters face difficult ethical decisions and struggle with their own weaknesses that trigger mistakes in judgment at crucial moments. In* L.A. Law, *the characters faced frustrations and failures as well as moments of moral achievement. These are often viewed with wry humor, creating multidimensional personalities that millions of viewers find involving.* L.A. Law *appeals especially to young, upscale viewers, the group advertisers most want to reach.*

SOURCE: NBC, Inc.

the networks focus on their new fall series, and in July the size of the summer audience rarely justifies blockbuster films. In February and May, however, the high name recognition and visibility of blockbuster films adds luster to a network's overall late-season program schedule.

The number of theatrical movies produced by the Hollywood studios declined in the 1970s as film production costs rose, but increased in the 1980s

as cable networks demanded more programs. The pay-cable networks frequently outbid the broadcast networks for top-quality theatrical films, forcing the networks to turn to related program types: made-for-TV movies and miniseries. Typically, a broadcast network's rental fee for a single showing of a major theatrical feature would more than pay for making a brand-new, modest-budget feature designed for television. Sets, props, and locations need not be lavish because the small screen loses so much detail. With extravagant promotion, one well-known star supported by unknowns suffices. Made-for-TV movies often win audience ratings comparable to those of the most popular theatrical films. In some recent seasons, the top made-for-TV movies commanded higher audience shares than any televised theatrical movie that year. By 1990, two-thirds of network movies were in the made-for-TV category. They not only competed well against cable and independent station movies, but sometimes served as pilots for prospective network series.

By the mid-1980s, the cable networks had also reacted to the scarcity and high cost of theatrical movies by starting to produce their own *made-for-cable* feature films. Basic cable networks such as The Discovery Network and CBN Family Network financed only documentaries and other low-budget programs, but the major pay-cable networks—HBO, Showtime, and Disney—plunged into the financing of *made-for-pay* prime-time entertainment movies. Production contracts give cable networks *premiere exclusivity,* the right to air the films first. Subscribers' willingness to renew monthly pay-cable channels depends heavily on the lure of original programs. In addition, pay-cable networks invest increasingly in original dramatic series, musical variety shows, and nightclub comedy. Nevertheless, feature films remain pay cable's bread-and-butter offering. Only by financing made-for-pay productions can they assure themselves a continuous stream of movies.

Miniseries are long-form programs, usually 8 to 12 hours in length, scheduled over successive nights. In 1977, *Roots,* a 14-hour adaptation of a best seller about the evolving role of blacks in American life since the time of slavery, as seen through one family's eyes, started the trend. It surprised the experts by drawing all-time-high audience shares, leading the networks to schedule miniseries in place of some blockbuster movies. Miniseries draw many viewers who do not normally watch series or movies on television, temporarily increasing the total number of households using television. Miniseries especially attract upscale professionals, compete well against cable movies, and can induce new viewers to sample other network programs.*

Miniseries, theatrical features, and made-for-TV movies impose special scheduling requirements on the broadcast networks. They do best starting at 8:00 P.M. or 9:00 P.M., when audience size peaks. They do poorly starting on the half hour because by then many viewers have already committed themselves to watching other television programs. They also need compatible lead-in programs, a difficult requirement because a movie slot's content and audience appeal change from week to week as the movies change, and a miniseries lasts only a few weeks. Lead-in and lead-out shows normally last all season, and are chosen to mesh with the entire year's schedule rather than specifically blending with a brief miniseries or succession of movies with varied appeals. See Exhibit 12–3 for ratings and audience shares of recent popular miniseries.

Cultural Programs   Public television once occupied a unique position in a programming game dominated by commercial interests. It served as a catchall for the cultural and other minority-interest programming that the commercial broadcasting networks claimed they could not afford to schedule.

---

*Although miniseries can cost a great deal (*War and Remembrance,* aired in two parts in 1988 and 1989, was said to have cost $110 million for the series and promotion), they bring prestige and occasionally high ratings while filling the large chunks of time once devoted to blockbuster movies. In spite of its large budget and cast of superstars, *War and Remembrance* did poorly in the ratings. On the other hand, *Lonesome Dove,* a western miniseries aired in four parts by CBS early in 1989, and produced at one-fifth the cost ($20 million), attracted critical acclaim and exceptionally large audiences (an average rating/share of 26/39). Western series programs have not been popular for decades, but *Lonesome Dove* had the benefit of outstanding writing and acting.

Intellectually challenging drama, nature films, science documentaries, and fine arts such as ballet and opera appeared almost exclusively on public television. All this changed with the development of cultural cable networks. Several thematic cable services specialize in programs of these types. As their reach increased, they bought up more and more of the specialized programs, leaving little that seemed exclusive to public television by the late 1980s. Bravo and Arts & Entertainment specialize in fine arts performances and foreign drama and films with artistic appeal; The Discovery Channel specializes in nature films and science documentaries; CNN and C-SPAN provide extended news treatments. Prestigious, award-winning PBS series such as *Masterpiece Theatre, Great Performances,* and *Nova* still made their mark, but public television lost its almost exclusive lock on such cultural programs.

Public television's long-running showcase, *Masterpiece Theatre,* gives Americans a glimpse of British video drama at its best. Scheduled as miniseries, historical programs based on real events became a mainstay of *Masterpiece Theatre,* starting in the 1970s with *The First Churchills.* Historical fiction, drawing on novels rather than the lives of real individuals, has proved even more popular. The most widely appealing series, *Upstairs, Downstairs,* detailed the doings of an Edwardian family (upstairs) and its servants (downstairs) for four successive seasons. Though some critics dismissed the series as merely high-class soap opera, *Upstairs, Downstairs* probably drew more viewers to public television than any other series with the exception of *Sesame Street.* Long after its original airing, the series continues to be popular in noncommercial syndication. Other adaptations from fiction on *Masterpiece Theatre* include *Good-bye, Mr. Chips, Silas Marner,* and *David Copperfield.* Journalist and critic Alistair Cooke introduces *Masterpiece Theatre* episodes. Delivered with great charm and wit, these introductions establish continuity and context for the episodes of one of the most culturally satisfying entertainment programs ever to appear on American television. In the late 1980s, Australian producers began contributing to *Masterpiece Theatre* with successes like *A Town Like Alice,* and more programs from other

EXHIBIT 12-3   Top-Rated Miniseries, 1977–1989

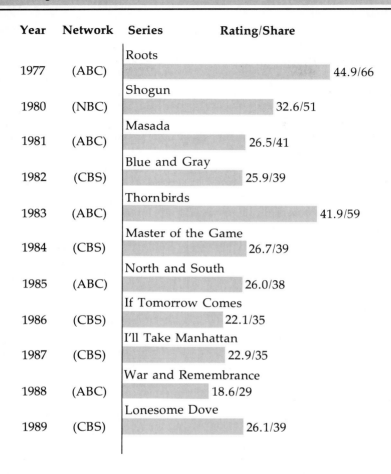

Year	Network	Series	Rating/Share
1977	(ABC)	Roots	44.9/66
1980	(NBC)	Shogun	32.6/51
1981	(ABC)	Masada	26.5/41
1982	(CBS)	Blue and Gray	25.9/39
1983	(ABC)	Thornbirds	41.9/59
1984	(CBS)	Master of the Game	26.7/39
1985	(ABC)	North and South	26.0/38
1986	(CBS)	If Tomorrow Comes	22.1/35
1987	(CBS)	I'll Take Manhattan	22.9/35
1988	(ABC)	War and Remembrance	18.6/29
1989	(CBS)	Lonesome Dove	26.1/39

The commercial networks have usually aired several miniseries each year since 1977, the year that ABC's Roots *captured the immense ratings and critical acclaim.* Roots *explored the history of author Alex Haley's family from the days of slavery to the present. The highest rated miniseries since have seldom attracted as many viewers as* Roots.

countries were expected to get their first U.S. exposure on public television during the 1990s.

PBS countered the criticism that too much public television fare came from Britain by developing *Great Performances,* a showcase for major American playwrights and musicians, often taped live before theater audiences. These performances helped to build U.S. audiences for opera and ballet, making artists such as Sills, Pavarotti, Horne, and Baryshnikov familiar personalities in millions of American homes. Cable television's active competition for cultural programs, however, creates a growing shortage of such fare for showing by American public broadcasting.

Diversity Issues One of the most persistent complaints about prime-time network programming concerns its sameness, its lack of diversity as to program types, themes, plots, production styles, and sources. Program genres rise and fall in audience popularity and, perhaps more crucially, vary in their popularity with network programmers. Networks risk so much on each program series that they take the safe route of copying successful shows again and again until each particular fad runs its course and another replaces it. Thus, spinoffs and clones reduce prime-time essentially to sitcoms, crime dramas, and movies. The networks' homogenizing influence also affects production styles; programs from one production company look much like those from another. Yet programmers desperately seek novelty. This seeming paradox comes from wanting to be different without taking chances. Occasionally, new ideas escape the network straitjacket, resulting in successes that surprise the programmers. *The Cosby Show,* one such surprise, became far more popular than industry experts originally predicted.

Cable television has brought only a limited increase in diversity. Several of the most popular cable networks seek the same mass appeal as the broadcast networks, following similar selection and scheduling practices on smaller budgets. USA Network, for example, treats dayparts like a broadcast network, scheduling reruns of broadcast network shows such as *Miami Vice* and *Murder, She Wrote* in prime time. Lifetime, a women-oriented cable network, obtained off-network shows such as *Spenser for Hire* and *The Days and Nights of Molly Dodd* for access and prime time. Needing more original programs, Lifetime commissioned additional episodes of *Dodd,* and the pay-cable network Showtime ordered more episodes of *Brothers,* but this practice only generates more episodes of program types already available to broadcast television viewers. Several specialized cable channels, however, expand on subject matter formerly only available in brief snippets on broadcast newscasts and entertainment programs. The Weather Channel, CNN Headline News, MTV, C-SPAN, and shopping services, for example, increase viewers' program choices at any hour.

12.2
Non-Prime-Time Entertainment

Non-prime-time breaks down into dayparts—early mornings, daytime, late night, and weekends—each of which carries a characteristic type of network program. Networks fill the early morning daypart with newscasts and talk, and weekends with sports, both discussed later. Soaps, games, and talk shows dominate daytime television just as they once dominated daytime radio. The late night period consists mostly of talk and comedy/variety programs. CBS once tried large blocks of movies in late night, then turned to series reruns; NBC introduced the comedy/variety series *Saturday Night Live* as far back as 1975. Music videos appeared in late night on weekends in the 1980s, filling extended network nighttime hours.

Although the broadcast networks put their best creative efforts into prime-time programming, the more stereotyped daytime programs yield a higher profit margin. Their extraordinary high production costs and their smaller number of commercial minutes make prime-time shows less efficient earners than daytime shows. ABC, for example, earns an estimated 25 percent of its revenues and 40 percent of its profits from daytime programming.

Soap Operas Among serialized drama formats, the *soap opera* (so called because in radio days, soap companies often owned and sponsored them) is the classic case of frugal expenditure of program resources. Notorious for the snail-like pace of their plots, these daytime serials use every tactic of delay to drag out the action of each episode. Soaps exactly suit low-cost television production because entire episodes often take place in a single location, involving only camera switches from face to face as actors utter emotionally laden dialogue. In the 1970s, the sponsors lengthened soaps from a half-hour to one-hour (doubling episode length increases production cost relatively little).

In recent years, soap-opera writers have accelerated plot development and risked plots dealing with once-taboo topics. Contemporary viewers apparently have less patience and more tolerance than their parents did. Drugs, social diseases, and family violence, once unmentionable, have become regular elements in such soaps as *The Young and the Restless* and *General Hospital.* Women and members of minority groups began appearing in more varied roles in the mid-1970s, although the distribution of occupations, races, and sex roles by no means reflects society's actual norms. More women characters in modern soaps have upper-income professions (medicine and law, with lots of free time for romantic involvements) than in society at large. Racial minorities remain underrepresented and restricted in their social interactions, though *Generations,* a trailblazing soap featuring close relations between a black family and a white family, emerged on NBC in 1989.

Controversial topics and new social roles in soap operas have been encouraged by changes in audience composition. Male viewership increased to over 10 percent of the audience. *Generations* (Exhibit 12–4) aimed at attracting the 20 percent of soap audiences who are black. *General Hospital* in the late 1970s and early 1980s and *The Young and the Restless* in the mid-1980s stimulated a faddish interest on the part of younger viewers. ABC launched *My Time for Me* during the summer of 1988 to lure young viewers during the school vacation. On-air promotion for NBC's *Santa Barbara* targeted the 15 percent of the 6 million daily soap watchers aged 15 to 24 years, trying to get the soap habit ingrained early. Still, the core of the soap opera audience remains housewives, an ideal target for manufacturers of household products, but a diminishing group as more women join the workforce. The extraordinary loyalty of dedicated soap opera viewers of any age makes them a favored commercial target. As intense in their dedication as sports fans, they support several fan magazines, avidly attend shopping center appearances of soap opera stars, and choose newspapers that give daily summaries of soap opera plots.

The loyalty of soap opera fans creates its own hazards for programmers, however. Although millions of Americans watch the Summer Olympics every four years, other millions stick to their habitual daytime viewing. To forestall an outcry from

EXHIBIT 12–4 *Generations*

A new daytime drama launched in 1989, Generations *tracks the family lives and careers of two intertwined Chicago families, the Marshalls and the Whitmores. The two families' links go back several generations; now, attorney Rebecca Whitmore has helped entrepreneur Henry Marshall launch Marshall's Ice Cream, a successful chain of five stores. The program reflects how people's lives today differ from those of their grandparents and mirrors our changing times in the format of a realistic, contemporary drama.*

SOURCE: NBC, Inc.

soap fans, the network that fills its days with Olympic events must insert special short versions of its most popular daily soaps with cliff-hanger endings, or risk losing viewers to the competing soaps. And the opposing networks take advantage of the irregularity of daytime programming during Olympic telecasts to launch their newest daytime efforts, hoping to snare displaced daytime viewers.

The most important afternoon hour on broadcast network television starts at 3:00 P.M., when viewing reaches its highest daytime level. At that hour, young children returning from school swell the stay-at-home audience. Network revenues depend heavily on the program scheduled at this hour. Daytime programs air about seven minutes more commercials than prime-time programs, allowing as many as sixteen commercial breaks in each hour. Constant switching of soap-opera plot lines from the doings of one character to those of another accommodates this large number of interruptions. As of the late 1980s, a gain of a single rating point was worth about $50 million annually in the daytime and as much as $65 million in prime time.*

The broad-appeal cable services such as Lifetime, superstation WTBS, USA Network, The Nashville Network, and CBN Family Network have yet to develop daytime soap operas that command the loyalty inspired by their broadcast counterparts. CBN made the most sustained attempt to launch a family-oriented soap opera, but it failed to capture an audience, perhaps because the program's religiously inspired "family" orientation inhibited its producers from dealing with the controversial subjects that seem essential to successful contemporary soaps.

Broadcast soap operas (as well as game and talk genres) have their counterparts on ethnic and foreign-language cable networks. For example, Univisión and Telemundo, two competing Spanish-language cable and broadcast networks, carry *telenovelas,* soap operas that reach tens of millions of Hispanics.†

Games Another classic parsimonious format, audience-participation *game shows,* became a staple of network radio more than a half century ago. One of the cheapest formats, they cost little in time, talent, effort, and money, once a winning formula has been devised. Game shows have the advantage over soap operas of limiting talent expenses to the host's salary and, in some cases, fees for show-business personalities, who usually work for minimum union scale for the publicity value of appearing on the show. Many games capitalize on the inexhaustible supply of amateurs willing to show off their abilities—or simply make fools of themselves. Most games run the half-hour length favored by the syndication market because it fits into an access slot and enables flexible scheduling.

During the 1980s, television game shows changed hosts and gimmicks with great frequency but continued to occupy a substantial portion of daytime network and syndicated television. By 1990, a new period of relative stability had been reached; old favorites among game shows earned higher ratings than new entries. A few games have great endurance. *Hollywood Squares,* for example, has been around since 1966 in various forms, first on a network, then in syndication. *The Price Is Right* started on network television in 1956, appearing on and off in daytime and prime time and in syndication in 30-minute and 60-minute versions.

Game shows now turn up on almost every cable network: MTV has *Remote Control*; The Nashville Network has country music quizzes; and ESPN has sports trivia such as *Scholastic Sports America,* pitting panels of college students from two universities against each other. USA Network blocks several hours daily with old game shows such as *Tic Tac Dough* and *The Gong Show.* Many modern game shows such as *Family Feud* use frivolous questions, often with risqué overtones. But the hit game show *Jeopardy* uses the older pattern of genuinely knowledgeable contestants armed with extensive memories. Its unique gimmick is to demand that

---

*These figures refer to the value of ratings increases on one network at the expense of the other two full-service broadcast networks; increases in network ratings that come from cable television audience losses or from growth in the number of viewers overall have much less direct monetary value to the broadcast networks (see discussion of shares and ratings in Chapter 14).

†Telenovelas (or *novelas*) differ from American soaps by ending in a few months rather than enduring for decades. They often serve mass educational as well as entertainment purposes. Typically, they instruct in socially desirable family behaviors and values, such as child care, husband/wife conflict resolution, and birth control.

contestants come up with *questions* to the answers already given by the MC instead of answers to the MC's questions. The top game hit of the 1980s, *Wheel of Fortune* (Exhibit 12–5), benefits both from the suspense element of the wheel's unpredictable stopping places and from the winning talent combination of MC Pat Sajak and his assistant, Vanna White. She won celebrity for a unique talent—that of "letter turner." Her primary role is simply to look beautiful while turning blocks on a board displaying the letters that contestants choose in their efforts to complete the words of a phrase or title.

A handful of specialists produce most of the successful broadcast and syndicated game shows. Goodson-Todman Productions, for example, grosses more than $50 million a year from game shows. Mark Goodson, the surviving member of the team formed in 1946, has pointed out that "soap operas and game shows are the greatest indigenous television forms, and they are alike in one important way. There are no endings. They go on and on and on" (quoted in Buckley, 1979).

Game-show profitability also hinges on enhanced commercial content. The giveaway format justifies supplementing the normal 16 minutes or so of advertising spots with additional short plugs for advertisers who donate prizes. Some advertisers even pay cash fees to gain brief visual and auditory plugs for their products. The television giveaway business supports several companies specializing as prize brokers, called *schlockmeisters* in the trade. They handle the collecting, warehousing, and dispatching of game-show prize merchandise. The advertiser pays the broker 40 percent of the retail value of the prizes. The prizes—whether cash or merchandise—come from the advertisers, costing the program producers nothing.

The broadcast networks schedule game shows in the late morning. Basic cable services such as WTBS and USA Network usually counterprogram with off-network situation comedy reruns; then cable turns this formula around, counterprogramming the broadcast networks' afternoon soaps with syndicated first-run game shows or movies. In addition, affiliates typically purchase first-run game shows to schedule in access time. Some cable subscribers can

EXHIBIT 12–5 *Wheel of Fortune*

An example of a highly utilized program, Wheel of Fortune, *aired first on daytime network television, then in a first-run syndicated version, and finally as an off network show syndicated to stations. Hostess Vanna White, looking beautiful in glamorous clothes, deftly turns letters of the alphabet as requested by game contestants. Co-host Pat Sajak's attempt in 1989 to become a talk show host did not succeed.*

SOURCE: Courtesy King World Productions.

see different versions of *Wheel of Fortune* several times daily (network, off-network, and first-run syndicated versions), illustrating the enormous popularity and durability of this hit game show. Every year, program prognosticators pronounce the death of *Wheel,* so far prematurely. Just in case, however, producers trot out dozens of new game-show ideas annually, hoping to hit upon the next invincible game.

Network TV Talk   In the 1950s programmers began extending network television into hitherto unprogrammed early morning and late evening hours, an extremely radical move at the time. "Morning television was available here and there," wrote a chronicler of the *Today* program, "but watching it was a taboo. . . . It was acceptable to listen to morning radio, but like sex and alcohol, television was deemed proper only after sundown" (Metz, 1977: 33). Throughout the 1980s, the *Today* show shared the 7:00 A.M. to 9:00 A.M. morning spotlight with the *CBS Morning News* (in various guises) and ABC's successful *Good Morning America.* Like NBC's program, *Good Morning America* adopted a variant of the magazine format, using informational talk as a primary ingredient. But *CBS Morning News* counterprogrammed by sticking closer to hard news in a traditional news format.

Although early morning programs also use the talk format, NBC's *Tonight,* a post-prime-time offering, is the quintessential network talk show. The television critic Les Brown called *Tonight* "the premier desk and sofa show" (1982: 430). *Tonight* started in 1954 as a showcase for the comic talents of Steve Allen. After a series of other hosts, including Jack Paar, Johnny Carson took over in 1962, becoming the perennial leader in late-night ratings. In 1979, after 17 years of monologues and interviews, Carson became restless and threatened to leave the show. Incredible though it may seem, considering that Carson's talent is virtually indefinable and his main previous experience had been as emcee of a quiz show, his threat shook both the NBC network and its parent company, RCA. According to estimates at the time, as much as 20 percent of NBC's income came from the 90-minute *Tonight* show; advertisers paid $25,000 for a 30-second ad reaching Carson's 15 million plus viewers. By 1979 Carson ranked as the highest-paid performer in television, with a salary reported to be on the order of $3 million a year.

In 1980 he signed a new three-year contract, reportedly at $5 million a year. When this contract was renewed in 1983, according to rumors his previous salary was doubled, and it has stayed at about that extraordinary level ever since.

Even more than the soap opera, Carson's type of talk show may qualify as a format unique to broadcasting. The British critic and playwright Kenneth Tynan pointed out that despite Carson's singular achievement in American television, many lesser pop-culture personalities have won far more attention in other countries. "The job at which he excels," said Tynan, "is virtually unexportable. . . . Most of what happens on the show would be incomprehensible or irrelevant to foreign audiences, even if they were English-speaking" (1979: 114).

That Carson has a unique quality seems evident from the fact that efforts to compete with him have always fallen flat. During his frequent absences from the show (in accordance with his extremely liberal contract), replacement emcees never equal Carson's audience share. The emergent Fox network had the temerity to lure away his most successful fill-in host, Joan Rivers, in 1987, scheduling her against Carson in a clone of *Tonight.* Predictably, her show proved a dud, lasting only a few months.

Cable television also takes advantage of the low production cost and flexibility of talk shows. Lifetime, for example, specializes in talk programs, carrying a dozen or so on health, consumer services, and the like. One well-publicized afternoon show, *Attitudes,* features two fashionable but zany women in an informal talk format that concentrates on fashion, beauty aids, and personal problems of women in their thirties and forties. On Sundays, Lifetime devotes its schedule entirely to medical programs, both talk/interviews and documentaries, aimed at physicians and other medical practitioners. In addition to *Larry King Live,* CNN regularly schedules talk shows on money management, as well as news interviews and discussions, the best known of which is *Crossfire,* an always acrimonious debate between opinionated opponents on hot political controversies. The religious networks rely heavily on inspirational talk programs, and sports channels on sports talk segments and interview shows.

Music Videos   Television paid little attention to popular music until 1981, when Warner Amex Satellite Entertainment Corporation formed Music Television (MTV), a basic cable network. MTV quickly became a 24-hour rock-video powerhouse. *Videos* are visual accompaniments to songs. Originally intended to promote record sales, they are now a television genre in their own right. Singers and performers act out song lyrics, interpret them, provide symbolic counterpoints, or otherwise create imaginative visual accompaniments for songs. As promotional tools, many videos come free of charge to any stations or networks that will play them. They have the added advantage of long-term reusability. But in 1984, MTV changed the ground rules by *paying* for exclusive rights to Michael Jackson's first *Thriller* video. MTV contracts for exclusive early *windows* (periods of availability) for the videos produced by several major record companies. In a barter arrangement, MTV offers free advertising time to the participating record companies. This strategy demolished music videos as a source of free programming, setting a precedent for network and station barter deals, trading commercial airtime for video programming.

MTV gained much influence with performers and record companies. The 24-hour availability of its program service and its tightly controlled song selection and rotation enabled it to target precise age groups. MTV targets teens and young adults aged 14 to 24, and its sister service, Video Hits One, targets adults aged 25 to 49. MTV's success had wide ramifications. Prime-time network programs, notably *Miami Vice,* added prominent musical elements. Competitors for the cable rock audience emerged, including local and regional rock video services, syndicated video countdowns and dance shows, and cable networks playing music videos other than rock, such as Country Music Television (CMTV). Even the broadcast networks scheduled MTV clones, especially in the weekend late-night time period.

By the mid-1980s, music videos on television had eaten into rock radio stations' audiences and threatened a key assumption about television's advertising practices. Several surveys indicated that most respondents aged 12 to 24 preferred MTV to a radio, and most young people in cabled homes said they always turned to MTV during commercial breaks in other television programs (Coleman, 1983: 60). Radio counterattacked by reaching out to rock music lovers in cars, at work, on the beach, while jogging with headphones, and so on. However, the grazing habits of television viewers with remote controls undermine the effectiveness of standard advertising practices such as clustering several spots in program breaks. A music video provides the perfect-length alternative to enduring the spots in a program's commercial break. In response, advertisers counteracted the lessened effectiveness of television spots by spreading their advertising budgets more widely, including a variety of media buys, thus weakening broadcast television's economic support.

Home Shopping   Since many people find in-person shopping entertaining, it follows that television programs devoted to remote shopping ought to attract audiences. Home Shopping Network and its several clones cable networks capitalized on this assumption, with instant success. They market popular consumer items, such as clothing, jewelry, home appliances, and novelty ware, claiming that bulk purchasing and low sales cost enable them to mark down prices dramatically. Cable systems carrying a shopping network receive a percentage of each sale consummated in their service areas.

This type of program represented a radical break with the broadcasting tradition, which used to hold that audiences could be asked to accept the intrusion of a small amount of advertising into their homes in exchange for a large amount of entertainment and information uncontaminated by commercialism. The pre-deregulation FCC took pains to maintain this arm's-length relationship by penalizing stations for "program-length commercials"—programs that so interweave commercial and noncommercial content that audiences cannot tell one from the other. The FCC reasoned that a broadcast station that devoted programs to advertising full time violated the public interest by displacing normal program functions.

Cable systems, however, can devote one or more channels to program-length commercials without denying subscribers normal program services on its other channels. Protected by deregulation, even some broadcast stations run syndicated home shopping programs, although broadcasting networks have not yet departed that far from the public-service tradition.

12.3
Network Sports Programs

For enthusiasts, sports give television and radio ideal subjects: real-life events that occur on predictable schedules and nevertheless are full of dramatic suspense. For the general audience, however, fictional drama and comedy have a wider appeal. Only a few play-off events, such as Super Bowl football and World Series baseball, rank among the all-time hit programs, and these have elements of pageantry and topicality that appeal to a broader audience than year-round sports fans.

Audience research suggests that more than half of the public watches professional football on television at least occasionally (Exhibit 12–6). Next in popularity come professional baseball and basketball, then big-stakes tennis and golf; after that the number of viewers falls off abruptly, with relatively few watching such sports as auto racing, soccer, and bowling, although enough watch to keep such events on network schedules. Network television strategists value sports programs mainly because they target the middle-class male group, which is not well reached by most other programs. Their appeal to such elusive consumers enables sports programs to command higher-than-normal advertising rates.

In the late 1960s, ABC's search for differentiation from its rival networks led to an all-out emphasis on sports. ABC pioneered the weekend sports *anthology* with its *Wide World of Sports* in 1961. By combining highlights of several sports events into a single program, the anthology genre avoids boring audiences with over-long coverage of minor sports or games that have only regional appeal. Even such esoteric sports as surfing and cliff diving receive coverage. ABC also introduced such novelties as instant replay, the controversial commentary of Howard Cosell, *Monday Night Football* starting in 1970, and extensive Olympic coverage. A decade after ABC introduced the genre, The Nashville Network adapted the sports anthology to a country-music cable audience, originating such shows as *American Sports Cavalcade* and *Celebrity Outdoors*. Most sports programs on broadcast television, however, consist of live contests between teams.

Weekend and Prime-Time Programs By 1990, television rights payments exceeded a billion dollars annually for on-the-spot coverage of sports events. In the early 1980s, the three major television networks paid $2.2 billion for a five-year deal with the National Football League (NFL) for the rights to selected professional games. In the mid-1980s, however, the broadcast networks learned the bitter lesson of cable television's impact on audiences. In this period, the once impregnable ratings for professional and college football declined as sports fans began to divide their attention among dozens of televised games. The networks responded in three ways: by diversifying into cable ownership (gaining outlets for sports and other original programming), by seeking exclusive rights to regular-season games accompanied by limits on competing local and regional telecasts of games (raising ratings for the national service), and by purchasing rights to sports mega-events for their image and promotional value.

Increasing its overall share of sports programming in 1984, ABC purchased the outstanding shares of ESPN (originally Entertainment and Sports Program Network), an all-sports basic cable network founded in 1980. ESPN became profitable by 1985 after Nabisco bought a part interest, enabling ESPN to purchase the rights to more popular sporting events. This 24-hour cable network carries first-rank sports events, including NFL football and major league baseball. It provides full-length coverage of events that ABC cannot schedule in their entirety. This pairing of broadcast and cable networks enhances their bidding power for rights to sports events. Following the ABC/ESPN success, in 1989 NBC also moved into basic cable, purchasing Tempo TV and SportsChannel America (jointly with Cablevision) to

EXHIBIT 12–6   Audience Interest in Televised Sports

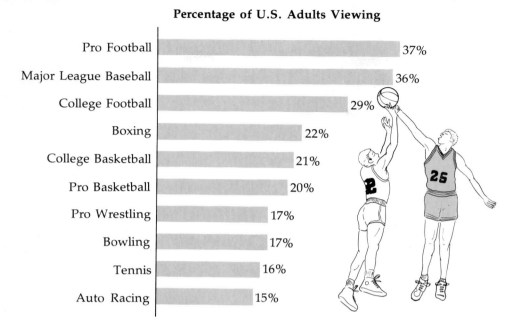

Percentage of U.S. Adults Viewing

Pro Football	37%
Major League Baseball	36%
College Football	29%
Boxing	22%
College Basketball	21%
Pro Basketball	20%
Pro Wrestling	17%
Bowling	17%
Tennis	16%
Auto Racing	15%

Professional football and baseball always capture the biggest sports audiences on television. Sports do best on weekend days; they usually do less well in ratings than entertainment series when scheduled in prime time.

create supplementary news and sports outlets on cable television for NBC. SportsChannel America introduced high school sports to national television in 1990, an innovative step which, if successful, could greatly expand the pool of televisable events.

The growth of sports on other cable networks, such as HBO, USA Network, The Nashville Network, and Univisión, as well as the superstations and regional pay sports networks, has been a major factor in reducing the value to the broadcast networks of all but exceptional or exclusive sports events. Combinations of sports-carrying cable networks reach, in the aggregate, more than half of all television homes with large numbers of events, decreasing

the broadcast networks' interest in carrying regular-season sports. Typically, national broadcasters now carry the end-of-season playoffs and championship games, leaving regular season events to cable networks and local broadcasters. CBS, however, surprised the television industry by spending more than $1 billion on major league baseball rights for the early 1990s and $243 million for the 1992 Winter Olympics—since CBS had not carried baseball for decades and last televised an Olympics in 1960 (Exhibit 12–7). From 1990 to 1993, CBS will televise 12 regular-season major league baseball games, the All-Star Game, both league championship series, and the World Series. Carrying these events will

EXHIBIT 12–7   U.S. Television's Rights Fees for Summer Olympics

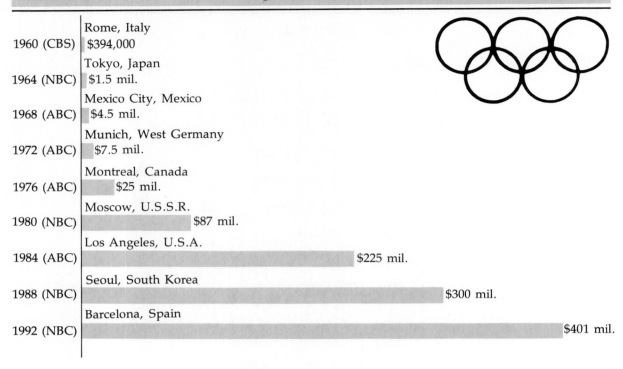

1960 (CBS)	Rome, Italy $394,000
1964 (NBC)	Tokyo, Japan $1.5 mil.
1968 (ABC)	Mexico City, Mexico $4.5 mil.
1972 (ABC)	Munich, West Germany $7.5 mil.
1976 (ABC)	Montreal, Canada $25 mil.
1980 (NBC)	Moscow, U.S.S.R. $87 mil.
1984 (ABC)	Los Angeles, U.S.A. $225 mil.
1988 (NBC)	Seoul, South Korea $300 mil.
1992 (NBC)	Barcelona, Spain $401 mil.

The rights-cost for televising the Summer Olympics has risen a thousandfold since 1960. The network winnning the rights also has large production costs, and not all of the programming will be timed ideally for U.S. prime-time viewing. Because of the cost increase, NBC agreed to share olympic programming with ESPN in 1992.

give the CBS network the prestigious sports image held by ABC and then NBC in the 1970s and 1980s. CBS protected its position by demanding exclusive rights to baseball on weekends and most weeknights, prohibiting cable networks, superstations, and local broadcast services from competing for the baseball viewer. Thus, CBS hoped to sustain its audience share (Exhibit 12–8).

Mega-events in the sporting world attract adult audiences that otherwise view little television. The Olympic Games, for example, attract millions of light television viewers who are especially inter-

ested in some aspect of the quadrennial event. This access to these infrequent viewers makes the Olympics a valuable showcase for promotional spots for regular prime-time programs. The networks pay far more for the Olympics than they can recoup in advertising revenues to enhance their worldwide images, to keep the premier events off cable and competing broadcast outlets, and to use the Olympics as a vehicle for promoting other programs. Annual mega-events such as the Super Bowl and World Series serve the same functions, especially because they normally occur just as the broadcast

EXHIBIT 12–8   Changing Network Sports Competition

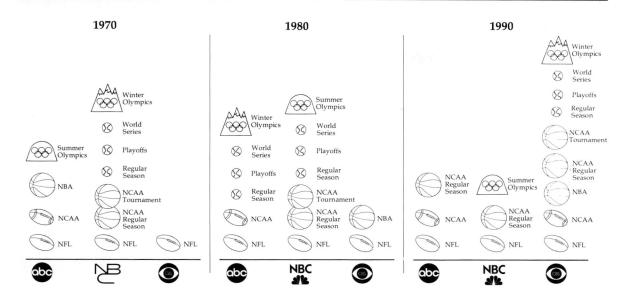

During the 1960s, ABC carried more sports programming than the other networks. NBC increased its sports coverage in the 1970s and 1980s, outbidding ABC for key events such as the 1980 and 1990 Summer Olympics. CBS stayed out of serious contention for sports viewers and sports advertising dollars for two decades. To improve its image with viewers and advertisers, CBS topped all network records in sports rights purchases for the 1990s.

SOURCES: William Oscar Johnson and William Taffee, "A Whole New Game," *Sports Illustrated,* Dec. 26, 1988–Jan. 2, 1989, pp. 34–36. Logos courtesy their respective organizations.

networks add new shows to their fall and winter lineups.

Sports on Pay Cable   Because costs for rights continue to rise, sports events are slowly migrating to pay cable, although basic services like ESPN and WTBS will remain major sports carriers for the foreseeable future. Some professional teams have been highly successful with home market distribution on pay channels, although several other attempts at regional pay sports channels have failed. These failures led sports promoters to smaller but safer distribution patterns. NHL hockey, for example, can be seen only on pay cable and only in the eastern states.

Events such as championship boxing and thoroughbred horse racing, which appeal strongly to relatively small but intensely devoted and willing-to-pay audiences, can be profitably scheduled on national pay-per-view television. Pay-per-view programs, seen only by means of addressable cable technology in homes, bars, and hotels, have proved lucrative for certain sporting events. More and more special events, particularly horse and car races, will move to pay-per-view in the coming decade, reducing the general public's access to these events. In 1990, over half of homes had cable service, but only 12 percent of all homes had pay-per-view. Although these numbers will rise, a large percentage of homes will never have cable service, nor will most people have access to pay-per-view in the 1990s.

Scheduling Problems   The seasonal nature of sports events and the limited control that stations and networks have over them give rise to scheduling complications. ABC made a daring innovation when it scheduled football in network prime time in 1969. It risked a long stretch of extremely valuable time on a single program with only selective audience appeal. Moreover, once football ended, replacement programs, preferably with similar audience appeal, had to be found, since much of the nonfootball audience had committed itself to viewing elsewhere.

All three broadcast networks fill weekend days with live sporting events but try to keep them out of prime time, except for ABC's Monday nights. Football scheduling is uncomplicated: college football games appear on Saturdays; professional NFL football appears on Sundays on two networks, which alternate coverage of the two leagues; and in the fall, ABC carries professional football games on Monday nights. In the late 1980s, ESPN also carried a package of late-season NFL games and college games on weekends, generally those the commercial broadcast networks did not want. Gaining the rights to these games, however, greatly enhanced ESPN's stature with advertisers and audiences, giving it the image of a major sports power. Professional NBA and NCAA college basketball playoffs and championships appear on the broadcast networks on weeknights during the spring, but otherwise, basketball appears mostly on Turner-owned networks and other superstations (WTBS carries all Atlanta Hawks games, for example) and regional cable services. Baseball causes more complications because of the large number of televised games.

Basketball and baseball present messier problems than football to television network schedulers. There are too many games and most of them are on weekdays and weeknights. Each professional baseball team plays 162 regular season games, and each NBA basketball team plays 82 regular-season games; each professional football team, however,

plays only 16 regular league games. The broadcast networks thus can carry professional football games because the events can be conveniently scheduled on Sundays and Monday nights. However, only a few regular-season baseball games appear on the broadcast networks. ABC and NBC carried major league games mostly on Monday nights and weekends in the late 1980s, at a financial loss because the ratings generated less revenue than the rights cost. Nonetheless, CBS picked up major league baseball rights for 1990–1993, scheduling carriage mostly on weekends. Generally, regular season sports get lower ratings than entertainment programs in prime time but capture the largest audiences on weekends. Thus, in rights contract negotiations, the networks bid for weekend events but avoid commitments to carry weeknight games (except, as always, ABC on Monday nights).

Issues in Televised Sports   Paradoxically, cable television both increases the amount of televised sports by expanding the number of services carrying games, minor sporting events, and sports-related programs, and decreases viewer access to those events. When games migrate from the broadcast networks to basic cable, they reach just over half of American homes; games that shift to pay cable can be seen by even fewer viewers. The loss of the supposed *right* to see certain games on "free" broadcast television generates hot debate. The courts, however, have sided with free enterprise, treating sporting events as just another commodity to be marketed to the owner's advantage.

Television also has an impact on event scheduling and how some games are played. Stations and network sometimes try to overcome the unpredictability of sports events by staging them expressly for television. Few quibble about such obvious entertainment events as the *NBA All-Stars, Legends of Basketball* (or baseball), and the like, but more subtle manipulations have raised questions.

Two problematic television-imposed practices are delaying starting times to permit viewing on both coasts and scheduling late-evening double-headers. Many games are played under lights on the East coast to maximize western audiences. Even more controversial are the 9:30 P.M. starts for college basketball games so that ESPN can carry double-headers on weekends. Indiana's coach Bob Knight has repeatedly denounced schedules that return college students to their dorms at 2 or 3 A.M. on school nights.

Another questionable practice is the arbitrary creation of time-outs for commercial breaks. Referees call such time-outs about every 10 minutes to accommodate advertising spots with football and basketball games. Artificial breaks can interrupt a team's momentum and adversely affect coaching strategies. Sports historian Benjamin Rader contends that television's need to attract occasional viewers has led to sports rule-changes for the sake of generating continuous excitement at the expense of the traditional balance between offensive and defensive strategies (Rader, 1985). NCAA rulemakers, for example, introduced the three-point shot in college basketball, a dramatic offensive effort that permits quick score changes in games that would otherwise tend toward balanced scoring—and perhaps dull television.

Still another type of sports manipulation affects the choice of games televised. Rights holders and game schedulers sometimes agree at the last minute to delay the start of a game in order to sign up more stations or cable systems. The financial interest in large audiences generates pressure to create last-minute *sports windows* during which large numbers of stations and/or systems can be assembled.* More commonly, however, blackout rules affect game carriage by mandating sell-outs before local television stations may acquire coverage rights. Television stations and sponsors sometimes short-circuit the

blackout rules by buying up the remaining tickets when a game is a few thousand short of a sell-out.

Ethical questions also arise because teams and sports associations insist on controlling the hiring of play-by-play and color announcers. This practice raises the issue of whether sports-events broadcasts are news, public relations, or entertainment. Consumer-oriented sports fans assert that broadcasters surrender control over their sports coverage because they need to please the people who govern the sale of coverage rights. A pre-deregulation FCC conducted an inquiry into biased sports reporting, reminding broadcasters that they have "a responsibility to refrain from engaging in or permitting others to engage in substantial deceptions or suppression of facts" in sports coverage (48 FCC 2d 237, 1974).

Television's tremendous impact on players' exorbitant salaries and widespread substance abuse create much larger concerns. During the 1970s, only a few superstars made salaries in the millions of dollars. As salaries have increased, the press has focused more attention on millionaire players, no longer hiding misdeeds like substance abuse and gambling. The widely acknowledged existence of racism in major sports, especially in coaching and management positions, also causes concern. In college sports, attention focuses on the low graduation rate of players, the frequent manipulation of college and NCAA rules, and event sponsorship by beer companies.

12.4
Network Children's Programs

Most television programs fall into recognized genres such as those already discussed: situation comedies, movies, soap operas, game shows, sports, and so on. The *children's* program category, however, encompasses virtually all genres. Cartoons dominate the children's category, but most adult program types also have their counterparts in children's programs.

---

*The term *sports window* differs slightly from *feature film window* mentioned in Exhibit 11–4. The sports term refers to events that are not initially scheduled for broadcast or cable showing, but that become last-minute television fare when, for a variety of reasons, a sufficient number of stations and/or regional cable networks make time available. This occurs when a particular player achieves special notoriety, an underdog team has a long winning streak, or a game is unexpectedly sold out at the last minute.

Broadcast Shows for Children Each commercial broadcast network programs about six or seven hours of children's television a week, nearly all on Saturday mornings, consisting largely of animated cartoons. More than 4 million child viewers watch the three networks regularly on Saturday mornings, and advertising aimed at them makes big profits for the networks. The networks value this audience so highly they alter the Saturday lineup in accordance with ratings trends just as rapidly as they change the prime-time schedule, canceling fading cartoons and adding new ones year round. Cartoons stripped daily by 150 or so stations can reach tens of millions of children several times a week, generating millions of dollars in product sales. Several half-hour cartoons can be re-edited into 90-minute theatrical features for theaters and videocassettes marketable in more than 100 countries around the world. Children's programs earn less than 10 percent of broadcast television's advertising revenues, but they represent good value because they run at times that might otherwise go unsold. Saturday mornings and early afternoons, though not especially attractive times for reaching adult groups, are crucial to toy, candy, and cereal manufacturers, and cartoons carry a heavy commercial load.

Toy, candy, and cereal manufacturers support most commercial children's programs; ice cream, soda pop, chewing gum, snacks, fast food, movies, video games, record companies, and bicycle manufacturers all market directly to children on television. Many syndicated children's shows operate as program-length commercials. Companies such as Mattel, Hasbro, and Tonka originate a line of toy products, then sponsor a television series featuring the toys. The most successful of these were *He-Man* and *Masters of the Universe* (Exhibit 12–9), *The Gobots, Transformers,* and *She-Ra: Princess of Power.*

Cable Channels for Children The three full-service commercial broadcast networks once accounted for nearly half of all hours of children's programs on television, but today cable television provides most children's programming to cabled homes. Of course, in homes without cable, the commercial networks remain the major providers. In

EXHIBIT 12–9   The Hero Business

Commercial and noncommercial stations produce less than 10 percent of the children's programs. In addition to the 2 1/2 hours offered weekly by the broadcast networks, syndicators market about four dozen animated series for children and two dozen or so half-hour live-action series, such as the successful character HE-MAN who is pictured above. The prices stations pay for children's programs depend on the same factors that affect the prices for sitcoms and other off-network and first-run shows—market size, station rank, previous ratings, and number of runs.

selling subscriptions to families with young children, cable systems emphasize their carriage of children's programs. For not-so-old parents who grew up watching a great deal of television themselves, this has proved a major selling point in persuading parents to subscribe.

Nickelodeon, Viacom's acclaimed cable network for children, originates several weekly hours of high-quality children's programming, avoiding violence as entertainment and favoring a broad range of role models. Altogether, Nickelodeon supplies 13 hours a day of children's programs, targeting the younger child in the mornings and teens in the late afternoons. In the evenings, Nickelodeon shifts to Nick at Nite, which schedules mostly off-network reruns and dance shows.

Nickelodeon's daytime programming array includes animated series, puppet and live-action comedies, off-network series, adventures, rock music videos, and magazine shows, divided about equally between syndicated programs and original, made-for-cable children's programs. Some of its long-running favorites include *Mr. Wizard, Against the Odds,* and *You Can't Do That on Television.* In addition to regular, ongoing series and movies, Nickelodeon imitates adult special programs by producing children's specials such as *Nickelodeon's Inaugural Ball,* commemorating President Bush's inauguration, and *Pop Warner's Football Superbowl,* highlighting the annual high school football championships.

Cloning adult programs at a level appealing to children has proved very popular with Nickelodeon's viewers, as have reruns of *Lassie* and *Dennis the Menace.* The cable network also finances dramatic and comedy series for children; it has gradually increased its total of original made-for-cable programs each year, but only slowly because of Viacom's purchase of Nickelodeon (along with MTV and VH-1) in the mid-1980s, which created enormous debt. Many of Nickelodeon's programs that started in the early 1980s remain on the air today, watched by a quarter of a million children at any one time. This is a small audience compared to the 3 million or so that watch a Saturday morning broadcast network cartoon, but in the aggregate, the cable services have greatly expanded television's total hours of children's programming to cabled homes.

USA Network also schedules programs for children, mostly syndicated cartoons or old off-network sitcoms, the same ones broadcast stations bid for. The Discovery Channel targets older children with original adventure and science programs, including shows on technology, history, and world exploration; these were available to more than 36 million cabled households by 1989. About one-third of Discovery's schedule consists of nature programs, which draw the highest ratings. Many of its shows use the anthology format, melding programs on a single theme from a variety of sources under a common title. For example, Discovery carries *Challenge,* an anthology about amateur adventurers and sports players; *A World in Conflict,* on World War II; and *The Race to Space,* on developments since Sputnik. Discovery, as the biggest buyer of nonfiction programs in the television business, has become a major contender for documentary films, acquiring more than 1,000 hours of nonfiction programming yearly. It provides a major addition to the total amount of nonfiction programming for the older child.

On pay cable, The Disney Channel programs for children in the daytime and the family in the evenings. This premium service draws on the large Disney studio library of films and off-network television series from the 1950s and 1960s, and originates several new adventure series for older children and feature films for all ages.

Noncommercial Programs Public broadcasting has a clear mandate to provide constructive, imaginative children's programs. Accordingly, public television stations fill a large portion of their daytime hours with in-school programs (paid for by school districts) and schedule additional special broadcast programs for children early in the morning and again in the afternoon.

Public television's most celebrated children's series, *Sesame Street,* uses a unique approach to programming for three- to five-year-olds. Ironically, all three commercial networks turned down the concept for *Sesame Street* in the late 1960s because they felt commercial sponsors would have little interest in a program narrowly focused on such a young age group. An independent, nonprofit corporation, Children's Television Workshop (CTW), launched *Sesame Street* in 1969. Funded initially by foundation and government grants, CTW now earns its own way, getting about half its income from the sale of articles that use the program's name and characters.

It is difficult to overstate the impact of *Sesame Street*. The series appeared just as the transition from "educational" to "public" television took hold, bringing the first large audiences to the service. *Sesame Street* targeted disadvantaged children, previously ignored by television. It aimed to help inner-city children prepare to learn reading and writing, and research showed that it worked. Children who watched *Sesame Street* at home often learned to read more quickly and easily than children who did not watch it. Preschool and primary teachers began to use broadcasts of *Sesame Street* during the school day, doing the previously unthinkable by incorporating a popular home program in the classroom. Its positive impact on reading skills improved the reputation of television generally by showing dubious parents and teachers how home viewing could aid education.

For the first time, CTW brought all the technical resources of television to bear on a series designed for children, backing the series with formative research establishing children's reactions to its educational elements. A wonderfully original set of large-scale puppets, the Muppets, became the program's hallmark. The episodes use very short segments to hold attention and employ a variety of formats, including "commercials" ("This segment of *Sesame Street* has been brought to you by the letters A and L and the numbers 3 and 7 . . ."). Even the entertaining Muppets and animated cartoon material serve an educational purpose (Exhibit 12–10). Noncommercial stations filled large portions of the day with repeats.

No series on either commercial or public television has been given the amount of scheduled air time as has *Sesame Street*. Throughout the 1970s, local stations have consistently devoted 29 percent of the weekday school-hour schedule, 14 percent of their weekend daytime schedule, and about 47 percent of their weekday after-school broadcast hours to *Sesame Street*. As the decade came to a close, an average 11.4 percent of the total broadcast hours of each public television station featured *Sesame Street*, with each program aired four times during the year (Sikes, 1980: 9).

By the 1990s, *Sesame Street* had taken on classic status as the pre-eminent program for three- to five-year-olds. CTW successfully reused segments of old episodes in new episodes, taking a kind of interchangeable-parts approach to production that stretched the series into its third decade and enabled it to serve its fifth and sixth generations of children, always with the same goal: to reduce the gap in basic reading (letters and numbers) and social skills between disadvantaged inner-city children and their suburban counterparts. Ironically, research showed that advantaged children benefited from the letter and number lessons even more than the original target audience.

Building on its initial success, CTW branched out with *The Electric Company* for older children, drawing on the production methods and research strategies of *Sesame Street* but using more advanced reading concepts. In 1980 CTW began a daily science program, *3-2-1 Contact,* in a half-hour format aimed especially at groups known to have little interest in science, particularly young females and Hispanic and black children. Later on, CTW began *Square One TV,* a math series for young children. As in *Sesame Street,* segments in these series can be pulled apart and reassembled for updating and reuse, stretching the production dollar as far as possible.

Because of their popularity and high production quality, CTW's programs create a dilemma for other producers of children's programs whose offerings frequently seem pale by comparison. Few of these producers have a budget anywhere near that of CTW, largely because of CTW's license revenue from *Sesame Street* characters. For the 1990s, the twenty-year-old *Sesame Street* added a new Muppet character, Blue Bird, a Japanese cast member, and the additional goal of encouraging an early interest in science. To enhance its revenues, CTW also began a commercial children's series for the pay-cable net-

EXHIBIT 12–10   Big Bird

Produced since 1969 by an independent, nonprofit corporation, the Children's Television Workshop (CTW), Sesame Street has become an institution for two generations of children in America. The show also is syndicated to dozens of other countries around the world. In most countries' versions, Big Bird is the most easily recognized star. Research shows that children who watch this program, which aims to educate through entertainment, learn to read more quickly and easily than those who do not watch Sesame Street.

SOURCE: Children's Television Workshop.

work HBO, *Encyclopedia.* Tagged by HBO insiders "Saturday Morning Live," the show targets 6- to 11-year-olds with a variety format that mixes animation and live action.

Other award-winning noncommercial children's programs include public broadcasting's *Villa Allegre* and *Carrascolendas,* bilingual series aimed at Hispanics and available only in cities with large Spanish-speaking audiences. Using live action with both children and adults, these half-hour shows attempt to ease the transition from Spanish-speaking family life to English-language public schools. For nearly three decades, another public television classic, *Mister Rogers' Neighborhood,* taught social skills to preschoolers, focusing on the very young child's values, feelings, and fears with gentle conversation and songs. Second in viewing popularity only to *Sesame Street,* it proceeds at a snail's pace that very young children happily endure, though it frustrates impatient older children and adults. The Smithsonian Institution enshrined Fred Rogers' sweater in its popular culture exhibit, commemorating his status with generations of children. Unfortunately, some children have no access to these cultural stepping-stones. Public television reaches more families than cable television, but still fails to reach about 25 percent of American households.

Children's Television Issues.   Children between 2 and 11 years of age watch an average of 25 hours of television weekly, and preschoolers watch as much as 28 hours a week. Most children will have spent more time watching television than in class by the time they graduate from high school. Children have such easy access to television, they consume so much of it, and it exerts such a powerful hold on their attention that the public has a special concern for the quality of children's programs. The main programming issues concern the appropriateness of what children watch, the impact of violent and aggressive content, the absence of a wide range of role models, and the pressure created by television advertising, especially ads for toys, candy, and sugar-coated cereals. The shortage of programs specifically designed for very young children creates particular problems, and commercial exploitation also raises public-interest questions. As a result, children's programs invite special regulation.

Most countries regulate children's programs in considerable detail; some forbid advertising to children altogether. The FCC first singled out children's programming for notice in 1960 when it listed children's programs among those program types to which broadcast licensees should pay particular attention because of their special public-interest significance. In 1988, Congress affirmed its concern by passing legislation setting limits on advertising in children's television programs. However, the president vetoed the bill on the ground that it conflicted with broadcasters' First Amendment rights (discussed in Section 18.1).

The very concept of "children's programs" remains ambiguous. Ratings companies and stations lump children as young as 3 years and as old as 11 years in a single category. The commercial services usually target children of school age, ignoring the preschooler. Programs for very young children cost more to research than programs for the older children that most advertisers want to reach, especially preteens and teenagers. Thus, programs targeting preteens and even teens have invaded children's schedules on many stations. Moreover, programs not intended for children nevertheless attract child audiences. About 9 million children watch prime-time television.*

---

*Stations have no compunction about scheduling adult programs at times when children normally watch television. As a scheduling strategy, for example, local independent stations often place off-network shows late on weekday afternoons (early fringe time), expecting that a high proportion of viewers will stay tuned, flowing through to the local news or entertainment shows that follow. The programs that draw these large, very youthful audiences include older situation comedies such as *Father Knows Best,* and cartoonlike adventures such as *Wonder Woman* and *The Hulk,* but they also include programs that are less appropriate for children, such as *Charlie's Angels.* At its peak, the prime-time version of *A Team* was watched by nearly 15 million children, as were shows like *Dukes of Hazzard,* and both capture enormous child audiences in syndicated rerun. However, being wary, the networks, stations, and ratings companies do not normally list these programs in the "children's" category that they report to the public and to Congress and the FCC when asked, even when the shows appear in times usually reserved for children.

12.5
News and Public Affairs

News does not usually attract large audiences, but it plays a significant role in establishing the medium's image. By assuming the serious function of conveying news and public-affairs programs, broadcasters took on a more important role than that of merely entertaining. They became, in effect, sharers with the print media in the Western world's tradition of press freedom. Not all broadcasters cared much about being part of a great free-speech tradition when doing so interfered with another great American tradition—that of making money through free enterprise. But in time, news programs changed from being money losers to money makers, ensuring the survival of broadcasting's special role as a bearer of information as well as entertainment. Most cable networks, on the other hand, specialize in either information or entertainment, with only a few of the largest adopting a comprehensive role comparable to that of the broadcast networks.

Broadcast Network News   The television networks weigh the cost of producing newscasts and documentaries against their benefits for network prestige and visibility. In the past, maintaining huge news staffs, far-flung facilities, and regular international satellite transmission cost more than the revenues they earned. Network news, for example, cost NBC $800,000 a day in the late 1980s, and lost about $55 million yearly. But competition from cable news services, growth in the popularity of information programs during the 1980s, and new, cost-conscious corporate managers encouraged the networks to add more news programs, to syndicate news footage to stations, and to diversify into cable. NBC purchased a cable network, now called CNBC, to get more mileage out of its news resources; CBS expanded into late-late newscasts; and all three networks began syndicating their video footage and feature stories to affiliated U.S. and foreign stations. Meanwhile, syndicated and cable informational programming also increased.

Fifteen minutes was the standard broadcast network newscast length until 1963, when CBS and

NBC expanded to a half hour (actually only about 22 minutes, after time for commercials and opening and closing announcements is subtracted). Despite the fact that the text of an entire half-hour network newscast would fill less than a single page of a full-size newspaper, the move to a half-hour format played a major role in elevating network television to the status of the most widely accepted source of news in the country.

In 1976, the dean of American television journalism, Walter Cronkite, argued strenuously, with widespread support from network management, for expansion of network evening news to a full hour. All three broadcast networks explored the possibility. CBS went so far as to relay a sample one-hour newscast to its affiliates in the hope of persuading them to accept the change. The affiliates nevertheless voted overwhelmingly against the expansion. They wanted to retain the evening lead-in slot (usually 6:00 to 6:30 P.M.) for their own highly profitable local newscasts while also retaining the 7:00 to 8:00 P.M. access hour for revenue-producing syndicated fare. This limitation meant that the networks could expand their evening news only by invading prime time at the expense of entertainment programs that earn far higher ratings than news.

However, CBS gradually expanded its *morning* news to a full hour. All three networks now schedule morning news or news magazine programs, as well as short news *summaries* throughout the day. In 1976 they began inserting one-minute *news capsules* in breaks between prime-time entertainment programs. These micro-newscasts usually consist of about 40 seconds of news, a 10- or 15-second commercial, and 5 to 10 seconds of announcements. On cable, on the other hand, *USA Updates* give only about 20 seconds to news, 10 seconds to a promo and identification, and 30 seconds to an advertising message. Because they are adjacent to high-rated entertainment, news capsules and summaries on the major networks draw the largest audiences of any regularly scheduled news reports. On days without important breaking events, the networks cut back on these capsules or, in the case of ABC, turn to shorts such as *Presidential Minutes,* a recounting of salient aspects of former presidents' administrations.

Late in 1979, finding that sizable audiences tuned to its temporary 11:30 P.M. nightly coverage of the crisis arising from the Iranian seizure of American embassy hostages in Teheran, ABC began a permanent late-night network news program, *Nightline,* featuring Ted Koppel. Each installment concentrates on one or two current news stories. For a time, ABC expanded *Nightline* to an hour, but in the absence of audience-attracting crises they found they could hold the audience for only 30 minutes. Charles Kuralt's *Sunday Morning* on CBS represents another network news expansion, condemned to low ratings by its schedule position but notable as a showcase for Kuralt's folksy style.

On the PBS network, *The MacNeil/Lehrer Newshour* provides some of television's best in-depth informational programming. Two hosts, Jim Lehrer, based in Washington, DC, and Robert MacNeil in New York City, quiz representatives of opposing views on significant current news topics. PBS began the *Newshour* as a half-hour program but expanded it to an hour in 1983, reflecting the trend toward longer news programs. Though acclaimed by critics, *The MacNeil/Lehrer Newshour* has not achieved widespread audience success, even by noncommercial standards. Public television stations have trouble finding schedule positions that do not face competition from commercial newscasts. The *Newshour* gains its largest audience shares when it is placed against entertainment programs; it does poorly against network evening newscasts. It also does better in the evening than in early fringe, but it must then compete for airtime with PBS's main evening program lineup. PBS relays *Newshour* starting every half hour over a three-hour period, allowing stations to downlink the signal whenever they choose. Public stations frequently juggle the program's start time to fit scheduling of adjacent entertainment shows, making it difficult for the *Newshour* to establish a steady viewing audience. Nonetheless, the kind of well-educated, upscale viewers this program attracts holds interest for newsmakers, and the program is monitored by journalists and other opinion leaders.

Dan Rather

Peter Jennings

Tom Brokaw

Lynne Russell

Bernard Shaw

EXHIBIT 12–11   Continued

Connie Chung

Jim Lehrer (left) and Robert MacNeil (right)

For more than two decades, the CBS Evening News *dominated the evening news ratings race. However, when Dan Rather succeeded Walter Cronkite, and Tom Brokaw became NBC's anchor for* NBC Nightly News *in the early 1980s, CBS lost ground to NBC. By the late 1980s, ABC's Peter Jennings on* World News Tonight *ran neck and neck with the ratings leaders. Although all three newscasts lose money, they have become the primary source of news for most Americans. These anchors rank among the most familiar and trusted broadcast personalities. As a result of foreign syndication of American network news, they have achieved worldwide recognition.*

SOURCES: For photos: Rather and Chung, CBS Newsphotos; Jennings, © 1989 Capital Cities/ABC, Inc.; Brokaw, NBC, Inc.; Russell and Shaw, Turner Broadcasting System, Inc.; MacNeil and Lehrer, MacNeil/Lehrer Productions.

In the early 1980s, the commercial broadcast television networks followed CNN's late-night lead by establishing their own middle-of-the-night newscasts: *News Overnight* on NBC, *Nightwatch* on CBS, and two "late, late" newscasts on ABC. They failed to justify their expense, however, and by 1985 only

CBS's *Nightwatch* remained, broadcasting at 3 A.M. nightly; ABC News scheduled reports after midnight only on weekends. The collapse of NBC's *News Overnight* encouraged many of its broadcast affiliates to pick up CNN Headline News for late-night closing broadcasts.

Cable News Networks Ted Turner made the risky decision to pioneer an all-news cable network in 1980. He began CNN as a fourth major television news service, providing domestic and international news in direct competition with ABC, CBS, and NBC. With a 24-hour schedule to fill, CNN can supply in-depth reportage and complete coverage of breaking news stories. Events such as shuttle launchings, presidential ceremonies, and personal interviews that the broadcast networks usually only summarize or highlight in half-hour evening newscasts, CNN often carries live and in full. It also fills the time between the weekday mornings and prime-time heavy news viewing periods with interview programs, half-hour shows on managing money and on the stock market, sports news programs, and debate programs such as *Crossfire*. Anchored by Bernard Shaw, CNN's two-hour *Prime News* counterprograms the broadcast network entertainment programs from 8 to 10 P.M., attracting a large nightly viewing audience. More than 2 million viewers tune in weekly to CNN.

Turner's companion news service, CNN Headline News, provides news headlines, fresh stories, and frequent updates on events in continuous half-hour cycles, much like all-news radio with pictures. Headline News appeals to viewers who prefer brief highlights to in-depth reportage. Its prime-time news anchor, Lynn Russell, became one of the best known female news anchors on television. More than half of all cable systems devote an entire channel to Headline News, in addition to one for CNN; others piggyback the Headline service on some other part-time service. By offering discounts and ready-made promotional support, Turner makes it more economical for cable systems to take all four of his services (CNN, CNN Headline News, WTBS, and TNT) rather than only two or three. Some independent broadcast television stations use Headline News in the overnight hours as a syndicated service, carrying a half hour, two hours, or more. In addition, CNN syndicates news footage and narrated stories to dozens of television stations for inclusion in local newscasts. It also supplies a radio network service called CNN Radio to hundreds of radio stations.

After an initial struggle, CNN teams attained parity with the broadcast news teams in such status indicators as receiving White House notices, participating in pooled coverage, obtaining major interviews, and securing space for cameras, crew, and reporters at major events such as political conventions and the Olympic Games. Without such access, CNN would have been overly dependent on the wire services and repeats of footage aired first by the broadcast networks. CNN moved from the red into the black by the end of the decade, becoming a profit center for Turner Enterprises.

Informational Networks Several cable networks that provide informational programming deserve mention as specialized sources of news for millions of Americans. Financial News Network is available to more than 30 million cabled homes with a continuous daytime television schedule of business and financial news. In the evenings, FNN supplies SCORE, an all-sports news service available to 20 million cabled homes. Other cable networks that carry large amounts of informational programming as well as entertainment include The Silent Channel, for the hearing impaired, and The Travel Channel, which carries 24-hour travel information as well as other feature material. Some cable systems also carry any one of several alphanumeric news services, such as AP News Wire or Update, supplying news headlines in text form. Consumer News and Business Service, NBC's cable channel, provides a mix of talk programs aimed at the family and at personal investment.

One of the most easily identifiable cable networks, The Weather Channel, supplies 24 hours of general and specialized weather news, inserting local weather conditions and temperatures within each region in hourly cycles. Segments on aviation weather, boating or skiing conditions, and world and domestic temperatures for travelers capture large short-term audiences. The Weather Channel also carries weather-related documentaries on such topics as natural resources (*Water Resources*) and emergencies (*Calm to Catastrophe*). This informational service reaches nearly 35 million homes, and although most viewing is for only brief periods of time, it attracts large cumulative audiences.

Public Affairs   In its station license forms, the FCC long distinguished "public affairs" as a separate class of programs defined as follows: "local, state, regional, national or international issues or problems, including, but not limited to, talks, commentaries, discussions, speeches, editorials, political programs, documentaries, minidocumentaries, panels, roundtables and vignettes, and extended coverage (whether live or recorded) of public events or proceedings, such as local council meetings, congressional hearings and the like." Until deregulation in the 1980s, heat from the FCC, critics, and Congress spurred the financing of topical *documentaries*. Though expensive to produce (by comparison to, say, talk programs), these rarely attract large audiences, and often cause a great deal of controversy. Nevertheless, the commercial broadcast television networks and most large stations maintain at least one weekly public-affairs discussion series, sometimes a news documentary series, and often minidocumentaries within newscasts (especially during ratings periods).

The most striking development in documentaries during the 1980s was the rise of *60 Minutes,* the weekly CBS magazine-format documentary series. In the 1979–1980 season it led all network programs in popularity, and since then it has generally stayed on the list of the top 20 programs every season. Its success violated all conventional wisdom about documentary programs, which had been considered repellent to mass audiences. One reason previous documentaries failed to achieve high ratings was the networks' tendency to position them in less favorable time slots and to deny them the luxury of stable scheduling. After years of wandering, *60 Minutes* finally achieved stability at a good hour—specifically because of the prime-time access rule, which opened the Sunday 7 to 8 P.M. time slot for nonentertainment network programs. Another factor may have been CBS's counterprogramming strategy; in the 1970s it typically scheduled *60 Minutes* against children's programs and movies. In the 1980s, *60 Minutes* followed live sporting events that included promotional spots featuring appeals to a male audience.

A stellar team of correspondents, originally Mike Wallace, Harry Reasoner, and Morley Safer, also con-

tributed to the *60 Minutes* success story. As a *New York Times* commentator put it:

> Their gray or graying hair, their pouched and careworn countenances, the stigmata of countless jet flights, imminent deadlines, and perhaps an occasional relaxing martini, provide a welcome contrast to the Ken and Barbie dolls of television news whose journalistic skills are apt to be exhausted after they have parroted a snippet of wire service copy and asked someone whose home has just been wrecked by an earthquake, "How do you feel?" (Buckley, 1978).

Later, Dan Rather joined the team; still later, Ed Bradley and Diane Sawyer balanced the cast with a black and a female correspondent. Rather left the show in the mid-1980s to become anchor of the *CBS Evening News,* the most prestigious news position a network can offer, and in 1989 Sawyer left for the greener pastures of ABC with a multimillion-dollar five-year contract. Nonetheless, *60 Minutes* remained among the top-rated programs.

The *60 Minutes* team, with chief producer Don Hewitt and a staff of some seventy producers, editors, and reporters, develops about 120 segments annually, some serious, some frivolous. The magazine format allows the program to treat a great variety of subjects in segments of varying lengths. The "confrontation" formula, a Mike Wallace specialty, also adds interest. Confronting his victims on camera with damning evidence of wrongdoing, Wallace grills them unmercifully. Some home viewers, already in the know, are fascinated by the victims' evasions, lies, and brazen attempts to bluff their way out of their predicaments; other viewers find Wallace's tactics ethically questionable. Corporations under *60 Minutes'* scrutiny often order their employees never to talk to Mike Wallace.

In the late 1980s, ABC's *20/20,* a magazine-format show similar to *60 Minutes,* moved into the pool of successful network prime-time shows. Although *20/20* rarely broke into the top 25, it coasted profitably with ratings in the 10s. Its costs are low in comparison with those of entertainment series, and it can be scheduled against ratings winners on competing networks and still attract a sizable audience. ABC concentrates most of its public-affairs programming in *Nightline,* its half-hour late-night news program hosted by Ted Koppel, and in its Sunday morning public-affairs program. To date, NBC has failed to develop a successful prime-time news magazine comparable to those of CBS and ABC.

Each of the three commercial broadcast networks schedules a public-affairs question-and-answer session with newsworthy figures on Sundays, usually around midday. Programs in that time period generally only get 2 or 3 rating points, but like the *MacNeil/Lehrer Newshour,* their importance lies in the people who appear on the shows and the people who watch. NBC's *Meet the Press,* dating back to 1947, has survived to become the oldest program on network television. CBS launched *Face the Nation* in 1954, and ABC began *Issues and Answers* in 1960, later replacing it with *This Week with David Brinkley.* Every politician of consequence appears on these Sunday public-affairs shows, and their remarks frequently become news on later network newscasts and in Monday newspapers. These programs reach important opinion makers and so have far more impact than their low ratings suggest.

CBS initiated *48 Hours* in the late 1980s, turning its cameras on a hospital, an election, a school, or the like for two days, attempting to reveal the underlying processes at work and the issues confronted daily by the participants. Narrated by Dan Rather, and operating with low budgets, episodes of the program varied from immensely evocative and insightful to awkward and insensitive. Programs in this realistic documentary style, using only minimal artistic contrivance and limited editing, typically attract 15 to 20 percent audience shares; they fill a need for information programs that is not met by traditional news and entertainment fare.

To offset the early negative image arising from frequent technical difficulties and often sleazy programs, the cable industry founded a nonprofit corporation, C-SPAN (Cable Satellite Public Affairs Network). C-SPAN I reached more than 40 million cabled homes by 1989 with live coverage of the House of Representatives, congressional hearings, and a variety of public-affairs programs. A second channel, C-SPAN II, reached more than 16 million cabled homes, carrying live coverage of the U.S. Senate and other public affairs programs and hearings. C-SPAN's two 24-hour services realize what idealists always thought electronic mass media should do—bring to the public serious, in-depth reporting of government in action.

Using an open-ended, no-frills, unedited format, C-SPAN's live cameras tell the story of Congress, showing the tense moments of party confrontation—such as the Tower "nonconfirmation" hearings in 1989—as well as empty House or Senate seats during dull afternoon speeches. It provides a forum for elected representatives to address both Congress and viewers at home, and gives at-home watchers a peek into the workings of Congress. In presidential election years, C-SPAN originates live coverage from cities outside of the Washington, DC area, and throughout the year it carries political interview shows, panel discussions, press conferences, and live or taped speeches by policy makers. It also pioneered national call-in programs and has expanded into satellite relay of events from abroad, such as the British House of Commons. About half of its nearly 5,000 hours of programming in 1988 consisted of live, original material. And it does all this on a budget of about $13 million a year with a staff of about 150 employees. As many as 20 million viewers watch C-SPAN over the course of a year, many of them politically active people who influence public opinion.

For its part, the Public Broadcasting Service provides a steady diet of public affairs with such award-winning programs as *Washington Week in Review, Nightly Business Report,* and *Frontline.* It also carries *The Constitution: That Delicate Balance,* an unusual series on questions of government and constitutionality in which distinguished American politicians, attorneys, judges, and public officials play roles in hypothetical news crises. The program has attracted such participants as former presidents, secretaries of state and of defense, heads of major corporations, and luminaries of the judicial world. The debate format places individuals at loggerheads over public-affairs issues, exposing contradictions and intricacies in the internal workings of contemporary American government. Combining live entertainment and education, it could be taken for college credit through the Annenberg/CPB Project, the program's funders.

Some public broadcasters regard extended public-affairs programming as the key advantage PBS offers as an alternative to commercial programming. Critics say the commercial networks devote too little time to news and public affairs, dilute information with too much entertainment, and evade real controversy. However, public and commercial broadcasters share the problem of getting support for serious programs. Businesses that underwrite PBS programs have no more appetite for controversial programs than do advertisers on the commercial broadcast and cable networks.

12.6
Commercial Radio Networks

Television competition devastated radio networks as full-service program suppliers, but the major networks survived by supplementing the local radio formats adopted by their affiliates. By 1970s, new full-service radio networks re-emerged to compete with locally originated music programming. Inexpensive satellite interconnection made this development possible. As of 1990, about 20 national radio networks competed for affiliates in the United States, providing predominantly news, talk, sports, or 24-hour music.

News   In 1968, the ABC radio network responded imaginatively to the needs of its formula-dominated affiliates. Recognizing the central role of audience segmentation in station programming, ABC designed four network services, each with a different type of audience in mind. Each service consisted of five-minute news-and-feature segments, styled to suit specific age groups and calculated to fit smoothly into the four most popular radio formats.

The success of this approach eventually encouraged ABC to offer seven such services. For example, ABC's Rock Radio complements the style of rock music stations targeting 18- to 24-year-olds with one-minute newscasts covering the entertainment world.

ABC's FM Network serves rock stations aiming at a different audience, 12- to 34-year-olds. Another ABC service, its Contemporary Network, also carries one-minute summaries of news, covering a wider range of topics suited to a broader audience. In contrast, ABC's Information service provides five-minute newscasts to fit within all-news and news/talk formats.

ABC gets maximum value from its relay facilities by cycling its short news feeds to its several sets of affiliates throughout each hour, using the remaining time to feed sports and features on a closed-circuit basis for later playback by the stations. Nearly 20 years passed before affiliate pressure persuaded CBS and NBC to copy ABC's innovative multiple networks. Westwood's Mutual Broadcasting System still programs a single feed, carried mostly by AM stations with information formats. Using a staff of about 50 reporters, producers, and editors based mostly in Washington, DC, and New York, Mutual supplies five minutes of news on the hour, 24 hours a day, and news on the half hour, varying from three minutes in daytime to two minutes in the overnight time period. In addition, Mutual supplies a minute-long update of headline news twice hourly at 25 and 55 minutes after the hour. Only about 800 of Mutual's 2,000 affiliates carry all or part of the news service.

The major network television news personalities also provide daily newscasts on radio. Some television journalists anchor specific radio news reports, such as morning drive reports; others pre-record particular news stories for later inclusion in scheduled newscasts. For example, a daily debate on hot political issues between Democratic Senator Ted Kennedy and Republican Senator Bob Dole, *Faceoff*, was one of Mutual's most popular features. Radio depends heavily on well-known voices to establish credibility and attract audiences for brief news reports. Network radio also broadcasts news and commentary by well-known journalists such as Paul Harvey, the longest surviving radio news personality and the leading radio ratings earner.

Talk and Sports   Two of the major networks also supply *talk formats* to radio affiliates. ABC's

Talkradio and NBC's TalkNet supply overnight talk and interview programs, mostly to AM stations in major markets. Sun Radio, a newcomer in 1988, supplies 24-hour talk programming, mostly to stations in the South. Mutual Broadcasting System distributes *The Larry King Show*, which originates in Washington, DC, the radio version predating the CNN television program *Larry King Live*. It is far and away the most popular talk show on radio, carried by nearly a thousand radio affiliates in the overnight time period. Another Mutual talk hit, *Dr. Toni Grant Show*, originating in Los Angeles, features a well-known psychologist taking live telephone calls in the evening hours.

Live sporting events featuring a well-known, long-established team usually come from *regional* sports radio networks, which supply live games to hundreds of stations within a state or larger region such as the Midwest or Southeast. The major national networks services, however, continue to seek play-by-play rights to games of national interest, filling their weekend schedules with live football, baseball, basketball, and some racing, tennis, and other events, varying with the season. Mutual has had the radio rights to national football for decades, featuring college games on Saturdays (especially Notre Dame games) and professional football on Sundays, supplemented by daily sportcasts and *Wide Weekend of Sports* twice on weekends. The sports component of radio networks is so important to affiliates that CBS paid $50 million for radio baseball rights for the early 1990s, nearly doubling the previous contract payment. In addition, the major networks supply sports specials and sports talk to block-schedule with games.

Music More than a score of radio networks featuring 24-hour music developed in the 1970s and 1980s. Stations often affiliate with a news network to supplement a music network. This double affiliation is possible because exclusivity operates only within one type of network service. Each of the largest surviving music networks, such as Westwood One, United Stations, Transtar, and Satellite Music Network, has more than a thousand radio affiliates. Perhaps the best known show on music radio, *Casey's Top 40 with Casey Kasem,* appeared on ABC for nearly 20 years until it shifted to Westwood One in 1989. Kasem's countdown technique, incorporating brief stories about the artists and their music, has become a radio standard.

Commercial radio networking and syndication sometimes appear indistinguishable to listeners, but each has its own characteristic type of content, delivery means, advertising procedures, and payment practices. The major networks supply news, sports, and specials, or all-talk or all-music by satellite, accompanied by national advertising; syndicators never supply news, concentrating instead on formatted popular music and music-related features on tape. Radio networks often pay compensation to major-market affiliates; syndicators usually charge for their programs, but on occasion, they will pay large-market stations to carry particular programs in order to justify producing the programs.

Summary

▌ Network programs are distributed to affiliates by the three major television broadcast networks, Fox, PBS, about fifty cable networks, and about two dozen radio networks.

▌ Prime-time programs, the most important part of network schedules, come mostly in weekly series and movie slots. New shows may be original ideas but are commonly spinoffs or clones.

▌ Series divide into family and nonfamily situation comedies, dramatic series, movies, and miniseries. Sitcoms target women 18 to 49 years and have great value in later syndication.

▌ Networks use both blockbuster movies and miniseries to clobber the competition during sweeps. Many movies have been shown too often on pay cable or rented on videocassette to interest the networks; thus miniseries and made-for-TV movies have special value. Miniseries raise HUT levels, and made-for-TV movies target precise audiences.

▌ Network soap operas attract fanatically loyal fans who resent disruptions of the daytime schedule for special events. The content of soaps has become progressively more controversial over the years, and the newest entries target younger viewers.

▮ Game shows, talk programs, and music videos are especially parsimonious television formats, showing on cable services as well as the broadcast networks. Shopping channels consist of long-form commercials, marketing personal and home items.

▮ The dramatic nature of sporting events makes many of them ideal for live network television, although only events with national appeal are suitable for network carriage. Annual mega-events will eventually shift to pay television, but the networks continue to carry many sponsored sports programs.

Sports are difficult for the broadcast networks to schedule, but ideal for cable television. Television's impact on both sporting events and athletes are active issues resulting from the commercial nature of television and the large sums it pours into sports rights.

▮ Toy, candy, and cereal manufacturers support much of the children's programming on network and local television, frequently creating cartoon series to market specific toys. Cable provides many programs for children.

▮ The success of *Sesame Street* altered the relationship between schools and television, showing that properly researched children's shows could have real educational impact.

▮ Network news has expanded beyond the evening news into the early morning and late night time periods, and now includes headline capsules within prime time. In-depth news reporting occurs regularly on PBS and CNN.

▮ Network public-affairs programs, though few in number and low in ratings, draw important participants and have an impact on other media and opinion makers.

▮ Radio networks, revitalized by the advent of low-cost satellite distribution, have adapted to formula radio by supplying brief newscasts targeted for specific age groups, and sports, talk, and 24-hour music suited to specific station formats.

CHAPTER 13

SYNDICATED AND
LOCAL PROGRAMS

Syndicated and local programs are the alternatives to network programs in broadcast and cable schedules (Exhibit 13–1). They piece out the one-third or so of affiliated television stations' schedules that are not cleared for network offerings. They fill entire schedules of nonaffiliated television stations, the independents. Local programs, though they play a significant role, occupy only a small percentage of total television schedules. For cable networks, syndicated programs supplement network-financed original cable productions. Local cable channels use mostly locally made programs or public domain programs (those for which the copyright has expired) to fill channels not occupied by cable networks or broadcast stations. Most radio stations have affiliation with one or more radio networks, but networks normally contribute only a small portion of radio station schedules, the bulk of which is filled by a mix of locally originated and syndicated material.

13.1
Syndication Basics

By nature a worldwide phenomenon, syndication occurs wherever broadcasting or cablecasting exists. The demand for programs always exceeds the local supply, so that only program resale and networking can overcome the limitations of local production. Most popular taped or filmed programs therefore go into syndication for sale and resale. News and most public-affairs programs are too timely to syndicate in the same manner as entertainment programs. However, news agencies may be considered as syndicators of original material, and the news departments of broadcast networks and cable news networks have begun syndicating their own news.

Distribution by syndication resembles network distribution in that the same programs go to many outlets, but syndication differs as to timing. Stations may schedule syndicated programs at any time according to the station's needs, whereas affiliated stations normally carry network programs as they come from the network.* Syndicators need no permanent relay interconnection with a permanent string of stations. They send their programs by various means to various stations according to market demand.

Some syndicated series have been running for more than 35 years, replayed scores of times. *Little*

---
*Occasionally syndicators stipulate specific time slots for certain prestigious programs, but they accomplish that simultaneity by advance planning, not by using permanent relay facilities.

EXHIBIT 13–1   Main Sources of Programs

Main Program Sources

Type of service	Broadcast TV networks	Cable TV networks	Affiliated TV stations	Independent TV stations	Local cable TV channels	Radio networks	Radio stations
Original production (studios/independents)	•	•					
Original production (networks)	•	•	•			•	•
Original production (local)			•	•	•		•
Off-network syndication		•	•	•			
First-run syndication			•	•			•
Movie syndication	•	•	•	•	•		
Record syndication							•

Both television and radio obtain programs from a variety of sources.

Rascals, a series edited from ancient *Our Gang* film shorts, started in television syndication in 1955 and can still be seen on independent stations. *I Love Lucy* (1951–1956), the quintessential off-network syndicated series, dates back to before color television and has been syndicated in virtually every country in the world. At times there have been as many as five *Lucy* episodes on the air on the same day in a single U.S. market.

Definition   The FCC defines a syndicated television program as follows: "any program sold, licensed, distributed, or offered to television stations in more than one market within the United States for non-interconnected [that is, nonnetwork] television broadcast exhibition, but not including live presentations" (47 CFR 76.5p). For practical purposes, programmers class all nonnetwork and non-local programs, whether live or not, as syndicated, including movies. Of the optional program-marketing methods listed in the FCC definition, *licensing* is used most frequently. The syndicator licenses the "buyer" (actually the lessee) to use a syndicated product (program or series) for a limited period. Off-network programs sold to cable networks technically are not "syndicated" according to the FCC's definition, since a cable network is not a station, but the same programs and marketing processes are involved. The cable networks, however, obtain program licenses for the national syndication market, not just for local markets.

Off-network syndicated programs have completed their contractual runs (usually two showings) on ABC, CBS, NBC, or Fox and have reverted to their owners, who then make them available for licensing to broadcast stations or cable networks. Sometimes early episodes of network series go into syndication while new episodes are still being produced for the network run.

The networks do not own these programs outright as a result of an FCC decision designed to prevent the networks from dominating entertainment program production and distribution. The rules prohibit networks from having a financial interest in the production of most of their entertainment programs and from syndicating *any* of their programs in the domestic market. (This topic is discussed in more detail in Section 17.2.)

Made-for-syndication programs are shows that are released initially to the syndication market and never shown on the networks. Programs intended for access time, such as games, magazines, and tabloid-news shows, are always first-run syndication products. Syndicators also license older movies in groups called "movie packages" to stations for replay after theatrical and any broadcast or cable network runs.

TV Syndication Process Television program *syndicators,* also called *distributors,* obtain distribution rights for a special or series from the program producer, which may be another branch of their own company or an independent producer. They then offer the shows *in syndication,* on tape or film, to stations or cable networks. The syndication companies send their product by mail, courier, or satellite relay. Individual stations, groups of commonly owned stations, and cable networks lease the right to a stipulated number of plays over a fixed period of time in a particular market, after which the rights revert to the syndicator.

Syndicators showcase new products at annual meetings of the National Association of Television Program Executives (NATPE) and at other national and international program trade fairs. The two major rating services, Arbitron and Nielsen, document the track records of syndicated programs already on the market, issuing special reports on the size and composition of the audiences attracted by current syndicated series. The most popular former network shows, such as *The Cosby Show* and *Three's Company,* play in most of the over-200 U.S. markets, reaching more than 95 percent of homes and thus rivaling network market coverage. Hit programs made especially for syndication, such as *Wheel of Fortune, Jeopardy,* and *Entertainment Tonight,* also appear in nearly 200 markets, but the majority of such made-for-syndication programs reach only about half of the television markets at any one time.

Rights normally give the buyer *exclusivity,* sole use of the product within the buyer's own market, for the term of the license. Only one cable network reaching across the nation or only one station in a local market can obtain a license for, say, a package of old *M*A*S*H* or *Miami Vice* episodes. However, syndicators may have enough episodes of a one-time network series on hand to split them into two packages. The station that gets a license to broadcast Package A gets exclusive rights only to Package A. Another station in the same market might get a license to show Package B; thus different episodes of the same series may be aired during the same period of time in the same market. Moreover, during the 1980s, a basic cable network and a superstation often obtained licenses for the same syndicated series, bringing identical episodes into cabled homes in a market where a broadcast station may have paid handsomely for sole rights. This duplication tends to divide the audience, diminishing the value of the broadcast station's "exclusive" rights. Currently, cable networks purchase a mix of exclusive and nonexclusive national rights, depending on their budgets and programming strategy.

In response to the duplication dilemma, in 1989 the FCC readopted *syndex* (syndicated exclusivity) rules that it had rescinded eight years before. Syndex rules empower broadcast television stations to force cable systems to delete duplicative syndicated programs. Cable systems must temporarily black out the superstation or other imported service, substituting another program. Syndex rules do not apply to two affiliates of the same network carried by a cable system or to very small cable systems, nor are all syndication contracts exclusive. In fact, obtaining exclusivity increases the price a station or cable network pays for syndicated program licenses and in many cases exclusivity would not be worth the extra cost.

Syndication and Prime-Time Access   The syndication market received a boost from the FCC's *prime-time access rule* (PTAR). Before 1971, the three major commercial television networks filled nearly all the best evening hours of their affiliates' schedules, leaving little opportunity for producers to sell programs aimed at the national market but not good enough (or lucky enough) to be selected by the networks. Only the fringe hours (those immediately preceding or following prime time) remained open for syndicated material on affiliated stations. Independent stations had time available but could not afford to pay for recently produced, high-quality syndicated shows.

In part to widen the market for original syndicated and local program production and in part to diminish the hold of the three commercial networks on the best audience hours, the FCC adopted the PTAR, effective in 1971. PTAR limits network entertainment programs to no more than three of the four prime-time hours. Prime time consists of the hours when the television audience reaches maximum size and hence is the time when stations can pay the most for programs. As defined by the FCC, it consists of the four evening hours between 7:00 P.M. and 11:00 P.M. Eastern and Pacific time (one hour earlier in Central and Mountain time zones, and varying during daylight savings). Regularly scheduled network newscasts do not count as part of the three prime-time hours that the networks may supply, as long as a local half-hour newscast precedes them. PTAR makes other exceptions, detailed in Exhibit 13–2.

In practice, the networks had already abandoned the 7:00 to 7:30 P.M. slot to their affiliates; PTAR therefore gave the affiliates only the additional half-hour between 7:30 and 8:00 P.M. One daily half-hour

may not seem like much for the networks to surrender. However, multiplying that half hour of access time by the 260 weekdays in a year and by the 150 affiliates in the top fifty markets yields an annual large-audience market of 39,000 half hours on major stations. Prior to 1971 syndicators and local producers had no access to prime time on the top affiliates except at the price of network pre-emption. PTAR therefore gave a significant new incentive to producers of nonnetwork programs.

With PTAR, the entire 7:00 to 8:00 P.M. hour became known as *access time.** Affiliates in the top 50 markets can fill access time with either locally produced programs or nationally syndicated nonnetwork programs. PTAR prohibits affiliates in the top 50 markets from airing former network shows during access time, but leaves all independents and the affiliates in the 150-odd smaller markets free to use one-time network material during access time if they choose. Since they generally find former network shows the most popular and most competitive syndicated programs, small-market stations that can afford them usually schedule off-network shows in access time.

To summarize: Most locally produced shows draw such small audiences that stations usually consider access time too valuable to expend on them. The great majority of access-time programming, therefore, consists of syndicated half hours, stripped at 7:00 P.M. and 7:30 P.M., Monday through Friday (see Exhibit 13–2 for special weekend variations). Affiliates in the top 50 markets, which are forbidden to use old network programs in access time, normally schedule shows made especially for syndication; other stations tend to schedule old network shows.

Programs produced especially for the access-time market have smaller budgets than network prime-time programs because (1) early prime time has less value in terms of advertising revenue than prime time from 8:00 P.M. onwards, (2) the many sellers of syndicated material (mostly games and magazine shows) scrambling to place their programs in access

---

*Television rating companies rate the access hour separately for stations and advertisers, identifying as prime time only 8 to 11 P.M. and ignoring the FCC's four-hour definition.

EXHIBIT 13–2 Prime-Time Access Rule Exceptions

As the FCC put it, PTAR aims "to make available for competition among existing and potential program producers, *both at the local and national levels,* an arena of more adequate competition for the custom and favor of broadcasters and advertisers" (25 FCC 2d 326, 1970, emphasis added). In practice, the great majority of stations fill access time with national-level syndicated programs.

Since PTAR aims at curbing the networks' control over prime-time *entertainment,* the rule also bars affiliates in the top 50 markets from scheduling *off-network syndicated shows* during access time, the period preceding the three hours of prime time—in practice, 7:00 to 8:00 P.M. East and West Coast time zones and 6:00 to 7:00 P.M. Central and Mountain zones. By the same token, the FCC did not want to discourage the networks from scheduling *nonentertainment* programs. PTAR therefore exempts from the ban network programs for young children (ages 2 through 12) as well as public affairs and documentary programs, except on Saturday nights. The FCC wanted to keep Saturday free of encumbrance by exemptions so as to encourage *locally produced* access programs at least

once a week (Saturday being at that time the traditionally favored time for locally produced programs). Networks tend to schedule their major public-affairs and documentary programs on Sundays; therefore, they usually take advantage of the exemptions to schedule such programs in Sunday access time. For example, because of PTAR, CBS moved *60 Minutes,* its prestigious news/documentary series, to the Sunday 7:00 to 8:00 P.M. time slot in 1975.

PTAR also makes exceptions for news specials dealing with currently breaking events, on-the-spot news coverage, broadcasts by and for political candidates, regular network newscasts when preceded by a full hour of locally produced news or public affairs programming, runovers of live sports events, begun in the afternoon, and special sports events such as the Olympic Games.

It must be borne in mind that the PTAR restrictions apply only to *affiliates* (including O&O stations) in the *top 50 markets.* This leaves independents in all markets and affiliates in the 150-odd smaller markets free to use off-network material during access time if they choose.

time usually win places only on relative short lists of stations, and (3) such programs have no track record, unlike off-network shows. Network shows, though, have assured placement on most affiliates during the most valuable segments of prime time.

13.2
Television Syndication Types

Commercially significant syndicated television product breaks down into three categories: off-network programs, first-run syndication programs, and theatrical films (feature films or movies). Barter syndication, an alternative method of defraying syndicated program license costs, contrasts with the usual cash payments. Prime-time syndication refers to especially prestigious first-run product designed to compete with the best of network programs.

Off-Network Programs The programs that do best on the networks usually also excel in syndication. Most stations schedule half-hour syndicated series because they attract a desirable demographic group (usually women 18 to 49 years) and permit scheduling flexibility. As the audience of working adults builds up during the important late afternoon time period, successive half-hour shows gain bigger audiences. Hour-long programs, on the other hand, do not attract many new viewers during their second 30 minutes. An off-network series typically earns a rating about 10 points lower in syndication on stations than it earned in its first network appearance. On cable networks, ratings for such programs may be even lower.

Broadcast stations fill two main time periods with off-network shows: early fringe and access time (if the station is not an affiliate in one of the top 50 markets). They strip both off-network sitcoms and hour-long adventure shows in late afternoons, with each station in a market usually choosing to block one programming genre or target one demographic group. Comedy sitcoms attract both children and adult women, and their half-hour length allows viewers who have newly arrived home to start a fresh program with minimum delay. Court shows and male-appeal programs such as *M*A*S*H* and *Barney Miller* provide an ideal lead-in to affiliates' local evening newscasts; in any event, stations usually put their "best" available syndicated program, often a recent off-network show, in the slot leading into local news.

Sixty-minute action-adventure series such as *Magnum P.I.* have also had success in the late afternoons because of their male demographics. Hour-long dramatic programs such as *Dallas, Dynasty, Falcon Crest, Knot's Landing,* and the like, however, have not succeeded in the late afternoon hour because: (1) they appeal to women rather than men, and women who are at home in the late afternoon often plan or cook the evening meal just then; (2) they do not appeal to children and teens, who usually control the television set in late afternoons; and (3) they require more regular viewing than late afternoons permit—viewers need to see virtually every episode of a series such as *Dallas* to keep up with the intricacies of the plot, but most adults view television irregularly in late afternoons.

Basic cable networks, however, have found some hour-long dramatic series appealing to cable viewers in access, prime time, and late fringe time periods. Lifetime, for example, successfully stripped *Spenser for Hire* in both access and late fringe; CBN Family Network stripped *Remington Steele* in late fringe, and USA Network stripped both *Miami Vice* and *Murder, She Wrote* in prime time. They obtained such series at relatively low per-episode rates because few stations had a suitable place in their schedules for hour-long programs without strong male appeal.

First-Run Syndication   Released initially to the syndicated market, *first-run syndicated shows* have never been seen on a network. Viewers can hardly distinguish the best first-run syndicated programs from network programs. For example, the daily 30-minute syndicated magazine show *Entertainment Tonight* (described in Exhibit 13–3) has much in common with such network magazine series as ABC's *20/20*. Indeed, programs discarded by the networks often turn up in first-run syndication. For example, ABC canceled *Fame* when its ratings declined, but it came back in first-run syndication with a mix of new (first-run) as well as off-network episodes. Similarly, MCA TV produced new episodes of *Airwolf* for USA Network. *Too Close for Comfort, Paper Chase,* and *The Days and Nights of Molly Dodd* also followed this network-to-first-run-syndication pattern.

The mass-appeal cable networks compete with the broadcast networks by purchasing first-run programs for prime time. Those programs that are attractive to women viewers have been especially successful on cable. Broadcast stations usually carry first-run syndicated shows only in access time because of their high cost. Distributors of first-run syndicated shows target the major-market affiliates, which, because of PTAR, must fill a daily high-audience hour with *nonnetwork* programs. Independents, on the other hand, stripped very little first-run material until inexpensive tabloid shows such as *A Current Affair* appeared.

In the late 1980s, many affiliates successfully stripped a mix of off-network and first-run syndicated court shows in early fringe. Court shows succeed best when they are blocked in late afternoon, and several relatively inexpensive first-run shows, such as *The Judge, Divorce Court, Superior Court,* and *The Supreme Court,* can surround hits such as *People's Court.*

Programs created especially for the access hour tend to use low-budget genres such as quizzes and games, interview programs, and magazines. The reigning king of access programs, *Wheel of Fortune,* with *Jeopardy* nipping at its heels, typically gets higher ratings than any competition in access time, including off-network shows. However, two game shows take care of only two half hours out of the six between 7 and 8 P.M. that the three top-market network affiliates collectively have to fill. Honorable mentions among access game shows include *Win, Lose or Draw* and the long-running *Family Feud,*

EXHIBIT 13–3   Entertainment Tonight

The weekday *Entertainment Tonight* and its Saturday wrap-up, *Entertainment This Week,* revolutionized the syndication business by proving that expensive, original, nonnetwork programs could be profitable for stations as well as for producers and syndicators. Until *Entertainment Tonight*'s success, programmers thought that only cheaply produced first-run access programs could make money for all participants. Previously, game shows had set the access-time standards for production budgets, license fees, and advertising rates.

Introduced in the late 1970s, *Entertainment Tonight* did not take off until Group W began delivering it by satellite in 1981. "Bicycling" (mail or courier videotape delivery) took too long for so topical a program. As a second innovation, Group W programmed a weekend wrap-up, *Entertainment This Week,* on the sixth day. The sixth show cost relatively little to produce, since it relies mostly on rerun segments dressed up with new introductions. An oddity in ratings calculations makes this single day's addition greatly increase the series' value. Stations enhance the five-day Monday-through-Friday ratings average by adding on the Saturday (or Sunday) rating. For example, if *Entertainment Tonight* averaged a 10 rating Monday through Friday and earned a 5 rating for the extra show on Saturday, it would be sold to advertisers as a 15 rating, making both its national and its local sales skyrocket.

Like most magazine shows, however, *Entertainment Tonight* suffers from the disadvantage of being unsuitable for reruns. Its topical nature makes each episode relevant only briefly. It provides a classic example of the constant innovation essential to keep a

series from going stale. Initially, *Entertainment Tonight* capitalized on the appetite for gossip, personality exploitation, and show-biz fluff. Later, the producer countered the program's lightweight image by introducing brief think-pieces, some hard news reporting, and more in-depth stories. Next, when ratings began to sag, the producer dropped many insider gossip segments for more substantial topics. *Entertainment Tonight*'s selling points include strong coverage of the rock music and video scene, behind-the-scenes looks at movies in production, appealing presenters, lively pace, and effective computer animation.

SOURCE: Photo courtesy Paramount Pictures.

Joker's Wild, and *Tic Tac Dough,* the mainstays of access in the early 1980s.

More sensational so-called reality shows emerged to challenge *Entertainment Tonight* and *PM Magazine,* which topped the access-hour magazine ratings during much of the 1980s. Pseudo-documentary magazine and talk shows, referred to as *tabloid TV,* such as *Geraldo* and *The Morton Downey, Jr. Show,* drew criticism for their muckraking approach and their sometimes sleazy topics. Downey, for ex-

ample, became notorious for titillation accompanied by loud attacks on his guests and audience members. Other tabloid programs rehashed sensational topics in pseudo-journalistic style, exploiting the public's curiosity about degradation, sexual misbehavior, and violence. Although critics attacked some episodes of programs such as *A Current Affair* for "going too far," audiences seemed ready to accept increasing doses of "reality," despite the criticism.

Barter Syndication In the 1970s a different way for stations to pay for some syndicated television programs emerged. Until that time, stations had normally paid cash for syndicated shows, but as program prices escalated, stations ran short of ready cash. Some program distributors responded by offering to trade (*barter*) programs for advertising time. They presold some of the advertising time in barter programs to national advertisers, filling about half the spot opening with preinserted ads before delivering the series to licensing stations. The stations obtained programs without disbursing cash, instead giving up ad time (which they might not have been able to sell anyway) and stood to gain if they could sell the remaining spots. Advertisers paid the syndicator or producer, getting cut-rate national advertising time and an assured place in programs of their own choosing.

At first barterers offered only once-a-week programs of little interest to most stations. Producer/syndicators of specials and weekly dance shows used to barter to get up-front commitments from advertisers that might help persuade waffling stations to take on untried shows at no cost. Generally, these were *full barter deals,* meaning that the producer/syndicator sold all the time and stations got a free program but no opportunity for profit. Later, nearly all first-run access programs were sold as *partial barter deals,* meaning that the station retained some minutes for spot advertising sales. Many animated and live-action children's shows, packages of movies, and other first-run strip series, such as the fringe-time hit *Star Trek: The Next Generation,* are partially bartered. Then syndicators discovered that former network hits could command both cash payments and advertising time from stations anxious to close a deal. Nowadays, most barter deals for off-network sitcoms are of this type, called *cash-plus-barter* or *barter-plus-cash.*

In the most common barter arrangement, the producer/syndicator presells two minutes of ads in each half hour, leaving four minutes for stations to sell. Alternatively, a national advertiser or ad agency obtains the rights to a program from the producer/syndicator, either by purchasing it or by underwriting a new production. The advertiser or agency then fills all the show's commercial time and syndicates it to stations in a full barter deal. In another variation, *time-bank syndication,* advertisers exchange programs for spot openings in other programs, usually to be scheduled at a later time. Toy manufacturers, for example, may bank spots during the year in order to intensify their pre-Christmas advertising.

Barter syndication came into its own as a method of financing program purchases when distributors of first-run access shows adopted it, notably for hit game shows such as *Wheel of Fortune* and *Jeopardy.* Soon barter included most syndicated daytime talk shows—*Oprah Winfrey* and *Donahue*—as well as first-run access magazine shows—*Geraldo, USA Today, Entertainment Tonight.* Then movie packages from major studios began including barter minutes, and finally even some off-network series offered barter minutes. *Cosby* was the first off-network series sold on a partial barter basis, and it shattered all revenue records for a syndicated program. Licensed mostly to affiliates as a lead-in to early evening news, *Cosby* earned more than any previous syndicated series. Adding all cash and barter revenue together, the show generated more than $600 million for its syndicator, Viacom Enterprises. At least $100 million came from the presale of a single minute of barter time.

Other Syndicated Materials Syndicators offer movies in packages of six or a dozen or more, usually grouping them by genre (horror, western, science fiction) and including some box-office successes along with lesser-known films. Stations and cable networks, and sometimes even cable systems, buy such packages, obtaining the right to show each move two (or sometimes more) times. Broadcast affiliates usually strip such movies in late-night and Saturday afternoon slots; independent stations and cable networks often schedule them in prime time and on Sundays.

Many of the national cable networks fill large portions of their schedules with syndicated programs, but syndication plays only a small role in *local* cable programming. Cable systems occasionally purchase the rights to old movies or series just as television stations do, though usually for much lower rates, in keeping with their smaller audiences. Few outside the largest markets have either the channel space or the advertising revenue to support such purchases. Cable television reaches more than half of all homes, but only a tiny fraction of the potential audience typically watches locally programmed cable channels.

Dozens of noncommercial syndicators supply instructional and educational programming for children and adults. Among the best known are the Agency for Instructional Technology (AIT) in Bloomington, IN, innovative producers of interactive videodisc programs for children; the Great Plains National Instructional Television Library (GPN) in Nebraska, producers of well-known classroom series for children; and the Annenberg/CPB Project, producers of several prime-time adult learning series. These nonprofit agencies license program series to public television stations for in-school use. Were commercial stations or cable networks to purchase the material, they would have to edit it drastically to make room for commercial slots. In any event, generally only noncommercial users can obtain the rights. However, commercial cable networks such as The Learning Channel and The Discovery Channel compete for many educational programs for children and adults, blurring the once-clear distinction between commercial and noncommercial types of programs.

Brief programs of less commercial significance also come from government, educational, corporate, and other sources. These are frequently offered without charge or period of license to stations, which use them as fillers.

13.3
Radio Syndication

Radio syndication once followed the same pattern as television syndication. Network entertainment shows went into syndication on radio stations fol-

lowing their network runs. After the rise of television, however, the major radio networks reduced production to little besides news and sports, genres with little rerun value. Nor do all-music radio networks offer many programs with replay value. Most syndicated radio programs are first-run features, produced especially for airing within particular music or talk formats, but such material often has a short lifetime, losing audience appeal after a few days or weeks.

News and Music Syndication   Radio depends heavily on two types of material that are not generally thought of as syndicated but that nevertheless fit the definition: recorded music and newswire services. Though stations may choose their own formats and produce their own programs, most would be lost without the music recordings and new services that provide the bulk of their program content. Even that limited degree of local production disappears when stations automate their operations and buy ready-made syndicated formats.

Brought about by developments in sound technology, the nationwide distribution of the elements of radio programming—recorded music, features, and often DJ voices—signals the approaching end of the traditional regulatory distinctions between local, syndicated, and network radio origination. So far, rapid blending of program sources cannot be achieved with the same ease in video as in audio; thus radio continues to lead television in evolving new distribution processes.

Role of Automation   Most radio and television stations use some degree of automation. Many repetitive operations in the program and production departments of radio stations lend themselves readily to automation. The daily program log, for example, normally requires only minor updating from day to day. Most of the items, such as commercials, public-service announcements, promotional spots, and station identification announcements, remain in place over long periods of time. Automated systems delete old material and add new without altering the rest. Advertiser billing also may be automated.

More sophisticated automation systems can carry out most programming, production, traffic, and engineering functions. For example, automated transmitter systems (ATS), first authorized by the FCC in 1977, automatically adjust power and modulation levels. If a serious malfunction occurs, the system shuts the transmitter down and sends an alarm signal to an engineer. Automated systems marry ideally with syndicated music formats, which demand precise control over content and timing. Modern radio automation uses microprocessor and digital memories, keyboards on which operators can type instructions in plain English, video screens that give the keyboard operator instructions and information on the status of the systems, and hard-copy printers that deliver information for the record, such as program and commercial logs.

Radio automation tends to break down distinctions between local and nonlocal programming. The degree of localism in radio music programming varies through three levels. In *live* programming, local DJs play the records and talk between songs, conduct contests, promote events, and so on. In *live-assist* programming, automatic equipment relays a syndicated music format with breaks for local DJs to add live patter between songs; this is mostly used only for large-audience dayparts. In the third type, *automated* programming, all music, commercial, and promotional content is automated without the help of live DJs or other local staff.

In a twist that combines the advantages of both syndicated formatting and the presence of a live radio personality, a single on-the-air disc jockey may speak for dozens of stations while playing a single music tape interspersed with commercials, weather, and announcements appropriate to each participating station's community. Using microprocessors and two-way interconnection, one orchestrator can command prerecorded tape cassettes of local advertisements and regional weather to play at each of dozens of stations (see Exhibit 13–4), occasionally interrupting with a chatty line or two heard only by that station's audience to establish the presence of a seemingly local, live DJ. This practice differs little from networking.

Format Syndication   So exacting has the art of music-program design and execution become that many radio stations employ the services of firms called *format syndicators* that provide not only program material but also a wide range of advisory services. In contrast to most radio networks, which supply only news headlines or sportcasts, format syndicators usually supply a full 24-hour schedule of music without national advertising or news. Stations that purchase syndicated formats usually also affiliate with a radio network for newscasts, which leaves them free to concentrate on selling their own advertising time.

Format syndicators distribute full program schedules tailored to particular audiences. There are more than a score of such companies, each supplying six or more targeted formats. Most format syndicators offer several rock music variations, ranging from new wave to hit songs to soft album cuts, that generally fit the major format classifications of CHR, AC, AOR and target narrowly defined demographic or psychographic groups. They also offer one or two country music formats, an easy listening or beautiful-music format, and perhaps even a classical music format. Bill Drake, of Drake-Chenault Enterprises, one of the most influential radio programmers, founded the oldest and probably the largest format syndication company in 1963. As examples of its eight formats, "Contempo-300" appeals to the 18- to 34-year-old age group and "XT-40" appeals to the 18- to 44-year-old age group.

Another successful format syndicator, Bonneville Productions, best known for a beautiful-music service designed especially for automated stereo FM stations, provides more than 100 one-hour tapes (minus time for local insertions). Each tape fits into a particular hour of the 24-hour broadcast day, carefully calculated to match the audiences available in each of eight different dayparts. In addition, the formula reflects changes between spring/summer ("happier, more up-tempo") and fall/winter ("more romantic"). The client station receives a manual of instructions along with the tapes, additional services such as a promotional kit, and ongoing advice based on monitoring of the station's output. Bonneville

EXHIBIT 13–4 Automated Cart
                Machines

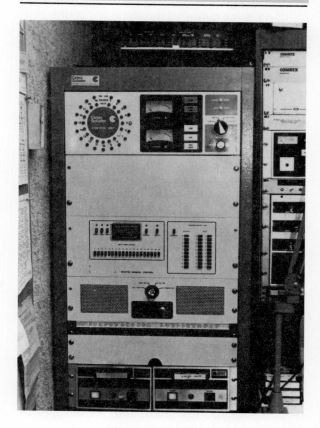

Automated tape cartridge (CART) machines help keep radio stations operating with limited staff. A combination of timing devices and carts pre-recorded with announcements, commercials, and music can provide entire dayparts. This machine, a central part of a Kansas network, can receive newscasts from other network stations for playback at late times.

SOURCE: WIBW Farm News.

aims its bland and unobtrusive sound primarily at women between the ages of 18 and 49, on the theory that women usually control the choice of station even when men in this age group are also listening.

Feature Syndication Ready-made program items packaged to fit within particular formats come from *feature syndicators.* They range from large companies supplying hundreds of feature programs and several syndicated formats to companies marketing only a few topical specials or a single series. These stand-alone programs, either series or specials, are interwoven with a locally or distantly produced DJ or talk/news format. Program types range from sets of religious sermons to series of domestic budget hints to play-by-play sporting events, distributed on tape or by satellite.

Weekly country and rock countdowns of hit songs are among the most popular syndicated programs, especially clones of Dick Clark's long-running *Top 40 Countdown* and Casey Kasem's *American Top Forty.* Stations normally schedule syndicated countdowns on weekends, filling long hours without paying for a live local DJ. Feature syndicators also supply brief telephone interviews with rock and country music celebrities, divided into one-minute segments for inclusion throughout the broadcast day. Such features add variety to otherwise predictable replays of fixed music playlists. Talk radio stations also vary their local sound with syndicated business, health, and other specialized reports voiced by well-known national announcers.

13.4
Syndicated Religion

At one time it would have seemed strange to include a section on religious broadcasting in a discussion of commercial radio and television programs. The networks and the larger stations used to regard religious programs as a public service, best scheduled as sustaining rather than commercial offerings. However, over the years, and at an accelerated pace since the 1970s, highly commercialized religious broadcasting began to replace sustaining programs. The *electronic church* became both conspicuously active and highly controversial.

Much has been written to explain the remarkable growth and political influence of the electronic church. In terms of numbers, it attracts a relatively

EXHIBIT 13–5   Audiences of the Ten Most Popular Religious Programs

	Number of U.S. Households Watching		
Program	In Feb. '87	In May '87	In May '88
Robert Schuller	1,256,000	1,158,000	1,145,000
Jimmy Swaggart	1,091,000	819,000	565,000
Oral Roberts	881,000	707,000	539,000
The World of Tomorrow	653,000	588,000	632,000
Old Time Gospel Hour	435,000	482,000	331,000
Kenneth Copeland	379,000	334,000	354,000
Dr. James Kennedy	363,000	385,000	367,000
The 700 Club	313,000	254,000	164,000
In Touch	230,000	177,000	191,000
Jim and Tammy Bakker	215,000	208,000	76,000

The 1st column shows the status before the Bakker/Swaggart scandals. Effects of the Bakker scandal seem reflected in the 2d column, the Swaggart scandal in the 3d column. Note that even before the scandals, some of best-known programs ranked below lesser-known programs.

SOURCE: A.C. Nielsen data, tabulated by Stephen Winzenburg, Florida Southern College.

small constituency, perhaps 6 to 10 percent of Americans (see Exhibit 13–5), mostly women over 50 years of age located in the south and west (Hoover, 1988: 63). However, their fervor and commitment make up for what they lack in numbers.

Origins   Preachers and religious organizations recognized the potential of radio broadcasting from its earliest days. Some started their own stations. The Mormons, for example, founded the predecessor of today's KSL (Salt Lake City) in 1922. Other church groups depended on time donated or sold by commercial stations and networks.

In the early days of broadcasting, the networks and the larger stations adopted a policy of scheduling "safe" religious programs in *sustaining* (donated, noncommercial) time, avoiding arguments with the many sects that clamored for access by dealing only with coalitions of Jewish synagogues and Catholic and Protestant churches. Frustrated at being excluded, the smaller sects and maverick in-

dividual preachers resorted to buying time, at first from small radio stations on which they could air their sermons, Bible lessons, commentaries, and pleas for donations with relative impunity. They nevertheless remained relatively unknown to the general audience until television projected them into the limelight. Again, televangelists started first on smaller, weaker stations. Larger stations tended to follow the industry's Television Code (now defunct—see Section 17.8), which recommended against selling time to "churches and religious bodies." But televised religious services in church settings, staged for dramatic visual effect, evolved naturally from the traditional revivalist tent shows and mass rallies that had long been a feature of American rural Midwestern and Southern urban life.

M. G. "Pat" Robertson exemplifies the new, television-bred generation of evangelists. Son of a U.S. senator and graduate of Yale Law School, he experienced a conversion, eventually obtained a UHF television station, and won a following with *The 700*

Club, a relatively low-key talk show featuring interviews with celebrities, healing sessions, and news "from a Christian perspective." Syndicated to scores of television stations (through the purchase of time), *The 700 Club* is the most visible part of the CBN (Christian Broadcasting Network) evangelistic empire. Its Virginia Beach headquarters embraces the CBN University, elaborate program-production facilities, satellite ground stations, a radio and television program distribution operation, and is the home of the advertising-supported CBN Family Network, one of the most widely distributed cable networks. CBN Continental Broadcasting, Inc., owns an FM station and two UHF television stations, all operated commercially. As this list suggests, Robertson expanded CBN far beyond its televangelistic origins.

In sum, the broadcast networks and stations produce a few religious programs working in cooperation with mainline churches and synagogues; they are scheduled as sustaining programs. In addition, religiously oriented television and radio stations, several religiously supported cable networks, and independent producers and syndicators specialize in religious programs. These programs may consist of formal sermons, talk and interviewing that are only vaguely religious in nature, or gospel singing and dancing elements in a variety show format. Popular evangelists star in the most conspicuous of the syndicated programs, usually recorded before live audiences in churches—some especially constructed and outfitted for television production. Robert Schuler, leader of the "positive thinking" school, built a "crystal cathedral," the most impressive of such church-studio complexes.

On the regulatory side, the FCC ruled in 1960 that stations could classify paid-for religious programs under "public service," a category normally limited to sustaining (noncommercial) programs. As further encouragement, the commission exempted paid-time religious programs from the prohibition then in effect against program-length commercials, which under the FCC definition could have applied to many such programs because they often revolved around pleas for money. Finally, the commission largely exempted religious programs from the right-of-reply requirements formerly imposed on other broadcasts by the fairness doctrine.*

Commercialization

Evangelists have obtained a virtual monopoly on television airtime for religion. As their purchases of time mounted, networks and stations cut back on giving sustaining time for religious programs, retaining only holiday specials. In 1988, after 40 years, CBS dropped the last of its traditional mainline programs, *For Our Times,* the only regularly scheduled network religious television program still on the air. By then, only 48 CBS affiliates out of over 200 carried the program. Similar clearance problems had occurred at the other networks.

Most stations welcomed televangelist time buyers because they often paid for otherwise unsellable, low-viewership hours. Moreover, the increased competition brought about by FCC liberalization of broadcast licensing and permissive cable television regulation forced television stations to scramble for revenue. Financial pressure made them willing to accept the small size of televangelist audiences and the problem of delays in payment (which often occurred because of the thin ice of donated revenue on which televangelists usually skate).

Televangelist-administrators can control production and mailing expenses to some extent, but they cannot shave the relentless bills from the stations from whom they buy time. Oral Roberts, for example, paid $19.5 million for time on 128 stations in 1987 to reach 800,000 households; Pat Robertson's *The 700 Club* paid $22 million for time on 93 stations to reach 200,000 households (Winzenburg, 1988). As these figures suggest, it costs so much to reach each donor household that the televangelists are under tremendous pressure to maintain a con-

---

*Fairness doctrine exemptions did not extend to personal attacks. One such attack gave rise to a major Supreme Court decision, the *Red Lion* case (discussed in Exhibit 18.4). Writer William A. Henry III tried unsuccessfully to get reply time to rebut some tendentious political programs on one of Pat Robertson's stations; "the run-around went on for months on every issue I pursued," he reported (Henry, 1987).

tinuously mounting cash flow. This accounts for the fervency of their appeals for money, accompanied by all-too-real threats of going off the air if donations fall short.

The televangelist movement relies heavily on the tax-exempt status of constitutionally protected religious activities. In addition to outright donations, many televangelists ask for "love offerings" for a variety of goods such as crosses, Bibles, cassette recordings, and pamphlets. Jimmy Swaggart, for example, in effect operates a "mail-order catalogue business in which items are offered for a fixed donation, which makes it a tax-deductible transaction" (Applebome, 1988). With so many millions of tax-free dollars passing through the mails, successful televangelists tend to take on for-profit sidelines such as Jim Bakker's gaudy theme park, Heritage USA, and to adopt the jet-and-limousine lifestyle of corporate executives. Questions about fiscal responsibility inevitably arise. Bakker, one-time star of the *Jim and Tammy Bakker Show* on the PTL cable network, flatly refused to give the FCC information about the disposition of funds solicited on his programs for a specific charity that a newspaper alleged he had misappropriated (71 FCC 2d 324, 1979). Bakker claimed that the inquiry violated the First Amendment guarantees of religious and speech freedom. The FCC dropped the case in a decision that later came under fire (see Exhibit 13–6).

It would be easy to overstate the significance of the electronic church. In the heady days of Ronald Reagan's first term as president, it seemed to some that nothing could stop a fundamentalist revolution. The failure of Jerry Falwell's Moral Majority to get its political agenda enacted, the defeat of Pat Robertson's bid for the presidential nomination, the Bakker and Swaggart scandals, and the national retreat from the high-water mark of Reagan neoconservatism seem to argue that televangelism, though still viable as a conspicuous and colorful source of broadcast and cable programs, will have relatively little political impact over the long haul. With the audience consisting of mostly already self-identified Christians, the evangelicals' goal of "converting unbelievers" stands little chance of wide-scale realization. Moreover, financial pressures drive once wholly religious cable program networks increasingly toward broad-appeal "family" programming.

13.5
Local Television Programs

Locally produced programs take up very little time in broadcast schedules; they make up less than 10 percent of all television programming, it is estimated. Most local television consists of news and some public-affairs programming. The local evening news ranks highest in importance among locally produced programs because of the revenue and prestige it brings.

Scheduling The commercial broadcast networks fill about 70 percent of their affiliates' schedules. Their programs occupy most of the early mornings, mornings, afternoons, prime time, and late evenings, as well as weekend days, although affiliates sometimes refuse to clear weak shows in the very early and late time periods. Affiliates have two key entertainment times to fill; early fringe, from 4 to 6 P.M. or whenever local news starts, and access (with zonal and season variations), 7 to 8 P.M. As previously explained, stations purchase high-priced syndicated programs to fill these two time periods.

Most affiliates originate a local early-evening newscast and a late-fringe newscast. Depending on the size of the market and when network news appears, local evening news may start as early as 4:30 or 5:00 or as late at 6:00 P.M. The larger the market, the more time the station is likely to devote to local news. After all, more happens in big cities. In addition, the higher the rank an affiliate holds within its market, the more time it will devote to local news. The number three affiliate in many markets feels pressure from cost-conscious management to cut back on news.

Local evening news may lead into network news or precede and follow network news in a *sandwich*. In the Eastern and Pacific time zones, network news

EXHIBIT 13–6   Trouble in Paradise

As early as 1979 rumblings could be heard from a storm brewing in the earthly paradise of the PTL's 2,300-acre Christian theme park, Heritage USA, from which Jim and Tammy Bakker used to broadcast their fund-raising talk show. Newspaper allegations that Bakker had misappropriated charitable funds for his personal use led the FCC to question Bakker's eligibility to continue holding a television license. The commission took no action then, but the issue arose again in 1982, when the PTL applied to the FCC to sell a debt-ridden station. The commission approved the sale by a 4–2 vote. According to a 1988 PBS documentary, *Praise the Lord,* the dissenting commissioners and an FCC staff member took strong exception to the decision, alleging that the majority papered over evidence of misconduct.

Bakker exulted over the air at having defeated the Devil and the FCC (he often spent hours on his program refuting "plots" to discredit his ministry). He embarked on a building frenzy to furnish his theme park with a grandiloquent hotel, campground, mall, huge wave-making swimming pool, water slide, and much more. A master of the art of high-pressure selling, Bakker peddled time-share rights to "lifetime partners" in the park's planned housing units. Showing off model rooms, cajoling prospects with daily warn-

ing that partnerships were almost sold out, he persuaded more than a hundred thousand "partners" to mail in checks for as much as a thousand dollars each in exchange for lifetime vacation rights at Heritage USA. For another building scheme, Bakker frequently exhibited a severely deformed person named Kevin as a come-on to secure donations to construct a Victorian mansion to house the handicapped. "People say we're exploiting you," Jim would say on the air to

usually starts at 6:30, preceded by local newscasts of a half hour to two hours in length. In the Central and Mountain time zones, and when parts of the country shift to daylight savings, schedules vary more. Network evening news may be scheduled as late as 7:00 P.M. or as early as 5:30, commonly within a local news sandwich. Late newscasts on affiliates typically appear at 11:00 P.M. and last a half hour. Many affiliates also schedule a half hour or hour of noon news. About 80 percent of affiliates also originate a half-hour newscast or magazine/talk show in the early morning on weekdays, preceding the network morning programs or pre-empting part of them if network ratings are weak.

Affiliates generally schedule local public-affairs shows on weekday or Sunday mornings. During election years or at times when important local issues arise, affiliates may increase their local programs, but typically they avoid scheduling them in the most valuable time periods, such as early fringe, access, or prime time.* Affiliates that produce regularly scheduled local nonnews shows usually choose a magazine/talk program for women, scheduled on weekday mornings.

Independent stations usually schedule their most popular programs against local programs on affili-

---

*An affiliate is more likely to pre-empt a weak network show in prime time than to pre-empt its own syndicated shows. Public-affairs programs sometimes show up in "syndicated program slots," however, when a hole occurs between the end of the contractual period for one series and the beginning of another.

EXHIBIT 13–6   Continued

Kevin. "Do you think you're being exploited?" Kevin would look up from his wheelchair and dutifully pipe a reply in the negative. The money poured in, and the house went up, but reportedly only Kevin ever lived in it—and only until the scandal necessitated his eviction.

The scandal erupted in mid-1987 when Bakker confessed to a sexual adventure with a woman to whom PTL had paid hush money. But this peccadillo looked insignificant among the avalanche of revelations that followed. Evidence of massive misappropriation of funds to support Jim and Tammy's self-indulgent lifestyle piled up; building came to a halt; contractors and commercial stations sued for unpaid bills; the Internal Revenue Service and the Justice Department investigated; Bakker resigned; the Assemblies of God church defrocked him. Another televangelist, Jerry Falwell, tried briefly, amid charges of a takeover, to save the floundering ministry (his stewardship was notable mainly for the bizarre televised scene of the normally dignified Falwell swooshing fully clothed down the Heritage USA water slide).

Before the end of 1988 a federal grand jury indicted Bakker and some of his cohorts, alleging that they diverted millions from PTL's charitable donations and defrauded thousands of "partners" whom the actual

Heritage USA facilities could never accommodate (just routine overbooking, like the airlines, Bakker claimed). As the rickety PTL financial structure collapsed, a veritable "holy war" broke out, with a half-dozen evangelical ministers excoriating one another. Another Assemblies of God minister, Jimmy Swaggart, condemned Bakker, only to be tagged himself with sexual indiscretions. A hard core of devoted supporters stoutly defended the self-confessed wrongdoers, but punishment from others came swiftly. Jimmy Swaggart's revenue fell by 49 percent, Jimmy Bakker's by 65 percent. Neither saw any inconsistency in continuing their ministries.

Shaken by the debacle, the National Religious Broadcasters' Association voted 324 to 6 to tighten the financial integrity aspect of its ethical code. Cable operators, embarrassed at having carried the PTL channel, supported mainline churches in founding a new, nonevangelical religious channel that barred fundraising. The new channel, VISN, opened in September 1988 and almost immediately won second place, after CBN Family Network, in penetration and popularity among the religiously oriented cable networks.

SOURCE: Photo from UPI/Bettmann.

ates, typically counterprogramming the affiliate evening news block with expensive off-network entertainment series to attract the nonnews audience. They usually fill prime time with movies or live sporting events. Independents tend to spread the cost of live sporting events by forming regional networks. One station may produce for the regional network, making sports "local" for that station. Many independents carry a syndicated newscast at 10 P.M. (EST) to attract early news viewers. The widespread availability of CNN, FNN, and Headline News, however, has diminished the value of this strategy. Only a small number of independents devote resources to local news or other local production.

If a cable system does any local production, and most do not, it generally offers a mix of council/

school board meetings, community reports, documentaries, and community productions, filling a part-day schedule and rerunning each item many times. Inclusion of local cable channels in program guides and newspaper television supplements has forced more standardized program scheduling, but the large number of one-time-only programs makes regular program patterns difficult to maintain.

Local TV News   As audiences for local newscasts grew in the 1970s, stations began investing heavily in news operations. Multimillion-dollar budgets for local television news departments in large markets became commonplace, enabling stations to purchase or lease helicopters, customized news vans loaded with minicams and topped with microwave relay dishes, movable satellite uplinks, automated newsrooms, computerized color weather maps, and other high-tech facilities for news gathering and presentation. Large stations developed their own investigative reporting and documentary units, expanding their coverage to nearby towns and cities. Satellite technology and networking enlarged the reach of local stations even further, minimizing time and distance constraints. By the mid-1980s, large-market stations routinely dispatched local news teams to distant places to get local angles on national news events, sending live stories back to the home base via satellite. So important had local news become, for network affiliates at least, that being number one in local news usually meant being number one in the market.

While helpful in expanding local news program length and in enlivening local production, improved news-gathering technology also has its down side. Critics point to overuse of live relays when thoughtful in-studio reports might be more informative. There is a natural tendency to show off technical capabilities to justify expensive equipment purchases. Some critics also think that the advantages of the local angle on national and international stories may be offset by the shallow reporting of personnel who lack the experience and background to handle such stories with authority.

Encouraged by their ability to fill more time with ENG-assisted stories and by the increased audience appetite for news, during the 1970s some stations lengthened local newscasts. Some stretched to 2 or $2\frac{1}{2}$ hours in length, notably those in Los Angeles, New York, and Washington, DC. As cable service penetrated those markets, however, CNN, Headline News, and FNN divided the news audience, driving broadcasters to cut back to shorter newscasts. Nonetheless, major-market affiliates generally produced an hour or more of early evening news, in addition to noon and late newscasts.

Independent stations have a tough time competing with affiliates for the news audience. Nevertheless, many produce a half hour of local news at 10:30 P.M., preceded by INN (Independent Network News) national news at 10:00. Independents draw on syn-

dicated materials from INN, CNN, NIWS, or Conus for international and national stories, supplemented by wire reports from the traditional news agencies (see Exhibit 11–7). *The Ten O'Clock News* (*The Nine O'Clock News* during daylight saving time) scheduled earlier than local late newscasts to attract viewers who are not willing to wait up for the 11:00 P.M. affiliate newscasts, has been INN's main service. The national newscast gets higher ratings, creating spillover viewers for local independent news. Local independents therefore generally follow INN with a half-hour of local news, rather than preceding it in the typical affiliate/network pattern.

News consultants brought a more entertainment-oriented style. For example, "happy talk" news jazzed up local news presentation with informal banter among members of the on-air news team—usually two news anchors, a sports reporter, a weather reporter, and various on-the-scene correspondents. Their synthetic light-heartedness created, as one critic put it, "an aura of exaggerated joviality and elbow-jabbing comradeship" (Powers, 1977: 35). In a similar vein, new directors contrived "happy news," stories lacking in hard-news value but inserted to relieve the gloom of real news by giving viewers the feeling that something good happened in the world that day.

Happy talk and happy news were encouraged by *new consultants,* marketing specialists who rose to prominence in the 1970s. Stations hired them to give advice on how to jack up local newscast ratings. Nowadays, few stations would alter the appearance or style of their newscasts without first seeking advice from a news consultant. Under contract to station management, news consultants move in with a battery of audience surveys and focus-group interviews to analyze public perceptions of a station's news presentation, content, and personnel. Consultants also examine organizational relationships within the station. Their advice can range from wholesale replacement of news anchors to the adoption of an on-the-air dress code. They have been accused of responsibility for more than a decade of Ken-and-Barbie-doll news anchors and for sexist and ageist recommendations favoring men over women and young over old as news presenters. By 1990, however, nonstandard looks had become more acceptable to the public, and able journalists could hope to survive consultant evaluations even without a youthful appearance.

Consultants disclaim any interference with professional journalistic judgments. Nevertheless, "action news," a format often recommended by consultants, emphasizes photographically interesting events, such as fires and accidents, and short, punchy news bites. In a book critical of news consultants, Ron Power concluded:

> When local stations create and choreograph entire programs along the guidelines supplied by researchers— toward the end of gratifying the audiences' surface whims, not supplying its deeper informational needs—an insidious and corrosive hoax is being perpetrated on American viewers. . . . The hoax is made more insidious by the fact that very few TV newswatchers are aware of what information is left out of a newscast in order to make room for the audience-building gimmicks and pleasant repartee (1977: 234).

Local news departments sometimes capitalize on the availability of *camcorders* (relatively inexpensive hand-held video cameras) to turn amateur photographers into "stringers." Stations have used amateur footage of earthquakes, tornados, train wrecks, convicted criminals out on bail and walking the streets, neighborhood riots, and traffic jams. Some stations solicit such stringer footage, paying a nominal fee of $50 to $250 per usable item. Even without solicitation, newsrooms receive miles of jiggly videotape from would-be news photographers, some of it useful to spice up local evening newscasts.

Cable Origination   Local cable systems rarely produce local newscasts. A major exception is *News 12 Long Island,* a 24-hour, cable-only all-news service produced solely for residents of Long Island's 108 towns and villages (see Exhibit 13–7). NBC is part owner of this service. Only about a quarter of the 8,000 cable systems in the United States originate programs of any kind. They offer either commercial *local origination channels,* programmed by cable operators themselves, or noncommercial

EXHIBIT 13–7   *News 12 Long Island*

New York's Long Island is home to America's only 24-hour local television news service. News 12 Long Island *reports events in the hundred or so communities on the island, generates feature stories about Long Island history, inhabitants, and customs, and interprets regional and national events in light of their impact on the area.*

SOURCE: Rick Young/News 12.

public-access channels, programmed by private citizens or nonprofit institutions such as schools and municipal governments. Channels run by cable operators, which are fewer in number nationally than access channels, carry local advertising and tend toward entertainment programs. In some communities they have been successful in generating revenue from high school sports, packages of old movies, and other low-cost syndicated shows. Ad-free channels open to community groups or schools focus on informational and cultural programs. About half of all local cable-only programs consist of public affairs, typically coverage of school board, city council, and county council meetings, hearings on community issues, and discussion or documentary programs on local political, environmental, and educational issues. Community calendars, updated daily, have been among local cable's biggest successes. They list local events and meetings that never get mentioned on the large broadcast stations. The other half of cable-only programs consists of entertainment, culture, fine arts, sports, children's cartoons, and sometimes religion.

Local cable channels can present public meetings more economically than broadcast stations can. Their equipment and staffs cost less, technical quality matters less, and they can ignore the tight scheduling of broadcast television stations and their dependence on advertiser, underwriter, or subscriber appeal. On a cable channel, meetings, hearings, and presentations on local issues can be carried to the bitter end without interruption. Live coverage of an issue important to just a few hundred residents may be justified on local cable channels but not on a broadcast station.

Increasingly, candidates for public office use cable channels for local political discussions. At election times, candidates for the House and Senate and state and local office fill large parts of cable schedules in major markets. Local cable programs also play a useful role between elections by enabling taxpayers to see and hear local officials in action at public meetings of city councils, school boards, and the like. Local cable channels also give local musicians, actors, dancers, video artists, and craftspeople a means of reaching an audience. Though as yet largely unstructured and amorphous, these types of specialized programs serve social goals that mass-audience commercial broadcasting cannot.

13.6
Local Radio Programs

By and large, radio stations retain much more local program autonomy than television stations and cable systems. Networks, once all-important, have receded into a secondary role. Although most stations depend almost totally on recorded music, they assemble it to fit their own program *formats*. Carefully crafted formats attuned to specific audience segments dominate radio programming to an extraordinary degree.

Music Formats   Radio is often characterized as a local rather than a national medium, especially in comparison to television. Although true in terms of advertising bases, this generalization overlooks the national scope of music recordings. Records and compact discs are syndicated media, simultaneously available all over the country. Rarely does a station have any exclusive play rights. Music promoters send free copies of most recordings to every station with an appropriate format, hoping for frequent airplay. Increasingly, stations mix syndicated formats and feature material with recordings and live DJ patter to create a unique local sound.

Most radio stations use modified blocking, changing format slightly to suit each daypart. For example, many stations schedule mostly news and weather/traffic information during drive times, shifting to recorded music at other times. Some promote disc jockey personalities; others suppress them. Most abide by rigid formulas, yet some favor free-form programming. Even the old-fashioned full-service program philosophy still has some followers, especially in very small towns. In major markets, however, stations typically adopt pure formats, continuing the same sound throughout the day and night. This strategy distinguishes each station from its competitors most effectively, since major markets have so many stations with similar formats.

Most parsimonious of all broadcast formats, the disc jockey show fully exploits the availability of recorded music, reducing production costs to the lowest possible level. The DJ format exploits per-

EXHIBIT 13–8   Major U.S. Radio Station Formats

Format	Total Stations	Percentage	AMs	FMs	Commercial	Noncommercial
Country & Western	2421	19%	1483	938	2410	11
Adult Contemporary	2325	18	1043	1282	2279	46
Religious/Gospel	1054	8	643	411	809	245
CHR/Top-40	984	8	188	796	891	93
MOR	729	6	560	169	706	23
Oldies/Classic rock	695	6	473	222	683	12
Diversified	614	5	153	461	192	422
AOR	486	4	56	430	333	153
Talk	408	3	352	56	360	48
Beautiful music	403	3	91	312	372	31
News	384	3	278	106	278	106
Classical	355	3	21	334	59	296
Jazz	296	2	27	269	66	230
Big Band/Nostalgia	259	2	216	43	248	11
Educational	259	2	13	246	7	252
Spanish	237	2	176	61	220	17
Urban Contemporary	193	2	86	107	176	17
Black	186	1	126	60	163	23
Agricultural	157	1	115	42	154	3
Progressive	127	1	4	123	14	113
	12,572	100%				

SOURCE: Based on data in *Broadcasting/Cable Yearbook,* 1989, p. F-120.

sonal DJ idiosyncracies and their interactions with the rapidly changing popular music scene. A form of expression once unique to radio, the DJ format has migrated to television through video jockeys (VJs) on MTV, *Night Flight, Night Tracks,* and other television shows.

Formats based on rock music predominate (see Exhibit 13–8). More fine distinctions are drawn among types of rock music than among most other musical genres. Rock formats include *adult contemporary* (AC), which uses a broad array of popular music and golden oldies to appeal to a broad range of adult listeners; *contemporary hit radio* (CHR), which uses playlists to tightly restrict songs to just the most recent hits appealing to teens and young adults; *album-oriented rock* (AOR), which mixes less popular songs from highly popular albums with rock classics; *oldies* or classic rock, which plays hits from the 1950s and 1960s; *urban contemporary* (UC), mixing rock and jazz, which favors black song writers, musicians, and singers with appeal for big-city listeners; and others such as *Top-40* and *new wave.* Of these, adult contemporary has been the most successful.

However, more stations play *country music* than any other type of music, and though Exhibit 13–8 shows it as a single format, by 1990 country was about ready to be subdivided into urban, country-and-western, oldies, and other specialties, just as rock had fragmented in the 1970s. Most country music stations are commercial AM stations. *Adult contemporary,* on the other hand, has been successful on both AM and FM stations. *Religious/gospel* radio, one of the top three formats (as shown in

Exhibit 13–8), shows a steady shift to the AM band as a commercial service. It finds adherents mostly in the South and Midwest but dominates Sunday mornings throughout the country. CHR has a somewhat larger playlist than Top-40, usually playing the most popular 100 or so songs. CHR and Top-40 are highly commercialized formats, concentrated in the FM band. MOR, in contrast, has survived mostly on commercial AM stations in very small markets. The most recent rock variant, oldies or, more commonly, classic rock, appeals to baby boomers, adults who listened to early rock as teenagers in the 1950s and 1960s. A broad form of *oldies* tends to survive on commercial AM radio, and the newer *classic rock* is promoted as an FM format targeting adult women.

Diversified, as a format, refers to the full-service AM station, which schedules a mix of news, talk, and some music, usually without commercials. Similarly, Spanish-language, black, and other ethnically oriented stations tend to mix music and informational programming as a commercial format, targeting specialized groups.

AOR has dropped in popularity as classic rock has risen, but it is still viable for at least one FM station in each major market because of its strong male appeal. *Beautiful music* and *easy listening,* broad-appeal formats using instrumentals or orchestrated music combined with popular songs, have adherents in most large radio markets. They saturate waiting rooms, elevators, department stores, and other public spaces. Several syndicated easy-listening music services without commercials, such as Muzak, go out on FM subcarriers that require special adaptors for reception.

Classical music appears mostly on noncommercial FM stations, but a few commercial and AM stations have adopted the format, especially in the largest markets. *Jazz,* on the other hand, though it has a devoted following, has not proved successful commercially. *Big band,* usually a syndicated format consisting of 1940s band music, has been successful mostly in large and mid-sized markets as a commercial AM format. In contrast, *Urban contemporary* is the major-market variant of rock and jazz that serves black city dwellers, whereas *black* mixes music and information to suit smaller, more rural

markets. *Progressive,* catch-all for secondary cuts on popular albums mixed with avant-garde rock music in loose formats once called "underground radio," is usually noncommercial and on FM radio, though a few commercial stations in the very largest markets have successfully adopted the format.

Information Formats   Although drawing a line between entertainment and information radio formats offers difficulties, four of the formats listed in Exhibit 13–8 are predominantly informational: talk, news, educational, and agricultural. Collectively, these formats occur on less than 10 percent of radio stations. Newly developed AM formats, such as *all-business* and *all-sports,* attempt to capture fresh audiences for AM radio as traditional AM listeners age and under-45 listeners turn to FM. Only about one-quarter of listening now goes to the AM band.

Radio uses informational programming both within music formats and as a stand-alone format. Within music programming, news may consist of as little as one-minute network headlines. Stations with *news/talk formats,* on the other hand, include local and network news headlines, in-depth newscasts, studio and remote interviews, informational feature stories, and telephone conversations with public figures and listeners. Although some music stations originate local news to supplement network news, they schedule it only in drive times. News on stations targeting teenagers has become a travesty, reporting the doings of celebrity rock stars while ignoring hard international and domestic news, which most young listeners consider boring.

The most popular informational format, *talk radio,* occurs almost exclusively on commercial AM stations. It combines telephone call-in and interview programs with feature material and local news. Talk content varies between the two extremes of sexual innuendo and serious political or social commentary. In major markets, *shock radio* deliberately aims at outraging conservative listeners by violating common taboos and desecrating sacred cows. Shock radio's contempt for adult authority and social tradition tends to attract very young listeners.

Most talk programming, however, focuses on local controversial issues, using guest experts and questioning by hosts and callers. The two-way telephone call-in show attracts an older and generally conservative class of listeners—people who have both the time and the inclination to engage in discussions with talk-show hosts. Program directors must take care lest a small but highly vocal group of repeat callers, often advocates of extremist views, dominate the talk and kill advertiser interest. Talk programs targeting younger listeners have been more successful with sports and shock talk and, in some major markets, classified advertising.

During the 1980s, talk radio emerged as an important public forum in the black community, although only a few of the 600 or so black-oriented stations adopted the format. Black talk stations provided a window through which candidates for public office, community organizations, and reporters could obtain a unique perspective on black public opinion. Politicians such as Harold Washington, Chicago's first black mayor, and the Reverend Jesse Jackson found that black talk radio gave them political input that they could not get through mainstream media.

The *all-news* format costs a lot to run, yet gets only low ratings compared with successful music formats. Actually, all-news stations devote only about a quarter of their time to hard news, filling the rest with informational and service features. They count on holding attention for only about 20 minutes at a time, long enough for listeners to arm themselves with the latest headlines, the time of day, weather tips, and advice about driving conditions. To succeed, this revolving-door programming needs a large audience reservoir that only major markets can supply.

Educational radio, overwhelmed by television and the growth of rock music, survives as a noncommercial FM format in some cities, usually as a public school service. Only about 2 percent of stations provide instructional programs for schools and other noncommercial institutions, such as churches. Radio's in-school function has been largely taken over by videocassettes, which provide visuals as well as sound under the classroom teacher's direct control.

Radio farm news plays an important role in modern farming. Office and factory workers find weather reports a convenience, but farmers find them essen-

tial. Many midwestern stations piggyback farm news on some major radio format. About 1 percent of stations, nearly all in the Midwest, carry a full-time *agricultural format,* nearly always on commercial AM. The U.S. Department of Agriculture distributes background information and taped radio and television series, as well as responses to telephone inquiries, by satellite to keep farmers current on federal policy and agricultural data.

Religious Radio   More than 50 religious organizations held station licenses in the 1920s, but like the educational licensees, most of them have since given up their grants. Only a dozen of these pioneer AM stations survive, but the later availability of FM channels encouraged a resurgence of *religious radio* stations, especially on the reserved noncommercial educational channels.

The practice of selling time to promoters of religious programming, a striking feature of modern commercial radio, has always been controversial, and some broadcasters still oppose it. Nevertheless, such sales amount to a multimillion-dollar business that even nurtures its own specialized advertising agencies. Much religious radio consists of old-fashioned back-to-the-Bible fundamentalist preaching, supplemented with church music, but recognized religious music formats exist: traditional gospel, contemporary Christian, Christian rock, Christian country, and others. About 8 percent of radio stations, most of them commercial, feature religious programming.

Community Radio   Noncommercial FM stations and cable-only FM services constitute *community radio.* In the 1960s, reacting against rigidly formatted radio and dissenting from establishment values, some small stations began the *underground* or *free-form* radio format. "Some great things were done," recalled one observer. "Tough, creative, unpolished, kinky scenes, but great. FM radio was a world full of surprises, like the world of early television" (Pichaske, 1979: 151). Such radio is now lumped under the *progressive* format, mixing live and recorded music and talk, usually at the whim of the presenter. Stations using antiestablishment formats have come and mostly gone, but the six-station Pacifica group described in Exhibit 13–9 has survived.

Some public stations also function as community radio outlets. The largest of them affiliate with the NPR and/or APR network, but they still must supply the bulk of their own programs. If not progressive music, public community stations often feature a classical, jazz, or diversified format. Small, low-salaried staffs supplemented by volunteers mean low overhead, enabling such outlets to present formats that would not be commercially viable. Most community stations, however, are not "public," having no affiliation with the Corporation for Public Broadcasting, NPR, or APR.

Some community radio facilities are nonlicensed, cable-only radio services, existing only as supplements to cable television. They operate on a shoestring, with all volunteers and wildly imaginative programming that wins devoted listeners. Hundreds of high school and college stations operate as low-power not-for-profit stations serving a campus or school. Some carrier stations may, however, sell advertising.

13.7
Program Critique

In this and the two preceding chapters, we have discussed broadcast and cable programs almost entirely from the industry viewpoint—as vehicles for commercial messages. This concluding section touches briefly on the consumers' viewpoint.

The viewer-listener perspective raises the question of whether commercial motives suffice as primary arbiters of program choice and quality. It brings up a fundamental issue around which debate has swirled ever since broadcasting began: how best to balance commerce and culture? Should the industry treat programs simply as "product"—articles of trade? Those who say that programs play a larger role in society regard them as broadly cultural, in the sense that they contribute to the intellectual, artistic, and moral quality of national life. Seen in that perspective, programs seem somewhat more than just devices for enticing audiences to expose themselves to commercial messages.

Wasteland vs. Toaster   Experts and critics agree that in the final analysis the industry sells not programs but *people*. Programs exist to attract attention to commercials. Nevertheless, as a practical matter, the industry must also think in program terms; television and radio can deliver people to advertisers only by supplying program services that interest people. Programs must have the motivating power to capture attention and to persuade consumers to invest in receivers and related equipment and, in the case of cable services, pay the monthly subscriber fees.*

As the preceding chapters show, given the need for programs that will continuously attract large numbers of viewers, the industry tends to concentrate on lightweight entertainment—the least demanding programs that have the most popular appeal and avoid serious controversy (except for superficial controversies that excite interest without challenging established beliefs). Until the 1970s, most responsible observers, including FCC members, seemed to take it for granted that the industry had a responsibility to rise above the lowest common denominator of audience tastes a significant part of the time. The Communications Act requires the FCC to consider the "public interest" in granting licenses and in making other decisions affecting broadcast licensees. The FCC interpreted this mandate as requiring something more than "naked commercial selfishness," as the Republican Secretary of Commerce, Herbert Hoover, put it at a 1925 radio conference at which he defended the notion of operation in the public interest.

The best-known critique of the industry's program performance from the public-interest viewpoint came from the FCC chairman appointed by the Kennedy administration, Newton Minow (1961–1963). In an address to the National Association of

---

*A TV set costs less than a microwave oven today, and the monthly cable subscriber fee costs less than a dinner for two. Radios sell for $10–12. These are hardly major investments for the generation that has grown up with cable television.

EXHIBIT 13–9   Pacifica Radio: Persistent Dissenter

The original inspiration for "free-form noninstitutional radio" came from Lew Hill, an idealist who initiated the movement when he found KPFA (FM) in Berkeley, CA, in 1949, under the umbrella of his Pacifica Foundation, so named because of Hill's lifelong devotion to pacifism (Trufelman, 1979). Pacifica later acquired a second station in Berkeley and others in Houston, Los Angeles, New York City, Washington, DC. Pacifica stations operate noncommercially, depending on listeners and foundations for financial support, supplemented by income from a news bureau and a tape syndication service.

The stations have scheduled such unusual features as the news read in Mandarin Chinese, a reading of all the Nixon Watergate tapes of the early 1970s, rec-itations of lengthy novels such as Tolstoy's *War and Peace* and Joyce's *Ulysses* in their entirety, and a two-hour opera improvised on the air by phone-in singers. Absurd though some Pacifica programs have been, and limited though their audiences have remained, they have played a role in shaking up established radio. Hundreds of stations have benefited, if only indirectly, from Pacifica's challenge to the safe, the conventional, and the routine. Protesters bombed Pacifica's Houston station, putting it off the air twice in the 1970s. Pacifica stations have consistently taken the lead in defending broadcasting from encroachments on its First Amendment freedoms, often a losing battle, as in the famous "seven dirty words" indecency case to which the Pacifica name is attached (described in Section 18.2).

Broadcasters in 1961, Minow challenged station owners and managers to sit down and watch their own programming for a full broadcast day. They would, he assured them, find a "vast wasteland" of violence, repetitive formulas, irritating commercials, and sheer boredom (1964, 52). The "vast wasteland" phrase caught on and became a part of the language of broadcasting.*

Fifteen years later, Minow (by then a lawyer in private practice and a PBS executive) told a panel at yet another NAB convention that he had no regrets; the vast-wasteland criticism had jolted broadcasters out of their complacency, at least momentarily. In the intervening years, said Minow, "there has been enormous improvement, particularly in the area of news and information" (Terry, 1976: 5).

Still later, in the 1980s, a Republican-appointed FCC chair, Mark Fowler, pointedly refrained from talking to the industry about program quality because, in his view, the FCC had no business interfering with the workings of the marketplace. He too coined a memorable descriptive phrase when, in addresses to industry groups, he equated television with a kitchen appliance—"a toaster with pictures." This dismissive phrase reflected the then-dominant theory in Washington, DC, that the economic laws of supply and demand suffice to ensure that commercial television will supply suitable programs: if it degenerates into a vast wasteland, blame not the industry but the audience.

Popular Taste vs. High Taste   Chairperson Minow exaggerated the low state of programming in order to challenge the industry to look critically at its own product. Few responsible critics would seriously make such a sweeping judgment about the entire commercial television output. Most would concede that television sometimes rises to peaks of excellence, though between the peaks lie broad valleys (vast wastelands?) of routine programs. How green the valleys are depends on the viewer's personal tastes.

Of course, a continuously available mass medium such as television cannot satisfy every taste. It must try to please the largest possible number of people most of the time. No other medium has faced such extraordinary demands. In meeting those demands, television made apparent something never before so blatantly exposed: the low common denomina-

*Television's impact has so diverted attention from radio that critical writing tends to ignore radio. Though the following discussion concerns television, much of it applies to commercial radio programs as well.

tor of mass *popular taste* as contrasted with the more cultivated standards of high taste. As Daniel Boorstin, an authority on American cultural history, put it:

> Much of what we hear complained of as the "vulgarity," the emptiness, the sensationalism, of television is not a peculiar product of television at all. It is simply the translation of the subliterature onto the television screen. . . . Never before were the vulgar tastes so conspicuous and so accessible to the prophets of our high culture. Subculture—which is of course the dominant culture of a democratic society—is now probably no worse, and certainly no better, than it has ever been. But it is emphatically more visible (Boorstin, 1978: 19).

The Middle Ground   Those who occupy the middle ground between the two extremes of programs-as-merchandise and programs-as-culture concede that it would be unrealistic to expect programs to rise above the lowest common denominator most of the time. As the most democratic of media, broadcasting necessarily caters to popular tastes; however, that mission need not preclude responsibility for serving minority tastes as well. Public broadcasting exists to compensate to some extent for the omissions of commercial broadcasting in this regard. But even public broadcasting has had to increase its popular appeal in order to attract program underwriters and broaden its subscriber base. So far, it has lacked the financial support it needs to offer an adequate alternative program service.

Promoters of the marketplace programming philosophy predicted that liberalizing the rules governing broadcasting and news services such as cable television would automatically do that job, diversifying programs and enhancing quality as it became possible for more and more services to cater to more specialized tastes.

The new options did indeed give viewers more choices, but only at an added price. Those who can afford cable or a satellite dish (more than half of homes by the late 1980s) can browse through scores of channels to find programs of interest; home video recorders (in two-thirds of homes) allow viewers to browse through the tape inventories of video

stores as well as to escape the tyranny of schedules by time-shifting programs.

So far, however, too many of the so-called new options have turned out to be merely repetitions of the old options. With few exceptions, they have failed to make the wasteland bloom. After all, cable and other optional delivery methods respond to the same marketplace imperatives that drive commercial broadcasting. Significantly, the shining exception in the public-affairs field, the program service that opens a window on government in action, C-SPAN, does not operate as a self-supporting commercial venture. The cable industry subsidizes C-SPAN as a public relations showcase of the good things television can do—when *not* constrained by the need to make money.

Popular Taste vs. Bad Taste   Though they have always catered to popular taste, for most of their history commercial broadcasters generally refrained from catering to the appetite for downright *bad* taste in programs. Conscious of their visibility and vulnerability to criticism and their public-service obligation under the law, most broadcasters fostered a sense of propriety in programming. In its now abandoned Television Code, the National Association of Broadcasters emphasized the role of television as a *family* medium, warning that "great care must be exercised to be sure that treatment and presentation are made in good faith and not for the purpose of sensationalism or to shock or exploit the audience or appeal to prurient interests or morbid curiosity" (NAB, 1978, 2).

That kind of sensitivity, along with the Television Code, has fallen victim to changing times. In fact, the code's statement of what *not* to do accurately describes exactly what succeeded on the air in the late 1980s. " 'Raunch' on a Roll," proclaimed a headline in a trade journal, *Broadcasting,* over a story about the rise of what it called *slobcoms*—sitcoms that "stretch the bounds of what's acceptable" (21 Nov. 1988). The Fox networks' *Married . . . With Children,* which occasioned the article, featured plotlines dealing with such touchy subjects as premenstrual syndrome, treated with outrageously vulgar humor. Despite complaints from some listeners and viewers, such programs drew relatively high ratings, at least momentarily. In the absence of any other criteria of evaluation, ratings assured widespread imitation of such programs and even deeper future excursions into raunchiness.

Many influences brought about this radical shift in program standards, among them:

▌ The FCC's laissez faire policy, which encouraged broadcasters to test the limits of public tolerance.

▌ Enforced abandonment of the NAB codes, which to some apparently implied that anything goes.

▌ Heightened competition, encouraged in part by FCC policies, requiring ever more strenuous efforts to capture audience attention.

▌ Cable television, which has never been constrained by legislated public-interest standards or a tradition of self-restraint.

▌ Corporate mergers that replaced experienced broadcast and cable executives with cost-conscious managers saddled with huge debts.

▌ Social changes in the direction of more open and permissive behavior, marked especially by violence, sex, and rebellion against conventional standards.

As the pendulum eventually swings in the opposite direction, reversing some of these trends, it will be interesting to see what happens. Will broadcast and cable programs regain their ability to satisfy popular taste without pandering to bad taste? Will competition from ever larger numbers of services improve or degrade program quality?

Summary

▌ Syndicated and local programs fill 30 percent of affiliate schedules and all of independent television station schedules, with local production limited mostly to news.

▌ Syndicated programs consist of off-network shows, first-run shows, and movies; they may be licensed for exclusive showing in individual markets.

▌ FCC rules prohibit the major commercial networks from owning most of their entertainment programs and from syndicating programs in the U.S. market. "Syndex" rules protect stations programs from duplication of their syndicated programs by cable networks or superstations.

▌ PTAR limits the commercial networks to three hours of prime time and prohibits affiliates in the top 50 markets from airing off-network programs

▌ Affiliates usually strip off-network shows in early fringe time and strip first-run syndicated shows in access time.

▌ Bartering involves trading commercial time for programs, sometimes with the station paying cash as well as time.

▌ Radio depends heavily on syndicated music and feature programs. Automation aids stations in using sophisticated program mixes that blur the line separating local, network, and syndicated production.

▌ Syndicators of religious programs purchase station time rather than requiring stations to purchase their programs. Stations produce very few religious programs today; most come from fundamentalist churches, using evangelical stars to attract audiences and raise the millions of dollars required to purchase television time.

▌ The proliferation of syndicated, politically colored religious programs, along with scandals involving some of their hosts, has raised questions about their spirituality.

▌ Most local television programs consist of newscasts. They often include "happy talk" to mitigate the impact of hard news events. New technology makes frequent local, national, and even international live relays available for local newscasts.

▌ Most radio stations use block formats. More radio stations program rock than any other music type. Most FM stations feature music, most AM stations information formats.

▌ Commercial broadcasters and cable operators view programs primarily as advertising vehicles. Some critics and consumers view them more as cultural vehicles. At issue is whether programs should be judged solely in economic terms or in terms of broader considerations of the public interest.

IMPACT

So far, we have examined broadcasting's history, technology, economics, and programming. Now we reverse perspective and look at electronic media more as cause than as effect. In order to do so, we first examine how research in this field tells us about audiences of electronic media, then look at some of what has been learned of the media's wider impact.

Effects, real or presumed, give significance to everything we have discussed thus far. That is to say, electronic media merit serious attention only *because they have consequences.* People buy and maintain receivers, advertisers buy time, donors help support noncommercial broadcasting—all in expectation of getting something of value in return. As we shall see in Part 6, Congress makes laws and the FCC issues rules and regulations, and other public and private forces seek to exert control—all on the assumption that media produce results, some good and some bad. Seen in this perspective, everything we have examined up to this point culminates in the study of what we know, don't know, and still need to learn about the effects of electronic media.

CHAPTER 14

AUDIENCE RATINGS AND APPLIED RESEARCH

In Parts 3 and 4 we discussed such audience-centered topics as dayparting, audience flow, program scheduling strategies, ratings, station and network economics, and advertising rates. All of these topics presuppose knowledge about audience size, composition, and habits. This chapter discusses ways of obtaining that knowledge.

Broadcasters need unbiased audience feedback. They need objective, consistent, and complete research to the extent that these ideals can be obtained in an imperfect world. For these reasons, broadcasters and advertisers employ independent companies to conduct most day-to-day audience research, using scientific methods for probing into human behavior and attitudes.* More than 50 such companies operate at the national level, many more at the local level. They use a variety of testing methods, first to assist in the preparation of programs and advertising messages, and later to assess the outcomes of these messages in terms of purchasing, brand recognition, and the image projected by performers, stations, networks, and programs. We hear mostly, however, about *ratings*—estimates of the sheer numbers of people exposed to given broadcasts.

*Audience measurement constitutes *applied* research. Theoretically oriented audience research, conducted mostly at universities and think tanks, is treated in Chapter 15.

We hear much about ratings because of the inherent drama in reports from the broadcasting battle front, telling which programs, stations, and networks claim to be ahead in the endless struggle for survival and supremacy. Because ratings play a decisive role in the selection of programs, they merit special study. For that reason most of this chapter focuses on that one area of audience study—the theory and practice of ratings research.

14.1
The Ratings Business

We seldom hear about magazine or newspaper ratings, because no national newspaper or magazine readership surveys appear on a regular basis. The Audit Bureau of Circulation and several other agencies conduct specialized print media research, but few outside print media hear about this research. On the other hand, practically everyone hears about Nielsen television ratings. In the network battle for ratings dominance, the rise and fall of prime-time programs makes news. But broadcasting and cable have no readily countable physical output. Program "publishing" goes on continuously, with audiences flowing at will from one program to another. Thus the need for highly specialized research.

Arbitron and Nielsen   Two ratings firms, Arbitron and Nielsen, dominate the ratings business as the usual sources of measurements used by electronic media and the advertising community. The two companies have been locked in methodological and commercial competition for decades. Other competitors focus more on limited types of research or have lasted only a few years.

The two services' revenues come mainly from subscriptions by individual stations and by advertising agencies. About 90 percent of all television stations subscribe to at least one of these two firms' reports, and those in the mid-size and largest markets usually subscribe to both. Station subscription rates vary according to station revenue, but actual rates are closely held proprietary information. Major ad agencies need to subscribe to both network and local-market ratings reports, some spending more than a half million dollars a year. Other purchasers of ratings reports include the networks, national sales rep firms, program suppliers, and syndicators. Most advertisers rely on their advertising agencies' subscriptions.

The Arbitron Ratings Company became a subsidiary of Control Data Corporation, a large conglomerate, in 1967. A. C. Nielsen Company, the largest market research firm in the world, became a subsidiary of Dun & Bradstreet in 1984. It has operations in a score of foreign countries as well as the United States. Broadcast ratings, though highly visible, are only a small portion of its market research activities, which mainly involve food and drug product marketing.

Local Market Ratings   Both Arbitron and Nielsen gather and publish television data for some 220 television markets. Arbitron provides data on 260 radio markets. Local reports reflect the relative position of each station among its competitors and estimate the size of the local audience for network, syndicated, and locally produced programs.

It would cost too much to collect data for local television ratings continuously. Instead, researchers gather data in short spurts known as *ratings periods.* The number of these periods per year varies according to market size, with as many as six or eight

scheduled for larger cities and as few as two for small markets. Ratings firms survey all, or nearly all, local radio markets at the same time twice yearly, and all local television markets four times annually. These less frequent, overall surveys, called *sweeps,* allow comparisons on a national scale, an important factor in the sale of national spot advertising, as discussed in Section 9.5.

Stations use local ratings reports as their primary tools in selling their time to advertisers and in evaluating their programming against that of their competitors. Sweeps supply an in-depth picture of network audiences, based on simultaneous individual market sampling. This information supplements the more frequent but less extensive television network ratings reports based on national metered samples, discussed later.

Arbitron and a company called Birch Radio provide radio market ratings reports (Nielsen stopped measuring radio use in 1964).

- *Arbitron* covers 260 radio markets in a 12-week spring sweep, remeasures 130 again in the fall, and surveys the 79 largest cities in summer and winter, for a total of four reports annually (Exhibit 14–1).

- *Birch Radio* covers 250 radio markets once or twice a year, with 109 larger markets receiving quarterly and monthly reports.

Both Arbitron and Nielsen produce television market ratings, using different means of measuring both markets and homes.

- *Arbitron* measures some 200 television markets four times a year in *sweep weeks* by means of written diaries; 13 markets with a combination of diaries and passive meters; and a growing number of big markets by people meter (each of these is described later). The meter cities are also provided with overnight "Arbitrend" reports. Arbitron measures metered markets several times a year in addition to sweep weeks.

- *Nielsen Station Index* (NSI), the major Nielsen local TV market measure, covers 219 markets, 192 by means of written diaries, the rest by means of a combination of diary and passive household

EXHIBIT 14–1   Local Market Radio Ratings Report

Specific Audience
MONDAY - FRIDAY   6AM - 10AM

			Persons 12+	Persons 18+	Men 18+	Men 18-24	Men 25-34	Men 35-44	Men 45-54	Men 55-64	Women 18+	Women 18-24	Women 25-34	Women 35-44	Women 45-54	Women 55-64	Teens 12-17
WAQI																	
MET	AQH	PERSONS	477	475	166	3	8	33	26	48	309	6	6	57	86	64	2
MET	AQH	RATING	1.8	2.0	1.5	.2	.3	1.5	1.7	3.5	2.4	.4	.2	2.5	5.1	3.7	.1
MET	AQH	SHARE	6.8	7.1	5.3	1.0	1.2	4.6	5.5	12.7	8.6	1.8	.9	8.5	16.2	12.9	.8
MET	CUME	PERSONS	1392	1384	556	8	27	145	68	150	828	19	33	181	199	199	8
MET	CUME	RATING	5.3	5.7	4.9	.6	1.2	6.7	4.4	10.9	6.3	1.4	1.4	7.9	11.8	11.4	.4
TSA	AQH	PERSONS	479	477	168	3	8	33	26	49	309	6	6	57	86	64	2
TSA	CUME	PERSONS	1418	1410	577	8	27	145	68	157	833	19	33	181	204	199	8
+WAQI-FM																	
WTHM-FM																	
MET	AQH	PERSONS	23	23	13	4		5		1	10	3		2	3	2	
MET	AQH	RATING	.1	.1	.1	.3		.2		.1	.1	.2		.1	.2	.1	
MET	AQH	SHARE	.3	.3	.4	1.3		.7		.3	.3	.9		.3	.6	.4	
MET	CUME	PERSONS	120	120	60	8		34		9	60	13		27	10	10	
MET	CUME	RATING	.5	.5	.5	.6		1.6		.7	.5	1.0		1.2	.6	.6	
TSA	AQH	PERSONS	23	23	13	4		5		1	10	3		2	3	2	
TSA	CUME	PERSONS	120	120	60	8		34		9	60	13		27	10	10	
WAXY																	
MET	AQH	PERSONS	206	204	83	4	30	43	4	1	121	16	42	14	31	9	2
MET	AQH	RATING	.8	.8	.7	.3	1.3	2.0	.3	.1	.9	1.2	1.7	.6	1.8	.5	.1
MET	AQH	SHARE	3.0	3.0	2.7	1.3	4.4	6.0	.8	.3	3.4	4.8	6.1	2.1	5.8	1.8	.8
MET	CUME	PERSONS	1213	1176	468	66	156	170	31	18	708	125	293	152	80	19	37
MET	CUME	RATING	4.6	4.8	4.2	5.0	6.7	7.8	2.0	1.3	5.4	9.3	12.1	6.6	4.7	1.1	1.8
TSA	AQH	PERSONS	235	232	95	4	40	44	5	1	137	17	43	20	39	9	3
TSA	CUME	PERSONS	1509	1433	618	66	285	185	37	18	815	137	321	195	90	19	76
WHQT																	
MET	AQH	PERSONS	265	217	85	37	26	11	2	7	132	49	58	14	11		48
MET	AQH	RATING	1.0	.9	.8	2.8	1.1	.5	.1	.5	1.0	3.6	2.4	.6	.7		2.3
MET	AQH	SHARE	3.8	3.2	2.7	12.1	3.8	1.5	.4	1.8	3.7	14.8	8.4	2.1	2.1		18.8
MET	CUME	PERSONS	1864	1355	629	196	240	105	28	32	726	355	204	101	55		509
MET	CUME	RATING	7.0	5.6	5.6	14.8	10.3	4.8	1.8	2.3	5.5	26.4	8.4	4.4	3.3		24.2
TSA	AQH	PERSONS	310	248	96	43	27	11	6	7	152	57	60	23	11	1	62
TSA	CUME	PERSONS	2212	1593	709	244	261	105	33	32	884	403	239	144	75	12	619

Footnote Symbols: * Audience estimates adjusted for actual broadcast schedule. + Station(s) changed call letters since the prior survey - see Page 5B.
Both of the previous footnotes apply.

MIAMI-FT. LAUDERDALE-HOLLYWOOD   **ARBITRON RATINGS**   166   **FALL 1988**

A small portion of one page from an Arbitron report covering one market in (season or date here). It covers morning drive time, showing cumes (ratings based on estimated total numbers of unduplicated listeners in each group over a 90-day survey period) for different audience demographic groups. Stations are listed alphabetically (only some shown here), with audiences for co-owned AM and FM stations shown both separately and combined.

SOURCE: © 1989 The Arbitron Company.

meters. Nielsen measures these markets four times a year in sweep weeks; additionally, it measures the larger markets up to seven times per year.

■ *Nielsen* planned to expand daily television viewing measurements to cover 22 major cities by 1990, using a computerized overnight measurement system, issuing on-line daily and printed reports once a week.

Network Ratings   Networks demand faster and more frequent reporting than do local stations. But in two ways network ratings are easier to obtain:

(1) not every market need be surveyed, as a sample of network markets yields a reliable picture of national network audiences, and (2) there are far fewer networks competing at any one time than there are stations. Unlike the situation in local ratings, network ratings providers have no competition: Nielsen issues the only television network ratings, and RADAR the only ratings for network radio.

▌ *Nielsen Television Index* (NTI) issues television network ratings every two weeks (Exhibit 14–2). Nielsen's regular network reports use a national sample of 4,100 people-metered homes, as described later.

▌ *RADAR (Radio's All-Dimension Audience Research),* financed by the networks that contract with Statistical Research, Inc., uses telephone recall interviews (discussed later). RADAR issues reports twice a year, each covering a sample week, based on surveys of 6,000 listeners. Unlike most telephone surveys, RADAR calls the *same* people each day for seven days in a row.

Syndicated-Program Ratings Syndicated television programs pose a special research problem. Although they are aired nationally, like network pro grams, they are not aired simultaneously in a predictable number of markets. Syndicated shows are seen in various markets at various times, yet program providers need to compare programs on a national basis in order to set per-episode licensing fees. Advertisers and stations also need comparative data. Using data from their market ratings reports, both Arbitron and Nielsen derive regular reports on the relative rankings of nationally syndicated programs.

The Nielsen *Cassandra* service, acquired in 1980, provides detailed audience demographic information for both first-run and off-network syndicated programs (as well as for network and some local programs). Cassandras allow researchers to compare household demographic information for the syndicated programs across markets, and collect and measure similar data on both lead-in and lead-out programs.

Special Studies Both Arbitron and Nielsen publish many supplementary reports, based upon data they gather in preparing their regular ratings reports. These supplements include analyses of minority-audience preferences and trends in ratings of particular program types. In addition, clients can order special reports tailored to their needs. For example, a local station might commission a study to determine how a new local program holds up against the competition, or a study to find out how much it appeals to specific audience subgroups. The special problems of cable and VCR and newer service audience measurements are discussed below in Section 14.7.

14.2
Collecting Set-Use Data

Whatever electronic medium they analyze, researchers use several methods for collecting the data on which to base ratings: diaries and passive household meters (the latter now obsolete, being phased out in the early 1990s), people meters, and two different kinds of telephone calls. Several other methods and combinations can also be used for special studies. Each has its own advantages and disadvantages.

Diaries and Passive Meters Arbitron and Nielsen researchers still use a written *diary* method for daily gathering of most market data. To gather radio data, Arbitron sends a separate diary to each person over 12 years of age in every sample household. Arbitron asks diary keepers to write down their listening times and the stations they tune to, keeping track of away-from-home as well as in-home listening for one week (Exhibit 14–3). Nielsen uses diaries for its Nielsen Station Index (NSI) market television ratings outside the largest cities, asking one person to take charge of reporting household viewing. Diaries suffer a key drawback: people often fill in inaccurate information, purposely (to show they have good taste in programs) or not (many

EXHIBIT 14–2   Nielsen National Ratings Report

A–6   *Nielsen* NATIONAL TV AUDIENCE ESTIMATES   EVE.WED. JAN.4, 1989

TIME	7:00	7:15	7:30	7:45	8:00	8:15	8:30	8:45	9:00	9:15	9:30	9:45	10:00	10:15	10:30	10:45		
HUT	63.5	64.3	64.1	64.9	65.4	66.4	66.2	66.8	66.7	67.1	65.7	64.9	62.7	60.7	58.7	55.9		

ABC TV

GROWING PAINS   HEAD OF THE CLASS   WONDER YEARS (R)   HOOPERMAN (R)(PAE)   ←————CHINA BEACH————→

AVERAGE AUDIENCE (Hhlds (000) & %)		18,440		17,360		13,110		12,020		12,570			
SHARE AUDIENCE %		20.4		19.2		14.5		13.3		13.9	13.9 *		13.8 *
		31		29		22		20		23	23 *		24 *
AVG. AUD. BY 1/4 HR %	19.5	21.4	19.2	19.3	14.8	14.2	13.0	13.6	13.9	14.0	13.9	13.7

CBS TV

←————TV 101————→   CBS SPECIAL MOVIE PRSNT AGATHA CHRISTIE'S "THE MAN IN THE BROWN SUIT" (PAE)

AVERAGE AUDIENCE (Hhlds (000) & %)	6,420			14,460								
SHARE AUDIENCE %	7.1	7.0 *		7.2 *	16.0	15.0 *		16.5 *		16.6 *		15.9 *
	11	11 *		11 *	25	22 *		25 *		27 *		28 *
AVG. AUD. BY 1/4 HR %	7.4	6.6	6.7	7.7	14.4	15.6	16.6	16.3	16.7	16.5	16.2	15.6

NBC TV

←————UNSOLVED MYSTERIES————→ (R)   NIGHT COURT (R)   BABY BOOM (R)   ←————TATTINGER'S————→

AVERAGE AUDIENCE (Hhlds (000) & %)	16,720				14,370		9,670		6,870			
SHARE AUDIENCE %	18.5	17.3 *		19.6 *	15.9		10.7		7.6	7.8 *		7.3 *
	28	26 *		29 *	24		16		13	13 *		13 *
AVG. AUD. BY 1/4 HR %	16.8	17.9	20.0	19.3	15.9	16.0	11.0	10.4	8.2	7.4	7.4	7.2

INDEPENDENTS
(INCL. SUPERSTATIONS)

| AVERAGE AUDIENCE | 17.4 | | 14.3 | | 12.0 | | 11.5 | | 11.6 | | 12.2 | | 12.8 | | 10.9 | |
| SHARE AUDIENCE % | 27 | | 22 | | 18 | | 17 | | 17 | | 19 | | 21 | | 19 | |

SUPERSTATIONS

| AVERAGE AUDIENCE | 5.6 | | 4.8 | | 3.9 | | 3.9 | | 3.7 | | 4.1 | | 4.2 | | 3.1 | |
| SHARE AUDIENCE % | 9 | | 7 | | 6 | | 6 | | 6 | | 6 | | 7 | | 5 | |

PBS

| AVERAGE AUDIENCE | 2.0 | | 2.4 | | 2.9 | | 3.1 | | 3.5 | | 4.0 | | 3.0 | | 2.7 | |
| SHARE AUDIENCE % | 3 | | 4 | | 4 | | 5 | | 5 | | 6 | | 5 | | 5 | |

CABLE ORIG.

| AVERAGE AUDIENCE | 7.5 | | 7.7 | | 7.7 | | 7.9 | | 8.7 | | 10.3 | | 9.0 | | 8.1 | |
| SHARE AUDIENCE % | 12 | | 12 | | 12 | | 12 | | 13 | | 16 | | 15 | | 14 | |

PAY SERVICES

| AVERAGE AUDIENCE | 2.9 | | 3.4 | | 3.7 | | 3.3 | | 3.9 | | 3.5 | | 4.3 | | 3.9 | |
| SHARE AUDIENCE % | 5 | | 5 | | 6 | | 5 | | 6 | | 5 | | 7 | | 7 | |

U.S. TV HOUSEHOLDS: 90,400,000   For explanation of symbols, See page B.

A ratings report for a weekday evening, comparing the prime-time appeal of the three national broadcasting networks with independent stations, superstations, Public Broadcasting Service, basic cable networks (shown here as "cable origination"), and pay-cable services. Shown for each broadcast network program is the average audience in TV households (of 90.4 million total early in 1989), the share of audience, and the average audience rating by quarter hour. Note that for the independent stations and nonbroadcast network services, ratings show only overall average audience and share of audience, as the figures are a combination of individual market ratings, often for different programs in different cities.

SOURCE: Nielsen Media Research, *Nielsen Television Index National TV Ratings, January 2–8, 1989.* Used with permission.

EXHIBIT 14–3   Local Market Diaries

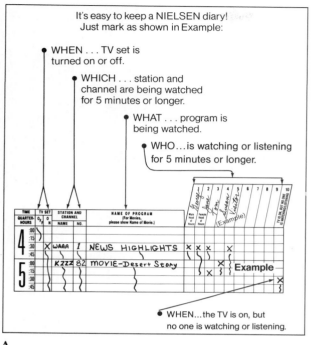

A.

B.

A. *Example page from a Nielsen television diary shows the information sought from sample families. B. A portion of an Arbitron radio diary uses a similar approach, but a notation of where listening takes place gives an additional dimension to radio research.*

SOURCES: (A) Nielsen Media Research and (B) © 1989 The Arbitron Company.

sample families fill in a diary in "catch up" style at the end of the week rather than as listening or viewing takes place).

The Nielsen passive household *meter* device, the Audimeter, was invented in 1936 and first used to report ratings in 1950.* Attached to each television set in a sample household, it automatically records when the set is on and to which channel it is tuned. The meter is called *passive* because it gives no indication as to who, if anyone, is actually watching. Nielsen therefore supplements its metered homes with another sample of diary homes, using the diaries to obtain demographic data on actual viewers. Nielsen issues market ratings based on the combined meter-diary sample. The passive meter was phased out of network rating use in 1987 with the activation of people meters, but remained in use for individual market ratings into the 1990s.

---

*The old meter is now called *passive* to distinguish it from the newer people meter, which requires an element of audience participation. The older meter registered that a receiver was in use without any special need for viewers to do anything other than watch.

EXHIBIT 14–4 Nielsen Network Ratings System

(A) The Nielsen national audience reporting system depends heavily on automation, from the home meter through the gathering, analyzing, and reporting processes. (A) The people meter used for network ratings consists of two parts: the hand-held unit on which each viewing member of the family and guests can "check in," using individual keys, and the base unit located on top of the television receiver that stores home viewing information.

A.

Continued on opposite page.

People Meters Changes in viewing habits caused by newer media technologies in the 1980s forced audience analysts to pay more attention to individual than to family viewing and listening habits. Advertiser interest and new computer capabilities prompted the development of the *people meter.* Like Nielsen's Audimeters, these electronic devices keep a record of receiver usage. In addition, however, the people meter serves the function formerly performed by diaries (as supplements to passive meters) by *simultaneously* collecting demographic data. It does this by requiring each viewer to "check in" and "check out" whenever he or she watches television by pushing a special handset button (Exhibit 14–4). Several extra buttons allow visitors in the household to check in and out as well. Data on both receiver use and viewer identity go by telephone line to a central computer containing basic household demographic data, stored earlier when the people meter was installed in the home.

Three firms, Nielsen, Arbitron, and AGB,* tested several people-meter variations in the mid-1980s.

---

*AGB, a British firm, developed the people meter and pioneered its use in Europe. After a Boston market test beginning in 1985, AGB began offering a national service in 1987, forcing Nielsen to do likewise. Unable to obtain sufficient broadcaster or advertiser support, however, AGB closed its U.S. operation in 1988 after a loss of nearly $70 million.

Nielsen began a three-year test of a people-meter sample in 1983 and began its people-meter national network ratings service in September 1987. Nielsen announced plans to begin market ratings with people meters in 1990 in New York and Los Angeles, adding two markets a year after that.

Arbitron, after conducting a market test in Denver starting in 1985, announced plans to introduce an enhanced version of the people meter in late 1989. Its "ScanAmerica" system uses people meters to obtain national network ratings, in direct competition with Nielsen, as well as local market ratings by late 1990 in selected cities. Arbitron touted ScanAmerica as a three-pronged *single-source* system providing ratings, demographic data on viewers, and a measure of the connection between program viewing and product purchasing. ScanAmerica directly correlates exposure to advertising with subsequent buying behavior (Exhibit 14–5). It began issuing network ratings in 1989.

Introduction of the AGB and Nielsen people meters created enormous controversy. Network ratings dropped in all time periods and ratings for many independent stations and cable channels rose. The networks understandably complained about methodological limitations of people meters, which appeared to slight such typical network heavy viewers as children and older people who might be intim-

EXHIBIT 14–4 Continued

B.

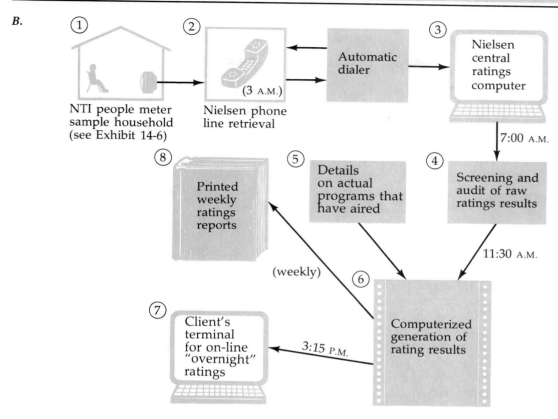

(B) *The Nielsen system begins with the individual sample household (1), whose people meter base unit results are (2) "read" over a telephone line (leased by Nielsen) at 3:00 A.M. local time each morning by a computer that sends the viewing results of the sample household into (3) the Nielsen central ratings computers. The collected raw ratings are (4) sent to the screening and audit process, where all ratings materials are assembled and (5) combined with the detailed program information constantly gathered by Nielsen. They are then sent for (6) computer generation of actual overnight ratings. By 3:15 P.M. the overnights are ready for (7) client (agencies, stations, networks) retrieval by computer terminal, and (8) weekly printed ratings reports. Nielsen diary and passive household meter markets go through a similar process to generate market-by-market reports.*

SOURCE: Photo courtesy Nielsen Media Research.

idated by (or others simply too impatient with) the computerlike button pushing the people meter required. Although overall viewing habits appeared, in fact, to be actually changing, the apparent drop in network viewing in 1987 could also have reflected the introduction of this new means of audience measurement by AGB and Nielsen people meters.

Coincidental Telephone Calls Many researchers consider the *coincidental telephone* method of data gathering the most accurate means of obtaining audience size information.* The term *coincidental* comes from the fact that researchers ask respondents what they are listening to or watching *during* (that is, *coincidental with*) the time of the call. Putting the question that way eliminates the memory factor and reduces the possibility of faking. The researcher asks whether the respondent has a set turned on at that moment, and if so, what program, station, or channel the set is tuned to, plus a few demographic questions such as the number, sex, and age of those watching.

Because the coincidental method provides only *momentary* data from each respondent ("What are you listening to or watching *now?*"), it requires a large number of calls, spaced out to cover each period of the day, to build up a complete profile of listening or viewing. Properly conducted, the coincidental call method requires large batteries of trained callers, making the method expensive. Nor can coincidental calls cover the entire broadcast day; information on audience activity after 10:30 P.M. and before 8:00 A.M. must be gathered later when the researcher asks respondents to recall the programs they listened to or viewed during these nighttime and early morning hours.

Though many research projects use coincidental telephone surveys, none of the major ratings companies relies on this method for regular reports, primarily because it costs too much for continuing, wide-ranging research. Nielsen does, however, offer a special coincidental service for customers who require quick answers to specific questions.

Telephone Recall Tricks of memory make the *telephone recall* method less reliable than the coincidental method, but it costs less because more

data can be gathered per call. RADAR, the only source of radio network ratings, uses telephone recall, collecting samples *daily* (by prearrangement) over a period of seven days, thus minimizing memory errors while attaining a week's coverage. RADAR employs *random digit dialing,* a technique for generating telephone numbers at random by computer. It designs a national sample of individuals (not households, in this case) based on random calls.

Personal Interview The use of in-person, door-to-door surveys based on probability samples has declined in recent years because knocking on strange doors in strange streets can be hazardous to the researcher's health. However, personal interviews are used with *convenience* samples (also called *judgment* or *purposive* samples) for studies other than ratings research that need not be based on probability sampling. Typically, interviewers question people on the street or in shopping centers, or, for car radio listening, at stoplights. Data gathered in these ways cannot be projected to the general population. If taken as statistically significant, such data can be very misleading.

Combination Methods If cost were no object, the most reliable and valid method of audience research would be some combination of the methods detailed above. Combinations of meters and diaries, or telephone calls with diaries or meters, help to provide added information while allowing checks on, and comparisons with, findings derived by different methods. People meters provide an equivalent of the diary combined with the meter efficiently, so long as respondents conscientiously push a button to signal their presence every time they watch the screen. In 1989, Nielsen announced it was developing (along with the David Sarnoff Research Center in Princeton) a "passive people meter" for introduction in the mid-1990s. Using image-recognition, the device was said to be able to "recognize" regular (family) viewers. Thus, the passive people meter could electronically record regular family members and others as guests, to tabulate who and how many were watching.

---

*The first radio ratings used telephone methods. The Cooperative Analysis of Broadcasting of 1930–1946 and the 1934–1950 Hooper ratings for network and local radio (the equivalent of Nielsen ratings in their time) relied on the telephone (Beville, 1988).

EXHIBIT 14–5   Arbitron ScanAmerica and Diary System

The ScanAmerica people-meter device introduced for national network ratings in 1989, and for market ratings a year later, has three parts—a set-top computer, a handheld scanner for indicating who is watching, and a "wand" that reads the universal product codes on purchases electronically. The wand is to be used by each household after shopping trips. It collects the product code information, which is downloaded into the set-top computer when the wand is reinserted into the slot designed for it. The set-top device is "read" in the early morning hours by automatic computer calls.

Most of Arbitron's market ratings are still based on diaries. (1) Telephone callers solicit households in each market to accept diaries. (2) Operators enter diary data into computers. (3) Program titles, previously collected and verified, are matched to the ratings. (4) Computers process survey results. (5) Checkers verify the results. (6) The Television Market Report *comes off the press. (7) Reports go out to stations, advertisers, agencies, and station rep offices.*

14.2 Collecting Set-Use Data   367

14.3
Sampling

No matter which research method one uses, around-the-clock monitoring of the private listening and viewing behavior of millions of people tuning to thousands of stations and scores of cable channels in more than 200 markets is an impossible task. The task becomes possible only with drastic simplification by means of *sampling*.

Sampling to Simplify   The *sampling* process simplifies three aspects of ratings research: behavior, time, and number of people.

▌ *Behavioral sampling.* Individual response to programs can vary over an endless range of observable human behavior. Researchers decided years ago on a minimum, universal, accurately measurable behavioral response: the simple acts of turning on a receiver, selecting a station, and later turning the set off. Each ratings company has adopted an arbitrary span of time (ranging from three to six minutes per quarter-hour) that the set must be turned on to count as being "in use" by an audience member.

This simple *set-use test* leaves out of consideration much that we would like to know about broadcast audiences. It tells us nothing about whether listeners liked a program, whether they understood what they heard or saw, whether they chose the program after considering alternatives or merely passively accepted it because it came on the channel already tuned in, whether one family member imposed his or her choice on others, and so on. Despite these ambiguities, most ratings use this set-use test.

▌ *Time sampling.* The second simplification used in ratings takes advantage of the repetitive daily and weekly cycles of broadcast and cable programming. A sample taken every few weeks or months from this continuous program stream suffices for most purposes. Ratings companies sample only network audiences and a few major-city audiences on a daily basis.

▌ *Number of people sampled.* The most controversial ratings simplification arises from using only a few hundred people to represent the program choices of thousands or millions of others. To those unfamiliar with sampling, it seems unreasonable to claim that set meters that record tuning in a few thousand homes could be used to assess the tuning behavior of more than 240 million people in some 90 million households. Sample sizes for the major surveys follow:

▌ *Arbitron radio market surveys:* 250 to 3,500 households per market, depending on market size.

▌ *Arbitron television market surveys:* 250 to 1,600 households per market, depending on market size (for the people meter, sample size will expand to between 600 and 1,000 households per market).

▌ *Nielsen Station Index (market) surveys:* up to 550 households (people meter ratings, introduced in 1990, will have somewhat larger samples—800 in New York, for example).

▌ *Nielsen Television Index (network) surveys:* previously 1,700 passive-meter homes, but increased for people meters to 4,100 homes by March 1989.

▌ *Arbitron national ScanAmerica surveys:* began in 1989 with about 1,000 households, expanding to 5,000 households by 1992.

▌ *RADAR national radio network surveys:* 6,000 persons.

Why Samples Work   The laws of chance, or *probability,* predict that *random selection* of a small sample (usually households) from a large population will make that sample representative, within a predictable degree of accuracy, of the entire population. Random selection means that, ideally, *every* member of the entire population to be surveyed has an *equal* chance of being selected. Major characteristics of the population as a whole will appear in such a sample in about the same proportion as their distribution throughout the entire population.

Audience research is but one of many areas of study in which a complete census would be impossible. The use of samples thus makes practical economic sense.

However, choosing at random is not as easy as it sounds. Reporters who intercept passers-by "at random" for street or shopping-center opinion interviews by news reporters, for example, get anything but a random sample. Systematic planning has to go into the making of random choices, strange as that may sound. Lotteries that involve drawing numbers at random meet the requirements of pure probability sampling from the population of lottery players. Sampling from less artificially defined populations always involves compromises on ideal randomness, calling for compensating corrections.

Sample Frames   To begin with, drawing a sample randomly from a large human population requires some way of identifying each and every member of the population by name, number, location, or some other unique distinguishing label. In practice, this usually means using either lists of people's names or maps of housing unit locations. Such listings are called *sample frames*. Ratings companies use either updated telephone directories or census tracts (maps showing the location of dwellings) as frames. But such frames never cover literally everybody; besides, they go out of date even before they can be printed.

Nielsen draws its national sample of metered television households from U.S. census maps by a method known as *multistage area probability sampling*. This method ensures that the number of sample members chosen from each geographic area will be proportional to the total population of each area. "Multistage" refers to step-by-step narrowing down of selection areas, starting with counties and ending with individual housing units, as shown in Exhibit 14–6. For its market-by-market ratings of stations, however, Nielsen uses special updated telephone directories, as do Arbitron and most other firms engaged in ratings research.

About 97 percent of U.S. households have telephones, making telephone directories the most readily available sampling frames. Directories have drawbacks, however: many listed numbers represent businesses rather than households and as many as 40 percent of the telephone subscribers in an area are not listed. *Random digit dialing* can solve the problem of reaching unlisted and newly installed telephones, but increases the number of wasted (unused or business address) calls, thus increasing survey cost.

Sample Turnover   Ideally, each time a company made a survey it would draw a brand-new sample so that imperfections in any one sample would not have a permanent effect. On the other hand, if the company uses expensive sampling and data-gathering methods, it cannot afford to discard each sample after only one use. Nielsen tries to retain each people-meter household in its national sample for no more than two years, but allows local market diary families to stay in samples for up to five. The company staggers its contracts with householders, replacing part of the total each year.

Choice of Sample Size   The researcher next decides how large a sample to choose. In general, the larger the sample, the higher its reliability. But reliability increases approximately in proportion to the square of sample size (the sample size multiplied by itself). For example, to double reliability requires a fourfold increase in size. Thus a *point of diminishing returns* soon arrives, after which an increase in sample size yields such small gains in reliability as not to be worth the added cost.

Researchers and their clients therefore have to balance the degree of certainty desired against the level of expense involved. At best, sampling yields only estimates, never absolute certainty; hence the question becomes how much uncertainty can be tolerated in a given sampling situation.

Sampling Error   The built-in uncertainty of all measurements based on samples arises from *sampling error*. This term refers not to mistakes made in gathering data, which constitute *non*sampling errors, but to the laws of probability. These statistical

EXHIBIT 14–6   Multistage Sampling in Practice

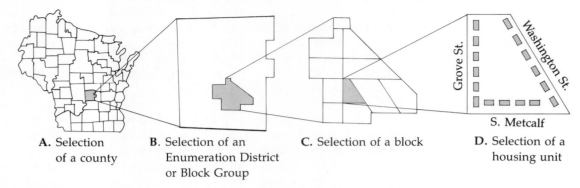

A. Selection
of a county

B. Selection of an
Enumeration District
or Block Group

C. Selection of a block

D. Selection of a
housing unit

The four steps show selection of a sample member on the basis of geography: (a) random selection of a county for the sample, (b) random selection of a specific district or block within the county; (c) random selection of a specific city block; and (d) random selection of a specific housing unit within a block. Official Census Bureau data provide the sampling frames.

SOURCE: Nielsen Media Research.

laws state that any given sample-based measurement would be equally correct if the sample size was increased or decreased by a known amount. Putting it another way, repeated sample measurements would vary among themselves, but the chances are that *most,* but probably not all, of the measurements would be *near* the real amount. The *probable* amount of statistical uncertainty in ratings (that is, the amount of sampling error to be expected) can be calculated in advance ("probable" because of uncertainty even about uncertainty!).*

Nonsampling errors arise from a legion of mistakes, both intentional and inadvertent. Such errors produce *bias* in the results. Bias can come from deliberate misrepresentation by respondents as well as from honest mistakes. Researchers may be consciously or unconsciously prejudiced. Failures to

fulfill sampling designs may occur, some avoidable, some not. The wording of questionnaires may be misleading; mistakes may occur in recording data and calculating results. Given all these pitfalls, some degree of bias arising from nonsampling error is inevitable when researchers sample large human populations.

Response Rate   Sometimes reports state sample size as the number of people (or households) the researcher contacted, but the key question should be how many actually *participated*. A 45 percent response rate indicates that only 45 out of 100 homes or individuals contacted actually participated. In practice, a *response rate* of 100 percent never occurs.

Ratings companies make special efforts to encourage participation of the preselected sample members and to ensure that those who agree to participate actually carry out their assigned tasks. Arbitron, for example, first writes a letter to prospective diary keepers, follows up with a telephone

*Public consciousness of sampling error has increased in recent years. News reports of survey results almost always add the provision, "Accurate within plus or minus so many percentage points." However, these disclaimers fail to reveal the *degree* of accuracy achieved within the stated limits.

call before and again during the sample week, and offers a small cash payment to encourage sample members to mail in completed diaries. Nielsen makes special efforts to encourage cooperation because it costs so much to recruit households and install and maintain meters. It encourages long-term cooperation by agreeing to pay half of any receiver repair costs as well as a small monthly cash payment. Throughout their five-year contracts, "Nielsen families" receive frequent mailings and personal visits from field representatives.

Despite such efforts, nonresponse remains a serious limitation on ratings accuracy. Some age groups, for example, have a particularly low response rate for radio diaries. Those who do return diaries may not represent those who do not. One or two diaries can make a critical difference in final market ratings and shares, especially in smaller markets. Overall, diary and meter methods yield a usable response rate of about 40 percent; the telephone method gets close to 75 percent. The number of such usable responses is termed the *in-tab sample*, the sample actually used to produce a given ratings report.

Typical kinds of nonresponses in the chief methods of data collection include:

▎ *Diaries:* refusal to accept diaries; failure to complete accepted diaries; unreadable and self-contradictory diary entries; drop-off in entries as the week progresses ("diary fatigue"); and failure to mail in completed diaries.

▎ *Passive (household) meters:* refusal to allow installation; breakdown of receivers, meters, and associated equipment; telephone-line failures.

▎ *People meters:* same drawbacks as passive meters, plus failure of some viewers (especially the very old and very young) to use the buttons to "check in" and "check out"—succumbing to "response fatigue."

▎ *Telephone calls:* busy signals; no answers; disconnected telephones; refusals to talk; inability to communicate with respondents who speak foreign languages.

Making Up for Sampling Deficiencies   No ratings company attempts pure probability sampling. Instead, researchers justify nonrandom sampling by taking into consideration the degrees and sources of nonrandomness. For example, *stratified sampling* ensures that samples are drawn in such a way as to represent known characteristics of the population in correct proportions. Prior research data, especially U.S. Census Bureau findings, make this procedure possible. Both Nielsen and Arbitron use stratified sampling to match the size of subsamples to the known population sizes of areas being sampled.

A similar corrective, applied to data after collection, minimizes known biases by *weighting* the results—giving extra numerical weight to the information received from certain sample members, corresponding to their known weight in the total population. All ratings services use weighting in an effort to improve the representativeness of their data. However, research that uses weighting assumes that the weight actually gives a representative picture of the population being measured. If data suffer from a high degree of nonresponse, as with some radio diaries in smaller markets, weighting can compound the bias caused by an unrepresentative sample.

14.4
Ratings Concepts

Market Delineation   The first step in ratings research is an accurate description of the local market covered by one or more stations. The broadcast advertising business depends heavily on a universally recognized, national system of clearly defined, nonoverlapping markets. The growth of cable television muddled this carefully constructed pattern; cable markets often include nonadjacent geographical areas. Spot sales planners need a market delineation system that avoids overlaps, so that they can group markets regionally or nationally without counting the same people more than once.

Arbitron's *Area of Dominant Influence* (ADI), first developed in 1965, has become the most widely accepted system for defining television markets, though Nielsen has its own version, called *Desig-*

nated *Market Area* (DMA). An ADI consists of one or more counties in which stations located in a central town or city are the most viewed (Exhibit 14–7). ADIs usually extend over smaller areas in the East, where cities are closer together, than in the West. Arbitron assigns each of the more than 3,000 counties in the United States to a single ADI, updating the assignments annually, although conditions change only slightly from one year to the next. ADIs range in size from No. 1 (New York City, with over 6.7 million television households) to No. 214 (Glendive, MT, with 5,200).*

Units of Measure   Another preliminary step in rating research is to define what will count as "one" when measuring the size of an audience. Researchers refer to this entity as the *elementary unit;* in broadcasting research it is usually defined as either a person or a household.

A *household* is defined as a group of persons who occupy any housing unit, including a house, an apartment, or a single room.† Researchers can count households more easily than individuals, because households stay in one place and are fewer in number. Households can consist not only of traditional family groups of two or more persons, but also multiadult and single-adult households. However, household-based sampling fails to account for viewing in hotels, dormitories, barracks, and institutions.

Television viewing has traditionally been a family activity, making the household a logical unit of measure, even though a majority of households now have two or more television sets, and much viewing takes place as a lone rather than a family activity. A single diary can be used to record the viewing or listening of all household members, or each individual can have a separate diary. Ratings reports based on household counts thus report more or less accurately on the individual viewing or listening of all people in that household *if* diaries or meters cover each receiver in the home and identify individual viewers.

Radio researchers prefer to count persons rather than households because (1) radio listening usually occurs as an individual activity, and (2) much radio listening takes place outside the home, especially in autos and workplaces. In the sections that follow, however, we will use the household as the elementary sampling unit unless otherwise noted.

Derivation of Ratings   A rating yields a *comparative estimate* of set tuning in any given market (or combination of markets, for network ratings) at any given time. More specifically, a rating is an estimate of the number of persons or households equipped to receive a broadcast signal who are in the audience of a specified station, network, or program, expressed as a percentage of some base.* The word *comparative* refers to the fact that a rating compares the *actual* estimated audience at a particular time with the *total possible* audience at that time. A rating constitutes an *estimate* because it measures only a sample of the audience; samples yield only approximations, never absolute measurements. A rating of 100 would mean that all (100 percent) of the households with sets in a market were tuned in to a particular station. But this unanimity can never happen: some people are not at home, some have broken receivers, and still others are otherwise occupied.

The most successful nonsports entertainment program of all time, an episode of the *Roots* miniseries in 1977, had a Nielsen rating of 51.5. The Super Bowl of 1983 achieved a rating of 48.6. Prime-

---

*Arbitron also uses two other terms to define slightly different market areas. The *home county* denotes a smaller area than an ADI, usually a station's county of license. Arbitron refers to some markets as *metros*. This term comes from *metropolitan statistical area* (MSA), a geographical region defined by the U.S. Department of Commerce for census and other statistical purposes, usually consisting of several counties around a central city core. Both the home and metro measures cover smaller areas than ADIs. On the other hand, *total service area* (TSA), the largest local region Arbitron reports, include 98 percent of a market's viewing or listening audience, thus covering counties outside an ADI. Published rating reports include maps of each area reported on, showing the differences between all these measures.

†In 1988 the U.S. Census Bureau estimated that the country had slightly more than 90 million households, averaging 2.64 persons per household.

---

*Definitions in this chapter generally conform to the National Association of Broadcasters' *Broadcast Research Definitions* (1988).

EXHIBIT 14–7 Arbitron Market Definition Terms

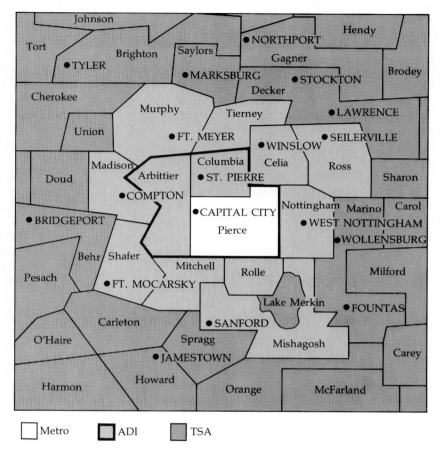

| Metro | ADI | TSA |

In this hypothetical state, the metro(politan) *area is defined as the "home" county of a station, while the* ADI (Area of Dominant Influence) *includes counties that listen primarily to the stations in "Capital City." The* TSA (Total Service Area) *includes nearly all listening to Capital City stations.*

SOURCE: © 1989 by Arbitron Ratings Company.

time television programs average a 17 rating; daytime programs average about 6. HBO averages a 2 prime-time rating in terms of all cable television homes and an 8 rating in terms of homes able to receive pay cable. Radio stations often earn ratings of less than 1, and rarely more than 2 or 3. Such low ratings make no meaningful distinctions among stations; radio therefore relies more on *cumulative* measures, discussed later in this section, under "Cumes."

Ratings calculations offer no problems. One simply divides the number of households in a sample tuned to a given program by the total television households in the sample. Thus, if in a sample of 400 households, 100 tune to a given program, you find the program's rating by dividing 100 by 400 (the 400 figure represents the full sample, and the 100 comes from diary reports for a specific program, station, or network). This equation yields 0.25, but you drop the decimal point, obtaining a rating of 25. Exhibit 14–8 graphically depicts the basic rating concepts.

You can *project* a properly derived rating. That is, expressed as a percentage, it can be applied to the total television population represented by the sample. Continuing with the above example, assume a total population of 100,000 television households, known from census data. Multiply this number by the rating with the decimal restored (0.25), and you have an estimated total audience of 25,000 households.

HUTs and Shares   Recall that a rating gives an estimate of the percentage of the total possible audience that was tuned to a particular program. You calculate a station's *share* of the audience, on the other hand, on the basis of *households using television* (HUT). A HUT of 55 indicates that in a given time period an estimated 55 percent of all television households actually tuned in to *some* station receivable in that market. In other words, HUT measurements refer to viewing in the market as a whole, not to any individual station or program receivable in that market. HUTs vary with daypart, averaging nationally about 25 for daytime hours and about 60 for prime-time hours. A HUT of 60 means that an estimated 60 percent of the television households in a measurement area have their sets turned on; the remaining 40 percent are not at home, busy with something else, or otherwise not part of the set-using group.

Radio research is usually based on persons rather than households, yielding a *persons using radio* (PUR) rather than HUT rating. PUR reports usually refer either to individual quarter-hours or to cumulative quarter-hours for a day or week.

You derive *shares* from HUT or PUR data. For television, divide each station's estimated viewing audience (in thousands) by the number of homes using television at that time, as shown in Exhibit 14–7. A station always has a larger share for a given time period than its rating for that time period. For example, top network prime-time programs usually average ratings of just over 20, but their corresponding shares amount to about 30. (The respective shares of the two record prime-time entertainment programs noted above were 71 and 69.)

Television programmers usually prefer to use share percentages in making programming decisions; salespersons usually prefer ratings as advertising sales tools. This difference arises because share percentages give programmers a more immediate estimate of their competitive position within one medium, whereas ratings more readily allow comparison of advertiser exposure on television with that in other media.

Time of day controls overall audience size. The availability of listeners within given dayparts varies little from day to day unless extraordinary events cause people to change their normal habits. But changes in program appeal can cause audience members to flow from one station to another, increasing or decreasing the audience share obtained by any particular program, even though the total audience (HUT) for that time period remains about the same.

Cumes   Radio gets such low ratings (because so many more stations divide the listeners, and because so many potential audience members opt for television instead) that advertising agencies use the larger share-percentage figures as a selling tool. *Cumulative audience* (cume) figures provide an even more favorable radio audience measurement. A radio signal reaches a relatively small number of people in any given quarter-hour, but over a period of many hours, or during the same period over a number of days, radio reaches a surprisingly large number of *different* listeners. A *cume rating* gives an estimate of the (cumulative) number of unduplicated persons tuning to a station over a period of time, expressed as a percentage of all potential radio listeners in a particular market. For example, during the two or four weeks that typically make up a rating

EXHIBIT 14–8   Ratings Concepts

A.

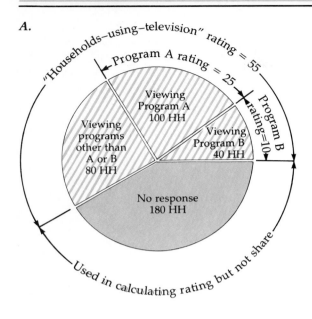

"Households–using–television" rating = 55

Program A rating = 25

Program B rating=10

Viewing
Program A
100 HH

Viewing
programs
other than
A or B
80 HH

Viewing
Program B
40 HH

No response
180 HH

Used in calculating rating but not share

A. *The pie shows television set-use information gathered from a sample of 400 households, representing a hypothetical market of 100,000 households.*

Note that program ratings are percentages based on the entire sample (including the "no response" households). Thus Program A, with 100 households, represents a quarter (25 percent) of the total sample of 400. The formula is 100 ÷ 400 = .25; the decimal is dropped when expressing the number as a rating.

Projected to the entire population, this rating of 25 would mean an estimated audience of 25,000 households. The formula is .25 (the rating with the decimal restored) × 100,000 = 25,000.

B.

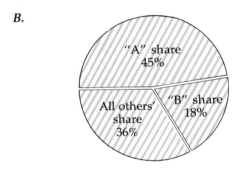

"A" share
45%

All others'
share
36%

"B" share
18%

B. *The smaller pie, 55 percent as large as the pie in A, represents only the households using television, in this case 80 + 100 + 40 households, or a total of 220 (expressed as a households-using-television or HUT rating of 55, as shown in A). Shares are computed by treating the total number of households using television, in this case 220, as 100 percent. Thus program A's 100 households divided by 220 equals about .445, expressed in rounded numbers as a share of 45.*

period, a person who listened several times to a particular station on different days would be counted as only one person in constructing a cume figure. A person listening only once during that period (tuning in just once during that week) would also be counted as one person, because a cume shows how many *different* people tuned to the station during a given period of time. The terms *reach* and *circulation* usually indicate cume audience measurements.

Demographics   Rating reports give audience composition in terms of gender and age. These *demographic breakouts,* or simply *demographics,* divide the overall ratings into subgroup ratings for men, women, teens (age 12–17), and children. Adult audience age-group categories typically consist of decade units (such as men 35–44) for radio and larger units for television (for example, women 18–34 or 25–49), although the "adults 12 +" category also occurs (Exhibit 14–9).

EXHIBIT 14–9 TV Audience Demographics and Time Spent Viewing

Hours of viewing per week

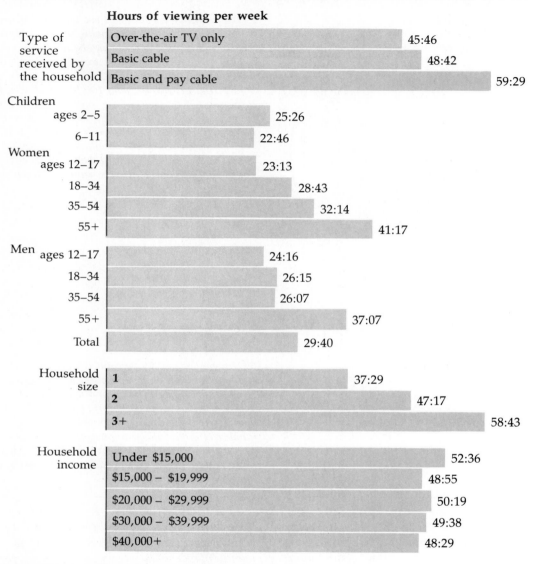

Many factors affect the amount of television watching in an average week. Note that weekly viewing hours increase with the presence of children in the home, with lower income, with pay cable, and with the age of the adult viewer. This information for November 1987 is the result of some of the first people-meter-based research: it shows a decline in amount of viewing for nearly all viewer categories from figures based on written diaries and passive household meters reported just a year earlier.

SOURCE: Nielsen Media Research, *1988 Report on Television*, pp. 7–9.

In advertising's stereotyped world, most products have appeal for specific groups (horror movies for teens, beer for men, denture products for the elderly, and so forth). Thus advertising agencies usually "buy" demographics rather than generalized audiences. Most advertisers would rather have an audience of moderate size with the right demographics for their product than a huge audience containing many members not likely to be interested in it.

14.5
Broadcast Audiences

Over years of intensive ratings research, a vast storehouse of knowledge about broadcast listening and viewing habits has been accumulated—this is surely the most analyzed mass media activity in history. After examining broadcast audiences in this section, we will take up cable and newer media audiences in Section 14.7.

Size Potential   The most fundamental statistic about radio and television audiences, called set *penetration* or *saturation,* is the percentage of all homes that have broadcast receivers. In the United States, radio and television penetration has long since peaked at between 98 and 99 percent. Indeed, most homes have several radios and more than one television set. In short, for practical purposes the entire U.S. population of over 90 million households constitutes the broadcast audiences' potential.

Actual Size   Of course, not all households have their sets turned on at the same time. HUT measurements, as previously explained, give an estimate of the percentage of television households actually using sets. Television viewing climbs throughout the day from a low in winter (when TV use is heaviest) of about 12 percent of households at 7:00 A.M. to a high of about 70 percent in the top prime-time hour of 9:00 P.M. to 10:00 P.M. The advent of cable has not altered these proportions, but VCR home video can interrupt both broadcast and cable viewing, making audience measurement more difficult.

Audience levels for television change predictably with the seasons; viewing peaks in January–February and bottoms out in June, reflecting the influence of weather on audience availability. Radio listening has a flatter profile than television, with the highest peak in the morning drive-time hours.

In the early years of broadcast television, many observers predicted that as the medium matured and its novelty wore off, the levels of set use would decline. Only in the late 1980s, however, with competition from cable and VCRs and introduction of people-meter methods, did the combined broadcast network share levels *really* drop off—from prime-time peaks of 90 to below 70 by the end of the decade. HUT levels remained stable, however—people continued to use their sets, but often to watch cable channels or playbacks from VCRs.

Size Stability   Long-term trends aside, in any particular season of the year people tend to turn on their television sets day after day in the same overall numbers, with no apparent regard for the particular programs that may be scheduled. Expressed in terms made famous by Marshall McLuhan, the *medium* matters more than the message.*

Paul Klein, a network programming expert, proposed a similar theory, that of the *Least Objectionable Program* (LOP). Half jokingly, he theorized that people stay with the same station until they are driven to another station by an objectionable program. But even if they find *all* programs objectionable, according to the LOP theory, they will stay tuned in to the *least objectionable* one rather than turning off the set entirely.

This accounted, wrote Klein, for the steady 90 percent of the prime-time audience gathered in by the three television broadcast networks in the 1970s. It also explained why seemingly excellent programs sometimes failed (because of being scheduled against

---

*Canadian communications theorist H. Marshall McLuhan (1911–1980), a cult figure in the 1960s, wrote a series of iconoclastic books about the impact of media on society. In the most important statement of his thinking, *Understanding Media* (1964), he explained his view that the nature and proliferation of media said more about society than any content carried by those media.

even better programs), and why seemingly mediocre programs sometimes succeeded (because they opposed even more objectionable mediocrities).

Whatever the reasons, ratings data confirmed that audience size remained stable, varying mostly because of changing dayparts and seasons. This constancy of the audience pool forced each network to focus its programming efforts on prying audiences loose from its two network rivals through counter-programming strategies. Rarely did a program forge ahead by enlarging the total sets-in-use figure; most succeeded only by diverting existing audience members from competing network programs.

In the 1980s, however, this static scene changed. Competition from independent stations, cable channels, and VCR viewing stimulated more complex and volatile audience behavior, creating problems for programmers and audience researchers, especially in prime time. The broadcast networks could no longer count on sharing 90 percent of the audience. Nevertheless, even with their aggregate prime-time share reduced to less than 70 percent, as it was by 1988, the three broadcast networks still had the most massive audiences of any medium and still constituted the most coveted national advertising vehicle.

Tuning Inertia　A corollary of LOP was *tuning inertia*. Whether because of viewer loyalty to a station or network or lethargy, audiences tend to let sets remain tuned to the same stations. Usually the proportion of flow-through viewers (those staying tuned to the same station) remained larger than those who flowed away to different stations. However, by the 1980s, remote-control devices and the large number of cable channels had modified this pattern. Tuning inertia (though still a factor in programming strategies) no longer had as predictable an effect on audience size as it had previously.

Tuning inertia affects radio audiences, too; in large markets with as many as 40 stations to choose among, listeners tend to confine their tuning to only two or three favorite stations.

Time Spent　The total amount of time people devote to listening and viewing also serves as a broad measure of broadcasting's audience impact. Perhaps this statistic arouses the most widespread concern among critics of the media. Any activity that takes up more time than sleeping, working, or going to school, they reason, surely has profound social implications.

Weekly average viewing per household, counting television, cable, and VCRs, reached more than 50 hours in the 1980s—on the order of seven hours a day. Of course, this total represents the sum of viewing by all members of households. As a group, women spend the most time viewing, following by children aged 2 to 11. Teenagers and college students view the least. But on the average, all age groups view close to the same number of hours per week; the differences between groups depend more on the accessibility of receivers than on deliberate choice. Thus women at home have more access than men at work; active teenagers have less access than younger children, who spend more time at home.

Demographic Influences　Averages, however, conceal differences of detail. Demographic differences profoundly influence audience set-use behavior. The following demographic variables, listed here along with examples of generalizations derived from audience research (Exhibit 14–8), hold special interest for broadcasters:

▫ *Age.* Among adults, viewing increases with age.
▫ *Education.* Viewing decreases with education.
▫ *Ethnic origin.* Blacks view more than whites.
▫ *Family size.* Large families view more than small families.
▫ *Occupation.* Blue-collar workers view more than professionals.
▫ *Place of residence.* Urbanites view more than rural dwellers.
▫ *Sex.* Women view more than men.

As a practical example of how broadcasters use demographic data, radio programmers take into account the fact that age strongly influences format preferences. Contemporary music formats appeal most to people in their late teens and twenties; classical, country, and MOR formats to people in their thirties and forties; and old-time music, news, and talk formats to people in their fifties and older. Interest in radio news and talk formats increases markedly with age. NCAA championship basketball games attract a much larger percentage of teenagers than other sports events. Gender is also important—for most sports events, male viewers outnumber females.

Advertisers will pay higher prices to reach specific audiences known to buy their products than to reach undifferentiated audiences. The more precisely an advertiser defines target audience demographics, the higher the per-viewer cost of reaching that audience.

14.6
Use and Abuse of Ratings

Ratings represent valid estimates that serve a useful purpose for programmers and advertisers. However, they easily lend themselves to abuse. Either through ignorance or deliberate misrepresentation, those who use ratings sometimes present them as hard-and-fast measurements instead of only estimates. Further, some unscrupulous users attempt to interfere with research procedures in order to influence their outcomes.

Ratings Investigations Complaints about the reliability of ratings mounted to such a pitch in the early 1960s that Congress launched an investigation. The House Commerce Committee commissioned a study of the statistical methods used in ratings research. Issued in 1961, the *Madow Report* stated that critics of ratings put too much emphasis on sample size and that more emphasis should be put on improving research methods and determining the significance of nonresponse (House CIFC, 1961: 1963–1965.)

While Congress conducted hearings, the Federal Trade Commission made its own investigation. The FTC ordered the ratings companies to account for noncooperation in sampling, to cease making misleading claims about sampling, to cease mixing data from incompatible sources, and to discontinue arbitrary, often unspecified, "adjustments" of research findings.

Industry Self-Policing In response to the barrage of criticism about ratings, the industry set up the Broadcast Rating Council in 1964 (changed in 1982 to the Electronic Media Rating Council, or EMRC) as an independent auditing agency representing ratings users. The EMRC accredits ratings services that meet its standards and submit to annual auditing. It also ensures full disclosure of methods in ratings reports. Nowadays, the ratings services disclose their methods fully, withholding from public scrutiny only some details of the way they edit the raw data they collect from diaries and meters. Every ratings report contains a supplement acknowledging the multiple limitations involved in a sampling. Arbitron, for example, lists 11 limitations in a page-long discussion of criteria for reporting station audiences.

But this candor did not stop criticism. More recent complaints have focused on such problems as the persistent failure of stations and networks to acknowledge the factor of sampling error, the tendency to underrepresent segments of society most difficult to sample, and the station practice of trying to inflate ratings during sweep weeks by program-scheduling tricks. Confusion over the introduction of the people meter compounded the problem in the late 1980s.

Reliability of Ratings Perhaps the major misunderstanding about ratings arises from the tendency to think of them as precise measurements, rather than merely *estimates*. Users of ratings often act as though differences of even fractions of a rating point have crucial significance, when in fact sampling error makes such precision impossible. Even repeated measurements of programs over time can only slightly reduce sampling error, not eliminate it.

It is important to keep in mind that ratings by their very nature can give us only limited information about audiences—and give it with only limited certainty. Hugh M. Beville, Jr., a former head of the Broadcast Rating Council, gives four warnings that every ratings user should heed (Beville, 1981):

- Ratings are approximations.
- Not all ratings are equally dependable.
- Ratings measure quantity, not quality.
- Ratings measure [set use], not opinion.

Validity of Ratings   *Validity* in research refers to the degree to which findings actually measure what they purport to measure. Ratings purport to measure the *entire* broadcast audience, but in practice they can only account for the broad middle-range majority of that audience. People at ethnic, economic, and geographic extremes have less chance to be solicited by, or inclination to cooperate with, ratings services than people in the middle range. Thus ratings tend to underrepresent the very rich, the very poor, and ethnic minorities. In recent years, both Arbitron and Nielsen have made special efforts to persuade minority respondents in their samples to participate fully.

The fact that television ratings use households rather than individuals as their measurement unit also affects validity. About a quarter of today's households consist of lone individuals whose lifestyle (and therefore broadcast use) patterns often differ from those of multiperson households. Also, household samples omit residents of group quarters such as college dormitories, much to the distress of stations in college towns.

Tampering and Hypoing   Ratings procedures can be vulnerable to tampering; someone who can influence the viewing habits of even a few sample households in a sample can have a substantial impact on the resulting ratings. Rating companies therefore keep the identity of sample households a closely held secret. Still, a few cases of outright manipulation of viewers have been made public, causing ratings services to junk reports for some programs, and even entire station or market reports for a given ratings period.

A far more widespread industry practice known as *hypoing* also skews ratings. Hypoing refers to the deliberate attempts of television stations or networks to influence ratings by scheduling extraor-dinary programs and promotional efforts during ratings sweeps. Radio stations hypo with listener contests. Both the FTC and the FCC have investi-gated hypoing, with little effect. In fact, the hypoing effects may cancel themselves out, since most sta-tions resort to it. Stations feel compelled to play the hypoing game because their competitors do.

Qualitative Ratings   Ever since ratings began to dominate programming strategies, critics have complained that the ratings system encourages me-diocrity by emphasizing sheer size to the exclusion of *qualitative* program aspects. Time and again, pro-grams that are seemingly of above-average quality receive enthusiastic reviews and substantial audi-ence followings, but fail to meet the rigid minimum-share requirements for commercial survival. Critics question whether programs that are merely toler-ated by large audiences should automatically win out over programs that attract smaller but intensely interested audiences. The quantitative ratings ap-proach decrees this kind of judgment; the system favors the "least objectionable" programs over the best possible programs.

In Britain and some other countries, laws require broadcasters to conduct research on qualitative as-pects of their programs and to take audience pref-erences into consideration in program decision making. U.S. public broadcasters have worked to establish a qualitative ratings system. Noncommer-cial broadcasting must, by virtue of its role as an alternative system, find evidence to support the need for its services, which often have strong appeal, but to a limited number of people. The only qualitative ratings that U.S. commercial broadcasters have shown interest in supporting aim at measuring the likability of performers.*

---

*Market Evaluations, Inc., regularly estimates image ratings of major performers, based on national samples of a thousand fam-ilies. Using mail questionnaires, the firm constructs both famil-iarity and likability ratings (the two do not necessarily coincide). The same company conducts the better-known TvQ (for TV Quo-tient) research on the popularity of specific programs. This qual-itative research uses questionnaires to determine the level of program appeal to different demographic groups.

14.7
Research on Newer Media

The emergence since the early 1970s of new ways of delivering programs to the home has complicated the researcher's task. Researching cable television audiences parallels somewhat the patterns familiar in broadcast research, but videocassette recorders present novel problems that are entirely different from those of broadcasting.

Cable Unlike broadcasting, cable television has objective information on its potential audience: its subscription records. By 1987, these records showed that cable penetration exceeded half of U.S. households. However, the number of subscribers tells nothing about actual cable use. Because of cable's many channels, its total audience is subdivided into many small groups, posing severe measurement difficulties. Cable systems that enjoy addressability (the ability to control and record access to each subscribing household) solves this problem, but few systems yet have that ability.

Nielsen introduced audience reports for a few national cable services in 1979, gradually increasing the amount of information provided on the basic and pay networks. These efforts led in 1983 to the Nielsen HomeVideo Index (NHI), set up to improve means of measuring the new services' audiences. Four times a year, NHI issues *Pay Cable Report*, covering all television activity in a sample limited to pay-cable subscriber homes. It provides national audience data for each of the larger national cable networks. Since the inception of people-meter methodology in 1987, Nielsen's national TV audience estimates have included ratings for superstations, cable origination, and pay services (see Exhibit 14–2). By the mid-1980s, this research showed clear evidence of the national cable services' impact on broadcast networks. The first detailed indications of the dimensions of that impact came with the start of national people-meter reports:

A comparison between the people meter sample and the old Nielsen meter showed a nine percent decline for ABC, CBS, and NBC and a 34 percent increase for cable-originated networks like CNN. And the discrepancy is not simply a function of the introduction of a new measurement technology. It is clear that viewers, not the meter, are causing the changes in the marketplace (Sieber, 1988: 72).

Local cable audiences proved more difficult to measure than national audiences. Cable franchise areas are defined by political boundaries, often comprising only a single county or even just part of one. Broadcast signals ignore political boundaries, creating larger market areas. Most individual cable systems are too small to attract enough advertiser interest to provide financial support for audience research. Nielsen and Arbitron included local cable viewing only in markets where cable audiences reached their minimum television reporting level, usually a share percentage of 3 or more. This criterion meant that cable measurements appeared in only about half of Nielsen and Arbitron local market reports. Cable system operators and national cable program suppliers continued to complain that broadcast-based research methods significantly underreported cable viewing, although people-meter reports appear to dispel most of their objections.

VCRs Home VCR penetration reached 60 percent by 1989, surpassing that of cable. The VCR presents novel problems for media research. Time shifting enables VCR owners to control the time at which they watch broadcast or cable programs. VCRs also encourage the evasion of commercials by zipping or zapping (see Sections 4.4 and 9.1). A recorded program and its advertisements may be seen several times and by different viewers, but ads may be seen only once if at all. Nielsen research on VCR phenomena is summarized in Exhibit 14–10.

14.8
Other Applied Research

Nonrating research probes into the subjective reasons for predicted as well as past audience behavior. It tries to find out what people like and dislike, what

EXHIBIT 14–10   VCR Use

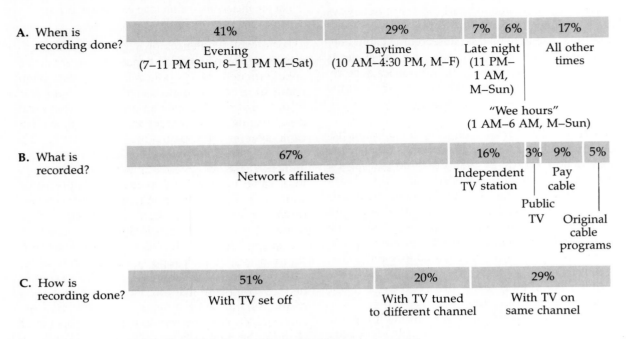

A. When is recording done?

41%	29%	7%	6%	17%
Evening (7–11 PM Sun, 8–11 PM M–Sat)	Daytime (10 AM–4:30 PM, M–F)	Late night (11 PM–1 AM, M–Sun)		All other times

"Wee hours" (1 AM–6 AM, M–Sun)

B. What is recorded?

67%	16%	3%	9%	5%
Network affiliates	Independent TV station		Pay cable	

Public TV   Original cable programs

C. How is recording done?

51%	20%	29%
With TV set off	With TV tuned to different channel	With TV on same channel

Research on use of home videocassette recorders in late 1988 demonstrated that the VCR is most often used for "time shifting." Taping is usually done in the evening to record programs on network affiliates, and is done when the receiver is not otherwise being used.

SOURCE: Nielsen Media Research, *1989 Report on Television.*

interests them and what bores them, what they recognize and remember, and what they overlook and forget. To study such subjective reactions, investigators usually use *attitudinal* research methods, which reveal not so much people's actions (in this case, set use) as their reactions—their *reasons* for action, as revealed in their attitudes toward programming.

Focus Groups   Commercial attitudinal research often makes no attempt to construct probability samples, because it usually does not try to make quantitative estimates that are projectable to entire populations. Instead, investigators choose respon-

dents informally, assembling small panels called *focus groups*. Investigators gain insights about people's motivations through informal discussion-interview sessions.

Program *concept* research, for example, tries out ideas for programs. A focus group's reactions to a one-page program description can help programmers decide whether to develop an idea further, to change some of its details, or to drop it entirely. Advertisers often test concepts for commercials before making final commitments to full production. These tests may use simple graphic storyboards, or they may employ *photomatics,* videotaped versions of the original storyboards with camera effects and sound added to make them look and sound something like full-scale commercials.

To test new or changed programs, researchers show pilot versions to focus groups. The people watch, give their reactions, and sometimes discuss the reasons for their attitudes with a session director. Frequently videotapes are made of these discussions to enable writers and others to study the reactions further.

Minute-by-minute reactions to a program can be studied using a *program analyzer,* a device first developed in the 1940s that enables test-group members to express favorable, neutral, or unfavorable reactions by pushing one of several buttons at regular intervals on cue. The machine automatically sums up the reactions of the entire test group, furnishing a graphic profile. A follow-up discussion can then probe for explanations of changes in audience interest at given moments in a script as revealed by peaks and valleys in the graph.

Theater vs. In-Home Testing The motion picture industry has long used theater previews to gauge audience response. Several firms specialize in staging similar theater previews of television programs and commercials. Investigators sometimes test advertisements under the pretext of testing programs, the commercials seeming to appear only incidentally. Viewer reactions emerge in questionnaires or discussions.

All such staged previews have the disadvantage of being conducted in an environment quite different from that of the home. Cable television has introduced a testing method that allows researchers to test viewers in their normal surroundings, using their own receivers. One research firm owns several small cable systems that it uses for research on commercials. One group of subscribers receives one version of test materials, and a second group gets a different version. The company asks the subscribers to keep diaries of their purchases, thus giving concrete evidence of the influence commercials have on actual buying behavior.

Physiological Testing Most methods described so far depend on introspection by panel members. In an attempt to eliminate the element of subjectivity and to monitor responses more subtly, researchers have identified a number of involuntary physical reactions that give clues to audience response. Reactions that have been measured for this purpose include changes in brain waves, eye movements, pupil dilation, breathing, pulse rate, voice quality, perspiration, and sitting position (the "squirm test").

For example, a number of researchers have capitalized on the two-sided nature of the human brain. Each side has its own specialized functions and reacts to different stimuli. Reasoning ability seems to be located in the brain's left side, and emotions in the right. It follows that commercials for products that have emotional appeal should primarily, if correctly oriented, stimulate the right side of the brain more than commercials that appeal mainly to logical considerations. Commercials shown to viewers wired for brain-wave recording can be tested to find out whether the messages elicited the desired brain-wave responses.*

Test Markets Test markets realistically appraise the effectiveness of advertising, but they require complex, expensive planning. Researchers select two or more markets, distant from each other but well matched demographically. Viewers in each market then see a different version of a proposed national advertising campaign, carried either on a broadcast television station or on a cable channel. Researchers judge the effectiveness of each local version by its influence on product sales. They measure sales by keeping track of the physical movement of goods in the market or (more easily) by using *direct marketing,* offering the product for sale only through broadcast or cable advertising.

---

*In the 1950s, *subliminal* advertising caused a flurry of interest. Such ads consisted of simple messages of a word or two flashed on a movie theater screen so briefly as to go unnoticed. Such messages appear to have an impact below the conscious level (hence, "subliminal"—below the threshold). Subliminal messages apparently stimulated audiences to buy greater quantities of popcorn or other foods mentioned in the messages. Fear that unsuspecting audiences would be subjected to this type of thought control led the FCC to ban it.

Research on Children Several companies specialize in analyzing children's likes and dislikes and how they influence adult purchasing decisions. Marketers know that children have an impact on what brands or products adults will buy. One research firm gains insight into children's preferences and motivations by turning a group of kids loose in a miniature supermarket. As the children go on a shopping spree, researchers secretly observe and record their behavior. Such firms avoid publicity, both to keep results confidential and to avoid criticism for taking what some would consider an unfair advantage of children.

Audience Response Telephone calls and letters from listeners or viewers about programs, performers, and commercials provide additional audience information. Indeed, at first broadcasters relied entirely on voluntary mail from listeners for audience information. But people who write or call a station are not a statistically representative sample of the entire audience. Research has shown that letter writers differ significantly from the general population in terms of race, education, income, type of job, age, and marital status—all differences important to advertisers and programmers. Further, letter-writing campaigns for or against a given point of view, product, or service can give misleading impressions about general audience reaction.

For these reasons, stations take telephone calls less seriously than systematically gathered data. Nevertheless, a few strong letters of complaint, especially if they give the impression of a spontaneous response rather than merely ready-made form letters, do get attention, since broadcasters and advertisers know that a few complaints of a focused kind probably represent a sizable number of dissatisfied listeners or viewers.

Summary

▌ There are two main kinds of applied audience research: studies that generate program ratings and studies that test the appeal of programs or advertising.

▌ Audience research methods for electronic media differ from research methods for print media circulation, because electronic media audiences are more difficult to count than print media readership.

▌ Ratings measure audience size in both local and national markets. The most commonly used market delineation is the area of dominant influence.

▌ Arbitron and Nielsen are the two important national ratings research companies. Arbitron does market surveys for both radio and television, and began a network service in 1989, whereas Nielsen does network and market surveys for television only.

▌ Data for ratings are usually gathered by written diaries, passive household meters, people meters, telephone calls, or a combination of these. Each method has its strengths and weaknesses.

▌ Ratings are estimates, in the form of percentages, of the proportion of the total possible audience that is tuned to a particular program. These data help in developing HUT (households using television), PUR (people using radio), and audience-share statistics. When audiences are small, as in the case of radio, cumulative data can be used to show the aggregate reach of a program over a period of hours, days, or weeks.

▌ In addition to showing audience size, ratings, especially those gathered with people meters, can supply information on audience composition in terms of sex, age, and other demographic characteristics.

▌ All ratings make use of three kinds of sampling: behavioral (usually set tuning), time (most are conducted periodically, not continuously), and number of people included (all ratings are based on relatively small, representative cross sections of populations).

▌ Accurate sampling requires the use of good sample frames, the systematic random selection of sample members for representativeness, high response rate, and avoidance of bias. All measurements based on sampling are subject to sampling error. In addition, sampling inevitably falls short of the ideal, causing additional nonsampling errors.

▌ Within given time frames (dayparts), the size of the broadcast and cable audience remains remarkably stable, with audience members tuning from channel to channel rather than turning sets on and off.

▌ Ratings provide a reasonably accurate picture of broadcast audiences as long as the rather severe limitations on their accuracy and significance are kept in mind.

▌ Development of audience ratings for cable, VCRs, and newer services is still in relative infancy. Among the problems faced are the large number of chan-nels available, the rising use of nonbroadcast material on home VCRs, and multiple channels with the same material.

▌ Other applied research tests commercials, programs, and the popularity of performers, both during program planning and after production. Such research often relies on small focus groups, probing the reactions of test subjects for personal motives and attitudes.

CHAPTER 15

SOCIAL EFFECTS

The previous chapter dealt with one particular set of effects as revealed by ratings and other market-research findings—audience behavior in terms of set tuning and other readily measurable effects. In this chapter we turn from market effects to less easily measured yet more important consequences of radio and television: their political and social effects.

15.1
Effects Research

Even without benefit of research, people have always assumed that radio and television have effects, both good and bad. These assumptions take on practical significance when decisions must be made concerning how these media should be regulated. For that reason, as well as for reasons of pure scientific curiosity, scholars have spent a great deal of time and money analyzing media effects.

Research and Policy-Making When Congress wrote the Radio Act of 1927 and the Federal Radio Commission first began writing rules to put the act into effect, neither the legislature nor the commission had the benefit of social and economic research on the effects of mass media. They relied primarily on legal-historical considerations and sheer guesswork. Today, however, major policy decisions rely on research to support their goals and assumptions, and to predict the probable outcome. For example:

- In defending a hands-off policy with regard to radio station format changes in the 1970s, the FCC used a study of the formats available in major markets as evidence that competition alone would ensure sufficient format variety.

- Congressional concern about the possible adverse effects of violence in programming led in 1969 to the allocation of a million dollars to the surgeon general for research studies, and to funding for a follow-up survey a decade later.

- To justify its radio deregulation proposals in 1979–1981, the FCC used research on current practices of radio stations to support its theory about the effects of competition.

During the 1970s the FCC came increasingly under the dominance of economic theorists in making decisions about the future of broadcasting. Research on the economics of broadcasting and cable television, along with predictions of their future interrelationships, became a growth industry. Foundations began funding such research and economists at major universities and research centers undertook numerous projects. By the 1980s, the FCC came to rely increasingly on economic theory and research in making the case for its regulatory decisions.

When Congress holds hearings on proposed new legislation or the FCC considers proposed new rules, private interests present their views. Representatives of the broadcasting industry usually buttress their arguments with surveys of prior research on the topic, frequently adding specially commissioned research of their own. Consumer organizations, too, have learned that good intentions and moral fervor do not get serious attention from government and industry. Their claims need to be supported by the kind of hard evidence that research alone can supply. Typical examples of research undertaken by private sponsors follow:

- Critics of broadcast news regularly conduct or cite content analysis studies to support their allegations of news bias.

- Action for Children's Television has for 20 years conducted content analysis research to support its petitions for improvements in children's programming.

- Commercial broadcasters surveyed existing research to demonstrate to Congress and others in the 1980s that bans on broadcasting advertising of alcohol or legal drugs would do little to curb excessive use of these products.

Early Findings   *Mass propaganda* efforts were first widely used during World War I (1914–1918), before the broadcasting era. Written and pictorial propaganda whipped up mass hysteria on both sides. After the war the extent of deception by propagandists was revealed, showing how unscrupulously people had been manipulated. It seemed as if a sinister new weapon had been found, capable of almost any excess. The advent in the 1920s of a potential new propaganda medium, radio broadcasting, along with the emergence of a potential new political threat, the recently installed communist regime in Russia, made the prospect of propaganda manipulation all the more alarming. This heightened concern about the effects of mass persuasion stimulated funding for research focused on analyzing the social and psychological dynamics of propaganda.

The concept of media effects that developed in the 1920s visualized propaganda messages as so many bullets of information (or misinformation) aimed at passive multitudes. Researchers assumed that the messages penetrated individuals, causing specific reactions. Accordingly, the concept later became known, somewhat derisively, as the *bullet* or *hypodermic injection* theory of communication effects.

By the end of the 1930s and with the approach of World War II, researchers realized that the bullet theory of propaganda effects had erred in treating the receivers of messages as mere passive targets. They found that, far from passively absorbing injections of propaganda, audience members act upon messages as individuals. The effects of messages therefore depend on a great many variables within and among the individual members of audiences.

Researchers labeled these factors, many subjective and therefore not directly observable, *intervening variables*. They come between messages and effects, varying the effects according to each individual's previously acquired attitudes, traits, experiences, social situation, and so on. Intervening variables explain why an identical message can have different effects on different people.

During the 1940s, World War II stimulated renewed interest in propaganda studies. A team of researchers at Yale University received a government grant to study the effects of orientation films the Army used to indoctrinate new recruits. The research focused on measuring *attitude change, a type of effect that lent itself readily to laboratory tests.* The Yale researchers asked such questions as: What is the most effective source for persuasive messages? What order of presentation of an argument works best? Is it better to ignore counterarguments in a campaign of persuasion, or to try to refute them? How do people's group affiliations affect their persuadability? To what extent do group pressures affect the independence of individual decision making?

The Yale studies ushered in a new phase of effects research. According to one estimate, they laid the groundwork for "a new scientific rhetoric, in which there was an attempt to set forth principles of communication effects in scientific terms backed by scientific evidence" (Schramm, 1973: 221).

One of the most influential discoveries concerning intervening variables was the importance of the personal influence of *opinion leaders,* as contrasted to the impersonal influence of the media. The flow of influence from the mass media, researchers found, often passes through leaders to followers rather than affecting all individuals directly.

During the 1940s a team of sociologists at the Columbia University Bureau of Applied Social Research, led by Paul Lazarsfeld, developed a theory about personal leadership vis-à-vis media influence. In 1955, Lazarsfeld and an associate painstakingly tracked down decisions people had made about movie-going, food buying, dress selection, and public issues, ascertaining whether the media or opinion leaders had been more influential (Katz & Lazarsfeld, 1955). For most people, personal influence played a larger role in each type of decision than the influence of radio, newspapers, magazines, and books. Other experiments and field investigations confirmed and refined this *two-step flow* hypothesis of media influence.

The two-step flow theory had great impact on mass media research in the ensuing 20 years. As one scholar put it, the Lazarsfeld concept "turned the mainstream of media effects thinking away from man as an atom to man as a member of many groups, each providing a context and sometimes a screening mechanism for receiving messages" (Kline, 1972: 22).

Selective Effects   Lazarsfeld and his associates found that the media did not influence even opinion leaders in direct proportion to the amount of persuasive content in the media. Media consumers, it appears, pay attention to communications that fit their established opinions and attitudes but ignore communications that challenge or contradict their established mind set. Because of this factor of *selective exposure,* media tend to reinforce people's existing views, rather than converting them to new viewpoints.

Existing mind sets influence how people perceive the communications they select for attention. Several people who select the same communication may interpret it in several different ways. Though the stimulus remains constant, the response varies. This variable, called *selective perception,* shows that people interpret messages based on their established opinions and attitudes rather than receiving them passively (as the old bullet theory had supposed).

Selective perception accounts for the *boomerang effect.* Experiments showed that highly prejudiced people tend to misinterpret messages containing evidence against their prejudices. They distort the evidence or sift out those elements that reinforce their existing attitudes, rather than allowing the message to reduce their hostile feelings. Thus propaganda can boomerang, producing exactly the opposite of the intended effect (Cooper & Jahoda, 1974). As a classic example of the boomerang effect, many viewers misread the antibigotry message of the Archie Bunker character in *All in the Family* in the 1970s. They saw in it an endorsement of the very prejudices that producer Norman Lear intended to satirize.

Even in the absence of prejudice, people under emotional stress may have difficulty accepting evidence that contradicts an existing mind set. Striking examples of this kind of selective perception occurred during the panic caused by the famous Orson Welles Halloween 1938 radio broadcast of an imaginary invasion from Mars. The radio dramatization simulated news reports, creating a realistic atmosphere that fooled a number of listeners, despite explicit warnings in the introduction to the drama. A sociological study of the panic revealed how some of the listeners tried to check on the authenticity of the broadcast; even when presented with evidence that it was fiction, however, they turned the facts around to support their conviction that the invasion was real:

"I look out of the window and everything looked the same as usual so *I thought it hadn't reached our section yet.*"

"We looked out of the window and Wyoming Avenue was black with cars. *People were rushing away, I figured.*"

"My husband tried to calm me and said, 'If this were really so, it would be on all stations' and he turned to one of the other stations and there was music. I retorted, 'Nero fiddled while Rome burned' (Cantril, 1940: 93).

Such stubborn refusal to forsake an existing mind set suggests that people have a kind of internal gyroscope that tends to maintain a consistent set of attitudes, opinions, and perceptions. Psychologists developed several versions of a concept known generally as *congruence theory* to account for this tendency, which acts as an intervening variable in determining the effects of communications.

In brief, congruence theories hold that a person's internal state of mind normally has the property of balance or congruence. A message that contradicts established opinions causes dissonance, lack of congruity, or imbalance. An effort to restore balance (conscious or unconscious) follows. It might take the form of rejecting the message (alleging that the source is "unreliable," for example), distorting the message to make it fit the existing mind set (the stations playing music are just fiddling while Rome burns), or, least likely, adjusting the balance by accepting the new idea and incorporating it into the existing mind set (conversion to a new point of view).

The theories and concepts so far reviewed came out of the social sciences. A fresh way of looking at communication came from the engineering field with publication of the book *The Mathematical Theory of Communication* (Shannon and Weaver, 1949). This theory looks at information from the point of view of transmission systems and therefore uses such familiar broadcast engineering terms as channel capacity, noise, encoding, decoding, and bit (Exhibit 15–1). Information theory contributed valuable insights and concepts to the study of mass communication. For instance, the concept of *feedback* (Wiener, 1950) came from information theory. The thermostatic control on a heating or cooling system illustrates feedback in the engineering sense. As the system delivers air to a room, a thermostat senses changes in room temperature. When it senses a critical temperature (according to the settings on the thermostat), it instructs the machine to turn itself off or on, as the case may be. This feedback of information and its insertion into the system

on continuously, maintaining the temperature within programmed limits.

Similarly, communicators modify their messages in response to information that comes back from audiences. In face-to-face communications, visual and auditory cues continually tell speakers about audience reactions. Speakers respond by adjusting what they say and how they say it from moment to moment—heating up or cooling down their rhetoric, so to speak. Lacking this sensitive and immediate give-and-take, mass media operate at a disadvantage. It takes time to obtain feedback and to modify the media product accordingly. The fact that tape or film freezes programs in a permanent form makes subsequent modification slow and difficult. Yet even recorded material can be modified by editing, explanatory introduction, or ultimately cancellation.

Research Topics   Communication involves a chain of events and so can best be regarded as a *process,* as suggested by the simple model in Exhibit 15–1. A communicator initiates a process that produces an end result—if indeed definable effects occur. Study of the process can be directed to any one, or any combination of, five different stages in the process: (1) *originators* of messages, (2) *contents* of messages, (3) *channels* through which messages travel, (4) *audiences* that receive messages, and (5) the *effects* of messages. A pioneer communications researcher, Harold Lasswell, summarized these stages by saying that the objects of research could be identified by posing the question: "*Who* says *what* in which *channel* to *whom* with what *effect?*"*

The commercial audience research discussed in Chapter 14 concerns the "whom" factor of Lasswell's paradigm. Ratings give information on media use, also called *media exposure* or *time-spent* data.

---

*Adapted from Smith, Lasswell, & Casey, 1946: 121. It should be understood that this single-sentence formula intentionally simplifies the communication process. A later commentator, for example, proposed that a more complete statement would ask three additional questions: *why?* (policy studies), *how?* (studies of communication techniques), and *who talks back?* (studies of feedback process).

EXHIBIT 15–1 Information Theory Model of Communication Process

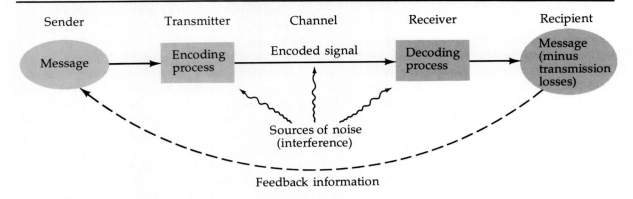

The model can be adapted to describe many modes of communication, from those with no technology (two people talking together) to the most complex (satellite relays of scrambled video signals).

Breakdowns of audiences into demographic sub-categories give further details about the "whom" of broadcast communication.

Researchers study the "who" of communication to find out about the sources of media content. In broadcasting, the sponsor-identification law mandates identification of the sources of paid material; otherwise broadcasters have no obligation to reveal the identity of originators (though talent contracts require listing of credits).

Shapers of content (the "what" of Lasswell's question) act as *gatekeepers*. The term originated in social psychology, but a study of the role newswire editors play in controlling the flow of syndicated news copy applied it to mass communications (White, 1950). Some scholars prefer the less picturesque but more inclusive term *information control*. Government regulation, industry codes, and network clearance represent types of gatekeeping, as do the selection, placement, and editing of broadcast material. Gatekeeping studies seek to answer questions about how the controls operate, where the gates in the flow of information occur, and what effects they have on the content by the time it finally reaches

its destination. Not only individuals but also institutions play a gatekeeping role in mass media.

Take the allegation of news bias on the part of television networks. Does a "handful" of biased editors and commentators personally control network television news, as alleged in a famous 1969 speech by then vice president Spiro Agnew?* Edward Epstein studied the network news divisions intensively as gatekeeping institutions, concluding that Agnew's allegation had no merit. Although key "visible" news staff members doubtless exercise considerable influence, the traditions of their craft and institutional gatekeepers beyond their control have more influence. Such background influences include the economic organization of the networks, the nature of news-gathering machinery, the technology and budgets available, the role imposed by the network-

*Agnew attacked the networks for the practice of "instant analysis," the dissecting of presidential speeches by commentators immediately after delivery. Learning from the advance release of Agnew's address that they were to be attacked, the networks canceled regular programs to carry it, "providing the greatest political windfall ever enjoyed by a vice-president" (Lippman, 1971: 192).

affiliate relationship, and many other factors not directly controllable by any individual (Epstein, 1973b).

Other areas in which gatekeeping research assists in policy decisions include the effects of cross-media and group ownership on programming decisions; the influence of advertisers on program content; the roles of professional criticism and of industry self-regulation; and the impact of government regulation on programs.

As to the "which channel" question, research shows that media channels differ among themselves as to psychological impact because audiences form attitudes and expectations regarding each information medium. They interpret what each medium sends accordingly. The Television Information Office (TIO), an organization supported for three decades (1959–1989) by the broadcast industry, commissioned the Roper Organization to conduct annual image studies of television. Roper reported on 16 national opinion polls, using many of the same questions each time so that trends could be monitored. For example, on a question about comparative performance of social institutions, respondents consistently increased their confidence in television—59 percent said television was doing an "excellent" or "good" job in 1959, 74 percent in 1984. Rankings of other media, schools, and government activity declined or stayed the same in esteem during the same period (Roper, 1984: 14).

Another key question in the Roper series dealt with media credibility, asking respondents which of several media they would believe in case of conflicting news reports. Since 1961, they consistently chose television over other media by a wide margin. In 1988, 49 percent chose television, 26 percent newspapers, and 7 percent radio as the most credible medium (Roper, 1989: 15).

In researching the "to whom" question, scholars use more detailed personal and social-group indicators to study the composition of broadcasting audiences than does ratings research. In particular, the child audience has been extensively analyzed, using such variables as race, intelligence, social class, home environment, and personality type. These analyses relate audience characteristics to effects. Researchers ask such questions as: What types of children will be most likely to believe what they see on television? What types will imitate what they see?

Finally, Lasswell's "with what effects?" culminates his questions because communicators, content, channels, and audiences all interest us precisely because they help determine the ultimate outcomes of communicating. Joseph Klapper summarized the status of effects theories as of 1960 in an influential book, *The Effects of Mass Communication.* After studying more than a thousand research reports, Klapper reached the tentative conclusion that ordinarily communication "does not serve as a necessary and sufficient cause of audience effects, but rather functions among and through a nexus of mediating factors and influences." The media largely *reinforce* existing perceptions and beliefs. They might persuade people to buy a product, but not to change a political allegiance or to adopt a new religion. The broadcasting industry welcomed this conservative conclusion, known as the *law of minimal effects,* because it gave apparent scientific sanction to the industry's rejection of consumer arguments that programs could be blamed for causing antisocial behavior.

During the 1970s, opinion began to shift away from the minimal effects concept, largely because of intensive research on the effects of violence (discussed in Section 15.7). However, researchers now tend to avoid talking about effects as such. The very word *effects* implies an oversimplification of what is now understood to be an extremely complex process. Without denying that specific media content might under specific conditions have specific effects on some specific people, researchers prefer to speak in terms of the *association* of certain inputs with certain outputs. They avoid going so far as to imply a simple, straight-line cause-effect relationship. Exhibit 15–2 summarizes the stages of research development, from the simplistic cause-effect concept of the early studies to the contemporary interest in looking more deeply into the antecedents of effects.

EXHIBIT 15–2   Evolution of Research on Media Effects

Stage	Prevailing viewpoint	Empirical basis
1	Mass media have strong effects	Observation of apparent success of propaganda campaigns Experiments demonstrating immediate attitude change after exposure to messages Evidence of selective perception—persons ignore messages contrary to existing predispositions
2	Mass media largely reinforce existing predispositions, and thus outcomes are likely to be the same in their absence	Evidence of personal influence—persons are more influenced by others than the mass media Evidence of negligible influence on voting No relationship observed between exposure to mass media violence and delinquent behavior among the young
3	Mass media have effects independent of other influences which would not occur in the absence of the particular mass media stimuli under scrutiny	Evidence that selective perception is only partially operative Evidence that media influence by setting the context and identifying the persons, events, and issues toward which existing predispositions affect attitudes and behavior Evidence that television violence increases aggressiveness among the young
4	Processes behind effects so far studied may be more general, suggesting new areas for research	New research is finding that under some circumstances television may influence behavior and attitudes other than those related to aggressiveness.

SOURCE: George Comstock et al., 1978: 392.

The People Problem   In designing research projects to study media effects, investigators face the frustrating problem that many effects consist of *subjective responses* that are beyond the reach of direct observation and measuring instruments. How can one *objectively* measure human attention, understanding, learning, likes and dislikes, and opinion formation? Some of these effects do produce observable physical cues—for instance, brain waves and other involuntary physical signals can be detected—but these signals usually reveal little about subjective experiences in human terms.

Even when communications effects emerge as overt, observable responses, a subjective link never-theless intervenes. In tracing the sequence of events from cause to effect, researchers lose the trail when it disappears into the subjective consciousness of the people being studied. What goes on inside the human brain certainly influences the final outcome, but it cannot yet be directly studied by the researcher.

For these reasons, most research on effects relies in whole or in part on questioning people about their subjective experiences rather than observing their reactions. Self-reporting, however, is not altogether reliable. People may be unwilling or unable to tell the truth about their inner experiences, or if willing they may be forgetful or unaware of their own subconscious motivations. Furthermore, listening and viewing usually occur privately, often in situations which prohibit the intrusion of an outside observer. Consequently, data gathering, whether based on self-reporting or direct observations, almost always introduces an element of artificiality, referred to in the research literature as *intrusiveness.*

Methods of Research Investigators use four major types of research: sample surveys, content analysis, laboratory experiments, and field studies or experiments. Each has its own pluses and minuses in terms of the extent of its reliance on subjective data, its intrusion on the spontaneity of respondents, and—most important for researchers hard pressed to finance their projects—its cost. See Exhibit 15–3 for further analysis.

Sample surveys The research strategy most familiar to the general public is the sample survey, used in opinion polls and audience rating reports. Such surveys can estimate characteristics of entire populations through use of very small random samples. An additional advantage, as with ratings, is that data are gathered in the settings in which listening or viewing normally takes place. Commercial ratings services use sample surveys to measure the most basic and objective behavior: set tuning, without reference to the effects of actual listening or viewing that may ensue after the set is on. Sample surveys thus tell us nothing about the *causes* of tuning. This is the major weakness of the survey strategy: "causal implications typically cannot be determined" (Comstock et al., 1978: 493).

Content analysis The classification of programming into various categories constitutes a simple form of *content analysis.* On a more sophisticated level content analysis categorizes, enumerates, and interprets items of message content. Broadcasting researchers have used content analysis to study advertising copy, censors' comments, cross-national program comparisons, television specials, specific types of new content, violent acts in programs (Exhibit 15–9), and the portrayal of minorities in tele-

vision dramas, as examples. We are also interested in content details that reveal what electronic media are saying or implying about various subjects. One problem is deciding how to define the content categories to be studied and compared. Researchers usually apply their own ideas of meaning to television programming, personal conversations, and other communications. Thus they are interpreting the message when in fact they may misunderstand or fail to perceive the importance of context—the private history and set of circumstances experienced by a viewer that no researcher can see.

Laboratory experiments Regarded as the classic strategy for conducting behavioral research, laboratory experiments enable investigators to control various experimental factors precisely and to exclude extraneous events and influences. Both subjectively reported and objectively observed data can be derived from such experiments. For decades, the most popular experimental variable used in studying communication was *attitude change.* A group of people is tested for current attitudes on a given topic. The experimenter then exposes them (either in a face-to-face talk or via a recording) to a persuasive message on that subject. A second test then determines if any change in attitude has occurred. One trouble with this approach is that attitudes measured in a laboratory situation do not always govern real-life actions. People often say one thing but then do another. This discrepancy has been noted in differences between expressed television program preferences and actual television viewing. Moreover, lab experiments put people in artificial situations that bear little resemblance to the complex situations in which they actually experience the media.

Field studies Research projects done in more naturalistic settings, known as *field studies,* record behavior in the real world without intruding into the situation or otherwise influencing the participants. In studying the impact of violent programming, for example, field-study researchers observe children in their normal home or school environment rather than moving them into a lab setting. A

EXHIBIT 15–3 Characteristics of Major Research Strategies

Strategy	Subjectivity	*Typical level of* Intrusiveness	Cost
Sample survey	high	moderate	variable
Content analysis	moderate[b]	nil	moderate
Laboratory experiment	variable	high	low[c]
Field study	low	low	high
Field experiment	low	moderate	high

[a]Costs of a simple local telephone survey can be low, but national telephone surveys employing sophisticated sampling and data gathering procedures (such as the commercial ratings services use) can be very high.

[b]Subjective in that coders make judgments in classifying content items.

[c]Cost can be high if sophisticated testing equipment or elaborate simulations are employed.

compromise between the tight controls and artificial context of the laboratory experiment and the unstructured naturalism of the field study can be achieved in *field experiments*. Here, researchers set up situations for testing in field or real-life situations. However, these experiments cost a great deal of time and effort to arrange, and some of their methods can be just as questionable as those used in laboratories. Thus they are relatively rare.

15.2
Advertising Effects

No consequence of broadcasting and cable has been more measured and manipulated than the effects of advertising. Advertisers demand, and get, measurable results, as described in the chapter on ratings. Here we focus on the broader, long-range social consequence of advertising rather than on its immediate business applications.

Advertising as Subsidy Advertising plays a useful social role by reducing the direct costs of media to the public. In the case of electronic media, for example, advertising appears to pay the entire

cost of the service (except for pay cable and other viewer-supported services). However, consumers eventually pay the full cost of media, because the final prices of consumer goods and services include advertising costs. In addition, audience members have to purchase, operate, and maintain radio and television sets. This public investment, combined with the fact that broadcasting uses the public frequency spectrum, gives the consumer more equity in radio and television than in other media. Advertiser-supported cable television exacts a triple price, adding a subscriber fee to advertising and receiver costs.

Power of Advertising Does advertising impose a penalty on consumers by generating a desire for unnecessary purchases—what economist John Kenneth Galbraith termed the *synthesizing of wants*? Electronic media advertising can stimulate widespread demand for goods and services for which consumers had no prior need. Advertising can build overnight markets for virtually useless products or "new and improved" versions of old products.

Critics often assume from these successes that advertising can overcome almost any defense a consumer can muster. Advertising practitioners find themselves wishing it were only so. The failure of a high proportion of new products each year hardly supports the assumption that advertising is all-powerful.

Not only do many products fail to catch on, but leading products often give way to competitors, despite intensive advertising support. Marketers recognize the transfer of *brand loyalty* as an ever-present threat. In fact, much television and radio advertising simply aims at keeping brand names visible and viable in the marketplace.

Advertising to Children   The possible effects of commercials in children's programs raise special issues of fairness and equity. Children start watching television early and find commercials just as fascinating as programs. Action for Children's Television and other consumer organizations believe that commercials take unfair advantage of young children who are not yet able to differentiate between advertising and programs.

Consumer groups also complain that commercials aimed at children urge consumption of sugared foods and beverages. One study quoted by the FTC staff examining the issue in the 1970s counted more than 7,500 network food commercials aired during the daytime weekend children's programs in the first nine months of 1976 (excluding ads for fast-food outlets). Of these ads, half promoted breakfast cereals and a third pushed candy, gum, cookies, and crackers. The staff concluded that the FTC had ample authority to ban such advertising. But the recommendation galvanized industry lobbyists and eventually precipitated a congressional crackdown on the idea of banning children's television advertising. The FTC has not considered the issue since.

The FCC's Children's Television Task Force (FCC, 1979) and a panel of experts funded by the National Science Foundation (Adler et al., 1980) also conducted studies. The FCC group reported that some progress had been made during the 1970s in eliminating selling by program hosts and in cutting back on commercial time in children's programs, but that the industry had a long way to go. The task force recommended encouraging alternative nonbroad-cast sources of entertainment for children. This advice reflected the emerging deregulatory trend; instead of forcing the industry to change its practices by regulation, the FCC relied instead on consumer self-discipline to prevent harmful effects.

Action for Children's Television, the most vocal consumer group, contested the FCC viewpoint before both the commission and the courts. A series of court decisions brought the FCC's refusal to set specific limits on advertising in children's programs back before the commission for reconsideration at the end of the 1980s. ACT and others pressured Congress to pass a law limiting the amount of advertising in children's programs. Despite President Ronald Reagan's veto of the bill in 1988, the issue seemed likely to come up again in subsequent years.

15.3
News Impact

Since most people in the United States depend primarily on television for news (Roper Organization, 1987: 4), it seems safe to assume that television journalism has important effects. Presumably, most of us perceive the world beyond our neighborhoods pretty much the way the media present it to us, especially the video media.

Gatekeeping   Only a tiny fraction of the events that occur in the world on any given day end up on our plate as "the news of the day." On its way to becoming the neatly packaged tidbits of the evening news, the raw reportage of events passes through the hands of many *gatekeepers.* Some open and close gates deliberately, deciding which events to cover in which places and how stories should be written, edited, and positioned in the news presentation. Some gatekeeping occurs inadvertently, depending, for example, on the accessibility of news events and the availability of transportation or relay facilities. Some gatekeeping has an institutional and an ideological bias. Institutional biases can come from network organizations, for example, and ideological biases from individual allegiances to political, social, economic, or religious beliefs. Thus the media profoundly affect the material they transmit, both deliberately and inadvertently.

Involuntary gatekeeping comes from the fact that television demands pictures. This elementary need tends to bias the medium toward covering events that have intrinsic visual aspects, despite the fact that much news has no inherent pictorial content. Effects of visual bias in television news include (1) a preference for airing stories that have good pictures and (2) a forced effort to illustrate nonvisual stories with essentially irrelevant stock shots, as when scenes of bidding on the floor of the stock exchange illustrate a story on financial trends. To counter this tendency, news directors increasingly use computer-based graphics to illustrate nonpictorial stories with meaningful animated symbols, charts, and other "visuals."

Agenda Setting   One example of the filtering and shaping process of gatekeeping is control over which subjects will be presented to audiences. Gatekeeping focuses our attention on selected events, persons, and issues that are temporarily in the news. The list changes frequently as old items drop out and new ones claim attention. Researchers term this overall process of selection and ranking *agenda setting,* one of the primary ways in which media affect our perception of the world (Exhibit 15–4).

A related effect is derived from *prestige conferral.* The very fact that an event appears on the current news agenda gives it an aura of importance. Well-known anchors and correspondents lend glamour and significance to the events and persons they cover. Commenting on how television coverage has exaggerated the importance of the state primary elections that come earliest in national political campaigns, former presidential news secretary Ron Nessen pointed out that television acts as a kind of giant megaphone, greatly amplifying the significance of some events (Nessen, 1980). If the story were not important, would Dan Rather, Tom Brokaw, and Peter Jennings be covering it? Conversely, can an event really matter if the networks choose not to cover it?

In 1984–1985, for example, television helped focus U.S. and world attention on starvation in parts of Africa. The drought-caused human disaster had been building for two years before a BBC film team's report appeared on a November 1984 *NBC Nightly News.* The grim scenes of Ethiopian refugees, soon repeated on other television news programs, created a public outcry that vastly increased the aid effort. In mid-1985, *Live Aid,* an unprecedented satellite-fed 16-hour rock music marathon seen in more than 80 countries, led to promised contributions of some $75 million dollars. Television opened the gate and set the agenda for expanded aid efforts.

Media News Staging   Television's need for images creates an ever-present temptation to enhance the pictorial content of news stories artificially. Even when news crews make no move to provoke reactions, the very presence of cameras in tense situations tends to escalate or sensationalize ongoing action.

Legitimate exercise of news judgments in the editing process can raise awkward problems for conscientious broadcasters. News documentaries have often been charged with bias and tampering with the facts, as was argued in the Westmoreland v. CBS case discussed in Exhibit 18–2.

As a practical matter, a certain amount of artifice is accepted in news coverage. In televised interviews, for example, the camera usually focuses on the interviewee the entire time. Shots of the interviewer are usually taken afterward and spliced into the interview, to provide a visual give-and-take. This tactic allows a single camera to cover interviews. The FCC recognized the need for this kind of latitude, rejecting claims that the networks had staged fake news stories at the riot-plagued 1968 Democratic national convention in Chicago:

> In a sense, every television press conference may be said to be "staged" to some extent; depictions of scenes in a television documentary—on how the poor live on a typical day in the ghetto, for example—also necessarily involve camera direction, lights, action instruments, etc....Few would question the professional propriety of asking public officials to smile again or repeat handshakes while the cameras are focused upon them (FCC 1969: 656).

Pseudoevents Outright staging of events by the *subjects* of news occurs when press agents and public relations counselors seek to plant information in the media or to create happenings designed to attract media coverage. Daniel Boorstin (1964) coined the term *pseudoevent* to describe these contrived happenings, analyzing the many forms they take, such as press conferences, trial balloons, photo opportunities, news leaks of confidential information, and background briefings "not for attribution."

Not all preplanned events deserve condemnation. For a newsworthy figure such as a president, a certain amount of ceremonial event-making is expected. The events that deserve denigration as pseudoevents are deliberate attempts to palm off fabricated nonevents as genuine news. Organizations that are interested in maintaining a favorable public image constantly churn out self-serving material in the guise of news. Government departments no less than private organizations exploit pseudoevents.

Conscientious broadcast news departments avoid using self-serving news handouts. But free *news clips* tempt stations that are short on photographic material. These short items supplied by business and government public relations departments contain pictorially interesting material in which the real message is unobtrusively buried. For example, a dramatic sequence of helicopter shots showing offshore oil drilling that could be used to illustrate an energy story might just incidentally show the name of the company engaged in the drilling. Or a film about high school training in auto mechanics might happen to feature students working on a particular make of car (Kiester, 1974).

Publicity Crimes News staging for self-publicity took a vicious turn when terrorist organizations began committing crimes to gain news coverage. In the 1980s, small and desperate political or religious groups seeking world attention perpetrated events of seemingly random violence against usually innocent third parties with increasing frequency. Such *publicity crimes* paradoxically transform pseudoevents into real events. Bombings of airport terminals, hijackings, and kidnappings, the most common kinds of terrorist stories in the 1980s, posed

The top-rated Sunday evening news magazine program, which first aired in 1968, now stars journalists (clockwise from left) Ed Bradley, Mike Wallace, Steve Kroft, and Harry Reasoner. In the front row are Morley Safer and Meredith Vierra. Its popularity and role as an agenda setter give 60 Minutes *stories considerable impact.*

SOURCE: CBS News Photo.

difficult ethical dilemmas for the news media. The very act of reporting a publicity crime transforms the media into accomplices in the crime, and the avidity with which the public awaits the latest news about it makes members of the public accomplices as well.

Publicity crimes reached bizarre new heights with the taking of American hostages in the Middle East—American embassy personnel in Iran in 1979, TWA airline passengers in Beirut in 1985, and other hostages in Beirut in the late 1980s. The Iranian episode lasted 444 days, contributing to the downfall of the Carter administration. Never before had American broadcasters faced such a news dilemma. Every time they showed footage of street rallies with Iranian marchers burning American flags or of hostages paraded before cameras to mumble transparently grudging "praise" for their captors, the American networks gave the terrorists priceless publicity.

In the 17-day TWA standoff in Beirut six years later, newscasters developed every possible angle of the story, including seemingly intrusive interviews with hostage families. Intense network competition increased emphasis on the crisis. Even before it finally ended, a hue and cry went up that television's massive coverage encouraged future terrorists by providing them with an unedited national forum. Criticism centered largely on the indiscriminate relaying of news conferences staged and controlled by the terrorists. The media appeared captive to terrorist manipulation.

Airing of counterterrorist plans during the Beirut crisis led some to argue that television made a difficult situation worse by giving away knowledge of future U.S. responses. Later, however, the news media revealed that they had in fact shown restraint in not disclosing certain U.S. countermoves.

Effects on People Covered   Media coverage of the celebration over the return of the Iranian hostages in 1981 and of those from the TWA plane in 1985 raised questions about the effects of media coverage on those returning. Some critics even speculated that the overwhelming barrage of media attention might cause more psychological trauma than the imprisonment itself.

In less unusual situations, media coverage undoubtedly does affect news subjects. For example, many people featured in *60 Minutes* reports have ended up paying fines or going to jail after on-camera exposure by reporters such as Mike Wallace (Kowet, 1979). Though the coverage itself did not cause the penalties, the cameras and reporters called attention to the subjects' earlier actions in compelling fashion.

More widespread but also more ambiguous effects on news subjects may occur when television covers court trials (Exhibit 18–3). For years legal authorities banned cameras and microphones in

virtually all courtrooms. The ban arose from the assumptions that (1) broadcast coverage would affect the behavior of witnesses, lawyers, and defendants, and that (2) these effects would be detrimental to the judicial process. Experience later showed, however, that once the novelty of being photographed wore off, subjects of coverage betrayed little reaction. They eventually accepted the equipment and crew as a normal part of the environment.

Three factors account for this minimal effect. Equipment became smaller and less obtrusive than it was when the ban first went into effect. Broadcast news crews became more professional and more sensitive to the need to avoid disruption. Also, society became more tolerant, even expectant, of broadcast access to official activities. Increased public access has been specifically mandated by *sunshine laws* (which require many official bodies to meet in public) and the *Freedom of Information Act* (which mandates access to many types of government information formerly withheld from public scrutiny). These changes suggest that although news coverage may have unwanted effects, they may not be as unfavorable as at first supposed.

15.4
Political Effects

Politicians recognized from the outset that broadcasting had significant implications for the electoral process. They saw to it that they would have fair access to the new medium when running for election. Beyond this self-serving consideration, broadcasting had obvious importance as a means of facilitating democratic processes.

Crisis Management   In times of crisis, open communication allays panic and eases the stress of transition. The electronic media, with their immediacy and instant national scope, can play a vital role in managing crisis situations.

The first great test of television's role in such a crisis came in November 1963, when President John F. Kennedy was assassinated in Dallas. Canceling commercials and commercial programs for "the most massive and the most concentrated broadcasting coverage in history," the networks won praise for competence, sensitivity, and dignity in handling the crisis (*Broadcasting,* 2 Dec. 1963).

Since then, the media have risen to the occasion of other national crises with equal distinction. For example, the broadcast networks covered the historic House Judiciary Committee hearings on impeachment charges against President Richard Nixon in full in the summer of 1974. For 54 days, they rotated the assignment day by day. It was the first time the House had permitted television coverage of any of its committee hearings, and the experience helped pave the way for full television coverage of House activity, as discussed later in this section.

Election Campaigns   Almost from its beginning, broadcasting has exerted a powerful influence on political campaigning. Radio speeches by Calvin Coolidge, whose low-key delivery suited the microphone, may have been a factor in his 1924 reelection. Radio became especially important to Democratic candidates because it gave them a chance to appeal directly to voters, going over the heads of the newspapers, most of which were controlled by Republicans. Franklin Roosevelt used radio masterfully in his four presidential campaigns, starting in 1932.

Television brought Madison Avenue sales techniques to the presidential campaign of 1952, when a specialist in the hard-sell commercial, Rosser Reeves, designed spots for Dwight Eisenhower. The commercialization of political campaigns has increased ever since. By 1968, when Richard Nixon won the presidential election, television had become—and remains—the most important factor in political campaigning.

Since 1968, national party conventions have been completely restaged to make them more effective as television programs. Convention managers time events to the second, with a certain number of minutes allowed for so-called spontaneous demonstrations. They leave little to chance, and by 1988 had the ironic effect of forcing the networks to reconsider just how much news value they had. Network

officials said that the predictability of the 1988 conventions and their consequent low viewer interest might well make them the last to be covered outside of normal news programming hours.

Starting in 1960, televised debates between presidential candidates began to steal the spotlight from the conventions as campaign highlights. This tradition began with the 1960 confrontation between candidates Kennedy and Nixon, made possible by a special act of Congress exempting their televised appearance from the law guaranteeing equal opportunities to opposing candidates. Often called the "Great Debates" (though in fact neither great nor debates), these carefully choreographed contests may have decided that close race. Exhaustive research suggests that Kennedy came across to viewers as more precise and visually crisp than Nixon (Rubin, 1967).

After the Kennedy–Nixon confrontations, presidential debates lapsed for 16 years, mainly because the incumbent president would not agree to face his opponent. Then, in 1976, President Gerald Ford, running for national office for the first time, agreed to debate Democratic nominee Jimmy Carter, who won the election. A pattern seemed to be in the making four years later when President Carter agreed to debate GOP nominee Ronald Reagan, and once again the incumbent lost. But the pattern reversed in 1984, when President Reagan faced Democrat Walter Mondale. Many believed that Reagan lost the first debate but came back much stronger in the second, recovering the momentum of his campaign and going on to win a landslide reelection.

The two 1988 televised debates between President George Bush and Democratic nominee Michael Dukakis seemed to have little overall impact on the election's outcome. Bush came across as "lean and mean," whereas Dukakis seemed wooden and cold in some of his responses. The single vice presidential debate showed up the weakness of the ill-informed Dan Quayle.

Given the power of television to influence campaign outcomes, it might seem a foregone conclusion that candidates with the most money to buy the most time and the best media consultants would inevitably win elections. But experience has shown

EXHIBIT 15–5   Televised Election Debates

A.

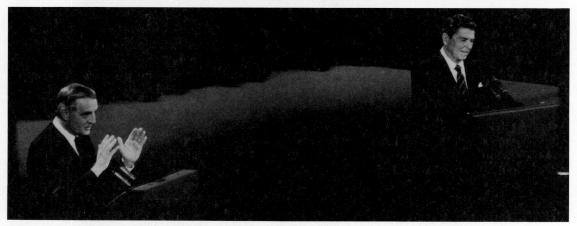

B.

C.

Nationally televised presidential debates have become standard campaign rituals. (A) John F. Kennedy debates Richard M. Nixon in one of four confrontations in 1960, with Howard K. Smith of CBS as moderator. The next debate would come only after 16 years, when Jimmy Carter debated—and beat—Gerry Ford. (B) Walter Mondale faces Ronald Reagan in the first debate of the 1984 campaign. (C) Michael Dukakis debated Vice President George Bush in the 1988 race. The format changed only slightly over nearly three decades.

SOURCES: (A) CBS News Photo; (B) and (C) UPI Bettmann News photos.

that candidates with the greatest access to television do not always win. One reason may be that television provides coverage in two different forms—as undisguised partisan advertising and as objective news and public-affairs coverage. Bona fide news and public-affairs programs about candidates have a credibility that 30-second advertising spots and candidate-controlled appearances can never obtain.

Moreover, critics may have overstated the extent to which candidates rely on broadcasting. A study commissioned by the National Association of Broadcasters analyzed officially reported 1986 campaign expenditures by federal Senate and House candidates. It indicated that although broadcasting claimed the biggest slice of their $400 million combined campaign budgets, it accounted for only a quarter of the total. Senate candidates spent more than House candidates, more than a third of their total budget. Mail expenses came second among media costs (NAB, 1988).

The impact of television coverage on presidential campaigns becomes especially controversial on the evening of national election days. Early television reports of voting trends in the eastern states have been blamed for the lower voter turnout in the West. Many members of Congress have felt that early predictions and candidate concessions of defeat adversely affect state elections, although few research findings have been reported. The networks agreed in 1985 not to air predictions of a state's results until after the polls in that state had closed. By and large they adhered to that promise in reporting results of the national elections of 1986 and 1988.

Presidential Television   After the campaign, the elected American president enjoys almost insurmountable advantages over political opponents in exploiting the media. Other branches of government and members of opposing parties can do little to counterbalance the pervasive influence of *presidential television*. Presidents have endless opportunities to manufacture pseudoevents to support their policies or to divert attention from their failures. No matter how blatant the exploitation by presidents and their staffs seem, editors dare not ignore presidential events. Virtually everything the head of state says or does has inherent news value.

Presidents often make foreign visits to other heads of state as a diversionary tactic. President Kennedy seems to have been the first to capitalize on this ploy: "The farther he was from Washington, the less he was seen as a partisan political figure and the more he was viewed as being President of all the people" (Halberstam, 1979: 316). President Nixon used the same tactics, making several overseas trips at the height of his domestic Watergate troubles.

As their single most powerful weapon, incumbent chief executives can call upon the broadcast networks to provide simultaneous national coverage of a presidential address (Exhibit 15–6). The emergence of CNN's two news networks has added to a president's impact by providing still more White House coverage for cable viewers. National addresses can give the president a gigantic captive television audience—a virtual monopoly of access to some 70 percent of the potential viewers. Moreover, opinion surveys suggest that such exposure usually pays off in increased acceptance of presidential policies.

No law requires networks to defer to presidential requests for time. Indeed, not until President Lyndon Johnson's administration (1963–1969) did such requests become customary. From 1966 through 1984, the networks gave time for more than 80 presidential speeches, and rejected just four (two by CBS, and one each by ABC and NBC). Perhaps because of the Nixon administration's Watergate troubles, network news divisions began to evaluate such requests more critically after 1974. Presidents Nixon, Ford, Carter, and Reagan were each turned down at least once when requesting time.

Ronald Reagan used broadcasts more effectively than any president since Franklin Roosevelt in the 1930s. A one-time radio sports announcer and a long-time veteran of political broadcasts, Reagan gave unusual attention to radio, recording a weekly radio address for Saturday airing throughout his two terms. Other media often quoted his radio remarks.

All presidents since the broadcasting era have

EXHIBIT 15–6   Presidential Television

Number of prime-time appearances

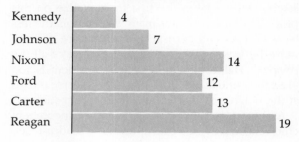

President	Appearances
Kennedy	4
Johnson	7
Nixon	14
Ford	12
Carter	13
Reagan	19

Hours of prime-time airtime

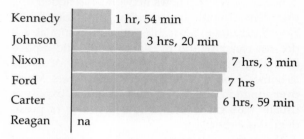

Kennedy	1 hr, 54 min
Johnson	3 hrs, 20 min
Nixon	7 hrs, 3 min
Ford	7 hrs
Carter	6 hrs, 59 min
Reagan	na

These figures cover the first 19 months in office for Presidents Kennedy, Johnson, and Nixon; the first 15 months for Ford; and the first 25 months for Carter and Reagan. Figures include both news conferences and other appearances.

SOURCE: Sterling, 1984: 177.

been accused at times of dodging direct confrontations with the press, preferring carefully orchestrated appearances controlled by the White House. For example, presidential "photo opportunities" create a favorable picture-taking environment, but usually ban questions from reporters. Ronald Reagan was prone to embarrassing errors when replying to questions in unscripted situations, obliging his staff to follow up with hasty "clarifications." This weakness kept Reagan even more isolated from give-and-take situations with reporters than previous chief executives. Frustrated by their lack of access, White House correspondents resorted to shouting questions at the president as he crossed the White House lawn to and from the presidential helicopter—an undignified practice encouraged by presidential remoteness but useful to the administration as a way of making reporters appear uncouth.

Congressional Television During television's formative years, older politicians such as House Speaker Sam Rayburn dominated Congress. Rayburn had no love for the press. When handed a petition from journalists asking for more radio and television access to cover the House, Rayburn simply muttered an obscenity and tore up the paper. Lack of television coverage limited the public impact of the House. Only when the president came to address a joint session did television enter Congress: "Then the congressmen could be seen dutifully applauding, their roles in effect written in by the President's speech writers" (Halberstam, 1979: 250).

The Senate, unlike the House, began allowing television coverage of its committee hearings (subject to committee chair approval) as early as the 1950s, leading to some notable television public affairs coverage that had repercussions on the careers of participants.* The first televising of a House committee's deliberations came only in 1974, when the Judiciary Committee debated the Nixon impeachment resolution. But for decades neither

---

*In 1951, his role in televised hearings on organized crime catapulted Senator Estes Kefauver (D–TN) onto the Democratic ticket in the following year's presidential campaign. The televised Army–McCarthy hearings in 1954 led to the censure of the Wisconsin senator by his colleagues and ultimately to the end of McCarthyism, the far-right communist witch-hunt that he led. Investigation of Teamster union officials began with Senate hearings in 1956–1957, showing the talents of a young government attorney named Robert Kennedy. The 1973 Watergate hearings chaired by folksy but astute Senator Sam Erwin (D–NC) made him a star, and the 1974 Nixon impeachment proceedings propelled many congressmen to fame. Hearings on the "Iran-Contra" scandal during the Reagan administration made a national folk hero out of Marine Lt. Col. Oliver North when he testified for three days in mid-1988.

congressional body allowed broadcast access to its legislative sessions on the floor.

In 1966 Congress began a counterattack on presidential television. That year, Senator William Fulbright, chairperson of the prestigious Foreign Relations Committee, boldly questioned White House policy on the Vietnam War in televised hearings before his committee:

Television had confirmed the legitimacy of the President, made his case seem stronger than it was, and made the opposition appear to be outcasts, frustrated, angry, and rather beyond the pale. The Fulbright hearings gradually changed this balance. Like the Ervin ["Watergate"] hearings some seven years later, they were the beginning of a slow but massive educational process, a turning of the tide against the President's will and his awesome propaganda machinery. (Halberstam, 1979: 506)

Although bills to authorize radio coverage of House debates had appeared regularly since 1941, approval for live television as well as radio coverage finally came only in 1979. Even then, the House refused to let outsiders run the show, but established its own closed-circuit television system run by House employees. Broadcasters could carry the signal, live or recorded, at will. Unenthusiastic about coverage they do not themselves control, commercial broadcasters use only occasional excerpts of House debates. Cable subscribers, however, see gavel-to-gavel coverage on C-SPAN, the cable industry's noncommercial public-affairs network.

House coverage became briefly controversial in 1984 when television cameras began to pan the House floor during speeches. Before that they had focused only on podium speakers. The Democratic House leadership used this ploy to embarrass Republican speechmakers delivering addresses for home consumption to a virtually empty House chamber.

The overall favorable record of House television encouraged the Senate to experiment with live radio coverage in 1978 when National Public Radio carried some 300 hours of debate on the Panama Canal treaties. Finally, in 1986, the Senate approved television coverage of all floor sessions. Congress had at last achieved a degree of video parity with the White House. C-SPAN officials regarded this move as important enough to justify adding a second channel to its service, C-SPAN II (Exhibit 15–7).

By the 1980s, both Congress and the administration had developed sophisticated facilities for exploiting television. The House and Senate maintained fully equipped studios for the personal use of members, and the White House could make news feeds and interviews available on short notice from its own studio facilities, as well as handling call-in interviews from local stations.

15.5
Television and War

Radio broadcasting played a highly supportive role in helping to build both civilian and military morale during World War II. Television's first experience of war came with the Vietnam conflict (the Korean War of 1950–1953 occurred during the formative years of television news, when live coverage from such a remote distance was impossible). Television made Vietnam a "living room war," in the words of *New Yorker* critic Michael Arlen (1969). Television affected both national morale and government policy in that conflict and in the later Central American guerrilla wars.

Vietnam   David Halberstam, who won a Pulitzer prize for his work as a war correspondent in Vietnam, supports the thesis that television had a decisive impact. "The war played in American homes and it played too long" (Halberstam, 1979: 507). In total, this longest war in United States history played in living rooms for 15 years. CBS sent its first combat news team to Vietnam in 1961, and news photography of the final evacuation of Saigon, showing desperate pro-American Vietnamese being beaten back as helicopters lifted off the landing pad atop the U.S. Embassy, came in 1975.

During the earlier years of the Vietnam War, coverage tended to be "sanitized," stressing U.S. efficiency and military might and playing down the gore and suffering of actual combat. Little military

EXHIBIT 15-7   C-SPAN and Congress

A.

B.

(A) Speaker of the House Thomas Foley opens a session of U.S. House of Representatives floor debate as covered by official congressional technicians and carried live by the cable industry's C-SPAN network. (B) In 1986, C-SPAN opened a second channel to cover the U.S. Senate, where speeches were often addressed to a nearly empty Senate chamber.

SOURCE: Nan M. Gibson/C-SPAN.

censorship had been imposed, as it had been in all previous wars, but in this undeclared war, the generals and the White House had public relations uppermost in their minds. Field commanders went to great lengths to obtain the kind of optimistic coverage expected by the administration back home.

A new, more violent phase of news coverage came as a result of the 1968 Tet offensive, which brought fighting to the very doors of the Saigon hotels where correspondents stayed. At that point, broadcast news coverage turned to combat realities. Vietnam became a real war in American living rooms, not the sanitized war of military public relations. Each network maintained its own news bureau in the field, with each bureau sending back two or three photographic stories and eight or ten radio tapes daily. In addition, many individual stations assigned reporters to the scene. Analyzing the contradictory

images projected by television news, critic Edward Epstein wrote in *TV Guide:*

> It is no doubt true that television was to a large extent responsible for the disillusionment with the war, as those in the media take relish in pointing out. But it is also true that television must take responsibility for creating—or at least, reinforcing—the illusion of American military omnipotence on which much of the early support of the war was based (1973a: 54).

Following the Tet Offensive by the North Vietnamese, several events combined to turn the U.S. opinion against the war. For one thing, the leading television journalist, CBS's Walter Cronkite, reported negatively on the war after a visit to Vietnam (as David Halberstam put it, for the first time a war had been declared over by an anchorman). Loss of Cronkite's support for the war solidified

President Lyndon Johnson's decision not to run for re-election.

At about the same time, two especially vivid photographic images from the battlefields became icons of American disillusionment. Correspondent Morley Safer was responsible for one, a film showing an American Marine holding a Zippo lighter to the straw thatch of a South Vietnamese hut, starting a fire that leveled 150 homes in the village of Cam Ne. The second image, recorded during the 1968 Tet Offensive, showed a South Vietnamese general calmly shooting a suspected Vietcong sympathizer in the head (Exhibit 15–8).*

Post-Vietnam Military Actions The role of broadcasting in the Vietnam conflict raised troublesome questions about future war reporting. Could a nation at war afford to allow television to bring home the horror of combat night after night? The 1983 terrorist bombing that killed some 240 Americans in the U.S. Marine barracks in Beirut seemed a case in point. U.S. television coverage of the bombing's aftermath undermined public support for the "peacekeeping" role of the Marines in Lebanon, making the venture politically untenable. The United States pulled its troops out of the area shortly thereafter.

On the other hand, would the U.S. public blindly support a war that was kept temporarily invisible by rigid military censorship? To the dismay of journalists, the U.S. invasion of the tiny Caribbean island of Grenada in 1984 suggested that it might. Alleging security concerns, the White House instructed the military to bar all press access to the initial assault. For the first 48 hours, the world knew what happened only from military press releases. Subsequent press disclosures of military bumbling in conducting the invasion and apparent official misrepresentation of the circumstances leading to the

---

*Controversy over the war and its coverage was revived a decade later when General William Westmoreland, once U.S. commander in Vietnam, brought suit against CBS for a *60 Minutes* report alleging a cover-up in reports of enemy troop strength, as discussed in Section 18.2.

invasion came too late to dispel entirely the aura of success and righteousness surrounding the Grenada "rescue" of American civilians allegedly endangered by the volatile political situation on the island (Hannan, 1988).

The U.S. public apparently largely supported the action and applauded the administration's decision to circumvent the press. Nevertheless, the strong criticism of this abrupt departure from the usual practice (for example, journalists landed in France on D-Day in World War II, an infinitely more sensitive security risk than the landing on Grenada) led to Pentagon agreement that in future military actions the authorities would set up a news pool to cover events from the outset.

When American fighter-bombers attacked targets in Libya in 1987, and again when an American navy vessel accidentally shot down an Iranian airliner over the Persian Gulf in 1988, the military reported in detail almost immediately after the conclusion of the actions. There were no news blackouts.

The Reagan administration's efforts to bring down the Sandanista regime in Nicaragua and the guerrilla fighting in several Central American countries served as testing grounds for television journalism's post-Grenada maturity. Controversy surrounded coverage of these conflicts. New Right politicians claimed that television weakened efforts to gain public support for "freedom fighters"; others, remembering Vietnam, said that aggressive television coverage might serve to keep American soldiers out of another prolonged, undeclared conflict.

A different problem emerges when the media try to cover a story in another country and the local government does not want the story reported. Weeks of peaceful student demonstrations in Beijing in the People's Republic of China in mid-1989 were widely covered by satellite-delivered reports on CNN and the networks—until Chinese officials "pulled the plug," fearing world reaction to live pictures of the military repression to come. Viewers then saw news reports based only on still photos, maps of the downtown part of the city, and reporters' voices via telephone circuit, rather than the on-the-spot live pictures they had come to expect. Still, even such

EXHIBIT 15–8   Televised War

A.

B.

The networks reported the Vietnam war nightly for more than a decade. Two famous visual images of the war still have impact years later. Both came from televised stories carried on evening network newscasts. (A) A marine touches the roof thatch of a South Vietnamese hut with his lighter to burn potential enemy hiding places. (B) The chief of the South Vietnamese police kills a Viet Cong suspect during the 1968 Tet Offensive.

SOURCES: (A) Courtesy CBS; (B) AP/Wide World Photos.

limited reporting prompted protest demonstrations by Chinese and others in cities around the world.

15.6
The Role of Entertainment

Entertainment, as well as news and public affairs, tends to reinforce the media's agenda-setting role. Any big news story that captures the headlines for long will soon become grist for comment in comedy series—or more usefully as the subject of a special drama or a miniseries and may influence future episodes of established series. Docudramas, those controversial blends of fact and fiction, are evidence of this tendency. By changing the facts around to suit the needs of drama, they add still more distortions to the already simplified version of reality presented to broadcast audiences.

Stereotypes   Fiction influences audience perceptions by reinforcing *stereotypes,* versions of reality that are deliberately oversimplified to fit in with preconceived images, such as the stock characters of popular drama: the Italian gangster, the inscrutable Oriental, the mad scientist, the bespectacled librarian.

Even authors who are capable of more individualized and realistic character portrayals resort to stereotypes when writing for television, to save time—both their own and that of the medium. Stories must unfold with the utmost efficiency to fit within the confines of half-hour and hour-long formats (minus time-outs for commercials, of course):

> Television dramas have little time to develop situations or characters, necessitating the use of widely accepted notions of good and evil. Since the emphasis is on resolving the conflict or the problem at hand, there is little time to project the complexities of a character's thoughts or feelings or for dialogues which explore human relationships. To move the action along rapidly, the characters must be portrayed in ways which quickly identify them. Thus the character's physical appearance, environment, and behavior conform to widely accepted notions of the types of people they represent. (U.S. Commission on Civil Rights, 1977: 27).

Stereotypical images on television help to establish and perpetuate those same images in the minds of viewers. As the U.S. Commission on Civil Rights put it, "To the extent that viewers' beliefs, attitudes, and behavior are affected by what they see on television, relations between the races and the sexes may be affected by television's limited and often stereotyped portrayals." The commission carefully avoided asserting flatly that such effects always occur, but it called for research to assess the extent to which they do occur.

World of Fiction   When researchers take a census of the characters in a body of television plays,* they find that the demographic characteristics of the fictional population invariably differ markedly from real people in the real world. Compared with life, the world of fiction has far more men than women, for example, most of them young adults, with few very young or elderly persons. Many have no visible means of support, but those who do work have interesting, exciting, action-filled jobs. Fiction therefore contains an unrealistically high proportion of detectives, criminals, doctors, scientists, business executives, and adventurers compared with the real world, where unglamourous, dull, and repetitive jobs dominate. Most people in the real world solve their personal problems undramatically, even anticlimactically or incompletely, using socially approved methods. Fictional characters tend to solve their problems with decisive, highly visible acts, often entailing violence.

Of course, none of this should surprise us. Fact may be stranger than fiction, but fact does not occur in neatly packaged half-hour episodes, with periodic commercial interruptions.

Socialization   Nevertheless, the make-believe world of radio and television serves as a model of reality for countless people, especially for children at the very time when they are eagerly reaching out to learn about the world. Those who are too young to read, those who never learned to read or acquired the habit of reading, and those who have little access to printed sources of information and entertainment all depend heavily on radio and television to inform them of the world outside their own immediate surroundings.

Dramatic fare has special influence because viewers and listeners identify with heroes, participating vicariously in their adventures. Research indicates that young children are especially vulnerable. They tend to believe what they see on television, making no distinction between fact, fiction, and advertising. Disadvantaged children tend to believe fiction more readily than those whose lives contain more opportunities for learning.

Given the enormous amount of time most children spend watching television, broadcasting has become a major agent of *socialization*—that all-important process that turns a squalling infant into a functioning member of society. Socialization, though a lifelong process, occurs intensively during the first few years of life, the time when children begin to learn the language, the meticulously detailed rules of behavior, and the value system of their culture.

In the past, socialization has always been the jealously guarded prerogative of family and religion, formalized by education and extended by peer-group experiences. The intrusion of a new, external agent of socialization represents a profound change. Of course, broadcasting functions as part of national culture, too, but it comes from beyond the immediate circle of the family and its community-linked supports. It imports ideas, language, images, and practices that may be alien to the local culture.

The question of how the intrusion of broadcasting has affected the socialization process has been widely researched and debated. Broadcasting can, of course have good (prosocial) and bad (antisocial) effects. Producers researched and designed such programs as *Sesame Street* and *Fat Albert and the Cosby Kids* with prosocial effects in mind. Follow-up research indicates that such programs do in fact succeed in achieving prosocial results.

---

*Such censuses have often been made of fictional populations in the course of content analysis studies, useful for describing the messages implicit in media content.

Much more effort, however, has gone into research to prove the existence of antisocial consequences of television program content, especially the effects of violence. In the late 1980s, there was a flurry of concern about the negative social impacts of some popular song lyrics (as well as music videos) that appeared to condone drugs or violence. A related topic, the effects of pornography, has been also studied intensively. This research is not discussed here because pornography, as legally defined, has so far been effectively excluded from broadcasting, although it plays a minor role in pay cable. The moralistic campaigns against sex in broadcast television that erupt periodically target programs that do not remotely approach legally preventable pornography.

Significance of Time Spent   One cannot help feeling that any activity that takes up as much of people's time as radio and television do must have profound effects. At the very least, time spent watching or listening could have been spent in some other way—perhaps on some useful, constructive activity. Some critics take it for granted that *anything* active would be more beneficial than passive absorption. This criticism seems to imply a moral judgment, the unstated feeling that it is wrong for people to waste their time staring like zombies at the television tube. Long ago one of the pioneers of social research, Paul Lazarsfeld, noted this tone of moral criticism. He pointed out that intellectuals who had fought for shorter hours and other labor reforms unconsciously resented the fact that the masses failed to take constructive advantage of their hard-won leisure. Instead they "wasted" it in passive enjoyment of broadcasting (Lazarsfeld and Kendall, 1948: 85). But it has not been demonstrated that listening and watching necessarily displace more useful and active forms of recreation. In the absence of radio and television, people would do other things with their time, of course, but these would not necessarily be better or more beneficial things. And in fact, many people keep their radios or television sets turned on while doing other things.

In any event, all those hours of passive listening and watching may be far less significant than they seem. Subjectively, time is relative, dragging on interminably in some circumstances, passing all too quickly in others. Each hour on the clock has exactly the same value; not so each hour of human experience. It follows that the huge amount of time that audiences devote to broadcasting may have far less psychological significance than the sheer number of hours suggests.

Play Theory   Nor can we assume that time spent passively listening and watching has value only if it is devoted to programs that uplift, educate, and inform. People also have a need to simply pass time painlessly. That, after all, is what *pastimes* are for, and electronic media are the most universal pastimes.

Media effects researchers usually study the media from the point of view of serious, socially significant consequences, such as those discussed thus far. They want to know how broadcasting affects buying, voting, stereotyping, learning, aggression, and so on. A researcher who stands out as a notable exception to this rule concluded that "at best mass communication allows people to become absorbed in *subjective play.*" Playing does not merely substitute for some valuable activity, but counts as a valuable activity in itself. It is vital to all human life—"thousands of customs, devices, and occasions are employed to gratify playing in every culture of the world, in all history" (Stephenson, 1967).

Unfortunately, researcher William Stephenson linked his play theory to an idiosyncratic research method that failed to gain widespread adoption. For that reason, his play concept has not received the attention it deserves. One commentator concluded, "After once exposing oneself to this brilliantly conceived theory, one can never again ignore the importance of the play-pleasure elements in communication" (Schramm, 1973: 26).

"Glow and Flow" Principle   The play theory helps to explain the widely acknowledged fact that programs seem of secondary importance as long as something fills the screen. Early in television history, a commentator observed that "it is the television set and the watching experience that entertains. Viewers seem to be entertained by *the glow* *and the flow*" (Meyersohn, 1957: 347, emphasis added).

In a landmark study of television audience attitudes, Steiner found that most of the people surveyed said they were more satisfied with television as a *medium* than they were with specific *programs*. He noted that "A large number of respondents were ready to say television is both relaxing *and* a waste of time" (Steiner, 1963: 411). Similar studies of attitudes made one and two decades later indicated that this ambivalence persisted (Bower, 1973, 1985).

The glow-and-flow principle comes sharply to the fore in situations where electronic media become the only companions people have. When Steiner asked respondents to describe the satisfactions they derived from watching television, he sometimes received moving testimonials such as this:

> I'm an old man and all alone, and the TV brings people and talk into my life. Maybe without TV, I would be ready to die; but this TV gives me life. It gives me what to look forward to—that tomorrow, if I live, I'll watch this and that program (Steiner, 1963: 26).

At extreme levels of deprivation, in hospitals and similar institutions, television has a recognized therapeutic function as the most valuable nonchemical sedative available.

Electronic media answer a compelling need of the mass audience simply to kill time painlessly, to fill an otherwise unendurable void. The media give people a way of *performing leisure*. But social critics worry that while we relax with our guard down watching television, the violence portrayed in many programs may have antisocial effects.

15.7
Impact of Violence

Concern that the portrayal of violence and crime might have antisocial effects dates back to well before television. The first systematic research on the effects of media violence dates from the 1930s, when a foundation underwrote a series of studies on the impact of feature films (Jowett, 1976: 220). Concern about the potential effects of violence shifted to radio and comic books in the 1950s, and later to television and rock videos. Along the way, emphasis shifted toward buttressing conclusions about effects with scientific evidence and some sort of explanatory theory, rather than merely taking effects for granted.

Direct Imitation   We occasionally see news reports of real-life violence that has apparently been modeled on similar actions in films or television programs. A child watches Superman fly and tries to do the same thing, with disastrous results. It seems natural to assume that such imitation proves that televised violence sometimes *causes* violent behavior. Exhaustive research demonstrates, however, that viewing a violent act at most serves as a *contributing factor* to any subsequent imitation of that act. In other words, the act of viewing takes place within a larger *context*—one's background, education, predispositions, and the like. Taken together, all these influences may, in some circumstances, lead to violent behavior.

A particularly repellent example of apparent imitation led to an unprecedented lawsuit. In 1974 NBC broadcast a made-for-television film called *Born Innocent,* in which inmates of a detention home for young delinquents "raped" a young girl with a mop handle. Four days after the telecast, older children subjected a nine-year-old California girl to a similar ordeal, using a bottle. Parents of the child sued NBC, asking $11 million in damages for negligence in showing the rape scene, which, they alleged, had directly incited the attack on their daughter.

The case raised a major issue: could broadcasters be held legally responsible for the reactions of audience members to their programs? Network attorneys persuaded the trial judge to define the issue as a First Amendment question, rather than as one of negligence. The case collapsed when it thus became impossible to show that NBC had surrendered its First Amendment protection by *deliberately inciting* the children to attack their victim (Cal., 1981: 888).

Generalized Violence Effects   Public concern about media violence arises primarily from possible generalized effects rather than from the risk of occasional direct imitations. Critics assume that adverse social effects are far more widespread and pervasive than isolated instances of imitation. This point of view emerged in another much-publicized court case in 1977.

The State of Florida charged a 16-year-old Florida boy, Ronnie Zamora, with murdering an elderly neighbor during an attempted robbery. The boy's attorney tried to build his defense on the argument that Zamora could not be held responsible for his violent behavior: he had become a television addict, "intoxicated" by the thousands of murders he had seen enacted on the screen. The trial judge rejected this argument, and the jury convicted the boy of murder. Though ill-considered, his lawyer's attempt to blame television for the crime drew its inspiration from the findings of research on the generalized adverse effects of televised violence that had accumulated during the 1970s.

The Surgeon General's Scientific Advisory Committee on Television and Social Behavior sponsored a large group of studies in 1969–1971. Congress allotted a million dollars for the research, which resulted in 1972 in five volumes of reports and papers. When questioned by a Senate Committee, the Surgeon General said flatly:

> The broadcasters should be put on notice. The overwhelming consensus and the unanimous Scientific Advisory Committee's report indicates that televised violence, indeed, does have an adverse effect on certain members of our society. . . . [I]t is clear to me that the causal relationship between televised violence and antisocial behavior is sufficient to warrant appropriate and immediate remedial action (Senate CC, 1972: 26).

A comprehensive analysis of the research literature, commissioned by the committee, established that, of all the types of television effects that had been studied, television's linkage to aggression had been the most intensively analyzed. The fact that every research method available had been employed in the study of televised violence made the cumulative evidence of its effects especially persuasive. The researchers later summarized their findings in these words:

The evidence is that television may increase aggression by teaching viewers previously unfamiliar hostile acts, by generally encouraging in various ways the use of aggression, and by triggering aggressive behavior both imitative and different in kind from what has been viewed. Effects are never certain, because real-life aggression is strongly influenced by situational factors, and this strong role for situational factors means that the absence of an immediate effect does not rule out a delayed impact when the behavior in question may be more propitious (Comstock et al., 1978: 13).

As a result of this work, and other studies done in the years since (including a revisit a decade later by some of the same researchers involved in the 1972 report), Congress and private groups pressured the FCC to limit televised violence. Chiefly for fear of violating the First Amendment and because of the trend toward deregulation, no lasting governmental action ensued.

Violence and Perceptions of Reality   During the 1967–1968 television season, George Gerbner and his associates at the University of Pennsylvania began conducting annual analyses of television violence. From these data they constructed "The Violence Profile," based on a content analysis that enumerated every violent act in a sample week of prime-time and weekend morning network entertainment programs (Exhibit 15–9). In this way they tracked changes in the level of violence from year to year according to network and program type. The Gerbner data indicated, for example, that animated cartoons depict a higher percentage of violent acts that any other program category (the coding system counted comic as well as serious acts of violence).

Gerbner theorized that violence in programs creates anxiety in viewers because they tend to perceive the real world in terms of their television experiences. Viewers identify with victims of violence in fiction who resemble themselves. Gerbner found that the elderly, the poor, and blacks have high "risk ratios," or *expectations* of becoming victims. This anxiety effect, he said, may be a more important byproduct of television violence than the imitation effect.

EXHIBIT 15–9   Trends in Television Violence, 1971–1985

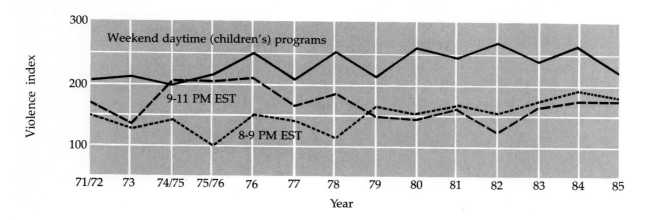

The scale from 0 to 300 on the left refers to the Gerbner "violence index," a measurement of the level of violence in programs that combines values for three variables: "the extent to which violence occurs at all in the program sampled, the frequency and rate of violent episodes, and the number of roles calling for characterization as violents, victims, or both." The dip in the 8–9 P.M. index in 1975 reflects the introduction of the family viewing hour restraints in that year (see Section 16.8). Notice that the index level for children's programs generally runs much higher than that for adult programs.

SOURCES: From "Television's Mean World," by George Gerbner, et al., in a report published for Annenberg School of Communications, University of Pennsylvania, 1986.

Desensitization   The Gerbner risk-ratio hypothesis reverses an older hypothesis that predicts that people exposed to fictional violence will become *desensitized*. According to the latter view, when the experience of violence in fiction becomes routine, people grow indifferent to real-life violence. The many instances of callousness in the face of urban violence that can be cited lend color to this hypothesis.

A related hypothesis holds that television depicts violence unrealistically because it has been deliberately *sanitized* in conformance with self-imposed codes. The consequences of fictional violence seem so neat and clean that viewers remain indifferent. They do not see what happens when real people get hurt. Audiences never see or hear the revolting, bloody aftermath, the screams of agony. Joseph

Wambaugh, a one-time police officer who became a writer of police stories, withdrew from a television series based on his writings because the producers treated violence so unrealistically, saying, "If they had a cop kill someone on TV, you never saw the blood. You never saw the face shot away. And you never saw the cop throwing up afterwards." Wambaugh put his finger on a seemingly insoluble dilemma: such graphic consequences should perhaps be seen for the object lesson they would convey, but the public and hence the media would never tolerate showing them.

In Defense of Violence   Given the range and depth of research evidence showing the antisocial effects of television violence, the television industry has found it increasingly difficult to defend its widespread use. Yet for television to serve as a medium for serious artistic expression for adult viewers, it cannot ban violence. After all, violence occurs in all forms of literature, even fairy tales for children. Bodies litter the stage when the curtain falls on some of Shakespeare's tragedies. Popular entertainment and sports have always featured violence.

Writers would face a difficult challenge if they had to meet television's relentless appetite for drama without resorting to violent clashes between opposing forces. A study of attitudes and opinions held by those responsible for network entertainment—the writers, producers, network executives, and program standards chiefs—supports this position (Baldwin & Lewis, 1972). A playwright expressed the problem by pointing out that authors have at their disposal four basic types of conflicts around which to build dramatic plots:

▌ *Man against nature:* "This is usually too expensive for television."

▌ *Man against God:* "Too intellectual for television."

▌ *Man against himself:* "Too psychological, and doesn't leave enough room for action."

▌ *Man against man:* "This is what you usually end up with."

Only one of the four lends itself to the limitations imposed by television, and that happens to be the one most likely to involve personal violence.

Defenders of current practice argue that violence in television merely reflects violence in real life. To ignore it or to pretend that it does not exist would restrict writers unreasonably. However, comparison of American culture with other cultures does not seem to bear out the assumption of a positive correlation between real and fictional violence:

> If television were the sole determinant of violent behavior, it would be difficult to explain the disparity in aggravated assault rates (almost 8 to 1) between Boston and Montreal, since these cities are both saturated with the same and similar television programs. This does not mean that there is no relationship between television violence and actual violence; it simply means that such a relationship cannot be defined explicitly at present (Kutach, 1978: 118).

Japan offers an interesting example in this connection. Crime statistics indicate that Japan has a much lower level of social violence than the United States. Yet Japanese television regularly imports the most violent of U.S. action dramas. Moreover, these imports seem mild compared to the ferocity seen in home-grown Japanese television plays.

Another justification of violence in programming holds that witnessing staged violence does good by defusing people's aggressive instincts. The ancient Greek theory of *catharsis,* as propounded by Aristotle, held that stage tragedy cleanses the emotions of the viewer through pity and fear. According to the analogous modern argument, fictional violence will drain off television viewers' aggressive feelings. Most experimental studies, however, suggest that seeing fictional violence arouses viewers' aggressive feelings rather than purging them (Comstock et al., 1978: 237).

Summary

▌ Early propaganda research relied on the simplistic bullet or hypodermic injection theory of communication effects. Post–World War II researchers examined the personal influence of opinion leaders who used media. Still later they studied the importance of selective exposure to and perception of media messages.

▌ Information theory applied engineering concepts to communication research in the 1950s. Klapper's 1960 survey showed that media largely served to reinforce audiences' existing beliefs and perceptions.

▌ As a medium of advertising, television can have a powerful impact on consumers, especially children. But as numerous business failures demonstrate, advertising alone cannot always create demand.

▌ Electronic media journalists largely define our world for us by a combination of gatekeeping and agenda setting. Media coverage can confer prestige, and by the same token can be exploited by the staging of pseudoevents. Terrorists who commit publicity crimes in order to gain attention present the media with the special dilemma of supporting terrorism simply by covering terrorist activities.

▋ Broadcasting, especially television, has long exerted a strong influence on U.S. election campaigns. Televised debates have been a regular feature of national campaigns since 1976. Congress opened itself up to regular television coverage, in part as a counterbalance to presidential television.

▋ Television coverage of the long and frustrating Vietnam War had a strong impact on American policy and American viewers. More recent war coverage has had a direct impact on the making of foreign and military policies.

▋ Television entertainment, which draws most of the audience most of the time, tends to reinforce stereotypes and to give a false impression of everyday life and work. Nevertheless, television can play positive roles in the socialization of children and in providing a needed leisure-time activity.

▋ The extent to which television contributes to violent behavior remains controversial even after massive research. The research indicates that the medium can at least be a contributing factor to violent action on the part of some people in some circumstances. It may also serve to desensitize others to violence. Violence on television can also heighten people's expectation of real-life violence.

CONTROLS

PART 6

Thus far we have explored the electronic media's historical development, physical limits, economic structure and support, programming, and audience research and impact. We turn now to the constraints society places on these media, especially on traditional broadcasting.

Chapter 16 reviews the formal laws and agencies that govern the electronic media, assessing the social control exerted by the nation's political climate, through public opinion and organized pressure groups, the educational system, and industry self-regulation. Chapter 17 discusses the single most important regulatory function—the licensing of stations and franchising of cable systems. It also traces the deregulatory trends that peaked in the 1980s. Chapter 18 then reviews the controversial constitutional issues that arise when formal controls are put into effect.

CHAPTER 16

REGULATION: LAWS
AND AGENCIES

The regulation of electronic media begins with establishing a constitutional basis on which to erect the statutory or legislative controls. These controls are embedded in the Communications Act, which defines the role of the Federal Communications Commission. This chapter also reviews other major agencies of control, both governmental and private, then describes some of the informal means society uses to influence the conduct of electronic media.

16.1
Federal Jurisdiction

The U.S. Constitution gives the federal government power over such areas as international relations and war-making, leaving all powers not specified as federal to the states. Before broadcasting could be regulated, it had to be decided whether it belonged under state or federal jurisdiction. Congress therefore had to find a constitutional justification for federal regulation of broadcasting, although broadcasting emerged long after the Constitution was written.

Broadcasting as Commerce The specific constitutional justification for Congress's taking control of radio comes from Article I, Section 8(3), which gives Congress the power "to regulate commerce with foreign nations, and among the several states." This, the well-known *commerce clause,* has played a vital role in U.S. economic development,

preventing individual states from undermining the unity of the nation by erecting internal trade barriers. Although not involving the exchange of tangible goods, the exchange of information by mail and wire had long been accepted as commerce under the Constitution. Thus, a statute governing radio could be regarded as justified by the commerce clause. That statute forms a link in a chain of responsibility extending from the Constitution to the people, as shown in Exhibit 16–1.

The commerce clause gives Congress jurisdiction over *interstate* and *foreign* commerce, but not over commerce within individual states. However, electromagnetic waves have an inherently interstate nature. Even radio services designed to cover only a limited area within a state—a radio-operated taxi-dispatching service, for example—cannot be stopped short at state boundaries. Zones of radio interference extend unpredictably far beyond zones of service. Wire communication, on the other hand, can be cut off precisely at any geographical boundary.*

---

*Either state or federal regulation governs telephone and related *common-carrier* services, depending on whether a given service crosses state lines. States have their own utility commissions that approve changes in telephone rates and service for in-state systems. Systems that cross state lines, however, need federal approval of changes in rates. In the mid-1980s, such regulation affected AT&T, the dominant long-distance carrier, and the *interstate* operations of the seven regional Bell Operating Companies.

EXHIBIT 16-1 Chain of Legal Authority

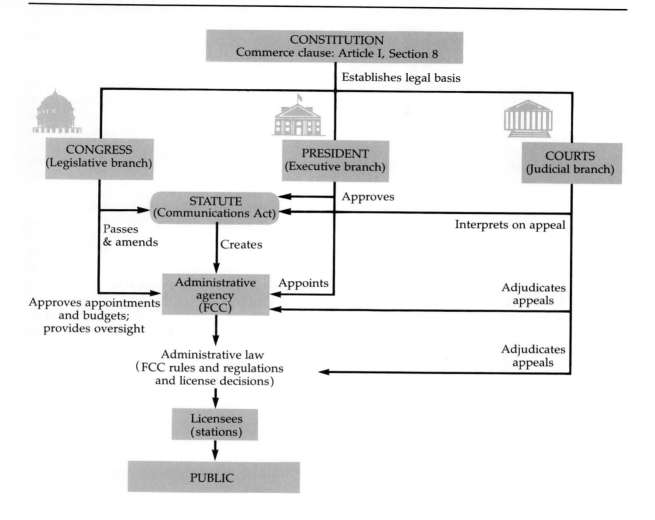

All three branches of government play a role in controlling electronic media under
the general umbrella of the Constitution.

Delegated Congressional Authority It
would be impossible for Congress itself to attend to
the endless details of regulation in specific fields.
Starting with the Interstate Commerce Commission
in 1887, Congress has delegated to a series of *independent regulatory agencies* the authority to supervise and regulate such often complex areas as commerce, power, transportation, labor, and finance.

Congress established the Federal Radio Commission in 1927 and its successor the *Federal Communications Commission* (FCC), in 1934 to act on
its behalf. Congress retains the power to regulate

communications, but assigns day-to-day authority to the FCC.

Although the president appoints the FCC commissioners, with the advice and consent of the Senate, the FCC remains a "creature of Congress." Congress defined the FCC's role in the Communications Act of 1934. Only Congress can change that role formally by amending or replacing the act, but the incumbent commissioners have considerable leeway in determining the regulatory atmosphere. The House and Senate subcommittees on communications constantly monitor the FCC, which must come back to Congress annually for budget appropriations. Moreover, since 1983 Congress has reauthorized the very existence of the commission every two years.*

Congress gave the FCC the power to adopt, modify, and repeal rules and regulations concerning interstate electronic media. These rules carry the force of federal law, deriving their power from Congress through the Communications Act. Any FCC rule not fully justified by the act can be nullified by successful appeal to the courts. Thus an understanding of the Communications Act is vital to an understanding of the FCC's day-to-day role.

16.2
Communications Act

As was described in Section 2.10, the Radio Act of 1927 brought to an end a period of chaotic development that dramatized the need for federal regulation. In the 1927 act, Congress for the first time crafted a statute—and created an agency—concerned explicitly with broadcasting.

Passage   The Radio Act of 1927 imposed order on broadcasting, but left control of some aspects of radio and all interstate and foreign *wire* communication scattered among several federal agencies. The Communications Act of 1934 brought wire as well as wireless communication under the control of the FCC, which replaced the FRC. This had minimal effect on broadcasting, however, because Congress simply re-enacted the broadcasting provisions of the 1927 law as a part of the 1934 act. Thus the framework of broadcast law dates back more than 60 years to the early development of radio. Although the Communications Act has been amended many times, its underlying concepts remain unchanged.

The very first paragraph of the 1934 act sets forth the underlying reasons for the creation of the FCC and the repeal of the 1927 act. Congress took action "to make available, so far as possible, to all the people of the United States a rapid, efficient, nationwide and world-wide wire and radio communication service with adequate facilities at reasonable charges."

Organization of Act   The Communications Act of 1934 consists of seven major parts called *titles*.* They cover the following general subjects:

I. Definition of terms; provision for setting up and operation of the FCC.
II. Common carriers.
III. Broadcast licensing, general powers of the FCC, program controls, public broadcasting.
IV. Hearings on and appeals from FCC decisions.
V. Penal provisions.
VI. Cable television.
VII. War emergency powers of the president; other general provisions.

---

*The change from permanent to temporary status of the independent regulators resulted from congressional displeasure with the aggressive regulatory policy of the Federal Trade Commission during the 1977–1981 Carter administration. Congress wanted more deference from the regulatory agencies. The reauthorization process lets Congress tack changes onto the Communications Act more easily when it wants to slow down or speed up FCC actions.

---

*Until late 1984, the act had six titles. However, when Congress passed the Cable Communications Policy Act of 1984, it became a new Title VI, making the existing VI Title VII. References to Title VI published before 1985 refer to what we now know as Title VII.

Definition of Broadcasting As related earlier, in the early 1920s AT&T tried to treat broadcasting as a common carrier, a communication service open to all comers without concern for what they communicate over the facilities. Telephone companies, the most familiar examples of common carriers, have been joined by other services using satellites, microwaves, optical fiber, and other high-technology devices that also fall under the common-carrier classification. Historically, common-carrier rates have been subject to government approval, by the FCC in the case of interstate operations and by the states for intrastate service, although with deregulation the extent of rate controls has been reduced.

If broadcasting were classed as a common carrier, programming would be entirely at the discretion of those who bought time on stations and networks, which in turn would probably be obliged to charge fixed prices in accordance with an FCC-approved tariff (rate scale). This common-carrier concept of broadcasting disappeared in 1926 when AT&T sold WEAF. The Communications Act formalizes the distinction in §3: "a person engaged in radio broadcasting shall not, insofar as such person is so engaged, be deemed a common carrier." The same section defines the term *broadcasting* as "the dissemination of radio communications intended to be received by the public directly or by intermediary or relay stations."

The key phrase "intended to be received by the public" excludes from the definition of broadcasting any private radio communication service aimed at individuals or specific groups of individuals. Yet radio communications that are not intended for the general public can be *received* by anyone who has the right kind of receiver. People can tune in to police, ship-to-shore, satellite, and other nonbroadcast transmissions for their own entertainment. But those who send such messages do not *intend* them for the general public; moreover, the Communications Act's §705(a) on "unauthorized publication or use" forbids the disclosure of nonbroadcast messages to people for whom they were not intended. Congress, the courts, and the FCC have also made it illegal for people to intercept for their own use nonbroadcast signals such as pay television. Nor may broadcasting be used to send private messages that are not intended for the general public. Thus, people who greet their families over the air during broadcast interviews are technically violating the law.

Finally, §3 of the act defines *radio communication* as "transmission by radio of writing, signs, signals, pictures, and sounds of all kinds, including all instrumentalities, facilities, apparatus, and services . . . incidental to such transmission." By giving the word *radio* such a broad definition, Congress made it possible for the radio provisions of the act to cover television when it became a licensed service nearly 15 years after adoption of the 1927 act.

Provision for FCC The president appoints the five FCC commissioners, with the advice and consent of the Senate. Congress sought to minimize economic and political bias on the part of the commission by allowing no more than three members from the same party.

§4 of the act gives the commission broad power to "perform any and all acts, make such rules and regulations, and issue such orders . . . as may be necessary in the execution of its functions." In a few instances Congress tied the commission's hands with hard-and-fast requirements, such as a limit on the terms of broadcasting licenses and the restriction on alien ownership of broadcast stations. But most provisions of the act give the commission wide latitude in applying its own experience and (presumably) expert judgment to the particular facts presented by each case.

Congress used a highly flexible yet legally recognized standard—public interest, convenience, or necessity (PICON)—to limit the commission's discretion when it makes a decision that is not dictated by specific requirements of the act. PICON occurs in every key section of the broadcasting parts of the act. For example, §303 begins: "Except as otherwise provided in this Act, the Commission from time to time, as *public convenience, interest, or necessity* requires shall. . . . (italics added)" The section goes on to list 19 functions, ranging from the power to classify radio stations to the power to make whatever rules and regulations are necessary to carry out the provisions of the act. The public-interest phrase similarly occurs in the crucial sections dealing with the grant, renewal, and transfer of broadcast licenses.

Defining Public Interest   Most people think of the public-interest clause as being aimed directly at broadcasters, forcing them to operate "in the public interest." In turn, broadcasters tend to picture themselves as constantly faced with excruciating dilemmas as to what the public interest requires.

Of course the act aims ultimately to ensure that broadcast licensees operate in the public interest, but it does not leave them adrift on a sea of doubt as to how to interpret the phrase. That task devolves upon the commission. As an appeals court put it:

> The only way that broadcasters can operate in the "public interest" is by broadcasting programs that meet somebody's view of what is in the "public interest." That can scarcely be determined by the broadcaster himself, for he is in an obvious conflict of interest. . . . the Congress has made the F.C.C. the guardian of that public interest (F, 1975a: 536*).

Because Congress chose the public-interest standard to give the FCC maximum flexibility in meeting new and unforeseeable situations, it invites charges of vagueness. But as an appeals court judge pointed out decades ago:

> It would be difficult, if not impossible, to formulate a precise and comprehensive definition of the term "public

---

*The full names and citations of all cases mentioned in the text can be found in the bibliography at the end of the book. Cases are listed chronologically (with suffix letters when there is more than one entry per year) under one of the four most common abbreviations used in Chapters 16–18: (1) **F**, indicating the *Federal Reporter,* the official multi-volume record of U.S. Appeals Court cases; (2) **FCC**, meaning the Federal Communications Commission; (3) **FCCR**, representing the *FCC Reports* (changed in 1986 to the *FCC Record*); and (4) **US**, meaning decisions of the Supreme Court as found in *United States Reports,* its official record. The page given in the text is that for the specific quotation; the citation list shows the page on which the case actually begins.

interest, convenience, or necessity," and it has been said often and properly by the courts that the facts of each case must be examined and must govern its determination (F, 1946: 628).

In sharp contrast, the 1984 cable act amendment nowhere uses the phrase "public interest." It gives the FCC discretionary powers that might well have been made subject to the public-interest test, but Congress did not mandate the use of that test. On the whole, the FCC has far less latitude in dealing with cable than with broadcasting.

16.3
Communications Act Revision

The cable amendment of 1984 is the most substantial example of a process that has gone on regularly since the passage of the 1934 act—revisions and updates of the act by amendment. Although the basic principles of the act have changed little, many of its specifics have been modified to meet the modern needs of a much larger and more complicated electronic media industry.

Amendments   Not counting changes to the original 1927 law prior to adoption of the 1934 act, by the late 1980s the statute had been amended more than a hundred times.

Amendments seek to (1) correct unforeseen weaknesses, (2) adapt to new conditions or introduce new subjects of regulation, and (3) curb certain actions the FCC has taken under the broad grant of discretionary powers given it under the act. Examples of each type of amendment follow:

▍ *Type 1:* The unforeseen effect of the equal-opportunity or "equal-time" provision for political candidates on news coverage of those candidates led in 1959 to the amendment of §315 to exempt bona fide news programs in which candidates appear.

▍ *Type 2:* To encourage low-power television and other new services, Congress in 1982 gave the FCC power to use lotteries to hasten the process of selecting licensees from among mutually exclusive applicants. Since then, further amendments have required the FCC to encourage new technologies and, as discussed further below, an entire title on cable television was added in 1984.

▌ *Type 3:* Objecting to the way the FCC used its discretionary powers to curb trafficking in licenses, Congress in 1952 adopted an amendment forbidding the FCC from interfering with the freedom of station owners to select buyers for their stations when they decided to sell.

Rewrites   Despite its longevity, the act has not lacked critics. Rumblings of discontent gained strength from a general sense of disillusionment with government overregulation that emerged in the 1970s. From 1977 through 1981, some in Congress made serious attempts to scrap the 1934 act in favor of entirely new legislation that would fully take into account the many new media and common-carrier services developed since 1934. Called *rewrites,* these legislative proposals went far beyond the kinds of patching-up done by both earlier and subsequent amendments. The efforts failed, largely because the many affected groups (broadcast, cable, and common carrier) could not come to a consensus on change.

The failure to adopt a comprehensive rewrite left the public-interest goal in place, as an ideal, though impractical, and the commissioners appointed by President Ronald Reagan in the 1980s largely ignored it. The attempted rewrites served several purposes, nevertheless. They educated key members of Congress on the growing problems of communication regulation, previously a subject that was not high on the congressional agenda. They laid the groundwork for the extensive deregulation that occurred in the 1980s. And they prepared the way for new legislation needed to deal with specific problems, such as comprehensive new regulations for cable television.

1984 Cable Act   For decades the legal status of cable television under the Communications Act remained uncertain. Much cable programming comes directly off the air from television stations, linking cable closely to broadcasting, yet cable systems deliver programs by wire over closed circuits, not by radio waves. Cable systems usually cover limited *intra*state areas and hence do not fall under federal interstate wire communications law, yet cable television uses *inter*state satellite networks to obtain much of its program material, and some systems rely on interstate microwave relays to pick up distant television stations. Cable operators sometimes act like neutral common carriers, as when they offer local access and leased commercial channels.

The 1984 cable act, which amended the Communications Act by adding a new Title VI, finally clarified the issue by defining cable television as *neither* a common carrier *nor* a broadcasting service. The FCC has some responsibilities for cable, but has far more for broadcasting and interstate wire services. States also have some authority over cable (generally, the right to establish statewide standards for franchising), but with the 1984 act Congress limited their right to regulate cable programming and subscriber rates. The cable act provides national standards for the franchising process that takes place at the local level (discussed further in Section 17.4).

16.4
FCC Basics

The independent Federal regulatory agencies play a unique role in Washington, blurring the lines separating the legislative, executive, and judicial branches of government. As a "creature of Congress," the FCC acts on behalf of the legislative branch. When it makes regulations, it acts in a quasi-legislative capacity. It also functions as an executive agency, putting the will of Congress into effect. And when the FCC interprets the 1934 Communications Act, conducts hearings, or decides disputes, it takes on a judicial role.

Budget and Organization   For fiscal 1989, Congress appropriated just over $100 million for the FCC. This budget makes the commission one of the smaller federal agencies, employing about 1,800 persons. The Field Operations Bureau, Common Carrier Bureau, and Mass Media Bureau have the largest staffs, about 400 members each. The unit of most interest here, the Mass Media Bureau, has four divisions, the duties of which can be summarized as follows:

- *Audio services.* Directs the processing of applications for construction permits, licenses, and license renewals for radio stations and related auxiliary operations.
- *Video services.* Directs the processing of applications for construction permits, licenses, and license renewals for television stations and related auxiliary operations. Maintains a small staff for the FCC's few remaining cable television responsibilities.
- *Policy and rules.* Handles FCC proceedings that produce new rules and conducts economic studies needed for policy-making decisions.
- *Enforcement.* Processes public complaints, ensures compliance with statutes and rules, issues interpretations of rules, and represents the bureau in hearings within the commission.

Several offices provide general services for all FCC operational bureaus: the Office of Plans and Policy, largely an economic research unit; the Office of the Chief Engineer, which provides the FCC's engineering expertise and runs the FCC laboratory that grants *type acceptance* of broadcast transmitters and other equipment; and the Office of General Counsel, which represents the FCC before other agencies and the courts and gives the commission internal legal advice.

Commissioners The president nominates FCC commissioners, who are subject to approval by the Senate. The five members* serve five-year terms and may be reappointed. Commissioners must be citizens, may not have a financial interest in any type of communications business, and must devote full time to the job. They meet several times each month in sessions open to the public. Robert E. Lee holds the record, having served for 28 years (1953–1981). The first woman commissioner, Frieda Hennock,

---

*Until 1982, there were seven commissioners, each appointed to a seven-year term.

served from 1948 to 1955. The next woman was not appointed until 1971, but since 1979 at least one commissioner has been a woman. The first black commissioner was Benjamin Hooks (1972–1977), a Memphis attorney and county judge. Hispanics as well as blacks have been appointed since then.

The five-year term, contrasted with the presidential term of four years, makes it unlikely that an incoming president could change all commissioners at once since only one commissioner's term expires each year. However, members often resign before serving a full term (replacements fill only the unexpired period of the term), with the result that two or more seats may come up for appointment in a given year. Additionally, the act gives an incoming president an immediate impact on the commission by allowing him to designate one of the existing members as chair.

Commissioners seldom originate policy. The commission staff generates policy initiatives, with the commissioners shaping and sometimes rejecting or altering proposed staff drafts of commission orders. Each commissioner has three assistants to help analyze the flood of complex issues presented at each meeting.

Strict *ex parte* rules govern contact with industry figures. Such rules require a public record of meetings between judges (or, as in this case, those acting in judicial roles) and individuals directly affected by a decision's outcome. To avoid unfair last-minute one-sided presentations, FCC commissioners may not meet with anyone concerned other than FCC staff members in the week prior to any FCC public meeting at which decisions will be voted upon. (The commissioners are often referred to collectively as "The Eighth Floor" for their location atop the FCC headquarters building in downtown Washington.)

Staff Role References to "the commission" usually signify not only the five commissioners but also the senior staff of the FCC's various divisions. Staff members handle most applications, including inquiries and complaints, which seldom need to come to the commissioners' personal attention. The staff handles the thousands of letters of complaint and comment from the public, as well as applications

EXHIBIT 16–2   FCC Organization

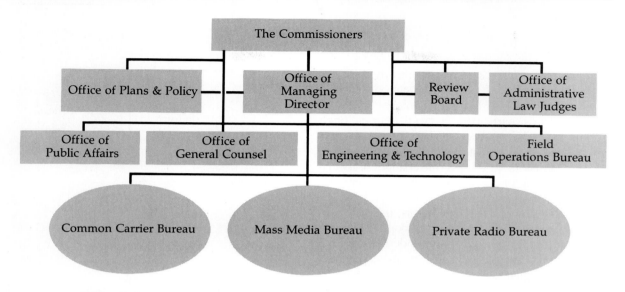

Twelve main units do the work of the FCC. The bureaus shown as ovals do the main work of authorizing services, and the other entities provide support to the three main authorizing bureaus and the commissioners. (The Field Operations Bureau, shown as a square, acts as the FCC's inspection/enforcement arm.) The managing director handles all personnel, budget, and administrative matters.

and forms from the industries the FCC regulates. Deregulation reduced the paperwork burden considerably during the 1980s.

Except for top administrators, whom the chair appoints, the staff is part of the federal civil service. Many staff members serve for decades, developing in-depth expertise on which commissioners depend. A researcher who spent several years closely observing the commission, noted that "staff members who are accomplished politicians and wily empire builders may find themselves with greater power than any single commission member . . . key staff members have the power to decide what information to bring to the commission's attention and in what form" (Cole and Oettinger, 1978: 11).

To make decisions, the staff needs formally delegated authority from the commissioners and guidance by *processing rules*. These rules spell out which decisions may be settled at the staff level and which need to be considered by the commissioners themselves. Commissioners decide agenda items either at an open meeting or *on circulation,* in which case an item circulates among the five members for action, before being made public. Staff recommendations accompany all items forwarded for formal commission consideration. The staff thus exerts a pervasive influence, not only on day-to-day operations but on long-term policy, in some ways reducing the commissioners to creatures of the staff.

Rule-Making Process   The rule-making function generates the large body of administrative law called FCC *rules and regulations* (there is really no difference between the two—the term is traditional). When the commission receives a petition to undertake a certain action or when it acts on its own, it may issue a *notice of inquiry* for a subject that needs preliminary comment and research, a *notice of proposed rule making* for a matter on which it offers specific new rules for public comment, or a combination of both. These notices invite comment from interested parties, mostly attorneys representing affected individuals, stations, companies, or industries. A few public-interest and consumer groups participate as well. Parties often submit extensive research studies to buttress their arguments for or against the FCC's intended action. On rare occasions, proposed rule changes of special significance or of a controversial nature may be scheduled for oral argument on "The Eighth Floor."

After digesting outside comments, the staff prepares a proposed decision for the commissioners, usually in the form of a recommended *report and order* announcing the new rule, with background discussion explaining and defending the decision. Once the FCC adopts or modifies the proposed report and order, that action becomes subject to petitions for reconsideration by the commission and/or appeal to the U.S. Court of Appeals for the District of Columbia Circuit, as shown in Exhibit 16–3. Indeed, in controversial matters, one party or another appeals nearly every "final" FCC decision, sometimes delaying implementation by months or years.

In some situations, rule making would be too cumbersome, too restrictive, or simply too difficult to defend. In such cases, the FCC may resort to less formal *policy making* instead—that is, summarizing past actions and laying down general guidelines instead of hard-and-fast rules.

Adjudication The second major class of FCC decision making is *adjudication*. This procedure settles specific disputes, whether between outside parties (rival applicants for a television channel, for example) or between the FCC and an outside party (the Mass Media Bureau versus a broadcast owner who protests the imposition of a fine, for example). The staff may settle the simpler disputes summarily, but many become the subjects of *hearings*.

EXHIBIT 16–3 FCC Rule-Making Process

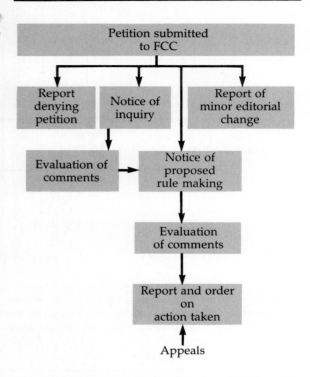

A petition for a new rule or a change of existing rules can come from the general public (rare), the regulated industries (common), another part of the executive branch, or a unit within the FCC itself. Parties who are dissatisfied with denials or new rules often appeal for reconsideration by the FCC and, if still not satisfied, to the courts. Each step of the process must be documented in the Federal Register so that all interested parties can keep themselves informed of rule-making actions.

Broadcasters want to avoid hearings at all costs. They nearly always take place in Washington, require expensive legal representation and much documentation, and can take a long time. And unexpected additional problems may arise while the licensee is in Washington, undergoing the scrutiny of a hearing.

Informal FCC Regulation In addition to formal rule making and adjudication, the FCC can influence licensee conduct through public statements in meetings, speeches, and articles and through personal contacts with licensees or their attorneys. This indirect "raised eyebrow" approach conveys an implied threat: "If you don't put your own house in order, the government may step in and do it for you." Carried further, the raised eyebrow technique of regulation can become *jawboning,* or coercive persuasion.

In the mid-1970s, for example, the FCC found itself under intense pressure from Congress and public groups to do something about the exposure of children to increasing amounts of violence and sex. Aware that a direct assault on the problem would certainly trigger First Amendment complaints, the commission jawboned the NAB, which then had a code of self-regulation, into "voluntarily" adopting *family viewing time* standards for program content. Industry representatives agreed in 1975 not to schedule "entertainment programming inappropriate for viewing by a general family audience" until after the first two hours of prime time, unless advisories were shown warning viewers that family standards might be violated.

Writers and directors challenged the FCC–industry agreement in court, alleging violation of the First Amendment. In 1979, a federal district court judge held that the policy did in fact violate the First Amendment because the government (that is, the FCC) had clearly coerced the industry into agreement (F Sup, 1976: 1134). An appeals court overturned that decision on other grounds (F, 1979: 355), and the parties concerned finally settled out of court in 1984. In the meantime, the now-deregulation-minded FCC took the opposite direction— urging broadcasters and licensees of other electronic media to protest government controls on programming and persuade their representatives in Congress to loosen or eliminate restrictions in the Communications Act.

FCC Critique Over the years, the FCC has been among the most frequently analyzed and scathingly criticized of the federal regulatory agencies. Official investigations and private studies of the commission and its methods reached negative conclusions with monotonous regularity. A few of the recurrent criticisms follow:

▪ The politically controlled process for choosing commissioners often fails to come up with qualified people. FCC appointments do not rank high in the Washington political pecking order. The president often uses appointments to regulatory commissions primarily to pay off minor political debts.

▪ As a consequence, commissioners tend to lack the expertise and sometimes the dedication assumed by the Communications Act. Most appointees have been lawyers. People with experience in engineering, the media or common carriers, or in relevant academic specialties have rarely been appointed.

▪ Commissioners' hopes for future employment with regulated industries undermine their concern for the public interest. Not many stay in office long enough to attain great expertise; the more ambitious and better qualified appointees soon move on to higher-paying positions, usually in private law practice.

▪ Taken as a whole, the regulatory process had an air of make-believe. Until the late 1970s, it set high-sounding public-interest goals that neither the broadcast industry nor the commission seriously tried to achieve. Since then, deregulation has gone to the opposite extreme, eliminating not only the pretense but also concern for protecting the larger public interest on the part of government.

16.5
Enforcement

Congress initially relied solely on the threat of license loss as the means of enforcing the Communications Act. The FCC can either refuse to renew a license or revoke it. In practice, however, penalties of such finality seemed too extreme for the types of infractions that most often occurred. Accordingly, in the early 1960s, Congress amended the act to allow for fines and shorter-term license renewals.

FCC Appeals and Hearings   A fundamental safeguard of individual liberties under the Constitution, the *due process* clause of the Fifth Amendment, guarantees that the government may not deprive a person of "life, liberty, or property without due process of law." Among many other things, this means that the FCC (as part of "government") may not use its powers arbitrarily. Fairness, the goal of due process, requires that applicants and petitioners have ample opportunity to argue their cases under nondiscriminatory conditions, and parties that are adversely affected by decisions must have the right to appeal for re-hearings and for review by authorities other than the ones that made the initial decisions. Many due process rights are protected by the Administrative Procedure Act adopted by Congress in 1946. The act specifies how administrative agencies, including the FCC, must conduct their proceedings to preserve due process for all participants.

When an issue arises that requires presentation of opposing arguments, the FCC may hold a *hearing* to settle the dispute. Senior staff attorneys called *administrative law judges* (ALJs) preside over initial FCC hearings. They conduct the proceedings somewhat like courtroom trials, with sworn witnesses, testimony, evidence, counsel for each side, and so on. Initial decisions of ALJs (who act as both judge and jury, in contrast to usual courtroom trials) are reviewed, first by the FCC's Review Board and then by the commissioners themselves. When opposing sides exploit all possibilities for reviews and appeals, final decisions can take a long time.*

Procedural rules head off frivolous interventions and intentional delays by carefully defining the cir-

cumstances that justify hearings and the qualifications of parties entitled to *standing*. For example:

- The Communications Act requires the commission to advise unsuccessful license applicants of its reasons for rejecting their applications. The applicant may reply, and if the commission still decides against the applicant, it must then set the matter for a hearing, "specifying the particular matter and things at issue" (47 USC 309 [e]).

- On the other hand, if the commission grants a license application *without* a hearing, for the ensuing 30 days (after a public notice announcing this action) the grant remains open to protest from "any party in interest"; if the FCC finds that the protesting parties raise pertinent issues, the commission must then postpone the effective date of the grant and hold a hearing.

- If the commission wishes to fine a licensee, §312 and 503 require the FCC to invite the licensee to "show cause" why such action should not be taken.

Court Appeals   Even after all the safeguards of FCC hearings and re-hearings have been exhausted, the Communications Act gives people adversely affected by FCC actions a further recourse. Section 402 provides that appeals concerning station licenses must go before the U.S. Court of Appeals for the District of Columbia Circuit, in Washington, DC. This court consists of nine judges, but panels of only three judges hear most cases. The court may confirm or overturn commission actions, in part or in whole. It may also *remand* a case, sending it back to the FCC for further consideration in keeping with the court's interpretation of the Communications Act and other laws. Appeals to the court from FCC decisions in cases that do not involve licensees may be initiated in any of the 12 other U.S. Courts of Appeals. Each serves a specific region of the country,

---

*The longest-running case in FCC annals began in 1941. Among other things, it entailed arguments over nighttime use of the 770-kHz AM radio channel used by both KOB in Albuquerque and WABC in New York. After more than 20 years of appeals, the FCC in 1977 again confirmed WABC's primary status on the channel. KOB's "final" objections appeared to be quashed by a

1980 appeals court affirmation of the FCC order that the Supreme Court declined to review. In 1981, however, KOB's irrepressible licensee filed a new petition asking the FCC to reclassify the channel, giving him yet another avenue of appeal. That also failed, and in 1986 the station was sold. For another example of marathon proceedings, see Exhibit 17–1.

called a circuit; hence they are known as *circuit courts of appeal.*

From any of the federal circuit courts, final appeals may be taken to the Supreme Court of the United States. A request for consideration by the Supreme Court, called a *writ of certiorari,* may be turned down *("cert. denied").* If that happens, the appeal process can go no further. Refusal to hear a case does not necessarily mean that the Supreme Court agrees with the lower court's finding, but the earlier decision holds nonetheless, though without standing as a compelling precedent.

Loss of License   From the FCC's creation in 1934 through 1987, only 141 stations lost their licenses. *Nonrenewal* accounts for 102 of these losses. Outright *revocation* without waiting for the current license to expire occurs rarely—only 40 times in 53 years. The average rate of *involuntary deletions,* the term for both nonrenewals and revocations, was a mere three stations per year. FCC records show no revocations and only 10 nonrenewals in the 1980s. In short, though an ever-present background threat, loss of license hardly ever becomes a reality.

Nonrenewal of broadcast licenses occurs more frequently than revocation because the burden of proof for showing that the renewal would be in the public interest falls on the licensee. In contrast, revocation puts the burden of proof on the FCC. A review of reasons for involuntary deletions shows that program infractions such as news slanting occur only rarely. In the great majority of cases, the FCC cites nonprogram violations related to character standards (such as misrepresentation and concealment of ownership), technical violations, and fraudulent billing of advertisers. One can safely assume that the almost complete absence of program infractions does not mean that the deleted stations had faultless program records; more likely, the FCC felt it was on safer constitutional ground when exacting the maximum penalty for nonprogram violations.

In most cases of license revocation or nonrenewal, loss of license climaxed a sorry history of willful misconduct by a station. Most deleted stations have been obscure radio outlets that were guilty of long lists of misdemeanors and lacking in any redeeming qualities. The FCC often treats transgressors with extraordinary leniency as long as they candidly admit error and contritely promise reform.

Some key cases of loss of license have already been mentioned: stations deleted for program excesses in the 1930s and television station WLBT's loss of license in 1969 for failing to serve the black population in its area. Exhibit 17–1 notes RKO's loss of a television license because of illegal business practices by its parent company as well as by its management. The following cases show other types of behavior that the FCC has found egregious enough to warrant the increasingly rare penalty of license deletion:

■ *Fraudulent billing.* An appeals court upheld the FCC's 1978 denial of renewal to a Berlin, NH, AM radio station charged with double-billing over $22,000 in overcharges to national advertisers. Claiming that the two other stations and the newspaper in his market did the same thing, the owner pleaded "business necessity"—a candid acknowledgment that market forces do not always operate in the public interest. The court concluded that "It appears to us that the Commission has not been giving sufficient consideration to the fraudulent conduct implicit in double billing as the serious *criminal* violation it constitutes" (F, 1979d: 869). Nevertheless, in 1986 the FCC deleted its rules against fraudulent billing, asserting that competing stations would keep one another in line, and that the Federal Trade Commission and the courts would be appropriate forums for action if need be.

■ *Staging of news.* The FCC denied the renewal of a Tucson, AZ, AM station in 1980 because of an irresponsible promotional stunt. When a recently employed DJ temporarily left town on personal business, station management concocted a story that he had been kidnapped. The station broadcast "news" of the kidnapping over a period of five days, even faking a police interview. Listeners flooded the Tucson police lines with calls. A local television station finally exposed the hoax. The FCC would not allow the absentee owner to shift responsibility. "A licensee cannot expect to be insulated from the irresponsible conduct of a vice-president and director" (FCCR, 1980c: 865).

■ *Equal employment and contest violations.* In early 1989 the FCC refused to renew the license of a Fredonia, NY, AM station, citing deliberate mis-representations by the licensee to the commission about an equal employment opportunity decision and a station contest prize that was promised but not given. Initial complaints from local groups had been filed in 1981, and an administrative law judge found against the station in mid-1986. It took nearly three years before the full commission took final action (FCCR, 1984: 2553).

The drop-off in the pace of involuntary deletions appears to be a result of the liberalized standards that flow from deregulation. Whereas the 1960s saw 29 denials and the 1970s 44 (not counting stations later regained by their licensees), through late 1987 only 10 stations had been denied renewals in the 1980s. The last license revoked at other than renewal time dates back to 1977.

When hearings delay a renewal, the license remains in effect pending resolution of the case. Even after a station loses its final appeal, the FCC gives it a grace period in which to wind up its affairs. Following this period, a new applicant may arrive on the scene to pick up the pieces and make a fresh start, or the commission may appoint an interim operator if comparative hearings delay the grant of the channel to a new licensee.

Lesser Penalties   Not all offenses, of course, warrant the capital punishment of license loss. For lesser offenses, the FCC inflicts the milder sanctions of short-term renewals, conditional renewals, forfeitures (fines), or letters placed in the station file.

Short-term renewal (usually for a year or two instead of the full renewal term) puts the licensee on probation, so to speak, pending the correction of deficiencies that were evident during the preceding license period. *Conditional renewal* might also be granted, pending correction of some specific fault. Either sanction can have a "green light" effect of encouraging competing applications at re-newal time. Both sanctions have been applied in the deregulatory 1980s.

The FCC can also impose penalties for day-to-day infractions of the rules without waiting for the end of the license period. These take the form of *forfeitures* ranging up to $20,000. Most forfeitures come from technical violations, few from program violations. When contrasted with the nearly 12,000 stations on the air, the low number of fines reflects the FCC's generally lenient treatment of licensee wrongdoing. Commissioners tend to sympathize with the tribulations of marginal radio stations struggling to survive, the ones most likely to commit punish-able infractions.

16.6
Copyright Law

In addition to the Communications Act of 1934, another federal statute strongly affects operations of the electronic media, the Copyright Act of 1976.

Basics   The Constitution recognizes the fundamental importance of encouraging national creativity. Section 8, the same passage that gives Congress the right to regulate interstate commerce, also calls on it to:

> promote the progress of science and the useful arts, by securing for limited times to authors and inventors the exclusive right to their respective writings and discoveries.

This provision resulted in the patent and copyright laws that enable investors and other creative people to profit from their achievements while also assuring reasonable public access to those achievements.

When broadcasting began, authors and composers had to rely on the Copyright Law of 1909, which dealt primarily with printed works and live performances. Congress amended the 1909 law from time to time to adapt it to the numerous recording, duplication, distribution, and reproduction technologies that emerged. But the old act never caught up with the times, and after two decades of study and debate, Congress passed the Copyright Act of 1976, effective for works published in 1978 and later.

Salient provisions of the 1976 act, administered by the Copyright Office, part of the Library of Congress, can be summarized as follows:

▪ *Purpose*. Copyright holders *license* others to use their works in exchange for payment of *royalties*. "Use" consists of making public by publishing, performing, displaying, and the like.

▪ *Copyrightable works*. In addition to traditionally copyrightable works—books, musical compositions, motion pictures, and broadcast programs—such works as sculptures, choreographic notations, computer programs can also be copyrighted. Things *not* copyrightable include ideas, slogans, brand names, news events, and titles (brand names, logos, and slogans can be protected under trademark regulations).

▪ *Length of copyright*. In general, a copyright lasts for the life of the work's creator plus 50 more years. After that, a work enters the *public domain* and can be used without securing permission or paying royalties.

▪ *Compulsory licensing*. In some cases copyright owners *must* license their works on a fixed-royalty basis. The 1976 law mandated compulsory licensing of cable systems, for example. Owners of copyrighted material who license television stations to use their works must grant *retransmission rights* to cable systems that lawfully pick up such programs off the air and deliver them to subscribers. Cable systems, in turn, must pay a preset small proportion of their revenue for these uses.*

▪ *Fair use*. Absolutely rigid enforcement of copyright restrictions would defeat the object of copyright law—the promotion of new creative activities. It would prevent, for example, a student from photocopying a magazine article, or a scholar from quoting other writers without securing permission. The new act retained the traditional copyright concept of *fair use*, which permits limited uses of copyrighted works without payment or permission for certain educational and critical or creative purposes (such as reviews of books and musical works).

Each of these provisions proved controversial, with electronic media often struggling among themselves as well as with copyright owners for favorable interpretations.

Music Licensing   Radio and television stations continue to obtain rights to play recorded music by reaching agreements with copyright licensing organizations ASCAP, BMI, and SESAC.* Most stations hold *blanket licenses* from these agencies, which allow unlimited use of any music in their catalogs in return for payment of an annual percentage of the station's gross income. Though some radio stations, especially those with news and talk formats, pay on a per-use basis, most radio and all television stations and networks hold blanket licenses.

Over the years, payment rates and billing systems have been the subjects of court battles between broadcasters and the performing-rights societies. Stations cooperate in hiring "all-industry" negotiating groups that annually negotiate rates with ASCAP and BMI (SESAC is less important). Deadlocks often result, usually ending in court proceedings, but rates climb each year nevertheless. Early in 1985 the Supreme Court let stand an appeals court ruling that the blanket station license did not violate antitrust laws, as television broadcasters had contended in a six-year legal battle (F, 1984: 217). Television networks had earlier lost the same battle.

Cable and Copyright   The Copyright Act established a Copyright Royalty Tribunal (CRT). In the case of cable television, the CRT has three major

---

*Copyright owners of broadcast programs that are imported from distant markets by cable systems receive two payments, one from the initial carrier (the network, or, in the case of syndicated programs, the station) and another from the cable system as a retransmitter.

*ASCAP, the American Society of Composers, Authors and Publishers, was founded in 1914 by, among others, composer Victor Herbert. BMI, Broadcast Music Inc., was set up originally by the broadcast industry in 1939–1940 as a means of balancing ASCAP's demands. It is now independently controlled. SESAC, the Society of European Stage Artists and Composers, is a relatively minor source for American media.

EXHIBIT 16–4   The Copyright System

A. Music Licensing System

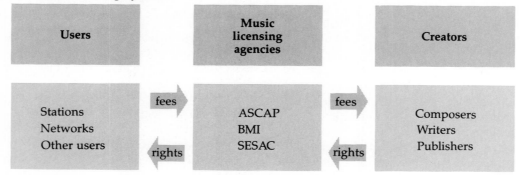

B. Cable TV Compulsory License System

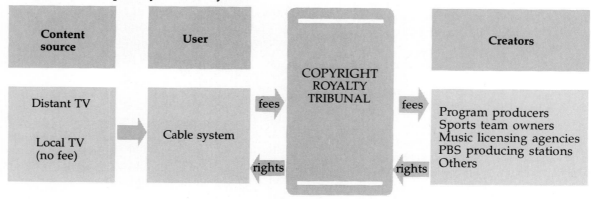

(A) The music licensing system has not changed substantially in more than a half century. Broadcasters and others obtain the right to use music by paying fees to the music licensing organizations ASCAP, BMI, and SESAC. They pass the fees on to the actual creators and publishers of the music.

(B) The more complicated compulsory license system for cable television, based on provisions of the 1976 copyright act, assesses cable systems fees based on the systems' overall revenue and the number of distant signals they import. The Copyright Royalty Tribunal, an agency of government separate from the Copyright Office, collects the fees and decides how much should go to each of the many different owners of copyrights.

tasks: to establish the rates cable must pay for use of imported distant television broadcast signals, to pool the revenue, and to divide the pooled royalty money among the copyright holders. The process of apportioning payments has been snarled in legal proceedings from the day the CRT began work. In dividing the royalties for 1978, the CRT managed to make everybody unhappy. It awarded broadcasters just over 3 percent of the royalty money (to be distributed through a quasi-independent committee set up by the NAB); program syndicators got the lion's share, or 75 percent, sports rights holders 12 percent, PBS just over 5 percent, and the music licensing agencies about 5 percent. Appeals filed by some of these parties delayed payment. Over the next decade, the portion allotted to commercial television increased to 5 percent, but broadcasters and other aggrieved parties regularly tied up the annual proceedings in further court appeals.

The 1976 Copyright Act set up a complicated royalty system for payment by cable-television systems to copyright owners. This system represented a tradeoff between broadcasters and copyright holders, mainly Hollywood film studios. Both assumed that in return for their agreement to the royalty plan, the FCC would sharply limit cable-system carriage of TV signals. The FCC's 1980 removal of rules limiting cable-system use of distant television signals jeopardized that copyright compromise. Cable systems could then import whatever signals they wanted, leading to a great increase in the retransmission of copyrighted programming without additional copyright payments.

The CRT added similar controversy in fixing the copyright royalty rate that cable systems had to pay for using distant television station programs. Copyright holders and broadcasters complained about extremely low levels of payment; some cable systems paid as little as a few hundred dollars a year. In 1981, the CRT raised the rates to meet these complaints and to compensate for inflation. Cable systems importing distant signals in the late 1980s had to pay just under 1 percent of their gross revenues to the CRT every six months, the total amount paid depending on the number and type (independent stations cost more) of stations carried.

Throughout its short history, the CRT has lacked sufficient staff and expertise to carry out its contentious assignments. In 1982, the agency's chairperson called the whole process unworkable and unfair, and urged Congress to reconsider the treatment of cable in the copyright act. A successor repeated the same charge in 1985. Bills introduced in Congress called for changes in or replacement of the CRT and changes in cable's compulsory license system. By the end of the decade, Congress still had changes under consideration.

Piracy The 1976 Copyright Act allows limited use of copyrighted materials without payment under the fair-use principle. Not everyone agrees on what constitutes fair use. Fair use controversies have involved issues in reception of cable television or satellite programs without payment of required fees and unauthorized recording of broadcast and other media.

Until the mid-1980s, *signal piracy* chiefly involved illicit hookups to cable television feeder lines, enabling cable reception without payment of monthly subscriber fees. As pay cable developed, illegal "black boxes" (decoders) made possible reception of even scrambled signals. The cable industry estimated that at least 10 percent of cable homes had illegal hookups, with the proportion rising to perhaps 25 percent in urban areas. Over-the-air subscription television suffered from the same problem. The cable industry found technical solutions to the problem of direct theft of pay-cable services by switching from easily circumvented "traps" for pay channels to much more secure addressable converter systems. But it appears that any scrambling system can be broken.

Pirated cable reception violates §705 of the Communications Act, which defines penalties for unauthorized "publication" of communications *intended* for reception only by subscribers paying to use special unscrambling devices. Cable systems prosecuted violators under the provisions of §705 and publicized the resulting felony convictions, which entailed jail terms and fines of up to $25,000 for the first violation and $50,000 for subsequent violations. Several widely publicized cases led to convictions and stiff fines. More than half the states passed anti-piracy laws prohibiting the manufacture, sale, or use of unauthorized decoders or antennas.

Piracy increased when the prices of television receive-only (TVRO) Earth stations began to fall, making them affordable by ordinary households.

By 1989 on the order of 2 million TVROs received basic cable and pay networks directly from satellites. Both pay and basic cable operators began to scramble satellite signals to protect their investments from pirates. The cable industry and pay-system operators complained of the fast-growing home receiver antenna industry and the freeloading users in hearings before Congress. As a result, Congress modified §705 as a part of the 1984 cable act.

As amended, §705 allows an individual to pick up any *nonscrambled* satellite programming *if* the cable programmer does not market directly to individuals (or, if it does, if the individual has obtained authorization, usually for a fee). The authorization applies only to satellite programming intended for personal use, not for resale. Since the cable industry has no way of marketing its services economically to such a scattered audience, in the late 1980s a number of third-party brokers assembled packages of cable services for sale to TVRO users.

A second major fair-use issue concerned home video recording off the air, off cable, or from rented cassettes. In 1976, a number of program producers brought suit against Sony, the pioneering manufacturer of home video recorders, for "indirect" copyright infringement.* A district court found in favor of Sony, concluding that home recordings that were not sold for a profit fell within the fair-use provision of that new copyright law. The Supreme Court confirmed the decision by a five-to-four vote (US, 1984a: 417). The high court cited audience research showing that people record broadcast signals primarily for time-shifting purposes, which it regarded as a "fair use."

The decision left unresolved the legality of recording cable or pay programming, however, for the Sony case covered only recording of over-the-air or "free" broadcast material. The legality of showing a taped copy of a copyrighted film or program to a group outside the home remained in question, a problem intensified by the growth of video rentals. Hollywood producers pressured Congress to once more modify the copyright act to extract indirect royalty payments from those who did home recording, such as a surcharge on recorders or blank tapes at the time of purchase, or on rental fees paid by customers to video rental stores.

The Sony case, the unexpected proliferation of TVROs, and the growth of the video rental business all illustrate the difficulty of keeping copyright laws abreast of technology and its newer applications.

16.7
Other Laws

International treaties, the law of the press, trade law, antitrust regulation, lottery and obscenity restrictions, and labor law covering affirmative action, also affect the electronic media. Broadcasters and cable-system operators also encounter state and local laws.

Treaties　Agreements between the United States and other nations concerning radio and wire communication have the status of treaties. After the executive branch reaches treaty agreements with foreign countries, ratification by the Senate gives these treaties the force of federal law. §303 of the Communications Act assigns the FCC the task of carrying out treaties that affect its work.

The United States and its neighbors have entered into separate regional treaties governing AM, FM, and television broadcasting. AM agreements cover the widest territory, because long-distance sky-wave propagation affects the scattered islands of the Caribbean as well as the two common-border nations, Canada and Mexico. Agreements on FM and television have long been in place with Canada and Mexico.

As a member of the International Telecommunication Union (ITU), the United States participates in worldwide regulation. The increased number and importance of ITU meetings since the 1970s has heightened the U.S. Department of State's concern with international telecommunications policy. Once handled by a minor office, telecommunications and information policy were elevated to bureau level in

---

*"Indirect" because Sony provided the *means* of infringement—the machines that made possible such recording in violation of copyrights.

the mid-1980s. During the Reagan administration (1981–1989), major conflicts arose from time to time over whether the National Telecommunications and Information Administration (NTIA) or the State Department had authority to lead American international telecommunications policy.* The FCC provides technical expertise and helps coordinate private sector participation.

Law of the Press   Electronic media share with print media a body of laws, precedents, and privileges known as the law of the press. Press law relies heavily on common-law traditions, case-law precedents, and constitutional theories built up over many generations. In contrast, electronic media are governed by more recent statutes.

Nevertheless, much of press law affects electronic media owners and programmers. Typical areas of common concern include libel, obscenity, fair trial, freedom of access to information, right of privacy, labor laws, advertising regulations, copyright, and reporters' privileges. The last includes the asserted right of news personnel to withhold the identity of news sources and to refuse to surrender personal notes, including any audio and video "outtakes." Many aspects of press law fall under state jurisdiction. Several press laws are discussed further in Section 18.2.

Advertising Regulation   Like the Communications Act, the 1914 act creating the Federal Trade Commission established a regulatory agency to oversee an aspect of interstate commerce. The similarity between the two acts stops there. The Com-

munications Act set out to regulate use of a specific technology with little legal precedent. The FTC act, however, applies to a field that has a long tradition of common law, which greatly complicates its regulatory activity.

As originally enacted, the FTC law was aimed at protecting businesses from unfair competition, not consumers from unfair business practices. Consumers had to look out for themselves in accordance with the doctrine of *caveat emptor*, "let the buyer beware." Not until the 1930s did the Supreme Court declare that "the rule of *caveat emptor* should not be relied upon to reward fraud and deception" (US, 1937: 112).

A 1938 amendment to the FTC act made it unlawful to use "unfair methods of competition in commerce, and unfair or deceptive acts or practices in commerce" (15 USC 45). The amendment gave the FTC a basis for attacking deceptive broadcast advertising, even if no harm to a competitor could be shown. This change gave consumers a needed weapon, for the Communications Act gives the FCC no authority to punish licensees for unfair advertising, except insofar as a licensee's character qualifications might be brought into question as a result of FTC actions.

Thus the FCC leaves most broadcast advertising regulation to the FTC. The FCC expects broadcasters and cable-system operators to cooperate with the FTC. In the past, the FTC has also acted against misleading broadcast ads but as a result of the deregulatory atmosphere of the 1980s, it stopped asserting that authority.

Only one product has been formally banned from the airwaves—cigarettes. In 1965, as a result of the first of what became an annual series of reports from the U.S. surgeon general on the health dangers of smoking, Congress issued a law mandating health warnings on all print and broadcast cigarette ads (15 USC 1333 [2]). Five years later, Congress banned advertising of cigarettes or little cigars on radio or television, effective January 1, 1971 (15 USC 1335). Smokeless tobacco was added to the broadcast ban in 1986. Broadcasters claimed that they had been unfairly singled out because cigarette ads continued to appear in print media. The health warnings and

---

*NTIA, an agency of the U.S. Department of Commerce, was established in 1978, growing out of the former Office of Telecommunications Policy in the Executive Office of the President. NTIA acts as the president's chief advisor on telecommunication questions and as spokesperson for the administration. NTIA plays three important roles: (1) a research "think tank;" helping to develop policy initiatives and prepare filings with the FCC in its proceedings; (2) assigner of spectrum to federal users, through the Interdepartmental Radio Advisory Committee; and (3) a disbursement agency for facility grants in support of expanding public telecommunications systems. NTIA has about 200 employees and an annual budget of some $14 million, plus $25 million for the grants.

the broadcast ban may be having an effect; cigarette smoking declined in the ensuing decade.

Antitrust Laws   The Sherman Act of 1890, the first of two major American antitrust statutes, reflected the same philosophy of protecting businesses from each other as the FTC act. In 1914, the same year it passed the FTC act, Congress complemented the Sherman Act with the Clayton Act. Together, the two antitrust acts aim to prevent the creation of monopolies. They provide the basis for government actions such as the one that led to the 1984 breakup of AT&T.

Courts have long held that despite the First Amendment, business laws such as antitrust statutes may be applied to the media. §313 of the Communications Act requires the FCC to consider revoking licenses held by companies found guilty of violating antitrust laws. However, the deregulatory atmosphere of the 1980s weakened enforcement of the antitrust laws (the move to break up AT&T had been initiated years earlier). The Justice Department rarely questioned the huge media mergers and takeovers of the 1980s and the trend toward ever-larger combinations in the cable industry. Yet these mergers tended to undermine the First Amendment goal of preserving competition in ideas by ensuring diversification of media ownership.

Lottery and Obscenity Laws   In 1948, Congress removed passages that forbade lottery advertising and obscenity in broadcasting from the Communications Act and inserted them in the U.S. Criminal Code. However, the FCC still had to develop its own rules against both obscenity and lottery advertising in order to invoke these Criminal Code provisions.

▌ *Lotteries.* Broadcasting advertising for or information about lotteries may subject a licensee to a fine of $1,000 and/or a year's imprisonment for each day's offense (15 USC 1304). The FCC usually issues lesser fines. This law created a dilemma for broadcasters when individual states began legalizing their own state lotteries. Congress therefore amended the law to permit licensees to carry state-government-operated lottery information and advertising, but only within their own and adjacent states. Efforts to get Congress to liberalize the antilottery statute to allow advertising of charitable and nonprofit lotteries finally achieved success with a more flexible law taking effect in early 1990.

The antilottery statute has a wider impact on broadcasters because they so frequently use *contests*, both in advertising and in promotional campaigns. Care must be taken that such contests do not turn into lotteries in the legal sense. The presence of three elements turns a harmless contest or promotion into an illegal lottery: a *chance* to win a *prize* for a *price*. A contest that requires participants to pay any kind of fee or calls for them to go considerably out of their way (*price* or *consideration*), that chooses the winner by lot (*chance*), and that awards the winner something of value (*prize*) constitutes a lottery and can get a station into serious trouble.

▌ *Obscenity.* "Whosoever utters any obscene, indecent, or profane language by means of radio communication shall be fined not more than $10,000 or imprisoned for not more than two years, or both" (18 USC 1464). The FCC requested an amendment that would broaden this law to cover visual presentation as well as language, but Congress took no action. Cases arising from this potentially significant source of program control are discussed in Section 18.2.

Equal Employment Opportunity   Broadcasting, once one of the most discriminatory fields of employment, substantially improved its record during the 1970s as a result of the Civil Rights Act of 1964, which prohibits discrimination in employment practices by any firm with 15 or more employees. In 1969, the FCC incorporated federal Equal Employment Opportunity (EEO) requirements into its own rules, becoming the first federal administrative agency to take such action. Later, such a Communications Act amendment extended EEO requirements to cable. Details are found in Section 17.2.

State and Local Laws   Under the Constitution, federal laws prevail over state laws in areas designated as federal matters. This means that a state law cannot rise above the Communications Act. Nevertheless, state laws govern many broadcasting activities that are not covered by federal statutes.

Scores of state laws affect broadcasting, especially those concerned with (1) individual rights (libel, privacy, and free press—fair trial limits on broadcast coverage of trials, for example), (2) advertising (laws controlling advertising of specific products and services), (3) noncommercial broadcasting (many states have commissions to coordinate statewide public radio and television activities), and (4) business operations (state taxes, for example).

Many states govern aspects of cable television. Most state cable laws regulate franchising or cable right-of-way disputes, theft of service, and the attachment of cable lines to telephone poles. Municipalities, too, have enacted many local regulations on cable franchising. However, a 1984 amendment to the Communications Act limits state and local authority, as discussed in Section 17.4.

16.8
Informal Controls

Many forces outside the formal regulatory structure also influence the conduct of electronic media owners. Some consist of lobbying and participating in hearings and court cases, whereas others consist of more direct social and economic pressures to force changes in the conduct of media operators.

We have seen how all three branches of government (executive, legislative, and judicial) participate in the formal regulatory process. These forces divide the FCC's allegiance. It finds itself under constant and often conflicting pressures not only from Congress, the White House, and the courts, but also from the industries it regulates, lobbyists representing special interests, and the general public.

Federal Micromanagement of FCC Operations   Although Congress gave the FCC a mandate

in the Communications Act of 1934 to act on its behalf, it continually brings the commission up short if it wanders far afield. In addition to the Senate's approval of nominations to the FCC and congressional control of the all-important federal budgeting process, Congress conducts frequent hearings on the commission's performance and plans. In fact, it tends to second-guess the FCC on virtually every major regulatory issue that arises. This detailed oversight is known in Washington as *micromanagement*.

The rapid changes of the 1980s made Congress even more active in shaping telecommunications policy. After the FCC announced plans to narrow the "window" during which broadcasters might program indecent material, Congress, under pressure from right-wing groups and in the midst of an election campaign, passed a law late in 1988 ordering the FCC to eliminate the window and flatly ban indecent programming at any time, despite the fact such a ban appears to violate the First Amendment. The FCC had no choice but to comply, despite threats of court appeals from many sources. Congress also protects its own special interests by vigilantly watching the laws affecting politicians' rights to use broadcasting in campaigns.

The White House has found ways, usually indirectly, to influence broadcasting ever since the 1920s. Franklin Roosevelt occasionally asked the FCC to pass on to the radio networks his dissatisfaction with the way they handled stories on the New Deal. Such intervention reached new heights with President Richard Nixon's Office of Telecommunications Policy, which spent much of its time in the early 1970s trying to get sympathetic news treatment of administration activities and goals. In the mid-1980s, the White House also played a role in short-circuiting an FCC plan to drop rules that curb the networks' control over program production, rules originally adopted to keep the networks from dominating the program market. The Hollywood producers, who stood to lose business if the change went through, applied pressure on President Ronald Reagan, who had long-term ties with the movie industry. The president, in turn, called in the FCC chair for an unprecedented "informational" talk. Congress, responding to Hollywood lobbyists, added its pressure. The FCC withdrew its plan to deregulate the networks' program-making role.

Most such efforts to influence the FCC take place behind the scenes, which makes them difficult to document. Broadcasters sometimes publicize such pressures as one means of protecting their position while also seeking support from other media. But the overall effect of White House pressure remains hard to gauge.

Consumer Action   The *boycott* is the most immediate action ordinary citizens can take to try to influence broadcasters' behavior. Lobbying Congress to intervene can take a long time. Boycotts usually involve a threat to refuse to buy advertised products. In a pluralistic society, boycotters have difficulty achieving sufficient consensus and discipline to do substantial economic damage. Were it not for the fact that advertisers and broadcasters often surrender without attempting to call the boycotter's bluff, boycotts would rarely have any discernible success.

Boycotts most often arise because programs or proposed programs offend church groups, ethnic minorities, or single-issue groups. Here are examples of each:

▪ *Church groups.* A widely publicized attack on immorality on television emerged in the early 1980s, spurred by the success of fundamentalist religious broadcasters in the 1980 political campaign. The Coalition for Better Television, a joint venture of several fundamentalist groups, threatened to boycott advertisers whose commercials appeared in offending programs. The coalition set up a national panel of monitors to evaluate levels of sex, profanity, and violence in television programs. It kept monitors' identity secret, and released no data on the validity of the methods it used. The networks and others denounced the coalition's goal of forcing its views on the rest of the public, but the advertising community, as usual, proved more timid. Procter & Gamble, the biggest television advertiser, announced that it had withdrawn ads from 50 program episodes alleged to be morally objectionable; other advertisers showed their concern by consulting with coalition leaders. With the exception of advertiser capitulation—markedly similar to sponsor compliance with blacklisting during the 1950s—the coalition had little impact.

▪ *Ethnic minorities.* Ethnic awareness and separatism increased during the 1970s. Common stereotypes of American Indians, Chinese, Irish, Italians, Japanese, Jews, Mexicans, and Poles have all come under attack. Cable and broadcast programmers now routinely edit old feature films to remove the gross ethnic slurs they often contain.

▪ *Single-issue groups.* Concern over abortion, gun control, and prayer in the schools heightened during the 1980s. Television and radio programs and ads debated all three issues. Protests on all aspects of these controversies stimulated widespread news coverage. Complaints under the fairness doctrine, which was then in effect, flooded the FCC. Ironically, a New York group's vociferous complaint about a local station's programs on nuclear power led the FCC to abolish the fairness doctrine (discussed in Section 18.5).

Even noncommercial broadcasting, which is supposedly freer to present a variety of points of view because it does not have to cater to the sensitivities of advertisers, has sometimes succumbed to group pressure. In 1984, PBS aired a highly acclaimed 13-part series on the Vietnam War, produced in cooperation with British and French firms. Though a decade had passed since the war ended, the role of the United States, and thus the series' depiction of that role, remained highly controversial. A conservative media watchdog group, Accuracy in Media (AIM), produced a 50-minute documentary "reply" to the PBS series, attacking both specific details and the overall program tone. PBS aired the AIM response in mid-1985, following it with a 45-minute discussion between producers and researchers of both programs. This attempt at defusing the controversy brought new complaints against PBS, charging it with having "given in" to its critics.

The single most important event that crystallized interest in broadcast reform came in the consumerism heyday of the 1960s. The WLBT case (Exhibit 16–5) gave a station's audience the legal right to file complaints on and participate in license renewal proceedings. Hundreds did, though with little long-lasting impact.

The FCC mandated in 1971 that stations keep license-renewal applications and other relevant documents in a station *public file*, readily available for public inspection. Three years later, the commission issued a *Broadcast Procedure Manual* (FR, 1974: 32288). It explained how the FCC handled complaints and how citizens could participate in its proceedings, detailing what intervening parties need to do to construct sound legal cases. Though now a quaint, outdated memento of pre-deregulatory attitudes, the manual is still supposed to form a part of every station's public file.

By the 1980s consumerism faced its most hostile political climate in 30 years. A reaction had set in against what many regarded as excessive government concern for consumer interests in such areas as the environment, occupational safety, and public health. Some consumer groups continued the struggle, but with diminishing returns. Consumer pressure helped to retain and even expand fair employment policies in electronic media, but consumer-interest activities suffered from budget cuts at both the FCC and FTC. Many once-active national consumer groups closed up shop, and those that remained seemed almost like anachronisms. On the local level, groups that once promoted public-service aspects of cable television faded when most municipal governments and cable operators failed to give them sufficient support.

Self-Regulation Many large industries adopt voluntary codes of conduct to cultivate favorable public relations and forestall abuses that might otherwise bring on government regulation. But industry codes also have a down side. Codes that affect the freedom to compete run afoul of the antitrust laws.

The National Association of Broadcasters began developing codes for radio program advertising practices as early as the late 1920s, and extended them to television in 1952. Necessarily voluntary, these codes used broad generalizations and lots of "shoulds" and "should nots," but left most decisions to the discretion of station management. Nonetheless, the codes reinforced generally observed standards, especially as to the amount of time broadcasters should devote to advertising. They were also designed in part to ward off FCC rules or congressional interventions.

Despite NAB precautions to avoid any hint of coercion, the Department of Justice brought suit against the Television Code in 1979. The suit alleged that the advertising time standards in the television code "artificially curtailed" advertising, repressing price competition and depriving advertisers of "the benefits of free and open competition." Late in 1982, a federal district court approved a consent decree by which the NAB disbanded its code-making activities.

The demise of industrywide NAB codes seemed to have little impact, however. For a time, the networks and many stations continued to follow their own internal standards, some even tougher than the NAB code had been. Marketplace competitive pressures seemed to help hold the line of the total amount of time devoted to advertising, but reliable research on trends in advertising quantity is lacking.

By the late 1980s, however, the networks had all but eliminated their program standards departments as part of their overall adoption to new and stringent budget controls. Broadcasters still announce most theatrical films as "edited for television," but the editing is more for length (to allow sufficient time for commercials) than to meet prescribed content standards.

Cable television enjoys more relaxed standards than broadcast television. Pay cable regularly shows films with uncut violence, profanity, and nudity. These episodes cause complaints, but nowhere near as many as such material on over-the-air television would elicit. Alleged obscenity in cable programming spurred several repressive state laws, but none survived First Amendment tests before the courts (as discussed in Section 18.2).

As to self-regulation by broadcast personnel, aside from engineers, the broadcast employees that come closest to being self-policing professionals probably

EXHIBIT 16–5   WLBT and "Standing"

Until the late 1960s, a broadcast station's audience members had no right to take part in regulatory proceedings concerning that station. That situation changed in a dramatic FCC and court case that demonstrated the value of planning a concerted citizens' effort backed by solid legal advice.

The case began in 1955 when a group of citizens made the first of a series of complaints to the FCC about the conduct of WLBT, a VHF television station in Jackson, MS. The group accused the station of blatant discrimination against blacks, who formed 45 percent of its audience, both in program content and in hiring practices. The FCC dismissed the citizens' complaints, saying that they had no legal right to participate in a licensing decision. When WLBT's license again came up for renewal in 1964, local groups obtained legal assistance from the Office of Communications of the United Church of Christ (UCC) in New York.

The UCC petitioned the FCC on behalf of the local groups for permission to intervene in the WLBT renewal application proceeding, but the FCC again rejected the petition, saying that citizens had no *legal standing* to intervene. At that time the commission recognized only signal interference or economic injury (to another broadcaster) as reasons to give parties the right to participate in renewal hearings. Thus only other broadcasters had standing to challenge existing licensees.

The UCC appealed to the Court of Appeals, claiming that the FCC had no right to bar representatives of the viewing public from intervening in renewals, or to award a renewal without a hearing in the face of substantial public opposition. The court agreed, noting the existence of ample precedent in nonbroadcast areas for allowing consumers legal standing to challenge administrative actions. The court directed the FCC to hold hearings on WLBT's renewal and to give standing to representatives of the public (F, 1966: 994). The FCC dragged its feet, fearing a flood of such petitions. Finally, the commission held a hearing and grudgingly permitted UCC to participate as ordered. However, the FCC once again renewed WLBT's license.

Frustrated with this implied approval of grossly discriminatory actions by the licensee, the UCC returned to court. In 1969, an exasperated appeals court reconsidered the case—14 years after the first complaints had been recorded. In the last opinion written by Warren Burger before he became Chief Justice of the Supreme Court, the court rebuked the FCC for "scandalous delay." It ordered the FCC to cancel WLBT's license and to appoint an interim operator pending selection of a new licensee (F, 1969d: 543). But ten *more* years passed before the FCC selected a new permanent licensee. Altogether, the case dragged on for more than a quarter of a century.

As the FCC had feared, the WLBT case triggered many petitions to deny renewal of other licenses. However, this "reign of terror," as a trade magazine put it, resulted in few actual hearings and still fewer denials. Of the 342 challenges filed in 1971–1973, only 16 resulted in denials of license renewal. An exacting standard of evidence established by the FCC and approved by the court ensured this high rate of petition failure. Only after an opponent presented overwhelming evidence would the FCC schedule a license renewal hearing (F, 1972: 316).

---

are those belonging to the Radio Television News Directors Association (RTNDA). Members subscribe to a Code of Broadcast News Ethics. The code stresses the importance of accurate and comprehensive presentation of broadcast news, no matter how such presentation might affect station or network public relations. Article 6 of the RTNDA code appears to mandate personal refusal by news directors to distort the news to suit their own political preferences or opinions or the whims of owners or managers:

> Broadcast journalists shall seek actively to present all news the knowledge of which will serve the public interest, no matter what selfish, uninformed or corrupt efforts attempt to color it, withhold it, or prevent its presentation.

Instances of news personnel denouncing attempts of owners to control the news occasionally surface, but not often. It appears that responsible journalists tend to leave stations that bring unethical pressures on them, rather than to openly challenge their employers.

Press Criticism   Coverage of broadcasting, cable, and related services in the trade and popular press often affects rule making. Congress, the White House, the FCC, and other agencies closely follow reporting about the media, seeking evidence of the impact of their actions. Certain prestigious writers and trade newsletters play a special role: how a new policy or rule "plays" in the trade press gives a foretaste of how the industry itself will react.

As for program criticism, reviewers in major newspapers and magazines seem to have more impact on news and public-affairs programs than on mass entertainment. Moreover, they influence producers of such programs more than they do the general audience. The agenda-setting role of critics can, however, sometimes focus government and industry attention on areas of controversy, such as violence, questionable advertising, and copyright violations. Tom Shales, the incisive television critic for the Washington *Post*, John O'Connor of the New York *Times*, and others can have an impact on network and program leaders as well as on Washington lawmakers.

Summary

▌ Electronic media come under the control of Congress because of the commerce clause in the U.S. Constitution. Through the Communications Act of 1934, Congress delegates supervisory responsibility to the FCC, using the broad guideline of the "public interest, convenience or necessity" to define the FCC's discretionary powers.

▌ Although many attempts have been made to rewrite or replace the 1934 Communications Act, notably the rewrite efforts of 1977–1981, amendments have been remarkably few for an act so old and a field going through such rapid change. Cable television is regulated by a 1984 addition to the Communications Act.

▌ The FCC consists of five presidentially appointed commissioners and a professional staff of about 1,800. It is organized into bureaus and offices, among which the Mass Media Bureau has jurisdiction over broadcasting and related media.

▌ The FCC imposes regulation through formally adopted rules, processing standards, guidelines and adjudicatory decisions. It also uses "raised eyebrow" and jawboning techniques to influence licensees.

▌ FCC commissioners are political appointees, usually with little experience in the communications field. Commissioners often serve for short periods and then move on to lucrative positions in the media industries.

▌ The threat of license loss is the FCC's ultimate enforcement weapon. However, the commission deletes few licenses through nonrenewal and fewer still through outright revocation. Lesser penalties include short-term renewals and fines. Few stations suffer any of these sanctions. Due process and the Administrative Procedure Act give those accused many avenues of appeal.

▌ The 1976 Copyright Act governs the controversial area of law that ensures creative artists payment for use of copyrighted works. When cable systems carry broadcast programs for which copyright fees have already been paid, copyright holders must grant compulsory licenses for which they receive reimbursement from fees paid to the Copyright Royalty Tribunal.

▌ The electronic media are also subject to many other laws, among them international treaties, the law of the press, advertising regulation, antitrust laws, bans on lotteries and obscene material, and equal employment opportunity rules.

▌ Regulation of broadcasting and cable is affected by White House and congressional intervention, court reviews of FCC actions, consumer activism (now in decline), network and station self-regulation, professional self-regulation and trade-press criticism.

CHAPTER 17

STATION AND SYSTEM LICENSING

The *authorizing* of service—licensing of broadcasting stations and franchising of cable television systems—is the single most important regulatory function. This chapter explores the process of federal station licensing and local government cable system franchising, comparing and contrasting the two. Most other regulation is derived from this process of authorizing services. The chapter concludes with a discussion of the deregulatory initiatives of the 1980s.

17.1
Station Licensing

In its central regulatory function, the FCC acts as a gatekeeper, using its licensing power to open the way to station ownership for some and close it for others. Sometimes it makes licensing decisions only after extensive investigation of would-be licensees and their plans; at other times it simply awards licenses by lot. In either case, licensing plays a key role in determining the nature of broadcast services, which inevitably reflects the character and standards of the people who own and operate the stations.

Channel Ownership   Neither nations nor individuals can literally "own" any part of the electromagnetic spectrum. In the early days of radio, some broadcasters claimed that they had acquired

perpetual squatter's rights to the channels they already occupied. Conscious of this potential problem for the success of broadcast regulation, Congress went to special lengths to prevent claims of channel ownership. One of the aims of the Communications Act is:

> to maintain the control of the United States over all the channels of interstate and foreign radio transmission; and to provide for the use of such channels, but not the ownership thereof . . . no such license shall be construed to create any right beyond the terms, conditions, and periods of the license (47 USC 301).

Congress stressed the point still further by requiring in §304 that each licensee sign a waiver "of any claim to the use of any particular frequency or of the ether as against the regulatory power of the United States because of the previous use of the same." And §309 requires every license to include the condition that it "shall not vest in the licensee any right to operate the station nor any right in the use of the frequencies designated in the license" beyond the terms of that license.

Finding a Channel   A would-be licensee must apply for specific facilities (channel, power, coverage pattern, antenna location, time of operation, and so on). Because the FCC has allotted all FM and television channels to communities in advance, the applicant consults the allotment tables to find a vacant channel (47 CFR 73.201, 73.603). Alternatively, the applicant may petition for a change in the allotment tables. In the case of AM channels, however, no such tables exist. Applicants must employ engineering consultants to search out locations where AM channels could be activated without causing interference.

By the 1970s, the most desirable commercial channels had long since been licensed, so that a would-be licensee nearly always bought an existing station. However, in the 1980s, new opportunities developed in both television and radio. In 1982, the commission approved a new service, low-power television (LPTV), whose channels fit in among current full-power allotments. LPTV stations use only low power and may not interfere with full-power television stations. The FCC created nearly 700 new FM allotments in the mid-1980s, made possible by improved technology that limits interference with stations already on the air. Finally, at the end of the decade, the FCC planned an internationally sanctioned extension of the AM frequency band to 1700 kHz, adding 10 new medium-wave channels on which the FCC could license several hundred more AM outlets.

Permits and Applications To assure that transmitters behave exactly as planned and authorized, the act requires would-be licensees to apply first for *construction permits* (CPs). The holder of a CP applies for a regular license to broadcast only after submitting satisfactory proof of performance of transmitter and antenna.

Applicants use FCC Form 301 to seek a construction permit; it must also be filled out for any substantial change in ownership (noncommercial applicants use Form 340). If granted, the permit allows the applicant to construct a new commercial station or to make changes in an existing station, such as relocating a transmitter or main studio. Form 301 requires disclosure of the financial, technical, and character qualifications of applicants (discussed in the following sections) as well as other technical information.

A CP gives its holder a limited time (usually 24 months for television and 18 for radio) to construct and test the station. The CP holder then uses Form 302 (Form 341 for noncommercial stations), basically a record of technical testing, to apply for a full license. With FCC permission, a permittee may begin on-air program testing pending approval of the license.

Licensee Qualifications Section 308(b) of the Communications Act allows only *U.S. citizens* who qualify as to *character, financial resources,* and *technical ability* to receive a license. Congress left the FCC wide discretion in implementing and interpreting these basic requirements. Section 310(b) forbids alien control of a broadcast license.

- *Character.* Applicants must have personal histories free of evidence suggesting defects in character that would cast doubt on their ability to operate in the public interest. Criminal records and violations of antitrust laws may constitute such evidence. Any previous history of misrepresentation to the FCC would prove to be an almost fatal defect. Close scrutiny of corporate licensees, might endanger scores of existing stations, as few large corporations have survived the corporate wars without blemish (see Exhibit 17–1).

- *Financial resources.* Form 301 requires applicants to certify that they have "sufficient" financial resources; the FCC has issued varied definitions over time as to what "sufficient" means. By the late 1980s, "sufficient" meant ability to construct and operate facilities for 90 days without reliance on revenues from advertising.

- *Technical ability.* Most applicants hire engineering consultants to prepare their technical applications. Such consultants specialize in showing how a proposed station will get maximum physical coverage (including primary service coverage in the proposed community of license) without causing objectionable interference to existing stations. Engineering plans must also show expertise in meeting FCC engineering standards.

Usually all competing applicants meet these minimum statutory qualifications for licenses. When that happens, the FCC exercises its right under the Com-

EXHIBIT 17–1   RKO—Licensee Qualifications Gone Wrong

In 1965, a license renewal challenge to Los Angeles television station KHJ began a bizarre series of events that tested two FCC licensing concepts: licensee "character" qualifications and the comparative renewal hearings process. KHJ-TV was one of 16 stations then owned by RKO General, a subsidiary of General Tire (renamed GenCorp in 1982). Although no serious complaints had been lodged against KHJ-TV during the preceding license period, the challenger had discovered that the parent of RKO General, General Tire, had been investigated by a federal agency for numerous alleged financial irregularities, including bribing foreign officials, maintaining secret overseas bank accounts, and misappropriating corporate funds. While such allegations, even if true, had no direct bearing on the operation of the Los Angeles station or of its parent, RKO General, they gave the opposing applicant, Fidelity Television, a chance to argue to the FCC that renewal should be denied on the ground that General Tire's alleged financial irregularities constituted "character" defects that disqualified it as a broadcast licensee.

Similar renewal challenges to the other RKO stations followed, against WNAC-TV in Boston in 1969, and WOR-TV in New York in 1972. Attacks on RKO's character qualifications snowballed, eventually placing all 16 of its licenses in jeopardy. In 1980, the commission declined to renew the Boston, New York, and Los Angeles TV stations. On appeal, RKO managed to retain two, losing the Boston outlet, then worth more than $200 million. In 1983, 18 years after the KHJ-TV case began, the FCC turned the whole affair (now including over 150 other applicants for RKO facilities) over to one of its Administrative Law Judges to make a definitive finding on the RKO character qualification issue, among others.

Delays and expense continued. It took the ALJ four years to explore such issues as whether RKO General had tried to deceive the FCC about the charges brought against General Tire, and whether such transgressions should endanger the broadcast stations which were not directly involved. While the legal fees and delay mounted, the head of General Tire, presumably the one responsible for its past irregularities, retired. This raised a new question: can character defects be ascribed to a corporation separate from its responsible officers?

Finally, in 1987, the ALJ concluded in a strongly worded report that renewal of all remaining RKO stations should be denied. RKO, he said, had set a record of dishonesty in dealing with the FCC. Of course, RKO appealed, admitting to only minor failings, pointing out that the changes in top management ensured future compliance with FCC rules, and stating its intention to sell all its stations as soon as the FCC cleared its licenses (owners may not sell stations while their licenses remain under investigation).

By 1989, after a quarter-century of hearings, appeals, court cases and remands—far more involved than the summary here—the RKO licenses still hung fire. RKO still operated all but two of its stations—the Boston TV station lost in the 1980 decision, and the New York TV station which had been sold (made possible despite pending renewal issues by a special act of Congress aimed at granting New Jersey its first commercial VHF channel).

Over the years, RKO had spent $27 million in legal fees. Adding up the expenses of all parties in the long series of disputes, the legal costs totaled close to $100 million. As for Fidelity Television, the company that had started it all back in 1965, it agreed to drop its application in favor of an offer of the Walt Disney studios to buy the station, with $103 million of the sale price going to Fidelity to cover its accumulated expenses. But even this was contingent on a final FCC decision as to RKO's overall status as a licensee. It *appeared* as this book went to press that the FCC would approve RKO's license renewals to allow the sales of all the stations which RKO had been lining up for several years to take place.

The marathon RKO case dramatizes the absurd lengths to which the character test of licensees, and the comparative renewal hearings process of the FCC can go when large complex corporate entities are involved.

munications Act to specify "other qualifications," using such tests as the degree of local ownership and the role of minorities and women in station management. These FCC-generated criteria become crucial when the commission has to choose among several competing applicants, as usually happens.

Mutually Exclusive Applications Before most desirable channels had been licensed, and even today when desirable channels become available because of deletions of existing licenses or changes in channel allotment rules, several applicants competed to obtain a license for the same market. The FCC calls such competitors *mutually exclusive* applicants. It makes a choice among them only after conducting comparative hearings, usually long-drawn-out and costly. They take place at FCC headquarters in Washington, DC.

A huge build-up of low-power TV (LPTV) construction permit applications occurred in the early 1980s. Responding to the FCC's request, Congress amended the Communications Act in 1982 to authorize the commission to select new (*not* renewal) LPTV licensees by means of a *lottery* system rather than by the time-consuming process of comparative hearings (47 USC 309[i]). Under the lottery system, the FCC could check an LPTV (or MMDS) applicant's qualifications to hold a license only *after* the applicant had already been chosen by the lottery. The FCC said it would use lotteries for regular broadcasting applications only when comparative hearings resulted in ties—which by 1989 had yet to happen. Critics object to lotteries, charging that they allow the FCC to evade its statutory responsibility to grant licenses only if the recipients show intention to serve the public interest.

The FCC intended the LPTV service as a means of diversifying television programming. In keeping with that goal, the lottery amendment included a provision giving a two-to-one *preference* to applicants more than 50 percent controlled by minorities and/or to applicants with no other media ownership interests. These minority and diversity preferences could be combined to give a minority-controlled entity new to the media field a four-to-one prefer-

ence.* The first LPTV lottery, held in September 1983, resulted in 23 grants, eight to minority applicants. By the end of the decade, many lotteries had been held for all markets, almost ending the application back-up for both LPTV and MMDS licenses.

Ironically, lotteries frustrated the goal of rapid license diversification by creating an unforeseen paperwork monster. Thousands filed the simplified application forms for the new services. By 1985, the FCC had been inundated by 20,000 LPTV, some 16,000 MMDS, and 5,000 cellular telephone applications.

Services Requiring No License Radio stations that use their subcarriers on their channels for auxiliary services that are not related to broadcasting and not received on regular radio receivers need not apply for licenses for such services. Nor do television stations need licenses to transmit teletext and related services. The FCC formerly required licenses for such services, but it deregulated them to encourage their wider use. Carrier current radio stations (found on many college campuses) also operate without licenses.

17.2 Monitoring Station Operations

In order to ensure operation in the public interest, as required by the Communications Act, the FCC would ideally monitor station operations constantly, ensuring fulfillment of licensee promises and compliance with regulations. It would be impracticable, however, for the commission to monitor some 12,000 stations in any detail. Instead, complaints from the

---

*The FCC conducts the lotteries by assigning a number to each applicant, mixing the numbers randomly before drawing enough of them to fill the current quota of licenses. It enhances the chances for both minority applicants and media newcomers by duplicating their numbers, thus doubling the chance their numbers will be drawn. An applicant who qualifies for preference of both counts enjoys the statistical benefit of quadruplicated numbers.

general public, competitors, and would-be competitors call attention to most transgressions. Insofar as the FCC does exercise oversight, the matters of concern tend to be easily identifiable and objectively verifiable—for example, engineering and employment practices, rather than less tangible matters, such as the quality and variety of programs.

Licensee Control over Programs From a regulatory viewpoint, it would seem pointless for a station owner to go through the licensing procedure only to turn over actual operation to some other party that had not met the same FCC tests. Ideally, the FCC would hold the licensee responsible for maintaining control over the station's programming. Licensees could not plead that because a program was in a foreign language, offensive material in an otherwise inoffensive program did not come to notice, or that a speaker made an unauthorized comment.

At one time the FCC took precisely this view of licensee responsibility, calling it a *nondelegable* duty. For example, the commission frowned on *time brokerage,* whereby owners sell blocks of time on their stations to brokers, who then resell it at a markup to third parties who provide programs for brokered periods. This practice can make it difficult for a licensee to supervise programs closely, thus verging on surrender of control. With deregulation, however, the FCC, while still paying lip service to the nondelegable duty of broadcasters, gave licensees far more autonomy; indeed, it even encouraged time brokerage as a desirable means of broadening access to the airwaves by enabling people who could not afford their own station to do their own broadcasts.

Employment Practices Applicants for CPs proposing to employ five or more persons full time must set up a "positive, continuing program of practices assuring equal employment opportunities." These *equal employment opportunity* (EEO) requirements refer to women in all cases, and to minority ethnic groups in cases where they form 5 percent or more of the work force in a station's or cable system's service area. The CP application includes guidelines for establishing EEO programs, which require statements about plans or practices with regard to:

▮ General EEO policy.
▮ The official responsible for implementing that policy.
▮ Methods of publicizing the policy.
▮ Methods of recruitment and training.
▮ An analysis of the racial composition of the population in the station's or system's service area (usually obtained from Census Bureau or Department of Labor records).
▮ Personnel promotion policies.

Stations and cable systems with five or more full-time employees must submit annual employment reports to the FCC. These reports must also be kept in the station's or cable system's public file, discussed below. The FCC reviews a licensee's recent EEO record when considering its application for license renewal. To help pin down EEO policy requirements, the commission has issued detailed processing guidelines (Exhibit 17–2).

In the early 1980s, political conservatives in the Reagan administration and at the FCC who opposed quotas in employment practices objected to the EEO guidelines. Nevertheless, Congress extended the broadcast EEO requirements to cable systems in the 1984 cable act. The FCC persisted in questioning the role of quotas until Congress ruled in an FCC budget bill that all EEO requirements *must* remain in place, making EEO one area where deregulation failed to have an impact.

Public File The FCC requires every broadcast station to maintain a *public file* in its community of license (47 CFR 73.3526, 73.3527). This requirement dates back to the 1970s, a period of consumer activism. When people wanting to challenge a station's renewal application need facts about the licensee's promises and performance in order to prepare a case against renewal, they can gather information from the station's public file. Applicants and licensees must assemble certain documents and keep

EXHIBIT 17-2   EEO and Station Size

Number of full-time employees	EEO requirements
1 to 4*	Need not file an EEO plan.
5 to 10	Stations will have their EEO programs reviewed by the FCC unless minorities and/or women are employed on a basis of half of their local labor force representation. In other words, if a market's labor force, as defined by the Census Bureau, is half black, at least a quarter of a licensee's employees in that market should be from that minority group. In the top job categories (officers and managers, professionals, technicians, and salespersons), the stations should have a minority employee ratio of at least one-quarter of that minority's market labor force representation. In the example used above, where half the labor force is black, the top four station job categories should be at least 12.5 percent black.
11 or more	Should employ at least half as many minorities and/or women as are represented in the local labor force overall *and* in the top four job categories (officers and managers, professionals, technicians, and salespersons).
50 or more†	Same as for stations with 11 or more employees; but in addition, EEO programs are regularly reviewed.

*This category includes many radio stations.
†Most of these are television operations.

them ready to show, during business hours, to any member of the public on request. As of the late 1980s, all stations, commercial and noncommercial, had to maintain such a file, retaining certain documents for seven years in the case of a radio station and for five in the case of television. Cable systems have to maintain a public file consisting only of employment-related documents (47 CFR 76.311[j][2]). The more inclusive broadcast public file includes:

- The latest construction permit or license application, including any for major changes.
- The latest license renewal application.
- Ownership reports and annual employment reports.
- The EEO model program (if required—see Exhibit 17–2).
- The now badly dated pamphlet entitled "The Public and Broadcasting—A Procedural Manual" issued by the FCC in 1974.
- A record of any political broadcast time requests for the past two years.
- A quarterly listing of programs the licensee believes provided the most significant treatment of community issues.
- Letters received from members of the public (to be kept for three years) and any agreement with citizens groups.

Deregulatory decisions such as the abandonment of formal ascertainment of community needs, the adoption of renewal applications in postcard form (Exhibit 17–3), and the deletion of programming guidelines reduced the material in the file, but broadcasters and other supporters of deregulation still regard it as a waste of time. Indeed, members of the public rarely ask to see it.*

Keeping Abreast of Regulations   While keeping one eye on the store, the licensee must direct the other toward Washington to keep up with the new FCC regulations and new interpretations of old ones. Trade organizations, trade publications, and a corps of communications attorneys in Washington help licensees with this task.

Lawyers who represent stations in FCC dealings belong to the Federal Communications Bar Asso-

---

*Broadcasting teachers at universities sometimes assign inspection of station public files as a student project. Often students get blank stares or flat refusals because some station personnel know nothing about the FCC public-file requirement.

EXHIBIT 17–3   Renewal Deregulation

FCC 303-S

United States of America
Federal Communications Commission
Washington, D.C. 20554

Approved by OMB
3060-0110

APPLICATION FOR RENEWAL OF LICENSE FOR COMMERCIAL AND NONCOMMERCIAL AM, FM OR TV BROADCAST STATION

1. Name of Applicant   Street Address

Call Letters   City   State   ZIP Code

2. Have the following reports been filed with the Commission:
(a) The Annual Employment Reports (FCC Form 395) as required by Section 73.3612 of the Commission's rules?
☐ Yes   ☐ No
If No, attach as Exhibit No. _____ an explanation.

(b) The applicant's Ownership Report (FCC Form 323 or 323-E) as required by Section 73.3615 of the Commission's rules?
☐ Yes   ☐ No   If No, give the following information:
Date last ownership report was filed. _____
Call letters of the renewal application with which it was filed. _____

3. Is the applicant in compliance with the provisions of Section 310 of the Communications Act of 1934, as amended, relating to interests of aliens and foreign governments?
☐ Yes   ☐ No
If No, attach as Exhibit No. _____ an explanation.

4. Since the filing of the applicant's last renewal application for this station or other major application, has an adverse finding been made, a consent decree been entered or final action been approved by any court or administrative body with respect to the applicant or parties to the application concerning any civil or criminal suit, action or proceeding brought under the provisions of any federal, state, territorial or local law relating to the following: any felony; lotteries; unlawful restraints or monopolies; unlawful combinations; contracts or agreements in restraint of trade; the use of unfair methods of competition; fraud; unfair labor practices; or discrimination?
☐ Yes   ☐ No   If Yes, attach as Exhibit No. _____ a full description, including identification of the court or administrative body, proceeding by file number, the person and matters involved, and the disposition of litigation.

5. Has the applicant placed in its public inspection file at the appropriate times the documentation required by Section 73.3526 or 73.3527 of the Commission's rules?
☐ Yes   ☐ No   If No, attach as Exhibit No. _____ a complete statement of explanation.

THE APPLICANT hereby waives any claim to the use of any particular frequency or of the ether as against the regulatory power of the United States because of the previous use of the same, whether by license or otherwise, and requests an authorization in accordance with this application. (See Section 304 of the Communications Act of 1934, as amended.)

THE APPLICANT acknowledges that all the statements made in this application and attached exhibits are considered material representations and that all the exhibits are a material part hereof and are incorporated herein as set out in full in the application.

CERTIFICATION

I certify that the statements in this application are true, complete, and correct to the best of my knowledge and belief, and are made in good faith.

Signed and dated this _____ day of _____ 19 ____

Name of Applicant _____

WILLFUL FALSE STATEMENTS MADE ON THIS FORM ARE PUNISHABLE BY FINE AND IMPRISONMENT, U.S. CODE, TITLE 18, SECTION 1001

By Signature _____

Title _____

One deregulatory benefit for broadcasters is demonstrated by the difference between (A) the more than 16-pound filing for renewal of four stations in Nebraska in 1971 and (B) the short stack of paper that was sufficient to renew the same stations in 1983. Seven staff members spent time developing the 1971 stack of material. (C) A key document in the change is the FCC's postcard renewal form.

SOURCES: *Broadcasting* magazine; FCC.

ciation (FCBA). It has about 1,500 members who handle both common carrier and electronic media matters. Most stations of any size retain an FCBA lawyer. Proximity to the commission and personal contacts with FCC staff members enable Washington lawyers to get things done faster than can distant licensees unfamiliar with federal bureaucratic labyrinths.

Most of a communications lawyer's routine work simply consists of keeping clients alert and properly informed. Very few of the thousands of applications, petitions, and other matters the FCC handles ever reach the point of being "designated for hearing," when formal legal representation becomes indispensable. Most lawyers mail out information regularly to their clients, reminding them of filing dates, informing them of new regulations, and interpreting recent FCC and court decisions. Trade association meetings, such as those of the National Association of Broadcasters, offer legal clinics. The NAB also publishes regularly revised primers on interpreting the rules governing broadcasts by political candidates, compliance with EEO guidelines, avoiding antilottery law violations and avoiding libel suits.

Checking on Licensee Performance   In the course of normal operations, a conscientious broadcaster experiences little official supervision or monitoring. Inspectors from the FCC's Field Operations Bureau check on technical aspects of station operations, but only occasionally and in random fashion. Questions about programming and commercial practices, if they arise at all, usually come to FCC attention through complaints from the general public, consumer groups, other licensees, and competing applicants at renewal time.

The Mass Media Bureau's Enforcement Division receives more public comments than any federal agency other than those dealing with environmental protection and consumer product safety. A complaints and compliance office came into being in 1960 in the aftermath of quiz and payola scandals. Originally planned as an active monitoring arm of the FCC, it settled into the more passive role of disposing in a perfunctory manner of the thousands

of cards and letters sent to the FCC each year by the general public.

Few complainants seem to understand the FCC's legal limitations. Most complaints have to be discarded simply because they ask the commission to violate the First Amendment by censoring material the writers personally dislike. The leading topics vary only slightly from year to year, often influenced by organized letter-writing campaigns as well as by program trends.

The most persistent letter-writing campaign, still evident 15 years later, began in 1975 in reaction to a petition asking the FCC to stop exempting noncommercial FM and television stations from the multiple ownership rules. It also asked for a freeze on licensing of such stations to government and religious groups, pending an investigation of the extent to which they complied with the fairness doctrine and fulfilled the educational purposes of the noncommercial allocations. The FCC rejected the petition less than a year after it had been submitted. That should have closed the episode, but the dismissal of the petition had no effect whatever on the flood of mail opposing it from those who had been misled into believing that the petition asked for a flat ban on all religious programs. By late 1988 more than 21 million complaints had been received by letter and telephone, and they continued to roll in despite efforts to stanch the flow. This mindless outpouring carried a double irony: not only had the petition long since been denied, but the writers had no understanding of what it would have accomplished even if it had been accepted by the FCC.

17.3
Station License Renewal

Under the Communications Act, licenses may be awarded for only "limited periods of time" (currently five years for television and seven years for radio) and must regularly come up for renewal, a requirement that greatly enhances the power implicit in the FCC's licensing authority. Although the FCC renews more than 98 percent of all licenses without asking any searching questions, licensees always feel the possibility of nonrenewal lurking in the background. Challenges to renewal applications can come not only from the FCC, but also from other would-be licensees who would like to displace the incumbent license holder and from dissatisfied citizens in the licensee's community. Even if the incumbent wins a contested renewal, defending it can be both expensive and time-consuming.

Application Routes The Communications Act stipulates that licenses shall be renewed *if the public interest, convenience, and necessity would be served* by renewal (§309). Before deregulation of renewal procedures, the application required mounds of documents showing how the licensee had served the public interest (Exhibit 17–3). In 1981, the FCC began phasing in a simple postcard-sized renewal form, submitted four months before the expiration of the current station license. The FCC staff investigates any minor problems by mail or telephone.

In deciding whether a renewal would be in the public interest, the FCC staff considers information that may have accumulated in a licensee's file as a result of complaints or penalties during the license period. Whether or not this evidence affects renewal decisions depends on the route the renewal application takes through the FCC bureaucracy. As shown in Exhibit 17–4, renewal applications take one of three basic paths: the *uncontested* route, the *petition-to-deny* route, or the *mutually exclusive* application route.

Some 98 percent of all renewal applications fall in the *uncontested* category. If there have been no serious complaints lodged against a station, no major penalties assessed against it during the preceding license period, and no objection filed, the FCC staff uses its delegated authority to renew the station almost automatically. In fact, consumer advocates complain that the Mass Media Bureau merely rubber-stamps uncontested applications, no matter how mediocre a station's past performance may have been.

The rare *petition-to-deny* renewal comes from a citizen group or other party that opposes an incumbent licensee without wanting to take over the license. Such groups claim that incumbents have failed to meet public-interest standards (most often allegations on EEO guidelines) and therefore should not be allowed to retain their licenses.

Mutually exclusive applications arise when would-be licensees try to displace incumbents, claiming they can do a better job in serving the public interest.

Contested Renewals Contested renewals present the FCC with difficult and controversial decisions. Two goals that may be desirable but are opposite compete for priority: (1) giving incumbent licensees a "legitimate renewal expectation," but at the same time (2) ensuring that incumbents nevertheless feel a "competitive spur" to strive to serve the public interest.

On the one hand, incumbent licensees need a reasonable assurance of continuity to justify investments in equipment, personnel, and programming. Without a strong expectation of renewal at the end of a license period, no prudent investor, commercial or noncommercial, would be willing to build a station.

On the other hand, if incumbent licensees feel assured of automatic renewal no matter how poor their program performance, they may be tempted to take the low road, wringing maximum profit out of their stations and giving no serious consideration to the public interest. Assured renewal would in effect give existing licensees a monopoly on channels, freezing out worthy competitors.

Even though the philosophy of the Communications Act plainly rejects this solution by stating that renewals must serve the public interest, not merely the private interest of the licensee, the deregulation of the 1980s had the practical effect of avoiding any serious effort to evaluate performance in terms of the public interest, creating virtually permanent licensees.

When it has to decide between incumbents and competing applicants, the FCC faces the dilemma of comparing apples and oranges—the incumbent's *actual* past record of service with a competitor's

EXHIBIT 17–4   License Renewal Routes

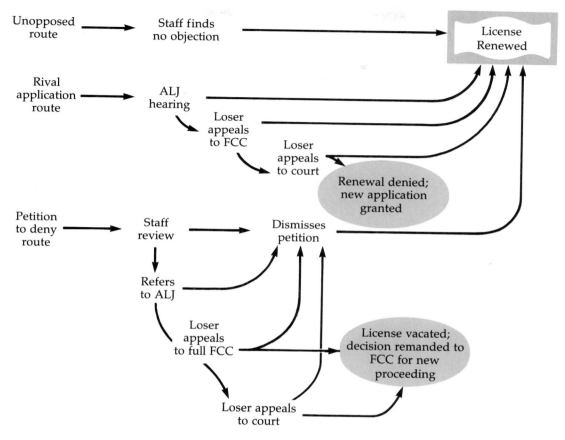

The great majority of renewals travel the unopposed route. Opposed applications, however, sometimes travel a long and rocky road before renewal or denial becomes final.

proposed future service. What sort of performance by an incumbent licensee should the FCC accept in preference to a would-be licensee's glowing promises to do even better if given a chance? Should merely average past performance assure renewal? Better than average performance? Superior performance? What evidence should the FCC weigh in grading past performance to decide whether an incumbent deserves a superior, passing, or failing grade? Significantly, all these questions involve programming. And programming is the one licensee role, admittedly crucial, the FCC least wants to appraise.

When faced with a comparative renewal, the commission relies in part on criteria issued a quarter-century ago for comparative hearings for new licenses (FCCR, 1965: 393). These include consideration of:

- Technical factors (for example, a proposed antenna location that would serve a larger area than the present one).

- Ownership and management issues (diversification of media ownership—not owning other media or not owning other media nearby; localism—active participation by the owner in management; and ownership by members of a minority).

- Past broadcast record (of the incumbent and, if applicable, the opposing applicant).

- Program service proposals (especially the amount and type of nonentertainment programming). Exhibit 17–5 illustrates a "David and Goliath" case in which all of these criteria played a part.

17.4
Cable Franchising

Cable licensing, called *franchising,* follows a totally different pattern from broadcast licensing. Franchises are issued by local rather than federal authorities because cable systems use streets and other public property that is subject to municipal jurisdiction rather than the electromagnetic spectrum.* Federal cable regulation deals only with broad subjects such as cross-ownership, equal employment opportunities, program obscenity, and technical standards.

Role of Local Authorities The cable act of 1984, incorporated as Title VI of the Communications Act (discussed in Section 16.3), established a loose federal regulatory framework for cable television. Key provisions of the law include:

- The act defines cable television as a one-way video programming service; it does not include two-way services (§602).

- Local franchising authorities may require public, educational, and governmental access ("PEG")

channels over which the cable operator has no editorial control (§611[a]). Some First Amendment experts question the constitutionality of this requirement.

- Cable systems with more than 36 channels must set aside 10 to 15 percent of those channels for *leased access* to parties other than the cable system owner. The cable owner sets rates for leasing the channels, but has no editorial control over programming on those channels (§612).

- Local franchise authorities may charge franchise fees of no more than 5 percent of gross cable system revenues (§622).

- Federal or state authorities may not regulate subscriber rates for basic cable service (§623). The statute incorporated the existing FCC ban on regulation of pay-cable rates.

- Local authorities may require that cable facilities and channel capacity be upgraded when granting franchise renewals (§626).

The cable act thus considerably limits the regulatory power of state and local authorities. Eleven states have cable statutes. They usually assign cable responsibility to existing public utility commissions but they have had little effect on the development of the medium. However, because cable systems nearly always have effective monopoly status within their service areas, they fall under state and community utility regulations, which govern installation, standards of service, and complaint procedures.

Franchising Process When a local franchising authority (city, town, or county) decides it wants cable service, it first develops an *ordinance,* describing the conditions under which a cable system will be allowed to operate. Drawn up in many cases with the advice of outside experts, ordinances typically stipulate

- The term of the franchise (usually 10 to 15 years, but sometimes more).

- The quality of service to be provided.

- Technical standards, such as the minimum number of channels to be provided, time limits on construction, and interconnection with other systems.

*The cable act does not cover cable systems that avoid using public rights of way (technically SMATV systems)—such as those that serve large apartment complexes and are entirely on private property. Neither state nor local authorities have the power to regulate such systems.

EXHIBIT 17–5 David v. Goliath—The Simon Geller Case

Simon Geller, the eccentric owner and sole staff member of classical music station WVCA-FM in Gloucester, MA, a fishing and resort community north of Boston, was a folk hero to his loyal listeners. Geller, who put his station on the air in 1964, adopted a wall-to-wall classical music format that ran 15 hours daily, interrupted only with barely enough advertising to keep the station solvent. In fact, many of his 90,000 appreciative listeners sent in donations to keep the station afloat. Geller did not let news or public-affairs programs interrupt the music; he felt that the Boston stations that put signals over the Gloucester area took care of those needs.

Grandbanke Corporation, a group owner of radio stations in Massachusetts, became interested in the potential of the Gloucester market. As no other FM channels were allotted to the small town, Grandbanke tried to buy Geller's station, offering to keep him on the payroll. Geller, for whom the station was a way of life, turned down the offer. Grandbanke thereupon filed a competing application for the facility when Geller's license came up for renewal. The corporation assembled a textbook set of management and program promises closely paralleling the FCC's 1965 comparative renewal criteria. It promised to devote nearly 29 percent of the station's overall schedule to news and public affairs, while retaining the classical music format the rest of the time. The management would work closely with Gloucester groups to air community issues.

The FCC administrative law judge who heard the case initially approved Geller's renewal. However, the commission, concerned about Geller's total lack of news and public affairs programs, set the case for an oral argument before making a final decision. Geller, who was unable to pay for an attorney, came to Washington and gave the FCC an emotional defense of his stewardship, noting that the station had to go off the air while he appeared before the FCC because there

was no one else to run it. Unmoved, the FCC found Grandbanke's several attorneys persuasive in proving that their client could better fulfill the public interest as defined by the FCC's 1965 statement.

Geller appealed the case, meanwhile keeping his station on the air. In 1985, the court of appeals returned the case to the FCC, telling the commission that it had been inconsistent in applying its own 1965 statement of comparative criteria to this case. Specifically, Geller should be awarded a preference for his absolute integration of ownership and management and for localism (the station was in Geller's two-room apartment). Finally, late in 1985, the FCC reversed itself and renewed Geller's license (FCCR, 1985c: 1443). David had faced Goliath in unequal combat and had won. In 1988, Geller had the last laugh: he sold his station for a cool million dollars—and not to Grandbanke—and retired to the movie theaters and delicatessens of the Upper East Side of Manhattan. The new owner promised to keep the classical format—and to hire 10 people to run the station 24 hours a day.

SOURCE: Rick Friedman/New York *Times* pictures.

- The franchise fee.
- PEG channel requirements, if any.

Bidders base their offers on the design and timetable, outlined in the franchise authority's *request for* *proposals* (RFP). Although franchisers usually grant a franchise to only one bidder, multiple awards (termed *overbuilds* if they cover the same region) are possible. Some cable operators have argued in court that cities should grant multiple franchises so long as space for additional systems remains available on telephone poles or in underground conduits. In 1990 the issue remained unresolved. During the 1980s, controversy arose when successful bidders made grandiose promises that they later could not fulfill, so that the franchise had to be renegotiated with a lower quality of service resulting. A few communities avoided such problems by choosing to operate cable systems themselves as a municipal service, an arrangement common in Europe.

Franchise Renewals As with original franchise awards, the local franchising authority, not the FCC, handles franchise renewals. The local authority need not find that renewal will serve the public interest or meet any other standard, but may simply renew a franchise without ceremony. If, however, the local authority wants to deny renewal, the Communications Act requires it to hold a hearing, in effect raising public-interest issues by deciding whether the incumbent operator has (1) complied with the law; (2) provided a quality of service that is "reasonable in light of the community needs"; (3) maintained the financial, legal, and technical ability to operate; and (4) prepared a renewal proposal that is "reasonable to meet the future cable-related community needs and interests" (§626). The act makes no mention of considering proposals from competing would-be franchisees during the course of renewal grants or renewal hearings.

17.5
Ownership Diversification

First Amendment theory, discussed in more detail in the next chapter, stresses the value of maintaining a marketplace in which ideas, information, and opinions from many diverse and antagonistic sources compete for acceptance. Under modern conditions, however, unregulated competition may lead to monopoly control. Government can play a positive First Amendment role by devising regulations that prevent media monopoly. *Diversification* of ownership and control therefore has been a major goal of FCC regulation. This type of *structural* regulation con-

trasts with the *behavioral* regulation discussed in the next chapter.

Examples of structural regulation include rules limiting

▌ The number and kind of stations licensed to any one owner.

▌ Concentration of control over program production and distribution.

▌ *Cross-media* ownership (stations, systems, and other media under common control).

Every broadcast station enjoys a limited monopoly, since its licensee has exclusive use of a given channel in a particular market. Cable presents a more far-reaching monopoly situation. Once viewers "go on the cable," installers disconnect antennas so that home owners receive broadcast stations *only* by cable. A cable operator thus has an effective monopoly on all video signals coming into a home, other than programs on rented or purchased tapes.

Multiple Ownership Because of the monopolistic nature of even a single station, the FCC limits multiple station ownership. Nationally, the *12-12-12 rule* confines a single owner to no more than 12 stations in each broadcast service: AM, FM, and television.*

During the 1980s the FCC eliminated a number of other ownership limitations, including the *anti-trafficking* rule that had required a licensee to hold a station at least three years before selling it; a limitation on regional concentration of ownership; and rules that defined passive financial holdings in broadcast companies as "ownership." These changes reflect the FCC's policy of relying more on mar-

---

*The FCC adopted the 12-12-12 rule in 1985. For 32 years before that, it had limited multiple ownership to no more than seven stations of each type. The commission, in view of the increase in the number of stations during the preceding three decades, wanted to deregulate limits entirely by 1990, but pressure from Congress and the film industry (which was concerned about network ownership of more stations) led to the 12-12-12 compromise. In the case of television, an owner is allowed to reach no more than 25 percent of the nation's population, even if fewer than 12 stations have that reach. Under certain conditions, combinations of stations controlled by members of minority groups can go as high as 14-14-14.

ketplace competition than on structural regulation to safeguard the public interest. Many financial analysts regarded the 12-12-12 rule as one reason for the explosive demand for broadcast and cable properties that sparked a media-merger mania beginning in 1985.

On the individual market level, the *duopoly* rule issued by the FCC in 1940 holds that no single owner can have more than one station of the same type (for example, more than one AM station) in the same market. Originally one owner could control a single-market AM-FM-TV combination, but the commission banned such combinations in 1970. Now one owner may have only one television station, one radio station, or one AM-FM combination in a single market. Individual exceptions often allow radio and UHF television station combinations to help strengthen the UHF service.

These broadcast ownership rules allow *grandfathering,* which exempts multiple ownerships that were already in effect in 1970 so long as the same owner has the stations. The FCC also grants waivers in specific cases.* Thus, restructuring of local ownership will take place only over time, as grandfathered groups are sold and broken up and as the FCC issues new licenses on a *one-to-a-customer* basis.

None of this regulatory complexity limits ownership of competing electronic media such as cable television systems. The possibility of a limit on *multiple-system operators* (MSOs) or a ceiling on how many cable subscribers one multiple-system operator may control has frequently been proposed to Congress, the Justice Department's Antitrust Division, and the FCC. But the deregulatory policy and cable industry lobbying have fended off such limits. LPTV stations also have no ownership limitation. Broadcasters argue that the 12-12-12 rule, because it affects only full-power radio and TV stations, flies in the face of the ideal of establishing parity among the media that are competing with one another for public acceptance and advertising revenue.

---

*These rules do not limit noncommercial station ownership, as the FCC wants to foster expansion of the noncommercial service. Some states have developed networks of FM and/or television stations under this exemption.

Cross-Media Ties   Every broadcast license or cable franchise granted to a local newspaper publisher automatically reduces diversification of media ownership. This reduction in alternative public sources of information (sometimes called media *voices,* as opposed to actual outlets, such as stations or systems) is especially undesirable in small communities, in which the only newspaper might own the only broadcast station or cable system.

The FCC issued rules banning newspaper-broadcasting *cross-ownership* in 1975, avoiding a confrontation with powerful newspaper interests by grandfathering all but a very few existing combinations. However, although the FCC and Congress have considered a limit on newspaper-cable cross-ownership on several occasions, none has been adopted.

Cable companies may not own or be owned by television stations or telephone companies (except in rural areas for the latter) whose coverage overlaps their cable coverage areas. According to the Communications Act, the FCC may set up other cross-ownership rules for cable if it chooses (§613). The FCC had first banned network ownership of cable systems and co-ownership of telephone companies and cable systems in 1970 to prevent older services from controlling programming to the detriment of the newer media.

At the end of the 1980s, however, a new cross-ownership controversy developed, one in which broadcasters and cable owners took the same side. They both feared that the FCC might allow telephone companies to own cable systems and possibly even broadcast stations in their telephone service areas. Bans against such cross-ownership kept the regulated common-carrier and media businesses apart, but telephone interests increasingly sought a share in the information business, to which the electronic media belong. More than one government research paper called for a "video dial tone" concept whereby telephone companies could own and operate at least the means of transmission, even if they were permitted no active role in programming.

The merger mania of the 1980s raised novel cross-media problems. A number of the takeovers and mergers created not only commonly owned collections of broadcast stations that were too large (more than 36 in all, or more than 12 of a particular type of service) but also new companies that owned both stations and cable systems or newspapers in the same market. The FCC granted short-term waivers to virtually all the companies affected to give them time to comply with cross-ownership rules by selling some of the properties.

In addition to FCC rules, antitrust regulations, though put on the back burner during the 1980s, play a potential role in media ownership regulation. FCC approval of joint ownership of stations or other media does not necessarily make the resulting combination immune from prosecution under the antitrust statutes. In the past, the Justice Department's Antitrust Division has often questioned, and sometimes gone to court to enjoin, FCC-approved mergers that appeared to lessen marketplace competition.

Minority Ownership   Initially the FCC declined to consider the minority status of owners as an aspect of diversifying media control. A series of court reversals in the 1960s and early 1970s, however, forced it to re-examine its position.

In the Orlando, FL, channel 9 case, the commission had refused to give much weight to the fact that one of the competing applicants had two black stockholders, despite the fact that about a quarter of Orlando's population was black. The FCC said it considered the Communications Act to be "color blind." An appeals court rejected this view, pointing out that it was consistent with the diversification principle "to afford favorable consideration to an applicant who, not as a mere token, but in good faith as broadening community representation, gives a local minority group media entrepreneurship" (F, 1973b: 937). As a result of this and other reversals, the FCC began to give an advantage to minority applicants.

In 1978, spurred by Carter administration policies on aid to minorities, the FCC took steps to enhance opportunities for members of ethnic and racial minority groups to become licensees:

▌ After prodding from the NAB, the FCC agreed to issue *tax certificates* to licensees proposing to sell stations to minority buyers. These certificates encourage such sales by allowing sellers to defer paying capital gains taxes on their profits; sellers can further defer the taxes if they purchase another station within two years (they must be paid when the "replacement property" is sold).

▌ The FCC also agreed to allow *distress sales* to minority groups. Normally the commission will not permit an owner whose license is in serious danger of nonrenewal to sell anything other than the station's physical assets. But to encourage sales to minority applicants, the FCC makes exceptions, permitting endangered licensees to recover some, but not all, of the market value of both tangible and intangible assets. For example, the FCC agreed in 1979 to drop fraudulent billing charges against a small AM station in Connecticut when the incumbent offered to sell the property to a minority group for 75 percent of its appraised value. The 75 percent figure became a *de facto* standard for future distress sales.

▌ In 1982, the commission gave further encouragement to minority participation in ownership. It allowed members of a racial minority holding as little as 20 percent of the equity in the licensee to take advantage of the tax certificates and distress sale rules, provided the minority owner had voting control. At the same time, the FCC made cable system sales also eligible for tax certificate consideration.

▌ Use of lotteries in choosing LPTV and MMDS licenses gave preference to minority ownership, as detailed in Section 17.1.

Although minority ownership of stations increased sharply after the 1970s (to about 300 stations in 1988 from about 50 a decade before), the National Black Media Coalition reported that to achieve ownership of stations in proportion to their actual numbers in society, some 1,250 broadcast stations would have to be owned by blacks, and about 450 by Hispanics. The industry has a long way to go before minorities achieve ownership parity.

Despite this record, the FCC briefly suspended the distress sale minority preference option in the late 1980s because of ideological opposition to "reverse discrimination," as opponents called the special breaks for minorities. However, pressure from Congress soon forced the commission to reinstate the rules encouraging minority ownership.

Network Ownership   As the chief producers, procurers, and distributors of broadcast programs, the television broadcast networks have long been the target of FCC structural controls. Network ownership of stations and of other media has been a specific subject of concern. Networks, like all other broadcast group owners, fall under the 12-12-12 rule. But they may not own cable systems as do many other group owners. However, the networks are permitted to cross-own cable program networks and cable programs.

The steady development of cable networks since the late 1970s has reduced the FCC's concern about the three-network bottleneck in national program origination. Nevertheless, several behavioral rules for television networks remain, strongly supported by elements of the broadcast and motion picture industries. Notable examples are the prime-time access and syndication/financial interest rules. Designed originally to increase diversity by maintaining the programming independence of network affiliate stations and opening the market to independent producers, these rules built up independent television stations and their program suppliers. Those elements of the business put pressure on Congress to make the FCC retain the rules.

17.6
Deregulation

In the preceding discussion of FCC licensing, it has frequently been necessary to refer to the deletion or softening of specific rules as a result of *deregulation*. The impulse to deregulate had more than one motive. On the least controversial level, deregulators simply wanted to discard outdated rules, to simplify unnecessarily complex rules, to ensure that those rules that remained on the books could actually achieve their objectives, and to lighten the

FCC's administrative load. Deregulation based on these motives began in the 1970s, supported by both Democratic and Republican administrations.

On a more controversial level, the impulse to deregulate also stems from ideological motives, arising from a specific vision of the government's proper role in national life. This vision minimizes the need for government intervention, advocating instead reliance on the economic marketplace as a nongovernmental source of control over private economic behavior. Deregulation of this type emerged as a major item on the national agenda when the Republican administration came to power with President Ronald Reagan in 1980.

Theory   The details of the wide-ranging theories about government spending and taxation, about marketplace competition and consumer choice, and about other economic activities that undergird contemporary deregulatory thinking are beyond the scope of the present discussion. But it should be realized that conservative policy makers, far from picking on telecommunications as a special target for deregulation, have applied similar reasoning to virtually every aspect of national life. Most people have become aware, for example, of the widespread repercussions from airline and banking deregulation.

In brief, deregulatory theory asserts that the competitive give-and-take of the marketplace can satisfy most regulatory goals without the need for government rules and bureaucratic supervision. Competition and consumer choice, the theory asserts, impose more sensitive, meaningful controls over economic activities than can government agencies. These private economic forces can stimulate production of better, more varied, and cheaper consumer goods and services without official guidance from above. Insofar as government regulation may be necessary, it should be tested by a cost-benefit formula to make sure that the losses arising from such regulation do not outweigh the gains.

As a case in point, the FCC explained its initial move to deregulate radio this way:

Producers (providers) of goods and services must be responsive to consumers' desires in order to compete successfully with rival producers. Consumers, by their choice of purchases, determine which producers (providers) will succeed. Moreover, not only does the competition among producers for consumers lead to the production of the goods and services that consumers want most, the same competitive process forces producers continually to seek less costly ways of providing those goods and services. As a result, parties operating freely in a competitive market environment will determine and fulfill consumer wants, and do so efficiently (FCCR, 1979c: 492).

The FCC did not go so far as to advocate abandoning *all* regulation. It divided rules into two categories, behavioral and structural. Behavioral regulation, which deregulators seek to discard or at least to minimize, controls what licensees may or may not do in conducting their businesses; structural regulation controls the overall shape of the businesses in which licensees engage and the terms on which would-be licensees can enter the marketplace. Rules requiring a licensee to carry a certain percentage of children's programs or to ban indecent program material would be examples of behavioral regulation; rules preventing a licensee from owning another related communications business or from owning more than X number of stations would constitute examples of structural regulation. The theory generally supports structural regulation because it can enhance competition by making marketplace entry easier and preserve competition by preventing monopoly.

Theorists admit that *market failure* can occur. Sometimes competition fails to produce the expected favorable results. For example, uncontrolled competition may eventually result in monopolies that suppress competition (airline control of most departures at "hub" airports in the late 1980s is one alleged example). Some public "goods," as economists call desirable things, may fall outside the realm of marketplace economics and therefore fail to materialize. If, for example, one grants that grand opera provides a desirable public good but costs too much to produce profitably on a commercial basis, it may be necessary to bypass the market by giving it government support.

This "public good" question arises with regard to public television: if the public declines to pay for it through subscriptions or other voluntary payments, is it so desirable a public good that the government should lend it support? Conservatives tend to answer "no," believing that public television offers nothing that private enterprise could not provide without need for government assistance.

Broadcasting Deregulation In the mid-1970s the FCC did away with many minor rules, but during the 1980s it began removing more substantive rules, focusing first on commercial radio, which with more stations is a naturally more competitive industry (Exhibit 17–6). In 1981, after an inquiry begun four years earlier, the commission deleted four of its long-standing constraints on radio licensees:

▌ The prescribed formal process for *ascertaining local community needs* that stations had to go through as a basis for making programming decisions; only the requirement of having a general knowledge of the local community remains.

▌ Rules for *program-log* keeping.

▌ Guidelines maintaining at least a certain level of *nonentertainment programs*.

▌ Guidelines on the maximum allowable amount of *advertising time* on the air (FCCR, 1981b: 968).

These steps caused heated controversy, especially because some observers mistakenly thought the FCC had previously imposed formal rules (rather than guidelines) on programs and advertisements. For example, many mistakenly feared that deregulation might mean the end of religion on the air, thinking that the FCC had always required such programs.*

Having paved the way with commercial radio deregulation, the FCC followed by deregulating edu-

---

*The FCC had delegated authority to enforce guidelines on nonentertainment programming and advertising to its licensing staff. Contrary to general opinion, the FCC never had *rules* mandating specific amounts of nonentertainment programming or limiting the maximum amount of advertising time. Instead, it had set up *guidelines* and allowed its staff to grant applications unless licensees failed to follow the guidelines. Violators' applications had to go before the full commission to explain their actions. In practice, the guidelines became virtual quotas because applicants sought to avoid the close scrutiny and delay that would result if the staff referred a decision upstairs to the commission.

EXHIBIT 17–6   Deregulatory Summary of the 1980s

FCC Regulations	*Post-Deregulatory Status*

A. Licensing

License lasts three years for radio and TV stations alike	License lasts 5 years for television, 3 for radio (action by Congress, 1981)
Comparative hearings required for any competing applications	Lottery allowed for newer services (LPTV, MMDS, etc.; action by Congress, 1982)

B. Ownership Limits

Ownership limit of 7-7-7 (AM-FM-TV) stations	Limit raised to 12-12-12 (action by Congress, 1985)
Trafficking rule: Must hold a station at least three years.	No minimum holding time; may sell at any time (action by FCC, 1982)

C. Programming

FCC application processing guidelines to staff call for minimum amounts of non-entertainment programming	No quantitative program guidelines (action by FCC: radio-1982, television-1985)
Specific rules for ascertaining local program needs (ascertainment)	No rules remain, just generalized requirement to "know" community of license (action by FCC: radio-1982, television-1985)
Guidelines (not rules) on maximum amounts of advertising per hour	No guidelines or rules on amount of advertising carried (action by FCC: 1982-radio, 1985-TV)
Controversial issues must be aired and opposing sides treated fairly	Fairness Doctrine dropped (action by FCC, 1987)

D. Cable Carriage

Cable systems must carry all local TV stations	Must carry rules dropped (action by U.S. Appeals Court, 1985, 1987)
Syndicated exclusivity rules allow stations to enforce contract provisions on syndicated programs	Rules dropped (action by FCC, 1980) but then reinstated (action by FCC, 1988)

E. Technical Rules

FCC had traditionally selected a specific technical standard for new services (color TV, FM stereo, etc.)	With AM stereo decision (1982), FCC generally leaves standards to marketplace forces.
All stations must have access to a First Class engineer	Engineers no longer ranked by class (action by FCC, 1981)
Many specific rules on technical operations	Stations use own methods for maintaining signal quality and avoiding interference (actions by FCC)

The list covers only the salient changes in broadcasting and cable rules. The FCC modified or eliminated many other broadcasting and cable rules during the deregulation drive of the 1980s. Unchanged, however, are rules on equal employment opportunity and political broadcast access, among others.

cational radio and television (FCCR, 1984c: 746) and then commercial television (FCCR, 1984d: 1076). In each case, the commission lifted mandated procedures for ascertaining community needs and for program logs; for commercial television, it lifted the programming and advertising guidelines parallel to the previously mentioned radio guidelines.

In some cases the FCC substituted less demanding procedures for detailed and onerous regulations. For example, though it rescinded explicit steps that licensees had to take to ascertain public needs in their communities, it now required them to place in their public files quarterly statements of community problems and issues and a list of programs the licensee had offered to deal with those problems (FCCR, 1984a: 930).

Television networks underwent an intensive FCC special inquiry in 1979–1980, the third and perhaps last broadcast network study. A special staff exhaustively researched the potential for new television networks, the FCC's jurisdiction over networks,* issues of station and cable-system ownership, the impact of existing FCC network rules, and the degree to which cable and newer media had broadened competition. This staff report concluded that prior network regulation had utterly failed to bring about its stated goal of fostering increased diversity of programming; instead, it had stifled competition, often by protecting the networks from the inroads of such new technologies as cable. It recommended that the commission undo most of its existing network rules (FCC, 1980b: 491).†

When the commission tried to follow the special-inquiry network deregulation recommendations, however, industry lobbyists brought the effort to a standstill. Program syndicators urged retention of

the prime-time access rule (PTAR) even though it does little to curb network domination of evening television time, as originally intended. The attempt to lift two related rules limiting network financial interest in and syndication of programs (the *syn/fin rules*) proved even more contentious. These rules restrict network ownership and distribution of programs once they complete their network runs (Section 13.3). In an unprecedented intervention, President Ronald Reagan directed his policy body, the National Telecommunications and Information Administration, to argue in favor of the rules, and NTIA pressured the FCC to change its plans to cancel these network restrictions.

Cable Deregulation   The FCC had more success in streamlining procedures and requirements for newer delivery services. As discussed in Section 4.1, cable television, as the first nonbroadcast mass electronic medium to develop, took the brunt of the FCC's traditional policy of protecting the broadcasting status quo. The commission sought especially to protect UHF television, which it feared would suffer irreparably from rapid cable expansion. A series of court reverses, followed by the economic rethinking noted above, caused the FCC to drop most of its cable regulation by 1980, as shown in Exhibit 17–7. Congress moved the same way in the 1984 cable act (Section 17.4).

By 1985, the most controversial FCC restriction on cable still in place was the *must-carry rule,* which required each cable system to carry the signals of all "significantly viewed" television stations within that system's coverage area. The FCC had intended to protect broadcasters from discriminatory treatment by cable operators and to help stations with weak signals, usually nonnetwork UHF and public stations, by equalizing the reach of all stations' signals in cable-covered areas.

---

*Bear in mind that the Communications Act gives the FCC no explicit power to regulate networks. Section 303(i) gives the commission the right to "make special regulations applicable to radio *stations* engaged in chain broadcasting" (emphasis added), but not to regulate networks directly. The FCC licensing process influences networks inasmuch as each network holds licenses for its several O&O stations.

†The FCC could not, however, undo the chief cause of the fact that there were still only three national television networks even though hundreds of new stations had been licensed since ABC,

CBS, and NBC had begun television operations. The FCC's post-freeze 1952 television channel allotment plan made it virtually impossible for a fourth network to recruit enough affiliates to compete effectively. The Fox network of the late 1980s demonstrated this; in 1989, three years after it started, its largely UHF station lineup reached only a fraction of the national audience served by the three traditional networks.

EXHIBIT 17–7 Cable Deregulation

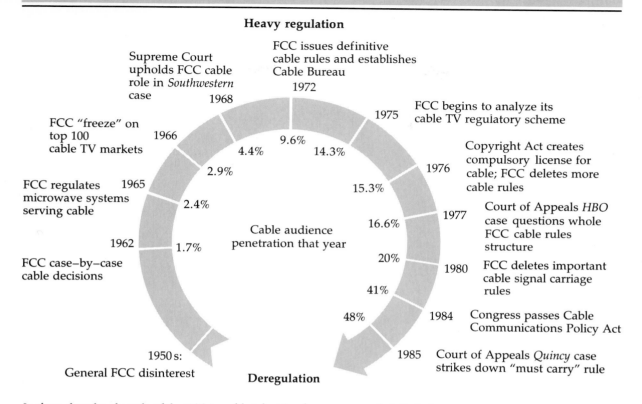

Heavy regulation

FCC issues definitive cable rules and establishes Cable Bureau
1972

Supreme Court upholds FCC cable role in *Southwestern* case   **1968**

FCC "freeze" on top 100 cable TV markets   **1966**

FCC regulates microwave systems serving cable   **1965**

1962
FCC case–by–case cable decisions

1950s:
General FCC disinterest

1975
FCC begins to analyze its cable TV regulatory scheme

1976
Copyright Act creates compulsory license for cable; FCC deletes more cable rules

1977
Court of Appeals *HBO* case questions whole FCC cable rules structure

1980
FCC deletes important cable signal carriage rules

1984
Congress passes Cable Communications Policy Act

1985
Court of Appeals *Quincy* case strikes down "must carry" rule

Deregulation

Cable audience penetration that year

1.7% 2.4% 2.9% 4.4% 9.6% 14.3% 15.3% 16.6% 20% 41% 48%

In three decades, the role of the FCC in cable television has come nearly full circle from virtually none to heavy interference and back to virtually none. As cable expanded, so did broadcaster fear of the service. Since 1975, cable regulation has been steadily relaxed for reasons discussed in the text, culminating in the strongly deregulatory 1984 cable act, which curbed regulation by the states and local communities as well as by the FCC.

The must-carry rule, however, penalized cable systems, especially those with a small channel capacity. Mandatory television signals filled many of their available channels, leaving few for cable-specific programs. Systems whose service areas straddled two or more broadcast markets sometimes had to carry several affiliates of the same network, stations that duplicated all but a few local programs.

When the FCC charged Ted Turner, as an operator of satellite-delivered program services, and a small cable system owner with violating the must-carry rule, both challenged the rule in court. They claimed it not only deprived subscribers of program options but also violated the First Amendment rights of cable operators. In 1985 an appeals court agreed that the rule as written violated the Constitution (F, 1985: 1434). The FCC rewrote the rule, requiring cable systems to carry most local broadcast signals for five years, until 1991. In 1987, the same appeals court also found this version unconstitutional, whereupon the FCC gave up and withdrew the must-carry rule (F, 1987: 292).

Cable operators could then pick and choose among television stations in filling their channels. Broadcasters remained concerned that they might lose access to the majority of their television audience, for by 1988 cable reached more than half the TV households. Cable systems did drop some of the many independent and public stations available in larger markets. In some cases television stations paid cable systems to continue carrying their signals.

TVRO Deregulation   Although its full impact was not foreseen at the time, the FCC's 1979 decision to deregulate the licensing of television receive-only (TVRO) antennas had far-reaching effects. The commission had required a complicated and often expensive licensing process for TVRO antennas, nearly all of which then belonged to cable systems or broadcast stations. Elimination of licensing meant that anyone could buy or build an antenna without red tape. Demand for antennas increased, prices came down, and demand surged further. TVRO deregulation directly fueled the expansion of satellite-delivered programming. On the other hand, TVROs also led directly to signal piracy (Section 16.6).

Technical Standards   Though the electronic media agreed with most aspects of the previously described broadcast and cable behavioral deregulation, they became uneasy when the FCC began *technical* deregulation. The issue came to the fore when the commission declined to select a specific technical standard for AM stereo. In 1982, for the first time in its history, the FCC refused to select a specific technical standard, a decision that became a precedent for future refusals to impose standards (Exhibit 17–8).

Similar nondecisions regarding DBS, teletext, television stereo, and other standards followed, indicating that economists had superseded engineers in commission policy making, even in largely technical matters. The "marketplace" in each case actually consisted, of course, not of consumers buying

receivers, but of station owners, operators, and manufacturers choosing equipment. Broadcasters would have to decide for themselves which transmission standard to use, hoping that set makers would eventually gear up to supply receivers that consumers would buy.

Industry debate over the FCC's approach to technical standards rose to a fever pitch over high-definition television (HDTV). At issue were the same concerns: whether the government should help industry select specific standards, and whether selection of a standard stifled technical development. But the stakes were far higher—the probable replacement of all the country's television receivers in the 1990s if HDTV succeeded. The potential impact on manufacturing and trade stimulated Europeans to begin a crash program in the late 1980s to develop their own HDTV standard so as to hold off the already well-developed Japanese system and preserve a still-thriving European consumer electronics industry. Similarly, many in the United States saw selection of an HDTV standard as the key to possible revival of the American consumer electronics market, which had long since given way to foreign, mainly Japanese, competition.

In 1986, the FCC established an advisory committee to consider the many competing systems of HDTV and "advanced" television, test them all, and make recommendations for commission action. Under the leadership of former FCC Chair Richard Wiley, the group began to issue reports in 1987. Late in 1988, the FCC made its first HDTV decision: any system adopted in the United States had to be compatible with existing receivers and could use no more than the existing broadcast television spectrum allotments.

Broadcasters feared that such limitations might allow cable, satellite, and VCR to deliver HDTV long before compatible systems for over-the-air broadcasting could be developed. Such uneven development could reduce conventional broadcasting to second-class status or even lead to its eventual demise. Thus HDTV loomed as possibly *the* media standards issue that needed to be resolved during the 1990s, with billions of dollars riding on the outcome.

EXHIBIT 17–8   Technical Deregulation: The AM Watershed

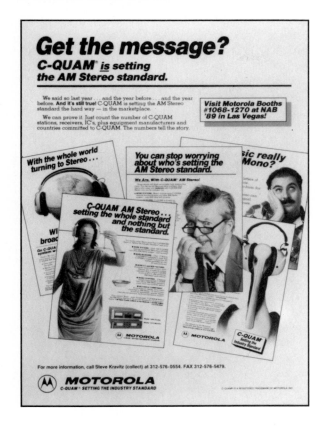

In April 1961, when the FCC approved an FM stereo standard, it turned down a parallel proposal for stereo AM in order to allow the then-weaker FM service to get a strong start. Less than two decades later, with the AM and FM roles reversed, AM stations sought to implement their own stereo system, to compete more effectively with now-dominant FM.

As they had done with FM and with television standards before that, manufacturers made comparative tests of several different systems as a basis for recommending the best system to the FCC as the legally mandated standard. However, the five AM stereo systems that emerged, though differing from one another in technical design (and thus mutually incompatible), offered little basis for choosing one over the others. The industry could not make a choice, and neither, apparently, could the FCC.

Early in 1980, the commission finally announced selection of the system developed by Magnavox. Broadcast engineers immediately challenged the system's technical quality and reliability, and questioned the validity of the testing process the FCC had used to reach its decision. The FCC thereupon withdrew its decision pending further research. Of the seven commissioners in 1980, only two voted against choosing a standard, arguing that the marketplace should decide such matters.

By March 1982, after several new commissioners had been appointed and with a quite different view of the government's regulatory role in ascendance, the commission voted six to one to approve AM stereo operations, but to leave the choice of system to the marketplace, setting only minimal standards to prevent interference (RR, 1982, 51:1).

By the end of the decade, only about 700 AM stations (of nearly 5,000) had started broadcasting in stereo. Most used a Motorola system, although 100 outlets clung to a system developed by Leonard Kahn. Many broadcasters felt that AM stereo had been fatally crippled by the lack of firm FCC standard setting. Because of antitrust laws, the industry could not simply get together and arbitrarily select a standard for all to follow. To do so would freeze out other standards, constituting restraint of trade in the eyes of the law. As related in the main text, however, the FCC saw the AM stereo nondecision as an important precedent to follow in standards cases that would come before it in future years.

SOURCE: Courtesy Motorola, Inc., AM Stereo.

New Services   The FCC's reluctance to mandate technical standards reflects the deregulatory concept that the market should lead technological development. For decades the commission had zealously protected traditional broadcasting, delaying the entry of new services and limiting competition. Examples of such FCC discouragement of new services include its early restrictions on cable television and its even longer delay of over-the-air subscription television.

In the 1980s, however, the FCC's deregulatory policy encouraged as many services as the market would bear, letting competition, not government, decide which new technologies should survive and how fast they should develop. The FCC's authorization of DBS services, discussed in Section 4.3, is a good example of this process. From the first filing for a DBS service in 1980 to final authorization in 1982, the commission moved with unaccustomed speed to authorize a wholly new service. Moreover, the agency moved ahead despite strong opposition from a broadcast industry fearful of potential competition. In this case, the market said, "No!" It decided that DBS as then conceived merely duplicated available services; consequently, this initial push for DBS in the United States failed.

In another case, the commission moved too fast, creating a huge application processing problem. The idea for LPTV became so popular in late 1980 that the FCC allowed applicants to file for the new service even before final technical and operational rules had been adopted. Inundated with an avalanche of applications, most of them mutually exclusive or otherwise defective, the commission had to impose a freeze. Congress's eventual approval of a lottery system, discussed in Section 17.1, permitted the FCC to break the logjam and get the first LPTV outlets on the air. In this case, deregulatory zeal delayed the emergence of a new service.

The FCC's permissive approach to newer technologies has so far failed to realize another deregulatory goal, the so-called *level playing field* among media services. Broadcasting, despite extensive deregulation, remains the most heavily regulated of the mass media. Cable, once pervasively controlled, now operates under little regulation. Some newer services, such as DBS and MMDS, have not been regulated at all.

Deregulation Critique Unquestionably deregulation has speeded up most FCC actions, eliminated outdated rulings, and encouraged development of new technology, giving audiences many more program choices. Take as a specific example the open skies policies that in 1972 allowed satellite companies to compete freely and in 1979 permitted anyone to set up a TVRO antenna to downlink satellite signals at will without the red

tape of an FCC license. Removal of such regulatory barriers benefited broadcasters, cable operators, and other users of satellite relays—as well as consumers.

Not all outcomes, however, have been so positive in the eyes of critics. Les Brown, a leading commentator on the electronic media, says flatly, "I find it hard to cite a single public benefit from the emancipation of the media business during [former FCC Chairman] Mark Fowler's . . . tenure" (Brown, 1987: 16). He cited as undesirable results less localism, less radio news, increased exploitation of children by television, and rising cable subscription rates. A senior FCC administrative law judge complained that the commission failed to enforce its regulations and no longer required full disclosure of station financing sources (*Broadcasting,* 18 November 1988: 72). The chair of the House subcommittee with the responsibility for overseeing the FCC commented on a study showing that the FCC suffered court reversals on a quarter of the appeals from its 1986–1988 decisions. He accused the FCC of zealously following a policy apparently "solely on the basis of ideology instead of reason and fact" (Markey, 1988).

Other previously mentioned criticisms of deregulatory decisions or approaches have included the following:

- The FCC vision of all human activity reduced to simplistic economic terms ("the marketplace") treats programs as the equivalent of manufactured goods (as in Mark Fowler's reference to television as a "toaster with pictures") without concern for their diversity, quality, or cultural content.

- Refusal to adopt a mandatory standard for AM stereo sound delayed its adoption, to the detriment of the declining AM broadcasting service (Exhibit 17–8).

- Wholesale abandonment of many types of record keeping as a money-saving tactic left huge blanks in the official records of broadcasting services. For example, discontinuation of annual financial reports in 1980 left us with no official knowledge of the financial health of broadcasters. Lack of program-log requirements has wiped out a once useful record of station performance (Section 17.2).

- Applicants for construction permits and licenses no longer have to include significant information that was once considered relevant to their qualifications to hold licenses (Section 17.1).

- FCC abandonment of the fairness doctrine poisoned relationships between Congress and the commission for years, delaying FCC appointments and other important actions (Section 18.5).

- With its acceptance of program-length commercials aimed at children, the FCC now considers allegations of harm only upon a specific showing of provable damage; a mere lack of benefit in such programs is regarded as irrelevant.

- With the abandonment of the antitrafficking rule requiring licensees to hold on to stations for at least three years, broadcasting became more subject to sheer profit-making tactics, with licenses being rapidly bought and sold for big overnight profits. Such deals often created high debt loads, forcing personnel layoffs and a decline in public-service programming to make room for more entertainment and advertising (Section 17.5).

- Deregulation tends to put business interests ahead of those of the public. The 1984 cable act, for example, curbed cities' right to control cable television subscription fees, allowing cable systems to raise rates freely, given their monopoly status in most markets. The cable industry disagrees, but some research indicates that as prices have increased, quality of service has not (Section 17.4).

Summary

- The authorizing or licensing of broadcasting stations and the franchising of cable television systems are the most important regulatory functions.

- Broadcast license applicants must be American citizens and qualify in terms of financial resources, technical ability, and character.

- Licensees do not own the spectrum channels they are licensed to use. In the 1980s, the FCC increased the number of broadcast stations by adding new AM, FM, and TV channels to those already in use.

- Broadcast licensees are responsible for enforcing equal employment opportunity programs, maintaining a public file that includes listings of community problems and related programs, and keeping up with FCC rule changes.

- Most broadcast license renewals are uncontested, and the licenses are granted almost automatically. Contested renewals usually arise because of competing applications. In deciding how to handle a contested renewal, the FCC must strike a balance between offering incumbents reasonable renewal expectancy and giving new applicants a chance to improve existing service.

- Local authorities franchise cable systems subject to regulations established by the 1984 cable act. A cable franchise usually runs for a decade or more and operates as a monopoly in its service area.

- FCC regulation of electronic media ownership is the major means of structural control—limiting the number of broadcast stations under any one owner, restricting cross-ownership, and limiting network control of programming. These rules aim at encouraging a diversity of viewpoints. Cable television is not subject to most such rules, except for cross-ownership restrictions.

- In the 1980s, the FCC took a strong deregulatory stance, abolishing long-existing rules and guidelines governing broadcasting and cable. It allowed new services to emerge with little or no regulation.

- The FCC's role in selecting technical standards for electronic media changed with the watershed decision on AM stereo in 1982. Since then, the commission has generally left technical standards to the marketplace. HDTV may be an exception because of its potential economic importance.

- Critics have expressed concern about the detrimental consequences of deregulation. The FCC's deletion of outmoded rules and removal of barriers to emergence of new media services have benefited consumers. However, deregulation has also encouraged a narrowly mercantile view of the electronic media that undervalues program quality and reduces the incentives to serve the public interest.

CHAPTER 18

CONSTITUTIONAL ISSUES

We turn now from discussing the practical day-to-day regulation of electronic media, mostly by the FCC, to the broader question of the constitutional limits on such regulation. The First Amendment prohibits federal regulation of speech—yet the Communications Act indeed imposes federal regulation on those who own or speak on broadcasting stations. This paradox is not unique to the treatment of electronic media. On many occasions the welfare of society calls for a balance between ideal freedom and the practical need to limit speech that might harm individuals or society as a whole. The essence of the First Amendment issues discussed in this chapter is defining the point of compromise between these contradictory goals.

18.1
First Amendment Basics

In staking their future on the Bill of Rights as a constitutional shield against government tyranny, the framers of the first ten amendments to the U.S. Constitution knew they were embarking on a risky experiment. They counted on people to rule themselves; the people thus need unhampered access to information, ideas, and opinions.

Freedom of speech and freedom of the press have as their goal a robust, wide-open *marketplace of ideas*. First Amendment theory holds that in such a marketplace, concepts and opinions from varied sources should compete for acceptance. As the Supreme Court noted in a major electronic media decision, "it is the purpose of the First Amendment to preserve an uninhibited marketplace of ideas in which truth will ultimately prevail, rather than to countenance monopolization of the market" (US, 1969: 390).

Although freedom of expression occupies only a part of one of the ten amendments that make up the Bill of Rights, it has had a pivotal role in the success of the U.S. political system (see Exhibit 18–1). In the words of the late Supreme Court Justice William O. Douglas, the First Amendment "has been the safeguard of every religious, political, philosophical, economic and racial group amongst us" (US, 1951: 584).

"No Such Thing as a False Idea" The constitutions of many other countries guarantee free speech, but they qualify that freedom by saying it must be used only "constructively," "responsibly," or "truthfully." Such provisos subvert the central meaning of the First Amendment, which makes no prior assumptions. "Under the First Amendment," said the Supreme Court, "there is *no such thing as a false idea.* However pernicious an opinion may seem, we depend for its correction not on the con-

EXHIBIT 18–1   The First Amendment

The First Amendment protects four fundamental rights of citizens that governments throughout history have had the most reason to fear and the greatest inclination to violate: freedom to believe, to speak, to gather together, and to ask rulers to correct injustices. The amendment conveys all this in only 45 words, of which just 14 guarantee freedom of expression:

> Congress shall make no law respecting an establishment of religion, or prohibiting the free exercise thereof; or abridging the freedom of speech, or of the press; or the right of the people peaceably to assemble, and to petition the Government for a redress of grievances.

These words limit not only Congress but also state and local governments, thanks to the Fourteenth Amendment, passed in 1868, which says, "No state shall make or enforce any law which shall abridge the privileges or immunities of citizens of the United States. . . ." Section 326 of the Communications Act of 1934 explicitly extends the First Amendment's protection to broadcasting:

> Nothing in this Act shall be understood or construed to give the Commission the power of censorship over the radio communications or signals transmitted by any radio station, and no regulation or condition shall be promulgated or fixed by the Commission which shall interfere with the right of free speech by means of radio communication.

science of judges and juries, but on the competition of other ideas" (US, 1974b: 339, italics added)—again, the marketplace metaphor.

The First Amendment encourages disagreement. "A function of free speech under our system of government is to invite dispute," wrote Justice Douglas. "It may indeed best serve its highest purpose when it induces a condition of unrest, creates dissatisfaction with conditions as they are, or even stirs people to anger" (US, 1949: 4). Anger certainly ensued in Dodge City, KS, in the 1980s when station KTTL (FM) broadcast daily hour-long sermons by two fundamentalist ministers attacking Jews, blacks, and other groups. They urged listeners to ignore police officers and attack such groups at will. The invective poured out in such abundance that several local groups protested renewal of KTTL's license, which expired in May 1983.

A huge media uproar resulted, with a congressional subcommittee hearing in August 1983 and extensive press coverage of the station owner's extremist conservative views favoring local armed vigilantes. In mid-1985, the FCC designated the license for a comparative hearing with another applicant for the same frequency. At the same time it imposed a forfeiture (fine) on the station for several rule violations. But in a controversial decision to renew, the FCC said that the First Amendment protected the broadcasts, offensive though they might be to many listeners (FCCR, 1985a). The commission found that because the material did not present a *clear and present danger* to the public, a test long since established by the U.S. Supreme Court, it qualified as protected speech (US, 1919: 52). Such incitement to take illegal or dangerous actions did not, as the FCC said in an earlier case, "rise far above public inconvenience, annoyance, or unrest" (FCCR, 1972c: 637).

Private vs. State Censorship   Many people assume that the First Amendment affords protection from *private* censors. But the amendment aims at protecting people from *government,* not from one another. Station, system, and network officials who edit, cut, bleep, delete, revise, and otherwise mangle programs may be guilty of bad judgment, excessive timidity, and other faults, but they do not violate the First Amendment. They may even go so far as to break FCC rules and federal laws without violating the amendment. Private censorship becomes a violation only when it results from government intrusion, known as *state action*. In promoting the "family viewing" concept in the 1970s, the FCC attempted to reduce television violence not by rule but by pressuring the television industry to regulate itself. When the NAB responded to pressure from the FCC by making changes in the Television Code, a court construed this indirect censorship as state action in violation of the First Amendment (F, 1979b: 355).

Religious Freedom Another First Amendment clause, also of particular interest to the electronic media, guarantees religious freedom. In addition to assuring the "free exercise" of religion, the amendment explicitly rules out the designation of any particular creed as the *established*—that is, state—religion. The Supreme Court has held that even the smallest step in the direction of state-enforced religion violates the First Amendment. The overt intrusion of television evangelists into the national elections of the 1980s (especially the candidacy of Pat Robertson for the GOP nomination in 1988) disturbed many people who were sensitive to First Amendment rights. However, the same amendment also protected the right of the evangelists to have their say.

Doubly protected by the freedom of speech and freedom of religion clauses of the First Amendment, a number of stations owned by religious groups have claimed near-immunity from commission requirements because they regard their right of religious freedom as absolute. Nevertheless, the FCC has generally regulated them just like any other licensees.

18.2
Unprotected Speech

Despite the uncompromising command "Congress shall make no law . . . ," U.S. legislative bodies do in fact make laws that punish *unprotected speech*. This term refers to defamation, obscenity, plagiarism, invasion of privacy, and incitement to insurrection.

Such punishable types of speech fall outside the First Amendment's protection from government interference, for they contribute nothing to the marketplace of ideas.

Libel The law of libel affords the best example of how the chilling effect of prospective punishment can undermine First Amendment goals.*

Criticism of those in power is a significant test of whether a society enjoys true freedom of expression. Democratic societies count on tenacious news reporting to uncover official wrongdoing, sloth, or incompetence, even at the highest political levels. Vigorous investigative reporting cannot flourish, however, in a society in which harsh, easily invoked libel laws threaten journalists with ruinous fines or imprisonment when they dare to criticize public officials.

Libel laws thus involve conflicting social interests. On the one hand, defamation should be punishable because society has an interest in protecting the welfare and dignity of the individual citizen. On the other hand, society also has an interest in exposing official corruption and incompetence. Harassing libel suits can have a chilling effect, serving as a screen to protect dishonest politicians.

Upon seizing power, a dictator first suppresses the freedom of the media to criticize the new regime—even though one of the complaints against the old regime may have been the lack of freedom to criticize. In the United States, however, not only politicians but all public figures must be prepared to face harsh, sometimes even unfair and ill-founded criticism from the media without being able to retaliate with easily won libel suits.

The leading case establishing the relative protection of the news media from such libel suits occurred during the civil rights protests of the 1960s.

*Libel is defamation by published words tending to bring upon its victim public hatred, shame, and disgrace. Spoken defamation is called *slander,* but because broadcasting spreads spoken words far and wide (and because the words are preserved in a script), broadcast defamation is treated as libel. If defamation can be proved, victims can sue for damages.

By chance it involved an instance of "editorial advertising," not investigative reporting. Supporters of the Montgomery, AL, bus boycott protesting segregation bought space in the New York *Times* for a full-page advertisement that criticized Montgomery officials. Some of the statements in the advertisement were false, although they apparently were not deliberate lies. One of the officials in question, a man named Sullivan, sued for libel in an Alabama court (since libel laws come under state jurisdiction, all libel suits have to be initiated at the state level). The court awarded Sullivan a half million dollars in damages, affirmed by the Alabama Supreme Court. On appeal to the U.S. Supreme Court, however, the *Times* won a reversal. Criticism of public officials, said the Court, had broad First Amendment protection. Even though some of the allegations against the unnamed officials were untrue, they did not constitute libel.

Argument over public issues, said the Court, should be "uninhibited, robust, and wide-open." It may include "vehement, caustic, and sometimes unpleasantly sharp attacks on government and public officials." Such freewheeling debate would be discouraged if, in the heat of controversy, the critic must pause to weigh every unfavorable word:

> The constitutional guarantees require, we think, a federal rule that prohibits a public official from recovering damages for a defamatory falsehood relating to his official conduct unless he proves that the statement was made with "actual malice"—that is, with knowledge that it was false or with reckless disregard of whether it was false or not (US, 1964: 279).

Subsequent libel cases broadened the term "public officials" to include anyone who, because of notoriety, could be classed as a public figure. People so classified have little chance of bringing a successful libel suit against the media. Even if stories about public figures are false, plaintiffs find it exceedingly difficult to prove deliberate malice.

In 1979, and again six years later, libel cases arising from television coverage of the Vietnam War focused on alleged malice toward well-known people. The first suit concerned a highly decorated combat officer, and the second the senior American military commander in Vietnam (Exhibit 18–2). Both suits grew out of interviews conducted by CBS reporter Mike Wallace.

In 1970, Colonel Anthony Herbert had accused the army of covering up atrocities committed by American troops during the Vietnam War. Wallace based his *60 Minutes* interview of Herbert on an investigation of Herbert's claims by program producer Barry Lando. Herbert sued Lando for libel, alleging that the program depicted him as a liar. He surprised CBS officials when, in order to find evidence of malice, he sought to determine Lando's "state of mind" while preparing the program. Herbert claimed that he needed to find out whether or not Lando personally believed he was lying. If he did not, the charges in the program would have constituted actual malice. Lando refused to answer such questions, claiming a journalist's privilege to keep news sources and editorial processes confidential. But on appeal, the Supreme Court upheld Herbert's claim, saying that denying a plaintiff access to material that could reveal the state of mind of the accused while preparing a news story would make it hard to prove actual malice as required by the New York *Times* case (US, 1979: 169).

This decision severely limited broadcast and print journalists' ability to defend libel suits. Complainants could now rummage through tape archives, correspondence files, and program outtakes to determine the state of mind of reporters and editors. The courts soon extended the ruling to other cases, making "journalists nearly as vulnerable for what they did not say as for what they did" (*Time,* 4 Mar. 1985: 94).

The Herbert decision contributed to the rising number of libel cases filed against the media by public figures. These suits often seek huge financial awards. Although the media usually win such cases, they spend a lot of money defending against them. More to the point, such suits tend to have a chilling effect on investigative reporting. In fact, some lawsuits seek just that—more "responsible" reporting of news and public affairs. Some critics feel that if most media libel cases went to arbitrators rather than judges and juries, this would result in public

EXHIBIT 18–2   The General vs.
              Television

General William Westmoreland, commander of American forces in Vietnam in the mid-1960s, claimed he had been libeled in a 1982 CBS documentary in which 60 Minutes reporter Mike Wallace interviewed him. After many months of testimony, when it became clear that he could not win, he dropped the case.

SOURCE: UPI/Bettmann Newsphotos.

court closed the case by ruling that Herbert had no grounds for bringing the libel suit in the first place. The Herbert v. Lando precedent regarding reporters' privilege remained, however.

The second case against CBS never reached a jury, but had far wider press coverage. On January 23, 1982, the CBS television network aired "The Uncounted Enemy: A Vietnam Deception," an hour-long documentary alleging that a military underestimate of enemy troop strength during the height of the Vietnam War in the late 1960s was deliberately undertaken to encourage support at home for pursuing the war. Interviews by Mike Wallace with the top American military commander in the war, General William Westmoreland, figured prominently in the program (Exhibit 18–2). In May, *TV Guide* published a long article accusing CBS News of violating reportorial standards and its own policies in an attempt to "get" Westmoreland (Kowet and Bedell, 1982: 10). CBS responded with a comprehensive internal investigation (Benjamin, 1984, 1988). This investigation found that the producers had in fact violated network news policies and standards, but it generally supported the cover-up allegation. In September, Westmoreland filed a $120 million libel suit against CBS, claiming that his reputation had been ruined by the program and its aftermath. Conservative foundations underwrote most of the $3 million cost of the five-month trial, which began in October 1984.

A year later, after it became clear that most of the testimony supported the CBS program, Westmoreland abruptly withdrew his suit. Apparently his backers, sensing that the verdict would go against the general, decided to cut their losses and settle for a mild apology from the network that admitted no wrongdoing.

The libel principle established by the New York *Times* case, that malicious intent must be proved, survived the Westmoreland case, as did most of CBS's journalistic credibility, but defending the suit cost the network millions.

Privacy Privacy as an individual right, though not spelled out in so many words in the Constitution, is implied in the Fourth Amendment: "The

correction of erroneous stories and more moderate monetary awards. Moreover, arbitration would consume far less time than libel suits and their appeals.

With the Supreme Court decision about questioning Lando in hand, Herbert pressed on for a trial on the substance of his case—the statements made in the CBS program that he felt libeled his reputation. Finally, early in 1986, a federal appeals

right of the people to be secure in their persons, houses, papers, and effects . . . shall not be violated." As a legal concept *invasion of privacy* is closely related to libel. Like libel laws, those on privacy vary from state to state. The law holds that an individual has several privacy rights: the right to physical solitude, to protection from intrusion on private property or into the details of one's personal life, to protection from being presented in a false light (for example, being said to support something one actually opposes), and to protection from unauthorized use of one's name or image for commercial gain. Investigative television reporters taking pictures of a restaurant kitchen that has been found in violation of local health standards, for instance, may run up against that establishment's right to control access to its own private property.

Taken together, the personal protections afforded by libel and privacy laws impose limits on media access. Although the courts have held that public officials, performers, and anyone involved in news events have a lesser right to privacy because of legitimate public interest in those persons or events, privacy laws still limit the media by generally supporting individual rights.

Obscenity Basics Prior to the 1930s, obscenity in literature and art could be arbitrarily suppressed at the whim of officials and censorship boards. The successful defense in 1933 of James Joyce's literary masterpiece *Ulysses* initiated a series of court decisions that protect the media from heavy-handed suppression by zealous moral watchdogs.

Current obscenity law goes back to the 1973 *Miller* case, in which the Supreme Court ruled on the constitutionality of a California state obscenity law. The decision emphasized that *community standards* vary from place to place: "It is neither realistic nor constitutionally sound to read the First Amendment as requiring that the people of Maine or Mississippi accept public depiction of conduct found tolerable in Las Vegas or New York City."

Nevertheless, warned the Court, state laws must carefully confine what they classify as obscene to "works which, taken as a whole, *appeal to the prurient interest in sex, which portray sexual conduct*

in a patently offensive way, and which, taken as a whole, do not have serious literary, artistic, political, or scientific value" (US, 1973b: 24, emphasis added).

The *Miller* case, along with some later cases that added minor modifications, restricted obscenity censorship to hard-core pornography, leaving it to the states to define obscenity—a task that is impossible to carry out to everyone's satisfaction. In any event, the law rules out abuses of power freely committed by censors in the past. For example, the First Amendment prevents censors from taking such arbitrary action as:

- Condemning an entire work because of a few isolated obscene words.
- Using outdated standards no longer common to the local community.
- Applying as a standard the opinions of hypersensitive persons, not typical of the general public.
- Ignoring serious artistic or scientific purpose in judging a work.

Generally speaking, the law requires the courts to consider the "average person" when applying contemporary community standards in assessing potentially obscene material. Of course, those standards will be stricter for material that is available to children.

Obscenity in Broadcasting Section 1464 of the U.S. Criminal Code makes punishable the utterance of "any obscene, indecent, or profane language by means of radio communication," but the FCC long remained in doubt as to its power to enforce that law. Because of the ready availability of broadcasting and cable in the home, especially to children, material acceptable in other media might be regarded as obscene, indecent, or profane by many in the audience. Furthermore, because broadcast and cable network services have national reach, they confront a great variety of local standards.

Broadcasting's traditional conservatism delayed its response to the tolerant social climate of the 1960s, but the liberalization of standards in other media had its effect. In the 1970s a "topless radio" fad triggered thousands of complaints to the FCC.

The format invited women to call in and talk on the air about intimate details of their sex lives. Although such talk shows are commonplace today, one blatant example in 1973 triggered a flood of complaints. The FCC imposed a $2,000 fine on an Illinois FM station in accordance with the Communications Act's §502, which explicitly authorizes fines for obscenity violations (FCCR, 1973: 919). The FCC had actually hoped that the station would contest the fine, thus precipitating a test case, but the station dutifully mailed in a check instead.

In 1973, the FCC finally got its test case. A noncommercial station, WBAI-FM in New York, included in a discussion of social attitudes about language a recording of a nightclub act by comedian George Carlin. Called "Filthy Words," the monologue satirized society's hang-ups about seven sexually oriented words not likely to be heard on the air. This time, though, they were heard—106 times in 12 minutes. The single complaint came from a man who, as it later turned out, was associated with a group called Morality in Media. He happened to hear the early afternoon broadcast while driving into the city with his teen-age son. The fact that the youth heard Carlin's language became a key element in the case.

On the basis of that lone complaint, the FCC wrote the station advising its management that the broadcast violated the obscenity statute. The FCC defined indecent content as that which, in a "potentially offensive fashion, according to contemporary community standards for broadcasting, depicted sexual or excretory activities or organs" when children were likely to be in the audience. The licensee, Pacifica (see description in Exhibit 13–12), challenged the ruling as a matter of First Amendment principle. The FCC received an initial setback in the appeals court, but won Supreme Court approval of its reasoning. Focusing its argument on the Carlin monologue as *indecent* rather than obscene, according to the Supreme Court's definition of obscenity, the FCC stressed the fact that the broadcast came at a time when children would normally be in the audience.

Children, said the commission, deserve protection from indecency, which the FCC defined as material that fails to conform to "accepted standards of morality." In reference to the court-approved "community standards" test, the commission slipped in a significant qualifier of its own, making it read "community standards *for broadcast media.*" Instead of meeting the First Amendment directly by flatly banning such material as the Carlin monologue, however, the FCC said it should be *channeled* to a part of the day when children are least likely to be in the audience.*

The channeling concept had a precedent in nuisance law, which recognizes that something that is acceptable in one setting could be an illegal nuisance in other settings. The Supreme Court agreed with the nuisance law rationale. Recalling that a judge had once said that a nuisance "may be merely a right thing in a wrong place—like a pig in the parlour instead of the barnyard," the Court added that if the FCC "finds a pig has entered the parlor, the exercise of regulatory power does not depend on proof that the pig is obscene." The Court also tacitly accepted the FCC's redefinition of community standards by adding the words "for broadcasting," saying, "We have long recognized that each medium of expression presents special First Amendment problems . . . And of all forms of communication, it is broadcasting that has received the most limited First Amendment protection" (US, 1978: 748). More on this special status of broadcasting is found in Section 18.3.

Fifteen years later, in 1987, a rising flood of complaints about perceived obscenity on the air caused the FCC to issue a policy statement announcing plans to enforce §1464 of the Criminal Code, the radio obscenity law. The commission reprimanded three stations for using overly explicit language, especially at times when children might be in the audience. In one case, another Pacifica station, this one in Los Angeles, had broadcast explicit excerpts from a play about homosexuals. In another, the University of California student station at Santa Barbara aired allegedly

---

*In assessing the channeling rationale, it should be borne in mind that ratings research data indicate that nearly as many children watch television in late prime time as in the traditional children's enclave, the Saturday morning hours.

indecent music and generally operated without adequate control by the licensee, the California Board of Regents. In the third case, the FCC found that radio DJ Howard Stern, a practitioner of "shock radio," used explicit language on a Philadelphia station in violation of §1464 (FCCR, 1987a: 2726). In an interview, the FCC's general counsel opined that marginal program material (indecent, perhaps, but not obscene) might be scheduled during the midnight to 6 A.M. period. For a number of years, the FCC had informally allowed such material to begin as early as 10 P.M. The narrower definition of allowable time led to a court appeal.

A number of broadcasters joined in challenging the FCC decision and in 1988 won a reversal of the commission action on the grounds that limiting indecent language to the midnight-to-6 A.M. hours violated the First Amendment. The court remanded to the FCC the question of how to best "promote parental—as distinguished from government—control" of children's listening (F, 1988: 1332).

Thereupon Congress entered this hotly controversial arena. In approving the FCC budget for the 1989 fiscal year, the legislators (perhaps mindful that they were in the midst of an election campaign) ordered the FCC to ban indecent material at *all hours* of the broadcast day. The FCC complied perforce, changing its rule to extend the ban on indecent programs in radio or television to the entire broadcast day. Observers questioned whether such a blanket ban would survive an appeal based on First Amendment principles.

Obscenity on Cable   Because states as well as the federal government regulate cable, obscenity in cable television has caused conflicts of jurisdiction as well as of substance. The Cable Communications Policy Act of 1984 provides for fines of $10,000 or up to two years imprisonment for anyone who "transmits over any cable system any matter which is obscene or otherwise unprotected by the Constitution" (47 USC 639). How this rule squares with the limits imposed on broadcasting and with First Amendment protections remained to be fully tested.

States have tried, however, to apply the Supreme Court's *Miller* and *Pacifica* decisions to questionable cable television content. Four court decisions in the mid-1980s, three of them initiated in Utah courts, concluded that state legislation banning cable obscenity violated the First Amendment. These courts threw out indecency statutes, finding them too broad in scope. Because cable does not use the open spectrum, the spectrum scarcity argument that had supported obscenity limitations in broadcasting could not be applied. The courts reasoned that cable is not as "uniquely intrusive" as broadcasting or as available to children because subscribers pay for the service. The judge in one case suggested that the real responsibility for preventing children from seeing such programming rested with parents (F, 1985b: 989), a finding that echoed the deregulator's argument against government intervention.

In 1986, the Supreme Court ruled unanimously that cable television *does* have First Amendment protection. But the Court also held that that protection must be balanced against what it called "competing social interests," without specifying what those interests may be or how that might be done (US, 1986: 488).

Obscenity-indecency law as applied to the electronic media will keep evolving as society's standards evolve. After three decades of increasing liberalization, during which many taboos fell and audiences grew more tolerant of explicit language and scenes on the screen, the time may have come for a swing to more conservative standards, to restrictions aimed at preserving "family values." The country's trend toward political conservatism in the 1980s inclined in that direction. Ironically, though, that conservative impulse contradicts another conservative article of faith—reliance on the marketplace to set the rules. No indication of a disappearing market for off-color programming was evident in the 1980s. The trend seemed to be toward more permissive interpretation of obscenity laws for cable as compared to broadcast programming. This difference no doubt arises from the fact that cable has nothing like the universal reach of broadcasting and comes into the home only after a conscious decision to subscribe that is reviewed monthly when the bill comes in. The all-out surrender to X-rated cable programs once feared by some has not occurred. Even such a mildly liberated home service as the Playboy pay-cable channel drew relatively few subscribers (so few, in fact, that in 1989 the channel switched to pay-per-view status).

Free Press vs. Fair Trial   Sometimes protecting the constitutional rights of individuals poses a challenge to the First Amendment rights of the press. The due process clause of the Fifth Amendment assures fair play to persons accused of crimes. The Sixth Amendment also spells out some of the elements of due process, among them the right to a public trial. Ordinarily, the news media freely cover trials, but coverage can subject defendants to such intense publicity that a fair trial becomes impossible. In this *free press vs. fair trial* confrontation, the constitutional rights of the press sometimes have to give way to the constitutional rights of defendants. Electronic media become deeply involved in this thorny issue when they attempt to air on-the-spot coverage of highly publicized trials or pretrial proceedings.

For decades there was virtually no live or recorded radio or television coverage of trials. The American Bar Association (ABA) recommended in 1935 that judges discourage broadcast and photo coverage because it tended "to detract from the essential dignity of the proceedings, degrade the court, and create misconceptions with respect thereto in the mind of the public." The 1960s trial of convicted swindler Billie Sol Estes in Texas (for a time one of only two states that did not follow the no-camera recommendation) seemed to support this stand; an appeals court reversed the lower court's guilty verdict because of the circus atmosphere created by 12 cameras and attendant lights and crews. The Supreme Court narrowly upheld the appeals court decision in the *Estes* case (US, 1965b: 532).

But during the 1970s, with less intrusive equipment, changing social standards, and more mature broadcast journalism practices, the ABA recommended that judges be given wider latitude in allowing photo and video coverage of trials. In 1981, the Supreme Court, although it bans cameras and microphones in its own proceedings, noted the improved technology, holding that "the risk of juror prejudice . . . does not warrant an absolute constitutional ban on all broadcast coverage" (US, 1981: 560). By the end of the decade more than 40 states had either allowed cameras in their courtrooms or conducted experiments to that end. But federal courts remained off limits to such coverage, despite repeated media attempts to breach that barrier (Exhibit 18–3).

18.3
First Amendment Parity

The framers of the First Amendment mentioned only "freedom of speech or of the press." They naturally could not imagine all the ways of amplifying speech and extending the press that future centuries would bring. The courts have therefore had to struggle constantly with questions concerning what the First Amendment words *speech* and *press* include in a modern context—speech amplified by public address systems, film, broadcasting and cable. Should all ways of expressing oneself and all forms of the "press" claim First Amendment rights equally?

Specifically, should government-regulated broadcasting, and by extension cable television and other methods of electronic program dissemination into homes, have *First Amendment parity* with unregulated media, especially the press? Until recent years, the answer has generally been "no." (See, for example, the judicial comments in the *Pacifica* case, quoted in Section 18.2.) It was taken for granted that just as some types of speech lack First Amendment protection from government interference, some media need less protection than others. Broadcasting, the argument ran, has unique attributes that justify imposing certain regulations that would violate the First Amendment if imposed on the press. Three main arguments supported this assumption:

▪ The scarcity of channels makes it necessary to reject some applications for licenses.

▪ In deciding which applicants deserve licenses in the public interest, the FCC must take their program plans or practices into consideration.

EXHIBIT 18-3   Trial by Television

A.   B.

C.

Broadcast coverage of court trials began with the 1925 Scopes case, and reached the height of overkill with (A) the 1935 trial of Bruno Hauptmann for the kidnap and murder of Charles Lindbergh's son. Reaction to that intrusive coverage by radio and film led to the ABA's "Canon 35," which banned trial coverage for decades. (B) An experiment in television coverage in the 1960s, Billie Sol Estes' trial for fraud, led to a Supreme Court reversal because of television intrusiveness. (C) The extraordinary 1973 hearings into the Watergate scandal demonstrated effective television coverage of an historic Senate investigation.

■ Broadcasting's intrusion into the home lays special obligations upon it that call for some government oversight to protect the public.

Scarcity Factor Not everyone who wants to own a station can do so because too many stations on the air cause intolerable interference, as occurred before passage of the 1927 Radio Act. Because of this *channel scarcity,* the government, as represented by the FCC, has to make choices among applicants.

Mutually exclusive applications make claims either to the same channel or to adjacent channels whose activation would cause interference. Only one license can be granted in such cases, thereby abridging the freedom of all other applicants. In contrast, print media suffer no such mutual exclusivity. Anyone who can afford it can publish without limit and without a license. Today the cost need not be very expensive—those who cannot afford presses can use desktop computer publishing or duplicating machines.

Developments in electronic technology have decreased the persuasiveness of the scarcity factor as a justification for regulating broadcasting. Opponents of traditional regulation point to the twentyfold increase in the number of stations since Congress wrote the 1927 act—from about 600 to over 12,000. They argue that even though demand for more channels in densely populated areas continues, cable television makes virtually unlimited numbers of additional channels available, converting scarcity into abundance. Some also suggest that all media should be counted in appraising the channel scarcity argument, in which case the diversity of nonelectronic information sources helps offset any electronic media scarcity.

In rebuttal to this view, other commentators point to the many applicants for any desirable stations that come on the market and the huge prices often paid for them, suggesting continued scarcity. Moreover, the availability of cable channels does not really relieve the scarcity of broadcast channels because cable channels reach only about half the population and so are not yet equal with broadcasting, which reaches virtually all the population. In any event, cable differs significantly from broadcasting in requiring subscription fees over and above the purchase, operating, and maintenance costs of receivers.

Licensing Factor When writing the law governing radio, Congress explicitly confirmed "the right of free speech by means of radio communication" (Exhibit 18–1). Nevertheless, the law instructed the FCC to grant and renew licenses only if to do so would serve the public interest. It also told the FCC to ensure that candidates for public office had equal opportunities to use broadcasting. Interpreting its duty to see that broadcasting serves the public interest, the FCC established guidelines for programming, particularly with regard to *localism* and *fairness.*

All such program restrictions limit licensees' freedom of speech. That fundamental contradiction came before the Supreme Court in the 1943 *NBC* case, in which broadcasters argued that the FCC had the right to regulate only *technical* aspects of broadcasting, and that any further regulation violated the First Amendment. But the Court emphatically rejected this argument, saying:

> We are asked to regard the Commission as a kind of traffic officer, policing the wave lengths to prevent stations from interfering with one another. But the Act does not restrict the Commission merely to supervision of the traffic. It puts upon the Commission the burden of determining the composition of that traffic (US, 1943: 215).

By "determining the composition of the traffic" the Court referred to the choices the FCC makes in *licensing.* In deciding which of several would-be licensees will best serve the public interest, the FCC necessarily takes program services into account. The courts have frequently cited the composition-of-the-traffic rationale of this landmark decision as legal precedent for upholding limited FCC control over programs.

Intrusiveness Factor The third argument for regulating broadcasting differently from newspapers and other media rests on its *intrusiveness.* It enters directly into virtually every home, becoming readily available to all ages and all types of people.

Material accepted as commonplace in other media would be regarded as intolerable in broadcasting, as noted above in the discussion of obscenity. Proponents of First Amendment parity argue that insofar as such distinctions need to be made, the marketplace can make them without interference from government. If people feel sufficiently outraged at objectionable material in broadcast or cable programs, they will make their feelings known to station and system operators and networks; they in turn will impose their own restraints in order not to lose public confidence. After all, broadcasters pass up valuable clients by refraining from advertising hard liquor, not because of any rule or law, but voluntarily, in their own self-interest.

To recapitulate, many in the electronic media claim that they should be just as free of government control as newspaper publishers and editors. Opponents—including some broadcasters—believe that a special public-service responsibility goes with the medium utilizing a limited spectrum (still in short supply, despite claims to the contrary), is licensed by the government, and has intimate access to virtually every home. So far, the social responsibility view seems in the ascendant; despite the inroads of deregulation, the Communication Act's public-interest standard has not been repealed, and Congress shows little sign of eliminating it in the near future.

18.4
Political Access

The Communications Act regulates programs most explicitly when they consist of broadcasts by candidates for public office. Congress correctly foresaw in 1927 that broadcasting would one day exert a major influence on voters. If the party in power could monopolize broadcasting (as now happens under authoritarian regimes elsewhere), candidates of opposing parties would stand little chance of winning elections.

Equal Opportunities for Candidates   In order to equalize the political benefits of broadcasting as nearly as it could, Congress wrote the *equal-time* provision (actually "equal opportunities") into the Communications Act:

> If any licensee shall permit any person who is a legally qualified candidate for any public office to use a broadcasting station, he shall afford equal opportunities to all other such candidates for that office in the use of such broadcasting station; *Provided,* That such licensee shall have no power of censorship over the material broadcast under the provisions of this section. No obligation is imposed under this subsection upon any licensee to allow the use of its station by any such candidate (47 USC 315a).

Originally, the "no obligation" clause in the last sentence gave licensees a chance to avoid demands for equal time by refusing *all* applicants for time. A series of amendments adopted to bring the Communications Act in line with the Federal Election Campaign Act of 1971 closed this option, at least for federal candidates. One of the 1971 amendments mandated allowing federal candidates to have time by adding as a new basis for license revocation:

> willful or repeated failure to allow reasonable access to or to permit purchase of reasonable amounts of time for the use of a broadcasting station by a legally qualified candidate for Federal elective office on behalf of his candidacy (47 USC 312a (7)).

A new subsection of the key §315 itself limits stations to imposing no more than their "lowest unit charge" on candidates (federal and nonfederal) in the weeks just before elections (details later in this section).

Candidates in the News   At first §315's equal-time mandate left licensees free to make their customary judgments as to newsworthiness, to distinguish between self-promotion and bona fide news in covering candidates' activities.* In 1959, however, the FCC surprisingly reversed its interpretation, ruling that even a bona fide news-related broadcast

---

*That newsworthiness is an acceptable guide in distinguishing self-promotion from real news is widely recognized. For example, an appeals court pointed out that in situations where publishing routine information about a lottery would be illegal, it would nevertheless be legal to treat the reactions of a big winner in a lottery as a news story (F, 1969: 990).

involving a candidate counted as a political "use" of broadcasting, triggering equal-time obligations (FCCR, 1959: 715).

This unexpected ruling came in response to a petition from a candidate for mayor of Chicago who was opposing the famed political boss Richard Daley, who was running for re-election. Every time Mayor Daley appeared in a broadcast news story, opponent Lar Daly claimed equal opportunities under §315. Ironically, Lar Daly had not the remotest chance of winning. A perpetual candidate, he ran with absolutely no success for many offices. He had, of course, a perfect right to do so, no matter how hopeless his case. Section 315 makes that very point—*all* candidates are to have equal opportunities, regardless of party or platform. But the ruling meant a blackout of news broadcasts involving Chicago's mayor during the race. Broadcasters would not give Lar Daly equal time to advance his doomed candidacy every time they covered the mayor opening a new shopping center.

Thus, in a strange subversion of congressional intent, the FCC's interpretation of §315 denied the public the right to receive political news of possible consequence. At the same time, it prevented licensees from using their right to make responsible judgments as to what qualifies as news. This affront to First Amendment principles (plus, no doubt, some self-interest) caused a furor, galvanizing Congress into action with unaccustomed speed. Though he again failed to win political office, Lar Daly won a small niche in broadcasting history as the gadfly who single-handedly drove Congress to make a significant change in the Communications Act. The amendment adopted in 1959 added the following to §315:

Appearance by a legally qualified candidate on any—
(1) bona fide newscast,
(2) bona fide news interview,
(3) bona fide news documentary (if the appearance of the candidate is incidental to the presentation of the subject or subjects covered by the news documentary), or
(4) on-the-spot news coverage of bona fide news events (including but not limited to political conventions and activities incidental thereto),

shall not be deemed to be use of a broadcasting station within the meaning of this subsection (47 USC 315a).

The amendment liberated news coverage from political equal-time harassments by future Lar Dalys, but it also left the FCC with many knotty problems of interpretation. Political candidates' rights are one of the most frequent subjects of inquiry from stations seeking interpretation of FCC rules. Some examples of the issues stations face:

▮ *Which candidates get equal time?* The rules apply both to candidates for party nomination in a primary election and to nominees in a general election. Equal opportunities can be claimed only by candidates for a specific office. For example, purchase of time by a candidate for Congress in a specific district entitles all other candidates for the same post in the same district to equivalent time, but not candidates for other districts or other offices.

▮ *Do presidential news conferences count as bona fide news programs?* Yes.

▮ *Do presidential candidate debates count as news?* Until 1975, political debates did not count as bona fide news exceptions to §315. After 1975, the FCC held that debates qualified as bona fide news events as long as third parties with no personal interest in the outcome controlled the event. Thus in 1976 and 1980 the League of Women Voters, a nonpartisan group, sponsored the debates. In 1983, however, the FCC ruled (and an appeals court upheld) that the electronic media could sponsor as well as cover such debates. The television networks themselves presented the two presidential and one vice presidential campaign debates in both 1984 and 1988. By weakening the chances of third party candidates to be heard, however, this exception to the equal opportunities requirement flies in the face of §315's intention.

▮ *Are regularly scheduled interview and talk programs exempt from equal-time requests?* Yes, including "infotainment" programs such as *Donahue* and *Oprah Winfrey*. Candidate appearances on *Today* and such news interview programs as *Meet the Press* have long qualified for exemption.

■ *How much time constitutes "reasonable access"?* Some stations tried to limit candidates to one-minute or five-minute political spots because their tightly regimented formats did not lend themselves to extended political speeches. But the FCC held that this violated the reasonable access provisions of §312(a)(7).

■ *May live news appearances be recorded for later playback and still be exempt?* For some time the FCC held that a broadcast aired within 24 hours of a news event would be considered on-the-spot coverage, and thus exempt. In 1983, it lifted this limit; thereafter licensees could use their own judgment.

■ *What constitutes a station's "lowest unit charge"?* This phrase in §315(b) defines the maximum rate licensees may charge candidates (federal, state, or local) who buy time for political purposes shortly before elections (45 days in the case of a primary, 60 days for a general election). Whereas a commercial advertiser might have to buy several hundred spots to qualify for the maximum quantity discount, a political candidate benefits from the maximum discount even when buying only a single spot announcement. When a station proposed charging a candidate more than five times its rate for a one-minute spot for a five-minute program on the grounds that program rates differ from spot rates, the FCC ruled that the lowest-unit-charge provision allows a rate no more than five times that of the one-minute spot.

■ *Is a candidate entitled to whatever time of the day he or she wants?* No. Candidates do not have the privilege of decreeing when they appear. Although the FCC has held that banning *all* political advertising in prime time violates §312's requirement of "reasonable access" for federal candidates, stations may keep political spots out of particular programs. For example, the FCC has allowed stations to bar political advertising on news programs.

■ *Must a station broadcast a candidate's use of obscene material?* No. When in 1984 *Hustler* publisher Larry Flynt threatened to use arguably obscene material in a possible campaign for the presidency, alarmed licensees asked the FCC for policy guidance. The commission held that the U.S. Criminal Code ban on obscenity overrode the "no censorship" provision of §315.

■ *May electronic media endorse political candidates in editorials?* Yes, but if they do, they must notify opposing candidates and offer reply time.

■ *Are cable systems held to the same regulations on political candidates as broadcast stations?* Regulations apply only to channels on which the cable operator *originates* programming. Cable systems are not responsible for political program decisions made by stations or services whose programs they carry but do not originate.

■ *May a licensee evade political broadcasting problems by banning all political advertising?* No. Section 312(a)(7) of the Communications Act requires broadcasters to provide "reasonable access" for candidates for federal office (House, Senate, president, and vice president). Any licensee that does not allow access by such candidates risks loss of license.

In sum, the electronic media play a major role in the electoral process. Elected officials fashioned the law in such a way as to assure candidates equal opportunities to use the media, and candidates spend a great deal of money taking advantage of those opportunities. In addition to providing this paid-for access, the media also have a responsibility to inform the electorate about political issues in a nonpartisan way. This tricky combination of enforced cooperation, profit making, and the obligation to journalistic objectivity will continue to create problems for those who operate the media.

18.5
Public Access

In order to enjoy First Amendment rights fully, citizens need to be able to listen to diverse voices in the marketplace, but they also need to have voices of their own. The notion of *public access* has reciprocal aspects—access both to what others express and to the means of expression for oneself or one's social group. The widespread availability of stations and cable systems in local communities can facilitate such two-way access. Mandated fair treatment of competing ideas furthers the access ideal.

Localism　The FCC encouraged localism in two ways: by distributing stations in such a way as to give as many localities as possible their own local outlets, and by rules that encourage the airing of locally produced programs reflecting community needs and serving community interests.

The Communications Act gives the FCC a localism guideline when it acts on applications for new broadcast stations:

> The Commission shall make such distribution of licenses, frequencies, hours of operation, and of power among the several States and communities as *to provide a fair, efficient, and equitable distribution of radio service* to each of the same (47 USC 307b, italics added).

Despite this policy of localizing station distribution, people in major American cities can choose from 40 or more stations, whereas people in rural areas often have little or no choice. Localism in station distribution, when governed by marketplace economics, inevitably leads to maldistribution—too many stations in rich, populous communities and not enough in underpopulated poor ones.

As cable penetration increased, it evened up the choices available in most urban and suburban areas. However, cable, too, underserves rural areas; moreover, it has no built-in public-service mandate to encourage local programming.

Ideally, local access to stations affords many opportunities for localized expression: public-service agencies can promote their objectives, partisans in local controversies can air their points of view, local governments and political candidates can inform the electorate, local educational and cultural institutions can broaden their community service, local firms can advertise, local talent can have an outlet, and so on. A station that offers such programs thus serves its area by affording it a means of community self-expression, giving it a broadcast voice as well as a broadcast ear.

Localism in this sense draws on the deep-rooted American political tradition of community auton-

omy. Idealists in the early days of radio looked to the new service to revive the fading spirit of the traditional New England town meeting. They hoped that, given local radio voices, communities would find new opportunities for grass-roots citizen participation in local affairs. Radio, they thought, might bring a new sense of community togetherness and awareness. Influenced by such thinking, the FCC pushed localism heavily in pretelevision days. The FCC's post-World War II "Blue Book" (FCC, 1946) and the program statement echoing its principles 14 years later (FCCR, 1960: 2303) urged stations to broadcast a wide variety of nonentertainment programming during any given week.

Such hopes faded as the forces of economic centralization inherent in broadcasting had their way. Networks and syndication swept away most local production. Licensing and renewal policies, discussed in Chapter 17, continue to hold localism up as a formal, though increasingly hollow, goal. For example, local residence counts as a point in favor of an applicant for a new station against an absentee owner. As late as 1980, FCC guidelines required applicants to provide information on the amount of local news, public affairs, and other nonentertainment programming in their license documents. By then, however, FCC concern for localism had become more procedural than substantive—and even the procedures disappeared over the next few years.

Broadcasters themselves often cite their unique ability to provide locally relevant programs when newer services threaten them. They argue that cable television and DBS rely almost entirely on national program services, whereas broadcasters still preserve the ideal of station-based localism.

Access for Ideas　Not everyone who wants to express ideas over the air can own a station or cable system, nor can everyone expect access to stations or systems owned by others. The FCC attempted to deal with this problem by assuring access to broadcasting for *ideas* rather than for specific *people*. But even access for ideas has to be qualified. It would be impracticable to force stations to give time for literally every idea that might be put forward. The FCC mandated access only for ideas about *contro-*

versial issues of public importance, thus stressing another First Amendment value. This approach had two advantages: (1) it allowed licensees to retain general responsibility for programming, leaving to their discretion decisions about which issues have public importance and who should speak for them, and (2) it obligated licensees, though in an unstructured way, to allow access to some ideas other than their own. Thus licensee First Amendment rights were generally preserved along with those of the public at large.

Fairness Doctrine Eventually the FCC elaborated its access concept into a formalized set of procedures called the *fairness doctrine*. In announcing this fairness concept in 1949, the FCC said:

> It is the right of the public to be informed, rather than any right on the part of the Government, any broadcast licensee or any individual member of the public to broadcast his own particular views on any matter, which is the foundation stone of the American system of broadcasting.
>
> This affirmative responsibility on the part of broadcast licensees to provide a reasonable amount of time for the presentation over their facilities of programs devoted to the discussion and consideration of public issues has been reaffirmed by the commission in a long series of decisions (FCCR, 1949: 1249).

Congress in 1959 lent reinforcing endorsement to the concept in an incidental way when it amended §315 to exempt bona fide news programs about political candidates from equal time requirements, as described in Section 18.4. After enumerating the four types of exempt news programs, the amendment goes on to mention the fairness doctrine concern, "controversial issues of public importance":

> Nothing in the foregoing sentence shall be construed as relieving broadcasters, in connection with [the exempt news programs], from the obligation imposed upon them under this Act to operate in the public interest and *to afford reasonable opportunity for the discussion of conflicting views on issues of public importance* (47 USC 315a, italics added).

The fairness doctrine obligated stations to schedule time for (A) discussions on controversial issues

of public importance and (B) the expression of opposing views when only one side of such an issue was aired. Both stations and the FCC largely ignored (A), focusing their attention on (B), the right of reply. In practice, therefore, most fairness doctrine complaints came as reactions to ideas that had already been discussed on the air, rather than as complaints about the failure to *initiate* discussion of issues. Stations needed to monitor their programs to make sure that if anyone introduced a controversial issue, opposing interests had a chance to reply. If licensees themselves introduced such issues in station editorials, they had to offer time for the expression of opposing views.

In complying with the fairness doctrine, licensees had great latitude in deciding whether or not a subject qualified as both a controversial issue and one of public importance, how much time should be devoted to replies, when replies should be scheduled, and who should speak for opposing viewpoints (except, of course, for those replying to personal attacks, as discussed on page 482).

In 1969, the Supreme Court upheld the FCC's fairness doctrine and its related personal attack and political editorializing rules in its landmark *Red Lion* decision (see Exhibit 18–4). By unanimously supporting the FCC in this case, the Court strongly affirmed the fairness doctrine concept in an opinion that emphasized four key principles relevant to broadcasting's First Amendment status (US, 1969: 367):

▨ *On the uniqueness of broadcasting:* "It is idle to posit an unabridgeable First Amendment right to broadcast comparable to the right to every individual to speak, write, or publish."

▨ *On the fiduciary principle:* "There is nothing in the First Amendment which prevents the Government from requiring a licensee to share his frequency with others and to conduct himself as a proxy or fiduciary."

▨ *On the public interest:* "It is the right of the viewers and listeners, not the right of the broadcasters, which is paramount."

▨ *On the scarcity factor:* "Nothing in this record, or in our own researches, convinces us that the

EXHIBIT 18–4   A Place and a Case called *Red Lion*

An unlikely small-town station, a long-lasting syndicated religious broadcaster, a writer, and a major political party figured in one of the leading Supreme Court decisions on the electronic media. During the 1960s, right-wing radio preachers inundated radio with paid syndicated political commentary. Backed by ultraconservative supporters such as Texas multimillionaire H. L. Hunt through tax-exempt foundations, these religious/political program series provided much-needed radio income in small markets.

The landmark case got its name from WGCB, a southeastern Pennsylvania AM/FM outlet licensed to

John M. Norris, a conservative minister, under the name Red Lion Broadcasting. In 1964, one of the Reverend Billy James Hargis's syndicated broadcasts, carried by the station, attacked author Fred Cook. Cook had criticized defeated Republican presidential candidate Barry

Fred Cook   **Billy James Hargis**

Goldwater and had written an article on what he termed the "hate clubs of the air," referring to the Hargis series, *Christian Crusade,* among others. Hargis charged Cook with communist affiliations and with attacks on

WGCB AM/FM, Red Lion, PA

[spectrum] resource is no longer one for which there are more immediate and potential uses than can be accommodated, and for which wise planning is essential."

Fifteen years later, in a footnote to another decision (US, 1984: 364), the Court implied that it would be receptive to a new case to reassess the relevancy of the scarcity factor in view of the increasing technological options. In the meantime, legal appeals continued against FCC fairness doctrine decisions.

Despite the fairness doctrine, some broadcasters used their stations to promote extreme positions on controversial issues, oblivious of the fact that as

licensees they had an obligation to offer opportunities for rebuttal. One of the most publicized instances of licensee one-sidedness, and the only case in which fairness violations led to loss of a license, again involved a religious broadcaster. The licensee of WXUR, a Media, PA, AM/FM radio station, defied the fairness doctrine and lied to the FCC about its intent to comply with the doctrine. Licensed to an organization headed by Carl McIntire, a cantankerous right-wing fundamentalist preacher, the stations carried his *Twentieth Century Reformation Hour,* a syndicated series noted for its intemperate attacks on opponents of his philosophy. In 1970, the FCC, after many citizen complaints, refused to renew the license, alleging not only fairness violations but fail-

EXHIBIT 18–4 Continued

the FBI and the CIA—the standard litany of accusations Hargis routinely made against liberals.

Cook accused the station of violating FCC rules by failing to inform him of a personal attack. When he wrote asking for time to reply, the station responded with a rate card, inviting him to buy time like anyone else. Cook appealed to the FCC, which agreed that he had a right to free air time for a reply. It ordered WGCB to comply.

It would have been easy for the Reverend Mr. Norris to grant Cook a few minutes of time on the Red Lion

station, but he refused on First Amendment grounds, appealing the commission decision. The court of appeals upheld the FCC, but Norris took the case to the Supreme Court. Once again the Court upheld the FCC.

Several years later, Fred Friendly, a former head of CBS news, but by then a Columbia University journalism professor, began looking into the background of this well-known case for a book about the fairness doctrine (Friendly, 1976). He discovered that Cook had been a subsidized writer for the Democratic National Committee and that his fairness complaint had been linked to a systematic campaign mounted by the Democrats to discredit right-wing extremists such as Hargis. According to Friendly, the Democrats set out to exploit the fairness doctrine as a means of harassing stations that sold time for the airing of ultraconservative political programs. Cook and the Democratic National Committee claim that Friendly had misinterpreted their activities, maintaining that Cook acted as a private individual, not an agent of the Democratic party.

Fred Friendly

ure to fulfill program promises and to ascertain local needs. An appeals court upheld the FCC action (F, 1972b: 16).

Few fairness complaints had such drastic consequences. The FCC dismissed most of them out of hand because complainants cited no legally definable controversial issue of public importance or failed to show how the overall programming of accused stations had in fact denied reasonable opportunities for opposing sides to be argued.

Demise of the Fairness Doctrine By 1985, the FCC, by then largely made up of Reagan administration appointees dedicated to deregulation, had joined the mounting chorus of opposition to the

fairness doctrine. After a lengthy proceeding, it reported:

> On the basis of the voluminous record compiled in this proceeding, our experience in administering the doctrine and our general expertise in broadcast regulation, we no longer believe that the fairness doctrine, as a matter of policy, serves the public interest. . . . Furthermore, we find that the fairness doctrine, in operation, actually inhibits the presentation of controversial issues of public importance to the detriment of the public and in degradation of the editorial prerogatives of broadcast journalists (FCCR, 1985b: 143).

However, the FCC concluded that it probably lacked the power to abolish the doctrine unilaterally. Did Congress's 1959 addition to §315 of the words "Nothing . . . shall be construed as relieving broadcasters . . . from the obligation imposed upon them under this Act . . . to afford reasonable opportunity for the discussion of conflicting views on issues of public importance" amount to a congressional *codification* (inclusion in a statute) of the doctrine? If so, that passage could prevent the FCC from eliminating the doctrine on its own motion. In a fairness doctrine case in 1986, a federal appeals court removed this doubt by concluding, "we do not believe that the language adopted in 1959 made the fairness doctrine a binding statutory obligation; rather it ratified the Commission's longstanding position" (F, 1986: 501). Thus armed, the FCC sent Congress the evidence it had accumulated against the doctrine, urging removal of all doubt by a Communications Act amendment expressly eliminating the doctrine.

In 1987, Congress pointedly ignored this FCC request, instead amending the Communications Act to give the fairness doctrine a firm basis *in law*. However, President Reagan vetoed the measure on First Amendment grounds, and its proponents in Congress failed to get enough votes to override his veto.

Later that year, the FCC issued the results of a congressionally mandated study on alternatives to the doctrine. Sticking to its guns, the commission concluded that an open marketplace of ideas made the fairness doctrine unnecessary. Acting on court remand requiring the FCC to reconsider an earlier fairness decision, the commission abolished the doctrine entirely (FCCR, 1987b: 5043). The personal attack and political editorializing rules, however, remained in place, as discussed below.

That should have ended the matter, but the FCC's defiance in ending a practice that Congress had gone on record as favoring enraged key legislators. They vowed to reinstate the fairness mandate, in the meantime making their dissatisfaction known by holding up approval of appointments to vacant FCC seats. Bills reinstating the doctrine were introduced early in 1989.

Right of Reply   Two specific fairness requirements, the personal attack and political editorial-izing rules, both adopted in 1967 and retained even after the fairness doctrine's demise in 1987, continued to cause special concern to opponents of FCC interference. These rules require stations to give those affected by explicit political editorials and personal attacks on-the-air copies of the relevant material within specified time limits.

The *personal attack* rule requires stations to inform individuals or groups of personal attacks on their "honesty, character, integrity or like personal qualities" that occur in the course of discussions of controversial public issues. Within a week of the offending broadcast, licensees must inform those attacked of both the nature of the attack and how replies can be made. Specifically exempted from the right of reply are on-the-air attacks made against foreigners, those made by political candidates and their spokespersons during campaigns, and those occurring in news interviews, on-the-spot news coverage, and news commentaries (47 CFR 73.1920)

The *political editorializing* rule stipulates that a candidate must be given a chance to respond when a licensee endorses any of his or her opponents. A station must inform the opposing candidate(s) within 24 hours of such editorial endorsements. The rule does *not* apply to use of a station's facilities by opposing candidates, a situation covered by the equal-time rules discussed in Section 18.4.

Access for Advertisers   Access by advertisers to broadcasting has been governed more by considerations of taste and public acceptance than by government regulation. However, cigarette advertising became the subject of a famous fairness doctrine complaint. In 1968, the FCC decided that the surgeon general's first report on the dangers of smoking and Congress's 1965 act requiring a health warning on cigarette packages, justified treating cigarette advertising as a unique fairness doctrine issue. Stations had to carry antismoking spots if they carried cigarette commercials. These counter-ads subsided after Congress banned broadcast advertising of cigarettes in 1971.

Editorial advertising or "advertorials," however, posed a different kind of problem. Traditionally, electronic media have declined to let advertisers use commercials as vehicles for comment on controversial issues. Owners argue that (1) serious issues cannot be adequately discussed in short announcements, and (2) selling larger blocks of time for editorializing by outsiders involves surrender of editorial responsibility.

The Supreme Court has upheld the principle of licensee journalistic discretion with regard to a fairness doctrine demand for access to editorial advertising:

> Since it is physically impossible to provide time for all viewpoints . . . the right to exercise editorial judgment was granted to the broadcaster. The broadcaster, therefore, is allowed significant journalistic discretion in deciding how best to fulfill the Fairness Doctrine obligations, although that discretion is bounded by rules designed to assure that the public interest in fairness is furthered (US, 1973a: 111).

Despite deletion of the fairness doctrine, the question of editorial advertising refuses to subside. Controversies arise periodically between advertisers and broadcasters. In several cases, ads that were turned down for television have appeared on cable or in print, with pointed comment about the refusal of broadcasters to sell time for such editorial advertising. The networks and their owned and operated stations remain, as a matter of company policy, the principal holdouts against selling time for issue advertising. A 1980 Television Advertising Bureau survey indicated that by that time nearly 90 percent of other television stations would at least consider accepting such ads on a case-by-case basis.

In a democracy, the fact that most of the population derives most of its knowledge of public affairs from the electronic media lays a special burden on those media. Ideally, they will ensure their audiences access to the full range of contemporary ideas. For advertising-supported media, the fact that commercials may be used to sell points of view as well as products and services adds another dimension to the access burden. The fairness doctrine was an attempt to ensure appropriate access for controversial viewpoints on significant public issues without unduly encroaching on the autonomy of station owners. Though the FCC finally reversed itself and abandoned its own doctrine, many critics of that action, including powerful members of Congress, hope to see the doctrine revived.

18.6
Fairness in News

News and public-affairs programs necessarily involve controversial issues, often leading to charges of unfairness by partisans. This makes it difficult for broadcasting and cable journalists to deal with serious issues if their corporate bosses prefer to avoid controversy. Yet these media cannot win public respect and First Amendment status without taking risks similar to those the press has always faced.

Editorial Discretion   The FCC and the courts generally assume that reporters and editors use *editorial discretion,* which calls for fair and considered news treatment of events, people, and controversies. No one believes that journalists always use the best judgment or that they totally lack bias or prejudice. First Amendment philosophy holds, however, that it is better to tolerate journalists' mistakes, and even prejudice and incompetence, than to set up a government agency as an arbiter of truth.

The Supreme Court has reaffirmed reliance on journalistic judgment. In confirming an FCC decision rejecting a fairness complaint, the court remarked:

> For better or worse, editing is what editors are for; and editing is selection and choice of material. That editors—newspapers or broadcast—can and do abuse this power is beyond doubt, but that is not reason to deny the discretion Congress provided. Calculated risks of abuse are taken in order to preserve higher values (US, 1973a: 124).

News Bias   Critics sometimes accuse the electronic media, and especially television network news departments, of *news bias.* Typically such charges come from political conservatives, who tend to regard the news media as too liberal in outlook. They argue that the cumulative effect of alleged liberal bias over time tends to build up one-sided perceptions of issues. Professional media gadflies like Reed Irvine, head of Accuracy in Media, regularly take up conservative causes against alleged media (usually television) bias, though since 1987 without the fairness doctrine as a weapon. Research studies based on program content analysis that support both sides of the bias question have appeared. The debate continues.

Partly because it has often scheduled more hardhitting documentary programs than other networks, CBS has been a frequent target of bias complaints from the political right. In the mid-1980s, critics took a new tack when conservatives tried to buy stock and take over the network to become, as one put it, news anchor Dan Rather's "boss." Instances of libel suits against CBS based on alleged bias in documentaries were discussed in Section 18.2.

Programs that take a point of view on news events, such as *60 Minutes,* almost inevitably provoke controversy. In preparing documentaries, producers sometimes resort to techniques that could be regarded as staging or rigging of news events. Such charges triggered both FCC and congressional investigations of "Hunger in America" (1969), "The Selling of the Pentagon" (1971), and the Westmoreland/Vietnam documentary (1982) discussed earlier. Individual employees sometimes used bad editing judgment, if not outright deception, but no blatant dishonesty was uncovered. Nevertheless, attacks on documentaries continue, made easier by the 1979 Supreme Court decision in the *Herbert* v. *Lando* libel case, discussed earlier in this chapter, because it gave plaintiffs the right to probe into editing processes.

18.7
Changing Constitutional Perspectives

The writers of the Constitution saw the marketplace of ideas in 18th century terms, as a forum in which small traders in the spoken and printed word competed on relatively equal terms. They expected a leisurely *self-righting* process to occur as citizens heard, read, and digested diverse viewpoints. Technological convergence and deregulation have changed all that, challenging previously accepted assumptions about how the First Amendment applies to mass communication.

In the late 20th century, numerous different media and media outlets compete for attention and consumer dollars, but more tends to become less in a marketplace dominated by giant corporations. Instantaneous corporate communicators blanket the entire nation, cutting down on the diversity of competing voices and narrowing the window of opportunity for the self-righting process to occur.

Diametrically opposed solutions have been proposed. On the one hand stands the *de*regulator, confident that the marketplace will regulate itself, given maximum competition and unconstrained consumer choice. On the other hand stands the *re*regulator, demanding that the government intervene once more to oppose monopolistic tendencies and to protect the public interest from the effects of unrestrained commercial competition. One wants all media to compete on an "even playing field," all equally protected from government interferences—in other words, First Amendment "parity." The other wants a more flexible interpretation of the First Amendment, one that takes into account the fact that different media have different natures in terms of their impact, reach, and accessibility. One side envisions the communication marketplace literally in economic terms; the other regards the marketplace as a metaphor, seeing mass communication more in cultural terms.

In this and earlier chapters many practical examples of this fundamental clash of views have been discussed: Should obscenity in broadcasting and cable have the same First Amendment protections it has on the newsstand and in the movie theater? Does the effect of violence as depicted in the electronic media have such damaging social effects as to justify tilting the regulatory playing field against it? Should electronic media have special responsibilities with regard to the airing of controversial issues of social importance? Does the impact of these media on children warrant special regulation?

The very capacity of broadcasting to survive in the traditional sense comes under question. Should communication media live or die solely according to their ability to survive competition in the economic marketplace? At one time broadcasting enjoyed special status as a uniquely democratic medium, worth preserving because it played an especially important informational role and made its services available equally to all at minimum cost. It received protection from the competition of cable television, a less democratic medium because it is more costly and far less universal than broadcasting. Broadcasting's special status evaporated with the new cable law of 1984 and subsequent court decisions. For example, the Court of Appeals decided that the must-carry rule forcing cable operators to carry all the broadcasting stations receivable in their franchise areas violated the operators' freedom of speech.

In sum, as the 20th century winds down, broadcasting in America as a public service, accustomed for its first half century to special regulation and in some ways favored treatment under the First Amendment, now faces a hostile climate. The continued conservatism of the FCC and the growing conservatism of the courts presage an era of intensifying media competition. In that environment, broadcasting's primacy as a mass medium and its special status as a service imbued with a unique public responsibility may continue to decline, despite the efforts of some in Congress to halt the trend.

Summary

▎ Freedom of speech and press have as their goal a robust and wide-open marketplace of ideas. The First Amendment protects even inflammatory, hateful, and false ideas from government interference, but it does not prevent private censorship unless it is carried out on behalf of the government.

▎ Unprotected forms of speech, such as libel, invasion of privacy, and obscenity, are punishable after the fact, but punishment must not be so easily imposed as to have a chilling effect on the freedom of speech and press in general.

▎ Attempts to broaden the ability of broadcast licensees to present some kinds of indecent material in late evening hours did not survive congressional oversight. Congress also included strong limits on cable programming of indecent or obscene material in the 1984 cable act.

▎ Former restrictions on cameras in courtrooms have given way in state courts, but electronic media are still not allowed in federal courts.

▎ Broadcasting has not had First Amendment parity with other media because of a scarcity of channels, the fact that the FCC must take programming into account in licensing decisions, and the medium's intrusive role in the home.

▎ Section 315 of the Communications Act requires equal opportunities for use of broadcast and cable facilities for opposing candidates for public office. Bona fide news and public-affairs programs are exempt. Section 312(a)(7) mandates access for candidates for federal office.

▎ At one time regulation of broadcast content was heavily influenced by FCC policies emphasizing service to local communities. Localism meant the right to hear—and express—ideas of interest to that community. Economic centralization of programming and ownership have to a considerable degree made localism obsolete.

▎ The fairness doctrine had its roots in earlier decisions, but was formalized in a 1949 FCC decision allowing station editorializing. It was enhanced by legislation in 1959, and was upheld by the *Red Lion* Supreme Court decision of 1969. In 1987, after intensive study, the FCC abolished the doctrine, although Congress has vowed to reinstate it.

▎ The personal attack rules and the political editorializing aspects of the fairness doctrine, both established in 1967, remained in force in the early 1990s.

▎ Only one commercial product—cigarettes—has ever been subject to provisions of the fairness doctrine. Few stations or systems will accept paid editorial advertising ("advertorials").

▎ When examining complaints about bias in news or documentaries, the FCC and the courts give heavy emphasis to broadcast and cable journalists' editorial discretion.

EPILOGUE

THE WORLD OF BROADCASTING

CHAPTER 19

GLOBAL VIEW

The study of broadcasting in America would be incomplete without some reference to broadcasting elsewhere. Radio's ability to ignore national boundaries (especially now that satellites can cover 40 percent of the globe from a single point in space) makes it essentially an international medium. Numerous international regulatory, trade, academic, and legal organizations facilitate global exchange of equipment, concepts, programs, techniques, and training. American influence in these areas touches virtually every foreign media system.

Each country starts with identical broadcasting potentialities, yet each capitalizes on them differently to serve the nation's particular needs and ambitions. "Every society," according to English media scholar Anthony Smith, "has to reinvent broadcasting in its own image, as a means of containing or suppressing the geographical, political, spiritual and social dilemmas which broadcasting entails" (1973: 50). Smith speaks of "containing" and "suppressing" because broadcasting can be a dangerous force, especially to governments that want to control citizen access to information.

19.1
Broadcasting and National Character

The very nature of the medium causes broadcasting to reflect national character. Three attributes, already discussed in a U.S. context, especially promote this mirrorlike relationship:

▌ Broadcasting invites political oversight because it uses public property, the electromagnetic spectrum that makes wireless communication possible. Each government interprets this duty according to its own political philosophy.

▌ Radio-frequency radiations interfere with one another, necessitating international as well as national regulation of physical aspects of transmission. Again, political philosophy affects the way in which a country chooses to regulate transmission.

▌ Broadcasting has political and social power because of its unique ability to communicate instantly with an entire nation and to penetrate the borders of other nations, bypassing officialdom by going directly to the people. No nation, whatever its politics, can afford to leave so powerful and persuasive an avenue of public communication unregulated.

These three considerations explain why broadcasting systems inevitably reflect differences in political philosophies. A country's economics, history, geography, and culture also influence broadcasting, but always with political overtones. As Anthony Smith put it, the way a country organizes its broadcasting system reveals "a strange, coded version of that country's entire political culture" (1973: 257).

19.2
Political Philosophies

The amount and kind of controls a nation imposes on broadcasting give a clue to the attitude the country's leadership takes toward its people. Ruling attitudes fall broadly into three orientations: the permissive, the paternalistic, and the authoritarian.

Permissive Orientation Broadcasting in America is the major exemplar of a predominantly *permissive* system. The profit incentive, minimally hampered by government regulations, encourages reaching as many people as possible as cheaply as possible. Operating within the permissive framework of the free-enterprise economic system, commercial broadcasting in the United States displays the qualities of pragmatism, materialism, expansionism, and aggressive competitiveness that characterize American marketing in general. Whatever critics may say (and many deplore the resulting program service), American commercialism achieves more lively, popular, and slickly finished broadcasting services than can be found elsewhere in the world.

Nevertheless, many countries disagree with the extreme permissiveness of U.S. commercial broadcasting. They deplore the commercialism that pays attention almost exclusively to what people *want* rather than what critics, experts, and government leaders think they *need.* In general, only countries within the U.S. sphere of influence, such as Central and South America, have adopted similar permissive, profit-driven systems with most broadcast facilities under private ownership. Since the advent of television, however, even these countries have retreated somewhat from their former easygoing, permissive approach in order to shape broadcasting more in accord with their national needs and goals.

Paternalism Most countries do not leave programming entirely to the interaction of commercial supply and demand. Lacking the avowed melting-pot character of the United States, they feel that broadcasting should play a positive role in preserving and enhancing their national cultures. They tend to put special emphasis on those all-important bearers of cultural tradition, official national languages. They also feel justified in mandating a balanced program diet. In particular, they stress the importance of regulating children's programs to ensure that they set positive, culturally relevant examples, responding more sensitively to the needs of the nation's children than to those of advertisers.

Most noncommunist industrialized countries subscribe to varying brands of *paternalism.* British broadcasting, the classic example, started with the deliberate goal of avoiding such American "mistakes" as commercialism. The British Broadcasting Corporation (BBC), a chartered, nonprofit corporation, carries no advertising on its stations, deriving nearly all its funds from annual receiving-set license fees imposed by the government (a small percentage of its budget comes from commercial activities such as program syndication abroad and the sale of publications). The government appoints the BBC board, but generally lets board members oversee the operation without political interference. Outsiders often mistake the BBC for a government service, but its charter, buttressed by long-standing tradition, assures its independence from both commercial and direct political controls.

True, the home secretary, the top public official responsible for broadcasting and cable in Britain, has certain "reserved powers." The secretary could go so far as to veto a particular program or class of programs, a sweeping power the U.S. Constitution and broadcasting law deny to any American official. The home secretary explicitly used this power for the first time with regard to a political issue* in 1988, forbidding either the BBC or commercial broadcasters from airing personal interviews with persons from Northern Ireland who were linked with paramilitary groups. The ban affected only *personal* appearances, on the theory that terrorists sought broadcast appearances to legitimize their activities. It did not affect members of Parliament from Northern Ireland in the course of election campaigns or

---

*The government used this power in a nonpolitical way once before: in 1964 it banned subliminal advertising.

EXHIBIT 19–1   Broadcasting House, London

In pretelevision days, broadcasters from all over the world journeyed to this famous art deco building in the heart of London as a kind of broadcaster's mecca. They came to see, confer, and receive training. The Eric Gill sculpture above the entrance represents Prospero, the wise magician of Shakespeare's The Tempest, *with Ariel, a sprite whose lightning speed symbolized radio. The BBC moved here from its original quarters on the Thames bank in 1932. Though Broadcasting House tripled the corporation's previous space, the new building proved too small for the BBC's activities even before its completion. The giant BBC television center is located in a London suburb.*

SOURCE: BBC copyright.

in parliamentary debate, nor did it affect newspaper coverage.

From its earliest days, the BBC adhered to a philosophy of "giving a lead," which meant programming somewhat ahead of popular taste at least part of the time. A well-articulated ideal of *public-service broadcasting* emerged from the BBC experience. As adopted in many democracies, it subscribes in general to the following principles:

▮ Balanced programming, representing all the main genres.

▮ Control by a public body, insulated from direct and total dependence on either political or commercial interests.

▮ A degree of financial autonomy, usually ensured by partial or complete dependence on receiver license fees.

▮ Service to the entire population, including rural dwellers and minorities.

▮ Political balance and impartiality.

▮ Respect for the artistic integrity of creative program makers.

This public-service philosophy of broadcasting, adapted to varying national circumstances, spread worldwide. Thousands of practitioners from scores of countries have visited the famous Broadcasting House in London (Exhibit 19–1) and have received systematic training and indoctrination from the BBC. Yet, despite being acknowledged as the most influential and imitated broadcasting service in history, the BBC never came even close to being replicated in a foreign country. Too much of its special character arises from the special character of the British nation, evidence of the fact that every system uniquely adapts the medium to its own national setting.

The advent of television and the turbulent political and social changes of the 1960s modified BBC paternalism. After 1955 it had to compete with an advertising-supported service,* albeit with strict limitations on advertiser influence over programs. In

---

*The enabling law for the new service went into effect in 1954, and the last of 15 regional companies comprising the Independent Television Network (ITN) began telecasting in 1962.

the 1980s, the U.S.-inspired deregulatory theory that swept the telecommunications world got an especially sympathetic hearing from Britain's conservative government under Prime Minister Margaret Thatcher. This influence led to still more competition for the BBC, even a threat to its very existence in its traditional form (Exhibit 19–3 outlines these developments).

Other national services modeled with varying degrees of fidelity on the BBC include Australia's ABC, Canada's CBC, and Japan's NHK.

Authoritarianism   Communist and many Third World countries take an *authoritarian* approach to broadcasting. The state itself finances and operates the system, along with other telecommunication services, using broadcasting to implement government policy. This means that governments own and operate the great majority of the world's broadcasting systems (Exhibit 19–2).

In the Soviet Union, the leading exemplar of broadcast authoritarianism, a committee responsible to the top echelon of political power runs broadcasting. Traditional Marxist doctrine holds that private ownership of the media inevitably results in capitalist exploitation; only government ownership can truly serve the masses in their own best interest.

The author of *The Great Soviet Encyclopedia*'s television article asserts that capitalist countries use television "in the interests of the ruling monopolistic circles to propagandize bourgeois ideology." He seemed not to realize that substituting the word *communist* for *bourgeois* would make the sentence an apt description of the Soviet system. With unconscious irony, in view of this statement, the Soviet writer goes on to say, "In the USSR and other socialist countries, television . . . demonstrates individual features of the socialist way of life, molds public opinion, and helps provide the ideological, moral, and aesthetic education of the masses" (Lapin, 1973: 484).

Because communist ideology stresses the importance of the media in mass political education, the Soviets embraced broadcasting early, embarking on a vigorous "radiofication" program. The Russian masses, however, failed to invest in home receivers

as eagerly as did Western audiences, partly no doubt because of low purchasing power, but probably also because government programs gave them little incentive to buy.

In order to enlarge radio coverage, communist countries rely heavily on state-subsidized listening by means of *wired radio*. This self-contradictory term refers to an audio forerunner of cable television, a system for receiving government broadcasts at local redistribution centers and forwarding them by wire to speaker boxes in homes, work places, and public squares. Redistribution centers usually have their own small studios for insertion of local material on a closed-circuit (nonbroadcast) basis to supplement programs received from distant regional or national capital transmitters. People rent speakers for a nominal monthly fee or listen in public without cost. About 15 percent of radio receivers worldwide are speaker boxes, although nowadays some listeners supplement them with their own radio receivers. In Eastern Europe the proportion of speaker boxes reaches 38 percent of all receivers (BBC, June 1988).

Soviet broadcasting's authoritarian outlook has meant that programs were chosen and production techniques were used with little regard for popular taste. Programs had a propaganda, or at best educational, goal; broadcasting officials paid scant attention to the marketing techniques that American broadcasters would employ to ensure that programs would be palatable and attractive. Programs emphasized political commentary, documentaries, classical music, ballet, and theater, with a sprinkling of innocuous light entertainment.

From a production standpoint, Soviet shows seemed stiff and constrained compared with American programs. A Columbia University professor, commenting on Soviet television after having seen it daily via satellite at the university, said in 1985, "On Soviet television, our students see women who, for goodness' sake, look like anybody's *mother* . . . I mean, they're often middle-aged, often a little dowdy, they may have wrinkles, they look far from picture perfect, and they don't look into teleprompters, because the Soviet Union doesn't have teleprompters" (*New Yorker,* 1985).

EXHIBIT 19–2   World Broadcasting Systems Ownership

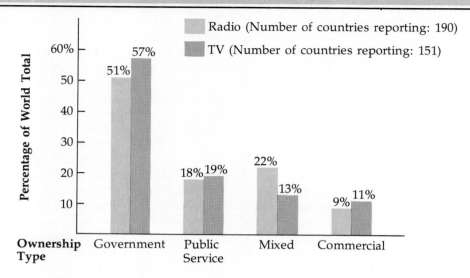

Government ownership *implies direct operation by the government, primarily paid for from tax revenues, but often with additional revenue from receiver license fees and advertising.* Public-service ownership *implies ownership by one or more public corporations, with some degree of insulation from direct government control (sometimes only on paper, however).* Commercial ownership *implies private control and full dependence on advertising revenue, with varying degrees of government control via station licensing and other laws.* Mixed ownership *implies a combination of two or more of the above. Deregulation has caused the number of mixed systems to rise since UNESCO gathered these data.*

Ownership patterns differ markedly among world regions: government ownership predominates in Africa and Asia, public service in Europe, and mixed in the Americas.

This tabulation treats each national system on equal terms, regardless of its audience size. In terms of people served, government, public corporation, and mixed television systems each potentially reach about equal numbers of receivers, with mixed systems somewhat ahead of the others. Solely commercial systems probably reach less than 1 percent of the world's aggregate receiver potential.

SOURCE: Based on data in UNESCO, *Statistical Yearbook, 1988* (UNESCO, Paris, 1988), Tables 10.1 and 10.3. Data are from 1985 reports to UNESCO, earlier for some countries.

Later that year the Soviet leader, Mikhail Gorbachev, announced a new policy of *glasnost* (roughly, "candor" or "openness"). A year after that the Chernobyl atomic energy plant disaster occurred, devastating not only the area surrounding the plant but also Soviet media credibility. In accordance with the established Soviet news code, the media suppressed coverage of the disaster, one of the biggest news stories of the decade. The government released a statement only after Sweden demanded an explanation of why nuclear radiation levels in its territory had reached dangerous heights.

Encouraged by the *glasnost* policy and embarrassed by its Chernobyl failure, Soviet broadcasting, along with other media, began a profound change; for the first time broadcasters covered hitherto banned subjects, such as domestic disasters, the Afghan war, and public criticism of government officials. Television news, hitherto notorious for stodgy, unimaginative production, began to brighten its image by using more open reporting. It even showed concern for production values, for example by using graphics and on-the-spot film inserts. Frequent United States–USSR broadcast "bridges" enabled Soviet and U.S. citizens to exchange views by satellite. The Soviets scheduled more live shows, spontaneous interviews (in place of the obviously rehearsed recitals formerly used), and telephone call-in shows, and extended schedules into early morning and late night segments. For the first time in the Soviet Union, broadcasting, that most democratic of media, began to fulfill its mission of pleasing and informing the public as well as lecturing and hectoring it.

The leading authoritarian broadcaster had not been magically transformed into a permissive model, any more than Marxism had been abandoned; but communist regimes began trying a less authoritarian approach, opening the media to U.S. influence. A similar, though more cautious, relaxation of broadcast authoritarianism occurred in China.

As for Third World countries, their citizens' woeful lack of purchasing power limits set penetration. Absence of central electrical supplies in rural areas and of relay facilities for networking further limits television growth. Neither receiver license fees nor advertising can bring in enough to support broadcasting. Most Third World governments therefore own and operate their systems out of necessity. In any event, leaders of these often shaky regimes feel that they dare not allow broadcasters free rein to communicate with the illiterate masses. In most cases, Third World authoritarianism thus arises more from pragmatic than from ideological motives.

Pluralistic Trend None of the three prototype regulatory regimes—permissive, paternalistic, and authoritarian—exists anywhere in pure form. The Soviet *glasnost* policy shows how even that very exemplar of authoritarianism finds reason to pay

some attention to what audiences really want. Extremes in any one of the three directions seem incapable of realizing broadcasting's fullest potential. Commercially motivated programmers imitate success, avoid controversy, concentrate on audience segments with the most buying power, and aim at the lowest common denominator of audience tastes. Authoritarian motives alone cannot succeed because they run counter to the inherently democratic nature of broadcasting—a medium that relies on uncoerced audience participation, in terms of both time and money. Paternalistic motives alone tend toward bureaucratic complacency, preference for the status quo, and contempt for popular tastes.

In the light of nearly three quarters of a century of experience, *pluralism* in broadcasting seems to offer the best chance of optimal development of the medium while minimizing its less desirable effects. Pluralism in this context means more than simple competition. If the same motives drive each competing service, they tend merely to imitate one another and drag one another down to meet the lowest levels of expectation. Ideally, pluralism means putting more than one motive to work, each on an approximately equal footing—in practice, usually a mix of commercial and public-service motives. Healthy competition between *differently motivated* broadcasting organizations stimulates creativity, encourages innovation, and gives audiences a range of genuine program choices.

British Pluralism A committee appointed by the British Parliament to look into the future of British broadcasting said in its 1986 report that when it consulted foreign broadcasting organizations:

> many of their senior officials were deeply envious of the British 'duopoly' and advised us to make no recommendations that would result in hastening the break-up of the present financial arrangements. They maintained that these arrangements were a necessary condition for the continuing production of the high quality television and radio programmes of the BBC which have earned international respect (Great Britain, 1986: 36–37).

"Duopoly" in this statement refers to the fact that so far two authorities have shared responsibility in

Britain: the British Broadcasting Corporation (BBC), responsible for noncommercial services, and the Independent Broadcasting Authority (IBA), responsible for commercial services.

The BBC has already been described. The IBA, a nonprofit chartered corporation, selects and supervises a number of companies that conduct commercial broadcasting operations in Britain. Like the BBC, the IBA owns and operates its own transmitters, so that commercial motives cannot distort geographical coverage by concentrating outlets in high-population areas. Unlike the BBC, however, the IBA has no programming function. Instead, it empowers private commercial companies to do the programming and sell the advertising.

Commercial programs come mainly from 15 regional program companies selected and regulated by the IBA, known collectively as ITV (Independent Television). Regionalization prevents any one company from dominating the commercial field. The IBA goes so far as to divide the lucrative London market between two companies, Thames Television (operating weekdays) and London Weekend. Regional franchising also prevents broadcasters from overemphasizing the national market in pursuit of profits. Thus Britain avoided the American commercial television pattern of domination by a few huge networks, national in scope and similar in program output.

Nevertheless, in order to realize the benefits of pluralism, commercial television in Britain needed to compete as a *national* network on a more or less equal footing with the BBC's two networks. To create a national commercial service, the IBA allows the 15 regional ITV companies to join forces most of the time in a cooperative national network. The five most lucrative companies furnish most of the programs,* although the ITV network relies on a commonly owned nonprofit subsidiary, Independent Television News (ITN), for its national and international news programs.

---

*U.S. viewers have become familiar with the names of some of these companies through British series seen on U.S. networks, such as Anglia Television (*Survival*), Thames Television (*The Benny Hill Show*), London Weekend (*Upstairs, Downstairs*), and Granada Television (*The Jewel in the Crown*).

In addition to the ITV companies, the IBA supervises a fourth British network, Channel Four, for which IBA again supplies the transmitter network. Channel Four acts as an "electronic publisher" in the sense that it originates no programs of its own but buys or commissions programs from others. It repeats a number of ITV programs, buys productions from independent producers, and obtains others from international syndicators. Channel Four successfully introduced American professional football to audiences previously dedicated to soccer.

Still another company, TV-am, owned by the IBA, conducts an early-morning "breakfast show" program prior to the start of the ITV schedule, using the same IBA transmitter network as the ITV group. The IBA also supervises some 50 independent local radio stations (ILRs). Though British viewers can choose from among only four domestic broadcast television programs, all four can be received throughout the territories, and at any one time each usually offers a distinctly different program, assuring genuine viewer choice. With no television equivalent of the ILRs, however, British viewers lack *local* television, although the ITV companies do supply regional programs.

As the quotation at the head of this subsection suggests, pluralism in Britain has worked—so far. The two competing national television services, those of the BBC and the IBA, have achieved approximate rating equality, yet the BBC maintains its dedication to offering alternatives to commercial programs and to serving cultural and intellectual minorities. The BBC-1 mass-appeal network confronts the ITV competition, whereas BBC-2 aims at smaller, more specialized audiences, as does the commercial Channel 4.

In radio, the BBC has retained its monopoly on national and regional services, operating four national networks plus regional services in Northern Ireland, Scotland, and Wales. Radio 1 features pop music, Radio 2 middle-of-the-road programs, Radio 3 serious music and talk, and Radio 4 news and current affairs. Some 40 local radio stations compete with the IBA-supervised ILR stations.

Despite the fact that in Britain "independent" means "commercial," the networks and stations supervised by the IBA do not practice the all-out commercialism of U.S. broadcasters. The IBA supervises and controls programs, schedules, and commercials in far more detail than does the Federal Communications Commission. In consequence, both the BBC output and that of the IBA-supervised companies qualify as public-service broadcasting.

British pluralism, admired though it may have been, has not escaped the winds of deregulatory change. Plans include new fifth and possibly sixth television networks, displacement of the IBA with a new, less authoritarian supervisory body, and pressure on the BBC to gradually wean itself away from the receiver fee as its revenue source in favor of some form of subscription television service. These plans, outlined in more detail in Exhibit 19–3, foretell the end of British broadcasting's "comfortable duopoly."

19.3
Legal Foundations

Broadcasting's physical nature makes not only domestic but also international laws necessary to prevent transborder interference and to facilitate international communication flow.

International Law   Most nations belong to the *International Telecommunication Union* (ITU), an affiliate of the United Nations, headquartered in Geneva, Switzerland. Since its members are sovereign nations, the ITU cannot force them to do anything; they join the ITU by treaty and may withhold their agreement to rules they oppose.

ITU members adopt both wire and wireless communication rules, standardizing terminology and procedures for international exchange of communications. For example, ITU members agree to *allocate* specific frequency bands to specific services. Thus AM radio, FM radio, television, and broadcast satellite service each has its own part of the spectrum. The ITU also allocates satellite positions in the geostationary orbit. With some regional variations, ITU allocations apply worldwide, facilitating international communication and trade in equipment. Exhibit 19–4 (pages 498–499) outlines the ITU's structure.

The ITU develops universal technical and operational *standards* through its International Radio Consultative Committee. Standardization helps to prevent interference, to maximize efficient use of the spectrum, and to maintain service quality. ITU standards thus play a significant role in facilitating international exchange of both technology and programs.

Although ITU standardization encourages internationalism, national chauvinism tends to impede it. If you take a portable radio receiver abroad, thanks to the ITU's allocations, you can pick up stations almost anywhere you land. However, this is not true of television receivers and other items of video equipment. Fourteen different monochrome technical standards and three color systems make it impossible in many cases to use television sets built in one country in another country without adding converters.

The three color television systems represent separate American, French, and German government decisions. Each of the three lobbied frantically to persuade other governments to adopt its version. Adoptions meant not only national prestige, but also tremendous profits from international sales, both present and future, by manufacturers of equipment using the favored system.

The advent of direct-satellite broadcasting and high-definition television opened the possibility of adopting new, universal, ITU-approved television signal processing standards. Certainly, satellite-to-cable and DBS services designed to cover several countries simultaneously cry out for such standards. Nevertheless, in 1988 the leading contenders (Europe, Japan, and the United States) were developing different HDTV standards. The world seemed once again on the road to adopting incompatible international television standards for both satellite-to-cable signals and HDTV.

Domestic Laws   In contrast to the American policy of licensing all stations to specific communities, most countries centralize control by using networks of repeater stations to carry identical national programs to everybody. Not many countries share the U.S. preference for autonomous local sta-

EXHIBIT 19–3   An End to the British Broadcasting Duopoly?

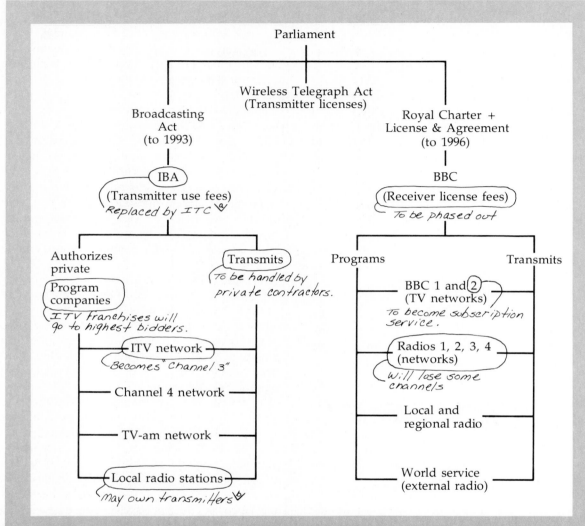

[a]ITC (Independent Television Commission) would take on an FCC-like role with respect to commercial television and DBS.

[b]A Radio Authority would lightly regulate commercial radio, including three new national networks and community stations. A Broadcasting Standards Council would work with ITC on setting taste, decency, sex, and violence standards.

tions, free to link up at will with national networks but nevertheless licensed to serve specific local areas.

U.S. broadcasters can invoke an elaborate machinery for review of and appeal from administrative decisions. In most countries domestic broadcasting laws give only limited opportunities for review and ap-

peal. For example, the two British authorities, the BBC and the IBA, can act quite arbitrarily in carrying out most functions without public hearings, reviews of decisions, or appeals to the courts.

In Europe, broadcasting cases arise in the courts infrequently. Those that do usually center on fun-

EXHIBIT 19–3   Continued

Until 1989, all British broadcasting fell under the control of one of two authorities, the BBC and the IBA. Legislative plans for that year, however, threatened to demolish this "comfortable duopoly," as it was often called. The government planned to introduce new competition, more private ownership, and lighter regulation—except with regard to obscenity, sex, and violence. The chart (left) shows the preregulation structure and some of the changes contained in an official 1988 legislative proposal (right).

- The BBC would continue as the "cornerstone of public broadcasting," deriving revenue from receiver license fees, at least until it can support itself from subscription fees.

- A new television network, Channel 5, would be programmed by companies controlling different dayparts. A possible sixth network, Channel 6, programmed along the same lines might be possible.

- Most services would have to fill 25 percent of their schedules with independently produced British productions.

- The ITC would regulate ownership, preventing overconcentration and ownership by religious and political groups. Private TVRO ownership (for reception of DBS programs) would be unregulated. Private companies would eventually build and maintain transmitters on contract; DBS operators would handle their own uplink transmissions. Local radio stations might assume responsibility for their own transmitters or contract with private firms.

- Channel 4 would continue its present role but would be responsible for its own ad sales, although not totally dependent on them.

SOURCE: Great Britain, Home Office, *Broadcasting in the '90s: Competition, Choice and Quality—The Government's Plans for Broadcasting Legislation.* Her Majesty's Printing Office, London, November 1988.

damental constitutional issues. In Italy, for example, the official broadcasting organization, RAI, went to court to suppress unauthorized cable television operations that cropped up in the 1970s. The Italian Constitutional Court ruled in 1975 that the RAI's legal monopoly covered only *network* broadcasting, and so RAI could not prevent *local* cable *or* broadcast operations by private owners. This ruling opened

the floodgates to thousands of private stations. Fifteen years later, these stations still operated without benefit of formal regulation because the Italian parliament, though always about to pass a new law, could not agree on the form it should take.

As this example suggests, statutes adopted to govern traditional broadcasting have proved inadequate to deal with new services, such as cable

EXHIBIT 19–4   International Telecommunication Union Structure

The International Telecommunication Union evolved from an organization founded to coordinate international use of the telegraph in 1865. A century later, by then also covering telephone and radio communications, it became one of the 18 specialized agencies of the United Nations.

The ITU coordinates and standardizes telecommunications worldwide and plays a leading role in helping developing nations improve their telecommunication facilities. Membership consists of most of the world's nations, each of which appoints an official national body or official to represent it in ITU matters. In the United States, the FCC has that role officially, but ITU decisions have such great national importance that both the State Department and the President's National Telecommunications and Information Administration participate actively in ITU meetings.

At one time the ITU dealt strictly with technical matters, apportioning frequencies on a first-come, first-served basis. With the emergence of the Third World, however, the Plenipotentiary Conferences and the Administrative Conferences have become politicized. Dissatisfaction emerged with the 1971 Space Conference, when newer countries complained that the ITU neglected their needs. They argue that spectrum and orbital position allocations should be planned for the long term, with some reserved for their future use. But the United States wants to use these resources immediately to meet current needs and to foster technological development.

The diagram below is a simplified outline of the ITU's complex organizational structure.

See next page for explanations of organizational chart (A), (B), (C), etc.

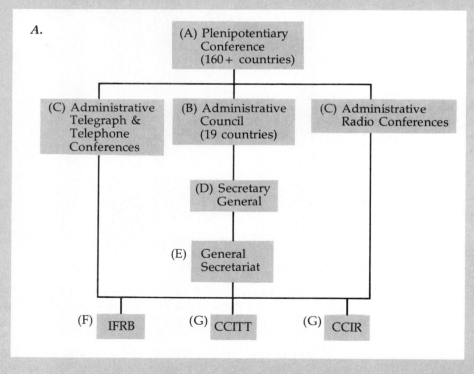

EXHIBIT 19–4   Continued

(A) Policy-making conferences, consisting of all member countries, meet about every five years. The Plenipotentiary Conferences endorse the governing statute of the union, the International Telecommunication Convention.

(B) The Administrative Council is a smaller elected administrative body that acts for the union between Plenipotentiary Conferences.

(C) The two conferences, one for radio and one for telegraph and telephone communication, meet as frequently as needed to revise regulations or draw up new ones on specific subjects. World Administrative Radio Conferences, called WARCs (or RARCs when they deal with only one of the ITU regions shown below), deal with the rules governing specific subjects, such as DBS satellites, AM radio, and short-wave radio.

(D) Appointed by the Administrative Council, the ITU Secretary General supervises the permanent staff, facilities, conferences, and represents the ITU before international bodies.

(E) The permanent staff, with offices in Geneva, Switzerland, prepares for and follows up the ITU's many meetings and publishes its numerous documents, including the *Radio Regulations,* which embody all the rules adopted by the ITU. It also issues the monthly *Telecommunication Journal,* which reports on ITU activities and publishes technical studies. Additional, highly specialized staff serve the bodies mentioned below.

(F) The International Frequency Registration Board keeps track of worldwide use of radio frequencies, in accordance with ITU allocations.

(G) The telegraph-telephone and the radio consultative committees (CCITT and CCIR) study technical problems and make recommendations for changes in regulations. The 1989 Plenipotentiary Conference added a third permanent unit at this level, the Telecommunication Development Bureau, which assists Third World countries.

As shown below, the ITU divides the world into three regions in order to adapt to varying geographic requirements. The table of frequency allocations lists frequencies by region, often with differences in allocations between regions.

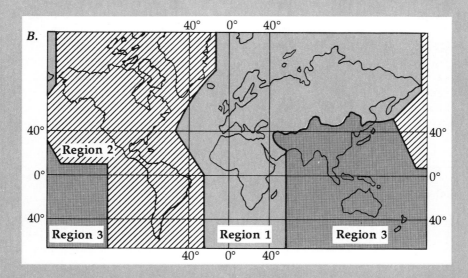

television, satellite relays, and direct-satellite broadcasting. In the United States, the FCC improvised cable regulation for years until Congress finally adopted comprehensive legislation in 1984. Britain adopted a new cable act in the same year. Many countries, however, are still wrestling with the problem of how to absorb the new communication technologies and how to deal with insistent demands for more private ownership, more localism, and more commercialism.

In Europe, the European Community (EC) complicates the problem by imposing another layer of regulation over national telecommunication laws. The EC aims to erase trade barriers among its 12 member countries, bringing about a true common market by 1992. The EC claims that broadcasting and the other media are among the services that should flow freely among its members. Already the European Court has begun to hear cases of alleged discrimination against cable program networks originating from foreign countries within the Community.

The traditional broadcasting organizations oppose some of the rules proposed by the EC, questioning whether an *economic* body has any business regulating *cultural* activities such as theirs. This controversy echoes arguments about U.S. deregulatory policy, whose proponents base their reasoning on economic theory, treating broadcast services as commodities. U.S. interests also question the authority of the EC over electronic media, foreseeing the possibility that while encouraging intra-Community program exchange, the EC may set up barriers against the importation of U.S. programs by EC member countries.

19.4
Access to the Air

Broadcasting's potential to inform (or disinform), to persuade, and to cultivate values has always made access to it a jealously guarded prerogative. Traditionally, access was limited to professional broadcasters, experts on subjects of public interest, people currently in the news, and politicians.

Political Access Politicians, as the ones who pass the laws governing broadcasting, have ample opportunity to ensure their own access. In political systems based on free elections, broadcasting plays a vital informational role. It can also pose a threat if the party in power takes advantage of its incumbency to monopolize access. Democracies have to devise ways of preserving fairness in political uses of broadcasting without at the same time crippling its role as a means of informing the electorate.

U.S. law, in keeping with the permissive orientation of the U.S. broadcasting system, allows liberal access by political candidates, requiring only *equal opportunities*. The weakest parties and candidates have the same access rights as the strongest—provided they can raise the money to buy time. Critics of the U.S. system point out that no other industrialized democracy permits such commercialization of elections.

Great Britain, for example, severely limits election broadcasts, emphasizing parties rather than individual candidates (in keeping with the parliamentary system, in which party membership plays a more important role than in the U.S. system). The two broadcasting authorities, the BBC and the IBA, confer periodically with representatives of the political parties to set up ground rules. In the recent past, only parties offering 50 or more parliamentary candidates received television time. Each party had one to five *free* broadcasts of five to ten minutes' duration. Individual candidates may plead their cases only under very limited conditions. These restrictions, plus the fact that British national election campaigns last only 30 days, mean that the British electorate escapes the interminable merchandising of candidates, and candidates do not need to beg for donations and accept money from lobbyists to pay for expensive advertising.

On the other hand, in Britain as in the United States, candidates and incumbents receive unlimited coverage in legitimate news programs. In such appearances, journalists rather than politicians choose the formats and run the shows, in accordance with normal canons of fairness and editorial judgment. The U.S. presidential candidate "debates" of 1988, in which the participating news professionals demeaned themselves by accepting ground rules contrived by the politicians, could not happen in Britain.

In other European countries, despite strict fairness regulations on paper, the ruling political parties often evade neutrality requirements by controlling appointments to the state broadcasting services and the regulatory agencies. In France the party in power has long regarded such appointments as the normal spoils of office. Successive statutory changes adopted by new administrations in 1982 (socialist) and 1986 (conservative) to insulate broadcasting from political influence had limited success.

Some of the West German states (which supersede the federal government in regulating broadcasting) attempt to ensure impartiality through a personnel policy called *Proporz* ("proportion"). It requires that appointments to key broadcasting posts mirror the political make-up of state legislatures. A broadcasting unit's chief executive officer who belongs to the ruling party would have a deputy belonging to the main opposition party. Italy's state-operated services, RAI, use a similar political balancing system called *lottizzazione* ("allotment"). This kind of calculated balancing helps ensure political neutrality but also tends to make broadcasters reluctant to come to grips with political issues, lessening the medium's usefulness to the voters.

Citizen Access   During the restless 1960s, people outside the ranks of broadcasters, journalists, and politicians began asking why ordinary citizens had no access to the airwaves. They argued that if the electromagnetic spectrum really does function like a national park or other natural resource, should not everybody get a chance to use it? This movement reflected the period's general rise in ethnic and regional consciousness, which is still being felt to this day.

Abetted by numerous domestic and external pirate radio stations, the access movement became widespread and vocal in the 1970s. Social reformers, artists, educators, small business people, and others with things to say to local audiences "shared a common mood and tone," said a UNESCO study of the movement, "at once romantic, radical, and missionary" (Berrigan, 1977: 15).

The movement had less relevance in the United States than in other democracies. The U.S. system's policy of local licensing accommodates a certain amount of local access. Broadcasting elsewhere tends to be more centralized. Access seekers could hardly expect national or regional networks to open their studios to them if they had nothing to say that was of national or regional significance. They tried instead to persuade the authorities to create new classes of local and community stations, exempt from the heavy regulation that governs more formal network services.*

Most democracies responded in the 1970s and 1980s by authorizing such stations. France, for example, legitimized more than a thousand small, privately owned FM stations following passage of a new broadcasting law in 1982. Many had started as pirate stations, which were rigorously suppressed by the French government. Italy has hundreds of small, private radio and television stations, the legacy of the previously mentioned 1975 court decision barring RAI from closing down nonnetwork private broadcasters.

Even some authoritarian regimes began to authorize local outlets. China, long noted for highly centralized control of broadcasting, including widespread use of wired-radio speaker boxes, began regionalizing and localizing its broadcast services in 1983, setting up stations down to the county level and encouraging local self-help in setting up radio stations and community antenna systems. In much of the Third World, however, the ever-present threat of political subversion and the divisive influence of tribalism tend to keep program control centralized in the capital city, with provincial transmitters merely relaying national network programs.

---

*As generally understood, the term *local* refers to stations that serve entire cities or towns, whereas *community* stations serve small, homogeneous groups, such as ethnic enclaves within cities. Community stations tend to be informal, minimally regulated, and shared by a number of separate small groups. The closest U.S. equivalent might be the Class D, 10-watt, noncommercial FM stations.

Group Access   Another way of dealing with demands for access is to shift the emphasis from the individual to the group to which the individual belongs. The U.S. fairness doctrine was an attempt to use this strategy with regard to controversies, obligating stations to give access to group-held ideas, though not to specific individuals.

The uniquely structured access system of the Netherlands has gone the furthest in ensuring groups their own programs on nationally owned broadcasting facilities. The government turns over most of the program time to citizen associations, some representing religious faiths, some nonsectarian in outlook. Even very small constituencies, such as immigrant workers or people from former Dutch colonies, can regularly obtain airtime.

Associations seeking recognition as regular daily broadcasters in the Netherlands set up nonprofit corporations, obtaining government-allotted production funds from receiver license fees; the associations also generate revenue for programs from their members by selling subscriptions to program guides. An umbrella organization, NOS, coordinates time sharing and itself produces certain programs of broad national interest, such as national and international news and major sporting events.

Although the associations operate noncommercially, advertising appears on the system, monopolized by a nonprofit government unit that turns the revenue over to the central program fund. In 1988, however, falling in with the universal trend toward deregulation, the Dutch began allowing some of the broadcasting associations to operate commercially.

19.5
Economics

Economics comes second only to politics in determining the shape of a country's telecommunication system. Primarily because of economic constraints, as qualified by political and cultural considerations, systems vary widely as to facilities, revenue sources, and the ability to produce home-grown programs.

Traditional Facilities   The world has some 212 broadcasting systems, of which only 35 lack television.* Receiver penetration (the number of receivers relative to population size) varies widely. The United States leads the major countries in television set penetration, with 745 television sets per thousand population, followed by Canada, with 497. U.S. leadership can be ascribed in part to economics—high living standards that make sets affordable to most of the population. However, other factors also play a role: strong motivation for set purchasing, aroused by highly attractive mass-appeal programming and by a national policy of licensing numerous localized stations.

In most communist countries, although their governments invest heavily in transmitters, relays, and production facilities, set penetration remains relatively low because of both consumer goods shortages and the low motivation supplied by government-controlled programming. The USSR, for example, had 270 sets per thousand population in 1988. China did not start television until 1958. Twenty years later it still had pitifully few receivers for a nation of over a billion population. Since adoption of more liberal policies in the late 1970s, however, television has expanded enormously, reaching an amazing 411 sets per thousand population by 1988—an ironic contrast with the USSR's low penetration, considering that the USSR helped China to introduce television.† Rapid expansion of China's domestic television set production facilitated this explosive growth.

In Third World countries, low purchasing power, lack of attractive programming, short television schedules, and paucity of local stations minimize set-buying incentives. Despite relatively high radio receiver penetration, a high percentage of the sets do not work because of battery shortages and humid

---

*This enumeration, based on listings in the *World Radio TV Handbook* (1989), includes dependencies as well as sovereign nations. Most of the 35 territories that lacked television as of that date were small islands.

†Figures on set penetration in this section come from estimates in the frequently updated "Worldwide TV Set Count," published in *Television/Radio Age International* (October, 1988: 147–150).

climates. Government investment in transmitters and production facilities can therefore be extremely uneconomic. It costs just as much in program and transmission expenses to reach a few scattered individuals as to reach the total population within a transmitter's coverage area. Lack of communications infrastructure, such as electric power, telephones, and relay facilities for networks, further impedes Third World broadcasting growth. However, a few of the oil-rich Middle East states have achieved high set penetration—for example, 401 per thousand population in Saudi Arabia and 349 in Kuwait.

Revenue Sources   Of the three main sources of broadcast funding (central government budgeting, advertising, and receiver license fees), most countries depend on the first, in whole or in part (Exhibit 19–2). Authoritarian regimes accept government ownership and support as natural, for in their view the media exist to serve the state. Third World countries, even if they would prefer to rely on advertising or receiver license fees to finance broadcasting, usually have no choice because those alternative sources cannot generate enough revenue. The communist countries generally impose only token receiver license fees. They would have difficulty in justifying fees the size of those in Western Europe, since the Marxist governments run the broadcasting services for the state's benefit rather than deferring to the public.

Broadcasting in most industrialized democracies depends in large part on license fees. Fees afford insulation both from direct government funding and from strong advertiser influence. They insulate only partly, however, because governments have a hand in making laws requiring payment of fees and in setting fee levels, and most fee-supported systems also depend on advertising for part of their revenue.

Western Europe's 1988 color television-set licenses* ran from the equivalent of about $42 a year

(Ireland) to as much as $220 (Switzerland). Britain's fee, on which the BBC depends, was $108. In most cases licensing of radio sets has been either dropped or combined with the television fee.

Receiver fees have the advantage of imposing a strong sense of public responsibility. Also, they insulate broadcasters from the taint of special influence that inevitably accompanies support by government or advertisers. Collection and enforcement costs absorb a relatively high proportion of the revenue. Great Britain has one of the more efficient systems, using the postal service as a collection agency. About 6.5 percent of the revenue goes to defray collection and enforcement expenses, and defaulters deprive the BBC of over 8 percent of its potential revenue (Great Britain, 1986: 11). NHK, Japan's equivalent of the BBC, employs its own collectors. They call personally on set owners, apparently experiencing little difficulty in persuading the law-abiding Japanese to pay up.

With the advent of color television, with its high production costs, systems relying heavily on fees began to have serious financial difficulties. As set penetration reached the saturation point, the license-fee revenue curve leveled off while operational costs kept rising. Fee levels always lag behind because the politicians, who control fee levels, delay the unpopular task of authorizing increases as long as possible. Some European fee-supported systems had to cut back production or turn to advertising for at least partial support. The staunchest holdouts against broadcast advertising welcome its support for modernized cable, subscription television, and direct-broadcast satellite services, even while fighting a rear-guard action to continue insulating traditional broadcasting from the influence of the marketplace.

European countries try to insulate programs from advertiser influence by strict regulations, including a ban on sponsorship* and limits on the percentage

---

*EBU Review regularly publishes a table of fees for the European region. These figures come from the May 1988 table, calculated at the October 1988 exchange rate (67 U.S. cents for one Swiss franc).

*Europeans unanimously forbid out-and-out commercial sponsorship (in which advertisers schedule commercials within their own programs), but there is a trend toward more liberal rules governing *program underwriting,* a limited form of sponsorship familiar to American viewers of public broadcasting.

of revenue that may be derived from advertising. For example, in the early 1980s, the Italian parliament allowed RAI to rely on advertising for less than a quarter of its budget.

Most European countries further protect programs on their public-service networks from commercial intrusion by scheduling all ads in a few special time blocks devoted exclusively to commercials, leaving the rest of the schedule free from interruption. Some keep advertisers at arm's length by still another method: appointing an official advertising agency with a monopoly on all sales. Italy, France, and Holland have such agencies for their public-service networks, for example.

Even the most stubborn holdouts against commercialism, the Scandinavian countries and Belgium, conceded that the new cable and direct-broadcast satellite services (discussed in Section 19.9) would need to resort to advertising for support. This foot-in-the-door commercialism began a general retreat from the purist no-advertising policy for most countries' national public-service broadcasting.

In the communist world, a similar retreat began. Though Marxist doctrine frowns on advertising as a capitalistic device for exploiting the workers, in practice communist countries found broadcast commercials useful for moving consumer goods that sometimes pile up because of central-planning errors. In a sharp change of policy, China began introducing Western-style advertising in 1979, in collaboration with U.S. companies such as CBS television. In the 1980s, the USSR, under the liberalizing influence of its own version of deregulation, *glasnost* and *perestroika,* also became more tolerant of advertising.

Program Economics Television consumes expensive program materials at such a rate that most countries, even highly advanced ones with strong economies, cannot afford to program several different television networks exclusively with home-grown productions. Britain is unusual in having four terrestrial television networks, although at the price of some program imports (voluntarily limited to 14 percent). Most countries have fewer national broadcast television networks, operating on limited schedules and depending on imports to varying degrees. In the smaller European countries, the dearth of programs from domestic sources stimulated cable television growth. Community antennas could pick up a half-dozen services from neighboring countries.

Shortages also account for the lively international trade in syndicated programs. The bulk of these programs come from the United States (as discussed in more detail in Section 19.9), with a relatively large number from Britain. However, communist and Third World countries increasingly display their wares at international program fairs. Brazil, for example, exports quantities of *telenovelas* (Hispanic soap operas) dubbed in Spanish, and Hong Kong exports programs in Chinese to the many places outside China where there are large Chinese settlements (including, of course, the United States).

No simple solution to the program shortage other than commercial syndication has emerged, although stratagems for alternative forms of cost and talent sharing have been developed. For example, the European Broadcasting Union (EBU), an association of official broadcasting services in Europe and nearby countries, shares programs through *Eurovision.* It arranges regular exchanges among its members, primarily of news, sports, and entertainment items. The East European communist countries have a similar association with its own program cooperative, *Intervision.* The East-West groups exchange programs with each other, with most of the material flowing from Eurovision to Intervision. There are associations of African, Arabic-speaking, Caribbean, and Asia-Pacific broadcasting systems that exist, but they have not yet developed their exchanges to the level of the Eurovision-Intervision operations.

Co-production has been increasingly used as another way of dealing with high program costs. Producers from two or more countries combine financial and often other resources to co-produce movies or television series, dividing the capital outlay and benefiting from the assured doubling of the market potential for the product.

19.6
Geography

A nation's size, shape, population distribution, nearness to neighbors, and historical development all affect the kind of broadcasting system it evolves. Geography plays an especially prominent role.

Coverage Problems Cost-effective coverage of a country depends on its shape as well as its size. The continental United States has the advantage of a relatively compact, unified land mass, surrounded mostly by large bodies of water (Alaska, Hawaii, and other offshore territories had to await satellites to enjoy coverage simultaneously with the mainland). These geographic factors make for efficient coverage and relative freedom from interference and spillover from neighbors.

Contrast this with the geography of Japan, an archipelago of mountainous islands spread over 2,000 miles of ocean. The Indonesian archipelago's 6,000 or so widely scattered inhabited islands with diverse populations speaking many different languages present even more formidable coverage problems. The USSR's territory extends so far in the east-west directions that its broadcasts have to be adapted to serve 11 different time zones (contrasted with the four zones of the United States). Such difficulties could not be tackled satisfactorily prior to satellite distribution of programs, and all these countries pioneered in satellite utilization. The USSR first employed satellites for domestic television relays.

Spillover Geography insulates most American listeners and viewers from spillover programs originating in foreign countries. Treaties with Canada, Mexico, and the Caribbean islands minimize transborder interference.

Geography has had a powerful influence on Canadian broadcasting, satellites, and cable. Most Canadians live fairly near the United States border, and so are ideally situated to pick up American radio and television signals. In addition, Canadian cable television companies deliver American programs to their subscribers, resulting in Canada's becoming one of the world's most cabled countries (more than 60 percent penetration). To limit U.S. cultural dominance, Canada imposes quotas on the amount of syndicated programming that Canadian broadcasters and cable operators may import and also subsidizes indigenous productions. The remoteness of its thinly populated northern regions motivated Canada to get an early start in the use of domestic satellites.

Geography both helps and hinders West European broadcasting. National systems suffer interference and spillover from neighbors because of the close proximity of many relatively small countries with highly developed broadcasting systems. Spillover helps, however, in supplementing the limited program resources of the smaller countries.

Spillover sometimes creates odd situations, as in divided Berlin, whose West German television reaches into surrounding East Germany. Citizens on each side of the Berlin Wall enjoy each others' programs, although their governments remain politically at odds and they have to buy converters to match their incompatible color systems. East German authorities, after trying fruitlessly to get their people to stop viewing Western programs, resigned themselves to living with the electronic invasion.

19.7
Programs and Schedules

Broadcasting's inherent technical, economic, and social characteristics made it inevitable that the same basic program formats would emerge and flourish throughout the world. News, commentary, public affairs, music, drama, variety, studio games, sports events—such program genres appeal everywhere. However, there are marked differences in the details of program content as well as in the balance among program types and the length of schedules.

News and Public Affairs National differences are especially evident in the treatment of news and public affairs. The main daily news presentation is a universally popular program fixture, but content and style differ from one country to another. Parochialism, chauvinism, and ideological biases affect the choice of news stories, their treatment, and their timing. Each country stresses its own national happenings, few of which hold interest for the rest of the world.

For these reasons, Third World leaders tend to agree with the traditional communist approach to news, which ignores timeliness, human interest, and Western "news values" generally. Since they have no need to compete with alternative domestic news sources, Third World journalists can afford to ignore marketability. Political correctness and educational values come first. They play down or omit stories about crime, accidents, civil disorders, and the personal lives of political figures. Third World government leaders reason that allowing broadcasters to report and edit according to Western standards would make the news depressingly downbeat, loaded with reports on food shortages, crop failures, black markets, industrial mismanagement, official corruption, breakdowns in public services, urban blight, and all the other horrendous problems that plague the less developed nations. Instead, most Third World leaders expect their journalists to look for news, or to devise news treatments, supportive of the government, praising its leaders, heralding the nation's accomplishments, and urging audiences to work hard at nation building.

Program Balance   Audiences everywhere prefer light entertainment to more serious content; accordingly, entertainment dominates broadcast schedules that are not controlled by policies that impose criteria other than popular demand. Aside from the United States, most industrialized democracies regulate broadcasting to ensure a certain balance between light entertainment and the news-information-culture-education program genres.

The expense and consequent paucity of homegrown productions make it difficult for Third World nations to regulate balance because they depend so heavily on foreign program sources. They find inexpensive but slickly produced popular entertainment hard to resist, even though these imports may throw schedules out of balance, emphasizing

light entertainment that plays up alien cultures. Communist systems, which traditionally viewed broadcasting as primarily an official instrument of education and persuasion, paid relatively little attention to popular preferences until *glasnost* caused more emphasis on production values and human-interest programs.

Schedules   Broadcast days of 18 to 24 hours, commonplace in the United States, occur in few other countries. Many radio services go on the air for a short morning segment, take a midmorning break before a midday segment, then take another break in midafternoon before the evening programs.

Television often commences late in the afternoon, going off the air by 11 P.M. Even in such a highly developed system as Britain's, the BBC did not begin 24-hour radio until 1979, when Radio 2 filled in the previously blank hours of 2 to 5 A.M. "Breakfast television" began in Britain in 1983, when both the BBC and a newly formed IBA commercial company first began offering early-morning programs. Extending programming into previously unused early-morning and late-night hours became one of the signs of change in the 1980s as new networks, stations, and cable systems heightened competition. European broadcasters held the first international conference on breakfast television in 1987, reported in the European Broadcasting Union's journal under the heading, "Morning Has Broken: An Idea Whose Time Has Come" (*EBUR, 1987*).

19.8
Transborder Broadcasting

Exploiting the ability of radio waves to surmount political boundaries introduced a potent new factor into relations among nations. Never before had it been possible to talk to masses of foreigners across even the most impervious of national boundaries. Broadcasting can inform and persuade people in closed societies that are impossible to penetrate with in-person messages. *External broadcasting* uses mostly short-wave radio (because of its long range) to send both official and clandestine programs to foreign countries, becoming an important ideological weapon both in warfare and in times of peace. More than 80 countries operate external services, although many have little more than symbolic importance. In 1988, the United States topped all external broadcasters in weekly time on the air, as shown in Exhibit 19–5.

Also ideologically motivated, religious groups recognized from the start that broadcasting gave them their first opportunity to get their messages directly to potential converts in societies dominated by other religions, sometimes despite official hostility. They have so saturated the short-wave bands that listeners can pick up Christian evangelism almost anywhere in the world 24 hours a day.

Other forms of transborder broadcasting have commercial motives: legal "peripheral" and illegal pirate stations.

BBC External Service   Colonial commitments abroad prompted the first external services. The Dutch and Germans started theirs in 1929, the French in 1931. After experimenting for several years, Britain's BBC formally launched external broadcasting (then called the Empire Service) in 1932. Broadcast entirely in English, it sought to maintain home-country ties with expatriates in the colonies and with residents in the dominions (independent ex-colonies such as Canada and Australia). Later on, the use of foreign languages in external services shifted their focus toward diplomatic and propaganda roles. The BBC began its foreign-language external broadcasts in 1938 on the eve of World War II, countering Italian radio propaganda in Arabic to the Near East. Soon Britain and the Axis powers became locked in a deadly war of words, using many languages.

During the war, foreign listeners came to regard the BBC as having the highest credibility among external broadcasters. It has retained that reputation ever since. Throughout the world, listeners tune to it automatically when they are in doubt about the authenticity of other sources. True, the British Foreign Office reimburses the BBC for the cost of the External Services (recently renamed the World

EXHIBIT 19–5   Ten Leading External Broadcasters

Rank	Country (languages)	Hours per week[a]
1.	United States[b] (50)	2,277
2.	USSR (81)	2,247
3.	China (47)	1,493
4.	Taiwan (17)	1,091
5.	West Germany (37)	821
6.	Egypt (30)	816
7.	United Kingdom (36)	751
8.	Trans World Radio[c] (61)	526
9.	Voice of the Andes[d] (14)	500
10.	Albania (21)	451

[a]Time rounded to nearest hour.
[b]Includes VOA and Radio Martí (1,199 hours), Radio Free Europe (630 hours), and Radio Liberty and Radio Free Afghanistan (448 hours).
[c]A religious broadcaster with transmitters located in Guam, Monaco, Netherlands Antilles, Sri Lanka, Switzerland, and Uruguay.
[d]A religious broadcaster with transmitters in Quito, Ecuador.

SOURCE: *Voice of America, 1988,* VOA, 1988, p. 55.

Service), but that ministry controls only the choice of languages, the hours of operation, and investments in new transmitters. Listeners understand that BBC commentators represent the independent, expert viewpoints of professors, foreign correspondents, and the like; they have more credibility than the civil servants presenting official government viewpoints that are found on other external services.

In the 1980s, the BBC, spurred by pressure to become more competitive, proposed mounting a television version of its World Service, a round-the-clock program in English. When the Foreign Office failed to come forward with the necessary funds for this new venture, the BBC began trying to recruit other backers.

Radio Moscow   The USSR, not having a colonial empire when broadcasting began, had different motives than the West for starting an external service. The Soviets used early radio to explain their recent revolution to sympathizers in Western Europe and to legitimize their regime among the family of nations. From the outset the Soviets recognized the importance of broadcasting in foreign languages as a means of gaining and influencing friends abroad. Radio Moscow began regular external services in 1929.

Radio Moscow uses fewer overseas relay stations than the major Western external broadcasters, although it has one in Cuba aimed at the Americas. Radio Moscow, like the external services of all communist states, tends to be relentlessly propagandistic.

Western studies of audience reactions in a variety of countries always show Radio Moscow's appeal running well behind that of the BBC and the VOA. However, in the 1980s Moscow lightened its tone, even before the 1985 *glasnost* policy took hold. It initiated a 24-hour daily service in English, appropriating the BBC "World Service" title.

Voice of America   The United States added its voice to the battle of words during World War II when President Franklin D. Roosevelt appointed a popular radio commentator, Elmer Davis, to head the Office of War Information (OWI). As a component of the OWI, the Voice of America (VOA) went on the air in February 1942. Wary of creating a propaganda agency that might be turned against the American people by the party in power, Congress forbade the VOA to release its programs in the United States, although anyone with a short-wave radio can pick up VOA programs aimed at overseas listeners. No such proscription exists in Britain, where the BBC external service, coming as it does from a nongovernment source, welcomes domestic listeners to its 24-hour World Service in English, which can be heard at home on regular AM radio sets.

The contemporary VOA functions as an arm of the United States Information Agency (USIA), the federal unit responsible for informational and cultural contacts with the rest of the world. In 1988, the VOA used 50 languages in addition to English, ranging from Albanian to Vietnamese (see Exhibit 19–5). Programs originate in Washington, DC, going overseas via leased satellite channels and VOA short-wave transmitters located in Greenville, NC, and several secondary U.S. sites. The VOA also leases sites in a dozen foreign countries, where it maintains transmitters for rebroadcasting programs to listeners in nearby areas.

VOA programs revolve around news and commentary but also use most of the other formats familiar in domestic radio, including a telephone call-in show (international listeners leave a message on a Washington, DC, answering machine and VOA staff members call back the listeners at VOA expense during production). News and public affairs items reflect official U.S. policies, but for the sake of credibility the VOA tries to observe the spirit of its original 1942 manifesto: "Daily at this time we shall speak to you about America. . . .The news may be good or bad. We shall tell you the truth." Truth telling continues to be VOA policy, despite occasional lapses when partisan officials appointed by the party in power bend the truth to suit momentary political objectives.

Adopting an aggressive information policy, the Republicans undertook a major VOA improvement and expansion plan during the 1980s. The USIA budget doubled between 1981 and 1988, much of it spent on updating long-neglected equipment and building new facilities (Exhibit 19–6). The VOA added languages and increased the number of overseas relay transmitters, especially in the Caribbean and Central America, where it set up standard AM transmitters to reach listeners with ordinary (non-short-wave) receivers.*

Worldnet   Because of its short range, television does not lend itself to external broadcasting as readily as does short-wave radio. The USIA, the VOA's parent agency, used to rely entirely on *placement,* persuading foreign broadcasters to carry American television programs on their own domestic services.

---

*According to BBC research, in most countries from about 30 to 75 percent of the households have short-wave receivers. Canada and the United States, which make little use of domestic short-wave broadcasting, have the lowest penetration, between 5 and 10 percent of all households.

EXHIBIT 19–6   VOA's Historic Control Center

The master control panel, with its clocks showing the time in different world target areas, has long been the centerpiece of public tours of the Voice of America facilities at 330 Independence Avenue, S.W. in Washington, DC. A modern, solid-state, computerized facility replaced this old-fashioned, hands-on control panel in the 1980s, but it remains on show as part of the tour.

SOURCE: Courtesy Voice of America.

In 1988, USIA information officers stationed in foreign countries succeeded in placing U.S.-sponsored program material on domestic television services in more than a hundred host countries.

In the 1980s, the USIA created *Worldnet,* a program service that harnesses satellites to extend the scope of external television. Worldnet transmits a daily *interactive* satellite exchange consisting of press conferences with important U.S. officials, intellectuals, and others, plus "passive" programs consisting of news and general information. U.S. diplomatic posts throughout the world pick up Worldnet on their own TVROs, as do some foreign cable systems and broadcast stations. By mid-1988, Worldnet reached TVROs erected at 137 U.S. diplomatic posts in more than 90 countries. The posts arranged access to Worldnet for media people and others in those countries.

Although Worldnet's interactive press conferences succeeded well in reaching foreign media professionals with the U.S. viewpoint, they reached only a limited general audience through the foreign cable systems and stations carrying them. U.S. Senate critics, regarding Worldnet as a grandstand play that drained funds away from the more conventional VOA external services, withheld funding for Worldnet's "passive" programs pending proof that they regularly reached at least 2 million European viewers. When it failed to convince the senators,* USIA made a deal with C-SPAN, the cable-industry-supported public-affairs network, to relay its 24-hour service over Worldnet facilities.

U.S. Surrogate Services In addition to conventional external radio services, the United States also engages in a special type of external broadcasting, *surrogate* domestic services. They simulate domestic services within target countries, attempting to bypass censored domestic media in those countries. Surrogate broadcasting seeks to substitute the sending country's view of the facts for the views promulgated by the target country's own broadcasters.

The two main U.S. operations of this type, Radio Liberty (RL) and Radio Free Europe (RFE), are aimed at the USSR and the East European communist states, respectively. They have studios and transmitters in Munich, West Germany, and additional transmitters in Israel, Portugal, and Spain. RFE/RL originated during the Cold War that followed World War II, covertly supported by the Central Intelligence Agency. The stations aimed to stir up dissent within, and undermine the credibility of, the target communist regimes. After the CIA connection became known publicly in 1973, Congress created a special agency, the Board for International Broadcasting (BIB), to supervise the operations. Congress funds them openly with annual appropriations. Broadcasting entirely in the languages of their target countries, RFE/RL choose domestic and foreign news from *their* perspective, not from the U.S. perspective as does the VOA, which also broadcasts to the same target areas.

In 1985 the United States introduced a new surrogate service, Radio Martí, aimed at giving the people of Cuba news and information free of Castro-regime bias. Congress declined to set up Radio Martí

as an independent surrogate service like RFE/RL. Instead, it became a special VOA service with its own supervisory board. It transmits from a previously existing VOA AM transmitter in the Florida keys as well as from U.S.-based short-wave stations.

Radio Martí started in May 1985, with an authorized staff strength of about 175. Supporters claim that it has had a powerful effect, creating dissatisfaction with the Castro regime by revealing facts concealed from the people, such as deaths of Cuban soldiers in Africa. Some observers think Radio Martí's impact caused the Castro regime to upgrade its own domestic services—an apparent positive benefit of pluralism.

In 1988 Congress authorized funds to experiment with a *television* version of Radio Martí, using a transmitter hung from a balloon tethered in the Florida keys. Although the scheme may sound far-fetched, such relay had actually been tried in the 1950s, prior to the start of Cuban television. A balloon-borne transmitter on the mainland relayed a major league baseball game to receivers on the island.

Commercial Transborder Services Several European ministates have operated *peripheral* stations for a long time, capitalizing on the unfilled demand for broadcast advertising and the appetite for alternative programs. Both audiences and advertisers, frustrated by severely regulated domestic services, welcomed these alternatives. Peripherals beam commercial services in the appropriate languages to neighboring countries. They specialize in popular music formats, sometimes supplemented by objective news programs, which are welcome in countries where the ruling political parties dominate broadcast news.

The Grand Duchy of Luxembourg, ideally located for peripheral transmitters at the intersection of Belgium, France, and Germany, gets much of its national income from international commercial broadcasting (Exhibit 19–7). Other notable transborder commercial stations operate in the German Saar (Europe No. 1), Monaco (Radio Monte Carlo), Cyprus (Radio Monte Carlo East), Morocco (Radio Mediterranean International), Yugoslavia (Studio

---

*USIA-sponsored research estimated that Worldnet's weekly cumulative adult average viewership in 11 European countries was little more than half a million (Burke-Inter/View, 1988: 5).

EXHIBIT 19–7   Luxembourg: Home of Peripherals

The tiny Grand Duchy of Luxembourg (GDL) granted a broadcasting monopoly to a hybrid government-private corporation, now known as RTL (Radio-Télé-Luxembourg), in 1930. In 1931, it began operating as what the French called a *radio périphérique* (peripheral radio). In those days, when official European radio services tended to be rather highbrow and stuffy, listeners far and wide heard its pop-music programs. Legend has it that Radio Luxembourg, received in Liverpool, England, gave the Beatles their first taste of pop music.

Today, RTL has high-power long-wave (2,000 kW), medium-wave (1,200 kW), and short-wave (500 kW) radio transmitters radiating across the borders carrying programs in English, Dutch, French, and German. It broadcasts television in both the PAL and SECAM systems in order to reach both French and German viewers. RTL holds shares in a number of European privately owned broadcasting services and owns extensive production facilities in Luxembourg.

Television's short range made it impossible for the GDL to repeat its radio coverage with the newer media, but it overcame this problem in part by setting up jointly owned broadcasting services in neighboring countries, notably RTL Plus in Germany (both a broadcast and a satellite-to-cable service) and TVi, French-speaking Belgium's first commercial broadcast channel.

The ITU's 1977 allocation of DBS orbital slots to European countries offered Luxembourg a chance to extend its television coverage to the whole of Europe. Two early attempts at establishing a DBS service in the GDL failed, but SES (*Societé Européenne des Satellites*), founded in 1985, finally succeeded, launching ASTRA in 1988—the first privately owned European communication satellite. The numbers on the map below indicate the width of the home television antennas needed to receive ASTRA in the zones defined by the contour lines.

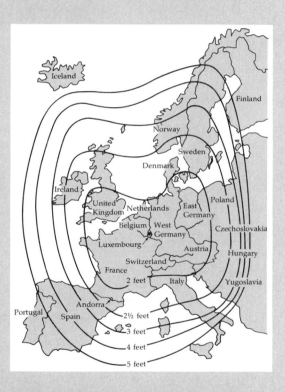

ASTRA contracted with a variety of direct-to-home and satellite-to-cable services to occupy its 16 channels, including Disney, Sky Channel (the pioneer European satellite-to-cable service), Eurosport, and MTV-Europe.

Koper/Radio Capodistria), and Gabon (Africa No. 1). Peripheral stations would have little motive for broadcasting to the United States, although powerful AM stations in Mexico, known as "border blasters," take advantage of Mexico's more liberal laws to circumvent U.S. regulations.

Peripherals, rather staid operations tolerated by some of their target countries (which even invested in them), still left commercial and program demands unsatisfied. This vacuum led to the emergence of *pirate* radio outlets.

The United States, because of its permissive system, its thousands of stations licensed to local communities, and its free-enterprise advertising, has not experienced pirate invasions of its airwaves except by occasional youthful pranksters. Less permissive systems have long been plagued by radio pirates operating stations on ships anchored offshore. Transmitting from beyond the territorial limits of their target countries, and therefore immune from domestic broadcasting laws, they violate licensing, copyright, and music performance restrictions.

The first offshore pirate began broadcasting from a ship anchored between Denmark and Sweden in 1958. Often U.S.-financed and always frankly imitative of American pop-music formats, advertising techniques, and promotional gimmicks, the pirates captured large and devoted youthful audiences. Some pirates made a lot of money, but only at considerable risk. They suffered from storms, from raids by rival pirates, and finally from stringent laws penalizing land-based firms for supplying them or doing any other business with them. Nevertheless, in spite of suppressive legislation, offshore pirates still crop up today.

The pirates whetted appetites for pop music, forcing national systems to take notice of hitherto ignored musical tastes. The BBC, as one example, reorganized its national radio network offerings, adding a pop-music network (Radio 1) imitative of the pirates. Some of the offshore DJs ended up working for the BBC and other established broadcasters. Pirate influence caused Holland to reorganize its broadcasting system, permitting two former pirate organizations to come ashore and develop into leading legitimate broadcasters.

More recently, commercial services have crossed national borders in satellite-to-cable networks and direct-to-home DBS broadcasting. These developments are discussed in the next section.

19.9
U.S. Global Influence

Aside from the special realm of public diplomacy, the United States exerts a powerful, worldwide influence on the electronic media in terms of technology, program expertise, and the economic concepts embedded in deregulatory theory. This pervasive influence has won foes as well as friends. American programs, for example, have the widest circulation of any in the world, attaining immense popularity with most foreign audiences; yet many foreign critics resent this U.S. influence, and their countries do everything they can to counteract it.

By the 1980s, however, American dominance, though still not seriously challenged, felt increasing competition. The Japanese had captured most of the consumer market for electronic media goods and led in DBS and HDTV technology. The European Common Market, scheduled to break down nationalistic trade barriers by 1992, threatened to become in time an even larger, more unified media market than the United States. Of the world's ten largest multimedia firms in 1989, only four were U.S. companies, and several of the six top foreign companies had substantial holdings in the American media.

Satellite Technology The United States took the technological initiative with an operational leap into space communication in 1965. In that year, the *International Telecommunications Satellite Organization* (INTELSAT) began relaying transatlantic communications traffic. INTELSAT relay satellites, stationed above the Atlantic, Indian, and Pacific Oceans, eventually made possible instant worldwide distribution not only of television programs but also of telephone conversations, news agency services, and business data.

Ever since, we have been able to see live televised scenes from distant overseas news events instantaneously.* More than a hundred countries share IN-TELSAT ownership, but the United States originated it, owns the largest percentage of its shares (about 25 percent), houses its headquarters (in Washington, DC), and until 1979 operated it on behalf of the rest of the consortium (through Comsat, the Communications Satellite Corporation).

Though primarily an international carrier, IN-TELSAT also leases satellite access at reasonable rates to Third World countries for *domestic* use. This enables the less-developed countries to set up their own internal satellite relay networks. With INTEL-SAT's aid, many vaulted directly into the satellite era, avoiding the need to erect costly microwave circuits throughout their territories. Among other things, this short-cut enabled them to feed daily national and international television news to transmitters throughout their territories, decades—even generations—before such national program distribution would have been possible using earthbound, presatellite networks. However, emerging private competition to INTELSAT in the provision of international satellite services may reduce its revenues, endangering its unique service to developing countries' domestic communications (Exhibit 19–8).

Communist countries have their own, much smaller international consortium, *Intersputnik,* serving only 14 countries. The USSR operates Intersputnik; nevertheless, it also uses INTELSAT services to reach noncommunist regions of the world.

Originally NASA, the U.S. government space agency, monopolized the West's capacity to launch communication satellites. By 1984, however, a consortium of European countries began to challenge NASA's monopoly with their own launch facility, Arianespace, named for Ariane, the rocket that launches the satellites. Ariane's launch site in French Guiana on the north coast of South America, near the equator, gives it better conditions for attaining equatorial orbit than does NASA's Florida location. Ariane contracts to launch satellites for other countries, as NASA did prior to the *Challenger* disaster. China and the USSR also opened their launch facilities to foreign commercial users.

Pioneering in domestic satellites (domsats), as opposed to international satellites, began in 1965 with the USSR's Molniya satellite series. Canada's Anik domsat series followed starting in 1972, preceding the first U.S. domsat, Westar, by two years. The 1970s also saw the launching of the first Third World satellite, Indonesia's Palapa, the forerunner of Europe's Eutelsat series, and the first Japanese satellite. France, first among the European countries with its own domsat, launched its Telecom in 1985, in part to enable relays to its overseas territories. Exhibit 19–9 (page 517) lists some of the foreign satellites used for broadcasting at the close of the 1980s.

DBS   Direct broadcast satellite (DBS) services took longer to emerge. A short-lived U.S. DBS service, USCI, went bankrupt in 1985 after only 17 months' operation. Without the benefit of a specialized high-power satellite suitable for easy home reception and lacking a wide choice of program channels, it could not compete with cable television.

DBS seemed more immediately promising in countries where it did not have to compete with deep cable-television penetration, such as Australia and Japan. Australia's AUSSAT, though a general-purpose satellite rather than a specialized DBS vehicle, transformed Australian broadcasting in the late 1980s by bringing programs to the remotest areas—regions too thinly populated to support cable. Japan forestalled cable by concentrating on DBS experiments. It led the world with the first full-time DBS service in 1987.

In Europe, cable not only had low average penetration but also offered relatively few channels, making DBS an attractive proposition, albeit mainly on a multinational basis. In 1989, Luxembourg launched ASTRA, Europe's first private DBS vehicle (see Exhibit 9–7). Other European DBS projects

---

*In earlier days, before videotape recorders and INTELSAT, the U.S. networks occasionally installed film processors in airplanes so that they could develop film of exceptionally newsworthy European events during the return trip across the Atlantic. Such strenuous efforts enabled them to show the coronation of Britain's Queen Elizabeth in 1952, for example, only a few hours after the event actually took place. This labored coverage contrasts with that of another royal event: the marriage of the Prince of Wales to Lady Diana Spencer in 1981, seen live all over the world, thanks to the global satellite system.

EXHIBIT 19–8   INTELSAT vs. "Separate Systems"

Comparing the successive generations of INTELSAT space vehicles gives a graphic picture of the remarkable growth of satellite communication within the short space of a quarter century. The table shows a dramatic increase in the number of transponders and voice channels (a conventional measurement of information capacity).

Several satellites of each model must be purchased to keep backup vehicles in reserve and to station ve-

Designation: INTELSAT	I	II	III	IV	IV-A	V	V-A	VI
Satellites Purchased:	2	4	8	8	6	9	6	5
First Launched:	1965	1967	1968	1971	1975	1980	1985	1989
Design Lifetime:	1.5 yrs.	3 yrs.	5 yrs.	7 yrs.	7 yrs.	7 yrs.	7 yrs.	13 yrs.
Bandwidth:	50 MHz	130 MHz	300 MHz	500 MHz	800 MHz	2,144 MHz	2,250 MHz	3,300 MHz
Voice Channels:	480	480	2,400	8,000	12,000	25,000	30,000	120,000

hicles above each of the three major oceans. Already orders for five *seventh* generation INTELSAT vehicles have been placed with Ford Aerospace. They will look like the diagram below right.

Some major components of Intelsat VII: (1) Ku-band steerable spot-beam antennas (suitable for small Earth antennas, such as those on mobile news vehicles); (2) antennas for larger footprints; (3) steerable C-band spot-beam antenna; (4) radiator to dissipate heat buildup aboard craft; (5) array of solar cells to generate electrical energy; (6) antenna for global footprint; (7) horns that direct signals to reflector at (9); (8) hinge to allow deploying (9) from folded position the reflector assumes during takeoff; (9) reflector fed by horns at (7), for large footprint.

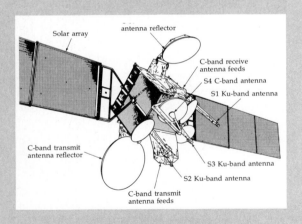

were also under way (see Exhibit 9–9). Thereafter it became a race between cable and DBS to see which could first sign up enough subscribers to justify the huge capital outlays. It seemed likely that only one contender could survive as a major service.

Cable TV   Europe had primitive cable television in the limited form of CATV (community antenna television) for many years before modern cable existed. These early systems merely extended domestic broadcast station coverage, sometimes

EXHIBIT 19–8   Continued

The globe below shows the differing footprints of INTELSAT V (F-15), located above the Atlantic Ocean and beaming to both the east and the west. Note that the west hemispheric beam (unbroken line) covers all of Africa and Western Europe.

The INTELSAT treaty requires member countries that launch their own international satellites to "coordinate" with INTELSAT to ensure that competing services do not harm it either technically or economically. A number of countries have obtained INTELSAT agreement, notably the consortium of European countries that operates Eutelsat, a regional satellite series that downlinks a number of satellite-to-cable program channels in Europe.

Prior to 1986, however, no competing satellite system had directly challenged INTELSAT for business on its most lucrative route, across the Atlantic between North America and Western Europe. In that year the FCC gave the go-ahead to several satellite companies that were planning to do just that. INTELSAT member nations opposed these plans for "separate systems," foreseeing that private competitors would skim the cream off the satellite business, lessening INTELSAT's earnings. This loss might force INTELSAT to modify its policy of averaging rates between heavily used and lightly used routes, a form of subsidy that enables Fiji, for example, to communicate with Australia for a fraction of what it would have to pay to cover the full costs of interconnection in the light-traffic Pacific region.

Moreover, INTELSAT normally downlinks and uplinks international traffic at only one or two teleports in each of the smaller countries; traffic to and from a teleport travels over conventional terrestrial circuits. This *ground segment* of a satellite communication link costs far more than the *space segment*. Centralized post and telegraph (PTT) telecommunication monopolies benefit from contracts that give them exclusive rights to these lucrative terrestrial segments of INTELSAT traffic. For this reason, government PTTs oppose private satellite companies that might bypass their facilities and link directly with consumers who erect their own Earth stations.

American satellite firms, strongly backed by the U.S. government, argue that INTELSAT's monopoly is inefficient, that its rates do not reflect actual costs, and that its sheer size makes it inflexible. Competition from smaller, nimbler satellite firms, they contend, would lower prices for all, enhance services, and encourage innovation. The first private U.S. "separate system" to launch a satellite, Pan American Satellite Corporation (PAS), planned to offer both domestic and international satellite services. It will link the United States and countries of the Hispanic world—Central

Exhibit continues next page.

adding a few channels for the purpose of carrying neighboring foreign broadcast networks. Most operated noncommercially, often owned by municipalities; they had few channels, no local origination, and no pay channels.

Modern cable developed most extensively in small countries such as Belgium (around 90 percent cable penetration by 1989) and the Netherlands (around 70 percent). Research indicates that audiences prefer home-produced programs, but small countries

EXHIBIT 19–8   Continued

and South America and the Caribbean—with Europe and serve their domestic needs as well.

(A) The PAS central beam focuses on Peru. Concentric rings delineate areas of different signal strength, with maximum strength at the center.

(B) The PAS south beam centers on Brazil. The "look angle" of the satellite from its position above the equator and west of the target areas distorts the maps.

PAS launched its first satellite in 1988, but experienced delays in finding "correspondents," firms or agencies at the foreign end of the circuits that were willing and legally able to enter into satellite services agreements. A U.S. international satellite system must have formal approval from foreign governments for any proposed linkups before it can obtain FCC licensing. Peru became the first PAS correspondent, soon followed by the Dominican Republic and Costa Rica on this side of the Atlantic and Britain, Ireland, Luxembourg, Sweden, and West Germany on the other, with more yet to come. CNN and other U.S. satellite-to-cable networks contracted with PAS to relay their programs to countries to the south.

A.   B.

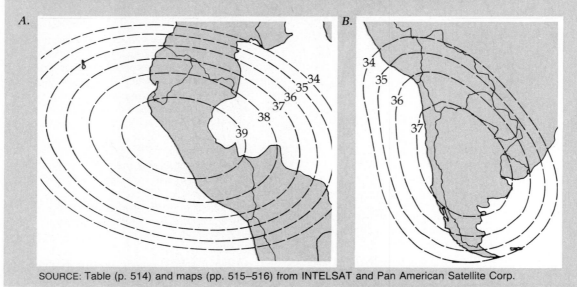

SOURCE: Table (p. 514) and maps (pp. 515–516) from INTELSAT and Pan American Satellite Corp.

can produce only a limited number of programs domestically; they necessarily draw on foreign producers to supplement their own resources.

In the larger European countries, however, cable progressed slowly. Extensive domestic broadcast program production held down the demand for alternative programs. In 1988 Britain had only 1.3 percent cable penetration and France less than 1 percent.

Although cable penetration continued to increase, public demand in the larger countries remained sluggish as long as basic cable systems could not offer a wide variety of high-interest programs. To become commercially viable in Europe, such networks had to cumulate a multinational audience—difficult to do in the face of national differences in language, culture, cable regulation, copyright law, and advertising practices.

The United States had led in the development of satellite-to-cable networks, starting in the mid-1970s. Such networks did not begin in Europe until 1982 with the launch of Sky Channel, a London-based English-language network. More than 40 such satellite-to-cable networks served Europe by 1989. Sky Channel then reached nearly 15 million households in 15 countries. Nevertheless, like all such European

EXHIBIT 19–9   Major Foreign Communication Satellites

Country	Name	First Launched	Remarks
Arab consortium	ARABSAT	1985	The League of Arab States developed Arabsat; however, the league's expulsion of Egypt for making a treaty with Israel diminished ARABSAT's usefulness by denying it to one of the countries potentially best able to use it for television.
Australia	AUSSAT	1985	Satellites completely transformed Australia's hitherto very unevenly distributed broadcast services.
Brazil	BRASILSAT	1985	Brazil pursued an aggressive space policy, having already installed an extensive ground-station network using INTELSAT before 1985.
Canada	ANIK	1972	One of the earliest countries to develop domsats, Canada uses them to reach remote settlements in the north.
China	STW	1984	An experimental satellite at that time.
European consortium	EUTELSAT	1983	Europe's first commercial telecommunications satellite, owned by PTTs. It delivers many cable network channels to systems throughout Europe.
France	TELECOM	1984	Designed for PTT services, but also carries domestic broadcast networks.
Great Britain	BSB	1989	A DBS satellite, rival to ASTRA. The government's insistence on private funding (and, originally, British manufacture of the satellite) delayed Britain's entry into the domestic satellite field.
India	INSAT	1984	A glitch in the first INSAT, launched in 1982, caused it to orient itself on the moon instead of Earth. Unable to receive instructions from the control station, it soon exhausted its fuel.
Indonesia	PALAPA	1976	The first Third World domestic satellite; it also serves neighboring countries.
Japan	BS ("Yuri")	1978	The first BS vehicle was used for DBS and HDTV experiments; regular services began with BS-2A in 1984.
Luxembourg	ASTRA	1989	The first European privately owned satellite, designed specifically for direct-to-home services.
Mexico	MORELOS	1985	One transponder relays U.S. cable programs to Mexican cable systems.
USSR	MOLNIYA	1965	Unusual because *nonsynchronous* (not in geostationary orbit) in order to reach Russia's far northern communities.

Each satellite is one of a series of at least two, with the second acting as backup or spare. Most have gone through several generations since the first in the series was launched. Many more national satellites were on the drawing boards or in the process of launch preparation when this table was drawn up in 1989.

networks, it still lost money. Some networks targeted only a single country, some several countries that had a common language (Exhibit 19–10). Cultural differences discouraged attempts to form true pan-European, multilingual satellite-to-cable program networks.

Beyond Europe, in the meantime, cable systems began to emerge in practically every other country. Canada has the highest cable penetration among large countries (some 70 percent), a development stimulated by Canada's proximity to U.S. program sources and aided by Canada's having its own domestic satellites to relay programs. Most other large countries installed cable slowly, usually only in a few major cities. Restrictive regulations, lack of skillful promotion, the high cost of cable installation, and difficulties in obtaining programs inhibited growth. Among the Caribbean islands, however, cable systems flourished on a small scale because that area falls within the footprints of U.S. domestic satellites. Island entrepreneurs could downlink American cable networks, often without benefit of licenses from the program owners.

Other New Technology   VCRs (home videocassette recorders) proved a boon to viewers in countries where broadcast services failed to satisfy demand. They represented a relatively inexpensive shortcut to programs banned from, or just not available on, national broadcast or cable channels. Dissatisfaction arose in some cases from heavy censorship—for example, in Saudi Arabia, puritanical Muslim standards severely limit movies and broadcast television. In communist countries, political censorship creates unfilled appetites that VCRs can satisfy. On the other hand, VCRs also abound in Britain, not primarily because of frustration with available programs but in order to *time-shift* desired programs to more convenient viewing hours.

In the Third World, VCRs help make up for the often inadequate television schedules and poor program quality of national broadcast television services. Few individuals can afford to buy VCRs outright, but rentals, club purchases, and paying customers in bars and on buses solve the cost problem. A worldwide underground market in VCRs and tapes defeats government attempts to limit sales and rentals.

British television engineers pioneered the transmission of text and graphic materials to television screens. The two British radio and television authorities, the British Broadcasting Corporation (noncommercial) and the Independent Broadcasting Authority (responsible for commercial companies), began broadcasting teletext services in 1974.

The French have had notable success with *Minitel,* a videotex service started by the PTT in 1981, originally as an electronic phone book. It grew to serve thousands of program providers; subscribers by the hundreds of thousands use it for banking, shopping, getting the news, sending messages to other subscribers, and many other purposes. France also has the world's most successful subscription television service, a broadcast network called *Canal Plus.*

Economic Influence   The industrialized world, and even to some extent the communist and Third Worlds, have been swept by the winds of change promoted by revisionist U.S. economic theories linked to the traditional American dedication to private ownership and free enterprise.

It would be claiming too much to give American influence sole responsibility for this trend, which no doubt reflects a worldwide evolutionary process. But foreign governments and industrialists studied the U.S. model intensively, and U.S. government officials and American industrialists zealously promoted deregulation and private ownership abroad. Whatever effect these moves might have on foreign economies, they would open up new markets for U.S. products, services, and investment capital.

Deregulation has been felt especially in the telecommunications realm, where it loosens highly centralized PTT (Post, Telephone, and Telegraph) monopolies. Their deregulation in turn affects broadcasting and cable television not only by example, but also because PTTs often control broadcast and cable engineering. PTTs usually hold exclusive rights to install and operate broadcast transmitters, thus separating the transmission from the programming functions. They also often mo-

EXHIBIT 19–10   Major European Multinational Satellite Program Channels

Channel Name (Place, Start Date)	Satellite(s)	Potential Households (Millions) (as of early 1989, listed by potential audience size)	Comment
Sky Channel (UK, 1983)	ASTRA, EUTELSAT	14.7	The pioneer European satellite-to-cable channel; commercial
Arts (UK, 1985)	EUTELSAT	14.7	Opera, dance, drama, jazz, classical music
Super Channel (UK, 1986)	ASTRA	13.9	English programs drawn from BBC and ITV (commercial companies) networks
TV-5 (France, 1984)	EUTELSAT	10.7	Programs in French from France, Belgium, Switzerland, and Canada; culturally oriented
MTV Europe (UK, 1987)	EUTELSAT, INTELSAT[a]	6.0	Modeled on U.S. videoclip network, owned in part by the owner of MTV-U.S., Viacom.
3Sat (W. Germany, 1984)	EUTELSAT	5.7	German-language co-venture by Austria, Switzerland, and West Germany; cultural orientation
Sat1 (W. Germany, 1985)	EUTELSAT	5.2	German publishers' channel; commercial
RTL-Plus (W. Germany, 1984)	INTELSAT	4.6	Started in Luxembourg; later primarily German-owned and headquartered in Germany
RAI (Italy, 1986)	EUTELSAT	3.6	Official Italian public-service networks[b]
CNN (USA, 1985)	ASTRA, INTELSAT	1.4	A U.S. export, Ted Turner's Cable News Network, at first seen mostly in hotels, embassies, government offices, etc.
Screensport (UK, 1984)	ASTRA, INTELSAT	1.2	Owned by UK's top newsagent and bookseller, WH Smith
Lifestyle (UK, 1985)	ASTRA, INTELSAT	1.1	Women's programs drawn from British and U.S. sources

[a]MTV Europe was on two Intelsat transponders.
[b]Each Italian government network, RAI 1 and RAI 2, had its own Eutelsat transponder.

This list comes from a roster of nearly 50 European satellite services in operation at the time, selected on the basis of their ability to reach more than a million homes in more than one country. EUTELSAT is operated by a consortium of European countries, INTELSAT by a world consortium, and ASTRA by a private company headquartered in Luxembourg. ASTRA, a DBS satellite, is described in Exhibit 19– 7. Cable television accounts for most reception, but some direct-to-home reception had already begun and was due to rise rapidly with the launch of ASTRA and the expected launch of the British DBS satellite, BSB.

SOURCE: Data from "Quarterly Connections" and "Datafile Channel Guide," *Cable and Satellite Europe,* February 1989, pp. 72–76.

nopolize cable laying in preparation for cable television, a field in which marketing and promotion can play a key role because consumers need a persuasive explanation of how this strange new service will benefit them. Because of their monopoly status, PTTs generally have no expertise in marketing; progress in cable installations therefore tends to languish under their leadership.

With deregulation, traditional centralized public-service broadcasting organizations began facing increased competition from cable television's satellite-distributed program channels, VCR rentals, and newly authorized, privately owned terrestrial broadcasting services. Public-service broadcasting units that depend partly on advertising revenue face competition not only for audiences but also for advertising revenue. The excessive competition that may result could lower program standards as rival services fight for survival.

Some observers thought that this kind of downgrading had already begun in Britain, whose Conservative Prime Minister, Margaret Thatcher, matched President Ronald Reagan's commitment to deregulation and marketplace competition (Exhibit 19–3 gives details on Britain's plans for deregulation).

Deregulation moved even faster in France, previously noted for strict media control by the state. In 1986, a French conservative government took the unprecedented step of selling off France's leading public-service television broadcasting network, TF1, and authorizing competition from several other privately owned networks. Two years earlier, a French socialist government had begun licensing private stations and networks, where before all broadcasting had been government owned.

Similar, though usually less drastic, deregulatory measures have been adopted in other European countries, as well as in Australia, Canada, Japan, and New Zealand. In the Soviet Union, and to varying degrees in its client states, the policies of *glasnost* and *perestroika* represent parallel liberalizing moves in different political settings.

Program Syndication   U.S. programs, always dominant in the world syndication market, came to new prominence in the age of satellite-distributed

EXHIBIT 19–11	Program Bargains from U.S. Syndicators (selected countries)

	Cost Per Program (U.S. Dollars)	
Purchasing Country	Half Hour	Theatrical Movie
Iceland	300–400	500–1,000
Israel	550–650	1,200–4,000
Yugoslavia	500–750	2,500
Argentina	750–850	3,000–6,000
Turkey	800–900	3,000
Brazil	2,000–3,000	15,000–30,000
Japan	4,000–6,000	50,000–200,000
Italy	4,500–10,000	20,000–2,000,000
Great Britain	8,000–16,000	50,000–500,000
France	10,000–20,000	30,000–150,000
Australia	12,000–18,000	75,000–500,000

Prices for U.S. syndicated material vary widely according to potential audience and ability to pay. As an extreme example, note that a British outlet can pay up to 500 times as much for a feature film as an outlet in Iceland.

SOURCE: Based on data in "Global Programming Prices," *Variety*, 19–25 April 1989, p. 79.

cable, direct-broadcast satellite channels, and VCRs. These program-hungry new services vacuum up programs from whatever sources they can find. Enhanced demand meant new markets for American feature films and television series, intensifying fears of American cultural domination. Most countries try to limit foreign imports, but they still use U.S. syndicated offerings. Their low cost (because the original investments have already been largely recouped in the domestic U.S. market) and the almost sure-fire mass appeal of American programs make them hard to resist. Increased competition makes resistance even harder (Exhibit 19–11 shows typical prices paid for such programs).

U.S. dominance in the international syndication market led to charges of *cultural imperialism.* Third

World critics assert that the images and values depicted in typical U.S. prime-time dramas, for example, undermine pre-industrial cultures. Such shows encourage excessive consumption, materialism, and disregard for tradition. Moreover, every program purchased from abroad denies indigenous arts and crafts practitioners opportunities to develop their own talents and skills, thereby perpetuating dependence on foreigners. Nor do these complaints come only from the Third World; even highly developed nations with their own flourishing production resources put a ceiling on the amount of entertainment their national systems may import.

Free Flow, Balanced Flow Charges of cultural imperialism gained strength as a reaction not only to the dominance of American programs, but also to the impact of U.S. institutions, activities, and ideology. America's commercialism, deregulatory philosophy, telecommunications manufacturing, international news agencies, RFE/RL broadcasts, government-aid programs to developing countries, invasion of foreign economies by multinational corporations, pre-eminence in data banks and transborder data flows, and dominant ownership role in INTELSAT all add to the impression of overwhelming American influence. A leading American critic of U.S. international media behavior, Herbert I. Schiller, charged that

> messages "made in America" radiate across the globe and serve as the ganglia of national power and expansionism. The ideological images of "have-not" states are increasingly in the custody of American information media.... The facilities and hardware of international information control are being grasped by a highly centralized communications complex, resident in the United States and largely unaccountable to its own population (Schiller 1971: 147).

Even before the deregulation frenzy of the 1980s, the United States had long advocated a *free-flow* communication policy. At the outset of the United Nations in 1945, its members accepted without question the freedom of expression model of the U.S. Constitution. The phrase "free flow" occurs explicitly in the 1946 United Nations Declaration on Freedom of Information: "All states should proclaim

policies under which the free flow of information, within countries and across frontiers, will be protected."

However, both the world and its means of communication have changed drastically since the 1940s. More than 70 new nations, most of them extremely conscious of their prior histories as colonial territories of the Western powers, have since joined the United Nations.

The nonaligned nations, those claiming allegiance to neither superpower, see *neocolonialism* as threatening to drag emergent countries back into dependent status. What value does free flow have for us, they ask, when it runs almost entirely in one direction—*from* the United States and a few other industrialized countries *to* the Third World? We don't need free flow, they say, but *balanced* flow; we need news reporting that treats us fairly and in proportion to our numerical significance; we need our own access to the means of international communication.

Third World leaders complain bitterly that the West unduly influences international news because its agencies dominate worldwide news flow. Each day an estimated billion people see and hear Associated Press stories, for example. In covering the less-developed countries, the critics claim, Western editors and reporters seek mainly negative stories. They prefer colorful dispatches about riots, famines, natural disasters, and the antics of military dictators to quiet, upbeat stories about factories, dams, education, hospitals, agriculture, and the achievements of Third World intellectuals.

The West monopolizes the media, using the free-flow doctrine to stack the cards in its favor, say the critics. As a former VOA officer sympathetic to Third World complaints summarized it, one-way flow means that

> citizens of the less developed countries must depend on foreigners to a significant extent for the books they read, the television programs and films they watch, and the news stories they read. They rely on foreign foundations for scholarly research grants, depend on universities abroad for better quality higher education, and, indeed, must even learn a foreign language, most often English, in order to avail themselves of desired information (Read, 1976: 163).

UNESCO's Role   Third World opponents of the free-flow doctrine have used their preponderance of votes to advance their views in the United Nations and its specialized agencies, such as the International Telecommunication Union and the United Nations Educational, Scientific and Cultural Organization (UNESCO). The latter, which had made Third World communication a major subject of study and aid, became the main arena of debate (see Exhibit 19–12 for a description of UNESCO).

After several years' debate, UNESCO set up a commission to define a *New World Information Order* (NWIO, later also known as NWICO, New World Information and Communication Order). The NWIO called for revising the organization and control of the world's news flow, and indeed of public communications in general. Its report, issued in 1980, offered more than 80 recommendations (UNESCO, 1980). They turned out to be conciliatory, urging (for example) development of:

▪ National production capacity, to reduce dependence on foreign syndicated material.

▪ Mechanisms for dealing with consumer complaints about advertising.

▪ A nonprofit means of information and news dissemination with curbs on advertiser influence.

▪ Codes of journalistic ethics, self-generated by the profession.

Even though the report toned down the more strident NWIO demands, its implicit criticism of advertising, the profit motive, and other western values displeased many U.S. government and media leaders. Typically, the trade journal *Broadcasting* editorialized that the report

> is heavy with recommendations that go against the grain of press freedom. It advocates free access to news sources and professes to oppose censorship, but at the same time it urges news media to support—not merely report on, but support—social, cultural, economic and political goals set by governments (*Broadcasting,* 12 Jan. 1981).

The editorial concluded by recommending U.S. withdrawal from UNESCO. In 1984, the United States did just that, alleging wasteful spending as well as politicization of the organization (25 percent of its funding had come from the United States).

American defenders of UNESCO, including the nongovernment U.S. Commission for UNESCO, opposed withdrawal, pointing to the many benefits of membership and the inevitability of politics in such international agencies (USNCU, 1982). Defenders deplored cutting off American scholars from important UNESCO projects in science, education, and the international copyright field. They thought the U.S. press overplayed the free-flow controversy because of its vested interest in the press-freedom issue, and criticized its failure to publicize UNESCO's many less controversial activities.

The Media Box   In the NWIO controversy, the Third World joined hands with the communist world. Most Third World leaders approved state-controlled media devoted to educating the masses and preserving the political status quo. They feared that the Western free-flow media model would undermine their chances to become economically viable and culturally autonomous.

Undoubtedly the NWIO agenda includes legitimate grievances. Indeed, Western news agencies have become more sensitive to Third World feelings, and Western governments have increased their aid to Third World communications, since the NWIO controversy erupted.

In the matter of program exports, however, a look at the experience of Europe's small but well-financed media systems suggests that television program autonomy cannot realistically be expected in countries of limited size, especially if they lack the infrastructure and cultural resources needed to support television production. Such countries will always need to import a certain amount of programming.

A British media scholar, Jeremy Tunstall, in a book on media imperialism, rejects the position taken by Herbert Schiller, the American scholar quoted earlier. Schiller, he says,

> attributes too many of the world's ills to television. He also has an unrealistic view of returning to traditional cultures, many of which although authentic are also dead. In my view a non-American way out of the media

EXHIBIT 19–12   UNESCO's Communication Connection

Why should UNESCO, the United Nations Educational, Scientific, and Cultural Organization, become deeply embroiled in controversy over the mass communication media?

UNESCO, which started as a United Nations specialized agency in 1946, has as its primary goal enlarging freedom and human rights through cooperative efforts in educational, scientific, and cultural activities. These activities all crucially involve communication. The UNESCO constitution explicitly directs it to use mass communication to promote mutual understanding and to "recommend such international agreements as may be necessary to promote *free flow of ideas by word or image*" (italics added).

In its early years, UNESCO reflected without opposition the free-flow ideology of its members, then mostly Western, industrialized democracies (the USSR boycotted UNESCO until 1954, and most Third World countries had not yet emerged from colonialism). It therefore drew upon Western models as it went about the task of encouraging media development and the free flow of information. It conducted innumerable media seminars, conferences, workshops, and studies that led to a stream of pamphlets, books, and statistical summaries. It assisted in founding regional media training institutes, and financed the loan of experts to assist Third World countries in developing their own media training curricula.

By the 1970s, with more and more Third World countries becoming UNESCO members, the comfortable assumptions about the validity of Western media models came into question. At each successive General Conference (held every two years for the full membership), communist and Third World members raised more strident questions about the actual nature of free flow and the proper role of the media in combating racism and what they perceived as neo-colonialism. By the mid-1970s, UNESCO had become thoroughly politicized.

These developments seemed to reflect UNESCO's latter-day leadership (its first director general had been Julian Huxley, an outstanding British biologist). As UNESCO matured, it developed a top-heavy bureaucracy at its impressive Paris headquarters (photo above), led by a director general with a great deal of autonomy. In 1974 Amadou Mahtar M'Bow, a wily Senegalese whose French education developed a natural talent for bureaucratic infighting, became director general. According to his critics, he packed his staff with Third World ideologues, encouraged an anti-Western bias, and wasted UNESCO funds—the great majority of which came from Western member countries. He ran for a third term of office in 1987, but the withdrawal of the United States and other Western members had undermined his credibility. He lost out to a Spanish candidate. With the change in leadership, many hoped that the United States and other defectors would rejoin UNESCO. As of 1989 they had still not done so.

SOURCE: Photo from AP/Wide World Photos.

box is difficult to discover because it is an American, or Anglo-American, built box. The only way out is to construct a new box, and this, with the possible exception of the Chinese, no nation seems keen to do (Tunstall, 1977: 63).

Ironically, since Tunstall wrote that comment, even China has stepped tentatively into the Anglo-American "media box." Following the overthrow of the "Gang of Four" and the abandonment of its disastrous Cultural Revolution, China began cautiously importing Western television programs, advertising techniques, consumerist ideology, and even free-enterprise marketing. Similarly, the USSR's *glasnost* and *perestroika* policies have allowed it and its client states to look more favorably on American media concepts. Experience of Third World countries with their own attempts at running an international news exchange, development of their own production resources, and the beginning of their own sales of syndicated shows abroad has made the free-flow doctrine seem less threatening than it did when the NWIO movement first began.

Summary

▌ Although broadcasting has universal characteristics, each country's system develops its own unique features.

▌ Government attitudes toward their citizens have produced three basic broadcasting orientations: permissive, paternalistic, and authoritarian. The most effective systems have pluralistic features. Great Britain's serves as a model.

▌ Broadcasting laws, international and domestic, prevent interference and provide political, group, and individual access to facilities.

▌ The extent of broadcast receiver penetration varies widely throughout the world.

▌ Broadcasting revenues come mainly from government grants, advertising, and receiver license fees, or combinations of these sources. The high cost of programs is a central feature of the medium's economics.

▌ Geographical factors influence the nature and extent of broadcast systems.

▌ Program types are universal, but countries vary in the extent to which they strive for balance among types. Few countries can afford 24-hour broadcast schedules, although the amount of time on the air is increasing.

▌ Major countries exploit transborder broadcasting as a form of public diplomacy. The U.S. carries such broadcasting a step further by blanketing unfriendly countries with surrogate programs.

▌ The BBC's World Service is recognized as the most credible of the official external services.

▌ Religion and commerce also motivate transborder services.

▌ United States' influence has been especially felt in the fields of international satellite relays, cable television development, program syndication, and in deregulation.

▌ Other countries have played leading roles in developing teletext, subscription (broadcast) television, direct-broadcast satellites, high-definition television, and electronic consumer goods manufacturing.

▌ The free-flow doctrine supported by the United States has encountered opposition from the Third World and the communist world, both of which have promoted the New World Information Order as an alternative.

▌ The free-flow vs. NWIO controversy led to U.S. withdrawal from participation in UNESCO, but subsequent political events seem to have made the U.S. position on media policies more acceptable to those who opposed them.

FURTHER READING

A SELECTIVE GUIDE TO THE LITERATURE ON ELECTRONIC MEDIA

Christopher H. Sterling

This guide, organized by the chapter and section headings of the text, gives suggestions for further reading on most topics. Limited space allows for only representative selections from the rapidly growing literature of the field. Included are examples of the most significant book-length publications that should be readily available, and are of current interest as of mid-1989. Following the chapter-by-chapter sections are annotated brief lists of bibliographies and relevant periodicals. Although many of the books mentioned here are cited in the text, this guide independently assesses each title. Every work cited below and within the text is listed in full detail in the bibliography.

Chapter 1:
Key Concepts

(Because this chapter introduces concepts covered in more detail later on, citations for further reading are listed below.)

Chapter 2:
The Rise of Radio

2.1 Precedents Tebbel, *The Media in America* (1975) is a good print-oriented survey of media development; Csida and Csida, *American Entertainment* (1978) provides a text and picture scrapbook approach to popular culture as taken from the pages of *Billboard;* and Toll, *The Entertainment Machine* (1982) is a very useful general tracing of American show business, including vaudeville, in this century. A handbook of historical statistics and trends in all the media is found in Sterling and Haight, *The Mass Media* (1978). Emery and Emery, *The Press and America* (1988) is the best overall history of newspapers and magazines. Advertising's development is covered in Fox, *The Mirror Makers* (1984) and Pope, *The Making of Modern Advertising* (1983). The two standard histories of the phonograph are Gelatt, *The Fabulous Phonograph* (1977) and the more detailed and equipment-oriented Read and Welsh, *From Tin Foil to Stereo* (1976). Two useful histories of American film are Jowett, *Film* (1976) and Balio, *The American Film Industry* (1985). A highly insightful analysis of the telegraph, motion picture, and radio and their impact on the United States is in Czitrom, *Media and the American Mind from Morse to McLuhan* (1982). Stevens, *A History of News from the Drum to the Satellite* (1988) offers a broadstroke review of the changing definitions of news—and how best to disseminate it.

2.2 Wire Communication An early but still useful survey of electrical communication history is Harlow, *Old Wires and New Waves* (1936), covering telegraph, telephone, and radio. Davis, *Electrical and Electronic Technologies* (1981, 1983, 1985) provides a technical chronology by year and by topic.

Thompson, *Wiring a Continent* (1947) is the definitive history of the telegraph to the formation of the Western Union monopoly in 1866. Coates and Finn, *A Retrospective Technology Assessment: Submarine Telegraphy* (1979) is a fascinating analysis of the impact of the 1866 trans-Atlantic cable. Brooks, *Telephone* (1976) is an informal history of AT&T, while Pool, *The Social Impact of the Telephone* (1977) shows how that impact has fluctuated with time. Kleinfield, *The Biggest Company on Earth* (1981) looks at AT&T on the eve of its breakup. Development of telecommunications industry and policy is related in Brock, *The Telecommunications Industry* (1981). The actual breakup—and the reasons for it—are best related in Temin and Galambos *The End of the Bell System* (1987).

2.3 Invention of Wireless The premier study of patent conflict in radio is Maclaurin, *Invention and Innovation in the Radio Industry* (1949), which caries the story through to early television. The FTC, *Report on the Radio Industry* (1924) focuses on patents in the rise of RCA. Development of GE and Westinghouse is found in Passer, *The Electrical Manufacturers: 1875–1900* (1953) and Bright, *The Electric-Lamp Industry: Technological Change and Economic Development from 1800 to 1947* (1949).

The definitive treatment on early wireless is the two-volume work by Aitken, *Syntony and Spark: The Origins of Radio* (1976), which relates the work of Hertz and Marconi, and *The Continuous Wave* (1985), which continues the story to 1932. Leinwoll, *From Spark to Satellite* (1979) is a brief survey of radio development. Dunlap, *Radio's 100 Men of Science* (1944) provides short biographies of inventors discussed in the text. Jolly, *Marconi* (1972) is the most recent biography of the key inventor. One of the few really good company histories in this field is Baker, *A History of the Marconi Company* (1972). Tyne, *Saga of the Vacuum Tube* (1977) is a very detailed study of the subject to about 1930. Lacking modesty but providing human interest detail is de Forest, *Father of Radio* (1950). Compare it to Lessing, *Man of High Fidelity* (1956), a biography of Edwin Armstrong.

2.4 Early Wireless Service Because of the predominant role of the U.S. Navy in this period, Howeth's *History of Communications—Electronics in the United States Navy* (1963) is essential to an understanding of nonmilitary events and international and domestic regulation, as well as the cover topic. For the general role of shipboard radio, see Hancock, *Wireless at Sea* (1950), a Marconi company history of technical applications. Radio's role in the *Titanic* disaster is best told in Marcus, *The Maiden Voyage* (1969). The second part of Schubert, *The Electric Word* (1928) provides a useful account of radio on land and sea during World War I.

2.5 Radiotelephony Experiments Fessenden, *Fessenden* (1940) is a good biography of the inventor by his wife. See also deForest's autobiography and Aitken's two volumes under 2.3, above.

2.6 Government Monopoly: The Road Not Taken See Howeth under 2.4, the FTC report under 2.3, and the Archer histories discussed under 2.8, all of which detail the formation of RCA and the patent pool. For the final government ownership debate, see House, CMMF (1919).

2.7 The "First" Broadcast Station Inception of amateur radio is related in De Soto, *Two Hundred Meters and Down* (1936). The major histories of American broadcasting include Barnouw, *A History of Broadcasting in the United States* (1966–1970, three volumes), Sterling and Kittross, *Stay Tuned: A Concise History of American Broadcasting* (1990), and the anthology edited by Lichty and Topping, *American Broadcasting* (1975). All three cover both radio and television, beginning with technical developments and carrying to the 1970s, although each is arranged differently. Best analysis of "Broadcasting's Oldest Station" is the article of that name by Baudino and Kittross (1977).

2.8 Emergence of an Industry Ponderous and disorganized, but still of value for its detailed view of the "radio group" side of the debate, is the two-volume history by Archer, *History of Radio to 1926* (1938) and *Big Business and Radio*

(1939), both biased to RCA's point of view. For a counterbalancing, telephone-company view, see Banning, *Commercial Broadcasting Pioneer* (1946), for the story of WEAF to 1926. The most objective contemporary telling of these events is Schubert, under 2.4.

2.9 Network Evolution See the discussion of the early years of NBC and CBS in the Archer histories, under 2.8, and Bergreen, *Look Now, Pay Later: The Rise of Network Broadcasting* (1980). For biographies of the key leaders, see Bilby, *The General* (1986) and Paper, *Empire: William S. Paley and the Making of CBS* (1987), as well as Paley, *As It Happened* (1979). Best analysis of the early development of radio advertising is Hettinger, *A Decade of Radio Advertising* (1933), which includes data and documents to be found nowhere else. The first books on how to advertise within the new medium were Felix, *Using Radio in Sales Promotion* (1927) and Dunlap, *Advertising by Radio* (1929), both filled with fascinating detail about early network and station operations.

2.10 Government Regulation An overview of the period is provided in Rosen, *The Modern Stentors: Radio Broadcasters and the Federal Government 1920–1934* (1980). Howeth, under 2.4, covers the 1910 and 1912 acts. Best study of the 1927 act is Davis, *The Law of Radio* (1927). See also House CIFC, *Regulation of Broadcasting* (1958).

Chapter 3:
From Radio to Television

3.1 The Great Depression (1929–1937) For a year-by-year retrospective see Broadcasting Publications, *The First 50 Years of Broadcasting* (1981). See the general titles listed under 2.7 as well as MacDonald, *Don't Touch That Dial!* (1979) and Settel, *A Pictorial History of Radio* (1967), both of which stress network programming, as does Slide, *Great Radio Personalities in Historic Photographs* (1982) and Henderson, *On the Air: Pioneers of*

American Broadcasting (1988). Codel, *Radio and Its Future* (1930) is an anthology suggesting the likely direction of the industry. Hettinger and Neff, *Practical Radio Advertising* (1938) reflects organization and practices in the industry in the 1930s. For reference and specific data see U.S. Bureau of the Census, *Radio Broadcasting* (1935), the first in-depth national government survey; and *Broadcasting Yearbook,* an annual (under varying titles) beginning in 1935.

3.2 Early Radio Controversies Late in the 1930s, a spate of books criticizing radio's direction began to appear: Frost, *Is American Radio Democratic?* (1937) and Brindze, *Not to Be Told: The Truth about Radio* (1937) are examples. The most detailed narrative of radio's ASCAP and AFM troubles is found in Chapters 12–14 of Warner, *Radio and Television Rights* (1953). On the rise of LP recordings, see the works on the phonograph under 2.1. Several works detail radio's structure at its pre-television peak: Rose, *National Policy for Radio Broadcasting* (1940) is the best early analysis of structural and regulatory problems; White, *The American Radio* (1947) is a critical analysis pleading for more public service and education applications; and Landry, *This Fascinating Radio Business* (1946) describes network radio development and the peak years. The definitive official analysis of radio network structure and operations is FCC, *Report on Chain Broadcasting* (1941), which is analyzed in Robinson, *Radio Networks and the Federal Government* (1943). See as well the early chapters of Bergreen, under 2.9.

3.3 Television and FM Radio Emerge The best history of television's early technology is Abramson, *The History of Television, 1880–1941* (1987), while the rise of the industry through 1941 is related in Udelson, *The Great Television Race* (1982). For a life of Farnsworth, see Everson, *The Story of Television* (1949). For FM's development, see Lessing, under 2.3, and Siepmann, *Radio's Second Chance* (1946).

3.4 Broadcasting at War (1938–1946) A fascinating analysis of the impact of early radio news and commentary is found in Culbert, *News for Everyman* (1976), while a more popular treatment is Fang, *Those Radio Commentators!* (1977). Individual biographies abound—best of the lot is Kendrick, *Prime Time: The Life of Edward R. Murrow* (1969). For television developments, see Abramson, under 3.3.

3.5 TV Growing Pains A solid analysis of television allocation to the late 1950s is found in House CIFC, *Network Broadcasting* (1958). The famous "Sixth Report and Order" that ended the Freeze is found in its entirety in *FCC Reports,* Vol. 41. That same volume includes the 1950 and final 1953 color decisions.

3.6 Era of TV Dominance Two good general surveys of television development are Barnouw, *Tube of Plenty* (1975), and Greenfield, *Television: The First Fifty Years* (1977), a coffee-table illustrated program history with an intelligent text. Shulman and Youman, *How Sweet it Was* (1966) is the best picture treatment of the first 15 years of network TV programming; see also Marschall, *The Golden Age of Television* (1987). For network developments, see House CIFC under 3.5, Paley under 2.9, Metz, *CBS* (1975), Quinlan, *Inside ABC* (1979), and Campbell, *The Golden Years of Broadcasting* (1976) for NBC. O'Conner, *American History, American Television: Interpreting the Video Past* (1983) reviews specific programs and events in television history. For directories of network program series, see titles under 12.2.

3.7 Television's Impact on Radio Early college texts on the structure of the radio industry in this period include Sipemann, *Radio, Television, and Society* (1950), focusing on impact of the media, Wolfe, *Modern Radio Advertising* (1949), and Midgley, *The Advertising and Business Side of Radio* (1948). The changing structure of the industry under television is evident in three later texts or professional books: Head, *Broadcasting in America* (1956), the first edition of this textbook, Seehafer and Laemmar, *Successful Television and Radio Advertising* (1959), and Reinch and Ellis, *Radio Station Management* (1960). Network radio programming is described in Dunning, *Tune in Yesterday* (1976), an alphabetical guide to most program series; Stedman, *The Serials* (1977), dealing with the genre on radio, film, and television; and Wertheim, *Radio Comedy* (1979). General surveys of music and radio developments include Eberly, *Music in the Air: America's Changing Tastes in Popular Music, 1920–1980* (1982) and Passman, *The Deejays* (1971), both informal narratives dealing with personalities and musical trends on radio. Later radio music programming is detailed in Sklar, *Rocking America: How the All-Hit Radio Stations Took Over* (1984). See also citations under 13.6.

3.8 Ethical Crises of the 1950s Definitive treatment of the quiz scandals is in Anderson, *Television Fraud* (1978), which includes transcripts of several programs. Blacklisting is a topic now widely discussed—see Vaughan, *Only Victims: A Study of Show Business Blacklisting* (1972) for a good survey. Important contemporary books include the original broadcast blacklist, *Counterattack, Red Channels* (1950), Cogley's *Report on Blacklisting, Radio and Television* (1956), and Faulk's telling of his own case in a suspenseful narrative, *Fear on Trial* (1964).

Chapter 4:
Era of New Competition

Reference statistics on trends in broadcasting and cable are found in Sterling, *Electronic Media* (1984). Useful broad background on the topics in this chapter is in Compaine, *Understanding New Media* (1984), Gross, *The New Television Technologies* (1986), and Singleton, *Telecommunications in the Information Age* (1986).

4.1 Emergence of Cable TV Any book on cable prior to the early 1980s provides only a historical perspective. Land Associates, *Television and the Wired City* (1968) reflects one early view of cable's potential. Among books that outline history, the most useful is LeDuc, *Cable Television and the FCC* (1973), which carries the story through the 1972 rules. A good sense of the earliest days is in Phillips, *CATV: A History of Community Antenna Television* (1972). The beginning of the deregulatory era is covered in Rivkin, *A New Guide to Federal Cable Television Regulations* (1978). Hollowell, *Cable Handbook* (1975) shows widespread thinking on cable's role on the eve of pay cable's appearance.

4.2 Cable Becomes a Major Player

The history of satellite communications is well told in Winston, *Misunderstanding Media* (1986), Chapter 5. The important policy decisions leading to approval of domestic satellites are reviewed in Magnant, *Domestic Satellite* (1977). There is as yet no overall history of pay television or even pay cable. Ted Turner is profiled in Williams, *Lead, Follow, or Get Out of the Way* (1981). Most of the literature on interactive cable is in the form of research reports, but see Bretz, *Media for Interactive Communication* (1983) for a sense of the technical basics and applications, and *The Interactive Cable TV Handbook* (1984) for industry development. Whiteside's "Cable" (1985) is an excellent narrative of the development of cable television. Survey overviews of cable are found in Roman, *Cablemania* (1983) and Baldwin and McVoy, *Cable Communications* (1988).

4.3 Niche Options

The best study of STV is Howard and Carroll, *Subscription Television* (1980). For background on initial pay cable development, see Scott, *Bringing Premium Entertainment into the Home via Pay-Cable TV* (1977), and Technology & Economics, Inc., *The Emergence of Pay Cable Television* (1980). For the multiple channel services, see Frank, *Multichannel MDS* (1984). A substantial number of reports appeared during the original early 1980s' heyday of DBS—of them, the best are Taylor, *Direct-to-Home Satellite Broadcasting* (1980), and NTIA, *Direct Broadcasting Satellites: Policies, Prospects, and Potential Competition* (1981). See also Gross and Singletary listed at the beginning of this chapter.

4.4 Home Entertainment Center

There is a growing literature on the development of computers and microelectronics. A good survey is Augarten, *Bit by Bit: An Illustrated History of Computers* (1984). The development of video recording is detailed in Abramson, "A Short History of Television Recording" (1954 and 1973). Economic and political assessments of home video are found in Noam, *Video Media Competition: Regulation, Economics, and Technology* (1985). An excellent history of the development of the VCR is in Lardner, *Fast Forward: Hollywood, the Japanese, and the VCR Wars* (1987). A valuable annual assessment is the *Channels* magazine "Field Guide" to the new technologies, with short articles on each. EIA, *Consumer Electronics* is a free, annual booklet of statistics for and descriptions of trends among electronic media components. Of the many books available on teletext and videotex, a comprehensive assessment is in Tydeman et al., *Teletext and Videotex in the United States* (1982), while the technical basics are detailed in Martin, *Viewdata and the Information Society* (1982), and Aumonte, *New Electronic Pathways* (1987). HDTV is covered in Arlen, *Tomorrow's TVs* (1987).

4.5 Impact on Broadcasting

The network investigation report is in FCC (Network Inquiry Special Staff), *New Television Networks* (1980, two volumes), which lists a great deal of economic information on television network structure and operations today. Useful analysis of the modern radio business appears in Fornatale and Mills, *Radio in the Television Age* (1980); see also 3.7.

Chapter 5: Basic Physical Concepts

A. Background in Telecommunication Technology

A good dictionary of electronics terms may help in Chapters 5–7. One good dictionary is Graham, *The Facts on File Dictionary of Telecommunications* (1983). Forester, *High-Tech Society: The Story of the Information Technology Revolution* (1987) surveys basic technological change and options. See Langley, *Telecommunications Primer* (1983) for very clear diagrams and text; Martin, *Future Developments in Telecommunications* (1977), though dated, very clearly explains signal distribution; and Pierce, *Signals: The Telephone and Beyond* (1981), which details technical basics for the reader with no prior knowledge. Noll, *Introduction to Telecommunication Electronics* (1988A) combines clear diagrams and jargon-free information on the broader field for those with little prior training. The Editors of Time-Life Books, *Understanding Computers: Communications* (1986) offers especially creative and clear illustrations. The *McGraw-Hill Encyclopedia of Electronics and Computers* (1983) is a good technical reference.

B. Background in Broadcast Technology

Noll, *Television Technology Fundamentals and Future Prospects* (1988B) is a fine introduction to all of this material and assumes no prior knowledge. In-depth background on all topics discussed in this and the next chapter is in Crutchfield, *NAB Engineering Handbook* (1985), which *does* assume a technical background on the part of readers. Diamant, *The Broadcast Communications Dictionary* (1989) gives concise annotations of some 6,000 terms. Besen and Johnson, *Compatibility Standards, Competition and Innovation in the Broadcasting Industry* (1986) is the best study of the changing regulatory and engineering view of the role of technical standards in radio and television.

5.1–5.2 Electromagnetism and Electromagnetic Spectrum
Levin, *The Invisible Resource: Use and Regulation of the Radio Spectrum* (1971) remains the definitive study, dealing equally with technical, economic, and political aspects of the topic. A political scientist and an engineer's point of view are combined in McGillam and McLachlan, *Hermes Bound: The Policy and Technology of Telecommunications* (1978). Glatzer, *Who Owns the Rainbow? Conserving the Radio Spectrum* (1984) is a useful introduction to a complicated topic.

5.3, 5.4, 5.5, 5.7 Waves, Modulation, and Propagation
A fascinating discussion of the kinds

and impact of sound is found in Schaefer, *The Tuning of the World* (1977). Truax, *Acoustic Communication* (1985) deals with all aspects of sound. A good, illustrated discussion of sound modulation is in Beck, *Words and Waves* (1967).

5.6 Digital Signal Processing
Watkinson, *The Art of Digital Audio* (1988) offers a good discussion of the basics of digital. Noll (1988A), mentioned under note 5-A above, devotes a readable chapter to digital signals.

5.8 Antennas
See Crutchfield under the general Chapter 5 note, above.

5.9 Spectrum Conversation
See titles under 5.1. The official detailed record of frequency use and management in the U.S. in in NTIA, *Manual of Regulations and Procedures for Federal Radio Frequency Management* (regularly updated). OTA, *Radiofrequency Use and Management* (1982) relates U.S. to ITU spectrum decisions.

Chapter 6:
Traditional Broadcasting Technology

6.1 Gaining Access to the Spectrum
For information on the ITU, see titles under 19.3. General spectrum assignment information is found in the titles under 5-B.

6.2–6.4 Interference, AM, and FM
Details on current broadcast practice are in Crutchfield, under Chapter 5 note B.

6.5 Short-Wave Broadcasting
The standard, annually revised source book for all radio "hams" is the American Radio Relay League, *The Radio Amateur's Handbook*. In addition to *World Radio-TV Handbook,* under 19.6, Fallon, *Shortwave Listener's Handbook* (1976) details the hows, whens, and wheres of SW listening.

6.6–6.9 Television Much technical literature on television exists, including Noll and Crutchfield listed under the Chapter 5-B introductory note. One of the clearest introductions remains Fink and Lutyens, *The Physics of Television* (1960), which is directed at the layperson. Details and diagrams are found in Spottiswoode, *The Focal Encyclopedia of Film and Television Techniques* (1969), and Marsh, *Independent Video* (1974). Zettl, *Television Production Handbook* (1984) and Wurztel and Acker, *Television Production* (1989) are two comprehensive examples of works relating technology to practical production concerns. Hanson, *Understanding Video* (1987) discusses applications and impact of changing technologies.

6.10 Transmission and Reception An engineering text of value is Freeman, *Telecommunications Transmission Handbook* (1981). See Crutchfield, under the general Chapter 5 note.

6.11 Technical Innovations Periodical articles are important here, and one of the best sources is the *Journal of the SMPTE*. For ENG equipment, see Yoakam and Cremer, *ENG: Television News and the New Technology* (1988).

Chapter 7:
Program Storage, Distribution, and Delivery

7.1 Roles of Storage and Distribution A dated but interesting approach to topics considered in this chapter is found in Bretz, *A Taxonomy of Communication Media* (1970), which compares interrelationships between and applications of transmission and recorded technologies.

7.2–7.3 Sound and Picture Recording Alten, *Audio in Media* (1986) is a detailed how-to guide to this topic. A well-illustrated guide is Overman, *Understanding Sound, Video & Film Recording* (1978). Oringel, *Audio Control Handbook* (1989) relates technology of recording to practical production.

7.4 Terrestrial Relays See Crutchfield, under the Chapter 5-B note, and Freeman, under 6.10. For background on applications for fiber optic cable, see Chaffee, *The Rewiring of America* (1988).

7.5 Satellite Relays Good diagrams, photos, and clear text highlight Prentiss, *Satellite Communications* (1987), while Binkowski, *Satellite Information Systems* (1988) provides a lucid narrative description. Elbert, *Introduction to Satellite Communication* (1987) is somewhat more technical in approach. Alper and Pelton, *The Intelsat Global Satellite System* (1984) contains a wealth of understandable technical information. The annual reports of NASA, Comsat, and Intelsat provide good current data.

7.6 Over-the-Air Hybrids Arnall, *Instructional Television Fixed Service* (1984) reviews ITFS potential and problems. Biel, *Low Power Television: Development and Current Status of the LPTV Industry* (1985) discusses translators and low power.

7.7 Cable Television See Baldwin and McVoy, *Cable Communication* (1988); Grant, *Cable Television* (1983); and Harrell, *The Cable Television Technical Handbook* (1985).

Chapter 8:
Organization: Operations and Finance

A useful foundation for media structure in the U.S. is found in Turow, *Media Industries: The Production of News and Entertainment* (1984). Dated, but providing context and comparisons across media, is Owen, *Economics and Freedom of Expression* (1975). Vogel, *Entertainment Industry Economics* (1986) contrasts broadcasting with other media.

8.1 The Commercial Broadcast Station Three books broadly introduce management of electronic media and offer much on individual station structure and operation: Sherman, *Telecommunications Management* (1987); Marcus, *Broad-*

cast and Cable Management (1986); and McCavitt and Pringle, *Electronic Media Management* (1986). More recent and specific are Keith and Krause, *The Radio Station* (1989); O'Donnell, et al, *Radio Station Operations* (1989); and Hilliard, *Television Station Operations and Management* (1989); all useful and concise handbooks of current thinking about station management. Abel, et al., *RadiOutlook: Forces Shaping the Radio Industry* (1988) sheds light on the many different issues and factors comprising the world of commercial radio. Day-to-day reality is detailed in Hunn, *Starting and Operating Your Own FM Radio Station* (1988).

8.2 Commercial Broadcast Networks

The definitive analysis is the FCC (Network Inquiry Special Staff), *New Television Networks* (1980). The economic and political lessons of that two-year study are clearly brought out in Besen et al., *Misregulating Television: Network Dominance and the FCC* (1984), while Botein and Rice, *Network Television and the Public Interest* (1981) adds some research analyses to the debate over the role of networks. See also the titles noted under Chapter 12.

8.3 Cable Television

The standard annual reference directories of systems, networks, and owners are *Broadcasting/Cable Yearbook,* and *Television Factbook,* both of which include a large cable section, and some statistics. Baldwin and McVoy, noted under 4.2, is the best overall introduction to cable. Background data is in Sterling, listed under the general Chapter 4 note.

8.4 Capital Investment

The only comprehensive information on this topic can be found in the NAB's *Radio Financial Report* and *Television Financial Report,* issued annually. These reports detail expenses and investment for differently sized stations in differently sized markets, based on annual national sample surveys. Vogel, noted at the beginning of this chapter, sheds considerable light on investment issues. For titles on satellite, see 4.5 and 4.7.

8.5 Ownership Turnover

Each year in a late January issue, *Broadcasting* reviews major sales and transfers of broadcast licenses in the previous year. A clear and detailed guide to the process is Krasnow, et al., *Buying or Building a Broadcast Station* (1988). Industry structure and FCC rules, many dropped since then, are discussed in Besen and Johnson, *An Assessment of the Federal Communication Commission's Group Ownership Rules* (1984) and Sterling, in Compaine, *Who Owns the Media?* (1982). A strong attack on what is described as overly concentrated media ownership is in Bagdikian, *The Media Monopoly* (1987). Mayer, *The Knowledge Industry Publications 200* (1987) gives a detailed breakout of holdings of the major media firms in the early 1980s, along with some sense of corporate structure and operation.

8.6 Personnel

Useful descriptive guides to career options are found in Bishop, *Making it in Video: An Insider's Guide to Careers in the Fastest Growing Industry of the Decade* (1988); Reed and Reed, *Career Opportunities in Television, Cable and Video* (1986); and Blanksteen and Odeni, *TV: Careers Behind the Screen* (1987). See also National Textbook Co., *Opportunities in Broadcasting, Opportunities in Cable Television, Opportunities in Telecommunication* (1983–84). Many titles deal with jobs in the electronic media as a part of the larger media scene—Mogel, *Making it in the Media Professions* (1988) and Noble, *The Harvard Guide to Careers in Mass Media* (1987) are two of the best. The role of minority employment, as well as content in programming, are detailed in the U.S. Civil Rights Commission, *Window Dressing on the Set* (1977, 1979). The only book on broadcasting unions is Koenig, *Broadcasting and Bargaining* (1970).

Chapter 9:
Revenues: Sources and Profits

9.1–9.2 Advertising and Announcements

Readers may find a general advertising text a useful supplement to this chapter. Barnouw,

The Sponsor (1978) is a critical essay on the development of the advertiser's role in radio and television. Warner, *Broadcast and Cable Selling* (1986) offers a comprehensive review of the process. Heighton and Cunningham, *Advertising in the Broadcast and Cable Media* (1984) and Ziegler and Howard, *Broadcast Advertising* (1984) cover all aspects of the topic. Murphy, *Handbook of Radio Advertising* (1980) is one useful guide to the topic. Poltrack, *Television Marketing: Network, Local, and Cable* (1983) is a valuable guide to the buying and selling of video time. The content of television advertising is assessed in Geis, *The Language of Television Advertising* (1982) and, less formally, in Hall, *Mighty Minutes: An Illustrated History of Television's Best Commercials* (1984). Busch and Landeck, *The Making of a Television Commercial* (1981) describes the complex production process in detail.

9.3 Cable Advertising See Poltrack under 9.1; Jones et al., *Cable Advertising* (1986); and Kaatz, *Cable Advertiser's Handbook* (1985) for general discussions of cable's advantages and disadvantages. Batra and Glazer, *Cable TV Advertising* (1989) offers a scholarly analysis of how cable fits into the larger advertising picture and traces the development of home shopping. See also Roman, and Baldwin and McVoy, under 4.2.

9.4–9.6 Advertising Rates, Sales and Standards Warner, noted under 9.1, is most useful here. Duncan, *American Radio* (annual) provides comparative rate information for most radio markets. Regular issues of *Standard Rate and Data Service* reprint some radio, television, and cable rate cards for many markets—larger stations began in the 1980s to hold back on printing rate cards in SRDS. Grossman, *The Marketer's Guide to Media Vehicles, Methods, and Options* (1987) does a good job of placing electronic media in a broader advertising context. Children's television advertising is most comprehensively reviewed in the Federal Trade Commission, *Staff Report on Television Advertising to Children* (1978) which, even though nothing has come of it, makes a strong case for "government as parent." More recent, and favorable

to advertiser support, is Schneider, *Children's Television: The Art, the Business, and How It Works* (1987).

9.7 Alternative Revenue Sources Webb, *The Economics of Cable Television* (1984) reviews issues and structures of both basic and pay cable. For further reading on cable subscriber fees and home shopping networks, check the periodicals listed on pages 546–547.

9.8–9.9 Profit and Loss and Bottom-Line Broadcasting See the titles noted under 9.1, above.

Chapter 10:
The Noncommercial Alternative

Literature on noncommercial radio and television is surprisingly sparse, considering the number of stations on the air—and the heat of the controversies surrounding public broadcasting.

10.1 From "Educational Radio" to "Public Broadcasting" Gibson, *Public Broadcasting: The Role of the Federal Government, 1912–1976* (1977) shows the growing federal financial support function, while Blakely, *To Serve the Public Interest* (1979) provides an overall historical picture. CCET, *Public Television* (1967) contains the landmark Carnegie report. The shape of public broadcasting after a decade of the new structure is outlined in Wood and Wylie, *Educational Telecommunications* (1977) and Carter and Nyhan, *The Future of Public Broadcasting* (1976).

10.2–10.3 National Organizations and Stations The debate among the national public broadcasting organizations is discussed in Avery and Pepper, *The Politics of Interconnection* (1979) and Witherspoon and Kovitz, *The History of Public Television* (1987). A good assessment of the early political battles is found in Stone, *Nixon and the Politics of Public Television* (1987). The second Carnegie report—very useful for statistics and background information on the first decade of the CPB-

PBS-NPR organization—is CCFPB, *A Public Trust* (1979). The many statistical reports issued by the Corporation for Public Broadcasting (1111 16th St. N.W., Washington, D.C. 20036), especially *Status Report on Public Broadcasting* (title varies, regularly revised), and the CPB *Annual Report,* which details spending and the overall shape of public radio and television, are invaluable. The most detailed discussion of public radio is found in NAPTS, *Public Television and Radio and State Governments* (1984), two volumes). The annual CPB, *Public Broadcasting Directory* details stations and support organizations.

10.4 Economics of Public Broadcasting
Current economic information will be found in the most recent hearings before the House Committee on Energy and Commerce, on the budget request of the Corporation for Public Broadcasting, and in the CPB *Annual Report.* The TCAF reports on alternative financing for public telecommunications (1982 and 1983) provide invaluable sources of data on the advertising experiment and other funding ideas.

10.5 Program Sources
The instructional role of educational media is assessed in Johnson, *Electronic Learning From Audiotape to Videodisc* (1987) and Hudspeth and Brey, *Instructional Telecommunications* (1986).

10.6 Rethinking the Role of Noncommercial Broadcasting
Two early and thought-provoking traditional analyses of what public television should be are found in Blakely, *The People's Instrument: A Philosophy of Programming for Public Television* (1971) and Macy, *To Irrigate a Wasteland* (1974).

Chapter 11:
Programming Basics

There are a number of books useful for Chapters 11, 12, and 13. Among them, Eastman et al., *Broadcast/Cable Programming* (1988) is the most inclusive assessment dealing with strategies for all types of stations and systems. Brown, *Les Brown's Encyclopedia of Television* (1982) is a good reference with entries on all aspects of programming. An overview of commercial television viewing is found in Gitlin, *Watching Television* (1986). For radio, see Keith, *Radio Programming* (1987).

11.1 Economic Constraints
The best discussion of network program economics is found in the FCC Network Inquiry report, under 4.5. Included are documents and analyses of network-affiliate contracts, compensation schemes, program procurement, etc. While dated, much of the overall view in Owen, et al., *Television Economics* (1974) remains valid.

11.2–11.3 Types and Sources of Programs
See notes for Chapters 12 and 13. See also Eastman et al., above.

11.4 News and Sports Sources
Books on network news are noted under 12.5, while sports are covered under 12.3.

11.5 Scheduling Practices
Several books describe the seasonal programming process in television, among them Christensen and Stauth, *The Sweeps: Behind the Scenes in Network TV* (1984); Gitlin, *Inside Prime Time* (1984); Levinson and Link, *Stay Tuned* (1981); and Cantor, *Prime-Time Television* (1980). All of them deal with the institutions and major players in program decision-making. Bedell's *Up the Tube: Prime Time Television and the Silverman Years* (1981) reviews trends through the career of the only man to hold high positions in all three networks. For more on the strategies discussed here, see Eastman et al., under the general note for this chapter.

11.6 Program Promotion
Promotion in broadcasting is assessed and described in Eastman and Klein, *Strategies in Broadcast and Cable Promotion* (1982), and Bergendorff et al., *Broadcast Advertising and Promotion* (1983).

Chapter 12:
Network Television and Radio Programs

Books on the programming process are listed under Chapter 11. Here we include titles on specific program types or formats—just a glimpse of a substantial literature on programs.

12.1 Prime-Time Entertainment As one might expect, there is a massive literature on this topic, with at least one book on any popular series. An overview of the prime-time programming process is Blum and Lindheim, *Primetime Network Television Programming* (1987). For series program reference, see Brooks and Marsh, *The Complete Directory to Prime Time Network TV Shows* (1988); for details of specific episodes, see the five-volume Gianakos, *Television Drama Series Programming* (1978–87) and Eisner and Krinsky, *Television Comedy Series: An Episode Guide to 153 TV Sitcoms in Syndication* (1984). Case studies of comedy programs are found in Adler, *All in the Family* (1979), which includes three scripts from the pioneering series of social satire, and Feuer et al., *MTM 'Quality Television'* (1984), which dissects a number of successful programs from one production house. A content analysis of drama program portrayals is found in Greenberg, *Life on Television* (1980). The continuing appeal of doctor shows is assessed in Turow, *Playing Doctor: Television, Storytelling and Medical Power* (1989). For a directory to all the made-for-TV movies and miniseries see Marill, *Movies Made for Television* (1984). The potential for cultural development on cable is reviewed in detail in Beck, *Cultivating the Wasteland* (1983).

12.2 Non-Prime-Time Entertainment Aside from the huge fan literature on soap operas, several scholarly studies shed analytical light on this enduring format. Stedman, under 3.4, is a history of serials in films and broadcasting. Matelski, *The Soap Opera Evolution* (1988) is a scholarly study of the plots, characters, and audiences of serials. Cantor and Pingree, *The Soap Opera* (1983) discusses the development, content, audience, and impact of such programs; Cassata and Skill, *Life on Daytime Television: Tuning-In American Serial Drama* (1983) offers a collection of content analyses; Allen, *Speaking of Soap Operas* (1985) reviews the production and consumption of the genre; and Intintolli, *Taking Soaps Seriously: The World of Guiding Light* (1984) is a detailed examination of a long running program. Fabe, *TV Game Shows* (1979) is dated but remains the best survey of that format. The two longest running talk shows are informally detailed in Metz, *The Today Show* (1977).

12.3 Network Sports Programs The first book on television sports programming was Johnson, *Super Spectator and the Electronic Lilliputians* (1971), based on a series of articles in *Sports Illustrated*. The early days of the most successful network sports coverage is related in Sugar, *"The Thrill of Victory:" The Inside Story of ABC Sports* (1978). Rader, *In Its Own Image: How Television Has Transformed Sports* (1984) is a critical commentary on what has been lost to sports because of TV coverage. Powers, *Supertube: The Rise of Television Sports* (1984) is a history of three decades' development of sports coverage. Klatell and Marcus, *Sports for Sale: Television, Money and the Fans* (1988) offers an insightful discussion of the interrelationships between teams and media. Chandler, *Television and National Sport* (1988) compares sports, audiences, and television coverage in Great Britain and the U.S.

12.4 Network Children's Programs A massive study of how much programming was provided for young children is FCC, *Television Programming for Children* (1979), which found little to cheer about. The historical research for that study appears in expanded form in Turow, *Entertainment, Education and the Hard Sell: Three Decades of Network Children's Television* (1981). A more popular treatment is found in Fischer, *Kid's TV: The First 25 Years* (1983), while the definitive directory is Woolery's two-volume *Children's Television: The*

First Thirty-Five Years, 1946–1981 (1983–84). Of the many guides for parents, Charren and Sandler, *Changing Channels: Living (Sensibly) with Television* (1983) is by far the best. For studies criticizing television fare for children, see Winn, *The Plug-in Drug* (1985) and Palmer, *Television and America's Children: A Crisis of Neglect* (1988).

12.5 News and Public Affairs Here again, the literature is huge and growing—some of it descriptive, some scholarly, and much highly critical. Mayer, *Making News* (1987) overviews the people, the business, and the impact of news. Matusow, *The Evening Stars* (1983) is a very readable narrative on development of the network news anchor. Gates, *Air Time: The Inside Story of CBS News* (1978) relates the story of both radio and television reporting. A content analysis of international news content in the 1972–81 period appears in Larson, *Television's Window on the World* (1984). Development of television documentary is related in Bluem, *Documentary in American Television* (1965), and, for the 1965–75 period, Hammond, *The Image Decade* (1981). Madsen, *60 Minutes: The Power and Politics of America's Most Popular TV News Show* (1984) traces the CBS program's development and weekly operations. Sanders and Rock, *Waiting for Prime Time: The Women of Television News* (1988) is an informal narrative of the increasing role of women in local and national television journalism. Donahue, *The Battle to Control Broadcast News* (1989) focuses on questions of freedom within and access to network broadcasts. More on the impact of electronic journalism is found under 15.3.

12.6 Commercial Radio Networks See titles under 3.7 and 4.5.

Chapter 13:
Syndicated and Local Programs

13.1–13.3 Radio and Television Syndication Erickson, *Syndicated Television* (1989) offers a four-decade narrative history of most series. See also Eastman et al. under general Chapter 11 notes.

13.4 Syndicated Religion Hadden and Swan, *Prime Time Preachers* (1981) suggests that conservative programs have nowhere near the audience they claim. Horsfield, *Religious Television: The American Experience* (1984) is a valuable study of the genre, with close analysis of the dramatic changes in religious programming after the late 1960s. Frankl, *Televangelism: the Marketing of Popular Religion* (1986) and Hadden and Shupe, *Televangelism: Power & Politics on God's Frontier* (1988) detail the crises that several of the TV figures went through in the 1980s. An excellent discussion of why people watch these programs is found in Hoover, *Mass Media Religion* (1988).

13.5 Local Television Programs A scathing attack on local station news programs is launched in Powers, *The Newscasters* (1977). Shaffer and Wheelwright, *Creating Original Programming for Cable TV* (1983) includes access programming.

13.6 Local Radio Programs Every two years a detailed content analysis of the major public radio stations appears as CPB, *Public Radio Programming Content.* Commercial radio music programs are assessed in Eberly and Sklar, under 3.7. Levin, *Talk Radio and the American Dream* (1987) explores the appeal of that format.

13.7 Program Critique Newcomb's *Television: The Critical View* (1987) is a respected collection of articles assessing television programs. Smith, *Beyond the Wasteland: The Criticism of Broadcasting* (1980) discusses the difficulty a critic faces in dealing with a transitory medium. Two works by Himmelstein, *On the Small Screen: New Approaches in Television and Video Criticism* (1981) and *Television Myth and the American Mind* (1985), review programming—the first by studies of selected critics, and the second in a unified essay. Orlik, *Critiquing Radio and Television Content* (1988) reviews the many ways the process can work. Adler's *Understanding Television as a Social and Cultural Force* (1981) offers original essays on programs and programming. Mander's *Four Arguments* *for the Elimination of Television* (1978) is, as the title suggests, highly critical.

Chapter 14:
Audience Ratings and
Applied Research

14.1 The Ratings Business The single most important book to supplement this chapter is the definitive work by a long-time practitioner: Beville, *Audience Ratings: Radio, Television, Cable* (1988). He reviews the major firms and their development, methods used, problem areas, and likely directions throughout the early application of people meters. For terminology, see NAB, *Broadcast Research Definitions* (1988).

14.2–14.3 Set-Use Data and Sampling Arbitron and Nielsen will, on request, provide detailed booklets on their radio and television data gathering and reporting methods.

14.4   Ratings Concepts A practical station workbook on how to use ratings is found in Fletcher, *Squeezing Profits Out of Ratings: A Manual for Radio Managers, Sales Managers and Programmers* (1985).

14.5   Audiences Changes in television audience makeup and preferences can be traced through Steiner, *The People Look at Television* (1963); Bower, *Television and the Public* (1973); and Bower, *The Changing Television Audience in America* (1985); which report, respectively, on parallel national surveys taken in 1960, 1970, and 1980. Barwise and Ehrenberg, *Television and Its Audience* (1988) does a good job in relatively few pages summing up audience research results in the U.S. and Great Britain. For radio and other audience data, see the section 6 Tables in Sterling, *Electronic Media* (1984). The definitive assessment of research on the television audience is Comstock, *Television and Human Behavior* (1978). Frank and Greenberg's two volumes of research, based on a national survey, are *The*

Public's Use of Television (1980), covering commercial stations and networks, and *Audiences for Public Television* (1982). Meyrowitz, *No Sense of Place: The Impact of Electronic Media on Social Behavior* (1985) is a readable survey covering all aspects of TV's role.

14.6   Use and Abuse of Ratings See Beville, especially Chapters 7, 8, and 9, under 14.1.

14.7   Research on Newer Media See Beville, Chapters 6 and 11, under 14.1, and Rice and associates, *The New Media: Communication, Research and Technology* (1984).

14.8   Other Applied Research Four recent works add greatly to our knowledge of research methods in mass communication. Dominick and Fletcher, *Broadcasting Research Methods* (1985) collects 20 original articles on all aspects of electronic media research, both scholarly and business-oriented. Broader instruction in methods across all media is found in Wymmer and Dominick, *Mass Media Research: An Introduction* (1987); Hsia, *Mass Communications Research Methods* (1988); and Tan, *Mass Communication Theories and Research* (1986). Fletcher, *Handbook of Radio and TV Broadcasting: Research Procedures in Audience, Program and Revenues* (1981) is a guide for station managers. Anderson, *Communication Research Issues and Methods* (1987) offers insight as to why research is done the way it is.

Chapter 15:
Social Effects

15.1   Effects Research Two books take a historical look at audience research developments: Lerner and Nelson, *Communication Research—A Half Century Appraisal* (1977) and Lowery and DeFleur, *Milestones in Mass Communication Research* (1988). A dated but still useful overview is Klapper, *The Effects of Mass Communication* (1960), updated to some degree by the reviews that appear every three or four years in *Annual Review of*

Psychology. An introductory survey to all this is found in Davis and Baran's *Mass Communication and Everyday Life: A Perspective on Theory and Effects* (1981). About every other year, another volume in the series edited by Dervin and Voigt, *Progress in Communication Sciences* (1979–89), provides insightful essays on various aspects of media impact. A good introduction to communication theory is DeFleur and Ball-Rokeach, *Theories of Mass Communication* (1988), while Blake and Haroldson, *A Taxonomy of Concepts in Communication* (1975) introduces the major terms and ideas. For current views, see McQuail, *Mass Communication Theory* (1983) and the graphic approach in McQuail and Windahl, *Communication Models for the Study of Mass Communications* (1981). For research methods, see 14.8.

15.2 Advertising Effects Any good survey of advertising can provide a current overview of research results. A critical survey is Shudson's *Advertising, The Uneasy Persuasion: Its Dubious Impact on American Society* (1984). For children's advertising impact, see Adler, *The Effects of Television Advertising on Children* (1980).

15.3 News Impact More and more works analyze all aspects of television news impact (see also titles under 12.5). The classic pseudo-event study is Boorstin, *The Image* (1964), while a useful agenda-setting study is McCombs and Shaw, *The Emergence of American Political Issues* (1977). Lesher's *Media Unbound: The Impact of Television Journalism on the Public* (1982) is based on the author's experience and interviews with news officials. Abramson et al., *The Electronic Commonwealth* (1988) reviews scholarly findings on the impact of new media technologies, especially on the political process.

15.4 Political Effects The best survey of work to 1975 is Kraus and Davis, *The Effects of Mass Communication on Political Behavior* (1976). Greenberg and Parker, *The Kennedy Assassination and the American Public* (1965) is a classic analysis of media in a national crisis. More recent crises are

reviewed in Nimmo and Combs, *Nightly Horrors: Crisis Coverage in Television Network News* (1985). Lang and Lang, *Politics and Television Re-Viewed* (1984) collects insightful research reports from MacArthur's 1951 return through Watergate events of the 1970s. The same authors' analysis of television impact during Watergate is *The Battle for Public Opinion: The President, the Press and the Polls During Watergate* (1983); for a detailed content analysis comparing print and television news coverage, see Lashner, *The Chilling Effect in TV News* (1984). Jamieson, *Packaging the Presidency: A History and Criticism of Presidential Campaign Advertising* (1984), can be combined with Tebbel and Watts, *The Press and the Presidency* (1985), which assesses noncampaign relationships for a full historical account. Diamond and Bates, *The Spot: The Rise of Political Advertising on Television* (1988) focuses on TV's unique role. An example of the large amount of literature devoted to media in specific campaigns is Robinson and Sheehan, *Over the Wire and on TV: CBS and UPI in Campaign '80* (1983). Swerdlow, *Beyond Debate: A Paper on Televised Presidential Debates* (1984) and Kraus, *Televised Presidential Debates and Public Policy* (1988) summarize what has been learned and how the process might be changed. The most comprehensive study of the struggle for TV coverage of Congress is Garay, *Congressional Television: A Legislative History* (1984).

15.5 Television and War Many works deal with the American experience in Vietnam, but two stand out for their study of media impact: Braestrup's *Big Story: How the American Press and Television Reported and Interpreted the Crisis of Tet 1968 in Vietnam and Washington* (1977) dissects the turning point in the war and American support of it; MacDonald's *Television and the Red Menace: The Video Road to Vietnam* (1985) assesses TV news coverage in the years before that war. Hallin, *The "Uncensored War": The Media and Vietnam* (1986), discusses wartime coverage before and after 1965 when American intervention dramatically increased, providing an assessment of media coverage on home audiences.

15.6 The Role of Entertainment Two interesting studies of minorities and the media are MacDonald, *Blacks and White TV: Afro-Americans in Television since 1948* (1983) and Greenberg, *Mexican-Americans and the Mass Media* (1983). Marc, *Demographic Vistas: Television in American Culture* (1984) reviews the general impact of television entertainment programming. Winn, *The Plug-In Drug: Television, Children and the Family* (1985) is sometimes overwrought, but suggests parental control of "kidvid" is crucial. Scholarly research on children's use of television is reviewed by Liebert et al., *The Early Window: Effects of Television on Children and Youth* (1988).

15.7 Impact of Violence The definitive study of how scholarly research can impact upon policy is Rowland, *The Politics of TV Violence: Policy Uses of Communication Research* (1983), which focuses on the first Surgeon General's committee. That committee's work is found in Surgeon General, *Television and Growing Up* (1972). The second such committee reported its work in National Institute of Mental Health, *Television and Behavior: Ten Years of Scientific Progress and Implications for the Eighties* (1982).

Chapter 16:
Regulation: Laws and Agencies

Note A: General Background Several books provide background for Chapters 16–18. For the history of early broadcast regulation, see titles under 2.10. In addition, two two-volume works are excellent for tracing broadcast policy development: Socolow, *The Law of Radio Broadcasting* (1939) and Warner, (1) *Radio and Television Law* (1948) and (2) *Radio and Television Rights* (1953). A chronological collection of the most important legal cases and other documents is in Kahn, *Documents of American Broadcasting* (1984). Ferrall, *Yearbook of Broadcasting Articles* (1980) shows in a collection of law journal articles the increasing complexity of broadcast regulation from 1959 to 1978. A more recent casebook on broadcast and cable regulation that includes extensive excerpts from FCC and court decisions as well as congressional actions is Carter et al., *The First Amendment and the Fifth Estate* (1989). An excellent primer to all the subjects discussed below is Krasnow, et al., *The Politics of Broadcast Regulation* (1982). For background on general media law, see the following, all regularly updated: Gillmor and Barron, *Mass Communication Law: Cases and Comment* (1984); Zuckman et al., *Mass Communication Law in a Nutshell* (1988), an inexpensive paperback; Carter, et al., *The First Amendment and the Fourth Estate* (1988); and Middleton and Chamberlin, *The Law of Public Communication* (1988). For a more journalistic than legal orientation of trends, see Pember, *Mass Media Law* (1984).

Note B: Staying Current While the documentation of administrative agencies, the courts, and Congress can seem forbidding to the uninitiated, here are some tips on staying current: A dated but still useful introduction is Le Duc, "Broadcast Legal Documentation" (1973). The definitive but unofficial source for keeping up with electronic media regulation is Pike and Fischer, *Radio Regulation,* a loose-leaf reporter service, updated weekly and indexed carefully. Instructions on its use appear in the "Current Service" volume. Decisions of the U.S. Court of Appeals for any circuit appear officially in the *Federal Reporter,* while Supreme Court decisions are reported officially in *United States Reports. Media Law Reporter* is another loose-leaf commercial service that rapidly reports legal developments. PLI, *Communications Law* provides an annual compendium of cases, decisions, and analyses of media issues over the previous year. The *NAB Legal Guide to Broadcast Law and Regulation* (1988) is a single-volume desk reference for station managers. The NAB *Broadcasting and Government,* updated twice yearly, and *Broadcasting* magazine, "Where Things Stand," which appears at the beginning of each issue, briefly summarize the current status of major issues, albeit with some industry bias.

16.1 Federal Jurisdiction Good treatments of First Amendment issues are found in Barron and Dienes, *Handbook of Free Speech and Free Press* (1979) and Tedford, *Freedom of Speech in the United States* (1985). Chamberlin, *The First Amendment Reconsidered: New Perspectives on the Meaning of Freedom of Speech and Press* (1982) discusses the impact of changing technology. In-depth analysis of early thinking about jurisdiction shows up in Chafee, *Government and Mass Communications* (1947).

16.2 Communications Act The official chronological compilation of all U.S. laws (legislation) on telecommunications from the 1910 Act to date is listed in U.S. Congress, House of Representatives, *Radio Laws of the United States,* which is revised by adding new material every few years. The compilation includes the 1962 Communications Satellite Act that created Comsat, the 1967 Public Broadcasting Act (part of Title III of the 1934 Act), and the 1984 Cable Act (a new Title VI of the 1934 Act). Of considerable historic interest is the book written by the senator most responsible for the 1934 act: Dill, *Radio Law* (1938).

16.3 Communications Act Revision The multivolume hearing transcripts on the various rewrite attempts, though voluminous, are useful for a broad view of issues on telecommunications and broadcasting. The process began with publication of House CIFC, *Options Papers* (1977), a very broad survey of possible courses of action for Congress and the FCC. This report led to seemingly endless hearings (through 1981) of value for their detailed record of changing industry and interest group positions. For the major hearings, see House CIFC, *The Communications Act of 1978: Hearings on H.R. 13015* (1979): House CIFC, *The Communications Act of 1979: Hearings on H.R. 3333* (1980), for the first and most comprehensive rewrite attempts; and Senate CCST, *Amendments to the Communications Act of 1934* (1980), which reflected the first serious interest in revision by that side of Congress.

16.4 FCC Basics A fascinating account of the development of the regulatory agency idea, told

through the lives of four key individuals, is in McGraw's *Prophets of Regulation* (1984). Kittross, *Administration of American Telecommunications Policy* (1980) collects important documents on development and criticism of the FCC. Obviously a key document for study is the FCC *Annual Report.* FCC rules and regulations are annually revised in the CRF (Code of Federal Regulations), *Title 47: Telecommunications.* Of the five volumes, the first deals with FCC organization and procedures, the second and third with common carrier regulation, the fourth with broadcasting, and the fifth with cable and emergency procedures. Proposed and final rules of the FCC appear in the daily issues of the FR (*Federal Register*), and are gathered chronologically in FCCR (*Federal Communications Commission Reports*, 1st and 2nd series through 1986, continued by *Federal Communications Commission Record* from that time forward). They accumulate at the rate of four to six fat volumes each year. See also Pike and Fisher under Note B. The appointment of FCC and FTC commissioners over a 25-year period is the subject of a fascinating study: Graham and Kramer, *Appointments to the Regulatory Agencies* (1976).

16.5 Enforcement See works on the FCC under 16.4. Hixson, *Mass Media and the Constitution: An Encyclopedia of Supreme Court Decisions* (1989) and DeVol, *Mass Media and the Supreme Court* (1982) both collect major decisions and commentary.

16.6 Copyright Law This is a complicated and changing field, so any books would contain general background rather than current specifics. Johnston, *Copyright Handbook* (1982) provides an excellent survey of the act and its provisions, as well as some of the early case laws. Strong, *The Copyright Book: A Practical Guide* (1982) is just that. The Copyright Office will provide useful information booklets and sample forms on request (Copyright Office, Library of Congress, Washington, D.C. 20559).

16.7 Other Laws For international treaties, see 19.3. Press law is covered in the general texts discussed under note 16-A. Two practical approaches to current EEO rules are Aird, *A Broadcaster's Guide to Designing and Implementing an Effective EEO Program* (1980) and the NAB legal guide, under note 16-A.

16.8 Informal Controls Cole and Oettinger, *Reluctant Regulators: The FCC and the Broadcast Audience* (1978) is an overview, though now very dated, of the policy-making process and the general Washington environment for policy. Specific case studies of the process are in Krasnow et al., *The Politics of Broadcast Regulation* (1982). Assessments of the most active years of citizen group action are offered in Grundfest, *Citizen Participation in Broadcast Licensing Before the FCC* (1976) and Guimary, *Citizen's Groups and Broadcasting* (1975). A good study of the limitations of self-regulation is Brogan, *Spiked: The Short Life and Death of the National News Council* (1985). A case study of government and industry self-regulation interaction is related in Cowan, *See No Evil* (1979) on the "family viewing" case. Of the increasing number of books on media ethics and self-regulation, the most useful are Fink, *Media Ethics in the Newsroom and Beyond* (1988); Christians et al., *Media Ethics: Cases and Moral Reasoning* (1987); and Rivers et al., *Responsibility in Mass Communication* (1980).

Chapter 17:
Station and System Licensing

17.1–17.3 Licensing, Operating, and Renewal The titles listed in note 16-A include material on the licensing process—the NAB legal guide being most specific. The *CITC Cable Books* (1982) offer a detailed guide to local cable television policy, especially franchising. Rice, *Cable TV Renewals and Refranchising* (1983) details that sometimes complicated process.

17.4 Cable Franchising PLI, *The New Era in CATV: The Cable Franchise Policy and Communications Act of 1984* (1985) combines the text of the Act, legal commentary on it, and the legislative

report urging its passage into a kind of handbook. The definitive legal work on cable is the three-volume Ferris et al., *Cable Television Law* (1984), which is updated twice a year.

17.5 Ownership Diversification See titles under 8.5. On the role of networks, see titles under 8.2.

17.6 Deregulation As yet, no book-length studies of electronic media deregulation have appeared. See the FCC annual report for its own report of yearly deregulatory actions. A number of works on telecommunications deregulation have appeared—one with specific comment on media is Derthick and Quirk, *The Politics of Deregulation* (1985). Tunstall, *Communications Deregulation* (1986) offers an insightful analysis of early deregulatory trends.

Chapter 18:
Constitutional Issues

18.1 First Amendment Basics See titles under 16.1 and 17.6.

18.2 Unprotected Speech See titles under note 16-A. Examples of the chilling effect occur in Watergate titles under 15.4. Detailed analysis of changes in libel law is in Smolla, *Suing the Press: Libel, the Media & Power* (1986) and Dill, *The Journalist's Handbook on Libel and Privacy* (1986). The Westmoreland Case is analyzed in Kowet, *A Matter of Honor: General William C. Westmoreland versus CBS* (1984), which takes a strong position on the general's side, and Brewin and Shaw, *Vietnam on Trial: Westmoreland vs CBS* (1987), which includes the trial and aftermath. Benjamin, *Fair Play: CBS, General Westmoreland,* and *How a Television Documentary Went Wrong* (1988) offers a fascinating view of the network's internal investigation. For the question of reporter privilege, see van Gerpen, *Privileged Communication and the Press* (1979). Spitzer, *Seven Dirty Words and Six Other Stories: Controlling the Content of Print and Broadcast* (1986) discusses reasons for control of some kinds of print and electronic media content.

18.3 First Amendment Parity Powe, *American Broadcasting and the First Amendment* (1987) makes a strong case for broadcast parity with print. See Parsons, *Cable Television and the First Amendment* (1987) and Shapiro et al., *'Cablespeech': The Case for First Amendment Protection* (1983), both of which argue for more freedom for cable television.

18.4 Political Access The NAB (and the FCC, although less often) regularly revises booklets guiding station managers on how best to treat access by political candidates. See also citations under 15.4.

18.5 Public Access A reasoned argument by an author combining both a law and network reporting background is Rowan, *Broadcast Fairness: Doctrine, Practice, Prospects* (1984), which contends that the fairness doctrine has outlived whatever function it had. A solid history of its development is found in Simmons, *The Fairness Doctrine and the Media* (1978). Two earlier works argue strongly for a public right of access to media: Schmidt, *Freedom of the Press vs Public Access* (1976) and Barron, *Freedom of the Press for Whom?* (1973), which is the key work promoting access. Written like a novel and relating the entire story of the *Red Lion* case is Friendly, *The Good Guys, The Bad Guys and the First Amendment* (1976). A survey of recent changes in the courtroom access issue is in Freedman, *Press and Media Access to the Criminal Courtroom* (1988).

18.6 Fairness in News For a viewpoint generally critical of the networks and establishment media, see the research monographs issued by such conservative think tanks as Accuracy in Media, American Enterprise Institute, and The Media Institute, all in Washington, D.C.

18.7 Unfinished Business For Mark Fowler's own assessment of his goals for the FCC, see Fowler and Brenner, "A Marketplace Approach to Broadcast Regulation" (1982). Le Duc, *Beyond Broadcasting: Patterns in Policy and Law* (1987) reviews recent trends and suggests needed changes.

Chapter 19:
Global View

The literature on international and comparative media systems has expanded greatly in recent years— we can include only the tip of it here.

19.1 Broadcasting and National Character The starting point for a broad-based philosophical discussion of broadcasting in different societies is Head, *World Broadcasting Systems: A Comparative Analysis* (1985). Rosen, *International Handbook of Broadcasting Systems* (1988) includes parallel information on 24 countries of all kinds. Howell, *World Broadcasting in the Age of the Satellite* (1986) takes a topical approach with some specific country examples. Several books offer original papers on the dramatic changes in European media systems in the 1980s: Rogers and Balle, *The Media Revolution in America & Western Europe* (1985). The role of newer media in Europe is assessed in Negrine, *Cable Television and the Future of Broadcasting* (1985) and *Satellite Broadcasting: The Politics and Implications of the New Media* (1988). Two multivolume paperback series detail specific countries from all regions of the world: ICC, *Broadcasting in . . .* and UNESCO, *Communication Policies in . . .*

19.2 Political Philosophies Material on American broadcasting is detailed under earlier chapters. Useful comparative studies of various developed nations, mainly in Europe, include Browne, *Comparing Broadcasting Systems: The Experience of Six Industrialized Nations* (1989); Kuhn, *The Politics of Broadcasting* (1985); Dyson and Humphreys, *The Politics of the Communications Revolution in Western Europe* (1986); and McQuail and Siune, *New Media Politics: Comparative Perspectives in Western Europe* (1986). The landmark study of European policies is Commission of the European

Communities, *Television without Frontiers: Green Paper on the Establishment of the Common Market for Broadcasting: Especially by Satellite and Cable* (1984). See also Head, and Smith, under 19.1. The development of British radio and television is well told in Briggs, *The BBC: The First Fifty Years* (1985) and Sendall, *Independent Television in Britain* (1982, 1983). For more on Soviet and related systems, see Mickiewicz, *Split Signals: Television and Politics in the Soviet Union* (1988) and Paulu, *Radio and Television Broadcasting in Eastern Europe* (1974). Chang, *Mass Media in China: The History and the Future* (1989) relates media changes in the most populous country in the world. See Tunstall, *The Media in Britain* (1983) for the broad context of pluralism, and Brown, *Commercial Media in Australia* (1986) for another example.

19.3 Legal Foundations

For material on U.S. media law, see notes under Chapters 16–18. British material is under 19.2. The ITU's operations are detailed in Codding and Rutkowski, *The International Telecommunication Union in a Changing World* (1982). A collection of important documents from world agencies is gathered and annotated in Ploman, *International Law Governing Communications and Information* (1982). The best, though now dated, comparative analysis of access policies is found in Berrigan, *Access: Some Western Models of Community Media* (1978). See also Head, under 19.1.

19.4–19.5 Economics and Geography

UNESCO is the standard source for information on all media in most countries. It publishes *World Communications* (1975), revised about every ten years and statistically updated in *Statistics on Radio and Television, 1960–1976* (1979), *Latest Statistics on Radio and Television Broadcasting* (1987), and *Statistical Yearbook* (annual). A good analysis of the development of the three conflicting systems of color television is in Crane, *The Politics of International Standards* (1979). The many European and British "pirate" broadcasters are detailed in Harris, *Broadcasting from the High Seas* (1977) and Hind and Mosco, *Rebel Radio: The Full Story of British Pirate Radio* (1985). Katz and Wedell, *Broadcasting in the Third World* (1977), though now dated, remains the best overview on that topic—see also Graff, *Communications for National Development: Lessons From Experience* (1983) for a sobering assessment. See also Head, *Broadcasting in Africa* (1974); Lent, *Broadcasting in Asia and the Pacific* (1978); Boyd, *Broadcasting in the Arab World* (1982); and Fox, *Media and Politics in Latin America* (1988); for detailed regional analyses.

19.6–19.7 Programs and Schedules

The standard annual of information on broadcasting systems and program schedules is *World Radio-TV Handbook*. Also issued annually but with a descriptive rather than directory approach, is Paterson, *TV and Video International Guide*. Worldwide exchanges are detailed in Wildman and Siwek, *International Trade in Films and Television Programs* (1989). See the items under pirate broadcasting under 19.4–19.5 to get a sense of audience dissatisfaction with licensed broadcasters' programming.

19.7–19.8 Transborder Broadcasting

There is a large literature on international propaganda, much of it based on World War II experiences. A good starting point is Browne, *International Radio Broadcasting* (1982), which covers major countries with a stress on more recent developments. Short, *Western Broadcasting over the Iron Curtain* (1986) provides 13 original studies of different countries' efforts. The story of BBC activities is in Mansell, *Let the Truth Be Told* (1982). Radio Free Europe and Radio Liberty are detailed in Mickelson, *America's Other Voice* (1983) and in the annual BIB reports. Soviet activity is reviewed in Shultz and Godson, *Dezinformatsia: Active Measures in Soviet Strategy* (1984). The rationale for beginning a transborder service, in this case Radio Martí into Cuba from the U.S., is found in the *Final Report* of the Presidential Commission on Broadcasting to Cuba (1982). Frederick, *Cuban-American Radio Wars* (1986) reviews the broader story of the airwaves conflict. Soley and Nichols, *Clandestine Radio Broadcasting* (1987) explores the many revolutionary and counter-revolutionary uses of media.

19.9 U.S. Global Influence For surveys of American policy and trends, see Barnett et al., *Law of International Telecommunications in the United States* (1988) and Fisher, *American Communication in a Global Society* (1987). INTELSAT information is found in Snow, *The International Telecommunications Satellite Organization* (1987) and Alper and Pelton, *The Intelsat Global Satellite System* (1984), as well as INTELSAT annual reports. Satellite policy more generally is discussed in White and White, *The Law and Regulation of International Space Communication* (1988) and Demac, *Tracing New Orbits: Cooperation & Competition in Global Satellite Development* (1986). Long, *World Satellite Almanac* provides annual reference on all aspects of the subject. Luther, *The United States and the Direct Broadcast Satellite* (1988) is a recent review of a controversial world debate. Ganley and Ganley, *Global Political Fallout: The VCR's First Decade* (1987) provides initial impressions of impact; Boyd et al., *Videocassette Recorders in the Third World* (1989) demonstrates the rapidly expanding role of the VCR in countries with limited internal electronic media; while Alvarado, *Video World-Wide* (1988) provides a Unesco-supported description of global patterns of video hardware and software distribution. McQuail and Siune, *New Media Politics: Comparative Perspectives in Western Europe* (1986) debates the spread of deregulation. A good deal of the literature on the crosscultural impact of Western media is highly polemical. The best international statement of the free versus balanced flow issue is found in Unesco's McBride Commission, *Many Voices, One World* (1980). Nordenstreng, *The Mass Media Declaration of Unesco* (1984) reviews that agency's increasing activity in this area, tilted toward the Third World viewpoint. A similar strong argument is Smith, *The Geopolitics of Information: How Western Culture Dominates the World* (1980). Western points of view are found in Tunstall, *The Media Are American* (1977), and a 20th Century Fund Task Force on the International Flow of News, *A Free and Balanced Flow* (1979). A counterargument, admonishing Third World nations not to let themselves be overwhelmed by Western media, is Hamelink, *Cultural Autonomy in Global Communications* (1983).

Bibliographies

This brief selected list includes the most useful media bibliographies for research or further reading on American electronic media. Libraries should have most of them. Full citations are in the bibliography. In addition, readers should check library availability of electronic data bases for more efficient literature searches.

Blum, *Basic Books in the Mass Media* (1980) is a standard overall annotated guide, divided by medium, and including foreign as well as domestic citations (new edition due in 1990).

Brightbill, *Communications and the United States Congress: A Selectively Annotated Bibliography of Committee Hearings, 1870–1976* (1978) is unique, covering all matters on media and common carrier communications.

Cassata and Skill, *Television: A Guide to the Literature* (1985) provides an intelligent assessment of books on the topic, well divided by subject categories.

Comstock, et al. *Television and Human Behavior* (1975) is a three volume bibliography of the research literature: a main list, 50 key studies with detailed annotations, and work then in progress, along with an integrative review.

Cooper, *Bibliography on Educational Broadcasting* (1942) is far more inclusive than the title suggests—it's the best annotated survey of pre-World War II literature on domestic broadcasting.

Cooper, et al. *Television and Ethics: A Bibliography* (1988) covers over 1,100 items through 1987 in well-annotated and indexed fashion.

Du Charme, *Bibliography of Media Management and Economics* (1986) Some 400 titles are divided into 35 subject categories with an author index. Not annotated, but often revised.

Fisher, *On the Screen: A Film, Television, and Video Research Guide* (1986) includes over 700 well-annotated entries divided by type of publication and indexed by subject and author.

Friedman, *Sex Role Stereotyping in the Mass Media* (1977) is the best annotated guide to this topic, with a great deal on television programming.

Garay, *Cable Television: A Reference Guide to Information* (1988) combines both reference text and some 400 specific bibliographic entries all arranged by topic.

Gordon and Verna, *Mass Communication Effects and Processes: A Comprehensive Bibliography, 1950–1975* (1978) is not annotated but covers a got of ground, providing some context for the electronic media studies.

Greenfield, *Radio: A Reference Guide* (1989) provides a narrative-style review of hundreds of books, periodicals, and documents.

Hill and Davis, *Religious Broadcasting: An Annotated Bibliography* (1984) details the increasing descriptive and research writing on this topic.

Johnson, *TV Guide 25 Year Index* (1979) is just that, covering the period 1953–77.

"Mass Communication," [title varies] in *Annual Review of Psychology* is appears every several years with a review article and appended list of research studies for the period covered. See Vol. 13 (1962): 251–184 for writings up to 1960; Vol. 19 (1968) 351–386 for research published in 1961–66; Vol. 22 (1971): 309–336 for the 1967–70 period; Vol. 28 (1977): 141–173 for 1970–76 research; and Vol. 32 (1981): 307–356 covering 1976–79 work. No more recent articles had appeared as this edition of BIA went to press.

Matlon, *Index to Journals in Communication Studies Through 1985* (1987) includes chronological tables of contents and subject/author indexes for 15 journals including those of the Speech Communication Association, *Journalism Quarterly,* and *Journal of Broadcasting.* Latter issued its own 25 year index in 1982.

McCoy, *Freedom of the Press* (1968 and 1979) is wide-ranging with excellent annotations covering two centuries.

Meringhoff, *Children and Advertising: An Annotated Bibliography* (1980) is one of the more complete guides to the topic.

NAB, *Broadcasting Bibliography* (1984) is an invaluable booklet of subject divided listings, plus current periodicals listing (new edition due in 1990).

Performing Arts Books: 1876–1981 (1981) is a massive card catalog which also has an index of serial publications.

Pringle and Clinton, *Radio and Television: A Selected, Annotated Bibliography* (1989) covers the 1982–86 period with some 1,000 annotated entries arranged by subject with good indexes.

Shearer and Huxford, *Communications and Society: A Bibliography on Communications Technologies and Their Social Impact* (1983) emphasises various kinds of impact of the electronic media.

Shiers and Shiers, *Bibliography of the History of Electronics* (1972) offers detailed annotations on the history of telegraph, telephone, radio, television and related services.

Signorielli, et al. *Role Portrayal and Stereotyping on Television* (1985) covers studies on women, minorities, aging, sexual behavior, health and handicaps.

Signorielli and Gerbner, *Violence and Terror in the Mass Media: an Annotated Bibliography* (1988) lists nearly 800 scholarly and research books and articles with an author index.

Sloan, *American Journalism History: An Annotated Bibliography* (1989) includes electronic media in later chapters.

Smith, *U.S. Television Network News: A Guide to Sources in English* (1984) is the most inclusive guide to the topic.

Broadcast-Related Periodicals

The following brief list includes the more important and/or useful electronic media-related periodicals, most of which should be in any good library. Given the rate of change in this field, these are the best sources for current developments.

Advertising Age (1929, weekly) a major trade paper, with details of new accounts and agency doings and periodic statistical summaries.

Broadcasting (1931, weekly) is the single most important trade paper for the business; although it usually takes a strong proindustry stance it is indispensable for understanding current events, especially those concerning management and relations with government.

Broadcasting Cable Yearbook (annual since 1935) is a directory of stations and systems, and support industries, with capsule information on regulation and other topics.

Cablevision (1975, weekly) provides the best coverage of all aspects of cable.

Channels of Communications (1981, bimonthly) offers criticism and analysis on all electronic media including the annual *Field Guide* summary of media status. Became primarily business oriented after 1986.

Columbia Journalism Review (1962, bimonthly) specializes in critiques of print and electronic journalism.

Critical Studies in Mass Communication (1984, quarterly) focuses on content studies and criticism across all media.

EBU Review (1949, monthly) provides in-depth articles and news notes on Europe's official broadcasting services.

Electronic Media (1981, weekly) focuses on programming and advertising aspects, often offering in-depth interviews and excerpts from books. Large tabloid format.

Federal Communications Law Journal (1946, triannual) specializes on detailed legal analysis of current concerns in regulation of electronic media by the FCC.

Gannett Center Journal (1987, quarterly) provides theme issues with a combination of research and commentary articles on all aspects of media.

InterMedia (1970, bimonthly) reviews worldwide communication trends and issues in short news pieces and longer essays, concentrating on Western Europe.

Journalism Quarterly (1924, quarterly) is made up of academic research on print and broadcast media, with excellent book review sections.

Journal of Broadcasting and Electronic Media (1956, quarterly) provides scholarly research on all electronic media.

Journal of Communication (1951, quarterly) has focused since 1974 on mass communication with research, opinion and reviews.

Public Opinion Quarterly (1937, quarterly) is a respected source of research on polls, media, opinion, measurement etc.

Telecommunications Policy (1976, quarterly) offer scholarly work on media and broader telecommunication concerns, emphasising U.S. and foreign policy development.

Television Digest (1945, weekly) provides excellent, highly condensed reports on electronic media and consumer electronics. Issues an annual, two-volume *Television Factbook*.

Television News Index and Abstracts (1972, monthly) lists the exact content of network evening newscasts, indexed by topic with an annual overall index.

Television/Radio Age (1953, biweekly), is the trade journal stressing advertising with in-depth special articles on news, FCC affairs, foreign developments, etc. See also the related, but separately published *Television/Radio Age International* (quarterly).

Topicator (1965, monthly) indexes broadcast and advertising periodicals with an annual index.

TV Guide (1953, weekly) is the standard guide to programs, with often excellent articles and an annual Fall Preview issue.

Variety (1905, weekly) is the major trade paper for show business: stage, screen, music, television, and foreign developments. Large, tabloid format.

BIBLIOGRAPHY

ABC *Nightline* (1984), December 21. Transcript.

Abel, John A., et al. 1970. "Station License Revocations and Denials of Renewal 1934–1969," *Journal of Broadcasting* 14 (Fall): 411–421.

Abramson, Albert, 1987. *The History of Television, 1880 to 1941*. McFarland and Co., Jefferson, NC.

————, 1955, 1973. "A Short History of Television Recording," *Journal of the SMPTE* 64 (February): 72–76; and 82 (March): 188–195.

Abramson, Jeffrey B., et al. 1988. *The Electronic Commonwealth: The Impact of New Media Technologies on Democratic Politics*. Basic Books, New York.

AD (Appellate Division, New York Supreme Court). 1963. *John H. Faulk v. AWARE, Inc., et al.* 19 AD 2d 464.

Adams, William, and Schreibman, Fay. 1978. *Television Network News: Issues in Content Research*. George Washington U., Washington, DC.

Adler, Richard P., ed. 1979. *All in the Family: A Critical Appraisal*. Praeger, New York.

————, et al. 1980. *The Effects of Television Advertising on Children: Review and Recommendations*. Lexington Books, Lexington, MA.

————, ed. 1981. *Understanding Television: Essays on Television as a Social and Cultural Force*. Praeger, New York.

Agostino, Don. 1980. "New Technologies: Problem or Solution," *Journal of Communication* 30 (Summer): 198–206.

————, and Eastman, Susan Tyler. 1988. "Local Cable Programming," in Eastman et al.: 347–369.

Aird, Enola. 1980. *A Broadcaster's Guide to Designing and Implementing an Effective EEO Program*. National Association of Broadcasters, Washington, DC.

Aitken, Hugh G. 1976. *Syntony and Spark: The Origins of Radio*. Wiley, New York.

————. 1985. *The Continuous Wave, Technology and American Radio, 1900–1932*. Princeton U. Press, Princeton, NJ.

Allen, Robert C. 1985. *Speaking of Soap Operas*. U. of North Carolina Press, Chapel Hill.

Alper, Joel, and Pelton, Joseph. 1984. *The Intelsat Global Satellite System*. American Institute of Astronautics and Aeronautics, New York.

Alten, Stanley R. 1986. *Audio in Media*. 2d ed. Wadsworth, Belmont, CA.

Alvarado, Manuel, ed. 1988. *Video World-Wide*. John Libbey, London.

American Radio Relay League. Annual. *The Radio Amateur's Handbook*. A.R.R.L., Newington, CT.

American University School of Communications. Dec. 1979. "Broadcast News Doctors: The Patient is Buying the Cure." AUSC, Washington, DC.

Anderson, James. 1987. *Communication Research: Issues and Methods*. McGraw-Hill Book Co., New York.

Anderson, Kent. 1978. *Television Fraud: The History and Implications of the Quiz Show Scandals*. Greenwood Press, Westport, CT.

Annual Review of Psychology. Annual. Annual Reviews, Inc., Palo Alto, CA.

Applebone, Peter. 1988. "Scandal Spurs Interest in Swaggart Finances," *New York Times* (27 Feb.): 8.

Archer, Gleason, L. 1938. *History of Radio to 1926*. American Historical Society, New York.

_____. 1939. *Big Business and Radio*. American Historical Company, New York.

Arendt, Hannah. 1964. "Society and Culture," in Jacobs: 43–52.

Arlen, Gary H. 1987. *Tomorrow's TVs: A Review of New TV Set Technology, Related Video Equipment and Potential Market Impacts, 1987–1995*. National Association of Broadcasters, Washington, DC.

Arlen, Michael J. 1969. *Living-Room War*. Viking, New York.

ARMS (All-Radio Methodological Study). 1966. *ARMS: What It Shows, How It Has Changed Radio Measurement*. National Association of Broadcasters, Washington, DC.

Arnall, Gail. 1984. *Instructional Television Fixed Service*. Corporation for Public Broadcasting, Washington, DC.

Aske Research Ltd. 1980. *The Effort of Switching Channels: Report Prepared for the Independent Broadcasting Authority*. Aske Research Ltd., London.

Astrachen, Anthony. 1975. "Life Can Be Beautiful/Relevant," *New York Times Magazine* (March 23): 12.

Augarten, Stan. 1984. *Bit By Bit: An Illustrated History of Computers*. Ticknor and Fields, New York.

Aumente, Jerome. 1987. *New Electronic Pathways: Videotex, Teletext, and Online Databases*. Sage Publications, Newbury Park, CA.

Avery, Robert K., and Pepper, Robert. 1979. *The Politics of Interconnection: A History of Public Television at the National Level*. National Association of Educational Broadcasters, Washington, DC.

Avery, Robert K., et al. 1980. *Research Index for NAEB Journals, 1957–1979*. National Association of Educational Broadcasters, Washington, DC.

Baer, Walter S. 1973. *Cable Television: A Handbook for Decision Making*. Rand Corporation, Santa Monica, CA.

Bagdikian, Ben H. 1971. *The Information Machines: Their Impact on Men and Media*. Harper and Row, New York.

_____. 1973. "Out of the Can and into the Bank," *New York Times Magazine* (Oct 21): 31.

_____. 1987. *The Media Monopoly*. 2nd ed. Beacon Press, Boston.

Baker, W.J. 1971. *A History of the Marconi Company*. St. Martin's Press, New York.

Baldwin, Thomas F., and Lewis, Colby. 1972. "Violence in Television: The Industry Looks at Itself," in Comstock and Rubenstein: 290–365.

Baldwin, Thomas F., and McVoy, D. Stevens. 1988. *Cable Communications*. 2nd ed. Prentice-Hall, Englewood Cliffs, NJ.

Balio, Tino. 1985. *The American Film Industry*. 2nd ed. U. of Wisconsin Press, Madison.

Bandura, A.D., et al. 1963. "Imitation of Film-Mediated Aggressive Models," *Journal of Abnormal and Social Psychology* 66: 3–11.

Banning, William P. 1946. *Commercial Broadcasting Pioneer: The WEAF Experiment, 1922–1926*. Harvard U. Press, Cambridge, MA.

Barnard, Charles N. 1978. "An Oriental Mystery," *TV Guide* (Jan. 28): 2.

Barnett, Stephen R., et al. 1988. *Law of International Telecommunications in the United States*. Nomos Verlagsgesellschaft, Baden-Baden.

Barnouw, Erik. 1966. *A Tower of Babel: A History of Broadcasting in the United States to 1933*. Oxford U. Press, New York.

_____. 1968. *The Golden Web: A History of Broadcasting in the United States, 1933–1953*. Oxford U. Press, New York.

_____. 1970. *The Image Empire: A History of Broadcasting in the United States since 1953*. Oxford U. Press, New York.

_____. 1975. *Tube of Plenty: The Development of American Television*. Oxford U. Press, New York.

_____. 1978. *The Sponsor: Notes on a Modern Potentate*. Oxford U. Press, New York.

Barron, Jerome A. 1973. *Freedom of the Press for Whom? The Right of Access to Mass Media*. Indiana U. Press, Bloomington.

_____, and Dienes, C. Thomas. 1979. *Handbook of Free Speech and Free Press*. Little, Brown, Boston.

Barthel, Joan. 1975. "Boston Mothers Against Kidvid," *New York Times Magazine* (Jan. 5): 15.

Barwise, Patrick, and Andrew Ehrenberg. 1988. *Television and Its Audience*. Sage, Newbury Park, CA.

Batra, Rajeev, and Glazer, Rashi, eds. 1989. *Cable TV Advertising: In Search of the Right Formula*. Quorum Books, New York.

Baudino, Joseph E., and Kittross, John M. 1977. "Broadcasting's Oldest Station: An Examination of Four Claimants," *Journal of Broadcasting* 21 (Winter): 61–83.

BBC (British Broadcasting Corporation). 1928–1987. *BBC Handbook* (title varies). Annual. BBC, London.

————, International Broadcasting Audience Research, 1988. "World Radio and Television Receivers" (June). BBC, London.

BBDO (Batten, Barton, Durstine and Osborn). Annual. *BBDO Audience Coverage and Cost Guide*. BBDO, New York.

Beck, A.H. 1967. *Words and Waves: An Introduction to Electrical Communication*. McGraw-Hill, New York.

Beck, Kirsten. 1983. *Cultivating the Wasteland: Can Cable Put the Vision Back in TV?* American Council for the Arts, New York.

Bedell, Sally. 1981. *Up the Tube: Prime-Time TV and the Silverman Years*. Viking, New York.

Bendinger, Robert. 1957. "FCC: Who Will Regulate the Regulators?" *The Reporter* (Sept.): 26.

Benjamin, Burton. 1984. *The CBS Benjamin Report*. The Media Institute, Washington, DC.

————. 1988. *Fair Play: CBS, General Westmoreland, and How A Television Documentary Went Wrong*. Harper and Row, New York.

Bennett, Robert M. 1981. "The Television Station's Future Identity." Keynote Address to National Association of Television Program Executives Annual Convention, March 16, New York.

Bergendorff, Fred, et al., 1983. *Broadcast Advertising and Promotion*. Hastings House, New York.

Bergreen, Laurence. 1979. "What's Edward VII Doing in 'The Incredible Hulk's' Time Slot?" *TV Guide* (Feb. 24): 25.

————. 1980. *Look Now, Pay Later: The Rise of Network Broadcasting*. Doubleday, New York.

Berrigan, Frances J., ed. 1977. *Access: Some Western Models of Community Media*. UNESCO, Paris.

Besen, Stanley M. 1973. "The Value of Television Time and Prospects for New Stations." Rand Corporation, Santa Monica, CA.

————, et al. 1984. *Misregulating Television: Network Dominance and the FCC*. U. of Chicago Press, Chicago.

————, and Johnson, Leland. 1984. *An Assessment of the Federal Communication Commission's Group Ownership Rules*. Rand Corporation, Santa Monica, CA.

————. 1986. *Compatibility Standards, Competition, and Innovation in the Broadcasting Industry*. Rand Corporation, Santa Monica, CA.

Beville, H.M., Jr. 1981. "Understanding Broadcast Ratings," 3rd ed. Broadcast Ratings Council, New York.

————. 1988. *Audience Ratings: Radio, Television, Cable*. 2nd ed. Lawrence Erlbaum Associates, Hillsdale, NJ.

BIB (Board for International Broadcasting). Annual. *Annual Report*. Government Printing Office, Washington, DC.

Biel, Jacqueline. 1985. *Low Power Television: Development and Current Status of the LPTV Industry*. National Association of Broadcasters, Washington, DC.

Bilby, Kenneth. 1986. *The General: David Sarnoff and the Rise of the Communications Industry*. Harper and Row, New York.

Binkowski, Edward S. 1988. *Satellite Information Systems*. G.K. Hall Publishers, New York.

Bishop, John. 1988. *Making It In Video: An Insider's Guide to Careers in the Fastest Growing Industry of the Decade*. McGraw-Hill, New York.

Bitting, Robert C., Jr. 1965. "Creating an Industry," *Journal of the SMPTE* (November): 1015–1023.

Blake, Reed H., and Haroldson, Edwin O. 1975. *A Taxonomy of Concepts in Communication*. Hastings House, New York.

Blakely, Robert J. 1972. *The People's Instrument: A*

Philosophy of Programming for Public Television. Public Affairs Press, Washington, DC.

————. 1979. *To Serve the Public Interest: Educational Broadcasting in the United States.* Syracuse U. Press, Syracuse, New York.

Blanchard, Robert O. "Put the Roper Survey on the Shelf—We Have Our Own Agenda," *Feedback* (Broadcast Educational Association) 29:3 (Summer 1988), 3.

Blank, David M. 1977. "The Gerbner Violence Profile," *Journal of Broadcasting.* 21 (Summer): 273–279.

Blankensteen, Jane, and Odeni, Avi. 1987. *TV: Careers Behind the Screen.* Wiley and Sons, New York.

Bluem, A. William. 1965. *Documentary in American Television; Form, Function, Method.* Hastings House, New York.

Blum, Eleanor. 1980. *Basic Books in the Mass Media: An Annotated, Selected Booklist.* 2d ed. U. of Illinois Press, Urbana.

Blum, Richard A., and Lindheim, Richard D. 1987. *Primetime: Network Television Programming.* Focal Press, Boston, MA.

Blumler, Jay G., and Katz, Elihu. 1975. *The Uses of Mass Communications: Current Prospectives on Gratification Research.* Sage Publications, Beverly Hills, CA.

Boorstin, Daniel J. 1964. *The Image: A Guide to Pseudo-Events in America.* Harper and Row, New York.

————. 1978. "The Significance of Broadcasting in Human History," In Hoso-Bunka Foundation. *Symposium on the Cultural Role of Broadcasting, October 3–5, 1978.* Summary Report. Hoso-Bunka Foundation, Tokyo: 9–23.

Booz, Allen and Hamilton, Inc. 1978. *Feasibility of a New Local Television Audience Measurement Service: Phase I Final Report.* Television Bureau of Advertising, New York.

Botein, Michael, and Rice, David M., eds. 1981. *Network Television and the Public Interest: A Preliminary Inquiry.* Lexington Books, Lexington, MA.

Bower, Robert T. 1973. *Television and the Public.* Holt, Rinehart and Winston, New York.

————. 1985. *The Changing Television Audience in America.* Columbia U. Press, New York.

Bowles, Jay. 1984. Telephone Interview, Blackburn and Co., Atlanta, GA. Nov. 9.

Boyd, Douglas A., ed. 1982. *Broadcasting in the Arab World.* Temple University Press, Philadelphia.

————, et al. 1989. *Videocassette Recorders in the Third World.* Longman, New York.

Boyer, Peter J. 1988a. *Who Killed CBS? The Undoing of America's Number One News Network.* Random House, New York.

————. 1988b. "NBC Tries a Quieter Way of Breaking into Cable TV," *New York Times* (June 6), D10.

Braestrup, Peter. 1977. *Big Story: How the American Press and Television Reported and Interpreted the Crisis of Tet 1968 in Vietnam and Washington.* 2 vols. Westview Press, Boulder, CO.

Bretz, Rudy. 1970. *A Taxonomy of Communication Media.* Educational Technology, Englewood Cliffs, NJ.

————. 1983. *Media for Interactive Communication.* White Plains, NY: Knowledge Industry Publications.

Brewin, Bob, and Shaw, Sydney. 1987. *Vietnam on Trial: Westmoreland vs. CBS.* Atheneum, New York.

Briggs, Asa A. 1965. *The Golden Age of Wireless, The History of Broadcasting in the United Kingdom,* Vol. 2. Oxford U. Press, Oxford.

————. 1985. *The BBC: The First 50 Years.* Oxford U. Press, Oxford.

Bright, Arthur A., Jr. 1949. *The Electric-Lamp Industry: Technological Change and Economic Development from 1800 to 1947.* Macmillan, New York.

Brightbill, George D. 1978. *Communications and the United States Congress: A Selectively Annotated Bibliography of Committee Hearings, 1870–1976.* Broadcast Education Association, Washington, DC.

Brindze, Ruth. 1937. *Not to Be Broadcast: The Truth about Radio.* Vanguard, New York.

Broadcasting. (Note: the articles listed here are mostly lengthy special reports. Citations to shorter specific articles are found only in the text.)

1963. "A World Listened and Watched." Special Report. (Dec. 2): 36.

1970. "A Play-by-Play Retrospective." Special Report. (Nov. 2): 74.

1979. "CBS: The First Five Decades." (Sep. 19): 45.

1979. "Minorities in Broadcasting: The Exception Is No Longer the Rule." Special Report. (Oct. 15): 27.

1979. "Children's Programming." Special Report. (Oct. 29): 39.

1980. "The Top 100 Companies in Electronic Communications." (Jan.): 35.

1980. "The Washington Lawyer: Power Behind the Powers that Be." Special Report. (Jun. 16): 32.

1981. "Faint Victory." Editorial. (Jan. 12): 106.

1983. "The Congressman and the Achilles Heel [Rep. Timothy Wirth]." Special Report. (Oct. 17): 43.

1984. "State of the Art: Technology," (Oct. 8): 54.

1984. "The New Order Passeth." (Dec. 10): 43.

1984. "Perspectives 1985." (Dec. 31): 72.

1985. "Broadcasting: Top 50 Advertising Agencies." Special Report. (Feb. 4): 40.

1988. "Broadcasting's Top 50 Advertising Agencies." Special Report (Mar. 21): 34.

1989: "Changing Hands." (Feb. 13): 41–54.

Broadcasting Publications, Inc., Annual. *Broadcasting/Cablecasting Yearbook.* (Title varies.) Author, Washington, DC.

————. 1981. *The First 50 Years of Broadcasting.* Author, Washington, DC.

Brock, Gerald W. 1981. *The Telecommunications Industry: The Dynamics of Market Structure.* Harvard U. Press, Cambridge, MA.

Broder, Mitch. 1976. "The Late Show Clocks 25 Years," *New York Times* (Feb. 22): D–29.

Brogan, Patrick. 1985. *Spiked: The Short Life and Death of the National News Council.* Twentieth Century Fund, New York.

Brooks, John. 1976. *Telephone: The First Hundred Years.* Harper and Row, New York.

Brooks, Tim, and Marsh, Earle. 1988. *The Complete Directory to Prime Time Network TV Shows: 1946–Present.* 4th ed. Ballantine Books, New York.

Brown, Allan. 1986. *Commercial Media in Australia: Economics, Ownership, Technology, and Regulation.* University of Queensland Press, St. Lucia, Queensland, Australia.

Brown, James A. 1980. "Selling Air Time for Controversy: NAB Self-Regulation and Father Coughlin," *Journal of Broadcasting* 24 (Spring): 199–224.

Brown, Les. 1971. *Televi$ion: The Business Behind the Box.* Harcourt Brace Jovanovich, New York.

————. 1977. *New York Times Encyclopedia of Television.* Times Books, New York.

————. 1982. *Les Brown's Encyclopedia of Television.* New York Zeotrope, New York.

Browne, Donald. 1982. *International Radio Broadcasting: The Limits of the Limitless Medium.* Praeger, New York.

————. 1989. *Comparing Broadcast Systems: The Experience of Six Industrialized Nations.* Iowa State University Press, Ames.

Buckley, Tom. 1978. "Popularity of '60 Minutes' Based on Wide-Ranging Reports," *New York Times* (Dec. 17): 99.

————. 1979. "Game Shows-TV's Glittering Gold Mine," *New York Times Magazine* (Nov. 18): 49.

Busch, H. Ted., and Landeck, Terry. 1981. *The Making of a Television Commercial.* Macmillan, New York.

Cal. (California Reporter). 1981. *Olivia N. v. National Broadcasting Co.,* 178 Cal. Rptr. 888 (California Court of Appeal, First District).

Campbell, Robert. 1976. *The Golden Years of Broadcasting: A Celebration of the First 50 Years of Radio and Television on NBC.* Scribners, New York.

Cantor, Muriel G. 1980. *Prime-Time Television: Content and Control.* Sage Publications, Beverly Hills, CA.

————, and Pingree, Susanne. 1983. *The Soap Opera.* Sage Publications, Beverly Hills, CA.

Cantril, Hadley. *The Invasion from Mars: A Study of the Psychology of Panic.* 1940. Princeton U. Press, Princeton, NJ.

Carey, William L. 1967. *Politics and the Regulatory Agencies.* McGraw-Hill, New York.

Casty, Alan, ed. 1968. *Mass Media and Mass Man.* Holt, Rinehart, and Winston Company, New York.

CCET (Carnegie Commission on Educational Television). 1967. *Public Television: A Program for Action.* Harper and Row, New York.

CCFPB (Carnegie Commission on the Future of Public Broadcasting). 1979. *A Public Trust.* Bantam Books, New York.

Carroll, Raymond L. 1980. "The 1948 Truman Campaign: The Threshold of the Modern Era," *Journal of Broadcasting* 24 (Spring): 173–188.

Carter, T. Barton, et al. 1988. *The First Amendment and the Fourth Estate: The Law of Mass Media.* 4th ed. Foundation Press, Westport, New York.

———. 1989. *The First Amendment and the Fifth Estate: Regulation of Electronic Mass Media.* 2nd ed. Foundation Press, Westport, New York.

Cassata, Mary, and Skill, Thomas, 1983. *Life on Daytime Television: Tuning-In American Serial Drama.* Ablex, Norwood, NJ.

———. 1985. *Television: A Guide to the Literature.* Oryx Press, Phoenix Press, Phoenix, AZ.

Cater, Douglass, and Nyhan, Michael. 1976. *The Future of Public Broadcasting.* Praeger, New York.

Chafee, C. David. 1988. *The Rewiring of America: The Fiber Optics Revolution.* Academic Press, Inc. Boston.

Chamberlin, Bill, and Brown, Charlene J. 1982. *The First Amendment Reconsidered: New Perspectives on the Meaning of Freedom of Speech and Press.* Longman, New York.

Chandler, Joan M. 1988. *Television and National Sport: The United States and Britain.* University of Illinois Press, Chicago, IL.

Chang, Won Ho. 1989. *Mass Media in China: The History and the Future.* Iowa State University Press, Ames, IA.

Charren, Peggy, and Sandler, Martin W. 1983.

Changing Channels: Living (Sensibly) with Television. Addison-Wesley, Reading, MA.

CFR (Code of Federal Regulations). Annual. 47 *CFR* 0.1 ff. *Telecommunications.* 5 vols. Government Printing Office, Washington, DC.

Chafee, Zechariah, Jr. 1947. *Government and Mass Communications.* U. of Chicago Press, Chicago.

Chagall, David. 1977. "The Child Probers," *TV Guide* (Oct. 8): 8.

———. 1978. "Can You Believe the Ratings?" *TV Guide* (June 24): 2; (July 1): 20.

Channels, Editors of. Annual. *Field Guide to the Electronic Media* (title varies). Author, New York.

Christensen, Mark, and Smith, Cameron. 1984. *The Sweeps: Behind the Scenes in Network TV.* Morrow, New York.

Christians, Clifford, et al. 1987. *Media Ethics: Cases and Moral Reasoning.* 2nd ed. Longman, New York.

Chu, Goodwin, and Schramm, Wilbur. 1967. *Learning from Television: What the Research Says.* National Association of Educational Broadcasters, Washington, DC.

Clancy, Thomas H. 1979. "Nine and a Half Theses on Religious Broadcasting," *America* (Apr. 7): 271–275.

Clift, Charles, III, et al. 1980. "Forfeitures and the Federal Communications Commission: An Update," *Journal of Broadcasting* 24 (Summer): 301–310.

Coates, Vary T., and Finn, Bernard. 1979. *A Retrospective Technology Assessment: Submarine Telegraphy—The Transatlantic Cable of 1866.* San Francisco Press, San Francisco.

Codding, George, and Rutkowski, Anthony. 1982. *The International Telecommunication Union in a Changing World.* Artech House, Dedham, MA.

Codel, Martin, ed. 1930. *Radio and Its Future.* Harper, New York.

Coen, Robert J. 1988. "Estimated Annual U.S. Advertising Expenditure, 1977–1987." (May) McCann-Erickson, Inc., New York.

Cogley, John. 1956. *Report on Blacklisting II: Radio-Television.* Fund for the Republic, New York.

Cole, Barry, and Oettinger, Mal. 1978. *Reluctant Regulators: The FCC and the Broadcast Audience.* Addison-Wesley, Reading, MA.

Commission of the European Communities. 1984. *Television without Frontiers: Green Paper in the Establishment of the Common Market for Broadcasting, Especially by Satellite and Cables.* Brussels, European Communities.

Compaine, Benjamin M., et al. 1982. *Who Owns the Media? Concentration of Ownership in the Mass Communications Industry.* 2d ed. Knowledge Industry Publications, White Plains, N.Y.

————, ed. 1984. *Understanding New Media: Trends and Issues in Electronic Distribution of Information.* Ballinger, Cambridge, MA.

Comstock, George, et al. 1975. *Television and Human Behavior.* 3 vols. Rand Corporation, Santa Monica, CA.

————. 1978. *Television and Human Behavior.* Columbia U. Press, New York.

————, and Rubenstein, E., eds. 1972. *Television and Social Behavior: Media Content and Control.* Vol. 1. Government Printing Office, Washington DC.

Coolidge, Calvin. 1926. *Message to Congress,* 68 *Congressional Record* 32.

Cooper, Eunice, and Jahoda, Marie. 1947. "The Evasion of Propaganda: How Prejudicial People Respond to Anti-Prejudice Propaganda," *Journal of Psychology* 23 (January): 15–25.

Cooper, Isabella. 1942. *Bibliography on Educational Broadcasting.* U. of Chicago Press, Chicago.

Cooper, Thomas W., et al. 1988. *Television and Ethics: A Bibliography.* G. K. Hall and Co., Boston, MA.

Counterattack. 1950. *Red Channels: The Report of Communists in Radio and Television.* Author, New York.

Cowan, Geoffrey. 1979. *See No Evil: The Backstage Battle Over Sex and Violence on Television.* Simon and Schuster, New York.

CPB (Corporation for Public Broadcasting, Washington, DC.).

Annual. *Annual Report.*

Annual. *Summary Statistical Report of CPB Qualified Public Radio Stations.* (Title varies).

Annual. *Summary Statistical Report of Public Television Licensees.* (Title varies).

Biennial. *Public Radio Programming Content by Category.*

Biennial. *Public Television Programming Content by Category.*

1981. *Status Report on Public Broadcasting.* (earlier editions: 1973, and 1977).

1987. *Public Broadcasting Directory, 1987–88.*

Crane, Rhonda J. 1979. *The Politics of International Standards: France and the Color TV War.* Ablex Publishing, Norwood, NJ.

Crutchfield, E.B. 1985. *NAB Engineering Handbook.* 7th ed. National Association of Broadcasters, Washington, DC.

Csida, Joseph, and Csida, June Bundy. 1978. *American Entertainment: A Unique History of Popular Show Business.* Billboard Books, New York.

C-SPAN. 1985. "Something Personal." Transcript. (Apr. 1): 1.

CTIC (Cable Television Information Center). 1982. *CTIC Cable Books: The Community Medium,* and *A Guide for Local Policy.* 2 vols. Cable Television Information Center, Arlington, VA.

Culbert, David H. 1976. *News for Everyman: Radio and Foreign Affairs in Thirties America.* Greenwood Press, Westport, CT.

Czitrom, Daniel. 1982. *Media and the American Mind from Morse to McLuhan.* U. of North Carolina Press, Chapel Hill.

Danielian, N.R. 1939. *ATandT: The Story of Industrial Conquest.* Vanguard, New York.

Davidowitz, Paul. 1972. *Communication.* Holt, Rinehart, and Winston, New York.

Davis, Dennis, and Baran, Stanley. 1981. *Mass Communication and Everyday Life: A Perspective on Theory and Effects.* Wadsworth, Belmont, CA.

Davis, Henry B.O. 1981–1985. *Electrical and Electronic Technologies: A Chronology of Events and Inventors.* 3 vols. Scarecrow Press, Metuchen, NJ.

Davis, Stephen. 1927. *The Law of Radio*. McGraw-Hill, New York.

Davison, W. Philips, and Yu, Frederick T.C., eds. 1974. *Mass Communication Research: Major Issues and Future Directions*. Praeger, New York.

DeFleur, Melvin, and Ball-Rokeach, Sandra. 1988. *Theories of Mass Communication*. 5th ed. Longman, New York.

de Forest, Lee. 1950. *Father of Radio*. Wilcox and Follett, Chicago.

Demac, Donna A. 1986. *Tracing New Orbits: Cooperation and Competition in Global Satellite Development*. Columbia University Press, New York.

Department of Commerce, 1922. "Minutes of Open Meeting of Department of Commerce on Radio Telephony." Mimeo.

————. 1924. *Recommendations for Regulation of Radio*. Government Printing Office, Washington, DC.

Derthick, Martha, and Quirk, Paul J. 1985. *The Politics of Deregulation*. Brookings Institution, Washington, DC.

Dervin, Brenda, and Voigt, Melvin., eds. 1979–1989. *Progress in Communication Sciences*. 9 vols. Ablex, Norwood, NJ.

De Soto, Clinton. 1936. *Two Hundred Meters and Down: The Story of Amateur Radio*. A.R.R.L., West Hartford, CT.

DeVol, Kenneth, ed. 1982. *Mass Media and the Supreme Court: The Legacy of the Warren Years*. 3rd ed. Hastings House, New York.

Diamant, Lincoln, ed. 1989. *The Broadcast Communications Dictionary*. 3rd ed. Greenwood Press, New York.

Diamond, Edwin, and Bates, Stephen. 1988. *The Spot: The Rise of Political Advertising on Television*. 2nd ed. MIT Press, Cambridge, MA.

Dick, Brad. 1987. "Who's Spending What." *Broadcast Engineering*. (Dec): 26.

Dill, Barbara. 1986. *The Journalists's Handbook on Libel and Privacy*. The Free Press, New York.

Dill, Clarence C. 1938. *Radio Law: Practice and Procedure*. National Law Book Co., Washington, DC.

Dizard, Wilson P. 1966. *Television: A World View*. Syracuse U. Press, Syracuse, NY.

————. 1988. *The Coming Information Age: An Overview of Technology, Economics, and Politics*. 3d ed. Longman, NY.

Dominick, Joseph R., and Fletcher, James F. 1985. *Broadcasting Research Methods*. Allyn and Bacon, Boston.

Donahue, Hugh Carter. 1989. *The Battle to Control Broadcast News: Who Owns the First Amendment?*. MIT Press, Cambridge, MA.

Drake-Chenault Enterprises Inc. 1978. "History of Rock and Roll." Drake-Chenault, Canoga Park, CA.

DuCharme, Rita, ed. 1986. *Bibliography of Media Management and Economics,* Media Management and Economics Resource Center, Minneapolis, MN.

Duncan, James. Quarterly. *American Radio*. Duncan Media Enterprises, Indianapolis, IN.

Dunlap, Orrin E., Jr. 1929. *Advertising By Radio*. Ronald Press, New York.

————. 1944. *Radio's 100 Men of Science*. Harper, New York.

Dunning, John. 1976. *Tune in Yesterday: The Ultimate Encyclopedia of Old-Time Radio, 1925–1976*. Prentice-Hall, Englewood Cliffs, NJ.

Dyson, Kenneth, and Humphreys, Peter. 1986. *The Politics of the Communications Revolution in Western Europe*. London. Frank Cass and Co., Ltd.

Eastman, Susan Tyler, and Klein, Robert. 1982. *Strategies for Broadcast and Cable Promotion*. Wadsworth, Belmont, CA.

Eastman, Susan Tyler, et al. 1988. *Broadcast/Cable Programming: Strategies and Practices,* 3d ed. Wadsworth, Belmont, CA.

Eberly, Philip K. 1982. *Music in the Air: America's Changing Tastes in Popular Music, 1920–1980*. Hastings House, New York.

EBUR (*European Broadcasting Union Review*). 1987. "Morning Has Broken: An Idea Whose Time Has Come." (Sep.): 12–30.

———. 1988. "Statistics on European Programmes and News Exchanges." (May): 27–39.

EIA (Electronic Industries Association). Annual. *Consumer Electronics.* Author. Washington, DC.

Eisner, Joel, and Krinsky, David. 1984. *Television Comedy Series: An Episode Guide to 153 TV Sitcoms in Syndication.* McFarland and Co., Jefferson, NC.

Elbert, Bruce R. 1987. *Introduction to Satellite Communication.* Artech, Norwood, MA.

Emerson, Thomas I. 1972. "Communication and Freedom of Expression," *Scientific American* (September): 163–172.

Emery, Michael, and Emery, Edwin. 1988. *The Press and America: An Interpretive History of the Mass Media.* 6th ed. Prentice-Hall, Englewood Cliffs, NJ.

Emery, Walter B. 1969. *National and International Systems of Broadcasting: Their History, Operation and Control.* Michigan State U. Press, East Lansing.

Ennes, Harold E. 1953. *Principles and Practices of Telecasting Operations.* Howard W. Sams, Indianapolis.

Epstein, Edward J. 1973a. *News from Nowhere: Television and the News.* Random House, New York.

———. 1973b. "What Happened vs. What We Saw," *TV Guide* (Sep. 29, Oct. 6, Oct. 13): 7, 20, 19.

Erickson, Hal. 1989. *Syndicated Television: The First Forty Years, 1947–1987.* McFarland, Jefferson, NC.

Ettema, James S., and Whitney, D. Charles, eds. 1982. *Individuals in Mass Media Organizations: Creativity and Constraint.* Sage, Beverly Hills, CA.

Eugster, Ernest. 1983. *Television Programming Across National Boundaries: The EBU and OIRT Experience.* Artech House, Dedham, MA.

Everson, George. 1949. *The Story of Television: The Life of Philo T. Farnsworth.* Norton, New York.

F (*Federal Reporter,* 2d Series). Government Printing Office, Washington, DC.
  1926 *U.S.* v. *Zenith Radio Corp.,* 12 F 2d 614.
  1929 *U.S.* v. *American Bond and Mortgage,* 31 F 2d 448.
  1931 *KFKB* v. *FRC,* 47 F 2d 670.

1932 *Trinity Methodist Church, South* v. *FRC,* 62 F 2d 850.
1946 *WOKO* v. *FCC,* 153 2d 623.
1948 *Simmons* v. *FCC,* 169 F 2d 670.
1962 *Suburban Broadcasters* v. *FCC,* 302 F 2d 191.
1966 *Office of Communication* v. *FCC,* 359 F 2d 994.
1968 *Banzhaf* v. *FCC,* 405 F 2d 1082.
1969a *N.Y. State Broadcasters Assn.* v. *U.S.,* 414 F 2d 990.
1969b *Kilby* v. *Noyce,* 416 F 2d 1391.
1969c *Nat. Assn. of Theater Owners* v. *FCC,* 420 F 2d 194.
1969d *Office of Communication* v. *FCC,* 425 F 2d 543.
1971a *Citizens Communication Center* v. FCC, 447 F 2d 1201.
1971b *Friends of the Earth* v. *FCC,* 449 F 2d 1164.
1972a *Stone et al.* v. *FCC,* 466 F 2d 316.
1972b *Brandywine-Maine Line Radio* v. *FCC,* 473 F 2d 16.
1973a *Yale Broadcasting Company* v. *FCC,* 478 F 2d 594.
1973b *TV 9* v. *FCC,* 495 F 2d 929.
1974a *Citizens Committee to Save WEFM* v. *FCC,* 506 F 2d 246.
1974b *NBC* v. *FCC,* 516 F 2d 1101.
1975a *Nat. Assn. of Independent TV Distributors* v. *FCC,* 516 F 2d 526.
1975b *Polish American Congress* v. *FCC,* 520 F 2d 1248.
1975c *Public Interest Research Group* v. *FCC,* 522 F 2d 1060.
1976 *Chisholm et al.* v. *FCC,* 538 F 2d 349.
1977a *Warner-Lambert Co.* v. *FCC,* 562 F 2d 749.
1977b *ACT* v. *FCC,* 564 2d 458.
1977c *Kuczo* v. *Western Connecticut Broadcasting Co.,* 566 F 2d 384.
1977d *Home Box Office* v. *FCC,* 567 F 2d 9.
1978a *Office of Communications* v. *FCC,* 567 F 2d 9.
1978b *Central Florida Enterprises* v. *FCC,* 598 F 2d 37.
1979a *American Security Council Education Foundation* v. *FCC,* 607 F 2d 438.

1979b *Writers Guild* v. *ABC,* 609 F 2d 355.

1979c *WNCN Listeners Guild* v. *FCC,* 610 F 2d 838.

1979d *Berlin Communications* v. *FCC,* 626 F 2d 869.

1980 *CBS Inc.* v. *ASCAP,* 620 F 2d 930.

1981 *RKO* v. *FCC,* 670 F 2d 215.

1984 *Buffalo Broadcasting Co.* v. *FCC,* 744 F 2d 217.

1985a *Quincy Cable TV Inc.* v. *FCC,* 768 F 2d 1434.

1985b *Jones* v. *Wilkinson* 800 F 2d 989.

1986 *Telecommunications Research and Action Center* v. *FCC,* 801 F 2d 501.

1987 *Century Communications Corp.* v. *FCC,* 835 F 2d 292.

1988 *Action for Children's Television et al.* vs. *FCC,* 852 F 2d 1332.

Fabe, Maxine. 1979. *TV Game Shows.* Doubleday, NY.

Fallon, Norman. 1976. *Shortwave Listeners Handbook.* 2d ed. Hayden, Rochelle Park, NJ.

Fang, Irving E. 1977. *Those Radio Commentators!* Iowa State U. Press, Ames.

Faulk, John H. 1964. *Fear on Trial.* Simon and Schuster, New York.

FCC (Federal Communications Commission). Government Printing Office, Washington D.C.

Annual. *Annual Report.* Government Printing Office, Washington DC.

1939 *Investigation of the Telephone Industry in the United States.* Government Printing Office, Washington DC.

1941 *Report on Chain Broadcasting.* Government Printing Office, Washington DC.

1946 *Public Service Responsibilities of Broadcast Licenses.* Government Printing Office, Washington DC.

1979 (Children's Television Task Force). *Television Programming for Children,* 5 vols. FCC, Washington, DC.

1980a *The Law of Political Broadcasting and Cable Casting: A Political Primer.* Government Printing Office, Washington DC.

1980b (Network Inquiry Special Staff). *New Television Networks: Entry, Jurisdiction, Ownership and Regulation. Final Report,* Vol. 1. *Back-ground Reports,* Vol. 2. Government Printing Office, Washington DC.

1980c *Staff Report and Recommendations in the Low Power Television Inquiry.* FCC, Washington, DC.

1984 *Equal Employment Opportunity Trend Report, Radio and Television* (30 Nov.)

1985 *Cable TV Equal Opportunity Trend Report* (5 Feb.)

1988 *Cable TV Equal Opportunity Trend Report* (29 Dec.)

1989 *Equal Employment Opportunity Trend Report, Radio and Television* (13 Jan.)

FCCR (*FCC Reports,* 1st and 2d Series, and *FCC Record*)

1949 *Editorializing by Broadcasting Licensees,* 13 FCC 1249.

1952 *Amendment of Sec. 3.606 [adopting new television rules] . . . Sixth Report and Order,* 41 FCC 148.

1959 *Columbia Broadcasting System.* In Interpretive Opinion. 26 FCC 715.

1960 *En Banc Programming Inquiry.* Report and Statement of Policy. 44 FCC 2303.

1965 *Comparative Broadcast Hearings.* Policy Statement. 1 FCC 2d 393.

1966 *Contests and Promotions Which Adversely Affect the Public Interest.* Public Notice. 2 FCC 2d 464.

1968 *Broadcasting in America and the FCC's License Renewal Process: An Oklahoma Case Study.* 14 FCC 2d 1.

1969a *Application . . . for Renewal of License of Station KTAL-TV, Texarkana, Tex.* Letter. 19 FCC 2d 109.

1969b *Complaints Covering CBS Program "Hunger in America."* Memorandum Opinion. 20 FCC 2d 143.

1970a *Nicholas Zapple.* Letter. 23 FCC 2d 707.

1970b *Complaint of the Committee for the Fair Broadcasting of Controversial Issues, Against Columbia Broadcasting System.* Memorandum Opinion and Order. 25 FCC 2d 283.

1970c *Amendment of Part 73 of the Commission's Rules and Regulations with Respect to Com-*

petition and Responsibility in Network Television Broadcasting. Memorandum Opinion and Order. 25 FCC 2d 318.

1971a *Licensee Responsibility to Review Records Before Their Broadcast.* Public Notice. 28 FCC 2d 409.

1971b *Complaint Concerning the CBS Program "The Selling of the Pentagon."* Letter. 30 FCC 2d 150.

1972a *DOMSAT.* Report and Order. 35 FCC 2d 844.

1972b *Cable Television.* Report and Order. 36 FCC 2d 143.

1972c *Complaint by Atlanta NAACP.* Letter. 36 FCC 2d 635.

1973 *Apparent Liability of Stations WGLD-FM* [Sonderling Broadcasting] News Release. 41 FCC 2d 919.

1974a *Handling of Public Issues Under the Fairness Doctrine and the Public Interest Standard of the Communications Act.* Fairness Report. 48 FCC 2d 1.

1974b *Practices of Licensees and Networks in Connection with Broadcasts of Sports Events.* Report and Order. 48 FCC 2d 235.

1974c *Children's Television.* Report and Policy Statement. 50 FCC 2d 1.

1975a *Applications for Renewal of Star Stations of Indiana.* Decision. 51 FCC 2d 95.

1975b *Inquiry into Subscription Agreements Between Radio Broadcasting Stations and Music Format Service Companies.* Report and Policy Statement. 56 FCC 2d 805.

1975c *Agreements Between Broadcast Licensees and the Public.* Report and Order. 57 FCC 2d 42.

1976a *Representative Patsy Mink et al. re WHAR. . . .* Memorandum Opinion and Order. 59 FCC 2d 987.

1976b *Development of Policy Re: Changes in the Entertainment Formats of Broadcast Stations.* Report, Statement of Policy, and Order. 60 FCC 2d 858.

1977a *Review of Commission Rules and Regulating Policies Concerning Network Broadcasting by Standard (AM) and FM Broadcast Stations.* Report, Statement of Policy, and Order. 63 FCC 2d 674.

1977b *Application of Sponsorship Identification Rules to Political Broadcasts, Teaser Announcements, Government Entities, and Other Organizations.* Public Notice. 66 FCC 2d 302.

1978a *Application for License Renewal by WPIX, Inc. and Construction Permit by Forum Communications.* Decision. 68 FCC 2d 381.

1978b *Commission Policy in Enforcing Section 312(a)(7) of the Communications Act.* Report and Order. 68 FCC 2d 1079.

1978c *Complaints Against Station KVOF-TV by Council on Religion and the Homosexual, Inc.* Memorandum Opinion and Order. 68 FCC 2d 1500.

1979a *PTL of Heritage Village Church (WJAN-TV).* Memorandum Opinion and Order. 71 FCC 2d 324.

1979b *Objectionable Loudness of Commercial Announcements. . . .* Notice of Inquiry. 72 FCC 2d 677.

1979c *Deregulation of Radio.* Notice of Inquiry and Proposed Rule Making. 73 FCC 2d 457.

1979d *Children's Television Programming and Advertising Practices.* Notice of Proposed Rule Making. 75 FCC 2d 138.

1980a *Rules and Policies to Further the Advancement of Black Americans in Mass Communications.* Memorandum Opinion and Order. 76 FCC 2d 385.

1980b *Application of RKO General, Inc. (WNAC-TV), Boston, Mass., for Renewal of Broadcasting License.* Decision. 78 FCC 2d 1.

1980c *Application of Walton Broadcasting . . . for Renewal of License.* Decision. 78 FCC 2d 857.

1980d *Cable Television Syndicated Program Exclusivity Rules [and] Inquiry into the Economic Relationship Between Television Broadcasting and Cable Television.* Report and Order. 79 FCC 2d 663.

1981a *Application of Faith Center. . . . Memorandum Opinion and Order. 84 FCC 2d 542.*

1981b *Deregulation of Radio.* Report and Order. 84 FCC 2d 968.

1981c *Stereo Broadcasters Inc.* Decision. 87 FCC 2d 87.

1982 *AM Stereophonic Broadcasting.* Report and Order. 51 RR 2d 1. (Report was never printed in official *FCC Reports*)

1984a *Deregulation of Radio.* Second Report and Order. 96 FCC 2d 930.

1984b *Amendment of Part 73 of the Commissions Rules and Regulations to Eliminate Objectionable Loudness of Commercial Announcements and Commercial Continuity over AM, FM, and Television Broadcast Stations.* Memorandum Opinion and Order. 56 *Radio Regulation* 390.

1984c *Revision of Program Policies and Reporting Requirements Related to Public Broadcasting Licensees.* Report and Order. 98 FCC 2d 746.

1984d *Revision of Programming and Commercialization Policies, Ascertainment Reports, and Program Log Requirements for Commercial Television Stations.* 98 FCC 2d 1076.

1985a *Cattle Country Broadcasting [KTTL-FM].* Hearing Designation Order and Notice of Apparent Liability. 58 *Radio Regulation* 1109.

1985b *Inquiry into. . . . the General Fairness Doctrine Obligations of Broadcast Licensees.* Report. 102 FCC 2d 143.

1985c *Application of Simon Geller.* Memorandum Opinion and Order. 102 FCC 2d 1443.

1987a *New Indecency Enforcement Standards to be Applied to all Broadcast and Amateur Radio Licenses.* Public Notice. 2 FCC Rcd 2726.

1987b *Complaint of Syracuse Peace Council Against Television Station WTVH.* Memorandum Opinion and Order. 2 FCC Rcd 5043.

1989 *Catoctin Broadcasting Corp. of New York (WBUZ),* Memorandum Opinion and Order. 4 FCC Rcd 2553.

Federal Radio Commission. Annual. *Annual Report.* 1927–1933. Government Printing Office, Washington, DC.

Felix, Edgar. 1927. *Using Radio in Sales Promotion.* McGraw-Hill, New York.

Fenby, Jonathan. 1986. *The International News Services.* Schocken Books, New York.

Ferrall, Victor E., ed. 1980. *Yearbook of Broadcasting Articles: 1959–1978.* Federal Publications Inc., Washington, DC.

Ferris, Charles, et al. 1983. *Cable Television Law: A Video Communications Guide.* 3 vols. Matthew Bender, New York.

Fessenden, Helen. 1940. *Fessenden: Builder of Tomorrows.* Coward-McCann, New York.

Feuer, Jane, et al., eds. 1984. *MTM 'Quality Television'.* British Film Institute, London.

Fink, Conrad C. 1988. *Media Ethics: In the Newsroom and Beyond.* McGraw-Hill, New York.

Fink, Donald G., ed. 1943. *Television Standards and Practice. . . .* McGraw-Hill, New York.

————, and Lutyens, David M. 1960. *The Physics of Television.* Anchor Books, Garden City, NY.

Fischer, Stuart. 1983. *Kids' TV: The First 25 Years.* Facts on File, New York.

Fisher, Glen. 1987. *American Communication in a Global Society.* 2nd ed. Ablex Publishing, Norwood, NJ.

Fisher, Kim N. 1986. *On The Screen: A Film, Television, and Video Research Guide.* Libraries Unlimited, Inc., Littleton, CO.

Fiske, Edward B. 1973. "The Oral Roberts Empire," *New York Times Magazine* (Apr. 22): 14.

Fletcher, James, ed. 1981. *Handbook of Radio-TV Broadcasting: Research Procedures in Audience, Program, and Revenues.* Van Nostrand-Reinhold, New York.

————. 1985. *Squeezing Profits Out of Ratings: A Manual for Radio Managers, Sales Managers, and Programmers.* National Association of Broadcasters, Washington, DC.

Foley, Joseph M. 1979. "Mass Communication Theory and Research: An Overview," In Nimmo, 1979: 263–270.

Forbes, Dorothy, and Sanderson, Layng. 1980. *The New Communicators: A Guide to Community Programming.* Communications Press, Washington, DC.

Forester, Tom. 1987. *High-Tech Society: The Story of the Information Technology Revolution.* MIT Press, Cambridge, MA.

Fornatale, Peter, and Mills, Joshua A. 1980. *Radio in the Television Age.* Overlook Press, Woodstock, N.Y.

Fowler, Gene, and Crawford, Bill. 1987. *Border Radio.* Texas Monthly Press, Austin, TX.

Fowler, Mark S., and Brenner, Daniel L. 1982. "A Marketplace Approach to Broadcast Regulation," *Texas Law Review* 60 (Feb.): 207.

Fox, Elizabeth, ed. 1988. *Media and Politics in Latin America: The Struggle for Democracy.* Sage Publications, Newbury Park, CA.

Fox, Stephen. 1984. *The Mirror Makers: A History of American Advertising and Its Creators.* Morrow, New York.

FR *(Federal Register)*

1974 *Program Length Commercials,* 39 FR 4042.
1974 *The Public and Broadcasting: A Procedure Manual.* Rev. ed. 39 FR 32288.

Frank, Peter. 1984. *Multichannel MDS: New Allocations, New Systems, and New Market Opportunities.* National Association of Broadcasters, Washington, DC.

Frank, Ronald E., and Greenberg, Marshall G. 1980. *The Public's Use of Television.* Sage, Beverly Hills, CA.

————. 1982. *Audiences for Public Television.* Sage, Beverly Hills, CA.

Frankl, Razelle. 1987. *Televangelism: The Marketing of Popular Religion.* Southern Illinois U. Press, Carbondale, IL.

Frazier, Gross, and Kadlec. 1986. *Independent Thinking: An Overview of the Independent Television Industry.* 1986. Author, Washington, DC.

Frederick, Howard H. 1986. *Cuban-American Radio Wars.* Ablex Publishing, Norwood, NJ.

Freedman, Warren. 1988. *Press and Media Access to the Criminal Courtroom.* Greenwood Press, Westport, CT.

Freeman, Roger L. 1981. *Telecommunications Transmission Handbook.* 2nd ed. Wiley, New York.

Friedman, Leslie J. 1977. *Sex Role Stereotyping in the Mass Media: An Annotated Bibliography.* Garland, New York.

Friendly, Fred. 1967. *Due to Circumstances Beyond Our Control. . . .* Random House, New York.

————. 1975. "What's Fair on the Air," *New York Times Magazine* (Mar. 30): 11–12, 37–48.

————. 1976. *The Good Guys, the Bad Guys, and the First Amendment: Free Speech vs. Fairness in Broadcasting.* Random House, NY.

F Sup *(Federal Supplement)*

1976 *Writers Guild et al.* v. *FCC.* 423 F Sup 1064.
1977 *CBS* v. *Stokely-Van Camp.* 456 F Sup 539.
1978 *U.S.* v. *NBC.* 449 F Sup 1127.
1979 *Universal City Studios* v. *Sony.* 480 F Sup 429.
1985 *Community Television of Utah* v. *Wilkerson.* 611 F Sup 1099.

Frost, S.E., Jr. 1937. *Is American Radio Democratic?* U. of Chicago Press, Chicago.

FTC (Federal Trade Commission)

1924 *Report on the Radio Industry.* Government Printing Office, Washington, DC.
1978 *Staff Report on Television Advertising to Children.* FTC, Washington, DC.

Ganley, Gladys D., and Ganley, Oswald H. 1987. *Global Political Fallout: The VCR's First Decade.* Ablex Publishing Corp., Norwood, NJ.

Garay, Ronald. 1984. *Congressional Television: A Legislative History.* Greenwood Press, Westport, CT.

————. 1988. *Cable Television: A Reference Guide to Information.* Greenwood Press, Westport, CT.

Gates, Gary P. 1978. *Air Time: The Inside Story of CBS News.* Harper and Row, New York.

Geis, Michael L. 1982. *The Language of Television Advertising.* Academic Press, New York.

Gelatt, Roland. 1977. *The Fabulous Phonograph: 1988–1977.* 2nd rev. ed. Macmillan, New York.

Gerbner, George. 1972. "Communications and Social Environment," *Scientific American* (Sep.): 153–160.

————, et al. 1977. "The Gerbner Violence Profile. . . ," *Journal of Broadcasting* 21 (Summer): 280–286.

_____, et al. 1984. *Religion and Television: A Research Report by the Annenberg School of Communication . . . and the Gallup Organization . . .* U. of Pennsylvania, Philadelphia.

_____, et al. 1986. *Television's Mean World: Violence Profile 14–15.* Annenberg School of Communications, Philadelphia.

Gianakos, Larry J. 1978–1987. *Television Drama Series Programming: A Comprehensive Chronicle.* 5 vols. Scarecrow Press, Metuchen, NJ.

Gibson, George H. 1977. *Public Broadcasting: The Role of the Federal Government, 1912–1976.* Praeger, New York.

Gillespie, Gilbert. 1975. *Public Access Cable Television in the United States and Canada.* Praeger, New York.

Gillmor, Donald M., and Barron, Jerome A. 1984. *Mass Communication Laws: Cases and Comment.* 4th ed. West, St. Paul, MN.

Gitlin, Todd. 1983. *Inside Prime Time.* Pantheon, New York.

_____. 1987. *Watching Television.* Pantheon, New York.

Glatzer, Hal. 1984. *Who Owns the Rainbow? Conserving the Radio Spectrum.* Howard W. Sams, Indianapolis.

Glynn, Eugene, D. 1968. "Television and the American Character," in Casty: 76–82.

Goldmark, Peter C., and Edson, Lee. 1973. *Maverick Inventor: My Turbulent Years at CBS.* Saturday Review Press, New York.

Gordon, Thomas F., and Verna, Mary E. 1978. *Mass Communication Effects and Processes: A Comprehensive Bibliography, 1950–1975.* Sage Publications, Beverly Hills, CA.

Graff, Robert D. 1983. *Communications for National Development: Lessons from Experience.* Oelgeschlager, Gunn and Hain, Cambridge, MA.

Graham, James M., and Kramer, Victor. 1976. *Appointments to the Regulatory Agencies: The Federal Communications Commission and the Federal Trade Commission (1949–1974).* Report to Senate Committee on Commerce. Government Printing Office, Washington, DC.

Graham, John. 1983. *The Facts on File Dictionary of Telecommunications.* Facts on File, New York.

Grant, William. 1983. *Cable Television.* Reston Books, Reston, VA.

Great Britain, 1977. *Report on the Committee on the Future of Broadcasting.* ["Annan Report."] Cmnd. 6753. Her Majesty's Stationery Office, London.

_____, 1986. *Report of the Committee on Financing the BBC.* ["Peacock Report."] Cmnd. 9824. Her Majesty's Stationery Office, London.

_____, Home Office. 1988. *Broadcasting in the '90s: Competition, Choice and Quality.* ["White Paper."] Cmnd. 517. Her Majesty's Stationery Office, London.

Green, Timothy. 1972. *The Universal Eye: The World of Television.* Stein and Day, New York.

Greenberg, Bradley S. 1980. *Life on Television: Content Analysis of U.S. Television Drama.* Ablex, Norwood, NJ.

_____. 1983. *Mexican-Americans and the Mass Media.* Ablex, Norwood, NJ.

_____, and Parker, Edwin B., eds. 1965. *The Kennedy Assassination and the American Public: Social Communication in Crisis.* Stanford U. Press, Stanford, CA.

Greenberger, Martin, ed. 1985. *Electronic Publishing Plus: Media for a Technological Future.* Knowledge Industry Publications, White Plains, NY.

Greenfield, Jeff. 1977. *Television: The First Fifty Years.* Abrams, New York.

Greenfield, Thomas A. 1989. *Radio: A Reference Guide.* Greenwood Press, Westport, CT.

Gross, Ben. 1954. *I Looked and I Listened.* Random House, New York (expanded edition issued in 1970).

Gross, Lynne Shafer. 1986. *The New Television Technologies.* 2nd ed. Wm. C. Brown, Dubuque, IA.

Grossman, Ann. 1987. *The Marketer's Guide to Media Vehicles, Methods, and Options.* Quorum Books, New York.

Grundfest, Joseph A. 1976. *Citizen Participation in Broadcast Licensing Before the FCC.* Rand Corporation, Santa Monica, CA.

Guimary, Donald L. 1975. *Citizen's Groups and Broadcasting*. Praeger, New York.

Hadden, Jeffrey K., and Shupe, Anson. 1988. *Televangelism: Power and Politics on God's Frontier*. Holt and Company, New York.

Hadden, Jeffrey K., and Swann, Charles E. 1981. *Prime Time Preachers: The Rising Power of Televangelism*. Addison-Wesley, Reading, MA.

Haigh, Robert W., et al., eds. 1981. *Communications in the Twenty-First Century*. Wiley-Interscience, New York.

Halberstam, David. 1979. *The Powers That Be*. Knopf, New York.

Hall, Jim. 1984. *Mighty Minutes: An Illustrated History of Television's Best Commercial's*. Harmony Books, New York.

Hallin, Daniel C. 1986. *The "Uncensored War": The Media and Vietnam*. Oxford U. Press, New York.

Hamelink, Cees. 1983. *Cultural Autonomy in Global Communications*. Ablex, Norwood, NJ.

Hammond, Charles M. 1981. *The Image Decade: Television Documentary 1965–1975*. Hastings House, New York.

Hancock, Harry. 1950. *Wireless at Sea: The First 50 Years*. Marconi International Marine Communication Co., Chelmsford, England.

Hanson, Jarice. 1987. *Understanding Video: Applications, Impact, and Theory*. Sage Publications, Newbury Park, CA.

Harlow, Alvin. 1936. *Old Wires and New Waves: The History of the Telegraph, Telephone, and Wireless*. Century, New York.

Harrell, Bobby. 1985. *The Cable Television Technical Handbook*. Artech House, Dedham, MA.

Harris, Paul. 1977. *Broadcasting from the High Seas: The History of Offshore Radio in Europe, 1958–1976*. Paul Harris Publishing, Edinburgh, Scotland.

Hayes, Thomas C. 1984. "Hollywood in Tumult, Booms," *New York Times* (29 Sep.): 19f.

Head, Sydney W. 1956. *Broadcasting in America: A Survey of Radio and Television*. Houghton Mifflin, Boston.

————. 1974. *Broadcasting in Africa: A Continental Survey of Radio and Television*. Temple U. Press, Philadelphia.

————. 1985. *World Broadcasting Systems: A Comparative Analysis*. Wadsworth, Belmont, CA.

Headen, R.S., et al. 1979. "The Duplication of Viewing Law and Television Media Schedule Evaluation," *Journal of Marketing Research*. 2: 29–36.

Heighton, Elizabeth J., and Cunningham, Don R. 1984. *Advertising in the Broadcast and Cable Media*. 2nd ed. Wadsworth, Belmont, CA.

Henderson, Amy. 1988. *On the Air: Pioneers of American Broadcasting*. Smithsonian Institution Press, Washington, DC.

Henderson, Bruce. 1979. "How Residuals Checks Surprise Actors," *TV Guide* (Dec. 22): 3.

Henry, William A. III. 1987. "Con Man of the Cloth," *Channels* (Jan.): 16.

Hettinger, Herman S. 1933. *A Decade of Radio Advertising*. U. of Chicago Press, Chicago.

————, and Neff, Walter J. 1938. *Practical Radio Advertising*. Prentice-Hall, New York.

Hickey, Neil. 1976. "The Case of the Missing Viewers," *TV Guide* (May 8): 4.

Hill, George H., and Davis, Lenwood. 1984. *Religious Broadcasting: An Annotated Bibliography*. Garland, New York.

Himmelstein, Hal. 1981. *On the Small Screen: New Approaches in Television and Video Criticism*. Praeger, New York.

————. 1985. *Television Myth and the American Mind*. Praeger, New York.

Hind, John, and Mosce, Stephen. 1985. *Rebel Radio: The Full Story of British Pirate Radio*. Pluto Press, London.

Hixson, Richard. 1989. *Mass Media and the Constitution: An Encyclopedia of Supreme Court Decisions*. Garland, New York.

Hoggart, Richard, and Morgan, Janet. 1982. *The Future of Broadcasting*. Macmillan, London.

Hollowell, Mary Louise, ed. 1975. *Cable Handbook*. Communications Press, Washington, DC.

————. 1983. *The Cable/Broadband Communi-*

cations Book, Volume 3, 1982–83. Communications Press, Washington, DC.

Holman, Robert G. 1984. Personal Correspondence (Nov. 5) Daniels and Associates, Denver.

Hoover, Herbert. 1952. *Memoirs*. 3 vols. Macmillan, New York.

Hoover, Stewart M. 1988. *Mass Media Religion: The Social Sources of The Electronic Church*. Sage, Newbury Park, CA.

Horowitz, Susan. 1984. "Sitcom Domesticus: A Species Endangered by Social Change," *Channels*. (Sept/Oct.): 22.

Horsfield, Peter G. 1984. *Religious Television: The American Experience*. Longman, New York.

House CIFC (U.S. Congress, House of Representatives: Committee on Interstate and Foreign Commerce. Note: Committee was renamed Committee on Energy and Commerce in 1981.) Government Printing Office, Washington, DC.

1958a *Network Broadcasting*. Report of the FCC Network Study Staff. House Report 1277, 85th Cong., 2d Sess.

1958b *Regulation of Broadcasting: Half a Century of Government Regulation of Broadcasting and the Need for Further Legislative Action*. 85th Cong., 2d Sess.

1960 *Responsibilities of Broadcast Licensees and Station Personnel (Payola and Other Deceptive Practices in the Broadcast Field)*. Hearings in 2 parts. 86th Cong., 2d Sess.

1963 *Broadcast Advertisements*. Hearings. 88th Cong., 1st Sess.

1963, 1964, and 1965. *Broadcast Ratings: The Methodology, Accuracy, and Use of Ratings in Broadcasting*. Parts 1–3. 88th Cong., 1st Sess.; Part 4, 88th Cong., 1st and 2d Sess.

1971 *Subpoenaed Material re Certain TV News Documentary Programs*. Hearings. 92nd Cong., 1st Sess.

1977 *Options Papers*. 95th Cong., 1st Sess.

1979 *The Communications Act of 1978: Hearings on H.R. 13015*. 5 vols. in 7 parts. 95th Cong., 2d Sess.

1980 *The Communications Act of 1979: Hearings on H.R. 3333*. 5 vols. on 8 parts. 96th Cong., 1st Sess.

House CMMF (U.S. Congress, House of Representatives, Committee on Merchant Marine and Fisheries). Government Printing Office, Washington, D.C.

1919 *Government Control of Radio Communication*. Hearings. 65th Cong., 3rd Sess.
1924 *To Regulate Radio Communication*. Hearings. 68th Cong., 1st Sess.

Howard, Herbert H., and Carroll, S.L. 1980. *Subscription Television: History, Current Status, and Economic Projections*. National Association of Broadcasters, Washington, DC.

Howell, W.J., Jr. 1986. *World Broadcasting in the Age of the Satellite*. Ablex, Norwood, NJ.

Howeth, L.S. 1963. *History of Communications-Electronics in the United States Navy*. Government Printing Office, Washington, DC.

Hsia, H.J. 1988. *Mass Communications Research Methods: A Step-by Step Approach*. Lawrence Erlbaum Associates, Inc. Hillsdale, NJ.

Hudspeth, DeLayne R., and Brey, Ronald G. 1986. *Instructional Telecommunications: Principles and Applications*. Praeger, New York.

Hunn, Peter. 1988. *Starting and Operating Your Own FM Station: From License Application to Program Management*. TAB Books, Blue Ridge Summit, PA.

IBA (Independent Broadcasting Authority). Annual. *Guide to Independent Broadcasting* [title varies]. IBA, London.

IIC (International Institute of Communication). 1976 ff. *Broadcasting in . . .* [various countries, by various authors.] Routledge and Kegan Paul, London.

Intinolli, Michael. 1984. *Taking Soaps Seriously: The World of Guiding Light*. Praeger, New York.

IRE (Institute of Radio Engineers). 1962. *Proceedings of the IRE*. 50 (May): entire issue on 50th anniversary, with articles covering 1912–1962.

Jacobs, Norman, ed. 1964. *Media for the Millions*. Beacon Press, Boston.

Jamieson, Kathleen Hall. 1984. *Packaging the Presidency: A History and Criticism of Presidential Campaign Advertising*. Oxford U. Press, New York.

Johnson, Catherine E. 1979. *TV Guide 25 Year Index: By Author and Subject*. Triangle Publications, Radnor, PA.

Johnson, Nicholas. 1970. *How to Talk Back to Your Television Set*. Little, Brown, Boston.

Johnson, William O., Jr. 1971. *Super Spectator and the Electronic Lilliputians*. Little, Brown, Boston.

Johnston, Donald F. 1982. *Copyright Handbook*. 2nd ed. Bowker, New York.

Johnston, Jerome. 1987. *Electronic Learning: From Audiotape to Videodisc*. Lawrence Erlbaum Associates, Hillsdale, NJ.

Jolly, W.P. 1972. *Marconi*. Stein and Day, New York.

Jones, Kensinger, et al. 1986. *Cable Advertising: New Ways to New Business*. Prentice-Hall, Englewood Cliffs, N.J.

Jowett, Garth. 1976. *Film: The Democratic Art*. Little, Brown, Boston.

Kaatz, Ronald B. 1985. *Cable Advertiser's Handbook*. 2d ed. Crain, Chicago.

Kahn, Frank J., ed. 1984. *Documents of American Broadcasting*. 4th ed. Prentice-Hall, Englewood Cliffs, NJ.

Kaltenborn, H.V. 1938. *I Broadcast the Crisis*. Random House, New York.

Katz, Elihu, et al. 1974. "Uses of Mass Communication by the Individual," in Davidson and Yu: 11–35.

————and Lazarsfeld, Paul F. 1955. *Personal Influence: The Part Played by People in the Flow of Mass Communications*. Free Press, Glencoe, IL.

————, and Wedell, George. 1977. *Broadcasting in the Third World: Promise and Performance*. Harvard U. Press, Cambridge, MA.

Keith, Michael C. 1987. *Radio Programming: Consultancy and Formatics*. Focal Press, Boston.

————, and Krause, Joseph M. 1989. *The Radio Station*. 2nd ed. Focal Press, Stoneham, MA.

Kendrick, Alexander. 1969. *Prime Time: The Life of Edward R. Murrow*. Little, Brown, Boston.

Kiester, Edwin, Jr. 1974. "That 'News' Item May Be a Commercial," *TV Guide*. (Oct. 5): 10.

Kittross, John M., ed. 1980. *Administration of American Telecommunications Policy*. 2 vols. Arno Press, New York.

Klapper, Joseph T. 1960. *The Effects of Mass Communication*. Free Press, New York.

Klatell, David A., and Marcus, Norman. 1988. *Sports for Sale: Television, Money, and the Fans*. Oxford U. Press, New York.

Klein, Paul. 1971. "The Men Who Run TV Aren't That Stupid . . . They Know Us Better Than You Think," *New York* (Jan. 25): 20.

Kleinfield, Sonny. 1981. *The Biggest Company on Earth: A Profile of AT&T*. Holt, Rinehart & Winston, New York.

Kline, F. Gerald. 1972. "Theory in Mass Communication Research," in Kline & Tichenor, 1972: 14–40.

————, and Tichenor, Phillip J. 1972. *Current Perspectives in Mass Communications Research*. Sage, Beverly Hills, Ca.

Knowledge Industry Publications. 1987. *The Knowledge Industry 200, 1987 Edition: America's Two Hundred Largest Media and Information Companies*. 2nd ed. Author, White Plains, NY.

Koenig, Allen E., ed. 1970. *Broadcasting and Bargaining: Labor Relations in Radio and Television*. U. of Wisconsin Press, Madison.

Kowet, Don. 1979. "Whose 'Truth' Can You Believe?" *TV Guide* (Sep. 22): 6.

————. 1984. *A Matter of Honor: General Westmoreland versus CBS*. Macmillan, New York.

————, and Bedell, Sally. 1982. "Anatomy of a Smear," *TV Guide* (May 29): 10.

Krasnow, Erwin, et al. 1982. *The Politics of Broadcast Regulation*. 3rd ed. St. Martin's Press, New York.

————, and Bentley, G. Geoffrey. 1988. *Buying or Building a Broadcast Station: Everything You Want-and Need-to Know but Didn't Know Who to Ask*. 2d ed. National Association of Broadcasters, Washington, DC.

Kraus, Sidney. 1988. *Televised Presidential Debates*

and Public Policy. Lawrence Erlbaum Associates, Hillsdale, NJ.

————, and Davis, Dennis. 1976. *The Effects of Mass Communication on Political Behavior.* Penn State U. Press, University Park, PA.

Kuhn, Raymond, ed. 1985. *The Politics of Broadcasting.* St. Martin's Press, New York.

Kutash, Irwin L., et al. 1978. *Violence: Perspectives on Murder and Aggression.* Jossey-Bass, San Francisco.

Land, Herman W., Associates. 1968. *Television and the Wired City.* National Association of Broadcasters, Washington, DC.

Landry, Robert T. 1946. *This Fascinating Radio Business.* Bobbs-Merrill, Indianapolis.

Lang, Kurt, and Lang, Gladys Engel. 1984. *Politics and Television Re-Viewed.* Sage, Beverly Hills, CA.

————. 1983. *The Battle for Public Opinion: The President, the Press, and the Polls During Watergate.* Columbia U. Press, New York.

Langley, Graham. 1983. *Telecommunications Primer.* Pitman Books, London.

Lapin, S.G. 1973. "Television Broadcasting," in *Great Soviet Encyclopedia.* Vol. 26: 484–486. Moscow.

Lardner, James. 1987. *Fast Forward: Hollywood, The Japanese, and the VCR Wars.* W.W. Norton, New York.

Larson, James. 1984. *Television's Window on the World: International Affairs Coverage on the U.S. Networks.* Ablex, Norwood, NJ.

Lashner, Marilyn A. 1984. *The Chilling Effect in TV News: Intimidation by the Nixon White House.* Praeger, New York.

Lasswell, Harold D. 1952. "Educational Broadcasters as Social Scientists," *Quarterly of Film, Radio, and Television* 7: 150:162.

Lazarsfeld, Paul F., et al. 1944. *The People's Choice: How the Voter Makes Up His Mind in a Presidential Campaign.* Duell, Sloan & Pearce, New York.

Lazarsfeld, Paul F., and Kendall, Patricia L. 1948. *Radio Listening in America.* Prentice-Hall, New York.

LeDuc, Don R. 1973. "Broadcast Legal Documentation: A Four-Dimensional Guide," *Journal of Broadcasting* 17 (Spring): 131–146.

————. 1987. *Beyond Broadcasting: Patterns in Policy and Law.* Longman, New York.

Leinwoll, Stanley. 1979. *From Spark to Satellite: A History of Radio Communication.* Scribner's, New York.

Lent, John A., ed. 1978. *Broadcasting in Asia and the Pacific: A Continental Survey of Radio and Television.* Temple U. Press, Philadelphia.

Lerner, Daniel, and Lyle Nelson, eds. 1977. *Communications Research: A Half Century Appraisal.* East–West Center, Honolulu.

Lesher, Stephan. 1982. *Media Unbound: The Impact of Television Journalism on the Public.* Houghton-Mifflin, Boston.

Lessing, Lawrence. 1956. *Man of High Fidelity: Edwin Howard Armstrong.* Lippincott, New York (Repr. Bantam Books, 1969).

Levin, Harvey J. 1971. *The Invisible Resource: Use and Regulation of the Radio Spectrum.* John Hopkins Press, Baltimore.

Levin, Murray B. 1987. *Talk Radio and the American Dream.* D.C. Heath, Lexington, MA.

Levinson, Richard, and Link, William. 1981. *Stay Tuned: An Inside Look at the Making of Prime-Time Television.* St. Martin's Press, New York.

Lichty, Lawrence W., and Topping, Malachi, eds. 1975. *American Broadcasting: A Source Book on the History of Radio and Television.* Hastings House, New York.

Liebert, Robert M., et al. 1988. *The Early Window: The Effects of Television on Children and Youth.* 3rd ed. Pergamon, New York.

Lindsey, Robert. 1983. "Home Box Office Moves in an Hollywood," *New York Times Magazine* (Jun. 12): 31–71.

Lippman, Theo Jr. 1972. *Spiro Agnew's America.* Norton, New York.

Little, Arthur D., Inc. 1969. *Television Program Production, Procurement, Distribution and Scheduling.* Arthur D. Little, Cambridge, MA.

Long, Mark, ed. 1985. *World Satellite Almanac: The*

Complete Guide to Satellite Transmission & Technology. CommTek Publishing, Boise, ID.

Lowery, Shearon, and De Fleur, Melvin L. 1988. *Milestones in Mass Communication Research: Media Effects*. 2nd ed. Longman, New York.

Lowry, Dennis. 1979. "An Evaluation of Empirical Studies Reported in Seven Journals in the '70s," *Journalism Quarterly* 56 (Summer): 262–268, 282.

Luther, Sara Fletcher. 1988. *The United States and the Direct Broadcast Satellite*. Oxford U. Press, New York.

McCain, Thomas. 1985. "The Invisible Influence: European Audience Research," *InterMedia* (Jul./Sep.): 74–78.

McCavitt, William E., and Pringle, Peter K. 1986. *Electronic Media Management*. Focal Press, Stoneham, MA.

McCombs, Maxwell E., and Shaw, Donald L. 1977. *The Emergence of American Political Issues: The Agenda-Setting Function of the Press*. West Publishing, St. Paul, MN.

McCoy, Ralph E. 1968. *Freedom of the Press: An Annotated Bibliography*. Southern Illinois U. Press, Carbondale, IL.

_____. 1979. *Freedom of the Press: A Bibliocyclopedia Ten-Year Supplement (1967–1977)*. Southern Illinois U. Press, Carbondale, IL.

MacDonald, Dwight. 1953. "Theory of Mass Culture," *Diogenes* 3 (Summer): 5, 13–14.

MacDonald, J. Fred. 1979. *Don't Touch That Dial! Radio Programming in American Life, 1920–1960*. Nelson-Hall, Chicago.

_____. 1983. *Black and White TV: Afro-Americans in Television since 1948*. Nelson-Hall, Chicago.

_____. 1985. *Television and the Red Menace: The Video Road to Vietnam*. Praeger, New York.

McDowell, Edwin. 1979. "Texaco and the Met: A Long Marriage," *New York Times* (Mar. 10): 25.

McGilliam, Clare D., and McLauchlan, William P. 1978. *Hermes Bound: The Policy and Technology of Telecommunications*. Purdue U. Office of Publications, West Lafayette, IN.

McGraw, Thomas K. 1984. *Prophets of Regulation*. Harvard U. Press, Cambridge, MA.

McGraw-Hill Encyclopedia of Electronics and Computers. 1983. McGraw-Hill New York.

McGuire, Bernadette, and LeRoy, David J. 1977. "Audience Mail: Letters to the Broadcaster," *Journal of Communication* 27 (Summer): 79–85.

McLuhan, H. Marshall. 1964. *Understanding Media: The Extensions of Man*. McGraw-Hill, New York.

Maclaurin, W. Rupert. 1949. *Invention and Innovation in the Radio Industry*. Macmillan, New York.

McQuail, Denis. 1983. *Mass Communication Theory: An Introduction*. Sage Publications, Beverly Hills, Ca.

_____, and Windahl, Sven. 1981. *Communication Models for the Study of Mass Communications*. Longman, New York.

_____, and Siune, Karen. 1986. *New Media Politics: Comparative Perspectives in Western Europe*. Sage Publications, Newbury Park, CA.

Macy, John Jr. 1974. *To Irrigate a Wasteland: The Struggle to Shape a Public Television System in the United States*. U. of California Press, Berkeley.

Madow, William G., et al. 1961. *Evaluation of Statistical Methods Used in Obtaining Broadcast Ratings*. House Report 193. 87th Cong., First Sess. Government Printing Office, Washington, DC.

Madsen, Arch. 1984. *60 Minutes: The Power and Politics of America's Most Popular TV News Show*. Dodd, Mead, New York.

Magnant, Robert S. 1977. *Domestic Satellite: An FCC Giant Step Toward Competitive Telecommunications Policy*. Westview Press, Boulder, CO.

Mander, Jerry. 1978. *Four Arguments for the Elimination of Television*. Morrow, New York.

Mansell, Gerard. 1982. *Let the Truth Be Told: 50 Years of BBC External Broadcasting*. Wiedenfeld and Nicolson, London.

Marc, David. 1984. *Democratic Vistas: Television in American Culture*. U. of Pennsylvania Press, Philadelphia.

Marcus, Geoffrey. 1969. *The Maiden Voyage*. Viking, New York.

Marcus, Norman. 1986. *Broadcast and Cable Management.* Prentice-Hall, Englewood Cliffs, NJ.

Markey, Edward J. 1988. "Statement Accompanying Congressional Research Service Letter to House Subcommittee on Telecommunications and Finance, Cases Involving the Federal Communication Commission That Were Reversed..." (21 Mar.) Library of Congress, Washington, D.C.

Marill, Alvin H. 1984. *Movies Made for Television.* New York Zoetrope, New York.

Marschall, Ken. 1987. *The Golden Age of Television.* Exeter Books, New York.

Marsh, Ken. 1974. *Independent Video: A Complete Guide to the Physics, Operation, and Application of the New Television for the Student, the Artist, and for Community TV.* Straight Arrow Books, San Francisco.

Martin, James. 1977. *Future Developments in Telecommunications.* 2nd ed. Prentice-Hall, Englewood Cliffs, NJ.

———. 1982. *Viewdata and the Information Society.* Prentice-Hall, Englewood Cliffs, NJ.

Martin, L. John, and Chardhau, Anju Grover. 1983. *Comparative Mass Media Systems.* Longman, New York.

Matelski, Marilyn J. 1988. *The Soap Opera Evolution: America's Enduring Romance with Daytime Drama.* McFarland, Jefferson, NC.

Matlon, Ronald. 1987. *Index to Journals in Communication Studies Through 1985.* 2nd ed. Speech Communication Association, Annandale, VA.

Matusow, Barbara. 1983. *The Evening Stars: The Making of the Network News Anchor.* Houghton Mifflin, Boston.

Mayer, Martin. 1987. *Making News.* Doubleday & Company, New York.

Meadows, A.J., et al. 1982. *Dictionary of New Information Technology.* Kogan Page, London.

Meeske, Milan D. 1976. "Black Ownership of Broadcast Stations: An FCC Licensing Problem," *Journal of Broadcasting* 20 (Spring): 261–271.

Meringoff, Laurene. 1980. *Children and Advertising: An Annotated Bibliography.* Council of Better Business Bureaus, New York.

Metz, Robert. 1975. *CBS: Reflections in a Bloodshot Eye.* Playboy Press, Chicago.

———. 1977. *The Today Show: An Inside Look....* Playboy Press, Chicago.

Meyersohn, Rolf B. 1957. "Social Research in Television," in Rosenberg and White: 345–357.

Meyrowitz, Joshua. 1985. *No Sense of Place: The Impact of Electronic Media on Social Behavior.* Oxford U. Press, New York.

Miami Herald. 1988. "U.S. Population," (Oct. 5): 9A.

Mickelson, Sig. 1983. *America's Other Voice: The Story of Radio Free Europe and Radio Liberty.* Praeger, New York.

Mickiewicz, Ellen P. 1988. *Split Signals: Television and Politics in the Soviet Union.* Oxford U. Press, New York.

Middleton, Kent R. and Chamberlin, Bill F. 1988. *The Law of Public Communication.* Longman, New York.

Midgley, Ned. 1948. *The Advertising and Business Side of Radio.* Prentice-Hall, New York.

Minow, Newton N. 1964. *Equal Time: The Private Broadcaster and the Public Interest.* Antheneum, New York.

———. 1985. "Being Fair to the Fairness Doctrine," *New York Times* (Aug. 27): A23.

Mogel, Leonard, 1988. *Making It in the Media Professions.* The Globe Pequot Press, Chester, CT.

Murphy, Brian. 1983. *The World Wired Up: Unscrambling the New Communications Puzzle.* Comedia, London.

Murphy, Jonne. 1980. *Handbook of Radio Advertising.* Chilton, Radnor, PA.

NAB (National Association of Broadcasters, Washington, DC.)
Annual. *Radio Financial Report.*
Annual. *Television Financial Report.*
Semiannual. *Broadcasting and Government.*
1978 *The Television Code.*
1982 *Cuban Interference to United States AM Broadcasting Stations.*
1984 *Broadcasting Bibliography: A Guide to the Literature of Radio and Television.* 2d ed.

1985 *Profile: Broadcasting, 1985.*

1988a *Television Employer Compensation and Fringe Benefit Report.*

1988b *Radio Employer Compensation and Fringe Benefit Report.*

1988c Media Watch," *Broadcast Marketing & Technology News* 5 (Dec.).

1988d *Broadcast Research Definitions.*

1988e (Political Broadcast Expenditures, press release)

1988f *RadiOutlook: Forces Shaping the Radio Industry.*

1988g *NAB Legal Guide to FCC Broadcast Regulations.* 3d ed.

NAPTS (National Association of Public Television Stations). 1984. *Public Television and Radio and State Governments.* 2 vols. NAPTS, Washington, DC.

Naisbitt, John. 1982. *Megatrends: Ten New Directions Changing Our Lives.* Warner Books, New York.

National Institute of Mental Health. 1982. *Television and Behavior: The Years of Scientific Progress and Implications for the Eighties.* 2 vols. Government Printing Office, Washington, DC.

National Science Foundation. 1976. *Social Services and Cable TV.* Government Printing Office, Washington, DC.

National Textbook Co. *Opportunities in Broadcasting* (1983); *Opportunities in Cable Television* (1984); and *Opportunities in Telecommunications* (1984), 3 vols. Author, Lincolnwood, IL.

NCTA (National Cable Television Association). 1985. *Cable Television Salaries . . . National Averages.* NCTA, Washington, DC.

Negrine, Ralph M. 1985. *Cable Television and the Future of Broadcasting.* St. Martin's Press, New York.

_____, ed. 1988. *Satellite Broadcasting: The Politics & Implications of the New Media.* Routledge, New York.

Nesson, Ron. 1980. "Now Television's the Kingmaker," *TV Guide* (May 10): 4.

Newcomb, Horace. 1987. *Television: The Critical View.* Oxford U. Press, New York.

_____, and Alley, Robert S. 1983. *The Producer's Medium: Conversations with Creators of American TV.* Oxford U. Press, New York.

Newsweek. 1963. "As 175 Million Americans Watched," (Dec. 9): 52.

New York Times. 1984. "Television Surpasses Radio News in Survey," (Sep. 1): Y13.

_____, 1985. "And Now, the Media MegaMerger." (Mar. 24):3:1.

New Yorker. 1985. "Talk of the Town," *The New Yorker* (16 Sep.): 29.

Nielsen Company, A.C. 1989. *The Television Audience, 1989.* Author, Northbrook, IL.

Nimmo, Dan, ed. 1979. *Communication Yearbook 3.* Transaction Books, New Brunswick, NJ.

_____, and Combs, James E. 1985. *Nightly Horrors: Crisis Coverage in Television Network News.* U. of Tennessee Press, Knoxville.

Nizer, Louis. 1966. *The Jury Returns.* Doubleday, New York.

Noam, Eli M., ed. 1985. *Video Media Competition: Regulation, Economics, and Technology.* Columbia U. Press, New York.

Noble, John H. 1987. *The Harvard Guide to Careers in Mass Media.* Harvard U. Press, Cambridge, MA.

Noll, A. Michael. 1988A. *Introduction to Telecommunication Electronics.* Artech House, Boston, MA.

_____. 1988B. *Television Technology: Fundamentals and Future Prospects.* Artech, Norwood, NJ.

Nordenstreng, Kaarle. 1984. *The Mass Media Declaration of UNESCO.* Ablex, Norwood, NJ.

NTIA (National Telecommunications and Information Administration, U.S. Department of Commerce).

Regularly Updated. *Manual of Regulations and Procedures for Federal Radio Frequency Management.* Government Printing Office, Washington, DC.

1981 *Direct Broadcast Satellites: Policies, Prospects, and Potential Competition.* Government Printing Office, Washington, DC.

Nye, Russel B. 1970. *The Unembarrassed Muse: The Popular Arts in America.* Dial, New York.

O'Connor, John E., ed. 1983. *American History/American Television: Interpreting the Video Past.* Ungar, New York.

O'Donnell, Lewis B., et al. 1989. *Radio Station Operations: Management and Employee Perspectives.* Wadsworth, Belmont, CA.

Ohio State University. School of Journalism. 1988. *1987 Journalism and Mass Communications Graduate Survey: Summary Report.* Ohio State University, Columbus, OH.

Oringel, Robert S. 1989. *Audio Control Handbook for Radio and Television Broadcasting.* Focal Press, Boston, MA.

Orlik, Peter B. 1988. *Critiquing Radio and Television Content.* Allyn and Bacon, Boston, MA.

Osborn, J. Wes., et al. 1979. "Prime Time Network Television Programming Preemptions," *Journal of Broadcasting* 23 (Fall): 427–436.

O'Shaughnessy, Hugh. 1985. *Grenada: An Eyewitness Account of the U.S. Invasion and the Caribbean History That Provided It.* Dodd Mead, New York.

OTA (Office of Technology Assessment). *Radiofrequency Use and Management: Impacts from the World Administrative Radio Conference of 1979.* 1982. Office of Technology Assessment, U.S. Congress, Government Printing Office, Washington, DC.

Overman, Michael. 1978. *Understanding Sound: Video & Film Recording.* Tab Books, Blue Ridge Summit, PA.

Owen, Bruce M. 1975. *Economics and Freedom of Expression: Media Structure and the First Amendment.* Ballinger, Cambridge, MA.

————, et al. 1974. *Television Economics.* Lexington Books, Lexington, MA.

Paley, William S. 1979. *As It Happened: A Memoir.* Doubleday, New York.

Palmer, Edward L. 1988. *Television and America's Children: A Crisis of Neglect.* Oxford U. Press, New York.

Paper, Lewis, 1987. *Empire: William S. Paley and the Making of CBS.* St. Martin's Press, New York.

Parsons, Patrick. 1987. *Cable Television and the First Amendment.* Lexington Books, Lexington, MA.

Passer, Harold C. 1953. *The Electrical Manufacturers, 1875–1900.* Harvard U. Press, Cambridge, MA.

Passman, Arnold. 1971. *The Deejays.* Macmillan, New York.

Paterson, Richard. Annual. *TV and Video International Guide.* Tantivy Press, London.

Paul Kagan Associates. Annual. *The Kagan Cable TV Financial Databook.* Author, Carmel, CA.

Paulu, Burton. 1967. *Radio and Television Broadcasting on the European Continent.* U. of Minnesota Press, Minneapolis.

————. 1974. *Radio and Television Broadcasting in Eastern Europe.* U. of Minnesota Press, Minneapolis.

————. 1981. *Television and Radio in the United Kingdom.* U. of Minnesota Press, Minneapolis.

Pember, Don R. 1984. *Mass Media Law.* 3rd ed. Wm. C. Brown, Dubuque, IA.

Performing Arts Books: 1876–1981. 1981. Bowker, New York.

Phillips, Mary Alice Mayer. 1972. *CATV: A History of Community Antennea Television.* Northwestern U. Press, Evanston, IL.

Phillips Publications. 1984. *Interactive Cable TV Handbook.* 1984. Author, Bethesda. MD.

Pichaske, David. 1979. *A Generation in Motion: Popular Music and Culture of the Sixties.* Schirmer Books, New York.

Pierce, John R. 1981. *Signals: The Telephone and Beyond.* Freeman, New York.

Pike and Fischer. *Radio Regulation*. Author, Washington, DC.

PLI (Practicing Law Institute, New York).
Annual. *Communication Law*.
1985. *The New Era in CATV: The Cable Franchise Policy and Communications Act of 1984*.

Ploman, Edward. 1982. *International Law Governing Communications and Information*. Greenwood Press, Westport, CT.

Poltrack, David. 1983. *Television Marketing: Network, Local, and Cable*. McGraw-Hill, New York.

Pool, Ithiel de Sola, ed. 1977. *The Social Impact of the Telephone*. MIT Press, Cambridge, MA.

————. 1983. *Technologies of Freedom*. Harvard U. Press, Cambridge, MA.

Pope, Daniel. 1983. *The Making of Modern Advertising*. Basic Books, New York.

Post, Steve. 1974. *Playing in the FM Band*. Viking Press, New York.

Powe, Lucas A., Jr. 1987. *American Broadcasting and the First Amendment*. U. of California Press, Berkeley, CA.

Powers, Ron. 1977. *The Newscasters*. St. Martin's Press, New York.

————. 1984. *Supertube: The Rise of Television Sports*. Coward-McCann, New York.

Prentiss, Stan. 1987. *Satellite Communication*. 2nd ed. TAB Books, Blue Ridge Summit, PA.

President's Study Commission on International Broadcasting ("Stanton Commission"). 1973. *The Right to Know*. Government Printing Office, Washington, DC.

Presidential Commission of Broadcasting to Cuba. 1982. *Final Report*. Government Printing Office, Washington, DC.

Pringle, Peter K. and Clinton, Helen H. 1989. *Radio and Television: A Selected, Annotated Bibliography, Supplement Two: 1982–1986*. Scarecrow Press, Metuchen, NJ.

Quinlan, Sterling. 1979. *Inside ABC: American Broadcasting Company's Rise to Power*. Hastings House, New York.

Rader, Benjamin G. 1984. *In Its Own Image: How Television Has Transformed Sports*. Free Press, New York.

Rather, Dan. 1987. "From Murrow to Mediocrity?" *New York Times* (10 Mar.): A27.

Ray, Michael L., & Webb, Peter H. 1978. "Advertising Effectiveness in a Crowded Environment." Preliminary Research Report. 78-113. Marketing Research Institute, Cambridge, MA.

Read, Oliver, and Welsh, Walter. 1976. *From Tin Foil to Stereo: Evolution of the Phonograph*. 2nd ed. Sams, Indianapolis.

Read, William H. 1976. *America's Mass Media Merchants*. Johns Hopkins U. Press, Baltimore.

Reed, Maxine, and Reed, Robert. 1987. *Career Opportunities in Television, Video and Cable*. 2nd ed. Facts on File, New York.

Reid, T.R. 1984. *The Chip*. Simon and Schuster, New York.

Reinsch, Leonard, and Ellis, Elmo. 1960. *Radio Station Management*. 2nd. ed. Harper, New York.

Rice, Jean, ed. 1983. *Cable TV Renewals & Refranchising*. Communications Press, Washington, DC.

Rice, Ronald, et al. 1984. *The New Media: Communication, Research, & Technology*. Sage Publications, Newbury Park, NJ.

Rivers, William L., et al. 1980. *Responsibility in Mass Communication*. 3rd ed. Harper & Row, New York.

Rivkin, Steven R. 1978. *A New Guide to Federal Cable Television Regulations*. MIT Press, Cambridge, MA.

Roberts, Donald F., and Bachen, Christine M. 1981. "Mass Communication Effects," in *Annual Review of Psychology*: 307–356.

Robinson, Michael J., and Sheehan, Margaret A. 1983. *Over the Wire and On TV: CBS and UPI in Campaign '80*. Russel Sage Foundation, New York.

Robinson, Thomas P. 1943. *Radio Networks and the Federal Government.* Columbia U. Press, New York.

Rogers, Everett, and Balle, Francis. 1985. *The Media Revolution in America and Western Europe.* Ablex, Norwood, NJ.

Roman, James. 1983. *Cablemania.* Prentice-Hall, Englewood Cliffs, NJ.

Roper Organization. 1989. *America's Watching: The 1989 TIO/Roper Report.* 16th Report in a Series. Television Information Office, New York (distributed by National Association of Broadcasters, Washington, DC.)

————. 1987. *Electronic Media Career Preparation Study: Executive Summary.* Author, New York.

Rose, Brian G., ed. 1985. *TV Genres: A Handbook and Reference Guide.* Greenwood Press, Westport, CT.

————. 1986. *Television and the Performing Arts: A Handbook and Reference Guide to American Cultural Programming.* Greenwood Press, Westport, CT.

Rose, C.B., Jr. 1940. *National Policy for Radio Broadcasting.* Harper, New York.

Rosen, Philip T. 1980. *The Modern Stentors: Radio Broadcasters and the Federal Government 1920–1934.* Greenwood Press, Westport, CT.

————. 1988. *International Handbook of Broadcasting Systems.* Greenwood Press, Westport, CT.

Rosenberg, Bernard, and White, David Manning, eds. 1957. *Mass Culture: The Popular Arts in America.* Free Press, Glencoe, IL.

Routt, Edd, et al. 1978. *The Radio Format Conundrum.* Hastings House, New York.

Rowan, Ford. 1984. *Broadcast Fairness: Doctrine, Practice, Prospects.* Longman, New York.

Rowland, Willard. 1983. *The Politics of TV Violence: Policy Uses of Communication Research.* Sage Publications, Beverly Hills, Ca.

RR (Radio Regulation): see under FCCR, 1982, *AM Stereophonic Broadcasting.*

Rubin, Bernard. 1967. *Political Television.* Wadsworth, Belmont, CA.

Rutkis, Denis S. 1976. "A Report on Simultaneous Television Network Coverage of Presidential Addresses to the Nation." (Jan. 12). Congressional Research Service, Washington, DC.

Sabine, Gordon A. 1980. *Broadcasting in Virginia: Benchmark '79.* Department of Communications, Virginia Polytechnic, Blacksburg, VA.

Sadowski, Robert P. 1974. "Broadcasting and State Statutory Laws," *Journal of Broadcasting* 18 (Fall): 433–450.

Safran, Claire. 1980. "Children's Television: What Are the Best—and Worst—Shows?" *TV Guide* (Aug. 9): 2.

Sanders, Marlene, and Rock, Maria. 1988. *Waiting for Prime Time: The Women of Television News.* U. of Illinois Press, Chicago.

Sarnoff, David. 1968. *Looking Ahead: The Papers of David Sarnoff.* McGraw-Hill, New York.

Saudek, Robert. 1973. "Omnibus Was Like Running Five Broadway Openings Every Week," *TV Guide* (Aug. 11): 22.

Schaefer, R. Murray. 1977. *The Tuning of the World.* Knopf, New York.

Schiller, Herbert I. 1971. *Mass Communications and American Empire.* Beacon Press, Boston.

Schmidt, Benno C. 1976. *Freeedom of the Press vs. Public Access.* Praeger, New York.

Schneider, Cy. 1987. *Children's Television: The Art, The Business, and How It Works.* NTC Business Books, Chicago.

Schofield, Lemuel B. 1979. "Don't Look for the Hometown Touch," *TV Guide* (Apr. 14): 39.

Schonfeld, Reese. 1983. "Pop News: TV's Growth Industry," *Channels* (Sep./Oct.): 33–38.

Schramm, Wilbur. 1973. *Men, Messages and Media: A Look at Human Communication.* Harper & Row, New York.

Schubert, Paul. 1928. *The Electric Word: The Rise of Radio.* Macmillan, New York.

Schultz, Richard H., and Godson, Roy. 1984. *Dezinformatisia: Active Measures in Soviet Strategy*. Pergamon-Brassey's, Washington, DC.

Schultze, Quentin J. 1988. "Evangelical Radio and the Rise of the Electronic Church, 1921–1948." *Journal of Broadcasting and Electronic Media* 32 (Summer): 289–306.

Scott, James D. 1977. *Bringing Premium Entertainment into the Home via Pay-Cable TV*. U. of Michigan Graduate School of Business Administration, Ann Arbor.

Seehafer, Gene F. and Laemmer, Jack M. 1959. *Successful Television and Radio Advertising*. 2nd ed. McGraw-Hill, New York.

Senate CC (U.S. Congress, Senate Committee on Commerce. Title of Committee has varied. Government Printing Office, Washington, D.C.)
1930 *Commission on Communications*. Hearings. 71st. Cong., Second Sess.
1944 *To Amend the Communications Act of 1934*. Hearings, 78th Cong., First Sess.
1948 *Progress of FM Radio*. Hearings. 80th Cong., Second Sess.
1972 *Surgeon General's Report by Scientific Advisory Committee on Television and Social Behavior*. Hearings. 92nd Cong., Second Sess.
1980 *Amendments to the Communications Act of 1934*. Hearings, 96th Cong., First Sess.

Sendall, Bernard. 1982–1983. *Independent Television in Britain*. 2 vols. Macmillan Press, London.

Sethi, S. Prakash. 1977. *Advocacy Advertising and Large Corporations*. Lexington Books, Lexington, MA.

Settel, Irving. 1967. *A Pictorial History of Radio*. 2nd ed. Grosset & Dunlap, New York.

———. 1983. *A Pictorial History of Television*. 2nd ed. Ungar, New York.

Shaffer, William Drew, and Wheelwright, Richard. 1983. *Creating Original Programming for Cable TV*. Communications Press, Washington, DC.

Shannon, Claude E., and Weaver, W. 1949. *The Mathematical Theory of Communication*. U. of Illinois Press, Urbana.

Shapiro, George H., Kurland, Philip B. and Mercurio, James P. 1983. *'CableSpeech': The Case for First Amendment Protection*. Law and Business, Inc., New York.

Shearer, Benjamin F., and Huxford, Marilyn. 1983. *Communications and Society: A Bibliography on Communications Technologies and Their Social Impact*. Greenwood Press, Westport, CT.

Sherman, Barry L. 1987. *Telecommunications Management: The Broadcast and Cable Industries*. McGraw-Hill, New York.

Shiers, George, and Shiers, May. 1972. *Bibliography of the History of Electronics*. Scarecrow Press, Metuchen, NJ.

Short, K.R.M. 1986. *Western Broadcasting Over the Iron Curtain*. St. Martin's Press, New York.

Shudson, Michael. 1984. *Advertising, The Uneasy Persuasion: Its Dubious Impact on American Society*. Basic Books, New York.

Shulman, Arthur, and Youman, Roger. 1966. *How Sweet It Was: Television—A Pictorial Commentary*. Shorecrest, New York.

Sieber, Robert. 1988. "Industry Views on the People Meter: Cable Networks," *Gannett Center Journal* 2 (Summer): 70–74.

Siepmann, Charles. 1946. *Radio's Second Chance*. Atlantic-Little, Brown, Boston.

———. 1950. *Radio, Television and Society*. Oxford U. Press, New York.

Signorelli, Nancy. 1985. *Role Portrayal and Stereotyping on Television*. Greenwood Press, Westport, Ct.

———, and Gerbner, George, comp. 1988. *Violence and Terror in the Mass Media: An Annotated Bibliography*. Greenwood Press, Westport, CT.

Sikes, Rhea G. 1980. "Programs for Children: Public Television in the 1970's," *Public Telecommunications Review* 8 (Sep/Oct): 7.

Silvey, Robert. 1974. *Who's Listening? The Story of BBC Audience Research*. George Allen & Unwin, London.

Simmons, Steven J. 1978. *The Fairness Doctrine and the Media*. U. of California Press, Berkeley.

Singh, Indu B., ed. 1983. *Telecommunications in Year 2000: National and International Perspectives*. Ablex, Norwood, NJ.

Singleton, Loy A. 1986. *Telecommunications in the Information Age*. 2nd ed. Ballinger, Cambridge, MA.

Sklar, Robert. 1984. *Rocking America: How the All-Hit Radio Stations Took Over*. St. Martin's Press, New York.

Slide, Anthony. 1982. *Great Radio Personalities in Historic Photographs*. Dover, New York.

Sloan, William David. 1989. *American Journalism History: An Annotated Bibliography*. Greenwood Press, Westport, CT.

Smith, Anthony. 1973. *The Shadow in the Cave: The Broadcaster, His Audience, and the State*. U. of Illinois Press, Urbana.

————. 1980. *The Geopolitics of Information: How Western Culture Dominates the World*. Oxford U. Press, New York.

Smith, Bruce Lannes, et al. 1946. *Propaganda, Communication and Public Opinion*. Princeton U. Press, Princeton, NJ.

Smith, F. Leslie. 1974. "Hunger in America Controversy: Another View," *Journal of Broadcasting*. 18 (Winter): 79–83.

Smith, Myron J. 1984. *U.S. Television Network News: A Guide to Sources in English*. McFarland & Co., Jefferson, NC.

Smith, Richrd A. 1985. "TV: The Light That Failed," *Fortune* (December): 78.

Smith, Robert R. 1980. *Beyond the Wasteland: The Criticism of Broadcasting*. Rev. ed. Speech Communication Association, Annandale, VA.

Smolla, Rodney A. 1986. *Suing the Press: Libel, the Media, & Power*. Oxford U. Press, New York.

Snow, Marcellus S. 1987. *The International Telecommunications Satellite Organization (INTELSAT)*. Nomos Verlagsgesellschaft, Baden-Baden.

Socolow, A. Walter. 1939. *The Law of Radio Broadcasting*. 2 vols. Baker, Voorhis, New York.

Soley, Lawrence C. and Nichols, John S. 1987. *Clandetine Radio Broadcasting: A Study of Revolutionary and Counterrevolutionary Electronic Communication*. Praeger, New York.

Spitzer, Matthew L. 1986. *Seven Dirty Words and Six Other Stories*. Yale U. Press, New Haven, CT.

Spottiswoode, Raymond, ed. 1969. *The Focal Encyclopedia of Film and Television Techniques*. Hastings House, New York.

SRDS (Standard Rate and Data Service, Skokie, IL) Monthly. *Spot Radio Rates and Data*. Monthly. *Spot Television Rates and Data*.

Standard & Poor. 1988. "Networks' Dynasty Dims," (4 July): 16.

Stedman, Raymond W. 1977. *The Serials: Suspense and Drama by Installment*. 2nd ed. U of Oklahoma Press, Norman.

Stein, Harry. 1979. "How 60 Minutes' Makes News," *New York Times Magazine*. (May 6): 28.

Steiner, Gary A. 1963. *The People Look at Television: A Study of Audience Attitudes*. Knopf, New York.

Stempel, Guido H., and Westley, Bruce H., eds. 1981. *Research Methods in Mass Communication*. Prentice-Hall, Englewood Cliffs, NJ.

Sterling, Christopher H. 1982. "Television and Radio Broadcasting," Chapter 6; and "Cable and Pay Television," Chapter 7 in Compaine et al., 299–450.

————. 1984. *Electronic Media: A Guide to Trends in Broadcasting and Newer Technologies, 1920–1983*. Praeger, New York.

————, 1988. "Billions in Licenses, Millions in Fees: Comparative Renewals and the RKO Mess," *Gannet Center Journal* (Winter): 53–53.

————, and Haight, Timothy R. 1978. *The Mass Media: Aspen Institute Guide to Communication Industry Trends*. Praeger, New York.

————, and Kittross, John M. 1990. *Stay Tuned: A Concise History of American Broadcasting*. 2nd ed. Wadsworth, Belmont, CA.

Stone, David M. 1985. *Nixon and the Politics of Public Television*. Garland, New York.

Stone, Vernon A. 1978. "News Staff Size, Turnover, and Sources Surveyed," *RTNDA Communicator.* 32 (August): 8.

Straubhaar, Joseph D. 1982. "The Decline of American Influence on Brazilian Television," Paper presented at V Ciclo de Estudos Interdisciplinares da Comunicao, Sao Paulo (September).

Strong, William S. 1984. *The Copyright Book: A Practical Guide.* 2d ed. MIT Press, Cambridge, MA.

Sugar, Bert Randolph. 1978. *"The Thrill of Victory": The Inside Story of ABC Sports.* Hawthorn Books, New York.

Surgeon General, Scientific Advisory Committee on Television and Social Behavior. 1972. *Television and Growing Up: The Impact of Televised Violence.* Government Printing Office, Washington, DC.

Swerdlow, Joel. 1984. *Beyond Debate: A Paper on Televised Presidential Debates.* Twentieth Century Fund, New York.

Tan, Alexis S. 1986. *Mass Communication Theories and Research.* Macmillan Publishing, New York.

Tannenbaum, Percy H., and Kostrich, Leslie J. 1983. *Turned-On TV/Turned-Off Votes.* Sage, Beverly Hills, CA.

Tannenwald, Peter. 1985. "Selling Off the Spectrum," *Channels* (July–Aug.): 41–43.

Taylor, John P. 1980. *Direct-to-Home Satellite Broadcasting.* Television/Radio Age, New York.

TCAF (Temporary Commission on Alternative Financing for Public Telecommunications).
1982. *Alternative Financing Options for Public Broadcasting.* Vol. 1.
1983. *Final Report.* Federal Communications Commission, Washington, DC.

Tebbel, John. 1975. *The Media in America.* Crowell, New York.

———, and Watts, Sarah Miles. 1985. *The Press and the Presidency.* Oxford U. Press, New York.

Technology & Economics, Inc. 1980. *The Emergence of Pay Cable Television.* 4 vols. NTIA, Washington, DC.

Tedford, Thomas L. 1985. *Freedom of Speech in the United States.* Southern Illinois U. Press, Carbondale.

Telemedia. 1983. "Where Does the Typical Station's Time Sales Dollar Come From?" (Nov./Dec.): 27.

Television Age International. 1985. "Worldwide TV Set Count," (February): 48–50.

Temlin, Peter and Galambos, Louis. 1987. *The Fall of the Bell System.* Cambridge U. Press, New York.

Terry, Clifford. 1976. "Vast Wasteland Revisited," *TV Guide* (Oct. 16): 4.

Thomas, Cal. 1988. "End of the Moral Majority?" (9 Nov.) Los Angeles Times Syndicate.

Thompson, Robert L. 1947. *Wiring a Continent: The History of the Telegraph Industry in the United States, 1832–66.* Princeton U. Press, Princeton, NJ.

Time-Life Books. 1986. *Communications: Understanding Computers.* Author, Chicago.

Toffler, Alvin. 1980. *The Third Wave.* Morrow, New York.

Toll, Robert C. 1982. *The Entertainment Machine: American Show Business in the Twentieth Century.* Oxford U. Press, New York.

Truax, Barry. 1985. *Acoustic Communication.* Ablex, Norwood, NJ.

Tunstall, Jeremy. 1977. *The Media Are American: Anglo-American in the World.* Columbia U. Press, New York.

———. 1984. *The Media in Britain.* Columbia U. Press, New York.

———. 1986. *Communications Deregulation: The Unleashing of America's Communications Industry.* Basil Blackwell, New York.

———, and Walker, David. 1981. *Media Made in California: Hollywood, Politics, and the News.* Oxford U. Press, New York.

Turow, Joseph. 1981. *Entertainment, Education and the Hard Sell: Three Decades of Network Children's Television.* Praeger, New York.

———. 1984. *Media Industries: The Production of News and Entertainment.* Longman, New York.

————. 1989. *Playing Doctor: Television, Story-telling and Medical Power*. Oxford U. Press, New York.

TV/Radio Age International 1988. "Worldwide TV Set Count." (Oct.): 147–150.

Tydeman, John, et al. 1982. *Teletext and Videotex in the United States: Market Potential, Technology, and Public Policy Issues*. McGraw-Hill, New York.

Tynan, Kenneth. 1979. *Show People: Profiles in Entertainment*. Simon & Schuster, New York.

Tyne, Gerald F. J. 1977. *Saga of the Vacuum Tube*. Howard W. Sams, Indianapolis.

Twentieth Century Fund. 1979. *A Free and Balanced Flow*. Lexington Books, Lexington, MA.

Udelson, Joseph H. 1982. *The Great Television Race: A History of the American Television Industry 1925–1941*. U. of Alabama Press, University, AL.

UNESCO (United Nations Educational, Scientific and Cultural Organization, Paris).
Various Dates. *Communication Policies in . . .* [various countries, by various authors] Annual. *Statistical Yearbook*.
1975 *World Communication: A 200 Country Survey of Press, Radio, Television, Film*.
1979 *Statistics on Radio and Television, 1960–1976*.
1980 *Many Voices, One World: Communications and Society Today and Tomorrow* ("MacBride Commission Report").
1987 *Latest Statistics on Radio and Television Broadcasting*.

US (*United States Reports*). Government Printing Office, Washington, D.C.
1919 *Schenk v. U.S.* 249 US 47.
1937 *FTC v. Standard Education Society*. 302 US 112.
1940 *FCC v. Sander Bros. Radio Station*. 309 US 470.
1942 *Marconi Wireless Telegraph Company of America v. U.S.* 320 US 1.
1943 *NBC v. U.S.* 319 US 190.
1949 *Terminiello v. Chicago*. 337 US 1.
1951 *Dennis v. U.S.* 341 US 494.
1959 *Farmers Educational Cooperative v. WDAY*. 360 US 525.
1964 *New York Times v. Sullivan*. 376 US 254.
1965a *FTC v. Colgate-Palmolive*. 380 US 374.
1965b *Estes v. Texas*. 381 US 532.
1968a *U.S. v. Southwestern Cable*. 392 US 157.
1968b *Fortnightly Corp. v. United Artists Television*. 392 US 390.
1969 *Red Lion v. FCC*. 395 US 367.
1973a *CBS v. Democratic National Committee*. 412 US 94.
1973b *Miller v. California* 413 US 15.
1974a *National Cable Television Association v. U.S. and FCC*. 415 US 336.
1974b *Miami Herald v. Tornillo*. 418 US 241.
1974c *Gertz v. Welch*. 418 US 323.
1978a *FCC v. National Citizen's Committee for Broadcasting*. 436 US 775.
1978b *FCC v. Pacifica Foundation*. 438 US 726.
1979 *Herbert v. Lando*. 441 US 153.
1981 *Chandler v. Florida*. 449 US 560.
1984a *Universal Studios v. Sony*. 464 US 417.
1984b *FCC v. League of Women Voters of California*. 484 US 364.
1986 *City of Los Angeles and Department of Water and Power v. Preferred Communications, Inc.* 476 US 488.

USACPD (U.S. Advisory Commission on Public Diplomacy). Annual. *Report to the Congress and the President of the United States*. Government Printing Office, Washington, DC.

U.S. Bureau of the Census. 1935. *Radio Broadcasting*. Government Printing Office, 1935.

U.S. Commission on Civil Rights. 1977, 1979. *Window Dressing on the Set: Women and Minorities in Television*. 2 vols. Government Printing Office, Washington, DC.

U.S. Congress, House of Representtives. Irregular. *Radio Laws of the United States*. Government Printing Office, Washington, DC (frequently revised).

USNCU (U.S. National Commission for Unesco). 1982. "A Critical Assessment of U.S. Participation in UNESCO," Department of State Pub. 9297. Government Printing Office, Washington, DC.

Van Gerpen, Maurice. 1979. *Privileged Communication and the Press: The Citizen's Right to Know Versus the Law's Right to Confidential News Source Evidence.* Greenwood Press, Westport, CT.

Vaughn, Robert. 1972. *Only Victims: A Study of Show Business Black-Listing.* Putnam, New York.

Vitale, Joseph. 1988. "Sad News at Black Rock, Good News from the Field," *Channels Field Guide 1988:* 36.

Vogel, Harold L. 1986. *Entertainment Industry Economics: A Guide for Financial Analysis.* Cambridge U. Press, London.

Warner, Charles. 1986. *Broadcast Cable and Selling.* Wadsworth, Belmont, CA.

Warner, Harry P. 1948. *Radio and Television Law.* Matthew Bender, Albany, NY.

———. 1953. *Radio and Television Rights.* Matthew Bender, Albany, NY.

Watkinson, John. 1988. *The Art of Digital Audio.* Focal Press, Stoneham, MA.

Weaver, Sylvester L. 1955. "The Form of the Future," *Broadcasting-Telecasting* (May 30): 56.

Webb, G. Kent. 1983. *The Economics of Cable Television.* Lexington Books, Lexington, MA.

Webster, James. 1985. "Program Audience Duplication: A Study of Television Inheritance Effects," *Journal of Broadcasting and Electronic Media* 29 (Spring): 121–133.

Webster, Lance, et al. 1983. *Advertising and Promotion.* Hastings House, New York.

Welch, Randy. 1985. "The Builder of Cable Empires," *Channels* (Jan./Feb.): 45.

Wenham, Brian, ed. 1982. *The Third Age of Broadcasting.* Faber and Faber, London.

Wertheim, Frank. 1979. *Radio Comedy.* Oxford U. Press, New York.

White, David M. 1950. "The 'Gate Keeper': A Case Study in the Selection of News," *Journalism Quarterly* 27 (Fall): 383–390.

White, Llewellyn. 1947. *The American Radio.* U. of Chicago Press, Chicago.

White, Rita Lauria and White, Harold M., Jr. 1988. *The Law and Regulation of International Space Communication.* Artech House, Norwood, MA.

Whiteside, Thomas. 1985. "Cable," *The New Yorker* (May 20): 45; (May 27): 43; and (June 3): 82.

Whitman, Alden. 1973. "William Benton Dies Here At 73, Leader in Politics and Education," Obituary, *New York Times* (Mar. 3): 1.

Whitney, Dwight. 1974. "Cinema's Stepchild Grows Up," *TV Guide* (July 20): 21.

Wildman, Steven S. and Siwek, Stephen E. 1988. *International Trade in Films and Television Programs.* Ballinger Publishing Co., Cambridge, MA.

Williams, Christian. 1981. *Lead, Follow, or Get Out of the Way: The Story of Ted Turner.* Times Books, New York.

Wilson, H. H. 1961. *Pressure Group: The Campaign for Commercial Television.* Rutgers U. Press, New Brunswick, NJ.

Wimmer, Roger, and Joseph Dominick. 1987. *Mass Media Research: An Introduction.* 2d ed. Wadsworth, Belmont, CA.

Winn, Marie. 1985. *The Plug-In Drug: Television, Children, and the Family.* 2d ed. Penguin Books, New York.

Winston, Brian. 1986. *Misunderstanding Media.* Harvard U. Press, Cambridge, MA.

Winzenburg, Stephen M. 1987. "How Televangelists Use their Air Time," Unpublished Paper, Florida Southern College.

———. 1988. "Swaggart's Sin Results in Increased Fund Raising on Program," (5 Apr.) News Release, Florida Southern College.

———. 1988. "On Understanding TV Evangelists," *Broadcasting* (18 Jul.): 25.

Witherspoon, John, and Roselle Kovitz. 1987. *The History of Public Broadcasting.* Current, Washington, DC.

Wolfe, Charles H., ed. 1949. *Modern Radio Advertising*. Funk & Wagnalls, New York.

Wood, Donald N., and Wylie, Donald G. 1977. *Educational Telecommunications*. Wadsworth, Belmont, CA.

Woolery, George W. 1983–1984. *Children's Television: The First Thirty-Five Years, 1946–1981*. 2 vols. Scarecrow Press, Metuchen, NJ.

World Radio-TV Handbook. Annual. Billboard, New York.

Wurtzel, Alan and Acker, Stephen R. 1989. *Television Production*. 3d ed. McGraw-Hill, New York.

Yoakam, Richard, and Cremer, Charles. 1988. *ENG: Television News and the New Technology*. 2nd ed. Southern Illinois U. Press, Carbondale.

Zettl, Herbert, 1984. *Television Production Handbook*. 4th ed. Wadsworth, Belmont, CA

Ziegler, Sharilyn K. and Howard, Herbert H. 1984. *Broadcast Advertising*. 2nd ed. Grid Inc., Columbus, OH.

Zoglin, Richard, and Ainslie, Peter. 1984. "Where's the Soaps," *Time* (Aug. 13): 96.

Zuckman, Harvey et al. 1988. *Mass Communications Law in a Nutshell*. 3d ed. West Publishing, St. Paul, MN.

INDEX

A & E. *See* Arts & Entertainment Network

ABC (radio network): affiliates of, 190 (table); breaks network recording ban, 56; divides into formula-specific subnets, 327; origin of, 59

ABC (TV network): affiliate clearance problems of, 195; cable TV investment of, 209; Capital Cities merger, 98–99; carries Army-McCarthy hearings, 78 n.; cuts news staff, 249; daytime programs of, 304; development of network, 72; news programs of, 321, 322 (photo), 323; sale of, 98–99; self-regulation by, 239–240; sports programs of, 310, 313 (graph), 314; takes ratings lead, 97–98, 194

ABSAT (ABC news coöp), 196

Absorption: atmospheric, 170; of sound, 114. *See also* Attenuation

Absorption, wave, as propagation factor, 124

A/B switch (cable TV/home TV antenna), 177, 192

AC. *See* Alternating Current

Access (to news): in courtrooms, 472, 473 (photo); & libel/privacy laws, 469. *See also* Access channels; Prime-time access; Access time

Access channels, cable TV: basics, 347–348; in franchise, 450–451; law requiring, 82

Access time (PTAR): & affiliate schedules, 343; basics, 333, 334 (exhib.); as daypart, 277, 278 (table), 279 (table); importance of, to affiliates, 289; programs made for, 335–336; & public affairs, 325; & syndication, 334, 335

Access to information, public, 478–479

Access to media: by advertisers, 482–483; by political candidates, 475–477, 500–501; by the public, 477–482, 501–502. *See also* Access channels; Fairness doctrine

Account servicing (sales tool), 234

Accuracy in Media (watch-dog group), 436, 483–484

Acoustics, 113–114

Action for Children's Television (ACT): & advertising, 240–241, 395; research by, 387. *See also Sesame Street*

Action News (format), 347

Ad hoc (temporary) networks, 189–190

Adapter: cable TV tuner as, 180

Addressability (of cable TV subscriber): & audience research, 381; & pay TV, 179; & signal piracy, 431; statistics on, 185 (table)

Adjacent channel interference, 131

Adlink (cable TV commercial interconnect), 198

Administrative Law Judge (ALJ), FCC, 426

Administrative Procedures Act, 42

Adult contemporary (radio format), 349 (table)

Advertising: in barter deals, 337; basics, 220–225; block scheduling of, 504; & boycotts, 436; by broadcasters, 292; on cable TV, 198, 227–228, 234; on carrier-current stations, 134; children's, 319–320; deceptive, 240; early doubts about, 42; editorial, 482–483; effects of, 394–395; in foreign countries, 510; in game shows, 307; influence on programs, 20; institutional, 43; jobs in, 217; as key topic of study, 14; local, 221 (graph), 222, 232; network, 222, 224, 230–232; nudity in, 239; & NWIO, 522; origins of radio, 46; participating, 226; by political candidates, 399, 401, 477, 500; products banned from, 482; radio, 221 (graph); pros and cons of broadcast, 223–225; on public broadcasting, 261, 265–266; rates, 193, 228–233; regulation of, 433–434; as revenue source, 14; salaries in, 213 (chart); selling of, 233–237; societal effects of, 394–396; standards of, 237–241; subliminal, 383 (n.); time limits on, 456, 457 (table); of tobacco, ban on, 433–434; transborder, 510, 511 (exhib.); volume, by medium, 221 (graph); in World War II, 63. *See also* Commercial(s)

Advertising agencies: basics, 235–237; jobs in, 217; government, 504; loss of TV network program control by, 72; as program producers 46–47; for religion, 351; and station operations, 186 (diag.)

Advertising Substantiation Program (FTC), 240

Advertorials, 482

Affiliation, network: & ad rates, 228; contract for, 192–196; primary vs. secondary, 191; profitability of,

245; in public broadcasting, 256, 258; switches in, 194, 210–211 (exhib.)

AFM. *See* American Federation of Musicians

Africa No. 1 (peripheral), 512

Afternoon (daypart), 278 (table)

AFTRA (American Federation of Television and Radio Artists): & blacklisting, 77; origins of, 217

Against the Odds (Nickelodeon), 317

AGB (research firm), 364–365

Agence France Presse (AFP), 285

Agency, advertising. *See* Advertising agency

Agency for Instructional Technology, 269, 338

Agenda setting: media role in, 396; by critics, 439

Agnew, Vice-Pres. Spiro, attack by, on networks, 390

Agricultural (radio format), 349 (table), 351

Airwolf, 284, 335

Albania (external service), 407 (table)

Alcoholic beverages, advertising of, 386

Alf, 291 (table)

All-business radio format, 350

All-channel receivers: FM, 75; TV, 68

All in the Family, 283, 388

All-sports radio format, 350

Allen, Fred (as vaudevillian), 32

Allocation, frequency: broadcast summary table, 145; conservation strategies, 127; defined, 130; by ITU, 495; for satellites, 167

Allotment, channel: of broadcasting services (summary), 145 (table); & licensing, 440–441; of TV channel 1, 131 n.; U.S. plan for TV, 65, 66 (map), 67–68, 130

Alphanumeric services (cable TV), 178, 324

Alternating Current (AC): basic concept, 115–116; role in TV synchronization, 142

All Things Considered (NPR), 259

AM radio: antennas, 134 (photo); channels, 145 (table); decline in technical quality of, 135 n.; formats on, 348–352; growth of, 52 (chart); international treaties on, 432; license application for, 441; & new competition, 102; public station growth, 253 (graph); stereo, 460, 461 (exhib.); technology of, 118–119 (diag.), 131–134; VOA overseas relay stations, 508

Amateurs, radio: role of in post-WWII era, 38; in early broadcasting, 40

American Bar Association, on courtroom TV, 472

American Cable (MSO), statistics on, 199 (table)

American Federation of Musicians (AFM): opposition to recordings, 56, 58; as umbrella union, 215

American Federation of TV and Radio Artists. *See* AFTRA

American Guild of Variety Artists (AGVA), 215

American Marconi, 35, 40

American Movie Classics (pay cable): ownership of, 204; use of movies by, 283; target of, 203

American Public Radio (APR), 259, 268

American Society of Composers, Authors and Publishers. *See* ASCAP

American Sports Cavalcade (ABC), 310

American Women in Radio & Television (AWRT), survey by, 213

Amos 'n' Andy, 55, 73

Ampex Corporation, 56

Amplifiers: cable TV booster, 162, 179; low-noise (LNA), 176 (diag.); repeater, 162, 163

Amplitude, wave, 112, 113 (diag.)

Amplitude modulation (AM), 118–119 (diag.), 120

Analog signals, 120, 158–159 (diag.)

Ancillary services: cable TV, 243; FM, 136; TV, 149–150; economics of, 244

Ancillary signals, TV, 149–150

Anglia Television (UK regional network), 494 n.

Anik (Canadian domsat), 513, 517 (table)

Annenberg, Walter, & *TV Guide,* 294 (exhib.)

Annenberg/CPB Project, 263, 338

Announcements: identification, 226; promotional, 227; public service, 227; station break, 226. *See also* Commercial(s)

Antenna(s), receiving: basics, 127; at cable TV headends, 178 (diag.); DBS, 176 (diag.); disconnected for cable TV hookup, 177, 452; TV, 147–149. *See also* TVRO

Antenna(s), transmitting: AM, 134 (photo); basics, 126–128; DBS, 173; FM, 135; microwave relay, 164 (diag.); satellite, 167, 171 (diag.), 174 (diag.), 514 (diag.); short wave, 137 (photo); TV, 147–149. *See also* TVRO

Antitrust actions: motion picture industry, 72, 203; NAB codes, 437; networks, 98, 203–204; patent pooling, 44

Antitrust laws: & AM stereo standard, 461 (exhib.); basics, 434; & mergers, 454

AOR (album oriented rock) radio format, 349 (table), 350

AP. *See* Associated Press

AP News Wire (alphanumeric), 324

Apogee kick motor, 171–172 (exhib.), 174 (diag.)

Appeals, legal: from FCC decisions, 418, 426–427, 462; in foreign countries, 496–497; in license renewals, 449 (chart)

Applications: for license, 441; mutually exclusive, 443, 448; renewal, 447–450

ARABSAT satellite, 517 (table)

Arbitration vs. trial (libel), 467–468

Arbitron (research firm): basics, 359, 360; market definition by, 371–372, 373 (exhib.), 367 (exhib.); samples used by, 368;

BBC-1 & -2 (UK TV networks), 494, 496 (diag.)
Beam-edge power (satellite footprint), 169 (diag.)
Beautiful music (radio format), 349 (table), 350
Beauty and the Beast (as hybrid genre), 300
Beirut massacre (marine barracks), 405
Belgium: cable TV in, 515; multilingualism of, 24; opposition to ads in, 504; program imports by, 25
Bell, Alexander Graham (telephone patent), 33
Bell Laboratories (AT&T subsidiary), 101
Bell System: antitrust suit, 100; origins of, 34. *See also* AT&T
Benny, Jack: signs with CBS, 73; as vaudevillian, 32
Benson (sitcom), 298
Bergen, Edgar: & Mae West incident, 53; signs with CBS, 73
Berlin, West (broadcasts to E. Germany), 505
Berlin Convention of 1906 (ships' radio), 46
BET (Black Entertainment Network), 209
Betamax (VCR), 92, 94
Bias: in documentaries, 396, 484; in news, 483–484; research on news, 387, 390; in sampling, 370; visual, of TV, 396. *See also* Libel
Big band (radio format), 349 (table), 350
Big Bird, 319 (photo)
Big Business: dominance over post-WWII wireless, 38; role in early broadcasting, 34; *See also* Mergers, Monopoly
"Big government:" regulation &, 22
Bill of Rights, 464
Billboard (announcements), 226
Billings, advertising: basics, 236–237; fraudulent, 427
Biltmore Agreement (ending press-radio war), 58
Binary number code (digital processing) 121, 122 (exhib.)

Birch Radio (ratings), 359
Bit (binary digit), 121 n., 122 (exhib.)
Black (radio format), 349 (table), 350
Black Entertainment Network. *See* BET
Blacker than black (TV picture signal level), 143 (exhib.)
Blacklisting, anticommunist, 76–77
Blackouts, sports, 315
Black Rock (CBS hq. building), 54 (n.)
Blair Television (sales rep), 234
Blanket license, music, 429
Blanking (TV signal), 141 (diag.), 143 (diag.), 144
Blockbuster (movie), 300–301
Block scheduling: of commercials, 225 n.; of programs, 289
"Blue Book" (FCC), 478
Blue Network (NBC radio): becomes ABC, 59; origin of, 44; starts newscasts, 58
Blue and Grey (miniseries), 302 (graph)
BMI (Broadcast Music Incorporated): challenges ASCAP, 56, 58; & music licensing, 429, 430 (chart)
Board for International Broadcasting, 510
Bonneville Productions (radio formats), 190 (exhib.), 339
Bookend (commercial position), 225
Boomerang effect of propaganda, 388
Boorstin, Daniel (scholar), 397
Booster rocket, satellite, 174–175 (exhib.)
Border blasters (Mexico), 512
Boresight (of satellite footprint), 169 (diag.)
Born Innocent (imitation effect), 409
Bottom line, the (accounting concept), 247–250
Boycott: as consumer stratagem, 436; of programmers, against MMDS, 89
Bradley, Ed (CBS News), 325

Brand loyalty, as advertising goal, 395
Brasilsat (Brazilian domsat), 417 (table)
Brattain, Walter (inventor), 92
Braun, Ferdinand (physics Nobelist), 35
Bravo (pay cable), 203, 302
Brazil: domsat of, 517 (table); PAS service to, 516; syndication by, 504; syndication to, cost of, 520 (table)
Breakfast TV, 506
Bridging (scheduling strategy), 289, 291
Brinkley, "Dr." J. R. (radio "doctor"), 54
British Broadcasting Corporation (BBC): basics, 489–491, 496–497 (diag.); deregulation of, 270; external services of, 507, 508; & Murrow wartime broadcasts from, 63 (exhib.); as PBS supplier, 268; & pirates, 512; political access to, 500; radio, 494, 512; teletext, 518; as TV pioneer, 60
British Marconi company: & BBC TV, 60; origin of, 35; sells U.S. subsidiary, 40
Broadcasting: as ad medium, 220–225; & bottom-line thinking, 247–250; & cable-TV crossownership, 198; capital investment in, 204; as commerce, 416; conservatism of, 53; culture vs. business issue, 270; definition of, 4, 6–7, 8 (exhib.), 419; as democratic medium, 493; under 1st Amendment, 471, 472, 474–475; flexibility of, 223–224; future of, 104, 460, 484–485; & home video center, 96 (diag.); as interstate commerce, 416; jobs in, 211–215; licensing of, 427–428; motion picture industry links, 32; & national character, 488–495; profitability of, 191–192, 206, 244–245; public-service role, 76; rate of early acceptance, 31; salaries in, 213 (chart), 214 (chart); self-regulation of, 437–439; short-wave, 136–138; station numbers, 128 n.;

survival of; & telco competition, 101–102; transborder, 506–512; uniqueness of, 470, 479, 485; vertical integration of, 203–204; world facilities of, 502–503. *See also:* Attributes of broadcasting; External broadcasting; Family medium; Public service broadcasting

Broadcasting (trade magazine): history of, 57 (photo); *Broadcasting/ Cablecasting Yearbook,* 185 n.

Broadcasting House (BBC), 490 (photo)

Broadcast Rating Council, 379

Broadcast Standards Department, NBC, 239–240

Brokaw, Tom (NBC News), 322 (photo)

Brokers: cable TV system sales, 209; prize, 307; spot ads, 234; station sales, 207; time, 233, 444; TVRO programs, 432

Brothers, 304

BS (Japanese DBS), 517 (table)

BSB (British Satellite Broadcasting), 517 (table), 519 (exhib.)

Burden of proof (in revocation cases), 427

Bureau of Applied Social Research (Columbia U.), 388

Burnett, Leo (ad agency), 236 (table)

Burns, (George) and Allen (Gracie), comedy team, 73

Bush, Pres. George (candidate debates), 399, 400 (photo)

Byte, 121 n., 122 (exhib.)

Caballero Radio Network, affiliates of, 190 (table)

Cable, coaxial: technology of, 162–163; & TV networks, 65, 69

Cable, fiber-optic, 163–164, 165

Cable, submarine: origins, 33; fiber-optic, 163–164

Cable Bureau (FCC), 459 (diag.)

Cable Communications Policy Act of 1984. *See* Cable TV Act

Cable Guide (publication), 292

Cable Health Network, 209, 239

Cable market of opportunity (CMO), 232

Cable Music Channel, 85, 256

Cable News Network (CNN): ad rates of, 232; basics, 324; in Europe, 519 (table); origins of, 86 (exhib.), 87; on PAS, 516 (exhib.); vs. PBS, 302; & presidential TV, 401; profitability of, 246; satellite relay of, 169 (exhib.); as station news source, 287, 288 (diag.); statistics on, 200 (table). *See also* CNN Headline News, CNN Radio

Cable One (cable TV time buyer), 237

Cable-only production, 283–285, 352

Cable-specific programs: & HBO, 86; key concept, 8–9; & TNT, 85 (exhibit)

Cabletelevision Advertising Bureau (CAB), 232, 234

Cabletext vs. teletext, 177

Cable TV Act (Cable Communications Policy Act of 1984): basics, 450; definition of cable in, 21; & EEO law, 444; & public interest, 420; & obscenity, 471; passage of, 421, 459 (diag.)

Cable TV networks: advertising on, 221 (graph), 227–228, 235 (table), 236 (table); capital investment in, 204–205; children's, 316–317; European, 519 (table); first-run programs on, 284; in foreign countries, 26, 516, 517, 519 (table); news & information channels, 324; production for, 283–285; profitability of, 246; & program diversity issue, 304; sale of, 208–209; scheduling strategies of, 290–292; statistics on, 200–201 (table). *See also networks by name*

Cable TV systems: advertising on, 222 (graph), 227–228; advertising sales, 234, 235 (table), 236 (table), 237; audience research on, 228, 362 (exhib.), 381; auxiliary services of, 243; basics, 196–198; capital investment in, 204–205; & broadcast channel scarcity, 474;

channels per system, 179; churn, 197; & copyright, 429–432; definition of, 21; as delivery system, 184; deregulation of, 458–460; emergence of, 80–82; & equal time rule, 477; as equalizer of UHF-VHF station coverage, 192; fiber-optic use by, 12 (exhib.), 164; First Amendment status of, 21, 471; in foreign countries, 514–516; franchising of, 450–452; growth of, 82–87, 459 (diagram); & home video center, 96 (diag.); interactive, 95, 179, 243; jobs in, 211–215; local origination by, 331 (chart), 347–358; market of opportunity (CMO), 232; as narrowcasting, 15; network fees, 198; network ownership of, 454; news on, 324; organization of, 196–204; origins of, ownership rules, 206–207, 450, 453; piracy of signals of, 431–432; & pole attachment, 163, 178 (diag.), 179, 205; profitability of, 245–246; program origination by, 197, 331 (chart), 347–348; programming of, 86–87; promise vs. performance, 209, 227; public file, 445; as "publisher," 21; radio channels on, 180 (exhib.); regulation of, 81–82; as research tool, 383; sales of systems, 208–209; sports programs on, 312–311; self-regulation of, 437; state & local regulation of, 434; subscriber fees of, 242–243 (diag.); systems statistics, 185 (table); technology of, 177–180; & telco competition, 101–102; TVRO use by, 167; as waveguide system, 128; Worldnet on, 519 (table). *See also* Cable TV Act; Cable TV networks; Community Antenna TV; Multiple-System Operators. *See also names of individual cable program networks*

Cable Value Network (home shopping), 209, 201 (table)

Cablevision Systems (MSO), 199 (table)

Cagney and Lacey: on cable, 282; & crime genre, 300

summarizing table, 145. *See also* Scarcity, channel

Channel as communication medium (information theory), 389

Channel 4 (UK network), 494, 496–497 (diag.)

Channeling of children's programs, 470

Channel 9 case, Orlando (minority ownership), 454

Channel 1 (TV), deletion of, 146 n., 145 (table)

Channels 5 & 6, UK plans for, 497 (exhib.)

Character qualifications, licensee, 441, 442 (exhib.)

Charged coupled device (CCD) camera, 139 n.

Charlie's Angels (as child fare), 320 n.

Charren, Peggy (ACT president), 241

Cheers: ownership of, 202; as sitcom, 298, 299 (photo); as studio product, 280, 282 (exhib.); syndication price of, 291 (table)

Chernobyl disaster (USSR), news of, 492

Child, Julia (TV cook), 267

Children: advertising to, 238–239, 240–241, 359; & indecency, 470–471; market research on, 384; network programs for, 278, 315–320; noncommercial programs for, 317–318; under paternalistic systems, 489; program issues, 319–320, 462; programs for, 315–320; research on media &, 391; socialization of, by TV, 407–408; violence in programs for, 411 (graph)

Children's Television Workshop (CTW): funding of, 268; basics, 318–319; merchandising by, 266, 267 (chart); as program source, 257 (chart)

Chilling effect: of fairness doctrine, 481; of libel suits, 466, 477

China: ads in, 504; censorship of news by, 404–406; external service, 517 (table); localization policy, 501; program imports by, 25

(exhib.); receiver penetration in, 502; satellites of, 175, 517 (table)

Chip, computer: origin of, 92, 93 (photo); as successor to transistor, 151

CHR (contemporary hit radio), 349 (table), 350

Chris Craft Industries (group owner), 189 (graph)

Christensen, Bruce (as PBS pres.), 265

Christian Crusade (religious series), 480 (exhib.)

Chung, Connie: career of, 216 (photo); at CBS news, 323 (photo)

Churn, cable-TV, 197

Cigarette ad ban. *See* Tobacco

Cinemax (pay cable), 203, 201 (table)

Circuit Courts of Appeal, broadcast litigation in, 426–427

Citation system of this book, 420 n.

Citizenship (as licensee requirement), 24 n., 441

Classic Rock (radio format), 349 (table), 350

Clayton Act (antitrust), 434

Clearance, network, 191, 193, 194–195

Clear and present danger test (SCOTUS), 465

Clear channel radio, 132, 133 (table), 156 n.

Clipping, network, 241

Clone programs: children's from adult shows, 317; of home shopping services, 309; of MTV, 309; & program diversity, 304; Rivers from Carson, 308; of sitcoms, 299–300

Closed captioning: as public service, 244; technology of, 151 (photo)

Closed-circuit TV: & business seminars, 266; jobs in, 219; wired radio as, 491

CNBC (Consumer News and Business Service) [cable TV], 320, 324

CNN. *See* Cable News Network

CNN Headline News: basics, 322 (photo), 323–324; & diversity, 304

CNN Radio Network (cable TV), 84 (exhib.), 324

Coach (as studio product), 280

Coalition for Better Television (consumer group), 436

Coaxial cable. *See* Cable, coaxial

Co-channel interference, 131

Code(s): binary, 121, 122 (exhib.); journalistic, 522; Morse, 33, 35 (exhib.); professional, 437; self-regulatory, 355

Codes, NAB: basics, 437; on broadcasting as family medium, 354; on commercial time standards, 238

Codification (rules into laws), 482

Co-financing, program, by cable TV, 284

Coincidental telephone research method, 366

Cold War, & blacklisting, 76

Colleges as public broadcast station licensees, 259–260, 267 (chart)

Colony Communications (MSO), 197

Color TV: basics, 142 (diag.), 143–144; & fee-supported systems, 503; national standards for, 68–69, 495; origins of, 68–69; receiver statistics on, 185 (table); technology of, 112, 142 (exhib.), 144, 149 (diag.), 150 (diag.)

Colorization (of feature films), 85 (exhib.)

Columbia Broadcasting System. *See* CBS

Columbia/Embassy (as syndicator), 291 (table)

Columbia Phonograph Broadcasting System (CBS forerunner), 46

Columbia Pictures, 282 (exhib.), 284 (table)

Columbia Records, sale of, 98

Comcast Cable (MSO), 209, 199 (table)

Command Communications, station purchase by, 208

Commerce, broadcasting as, 416

Commerce clause (Constitution), 416, 417 (chart)

Commercial(s) for: banned products, 225; in barter syndication,

337; basics, 225–226; early ban on, 42; inventory of, 224; issue oriented, 483; length of, 225, 227, 238; local cable interconnects for, 197–198; production of, 223, 227, 235–236, 243; proof of performance of, 237; on public TV, 265–266; station-break, 193; tracking services, 237; zapping of, 287

Commission, sales, 233

Commissioners, FCC: basics, 422, 423 (chart); legal provision for, 419–420; quality of, 425; rule-making by, 423–425

Common carrier(s): vs. broadcasting concept, 43, 419; & cable TV, 21; in Communications Act, 418; definition of, 4; FCC bureau for, 423 (chart); MMDS as, 88, 181; satellites as, 83; state vs. interstate, 416 n.

Common Market, The (Europe), 500, 512

Communications Act of 1934: & antitrust laws, 434; amendments to generally, 420–421; on appeals, 418, 426; basics, 418–420; in chain of legal authority, 417 (chart); on channel ownership, 440; on common carriers, 5; equal time rules of, 465 (exhib.), 476, 479; on foreign ownership of stations, 24; on mass media, 5; Lea Act (music), 58; on licensee qualifications, 441; on localism, 478; on lotteries, 434; origins of, 53; payola amendment, 241; on political candidates, 475–476; public broadcasting amendment to, 251, 254, 255 (exhib.), 263; & public interest concept, 352; quiz-rigging amendment, 76; on renewals, 447–448; on signal piracy, 432; on signal privacy, 431; & sponsor ID, 237–238; vs. state laws, 434; on UHF tuners, 68; wartime emergency provisions, 63 n. *See also* Federal Communications Commission

Communications Satellite Corporation (Comsat): & DBS, 91; as U.S. INTELSAT agency, 513

Community antenna TV (CATV): as cable TV forerunner, 80–82; in Europe, 514–515

Community radio: basics, 351–352; vs. local, 501

Community standards (in obscenity cases), 469

Compact disc (CD): origin of, 95; technology of, 158, 159 (diag.)

Compatibility, technical: HDTV with NTSC TV standard, 154; modern receivers with old standards, 102; monochrome with color TV, 68, 144. *See also* Standardization

Compensation, network to affiliate: & affiliate switches, 210–211 (exhib.); amount of, 222 (graph); contract terms for, 192–194, 195

Competition: AT&T vs. new telcos, 99–102; cable TV vs. broadcasting, 248, 268, 275, 285–286; cable TV vs. DBS (Europe), 514; cable TV vs. SMATV, 90; cable TV vs. telcos, 101–102; cable TV vs. VCR, 95; in deregulation theory, 455; effect on schedules, 506; excessive, 104; key concept, 22; intermedia, 17–18, 234, 235 (table); INTELSAT vs. private firms, 513, 514–515 (exhib.); internetwork, 97–98, 100 (exhib.); of the marketplace, 263–264; & network regulation, 458; in pluralistic systems, 593; public broadcasting vs. commercial, 14, 491, 520; radio vs. newspapers, 58; & program quality, 355; scheduling as weapon in, 289; start of radio, 42; & technology choice, 462; telcos vs. media, 101–102; VCRs vs. media, 246

Complaints to FCC, public: basics, 422–423; disposition of, 447; & licensing, 443–444

"Composition of the traffic" (SCOTUS), 474

Comprehensive programming, 16

Compression, signal, 136

Compulsory licensing (of copyrighted programs), 202

CompuServe (data base), 97

Computer(s): broadcasting use of,

11–12, 206–207 (exhib.); in CD recording, 159 (diag.); and commercial insertion (cable TV), 228; and convergence, 158; & DBS system, 96 (diag.); & graphics; home, 96 (diag.), 185 (table); & logging, 237; origin of, 92; in ratings research, 365 (exhib.), 367 (exhib.); role in station operations, 187; in teletext, 151 (exhib.); in TV receivers, 153; in two-way cable TV, 179; in video equipment generally, 161–162. *See also* Automation

Comsat (satellite series), 166 (diag.). *See also* Communications Satellite Corp.

Comstar (satellite series), 166 (exhib.)

Concept research, program, 382–383

Conflict, dramatic (as violence source), 412

Conglomerates: & cable TV, 198–199; Capital Cities as, 98–99; as media investors, 206

Congress: & Communications Act rewrites, 421; FCC oversight by, 417–418, 435; regulatory power of, 416–417; TV coverage of, 326, 399, 402–403, 404 (photo). *See also* C-SPAN; Hearings

Congruence theory (media effects), 389

Conrad, Frank, & KDKA origin, 40, 41 (photo)

Consent decree, acceptance of: by AT&T, 100–101; by motion picture industry, 72; by NAB re codes, 437; by networks, 98

Consent order, FTC, 240

Conservation, spectrum, 127–128

Constitution of the United States: Commerce Clause of, 416, 417 (chart); on copyrights and patents, 428; & electronic media issues, 468–484. *See also amendments by number*

Constitution: That Delicate Balance, The (PBS), 326

Construction permit (CP), 441, 445

Consultants: news, 186 (chart), 346–

studio, 282 (exhib.); RKO offer for studio of, 442 (exhib.); TV production of, 284 (table)

Disneyland (TV series), 73

Distant stations, retransmission of by cable TV, 81, 429, 430 (chart), 431. *See also* Superstation

Distortion in analog recording, 121, 158

Distress sales (minority buyer preference), 454

Distribution function, 191, 283

Distributor, syndicator as, 332

Diversification goal: of broadcast programs, 458; of cable TV programs, 285; of ideas (1st Amendment), 484; of information sources, 22; & minority ownership, 454; & new technology, 354. *See also* Ownership, diversification of

Diversified (radio format), 349 (table), 350

Divestiture: AT&T, 100–101; motion picture industry, 72

DJ. *See* Disc jockey

"Doctrine" term, as used by FCC, 21 n.

Docudrama: & agenda setting, 406; as hybrid genre, 278

Documentaries: bias charge against, 396; decline of, 325; science, 302

Dole, Sen. Bob, 327

Domsats (domestic satellites): origins of, 82–83; foreign, 513, 517 (table)

Donahue (as barter show), 337

Double billing (of coöp ads), 241

Douglas, Justice William O. (SCOTUS), 464–465

Downconverter (higher frequencies to TV receiver range): DBS, 176 (diag.); MDS, 88, 181; TVRO, 167

Dragnet (as crime drama), 300

Drake-Chenault Enterprises (format syndication), 339

Drama (as genre), 292 (table)

Dramedy (as hybrid genre), 278, 300

Drive times (as dayparts), 277, 278 (table)

Drop-cable (cable TV distribution), 178 (diag.)

Dr. Toni Grant Show (MBS), 328

Dubbing of imported programs, 24

Ducting, wave, 124

Due process, right of (5th Amendment), 472

Dukakis, Michael (as presidential candidate), 399, 400 (photo)

Dukes of Hazzard (as child fare), 320 n.

Dumont, Allen B. (CRT manufacturer), 69

Dumont Television Network & Army-McCarthy hearings, 78 n.

Duopoly (duplicate coverage) & NBC Blue network, 44, 59

Duopoly (shared authority of BBC & IBA in UK), 493, 496–497

DX (long distance) reception, 42, 45

Dynamic range of sound, 136

Dynasty, 335

Early morning (daypart), 304

Earth station, satellite, uplink costs of, 205. *See also* TVRO

Eastern Microwave (DBS packager), 243

Easy Listening (radio format), 350

Economics of electronic media: cable TV, 196–204; capital investment, 204–205; commercial networks, 189–196; key concepts, 13–15; public broadcasting, 260–266; research on, 386; stations, 184–188; world comparisons, 502–504

Economies of scale by groups & MSOs, 247

Edison, Thomas (inventor), 32, 36

Editorial(s): advertising, 238, 467, 482–483; & fairness, 479; political (by licensees), 477, 479, 482

Editorial control over non-common-carrier channels, 5, 23 (exhib.)

Editorial discretion, SCOTUS reliance on, 483–484

Educational (radio format), 349 (table), 351

Educational stations. *See* Public broadcasting

Education in media, 31, 218 (exhib.)

EEO. *See* Equal Employment Opportunities

$E = Mc^2$ (Einstein equation), 109 n.

Effect(s) of and on electronic media: of advertising, 394–396; basics, 378; on competing media, 17–20, 58; & demographics, 376 (graph); of entertainment, 406–409; on musicians, 55–56, 57; of news, 395–398; on political life, 398–406; as reason for study, 3; on sports, 314–315; time spent as, 378; of violence, 409–412; of war coverage, 403–406. *See also* Competition

Effective radiated power (ERP): of TV antenna, 147; of microwave relays, 163

EHF (extremely high frequency) band, 111 (table)

8XK (KDKA experimental predecessor), 40–41

Eisenhower, Pres. Dwight D., 399

Elections: de Forest report on, 39; KDKA report on, 41–42; media impact on, 399, 401. *See also* Equal time

Electrical transcription (ET), 56

Electric Company, The (CTW), 318

Electromagnetic energy, 109, 111 (table). *See also* Spectrum

Electron gun: in color receiver tube, 150 (diag.); in TV pickup tube, 139, 140 (diag.)

Electronic church, 340–343

Electronic mass media, definition of, 4–5

Electronic Media Rating Council, 379

Electronic news gathering (ENG): & affiliate autonomy, 196; basics, 286–287, 345–346; technology of, 151–153

casting, 262–263; satellite proposal of, 257

Foreign language radio, 349 (table)

Forfeitures. *See* Fines

Format(s): demographics of, 378–379; DJ, 348–349; hybrid, 16, 238, 300, 476; key concepts, 15, 17; local radio, 348–350; news, 346–347; opposition to change of, 215 n.; & political ads, 477; of program services, 278; radio network, 190 (table); radio station adoption of, 73–74; as station price factor, 208; syndication of, 292, 339–340

48 Hours (CBS), 326

For Our Times (CBS), 342

Foundations, public broadcasting support by 262–263, 267 (chart)

Fourteenth Amendment vs. 1st Amendment, 465 (exhib.)

Fourth Amendment (privacy right), 468–469

Fourth network issue (TV), 69, 98, 458 n. *See also* Fox network

Fowler, FCC Chair Mark: on commercials, 238; critique of, 462; "dinosaur" epithet of, 53, 78; "toaster" epithet of, 353, 462

Fox network (FBC): basics, 282 (exhib.); financial status of, 245; as group owner, 189 (graph); growth of, 458 n.; & network program rules, 98; origins of, 100–101 (exhib.); Rivers show on, 308; & vertical integration, 204

Frame: video, 138; sample, 369

Frame stores (video), 161

France: cable TV penetration in, 516; deregulation in, 520; external service of, 507; public ad agency in, 504; reliance of on foreign programs, 26; satellite of, 517 (table); satellite network of, 519 (table); STV network in, 518; syndication prices paid by, 520 (table); videotex in, 518

Franchising of Bell telephone companies, 34

Franchising of cable TV systems: basics, 450–452; in CATV era, 81; overbidding in, 246

Fraudulent billing, 241

FRC. *See* Federal Radio Commission

Frederick, Pauline (pioneer newsperson), 216 (photo)

Freed, Alan (rock innovator), 74

Freedom of Information Act, & news access, 398

Free flow doctrine (vs. balanced flow), 521–524

Free-form radio, 351, 352 (exhib.)

Free press vs. fair trial, 472, 473 (photo)

Freeze, TV (1948–1952), 65–68

Freeze-frame (VCR), 161

French Chef, The (PBS), 267

Frequency division multiplex, 128

Frequency modulation (FM): basics, 118–119 (diag.); & FM stations, 135; & TV sounds, 142 (diag.), 142–145, 143–144

Frequency of waves: basic concepts, 110, 112, 113 (diag.); carrier, 115–116, 118–119 (diag.); electromagnetic waves in general, 110, 111 (table); of household current, 115, 142; propagation effects of, 124; radio bands, 111 (table); relationship to wavelength, 115, 116 (exhib.); satellites, 167; sound, 112–115; vs. wavelength, 115, 116 (exhib.). *See also* Allocation, Spectrum

Frequency (repetition rate) standards, TV: field & frame rates, 138–139; scanning rate, 140–143

Friendly, Fred: as Murrow producer, 78; & Red Lion case, 481 (exhib.)

Fringe times: basics, 277, 288 (table), 289 (table); importance of, to affiliates, 289, 343; off-net shows in, 334

Frontline (PBS), 326

FTC. *See* Federal Trade Commission

Fuel, satellite: in external tanks on orbiter, 174 (diag.); as weight factor, 165 n., 172 (exhib.)

Fulbright, Sen. William, & congressional TV, 402

Full-service: networks, 190; stations, 348

Fundamental pitch (of sounds), 112–113, 114 (diag.)

Fund for Adult Education (Ford Foundation), 262–263

Fund for the Republic, blacklisting study by, 77

Fund raising by public broadcasting: 262 (graph), 266, 267 (diag.)

Gain, antenna: definition of, 127; microwave, 163; satellite, 167

Galaxy (satellite series): cable TV use of, 205; orbital location of, 166 (diag.)

Game shows: basics, 306–308; as genre, 278, 279 (table); quiz scandals, 75–76

Gamma rays (as electromagnetism), 111 (table)

Gannett (group owner), 189 (graph)

Gatekeeping (research concept), 390–391, 395–396

GE. *See* General Electric

Geller, Simon (renewal case), 451 (photo)

GenCorp (RKO owner), 442 (exhib.)

General/Administrative Department: in broadcasting, 184–185, 186 (exhib.), 188 (table); in cable TV, 196–197

General Electric: & alternator, 37; cable TV interests of, 245; RCA purchase by, 99; role of in early wireless, 34, 35; role of in TV development, 61

General Hospital (innovative soap), 305

General Motors, ad strategy of, 235 (table)

General support announcement (public broadcasting), 265

General Tire (as RKO owner), 442 (exhib.)

Generations (innovative soap), 305 (photo)

Generator, sync, 146 (diag.)

Generic scheduling, 16

Genre(s), program: basics, 278, 279 (table); children's shows, 320;

early radio, 42; early TV, 71 (photos); movie packaging by, 337; universality of, 505

Geography & broadcasting, 505

Geostationary orbit. *See* Orbit

Geraldo: as barter show, 337; as syndicated series, 248; as tabloid, 336

Gerbner, George (researcher), 410–411

Germany (pre-World War II), external service of, 507

Germany, West: cable TV reliance on U.S. programs, 26; external service of, 507 (table); regionalism in, 24 n.; satellite networks of, 519 (table)

Ghostbusters, 300, 282 (exhib.)

Ghosts (in TV pictures), 148, 153–154

Giga-, as metric prefix, 115

G.I. Joe (children's series), 241

Gillett Group (group owner), 189 (graph)

"Giving a lead" policy (BBC), 490

Glasnost: vs. deregulation, 520, 524; & production values, 506; & USSR news, 492

Gleason, Jackie (comedian), 71 (photo)

Global beam (satellite footprint), 167

Gobots, The (cartoon), 316

Goldberg (as independent production firm), 283

"Golden Age": of radio, 51; of TV, 69–72

Golden Girls, 282 (exhib.), 298

Golden West Stations, sale of KTLA-TV by, 208

Goldensen, Leonard (as ABC chair), 98–99

Gold Dust Twins (early commercial), 47

Gone with the Wind: on NBC, 300; Turner &, 84–85 (exhib.)

Gong Show, The (on USA Network), 306

Good Evening (APR), 259

Good Morning America (ABC), 308

Goodson-Todman Productions (game shows), 307

Gosden, Freeman ("Amos"), 55

Government funding of broadcasting: U.S., 262 (graph), 263–264, 267 (chart) world statistics on, 492 (graph)

Grades A and B (TV coverage contours), 149

Granada Television (UK regional network), 494 n.

Grandfathering (of ownerships), 453

Grazing (channel sampling), 224, 287, 309

Great Britain. *See* United Kingdom

"Great Debates" (presidential candidates), 399, 400 (photo)

Great Performances (PBS), 303 (graph)

Great Plains National Instructional Television Library, 268, 338

Greenwich prime meridian (orbital locations), 166 (diag.), 165 n.

Gremlins (as studio product), 282 (exhib.)

Grenada invasion, media censorship during, 405

Gross, Ben (radio critic), 53

Grossman, Lawrence (as PBS pres.), 256

Ground system, antenna, 134 (photo)

Ground wave(s), 124, 125 (diag.)

Group ownership: basics, 187–188, 189 (graph); & economies of scale, 247

Group W: as group owner, 189 (graph); Newsfeed Network of, 288 (exhib.); Television Sales Premiere Announcement Network of (spot sales), 134

Growing Pains (sitcom), 291, 298 (table)

G-Star (satellite series), 166 (diag.)

Guard bands, 142 (diag.), 145, 180 (diag.)

Guided waves, 128

Guidelines, FCC, 421, 456, 557 (table)

Guides, program, 292–295

Gulf Broadcasting, sale of station group by, 207 n.

Gunsmoke (as long-run series), 290

Habit formation (programming strategy), 290, 291

Hammock (scheduling strategy), 289

Happy Days, 282 (exhib.), 290

Happy Talk (news format), 346

Hard vs. soft interconnection, 197

Hargis, Billy James (radio preacher), 480 (exhib.)

Harmonics. *See* Overtones

Harvey, Paul (radio commentator), 327

Hauptman trial (cameras in courtroom), 473 (photo)

Hawaiian Heat (as clone), 300

HBO. *See* Home Box Office

HBO case (cable TV regulation), 459 (diag.)

HDTV. *See* High-definition TV

Head(s), recording: audio, 158–159; videotape, 160, 161 (diag.)

Headend, cable-TV system: location of, 178 (diag.); functions of, 86 (diag.), 177, 197; in two-way cable, 243

Headline News (CNN), d84 (exhib.)

Head of the Class, 280, 291 (table)

Hearing (human), physics of, 112

Hearings, congressional: on ads in public broadcasting, 265; on children's programs, 241; on Nixon impeachment, 399; on ratings, 379; televising of, 402 n., 403, 404 (photo); Watergate, 473 (photo)

Hearings, FCC: basics 424, 426; comparative, 443, 448–450, 457

Helical VTR format, 161 (diag.)

He-Man (children's series), as merchandising tool, 241, 316

Hemispheric beam (satellite footprint), 167

Hennock, FCC Com. Frieda, 422

Herbert case (libel), 467–468

Heritage USA (theme park), 343, 334–345 (exhib.)

Hertz, Heinrich (physicist), 34–35

Hewitt, Don (CBS News), 325

Jennings, Peter (ABC News), 322 (photo)

Jeopardy (game show), 306–307, 332, 337

Jim and Tammy Bakker Show (PTL), 341 (table), 343, 344–345 (exhib.)

Jobs, advice on for those seeking, 218 (exhib.). *See also* Employment

Johnson, Pres. Lyndon: & presidential TV, 401, 401 (photo); & public TV, 254

Joint Committee on Educational Television (JCET), 252

Journalistic judgment. *See* Editorial discretion

Journalist's privilege, 433, 467–468

Junk bonds, TBS &, 99

JWT Group (ad agency), 231 (table)

Kahn, Leonard (AM stereo system), 461 (exhib.)

Kaltenborn, H. V. (radio newsman), 63–64

Kate and Allie, 298, 291 (table)

Katz Television Group (sales rep), 234

KBEM, format of, 293 (exhib.)

KCBJ-TV (affiliation changes), 194

KDKA (as 1st station), 41–43

Kefauver, Sen. Estes, & hearings on TV, 40, 402 n.

Keillor, Garrison (APR), 259

Kemp, George (Marconi assistant), 35 (photo)

Kennedy, James (televangelist), 341 (table)

Kennedy, Pres. John F.: assassination of, 388–389; & presidential debates, 399, 400 (photo); & presidential TV, 401, 402 (graph)

Kennedy, Robert, & hearings on TV, 402 n.

Kennedy, Sen. Ted, 327

Key pad: & audience flow, 287; & people meter, 364; & tuning inertia, 378

KFKB (deleted Brinkley station), 54

KGEF (deleted Shuler station), 54

KHJ-TV: bought by Disney, 204; & RKO renewal case, 442 (exhib.)

Kilby, Jack (inventor), 92

Kilo- (as metric prefix), 115

Kinescope: color tube, 150 (diag.); as CRT, 149; future of, 153; recording, 69, 160

Kinetoscope (motion picture projector), 32

King, Larry (talk host), 308, 328

KJOI-FM, sale of, 208

Klapper, Joseph (researcher), 391

Klein, Paul (programmer), 377

KMBC-TV & sex discrimination suit, 213 n.

KMOX & IBEW, 217

Knots Landing, 335

KOB (long-running appeals), 426 n.

KOMU-TV (affiliation changes), 194

KNBN-TV, sale of, 100 (exhib.)

Knight-Ridder, MSO acquired by, 209

KNXT (launched C. Chung career), 216 (exhib.)

Korea & 1988 Olympics, 168 (diag.)

Koppel, Ted (ABC News), 321, 326

KQED: as producer, 267

KREX-TV: & translators, 177

KRIV-TV, sale of, 100 (exhib.)

KRLD, for record price (sold), 208

KSL (pioneer religious station), 341

KTLA-TV (sold for record price), 208

KTTL renewal case, 465

KTTV-TV, sale of, 100 (exhib.)

Ku-band satellites: Conus use of, 288 (exhib.); & DBS, 173, 176 (diag.); & home reception, 11 (ill.); news-gathering role of, 152; orbital location of, 166 (diag.); orbital spacing of, 167; PBS plans for, 258; power of, 170

Ku Klux Klan use of access cable channel, 23 (exhib.)

Kuralt, Charles (CBS News), 321

KVIL AM/FM (sold for record price), 208

L.A. Law (as crime drama), 300, 301 (photo)

Lando, Barry (CBS News), & journalist's privilege, 467–468

Language(s): bilingual sound, 150;

of external services, 447 (table), 508; in international cable TV, 26; & national culture, 489; regulation of, 24

Larry King Live (CNN), 308

Larry King Show, The (MBS), 328

Laser (light amplification by stimulated emission of radiation): CD use of, 158, 159 (diag.); fiber-optic cable use of, 163; video recording use of, 162

Lassie (on cable TV), 317

Lasswell, Harold (researcher), 389

Late night (TV daypart), 277, 278 (table), 279 (table)

Late Show, The (Fox), 100 (exhib.)

Latin American broadcasting, U.S. as model for, 25

Launch service, satellite: 170–172, 174–175 (exhib.)

Laverne and Shirley (as independent product), 283

Law: of advertising, 433–434; appeals provisions in, 426–427; copyright, 428–432; EEO, 434; lotteries, 434; obscenity, 434; press, 433; state & local, 435; treaties as, 432–433. *See also* Cable TV Act, Communications Act

Law of minimal effects, 391

Lazarsfeld, Paul (researcher), 388

LCD (liquid crystal display), TV receiver screen, 154

Lea Act (limiting union control over music), 58

Lead-in (scheduling strategy), 289, 302

Lear, Norman (as independent producer), 283

Learning Channel, The (children's fare on), 338

Least objectionable program (LOP), 377–378, 380

LED (light-emitting diode), 163

Lee, FCC Com. Robert E., 422

Legacy Broadcasting, station sale by, 208

Lehrer, Jim (PBS), 321, 323 (photo)

Letterman, David, & affiliate clearance, 194 n.

Made-for-TV movies: on cable TV, 301; in prime time, 298

Magazine format, 72

Magazines, ad sales of, 221 (graph)

Magazines, broadcast impact on, 17

Magnavox AM stereo system, 461 (exhib.)

Magnetic tape. *See* Recording, technologies of

Magnum, P.I., 283, 335

Mail, audience, 384. *See also* Complaints

Make-goods: on CPM shortfalls, 228; of missed commercials, 234; of preempted spots, 230; traffic dept. role in, 187

Malice, "actual" (as libel test), 467

Mamma's Family, price of, 291 (table);

Management, station, 187 (diag.), 188 (diag.), 214 (chart)

Man Called Hawk, A (as spin-off), 300

Marconi, Guglielmo (inventor), 35 (photo)

Marcus Welby, M.D., long run of, 290

Marine wireless, 36, 37 (exhib.)

Market: delineation of, 371–372, 373 (diag.); test (research tool), 383

Marketing: cable TV, 197, 203; of toys in children's programs, 316; jobs in, 218

Marketplace, economic: vs. culture, 484; failure of, 456; & fairness doctrine, 482. *See also* Competition, Deregulation

Marketplace of ideas, as 1st Amendment goal, 22, 464–465, 485

Market size: cable TV vs. broadcast, 81, 381; & profitability, 247; & station value, 208; & TV ad rates, 231 (graph), 192

Married with Children: as sitcom, 298; as slobcom, 354–355; & taste issue, 248

Martin, Mary, 71 (photo)

Mary Tyler Moore Show, The, 283

Marx, Groucho, signs with CBS, 73

Masada (miniseries), 303 (graph)

*M*A*S*H,* 282, 290, 335

Mass announcement service (telephone), 5

Mass appeal: of prime-time programming, 297; of programming generally, 15; & technologic innovation, 13–14; Weaver's touch, 72. *See also* Narrowcasting

Mass demand, economic role of, 13–14, 15, 154

Massification, 15

Mass Media Bureau, FCC, 421–422, 423 (chart)

Master of the Game (miniseries), 302 (graph)

Masterpiece Theatre: basics, 302; underwriting of, 264; production of, 267–268

Masters of the Universe (cartoon), 316

Matsushita (VHS system), 94

MATV (master antenna television). *See* SMATV

Maxwell, James Clerk (physicist), 34

M'Bow, Amadou M. (as UNESCO official), 523 (exhib.)

MBS. *See* Mutual Broadcasting System

MCA, Inc. (conglomerate), 204, 284, 291 (table)

MDS (multipoint distribution service). *See* MMDS

Meadows, Audrey, 71 (photo)

"Media," as plural word, 4 n.

Media General (MSO), revenue of, 199 (table)

Media mix (ad strategy), 235

Medium frequency band. *See* MF

Medium vs. message: the "glow & flow principle," 408–409; McLuhan theory, 377 n.

Meet the Press (NBC), 326

Mega- (as metric prefix), 115

Mega-events (sports), 310, 311, 312

Memory, computer, 158, 162

Merchandising, 186 (diag.), 268

Mercury Theater of the Air, The (Martian invasion), 53

Merger(s): of ad agencies, 235; of cable TV networks, 203, 209, 246; encouraged in 1980s, 220; impact of (on program quality), 355; mania for, 453–454; of Time-Warner, 199 (exhib.); of United Artists-United Cable, 199 (exhib.)

Meridians & satellite slot positions, 165 n.

Meters, audience measurement: passive, 363; people, 364–365, 371

Metromedia, sale of, 100 (exhib.)

Metropolitan Opera broadcasts (radio), 55

Mexico: domsat of, 517 (table); treaty with U.S., 432

MF (medium frequency) band: & AM radio, 131; external services on, 138 n.; propagation of waves in, 124–125

MGM: film library of, 85 (exhib.); as major studio, 282 (exhib.); TV productions of, 283 (table)

Miami Vice: on cable TV, 304, 335; as clone, 300; as movie studio product, 280; music use by, 309; in syndication, 291 (table)

Micromanagement of FCC (by Congress), 435

Microphone, 112, 118 (diag.)

Microwave relay(s): & cable TV, 82, 179, 459 (diag.); definition of, 111 (table), 116; & ENG, 152 (exhib.); vs. satellite, 164–165; technology of, 163, 164 (diag.)

Midband channels, cable TV, 180 (diag.)

Midday (radio daypart), 277

Middle-of-the-road (MOR) music format, 349 (table), 350

Miller case (obscenity), 469

Miniaturization, 82, 151–151

Miniseries: basics, 300, 301–302; as prime-time fare, 298

Minitel (French videotex), 97 n., 518

Minorities: & audience research, 361, 380; & EEO rules, 444–445; employment of, 213 (chart); preferential licensing of, 442, 443, 454–455; & public-service broadcasting, 490; in soaps, 305; stereotypes of, 436; & talk radio, 351; viewing time of, 378

Minow, FCC Chair Newton, 352–
353
Mister Rogers' Neighborhood (PBS),
319
MMDS (multichannel multipoint
distribution service): basics, 180–
181; capital cost of, 205; in home
video center, 96 (diag.); licensing
of, by lot, 443; origins of, 88–90;
subscription fees for, 243
Modem (modulator-demodulator),
117
Modified Final Judgment (MFJ) in
AT&T case, 100 n.
Modulation, 116–119, 158, 159
(diag.)
Molniya (Soviet domsat), 513, 517
(table)
Mondale, Walter (presidential candidate), 399, 400 (photo)
Monday Night Football (ABC), 310,
314
Moneyline (CNN), 232
Money machine, broadcasting as,
244–245
Monitor-Plus (ad monitoring service), 237
Monopoly, government, 39–40
Monopoly, private: & antitrust laws,
434; assured license renewals as,
448; by AT&T, 99–101; broadcast-
ing license as, 452; cable TV fran-
chise as, 196, 450, 452; CBS-NBC
networks as, 59; key concept, 22.
See also Antitrust actions
Moody Bible Network, 189
Moonlighting (ABC-produced
series), 279
MOR (middle of the road) radio
format, 349 (table), 350
Morelos (Mexican domsat), 517
(table)
Morning (TV dayparts), 282 (table)
Morning Edition (NPR), 259
Morse, Samuel F. B. (inventor), 33
Morse code: as binary system, 122;
origin of, 33; in radiotelegraphy,
35 (photo)
Morton Downey, Jr., Show, The: as
tabloid TV, 336; & taste issue, 248
Mosaic image (VTR capability), 161

Motion pictures: vs. HDTV, 154;
technology of, 138; & vertical integration, 203. *See also* Feature
films, Made-for-TV movies.
Motorola (AM stereo method), 102,
461 (exhib.)
Movie Channel, The (pay cable),
201, 203, 209 (table)
Movies. *See* Feature films
MPX (multiplex) TV receiver terminal, 150
Mr. Wizard (Nickelodeon), 317
MSO (multiple system operator):
basics, 198–204; & economies of
scale, 247; ownership rules, 453;
profitability of, 246;
MTM (independent producer), 283
MTV (Music TV): ad rates of, 232;
basics, 309; as cable specific, 87; &
diversity issue, 304; ownership of,
209; profitability of, 246; statistics
on, 200 (table); strip scheduling
by, 292
MTV-Europe, 511 (exhib.), 519
(table)
Multiple ownership. *See* Group
owner, MSO, Ownership
Multiple System Operator. *See* MSO
Multiplexing: of ancillary services,
244; on FM channels, 135, 136; &
MPX terminals, 150; technology of,
128; of TV color, 144
Multistage sampling, 369, 370
(diag.)
Municipalities & cable TV systems,
434, 452
Muppets, The, 318
Murder, She Wrote: on cable TV,
282, 304, 335; as crime drama,
300; reruns of, 232; as studio
product, 280; syndication price of,
275
Murdoch, Rupert: buys *TV Guide,*
294 (exhib.); & 20th Century Fox,
92, 282 (exhib.)
Murrow, Edwin R.: clearance for,
195; McCarthy program, 77–78;
World War II coverage by, 63, 64
(photo)
MUSE (Japanese HDTV system),
154

Music: on cable TV, 202; formats, local radio, 348–352; licensing, 186
(diag.), 429; live era (radio), 55–
58; radio impact on, 32; radio
network, 328; rotation of (radio
format), 292, 293 (graph); syndicated (radio), 338; union battle
to control, 56, 57; videos, 304, 309.
See also MTV
Must-carry rule: elimination of, 192,
457–460; origin of, 82
Mutual Broadcasting System (MBS):
affiliates of, 190 (table); failure of
to start TV network, 73; news on,
327; origins of, 55; triggers network investigation, 59
Mutually exclusive applications: basics, 443; for post-freeze VHF TV
channels, 68; for renewals, 448,
449 (chart); & speech freedom,
474
Muzak (background music service),
244
MW (medium wave) band. *See* Medium frequency
My Two Dads (sitcom), 298

NAACP (National Association for
the Advancement of Colored Peo-
ple), opposition of to *Amos 'n'
Andy,* 55 n.
NAB. *See* National Association of
Broadcasters
Nabisco, interest of in cable TV,
209, 310
NABTS (North American Basic
Teletext Specification), 150
Narrowcasting: cable TV vs. broad-
casting, 209; key concept, 15; by
pay cable, 203
NASA (National Aeronautics and
Space Administration): & satellite
launching, 170, 174–175 (exhib.),
513; launch costs of, 205
Nashville Network, The, (as cable
specific), 87
National Association of Broadcast
Employees and Technicians
(NABET), 217
National Association of Broadcast-
ers (NAB): & family viewing stan-

dard, 425; job survey by, 217; legal clinics of, 447; & liquor ads, 239; opposition to public broadcasting ads, 265; management &, 185; origin of, 56. *See also* Code, NAB

National Association of Television Program Executives: job survey by, 218 (exhib.); meeting of as product show case, 332

National audience ratings: Arbitron system, 367 (exhib.); basics, 360–361; Nielsen system, 364–365 (exhib.); report example, 360 (exhib.); sample sizes, 368

National Black Media Coalition, 454

National Black Network, affiliates of, 190 (table)

National Broadcasting Co. *See* NBC

National Cable Television Association, 196–197

National Educational Television (NET) tape network, 252

Nationalism, role of in broadcasting, 24

National Public Radio (NPR): basics, 258–259; & Panama Canal treaty debate, 403; program output, 268

National Radio Conferences (1922–1925), 47, 49

National Religious Broadcasters (NRB), 345 (exhib.)

National sales representatives ("reps"): basics, 222–223, 234–245; jobs with, 217; networks as, 193; in station organization, 186 (diag.), 187

National spot advertising, 222–223, 233–234

National Telecommunications and Information Administration (NTIA): & ITU, 433; & public broadcasting, 262 (chart), 263, 264, 266, 267 (chart); & syn/fin rules, 458

National Television System Committee. *See* NTSC

Nature films as cultural genre, 302

Navy, U.S., claims on wireless of, 40

NBC (National Broadcasting Company): & *Born Innocent* case, 409; cable-TV interests of, 245, 310–

311, 320; cutbacks by, 248–249; entertainment programs of, 299 (photo), 301 (photo), 308; as group owner, 189 (graph); news & public affairs programs of, 322–327; profitability of, 244–245; radio programs of, 327–328; as reflecting RCA parentage, 54; Reuters interest of, 285; sale of, 99; self-regulation by, 239–240; sports program of, 168 (graph), 275, 312 (graph), 313 (graph); transponder time sales by, 205; tops TV competition, 98; in Weaver era, 72

NBC case (technical vs. program regulation), 474

Neocolonialism, 521

Netherlands: advertising in, 504; cable penetration in, 515; external service of, 507; group access in, 502; pirate influence on, 512

Netlink USA (satellite service), 204

Network(s), broadcasting generally: dominant role of, 7–8; & parsimony principle, 276; use of relays, 7; sales function of, 187; station ownership by, 454. *See also names of individual networks;* National audience ratings; National Public Radio; Public Broadcasting Service

Network(s), cable TV: basics, 198–202; children's programs on, 316–318; dominance of, 297; homes reached by, 200 (table); informational programs on, 324; mergers of, 209; statistics on, 200–201 (table)

Network(s), radio: decline of, 73; definition of, 190 n.; evolution of, 54–55; examples of, 190 (table); in foreign countries, 494, 496 (diag.), 501; interconnection of, 162; origins of, 43–46; programs on, 327–328. *See also* Networks, broadcasting; APR; NPR

Network(s), TV: advertising on, 222, 224, 230–232; affiliate compensation by, 222 (graph); affiliate numbers, 185 (table); affiliate relations of, 192–196; basics, 189–196; as

cable TV owners, 310; children's programs on, 315–320; competition among, 72–73, 97–98; consent decrees of, 98; cutbacks of, 285; decline in audience share of, 9, 97, 248–249; 290, 297–298, 377, 378, 381; definition of, 190; deregulation of, 193–194; feature films on, 279–280, 281 (diag.), 300–301; & financial interest rule, 279 n.; in foreign countries, 494–497; home shopping, 243; interconnection of, 162–163, 168 (diag.); news programs on, 285–286, 320–323; organization of, 190–191; origins of, 65; ownership changes of, 97–99; profitability of, 244–245; program costs of, 274–277; program procurement by, 280 (chart), 331 (chart); programming of, 287–308, 310–316, 321–323; regional, 328; regulation of, 193–194, 458; scheduling by, 290, 301–302; self-regulation by, 239–240, 437; sports programs on, 286; station ownership by, 454; syndication by, 458; unwired, 234. *See also names of individual networks;* National audience ratings; Public Broadcasting Service

Newhart (sitcom), 298

Newhouse (MSO), statistics on, 199 (table)

New Jersey ETV network, 265

New World Information Order (NWIO), 522–524

News: access to courts by, 398, 472, 473 (photo); affiliate autonomy in, 196; all-news radio, 351; bias in, 387, 390; block (daypart), 277; on cable TV, 178, 200–201, 343–347; computer use by, 206 (exhib.); consultants, 346–347 (chart); & deregulation, 462; vs. entertainment, 187; & equal time law, 475–477; fairness of, 483–484; farm radio, 351; in foreign countries, 492–493, 500–501, 505–506, 510; formats (radio), 349 (table), 351–352; & free-flow doctrine, 521–522; as information, 277; jobs in

Public file, station & cable system, 437, 444–445

Public interest: and bottom-line thinking, 247–250; in Cable TV Act, 452; & children's programs, 319–320; in Communications Act, 372, 475; & fairness doctrine, 21; definition of, 420; in license decisions, 448; vs. licensee rights, 479; in maritime emergencies, 37 (exhib.), 46; & network takeovers, 99; vs. profit motive, 220, 247–250; profitability &, 244; in Communications Act, 420; Supreme Court view of, 479; "Public interest, convenience, and [or] necessity" phrase (PICON), 14, 419–420. *See also* Public interest

Public investment in electronic media, 13, 204, 394

Publicity crimes, news coverage of, 397–398

Public radio stations: CPB qualified, 260; growth of, 52 (graph), 253 (graph); low power, 135 n., 260; rise of, 251–252. *See also* American Public Radio, National Public Radio, Public broadcasting

Public relations: jobs in, 213 (chart); as station function, 186 (diag.); vs. news, 397

Public-service announcements (PSAs), 226–227

Public-service broadcasting: basics, 490, 492 (graph); & deregulation, 26, 463, 520; key concept, 25–26

"Publishing, electronic": as cable TV function, 21; as UK Channel 4 function, 495

PUP (portable uplink), 205

PUR (persons using radio) rating, 374

Quadraplex VTR, 160

Qualitative vs. quantitative ratings, 20

Quantizing (of digital signal), 121, 122 (exhib.)

Quayle, Vice Pres. Dan (campaign debate), 399

Qube (interactive cable TV firm), 95

Quiz scandals, 75–76

Quotas: on independent productions, 497 (exhib.); on program imports, 24, 520

Rabbit ears (TV antenna), 127

Race and Reason (cable TV access), 23 (exhib.)

Race (black) music, 56

Race to Space, The (cable TV), 317

Racism in media: failure to serve black audience, 438 (exhib.); Ku Klux Klan program, 23 (exhib.); by radio preacher, 465; stereotypes, 436

RADAR (Radio's All-Dimension Audience Research), 361, 366, 368

Radiant energy, 109. *See also* Electromagnetism

Radio (generic sense), 109

Radio, technology of: AM broadcasting, 131–134; FM broadcasting, 134–136; short-wave broadcasting, 136–138; as transmission mode, 7 n.; precedent technologies, 31–34

Radio Act of 1912, 47

Radio Act of 1927: origins, 49; vs. Broadcasting Act, 53, 418

Radio Advertising Bureau (RAB), 234

Radio broadcasting: advertising on, 221 (graph); on cable TV, 179; in Depression years, 51–52; deregulation of, 102, 456–457; employment in, 212 (graph); evolution of, 51–59, 62; first station, 40–42; formats, 378–379; growth of, 52 (graph), 62, 63; local programs on, 331 (chart), 348–352; network development, 54–55; networks adjust to TV, 73; profitability of, 245; programs, 327–328, 348–352; public, 251–252, 260, 267–268; rating reports, 359–360, 361, 363 (exhib.), 368; Reagan's use of, 401; & religion, 351; schedules, 292–293; superstations (radio), 202; syndication in, 292, 308; vs. TV, 73–74; in UK, 494, 496–497 (exhib.); in World War II, 63–64. *See also* AM radio; APR; FM radio; Networks, radio; NPR; Programs, radio; Public broadcasting; Radio technology

Radio Capodistria (Yugoslavia), 510–511

Radio communication, legal definition of, 419

Radio Corporation of America. *See* RCA

Radiofication (USSR), 491

Radio Free Afghanistan (VOA), 507 (table)

Radio Free Europe (RFE), 507 (table), 510

Radio Group (1920s), 43, 44

Radio Liberty (RL), 507 (table), 510

Radio Luxembourg, 510, 511 (exhib.)

Radio Martí: 165 n., 508 (table), 510

Radio Mediterranean International, 510

Radio Monte Carlo, 510

Radio Moscow, 507–508

Radio networks. *See* Networks, radio

Radio 1, 2, 3, & 4 (UK networks), 494, 512

Radio stations. *See* AM radio, FM radio, Radio broadcasting

Radiotelegraphy, 35–37

Radiotelephony, 38–39

Radio-Television News Directors Association (RTNDA): job survey by, 213, 218 (exhib.); self-regulation by, 438

RAI (Italy), 496–497, 501, 519 (table)

Raiders of the Lost Ark (as Paramount product), 282 (exhib.)

Raised eyebrow regulation (FCC), 425

Random digit dialing (in research), 366, 369

Randomness in sampling, 368–371

Rate grid (sales tool), 230

Rates, advertising: basics, 228–233; network control of, 193; for political candidates, 477

Rates, time (in affiliation contracts), 192

Rather, Dan: as CBS anchor, 322 (photo); on news policy, 249; salary of, 212 n.; on *60 Minutes,* 325

Ratings: averages, 373; business of, 358–359; cable TV, 381; calculation of, 371–375; of children's programs, 320; data collection for, 361–367; & demographic data, 363–376; local, 359–360, 363 (exhib.), 368; national, 360–362, 364–365, 367 (exhib.), 368; qualitative, 380; reliability of, 379–380; & sampling, 368–371; of syndicated programs, 361; tampering with, 388; validity of, 380

Rayburn, Cong. Sam (congressional TV), 402

RCA, Inc.: and broadcasting, 44–45, 54, 60–61; color system adopted, 68–69; and cross-licensing, 40, 44; growth of, 54; movie sound system, 32; origins of, 40; as Radio Group member, 43; sale of to GE, 99; World's Fair TV demonstration by, 61

RCA Laboratories, 60 (exhib.), 61–62

Reach (audience measurement): basic concept, 18–19; cable TV network vs. stations, 283; of group-owned stations, 188, 189 (graph); & must-carry rule, 458

Reagan, Pres. Ronald: campaign of, 399, 400 (photo); & CPB funding, 254 (exhib.), 255 (exhib.), 263, 264; & deregulation, 455; fairness law veto by, 482; FCC, 435–436, 458; & FTC, 240; & presidential TV, 401, 402 (graph); radio use by, 401; veto of 'kidvid'' bill, 241, 320, 395

Reality programs, 336

Real-time attribute of broadcasting, 16–17, 488

Reasoner, Harry (CBS News), 325

Rebroadcasting, 173

Recall, telephone (research tool), 361, 366

Receiver(s): color vs. monochrome TV, 69; in DBS system, 176 (diag.); dial calibration of, 115; early radio, 41–42, 44; FM, 62, 75; HDTV, 13; & home video center, 96 (diag.); impact of convergence on, 157–158; improved TV, 102–104, 152–153; penetration of, U.S., 377; penetration of, world, 502; portable, 92,

93 (photo), 102, 142; transistor, 75; tuning of, 36; TV, 65, 143, 149–150, 154 (diag.); & VCR, 160. *See also* License fees, receiver; TVRO

Recording(s): advantages of, 70; kinescope, 69, 160–162; radio network ban on, 56, 63; & syndication, 338; as storage, 156; technologies of, 121, 158–160, 161 (exhib.); union opposition to, 56. *See also* Videocassette, Videotape

Red Channels (blacklist), 77

Red Lion case (fairness), 479–481

Red Network (NBC), 44

Reflection, wave: as common to sound and radio, 109; as propagation phenomenon, 124, 148 (diag.); sound, 114

Refraction, wave: (propagation phenomenon), 124, 125, 126 (diag.)

Regional: channels, AM, 132, 133 (table); sales reps, 324; sports radio networks, 328

Regionalism: in China, 501; of ITU, 499 (exhib.); in UK, 494

Registration (film synchronization), 144

Regulation: agencies of, 421–425, 429–431, 433–436; behavioral vs. structural, 452, 456; of cable TV subscription fees, 242; of early wireless, 46–47; federal jurisdiction over, 416–418; informal, 425; & political philosophy, 472, 474–475, 489–495; process of, 423–424; of programs, 474; protectionist, 81–82, 458. *See also* Cable TV Act; Communications Act; Deregulation; Federal Communications Commission; Federal Radio Commission; Radio Act of 1912; Radio Act of 1927; Self regulation

Reiss Media Enterprises (PPV), 242–243

Relay(s): coaxial, 162–163; definition of, 4; demands on spectrum by, 128; by external services, 508, 510; fiber-optic, 163–164; international, 168 (diag.); microwave, 163, 164 (diag.); network role of, 5, 7, 147; rebroadcast as, 173; satellite, 153 (diag.), 164–167.

See also Coaxial cable, Microwaves, Fiber optics, Satellites

Religion in broadcasting: & boycotts, 436; & complaints to FCC, 447; & fairness, 479–481; & First Amendment, 466; on radio, 54–55, 349 (table), 465, 351; *Red Lion* case, 479–481; on short-wave stations, 137; syndicated TV programs, 340–343; UK ownership ban on, 497 (exhib.); *WXUR* case, 480–481

Remand (legal action), 426

Remington Steele (on cable TV), 335

Remote Control (game show), 306

Remote pickups, 151–153, 162, 169 (chart)

Renewal, license: basics, 447–450; failure of, 427–428; conditional, 428; consumer opposition to, 437, 438 (exhib.), 465, 480–481; *Geller* case, 451 (exhib.); postcard form for, 446 (photo); short term, 428

Repeater amplifiers. *See* Amplifiers

Repetition (schedule strategy), 289

Reply, right of (fairness concept), 482

Report and Order (FCC document), 65 n., 424

Reporter's privilege. *See* Journalist's privilege

Repositioning (of TV channels on cable TV), 177 n.

Representative, national sales, 234

Request for proposals (RFP), cable TV, 451

Request Television (PPV), 201 (table), 242–243

Reregulation (as reaction to deregulation), 484

Reruns. *See* Off-network programs

Research, audience: cable TV as tool, 383; fraudulent use of, 388; key concepts, 18–20; need for, 358; non-rating, 381–384; program ratings, 358–381; & sales, 233–234. *See also* Effects, Ratings

Research on media effects: evolution of, 387–391; methods of, 392–394; need for, 386–387; policy role of, 396–397; topics of, 389–392. *See also* Effects, media; Advertising, effects of

EVENTS IN

1910
First wireless legislation

1912
Radio Act provides first regulations for local stations

1916
DeForest broadcasts election returns

1917
U.S. Navy takes over all wireless transmitters during World War I

1919
Formation of RCA and initial commercial patent pool

1920
KDKA begins operation as first regular broadcast station

1922
Radio boom: about 500 stations on the air

1922–25
Hoover hosts four radio conferences seeking order in the new industry

1926
NBC begins network operation; adds second network a few months later; CBS follows in 1927

1927
Congress passes Radio Act of 1927 creating Federal Radio Commission

1929
Crossley's CAB initiates ratings for radio networks

1930

1931
Radio sets are in more than half the nation's homes

1934
Communications Act creates Federal Communications Commission, replacing FRC; beginning of Mutual network

1938
"War of the Worlds" broadcast causes panic which illustrates growing impact of radio

1940

1941
FCC approves regular FM and TV broadcasting; issues report more strongly regulating network broadcasting; war causes 1942–45 hiatus in all broadcast development

1943
In *NBC* v *U.S.*, the Supreme Court generally upholds FCC regulation of broadcasting

1945
Post-war reallocations move FM radio "upstairs" to present band

1948
First TV networks and many stations going on the air; FCC initiates TV Freeze to study interference problems

1949
Inception of CATV; invention of transistor; Nielsen takes over Hooper as major supplier of network TV ratings

1950

1951
First coast-to-coast television network broadcasts; radio available in more than half the nation's cars

1952
FCC *Sixth Report and Order* reserves channels for educational TV and allots UHF channels

1953
FCC approves color TV standards

1954
Television, available in more than half the nation's homes, covers Army-McCarthy hearings

1956
First use of videotape by television broadcasters

1958
Quiz show scandals in network television

1959
Invention of integrated circuit ("chip")